W9-APR-473

Classical Music

THE ROUGH GUIDE

Other Rough Guides music reference titles:

The Rough Guide to World Music
The Rough Guide to Jazz
The Rough Guide to Rock
The Rough Guide to Reggae
The Rough Guide to Opera

Credits

Text Editor: Joe Staines
Project Editor: Jonathan Buckley
Series Editor: Mark Ellingham
Typesetting: Helen Ostick
Proofreading: Nikky Tywman
Picture Research: Vanessa Kelly
Design: Henry Iles

Acknowledgements

Thanks to all those who have assisted in the creation of this guide, in particular Celia Ballantine at Hyperion, Victoria Bevan at Harmonia Mundi, Alf Goodrich at Nimbus, Roger Mills at Auvidis, Paul Westcott at Chandos, Nicole Bachmann at Collins, Jo Carpenter at Naxos, Jo Nicholson at Polygram, Emily Robins and Carol Lowry at Sony, Sarah Christie at EMI, Tara Guha and Talia Hull at Warner, Ivor Phuell at Complete, Tonia Franklin, Elbie Lebrecht, Rebecca Meitlis, Lewes Music Library and James McConnachie. Thanks also to those who contributed to the first edition of this book – Matthew Rye, Simon Broughton, Gavin Thomas, Jonathan Webster, David Doughty and Kim Burton.

Publishing details

Published September 1998 by Rough Guides Ltd, 62–70 Shorts Gardens, London WC2H 9AB
Distributed by the Penguin Group:
Penguin Books Ltd, 27 Wrights Lane, London W8 5TZ
Penguin Books USA Inc., Hudson Street, New York 10014, USA
Penguin Books Australia Ltd, 487 Maroondah Highway, PO Box 257, Ringwood, Victoria 3134, Australia
Penguin Books Canada Ltd, 10 Alcorn Avenue, Toronto, Ontario M4V 1E4, Canada
Penguin Books (NZ) Ltd, 182–190 Wairau Road, Auckland 10, New Zealand

Typeset in Bembo and Helvetica to an original design by Henry Iles.
Printed in Spain by Graphy Cems.

No part of this book may be reproduced in any form without permission from the publisher except for the quotation of brief passages in reviews.

Text © The Rough Guides Ltd, 1998
All drawings © Guus Ong
All photographs copyright of credited photographers, agencies and record labels.

528pp.

A catalogue record for this book is available from the British Library.
ISBN 1-85828-257-8

Classical Music

THE ROUGH GUIDE

Written by
Joe Staines, Nick Kimberley,
Barry Witherden, Matthew Boyden,
Andy Hamilton, Stephen Jackson,
Mark Prendergast, Sophie Fuller,
Richard Chew and Jonathan Buckley

Edited by
Joe Staines and Jonathan Buckley

THE ROUGH GUIDES

CONTENTS

INTRODUCTION

Though few of them make much effort to entice a new audience to their product, the recording companies continue to pour out a flood of classical music. The catalogue of current classical CDs runs to more than two thousand tightly packed pages, and lists nearly three hundred composers before reaching the second letter of the alphabet. An average month sees some four hundred recordings added to the pile. **THE ROUGH GUIDE** to **CLASSICAL MUSIC** attempts to make sense of this overwhelming volume of music, giving you the information that's essential whether you're starting from the beginning or have already begun exploring.

As well as being a buyer's guide to CDs, this book is a who's who of classical music, ranging from Hildegard of Bingen, one of the great figures of twelfth-century European culture, to Michael Torke, born in Milwaukee in 1961. Of course we've had to be selective, both with the composers and with their output – Domenico Scarlatti, for example, was a fascinating musician, but no book of this scope could do justice to each of his five hundred keyboard sonatas. Gaetano Donizetti wrote more than seventy operas, but you wouldn't want to listen to all of them. We've gone for what we think are the best works by the most interesting composers, mixing some underrated people with the big names, and highlighting some we think you should keep an eye on.

When it comes to CDs the situation requires even greater ruthlessness. Beethoven may have written only nine symphonies, but there are more than one hundred versions of the fifth in the catalogue, and scores of recordings of all the others. Several of these CDs should never have been issued – they are there simply because any up-and-coming conductor has to make a Beethoven recording as a kind of calling card, regardless of any aptitude for the music. However, a fair proportion of the Beethoven CDs are worth listening to, because a piece of music as complex as a Beethoven symphony will bear as many different readings as a Shakespeare play.

Although there are recordings that stand head and shoulders above the competition, no performance can be described as definitive, which is one reason why we have often recommended more than one account of a work. Whereas all our first-choice CDs make persuasive cases for the music, some of the additional recommendations are included because they make provocative counter-arguments. Where price is a consideration, we've also listed a lower-cost alternative whenever appropriate – thus we might suggest a mid-price boxed set of symphonies as an alternative to buying them as full-price individual CDs. Finally, in many instances we've picked an outstanding pre-stereo performance as a complement to a modern recording.

These "historic" reissues are the one reliable growth area in the classical music industry, and their success is not due to mere nostalgia. There are some great musicians around today, but there's also a lot of hype in the business, with many soloists owing their success more to the way they look than to the way they play – and, conversely, many superlative musicians who remain obscure because they don't project the requisite glamour. It's in the area of orchestral music and opera that the situation is especially bad, notwithstanding the technically immaculate quality of many digital recordings. Orchestral musicians are now trained to a very high standard, but only a few of the top-class orchestras enjoy the sort of long-term relationship with an individual conductor that can mould a distinctive identity. The same goes for opera companies, which used to have a stable core of singers and musicians working under the same conductor for years. Now there's a system based on jet-setting stars, who might be performing in London one night, New York the next, then in the recording studio for a few days to record something with people they hadn't met until the day the session started. You don't necessarily get a good football team by paying millions for a miscellaneous batch of top-flight players, and you don't build a good musical team that way either.

Musically, then, new is not always best. And don't assume that a recording made more than thirty years ago will sound terrible. Sound quality won't match that of digital CDs, but you'll be surprised at how good it can be – indeed, many people prefer the warmth of the old analogue sound to the often chilly precision produced by modern studios. (We've warned you if surface noise or tinny quality might be a hindrance to enjoyment.) In short, you'll be missing a lot if you insist on hi-tech – few recent releases can match Vladimir Horowitz's 1940 account of Tchaikovsky's *Piano Concerto No. 1*, for instance, or Josef Hofmann's versions of the Chopin piano concertos from the 1930s.

How this book works

Immediately after this introduction you'll find a list of all the composers covered in the guide, arranged chronologically, so you can see at a glance who fits where. If you find you like the music of Palestrina, you could check the list and decide to listen to Byrd, his contemporary. Things are more complicated with the stylistically diverse twentieth century: Xenakis and Arnold may have been born just a year apart but their music seems to come from different worlds. When a musical connection does exist, as in the case of Schoenberg and Berg, or Pärt and Tavener, a cross-reference in the text will point you in the right direction. At the end of the book there's a detailed glossary, defining all the technical terms we've used.

Between lies the bulk of the guide, an A to Z of composers from John Adams to Alexander Zemlinsky. Each entry starts with an introduction to the composer's music, usually with an outline biography. (Many composers were too busy writing music to lead interesting lives, but if there's a story to tell we tell it.) That's followed by a run-through of the main compositions, with subheadings for individual works that need detailed discussion. These subheadings follow the same basic order, moving from largest-scale works down to the smallest: thus operas precede symphonies and concertos, which in turn precede chamber works and solo instrumental music. With the most important figures – such as Haydn, Mozart and Beethoven – we've generally grouped the music under generic headings (eg "Symphonies"), giving an introduction to each composer's work in that genre before going on to the most important individual pieces, which are then arranged chronologically.

Under each heading you'll find a short discussion of the piece or pieces to which the heading refers, followed by recommended recordings of those pieces, and a review of each CD. The CD details conform to a regular format: soloist first; then orchestra (and/or choir); then conductor, with the record company and serial number in parenthesis. (The serial number is generally the same in Europe as in North America, except that the -2 suffix is usually dropped in North America.) You'll have to get your store to order many of the CDs we've recommended, as most stores stock just the best sellers and the new releases. What's more, some of the major companies have begun targeting what they regard as non-mainstream material at a specific audience. Thus the EMI recording of Samson François playing Ravel will be easily available in France but only available as a special import in Britain and the US. Ordering should not be a problem, however, and you should be able to get hold of eighty percent of our recommendations within ten days of asking for them, with imports taking perhaps a week longer. Should you find that a listed CD is not in your store's catalogue, get them to check that the performance has not been repackaged under a different serial number – the major companies are pretty quick to delete slow-moving items, before eventually reissuing them, either at a lower price or combined with different music.

Each CD listing in the book is preceded by a symbol indicating the price of the CD, as in the following examples of recordings of Vivaldi's *Four Seasons*:

● **Freiburg Baroque Orchestra; Goltz** (Deutsche Harmonia Mundi 05472 77384-2; with *Violin Concertos Op. 8, Nos. 5 & 6*) = over £10 or $13.

◑ **Raglan Baroque Players; Kraemer** (VER 5 61172-2; with *Violin Concertos Op. 8, Nos. 5, 6, 10 & 11*) = £7–10 or $8–13.

⊙ **English Chamber Orchestra; Garcia** (ASV CDQS 148; with other Vivaldi concertos) = under £7 or $8.

The pricing of CDs is a contentious subject. The difference between prices in North America and Britain is explained by differences in taxation and mark-up margins, but you'll come across the argument that top-price CDs are still overpriced in both markets. Certainly some CDs are too expensive – occasionally a label will recycle a best-selling vinyl disc as a full-price CD with little more than half an hour's music on it. That said, the vast majority of CDs are good value. The catalogues of the multinationals are bursting with CDs that pack the contents of two former LPs onto a single eighty-minute disc, often at mid-price or lower. As well as this you'll find that big stores often have special promotions, while many smaller outlets can beat the average prices of the megastores, and there are plenty of mail-order companies selling CDs at a discount.

On top of all this, in recent years there's been an explosion of budget labels, led by Naxos. Don't think that a CD can't be any good if it hasn't got a famous face on the cover – the commitment you get on many of the budget-label performances often outweighs the finesse of the major-league players, and in several instances they win on all fronts. The success of these relative newcomers has spurred the big companies to put more effort into their own budget-price series – every big company now has a range of CDs costing less than half the top price, and two-for-the-price-of-one packages are increasingly popular. All in all, the CD format has made it easier than ever to accumulate a classical collection at moderate cost and, though alternative recording technologies do surface from time to time (such as the short-lived DAT), for the foreseeable future the CD will remain the dominant format.

CHRONOLOGY OF COMPOSERS

Born before 1400

Hildegard of Bingen	1098–1179
Pérotin	1160–1225
Guillaume de Machaut	1300–1377
John Dunstable	c. 1390–1453

Born 1400–1500

Guillaume Dufay	1400–1474
Johannes Ockeghem	1410–1497
Josquin Desprez	1440–1521
Antoine Brumel	c. 1460–1515
John Taverner	1490–1545

Born 1500–1600

Thomas Tallis	c. 1505–1585
Giovanni Palestrina	1526–1594
Roland de Lassus	1532–1594
William Byrd	c. 1537–1623
Tomás Luis da Victoria	1548–1661
Giovanni Gabrieli	1557–1612
Carlo Gesualdo	1561–1613
John Dowland	1563–1626
Claudio Monteverdi	1567–1643
Gregorio Allegri	1582–1652
Orlando Gibbons	1583–1625
Heinrich Schütz	1585–1672

Born 1600–1700

Giacomo Carissimi	1605–1674
Jean-Baptiste Lully	1632–1687
Heinrich Biber	1644–1704
Alessandro Stradella	1644–1682
Marc-Antoine Charpentier	1645–1704
Arcangelo Corelli	1653–1713
Johann Pachelbel	1653–1706
Henry Purcell	1659–1695
Alessandro Scarlatti	1660–1725
François Couperin	1668–1733
Tomaso Albinoni	1671–1750
Antonio Vivaldi	1678–1741
Georg-Philipp Telemann	1681–1767
Jean-Philippe Rameau	1683–1764
J.S. Bach	1685–1750
George Frideric Handel	1685–1759
Domenico Scarlatti	1685–1757

Born 1700–1800

Giovanni Battista Pergolesi	1710–1736
C.P.E. Bach	1714–1788
Christoph Willibald Gluck	1714–1787
Joseph Haydn	1732–1809
Luigi Boccherini	1743–1805
Muzio Clementi	1752–1832
Wolfgang Amadeus Mozart	1756–1791
Ludwig van Beethoven	1770–1827
Johann Hummel	1778–1837
Nicolò Paganini	1782–1840
Carl Maria von Weber	1786–1826
Giacomo Meyerbeer	1791–1864
Gioachino Rossini	1792–1868
Gaetano Donizetti	1797–1848
Franz Schubert	1797–1828

Born 1800–1825

Vincenzo Bellini	1801–1835
Hector Berlioz	1803–1869
Johann Strauss the Elder	1804–1849
Mikhail Glinka	1805–1857
Felix Mendelssohn	1809–1847
Frédéric Chopin	1810–1849
Robert Schumann	1810–1856
Franz Liszt	1811–1886
Giuseppe Verdi	1813–1901
Richard Wagner	1813–1883
Charles-François Gounod	1818–1893
Jacques Offenbach	1819–1880
César Franck	1822–1890
Anton Bruckner	1824–1896
Bedřich Smetana	1824–1884

Born 1825–1850

Johann Strauss the Younger	1825–1899
Alexander Borodin	1833–1887
Johannes Brahms	1833–1897
Camille Saint-Saëns	1835–1921
Leo Delibes	1836–1891
Georges Bizet	1838–1875
Max Bruch	1838–1920
Modest Mussorgsky	1839–1881
Pyotr Il'yich Tchaikovsky	1840–1893
Emmanuel Chabrier	1841–1894
Antonin Dvořák	1841–1904
Jules Massenet	1842–1912
Arthur Sullivan	1842–1900
Edvard Grieg	1843–1907
Nicolai Rimsky-Korsakov	1844–1908
Gabriel Fauré	1845–1924
Hubert Parry	1848–1918

Born 1850–1875

Engelbert Humperdinck	1854–1921
Leoš Janáček	1854–1928
Edward Elgar	1857–1934

Ruggero Leoncavallo	1857–1919
Giacomo Puccini	1858–1924
Ethel Smyth	1858–1944
Isaac Albéniz	1860–1909
Gustav Mahler	1860–1911
Hugo Wolf	1860–1903
Claude Debussy	1862–1918
Frederick Delius	1862–1934
Pietro Mascagni	1863–1945
Richard Strauss	1864–1949
Paul Dukas	1865–1935
Alexander Glazunov	1865–1936
Carl Nielsen	1865–1931
Jean Sibelius	1865–1957
Ferruccio Busoni	1866–1924
Erik Satie	1866–1925
Umberto Giordano	1867–1948
Enrique Granados	1867–1916
Hans Pfitzner	1869–1949
Franz Lehár	1870–1948
Alexander Zemlinsky	1871–1942
Alexander Scriabin	1872–1915
Ralph Vaughan Williams	1872–1958
Sergei Rachmaninov	1873–1943
Max Reger	1873–1916
Gustav Holst	1874–1934
Charles Ives	1874–1954
Arnold Schoenberg	1874–1951
Josef Suk	1874–1935

Born 1875–1900

Maurice Ravel	1875–1937
Manuel de Falla	1876–1946
Franz Schreker	1878–1934
Marie-Joseph Canteloube	1879–1957
Ottorino Respighi	1879–1936
Béla Bartók	1881–1945
Percy Grainger	1882–1961
Zoltán Kodály	1882–1967
Igor Stravinsky	1882–1971
Karol Szymanowski	1882–1937
Edgard Varèse	1883–1965
Anton Webern	1883–1945
Alban Berg	1885–1935
Heitor Villa-Lobos	1887–1959
Frank Martin	1890–1974
Bohuslav Martinů	1890–1959
Sergey Prokofiev	1891–1953
Arthur Honegger	1892–1955
Darius Milhaud	1892–1974
Lili Boulanger	1893–1918
Paul Hindemith	1895–1963
Carl Orff	1895–1982
Erich Korngold	1897–1957
Hanns Eisler	1898–1962
George Gershwin	1898–1937
Viktor Ullmann	1898–1944
Francis Poulenc	1899–1963

Born 1900–1925

Aaron Copland	1900–1990
Kurt Weill	1900–1950
Joaquín Rodrigo	1901–
William Walton	1902–1983
Aram Khachaturian	1903–1978
Michael Tippett	1905–1998
Elisabeth Lutyens	1906–1983
Dmitri Shostakovich	1906–1975
Elizabeth Maconchy	1907–1990
Elliott Carter	1908–
Olivier Messiaen	1908–1992
Grazyna Bacewicz	1909–1967
Samuel Barber	1910–1981
John Cage	1912–1992
Benjamin Britten	1913–1976
Witold Lutosławski	1913–1994
Leonard Bernstein	1918–1990
Malcolm Arnold	1921–
Iannis Xenakis	1922–
György Ligeti	1923–
Luigi Nono	1924–1990

Born 1925–present

Luciano Berio	1925–
Pierre Boulez	1925–
Morton Feldman	1926–1987
Hans Werner Henze	1926–
György Kurtág	1926–
Einojuhani Rautavaara	1928–
Karlheinz Stockhausen	1928–
Toru Takemitsu	1930–1996
Sofia Gubaidulina	1931–
Henryk Górecki	1933–
Krzysztof Penderecki	1933–
Harrison Birtwistle	1934–
Peter Maxwell Davies	1934–
Alfred Schnittke	1934–
Nicholas Maw	1935–
Arvo Pärt	1935–
Steve Reich	1936–
Philip Glass	1937–
Louis Andriessen	1939–
Jonathan Harvey	1939–
Michael Nyman	1944–
John Tavener	1944–
John Adams	1947–
Poul Ruders	1949–
Judith Weir	1954–
Magnus Lindberg	1958–
James Macmillan	1959–
George Benjamin	1960–
Mark-Anthony Turnage	1960–
Michael Torke	1961–

JOHN ADAMS

(1947–)

Like Philip Glass and the other Minimalists with whom he is often bracketed, John Adams has set out to reverse the influence of modernist cerebralism, to make it ok for composers to write unashamedly tonal music again. For Adams, "tonality is not just a cultural invention, but a natural force, like gravity". But unlike any thoroughgoing Minimalist, Adams writes fairly eventful music which in a way is reminiscent of Charles Ives: never coy about using vernacular and "banal" elements, he is a crusading synthesist who is quite happy to openly borrow from sources as wide-ranging as jazz, Arabian music, church music and folk tunes.

BETTY FREEMAN/LEBRECHT COLLECTION

John Adams

Adams' father was a dance-band saxophonist and, as a boy, he was encouraged by both parents to listen to a huge variety of music, ranging from Mozart to Duke Ellington. (One of Adams' most cherished boyhood memories was of being taken to an Ellington concert and put up on the piano stool next to the jazz maestro.) When Adams arrived at Harvard in the late 1960s he was swept up by the radicalism of the times, and was particularly fascinated by William Burroughs' use of "vernacular, junkie language", which directly inspired him to develop a musical language that "didn't make a distinction between high art and low art, highbrow and middlebrow and lowbrow". An even greater influence in those years was the composer John Cage (see p.97), whose *Silence*, a delightfully eccentric Zen-like collection of essays, gave Adams the courage to find his own voice as a composer.

After graduation, he headed west to San Francisco, where he encountered the Minimalist works of Steve Reich, Terry Riley and Philip Glass for the first time. Adams was immediately drawn to Minimalism's resolute reliance on tonality, its insistent, hypnotic rhythms, and its absorption of Balinese, African, Indian and other non-Western musics. Yet, while Adams still stands by the view that Minimalism is "the most important stylistic development in Western art music since the Fifties", he soon saw the limitations of a technique that placed so much emphasis upon repetition. With *Shaker Loops* (1978) he heralded what he termed "post-minimalism", a style characterized by a more fluid and layered sound, and greater dynamic contrasts.

With his three-act opera *Nixon in China*, premiered at Houston in 1985, Adams really hit his stride. The choice of subject – President Nixon's visit to Peking in 1972 – was a daring departure for a genre that tends to fall back on ancient history or mythology for its plots, and Adams' music showed the potential of a style that amalgamated Minimalist procedures with more dramatic forms of writing. Sections of *Nixon* display the same sort of highly kinetic repetitive rhythms as you'll hear in Philip Glass, but it also has stretches of witty pastiche and parody. Audience response to *Nixon in China* was very positive. Critics, however, were divided, some declaring *Nixon* the most accomplished new opera since *Peter Grimes*, others condemning it for relying too heavily on mere spectacle. European critics were notably less enthusiastic than their US counterparts, but with his second opera, *The Death of Klinghoffer* (see overleaf), Adams began to get a more enthusiastic press on both sides of the Atlantic.

THE DEATH OF KLINGHOFFER

The Death of Klinghoffer (premiered in March 1991), is similar to *Nixon in China* in that it tackles an event from very recent political history – the hijacking by Palestinian terrorists of the ocean liner *Achille Lauro*, and their murder of one of the passengers, Leon Klinghoffer. Adams created it in partnership with the librettist Alice Goodman and the director Peter Sellars, the team responsible for *Nixon*, but there the similarities between the two operas end. While *Nixon in China* was essentially a comedy, *Klinghoffer* is preoccupied with the deep religious and economic conflicts that drove the terrible events of October 1985. Whereas *Nixon in China* is for the most part naturalistic in pace and setting, the dramaturgy of *Klinghoffer* is based, according to Adams, on largely static models, encompassing Bach's Passion settings, Greek tragedy, and Persian and Japanese drama. *Klinghoffer* is too raw to make for a comfortable night at the theatre, but it is an emotionally riveting experience, and Adams' most impressive achievement to date.

O Maddalena, Felty, Hammons, Young, Perry, Sylvan, Friedman, Nadler; Lyon Opera Chorus & Orchestra; Nagano (Elektra Nonesuch 7559-79281-2; 2 CDs).

It's clear right from the opening orchestral F minor chords that Kent Nagano has a tight grip on this piece, and the entire performance turns out to be deep and searching. The expressiveness of the Lyon Opera Orchestra is remarkable, while the soloists give performances of real stature, with James Maddalena, as the ship's philosophical captain, and Sanford Sylvan, as Klinghoffer, particularly outstanding.

SHAKER LOOPS

Shaker Loops grew out of *Wavemaker,* a string quartet in which Adams tried to merge the repetitive processes of Minimalism and his own interest in waveforms. Its premiere was a failure, and Adams used his classes at San Francisco Conservatory as a means of salvaging something from it. Renamed, radically amended, and expanded to a septet, *Shaker Loops* appeared in 1978. Its new title was inspired by the Minimalist tape-loop works of the 1960s (eg *It's Gonna Rain* by Steve Reich, see p.336); a pun on the musical term for a rapid tremolo; and the state of religious ecstasy attained by members of the Shaker sect.

Shaker Loops is characterized by ceaseless motion even in the slower sections, where the lines drift like mist in a forest breeze. The restless first and fourth parts (*Shaking and Trembling* and *A Final Shaking*) frame the slow and languid glissandi of the second (*Hymning Slews*) and the lyrical character of the third (*Loops and Verses*), which moves towards a "wild push-pull section" – what Adams calls "the emotional high point" of the work.

O Orchestra of St Luke's; Adams (Nonesuch 7559 – 79360-2; with *Violin Concerto*).

In 1983 Adams expanded the instrumentation of *Shaker Loops* further, producing a version for string orchestra. This has become one of Adams' most popular scores, and was used in the film *Barfly*. This 1988 recording by Adams himself must be regarded as authoritative (though Edo de Waart's vibrant recording with the San Francisco Symphony Orchestra is equally impressive).

O Ensemble Modern; Edwards (RCA 09026 68674 2; with *Chamber Symphony* & *Phrygian Gates*).

For those who think they might prefer the purity of the septet version (for three violins, two cellos, viola and bass) this recording by the Ensemble Modern is excellent. Crisply and energetically performed, the music achieves a greater clarity with little loss of power.

THE VIOLIN CONCERTO

Co-commissioned by the New York City Ballet, the LSO and the Minnesota Orchestra, the *Violin Concerto* was created with the knowledge that it would be choreographed, and this influenced its form as well as its content and character. It may seem odd that, writing music for dancing, Adams should tone down the strong rhythmic character of his style, but the violin part moves through the three movements in an endless line that weaves its way in and out of the orchestral texture. Though he follows the outline of the traditional concerto – a rhapsodic beginning, a slow central movement (*Chaconne; Body Through Which the Dream Flows*) and an energetic climax (*Toccare*) – the violin is always an active presence, flowing through the body of the orchestra rather than engaging with it in the usual dialogue.

O Kremer; London Symphony Orchestra; Nagano (Nonesuch 7559-79360-2; with *Shaker Loops*).

The world premiere of the concerto was performed by Jorja Fleezanis in 1994, but Gidon Kremer was the soloist in the European premiere six months later, so it's hardly surprising he sounds thoroughly steeped in the music. Kremer's playing is sleek, sinuous and supple, and his tone glows richly against the varied orchestral background.

HARMONIELEHRE

Despite his insistence on the significance of Minimalism, Adams was never really a pure Minimalist: his music had too much harmonic momentum, too much timbral lushness – factors which gave classic early pieces like *Harmonielehre* their exhilarating feel. The opening movement, inspired by a dream in which Adams saw a gigantic tanker rise from San Francisco Bay and hurtle into the sky, begins with shattering chords dominated by brass and percussion. The second movement (*The Anfortas Wound*, a reference to the stricken guardian of the Holy Grail in Wagner's *Parsifal*) is completely different: its harmonic and melodic idiom recalls the late Romanticism which Schoenberg believed signalled the end of tonal music. Indeed *Harmonielehre* is the title of Schoenberg's 1911 treatise on harmony in which he spelled out his new radical departure (by purloining the title, Adams states his faith in tonality as a still living tradition). In the last movement (*Meister Eckhardt and the Quackie*) Adams pictures the medieval mystic flying through the air with Adams' daughter riding on his shoulder, and interweaves the minimalism and the neo-Romanticism of the previous movements into a marvellous fusion – a celebration of the key of E flat.

⊙ City of Birmingham Symphony Orchestra; Rattle (EMI CDC 5 55051-2; with *The Chairman Dances, Tromba Lontana & Short Ride in a Fast Machine*).

Simon Rattle regards Adams as one of the most significant composers of modern times, and in this vigorous performance he certainly seems to be putting his energy where his enthusiasm is. The CBSO plays with wonderful punch and precision in the minimalist episodes, and a languid grace in the neo-Romantic passages.

ISAAC ALBÉNIZ

(1860–1909)

Isaac Albéniz, a crucial figure in the creation of a distinctively Spanish classical musical idiom, is associated primarily with works for the piano, and above all with *Iberia*, a suite of twelve piano pieces composed between 1906 and 1909. It's hardly surprising that the majority of his pieces were written for that instrument, given Albéniz's extraordinary gifts as a performer.

Born into a musical family, Isaac made his public debut at Barcelona's Teatro Romea at the age of 4, where some members of the incredulous audience supected that some kind of fraud was being perpetrated. At 7 he auditioned at the Paris Conservatoire, where he was praised by Professor Marmontel – the teacher of both Bizet and Debussy – but was considered too young to become a student. In 1869 he enrolled at the Madrid conservatory but at the age of 10 he suddenly ran away from home and supported himself by giving concerts in various cities in Castile. A couple of years later he topped that escapade by stowing away on a ship to South America, travelling to the USA via Argentina, Uruguay, Brazil, Cuba and Puerto Rico, earning his bread by playing piano in so-called "places of entertainment".

GUUS ONG

Although he returned to Spain and became a diligent student, Albéniz never fully exorcized his wanderlust and spent much of the rest of his life moving between Barcelona, Madrid, Paris and London. On one trip in 1880 he followed his idol Liszt through Weimar, Prague, Vienna and Budapest, gaining invaluable instruction along the way. The fulcrum of his nomadic existence for much of the 1890s was Paris, where he taught piano and struck up friendships with, among others, Debussy. His encounters with the new wave of French composers, headed by Debussy and Ravel, were immensely productive – and the relationship was not the one-way process it's sometimes depicted as having been, as Albéniz contributed much to the emergence of impressionist music.

But the most significant influence on Albéniz came from the musicologist and folk-song collector

Felipe Pedrell. Albéniz's earliest compositions were overindebted to Liszt, but after meeting Pedrell he began to explore and experiment with Spanish folk idioms. As the nineteenth century came to a close, it was Albéniz's music above all that defined everything that was exciting about modern Spanish piano writing. Pieces like *La Vega*, the *Cantos de España* and *Suite española* are bursting with national colour, evoking the sound of guitars, flamenco rhythms, and dances like the Sevillana and Corranda.

Although enough survives of Albéniz's output to get a good overview of his achievements, biographers have been thwarted in their attempts to devise a definitive catalogue of his works owing to the fact that his manuscripts were so widely dispersed during his lifetime, with the result that many pieces have gone missing. Equally unfortunate is the fact that there are no recordings of Albéniz playing the piano – his death at the early age of 49 just preceded the spread of the earliest gramophones.

IBERIA

Everything in Albéniz's life had been building up to his twelve-part *Iberia* suite, and in the last three years of his life he obsessively worked on this music to get it just right. *Iberia* was immediately recognized as the most important Spanish work for solo piano, a status it still retains, and its bold sonorities and harmonies were an inspiration for that country's young composers. In this single work Albéniz conjures up the presence of a whole array of different regions, ranging from Seville to Cadiz and Madrid, capturing the musical essence of each local culture not by merely aping and embellishing its tunes, but through a subtle snatch of rhythm here and the faintest outline of a melodic refrain there.

⊙ de Larrocha (EMI CMS 7 64504 2; 2 CDs; with various other Albéniz piano works).

Although there are no recordings of Albéniz playing his own music, we have the next best thing in Alicia de Larrocha who learned piano from Frank Marshall, a pupil of Albeniz's friend Enrique Granados who in turn studied with Pedrell. This EMI set – which offers a substantial overview of the rest of Albéniz's output – was made in 1962, when de Larrocha was full of youthful ardour and prepared to take risks.

⊙ de Larrocha (Decca 417 887-2; 2 CDs; with *Navarra* & *Suite española*).

For a more sonically spectacular (and digital) performance, the recording de Larrocha made for Decca 25 years later is remarkably vivid, if not quite as volatile as the earlier set.

TOMASO ALBINONI

(1671– 1750)

Albinoni is almost entirely known for a piece of music he didn't actually write. The famous *Adagio in G Minor* was not merely reconstructed by the Italian musicologist Remo Giazotto, as is usually acknowledged after Albinoni's name – it was pretty well written by him in its entirety. Giazotto came across the manuscript in a library in Dresden just after World War II. The music consisted of a bass line, a few bars of the violin part, and nothing more. Deciding that what he'd found was a church sonata, Giazotto scored the piece for organ and strings. The result is a work of solemnity and affecting simplicity, which has proved an astonishingly durable favourite, almost on a par with Vivaldi's *Four Seasons* (which was rediscovered around the same time, but is entirely genuine). If, as is rumoured, Giazotto owns the copyright to the *Adagio*, he must by now be very rich indeed.

Approaching Albinoni's genuine compositions after the lushness of the *Adagio* can come as a shock. On the whole it is bright, lively and melodious music, with more than a passing resemblance to that of Vivaldi, his great contemporary and fellow Venetian. Unlike Vivaldi, Albinoni didn't have to compose to earn his living. As the eldest son of a highly prosperous paper merchant, he approached music as a committed amateur, but soon made his mark as an opera composer, writing over fifty works (of which few have survived intact). In 1721 the family business, part of which he had inherited in 1709, was successfully claimed by one of his father's many creditors, but this loss of income coincided with the most successful period of Albinoni's career. His operas were being performed outside Italy, and he was invited to supervise one of them, *I Veri Amici* (The True Friends) at the Bavarian court in Munich. He even received the accolade of having three themes used as the subjects for fugues by J.S. Bach – perhaps the pinnacle of his reputation until the resurrection of the *Adagio*.

◑ **Adagio in G Minor: I Musici** (Philips 410 606; with Pachelbel's *Canon*, etc).

Performances of the *Adagio* range from the overblown (Herbert von Karajan's high-kitsch version being notorious) to briskly efficient versions from early music groups. This recording by the Italian string orchestra I Musici makes a satisfying compromise. The pace is slow without being ponderous, and the string sound is generous but not too big. As is usually the case, the *Adagio* is coupled with a selection of Baroque favourites, including Pachelbel's *Canon* and Boccherini's *Minuet*.

○ **Albinoni and Vivaldi Wind Concertos: Goodwin; The King's Consort; King** (Hyperion CDA 66383).

After the spurious *Adagio*, the most recorded of Albinoni's works are the two sets of oboe concertos Opus 7 and Opus 9. The King's Consort recording combines three of the concertos from Opus 9 and a concerto for trumpet, three oboes and bassoon by Albinoni with three wind concertos by Vivaldi. It makes for a well-balanced programme: Vivaldi is clearly the more brilliant of the two composers, but Albinoni excels in the slow movements, which are consistently lyrical and – in the D minor oboe concerto and the G major concerto for two oboes – outstandingly beautiful. Paul Goodwin, a Baroque oboe specialist, combines a fine tone with a marvellously assured sense of phrasing.

GREGORIO ALLEGRI

(1582–1652)

The Sistine Chapel was built by Pope Sixtus IV to aggrandize not just himself and his family but the very office of the papacy itself. Subsequent popes contributed to its visual splendour, most notably through the frescoes of Michelangelo, but much of the chapel's fame derived from its music. The choir became a yardstick for choral excellence, and contributed to the refinement of polyphonic singing which culminated in the spirtualized serenity of Palestrina (see p.295). Its most celebrated work, however, came from an obscure composer of the next generation, Gregorio Allegri, whose setting of the *Miserere Mei* (Psalm 51 in the English Bible) was performed three times during Holy Week from the year of its creation until 1870. So renowned did this work become that its music was a closely guarded secret and illicit copyists were threatened with excommunication – though this did not stop the 14-year-old Mozart transcribing it from memory after hearing it once.

In fact the reputation of Allegri's *Miserere* derived not so much from the music itself – a simple harmonized chant – as from the astonishingly ornate embellishments improvised by members of the choir. This skill was gradually lost over the centuries so that the version that we usually hear today is one using ornamentation fixed around the end of the eighteenth century. It may be less dramatic than original performances, but its embellishment – above all the climactic top C – makes it one of the most rarefied and ethereal pieces in the whole of Catholic church music.

Allegri's musical career began in 1591 as a chorister at Rome's San Luigi dei Francesi, where he took lessons with the *maestro di cappella* Giovanni Bernardino Nanino, a follower of Palestrina. When his voice broke, Gregorio was replaced by his younger brother Domenico, but he returned as an alto in 1601. About four year laters later, he took holy orders and left Rome, taking up positions as composer and singer at the cathedrals of Fermo and Tivoli. After a brief spell as *maestro di cappella* of Santo Spirito in Sassia, Rome, Allegri joined the papal choir at the end of 1629. He retained the position until his death – some 22 years later, and was elected *maestro di cappella* by his colleagues for the Holy Year of 1650.

In his previous appointments Allegri had adopted the new more expressive style of composition (the *seconda prattica*), but in the papal chapel, where no instruments were permitted, he returned to the *stile antico* (or *prima prattica*) as exemplified by Palestrina. Very little of this music has been recorded. At its best, as in the six-part *Missa Vidi Turbam Magnam*, Allegri breathes new life into the old forms with a wide range of contrasted voice groupings and a masterful control of sonority.

MISERERE

The *Miserere*, a penitential psalm much concerned with sin, was performed at Lauds on the three days before Easter. These were Tenebrae services – as they progressed, the candles which illuminated the chapel were extinguished one by one until, in almost complete darkness, the *Miserere* was performed. In Allegri's setting the verses of the psalm alternate between plainsong (the even verses) and *falsobordone* or harmonized chant (odd verses). A further subdivision occurs: the *falsobordone* is performed in a five-part version and a four-part version by different choirs. Originally the *falsobordone* sections were a vehicle for improvised embellishments of a highly virtuosic nature in which the castrati in particular excelled. In the eighteenth century these were described by Charles Burney as "... certain customs and expressions ... such as swelling and diminishing the notes altogether; accelerating or retarding the measure, singing some stanzas quicker than others. . ." But already the tradition of improvisation was lost and what Burney is describing is really an interpretation of Allegri's simple harmonies onto which the embellishments had been fixed. Burney introduced the work to England but its resurgence in modern times is due to the recording made by King's College Choir in the early 1960s.

◑ **Goodman; King's College Choir; Willcocks** (Decca 421 147-2; with Palestrina's *Stabat Mater*).

Thirty or so years on and this performance still packs a punch. The treble soloist Roy Goodman (now a well-known conductor) had been cavorting around the football pitch minutes before this recording was made, but he still produced an effortless purity of tone and incisiveness which has never been bettered. The sound is warm and natural for such a notoriously difficult acoustic.

O A Sei Voci (Astrée Auvidis E8524; with *Missa Vidi Turbam Magnam & Motets*).

An entire disc of music by Allegri is something of a rarity. A Sei Voci (in fact a choir of ten voices) present a cross-section of Allegri's work, including a sparkling reading of the *Missa Vidi Turbam Magnam*. There are two versions of the *Miserere* – the familiar modern edition, and one which attempts to reconstruct seventeenth-century ornamentation. The two versions are strikingly different: the ornamented version is as quirkily animated (with some odd harmonies which recall Bulgarian women's choirs) as the other is serenely predictable.

LOUIS ANDRIESSEN

(1939–)

Louis Andriessen, Holland's foremost living composer, has a reputation as a musical iconoclast. He was one of the first European composers to break with modernism, developing a musical language which combines the hypnotic textures of Minimalism, the rhythmic dynamism of Stravinsky, and the mathematical structures of J.S. Bach. Jazz is another important influence, especially bebop and boogie-woogie – music which he admires both for its coolness and its classicism. During the past twenty years Andriessen has combined his work as a composer and pianist with a teaching post in The Hague, and has become a guru to a whole generation of radical young composers.

Born in 1939 in Utrecht, Andriessen studied at The Hague Royal Conservatory with his father Hendrik and with Holland's first serial composer, Kees van Baaren, before further studies with Luciano Berio (see p.53). During the 1970s his left-wing politics led him to write for ensembles other than the conventional symphony orchestra and he created some of his most radical utterances. Two pieces, *De Volharding* (Perseverance, 1972) and *Hoketus* (1975–77), led to the formation of ensembles named after those pieces, which blurred the distinctions between "high" and "low" culture. De Volharding consisted of jazz musicians equally at home at political rallies and in the concert hall, while Hoketus were a heavily amplified group of classically trained rock musicians whose aim was to play loud, fast and dirty. Hoketus has since disbanded, but the piece of that name remains widely performed: its searing rhythmic drive and unique sound world (saxophones, electric pianos, congas, bass guitars, panpipes) defined a new branch of urban minimalism – a far cry from the cool, laid-back quality of much American minimal music of the time.

With *De Staat* (1973–76) Andriessen began a series of pieces for large ensemble which culminated in his monumental music theatre work, *De Materie* (Matter, 1985–88) – an exploration of the relationship between spirit and matter in four interdependent non-narrative works. Andriessen continues to compose on a large scale. His artistic collaboration with the British film-maker Peter Greenaway has recently resulted in the operas *Rosa* (1991) and *Vermeer* – scheduled for performance in 1999.

DE STAAT

Andriessen wrote *De Staat* as a contribution to the discussion about the place of music in politics: "The moment the musical material is ordered . . . it becomes culture and, as such, a given social fact." Using extracts from Plato's *Republic* which warn of

VAN ZUYLEN/LEBRECHT COLLECTION

Louis Andriessen

the socially disruptive influence of certain types of music, *De Staat* is scored for four women's voices and twenty-five instrumentalists. The austere opening of the work – a series of canons for four oboes – has the remote and precise beauty of a mosaic. Flatulent low brass break up this restrained beginning and, throughout the work, stark contrasts of instrumental timbre are cleverly employed as if to illustrate Plato's dictum "beware of changing to a new kind of music, for the change always involves far-reaching danger". This piece frequently sounds dangerous, with its proliferation of frenzied ostinatos between cool incantatory choruses. The influence of Stravinsky and Bach is evident in the clear textures and motorized rhythms, yet the complex harmonic language and raw intensity of the work are very much Andriessen's own.

⊙ Schoenberg Ensemble; de Leeuw (Nonesuch 7559-79251-2).

The Schoenberg Ensemble and Reinbert de Leeuw have given the premieres of many of Andriessen's works for large ensemble over the past ten years. Their playing on this 35-minute CD, in a work which makes huge demands on the stamina and rhythmic accuracy of the performers, is both exciting and technically superb.

DE STIJL

Written for the group Kaalslaag, and completed in 1985, *De Stijl* forms the third part of *De Materie*. Andriessen conceived the overall stucture of the work as a translation into musical terms of the geometrical proportions of Mondrian's painting, *Composition with Red, Yellow and Blue* (1927), creating the text by juxtaposing writings on mathematical theory with reminiscences about Mondrian and his penchant for dancing. Much of the work's bristling energy is derived from the heavily amplified big band, which includes electric guitars, synthesizers, "heavy metal" percussion (ie four car bumpers) and boogie-woogie piano. Over a battery of strident and compulsive dance rhythms, a choir of female voices intones impassively. The perpetually restless energy of the instrumentalists conjures up more of a living and unpredictable presence than the vocalists, and despite the long, drawn-out chords that end *De Stijl* this is a work which is both exhilarating and unnerving.

⊙ Schoenberg/Asko Ensembles; de Leeuw; Orkest de Volharding; Hempel (Nonesuch 7559-79342-2; with *M is for Man, Music and Mozart*).

This performance of *De Stijl* (also available on a complete recording of *De Materie*) is even more hard-drive than *De Staat* and conveys much of the power of what Andriessen calls "the terrifying twenty-first century orchestra". It is coupled with the music for Peter Greenaway's film *M is for Man, Music and Mozart*, in which the soprano Astrid Series' vibrato-free voice is the perfect vehicle for Greenaway's icy lyrics.

MALCOLM ARNOLD

(1921–)

Like Robert Simpson, Malcom Arnold is one of the most traditional of modern English composers. Although there are traces of jazz (which he loves) in some of his music, his output is based almost exclusively on strong engaging melodies supported by diatonic harmony, and it has found a stable if static audience. Still writing well into his seventies, Arnold has produced a vast amount of orchestral music, including dozens of concertos, overtures, film scores, dances and suites, in which he displays an enviable skill as an orchestrator.

To some extent his traditionalism, his apparent facility, and the ease with which he moves from so-called light music to more "serious" genres, has meant that his critical fortunes have wavered more dramatically than most. The biggest patron of music in Britain, the BBC, practically ignored Arnold throughout the 1960s, when the Controller of Music, William Glock, instigated a policy favouring serialism and the avant-garde. The composer's own capacity for self-destruction also led to many creatively lean periods: alcholism caused the collapse of both his marriages and in 1981 he was hospitalized following a complete mental breakdown.

His music reflects the complexity and contradictions of his life. His years as a trumpeter, principally with the London Philharmonic, gave him a thorough grounding in the fundamentals of orchestration. His eclecticism is revealed in the fact that two of his greatest musical heroes are Berlioz and Louis Armstrong (whose playing inspired Arnold to take up the trumpet), but more apparent influences – particularly in his symphonies – are Mahler and Shostakovich: both composers with a tendency to set up stark, often contradictory, contrasts of mood in their works, a strategy equally evident in Arnold's large-scale work.

ORCHESTRAL MUSIC

Some of Arnold's most appealing music is to be found in his series of national dances, a continuing sequence of pieces derived from the folk songs of various countries. These tuneful orchestral showpieces, designed to entertain the perfomer as much as the listener, make the most immediate introduction to Arnold's music.

Much of Arnold's symphonic writing (his most substantial achievement) relies on the use of extremely startling contrasts of mood. Time and again, music that seems to establish one kind of emotional landscape will be bluntly interrupted – or ironically undermined – by something alien to it. This usually takes the form of direct contradiction: the tranquil up against the strident, the sentimental mocked by the mischievous. The impact of these contrasts is occasionly lessened by Arnold's tendency to overuse them, but it's apparent straight away in his *Symphony No. 1* (1949) whose dynamic first movement has a typically Arnoldian sense of an unresolved struggle between conflicting forces. The best known of the symphonies, the sombre fifth (1961), also abounds in paradoxes right from the first movement, in which the prevailing mood of unease has glints of lyricism shining through it. Even more startling is the Andante, seemingly a parody of a Mahler slow movement but becoming increasingly unstable as it progresses.

O English, Scottish, Cornish and Irish Dances: Philharmonia Orchestra; Thomson (Chandos CHAN 8867).

Bryden Thomson's recording of the *English, Scottish, Cornish and Irish Dances* is spontaneous and brimming with life. The recording is clear and well-focused and the playing of the Philharmonia is very light and responsive. It's part of a series of Arnold's music made by the Chandos company, which includes recordings of all nine symphonies by Richard Hickox.

O Symphonies Nos. 1 & 5: Royal Philharmonic Orchestra; Handley (Conifer 75605 512572-2).

It's a measure of the depth of the recent Arnold revival that no fewer than three complete symphony cycles are now available, all of which are extremely fine. Handley on Conifer is the more measured of the three, with an approach that is warmer and more expansive than his rivals on Naxos and Chandos. These two symphonies make a good starting point before moving on to the more acerbic world of the seventh and eighth symphonies.

GRAZYNA BACEWICZ

(1909–1969)

Poland's most important composer between Szymanowski (see p.419) and Lutosławski (see p.228), Grazyna Bacewicz was born in Łodz into a musical family – her brother Kiejstut was a fine pianist with whom she frequently performed – and began studying at the Warsaw conservatory in 1928. She continued her musical education in Paris with two of the most influential teachers of the period, Carl Flesch for violin and Nadia Boulanger for composition. She was unfortunate to be entered for the Wieniawski violin competition in 1935, the same year as David Oistrakh and Ginette Neveu, two of the greatest violinists of the century. She did well enough, however, to gain a first-class distinction and went on to have an outstanding career as a soloist, being especially noted as an interpreter of the first violin concerto of her fellow countryman and mentor Karol Szymanowski.

Unsurprisingly much of her best writing is for the violin. She wrote no fewer than seven violin concertos and five sonatas for violin and piano, but even her orchestral writing tends to locate the dynamic drive in the string section. The music composed before 1960 is often described as neo-classical and, though she disliked the term, it adequately summarizes her emphasis on clear contrapuntal lines, the general brightness of her sound-world, and her avoidance of sentimentality. That is not to say her work lacks emotion – for example, the slow movement of the concerto for string orchestra, one of her best works, contains a sensuous and haunting cello part set against soft but rhythmically insistent high strings. Occasionally the momentum flags and the writing can sometimes seem a rather schematic interchange of voices, but on the whole she maintains a firm grip on the proceedings. From 1960 her work was marked by an attempt to assimilate some of the sonorities of the avant-garde, particularly those techniques, such as glissandi and clusters, often associated with her younger compatriot Penderecki (see p.300). The CD reviewed below makes a good introduction to her work.

⊙ Sonata No. 4 for Violin and Piano; Piano Sonata No. 2; Concerto for String Orchestra; Violin Concerto No. 7: Statkiewicz; Utrecht; Zimerman; Janowski; Polish Chamber Orchestra; National Philharmonic Orchestra Warsaw; Maksymiuk; Markowski (Olympia OCD 392).

There is a wide variety of music on this disc, ranging from an electrifying account of the brilliant *Concerto for String Orchestra* (1948) to a live performance of the *Violin Concerto No. 7* (1965), a work high on atmospheric effects if rather lower on coherence. In general the earlier works are the most memorable, with an infectious wit and vitality. The *Piano Sonata No. 2*, here given a bravura performance by Krystian Zimerman, is a virtuosic catalogue of pianistic tricks, at times reminiscent of Ravel but with a rather more restrained harmonic palette. Better still is the *Violin Sonata No. 4* (1949), a work similar to Bartók in its abrasive energy, but in no way derivative. It has an unnervingly edgy slow movement in which a lilting but anguished lullaby is framed by defiant-sounding broken chords on the piano.

STRING QUARTET NO. 4

As well as the five violin sonatas, Bacewicz wrote a wide variety of chamber music throughout her life, including seven string quartets. In 1951 her *String Quartet No. 4*, written the previous year, won first prize at the International Composers Competition in Liège. This is an arresting three-movement work in an adventurous and individual voice, with a powerful opening movement in which contrasts are set up between darkly contemplative music and a more abandoned rhapsodic style. Much of Bacewicz's chamber music reveals, in the words of Adrian Thomas, "a tougher more challenging musical idiom" than her more public orchestral work. There are passages of serial writing in *String Quartet No. 7* (1965), for example, as well as a fascinating exploration of different textures and timbres.

⊙ The Maggini Quartet (ASV CD DCA 908; with Szymanowski, *String Quartets Nos. 1 & 2*).

The Maggini Quartet give a bold and passionate performance of the fourth quartet and really do justice to its striking sonorities. This well-planned disc allows the listener to hear the best of Bacewicz's quartets alongside those of her mentor Szymanowski.

CARL PHILIPP EMANUEL BACH

(1714–1788)

Of Johann Sebastian Bach's twenty children, three were outstanding musicians in their own right. Of these three – Wilhelm Friedmann, Johann Christian and Carl Philipp Emanuel – the last was the most influential as a composer, creating a bridge between the exuberant Baroque style of his father and the Classical style of Haydn and Mozart. While always acknowledging a great debt to his father (his only teacher), he came to reject the complexity of polyphonic music, preferring a much more subjective and dramatic approach, full of unexpected and odd shifts in harmony, and with an emphasis on melody – a style known as *empfindsamer Stil* (expressive style).

Although C.P.E. Bach's educational background was broader than his father's – he trained as a lawyer and preferred the company of writers and intellectuals to that of musicians – he suffered a similar hard grind as a musician: in his case nearly thirty badly paid years as a keyboard player at the court of Frederick the Great at Potsdam. Frederick's taste was conservative, and the experimental nature of much of C.P.E. Bach's music meant that he never won preferment – indeed his principal duty seems to have been to accompany Frederick, a keen amateur flautist, on the harpsichord. Perhaps it was to widen his fame outside the narrow confines of Potsdam that he published his *Essay on the True Art of Playing Keyboard Instruments*, a highly influential treatise which was used as a teaching aid by both Mozart and Beethoven. In 1767, upon the death of his godfather, Georg-Philipp Telemann, the restless C.P.E. Bach succeeded him as music director of the five principal churches in Hamburg. His workload was enormous but, away from his church duties, the freer atmosphere of the commercial city-state made the last twenty years of his life much more stimulating.

KEYBOARD MUSIC

C.P.E. Bach's favourite keyboard instrument was the clavichord, a soft and delicate-sounding instrument whose strings were struck like those of the piano, rather than plucked like the harpsichord, and whose dynamics could therefore be controlled by touch. He was an immensely sensitive performer, famed above all for the emotional intensity of his improvisations, a quality most evident in his fantasias and the slow movements of his sonatas, which are more harmonically quirky and unconventional than those of his great successors Haydn and Mozart.

⊙ Sonatas and Rondos: Bärtschi (Jecklin-Disco JD 683-2).

Surprisingly, C.P.E. Bach's keyboard music has not been taken up by pianists in the same way as his father's or Domenico Scarlatti's. That it can sound equally convincing on the piano is proved by this fine recital by Werner Bärtschi, who plays four sonatas, two rondos and a fantasia from various stages in C.P.E. Bach's career. Bärtschi's playing is cleanly articulated and he possesses a sufficiently delicate touch to do justice to the evasive, will-o'-the-wisp nature of this subtle and beautiful music. He's at his most sensitive in the first piece on the disc, the G minor sonata of 1746, in which the sudden changes of mood and speed are very deftly handled.

CHORAL MUSIC

The sheer volume of music that C.P.E. Bach had to provide for the Hamburg churches inevitably had a deleterious effect on its quality – as well as composing in a hurry, he also was obliged to knock together composite works using music by his relations and by Telemann. Of his later works the oratorio *Die Israeliten in der Wuste* (1769) is worth hearing, but his choral masterpiece is an earlier work, the *Magnificat* of 1749. The opening words of praise of the Virgin Mary are set with a thrilling energy that looks back to the Baroque, especially to the setting of the same words by his father. However, apart from a fugal final chorus, this is not a contrapuntal work but one whose impact derives from its operatic arias and its vigorous choruses.

⊙ Magnificat: Gachinger Kantorei Stuttgart; Bach-Collegium Stuttgart; Rilling (Hanssler 98.970; with J.N. Bach, *Missa Brevis*).

Rilling is a veteran conductor of Baroque choral music, and this recording from the mid-1970s still sounds fresh and lively, with clear and incisive singing from the chorus. The soloists are extremely fine, with the soprano Arleen Auger excelling in her long and tender aria *Quia respexit humilitatem*, while the alto, Helen Watts, and tenor, Kurt Equiluz, provide one of the work's highlights in their dynamic duet *Deposuit potentes* (He has put down the mighty). The *Magnificat* is coupled with an interesting but considerably less exciting *Missa Brevis* by Johann Nikolaus Bach, J.S. Bach's second cousin.

THE SYMPHONIES

With their emphasis on the emotional manipulation of the listener, the symphonies of C.P.E. Bach exemplify the *empfindsamer Stil* just as much as his keyboard pieces. They are intense, compact works whose three movements tend to follow a pattern: fast and agitated, followed by slow and sorrowful, and concluding fast and cheerful. The best and most adventurous of them, the six *Hamburg Symphonies* were commissioned by Baron van Swieten (later a patron of Mozart), who allowed the composer a completely free hand. The result is startlingly original: audacious changes of key, sudden contrasts in dynamics and complete breaks in the musical flow all contribute to the music's restless excitement.

O The Six Hamburg Symphonies: C.P.E. Bach Chamber Orchestra; Haenchen (Capriccio 10 106).

The volatility of these symphonies makes them difficult to perform without sounding incoherent, but Haenchen and the C.P.E. Bach Chamber Orchestra avoid the pitfalls by taking the mood-swings completely seriously: their fast movements really rattle along, while their slow movements have a languidness that seems entirely authentic. Occasionally they are overenthusiastic and the ensemble becomes a little ragged, but this is a small price to pay for such energy and commitment.

THE CELLO CONCERTOS

The three delightful cello concertos of C.P.E. Bach are thought to date from around 1750. They are unlikely to have been composed for Potsdam and may have been first performed by Berlin amateurs with Christian Schale (the court orchestra cellist) as soloist. Their outer movements, which display the kind of restless, stop-start energy of the *Hamburg Symphonies*, follow the pattern of Baroque concertos by having alternate solo and tutti sections. The striking slow movements are notable for their poetic solo lines, which seem to aspire to the intensity of vocal expression. In particular, the melody of the doleful slow movement of the A minor concerto is made up of short-breathed phrases that seem to suggest sighing or even sobbing.

◑ Bylsma; Orchestra of the Age of Enlightenment; Leonhardt (Virgin Classics VM5 61401 2).

Anner Bylsma is the doyen of Baroque cellists, and this disc shows him at his best, with performances of great sensitivity especially in the slow movements, which he draws out with great tenderness. The orchestral support is a little disappointing on account of its rather brash approach to the fast movements, but this disc is worth buying for Bylsma's playing alone.

JOHANN SEBASTIAN BACH

(1685–1750)

Johann Sebastian Bach is unquestionably the greatest composer before Mozart, and arguably the greatest ever. On one level, his music is an example of supreme craftsmanship, mastering with mathematical precision the formal problems of counterpoint, producing keyboard music in which as many as five separate lines of argument are simultaneously sustained. Yet this is also music of the deepest humanity, and not just in the most overtly dramatic of Bach's works, such as his depiction of Christ's suffering in the *St Matthew Passion*. To listen to a complete performance of the *Goldberg Variations* – as purely abstract as anything he wrote – is to participate in a journey of extraordinary transformations, in which the final return of the original theme is a deeply moving and satisfying experience.

Bach came not so much from a musical family as from a musical dynasty: the line of musical Bachs begins all the way back in the sixteenth century and extends to the middle of the nineteenth, when it finally comes to an end. And to a large extent, despite his superior talent, Johann Sebastian's career was no more distinguished than those of several of his forbears. For Bach there was to be none of the international experience and renown of his great contemporary Handel.

After spells as church organist at Arnstadt and Mulhausen, Bach's first important position was at Weimar, where in 1708 he became the court organist and a chamber musician to the duke, Wilhelm Ernst. When eight years later a disgruntled Bach overinsistently applied for permission to leave, having been passed over for the senior post of Kapellmeister, the duke's response was to jail him for one month for his impertinence. (Disagreements with employers were to occur throughout his career.) The position he was attempting to leave for, and which he took up in 1718, was Kapellmeister at the small court of Prince

LEBRECHT COLLECTION

Johann Sebastian Bach

Leopold of Anhalt-Cöthen. Here he composed most of his instrumental and orchestral music, since the prince belonged to the Calvinist church, whose austere services employed little music beside psalm singing. When the prince married, his enthusiasm for music waned and in 1722 Bach applied to be cantor at the Thomasschule (the school of St Thomas) in Leipzig – rather reluctantly, since it seemed like a demotion. He got the position, but only after his friend Telemann (see p.434), among others, had turned the job down.

Bach was to spend the last 27 years of his life dealing with the gruelling workload at Leipzig, where his duties were almost impossibly demanding. As well as teaching at the Thomasschule (his primary task), he was also responsible for the music for the church of St Thomas and three of the town's other churches, and on top of that was expected to provide music for important civic occasions. In his first six years there he composed a staggering amount of music, including five cycles of cantatas for the main services in the Lutheran Church calendar, and his two magnificent settings of the Passion. He also found time, during the Leipzig years, to father thirteen children by his second wife Anna Magdalena (of whom only six grew to adulthood) to add to the four surviving children of his first marriage.

Such were the stresses of work that by 1729 there was sufficient friction between Bach and his employers for him to consider moving on once again. Among the problems, according to Bach, was the fact that "the place is very expensive and the authorities are hard to please and care little for music". In the end he stayed put, but he diversified his compositional activities, most significantly by writing for the Collegium Musicum of Leipzig, a musical society of students and professionals, originally founded by Telemann, which met and performed in Zimmermann's popular coffee house.

He died in July 1750, leaving unfinished his last extended project, a complex and theoretical exploration of counterpoint called *The Art of Fugue*. Even before his death he was regarded as hopelessly old-fashioned and was attacked for his "turgidity" by a leading critic Johann Adolphe Scheibe. Bach's work remained under-performed – though not completely neglected – until well into the nineteenth century, and the most talented of his sons, Carl Philipp Emanuel (see p.10), was to develop a style markedly different from that of his father.

CHORAL MUSIC

The Lutheran church had always regarded music as an integral component of its liturgy, with a strong emphasis on congregational participation in the form of hymns or chorales, often to words and music by Luther himself. The music for the main Sunday service, which could last as long as five hours, consisted of a motet, the Lutheran Mass, several chorales (a type of hymn) and a cantata. Then there was the music for special occasions, like the settings of the Passion for Easter. In Leipzig, where the bulk of his choral music was written, Bach was responsible for providing the music (which meant writing most of it) for all four churches, of which St Thomas and St Nicholas were the most important. Most of his singers and some of the instrumentalists required would have come from the Thomasschule, with the rest recruited from the town. Standards would thus have been extremely variable, but this did not prevent Bach from writing consistently rich and exhilarating works that often make great demands on the singers.

Chorales and the setting of biblical texts were the dominant musical forms in the Lutheran Church until about 1700, when the theologian-poet Neumeister published a collection of religious verses in German that were intended to be sung. These so-called cantatas were not narrative pieces, but rather commentaries on the biblical texts used in the service – most importantly on the Gospel reading. Texts were extremely pious, often emphasizing God's mercy in the face of the abject nature of man. All the major German composers wrote them, but no one wrote music as ambitious or as lavish as Bach's, in which recitatives and arias, choruses and chorales were often combined together into one dramatic whole. About three-fifths of Bach's cantata output, over two hundred works, has survived but they remain the least known of his music, partly because of their number but also because their often morbid texts do not appeal to modern tastes. Bach also wrote several secular cantatas, either to celebrate civic or royal occasions or – as in the so-called "Coffee" and "Peasant" cantatas – purely as quasi-operatic entertainments. Not all the cantatas are as good as each other, some contain unidiomatic and occasionally meandering vocal lines, but the best are masterpieces and should not be ignored.

Among Bach's most celebrated choral works are the *B Minor Mass* and his settings of the Passion, written for performance each year at Easter time. As in his cantatas, Bach took an already existing genre – in this case the musical setting of the gospel accounts of Christ's suffering and death – and turned it into a monumental epic which emphasized, above all, the human dimension of the story. Passion settings had existed since medieval times but from the mid-seventeenth century additional texts were added to the basic narratives as meditations and commentaries on the proceedings. Again, like the cantatas, the Passions aroused mixed feeling in their listeners. Many disapproved of what they perceived as an opera performance in a sacred setting, and indeed the swift changes of mood, from the consoling tone of the chorales to the sheer viciousness of some of the crowd choruses, is shockingly direct in the way it involves and implicates the listener in the story. According to Bach's obituarist, he wrote a total of five Passions but only two, the Passions of St Matthew and St John, have survived.

THE CANTATAS

One of the most famous of all Bach's cantatas is the rousing eightieth cantata, *Ein' feste Burg* (A Mighty Fortress), originally written in 1715 but revised for use at Leipzig in 1723 (numbering does not signify the order in which the cantatas were written). It is a typical example of a cantata in which Bach uses a simple chorale tune (in this case one by Luther) around which to build a large and magnificent musical edifice. On one level the cantata is a set of variations on a theme with which the congregation were completely familiar: from the opening chorus, in which the voices create an elaborate fantasia around the chorale, through various permutations of soloist and thematic material until the final singing of the chorale, in which the congregation may well have joined.

As well as large-scale works involving combinations of soloists and chorus, Bach also wrote a number of solo cantatas of which the best is *Ich habe genug* (It is enough). The text is a response to the biblical story of Simeon who, having seen the Christ child, felt he could die in peace. It is one of Bach's most intensely personal and consolatory works, with the opening words reiterated throughout its length. A solo oboe magically interweaves itself around the vocal line in the yearning opening aria (a very characteristic device in the more lyrical cantata arias); the second aria is a gentle, reassuring lullaby; the third, a joyous welcoming of death.

Cantata No. 106 (known as "Actus Tragicus") is not part of the cycle of cantatas written for the liturgical year but a funeral cantata written for a specific memorial service, possibly that of Bach's uncle Tobias Lämmerhirt who died in 1707. If this early date is correct, it would signal a turning point in Bach's choral music, for this is a mature and profound work which, like *Cantata No. 82*, creates a remarkable mood of calm serenity and consolation from its very beginning. Bach's talents as a subtle dramatizer of words (mainly from the Bible) is everywhere apparent. At the heart of the work a beautiful tenor arioso gives way to an admonitory bass aria, which leads to a sombre choral fugue, which diminishes into a lone soprano voice exclaiming the word "Jesu!" – a moment of touching vulnerability and an expressive masterstroke.

No. 140, *Wachet auf* (Sleepers Wake), and No. 147, *Herz und Mund* (Heart and Mouth), are two of the most popular of all the cantatas. The theme of the first is that of the soul eagerly anticipating the arrival of Christ like a bride awaiting the bridegroom. The joyous, expectant mood is established in the opening chorus by the underlying restless rhythm over which Philipp Nicolai's soaring chorale tune is spun out by Bach into ever richer configurations. *Herz und Mund*, more monumental and varied in mood, is a meditation on receiving Jesus – into the womb of the Virgin Mary and into the hearts of man. It is famous for the chorale that closes each of its two sections, a melody popularly known as *Jesu, Joy of Man's Desiring*.

O Complete cantatas: Amsterdam Baroque Choir and Orchestra; Koopman (Erato – 5 volumes so far).

The complete cantatas are currently available in two performances: the pioneering set on Teldec, directed by Nikolaus Harnoncourt and Gustav Leonhardt, and a set of individual discs on the German label Hänssler, directed by

Helmuth Rilling. The Harnoncourt/Leonhardt discs now sound rather bald and prosaic. Rilling's performances have more warmth and emotion but the sound quality in many of the recordings is dry and ungiving. Better than either of these is the ongoing series on Erato directed by Ton Koopman, which has now reached its fifth volume, and a fine cycle of Japanese forces on the Bis label. So far Koopman just has the edge, though there's very little in it. Koopman's characteristic buoyancy of approach is much in evidence, as is the way he allows his soloists their own interpretative space. It's a series certainly worth thinking about collecting, perhaps after investigating some of the better-known cantatas listed below.

O Cantata No. 80: Schlick, Lesne, Crook, Kooy; Ghent Collegium Vocale; Herreweghe (Harmonia Mundi HMC90 1326; with *Magnificat*).

Herreweghe's approach emphasises the way the strands of polyphony move in and out of each other like living organisms. There's very little aggression in his performances and some may find them underdramatized. For me he makes just the right emphasis on musical sense without recourse to self-seeking stylistic idiosyncrasies.

O Cantata No. 82: Hotter; Philharmonia; Bernard (EMI CDH7 63198-2; with Brahms Lieder).

This cantata is frequently a showcase for singers who don't usually sing Bach. Few have brought such a degree of sensitivity to it as the great bass-baritone Hans Hotter in this 1950 recording. Renowned as a Wagnerian and as a Lieder singer, his awareness of textual meaning is effortlessly conveyed through an unforced shaping of Bach's long lines. One of the great Bach recordings.

O Cantata No. 82: Argenta, Mertens; La Petite Bande; Kuijken (Accent ACC 9395; with *Cantatas BWV 49 & 58*).

Mertens is not in the same league as Hotter but, like him, he lets the music convey the meaning. What is special about this performance is the way the voice is integrated with the subtle orchestral playing of La Petite Bande. In addition the two cantatas for soprano and bass, which function as a kind of musical conversation, are given powerfully concentrated performances by the well-matched soloists.

O Cantata No. 106: Argenta, Chance, Rolfe Johnson, Varcoe; Monteverdi Choir and English Baroque Soloists; Gardiner (Archiv 429 78-2N; with *Motet BWV 118b & Mourning Ode BWV 198*).

This gentle and reassuring work here gets a suitably sensitive performance. Gardiner is a Bach interpreter who usually prefers to point up the drama of the choral works, but although there is much spirited singing – notably in the final God-glorying chorus – what most impresses is the eloquent restraint of the whole piece, which establishes exactly the right mixture of seriousness and joy.

O Cantatas Nos. 140 & 147: Monteverdi Choir; Gardiner (Archiv 431 809-2).

This is a wonderful recording of two of Bach's most popular cantatas. In particular the choral singing has an energy and a bounce which is positively uplifting. This disc would make the perfect introduction to the cantatas as a whole.

THE ST MATTHEW PASSION

Written in the late 1720s, the *St Matthew Passion* is Bach's grandest and arguably his greatest work. The narrative, taken from chapters 26 and 27 of St Matthew's Gospel, is sung in a highly expressive recitative by a tenor Evangelist. Direct speech is allocated to soloists; a bass singing the role of Christ and the remaining "characters" distributed among a range of voices. The most animated and contrapuntal music is given to the chorus in their capacity as crowd. Throughout the narrative Picander's additional words (for both soloists and chorus) balance the urgency of the story and provide an element of inward meditation which is highly personal. The prevailing mood of the work is more contemplative than dramatic and, though a terrible feeling of tragedy pervades the music, there is also an overwhelming sense of community that binds all the participants together, in particular through the vehicle of the Passion chorale which punctuates the drama at five separate points.

O Rolfe Johnson, Schmidt, Bonney, Monoyiof, Von Otter, Chance, Crook, Bär, Hauptmann; London Oratory Junior Choir & Monteverdi Choir; Gardiner (Archiv 427 648-2; 3 CDs).

The *St Matthew Passion* has been staged several times this century and Gardiner's ardently dramatic interpretation immediately makes you realize why. His speeds are faster than most but always in the service of narrative momentum, as is his use of an extreme dynamic range. The soloists, who seem to have been selected for their clear and open delivery, are uniformly excellent and match the bright and incisive style of the chorus. If this sounds too strident an approach, then rest assured that the more contemplative moments have all the requisite tenderness and sensitivity. All in all, a remarkable achievement.

◑ Pears, Fischer-Dieskau, Schwarzkopf, Ludwig, Gedda, Berry; Philharmonia Choir and Orchestra; Klemperer (EMI CMS 7 63058 2; 3 CDs).

Klemperer's *St Matthew Passion* is one of the great Bach recordings of the last forty years. It does sound very old-fashioned: forces are big and speeds slow to the point of stateliness, but what makes this account unrivalled in its grandeur and solemnity is Klemperer's ability to control a large chorus, and his unfailing sense of the shape and direction of a phrase. The choice of soloists is inspired, and a devotional intensity is sustained through the whole work, making the final chorus *Wir setzen uns mit Tränen nieder* (We sit down in tears) almost unbearably powerful.

THE ST JOHN PASSION

The *St John Passion*, first performed on Good Friday 1724, has, until recently, been judged the lesser of the two extant Passions. It is certainly on a smaller scale, and is more concise and concentrated with the gospel text dwelling in greater detail on the cruelty of the crowd and the dilemma of

JIM FOUR/DGG

John Eliot Gardiner

Pilate. The additional texts, selected from a number of authors, adds up to a less coherent whole than Picander's *St Matthew* additions. Even so, it is a remarkably powerful work, particularly so in its dramatic crowd scenes.

⊙ Argenta, Holton, Rolfe Johnson, Varcoe, Hauptmann, Chance; Monteverdi Choir; Gardiner (Archiv 419 324-2; 2 CDs).

Gardiner's bright, forceful style is admirably suited to the *St John Passion*. As usual the Monteverdi Choir are superbly flexible and versatile: sinister and aggressive in the choruses at the Crucifixion, powerful but tender in the chorales. They are matched by the fine soloists, with Anthony Rolfe Johnson immensely authoritative as the Evangelist and a pure-toned Nancy Argenta outstanding in the soprano arias.

THE MAGNIFICAT

A Magnificat is a musical setting of the Virgin Mary's words of joy ("My soul doth magnify the Lord") to her cousin Elizabeth, after she had conceived. Bach's first setting, his only surviving one, was written for the Christmas celebrations of 1723, and is one of the most Italianate of all his choral works, with a splendid Vivaldi-like blast of rippling semiquavers in the opening chorus. It is broken up into sections like a cantata, and involves soloists as well as a chorus, providing them with some melodies that are disarmingly simple and direct by Bach's normally complex standards.

⊙ Ghent Collegium Vocale; Herreweghe (Harmonia Mundi HMC90 1326; with *Cantata BWV 80*).

Herreweghe is one of the finest recent interpreters of Bach's choral music. There's a fluidity in evidence, a sense of the polyphonic lines all flowing together in one direction, that is completely captivating. His judgement of the balance between voices and instruments is exemplary: he treats them as part of one integrated texture, highlighting where appropriate. Especially telling is the soprano solo *Quia respexit humilitatem*, which is effectively a duet between the soprano and a highly vocalized oboe line.

THE CHRISTMAS ORATORIO

Though there is a narrative to the *Weichnachts-Oratorium* or Christmas Oratorio, this is not really an oratorio at all, but a series of cantatas to be performed at the six services that begin with Christmas day and end with Epiphany (January 6). Plundered from already composed secular cantatas, it would never have been performed as a single work in Bach's time though it forms a musically unified whole. The author of the text is unknown – it was probably Picander, the author of the *St Matthew Passion* and many of the cantatas – and, although not as theatrical as the passion settings, the joyfulness of the text is perfectly evoked by some thrillingly exuberant music. Nowhere is this more evident than in the work's brilliant opening, which combines kettledrums, a fanfare and a rousing chorus to the words "Jauchzet, frohlocket!" (Rejoice, Exult!).

⊙ Larsson, von Magnus, Prégardien, Mertens; Amsterdam Baroque Choir and Orchestra; Koopman (Erato 0630 14635-2; 2 CDs).

Koopman's approach is to treat this work as one of varying moods and colours without resorting to theatricality. The forces are quite small-scale but there is an intensity to the choral singing which is never overstrained. The recording also boasts, in Christophe Prégardien, the most sweet-toned and convincing Evangelist – direct, unfussy and sincere.

⊙ Schlick, Chance, Crook, Kooy; Collegium Vocale; Herreweghe (Virgin VCD 7 59530 2; 2 CDs).

Herreweghe instantly captures the prevailing festive mood of the work with a sparkling opening, in which the instrumentalists acquit themselves brilliantly. Howard Crook makes a strong and sympathetic Evangelist, and there are no weak links among the other soloists. As with Koopman, the dramatic elements are never overplayed, in keeping with the innocent world of the story.

THE B MINOR MASS

Like the *Christmas Oratorio*, the *B Minor Mass* is a composite work largely put together over two decades from cantata movements, and it was possibly intended as a compendium to show off Bach's skill as a choral composer, rather than as a piece for a specific occasion. Bach sent the Kyrie and the Gloria to the Catholic Elector of Saxony in 1733, along with a letter complaining about his Leipzig employers, and asking for a job, which he did not get. From such unpromising beginnings emerged one of his greatest works. Its first chorus, a stately fugue, establishes the sense of solid and unshakable faith with which the work is imbued. Not all the music is so solemn, however. The glorious Sanctus is an animated rush of energy for six-part choir and high trumpets, with rhythms that suggest dancing rather than worship.

⭘ Argenta, Denley, Tucker, Varcoe; Collegium Musicum 90; Hickox (Chandos CHAN 0533/4; 2 CDs).

Hickox doesn't follow recent tendencies to scale the choral forces right down (sometimes to one voice per part); instead he uses a medium-sized choir that's able to provide clear and bright textures in the Kyrie, but can also pile on the power where necessary – for instance at the beginning of the Gloria. The Kyrie's fugue, which can sound dull and meandering if badly phrased, is here built and shaped with real attention to detail. Similarly the Sanctus, which can be made to swing too much, here sounds controlled and radiant.

⭘ Schlick, Wessel, de Mey, Mertens; Amsterdam Baroque Choir and Orchestra; Koopman (Erato 4509-98478-2; 2 CDs).

There is very little to choose between this and the above recording. Koopman's producers have allowed the acoustic of the Amsterdam church where it was recorded to soften the impact of the voices, making for a more intimate and subdued performance. The result is closer in spirit to a liturgical occasion than Hickox's more bright and energetic concert-hall approach.

ORCHESTRAL MUSIC

It was at Weimar that Bach first came into contact with the Italian style of concerto in which a large instrumental ensemble played in alternation with a smaller group of soloists. It was exemplified by the concertos of Vivaldi, several of which Bach arranged for solo keyboard and as concertos. However, it was at Cöthen that he composed his first original concertos, though these were still largely based on the Vivaldian model. This consisted of three movements (fast–slow–fast): an aria-like slow movement, and outer movements that were characterized by vigorous forward-driven rhythms in which thematic material (the ritornello) repeatedly returned. As well as the concertos mentioned below, he also wrote several that survive only in part – mostly for oboe, some of which have been reconstructed for performance. If the dynamism of the concertos was inspired by Italian models, then the elegance of the four *Orchestral Suites* shows the influence of French forms which by the end of the seventeenth century were highly popular in German aristocratic circles. Bach almost certainly composed all four while at Cöthen, though it is also likely that they were later adapted, along with various concertos, for performance by the Collegium Musicum at Leipzig.

THE BRANDENBURG CONCERTOS

First printed in 1721, the six *Brandenburg Concertos* were dedicated to the Margrave of Brandenburg, who had commissioned them after hearing Bach play two years earlier. All but the first, and possibly the third, were written at Cöthen, and they were undoubtedly conceived primarily for the court orchestra since the unusual orchestration of several of them is known to have matched the players at Bach's disposal there. Largely assembled from other compositions – some of them written around the same time, others earlier – the *Brandenburgs* were probably intended to demonstrate the potential of the concerto form. From the jubilant first to the intimate sixth concerto, Bach develops his thematic material in a more complex and extended fashion than Vivaldi does, and the relationship between the soloist and the orchestra similarly breaks new ground – the extended role of the harpsichord in the fifth sounds in places like an anticipation of Mozart's piano concertos.

◑ Amsterdam Baroque Orchestra; Koopman (Erato 0630 13733-2; 2 CDs).

Koopman is one of the most versatile and exciting of present-day Bach interpreters. Although his approach is essentially an "authentic" one, this recording seems primarily concerned with communicating the sheer exuberance of these pieces. Koopman tends to favour quite snappy tempos, especially in the fifth, but the flair of his soloists means that there is never any sense of rush.

⭘ Il Giardino Armonico; Antonini (Teldec 4509 9844-2; 2 CDs).

This is an even more dynamic performance by a young group based in Italy. Ensemble is extremely tight, tempos even faster than on the Koopman discs (above) and there is some extremely vivid tone colour, especially in the brass section. There are occasional moments of eccentricity but what is lost in subtlety is gained in the sheer panache and evident enjoyment of the playing.

⊙ Bruggen, Kuijken, Bylsma; Leonhardt (Sony SB2K 62946; 2 CDs).

Dating from the mid-1970s, this is a star-studded ensemble directed by the veteran harpsichordist Gustav

Leonhardt. Performances are characterized by a straightforward, unflashy but highly sensitive approach which allows the music to speak for itself.

THE VIOLIN CONCERTOS

The two *Violin Concertos*, in A minor and E major, and the marvellous *Double Violin Concerto in D Minor*, also probably date from Bach's Cöthen period, although it is by no means certain. The E major concerto, which opens with three bold chords (a classic Vivaldian device), comes close to the buoyant mood of the *Brandenburgs*, and also contains one of Bach's most inspired and poignant slow movements, in which the delicate solo melody is framed by slow and sombre music in the lower strings. Best of all is the *Double Concerto*, a marvel of contrapuntal inventiveness, with the imitative solo lines weaving in and out of each other with a playful brilliance in the outer movements, and with a fulsome lyricism in the slow movement.

○ Podger, Manze; Academy of Ancient Music (Harmonia Mundi HMU 907155).

This is an original instrument performance, but in Andrew Manze the Academy have a leader/director of such chutzpah that such designations seem irrelevant. It's not that the music is simply revealed in a fresh light (which it is) but that the sheer enjoyment that the soloists exude is truly infectious. Ornamentation genuinely decorates a line, and there is an almost improvisatory swagger to the proceedings. The sound is just a little too close.

○ Perlman, Zuckerman; English Chamber Orchestra; Barenboim (EMI CDC 7 47856-2).

This recording dates from the late 1960s when Perlman, Zuckerman and Barenboim frequently played together, and there is a rapport and a freshness to this music-making which is genuinely thrilling. Perlman plays the solo concertos with his characteristic sweetness and fullness of tone, which is especially telling in the wonderfully vocal slow movements, and there is a competitive edge to the swagger that both soloists bring to the *Double Concerto*.

THE HARPSICHORD CONCERTOS

Most of Bach's harpsichord concertos started life in another form, usually as concertos for different instruments and, in one case – the *Concerto for Four Harpsichords* – as a concerto by Vivaldi. Transcribing them from a single-line instrument (or intruments) to one capable of playing polyphonically, meant that their textures became denser and the elaboration of their thematic ideas more complicated, so that the piece often undergoes a complete change of character. Several of these harpsichord concertos were written for the Collegium Musicum of Leipzig, and would have been performed with Bach himself at the keyboard.

◑ Amsterdam Baroque Orchestra; Koopman (Erato 4509 91930-2; 2 CDs).

As in the *Brandenburgs*, the most impressive aspect of these performances is their energy and lightness. Koopman takes a refreshingly flexible attitude to his solo part, treating ornamentation in a way that sounds both idiomatic and spontaneous. The balance between soloist and orchestra is near perfect, with the harpsichord seeming to move effortlessly in and out of the orchestral fabric.

THE ORCHESTRAL SUITES

In Baroque music a suite consisted of a set of contrasting movements based on dance forms. All four of Bach's *Orchestral Suites* begin with the kind of grandiose and stately overture that suggests a debt to French music, in particular to Lully. But even here Bach makes the form his own, by writing the fast middle section of each overture in the more complex style of the Italian concerto. But generally the overall mood of the suites evokes the easy-going elegance of court music: the german dance form – the allemande – is discarded, and the optional forms of bourrée, gavotte and minuet begin to dominate. Bach's melodic invention, especially in suites 2 and 3, is at its most easy and inspired – notably in the serene air from *No. 3* (the famous "Air on a G string") and the electrifying flute solo (the *Badinerie*) from *No. 2*.

○ Amsterdam Baroque Orchestra; Koopman (Deutsche Harmonia Mundi RD 77864; 2 CDs).

This is one of Koopman's best recordings. The mixture of formal elegance and excitement which these works require is perfectly achieved by a wonderful nobility of phrasing and finely judged speeds. The result is an unruffled and flawless ensemble which serves to highlight the more dazzling moments – like Wilbert Hazelet's flute playing in Suite no. 2.

KEYBOARD MUSIC

Bach's renown in his own lifetime was less as a composer than as a keyboard player, both at the harpsichord and at the organ. His great ability was summarized in his obituary: "How strange, how new, how beautiful were his ideas in improvising. How perfectly he realized them! All his fingers were equally skilful; all were capable of the most perfect accuracy in performance." Such skill and knowledge could be put to a variety of uses. Not only did Bach write music in every known form of his time (both for performance and for education), but he was also known for his ability as a designer of organs, and at Cöthen was expected to carry out all the repairs on the court harpsichords. Bach would have played on a range of keyboard instruments: the soft-toned clavichord, the strings of which sounded by being hit, as well as the fuller-toned harpsichord, the strings of which were plucked. Nowadays argument rages as to whether Bach's music sounds better played on the harpsichord or the modern piano. It undoubtedly sounds good on both, but the tone and volume of a piano (unlike the harsichord) is modified by the pressure of the fingers, thus allowing a performer a wider range of sounds with which to explore the intricacies of Bach's contrapuntal style.

THE WELL-TEMPERED CLAVIER

The Well-Tempered Clavier consists of two books of twenty-four preludes and fugues, each book working through the twelve major and twelve minor keys. Intended as a sort of manual of keyboard playing and composition, the *Well-Tempered Clavier* is Western music's first systematic exploration of harmony, and remains unequalled in the profligacy of its inventiveness. The fugues, written in as many as five voices, use devices such as inversion (turning the melody upside down) and augmentation (lengthening the duration of notes) to produce a texture so dense that in places it is difficult to discern the melodic pattern that's common to these individual voices. Yet these are not desiccated academic studies. They are full of sprightly dance-like passages and strong, concise melodies, and the preludes that introduce each fugue can be seen as prototypes for the poetic distillations of Chopin's *Préludes* and *Études* – indeed, Chopin revered the "48", as it's often known. Of the two books, the slightly earlier first book is marginally more playful and inventive. (And "Well-Tempered", by the way, refers to the method of tuning the instrument so that the twelve semitones of the chromatic scale are an equal distance apart in terms of perceived pitch. If you tune a keyboard using strict mathematical principles rather than the evidence of your ears, you end up with scales that sound out of tune.)

○ Nikolayeva (Mezhdunarodnaya Kniga MK 418042 [2 CDs] & MK 418043 [2 CDs]).

Tatiana Nikolayeva exploits the full range of the piano's sonorities: a crisp, hard touch is used for the more rhythmically motorized preludes yet there are no qualms about using the sustaining pedal to add colour and warmth to the sound. Her speeds can be slow, especially in some of the fugues, but the shape and direction of a piece is never in any doubt.

◑ Gould (Sony SM2K 52600 [2 CDs] & SM2K 52603 [2 CDs]).

Glenn Gould's account is very different. As with all his Bach performances he doesn't touch the pedal, preferring a shallow sound that emphasizes line above tone. And he has some odd ideas about tempo – some fugues played so slowly that they almost fall apart, others taken at a speed your ears can only just keep up with. This set was hailed as "one of the greatest piano recordings of the century"; for Bach authenticists it's one of the most maddening. (Incidentally, a recording of Gould's version of the first prelude of Book I was placed on board the *Voyager* space-shot, in order that any alien civilization intercepting the machine would gain some idea of the capabilities of the human species.)

◑ Tilney (Hyperion CDA66351-4; 4 CDs).

Colin Tilney plays all of Book 1 on a clavichord (a soft-toned keyboard instrument whose strings are struck) and Book II on a harpsichord (a hard-toned keyboard instrument whose strings are plucked). The result, in Tilney's skilful hands, merely reveals how receptive these works are to a range of interpretations. The very first prelude (the most famous) has a delicate finesse which makes its harmonic progressions sound all the more subtle.

THE GOLDBERG VARIATIONS

This set of thirty variations on a theme were supposedly commissioned by Baron von Keyserling – the Russian ambassador to the Dresden court – in order to relieve the wearisome hours of his insomnia, and were named after the baron's harpsichordist, who was to play them. The work begins with a highly ornamented but rather demure theme, around whose bass line Bach proceeds to fashion an astonishing series of transformations, from the ebullient to the introspective. The variations are grouped in threes, each group ending with a canon, except for the very last variation which is a quodlibet – a rousing piece which combines two popular songs. The epic scope of the work is due not simply to its length, but to its enormous variety – both stylistically and in terms of mood – and the way the whole work is held together by the constant underlying presence of the original thematic material.

◑ **Gould** (Sony SMK 52619).

Glenn Gould's 1955 recording of the *Goldberg Variations*, his debut release, revolutionized people's perception of how Bach should be played, and established the pianist's reputation as one of the great Bach interpreters. His 1982 recording, released shortly before his death, is even more remarkable for the vivid precision of his touch, and the way that each line of the music is so clearly articulated. Speeds are sometimes idiosyncratic, but you'll be swept along by Gould's verve and enthusiasm. One possible drawback (though one you get used to) is his habit of quietly singing along, rather tunelessly, as he plays.

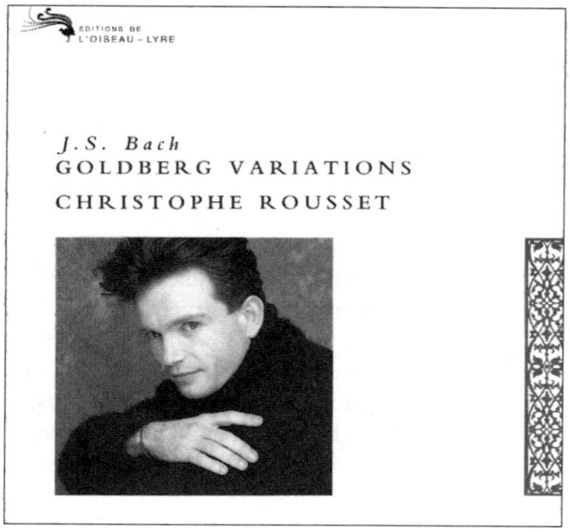

○ **Rousset** (L'Oiseau-Lyre 444 866-2).

This is a refreshingly forthright and decidedly wide-awake performance on a suitably bright-sounding instrument (a Paris-made harpsichord of 1751). Christophe Rousset's speeds tend to be brisk and he limits his changes of registration, letting the instrument do the work in crisp and buoyant style. If you're seeking a solemn and reverential account of this masterpiece then this recording should be avoided, but if you want something alive and animated give it a listen.

THE ENGLISH AND FRENCH SUITES

The titles of the *English Suites* and *French Suites* were not chosen by Bach, and their significance is unclear, as they do not define any substantial differences between these two sets of dance movements. Written purely for enjoyment rather than for instruction, they follow approximately the same format, with a steady allemande followed by a more rapid courante, a stately sarabande and an extremely lively gigue, sometimes with additional short movements – such as a bourrée – inserted between the sarabande and gigue. The *English Suites*, however, begin with a prelude which is often, as in the third suite, a large-scale concerto-like movement. The *French Suites* are less grandiose: the sarabandes and briefer additional movements are less contrapuntal than the equivalents in the *English Suites*, and bear a slight resemblance to the easy-going and flowery style of Couperin, with whom Bach is known to have corresponded.

◑ **English Suites: Gould** (Sony SM2K 52606; 2 CDs).

◑ **French Suites: Gould** (Sony SM2K 52609; 2 CDs; with *Overture in the French Style*).

Though there was no shortage of objectors to Glenn Gould's cavalier treatment of the printed page, nobody could match the clarity that he brought to Bach's multi-stranded keyboard music. These two sets show Gould at his most enjoyable – astonishingly fleet-fingered and full of argumentative intelligence.

THE PARTITAS & THE ITALIAN CONCERTO

The six keyboard *Partitas* were the first works of Bach to be published during his lifetime. Intended to form the first part of a *Clavierubüng* (Keyboard Exercise), the *Partitas* are an obvious development from the *English Suites* and *French Suites* and progress in difficulty and grandeur as the series unfolds. A partita is essentially the same as a suite, being a collection of movements based on dance forms. Bach's six are among the last great examples of a genre which was already beginning to be superseded by the sonata. They are all highly individual works: from the sprightly delicacy of No. 1 to the monumental No. 6, each contains its own assortment of *galantarien*, optional movements, like the minuet, which were added to the core movements of allemande, courante, sarabande and gigue, and each begins with a different form of opening movement.

In 1735 the second part of Bach's *Clavierubüng* appeared, which contained two works: a partita, published as *An Overture in the French Manner*, and the *Italian Concerto*. Here the emphasis is on contrast, both works mimicking orchestral music of two different national styles: the concerto in a major key, and the Partita in a minor one. The *Italian Concerto*, one of the most popular of Bach's keyboard works, is a clever translation of a typical three-movement Vivaldian concerto into keyboard form. Bach specifically indicates that it should be played on a two-manual harpsichord; the main manual representing the orchestra, the other, softer, manual representing the soloist. The middle slow movement in particular has a long solo part, rich in ornament, that is highly suggestive of a lyrical oboe line.

● Six Partitas: Rousset (L'Oiseau-Lyre 440 217-2; 2 CDs).

Sparkling accounts of the *Partitas* from Rousset, full of spring and excitement. Again his instrument has a bright, forward sound but he uses a greater variety of registration than in his *Goldberg Variations,* finding just the right tone and touch for the great range of moods that are present.

◑ Six Partitas: Gould (Sony SM2K 52597; 2 CDs).

Recorded in the late 1950s and early 1960s, this sequence is a typically thrilling, strong-willed and occasionally strange Gould production. Critics (and later Gould himself) expressed reservations about its tendency to overassertiveness, but no other pianist conveyed so powerful an impression of passionate analytical intelligence.

● Italian Concerto: Rousset (L'Oiseau-Lyre 433 054-2; with *Chromatic Fantasy and Fugue* & *French Overture*).

As well as a brilliant account of the Italian concerto, Rousset gives a fleet-fingered performance of one of Bach's most mercurial keyboard pieces, the *Chromatic Fantasy and Fugue*, making this a near ideal introduction to Bach on the harpsichord.

ORGAN MUSIC

While organist at Arnstadt, Bach requested four weeks' leave to walk to Lübeck (some 300km) in order to hear Dietrich Buxtehude, then the greatest organist in Germany. Much of Bach's early organ works show the influence of the older man, but a more dynamic style, and one with a greater sense of continuity, was forged, once again, as a result of Bach's contact with the music of Vivaldi. Bach composed a wide range of organ works, of which the best known and most exciting are the spectacular fugues, often preceded by a short prelude or a more virtuosic toccata. Closer to the heart of the Lutheran Church tradition are the chorales and chorale preludes, works based on the unaccompanied hymns sung by the congregation and played as introductions to them: Bach's ability to create florid improvisations on these simple tunes drew complaints from his congregation on more than one occasion. (Incidentally Bach's most well-loved and oft-played organ work, the *Toccata and Fugue in D Minor*, is now thought by most modern scholars to be neither by Bach nor originally written for the organ.)

● The Organ Toccatas and Passacaglia: Herrick (Hyperion CDA 66434).

Christopher Herrick is near to finishing his cycle of the complete organ music of J.S.Bach. The problem of achieving both unity and variety in the series has been cleverly achieved by recording each disc on a different Swiss organ, all of which were made by Metzler. This disc makes a good introduction both to Bach on the organ and to the series in general. Herrick eschews anything too thunderous or heavy and the result is refreshingly clear and direct, if sometimes a little undercharged.

◑ Great Organ Works: Koopman (Teldec 0630-17369-2).

Ton Koopman is also well into his second complete cycle. He also is recording each disc on a different organ, all of which were extant during Bach's lifetime. This disc, a sampler for the series, is an almost identical programme to the Hyperion disc. Koopman is not such a careful player as Herrick, but arguably he has more flair. He prefers a more dramatic improvisatory style, building each piece to strong climaxes through changes of registration and dynamics.

THE ART OF FUGUE

Bach's very last work is one of his most baffling. The *Art of Fugue* is a collection of fugues and canons which display the full gamut of transformational techniques including augmentation and diminution (lengthening and shortening the duration of notes), inversion (whereby the melody is stated as a mirror image of itself) and retrograde (back to front). The generally accepted theory that the work was intended as an intellectual exercise rather than for performance is borne out by the fact that no instruments are specified in the score. It may have been created for the members of the Corresponding Society of the Musical Sciences, a society formed by Bach's former pupil Lorenz Mizler, which explored music's theoretical basis in mathematics. But although the *Art of Fugue* (the title was not Bach's own) reveals Bach in his most academic and puzzle-solving guise, it is no mere pedantry and there is much here of great energy and inspiration.

● MacGregor (Collins 70432; 2 CDs; with Nancarrow, *Three Canons for Ursula* & *Three Player Piano Studies*).

Since Bach did not specify any instrumentation, the big question is: what instrument or instruments should the *Art of Fugue* be played on? Most recordings are keyboard versions, and of these the most exciting in recent years has been by Joanna MacGregor on the piano. Although she clearly relishes the contrapuntal complexity of these pieces, there is also a warmth and a flexibility to her playing that makes this great work leap from the page.

OTHER INSTRUMENTAL MUSIC

The main forum for Bach's orchestral and instrumental music was Cöthen and the Collegium Musicum at Leipzig. Cöthen possessed a wealth of talented instrumental players: Prince Leopold himself was a gifted amateur who played the harpsichord, the violin and the viola da gamba.

Oddly enough, apart from the keyboard music outlined above, there is not a great deal of instrumental music from this, or any other, period of Bach's career, and much of what has survived is of dubious authorship. Undoubtedly the greatest of the non-keyboard instrumental pieces are the three partitas and three sonatas for unaccompanied violin and the six suites for unaccompanied cello, works which push the expressive and technical possibilities of their respective intruments to unprecedented extremes.

THE VIOLIN SONATAS & PARTITAS

Although a stringed instrument is capable of playing two notes at the same time, one expects a work for a solo stringed instrument to produce a single line of music, without much harmony and without counterpoint. The extraordinary achievement of Bach's violin sonatas and partitas is that harmony and counterpoint are implied by the device of frequently spreading the component notes of a chord – and for the second movement of each sonata Bach provides a fully realized fugue. Listening to these works for the first time it is difficult to believe that you are only hearing just one instrument. At the same time this is not simply intellectual wizardry: these works abound with vivid melodies and, in the famous chaconne from the *D Minor Partita*, some of the most deeply emotional moments in all of Bach's music.

◑ **Complete Sonatas and Partitas for Solo Violin: Grumiaux** (Philips 438 736-2; 2 CDs).

These pieces are the Everest of the violin repertoire, extremely difficult to play and of course utterly exposed, with no orchestra or piano to cover mistakes. Grumiaux makes it all sound terribly easy: his playing is clean and (above all) incisive, with a stylish sense of line, and double-stopping (the playing of chords) that is boldly and clearly articulated. By employing an occasionally springier touch he also suggests the dance origins of many of the movements – the gigue from the second *Partita* is especially lively.

○ **Complete Sonatas and Partitas for Solo Violin: Huggett** (Virgin Classics VCD5 45205-2; 2CDs).

Unlike the cello suites, these works have not been recorded by many Baroque specialists. But even with stiffer competiton, Monica Huggett's performance would still be outstanding. There's a real sense of her stamping her personality on the work, not in a self-seeking way but out of a really close feeling for the music. It's clearly the same music as that played by Grumiaux but, instead of an emphasis on a clear steely line, the music is made to sound more rounded and flexible and less obviously virtuosic.

THE CELLO SUITES

There is no fugal writing in the *Cello Suites* but they share with the unaccompanied violin works the same capacity to create a multi-textured sound from a single-voiced instrument. A spectacular example of this is the prelude of the first suite, in which succeeding chords are separated out into their individual notes – what you hear is both the gently rocking, forward momentum of the separated notes, and the underlying harmonic structure. The last two suites are the most technically demanding: *Suite No. 5* involves unconventional tuning, or *scordatura*, while *No. 6* is written for a five-stringed instrument, rather than the usual four-stringed one. Like the violin works, these are virtuosic pieces – the first ever written for cello – and may have been composed for one of the most talented of the Cöthen players, the cellist and viola da gamba player Christian Ferdinand Abel.

◑ **Starker** (Mercury 432 756-2; 2 CDs; with *Viola da Gamba sonatas*).

Janos Starker has recorded these works at least four times, the best of which – made in the late 1950s for EMI – is only available as part of a six-CD set. This slightly later performance is still pretty remarkable, however, possessing a sinewy vigour and a dynamism which revolutionized the playing of these works.

◑ **Bylsma** (RCA RD 70950; 2 CDs).

Anner Bylsma has recorded the *Cello Suites* twice, both times on Baroque instruments that employ gut rather than metal strings, thus making for a warmer and more diffuse sound. This suits his style of playing, which tends to stress the delicacy and intimacy of these pieces, rather than their difficulty. He is a master of phrasing and of touch, with subtle shifts of emphasis that can refashion a phrase in a bold but utterly convincing manner.

THE FLUTE SONATAS

By the early eighteenth century the transverse flute (as opposed to the recorder) had become hugely popular, and there was a continuous demand for new music for it. Of the six flute sonatas traditionally ascribed to Bach, two are now thought to be highly doubtful, though both are delightful works. The genuine ones are marked by the intricacy of the writing, in which the equal importance of each line (the flute part, and the bass and right-hand harpsichord lines) make them closer to trio sonatas than to solo ones. They are generally characterized by cool restraint, rarely matching the energy or dynamism of the unaccompanied violin or cello pieces, yet there is much of great beauty in this tightly reined music, notably the *B Minor Sonata* where flute and keyboard function as equals.

⊙ **Bennett; Malcolm** (ASV CD QS 6108).

William Bennett possesses a full and controlled tone, and makes an eloquent and refined soloist, especially impressive in the long elegant phrases of the *E Minor Sonata*. The dynamic control of these performances makes them livelier than most – a fine example is the way the emphasis shifts from instrument to instrument in the first movement of the *B Minor Sonata*.

THE MUSICAL OFFERING

In 1747 Bach, still with a reputation as a brilliant keyboard improviser, travelled to Potsdam at the request of King Frederick the Great of Prussia. He arrived in the evening just as the king (a talented flautist) was beginning his regular concert with his court musicians, among whom was Bach's second son Carl Philipp Emanuel. The older Bach requested a theme from the king on which he improvised a three-part fugue, later improvising a six-part fugue on a theme of his own devising. Back in Leipzig the king's theme was written up and extended into a work containing a three- and a six-part ricecar (or free improvisation) for keyboard, and a trio sonata in four movements for flute, violin and continuo, together with ten scholarly canons. The whole thing, lavishly printed, bound and presented to the king as a *Musical Offering*, can be seen as a sophisticated calling card – Bach flexing his musical and intellectual muscles with, perhaps, half an eye on a possible royal appointment.

O B. Kuijken, S. Kuijken, W. Kuijken; Kohnen (Deutsche Harmonia Mundi 05472 77307 2).

The three Kuijken brothers and Robert Kohnen play this music with a refined elegance and grace. The sound is a little forward, but this merely increases the intimate quality of their performance.

SAMUEL BARBER

(1910–1981)

Right back in the 1930s, when Samuel Barber was being lauded in some quarters as one of the most talented American composers of his generation, his music was being labelled as utterly anachronistic by modernists. Totally unperturbed, Barber went on writing in his neo-Romantic vein, turning out essentially dramatic and lyrical works in a tonal language rooted in the late nineteenth century. In the 1970s, with a large and varied body of work behind him, Barber was able to state with a certain satisfaction, "it is said that I have no style at all but that doesn't matter. I just go on doing, as they say, my thing. I believe this takes a certain courage."

It's hardly surprising that many of Barber's compositions are vocal settings – he was an excellent baritone, and as a young student at the Curtis Institute he entertained notions of becoming a professional singer. By the time Barber graduated in 1932 he was already a confident composer with several highly accomplished works under his belt, including *Dover Beach* (a song singled out for praise by Vaughan Williams) and the *Serenade for String Quartet*. From the start his music exhibited many of the Barber hallmarks, notably extended lyrical lines and a remarkable facility for instrumental colour and text-setting. Barber was never coy about wearing his heart on his sleeve – his music was always first and foremost to do with the expression of profound personal emotion, a quality which soon got him noticed, not least by Toscanini. Once Toscanini had performed the *Adagio for Strings* in 1938, Barber never looked back. Numerous awards came his way, including Pulitzer prizes for the opera *Vanessa* (1958) and for his *Piano Concerto* (1962), and it must have seemed as though his star would never stop rising.

The bubble was to burst, however, with the failure of Barber's biggest work of the 1960s, the full-scale Shakespearean opera *Antony and Cleopatra*. Franco Zeffirelli's libretto was decidedly over-the-top, as was his production for the 1966 premiere, which with all its live animals and hundreds of extras looked like a second-rate Cecil B. de Mille movie. The opera was revised by his lifelong companion Gian Carlo Menotti, and restaged in 1975 at the Juilliard School in New York, but never found many admirers. Although Barber had a spate of commissions in the early 1970s, his writing tailed off at the close of the decade, due in no small part to the cancer that was to kill him.

ADAGIO FOR STRINGS

Barber's name is synonymous with one composition, the undeniably beautiful *Adagio for Strings* which began life as the slow movement of his 1936 *String Quartet*. Two years later Barber arranged it for string orchestra and, with the help of Toscanini, it lodged itself indelibly in the American psyche. With its slow-building melodic lines, breath-like pauses and general mood of subdued sadness, it is not difficult to see why it has taken on the status of a twentieth-century classic. It was broadcast at the death of President Roosevelt and more recently provided catharsis in Oliver Stone's Vietnam film *Platoon*. Unfortunately the *Adagio* has tended to overshadow all Barber's other work, but there is now an increasingly wide cross-section of his music appearing on CD.

O Atlanta Symphony Orchestra; Levi (Telarc CD-80250; with *Knoxville, Essays Nos. 1 & 2, School for Scandal Overture & Medea's Dance of Vengeance*).

This is a broodingly atmospheric account of the *Adagio*, with Levi perfectly judging the work's dark ebb and flow and resisting the temptation to underline the pathos. The disc also includes a selection of Barber's better-known orchestral works, including the two concentrated *Orchestral Essays*, as well as a delightfully fresh performance of *Knoxville: Summer of 1915* (see opposite).

THE VIOLIN CONCERTO

Barber's Violin Concerto was commissioned in 1939 by the businessman Samuel Fels for his young protégé the violinist Iso Briselli, who rejected it as too easy when Barber submitted the first two movements. It is true that, though unabashedly Romantic in tone, the Allegro and Andante contain no technical fireworks. What they do possess is a rhapsodic exuberance in the Allegro and a defiantly vocal melancholy in the Andante. There's a Mendelssohnian fervour to both movements, but it's saved from being a nineteenth-century pastiche by Barber's characteristic spare and loose-limbed orchestration. For the finale (marked "Presto in moto perpetuo") Barber tapped into a more modern, though hardly avant-garde, vein in which woodwind and brass scuttle alongside the frenetic soloist as if in pursuit. Briselli rejected this movement as unplayable and the work was eventually premiered by Albert Spalding and the Philadelphia Orchestra in 1941.

O Shaham; London Symphony Orchestra; Previn (Deutsche Grammophon 439 889-2; with Korngold, *Violin Concerto & Much Ado About Nothing)*.

It's an interesting coupling to set the Barber concerto alongside that of Korngold. Both are Romantic works but Barber seems to have more of a modern take; it's more neo-Romantic than Korngold's blatant heart-tugging. Gil Shaham and André Previn make an excellent team, bringing out the brilliance and vivacity of the Barber rather than milking its more emotional side.

KNOXVILLE: SUMMER OF 1915

When, in 1947, the soprano Eleanor Steber asked Barber for a new work for her to perform with the Boston Symphony Orchestra, the composer turned to the prose and poetry of James Agee, which he had recently been reading. The result was *Knoxville: Summer of 1915*, an unashamedly nostalgic evocation of a child's view of small-town family life, as American as Thornton Wilder's *Our Town* or Frank Capra's *It's a Wonderful Life*. Barber sets Agee's prose poem (a mix of the simple and the overly poetic) in a largely syllabic and straightforward manner which stays close to the rhythms and inflections of the original. Musically it is dominated by a gentle rocking melody – suggesting a lullaby – that frames the work. A more animated middle section (representing the clatter of the streetcar) leads into a brief rhapsodic passage as night falls. Barber's restraint and real identification with the material means that sentimentality is avoided and a genuinely moving picture emerges.

O McNair; Atlanta Symphony Orchestra; Levi (Telarc CD-80250; with *Adagio, Essays Nos. 1 & 2, School for Scandal Overture, Medea's Dance of Vegeance*).

Knoxville is a marvellous vehicle for a lyric soprano (preferably an American one) but it's not that easy to bring off. Sylvia McNair has a beautiful, full and rounded voice and does as well as any at expressing the easy-going, everyday innocence of the work, especially in the opening. Just occasionally, in the more rapturous passages, the words get lost, but overall her enunciation is good and this is the best of recent recordings.

SONGS

Perhaps the most attractive of all Barber's works are his songs, in even the earliest of which – such as *Slumber Song of the Madonna* (1925) – he shows an impressive facility with vocal colour and word-setting. By the time of *Dover Beach*, for string quartet and baritone, he was completely in control of the medium, exploring rich harmonic textures and complicated polyphony. His range of expression is unrivalled among modern songwriters, encompassing every mood from Schubertian tenderness and simplicity (as in *A Nun Takes the Veil*, 1937) to the artfully decadent (as in the café-style *Solitary Hotel*, 1968–69).

⊙ The Songs: Hampson, Studer, Browning; Emerson Quartet (Deutsche Grammophon 435 867-2; 2 CDs).

The DG set of Barber's songs is a splendid chronological survey, excellently performed by all involved. Thomas Hampson is especially fine, effortless in Barber's protracted lyrical melodies yet intensely dramatic where necessary.

BÉLA BARTÓK

(1881–1945)

During the first two decades of the twentieth century, the tonal basis of classical music – the tyranny of major and minor keys, as Stravinsky termed it – finally collapsed. For Schoenberg and his Viennese followers, the logical progression from the lush ambiguities of Wagner was the development of serialism, replacing the exhausted principles of tonality with the rigours of the twelve-tone system. Béla Bartók, however, found another way out of the impasse, producing music in which the Germanic tradition was given new life by incorporating it into a strongly nationalist style. In this he was, of course, not unique. Nationalism had been an increasingly powerful force since the European wave of revolutions in 1848, and received crucial impetus with the outbreak of worldwide conflict in the 1910s, as can be heard in the work of such diverse figures as Dvořák, Prokofiev, Janáček, Grieg, Sibelius and Vaughan Williams. But no other composer managed to produce work in which folk elements were absorbed into music of such power and modernity.

Bartók's early music was the product of years of studying the German tradition at the Budapest Academy. Bearing the imprint of Wagner, Brahms, Liszt and Strauss, it was traditional, slightly old-fashioned and full of unfettered melodic expression. In 1902 Bartók was inspired by a performance of Strauss's *Also Sprach Zarathustra* to write his own tone poem *Kossuth*, but for all his composing ambitions he spent the next five years pursuing the career of a travelling piano virtuoso, specializing in the music of Liszt. The partial exorcism of these Romantic influences began in 1905, when he interrupted his touring to begin an exploration of Hungarian peasant music; the following year, he and his friend Kodály (see p.210) published a collection of twenty Magyar songs. However, his own music was persistently rejected and in 1907, recognizing the futility of life as a composer, he took a position as head of piano studies at the Budapest Academy, where he continued his ethnological studies. Bartók's immersion in Hungarian folk traditions – and his discovery of Debussy's impressionism – encouraged him to look beyond the confines of purely tonal expression and he developed a fascination with dissonance, a feature of nearly all his music written after his extraordinary opera *Duke Bluebeard's Castle* (1911).

Bartók was not the first composer to write "Hungarian" classical music, but, whereas Brahms and Liszt had written pieces in a style that was

LEBRECHT COLLECTION

Béla Bartók (left) with Zoltán Kodály, 1918

Hungarian in atmosphere rather than substance, Bartók marked a clear break with tradition by treating his folk melodies and rhythms as truly raw material, emphasizing their "primitive" elements. On the other hand, though his music was often aggressive and harsh, its essential language never diverged from tonality, and the structural principles of his greatest compositions – such as the astringent string quartets – justify the description of Bartók as one of the last and most original Romantic composers. His ardent nationalism and his refusal to adopt the methods of the Second Viennese School placed him outside the mainstream of the European avant-garde, and Bartók's name did not feature prominently on concert programmes during his lifetime. His successes in the USA, where he spent the last five unhappy yet productive years of his life, were engineered by extremely prominent performers whose advocacy did more to persuade the promoters and press than did than the music itself. He remains a slightly eccentric figure in the history of modern music – his music is now featured widely in concert halls and record catalogues, but he's the least influential of this century's indisputably great composers. There is no school of Bartók.

DUKE BLUEBEARD'S CASTLE

Bartók composed only three stage works: the two ballets, *The Wooden Prince* and *The Miraculous Mandarin*, and the one-act opera *Duke Bluebeard's Castle*. *Bluebeard's Castle*, the finest of the three, is a disturbing, static drama with just two characters – Bluebeard himself (bass/baritone) and his new wife, Judith (soprano). The opera, written in 1911, represents Bartók's departure from his intoxication with German music in general and Richard Strauss in particular, though his debt to Strauss's chromatic indulgence is revealed in the Romantic grandeur of the music he assigns to Judith. Her sinister husband sings in contrastingly dour and stark tones, setting up a tension that is quintessentially Bartók.

The action of this deeply disturbing tale is simple. Against his wishes, Bluebeard allows his new wife to open the seven doors that open onto the hall of his castle. Behind each door she discovers something terrible – from a torture chamber to a magic garden where the roses are spotted with blood – until finally she realizes that she is to be imprisoned forever, along with his three other wives, behind the seventh door. The opening of the fifth door is an awesome moment: as it opens, Judith is confronted by a blinding ray of sunshine, an event for which Bartók found one of his greatest inspirations – a simple but amazingly effective C major chord, from which develops some of the opera's most stunning music. This scene is a staggering visual coup, but *Bluebeard*'s general lack of narrative incident makes it one of the few operas that's as effective on disc as it is on stage.

O Ramey, Marton; Hungarian State Orchestra; Fischer (Sony MK4523).

This graphic and intense work makes enormous demands on its performers, but as it has a cast of just two and can be fitted on a single CD it's frequently been recorded. The Sony (formerly CBS) recording is arguably the best of the nine versions currently available. Eva Marton delivers a rainbow of vocal colours, and Samuel Ramey similarly makes the most of his role's potential. Adam Fischer directs the whole thing with a sometimes overwhelming passion; especially in the finale, he creates a translucent sound that highlights the mastery of Bartók's orchestrations and chillingly conveys the horror of the story.

◑ **Berry, Ludwig; London Symphony Orchestra; Kertész** (Decca 443 571-2).

Kertész's vision of *Bluebeard* is entirely different from Fischer's: here all is febrile, restless and edgy. He pays a great deal of attention to detail which, with his manic and fluctuating tempi, makes the score sound less flowing than it really is – but it is an approach that works well. The husband-and-wife team of Walter Berry and Christa Ludwig sing with their usual strength and commitment, though the former's tone occasionally seems too smooth and generous.

THE MIRACULOUS MANDARIN

Bartók, whose introspection bordered on the pathological, was clearly attracted to stories of loneliness and alienation in which the power of love could both redeem and destroy. In 1917 he read the scenario for a ballet, *The Miraculous Mandarin*, in the Hungarian literary magazine *Nyugat*. Bartók immediately decided to set it to music, enthusiastically describing the grisly tale to a journalist as "beautiful". The plot tells of three thugs who force a young girl to lure passers-by into a room where they will rob them. After two unsuccessful attempts, a strange Chinese man appears. The girl arouses his desire by dancing. The men try to kill him but he will not die. Only when the girl satisfies his desire do his wounds begin to bleed and he dies.

Like *Duke Bluebeard's Castle*, *The Miraculous Mandarin* exudes a disturbingly tangible claustrophobia and an almost suffocating sexual tension. The work's swirling, restless energy and profusion of jagged cross-rhythms clearly owe much to *Petrushka* and the *Rite of Spring* but, whereas Stravinsky's rawness conjures up the exotic, Bartók evokes a much more modern vision – an alienating cityscape of glaring lights and blaring klaxons. This is certainly his most aggressive score, with only the beguiling and virtuosic clarinet solos of the three enticement scenes offering much in the way of lyricism. The nightmarish and percussive violence of the score is made bearable by the brilliant richness of the orchestral colouring, which, though consistently sinister, has several highly sensuous moments.

○ **Hungarian Radio Chorus; Budapest Festival Orchestra; Fischer** (Philips 454 430-2; with *Hungarian Sketches*, *Romanian Folk Dances*, etc).

Fischer gets a finely detailed and energetic performance from his Budapest players. There is clarity and bite in abundance – qualities which also serve the orchestral dances well – and the solo passages are excellent. The seduction scenes, in particular, are beautifully played by an uncredited clarinettist.

THE PIANO CONCERTOS

Bartók was an excellent pianist and his first two piano concertos, dating from 1926 and 1931, were clearly written to suit his own particular style of playing. In both concertos, Bartók treats the piano as primarily a percussive instrument, and their raw ferocity can still shock listeners as much as they did at their first performances. Unlike his violin concertos, there is no lyricism or Romantic lilt here – you might be seduced by the music of these other works, but the first two piano concertos batter you into submission.

The third piano concerto was one of Bartók's final pieces and was left incomplete at his death – after the final seventeen bars had been completed by a former student Tibor Serly, the work was first performed on February 8, 1946. Written for Bartók's wife Ditta, the third concerto is considerably less aggressive and more classical in form – indeed it is one of the most conventionally constructed works he wrote. The music reflects the composer's contentment at the very end of his life: America may not have turned out to be the land of milk and honey, but the Nazis had been defeated and he had been restored to all his official musical posts in his absence, encouraging him to consider a return to his native Hungary.

O Piano Concertos Nos. 1 & 2: Pollini; Chicago Symphony Orchestra; Abbado (Deutsche Grammophon 415 371-2).

For performances of the first two concertos, Pollini's assertive and scintillating accounts are unbeatable. His brilliance and dynamic virtuosity are well matched by Abbado and the Chicago Symphony Orchestra, and the recording has the sense of occasion that you usually associate with a live performance.

⊙ Piano Concertos Nos. 1-3: Jandó; Budapest Symphony Orchestra; Ligeti (Naxos 8.55071).

This is one of Naxos's best achievements. Jandó, their chosen pianist for all the major piano repertoire, is clearly very much at home with Bartók. These are vigorous, idiomatic accounts which hold their own with the best.

THE VIOLIN CONCERTOS

Bartók wrote his two-movement first violin concerto in 1908, soon after returning from his first folk-song-collecting expedition to Transylvania. This headily Romantic piece was written for the young violinist Stefie Geyer, but sadly she did not reciprocate the emotion so clearly expressed in the lovely first movement, and she left the composer shortly after the work's completion. Bartók duly shelved the concerto, which remained unperformed until two years after Geyer's death and fifty years after it was written.

Thirty years after the troubled inception of this first concerto, the Hungarian violinist Zoltán Székely asked Bartók to have another go. The composer preferred to write an extended set of variations but Székely maintained that, as he was paying for the work, he should get what he asked for. Not wishing to be defeated, Bartók then cheated by writing a three-movement concerto which is, in fact, an extended set of variations – though it requires close analysis to find the relation between the opening pizzicati and the finale. It has its moments of dissonance, but predominently this concerto is as melodic as the earlier one, and repeated listening reveals a flood of ideas that seem to tumble over each other.

O Violin Concertos Nos. 1 & 2: Midori; Berlin Philharmonic Orchestra; Mehta (Sony SK45941).

Midori's recording of the Bartók concertos was the one that showed that the Japanese-American whizz kid amounted to a lot more than just an amazing technique: this disc is a marvel, her interpretations are well measured, understated and deeply thought out.

◑ Violin Concerto No. 2: Menuhin; Dallas Symphony Orchestra; Dorati (RCA 09026 61395-2; with Lâlo, *Symphonie espagnole*).

Menuhin's 1946 recording of the second concerto is less intimidating than Midori's high-octane performance: it's a profoundly lyrical reading, with Menuhin producing an astonishingly sweet and luxurious tone.

CONCERTO FOR ORCHESTRA

The genre of the "concerto for orchestra" was a twentieth-century invention inspired by the rapidly increasing technical abilities of American orchestras in the period after World War I. Kodály and Lutosławski both wrote pieces in this format, but neither quite matches Bartók's intricately constructed showpiece, which gloriously displays the virtuoso talents of each of the orchestral sections.

One of the composer's last works, the *Concerto for Orchestra* was commissioned by the conductor Serge Koussevitzky in 1943, whose Boston Symphony Orchestra gave the first performance at the end of the following year, an event received with great acclaim. The five movements present a gradual transition from the severity of the first to a life-affirming finale, with interruptions along the way – thus the satirical and light-hearted second movement is followed by a *Song of Death*, which in turn gives way to an Intermezzo that has a dig at Shostakovich by quoting his seventh symphony.

O London Symphony Orchestra; Dorati (Mercury 432 017-2; with *Dance Suite*, *Two Portraits* & excerpts from *Mikrokosmos*).

Antal Dorati, a friend of Bartók's, recorded the *Concerto* several times. His best version, made in 1962, is superb, combining fierce energy and rhythmic momentum with extremes of colour. The LSO play with great virtuosity, especially in the daunting finale. Coupled with the *Concerto* is a shuddering account of the *Dance Suite* and *Two Portraits*, the latter an early work that Bartók derived from the first movement of his first violin concerto.

◑ RIAS-Symphonie-Orchester Berlin; Fricsay (Deutsche Grammophon 447 443-2; with *Music for Strings, Percussion and Celesta*).

Ferenc Fricsay was another close associate of the composer's (he conducted a Bartók premiere as a 22-year-old), and this 1957 performance is imbued with a profound knowledge of every intricacy of this great piece. The sound quality is remarkably vivid, and at mid-price this coupling is a real bargain.

MUSIC FOR STRINGS, PERCUSSION AND CELESTA

Commissioned by one of this century's most important patrons, Paul Sacher, and first performed by him and his Basel Chamber Orchestra in 1937, *Music for Strings, Percussion and Celesta* is one of Bartók's most unorthodox, complicated and demanding works. It's written in four continuous movements, lasts around thirty minutes, and is scored for a unique ensemble: two groups of strings, a phalanx of percussion instruments including cymbals, drums, tam-tam, timpani and xylophone, plus piano, harp and celesta, a piano-like instrument with metal bars instead of strings. It's an extremely eerie piece of music (Kubrick used it on the soundtrack of *The Shining*), and a seminal one, too – its monothematicism (ie the whole thing is generated from a single theme), and its emphasis on rhythmic power rather than on melody, established a mature style from which Bartók did not stray until his last five years.

◑ **RIAS-Symphonie-Orchester Berlin; Fricsay** (Deutsche Grammophon 447 443-2; with *Concerto for Orchestra*).

Throughout his career Fricsay was famed both as an interpreter of Bartók's music and as a fastidiously precise director of his orchestras. His reading of the *Music for Strings, Percussion and Celesta* (dating from 1953) won awards when it was first released, and still has very few rivals.

○ **Oslo Philharmonic Orchestra; Jansons** (EMI CDC7 54070-2; with *Concerto for Orchestra*).

Mariss Jansons' strong rapport with the Oslo orchestra has produced several fine recordings, and this is one of the best. Jansons brilliantly conjures the translucent texture demanded by Bartók and he doesn't labour the work's thematic reinventions. The coupled performance of the *Concerto for Orchestra* is a good one, but sounds a fraction too slick when compared to the Dorati version.

THE STRING QUARTETS

Bartók's six string quartets are his greatest achievement and span his entire creative life: the first was completed in 1908, the second in 1917, the third in 1927, the fourth in 1928, the fifth in 1934 and the last in 1938. As with Beethoven and Shostakovich, Bartók translated his deepest and most personal thoughts into his quartets, and each of the six is the purest distillation of his immersion in folk song. The two central quartets, the third and the fourth, have the most astringent and difficult music, but they are also the two most challenging and exciting to listen to. The third is a short, highly concentrated exercise in expressionism that teeters on the brink of atonality. Though Bartók was not a string player, he manages to create an astonishing variety of deeply anguished and mysterious sounds, culminating in the hard-driven and cathartic finale. The sections of the third's single-movement structure form a palindrome; a pattern repeated in the fourth quartet, a more expansive and less introspective work. At its heart is an extraordinary slow movement, full of the wild "night sounds" of nature – rustling trees, birdsong, the movement of insects. It's followed by a short Scherzo entirely made up of manic pizzicato strumming. The finale is one of the most disturbingly driven and dissonant works in the whole of quartet literature.

◑ **Quator Végh** (Auvidis Valois V 4809; 3 CDs).

This is some of the liveliest, most committed and spontaneous quartet playing on disc. Some have carped at an occasional roughness around the edges, but it's hardly noticeable if you allow the sheer energy and joy of the playing to take you over. Also available as individual discs.

○ **Lindsay Quartet** (ASV CD DCS 301; 3 CDs).

The Lindsay Quartet, like the Vegh, take risks in the service of the music's spirit rather than subject each bar to excessive analysis and rehearsal. Not everything is exactly in its place, but this doesn't really matter, as you're left marvelling at what Bartók wrote rather than at the prowess of the performers. It's only available as a box set.

THE VIOLIN SONATA

After the string quartets, Bartók's most important chamber music is his *Violin Sonata*, Op. 117, one of the greatest works ever written for unaccompanied violin. It was commissioned by Yehudi Menuhin in 1944, the year after Bartók had praised Menuhin's performance of the composer's first sonata for violin and piano. Although it was written in America, a period of almost unrelieved unhappiness for Bartók, the sonata is an incredibly positive piece of music, showing an understanding of the violin's capabilities that's extraordinary for a composer who didn't play this difficult instrument. With the exception of Ysaye's six sonatas, Bartók's was the first sonata for solo violin to be written since Bach's, and the example of Bach's compositions is never far away in this neo-classically structured piece. Bartók's imagination was inspired by these self-imposed restraints – with its strange cross-rhythms and harmonics, the sonata gives the violin a wholly original voice.

○ **Nikkanen** (Collins CD1203-2; with *Sonata No. 1 for Violin and Piano & Romanian Folk Dances*).

The young Kurt Nikkanen gives a wonderfully assured performance which is technically so secure that the sonata's demands are taken for granted, allowing his expansive vision of the piece to surface unhindered.

SOLO PIANO MUSIC

Like Prokofiev and Rachmaninov, Bartók was a brilliant pianist, destined to lead the life of a virtuoso until he met Kodály and turned his attention to ethnomusicology. His piano music reflects a complete understanding of the piano's possibilities – in particular its percussive aspect – and is frequently shot through with the quirky rhythms and modality of the folk music he collected. Several of his piano works, like the *Six Romanian Folkdances* (1915), are, in fact, relatively simple arrangements of folk music, but in other instances, having imbibed the spirit of a musical region, he produced complex works of an extreme originality. The short, popular *Allegro barbaro* (1911) is a case in point: its swirling rhythms are like an encapsulation of every wild, Eastern European dance one has ever heard. But even in more tightly structured works, like the *Suite* (1916) or the *Sonata* (1926), propulsive rhythms and modal melodies never disappear for long. *Out of Doors* is another work that dates from 1926 (sometimes called his piano year). Though not strictly programmatic, it's clearly meant to evoke rustic sounds and sights from croaking frogs to droning bagpipes. Bartók also wrote a number of lively pedagogical works, of which *Mikrokosmos*, in six progressively difficult volumes, is the most famous.

○ Works for Piano Solo Vol. 2: Kocsis (Philips 44 016-2).

Zoltán Kocsis is a Hungarian pianist absolutely steeped in the music of Bartók (he edited the Hungaraton CD set "Bartók at the Piano"). He is therefore a good choice for Philips' enterprising project to record all Bartók's piano music. Like Bartok himself, Kocsis doesn't accentuate the toughness of this music but instead adopts a varied approach which is flexible and giving when necessary. There are four discs completed so far; volume 2, with an absolutely sparkling account of the *Suite*, makes a good one to start with.

SONATA FOR TWO PIANOS AND PERCUSSION

About a year after writing the *Music for Strings, Percussion and Celesta*, Bartók recieved a commission from another Basle group to write the *Sonata for Two Pianos and Percussion*. Like the earlier work, this is very much an exercise in exploring the specifically percussive timbres of the piano and the expressive capacity of percussion – a fascination that can be traced back to the slow movement of his *First Piano Concerto* (1926). Once again the relationship of the two pianos – placed on either side of the platform – to the percussion section is that of first among equals. There is also a similar mood of mystery to the work, not least in the brooding build-up of its opening section, and the weirdly funereal march that constitutes the slow movement. There is something almost anthropomorphic about the the disconcertingly varied range of voices in this movement – Bartók may have stopped writing for the theatre but he hadn't lost his sense of drama. The final movement is a madcap romp with a witty xylophone part that recalls Shostakovich at his most exuberant.

○ Argerich, Freire, Sadlo, Guggeis (Deutsche Grammophon 439 867-2; with Ravel, *Ma Mère l'oye* & *Rapsodie espagnole*).

Like Kocsis, Martha Argerich and Nelson Freire play down the idea of Bartók the uncompromising modernist and instead give us Bartók the magician, effortlessly conjuring up a world of exotic and frequently lush sounds. This is a performance which brings an added dimension to the music, making it miraculously alive as never before on disc.

LUDWIG VAN BEETHOVEN

(1770–1827)

Beethoven the demigod, the tragic yet otherworldly genius, scornful of society and oblivious of life's trivialities, is the product of almost two centuries of mythologizing. Dubious biographies with titles such as *Beethoven, the Man Who Freed Music* and *Beethoven, Life of a Conqueror* are typical of the awestruck image-creation that has been going on since the composer's day, extrapolating an astounding character from the astounding music. Yet the facts of Beethoven's life – such as are known for certain – create a rather more complicated and disturbing picture.

Born in the elegant but provincial city of Bonn, Beethoven's earliest musical training was at the hands of his singer father, a hard and unbending man whose decline into alcoholism made Ludwig the virtual head of the family during his teenage years. In 1787 a brief spell of study with Mozart in Vienna was interrupted by the death of his mother, but he returned there on a permanent basis three years later and began studying again – first with Haydn (from whom he "never learned anything"), then with Albrechtsberger and finally with Salieri, who taught him Italian vocal style. In Vienna, the musical capital of Europe, Beethoven rapidly established himself as a virtuoso pianist of the highest calibre: his initially rough style was refined after hearing the pianist Johann Sterkel and thereafter his pianistic supremacy was rarely challenged. He was admired, above all, for his amazing powers of improvisation, whether it be on a given theme or in developing an idea within a sonata movement.

Beethoven's success, however, was clouded by hearing difficulties, which had begun troubling him as early as 1797. In 1802, when medical treatment brought no improvement, he took himself off to the nearby village of Heiligenstadt for a rest cure. When this too proved fruitless, Beethoven, in near-suicidal depression, wrote a desperate and poignant letter to his two brothers explaining why he hadn't told them of his affliction earlier and outlining what he saw as his future as "an outcast; I can enter society practically only as true necessity demands". Only his art prevented him from taking his life: "it seemed to me impossible to leave the world until I had brought forth all that I felt was within me".

All the stories of Beethoven's misanthropy, his eccentricity and wildness, date from the decline in his hearing, which frequently caused him acute physical pain. Never the easiest of men, his frustration and anger at his condition made him intensely prickly, and the patience of his friends and family was frequently tested. Karl, his nephew and ward, was so oppressed by his uncle's heavy hand (Beethoven forbade him from seeing his mother) that he attempted suicide in order to be free of him. Even so, the power and charm of the composer's personality was such that he had a number of close relationships with women, though most of them were married nobility and therefore unattainable. The identity of Beethoven's greatest love, his "Immortal Beloved", remains a mystery to this day. The most likely candidate seems to be Antonie Brentano, whose youngest child Beethoven might just conceivably have fathered.

LEBRECHT COLLECTION

The young Beethoven

Despite moving within an aristocratic milieu, Beethoven's attitude to the upper classes was ambivalent. He was at heart a republican, and though nearly all of his patrons were titled – beginning with Count Waldstein in Bonn – he would not be condescended to. He ended his close friendship with the generous Prince Lichnowsky in 1806 by declaring: "There have been, and will be, thousands of princes. There is only one Beethoven." Whereas Mozart and his predecessors were craftsmen who supplied a commodity to a paying master, Beethoven insisted on asserting his independence and the absolute importance of self-expression: "What is in my heart must come out and so I write it down."

If Beethoven's confidence as a performer was gradually diminished by his deafness (he finally stopped playing publicly in 1815), then his imaginative powers as a composer grew greater and greater. Cushioned by an annuity provided in 1808 by his friend and pupil the Archduke Rudolph and two other nobles, his maturity as a composer was signalled two years earlier by the *Eroica* symphony, arguably the most significant single work of his entire life. As a broad generalization, Beethoven prior to the *Eroica* had been a composer of the eighteenth century; with this symphony music entered the age of Romanticism.

The post-*Eroica* decade produced a succession of masterpieces, including the opera *Fidelio*, the *Rasumovsky* string quartets, the *Violin Concerto*, the fourth and fifth piano concertos, symphonies four to eight, and some magnificent works for solo piano – notably the *Waldstein* and *Appassionata* sonatas. These "middle period" works, containing most of Beethoven's great melodic writing, have remained the most popular, but in terms of intensity and originality the finest was yet to come. Around the middle of the 1810s, his retreat from the outside world almost complete, Beethoven commenced perhaps the greatest continuous cycle of composition in history: the last five piano sonatas, the last five string quartets, the *Diabelli Variations*, the *Missa Solemnis* and, most famous of all, the gargantuan *Symphony No. 9*, all come from this, his so-called "late period". Never doubting the validity of his ground-breaking departures from convention, his last music is without precedent, characterized by ever greater abstraction and contrast; by the proximity of episodes of stridency and violence with lyrical passages that seem to melt into silence; by a sense of agonizing self-revelation.

As Beethoven plumbed the depths of introspection, his fame grew so far that, by 1824, when his final symphony was given its first performance, his name and music were international in a way that not even Mozart's had been. When he died, aged 57, obituarists recorded that a terrible storm had raged in Vienna, and that the dying man had shaken his fist at the heavens as thunder and lightning struck the town.

OPERA – FIDELIO

Although Beethoven dallied with numerous operatic plans from 1800 to 1815, he completed only one opera – *Fidelio*. It is, however, one of the greatest of all German operas and, in its mastery of Mozartian "realism", it can be seen as the apotheosis of eighteenth-century operatic style. With its themes of unselfish love, loyalty, courage, sacrifice and heroic endurance, *Fidelio* is furthermore the nearest thing Beethoven ever produced to an explicit political-philosophical creed.

The plot, said to be based upon an event during the French Revolution, concerns the unjust imprisonment of Florestan, husband of Leonore, who attempts to free him by disguising herself as a man and entering the service of Pizarro, the prison governor. Pizarro, a veritable emblem of *ancien régime* repression, tries to have Florestan executed before the arrival of Don Fernando, the minister of state, but his plot is thwarted by Leonore. Don Fernando arrives at the prison, sets Florestan free and duly punishes Pizarro. This simple narrative gives rise to some astonishing moments, perhaps the most powerful being the prisoners' chorus, a slow and deeply moving song of solidarity that opens with a simple set of shifting chords quite unlike anything ever written before.

The first performance in 1805 was not a success, owing partly to the simple fact that many people found the opera too long and too demanding. Even the subsequent heavy revisions did not give *Fidelio* the popularity of Mozart's more ingratiating operas, and it remains a woefully under-staged masterpiece. If you ever get the chance to see it in the opera house, you should jump at the chance – few other operas can match its sustained seriousness and intensity.

○ Ludwig, Vickers, Frick, Berry, Crass, Hallstein; Philharmonia Orchestra and Chorus; Klemperer (EMI CMS 769324-2; 2 CDs).

Klemperer's intense, slow-moving performance of *Fidelio* (made for EMI in 1961) is a very fine achievement, with Jon Vickers a splendid Florestan and Christa Ludwig unrivalled in the role of Leonore. Throughout his long career Klemperer had a profound affinity with this opera and, although at the time of this recording he was old, semi-paralysed and bearing the scars of sixty percent burns, his resolve and integrity produced an awe-inspiring performance.

○ Flagstad, Patzak, Schöffler, Greindl, Schwarzkopf; Vienna State Opera Chorus; Vienna Philharmonic Orchestra; Furtwängler (EMI CHS7 64901-2; 2 CDs).

There are two recordings boasting Furtwängler's name: an EMI studio session of 1952, and this one, taped at the Salzburg Festival two years earlier. The sound is far from perfect, but this recording has the sort of atmosphere that a studio session can never generate. Slow and fearsomely weighty, Furtwängler's tempi make terrible demands on his singers and yet they all rise to the challenge. Flagstad is a massive-voiced and deeply heartfelt Leonore, and it's to Julius Patzak's great credit that he doesn't seem spineless alongside her. The chorus is magnificent and Furtwängler's reading of *Leonore No. 3* (inserted before the finale) is tremendously exciting.

SACRED MUSIC

Beethoven's distinctly personal Christian faith, a faith that denied conventional observances and public display, was sorely tested throughout the years of his deafness, but two Masses came out of this period. The first of these, the *Mass in C*, is a fine work; the second, known as the *Missa Solemnis*, is the nineteenth century's finest.

Early in June 1819 Beethoven wrote to his pupil Archduke Rudolph who was to be installed as Archbishop of Olmütz the following year: "The day on which a High Mass composed by me will be performed during the ceremonies solemnized by Your Imperial Highness will be the most glorious day of my life." Soon afterwards he began work on his D major Mass, the *Missa Solemnis*, but this mighty, uncompromising work was not finally completed until 1823.

There's no piece of religious music to compare with the *Missa Solemnis*, for this is a composition that externalizes its creator's struggle to achieve inner peace, with extraordinary dynamic contrasts and passages that make enormous demands of the soloists. Perhaps the most remarkable section is the Benedictus, a huge, Gothic conception culminating in a ten-minute violin solo of extreme beauty that leads, like some massive papal procession, into the Agnus Dei, a section that incorporates an episode of brash, almost militaristic declamation. The polar opposite of most Masses, it's a disconcertingly exposed work, sometimes tranquil, sometimes strenuous, but always profoundly spiritual.

◑ Missa Solemnis: Janowitz, Ludwig, Wunderlich, Berry; Berlin Philharmonic Orchestra; Karajan (Deutsche Grammophon 423 913-2; 2 CDs; with Mozart, *Mass in C*).

Among the many recordings of the *Missa Solemnis* there are few serious rivals to this, one of Karajan's best recordings, featuring one of the finest vocal quartets of the century. It's not perfect – the tempi are sometimes too slow, the balance is odd in places, and the solo violin tends to wander out of tune – but the pathos and weight of the performance are desperately moving. The singing is magnificent (Janowitz and Wunderlich in particular), and Karajan's direction is consistently expressive.

○ Missa Solemnis: Mannion, Remnert, Taylor, Hauptmann; Choeurs de la Chapelle Royale et du Collegium Vocale; Orchestre des Champs-Elysées; Herreweghe (Harmonia Mundi HMC 90155).

This is a very different approach, which succeeds in blowing the cobwebs off what can be an unwieldy giant. Herreweghe's forces are smaller than Karajan's and none of his soloists are big stars, but he succeeds because he faces up to the Mass's striking originality and doesn't try to homogenize its stylistic richness. A superb recording in a fine acoustic which really captures both the restless energy and the grandeur of this great work.

THE SYMPHONIES

With a mere nine symphonies, Beethoven revolutionized the orchestra and overturned all previous attitudes to symphonic form. The first two, completed in 1800 and 1802 respectively, are openly based upon the examples of Mozart and Haydn, but the third – the *Eroica* – heralded an entirely new concept of scale. Numbers five through to nine increasingly free the structure from classical restraints and move swiftly towards the more Romantic, subjective approach that was to prevail in mid-nineteenth-century Europe. Beethoven completed his *Ninth Symphony* in 1824; just six years later, Berlioz completed his first symphonic work, the *Symphonie Fantastique*. The first complete recorded cycle of the symphonies was made in the 1930s by Felix Weingartner. Since then over fifty conductors have recorded these immense works, though frankly some of them shouldn't have bothered. There are, however, a few whose overview justifies the cost of buying the full set.

○ Complete Symphonies: Philharmonia; Karajan (EMI CMS 7 63310-2; 5 CDs).

First choice is the first of Karajan's four cycles, recorded with the Philharmonia in the 1950s – this is Karajan at his best and is far superior to his other sets.

O Complete Symphonies: Chamber Orchestra of Europe; Harnoncourt (Teldec 2292-46452-2; 5 CDs).

For a more modern interpretation, Harnoncourt's 1990 set is outstanding for the way it assimilates much of the discoveries of the period-instrument brigade without making a fetish out of it – these are powerful and highly expressive performances.

O Complete Symphonies: Vienna Philharmonic Orchestra; Furtwängler (EMI CHS7 63606-2; 5 CDs).

If interpretative vision matters to you more than sound quality, then Furtwängler's postwar cycle will offer genuine insights, though the playing is variable since the "cycle" was put together from performances given over quite a long spread of time.

⊙ Complete Symphonies: London Symphony Orchestra; Morris (Carlton 30368 01157, 01197 & 01207; 6 CDs).

At budget price, Wyn Morris's fine recordings with the LSO (in three double CDs) are excellent value: tempi are occasionally eccentric, but the orchestral playing is magnificent, with the recording of the ninth especially fine.

SYMPHONY NO. 1

Though neither of Beethoven's first two symphonies is comparable to the majesty and innovation of the *Eroica*, it is a mistake to look upon them as mere preludes to that amazing piece – by the time Beethoven came to write the first symphony he was already 30 and had a considerable body of music to his name. *Symphony No. 1* clearly reflects Haydn's towering presence in late eighteenth-century Vienna, but Beethoven brought his own, rough-edged manner to the old master's style – Beethoven's fingerprints are especially in evidence in his reworking of Haydn's trick of slow introductions to the outer movements.

O Chamber Orchestra of Europe; Harnoncourt (Teldec 9031-75708-2; with *Symphony No. 3*).

Coupled with an outstanding performance of the *Eroica*, Harnoncourt's reading of *Symphony No. 1* brings out the wit and sprightliness of the piece in an utterly winning manner. Tight ensemble and an overriding sense of energy, which characterize the COE's approach to the cycle as a whole, is here employed with a control and a lightness of touch which is in marked contrast to the later more grandiloquent symphonies.

SYMPHONY NO. 2

The *Symphony No. 2* grew out of a period of intense despair as Beethoven struggled to come to terms with his increasing deafness. Amazingly, it's a work that bears little sign of this torment – rather, it bubbles with life and optimism. This is more obviously a piece by Beethoven than is the first symphony – the leg-pulling Scherzo, for example, is unmistakably his, with its innovative scoring and its unexpected exchanges, stops and starts. On the other hand, the finale – while maintaining the mood of the preceding movement – plainly looks to the eighteenth century as it slips into a polyphonic style that owes considerably more to Bach than to Mozart or Haydn.

O North German Radio Symphony Orchestra; Wand (RCA RD60058; with *Symphony No. 4*).

The live cycle by the veteran German conductor sparkles with life and the sheer joy of music-making, nowhere more so than in the performance of *Symphony No. 2*. Speeds are lively without sounding rushed, and the bright sound quality heightens the effect of spontaneity and celebration.

SYMPHONY NO. 3

Beethoven's *Symphony No. 3* is better known as the *Eroica*, a title thoroughly befitting what many people consider the greatest symphony ever written. Completed in the spring of 1804, this amazing score contains the very foundations of Romanticism in its grandiose gestures and burgeoning themes, and in its unprecedented scale – the outer movements are enormous structures that virtually ignore the accepted conventions of sonata form.

The thunderous opening chords – like those launching the fifth symphony – are some of the most recognizable in all music, and the last movement is the most exciting and thrilling of all his symphonies. On the way to this finale one crosses extremes of exultation and misery that belong to a world unknown to the music of the eighteenth century. Another crucial characteristic of the *Eroica* is its anticipation of programme music – ie music with a narrative. That said, the extra-musical references are more elusive than those to be found in Berlioz or Strauss, for example. Some have suggested that the second movement's funeral march was inspired by a real-life cortège or by a poem describing one, while others – on slightly surer ground – have inferred that the references to English and Hungarian music in the last movement were intended as tributes to the nations uniting to defeat Napoleon (the symphony's dedicatee until he went and crowned himself emperor, whereupon Beethoven tore the title page in half and rededicated it to Prince Lobkowitz).

O Chamber Orchestra of Europe; Harnoncourt (Teldec 9031-75708-2; with *Symphony No. 1*).

From the very beginning this performance announces itself

as an electrifying one. The opening movement is highly dynamic, with the great clattering chords being given an extra impact by the use of natural trumpets. The Funeral March – the emotional heart of the work – achieves an astonishing aura of dignified despair, while the triumphant finale has a fluidity and flow which few other conductors have matched.

O San Francisco Symphony Orchestra; Blomstedt (Decca 430 515-2; with *Symphony No. 1*).

Blomstedt's performance of the *Eroica* is at times over-cautious, but it has an impressively purposeful clear-sightedness, especially in the opening two movements. Where other conductors have swamped the music beneath aggression and bombast, his unerring sense of structure and steady tempi imbue the performance with true dignity.

SYMPHONY NO. 4

Beethoven's fourth symphony, completed in 1806 and performed the following year, is often dismissed – along with the other even-numbered symphonies – as one of his "lighter", unclouded pieces. The categorization is hard to fathom, as the symphony shares its mysterious key of B flat with some of Beethoven's most profound music – the *"Archduke" Piano Trio*, the *Piano Sonata No. 29* and the *String Quartet No. 13*. This neglected symphony is a witty yet often disturbing creation, with an opening movement that recalls the titanic strength of the first movement of the *Eroica* and an Adagio not far removed from the *Eroica*'s funeral march.

O Bavarian State Orchestra; Kleiber (Orfeo C100841H).

This Orfeo CD, recorded live with the Bavarian State Orchestra, is a truly remarkable performance. Kleiber's rhythmic flexibility verges on the extreme, but he maintains a flowing, uninterrupted sense of line that holds the music together no matter what his chosen pulse. Though it contains little over half an hour's music, this CD is special enough to justify the full price.

SYMPHONY NO. 5

The first five bars of the fifth symphony – perhaps the most famous musical motif ever written – are so terrifyingly direct that commentators have been unable to resist attributing some autobiographical "meaning" to them. "Fate knocking at the door" is a more noble interpretation than the one that links the orchestral hammering to the arrival of Beethoven's bad-tempered cleaner, but this exceptional work really doesn't benefit from any narrative additions. Those opening beats provide the impetus for a first movement that is as concentrated as anything in symphonic literature, and the unrelenting forward motion is maintained right through the whole symphony. The impact of the finale – again announced by united chords – is heightened by the addition of trombones, piccolo and contrabassoon, instruments that heralded enormous advances in orchestration. The headlong rush into C major at the close is almost as euphoric as in the *Eroica*, concluding with emphatic chordal repetitions that still sound shocking.

◑ Vienna Philharmonic Orchestra; Kleiber (Deutsche Grammophon 447 400-2; with *Symphony No. 7*).

There are numerous fine recordings of the fifth, but two – by Carlos Kleiber and Victor de Sabata – really stand out. Kleiber's version is one of the most celebrated recordings since the war. The last movement may be slightly undercharged, but the drive that Kleiber imparts to the first movement and the Scherzo are unequalled by any other conductor in the studio – this is one of the very few performances that doesn't make this symphony sound hackneyed music. De Sabata's live recording with the New York Philharmonic is an incandescent performance despite poor sound; unfortunately it is not currently available.

SYMPHONY NO. 6 – THE PASTORAL

It is remarkable that the fifth and sixth symphonies were both written in 1808 and were performed on the same evening shortly before Christmas the same year. Subtitled the "Pastoral" in response to its obvious representation of the countryside, the *Symphony No. 6* is replete with characteristic Beethoven touches, with a profusion of contrasting ideas following hard on each other's heels, but is completely unlike its Promethean predecessor in atmosphere. Its five highly melodic movements are predominantly sunny, and Beethoven attached unambiguously bucolic titles to each of them – "Awakening of joyful feelings on arrival in the country", "Merry-making of the country folk" and so on. He was anxious, though, that the symphony should not be taken as a sequence of naïvely descriptive episodes – as he wrote in his notebook, "the meaning of the work is obvious without verbal description". Of all Beethoven's symphonies, the sixth is the one that most clearly looks forward to the tone-poems of the late nineteenth century.

⊙ NDR Sinfonieorchester; Wand (RCA 61930-2; with *Symphony No. 5*).

This CD came as a surprise when it was released late in 1993. Günther Wand was 80 when he made this live recording but his performance is bursting with energy. Some of Wand's earlier work was excessively concerned with fidelity to the score, but here he delivers a fresh and personal view of a piece that can too often sound hackneyed.

SYMPHONY NO. 7

The seventh symphony, composed during 1812, plainly reflects the terrible circumstances in which it was written. The Napoleonic wars were wreaking havoc across Europe, Beethoven's deafness was far advanced and, to make things worse, he was in love with a woman who was already married – recognizing the futility of his affections, he wrote letters to her which he never sent. Amongst this anguish he created the gigantic *Symphony No. 7*, a work that was one of Beethoven's notable financial successes.

It opens – as does the first – with a slow introduction, but this one leads into a thrilling Vivace, in which Beethoven juxtaposes rhythms derived from Sicilian dance music with a cleverly syncopated theme. The following Allegretto is an almost unrelievedly doom-laden episode, with its relentlessly repeated statements of grief and mourning. An austere Presto then precedes an Allegro of manic fury, which is dominated by monumentally grand themes, the orchestral texture being dominated by the timpani and horns.

◑ Vienna Philharmonic Orchestra; Kleiber (Deutsche Grammophon 447 400-2; with *Symphony No. 5*).

Carlos Kleiber's astounding vision of the seventh, now coupled with the fifth (see above), is the most thrilling performance of this symphony on disc. As with most of his work, there is a tautness to his conducting that keeps the tension running high, but never out of control. His is one of the few performances that takes the Allegretto at the tempo Beethoven intended, maintaining a sense of momentum rather than – as is more usual – milking the pathos with a slow-paced approach.

SYMPHONY NO. 8

The eighth symphony – often disparagingly known as the "Little" Symphony – was written at the same time as the heroic seventh, though you'd never guess it. This is a much lighter piece, with a vein of humour that's apparent from the start. The polite-toned first movement, which at first hearing might seem something of a regression into nostalgia, is a self-consciously slight piece of music in which Beethoven makes fun of the recently invented metronome, a mechanism recently devised by his friend Johann Maelzel. The sense of fun continues throughout the Scherzo (for once a genuinely jokey movement), the Trio and, finally, into a bizarrely constructed Finale, in which Beethoven plays one last trick by beginning the coda extremely early, and using it to create entirely new themes rather than bring the music to a swift conclusion. Formally, this is Beethoven's oddest symphonic creation; it's also his most entertaining.

◑ Royal Philharmonic Orchestra; Beecham (EMI CDM7 63398-2).

Thomas Beecham, one of the wittiest men ever to wield a baton, was a natural for this remarkable work. It's a typically enthusiastic performance, encouraging his players to relax into the music to produce an account that contains nothing pompous or heavy-handed.

SYMPHONY NO. 9

The idea of setting Schiller's *Ode to Joy* came to Beethoven as early as 1793, but it was not until the winter of 1823–24 that he completed the work for which that poem provided the climax – the *Symphony No. 9*, or *Choral Symphony*. Beethoven's most grandiose work, it heralded the epics of Wagner and Berlioz, and has entered the Western consciousness to such an extent that, over a century and a half later, it was the obvious choice as the anthem of the European Community – a tepid political approximation to the universal community celebrated in Schiller's text and Beethoven's triumphant music. It's a work so stupendous that later composers felt a superstitious dread of completing their ninth symphony, as if it were tempting fate to attempt to venture beyond the number marked by Beethoven's final work in the genre. For others, however, the ninth symphony was a catalyst. Beethoven's fusion of poetry and orchestral music was the starting point for Wagner's obsession with the development of an art form that would make possible the expression of unbounded feeling and, when he laid the foundation stone of his theatre at Bayreuth, Wagner celebrated the occasion with a performance of the *Symphony No. 9*, paying homage to a score that was the foundation stone of his own life's work.

Lasting over an hour, the four movements of the ninth symphony are extraordinarily diverse and can be a desperately draining experience. The long opening movement – combining innovative orchestration with formal restraint – leads to a fiery Scherzo, an amazing piece of music that seems to be on the brink of being forced apart under its own head of steam. Nothing in these two movements prepares one for the massive spirituality of the Adagio – almost unbearably moving in its troubled tranquillity, this one section of the ninth can lay claim to being the most influential forerunner of Romantic expressionism. The finale, a colossal conceit for four soloists, a chorus and full orchestra, is the symphony's centre of gravity – indeed, it quite explicitly declares its primacy, summoning quotes from the previous movements only to reject them in favour of the titanic outburst of the *Ode to Joy*. Beethoven's concept of the symphony as a cogent unit with an overriding dynamic that propels the audience towards the climactic last movement here reaches its glorious fruition.

O Briem, Höngen, Anders, Watzke; Bruno Kittel Choir; Berlin Philharmonic Orchestra; Furtwängler (Music and Arts CD 653).

If you're not fussy about sound quality, then buy Wilhelm Furtwängler's March 1942 performance, live from Berlin. This is the greatest of his ten recordings of the symphony (five of which are currently available), and one of the greatest recordings ever made. It's a reading unlike any other, imbued with religious devotion and yet full of anguish and torment – his vision of the last two movements is terrifying, absolutely unencumbered by mere accuracy.

◑ Rodgers, Jones, Bronder, Terfel; Royal Liverpool Choir and Orchestra; Mackerras (EMI CD-EMX 2186).

At the opposite end of the spectrum from Furtwängler comes this performance by Mackerras, which is remarkable for the extent to which the conductor refuses to impose a "reading" on the work: this is a performance where respect for the score is absolutely paramount. The result is neither bland or anonymous; rather, it is fresh and consistently exciting. Like Harnoncourt, Mackerras has learned from current scholarship about performance practice, and the result is a performance high on joy and low on solemnity.

THE CONCERTOS

Beethoven's first concerto was composed for the piano in 1795 and his last, again for piano, in 1809. In between he composed a further three concertos for piano, one for violin and one for piano trio – one of the very few ever written for violin, cello and piano, and the only Beethoven concerto to fall short of greatness. The concerto for solo violin, on the other hand, is a highly melodic masterpiece with a sense of cohesion and an understanding of the instrument that has remained unequalled. Each of the piano concertos is a microcosm of the composer's style at the time of its composition, and show the evolution in his conception of the relative roles of orchestra and soloist. The piano finally triumphs in the opening bars of the fifth, the *Emperor Concerto*, a work written for an ideal instrument that would not become a physical reality until the time of Brahms's *Piano Concerto No. 1*.

THE PIANO CONCERTOS

Beethoven's piano concertos were the first to challenge the formula of the eighteenth century. Until Beethoven's emergence, the piano repeated or developed an opening theme played by the orchestra, and sometimes took over the material on its own – but never did it battle openly with the "accompaniment". Beethoven recognized the form's potential for dramatic conflict and gave the protagonists material to be played independently of each other, but working towards a common goal. With Beethoven the concerto ceased to be a series of delicate exchanges between soloist and orchestra.

All five concertos are in three movements, with a slow and intense central movement being followed by a finale of generally boisterous, upbeat temperament. All five are splendid creations, but the *Emperor* stands clear of the others – Beethoven would not have approved of the title, but it does justice to the stature of the piece. The piano can now more than stand up to the orchestra, which here, with a few chords, does little more than make a harmonic statement of key to announce the soloist's entry. The piano then lets loose a flood of sound that washes over the orchestra before attacking a cadenza of great difficulty which, eventually, allows the orchestra back in to pursue a standard sonata-form exposition. The slow movement is the most touching and beautiful of all those to be found in the piano concertos (though the fourth concerto runs it close), and leads into the animated Rondo finale by a "bridge" of mystical, lightly touched chords.

⊙ Piano Concertos Nos. 1–5: Pollini; Berlin Philharmonic Orchestra; Abbado (Deutsche Grammophon 439 770-2; 3 CDs).

Maurizio Pollini has twice recorded all five concertos. The more recent cycle, a live set made with Abbado, is more \a real partnership than his earlier set. These are not perfect recordings, but Pollini's technique is so fine that slight irritations caused by close miking and occasionally anonymous orchestral playing never get in the way. Some find Pollini's obsession with accuracy off-putting, but on balance this is the best cycle of recent years.

◑ Piano Concertos Nos. 1–5: Backhaus; Vienna Philharmonic Orchestra; Schmidt-Isserstedt (Decca 433 891-2; 3 CDs).

Wilhelm Backhaus played his first tour as a boy of 16 in 1899; his complete set of the Beethoven concertos for Decca was made towards the end of his life, but is remarkable for the freshness and forcefulness of his playing. The sound quality is a bit dated and some of Backhaus's slow tempi may be slightly frustrating but this is a brilliantly thought-through cycle, full of personality.

⊙ Piano Concerto No. 1: Michelangeli; Vienna Symphony Orchestra; Giulini (Deutsche Grammophon 419 248-2; with *Piano Sonata No. 4*).

The second to be written, *No. 1* is the most quixotic and lively of the early concertos. Michelangeli might not be an obvious choice for this work (several critics loathed this recording) but, in tandem with Giulini, he really lets his hair down, bringing out the work's wit and energy – above all in the brilliant and carefree finale.

◑ Piano Concerto No. 2: Argerich; London Sinfonietta (EMI CDM7 63575-2; with Haydn *Piano Concerto No. 11*).

Argerich's earlier recording of the second concerto, which she conducts from the keyboard, is to be preferred to her recent recording with Sinopoli: there's a lightness and crispness of articulation to her playing which makes the concerto – the first to be written – come alive in a way that rarely happens.

⊙ Piano Concertos Nos. 3 & 4: Kovacevich; BBC Symphony Orchestra; Davis (Philips 426 062-2).

Stephen Kovacevich (formerly Stephen Bishop) is one of the great Beethoven pianists of the last thirty years. His recordings of the concertos with Colin Davis, available individually, are all good but this is the best of the set. Where Pollini is all precision, Kovacevich is expansive and poetic. His treatment of the magnificent slow movement of the fourth possesses a clarity and an intensity which is awe-inspiring.

◑ Piano Concerto No. 5: Kempff; Berlin Philharmonic Orchestra; Leitner (Deutsche Grammophon 419 468-2; with *Piano Sonata No. 32*).

Perhaps the best single CD of the *Emperor* is the one from Wilhelm Kempff, no show-stopping virtuoso but a musician with a deep affinity with Beethoven's music. Eschewing the overblown gestures that some pianists resort to in the *Emperor*, he is strong without being overassertive, and in the slow movement he achieves a liquid sonority which, with Leitner's beautifully phrased accompaniment, is highly affecting.

⊙ Piano Concerto No. 5: Levin; Orchestre Révolutionnaire et Romantique; Gardiner (Deutsche Grammophon 447 771-2; with *Choral Fantasy*).

There are now many "period instrument" pianists around prepared to take on the Beethoven concertos, but so far only Robert Levin has produced results that can compete with the best. Sensitively partnered by Gardiner, Levin uses an 1812 piano which is both harder-sounding and more limited in volume than a modern piano. In the slow movement this means a less singing line than usual, but the piano's reticence and frailty in the face of the orchestra is oddly touching. Worth investigating.

THE VIOLIN CONCERTO

Beethoven's *Violin Concerto* was first performed on December 23, 1806 by Franz Clement, who hadn't seen the piece before its premiere, let alone rehearsed it. It was surely for this reason that the press found little to praise in the work – except Clement's "entertainment" between the first and second movements, when he played a sonata of his own composition on one string, with the violin held upside down. The concerto remained lost in obscurity until Joseph Joachim rescued it as a child and gave a series of memorable performances with Mendelssohn conducting.

The first movement – based upon a series of four crotchets first tapped out on the timpani – is a grand construction lasting over twenty minutes alone, but it contains music of such beauty that you might wish it lasted twice as long. The Adagio is even more exquisite, featuring one of the composer's most inspired tunes, and the finale offers superb counterplay between orchestra and soloist – a sparring relationship that, in essence, makes this the first Romantic violin concerto.

⊙ Perlman; Berlin Philharmonic Orchestra; Barenboim (EMI CDC7 49567-2; with *Two Romances*).

Izthak Perlman has recorded this work more than once; his 1986 CD – a "live" version edited from a several concerts with studio patching – is one of his very best performances on record, if slightly dry-sounding. It's particularly notable for Perlman's brilliantly lyrical playing of Kreisler's imaginative cadenza to the first movement.

◑ Menuhin; Philharmonia Orchestra; Furtwängler (EMI CDH7 69799-2; with Mendelssohn, *Violin Concerto*).

Made in 1954, this is one of Furtwängler's very last recordings and it makes an eloquent swan song. Menuhin – perhaps the work's greatest modern interpreter – is on his very best form: the tone is sweet but never simpering, and the sense of line assured and firm. It's an amazing partnership which generates a real quality of a unique moment in time.

○ Heifetz; Philharmonic Symphony Orchestra; Rodzinski (Music and Arts CD 3873; 2 CDs; with concertos by Korngold, Brahms, Mendelssohn and Sibelius).

Heifetz's live recording, made on January 14, 1945, is the stuff of dreams. His tone and delivery are light and unfussy, yet Heifetz's prodigious technical proficiency never dominates the performance – it's the music one remembers.

THE TRIPLE CONCERTO

The so-called *Triple Concerto* for violin, cello and piano is something of an oddity and until quite recently was regarded as one of Beethoven's weaker (or lighter) works. It certainly lacks the dramatic impact of the violin concerto, and seems to look back to the slightly earlier genre of the Sinfonia concertante, in which the soloists were more closely integrated with the orchestra. The relative easiness of the piano part reflects the fact that an "amateur" pianist, the Archduke Rudolph, gave the first performance with two professionals, Seidler and Kraft, on violin and cello.

There's a strange and elegiac quality to the concerto's opening, and the cello's statement of the sombre main theme makes you regret that Beethoven didn't write a concerto for that instrument alone. If the first movement slightly outstays its welcome, then the second – again in subdued mood – simply serves as a dark introduction to the bravura finale, an energetic polonaise which really wears its dance origins on its sleeve.

○ Beaux Arts Trio; Leipzig Gewandhaus Orchestra; Masur (Philips 438 005-2; with the *Choral Fantasia*).

Using a chamber group as soloists for this work has the obvious advantages of tight ensemble and a built-in rapport between the players. That's certainly the case in this performance, which under Masur's dynamic direction packs considerably more of a punch than usual. The cello part, which really dominates the solo writing, is played with great warmth and feeling by Peter Wiley. The coupling of the *Choral Fantasia*, a trial run for the ninth symphony, is an added bonus.

CHAMBER MUSIC

Chamber music is, by definition, an intimate and personal means of expressing musical ideas, and much of Beethoven's most beguiling music can be found in small forms like the piano trios (for piano, cello and violin) and the violin sonatas (for piano and violin). But Beethoven's restless and probing mind meant that nearly every chamber genre that he attempted more than once had its formal limits challenged and extended. Thus many works have a complexity and a depth of feeling that have led some critics to describe them as symphonic in scope. Examples would include the *Archduke Trio* and the *Kreutzer Sonata* for violin and piano. This sense of development, of pushing a genre to its formal and emotional limits, is most dramatically exemplified in the string quartets, which range from the utterly conventional to works so subjective and experimental that Beethoven's contemporaries could scarcely acknowledge them as music at all.

THE PIANO TRIOS

Beethoven's first published works – his Opus 1 – were three trios for piano, cello and violin, and already they show a marked advance on Haydn's trios in the comparative independence of the three parts. Their freedom from Haydn's frequently oppressive formality looks forward to the first mature trios, the pair that comprises Op. 70: displaying all sorts of harmonic twists, thematic innovations and structural idiosyncrasies, these trios make much of the piano part and contain plenty of those dramatic outbursts that are typical of Beethoven's middle period. Even more arresting is first of the two Op. 70 trios (1808), nicknamed the *Ghost* because of its mysterious and haunting Largo; its sibling boasts a cheerful, bombastic finale that's the most entertaining music Beethoven composed for this combination of intruments.

The so-called *Archduke Trio*, Op. 97 (1811), was Beethoven's last full-scale work for piano trio, and is typically conclusive. The third movement is its centre of gravity: a highly moving set of variations, with the cello dominating the thematic content, it opens with a hymn-like theme and progresses to a coda which magnificently sums up the movement's ideas. The finale might be less powerful than that of Op. 70 No. 2, but it nevertheless has a sweeping rhythmic power.

○ Piano Trios Nos. 1–11: Beaux Arts Trio (Philips 436 948-2; 3 CDs).

The Trio Zingara have made the best recorded overview of the complete trios, but their set (on the Collins label) is not currently available. Nearly as good, if at times a little hectic, are these 1965 recordings, by the great Beaux Arts Trio. Their trademark is a rich and full tone and the kind of rapt and attentive ensemble that only comes from playing together a long time.

◐ Piano Trios Nos. 5 & 7: Szeryng, Fournier, Kempff (Deutsche Grammophon 429 712-2).

The *Ghost* and *Archduke*, the best known of all the trios, are often coupled together on one disc. A later incarnation of the Beaux Arts Trio recorded them in the late 1970s, but for a rather different approach try this recording by three outstanding soloists, two of whom – Szeryng and Kempff – were particularly renowned Beethoven interpreters. It's more introspective playing than that of the Beaux Arts, but what you lose in tonal sheen you gain in a kind of steely intensity and concentration.

THE VIOLIN SONATAS

Beethoven was the first composer to write sonatas for "Piano and . . ." as opposed to the classical norm of sonatas for ". . . and Piano", an arrangement that had subjugated the keyboard to the role of accompanying instrument. In Beethoven's violin sonatas the piano carries as much responsibility for the musical argument as the violin, and many of his violin sonatas are fearsomely difficult for the pianist.

Of the ten violin sonatas, *Sonata No. 5*, subtitled the *Spring*, and *Sonata No. 9*, known as the *Kreutzer*, are recorded and performed almost to the exclusion of the remaining eight. They do indeed warrant the attention, yet they are very different pieces indeed. As its nickname suggests, the *Spring* sonata is a light-hearted and airy work: opening with one of the most charmingly lyrical of all Beethoven's melodies, it's a piece that demands beauty of tone rather than trailblazing virtuosity. The *Kreutzer*, on the other hand, might initially seem to require nothing but virtuosity. Named after a leading French violinist who never played it, it was premiered by the Afro-English violinist George Bridgetower, who Beethoven greatly admired but later fell out with. Both parts are fiendishly difficult, although the piano is very much the dominant party and carries much of the weight – especially in the first movement. The passionate exchanges and heavy counterpoint of this movement are particularly dramatic and inspired Tolstoy to write his novella, *The Kreutzer Sonata*, about a wife-murderer in which music is condemned as being a powerful and morally subversive force. (Tolstoy's story in turn inspired Janáček to write his brilliantly disturbing *String Quartet No. 1* – see p.208.)

◑ Complete Sonatas for Piano and Violin: Szeryng, Haebler (Philips 442 625-2; 4 CDs).

If you're seeking a complete set of the sonatas then Szeryng and Haebler take the honours in the face of some pretty stiff competition. They are at the best in the more lyrical moments with Szeryng's sweet but incisive tone and unerring sense of line especially effective in the *Spring Sonata*. The one disappointment is the *Kreutzer*, which is just a little undercharged – but it's a notoriously difficult piece to really bring off.

◑ Sonatas Nos. 5 & 9: Perlman, Ashkenazy (Decca 410 554-2).

Several performers couple the most famous two sonatas on one disc single. Perlman and Ashkenazy achieve the best results because both performers have a wide enough emotional range in their playing to encompass the very different moods within these pieces.

◐ Sonatas Nos. 9 & 10: Kremer, Argerich (Deutsche Grammophon 447 054-2).

The most breathtaking performance of the *Kreutzer*, by Josef Szigeti with Bartók at the piano, is not currently available. Equally passionate if not quite so demented are Gidon Kremer and Martha Argerich, who have recorded the whole cycle but only really come into their own with the *Kreutzer*. There is an almost palpable air of unease in the violin's opening broken chords, which builds into an almost unbearable tension. Undoubtedly both performers push the work to extremes but the result is overwhelming.

THE STRING QUARTETS

The string quartet genre had come to prominence during the latter half of the eighteenth century, when Mozart and Haydn started to produce quartets of exceptional quality. Beethoven's first set of six quartets (Op. 18) bear his individual stamp but are clearly written in the shadows of his great predecessors. His seventh quartet, Op. 59 No. 1 (1806) – first of three quartets named after Count Rasumovsky, their dedicatee – is the turning point and initiates a departure from accepted rules quite as radical as that brought about by the *Eroica* symphony. The subsequent middle-period quartets are characterized by slow introductions, lengthy four-movement structures, complicated dramatic counterpoint and the development of an elaborate sonority far removed from the decorous formality of Haydn. Even more startling are the last five quartets. As spare and intense as the last five piano sonatas, these astonishing compositions are marked by an increasing predilection for a polyphonic style, evident not only in movements that are overtly fugal but also in episodes where the four separate parts finally become thematically indivisible, creating a sense of four minds combining for the perfect expression of a single idea.

◑ Complete String Quartets: Végh String Quartet (Auvidis Valois V440; 8 CDs).

Recorded in the early 1970s, the Végh Quartet performances remain at the top of the pile despite some stiff opposition. Led by an outstanding violinist, Sandor Végh, there is a constant sense of exploration in these readings as if the players were determined to penetrate to the very heart of the music. Some may find Végh's audible huffing and puffing a little off-putting, but it's a small price to pay for such deeply felt and committed playing.

O Complete String Quartets: Lindsay String Quartet (ASV CD DCS305 [3 CDs], CD DCS 207 [2 CDs] & CD DCS403 [4 CDs]).

One of the most searching and original cycles comes from the Lindsay Quartet. These recordings are at times eccentric and occasionally melodramatic, but they have an electric sense of occasion normally found only in the concert hall. Leaving little to editing or post-production, the Lindsays possess an urgency that touches every movement – even the earliest quartets are given a new lease of life by their vital sense of discovery.

O Complete String Quartets: Emerson String Quartet (Deutsche Grammophon 447 075-2; 7 CDs).

Both the above sets regularly sacrifice precision and finesse in the pursuit of maximum expression. If you think this might bother you, then a better choice would be the Emerson Quartet, a group whose technical expertise and panache is truly breathtaking. There are occasions, especially in the late quartets, when the perfection of the playing seems to contradict the raw and vulnerable spirit of the music, but theirs is, nonetheless, a very fine achievement.

THE EARLY AND MIDDLE QUARTETS

There is a lot of fine music in Beethoven's first six quartets, but the debt to his great predecessors is everywhere apparent, and only in the melancholy last movement of *Quartet No. 6* does a unique voice really emerge. Perhaps the best place for the newcomer to start is the *Quartet No. 7*, the first of the quartets dedicated to Count Rasumovsky, written when Mozart and Haydn's influences were completely assimilated. The *Quartet No. 7* still respects the classical forms, but employs such idiosyncratic harmonic and melodic devices that, at the first performance, the instrumentalists laughed at what they were expected to play and the audience launched an angry protest. The middle two movements epitomize Beethoven's innovative writing: the Scherzo juggles numerous ideas, each passing within sight of the others but never uniting, while in the impassioned and poignant third movement, Beethoven reverses the accepted hierarchy of the opening motifs – the first being lithe and elegant, with the second taking on the punchy, dominant role normally given to the opening statement. Apart from the second and third *Rasumovsky* quartets, the other middle-period pieces are the tenth, known as the *Harp* (1809) because of the pizzicato exchanges in the first movement, and the eleventh, the *Serioso* (1810) – unlike most, a title ascribed by Beethoven – which is the last and most powerful quartet before the final five.

O String Quartets Nos. 1–9: Végh Quartet (Auvidis Valois V4401, V4402, V4403 & V4404).

The Végh Quartet recordings can also be purchased as individual discs – a good way of getting to know the works gradually. Their playing of the early and middle quartets is characterized by a robustness which brings out the frequent playfulness of these pieces as much as their seriousness. In the more contemplative slow movements there is a raptness and an empathy between the players which few other quartets achieve.

THE LATE QUARTETS

Beethoven began the late quartets in 1822, after a gap of twelve years, prompted by an amateur cellist Prince Galitzin who commisioned the first three. Each of the five is a titanic piece but two of them, the *Quartets Nos. 13* and *14*, reach levels of profundity astonishing even for Beethoven. *Quartet No. 13* contains some of the most troubling of all Beethoven's music – the achingly beautiful *Cavatina* and the torrential last movement, *Grosse Fuge* (Great Fugue). The Schuppanzigh Quartet, who gave the first performances, were quite unable to understand this music, and refused to play the *Grosse Fuge* – their protests over its impossible technical demands allegedly prompted Beethoven to remark "what do I care about you and your fucking fiddles".

In the Schuppanzigh's defence, the fugue is a terrifying piece. Running to 745 bars and lasting over twenty minutes, it reaches new extremities of anguish and violence, making terrible demands of the four performers. Beethoven agreed to write an alternative ending for the quartet and, in a moment of exasperation, gave the musicians a feeble replacement finale that bore no relation to the remainder of his late music. Beethoven claimed that the *Grosse Fuge*, published separately as Op. 133, was the "the high point to my entire chamber music" but arguably *Quartet No. 14* is an even greater work. It begins with a slow and gentle fugue which builds to an almost unbearable intensity and has at its core a set of variations of increasing complexity. All of these last quartets communicate a sense of the composer thinking out loud, with the listener as a kind of privileged eavesdropper. They are frequently difficult, though not as relentlesly serious as some have suggested, but what makes them so satisfying is precisely the demands that they make: this is music which, unlike some, calls for an active and concentrated listening response before it will yield up its magic. It is certainly worth the effort.

O String Quartets Nos. 10–16: Végh Quartet (Auvidis Valois V4405, V4406, V4407 & V4408).

The Végh Quartet approach the late quartets with exactly the right balance of spontaneity and respect – knowing just when to step back and let the music speak for itself. Similarly, the ensemble sometimes stresses the individuality of the players and at other times their unanimity. It is this consistent sensitivity which makes them so outstanding – the light and shade of these great works is never exaggerated.

◑ **The Late Quartets: Busch Quartet** (EMI CHS5 65308-2; with *String Quartets Nos. 1 & 9, Violin Sonata No. 3,* etc; 4 CDs).

The Busch Quartet were one of the last quartets to play in a style that had its foundations in the nineteenth century. In this set, recorded in the 1930s, they produce a tone quite unlike modern quartets, with occasional swoops between the notes, but on the whole only using vibrato when the music demands a sweetening of the texture. The recorded sound is not brilliant and the absence of the *Grosse Fuge* is a drawback, but the sheer sense of immediacy and of struggle within the group makes for many electrifying moments.

PIANO MUSIC

Just as Beethoven's string quartets are the finest body of quartets created by one person, so his piano sonatas are the summit of that instrument's repertoire. All 32 sonatas are masterpieces, while his final major work for solo piano, the *Diabelli Variations*, represents a profound summation of his lifetime's work.

The crucial thing to remember when listening to these works is that every note that Beethoven wrote for the piano was written solely with himself in mind. Beethoven's independence and self-reliance colour each of the 32 sonatas, from the three pieces that comprise Op. 2, begun when Beethoven was only 23, to the final Opus 111, a composition so extraordinary that Thomas Mann devoted part of his *Doctor Faustus* to an exposition on its form. His attitude towards the piano was typical of his attitude towards all instruments, in that everything he wrote posed a challenge to the piano's resources. In fact piano technology was progressing at an astonishing rate during this period: the range of notes was extended by two and a half octaves, the sustaining pedal was developed and there was a marked difference between the light-toned Austrian instruments (which Beethoven seems to have preferred) and the heavier actions of French and English pianos. Even so, with the last five sonatas Beethoven went as far as the instrument could possibly take him, and then looked towards the string quartet as the ultimate means of expression.

As with the symphonies and the quartets, you should really listen to the whole of the piano sonatas, and the easiest way to do that is to buy one of the cycles listed below. However, if want to get to know them slowly, begin with the ones we've singled out – they are not necessarily the greatest, but each one vividly characterizes certain crucial aspects of Beethoven's approach to the form.

O Complete Piano Sonatas: Goode (Elektra Nonesuch 7559-79328-2; 10 CDs).

Richard Goode's cycle is at its best with the last five sonatas, which are available in a separate box (the rest of the cycle is divided into two four-CD sets). The middle-period sonatas sometimes suffer from a percussive and over-weighted strength, while his playing of the early sonatas suggests that Goode is happier with profound introspection than with humour. Despite these limitations, this is a personal and very revealing cycle that can stand up to any of the existing competition – it's also well recorded and superbly annotated.

⊙ **Complete Piano Sonatas: Lill** (ASV CDQS 6055–6064; 10 CDs).

There is no better overview of the sonatas than John Lill's retrospective for ASV – available as ten separate CDs at budget price (there's no boxed set). Don't think that the price tag means you're getting cheap performances – Lill might not possess the breathtaking technique of a Pollini or a Gilels, but he has a powerful grip on these noble pieces, especially the middle-period sonatas. Lill's performances are instantly recognizable, chiefly because of the definition he brings to the rhythmic idiosyncrasies that many pianists simply gloss over.

⊙ **Complete Piano Sonatas: Perl** (Arte Nova 74321 40740-2; 10 CDs).

Amazingly there exists another outstanding complete set available at budget price (also available as individual CDs). Alfredo Perl is a young Chilean pianist with an amazing technique and plenty of passion. Like Lill, he never shies away from the more weird and quirky aspects of these sonatas and he is especially strong in the most turbulent sonatas, like the *Appassionata*. Occasionally the more lyrical and introspective moments evade his grasp, but in the end the sheer energy of his playing sweeps you away.

SONATA NO. 8 – THE PATHÉTIQUE

The *Pathétique*, the most important of Beethoven's early sonatas, was written in 1798–99 during his "C minor period", when this was almost the only minor key he used for important works – other examples being the *Piano Concerto No. 3, String Quartet No. 4* and the third of the Op. 1 piano trios. It's a key well-suited to the expression of pathos – hence one element on the title that Beethoven gave to this work – *Grand sonata pathétique*. The other component of the title – the sonata's scale – has less to do with mere length than with the size of the sound, for the orchestral sonority of the *Pathétique* must have placed a great deal of strain on the instruments of the day. Showing obvious signs of Beethoven's dissatisfaction with the rigidities of classical form, this is a mighty, sometimes desperate work, reflecting Beethoven's awareness of the deterioration in his hearing. There's a terrible sense of loneliness in the weightily solemn central movement, a section which – as in the *Appassionata* – is framed by contrastingly dramatic outer movements.

◑ **Gilels** (Deutsche Grammophon 439 426-2; with *Sonatas Nos. 23 & 31*).

The Russian pianist Emil Gilels was revered for his granite-like performances of Beethoven's music, and he was never more impressive than on this Deutsche Grammophon recording of the *Pathétique*. He adopts slower than average tempi but the playing never drags, such is his grasp of the music's structure. His tone is expressive and resonant throughout, notably in the central Adagio, where his massive, weighted sound produces such an atmosphere of terrible oppression that the finale comes as a welcome relief. Coupled with an equally brilliant *Appassionata*, this CD is exceptional value.

SONATAS NOS. 13 & 14 (THE MOONLIGHT)

By the end of 1801 Beethoven had completed a further seven sonatas, including the two sonatas of Op. 27. The second of these, the so-called *Moonlight Sonata*, opens with Beethoven's most famous piano passage, a dreamy, melancholic movement that's now too well-known to be heard as the revolutionary idea it was. By labelling this sonata and its twin as "Quasi una fantasia" (Like a Fantasy), Beethoven was explicitly differentiating his work from the weighted, formal structures of his predecessors, and by opening the *Moonlight* with a slow movement he was instantly establishing a sound-world in which the certainties of classical form no longer applied. The second movement, an Allegretto, was described by Liszt as a "flower between two abysses" and it really is little more than an interlude before the stormy finale – a movement built upon a rhythmic idea rather than a melody.

The other Op. 27 sonata is also a marvellous work, but has never achieved the same popularity, perhaps through the lack of so memorable an opening. Comprising four movements that are unbroken in performance, it's a strangely prophetic work – with its inward-looking freedom of construction, and its alternating moments of unannounced restfulness and sudden near-dementia, it looks forward to the late sonatas.

O Pollini (Deutsche Grammophon 427 770-2GH; with *Sonata No. 15*).

There are over one hundred recordings of the *Moonlight* in the current catalogue, and many of them just run through the music as if it were little more than a Romantic scribble. With Pollini you certainly don't get anything wishy-washy:

POLYGRAM

Maurizio Pollini

this performance is well thought out and fanatically secure in its technique. The other two sonatas on the CD are similarly serious and thoughtful, but his performance of Op. 27 No. 1 has an extra degree of warmth and emotional involvement.

SONATA NO. 21 – THE WALDSTEIN

In 1804, Beethoven generously repaid the support he'd received from Count Ferdinand von Waldstein by dedicating a piano sonata to him. Written a year after the *Eroica*, the *Waldstein* is a similar landmark in the evolution of its genre, accelerating the dissolution of conventional cyclic forms and pushing towards a great expansion in scale. The *Waldstein* had begun as a relatively normal three-movement sonata, albeit one with a monumental opening movement constructed from an audaciously simple rhythmic conceit – the whole movement is generated by just two bars of chopping quavers. The masterstroke of Beethoven's rewriting was to remove the central movement and replace it with a slow and haunting section which is little more than an introduction to the Rondo finale. Where an eighteenth-century sonata would pause for contented reflection, the *Waldstein* merely halts long enough to catch its breath before hurrying onward.

O Kovacevich (EMI 7 54896-2; with *Sonatas Nos. 24 & 31*).

The weight and tension of Kovacevich's playing is the product of many years' experience, and there is nothing flashily impressive about this performance – though his uninhibited prestissimo ending to the finale is as thrilling as any crowd-pleasing virtuoso could muster. The accompanying performance of the Op. 110 sonata is stupendous (see below), and the recorded sound is faultless.

O Gilels (Deutsche Grammophon 419 162-2; with *Sonatas Nos. 23 & 26*).

The recordings on this disc were made in the first half of the 1970s, and instantly acquired the status of classics. Both fastidious and fiery, Gilels' *Waldstein* is one of the peaks of an extraordinary career.

SONATA NO. 23 – THE APPASSIONATA

In the opinion of Beethoven his greatest sonata was the *Sonata No. 23* (1804), a titanic four-movement work of unprecedently extreme emotional and technical challenges. The initial Allegro and the succeeding Andante (a huge set of variations) are magnificent creations, but it is the last movement that justifies the name *Appassionata*, which was bestowed on it a few years after Beethoven's death. This tempestuous finale is introduced by crashing, repeated chords which are followed by a simple series of semi-quavers, in turn punctuated by shockingly violent outbursts. After a number of unexpected pauses, introduced by aggressive high-speed octave passages, comes the coda – one minute of uninterrupted, surging mayhem. This final section is extraordinarily difficult to play and is always disturbing, no matter how often you listen to it. Its first audience must have been utterly perplexed.

⊙ **Ogdon** (Pickwick PCD828; with *Sonatas Nos. 8 & 14*).

John Ogdon's *Appassionata* is error-strewn and imprecise, but this is the only sort of playing that really does justice to the music's terrifying demands. Creating a sense of furious tension through his barely perceptible gradations of dynamics, he over-pedals and smashes the keys with such anger that, quite simply, there is probably no more exciting performance of Beethoven's piano music on record.

◑ **Gilels** (Deutsche Grammophon 439 426-2; with *Sonatas Nos. 8 & 31*).

Emil Gilels' 1974 version is the perfect foil to Ogdon's manic energy. Where Ogdon is abandoned, Gilels is more controlled and incisive, producing sharply distinguished rhythmic punctuation and, when necessary, a biting, metallic piano sound. This performance is so celebrated that it's also been released on another coupling, with the *Waldstein* and *Les Adieux*.

SONATA NO. 26 – LES ADIEUX

No. 26 is unique among Beethoven's piano sonatas in being the only one which contains a specific programme, or exterior reference, woven into its structure. The "farewell" of its title is to Beethoven's friend and pupil Archduke Rudolph who, between 1809 and 1810, was forced to leave Vienna because of the advance of Napoleon's army. (The cannon fire during this dark time caused Beethoven to take refuge in a cellar in order to protect his ears.) In fact there is nothing overtly pictorial in the music; rather the three movements establish the appropriate moods indicated by their titles ("Farewell", "Absence" and "Return"). In the case of the first, the central motif is based on three notes G-F-E flat which in German spells Le-be-wohl – "Farewell". The second, Andante espressivo, has a wonderfully understated poignancy with gleams of light shining through, which finally breaks into a fast movement of undisguised elation.

◑ **Kempff** (Deutsche Grammophon 419 053-2; with *Sonatas Nos. 21 & 23*).

Kempff, in his second set of Beethoven sonatas, provided a refined antidote to the kind of Beethoven-playing which is all sound and fury. His playing is restrained, elegant and lyrical – qualities particularly suited to *Les Adieux*, with its subtle changes of mood and inflection. His gentle but penetrating reading is particularly good at bringing out the bittersweet quality of the slow movement.

O Gilels (Deutsche Grammophon 419 162-2; with *Sonatas Nos. 21 & 23*).

Gilels adopts a more heroic stance, but there's no bluster to this technically peerless playing – coupled with stupendous accounts of the *Waldstein* and *Appassionata* sonatas, this performance on its own confirms Emil Gilels as one of the most remarkable of all pianists.

THE LATE SONATAS

With his last five sonatas, Beethoven took keyboard writing into a new realm, and at their completion he almost decided to finish with the piano for good, declaring that it was an "unsatisfactory instrument" – though he went on to compose the *Diabelli Variations*. A brief glance at some of the movement headings gives a good idea of what the composer was looking for in his music – the words *appassionato*, *molto sentimento*, *espressivo* and *dolente* litter the scores. Striving for absolute expression, Beethoven ventured into a complex revaluation of tradition, in which the standard forms of classical music were invested with extraordinary emotional potency. The impetus of each sonata's musical argument propels one towards the final movement, and the finales of Op. 109 and Op. 111 are in variation form, while the finales of Op. 106 and Op. 110 are fugal. Beethoven had, in effect, come full circle: tormented by the most unclassical of feelings, he followed the old paths in search of new freedoms.

Beethoven's longest and most difficult sonata is the twenty-ninth, Op. 106, subtitled the *Hammerklavier* – technically a pointless title, since *Hammerklavier* is German for "pianoforte", but one that has appropriately aggressive connotations. No other sonata covers as vast a terrain as this one. Once you've recovered from the percussive opening movement, you find yourself in a strange lopsided march that is then hammered by petulant chords before expiring mid-phrase. After that comes a slow movement of heart-wrenching intensity, in which the music persistently ebbs away to the verge of silence; the desperate conclusion is a colossal fugue, an almost unmanageably complex construction which is attacked by Beethoven almost as if he wants to beat it into submission.

The last sonata, Op. 111, is the most mysterious. It contains only two movements, a disconcertingly unclassical structure that has prompted much speculation. In Thomas Mann's *Doctor Faustus*, one of the characters gives a lecture entitled "Why did Beethoven write no third movement to Op. 111?" – and the answer, in a nutshell, was that the second movement had effectively nailed the sonata form into its coffin. This second movement is a monumental set of variations based upon a beguilingly simple "Arietta" theme that becomes the basis for some of Beethoven's most agonized, most serene and most eccentric writing – including one heavily syncopated section which sounds like a jazz break. As the piece comes to a close, the exhausted pianist is required to play a huge series of trills, turning a device that in the eighteenth century was merely a decorative convention into a devastatingly moving episode, a suggestion of refuge after the preceding storms.

◑ **The Late Sonatas: Pollini** (Deutsche Grammophon 419 199-2GH2; 2 CDs).

Pollini's technically overwhelming set of the last five sonatas is rightly famous, admired even by those who generally find his perfectionism too clinical. The performance of Op. 101 is insurpassable in its delicacy, while the *Hammerklavier* gets the full powerhouse treatment – it might seem overdone, but this is surely how the composer imagined the music would sound on a piano more muscular than the ones at his disposal.

O The Late Sonatas: Goode (Elektra Nonesuch 7559-79211-2; 2 CDs).

Richard Goode is a less exciting musician than Pollini, but comes into his own with the more contemplative element of these sonatas. It would be ideal – if expensive – to have both versions, in order to hear how this inexhaustible music can be read in such different but highly convincing ways.

O Sonata No. 31: Kovacevich (EMI 7 5489620; with *Sonatas Nos. 21 & 24*).

Op. 110 gets an incredible performance from Kovacevich: there's a profound and intense concentration about his playing which culminates in an almost spiritualized reading of the fugal last movement.

THE BAGATELLES

Of the shorter pieces that Beethoven wrote for the piano, the three sets of *Bagatelles* (24 in total) are the best known. A bagatelle literally means "a trifle" and, though such pieces are predominantly light, in Beethoven's hands they become finely wrought and highly characterful works which look forward to the concentrated piano miniatures of such Romantic composers as Chopin and Schumann. All three sets exhibit strong contrasts and a range of moods between the individual pieces, but only the last set, *Six Bagatelles* (Op. 126), was actually conceived as a cycle. Composed in 1824 they are close in style to the late sonatas in their complexity, quixotic mood changes, and in the way rhythmic predictability is constantly undermined. The *Bagatelles* have long proved highly popular with amateur pianists, although the best-loved *Bagatelle* of all, a piece known as "Für Elise", was written as a single work.

◑ **Bagatelles 1–24: Kovacevich** (Philips 426 976-2).

Kovacevich plays these pieces with great enthusiasm and a natural spontaneity. He finds poetry and fantasy in even the simplest pieces, investing them with a warmth and a charm which is completely captivating.

◑ **Bagatelles 1–25: Brendel** (Philips 456 031-2).

Brendel's approach is less mercurial than that of Kovacevich: his readings bring out the vigour and the fluidity of these pieces. Similarly his "Für Elise" is pointedly unsentimental but exquisitely shaped.

THE DIABELLI VARIATIONS

Beethoven's *Thirty-Three Variations on a Theme by Diabelli* were completed in 1823 in response to a commission from publisher and composer Anton Diabelli. Thinking he'd hit upon a way to make a fast buck, Diabelli asked fifty composers to submit a variation on a theme that Diabelli had written, with a view to publishing the results as a composite creation. He received one from Schubert, one from the 11-year-old Liszt, and thirty-three from the insulted Beethoven. Diabelli had never seen the like of them before, but, immediately recognizing their greatness, he published them as a separate album. In this incredible work, Beethoven realized a new mode of variation in which each variation radically reinterpreted the original theme, instead of merely parodying it or playing upon its basic framework. At the end of the *Diabelli*'s colossal trajectory, in which a host of musical forms has been quoted and transformed, Beethoven comes up with an astonishing gesture of reconciliation – a Haydnesque theme ending in a simple C major chord.

◑ **Kovacevich** (Philips 422 969-2).

Stephen Kovacevich's recording of the *Diabelli* is a classic, as free-flowing as Beethoven's approach to the variation form. His playing is muscular yet supple, accentuating the integrity of each variation without sacrificing the sense of overall structure. That final chord, which can make or break a performance of the *Diabelli*, is like a goal reached at the end of a long, long journey.

◑ **Buchbinder** (Teldec 0630-17388-2; 2 CDs; with additional variations by Schubert, Liszt, Hummel and others).

As well as Beethoven's 33 variations, this recording includes all the other pieces that Diabelli received from the various composers he commissioned. It's saved from being a mere curiosity because Rudolf Buchbinder is such a fine Beethoven pianist and gives a compelling performance that only just falls short of the brilliance of Kovacevich. The other pieces, which range from the trite to the charming, give a wonderful picture of the state of piano writing in the 1820s, and serve to highlight Beethoven's incredible originality.

VINCENZO BELLINI

(1801–1835)

It can be difficult to appreciate what it was that made Vincenzo Bellini so remarkable, as modern audiences tend to have a problem with his abundance of oom-pah-pah orchestral passages, bombastic choruses and solo histrionics. But it's worth persevering, for there's more to Bellini than first meets the ear. Italian opera composers immediately prior to Bellini saw themselves primarily as creators of melodies, and those melodies had little or no connection with the words that the singers were singing. Effectively, the libretto and the orchestra were operating independently of each other. Bellini set about writing intense yet melodic music which related closely to the attitudes and sentiments of his characters, thus laying the foundations for the dramatic masterpieces of Donizetti, Verdi and Puccini. Whereas Rossini and his predecessors had relied on formula, enabling them to dash off an opera in seven days, Bellini took time and effort over his work, struggling towards a poised and well-proportioned form that appealed to the emotions as well as to the ear. He was, as Wagner wrote after Bellini's death, "all heart".

Born three years before Beethoven completed the *Eroica*, Bellini lived for only 34 years, leaving his eleventh opera incomplete. His first great success was *Il Pirata*, commissioned by La Scala in 1827 and written (as were *I Puritani* and *La Sonnambula*) for the expressively lyrical voice of Giovanni Rubini, a man famous all over Europe as "the King of Tenors". Bellini's music is the summit of the bel canto style, requiring voices of massive flexibility and range – and, as far as the lead roles are concerned, enormous stamina. Even though the tenor parts are now transposed downwards, as they were written for falsetto voices rather than the full chest voice of the present day, Bellini's male leads are among the most demanding in the repertoire.

In 1831 he wrote his masterpiece, *Norma*, which ever since has been the vehicle for some of the world's greatest sopranos – Maria Callas, Montserrat Caballé and Joan Sutherland have all excelled in the title role. This fabulously emotive score, in which the words carry as much of the meaning as does the music, and the pace of the action is dictated by dramatic necessity, clearly represented a turning point in the development of Italian opera. The passionate ecstasy and elegiac melancholy of Bellini's music, allied with his fragile good looks, led to his idolization as the very personification of Romanticism, though not everyone was susceptible to his charm. The German poet Heinrich Heine wrote of him acidly: "he was coquettish, ever looking as though just removed from a bandbox . . . his features had something vague in them, a want of character, something milk-like; and in this milk-like face flittered sometimes a painful-pleasing expression of sorrow. The whole man looked like a sigh in pumps and silk stockings."

Bellini's early death compounded the Romantic myth. Exhausted by the effort of composing *I Puritani*, he fell ill and died, alone, in a dreary house in a suburb of Paris, where his last opera had just had its premiere. Rossini was among the bearers of the funeral shroud at the Requiem Mass; Bellini was later buried in the cathedral of his native Catania.

LA SONNAMBULA

As its title suggests, the plot of *La Sonnambula* (The Sleepwalker) is not exactly a model of plausibility. Amina is to marry Elvino. Lisa also loves Elvino but agrees to entertain Count Rodolfo, a handsome lord recently returned from abroad. Unknown to everyone, Amina is a sleepwalker, and she winds up, all unwitting, in the bed of Rodolfo. Elvino then agrees to marry Lisa, but Rodolfo attempts to explain the mistake. Everyone scoffs at his story but, as they do, Amina is seen walking along the roof of a mill, which collapses as soon as she is safely across. Elvino and Amina duly marry. Bellini's essentially simple music transforms this tale into a touching rustic idyll. *La Sonnambula* contains a substantial amount of beautifully expressive writing for soprano and tenor, especially in the second act, and the role of Amina features some real show-stopping coloratura singing.

O Sutherland, Pavarotti, Ghiaurov, Buchanan, Jones, Tomlinson, de Palma; London Opera Chorus; National Philharmonic Orchestra; Bonynge (Decca 417 424-2DH2; 2 CDs).

Richard Bonynge's recording is blessed with the incredible voice of the young Luciano Pavarotti as Elvino. His voice has the texture and confidence of a singer at the height of his powers, and his phrasing is pure and enthrallingly musical. Pavarotti's pairing with Joan Sutherland works wonderfully – her singing might occasionally be over-stylized but she revels in Bellini's expressive artistry.

I PURITANI

The excessively complicated plot of *I Puritani* is set in England at the time of the Civil War, the action revolving around two rival families – one Roundhead, the other Cavalier. Yet, for all its complexity, the libretto provided Bellini with considerably more substantial characters than *La Sonnambula*, and it inspired him to create some of his most perfect and demanding music for the tenor voice. The first act's *A te, o cara* is one of his most beautiful solo arias, while the final act's *Vienni, fra queste braccia* demands two high D naturals – two full notes higher than the penultimate note of *Nessun Dorma*. Elvira, the soprano lead, is less involving than Amina or Norma but suffers no dearth of lyrical music, and the concluding *Credeasi, misera!* is one of the saddest, most affecting tenor/soprano duets ever written.

O Sutherland, Pavarotti, Ghiaurov, Cappucilli, Luccardi; Royal Opera House Chorus; London Symphony Orchestra; Bonynge (Decca 417 588-2DH3; 3 CDs).

This recording boasts four of the protagonists featured in Decca's *La Sonnambula* and they are similarly effective here. Pavarotti steals the show with an awesome performance of seemingly effortless flair – in fact, this is some of the greatest bel canto tenor singing on record. Sutherland is slightly self-conscious at times, as if in awe of her partner's abilities, but she produces some wonderful moments, not least when singing of her supposed betrayal. Again, Bonynge encourages her to take all sorts of liberties with the tempo and pulse, but Sutherland and Pavarotti work well together, and the recording is slightly more atmospheric than their *Sonnambula*.

NORMA

Norma is Bellini's greatest opera, its glorious music triumphing in the face of a plot that degenerates into near farce. The action takes place in Gaul during the Roman occupation. Pollione, a Roman, has abandoned the Gaul high priestess Norma and their two children in favour of another priestess, Adalgisa. Discovering Pollione's infidelity, Norma moves to kill her children but is unable to go ahead with the terrible deed. Adalgisa implores Pollione to return to Norma but fails. Norma then incites war between the Gauls and Romans, a conflict which leads to Pollione's capture and death sentence. Norma, still in love with her husband, offers her life in exchange for his, and mounts the funeral pyre, where Pollione joins her.

From this raw material Bellini creates a lyric drama which, in the last act, takes on a true tragic

EMI/NEVVECELLE

Maria Callas

grandeur. Bellini's mastery of long and deeply expressive melodies is at its most sublime in *Casta Diva*, the ultimate bel canto soprano aria, and in the soberly moving soprano/tenor duets *In mia man* and *Qual cor tradisti*. It's no overstatement to say that the final act is the greatest example of dramatic bel canto ever written.

◑ **Callas, Corelli, Ludwig, Zaccaria, de Palma, Vincenzi; La Scala Orchestra and Chorus; Serafin** (EMI CMS7 63000-2; 3 CDs).

Norma is the most recorded of Bellini's operas and there are presently more than ten versions of it on CD. The title role is also one of the most difficult to bring to life, as it demands a soprano who can act as well as she can sing. Maria Callas possessed this combination of qualities, and dominated the role during the late 1950s and 1960s. She recorded *Norma* twice for EMI, both times conducted by Tullio Serafin with La Scala's forces, but this later performance (1960) also boasts the amazing Pollione of Franco Corelli. Here is some of the most impressive Bellini tenor singing on record and one of those very rare occasions when Callas was almost outshone by her leading man.

◑ **Callas, Filippeschi, Stignani, Rossi-Lemeni, Caroli, Cavallari; La Scala Orchestra and Chorus; Serafin** (EMI CDS7 47304-8; 3 CDs).

Callas's earlier recording (1954) is a powerful, frequently astonishing display of theatrical singing, with the blood-curdling outbursts balanced by moments of tender introspection. Mario Filippeschi was an underrated singer, but his open-throated tenor is ideally placed for Pollione and there is something hypnotic in his old-fashioned melancholic sound. Serafin is in marvellous form, inciting a searing account from singers and musicians alike.

GEORGE BENJAMIN

(1960–)

We are disappointed when our prodigies turn out to be less prolific than they are prodigious, but in George Benjamin's case disappointment fades in the face of painstakingly consummate craftsmanship. In seeking different techniques for every piece, Benjamin eschews reach-me-down grids and systems, and his work-list contains barely an hour of music written in the 1990s (compared with some ninety minutes written during the first five years of his career). Yet if composing seems not to have become easier as he gets older, there is no sense, in listening to his music, of grinding labour, only of a sensuous delight in organizing sound, although Benjamin himself has said, "Sound is lovely, but unless it is somehow more than itself, it's of no interest."

Benjamin began composing at the age of 9, although his infantilia do not see the light of day. In 1974 he began studying with Peter Gellhorn, followed in 1976 by studies at the Paris Conservatoire with Olivier Messiaen (composition) and Messiaen's wife, Yvonne Loriod (piano). For a whole year, study with Messiaen consisted of writing thousands of chords, exploring the nuances and possibilities of harmony. The discipline bore fruit when, in 1978, he premiered his *Piano Sonata*, a work luxuriating in the colouristic world of Debussy and Ravel.

In 1980 Benjamin became the youngest composer to have a work (*Ringed by the Flat Horizon*) performed at the BBC Promenade Concerts. It was apparent that a major talent was emerging; an impression confirmed by *A Mind of Winter* (1981) and *At First Light* (1982), two of the most magical works of the 1980s. There followed a period of intensive study in Pierre Boulez's research centre IRCAM, from which Benjamin emerged in 1987 with *Antara*, in which the sound of Peruvian panpipe buskers is electronically manipulated to produce a kind of idealized panpipe, the sonic foundation for the live instruments, including anvils and bells alongside flute, trombones and strings.

So far, *Antara* is Benjamin's last encounter with computers and electronics: "In the end I'm an instrumental composer," he confesses; "I value the relationship from the arm to the instrument to the ear." That relationship is beguilingly explored in *Upon Silence* (1990), which fashions the antique sound-world of viol consort (in combination with a vocalist) into something fresh and modern. Although Benjamin plans an opera, it is perhaps his vocal writing that is least successful: the voice too readily becomes an abstract instrument, rather than a communicator of human, verbal meaning. Nevertheless *Upon Silence* (which also exists in a version for modern strings) is remarkable, not least in the way tempo fluctuates to produce sudden, unexpected eddies of musical time. And indeed *Sudden Time* (1993) was Benjamin's next major composition, a large orchestral work exploring the contrasts between the elasticity of "dream time" and the more rapid motion of "real time". That was followed in 1995 by *Three Inventions*, in which Benjamin's ear for sonority showed yet further refinement, revealing an ever-developing expressivity that promises great, if not numerous things for the future.

From early in his career, Benjamin has conducted his own and, later, other composers' works, and he acknowledges that conducting music he hasn't written has sometimes provided "seeds of thought". He continues to teach in London, where he is a significant *éminence grise* on the new music scene. Since 1995 he has acted as the principal artistic consultant for the BBC's celebration of twentieth-century music, "Sounding the Century". Meanwhile he has in Nimbus Records a champion prepared to commit almost every note he has written to disc.

EARLY WORKS

The three major works of Benjamin's youth – *Ringed by the Flat Horizon*, *At First Light* and *A Mind of Winter* – all show his acute feeling for harmonic and instrumental colours, a fluid approach to form and a sensual delight in sounds for their own sakes. What's more, they demonstrate an amazing ability to translate visual or poetic images into vivid music. The hazy radiance of Turner's painting *Northiam Castle: Sunrise* provided Benjamin's visual stimulus, and there is something that might be called Turneresque in Benjamin's instrumental response. Sounds emerge from musical textures just as objects emerge from the mist in Turner's painting, and as they appear we're not sure whether they are benign or menacing. So detailed is Benjamin's deployment of his forces (the score calls for "large newspaper" and "ping-pong ball with flat-bottomed glass") that it's hard to believe there are only fourteen players producing the delicate interplay between shimmering background and sometimes raucous foreground.

O At First Light; A Mind of Winter; Ringed by the Flat Horizon: Walmsley-Clark; London Sinfonietta, BBC Symphony Orchestra; Benjamin, Elder (Nimbus NI 5075).

In this lucid performance, Benjamin conducts the London Sinfonietta, who premiered the piece under Simon Rattle. The CD also includes Mark Elder conducting a no less persuasive account of *Ringed by the Flat Horizon*, while Penelope Walmsley-Clark is the fearless vocal soloist in *A Mind of Winter*, a setting of Wallace Stevens' poem *The Snow Man*.

SUDDEN TIME & THREE INVENTIONS

The mid- to late 1980s was an exceptionally lean period for Benjamin, one in which he took stock

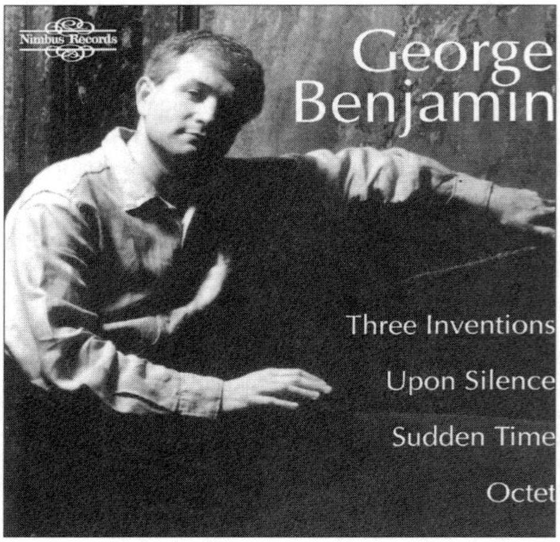

and attempted to move his music into a new – more dynamic – direction. *Sudden Time*, an orchestral work conceived in 1983 but not completed for another decade, was the result. The title refers to a poem by Wallace Stevens: "It was like sudden time in a world without time", and Benjamin recalls how the work was inspired "by a dream I once had in which the sound of a thunderclap seemed to stretch . . . before circulating, as if in a spiral, through my head. I then awoke, and realized that I was experiencing the first second of a real thunderclap." This sense of time simultaneously condensed and extended is magically realized through a refined choice of instrumental colouring delicately deployed. Benjamin's orchestral fabric is even more delicately woven in his next major work *Three Inventions*. There is an acute sense of musical drama, in the way the flugelhorn induces an orchestral hush in the first *Invention*, for example; or in the evanescent gong-strokes and mighty bass-drum blows which punctuate, and eventually terminate, the third. Perhaps with this work, Benjamin comes closest to the kind of narrative tension he'll need to generate if and when he writes his opera.

O Three Inventions; Sudden Time; Upon Silence; Octet: Bickley; Fretwork; London Sinfonietta; London Philharmonic Orchestra; Benjamin (Nimbus NI 5505).

Benjamin and the London Sinfonietta again, with John Wallace taking the mournful flugelhorn solo in *Three Inventions*. The disc also includes performances of both versions of *Upon Silence* – one for viol consort, one for modern strings (Susan Bickley the excellent soloist singer in both) and the *Octet* from 1979. This collection offers the single most succinct demonstration of Benjamin's talent.

ALBAN BERG

(1885–1935)

Despite their reputation, the composers known as the Second Viennese School (Schoenberg, Berg, Webern) did not turn their back on the past. Following Schoenberg's lead, they saw the twelve-tone system of composition (see p.355) not as a negation of tonality, but as its logical development. This is nowhere more apparent than in the music of Alban Berg, which marries an expressive richness – the equal of any late Romantic music – to a complexity that even now retains some of its coded secrets.

Berg already had a substantial body of songs to his credit when, in 1904, he enrolled in Schoenberg's classes. Anton Webern had already signed up; the two were to remain close friends. Over the next seven years, Berg's music achieved astonishing maturity under Schoenberg's watchful eye: there can be few more masterly works labelled "Opus 1" than his *Piano Sonata* (1908), and the last piece he wrote while a Schoenberg student, the *String Quartet* (1910), remains a cornerstone of twentieth-century quartet literature. Meanwhile, the last of his *Four Songs* (1910) was his first atonal work.

Shortly before Schoenberg's move to Berlin in 1911 put an end to Berg's studies, Berg attended Mahler's funeral, and later the Munich premiere of Mahler's *Das Lied von der Erde*. Within weeks he had begun composing his first orchestral work, the *Five Orchestral Songs on Picture-Postcard Texts* by Peter Altenberg (Altenberg was known in Viennese intellectual circles as "the Socrates of the coffee house"). When Schoenberg premiered two of these songs in Vienna in 1913, a riot ensued. Schoenberg himself soon added his voice to the detractors, suggesting that Berg would do better to write longer, more discursive pieces than these songs, and the epigrammatic *Four Pieces for Clarinet and Piano* which followed.

Chastened, Berg duly embarked on his *Three Orchestral Pieces*, which were much more what

LEBRECHT COLLECTION

Alban Berg (centre front) during rehearsals for the first run of *Wozzeck* at the Berlin Staatsoper

Schoenberg had in mind. Meanwhile, shortly before war broke out in 1914, he was in the audience for the Viennese premiere of *Woyzeck*, a play written eighty years earlier by Georg Büchner. Immensely moved, Berg vowed to make an opera from the play. War and military service interrupted his work, and it was not until 1922 that he completed *Wozzeck* (as the play was then, and the opera still is, known). Excerpts were successfully performed in 1924, by which time Berg was working on his *Chamber Concerto*.

Erich Kleiber conducted the premiere of *Wozzeck* in Berlin in 1925: it required 34 full orchestral rehearsals, so revolutionary was Berg's language, both musical and dramatic. Performances followed throughout Europe and the United States. It was the first international success for an atonal work from the Schoenberg school, and Berg confirmed his growing status with the *Lyric Suite* (1927). Then in 1929 he signed a contract for the rights to the "Lulu" plays (*Earth Spirit* and *Pandora's Box*) of Franz Wedekind, which had enjoyed a *succès de scandale* ever since *Pandora's Box* was banned in 1904 (Berg saw a private performance in 1905). Work on the opera *Lulu* had begun before Berg signed the contract; now it proceeded apace.

With the Nazis a growing threat, the whole country, as Berg wrote, was "dancing on a volcano". Hitler became Chancellor in January 1933, Schoenberg left Berlin in May, finally emigrating to the United States in October. In May 1934, Berg wrote to Webern that he had finished *Lulu*, bar some finishing touches. Nearly a year later, he set the opera aside to compose the *Violin Concerto* in memory of Manon Gropius. Soon after completing what is now his most popular work, Berg was stung by an insect. An abscess developed, the infection worsened, and on Christmas Eve 1935 Alban Berg died of general septicaemia. He was just 50 years old.

WOZZECK

Fragmentary, hallucinatory and profoundly pessimistic, Georg Büchner's play *Woyzeck* (left incomplete when the playwright died in 1837, aged 23) is an astonishingly prescient piece, "the first real tragedy of low life" according to George Steiner. When Berg saw the Vienna premiere in 1914, he knew that he had a subject for his first opera and, although he did not serve at the front, his experiences of World War I only confirmed his realization. *Wozzeck* tells, with cinematic immediacy, the story of a simple soldier's brutalization and humiliation by a sadistic and repressive system; pushed to the brink, Wozzeck kills his wife, then himself.

Wozzeck is Berg's most Expressionist work, with a largely dissonant score that creates an atmosphere of mounting paranoia and oppressiveness. The opera's musical structure is formidably complex, but as Berg himself wrote, "there must not be anyone in the audience who, from the moment the curtain rises until it finally descends, notices anything of these various fugues, inventions, suites and sonata movements, variations and passacaglias. Nobody must be filled with anything except the idea of the opera." In a performance which does justice to the music, Berg's wish is fulfilled: the form of *Sprechgesang* (speech-song) he evolves suits the characters' halting attempts to communicate, while the orchestra tells us everything they can't express.

○ Waechter, Silja, Winkler; Vienna Philharmonic Orchestra; Dohnányi (Decca 417 348-2; 2 CDs; with Schoenberg, *Erwartung*).

Eberhard Waechter's characterization of Wozzeck is a terrifying portrayal of fear and desperation. Through varying the quality of his voice he gives a chilling impression of Wozzeck's instability without resorting to the sort of barking and wailing found on some other recordings. Anja Silja's Marie, a powerfully lyrical reading, perfectly matches Dohnányi's visceral view of the score.

◑ Harrell, Farrell, Mordino; New York Philharmonic; Mitropoulos (Sony MH2K 62759; 2 CDs; with Schoenberg, *Erwartung*, Krenek, *Symphonic Elegy*).

Although most of the singers play free with Berg's notation, this is a superbly dramatic performance (recorded live in 1951), underpinned by Dimitri Mitropoulos' rhythmic precision. Mack Harrell's Wozzeck is a decent man driven over the edge by a cruel system, incarnated in Joseph Mordino's Captain – a spine-chilling caricature straight out of one of Georg Grosz's notebooks. The Krenek elegy (for Anton Webern) is a real rarity, well worth discovering.

LULU

Berg's second opera was incomplete at his death, his substantial sketches hidden, almost as a sacred relic, by his wife Hélène. Only the first two acts were performed at its 1937 Zürich premiere, with a mainly pantomimed episode from Act 3 concluding the work. For forty years, the work survived as a two-act torso, but when Hélène died in 1976 Friedrich Cerha undertook the completion, which required less intervention than Berg's widow had suggested. The third act was crucial to Berg's plan of the opera as a kind of palindrome, the turning point occurring in Act 2 Scene 1, where a silent film depicts Lulu's arrest, trial and imprisonment. Pierre Boulez conducted the Paris premiere of the completed *Lulu* in 1979.

While Strauss's *Salome* epitomizes the fantasy of the destructive allure of female sexuality, Berg's *Lulu* is a rather more complex and human representation of that *fin de siècle* archetype the *femme fatale*. Lulu is both a self-determining, modern woman who uses her sexuality as a weapon, and at the same time the victim of the men, and women, who objectify her (the libretto even hints at childhood abuse). The last act finds her reduced to walking the streets of London, where she finally falls victim to Jack the Ripper. Berg's flexible twelve-note technique produces music that is tough and lyrical, expressionist and dramatic. The harmonies are richer than in *Wozzeck*, the musical and dramatic shape more immediately appreciable, thanks in large part to the theme associated with Lulu, a point of reference throughout.

⊙ Stratas, Mazura, Riegel, Minton, Tear; Paris Opera Orchestra; Boulez (Deutsche Grammophon 415 489-2; 3 CDs).

This studio recording, which largely recreates the 1979 premiere performance, is one of the highlights of Boulez's conducting career. There is a freedom and spontaneity to the performance, an ease and inevitability to the changes of pacing and subtleties of rubato that is simply breathtaking. Teresa Stratas, famous for playing neurotic heroines, has long been associated with Lulu, and her interpretation is exceptional.

⊙ Wise, Fassbaender, Schöne, Straka; Orchestre Nationale de France; Tate (EMI CDS 7 54622-2; 3 CDs).

Jeffrey Tate's live recording followed a production at the Chatelet in 1991. It has more slips than the Boulez but arguably there is a little more emotion and theatricality in evidence. Tate also gets a commanding performance in the title role from Patricia Wise, the Lulu *de nos jours*, and from Brigitte Fassbaender – compelling as Lulu's lover, the Countess Geschwitz.

SONGS

As you might expect of one of the greatest opera composers, Berg also wrote some extremely fine songs. Many of the earliest pieces (those without opus numbers) are, as Schoenberg suggested, "in a style between Wolf and Brahms", but with the set known as *Seven Early Songs*, written under Schoenberg's tutelage between 1905 and 1908, a more distinctive voice emerges. Originally written for piano accompaniment, they achieve greater impact in Berg's 1928 orchestration.

More remarkable still are the *Altenberg Lieder*, settings of texts which the poet Peter Altenberg sent to the Bergs on postcards from the Alps. A riot greeted the premiere of two of the songs under Schoenberg's baton in 1913: the audience didn't like the epigrammatic texts, or the use of a large orchestra to produce such quiet, chamber-like textures. Now, those very qualities are what make the songs so appealing. Also worth mentioning is Berg's concert aria *Der Wein*, which the composer saw as no more than an occasional piece, but which today seems to breathe the same air as *Lulu* (for a recommended recording, see below, under "Three Pieces for Orchestra").

⊙ Norman, Schein; London Symphony Orchestra; Boulez (Sony SK 66826).

It's regrettable that Jessye Norman so rarely records such repertoire. Her sumptuous voice revels in Berg's music, her attention to detail, and to the sense of the words, making her an ideal interpreter. In addition to the *Altenberg Lieder* and the *Seven Early Songs*, the disc also includes a handful of mostly early songs with piano accompaniment: Norman again excels.

THE VIOLIN CONCERTO

Few twentieth-century works are as wrenchingly moving as Berg's *Violin Concerto*, written in response to the death in 1935 of Manon Gropius, the 18-year-old daughter of Alma Mahler and the architect Walter Gropius. The violinist Louis Krasner had already commissioned a concerto from Berg, who broke off from *Lulu* to write the piece, dedicated "to the memory of an angel". Berg scholars, who enjoy nothing more than the composer's cryptological and numerological obsessions, have uncovered "a secret programme" of references to Berg's mistress, Hanna Fuchs-Robettin, and to Berg's illegitimate daughter, progeny of a youthful affair with a servant girl in the Berg household.

Be that as it may, the *Violin Concerto* needs no secret programme to work its magic. Reconciling the twelve-note system with traditional tonality, Berg quotes from a Carpathian folk tune in the opening movement, and from the Bach chorale *Es ist genug* (It is enough) in the second movement. The concerto begins as if the soloist were tuning the violin against the orchestra, but tension quickly mounts as the music becomes more agitated. As in *Lulu*, Berg then reverses the process, the music slowing, growing ever quieter until the Bach chorale steals in, and violin and orchestra sink into a mood of loss and resignation.

⊙ Mutter; Chicago Symphony Orchestra; Levine (Deutsche Grammophon 437 093-2GH; with Rihm's *Gesungene Zeit*).

Mutter's panache pays rich dividends in a work demanding a match between free fantasy and cast-iron discipline. Under James Levine, the Chicago orchestra provides sumptuous but delicate support.

⊙ Krasner; BBC Symphony Orchestra; Webern (Testament SBT1004; with *Lyric Suite*).

Krasner's version, accompanied by Webern, is the first recording ever made of this work and, despite the inevitable crackle on the transfer from 78s, this is a deeply moving performance with a wonderfully idiomatic authority.

THREE PIECES FOR ORCHESTRA

The *Three Pieces for Orchestra* were completed in 1915, shortly before Berg was conscripted into the Austrian Army's war effort, but they did not receive their first complete performance until 1930. It is difficult to understand why, since the music so clearly honours the example of Mahler – the composer whose work first pointed Berg towards orchestral composition. Yet the piece is mature Berg, a complex structure yielding a richness of musical incident that is both exhilarating and unsettling, as at first thin, then eventually massive sounds emerge from the opening silence. The world of *Wozzeck* is just around the corner.

⊙ Vienna Philharmonic Orchestra; Abbado (Deutsche Grammophon 445 846-2; with *Der Wein* and *Seven Early Songs*).

Abbado brings bite to the Vienna Phil's sheer lustrousness, working wonders in this dense score; the climactic March is hair-raising. In the accompanying orchestral songs, Anne Sofie von Otter is beautiful but a touch cool for the *Seven Early Songs*, but her aristocratic tones marry perfectly with the jazzy pungency of *Der Wein*, written while the composer was already at work on *Lulu*.

LYRIC SUITE

Berg's six-movement *Lyric Suite* for string quartet, written in 1925–26, contains, like the *Violin Concerto*, coded references to his affection for Hanna Fuchs-Robettin, as well as quotations from Wagner's *Tristan und Isolde* and from Zemlinsky's *Lyric Symphony* (see p.485). When, at his publisher's request, Berg prepared an arrangement for string orchestra, he orchestrated only movements two to four – the expressive core of the work. If in the process he smoothed away some of the quartet version's toughness, he also added an emotional richness, and the closing moments of the third movement (marked Adagio appassionato) are as touching as anything he ever wrote. It was premiered by Jascha Horenstein in Berlin in 1929.

⊙ Balleys; Deutsches Symphonie-Orchester; Ashkenazy (Decca 436 567-2; with *Seven Early Songs*, *Altenberg Lieder* and *Three Orchestral Pieces*).

Some details go missing in Ashkenazy's account, but his is a forthright performance, less heated than the Alban Berg Quartet's recording of the quartet version (see below). In the songs, Brigitte Balleys, lighter of voice than Jessye Norman, is perhaps even more subtle: like Ashkenazy, she avoids exaggeration in music that readily invites it.

THE CHAMBER CONCERTO

Its short score completed on Berg's fortieth birthday (February 9, 1925), and dedicated as a belated fiftieth birthday present to Schoenberg, the *Chamber Concerto* also marks the twentieth anniversary of the friendship between Berg, Schoenberg and Webern. No wonder, then, that to honour these associations Berg derived the work's opening motifs from the composer's names (the German system of notation favours such musical tributes). By restricting the concerto's accompaniment to thirteen wind instruments, Berg produced some marvellously unusual colourings, while the solo parts for piano (first movement), violin (second movement) and, finally, both together, are virtuoso showpieces.

◑ **Barenboim, Zukerman; Ensemble InterContemporain; Boulez** (Deutsche Grammophon 447 405-2; with Stravinsky's *Dumbarton Oaks, Instrumental Miniatures & Ebony Concerto*).

There's a fruitful tension here between the soloists' expansive romanticism and the no-nonsense rigour of Boulez, a tension that matches the conductor's statement, "what I find most striking [in Berg's music] is the combination of immediate expressiveness with outstanding structural powers".

THE STRING QUARTET

Effectively marking Berg's graduation from Schoenberg's class, the *String Quartet* is the composer's first conclusive foray beyond tonality. Like the *Piano Sonata*, it displays great rhythmic flexibility and a broad expressive range, immediately apparent in the way the blunt opening statement quickly softens into a kind of question. There are moments of aching lyricism, but also bursts of fiery declamation, both stretching the players' techniques: it at times feels as if the young Berg is trying to fit everything he knows into one piece, but the quartet deserves its status as a twentieth-century classic.

○ **Alban Berg Quartet** (EMI CDC5 55190-2; with the *Lyric Suite*).

If the Berg Quartet misses something of Berg's sensuality, there is compensation in their fearless attack on the more expressionistic passages: nowhere to hide here. The coupling is Berg's other great work for string quartet, the *Lyric Suite* in its original form (Berg's first piece to deploy Schoenberg's twelve-tone method), given a no less persuasive treatment.

THE PIANO SONATA

The hegemony enjoyed by tonality was already decaying when, in 1908, Berg completed his Opus 1. As Pierre Boulez wrote of the piece, Berg "feels the attraction of the distant future, but is still tied to the recent past". There are traces of Liszt and, unsurprisingly, of Schoenberg, but there is already originality in the way Berg manipulates tiny fragments of melody and rhythm into a statement dense with dramatic gesture and packing a powerful emotional punch, not least in the closing moments, which seem to imply not so much rest as exhaustion.

○ **Pollini** (Deutsche Grammophon 423 678-2; with Debussy's *Études*).

Not everyone enjoys Maurizio Pollini's crisp attack: he plays the sonata much faster than, for example, Glenn Gould, who recorded this "music from the twilight of tonality" several times. But Pollini's cerebral clarity pays dividends in a work that, though short, makes great demands on the player if the lines are to emerge uncongested.

LUCIANO BERIO

(1925–)

Of all the leading figures of his generation, Luciano Berio is the most prodigal and encyclopedic, drawing on a range of influences that reaches from the poetry of Dante to the politics of Martin Luther King, and from the operas of Monteverdi to the sonorities of modern jazz. His output includes beautiful settings of traditional folk songs, yet has also embraced all the major musical developments of its time, including electronic music, music theatre, and works using quotation and collage – hence the common critical description of him as an "omnivore". Above all his music possesses a dynamic lyricism which links him to the great Italian tradition of Verdi and Puccini.

Berio's formative years, the 1950s, were spent as much in the studio as in the concert hall, and in early works such as *Omaggio a Joyce* and *Visage* he produced some of the seminal electronic music of the period. Both these pieces incorporate the recorded voice of Berio's then wife, Cathy Berberian, a mezzo-soprano whose vocal gifts were matched by a vivid stage presence which was exploited to the full in other works Berio wrote for her – *Recital*, for instance, in which the performer is asked to enact the nervous breakdown of a neurotic concert singer. But Berio's vocal music is not just concerned with theatrical role-playing or with recreating the beauties of Italian bel canto for the twentieth century. It's also interested in the very nature of language and speech, as in *Circles* (another piece written for Berberian), in which the singer's movement in a circle around the stage is mirrored by a musical circle in which three poems by e.e. cummings are progressively deconstructed into their constituent phonetic parts and then reconstructed. A similar idea underpins the beautiful *O King* (1967) for mezzo and five instruments, in which the words "O Martin Luther King" are gradually constructed out of their vowel sounds.

O King was later incorporated into *Sinfonia* (1969), one of three major vocal and orchestral works from the 1960s – with *Épiphanie* (1962) and *Laborintus 2* (1965) – that perfectly demonstrate the omnivorousness of Berio's music. *Épiphanie* sets words by Proust and Brecht (among others) in a variety of vocal styles ranging from the extravagantly ornamented to the monotonously spoken, interleaved with orchestral movements, while *Laborintus 2* uses speaker, singers, orchestra and jazz musicians to explore a welter of texts organized around the poetry of Dante. Most extraordinary of all is the third movement of *Sinfonia*, where a musical and verbal labyrinth is built around the third movement of Mahler's *Symphony No. 2* and passages from Samuel Beckett's *The Unnameable*. Berio's appropriation of other people's words and music hasn't always aspired to the complexity found in *Sinfonia*, however. *Folk Songs* (1964), his transcriptions for soprano and ensemble of folk songs from around the world (including one by Berio himself), has proved one of his most popular and accessible works, and was followed, in the 1980s, by transcriptions of works by de Falla, Mahler and Brahms – and, in *Rendering*, by the completion of unfinished symphonic sketches by Schubert. Folk music has become an important source of material in more recent works such as *Voci* (1984), a haunting recomposition of Sicilian folk melodies for viola and orchestra, and, more elaborately, in *Ritorno degli snovidenia* (1977), for cello and orchestra.

Berio's taste for recomposition and collage runs throughout his work, as does his love of the theatrical. This theatrical element looms large in the *Sequenza* cycle, a series of solo pieces which launch an innovative and sometimes zany investigation into the virtuosic and dramatic possibilities of musical performance, ranging from the vocal extravangazas of *Sequenza III* for voice to the instrumental bufoonery of *Sequenza V* for trombone. Later, some of these pieces were themselves recomposed in yet another cycle of works, called *Chemins*, in which new layers of musical "commentary" are added to the original *Sequenza*.

Such "commentary" techniques, both literary and musical, also appear in the first of Berio's three "operas", baldly entitled *Opera* (1970), which uses the techniques developed in *Épiphanie, Laborintus II* and *Sinfonia* to interweave three distinct narratives drawn from the sinking of the *Titanic*, Monteverdi's *Orfeo* and a contemporary American drama about the care of the dying. *Opera* suffers from a certain musical and dramatic incoherence, but in his two later operas, *La vera storia* ("The True Story"; 1981) and *Un re in ascolto* ("A King Listens"; 1984) Berio has achieved a remarkable synthesis of extended theatrical techniques and large-scale musical means, albeit one which owes little to traditional operatic models. These works show Berio transforming the experimental fervour of his earlier work into a musical language of greater restraint and consistency, a process that can be charted through works such as the dazzling piano concerto *Points on the curve to find . . .* (1974), the magnificent orchestral piece *Formazione* (1987), or the beautiful transitions of his Schubert "restoration", *Rendering* (1988–90).

WORKS FOR SOLO VOICE

As Berio expert David Osmond-Smith puts it, "the seminal works of the early 1960s were written not for 'the voice', but for a voice: that of Cathy Berberian" – the American singer who was married to Berio from 1950 to 1966. Three poems by e.e. cummings provided the text for *Circles* (1960), a piece for voice, harpist and two percussionists. Perhaps Berio's most-performed work is *Folk Songs* for voice and septet (1964), a delightful selection of numbers from around the world that makes a marked contrast with *Sequenza III* (1966), an acrobatic display of phonetic materials which belongs with a series of instrumental works of the same name. *Recital I for Cathy* (1972) is an extraordinary piece of music theatre, a "deconstructed recital" in which the soloist tries to work through her repertoire with a chamber orchestra while giving a Beckett-like stream-of-consciousness commentary.

⭘ Circles; Sequenza I, III, V: Berberian, Nicolet, Globokar (Wergo WER 6021-2).

Berberian's unique variety of vocal theatre inspired some of the composer's most distinctive works, and is superbly captured in this historic recording from 1967. The punctuations of carefully specified kinds of laughter on *Sequenza III* are phenomenal. Digital transfer is exceptionally vivid; the disc in addition has Vinko Globokar on trombone in *Sequenza V* and Aurèle Nicolet on flute in *Sequenza I*.

◑ Recital I for Cathy; Folk Songs: Berberian; London Sinfonietta; Juilliard Ensemble; Berio (BMG 09026 62540 2; with songs by Weill).

Further classic recordings from Berberian. Her performance of *Recital I* is a *tour de force* which it is hard to see anyone else matching. *Folk Songs* has received several interpretations on disc but Berberian is clearly authoritative. She also shows great empathy in the three Kurt Weill songs. An indispensable disc.

SINFONIA

Sinfonia (1968–69), for eight amplified voices and orchestra, was part of a wider pattern of response to the crisis in avant-garde music. Many composers turned to quotation from their illustrious forebears as part of a postmodern turn towards "meta-music" – music about music. The third movement of *Sinfonia* is one of the most famous and remarkable such responses to the music of the past. As Paul Griffiths puts it in *Modern Music and After*, it is a wash of verbal quotations contained within a musical quotation – the Scherzo from Mahler's *Symphony No. 2*. This movement is virtually borrowed wholesale, and there are other briefer quotations from Mahler and Debussy. Against this, the vocalists quote from Samuel Beckett's *The Unnameable*. The result is a chattering, dazzling melee of sounds. The remaining four movements provide a setting for this centrepiece in similar vein – the second movement is a tribute to Martin Luther King.

O New Swingle Singers; Orchestre National De France; Boulez (Erato 2292-45228-2; with *Eindrücke*).

This is a recording of great impact and immediacy. Berio's music loses more than most by translation to disc, but Boulez minimizes the loss in a taut performance which displays a dazzling sonic palette.

RENDERING

In *Rendering* (1988-90), Berio realizes in Schubertian style Schubert's late sketches for a tenth symphony, a process he compares to "the modern restoration of frescoes that aims at reviving the old colours without, however, trying to disguise the damage that time has caused, often leaving inevitable empty patches in the composition". Instead of "empty patches", however, Berio has interpolations of ruminative material often loosely based on other Schubert works, the tinkling of a celeste marking the joins.

O Houston Symphony Orchestra; Eschenbach (Koch 3-7382-2; with Schubert's *Grand Duo*).

A beguiling performance that well captures the gauzy character of the non-Schubert interludes, and effortlessly manages the transitions between these and the more propulsive Schubert material. This is a deceptive work that repays repeated listenings; this is less true of Joachim's workmanlike 1855 orchestration of Schubert's *Grand Duo* for piano, also included here.

CONCERTOS

Except for *Points on a curve to find. . .* (1974) – a concerto-like work for piano and 22 instrumentalists – Berio's major explorations of the concerto genre belong to a project titled *Chemins*. This is an orchestral progression from *Sequenza*, the title indicating the proliferating "paths" from the original line of the solo piece. Thus *Chemins II* for viola is based on *Sequenza VI* for the same instrument, while *Chemins IV* for oboe is based on *Sequenza VII*. One of the most engaging components of this sequence is *Corale* (1982), an orchestration of *Sequenza VIII* for solo violin from 1975, with an identical solo part. The work has Mediterranean expressiveness and calls for breathtaking virtuosity.

O Chemins II & IV; Corale; Points on the curve to find. . .: Ensemble Intercontemporain; Boulez (Sony SK 45862; with *Ritorno degli snovidenia*).

This disc represents a denser, less immediately accessible side of Berio's output, but repeated listening brings out its richness. The high points are the "violin concerto" *Corale* and a characteristically lucid performance by Pierre-Laurent Aimard of the hugely complex "piano concerto", *Points on the curve to find...*

HECTOR BERLIOZ

(1803–1869)

The life of Hector Berlioz – as related in his dazzling, if overimaginative memoirs – is classical music's Byronic epic. Yet this quintessential Romantic began rather inauspiciously, in the backwater of Grenoble. Whereas most musical giants displayed prodigious gifts in childhood, Berlioz learned neither the piano nor the violin, though he did develop an enthusiasm for the flute and, later, the guitar. Notwithstanding his lack of practical musical ability, he wanted to pursue a career in music, but his father insisted that he enter the medical profession. Berlioz did as he was told, but in 1822, while studying at the Paris Medical School, he began to take serious music lessons for the first time.

Owing to the fact that his father's allowance was forthcoming only for as long as he remained at school, Berlioz hesitated over making a serious break until 1826, when he mustered the courage to leave the medical school and enter the music conservatory. His subsequent development was bewilderingly fast, and was actually aided by his inability to play the piano well – other composers tended to work out their ideas at the piano, but Berlioz found himself free of such creative limitations and soon realized that the orchestra and large ensembles were his true métier.

In 1827 he experienced one of many life-changing events when he went to see a performance of *Hamlet*. Even though his English was far from fluent, the play hit him "like a thunderbolt", as did the beauty of the leading lady, Harriet Smithson. It was to be the start of a lifelong addiction to the Bard and an equally intense, if less durable, passion for Miss Smithson (they married in 1833 and separated nine years later). During the first five months of 1830 – having in the interim immersed himself in Goethe's poetry and attended a revelatory series of Beethoven concerts in Paris – he composed his *Symphonie Fantastique*, a huge orchestral piece in which he attempted to sublimate his passion for the actress; its subtitle, "Episodes in the life of an artist", betrays an autobiographical element that was never far below the surface of Berlioz's music.

Not long after, Berlioz finally succeeded in winning the *Prix de Rome*, a scholarship given to artists to enable them to study at the Villa Medici in Rome – and Italy was duly to become another of his great inspirations. Berlioz proceeded to produce a string of similarly colossal and innovative works that secured the admiration of composers such as Liszt, Paganini and Chopin, but had difficulty obtaining a wider audience, not least because his music usually demanded very large and expensive forces.

The work that posed the greatest problems in this respect was his penultimate opera, *Les Troyens*, a five-act, four-hour monster which the Paris Opéra refused to produce in its entirety. Berlioz then divided the work into two parts and, eventually, he saw the second of these, *Les Troyens à Carthage*, staged at the Théâtre-Lyrique in 1863. As with so many of his works, the performance was a grand failure, but this failure hit him harder than any.

LEBRECHT COLLECTION

Berlioz in 1846, the year *Faust* was first performed

He found occasional solace through conducting, but his last seven years were overshadowed by illness, despair and resentment at his country's inability or unwillingness to recognize his talent – a situation that has not really changed, for Berlioz is far more widely respected abroad than he is at home. His music was doubtless very strange for its time, with its irregular rhythms and almost boastfully complicated orchestration, and certainly it can be pompous and overblown. However, Berlioz is one of music's great originals, spurning traditional formulas to blend literary, pictorial and musical elements into highly energetic and highly personal creations.

STAGE WORKS

Of Berlioz's five stage works, two are masterpieces – the classically inspired *Les Troyens*, and his homage to Goethe, *La Damnation de Faust*. The early *Les Francs Juges* is lost, apart from a lengthy overture which is sometimes programmed in orchestral concerts. *Benvenuto Cellini*, the story of the intrigues surrounding the Renaissance sculptor and his rivals, gets an occasional performance and recording, but is too lengthy for its content, although Berlioz created one of his best overtures – *Le Carnaval Romain* – out of its carnival scene. His late Shakespearean comedy, *Béatrice et Bénédict*, a hotchpotch of styles with heavy reliance on spoken scenes, has never been a success, despite containing one or two musical highlights and an attractive overture.

LA DAMNATION DE FAUST

Berlioz read a translation of the first part of Goethe's *Faust* in 1828 and fell under its spell at once. He immediately set to work on eight *Scenes from Faust*, which he sent to the poet for approval – a bad move, as it turned out. Goethe showed the score to a composer friend who was appalled by Berlioz's outrageous music, and the result was that Berlioz withdrew the work. Many years later, he reworked the scenes into *La Damnation de Faust*, a hybrid work, more closely resembling an oratorio for concert performance than an opera – Berlioz himself called it a "dramatic legend". It was produced at the Opéra-Comique in 1846, then in Drury Lane two years later, after which Berlioz planned a further revision to make the work a true opera – it's almost impossible, for example, to stage the *Ride to Hell* and *Pandemonium*. However, the Drury Lane opera company for which the opera was to be written soon went bankrupt, and so *La Damnation* remained as it was.

Berlioz sticks much closer to his source than many composers have – Gounod, for example, concentrated merely on the Faust and Gretchen scenes in his *Faust*. Not only does he retain the narrative scope of the original text, he tackles its supernatural and philosophical apsects too, and in this respect *La Damnation* resembles Busoni's version of the legend (see p.94). Temperamentally, however, there's a world of difference between Busoni's cerebral opera and Berlioz's kaleidoscopic work, which crams an extraordinary range of music into its two-hour span. Between the crashing "Hungarian March" of the opening scene and the climactic ride to hell, there's a rowdy tavern scene, a supernatural ballet as Faust dreams of Marguerite (Gretchen in the original), a love scene, a mad aria and a great pantheistic invocation of nature, one of the most advanced parts of this amazingly vivid score. No previous work for the stage had risked such violent contrasts, and few subsequent composers could bring them off so successfully.

O Veasey, Gedda, Bastin; Ambrosian Singers; London Symphony Orchestra; Davis (Philips 416 395-2; 2 CDs).

Despite being recorded over twenty years ago, this Philips set is wonderfully vivid. Colin Davis is masterful in portraying the tender moments of Marguerite's despair as well as the vast climaxes of the "Hungarian March" and the ride to hell. Josephine Veasey is a poignant heroine, Nicolai Gedda a magnificent Faust, and Jules Bastin a suitably evil Mephistopheles.

LES TROYENS

Berlioz's epic tale of the Trojan War was written in the late 1850s but brought together the obsessions of several decades – primarily the poetry of Shakespeare and Virgil, and the operas of Gluck, whose finely structured libretti provided a model for the text of this most un-Gluck-like extravaganza. Berlioz never lived to see *Les Troyens* performed complete: after five years of waiting for the Paris Opéra to agree to a production, he split the opera in two and let the second section, *Les Troyens à Carthage*, be performed at the smaller Théatre Lyrique. The first part, *La prise de Troie*, wasn't performed until 1890, by which time *Les Troyens* had pretty well fallen into oblivion as a unified work. It wasn't until 1957 that a nearly uncut version was played in one evening at Covent Garden, a premiere that put paid to the notion that the piece was even more unwieldy than Wagner's later operas. *Les Troyens* is nonetheless too expensive to be performed regularly – you're more likely to see semi-staged concert performances than full-dress opera-house productions.

The opera begins in war-ravaged Troy, quickly introducing the prophetess Cassandra, the pivotal figure of the first two acts (ie *La Prise de Troie*), and the role with perhaps the noblest music in the entire score. The whole of this first part of *Les Troyens* is full of grandiose and doomstruck music, its highlights being Cassandra's aria, the procession of the widowed Andromache, the entry of the wooden horse, the ghost scene in Aeneas's tent and finally the mass suicide of Cassandra and the Trojan women.

Berlioz creates a wholly different sound-world for the sensuality of the court of Queen Dido at Carthage, where Aeneas and his party arrive after fleeing the conflagration of Troy. These final three acts progress at a slower and more luxuriant pace. After the celebratory first act comes the best-known music of the opera, the symphonic interlude known as *The Royal Hunt and Storm*, commencing a succession of beautiful set pieces that culminates in a great love duet for Aeneas and Dido, set to words from Shakespeare. The final act brings the Aeneas's desertion of Dido and her suicide, a scene redolent of the majesty of Gluck.

⭘ Veasey, Vickers, Lindholm; Royal Opera House Orchestra and Chorus; Davis (Philips 416 432-2; 4 CDs).

This set, featuring the cast of the 1969 Covent Garden performances, demonstrates Davis's unrivalled ability to project Berlioz's wonderful melodies, often quirky rhythms and rich orchestral colours. Josephine Veasey is a full-sounding Dido, Berit Lindholm a powerful Cassandra and Jon Vickers is simply the perfect Aeneas – no one since has brought the sheer power and nobility to this most difficult of roles.

CHORAL AND VOCAL WORKS

Berlioz wrote a considerable amount of vocal music apart from the operas, including a number of cantatas (several of which are lost), some lovely orchestral songs and two large-scale religious works – the *Grand Messe des Morts* and *L'Enfance du Christ* (The Childhood of Christ). Written in 1837 and 1850–54 respectively, they are total opposites in style – the *Grand Messe* is a hyperbolically massive affair, *L'Enfance* a gentle series of musical tableaux.

GRAND MESSE DES MORTS

The *Grand Messe des Morts* (1837) is unique in being a Requiem created by a man of no real religious belief. It is doubly strange in that it is written almost entirely for chorus and orchestra – there's just one soloist, a tenor, and he appears in one movement only. Comparable to Beethoven's *Missa Solemnis* in its dynamic extremes, the *Grand Messe* is famed primarily for its use of four brass bands in the *Tuba Mirum* movement, placed at the four compass points to conjure the Day of Judgment in an ear-splitting display. Certainly nothing else in the work matches the theatricality of this moment, but there is much to admire in this austerely grand and sometimes lurid composition.

◑ Dowd; Wandsworth School Boys Choir; London Symphony Chorus and Orchestra; Davis (Philips 416 283-2; 2 CDs; with *Symphonie funèbre et triomphale*).

Though Bernstein's fine recording is no longer available, this makes a more than worthy substitute – though tenor Ronald Dowd for Davis is not as dramatic as Stuart Burrows for Bernstein. The Philips engineers capture better than most the full impact of the brass bands.

L'ENFANCE DU CHRIST

L'Enfance du Christ is so distinctly archaic in style that it hardly seems possible that it's written by the composer of the *Grand Messe*. A self-confessed agnostic, Berlioz presents the story of the young Christ as a legendary narrative rather than as an uplifting religious experience. The work is in three sections: the first centres on the birth of Christ and the predicament of King Herod; the second is a pastoral interlude in which the Holy Family flee into Egypt, a scene containing some of the composer's most placid music; and the final part depicts the hospitality given to them in Egypt, an episode featuring some fairly crass scene-painting but a serene choral ending.

⭘ Gens, Agnew, Naouri, Lallouette, Caton; La Chapelle Royale; Collegium Vocale; Orchestre des Champs Élysées; Herreweghe (Harmonia Mundi HMC 901632-33; 2 CDs).

This live performance on period instruments is an absolute revelation. The soloists are all French (with the exception of Paul Agnew's narrator) and the combination of native singers and the more pungent sonorities of the instruments (especially the woodwind) creates some wonderfully rich, individual sounds, which Herreweghe shapes with great subtlety.

LES NUITS D'ÉTÉ

Les Nuits d'été (Summer Nights), a cycle of six songs to words by Théophile Gautier, was first written in 1841 as a composition for voice and piano. A couple of years later Berlioz orchestrated the third song, *Absence*, and in 1856 he decided to make orchestral versions of the other five. It is impossible to overstate the importance of this piece to French music: whereas Beethoven, Schubert and Schumann had already established the concept of the song cycle in Germany, it was Berlioz who single-handedly introduced the form to France. Yet its novelty is but a small part of the appeal of *Les Nuits d'été*, for these are among the loveliest songs of the nineteenth century, thanks to music that's completely attuned to the melancholic languor of Gautier's poems.

⭘ Crespin; Orchestre de la Suisse Romande; Ansermet (Decca 417 813-2; with other French songs).

Berlioz originally wrote the songs for different voice types but nowadays they are usually sung by a soprano – and it's difficult to find a voice that's exactly right for all these songs, as the opening and concluding songs are of a lightness that contrasts with deep sorrow expressed in the longer central pieces. The most celebrated of all the solo versions is that of Régine Crespin, who was at the height of her powers as a dramatic singer when this recording was made in 1963.

◑ de los Angeles; Boston Symphony Orchestra; Munch (RCA GD60681; 2 CDs; with *Roméo et Juliette*).

Victoria de los Angeles gives a marginally more subtle and telling performance than Crespin, but it's only available on a two-CD set coupled with a fine account of the dramatic symphony *Roméo et Juliette*.

ORCHESTRAL WORKS

Berlioz's early overtures – especially *Le Corsair* and *Le Carnaval Romain* – generate a certain fidgety excitement, but there's no disputing which two compositions stand out as the best of his small output of orchestral work: the *Symphonie Fantastique*, the first and greatest Romantic symphony, and *Harold en Italie*, a sort of travelogue for viola and orchestra.

SYMPHONIE FANTASTIQUE

Both as a first symphony and as a work by a 27-year-old, the *Symphonie Fantastique* is a staggering achievement. Written just three years after Beethoven's death, at a time when he was still regarded as a radical, this hour-long and five-movement work took several steps beyond Beethoven's symphonic structures. For one thing, this is the first symphony to make thorough use of the *idée fixe*, a single melody that reappears in different guises throughout the work – a concept that is the forerunner of the leitmotifs in Wagner and Richard Strauss. Furthermore, although composers had written scenic music before the *Symphonie Fantastique* (eg Beethoven's *Symphony No. 6*) and simple musical onomatopoeia had been common for centuries (eg Vivaldi's *Four Seasons*), no composer had used instrumental music to present so specific a narrative drama. In short, this symphony is an opera without words.

Mythologizing Berlioz's neurotic obsession with Harriet Smithson, the "plot" of the *Symphonie Fantastique* is an opium-induced phantasmagoria, in which the hero imagines the torrid progress of a love affair that ends ultimately in his execution for the murder of his lover. Berlioz supplies subtitles to explain events: *Reveries – Passions*; *A Ball*; *Scene in the Country*; *March to the Scaffold* and *Dream of a Witches' Sabbath*. The *idée fixe* runs chillingly through each movement and reaches its gruesome climax when it is coupled with the terrifying Dies Irae plainchant – Romanticism's ultimate musical theme.

○ Vienna Philharmonic Orchestra; Davis (Philips 432 151-2).

The symphony, with its vast forces, wild rhythms and extremes of loudness and softness, is a *tour de force* of orchestral writing and no one knows it better than Sir Colin Davis. His third recording of it, with the Vienna Philharmonic, has the advantage of superb sound and excellent playing.

◑ Detroit Symphony Orchestra; Paray (Mercury 434 328-2; with *Hungarian March*, *Roman March*, *Corsair Overture* and *Roman Carnival Overture*).

This is an absolutely spine-tingling account by an orchestra and conductor completely of one mind. They present Berlioz as the high priest of Romanticism: brooding, darkly imaginative and with a ferocious energy which borders on the demented.

HAROLD EN ITALIE

Although it was composed in 1834, the gestation of *Harold en Italie* began three years earlier, when Berlioz was travelling through Italy after winning the Prix de Rome. While crossing from Marseilles to Leghorn, he had met a sea captain who claimed to have ferried Byron – author of the immensely popular *Childe Harold's Pilgrimage* – around the Greek islands. That gave Berlioz his initial ideas for the piece, but the catalyst was Paganini, who approached him for a viola concerto; Berlioz accepted the commission, then promptly abandoned the idea of a strict concerto in favour of what amounted to a symphony with obbligato viola.

The work was based, as Berlioz wrote, upon his "impressions recollected from . . . wanderings in the Abruzzi mountains", and the solo viola was conceived as a portrayal of "a kind of melancholy dreamer in the style of Byron's *Childe Harolde*". Paganini was unimpressed. He had asked for a concerto and expected something to display his notorious abilities: when he realized that there was nothing even vaguely difficult in the score he refused to play it. The two duly fell out, but when Paganini heard the work performed he threw himself at Berlioz's feet to beg forgiveness and later sent the composer a note comparing him to Beethoven – enclosed was a gift of 20,000 francs. Berlioz needed the money and they became friends once again, but Paganini never played his commission.

Again, the work is in five movements and is dominated by a central thematic idea (Harold's theme), but Berlioz now takes the *idée fixe* a stage further – whereas in the *Symphonie Fantastique* the *idée fixe* recurs unchanged, here the "Harold" idea appears in every movement but serves as the basis for thematic development. The rhythmic pungency of *Harold en Italie* is even more engaging than the symphony, and the melodies – especially in the adrenaline-pumping finale – are much more immediate. In effect Berlioz's second symphony, it has proved less popular than the first, but is musically its superior, for, whereas the drama of the *Symphonie Fantastique* can sound close to orchestral gimmicry, here everything takes second place to the thematic content, and it is Berlioz's genius for melody and harmony that remains uppermost.

⊙ Imai; London Symphony Orchestra; Davis (Philips 416 431-2; with *Tristia*).

Davis correctly sees the piece as more a symphony than a concerto, and Nobuko Imai is an excellent partner, always playing the viola as part of the integral musical soundscape, never clamouring for the limelight. Excellently recorded, the disc also has a fascinating fill-up in the little-known *Tristia* pieces.

LEONARD BERNSTEIN

(1918–1990)

Leonard Bernstein's big break is the stuff of legend – substituting for the sick maestro Bruno Walter for a New York Philharmonic concert on November 14, 1943, he became famous overnight, launching a meteoric and controversial career as a conductor. For some, Bernstein got right to the heart of Beethoven, Mahler and the other great symphonists, giving himself unreservedly to the music's emotional pulse; for others, he was a self-indulgent showman, besotted with himself and with the audience's applause. Yet conducting was but one strand of a career that was remarkably varied and at the same time consistent.

From the mid-1950s Bernstein presented dozens of TV programmes – most famous being the *Young People's Concerts* (1958–73) – in which he played and brilliantly explicated the works that he so manifestly loved. The basis for Bernstein's lectures was his belief, very similar in its thrust to Noam Chomsky's theories of speech structure, that all music is rooted in a universal language that is basically tonal. This belief was fundamental to his own compositions, in which Bernstein strove to forge a connection between art music and the music of the American people. More specifically, he felt that jazz was the essential sound of the USA – though the jazz you hear in Bernstein's music is not so much a direct legacy of Duke Ellington or Jelly Roll Morton, but jazz as reworked by Aaron Copland.

As a composer his greatest successes were in music for the stage, and he created a string of hit shows that culminated in *West Side Story* (1957), a classic of American musical theatre. His theatrical instincts frequently spilled over into his concert works, Bernstein himself admitting to "a deep suspicion that every work I write, for whatever medium, is really theatre music in some way". Such compositions as his three symphonies, *Jeremiah*, *The Age of Anxiety* and *Kaddish*, are indeed profoundly dramatic, but they also draw sustenance from Bernstein's Jewish heritage, with its basis in synagogue chant.

As the 1960s progressed, Bernstein came under increasing fire from radical young musicians, for whom the serialist principles of Schoenberg, Berg and Webern, and their hardline successors Boulez and Stockhausen, were the new orthodoxy. Although Bernstein fought a vigorous rearguard action against the dogmatic rejection of the general public's taste, he began to lose his confidence as a composer, preferring instead to develop his role as the guardian of what he felt was best in music. Bernstein's liberal humanism, sincere though it was, didn't always endear him to the younger generation either. Most notoriously, his fund-raising evening for the Black Panther movement backfired calamitously when Tom Wolfe made it the subject of his most celebrated article, *Radical Chic*.

Yet even in the face of vilification Bernstein never relinquished his musical values, and his principles have come to be more relevant now than they were at the time. There may be some truth in the accusation that Bernstein's own music is often nothing more than immensely skilled pastiche, but it's equally true that he could be seen as the precursor of a generation of American composers – Adams, Glass, Reich and so on – who are as effusively theatrical, eclectic and tonal in their leanings as Bernstein was.

WEST SIDE STORY

Of all Bernstein's music, it's the stage works that sum up best what he was all about, and of these

SONY

Leonard Bernstein

West Side Story is the most consistently tuneful. Transposing *Romeo and Juliet* to the gangland of New York's West Side in the 1950s, it was not a huge success at its premiere – its reputation soared after the release of the film version in 1961. Though *West Side Story* is full of great songs, including *America*, *Maria* and *Tonight*, it's equally remarkable for the quality of its dance music (which Bernstein later rearranged as a concert suite) and for its decidedly downbeat ending, breaking one of the cardinal rules of music theatre.

◑ **Nixon, Bryant, Tamblyn, Wand, Chakiris; chorus and orchestra; Green** (Sony SMK48211).

There are now a handful of recordings of *West Side Story*, but for those wanting the authentic buzz of the original the best place to go is to the film soundtrack. It's not the complete score but it's more than just highlights and it packs more of a punch than any subsequent version.

○ **Te Kanawa, Carreras, Troyanos, Horne, Ollman; chorus and orchestra; Bernstein** (Deutsche Grammophon 415 253-2; 2 CDs; with *On The Waterfront, Symphonic Suite*).

Bernstein's own recording of the complete score remains controversial because of the way it gives the piece the full-blown operatic treatment. Many will find the voices of Kiri Te Kanawa and José Carreras rather lifeless and overpolished in this repertoire. There's no doubt that Bernstein taps his soloists' ability to elicit the kind of subtle vocal effects that would not be possible from Broadway singers, but whether such vocal finesse is appropriate is a moot point.

HEINRICH BIBER

(1644–1704)

In the seventeenth century the violin consolidated its position as expressively the most wide-ranging of non-keyboard instruments. This was an age of great violin makers, like Amati and Stradivari, as well as outstanding performers like Corelli (see p.111). Italy was the centre of instrumental prowess, but the finest of all seventeenth-century virtuosi was Heinrich Biber, who spent most of his working life in Salzburg. A composer as well as a performer,

Biber was fascinated by the doctrine of the affections: the belief that emotional states such as tenderness, fear and anger could be given direct musical expression. Many Baroque composers pursued this idea but none did so with such a degree of quirkiness, flair and sheer experimental verve as Biber. Above all else in his violin sonatas, he reveals an astonishing combination of profound feeling and technical wizardry that suggests a brilliant improviser at work.

Biber was born in Warttenberg in Bohemia but probably received his early training in Vienna under Johann Schmelzer, the leading Austrian violinist of the day. Some time around 1668 he entered the service of Archbishop Karl von Liechtenstein-Kastelkorn, a music lover whose castle in Moravia boasted a fine musical establishment. In 1670, while on official business, Biber mysteriously abandoned his position while in Salzburg and entered the employ of another powerful churchman, the Prince-Archbishop of Salzburg, Maximilian Gandolph. He was to remain there for the rest of his life: beginning as a court violinist and rising to the rank of court Kapellmeister and cathedral choirmaster in 1684 before his eventual ennoblement in 1690. In his later years his duties included writing a substantial amount of large-scale choral music for the cathedral, among which the *Requiem in F* is outstanding. Despite his renown as a performer, there is no evidence to suggest that he travelled anywhere much farther than Munich. Nor was there any known contact with other major composers, apart from his colleague at Salzburg, George Muffat (a student of both Lully and Corelli), who shared Biber's enthusiasm for writing sonatas.

THE VIOLIN SONATAS

The normal tuning of instruments of the violin family is in intervals five notes apart (fifths). However, much of Biber's music employs a device called *scordatura* whereby an instrument is tuned differently from piece to piece. This was done for a variety of reasons: to extend the possible range of notes, to make certain chords playable, and to change the character of the instrument by creating new sonorities. In *The Mystery Sonatas*, composed for a religious ceremony celebrating the Rosary, Biber takes the use of *scordatura* to imaginative extremes. Each sonata corresponds to an event in the life of Jesus or the Virgin Mary and, though they employ stylized dance forms and sets of variations, each attempts to evoke a particular devotional mood and sometimes to create a particular scene – such as the fluttering of angelic wings in No. 1 (*The Annunciation*) or the rising of the sun in No. 11 (*The Resurrection*). The set ends with a passacaglia for unaccompanied violin, the earliest known extended work for solo violin and an obvious forerunner of J.S. Bach's great *Chaconne*. In the other outstanding set of violin sonatas of 1681, *scordatura* is rarely used: they are, nevertheless, highly inventive and technically demanding works. Once again, sets of variations abound, as does brilliant passage work, often over a sustained note in the bass part. Certainly, these works are occasionally flashy for the sheer hell of it, but more often their sudden changes of mood reveal a brilliant, restless and essentially improvisatory musical temperament.

O The Mystery Sonatas: Holloway (Virgin VCD 7 90838-2; 2 CDs).

This is the better of the two available recordings. John Holloway's sinewy and rather bare violin tone is well-suited to the generally austere nature of the music. Though it is possible to ignore the religious aspect of these sonatas, and to listen to them individually, Holloway communicates a real sense of progression so that the cumulative effect of the full set, culminating in the solo passacaglia, is extremely powerful. Each sonata employs a different continuo combination and there is highly sympathetic support from the keyboard player Davitt Moroney and the versatile ensemble Tragicomedia.

O Eight Violin Sonatas; Sonata Representativa; Two Passacaglias: Romanesca (Harmonia Mundi HMU 906 134.35; 2 CDs).

Andrew Manze, the violinist of Romanesca, is a Baroque specialist whose panache and lack of inhibition are perfectly suited to this music. He is particularly adept at an almost throwaway manner with Biber's more filigree passage work and displays an appropriately wide range of tone colour for this lively and colourful music. The slight fluctuations of mood are judged with all the nonchalant ease of a good jazz musician, and Manze even manages to make the *Sonata Representiva* (short animal portraits) seem more substantial music than it is. Overall, a superb achievement.

HARMONIA ARTIFICIOSA-ARIOSA

As well as vehicles for his own prodigious virtuosity, Biber also wrote music for larger ensembles. Most of these chamber works employ conventional string tuning, the exception is one of his most striking works the *Harmonia artificiosa-ariosa*, a collection of seven partitas for two instruments and bass, six of which employ *scordatura* tuning. These are magical works: more tightly formed and less capricious than the violin sonatas but with a similar depth of feeling and abounding in contrapuntal vigour and strange harmonies.

Biber was an exact contemporary of Pachelbel (see p.293) and there are moments in these works which resemble the latter's famous *Canon and Gigue*. Biber, however, was a more sophisticated composer and the partitas' many variations display an endless capacity for unpredictable invention. Particularly spectacular are the air and thirteen variations of *Partita VI* (the non-*scordatura* partita), which include a canon in which the voices are only separated by half a beat's difference.

⊙ The Rare Fruits Council (Auvidis E8572).

The bizarrely named Rare Fruits Council attack this music with an almost brutal energy and with an appropriately ripe sound. Their approach brings out the weird and wondrous aspects of the music: accents are occasionally over-stressed, speeds are sometimes precipitously fast, and slow movements treated with luxuriant sensuousness. Even so, this is the best of the three available recordings because the occasional exaggeration suits the quixotic nature of the music and the group's enthusiasm for it is completely infectious.

HARRISON BIRTWISTLE

(1934–)

Despite acknowledged debts to Stravinsky and Varèse (see p.410 & p.444), Harrison Birtwistle's music sounds as if it has sprung into being from a point outside the mainstream of European music, evoking the stylized ceremonies of Greek tragedy, the ritual violence of ancient myths, and the bleak and depopulated landscapes of rural England. Many of Birtwistle's compositions have the massive, rough-hewn quality of a prehistoric monument, but he can also produce music of spare lyrical beauty and, on occasion, haunting delicacy.

During the 1950s, when Birtwistle began his musical studies, the English scene was dominated by the shadow of Vaughan Williams (see p.388) and other such pastoral composers, while recent events in European music were generally regarded with reactionary disdain. It was in this claustrophobic environment that the "Manchester School", consisting of composers Birtwistle, Alexander Goehr and Peter Maxwell Davies (see p.250), plus conductor Elgar Howarth and pianist John Ogdon, began their careers, looking to the latest developments on the continent for inspiration. Birtwistle bided his time, studying clarinet and keeping his ambitions as a composer to himself until 1957 when, with the wind quintet *Refrains and Choruses*, he launched himself as the most distinctive voice among his illustrious contemporaries. Here, immediately, is a fully formed style. It's strikingly raw and hard-edged music, and it unfolds not by any conventional development but as a series of static blocks, evoking a kind of imaginary rite.

Birtwistle scored his first major critical success with the ensemble piece *Tragœdia* (1965) – the title, meaning "goat dance", is drawn from Greek drama, one of the principal influences on Birtwistle during this period. Birtwistle's works of the 1960s culminated in the notorious chamber opera *Punch and Judy*, which was premiered at the Aldeburgh Festival in 1968, when Benjamin Britten – guiding light of the festival – was among those who walked out in disgust or incomprehension. Here the ritual violence of purely instrumental works such as *Tragœdia* is transferred to an explicitly theatrical context, depicting the gruesome encounters of Punch and Judy. What is typical of this and subsequent works for the stage is the lack of progressive narrative: the story is not told in sequence from beginning to end, but re-enacted over and over again, each time from a slightly different angle (Punch commits no fewer than four murders), creating a tension between the heated, murderous subject matter and its cool, rather distanced presentation.

The work that really signalled the arrival of Birtwistle as one of the major composers of his generation was *The Triumph of Time* (1972), a monumental orchestral procession inspired by Brueghel's depiction of the remorseless progress of Time and Death. After this came a series of masterful works such as *Silbury Air*, *Secret Theatre*, *The Fields of Sorrow* and, in 1984, *The Mask of Orpheus*, an opera which, with its mythologized, masked characters, represents the summation of Birtwistle's love of hieratic structures and repetitive narratives. Since the long-postponed premiere of *The Mask of Orpheus* in 1986, Birtwistle has increasingly turned his attention to opera. In 1988 came the "mechanical pastoral" *Yan tan tethera*, a supernatural tale of two shepherds, their sheep and the devil, followed in 1991 by the monumental opera *Gawain*, in which he counterpoints the Arthurian hero's trials against the circularity of the seasons, while finding a musical structure to propel the narrative forward.

RICHARD KALINA/BOOSEY & HAWKES

Harrison Birtwistle

mixes violence, humour and lyricism to present Punch, the serial killer.

Birtwistle laboured from 1973 to 1984 on his "lyric tragedy" *The Mask of Orpheus* (1986), arguably his greatest work. Vast and unwieldy, the opera presents the story of Orpheus and Eurydice, not cleansed as it was in Baroque operas, but as a tale of fundamental violence and tragedy; and it tells that tale over and over again, viewing it and reviewing it from every possible angle in 42 "trinities of action". It is a work like no other, yet it also seeks to encompass the whole history of opera, music, dance, theatre, and language itself. The principal characters appear in three guises – the mythical, the heroic and the human – and each is played by three performers: a singer (with a puppet double), a dancer and a mime. There is also an elaborate electronic score. On paper this sounds impenetrable; if performance does not make everything crystal clear, it nevertheless carries a powerful physical weight that transcends narrative clarity.

Birtwistle's most recent opera mingles myths ancient and modern: the characters of *The Second Mrs Kong* (1994) include not only Orpheus and Eurydice, but also Vermeer, King Kong and a beauty queen. If the libretto is tortuous, Birtwistle's score is looser, less dense than we've come to expect: there is some dazzlingly witty writing for accordion and saxophone, for example, though whether this marks the birth of a new theatrical language remains to be seen.

Despite this commitment to opera, Birtwistle has found time to complete other commissions, including the massive *Earth Dances* (1986), and "concertos" (the label is barely adequate) for trumpet (*Endless Parade*; 1987), piano (*Antiphonies*; 1993) and saxophone (*Panic*; 1995), works in which the savagery of earlier pieces seethes, volcanically, beneath an often richly poignant lyricism.

THE MASK OF ORPHEUS

As early as *Tragœdia* (1965), it was apparent that Greek drama was to provide one point of reference for Birtwistle's theatre music: in this, he shares common ground with the earliest opera composers, who were likewise attempting to recreate ancient models in their musical fables. Tellingly, though, Birtwistle's first opera, *Punch and Judy* ("comical tragedy or tragical comedy" in the composer's description) took the seaside puppet show as its subject, with a libretto that

◑ Garrison, Bronder, Rigby, Owens, Angel; BBC Singers and Symphony Orchestra; Davis (NMC D050; 3 CDs).

It was brave of Andrew Davis to revive the opera in 1996, albeit in semi-staged form; and braver still of NMC to issue this live recording of a piece that cries out for theatrical presentation to make sense of its convolutions. Excellent documentation casts light where it can, but in the end it's the sheer commitment of all involved that carries the listener to a point where the score's fathomless riches overcome all doubts.

THE TRIUMPH OF TIME

The Triumph of Time represents the classic instance of how Birtwistle was able to achieve a structure that has nothing to do with traditional ways of sustaining an extended piece of music. Birtwistle often describes his works as "imaginary landscapes", a particularly apt description for *The Triumph of Time*. Listening to this thirty-minute orchestral procession is rather like moving through a landscape, viewing the same landmarks from ever-changing perspectives. And the landscape we are observing is also that of Time itself, in which past, present and future coexist. Two instruments stand out from the constant, slow-moving flux: a brief fragment of melody for soprano saxophone occurs and reoccurs, while a more elaborate cor anglais solo floats free to remind us of Birtwistle's lyrical gifts, all the more moving for never being overindulged.

⊙ Philharmonia; Howarth (Collins Classics 13872; with *Gawain's Journey*).

Elgar Howarth has been a doughty champion of Birtwistle's music from the beginning of the composer's career, and here produces a performance of subtlety and power in equal measure. In the wrong hands, a work like *The Triumph of Time* can seem merely static; Howarth ensures that there is a sense of movement, albeit according to Birtwistlean laws. *Gawain's Journey*, although free-standing, acts as a kind of digest of the opera from which it derives, vocal parts reassigned to solo instruments.

EARTH DANCES

Just as the Earth's continents are in perpetual, imperceptible motion, so here the strata of Birtwistle's orchestra shift and shuffle around each other in ever-changing patterns. Sometimes the strata stack up immensely; at other moments, they thin to the most diaphonous textures; but always there is the sense of returning to the same point, only to discover that the view has changed in the interim. Though it is only distantly related to Birtwistle's works for theatre, there is palpable menace in this massive (forty-minute) score.

⊙ Cleveland Orchestra; Dohnányi (Argo 452-104-2; with *Panic*).

It's a mark of Birtwistle's hard-won status that American orchestras, often conservative in their choice of modern repertoire, are now playing, sometimes even commissioning, his music. Here, Christoph von Dohnányi's aristocratic orchestra tussles mightily with the Lancastrian grit of one of Birtwistle's grandest structures, giving a performance both lustrous and wild. The accompanying *Panic* (performed by Andrew Davis with the BBC Symphony Orchestra), more boisterous, often jazzy in a free-form kind of way, is the work that jammed BBC switchboards when it was performed at the Last Night of the 1995 Proms: Birtwistle is rather proud of the alleged ten thousand complaints it occasioned.

GEORGES BIZET

(1838–1875)

Like so many nineteenth-century opera composers, Bizet attained immortality through a single score – *Carmen*. He completed its fourth and final act in 1874; a year later he was dead.

Bizet packed a lot into his short life. By the age of nine he had entered the Paris Conservatoire and within months was winning every major prize for piano, organ and composition. In 1857, aged 19, he won the coveted Prix de Rome, which set him on a steady course to security and fame. An example of his abilities at this time can be found in his *Symphony in C major*, an astonishing work which reflects the influence of Gounod, whom Bizet had befriended in 1856.

His first major opera, *Les Pêcheurs des Perles* (The Pearl Fishers), was produced at the Opéra Comique in 1863. It was written to an appalling libretto whose authors later admitted that, had they been aware of Bizet's talents, they would not have saddled him with such a "white elephant". However, the public warmed to Bizet's sensual and melodic music, and *Les Pêcheurs des Perles* became one of Bizet's very few immediate successes – though its continued survival is primarily due to one lovely duet for tenor and baritone. He went on to compose a number of comic and dramatic operas, many of which were left incomplete, and none of which suggested anything more remarkable than proficiency. Then in 1872 Bizet began to take an interest in Prosper Merimée's short novel *Carmen*; the Opéra Comique, however, was far from enthusiastic – they didn't want death on their stage, and neither were they keen on a project dominated by thieves, gypsies and cigar-makers. Despite these misgivings, the manager finally committed himself to a production and on March 3, 1875, *Carmen* was given its premiere.

Bizet described the result as "a definite and hopeless flop" (an exaggeration) and, ever prone to psychosomatic illness, took to his bed. Four hours after the curtain had fallen on the 33rd performance, he died from the second of two major heart attacks.

CARMEN

Carmen is the first "realistic" French opera, and its merging of intense local colour with well-crafted tragic drama attracted praise from influential quarters: Wagner wrote of it, "Here thank God . . . is somebody with ideas in his head"; both Brahms and Tchaikovsky adored it; and Nietzsche used the opera as a stick with which to beat Wagner, suggesting that he adopt some of Bizet's healthy Mediterranean philosophies. However, the hot-blooded characterization of Carmen, and of her rival lovers Don José and Escamillo, scandalized the first audiences, as did the tragic ending, in which Don José murders the heroine.

Bizet's evocation of the opera's Spanish locales displays amazing abilities as an orchestrator, while the plentiful magnificent arias are so adroitly and economically woven into the plot that you come away with the sense that nothing could possibly be added or taken away. It is hard to imagine how critics could have attacked *Carmen* for being tuneless – it boasts more memorable tunes than any other French opera except Gounod's *Faust*, which remains the only French opera more popular than *Carmen*.

⊙ Berganza, Domingo, Cotrubas, Milnes; Ambrosian Singers; London Symphony Orchestra; Abbado (Deutsche Grammophon 419 436-2; 3 CDs).

This is a superbly professional *Carmen* and the most Spanish ever recorded. Placido Domingo makes a smooth but powerful Don José, while Teresa Berganza is a very sexy Carmen, suggesting a youthful capriciousness that's absent from most interpretations. Sherill Milnes delivers the "Toreador Song" with real oomph, and Ilena Cotrubas is a vibrant, if unusually weighty Micaëla.

⊙ Price, Corelli, Freni, Merrill; Vienna Boys Choir, Vienna State Opera Chorus; Vienna Philharmonic Orchestra; Karajan (RCA GD86199; 3 CDs).

Though he's less than comfortable with the French language, Franco Corelli makes an outstanding Don José. His massive voice is incomparably thrilling, and he produces an outstandingly tragic portrayal. He sings opposite Leontyne Price, not the most characterful Carmen, but with an effective sense of malice to the part. Karajan's approach is exciting if unsubtle, but with Mirella Freni and Merrill in marvellous form this set is the most entertaining introduction to Bizet.

SYMPHONY IN C MAJOR

Bizet's finest orchestral score, the *Symphony in C major*, was composed in 1855, when he had only recently turned 17 – though it was not performed until 1935 when the conductor Felix Weingartner discovered the manuscript in Paris. Like its model, Gounod's *Symphony No. 1*, Bizet's work makes no claims to originality, but it's a fresh, ingenious and uninhibited piece, something like a French version of Schubert in its beautiful melodic writing (though Bizet could not have known Schubert's large-scale works). Like Mendelssohn's early music, this is more than mere juvenilia.

⊙ Royal Philharmonic Orchestra; Beecham (EMI CDC 7 47794-2; with *L'Arlésienne Suites*).

Beecham's charming and light-footed account of the symphony is full of wit and colour. His moulding of Bizet's intricate architecture is unfailingly sure and the orchestra responds to his demands with engaging immediacy.

LEBRECHT COLLECTION

Bizet in his early twenties

L'ARLÉSIENNE SUITES NOS. 1 & 2

In 1872 Bizet wrote the incidental music for Alphonse Daudet's play *L'Arlésienne*, a tragedy set in the author's native Provence about a man who kills himself because of his unrequited love for a girl from Arles. Bizet's discreet and sensitive music did not guarantee the play's success and it closed after a few weeks. Rather than waste the music, Bizet took four of the pieces and turned them into a concert suite which proved extremely popular, and soon after his death, his friend Ernest Guiraud made a second suite, again of four pieces, which included a minuet based around a duet from Bizet's opera *La Jolie Fille de Perth*. Both are frequently performed and contain a wealth of sparkling and inventive music: particularly delightful is the Prélude from *Suite No. 1* in which a set of variations around a strident melody is followed by a plaintive solo for the (then new) saxophone.

⊙ Royal Philharmonic Orchestra; Beecham (EMI CDC 7 47794-2; with *L'Arlésienne Suites*).

Beecham gives an equally lively performance of the two *L'Arlésienne* suites. Again the aprroach is nimble and stylish, but he also communicates a strong sense of dramatic spontaneity.

LUIGI BOCCHERINI

(1743–1805)

Though Boccherini was a highly successful cellist and a prolific composer – especially of chamber music – he is largely known today for just one work, the Minuet from his *String Quintet in E*, a piece that gained a new lease of life when it was used on the soundtrack of the classic comedy film *The Ladykillers*. He was almost an exact contemporary of Haydn, and his music possesses a similar classical elegance and charm – indeed, the Minuet bears a marked resemblance to Haydn's equally popular Serenade. It is true that he rarely matches the depth or passion of the older composer, but to dismiss him, as the violinist Giuseppe Pupo did, as "Haydn's wife" is grossly unfair. His music might occasionally be insipid, but it's full of good tunes, always pleasant, and sometimes startlingly original.

Boccherini was born in Lucca, the son of a double-bass player and cellist, who gave him his first lessons. His early career was spent as a cello virtuoso, and he took part in the first ever public string quartet concerts in Milan in 1765 at the same time forming a friendship with one of the violinists, Filippo Manfredi. The two decided to tour together, travelling to Paris in 1767 and then onto Madrid a year later, where Boccherini gained the patronage of the Infante Don Luis, the king's younger brother. He was to remain in Madrid for the rest of his life, serving Don Luis until 1785 and then the Benavente-Osuna family until 1798, while at the same time providing music for Prince Frederick-William of Prussia.

His final years were full of misfortune. The Parisian music publisher Pleyel took advantage of Boccherini's good humour and generosity, refusing to return manuscripts and demanding changes in his style to match public taste. Two daughters died in 1802, and his wife and another daughter in 1805 – events that almost certainly contributed to his mental decline. He died in poverty, although ironically his music was to enjoy a real vogue almost immediately after his death.

CHAMBER MUSIC

"There is perhaps no instrumental music more ingenious, elegant and pleasing, than his quintets," wrote Charles Burney in 1770. Boccherini went on to write over a hundred of them plus nearly as many string quartets, so it is unsurprising that a lot of his chamber music is bland and repetitious. That said, several of his chamber pieces involve the interesting imitation of non-musical sounds, like birdsong, in his quintet *L'Ucelliera*, or – even more strikingly – street sounds in the quintet entitled *Night Music in the Streets of Madrid*. Unfortunately, these pieces are available only on CDs that are largely devoted to fairly uninteresting music; for a decent recording of the famous Minuet from the *String Quintet in E*, you're best advised to buy the Baroque compilation CD recommended on p.65.

You can, however, buy a fine CD of the delightful guitar quintets, which were arranged for the Marquis of Benavente, a talented amateur guitarist, and evoke the sunny, easy-going atmosphere of the early paintings of Goya. One remarkable aspect of these quintets is the variety of effects that Boccherini spins out of this combination of instruments. In some pieces the guitar is clearly the dominant voice; in others, like the boldly dramatic first movement of the first quintet, it is the violin that prevails. The most extraordinary single piece, though, is the last movement from the fourth quintet where, after a slow introduction, a full-blooded fandango lets rip, complete with strumming guitar, insistent rhythmic repetitions and even castanets.

◑ **The Guitar Quintets: Romero; Academy of St Martin in the Fields Chamber Ensemble** (Philips 438 769-2; 2 CDs).

This is a fine introduction to Boccherini's music. Delicacy and wit predominate, but Pepe Romero and the Academy chamber players are not afraid to let go where necessary – the performance of the *Fandango Quintet* is particularly thrilling.

THE CELLO CONCERTOS

Boccherini wrote at least eleven cello concertos, and all of them were written for himself to perform – thus they often make difficult technical demands on the soloist, with much of the solo writing not just richly ornamented but also placed consistently high in the register. As with most of his music, the prevailing mood of these works is of an easy gracefulness and poise. In the nineteenth century a cellist named Grützmacher took movements from two of the best concertos and arranged them into a single work, a romanticized hybrid that is still, after the Minuet, Boccherini's best-known work.

⊙ Three Cello Concertos; Aria Accademica: Coin, Almajano; Ensemble Baroque de Limoges (Astreé E8517).

The cello concertos on this disc include the two tampered with by Grützmacher, here performed in their original versions in B flat major and in G major. The highlight of the latter is a lugubrious but lyrical slow movement, which is shaped and controlled by Coin with a beguiling restraint. The third concerto, in D major, has some wonderfully ornate passage work in its slow movement, while the disc's fill-up is a brilliantly virtuosic concert aria for soprano in which the cello part dominates the orchestral writing.

ALEXANDER BORODIN

(1833–1887)

Like many of his Russian contemporaries, Borodin was essentially an amateur composer, in the sense that he had a flourishing career in a completely different field and composed in his spare time – which accounts for both his relatively small output and the high proportion of works that he never found time to finish. Yet Borodin made a distinctive contribution to the Russian musical nationalist cause in the 1870s and 1880s. In addition to his fertile melodic talent, he had a good ear for exotic orchestral sounds, and created some pungent harmonic writing that gives his music a real strength and originality.

GUUS ONG

He was the illegitimate son of a Georgian prince and by the tradition of such things was given the name of one of the prince's serfs. Despite displaying a childhood passion for music, he trained as a chemist and physician and it was as an academic chemist that he first made his name, engaging in important research as a professor at the Academy of Medico-Surgery in St Petersburg.

Although he had been attempting to compose since his teens, he began to exploit his compositional skills only when, as a young man, he came under the influence of Mily Balakirev (1837–1910), the figurehead of a group of radical musicians based in St Petersburg (the others were César Cui, Modest Mussorgsky and Nikolai Rimsky-Korsakov). He refused to contemplate cutting down on his scientific responsibilities, and the five years it took for him to complete his first work, his *Symphony No. 1*, set the pattern for his rate of composition. Characteristically, he worked on the opera *Prince Igor* for some eighteen years, from penning the first ideas in 1869 to his death in 1887, when it was still not complete. In the meantime, he did manage to finish one of his most popular works, his *Symphony No. 2* (after nearly seven years' work), though its successor, begun in 1885, also remained incomplete on his death and, like much of the opera, was made performable by Alexander Glazunov (see p.159).

PRINCE IGOR

Borodin's first and only complete opera, *The Bogatyrs* (1867), was an unsuccessful comic parody of grand opera and was followed by an equally futile bid to write a serious opera, *The Tsar's Bride*. But in *Prince Igor*, rambling though some of it may be, he created a worthy counterpart to Russian opera's greatest historical tragedy, Mussorgsky's *Boris Godunov* (see p.280). It is more an opera of tableaux than of forward-moving action, and gave Borodin the chance to demonstrate his flair for oriental imagery and orchestral colour, best demonstrated in the orchestral highlights that, despite the opera's rarity on stage, have always been popular in the concert hall and on record. The overture, reputedly written by Glazunov from memories of Borodin's piano improvisations, is a vivid foretaste of what's to come; the other famous excerpts – a *Polovtsian March*, the *Dance of the Polovtsian Maidens* and the choral *Polovtsian Dances* – all come from the scene set in the encampment of Igor's enemies.

⊙ Prince Igor: Kit, Gorchakova, Grigorian, Ognovenko, Minjelkiev; Kirov Theatre Chorus and Orchestra; Gergiev (Philips 442 537-2; 3 CDs).

Recorded in conjunction with a 1993 production at the Kirov, this is by far the best *Prince Igor* ever recorded. Gergiev gives a dynamic, sometimes ferocious reading of the score, animating even the weakest scenes. Mikhail Kit's ringing bass lacks definition, but he is a formidable presence as Igor. Galina Gorchakova's dramatic soprano has a glorious bloom and she brings both dignity and sweetness to Yaroslavna.

◑ Overture & Polovtsian Dances: Royal Liverpool Philharmonic Orchestra & Chorus; Mackerras (Virgin CUV 5 61135-2; with Mussorgsky, *Pictures at an Exhibition* & *Night on the Bare Mountain*).

The orchestral excerpts can be found on any number of Russian orchestral collections, but this account of the *Overture* and *Polovtsian Dances* from Charles Mackerras and the RLPO is as good as any.

SYMPHONIES AND ORCHESTRAL WORKS

Although Borodin in effect wrote only two and a half symphonies, they represent a significant contribution to the history of the form in Russia. Like Tchaikovsky's earlier symphonies, Borodin's employ typically Russian harmonies, melodies and rhythms against a fairly conventional Germanic formal background. *Symphony No. 1*, in particular, looks back to Schumann, one of Borodin's prime influences at the time, yet is a distinctly Russian work, particularly in the use of a folk song in the Scherzo and the oriental lyricism of the slow movement. *Symphony No. 2* – the best of them – represents his first fully mature work and demonstrates all his most characterful features: rhythmic drive, grandeur, nostalgia and exuberance. Much of it was derived from sketches for *Prince Igor*, and it inhabits the same world of epic romance. From reminiscences by his colleagues Borodin clearly had the whole of his *Symphony No. 3* in his head, but only completed the spellbinding second movement and sketched the first.

Of Borodin's other orchestral works only one is a self-contained original work for orchestra. *In the Steppes of Central Asia* is a marvellously rich tone poem depicting an oriental caravan (evocatively suggested by a cor anglais melody) crossing the central Asian plains with an escort of Russian soldiers.

⊙ Symphonies Nos. 1 and 2; In the Steppes of Central Asia: Royal Philharmonic Orchestra; Ashkenazy (Decca 436 651-2).

This is one of Ashkenazy's very best discs as a conductor. He's very much alive to the slow unfolding drama of both symphonies and gives a brilliantly colourful account of *In the Steppes*. He's undoubtedly helped by the Decca engineers, who produce an especially full and atmospheric sound.

⊙ Symphonies Nos. 1–3: CSR Symphony Orchestra Bratislava; Gunzenhauser (Naxos 8.550238).

The budget-price CD from Stephen Gunzenhauser and the authentically Slav-sounding Czechoslovak Radio Symphony Orchestra of Bratislava is among the most successful in the Naxos catalogue, with brilliant performances and a vivid recording quality that's better than several bigger-name companies.

THE STRING QUARTETS

Borodin's mature chamber music comprises two delightful string quartets. The second (1881) is by far the more popular, largely because of its slow movement, a ravishing, orientally flavoured Nocturne that has gained a separate life of its own in versions for string orchestra as well as in its original scoring. Its other three movements are no less striking, particularly the amiable Scherzo.

⊙ Borodin Quartet (EMI Melodiya CDC 7 47795 2).

The suitably named Borodin Quartet has recorded the second quartet several times, but the most successful is on this 1980 disc of both quartets, recorded in Russia and issued by EMI. This is a delightful, engaging performance, with a warm sound quality.

⊙ St Petersburg Quartet (Sony SMK64907).

Some of the EMI material originating on Melodiya has a habit of disappearing from the catalogue. This 1993 performance, though lacking that final ounce of finesse and style, has a great deal of charm and makes a worthy alternative to the Borodins' classic recording.

LILI BOULANGER

(1893–1918)

Lili Boulanger has been eclipsed by the reputation of her younger sister Nadia, one of the most influential teachers and musicologists of her time. Yet in her tragically short life she produced music that can stand comparison with virtually anything written at that time in France, and had she lived longer it's almost certain that she would have become one of the century's greats. Despite the advocacy of her sister and a phalanx of other musicians, she remains shamefully neglected.

The sisters came from a long line of musicians and were educated by their aristocratic Russian mother, establishing a cultural connection that was strengthened by the Parisian vogue for all things Russian following the first season of Diaghilev's Ballet Russes in 1909. In fact her music shows a greater debt to Debussy and her teacher and mentor Fauré than it does to Rimsky-Korsakov or Stravinsky. In 1913 Boulanger became the first woman ever to win the coveted Prix de Rome, which was awarded for her dramatic cantata *Faust et Hélène* (her father had also won the prize in 1835). This was one of her most substantial works, along with the unfinished opera *La Princesse Maleine* which, like Debussy's *Pelleas et Mélisande*, was based on a play by Maeterlinck.

Boulanger was an invalid for most of her life, seriously weakened by bronchial pneumonia at the age of 2 and eventually dying of cancer at the age of 24. Yet by all accounts she was also remarkably self-assured and determined, attributes that are mirrored in her music. In view of her illness, and the social context of a country mired in the hell of World War I, it's scarcely surprising that much of her small, largely vocal, output is often tinged with desolation.

CHORAL MUSIC

Boulanger was a Catholic and poured a deeply religious intensity into much of her choral music, even when she was not setting a sacred text. The finest of her several psalm settings is *Du fond de l'abîme*, a setting of the De Profundis for alto and tenor soloists, chorus and orchestra, composed between 1910 and 1917. This is a deeply felt and highly personal creation of great solemnity, thickly written but subtle in its handling of the combination of large forces and solo voice. Its outstanding quality only accentuates the tragedy of her premature death.

◑ **Du fond de l'abîme and other works: Dominguez, Amade, Menuhin, Curzon; Concerts Lamoureux; Markevitch** (EMI CDM 7 64281-2).

This classic disc still serves as the most complete introduction to Boulanger's music. As well as an intensely moving version of *Du fond de l'abîme*, it contains the lovely *Pie Jesu* (written on her deathbed) and some violin and piano pieces excellently played by Yehudi Menuhin and Clifford Curzon. The only drawback is the rather dated sound.

SONGS

Boulanger always loved the music of Fauré and many of her songs reveal his influence, particularly in the way the soloist and pianist are equal partners. Her outstanding work in this genre is *Clairières dans le ciel* (Clearings in the Heavens), a cycle for male singer of thirteen songs to poems by the symbolist Francis Jammes. Written during her residency in Rome in 1914, her music perfectly captures the bittersweet mood of the poems in which memories of a lost love are prompted by chance association with nature or everyday impressions. Word-painting and some exquisitely delicate piano writing make this an exceptionally effective and poignant cycle.

○ **Clairières dans le ciel: Hill, Ball; New London Chamber Choir; Wood** (Hyperion CDA 66726; with other songs and choral works).

Tenor Martyn Hill and pianist Andrew Ball give a highly sensitive and nuanced performance of the songs, while the New London Chamber Choir present five earlier choral works. The disc gives an excellent insight into the less despairng side of Boulanger's music.

PIERRE BOULEZ

(1925–)

The figure of Pierre Boulez has dominated the avant-garde of Western music since 1950. One of the century's finest composers, Boulez has also been one of its great conductors and most outspoken ideologists, whose ideas and polemics have alternately captivated and infuriated successive generations of musicians. Born in Montbrison in southeastern France, Boulez studied composition with Messiaen in Paris before bursting into spectacular compositional life in the late 1940s with works such as the first two piano sonatas and the cantatas *Le Visage Nuptial* and *Le Soleil des Eaux*. Marrying the rhythmic complexities of Stravinsky and Messiaen with the atonal vocabulary of Schoenberg and, particularly, Webern, Boulez achieved a distinctive new synthesis to which he added something completely his own – a sense of unbridled violence, as typified by the second piano sonata.

POLYGRAM

Pierre Boulez

Thus established as the *enfant terrible* of French music, Boulez embarked on a period of research into ways of writing music that would eradicate all traces of tradition, an enterprise he shared with other young turks such as Stockhausen and Nono – the so-called "Darmstadt School", named after the German town which hosted a summer school devoted to their ideals. It was Messiaen's uncharacteristically austere *Mode de valeurs et d'intensités* which showed them how, by systematically ordering pitch, rhythm and dynamics in strict numerical sequences, one could write "automatic" and almost completely impersonal music. And it was Boulez who produced – in *Structures I* for two pianos – the classic work of what has come to be known as total serialism.

Boulez, the figurehead of the hyper-modernist cause, promulgated the doctrine loudly not only in his own music but also in his denunciations of Schoenberg and Stravinsky, in both of whose later works he had come to see signs of a fatal compromise with tradition. However, it's impossible to ignore the suspicion that Boulez was always preaching what he would rather not practise. Ever since *Structures*, his music has been characterized by the way in which his natural gifts, which link him to Debussy rather than Webern, have increasingly succeeded in transcending his self-imposed ideological limits. Indeed his next major work, *Le Marteau sans maître*, already suggests the conflict between the hermetic demands of total serialism and a love of colour that's typical of French music.

Yet as the 1950s and 1960s progressed, Boulez's effortless creative confidence seemed to evaporate, though there was no slackening in his protean intellectual speculations. He flirted with electronics in *Poésie pour pouvoir*, with open-ended form in *Figures, Doubles, Prismes*, and with indeterminacy in the *Piano Sonata No. 3* – all backed up by elaborate theorizing but subsequently withdrawn, revised or left unfinished. The one project which seemed to sustain him during this stage of his life was the monumental vocal cycle, *Pli Selon Pli*.

It was at this time that Boulez emerged as a conductor of international standing and, although he has always denied it, one can hardly escape the conclusion that conducting has been at least partly a means of avoiding his creative impasse. By 1970 he was holding prestigious but onerous positions as chief conductor to both the BBC Symphony

Orchestra and the New York Philharmonic, and his composing had virtually dried up – the monumental orchestral work *Rituel* was the only finished work to emerge during the entire 1970s. History seemed to have marginalized the modernist cause and to have robbed Boulez of the revolutionary fervour which had fuelled his earlier achievements.

Then, in 1977, came the greatest public challenge of his career, when he secured a colossal government grant for the establishment of the Institut de Recherche et Co-ordination Acoustique/Musique (IRCAM), a futuristic musical laboratory buried under the Pompidou Centre in the heart of Paris. Overseen by Boulez, IRCAM would provide a hi-tech venue in which leading composers and scientists would work together to investigate the possibilities of technology in music, educating musicians and public in a setup complete with its own resident ensemble, the matchless Ensemble InterContemporain. In the history of music only Wagner previously had been able to command patronage on this scale, and expectations were high, the greatest one being of course that Boulez himself would use the resources of IRCAM to produce the masterpiece which seemed to be demanded by investment on such a massive scale. Boulez's response, *Répons* – premiered in 1981 and constantly revised since – seemed set to meet the demands of producing a huge public statement using the latest computerized gadgetry, but like so many of Boulez's works it remains under a cloud, unfinished and unrecorded. Since the massive undertaking of *Répons*, Boulez seems once more to have lost the ability to tackle fresh major projects. The works which have appeared include exquisite miniatures such as *Dérive* and *Memoriale* and further revisions and recompositions of earlier works, notably a sumptuous new version of *Le Visage Nuptial*.

Assessing Boulez's achievement is complicated not only by his status as the firebrand of modernism and by his manifold musical activities, but also by the chaotic state of his output. Some pieces have been temporarily or permanently withdrawn by him; others have been left unfinished (and perhaps unfinishable), or reissued in versions entirely different from the form in which they first appeared, or are still "in progress" half a century after they were begun. The most talented of all postwar composers has, it seems, been silenced by the contradiction between Boulez the uncompromising evangelist of hardline modernism, and Boulez the musician, whose extraordinary gifts – untrammelled by doctrine – could have produced work as seductive and evocative as anything in twentieth-century music.

⊙ Pli Selon Pli; Le Visage Nuptial; Le Soleil des Eaux; Figures, Doubles, Prismes; Rituel; Messagesquisse; Notations; Sonatine; Piano Sonata No. 1; Dérive; Mémoriale; Dialogue de l'Ombre Double; Cummings ist der Dichter: BBC Symphony Orchestra, Orchestre de Paris, Ensemble Intercontemporain; Boulez, Barenboim (Erato 4509-98495-2; 4 CDs).

This 4-CD set brings together some classic recent recordings by Boulez from 1981–90, all of them digital, but only one CD of which, *Pli Selon Pli*, is now available separately. Boulez is the leading interpreter of his own music, and his famous attention to detail leads to recordings of unrivalled clarity, In addition, Daniel Barenboim conducts the Orchestre de Paris in a memorable performance of *Rituel*. The recording quality is uniformly excellent.

LE MARTEAU SANS MAITRE

For *Le Marteau sans maître* (The Unmastered Hammer; 1953–55), perhaps his most extraordinary achievement, Boulez took as his starting point the surreal poetry of René Char, whose texts are set in four of the nine interlocked movements. These vocal movements are not song-like in any orthodox sense, and the orchestration of the work is equally novel: it's written for contralto voice, alto flute, viola, guitar, vibraphone, xylorimba – a kind of xylophone – and unpitched percussion. This ensemble opened up new possibilities for Western music at the time, and pioneered the "music of the whole world", which Stockhausen took as an ideal (though Boulez's attitude to non-Western music has been more condescending and not always well-informed). The insistent drumbeats and incantatory flute-lines owe as much to Africa as to Europe.

⊙ Le Marteau sans maître; Lontano; de la Martinez; Ponthus (LoreIt LNT 108; with *Piano Sonata No. 1*).

The fluid, darting quality of *Le Marteau* has been compared by Boulez to fish in an aquarium, and Odaline de la Martinez's dynamic interpretation well captures this iridescent and kaleidoscopic music.

PLI SELON PLI

Boulez's most monumental work, *Pli Selon Pli* (Fold by Fold) is a setting of sonnets by Mallarmé in five movements. Written in 1957–62, with the inevitable later revisions, it exudes a quality of hypnotic stasis, its fantastically sculpted vocal lines contrasting with brittle percussion sonorities. The first and last movements feature a large ensemble with voice only briefly present, while the three vocal "improvisations" include a central movement that's a song for soprano with nine-piece percussion ensemble. Boulez's work is sometimes hard to penetrate, but the dazzling orchestral colours on display here have an immediate appeal.

⊙Bryn-Julson; BBC Symphony Orchestra; Boulez (Erato 2292-45376-2).

A 1969 recording by the composer with the same orchestra has been reissued at mid-price on Sony, but digital transfer reveals some shortcomings in the analogue recording. The outstanding later performance is more expansive, and features Phyllis Bryn-Julson, the composer's favoured soprano.

RITUEL

Rituel, Boulez's memorial to his friend and colleague, Italian avant-gardist Bruno Maderna, is his major work from the 1970s, and perhaps the most accessible, despite its austerity and sombreness. Repetitive, obsessive, inexorable, almost machine-like, *Rituel* is scored for a large array of exotic percussion, elements of which maintain a beat, though they are often interrupted or in conflict with each other. In contrast to many of his works, *Rituel* was completed and left unaltered.

⊙BBC Symphony Orchestra; Ensemble Intercontemporain; Boulez (Sony SK 45839; with *Éclat/Multiples*).

The composer's recording from 1976 remains first choice, even though digital remastering exposes a certain amount of analogue "hiss". It has the expected clarity and, despite a more measured tempo than Barenboim on Erato, it is more incisive. Also featured is the chamber-work *Éclat/ Multiples*, premiered in 1970 and still "unfinished". *Éclat* is a brief but dazzling exploration of scintillating percussion sounds, later developed with added instrumentation into *Multiples*.

PIANO MUSIC

The piano sonatas stand either side of the brief foray into "total serialism" represented by *Structures I* for two pianos: the two-movement *Sonata No. 1* was written by the 21-year-old composer in 1946, and the more ambitious *Sonata No. 2* followed two years later. The furious keyboard assault represented by the first movement of the *Sonata No. 2* was described by Boulez as "percussion piano", but it is followed by a slow movement that has a gentleness unusual in his music. The notion of "mobile form" was pioneered by Boulez and Stockhausen at the same time, the latter in *Piano Piece XI* (1956), the former in his *Piano Sonata No. 3* (1955–57). This is one of the many Boulez works that remains "unfinished", and its use of indeterminacy means it "will never have a definite face". The performer's freedom is fairly limited, but the pianist selects the order of movements and some internal arrangements, as well as tempo and dynamics.

⊙Piano Sonatas Nos. 1–3: Henck (Wergo 60121-50).

Recording quality on Herbert Henck's 1980s Wergo recording is less good than on the rival set from Naxos, but the performance is even more impressive, with greater delicacy and a wider dynamic range. The *Sonata No. 2* is taken at a more measured pace, most notably the slow movement.

◑ Piano Sonata No. 2: Pollini (Deutsche Grammophon DG 447 431; with pieces by Stravinsky, Prokofiev & Webern).

Maurizio Pollini's taut and vehement recording of the formidable second sonata is the best performance of a Boulez keyboard composition yet recorded, and the rest of this set is of equal quality.

⊙Structures I & II for two pianos: Kontarsky; Kontarsky (Wergo 6011-2).

Alfons and Aloys Kontarsky are two of the leading pianists of the postwar avant-garde, and their remarkable recording is the only one currently available of *Structures I*. *Structures II* (1956–61) marks a reaction to the "automatic music" of its precursor, offering limited performer-freedom. Once you get over the complete lack of melody in these works, this can be curiously relaxing music.

JOHANNES BRAHMS

(1833–1897)

In the face of Liszt, Wagner and the "New German School" of music, it was Brahms who upheld the long-established ideals of the German tradition. He was not, however, the reactionary figure he's sometimes portrayed as being. No less a revolutionary than Arnold Schoenberg praised Brahms's combination of "economy and riches", and his best music (of which there's a great deal) generates a remarkable power from the tension between its seething emotions and the propriety of its classical structures.

As in the case with so many composers, Brahms's life lacked much in the way of incident.

LEBRECHT COLLECTION

Johannes Brahms

His childhood in Hamburg was devoted to study and it was not until he was 15 that he began to play in public. In order to make himself some money, he often played in brothels, a fact which various biographers have linked to Brahms's precarious later relationships with women. Whatever the cause of his notorious reticence and boorishness, Brahms always felt uncomfortable with women, but was able to see the positive side to his awkwardness – it saved him, he said, from "both opera and marriage".

One of the greatest influences on his life and music was the great violinist Joseph Joachim, whom he met in Hanover in 1853 while touring with another Hungarian violinist, the self-styled "gypsy" musician Eduard Reményi. Upon hearing the young Brahms perform some of his own work, Joachim gave him written introductions to Liszt and Schumann; when Schumann in turn heard Brahms play, he hailed the young man as a genius – not the first time he'd become overexcited by a new young artist, but on this occasion he was right. The ensuing friendship with Schumann and with Schumann's wife, the pianist Clara Wieck, did much to nurture Brahms's talent, but it was not until after Schumann's death, in 1856, that Brahms began to devote much time to composing.

In 1860 he put his name to a declaration – also signed by Joachim – that dissociated the signatories from the new trends championed by Liszt and his circle. This professed conservatism meant that success remained elusive for years, and it was not until 1869, when his *Deutsches Requiem* was first performed, that he was recognized as a major creative force. In 1872, having moved to Vienna, he succeeded Rubinstein as artistic director of the Gesellschaft der Musikfreunde, a post he held onto for only three years. From 1875 until his death, his time was dominated by composition, and by occasional engagements as a conductor or pianist.

The symphonies, all but one of the concertos and most of the chamber music for which he is now remembered were composed during this extraordinarily fertile quarter-century, years which saw Brahms drift ever further away from public life. He was happiest on his own. In 1885 Clara Schumann, his friend and rumoured lover, said of him: "To me he is as much a riddle – I might almost say as much a stranger – as he was twenty-five years ago." There is, however, little sense of distance in his work, which is some of the most profound, elegiac and unsentimental music of his century.

THE SYMPHONIES

Brahms's four symphonies are unique in that they are all products of the composer's maturity. The fear of comparison with Beethoven inhibited him so much that he struggled for decades with the idea of writing his first symphony, which finally saw the light only in 1876. Within a decade he'd completed his second, third and fourth, a sequence of greatly different compositions that encompass a vast range of styles, forms and emotional states. In the opinion of many, it's the most important body of symphonic music after Beethoven's. Hans von Bülow, conductor of the premiere of *Symphony No. 4*, declared that his favourite key was E flat, for its three flat notes (signified by the letter b in German) symbolized for him the trinity of Bach, Beethoven and Brahms.

◑ **Complete symphonies: Berlin Philharmonic Orchestra; Karajan** (Deutsche Grammophon 429 644-2; 3 CDs).

Karajan's 1978 DG cycle offers loving performances and fine recorded sound at mid-price. This is very much a traditionalist's view of Brahms: grandiose, at times a little pompous, but the richnesss of the string tone and Karajan's unerring sense of line and shape make for a very satisfying experience.

⊙ Complete symphonies: Scottish Chamber Orchestra; Mackerras (Telarc CD80450; 3 CDs).

In stark contrast to the seamless suavity of Karajan comes this fine set from Charles Mackerras. Using forces much closer in number to the orchestras that premiered these works means that textures are wonderfully clear, and the heavy-footed quality often associated with these symphonies has completely disappeared. An absolute revelation.

⊙ Complete symphonies: Vienna Philharmonic Orchestra; Berlin Philharmonic Orchestra; Furtwängler (EMI CHS5 65513-2; 3 CDs).

If it's drama and power that you're looking for, then Furtwängler provides it in large quantities. Recorded live in the late 1940s and early 1950s, these performances (all but the first with the Berlin Philharmonic) seethe with a brooding energy and an overriding sense of tragedy.

⊙ Complete symphonies: Royal Liverpool Philharmonic Orchestra; Janowski (ASV CDQS6 101–104; with overtures; 4 CDs).

If you want to get to know the symphonies for minimum outlay, the ASV budget-price set (not available as a box) has a lot to commend it – Janowski is an honest and clear-sighted conductor whose performances are full of enthusiasm.

SYMPHONY NO. 1

Although the first symphony was only received politely at its premiere in Karlsruhe, by the time it reached Vienna it was being nicknamed "Beethoven's Tenth", affirming Brahms's arrival in the ranks of the symphonic masters. The first movement does indeed owe something to Beethoven but it is in the last movement's second principal theme, announced in unison by the violins after the dark and ominous introduction, that the influence is clearest, in its allusion to the main theme from the last movement of Beethoven's ninth. The joyful thrill of this movement is unmatched by any of the other symphonies, as Brahms's relief at having finally managed to embark upon his first symphony finds outlet in a finale of awesome scale.

◑ Berlin Philharmonic Orchestra; Karajan (Deutsche Grammophon 447 408-2; with Schumann's *Symphony No. 1*).

Karajan recorded this music several times, but it's in this 1963 version that his pulse is strongest and most stable. The great moments are lithe, muscular and unswerving but there's also a greater degree of poetry than you find in most accounts.

◑ Philharmonia; Klemperer (EMI CDM 7 69651-2; with overtures).

Klemperer's reading of the first symphony is extraordinarily stately, but it's also majestic, with grandeur and warmth going hand in hand.

SYMPHONY NO. 2

When Brahms set about writing his second symphony he had the confidence to relax, and this work is a much more amiable piece than its predecessor. It repeated the success of the first in Vienna, and duly attracted more comparisons to Beethoven, acquiring the nickname "The Pastoral" in reference to Beethoven's sixth. The *Symphony No. 2* marked a crucial point in Brahms's career – on the back of its reception both his first and second symphonies were published, and he embarked on a series of triumphant European concert tours.

◑ Philharmonia; Klemperer (EMI CDM 7 69650-2; with *Alto Rhapsody*).

Lustrous playing, and from Klemperer a beguiling yet epic vision. An overwhelming sense of pastoral ease is summoned here, and everything works perfectly. Klemperer maintains a flow and a charged, noble grandeur which keeps its sense of yearning where lesser performances falter.

◑ Columbia Symphony Orchestra; Walter (Sony SMK 64 471; with *Symphony No. 3*).

Bruno Walter's interpretation of the second symphony had lost the edge of its youthful spontaneity when he came to make this 1960 recording, and compared to Klemperer there is a certain lack of essential simplicity. What you do get is a surmounting sense of joy, and this eager performance is beautifully sprung.

SYMPHONY NO. 3

The Viennese public had to wait another six years for the third symphony, and when it finally arrived it was received with even more enthusiasm than the first two. Eduard Hanslick, the vociferous anti-Wagner and pro-Brahms music critic, declared that it united the titanism of the first symphony with the untroubled charm of the second. It's certainly a magnificent achievement (some would say Brahms's greatest symphony), but it's not the most ingratiating composition. The third symphony is a tightly wrought piece and its drama is generally low-key – there are no fireworks here, but rather a mood of subdued confession. With this symphony it's essential to give the music time to work on you.

◑ Columbia Symphony Orchestra; Walter (Sony SMK 64 471; with *Symphony No. 2*).

The tragic music is not supposed to take flight, yet it does here – gloriously so. Walter's use of pivotal phrases to change the pace and emotional temperature allows him to suggest immense breadth of imagination and an autumnal resignation. With a spaciousness yet also, when necessary, an urgency Walter makes this music – above all else – seem to dance.

◑ **Philharmonia Orchestra; Klemperer** (EMI CDM7 69649-2; with *Symphony No. 4*).

This time it's Klemperer who takes second fiddle – only just – for he does not quite evoke Walter's depth of introspection or his sheer range. This is nonetheless a performance of wise humanity and granitic strength, which on Klemperer's own terms is superlatively judged.

SYMPHONY NO. 4

With the *Symphony No. 4* Brahms reached the culmination of his symphonic style – the outer movements are virtually symphonies in themselves, containing ideas that are almost too grand to be fully worked through. The vast opening movement is packed with huge and intoxicating melodic ideas, while the momentous finale, a passacaglia built upon a simple harmonic idea, has the same air of finality as the conclusion of Beethoven's ninth.

◑ **Vienna Philharmonic Orchestra; Kleiber** (Deutsche Grammophon 457 706-2).

Brahms's gravest symphony elicits from Kleiber one of the most memorable recordings of the digital era. It's a fair bet that Kleiber heard Furtwängler conduct this symphony, for this is a performance characterized by the same command of orchestral colour and electrifying dynamism. There is no serious competition.

THE CONCERTOS

Brahms wrote four concertos – two for piano, one for violin and one for violin and cello (the so-called *Double Concerto*) – and all except the last have become regular fixtures in the concert halls. Though each is quite distinct in character, they are united by Brahms's conception of the concerto as a symphonic form, in which the soloist becomes at times subservient to the independent-minded orchestra. Thus in the *Violin Concerto* the second movement is introduced by a theme that the soloist never gets to play, while in the *Piano Concerto No. 2* the third movement is dominated not by the pianist but by the principal cellist, whose long and beautiful theme is taken up by the rest of the orchestra. As in Beethoven's concertos, there are moments of antagonistic drama as the soloist and orchestra contend supremacy, but in Brahms the sense of unity prevails.

◑ **Complete Concertos: Kremer, Maisky, Zimerman; Vienna Philharmonic; Bernstein** (Deutsche Grammophon 431 207-2; 3 CDs).

This set is the only available overview of all four concertos in one boxed set. Naturally, it has its weaknesses – not least Bernstein's emotional hand-wringing – but his soloists are all in fine form. Good sound and orchestral playing all round, and good value.

THE PIANO CONCERTOS

Brahms began his first piano concerto at the age of 21, shortly after Robert Schumann's attempted suicide, as a tribute to Robert and to Clara, who had given the first performance of Schumann's piano concerto. Eventually the work was premiered by Brahms in 1859, three years after Schumann's death, and it was a disaster. Soon, however, with Clara's help, the work's quality was recognized and, even now, it remains the more popular of the piano concertos. Though it begins with an orchestral introduction that keeps the soloist out of the picture for some four minutes, it's a more flamboyant and virtuosic piece than the second concerto, building to a wonderful finale with a momentous and percussive principal theme that dominates from beginning to end.

The second concerto – one of the longest ever written – was composed some twenty years later, while Brahms was basking in the acclaim for his third symphony. Like that work, it shows the mellower aspects of the composer, particularly in the slow movement, with its innovative use of a second solo instrument (the cello) to carry the main theme. It's by no means a placid piece of music, however – the tussle between piano and orchestra in the second movement is one of the most exhilarating episodes in the entire concerto repertoire.

◑ **Piano Concertos Nos. 1 & 2: Gilels; Berlin Philharmonic Orchestra; Jochum** (Deutsche Grammophon 447 446-2; 2 CDs; with *Op. 116*).

Gilels' deeply humane performances are now coupled together with marvellously refreshed sound, and the combination will be hard to beat. This is playing which penetrates the music and possesses it from within: tender, fervent, striking for its refined judgement, and glowing with a majestic poise. The concertos are also available singly, at mid-price, in DG's Galleria series.

◐ Piano Concertos Nos. 1 & 2: Kovacevich; London Philharmonic Orchestra; Sawallisch (EMI CDC7 54578-2 [with *Lieder Op. 91*] & EMI CDC5 55218-2 [with *Lieder Op. 105*]).

Stephen Kovacevich's recent performances of the piano concertos with Sawallisch are passionate and declamatory, with an acute sense of architecture and real strength of purpose. Sawallisch allows his orchestra more freedom than most conductors – their last movement of the first concerto is just about the most exciting on record.

THE VIOLIN CONCERTO

For years Brahms promised to write a concerto for Joseph Joachim, but as with so many of his major projects he kept putting it off. Finally, spurred by the success of the second symphony, he set to work on the piece, taking guidance from Joachim as to what was possible for the instrument. Although it was originally conceived in four movements, Brahms was persuaded to drop one of the central movements to keep the concerto down to a more conventional length – the excised portion later reappeared as part of the second piano concerto. Essentially lyrical, the final version shares much of the second symphony's mood – the key of D major is common to both works, as it is to the Beethoven concerto which Brahms so admired. By the time of its premiere, on New Year's Day 1879, Brahms had become somewhat eccentric in his mode of dress, and the staid Leipzig audience watched in horror as the composer-conductor's trousers, tied up with an old necktie, began to slip. Fortunately the trousers remained on, but the verdict on the concerto was lukewarm. Its breakthrough came shortly afterwards, when Joachim introduced the work to England, and since then it's been one of the most popular concertos in the violin repertory.

◑ Heifetz; Chicago Symphony Orchestra; Reiner (RCA 9026 61742-2; with Beethoven, *Violin Concerto*).

From the most virtuosic of violinists, a supremely effortless and indeed – before its exhilarating finale – an almost undemonstrative performance. Heifetz's attack is crisp and vigorous, and yet he knew better than almost anybody how to make this music sing. There is the artlessness that conceals art in the darting invention and luscious cantabile of his fastidiously spun lines, and a touching candour in every bar.

◑ Little; Royal Liverpool Philharmonic Orchestra; Handley (EMI CD-EMX 2203; with Sibelius, *Violin Concerto*).

Little's outstanding debut CD is altogether warmer, faster and brighter than the Heifetz. It is elevated by a rare quality of rapport between soloist and conductor, so that the spontaneity of its insights is never in question. This is effortless playing, poised and sumptuous in tone if a little lacking in breadth. Alone amongst these recommendations, Little's first movement features Joachim's famous cadenza.

◑ Neveu; Philharmonia; Dobrowen (EMI CDH 7 61011-2; with Sibelius, *Violin Concerto*).

Ginette Neveu, who died in a plane crash in 1949 at the age of only 30, left what is perhaps the finest recorded version of this concerto. This is a marvellously poetic and dramatic performance, and it has been well transferred from original 78s – though inevitably the sound lacks the subtleties of modern engineering.

THE DOUBLE CONCERTO

The *Double Concerto*, like the *Violin Concerto*, owes its creation to Joachim, whom Brahms had alienated by supporting Joachim's wife during their unpleasant divorce. He conceived this concerto as a gesture of reconciliation, but it has to be said that another violin concerto might have been a more appropriate gift – in some ways, it is almost as if Brahms were baiting the violinist, as he gives nothing of great importance to the solo violin. Written after the symphonies and piano concertos, it's a particularly angular and aggressive piece, and in places is too thickly orchestrated. Yet, while this might not be his greatest work, it does feature some wonderful interplay between cello and violin.

◑ Oistrakh, Rostropovich; Cleveland Orchestra; Szell (EMI CDM 7 64744-2; with Beethoven, *Triple Concerto*).

There is no better case to be made for the concerto than this CD – Rostropovich and Oistrakh knew each other's style so well that they move through the music with a single mind. Their pugnacity might take some getting used to, but the bluster is mixed with lyricism of great beauty. It's coupled with a 1969 recording of the rather superior Beethoven *Triple Concerto*.

CHORAL WORKS

Brahms wrote many unaccompanied choral pieces for women's choral societies as well as a huge output of songs for solo voice, duet and other combinations. Much of this output was for amateur musicians and is of mixed quality, so very little of it is now recorded or performed except by amateur groups. Two works stand out from the rest: the *Deutsches Requiem* – his greatest vocal work and his first orchestral score to receive widespread praise – and the *Alto Rhapsody*, one of his most moving creations.

EIN DEUTSCHES REQUIEM

The idea of writing a Requiem Mass first came to Brahms after the death of Schumann in 1856, but for various reasons – not least of them his lack of true faith – the intention lapsed until 1865, when the death of his mother plunged him into inconsolable grief. Four years later he completed his tribute to her, *Ein deutsches Requiem* (A German Requiem), a Mass quite unlike any previous Requiem. Spurning the conventional Latin texts, Brahms set sections of Luther's translation of the Bible in a composition that was primarily intended to reconcile the living to their loss, and dwelt more on the hope of the Resurrection than on the fear of Judgment Day. It first appeared without its central and most beautiful section, the soprano solo which makes up the fifth movement.

⊙ Schwarzkopf, Fischer-Dieskau; Philharmonia; Klemperer (EMI CDC 7 47238-2).

Klemperer's famous 1961 recording is a highly reverential account with excellent solos from Fischer-Dieskau and Schwarzkopf and fine choral singing. For some tastes it's an approach that is too slow and clotted, but for many it's an awe-inspiring experience.

⊙ Margiono, Gilfry; Orchestre Révolutionaire et Romantique; Gardiner (Philips 432 140-2).

John Eliot Gardiner's more recent recording is at the other end of the spectrum. He uses period instruments and produces amazingly clear sound and textures; the soloists hardly match up to Klemperer's pair, but this is a thrilling and revealing performance.

THE ALTO RHAPSODY

The *Rhapsody for Alto, Chorus and Orchestra* – to give the *Alto Rhapsody* its full name – was written in a fit of despair. Brahms's feelings for Clara Schumann had subsided after her husband's death and he had transferred his affection to her daughter Julie – one of many such futile infatuations. Julie, oblivious to Brahms's motives, saw him merely as a benevolent uncle figure, and in 1869 she got married. As a wedding gift Brahms presented her with the *Rhapsody*, a setting of Goethe's poem *A Winter Journey in the Harz Mountains* – a thunderous example of Brahms's gift for self-pity, as Clara noticed even if her daughter did not. The mood of the piece is decidedly unmatrimonial, but the despairing bleakness of its opening is soon left behind – the point at which the chorus finally joins the soloist is one of the most heart-warming moments in all Brahms's output.

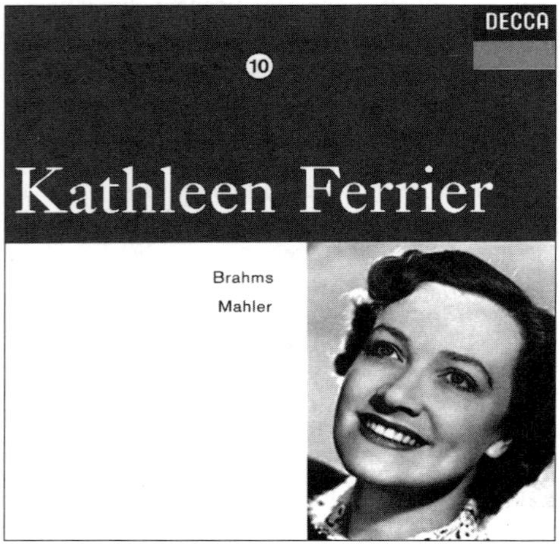

◑ Ludwig; Philharmonia; Klemperer (EMI CDM 7 69650-2; with *Symphony No. 2*).

The Klemperer–Ludwig performance is essential to any Brahms collection: Christa Ludwig, one of the century's greatest German altos, gets marvellously restrained orchestral accompaniment from the Philharmonia at its peak.

◑ Ferrier; London Philharmonic Orchestra; Krauss (Decca 433 477-2; with Lieder by Brahms and Mahler).

This historic recording, part of Decca's superb Kathleen Ferrier edition, is the only one in the same class as the Ludwig performance. Ferrier's plangent contralto transmits a profound sense of desolation and then blossoming joy.

CHAMBER MUSIC

Brahms was happiest at the piano, and was somewhat reluctant to explore the unknown territory of chamber music. His first ventures into the genre were undertaken partly to perfect his technique and partly as preparation for orchestral composition – they have not survived, as Brahms had a habit of destroying music of which he did not approve. It's remarkable then that his mature chamber music is among the greatest of the nineteenth century. Only Beethoven wrote so successfully for so many different ensembles: Brahms's output includes sonatas for violin, viola, cello and clarinet; trios for clarinet, horn and piano; sextets; string quartets; quartets for piano; string quintets; a piano quintet and – perhaps his masterpiece in this field – a quintet for clarinet and strings. There are no duds among this group, but the pieces we've singled out will take you to the heart of things.

THE CLARINET QUINTET

The astonishing *Quintet for Clarinet and Strings* is the finest of four clarinet pieces written for Richard Mühlfeld, a dazzling instrumentalist who also inspired Mendelssohn. Composed in the calming atmosphere of the alpine resort of Bad Ischl in 1891, the quintet seems to show that its morose and difficult creator had found peace in his final years – only Mozart's clarinet quintet can strike quite as deeply as this resonant masterpiece.

The unprecedented range of expression and unrivalled understanding of the solo instrument's capabilities give this piece a sense of completeness that few of Brahms's other chamber works can boast.

O Busch Quartet; Kell (Testament SBT 1001; with *Horn Trio*).

The playing of the Busch Quartet and Reginald Kell is the closest thing you'll hear to the sort of playing that Brahms would have heard. Giving the music's weighted counterpoint a rare freedom and sense of direction, this is one of the most moving Brahms recordings ever made.

O Gabrieli Quartet; King (Hyperion CDA 66107; with *Clarinet Trio*).

A modern alternative is Thea King's recording with the Gabrieli Quartet – it can't match the glowing humanity of the Busch and Kell version, but a strong point in its favour is that it's coupled with a fine performance of the genial clarinet trio.

THE PIANO QUINTET

In his 1853 article *New Paths*, Schumann described Brahms's chamber music as "symphonies in disguise". That description was never truer than it is for the Op. 34 *Quintet*, in which Brahms's own beloved instrument takes centre stage and roars, whenever the occasion demands it, like a lion. The *Quintet* was originally planned with two cellos – only for Brahms's friend, the violinist Joachim, to dismiss it as opaque. The introduction of a piano came to the rescue, by turns incisive, quizzical, introspective – driving the music on, interrogating and lightening the mellow confidences of the strings, whipping the finale from diffidence into defiant exultation. The work in its finished form has been seen as an attempt to combine the resonances of orchestral music with the differentiated textures of chamber music. It is certainly one of the masterpieces of Brahms's maturity.

O Quartetto Italiano; Pollini (Deutsche Grammophon 419 673-2).

Amongst modern single-disc sets, Pollini offers an interpretation which stands above the rest for its high drama: its impulsive accelerations and ominous pauses which shrink from a whisper, the moments of deliberation which suddenly explode into life. The piano line is meticulously articulated and there is an electrifying rapport between the strings.

THE STRING QUARTETS

In the nineteenth century, the rise of the symphony as a melting pot for innovation meant that chamber music had become displaced, except as a vehicle for the more intimate ideas. But Brahms kept his allegiance to a classical past, and for him the quartet remained an opportunity for experiments of striking originality. From his youth he admitted to having sketched chamber music, which he'd destroyed, and only in 1873 did he complete something he felt ready to publish. The first of this Opus 51 set has the striving spirit characteristic of his middle period; and with customary high craftsmanship Brahms toys with our expectations, as if discovering the medium of the quartet afresh. The *Third Quartet* (1876) harks back to the world of Mozart and Haydn. Yet, throughout the cycle, nostalgia is muted, and it serves only to allow Brahms's interplays and musical tensions to be resolved with greater impact.

O String Quartets Nos. 1 and 3: Borodin Quartet (Teldec 4509 90889-2).

O String Quartet No. 2: Borodin Quartet; Leonskaya (Teldec 4509 97461-2; with Brahms, *Piano Quintet*).

The Borodins' awareness of timbre, of texture and pulse, creates an atmosphere which carries a formidable charge. If Brahms's euphonious geniality is there, so too is his depth – that luminous inner world which his masterful fusion of craftsmanship and bittersweet introspection opens up. These are, in fact, supremely idiomatic interpretations, never too obvious, but with an underlying yearning. The same might be said of Brahms himself; and it is the subtle understatement of the playing which leaves a lump in the throat.

THE VIOLIN SONATAS

The three violin sonatas, written between 1878 and 1886, epitomize Brahms's remarkable ability to reconcile heartfelt expression with classical discipline. The first – in fact his fourth, as three earlier ones were destroyed – is the perhaps the most lyrical and is an outstanding example of his use of cyclic form: the whole work is unified by a single idea, three repeated notes that are first heard at the work's beginning. The second sonata exudes an optimistic and confident atmosphere, but the third – also written in the summer of 1886 – is a bleak, melancholic and introspective piece. Unlike its predecessors, the third sonata is in four movements, and, whereas the outer movements dominate the earlier sonatas, here it is the central movements that form the crux.

O Perlman; Ashkenazy (EMI CDC 7 47403-2).

Perlman and Ashkenazy give outstanding, mellow performances, complemented by the recording's rich and warm sound. This is some of the most contented music-making on any chamber-music disc.

THE STRING SEXTETS

Brahms's two sextets, both scored for two violins, two violas and two cellos, are among his finest works. The first, composed in 1858, is fairly straightforward in its construction, with an almost complacent feel that contrasts starkly with the deliberate contrapuntal introspection of the second, written six years later in absolute privacy – almost certainly in response to the failure of a friendship with one of his lady friends, Agathe von Siebold. Both works share a similarly constructed opening movement but it is in the finales that Brahms's expression most obviously differs. The first ends with cheerful exuberance while the second concludes with a turbulent and complex reworking of a single idea that, in well-disguised form, reappears throughout the other movements. In short, the second sextet is Brahms at his most engagingly melancholy.

⭘ Raphael Ensemble (Hyperion CDA 66276).

The Raphael Ensemble really warm to Brahms's typically independent part-writing – each of the players shines in these rich and enthusiastic performances, assisted throughout by a clear and spacious recorded sound.

SONGS

It was Brahms who, with Schumann, championed Schubert during the decades of his posthumous discovery. "There is not one of Schubert's songs", Brahms wrote, "from which you can't learn something." The partnership between soloist and accompanist, the way a human drama might unfold through the most economic of means, were things from which Brahms was quick to learn – adding his own sheen of delectable, sensuous vitality. At times Brahms's songs seem an ardent communion with the women whose long-term companionship he denied himself in life. But he also gained from Schubert an appreciation not only of Germany's lyric poets but of the rich body of folk material. The melodies of the *Deutsche Volkslieder*, which he composed throughout his career, are lifted from folk songs: the *Zigeunerlieder* ("Gypsy Songs") of Op. 103 (1888) perhaps take their "glorious swing" (as a female friend wrote) from the Hungarian poems which they set. He created few cycles, and the most famous of those he did, *Die schöne Magelone*, rather resolutely fails to hold together as a poetic narrative in the way that Schubert's two great cycles do.

⭘ Price; Johnson (RCA 09026 60901-2).

Full of warmth and sweetness, this recital makes a fine introduction to the world of Brahms's songs. Ideas spark between soloist and accompanist and an apparent lack of inhibition masks superlative judgement in matters of breadth and phrasing.

PIANO WORKS

Brahms was a formidable pianist and he wrote a large amount of music for the instrument throughout his creative life – for only on the piano, as he once told Clara Schumann, did he feel fully at ease and at home. Though there is more virtuoso display in his early piano works and more of an emphasis on chordal writing in the later ones, Brahms's piano style evolved only slightly once he had achieved maturity – there is not, as there is with Beethoven, a sense that this piano music traces the course of a long journey. You'll find some lovely melodies here, but an equally important aspect of most of the works listed below is their quasi-orchestral texture, a quality that again allies Brahms with Schumann. Brahms thought with all ten fingers, and the resulting music can sometimes seem distinctly heavyweight; but when played by a pianist with the requisite sensitivity to tone, Brahms's piano works are revealed as masterpieces of condensed, almost refractory writing.

As is the case with Schumann, Brahms's sonatas are relatively neglected, and his reputation as a composer for the piano rests almost exclusively upon a group of short, condensed pieces – the *Ballades* Op. 10, the two *Rhapsodies* Op. 79, and the piano pieces of Op. 117, Op. 118 and Op. 119.

◑ Complete Piano Works: Katchen (Decca 430 053-2; 6 CDs).

If you want to tackle all of Brahms's piano music, pick Julius Katchen's mid-price set from the mid-1960s – something of a heyday for Decca recordings. Avoiding any tendency to heaviness, his playing has invigorating refinement and spirit.

THE BALLADES AND RHAPSODIES

Listening to the four *Ballades*, composed in 1854 when Brahms was only 21, you can hear why Schumann so readily proclaimed him a genius. Inspired by the brooding fatalism of folk ballads (the first is inspired by the Scottish poem *Edward*, which described an act of matricide), all of them share a basic ternary structure. The first three are almost demonic in character, as Schumann remarked at the time, but the last and longest of the four is something quite different. A sighing Adagio of immense beauty, it seems to reveal an act of reticent and private soul-searching, almost an innocence, that was never again to be heard in Brahms's music. The two thrilling *Rhapsodies* in B minor and G minor (1879), are kindred spirits to the first three *Ballades* – marked "agitato" and "molto passionato", they are music of primal urgency, offset by lambent interludes of introspection.

◑ **Four Ballades: Gilels** (Deutsche Grammophon 447 407-2; with *Piano Quartet No. 1*).

It is Gilels's breadth and restraint which allows Brahms's crucial changes in voicing and pace to register. This is playing of profound composure and inner wisdom, whose measured sensibility permits a unique command and variegation of phrase and texture – whether in the shifting clouds of *No. 2*, the clipped pedalwork of *No. 3*, or the sullen fog of *No. 4*. This performance is also available, un-remastered, at budget price.

◑ **Two Rhapsodies: Argerich** (Deutsche Grammophon 447 430-2; with Chopin, Liszt, Ravel, Prokofiev).

There are many performances of these thrilling pieces, but none better than this. Argerich brings passion tempered by eloquence: each shift of nuance is given its proper intensity and context. Nobody has found a better sense of space for Brahms's reflected emotion, or allowed it to breathe and grow with a wider range of colour. This performance is also available, un-remastered, at budget price.

THE PIANO SONATAS

The three piano sonatas were what a 20-year-old Brahms carried under his arm for his first, historic meeting with Schumann. The third and best of them he had just penned; the other two he'd dashed off the previous year, with a young man's proud disdain for any humbling comparisons with Beethoven, or for that matter any other antecedent. For this is music which takes the notion of the sonata by the throat and shakes it into a gargantuan receptacle for teeming ideas: "that young eagle" said Schumann in his subsequent magazine editorial, seemingly staggered by this poetic onslaught, and eager to think that a successor to Beethoven might have arrived. Perhaps it was Robert's exuberant reception that induced Brahms's subsequent caution towards his own art, for he never wrote another sonata. Be that as it may, these works align a mastery of organization with the boundless fertility of one who revels in his own mastery of the mightiest of instruments.

○ **Piano Sonatas Nos. 1 and 2: Richter** (Philips 438 477-2; 3 CDs; with *Paganini Variations*, Schumann, *Fantasie*, etc).

Richter's grand manner may drain a little of the essential youthful impetuosity from this music, but it gets to the heart in so many other ways, seeking out Brahms's premature nostalgia as well as his fulminating grandeur. This is a live recital of the highest order, but for those preferring the safety of the studio Richter has recorded both sonatas on a single disc for Decca.

◑ **Piano Sonata No 3: Lupu** (Decca 448 129-2; *with theme and Variations in D minor* & Schubert, *Sonata in A Flat*).

Those who see either Lupu or Brahms as primarily soul-searching artists will be astonished by the display of fire here. The third sonata is a work bursting at the seams with ideas and Lupu's orchestral command of the keyboard is ideal to give it the cohesion it needs, as well as the toughness it demands.

LATE PIANO WORKS

Most intensely personal of all Brahms's piano compositions are the pieces gathered under the titles Op. 116, Op. 117, Op. 118 and Op. 119. Composed around 1892 for a failing Clara Schumann, these miscellanies of ballades, romances, rhapsodies and intermezzos (terms with no precise definition) offer a kaleidoscopic image of the composer, compacting an extraordinary range of emotion into a brief span. Each of these miniatures is a marvel of immediacy, making them perhaps the best place to start an exploration of Brahms's piano music.

◑ **Piano Pieces Op. 116: Gilels** (Deutsche Grammophon 447 446-2; 2 CDs; with the piano concertos).

Profoundly contemplative, this is playing almost beyond praise, with an extraordinary refinement and quality of judgement. The clarity with which Brahms's overlapping melodic strands and patterns of narrative tension are weighted, articulated and brought together is something to marvel at.

○ **Piano Pieces Opp. 117–119: Lupu** (Decca 430 053-2; with *Two Rhapsodies*).

Radu Lupu is a master of Brahms's late style, allowing each detail room to breathe, and defining all the varied inner voices that are so important to the Opp. 117–119 pieces. He may not be the most exciting pianist to have recorded these works, but his unshowy approach makes him one of the most revealing.

BENJAMIN BRITTEN

(1913–1976)

Benjamin Britten was simply the most prolific and most significant British composer since Purcell, with almost one hundred major compositions to his credit, ranging from full-scale operas to accessible but unpatronizing music for schoolchildren.

He was born in Lowestoft on St Cecilia's Day (November 22) – appropriately, as she is the patron saint of music. His mother, a keen amateur musician and singer, was the formative influence in his early years, and by the age of five he was already writing. Britten went on to take lessons from the composer Frank Bridge, who introduced him to the music of progressive European composers such as Bartók, Berg and Schoenberg. After studying at the Royal College of Music, Britten got a job with the Post Office film unit and wrote music for a number of innovative documentary films, a crucial experience in refining his technique as a dramatic composer. He also met and collaborated with the poet W.H. Auden, who was to be one of the most important influences of his life, reinforcing Britten's pacifism and providing the text for his first important song cycle, *Our Hunting Fathers* (1936).

Discontented with life in England, Auden emigrated to America in 1939, followed a few months later by Britten and Peter Pears, the tenor who was to be Britten's partner for almost forty years – it's hard to find a partnership that so dominated the creative output of a composer as did this one. Britten and Pears spent nearly three years in America, where Britten wrote his first big orchestral work, the *Sinfonia da Requiem* (1940), and his first dramatic work, the operetta *Paul Bunyan* (1941), to a libretto by Auden. This period in the States was crucial in bringing out Britten's profound attachment to his English heritage, and his feelings for his native East Anglia were heightened by an article he read on the Suffolk poet George Crabbe. He determined to go back to England and to set Crabbe's work as an opera.

Britten returned home in 1942 and had soon written some of his very best music – *A Ceremony*

NIGEL LUCKHURST/LEBRECHT COLLECTION

Britten (3rd from left) at the 1976 Aldeburgh Festival, with Peter Pears, André Previn and Elisabeth Söderström

of Carols and a song cycle for Pears titled *Serenade for Tenor, Horn and Strings*. But it was the opera *Peter Grimes* (1945), based on a story by Crabbe, that put him firmly on the map, establishing him not just as a brilliant composer but also a sincere commentator on social and political events, something that runs through most of his output. At the time of *Peter Grimes* there were only two established opera companies in Britain, so Britten turned to the medium of chamber opera and created his own company, the English Opera Group, to perform these small-scale pieces. They became the centrepiece of the annual Aldeburgh Festival, which Britten started in 1948 in the Suffolk seaside town he had made his home.

Throughout the rest of his life, in addition to writing works for Aldeburgh and for amateur groups and schoolchildren (*Noye's Fludde*, 1957, is the best of these), Britten received several major commissions, the greatest of which was the *War Requiem* (1961), composed for the consecration of Coventry Cathedral after its postwar reconstruction. Britten had been a conscientious objector during the war, and several of his works carry a pacifist message, the *War Requiem* foremost among them. A few years later the opening of the Snape Maltings just outside Aldeburgh allowed for larger-scale opera productions, and *Death in Venice*, the last of Britten's fifteen operas, was produced there in 1973. Giving Pears his most demanding stage role, *Death in Venice* was Britten's most public statement about his long-standing relationship with the singer.

Britten accepted a life peerage – the first musician to be so honoured – in 1976. He died in December of that year, of the heart disease that had weakened him in his last few years.

PETER GRIMES

Peter Grimes, which reopened Sadler's Wells theatre after the war in June 1945, marked a watershed for Britten and a rebirth for British opera. It was so widely publicized and well received that a bus conductor on the route to the theatre is reported to have announced "Sadler's Wells! Any more for *Peter Grimes*, the sadistic fisherman?"

The story is a grim one and reflects themes which frequently recur in Britten's music – innocence as a prey to violence and the outsider as prey to society. Grimes is a fisherman whose temperament and conduct have put him at odds with the Aldeburgh community in which the opera is set. At the outset he is acquitted of the murder of his young apprentice, who has died at sea. Here Grimes has music of great beauty and vulnerability that is sharply contrasted with the gossips and busybodies of The Borough. But we see his darker side as he bullies his new apprentice, who then accidentally falls to his death. Grimes sets sail in his ship and sinks it out at sea.

Though the action of *Peter Grimes* is focused on the ambiguous fisherman and his finely drawn social background, its magnificent orchestral score evokes another principal character, the sea itself. The opera's four vivid *Sea Interludes*, which allow for scene changes, have become concert pieces in their own right, and the music conjures up tempests throughout the piece. It's the sea that closes the opera as Grimes' boat disappears and the community resumes its daily routine, already forgetting its outcast.

⊙ Pears, Watson, Pease; Royal Opera House Chorus & Orchestra; Britten (Decca 414 577-2; 2 CDs).

Most of Britten's recordings of his own operas stand as classics, and nowhere is that truer than with *Peter Grimes*, recorded complete for the first time in 1958, with Peter Pears superb in the title role and Britten bringing a pacy energy to the score. Pears' singing of *Now the Great Bear and Pleiades* in Act I poignantly evokes the loneliness of the fisherman at the mercy of fate and the elements.

⊙ Rolfe Johnson, Lott, Allen; Royal Opera House Chorus & Orchestra; Haitink (EMI 7 54832 2; 2 CDs).

Anthony Rolfe Johnson, in the EMI recording of 1993, is almost as good at the poetic side of Grimes and brings out more of his ambiguities in his brutal treatment of the boy. Felicity Lott is a glorious Ellen Orford, the one person in the community sympathetic to Grimes, and the orchestral score comes across brilliantly.

BILLY BUDD

Britten's next large-scale opera was *Billy Budd*, composed for the Festival of Britain in 1951. Based on a story by Herman Melville, it recapitulates the maritime setting and several of the themes of *Peter Grimes*. Billy Budd, a sailor unjustly accused of murder, is driven to his execution by the vindictive Claggart and by Captain Vere, a decent man forced by circumstance to sacrifice him. The dual aspects of Grimes – the brutal and poetic – reappear in these latter characters, and again there is a sexual undercurrent to the action, with the suggestion of Claggart's stifled homosexual desire for Billy. *Billy Budd* was highly acclaimed at its first performances – some proclaiming it greater than *Grimes* – although it hasn't enjoyed the same popularity since.

⊙ Glossop, Pears, Langdon; London Symphony Orchestra; Britten (Decca 417 428-2; 3 CDs).

This is the only recording available of Britten's preferred revision from three acts to four. The three principals are well cast, though Michael Langdon is a little melodramatic as Claggart, and the orchestral sound is suitably dark and violent. The final scene of Billy's hanging is especially powerful.

THE TURN OF THE SCREW

Britten's next major opera, *The Turn of the Screw* (1954), inhabits a totally different world. Written for Britten's English Opera Group and premiered at La Fenice in Venice, it's the finest of his chamber operas, tailor-made for six singers and thirteen instrumentalists whose musical abilities Britten knew intimately. The libretto was written by Myfanwy Piper (wife of the painter John Piper, who designed the sets for many of Britten's operas), based closely on the story by Henry James. It tells of Miles and Flora, two children in a remote country house haunted by the ghost of Peter Quint, the man who may have sexually corrupted them. The exact nature of what went on between Quint and the children is unclear, as is the contribution made by the imagination of the children's governess. Britten described the opera's subject as the "nearest to me of any I have chosen (although what that indicates of my own character I shouldn't like to say!)."

Britten composed the opera at lightning speed, yet it is one of his most brilliant scores. It is very tightly constructed as a sequence of variations on a theme using all twelve notes of the chromatic scale, yet because it requires two child performers the music also has a wonderful simplicity and transparency – indeed, some nursery rhymes are cunningly woven into the score. The sheer range and delicacy of the sounds Britten gets from the chamber orchestra is quite remarkable.

O Lott, Langridge; Aldeburgh Festival Ensemble; Bedford (Collins 70302; 2 CDs).

This 1994 recording is so wonderful it even supersedes the version made under the direction of Britten himself. Felicity Lott is perfectly heroic yet vulnerable as the Governess and Philip Langridge menacing and seductive as Quint. The two children, Sam Pay and Eileen Hulse, are good too. Much of the special atmosphere of this piece is created by the orchestral textures, which have never sounded as luminous as here.

A MIDSUMMER NIGHT'S DREAM

A Midsummer Night's Dream, composed for Aldeburgh in 1960, is probably Britten's most immediately attractive major operatic score. The libretto is a drastically reduced version of Shakespeare's play, but it retains the plays three distinct groups of characters – the fairies, the rude mechanicals and the Athenian lovers who enter the wood – and gives each group its own distinctive musical characteristics. The most startlingly original music is that associated with the fairies, who have ethereal sliding strings, harps, tuned percussion and celesta; Oberon, the fairy king, is a countertenor while Titania, the fairy queen, is a coloratura soprano, so they both have an otherworldly quality to their voices.

The rude mechanicals (or "rustics" as Britten calls them) are depicted in a much more basic way, with an emphasis on instruments such as the bassoon and trombone. Their performance of *Pyramus and Thisbe* is a crude but hilarious pastiche of nineteenth-century grand opera: it was a topical joke aimed at Zeffirelli's production of Donizetti's *Lucia di Lammermoor* at Covent Garden – Peter Pears took the part of Flute/Thisbe and did a devastating imitation of Joan Sutherland, the star of the Zeffirelli show.

The Athenian lovers are portrayed in a more conventional musical language, although it is never pedestrian – the highlight is the four lovers' reconciliation at the beginning of Act III, a simple but astonishingly beautiful quartet.

O Deller, Harwood, Harper, Veasey, Pears, Hemsley, Watts, Shirley-Quirk; London Symphony Orchestra; Britten (Decca 425 663-2; 2 CDs).

Despite very strong competition from Richard Hickox, the Britten recording is still supreme. It was made in 1966 and contains several of the original singers, notably Alfred Deller, for whom the part of Oberon was created. This is pretty much an all-star cast and the orchestral textures sound marvellous, with Britten bringing out a sinister underside to the magical realm.

SONGS

Britten composed his precocious *Quatre Chansons Français* for soprano and orchestra at the age of 15, and song cycles were to form a prominent part of his output from then onwards. His first major cycle was *Our Hunting Fathers* (1936), which shows him as something of an *enfant terrible*, with its wild orchestral writing, strenuous vocal line and political message. W.H. Auden's text ostensibly deals with humanity's cruelty to animals, but the real subject is anxiety at the current situation in Europe – the *Dance of Death* specifically alludes to German persecution of the Jews.

More oblique is *Les Illuminations* (1939), a tightly structured setting of eight verses by Arthur Rimbaud, featuring some glorious effects from the strings – evoking the sound of bells, for instance, in *Phrase*. The cycle incorporates a nightmarish evocation of city life, a love song dedicated to a close friend and another dedicated to Peter Pears, but the precise meaning is elusive. The line that frames the cycle, "J'ai seul la clef de cette parade sauvage" ("I alone hold the key to this savage parade") suggests that it is probably autobiographical. It is certainly one of Britten's most attractive and inspired scores.

Perhaps Britten's finest cycle, the *Serenade for Tenor, Horn and Strings*, was written for Pears in 1943 and takes the night as its subject. Its unusual instrumentation was the result of Britten's admiration for the horn playing of Dennis Brain, who demonstrated the possibilities of using the instrument's natural harmonics rather than the valves for the mysterious scene-setting prologue. The technique gives the music an eerie, slightly "out of tune" sound which is highly effective.

Another important cycle, with a similar subject but a more expressionist mood, is the *Nocturne* of 1958. The work is related in theme and style to *A Midsummer Night's Dream* and begins with a Shelley poem about the creative power of dreams. Each of the songs is given a distinctive character by an instrument that's unique to it within the cycle, ranging from the dramatic timpani to the elegiac cor anglais.

◑ **Our Hunting Fathers; Serenade; Folksongs: Söderström, Tear; Welsh National Opera Orchestra, Northern Sinfonia; Armstrong, Marriner** (EMI CDM 7 69522 2).

Elizabeth Söderström's 1982 recording of *Our Hunting Fathers* was the work's first and it confirms it as one of Britten's most remarkable and uncompromising works. Robert Tear and Alan Civil, on the horn, are first-class soloists in this CD's idiomatic performance of *Serenade*, but the folk-song settings are slighter and rather mannered.

◑ **Les Illuminations; Serenade; Nocturne: Pears, Tuckwell; English Chamber Orchestra; Britten** (Decca London 436 395-2).

The reissue of Pears' recordings of these major song cycles represents the essential disc of Britten's vocal music, and not just for historical reasons. Of course Pears brings a special quality to this repertoire, but the technical and artistic quality of the whole disc is unbeatable.

O Les Illuminations; Serenade; Quatre Chansons Français: Lott, Rolfe Johnson; Scottish National Orchestra; Thompson (Chandos CHAN 8657).

On the Chandos disc a beautifully understated performance of the *Serenade* by Anthony Rolfe Johnson, with Michael Thompson on horn, is combined with Felicity Lott singing *Les Illuminations* – it was originally intended for a soprano. The youthful *Quatre Chansons Français* are also very beautiful.

CHORAL MUSIC

Britten's choral writing, another crucial part of his output, ranges from small-scale pieces for boys' choir to massive works like the *Spring Symphony* and the *War Requiem*.

The Hymn to St Cecilia (1942) for unaccompanied five-part chorus is quintessential Britten, with text (by Auden) and setting that emphasize not just the emotional and aesthetic power of music, but its erotic power as well. He followed it with one of his freshest pieces, *A Ceremony of Carols* (1942), for the economical combination of boys' voices and harp. A series of nine medieval lyrics, it's a simple, tuneful and inventive celebration of innocence.

The *Spring Symphony* (1949), commissioned by Serge Koussevitsky for the Boston Symphony Orchestra, is like the *Ceremony of Carols* writ large. Inspired directly by the experience of the Suffolk countryside, it sets a series of fourteen poems for soloists and chorus, evoking the progress of winter to spring and the onset of summer. Given the nature of the poems, it is a testament to Britten's ingenuity that the music steers well away from the hackneyed English pastoral tradition. The orchestra is large, but he scores the music for small and contrasted instrumental groups.

Britten's choral masterpiece is the *War Requiem* (1961), an altogether deeper and more complex structure than any of its predecessors, interweaving the Latin Mass (for soprano, chorus and orchestra) with nine poems by Wilfred Owen (for tenor and baritone soloists with chamber orchestra), with a third element in the form of a distant choir of boys' voices accompanied by an organ. Britten had a strong message and he wanted to tell it as strongly as possible: "My subject is War, and the Pity of War. The Poetry is in the pity . . . All a poet can do today is warn" is the Owen inscription on the title page. Owen himself is a symbol of the pity of war, as he was killed in the last days of World War I, and Britten chose some of his most powerful verses to set, culminating in *Strange Meeting*, in which a soldier encounters the enemy he has killed. Fundamentally this is a work of reconciliation, and Britten wanted this fact to be represented by the three soloists in the first performance: Peter Pears, Dietrich Fischer-Dieskau and Galina Vishnevskaya, from Britain, Germany and Russia respectively. In the event the Soviets wouldn't give Vishnevskaya a visa and the part was taken at short notice by Heather Harper, although the intended soloists recorded it the following year.

O A Ceremony of Carols; Missa Brevis; A Hymn to the Virgin and other works: Choir of Westminster Cathedral; Hill (Hyperion CDA 66220).

The best all-round recording of Britten's smaller-scale choral music is by David Hill and the Westminster Cathedral Choir. The voices are clear and pure and the acoustic gives the music just the right amount of bloom.

◑ Spring Symphony; Cantata Academica; Hymn to St Cecilia: Vyvyan, Procter, Pears; Orchestra & Chorus of the Royal Opera House, London Symphony Orchestra & Chorus; Britten, Malcolm (Decca 436 396-2).

The 1960 Britten recording of the *Spring Symphony* is tremendously vivid and comes with a performance of the *Cantata Academica*, a very high-spirited and ebullient piece written for Basle University in 1959. The performance of the *Hymn to St Cecilia* is rather overrich, however.

O War Requiem; Ballad of Heroes; Sinfonia da Requiem: Harper, Langridge, Shirley-Quirk; London Symphony Orchestra & Chorus; Hickox (Chandos CHAN8983/4; 2 CDs; with *Sinfonia da Requiem* and *Ballad of Heroes*).

There are currently six good recordings of the *War Requiem*. The original Britten recording is a classic, featuring as it does the trio of Pears, Fischer-Dieskau and Vishnevskaya, but equally impressive is this 1991 recording conducted by Richard Hickox. A work of this size and complexity really benefits from a clean modern recording, and it comes with soloists deeply rooted in the music. Heather Harper was soprano soloist for the premiere and Philip Langridge and John Shirley-Quirk are seasoned Britten performers. The set has generous fill-ups too.

ORCHESTRAL MUSIC

Britten wrote relatively little purely orchestral music, but some of it ranks amongst his best work.

The *Variations on a Theme of Frank Bridge* (1937) is a tribute to his teacher – Britten said that each of the movements portrayed a different aspect of Bridge's character. It is a tremendously confident and extrovert work, including affectionate pastiches of classical forms and a Viennese waltz, although it has its darker moments as well. It has deservedly become one of the composer's most popular works, as has the *Young Person's Guide to the Orchestra* (1946), a tribute to Henry Purcell, whom Britten always cited as his prime example in setting the English language – scores like *A Midsummer Night's Dream* resonate with the spirit of Purcell. The *Young Person's Guide* was written as the soundtrack for an educational film and is made up of a series of variations on a Purcell theme, presented by the different sections of the orchestra and culminating in an exuberant fugue.

In sharp contrast to the carefree mood of the *Young Person's Guide* is the *Sinfonia da Requiem* (1940), the closest Britten came to writing an orchestral symphony; written while he was in America, it is a mournful three-movement requiem for his parents and for the war dead of Europe. Outstanding amongst Britten's other orchestral scores are various suites extracted from his operas, especially the *Four Sea Interludes from Peter Grimes*.

O Young Person's Guide to the Orchestra; Variations on a Theme of Frank Bridge; Simple Symphony: English Chamber Orchestra; Britten (Decca 417 509-2).

Britten's recording of his most popular orchestral scores is bright and vivacious, making a good introduction to the lighter side of his music.

◑ Sinfonia da Requiem; Four Sea Interludes & Passacaglia from Peter Grimes; Young Person's Guide to the Orchestra: Royal Liverpool Philharmonic; Pešek (Virgin CUV 5 61195-2).

The Pešek recording of the *Sinfonia da Requiem* is powerfully conceived and extremely well played, and the same goes for the *Sea Interludes and Passacaglia*, which form a wonderful symphonic evocation of the world of Grimes. Including the *Young Person's Guide*, this is a very good cross-section of Britten's orchestral music.

O Variations on a Theme of Frank Bridge; Simple Symphony; Lachrymae: Tomter; Norwegian Chamber Orchestra; Brown (Virgin VC 5 45121-2).

Both the *Frank Bridge Variations* and the *Simple Symphony* are given wonderfully spritely and generous performances, but it's the passionate performance of *Lachrymae*, a work for viola and string orchestra inspired by Dowland, which makes this disc so special.

MAX BRUCH

(1838–1920)

Bruch is widely known just for his first violin concerto, which is perhaps unfair and certainly misleading. One of the late nineteenth century's most prominent German composers, he produced a large amount of tuneful, lush music that was completely out of step with the expressive innovations of Gustav Mahler, let alone the radical experiments of Schoenberg. His career was something of a procession along the establishment path, winning competitions, studying with well-respected figures, composing for the theatre, concert hall and church, and accepting various short-term positions until, in 1891, he was made

GUUS ONG

Professor at the Berlin Academy, where he taught composition until 1910. Like Pfitzner (see p.304), he lived out of academia's palm, producing music that was designed first and foremost to appease the institutions that supported him, and, secondarily, to entertain the public in the least demanding fashion.

His music made something of a comeback in the decade after his death, but with the Nazis' rise to power his work was suppressed, along with all other Jewish music. Though the bulk of his output remains in limbo, there's been something of a mini-revival of late: his symphonies and concertos are now well represented on record, and the most successful of his three operas, *Die Loreley*, has recently been staged by at least three different companies.

SYMPHONY NO. 3

Bruch's symphonic style owes much to Mendelssohn and Schumann, and even more to Brahms, whose influence is clear in the *Symphony No. 3* – the last and best of his three symphonies – written in 1887 two years after Brahms's fourth. That said, the symphony displays more complicated orchestration and a less rigid structure than you'll find in Brahms, and you'd have to have a hard heart not to find something intoxicating in the sweep of its old-fashioned melodies.

◑ **Symphonies Nos. 1–3: Leipzig Gewandhaus; Masur** (Philips 420 932-22; CDs; with *Swedish Dances*).

Kurt Masur's set of the symphonies is the best – he indulges Bruch's sweeping (sometimes rambling) lyricism, and brings a rewarding flexibility to the music. The sound is superb and the playing enthusiastic.

VIOLIN CONCERTO NO. 1

Bruch wrote a lot of music for the combination of violin and orchestra, including three concertos, of which the best is the *Violin Concerto No. 1* (1868). If you don't know this work by name you're almost certain to recognize it in performance. This is the quintessential Romantic showpiece, full of engaging themes and bravura writing that makes it as exciting as any violin concerto in the repertoire, when played well. It was dedicated to Brahms's friend the violinist Joseph Joachim, and again it has a Brahmsian sweep to it, though in fact it was written ten years before Brahms's own violin concerto.

◑ **Heifetz; New Symphony Orchestra; Sargent** (RCA 09026 61745-2; with *Scottish Fantasy and Vieuxtemps, Concerto No. 2*).

The finest version of Bruch's *Violin Concerto No. 1* is the historic account from Jascha Heifetz – the quality of his sound and his response to the music's inflections are stunning, and his phrasing encourages Sargent and the orchestra to wallow in the score's sensual beauty.

⊙ **Lin; Chicago Symphony Orchestra; Slatkin** (Sony SMK 64250; with Mendelssohn *Violin Concerto*, Vieuxtemps *Violin Concerto No. 5*).

For the classic coupling of the Bruch and Mendelssohn concertos, there is no finer modern recording than the one from Cho-Liang Lin and Leonard Slatkin, a performance that's particularly beautiful and intense in the slow movement of the Bruch.

THE SCOTTISH FANTASY

Bruch composed the *Scottish Fantasy* in 1879 for the virtuosic brilliance of Pablo de Sarasate. The style is far removed from the seriousness of the *Violin Concerto No. 1*, with Bruch spinning together Welsh, Irish and even Swedish popular folk tunes, in a manner that, at times, borders on the kitsch. "Auld Rob Harris" provides a suitably sepulchral opening, and through four linked movements the music moves its way towards an ebullient finale.

◑ **Heifetz; New Symphony Orchestra; Sargent** (RCA 09026 61745-2; with *Violin Concerto No. 1* and Vieuxtemps, *Concerto No. 2*).

Heifetz's playing of the *Scottish Fantasy* is no less brilliant than his account of the *Violin Concerto*. It's a performance that throbs with energy and a marvellous ebullient spontaneity. Sargent and the New Symphony Orchestra provide the perfect platform for Heifetz's magic.

O Meyers; Royal Philharmonic Orchestra; Lopez-Cobos (RCA RD 60942; with Lalo, *Symphonie Espagnole*).

Anne Akiko Meyers' entry floats spectrally above its orchestral backdrop. This is playing of high concentration and gentle distinction, for there is a melancholy behind the *Scottish Fantasy* which Meyers, perhaps more than anyone else, manages to catch.

ANTON BRUCKNER

(1824–1896)

For much of the earlier part of this century, Bruckner's name was routinely paired with that of Mahler: both were Austrian, both wrote vast symphonies and both have needed many years of proselytizing for their music to be truly appreciated. Apart from these similarities, however, they were very dissimilar people. Mahler the neurotic and adventurous composer-conductor has little fundamentally in common with Bruckner the pious church organist, who wrote his massively simple music to the glory of God.

Bruckner's grandfather and father were both village teachers. As the position traditionally went hand in hand with that of church organist, young Anton was surrounded by the worlds of the schoolroom and the church from an early age, and by the age of 10 he was deputizing for his father at the organ. He began receiving formal music education the following year, and in 1836 he was accepted as a choirboy at the monastery of St Florian near Linz in Upper Austria.

He spent 1840–41 in Linz itself, training to be a teacher, and landed his first position in a small village on the Bohemian border. But his true ambition was achieved when he gained a teaching post at St Florian, where he remained for ten years. During all this time he continued his musical education and composed his first works, mainly liturgical pieces. In 1855 he moved back to Linz to take up the position of cathedral organist and soon established himself as one of the greatest exponents of the instrument. His studies still continued, this time with the Viennese theoretician Simon Sechter, and he later took lessons in formal composition and orchestration with a teacher ten years his junior, Otto Kitzler.

It was through Kitzler that Bruckner found his true musical vocation, when the former gave a performance of Wagner's *Tannhäuser* in Linz. It proved a revelation. Bruckner had spent nearly forty years of his life learning all the theoretical rules of composition; his exposure to Wagner made him realize that his way forward was to break these rules, as Wagner had done, and to create in the symphony what Wagner had achieved in music drama. (He and Wagner subsequently became firm friends; something that the pro-Brahms Viennese faction used against him.)

Until this point, none of Bruckner's compositions had really stood out from the run-of-the-mill music written for day-to-day use in the Catholic Church. Now, as if to make up for lost time, he immediately began a series of truly original scores, including the *Symphony in D minor* (1863–64), which he later numbered No. 0, the three mature Masses (1864, 1865–66 and 1867–68), and his acknowledged *Symphony No. 1* (1865–66), all of them recognizably Brucknerian in scale and content. In the middle of this period, he suffered a mental breakdown and a bout of numeromania (an obsession with counting), and spent the spring and summer of 1867 in a sanatorium until he was fully recovered. The following year he moved to Vienna to succeed his old teacher Sechter at the city's music conservatory, where he taught theory and the organ, and later became a lecturer at the university.

Here, between 1871 and 1876, he composed his next four symphonies, beginning each one as soon as he had finished its predecessor. He then spent the next three years making revisions to these, before embarking on his next great creative surge, writing his *String Quintet* (1879), symphonies *No. 6* (1879–81), *No. 7* (1881–83) and *No. 8* (1884–87) and the *Te Deum* (1881–84). A further period of revisions followed – largely spurred on by friends seeking ways of making his music more successful – and this was the main reason behind his inability to complete his last symphony, *No. 9* (1891–96). He died in Vienna in October 1896 and in accordance with his wishes was buried beneath the organ at St Florian.

Throughout all his years in Vienna, Bruckner had to put up with continual barracking from the anti-Wagnerites and in particular the critic Eduard Hanslick, who wielded far-reaching powers in Viennese musical life. Only *Symphony No. 7* brought him unchallenged success and led to international recognition during his last decade. Some still carp at the crudities and naiveties that many of Bruckner's works apparently display, yet there was arguably no other composer who spent so many years studying his art before establishing his unique voice. He remained a devout Catholic for the whole of his life and his faith pervades all his music, though it was with the traditionally secular symphony – Gothic cathedrals in sound, as they have often been described – that his originality was established.

CHORAL MUSIC

Before Bruckner had any idea about how to write for an orchestra, he had excelled in his writing for choir with basic instrumental accompaniment. Indeed, his liturgical output exceeds his symphonic, though many of these early works are best left to the dedicated. Much more worthwhile are the mature Masses, which bring to the Mass tradition of Mozart and Haydn both the lyricism of Schubert and the austerity of Bach. On a grander scale is the *Te Deum*, a work Bruckner felt to be one his best. "When God finally calls me," he once said, "and asks 'What have you done with the talent I gave you, my boy?', I will present him with the score of my *Te Deum* and hope he will judge me mercifully."

MASSES NOS. 1–3 & THE TE DEUM

Bruckner wrote as many as seven Masses, but only the last three, dating from the 1860s and known confusingly as nos 1, 2 and 3, are performed with any regularity. These works were no more immune from Bruckner's revisionary practices than were his symphonies, and the third, in F minor, was reworked at least four times before he arrived at a definitive version. The first (D minor) and last have orchestral accompaniment, but the middle work (E minor) has only an accompaniment of wind instruments in response to the more austere sect for whom he wrote the work.

Bruckner's setting of the great hymn of praise to God, the *Te Deum*, was written between the seventh and eighth (1881-84) symphonies and is thus his most mature vocal composition. It is on the same scale as his symphonies, requiring four soloists, a choir, organ and orchestra, and, despite its key of C major, it has even been used, following Bruckner's own misguided suggestion, as a choral finale to the ninth symphony, which is in D minor.

◑ **Mass Nos. 1–3; Te Deum: Corydon Singers & Orchestra; Best** (Hyperion CDS4 4071/3; 3 CDs; with other choral pieces).

Matthew Best and the Corydon Singers have made their name in this music and these Hyperion discs provide some of the most intensely moving Bruckner available, sensitively performed and recorded. The discs are all available individually, but there is a discount if you buy the full set.

THE MOTETS

The motets span almost the whole of Bruckner's adult life. They are among the finest liturgical music of the last 150 years, in which Bruckner's love of Renaissance polyphony is fused with his own ripe chromaticism. Many are written to be performed without accompaniment and, as expressions of devotion, they possess a touching simplicity in their directness of expression. High points include the setting of *Ave Maria* in 1861, which marked the beginning of his stylistic maturity, and the more intense *Locus iste* (1869) and *Virge Jesse floruit* (1885).

⊙ **Corydon Singers; Best** (Hyperion CDA 66062).

Luxurious but pure singing from the Corydon Singers. Their radiant performances bring out the quiet sincerity of Bruckner's religious convictions without a hint of heaviness or sentimentality.

THE SYMPHONIES

Bruckner was 40 before he found his symphonic vocation, then went on to write ten symphonies on a scale not heard before. While his contemporary Brahms was happy to follow the example of Beethoven's classicism, Bruckner sought a much more modern and novel development of the form, an enterprise in which he was immensely influenced by the operas of Wagner. Bruckner's orchestral forces are on a truly Wagnerian scale – the late symphonies, for example, call for a quartet of Wagner tubas in addition to the already substantial brass section, and the music cries out for vast numbers of string and woodwind instruments.

Yet the music itself often betrays Bruckner's background as an organist. Huge sections of the symphonies concentrate exclusively on a particular combination of instruments, as if a particular selection of organ stops had been chosen; these blocks of sound often change abruptly, sometimes with a naive pause to divide them; themes are presented and developed in long strands that are often achieved by simply repeating phrases before moving on; climactic sections often find the full orchestra reiterating a single chord; and, at his most basic, Bruckner has the whole orchestra playing in unison – a dramatic stroke, but one which often sounds coarse and unsophisticated. So Bruckner is not the most subtle or natural of symphonists, but there is so much in the way of harmonic ingenuity, melodic sweep and sheer orchestral magnificence in his music that, despite its scale, diffuseness and clumsiness, it invariably repays your patience. The best works for a first try are symphonies *No. 4* and *No. 7*.

All of the symphonies except numbers 0, 5, 6 and 7 were subjected to revisions of varying degrees in an attempt to make them more acceptable to audience and critics, and this has resulted in the survival of several different versions of many of them. To make things worse, most were first published with further "improvements" by his followers and pupils. Their motives were good – they wanted to increase the symphonies' chances of performance – but their cuts and additions often harmed Bruckner's overall plan. Between the 1930s and 1950s two musicologists, Robert Haas and Leopold Nowak, each brought out a complete edition of Bruckner's scores, as far as possible restoring them to their original form, though each editor often had his own interpretation of that original state. It's recently been revealed that Haas was encouraged in his editorial policy by the Nazis, who urged him to go for more monumental readings; in a sense, Nowak's subtler and more refined versions can be seen as a denazification of the texts. Both versions are still very much in circulation.

◑ **Symphonies Nos. 0–9: Concertgebouw Orchestra; Haitink** (Philips 442 040-2; 9 CDs).

A recording of the complete symphonies won't necessarily provide you with the best performance of each work, but has the advantage in terms of convenience and cost, since all available sets are at reduced price, and make the best use of disc space. Haitink's cycle, recorded throughout the 1960s, did much to establish his reputation as a conductor of enormous integrity and power. His sense of structure is as good as anyone's, but he can also pull the stops out, as in his scintillating reading of the *Symphony No. 4*.

SYMPHONIES NOS. 0–2

Though less distinguished than the later symphonies, the first three nevertheless established many of Bruckner's most distinctive characteristics, from the sense of scale to the organ-like washes of orchestral sound and the construction of long expanses from short, repeated phrases. Bruckner's stylistic development was very much a gradual process, however, so there is often little to distinguish one symphony from the next.

Much of the music of *No. 0* postdates *No. 1*: Bruckner at first abandoned it then revised it before embarking on *No. 2*, but felt that the work now known as *Symphony No. 1* was worthier of the title, so relegated *No. 0* to its zero status. *No. 1* was the first to be performed, at a concert in Linz in 1868 conducted by the composer. Shortly afterwards, he moved to Vienna and from time to time over the next twenty or more years tinkered with the score of the work, finally producing a complete revision in 1891 (the so-called Vienna version) that left hardly a bar untouched. The second symphony was the first to be completed after his move to Vienna and before the anti-Wagner claque began directing its venom towards him. It had a successful first performance in 1873,

POLYGRAM

Riccardo Chailly

but his friend Johann Herbeck encouraged him to make changes and cuts, resulting in the 1877 version, though Robert Haas restored the cuts in his edition and it is this version that is invariably played today.

○ Symphony No. 0: Berlin Radio Symphony Orchestra; Chailly (Decca 421 593-2; with *Overture in G*).

Riccardo Chailly is the most persuasive conductor of the early symphonies, and in this radiant performance of *No. 0*, it stands revealed as no lesser a work than its better known companions.

○ Symphony No. 1 (1866 version): Chicago Symphony Orchestra; Solti (Decca 448 898-2).

Chailly's fine account of *No. 1* is currently out of the Decca catalogue, presumably to accommodate this performance by Solti. As might be expected, it's a supremely confident reading, dynamic but never forced or overdriven.

○ Symphony No. 2 (1877 version – ed. Haas): Concertgebouw Orchestra; Chailly (Decca 436 154-2).

Moving from the Berlin Radio Symphony Orchestra to Amsterdam, Chailly continues his survey with a thoroughly convincing account of the second. He is well served by Decca's bright but natural sound.

SYMPHONY NO. 3

In September 1873, Bruckner took an incomplete symphonic score to Richard Wagner at Bayreuth, along with the score of *Symphony No. 2*, to ask

Wagner which one he would like to have dedicated to him. He chose the unfinished piece, and from then on Bruckner always referred to his *Symphony No. 3* as the "Wagner Symphony". Its first version contained a string of quotations from Wagner's operas, but these were eradicated before the premiere in 1877, and Bruckner made a further revision in 1889. It is one of his most enjoyable early symphonies, full of original harmonic and melodic touches, and with a concluding section that, more than any of his other works, looks forward to the grandeur of Mahler.

◑ **Symphony No. 3 (1874 version): Frankfurt Radio Symphony Orchestra; Inbal** (Teldec 0630-14197-2).

Iliahu Inbal's richly rewarding recording with the Frankfurt Radio Symphony Orchestra uses the original 1874 version of the symphony, complete with Wagner quotations.

◑ **Symphony No. 3 (1889 version – ed. Nowak): Vienna Philharmonic Orchestra; Böhm** (Decca 448 098-2; 2 CDs; with *Symphony No.4*).

When it comes to the 1889 version, which has superseded that of 1877, the choice must fall on Böhm, who makes the most of the work's rich sonorities in a subtle performance.

SYMPHONY NO. 4 – THE ROMANTIC

Bruckner himself referred to his fourth symphony as the "Romantic", but when Bruckner uses the term he's not thinking of any Byronic human drama, but rather of the romanticism of nature. This symphony is in essence an allegorical representation of the Austrian countryside. Following the example of Weber's *Der Freischütz* (see p.472), in which the sound of the horn first acquired romantic connotations, Bruckner makes the instrument dominate this symphony: the opening movement features avalanches of brass tones, but the horn really comes into its own in the Scherzo, an evocation of a hunting scene that alludes to the rustic Austrian dance known as the *Ländler*. This movement first introduces a characteristic triplet rhythm which became known as the "Bruckner rhythm", so often did he use it subsequently.

There were as many as four versions of this symphony, though only three survive: the first from 1874, a revised one from 1878–80, when he added the "hunting-horn" Scherzo, and an unauthorized, bastardized version by his pupil Ferdinand Löwe, made in 1888 but long since superceded by the Haas edition of the 1878–80 (though there are still recordings available of this version).

POLYGRAM

Karl Böhm

◑ **Symphony No. 4 (1888 version): Vienna Philharmonic Orchestra; Böhm** (Decca 448 098-2; 2 CDs; with *Symphony No. 3*).

Although it uses the 1888 version, Böhm's recording is nevertheless a classic. The orchestra respond well to his direction, the horns, in particular, excelling themselves in the Scherzo. This performance is also available as a single CD.

◑ **Symphony No. 4 (1878–80 version): Berlin Philharmonic Orchestra; Jochum** (Deutsche Grammophon 427 200-2).

For a more "authentic" account, Jochum's is a fine example of his personal, yet faithful, way with Bruckner. Stridency and pomposity (the perils of Brucknerian interpretation) are avoided through the most sensitive of touches.

SYMPHONY NO. 5

This was the first of Bruckner's mature symphonies to survive in a single version and was his most monumental to date, being both longer and more finely worked-out than its predecessors. It has a sense of solemnity not found in the earlier symphonies, with a dramatic sense of conflict generated by the suggestion that passion is always being kept in check. Bruckner's characteristic use of rich brass chorales is here becoming an increasingly prominent feature, while the finale is a marvellously constructed amalgam of fugue and chorale.

○ **Berlin Philharmonic Orchestra; Wand** (RCA 09026 685023-2).

Gunter Wand is a conductor who became a recording artist rather late in his career. Perhaps that explains why his interpretations, of Bruckner in particular, seem so carefully worked out without being careful. This is his second recording of the fifth, and what is especially impressive is the way momentum is always maintained, even in the tricky last movement.

SYMPHONY NO. 6

Bruckner's next symphony proved to be a lighter, more congenial work than its predecessor – the equivalent, say, of Beethoven's eighth or Brahms's second. This is not one of his most frequently performed symphonies, perhaps because of its relative coolness and detachment, but it is typical Bruckner to the core, and again it required no revision on Bruckner's part.

◑ **Symphony No. 6 (ed. Haas): New Philharmonia; Klemperer** (EMI CDM 7 63351-2).

Made in 1964, this has long been regarded a classic among Bruckner recordings and wears its age well. Klemperer handles the New Philharmonia with a serene confidence, and both orchestra and conductor revel in the symphony's joyous climaxes.

⊙ **Symphony No. 6 (ed. Haas): New Zealand Symphony Orchestra; Tintner** (Naxos 8.553453).

Naxos's signing of the octogenarian Viennese conductor Georg Tintner is a real coup. The company intend to record all the symphonies with him (and different orchestras). This is the pick of them so far, a powerfully energetic account which moves along with an effortless grace.

SYMPHONY NO. 7

Symphony No. 7 is the work that brought Bruckner most success in his lifetime, and has always been his best-loved symphony. After *No. 6* the expansiveness is back, and the symphony begins with his broadest theme yet, a wonderful, noble, arching E major melody on the cellos, variously coloured by other instruments – Bruckner is supposed to have heard it in a dream, though it quotes from his *Mass No. 1*, which he was revising at the time. The work as a whole is intimately connected with Wagner, who died while Bruckner was working on the already funereal Adagio. As a tribute, he introduced the mellow sound of a quartet of Wagner tubas into this movement, and the heart-rending coda was written as a direct response to the news of his mentor's death in 1883.

O Berlin Philharmonic Orchestra; Karajan (Deutsche Grammophon 439 037-2).

Incandescent is the word to apply to Karajan's third recording (his last ever), which grasps more any other the music's unfolding symphonic architecture, and the inner calm which gives unity to an extraordinary range of utterance. The BPO always played this music sumptuously, but there is a particular transparency to their playing here.

SYMPHONY NO. 8

The *Symphony No. 8* is Bruckner at his grandest, most uplifting and most religious. At around eighty minutes long, with a slow movement lasting up to half an hour, it can seem daunting and diffuse on first hearing, but it repays repeated acquaintance for the sumptuousness of its orchestral sound and grandeur of its themes. Like nearly all his symphonies, Bruckner opens with pianissimo tremolo strings, an allusion to the opening of Beethoven's ninth, where similarly the music seems to emerge from nothingness – and the theme the strings accompany even matches the rhythm of Beethoven's at the same point. Bruckner completed his symphony in 1887 but then bowed to the inevitable pressure to make cuts, and a new version was completed in 1890.

O Symphony No. 8 (ed. Haas); Vienna Philharmonic Orchestra; Karajan (Deutsche Grammophon DG 427 611-2; 2 CDs).

Karajan recorded the symphony a number of times, always opting for the Haas version of the fuller 1887 text. His last account, with the Vienna Philharmonic Orchestra and issued posthumously, is the most powerful of them, with an unparalleled sense of communion between conductor, orchestra and music.

O Symphony No. 8 (ed. Nowak); Vienna Philharmonic Orchestra; Giulini (Deutsche Grammophon 445 529-2; 2 CDs).

Guilini opts for the Nowak edition is this rapt and highly charged reading. As is customary with Guilini's interpretations of the Romantic repertoire, the pace is stately to a degree which many find wearing, But he never loses sight of the overall scheme of things, nor does the slightest detail elude him.

SYMPHONY NO. 9

So preoccupied was Bruckner with making needless revisions of his earlier symphonies that he never managed to complete his last work in the form. Attempts have been made to furnish it with a finale from Bruckner's sketches, but it has long been accepted in the form of a three-movement torso. More approachable than *No. 8* (and, if completed, it would probably have been even longer), it is a musical summation of his life: the great Adagio subtly alludes to earlier works, while the symphony's drama expresses the resolution of his self-doubts in the solace of overpowering religious faith.

⊙ Vienna Philharmonic Orchestra; Giulini (Deutsche Grammophon 427 345-2).

In this astonishing live recording of 1988, Giulini adopts the broadest of tempi (particularly in the outer movements) but manages to keep everything perfectly balanced. Nothing ever sounds exaggerated or forced and the orchestra clearly revel in being allowed to produce the most sumptuous of sounds, which is beautifully captured by the DG engineers. A triumph for all involved.

◑ Berlin Philharmonic Orchestra; Karajan (Deutsche Grammophon 429 904-2).

Karajan excelled in Bruckner's late symphonies. His 1976 Berlin recording improved upon his performance of a decade earlier, reaching new heights of expression and ethereal drama.

ANTOINE BRUMEL

(c.1460–c.1520)

Antoine Brumel, born near Chartres around the middle of the fifteenth century, was one of the most respected musicians and composers of his time. Josquin's *Deploration sur la morte d'Ockeghem* mentions Brumel as one of four followers of Ockeghem who should "weep great tears of grief" at the loss of their "good father" (the others are Josquin himself, Pierre de la Rue and Loyset Compère), and although the theorist Glareanus sourly notes that Brumel excelled through his industry rather than his natural gifts, most writers of his period showered him with praise.

Like many of his contemporaries he travelled widely: probably beginning his career in the choir of Chartres Cathedral, he was last heard of in Italy, where he settled in Rome for some time. Brumel had a reputation as a difficult man to deal with, and this may be borne out by the rapidity with which he moved from job to job – for example, he held a post at Notre Dame in Paris for no more than a year before leaving in some haste. Nonetheless, he was sufficiently valued for Alphonso I of Ferrara, an important patron, to make more than one attempt to hire him. The duke finally succeeded in enticing him to his court in 1505 with the offer of a large salary augmented by a travel allowance. He remained there for five years before his move to Rome. Neither the date nor the place of his death are known.

SACRED MUSIC

Although we know of over fifty *chansons*, Brumel's greatest works are religious. Of his sixteen surviving settings of the Mass, which include one of

the earliest Requiems, the late *Missa de Beata Virgine* is probably his masterpiece. It may well have been written in competition with Josquin's setting, and suffers little in comparison, showing an easy control of counterpoint with a sometimes insouciant approach to dissonance, daring melodic and rhythmic invention and an immaculate sense of pacing. Brumel's particular gift for raising the tension towards the end of a movement as the voices chase each other in a flurry of cross-rhythms and ever-decreasing note-values before coming to satisfying rest is especially notable here. Unfortunately, at the time of writing there's no CD of this Mass, but there is a recording of the astonishingly assured and flamboyant *Missa "Et Ecce Terrae Motus"* for twelve voices, which mixes strict canonic techniques with free invention, contrasts of timbre and impressively full textures when all twelve voices are singing at once.

⊙ Missa "Et Ecce Terrae Motus"; Sequentia "Dies Irae": Huelgas Ensemble; van Nevel (Sony Vivarte SK 46 348).

The massive sonorities of this Mass are well served here by an acoustic that suits the grandeur of Brumel's conception without obscuring the complex interweave of the twelve voices. The energy of the writing and the powerful ostinati that are such a feature of his work are joyfully brought out by van Nevel's ensemble, who also convey the sense of awe at the mystery of the Incarnation, the very heart of the Mass. The inclusion of the solemn setting (the earliest known) of the Dies Irae from his *Requiem* is an extra treat.

FERRUCCIO BUSONI

(1866–1924)

Ferruccio Busoni is the forgotten man of twentieth-century music, a situation largely due to the diversity of his talents and his resistance to easy classification. The child of professional musicians, Busoni was born in Tuscany but spent most of his professional life in Germany where, although he always regarded himself as primarily a composer, his early fame was achieved as one of the greatest pianists of his generation.

Like Schoenberg – with whom he enjoyed a mutually respectful relationship – Busoni was a formidable theoretician, and his *Outline of a New Aesthetic of Music* (1907) established him as one of the leading figures of the avant-garde and the first musician to espouse microtonality (music with 36 notes to an octave) and electronic music. His theories on new music made him the target of musical conservatives, notably Hans Pfitzner (see p.304), who attacked him for his "sterile intellectualism". Yet Busoni was never able to escape the pull of tradition and his more daring notions were never incorporated into his own compositions. Instead he preferred to write music that looked back to the eighteenth century for inspiration, an approach he termed "Young Classicism" and defined as "the mastering, sifting and exploitation of all the achievements of preceding experiments".

Ultimately Busoni was hamstrung by his own analytical intelligence and by his reverence for the past, and is probably most likely to be remembered as a formidable pianist. The only works you are likely to come across regularly in the concert hall are his transcriptions of Bach for the piano, in particular his masterful version of the D minor *Chaconne* from the *Violin Partita No. 2*. There are, however, a few works in which Busoni manages to struggle free of the weight of history, and these are his gargantuan piano concerto and his operas. The stage works are not ingratiating pieces – Busoni hated the exciting realism of verismo opera, aspiring instead to create a hieratic music drama in which a perfect fusion of music and text would facilitate the spiritual elevation of the audience. The results can be turgid in places, but *Doktor Faust* in particular has moments of great power, and each of the operas is clearly the product of a questing intelligence.

ARLECCHINO & TURANDOT

Busoni's *Turandot* (based on the same source as Puccini's) was composed as a companion piece for his earlier one-act opera *Arlecchino*, and the two works were first performed together in 1917 under the heading *La nuova commedia dell'arte*. Brilliant examples of Busoni's eclectic but highly individual style, they are scored for modest forces, which Busoni uses with great economy and wit. The better of the pair is *Turandot*, with its thickly layered oriental melodies and general air of chinoiserie – though somewhat enigmatically Busoni breaks the oriental mood at the beginning of Act II, when he incorporates, of all things, the music of *Greensleeves*. The music for this neo-classical *Turandot* shows a complete mastery of the human voice; Busoni's vocal writing may be less memorable than Puccini's, but it's more effective as a component of a coherent theatrical experience.

⊙ Gessendorf, Selig, Dahlberg, Schafer, Kraus, Holzmair; Choir & Orchestra of the Lyon Opera; Nagano (Virgin VIRG 7777 593132-7; 2 CDs).

Kent Nagano's performances of Busoni's two comic operas are characterful and highly charged, even if much of the singing is not exceptional – Mechthild Gessendorf is a good Turandot, but Stefan Dahlberg's one-dimensional Kalaf is unable to convey much beyond the words. The recording is clear and well defined, although the chorus is allowed an overbearing prominence.

DOKTOR FAUST

Busoni began the libretto of *Doktor Faust* in 1914, basing it not on Goethe's poem but on an old

German puppet-play and on Marlowe's *Doctor Faustus*. The finished article, however, is a metaphysical drama that bears little resemblance – beyond its sixteenth-century setting – to Marlowe's semi-farcical creation. The barest outline is as follows. Having invoked Mephistopheles to help him gain "riches, power, fame" et cetera, Busoni's Faust runs away with the recently married Duchess of Parma, whom he abandons when she becomes pregnant. Later he meets the Duchess, now destitute, carrying the body of their child. Stricken by the scene, Faust offers his own life that the child might live; as Faust dies, defiant of God and the Devil alike, a young man rises from his child's corpse.

Completed after Busoni's death by Philip Jarnach (Puccini, who also died in 1924, similarly didn't complete his final opera), *Doktor Faust* is a work of immense power that confronts the complexities of the Faust legend more completely than any other operatic treatment of it. Though written in strict classical form, its orchestration is lush and inventive, and the heavily chromatic vocal parts infuse the rigid structure with a sweeping sensuousness not found in Busoni's other work for the stage. The text is difficult and the opera does demand repeated listening for its ideas and leitmotifs to have any effect, but, as with any twentieth-century progressive opera, a little effort reaps very great rewards.

◑ **Fischer-Dieskau, Cochran, de Ridder, Hildebrecht; Bavarian Radio Orchestra & Chorus; Leitner** (Deutsche Grammophon 427 413-2GC3; 3 CDs).

This is the only available recording of *Doktor Faust*, and it's so fine that it has probably dissuaded record companies from attempting to compete. Fischer-Dieskau's Faust and William Cochran's Mephistopheles are especially good – Cochran's purposeful and ringing tenor voice well balanced by Fischer-Dieskau's smooth but highly coloured baritone. Busoni makes less of the Duchess than the text might suggest, but Hildegard Hildebrecht sings the part with conviction and considered characterization. However, it is Fischer-Diskau's astonishing portrayal of Faust's final failure to find Christian redemption that steals the show. Keep the libretto in sight at all times – without it, the work makes almost no sense.

THE CONCERTO FOR PIANO AND ORCHESTRA

Busoni's *Concerto for Piano and Orchestra* is a massive creation, requiring the pianist to play almost continually for over an hour and – come the last movement – to do battle with a male chorus as well as a hundred-strong orchestra. It shows Busoni as a consummate synthesist: there is a great deal of Brahms's influence here (especially the opening theme) and a constant recourse to traditional Italian rhythms and melodies – each of the first three movements is built around folk songs, while the fourth is a highly developed quasi-Neapolitan song. The work contains perhaps Busoni's most accessible and memorable writing, with grand melodies that surge through the piano part and some fine passages of orchestration. The last ten minutes of the fifth and final movement are particularly beautiful, and the music's transformation into its conclusive glowing resolution is a remarkable achievement.

◑ **Ogdon; John Alldis Choir; Royal Philharmonic Orchestra; Revenaugh** (EMI CDM7 69850-2).

Ogdon's legendary recording for EMI is still unrivalled, although the same label's live performance with Donohoe is better recorded. Both pianists do the work justice, but Ogdon – who studied with Egon Petri, Busoni's favourite pupil and the pianist for the work's British premiere – has an unmatched grasp of the colossal structure. Ogdon's mighty technique is remarkable throughout, with some of his playing in the outer movements being almost beyond belief.

WILLIAM BYRD

(c.1537–1623)

William Byrd was called by his contemporaries "Britanniae Musicae Parens", the father of British music. It was a title he fully deserved: though writing in the Golden Age of English music, he stands out for his combination of sensuousness and formal precision. It was an achievement all the more remarkable since Byrd was a lifelong Catholic during one of the most violent periods of England's religious history. What saw him through was probably a combination of shrewdness, friends in high places (the Earl of Worcester and Lord Lumley, leading Catholics, were patrons), and his outstanding musical ability.

Little is known about his family background. He may have been the son of Thomas Byrd, a gentleman of the Chapel Royal and a colleague of Thomas Tallis (see p.423), with whom the younger

Byrd is thought to have studied. In 1563 he was appointed organist and choirmaster of Lincoln Cathedral, a post he held until 1572 when he moved to London to become joint organist at the Chapel Royal with Tallis. The two men also held the exclusive right to print and publish music and in 1575 they published *Cantiones Sacrae*, a collection dedicated to Queen Elizabeth and containing seventeen motets by each composer. After the enterprise's financial failure the pair petitioned the queen and were granted the lease of the manor of Longney in Gloucestershire. In his later years Byrd became more and more uncompromising about his religious beliefs and on several occasions he and his wife were fined for recusancy (failure to attend Church of England services). In 1593 he moved to a large property at Stondon Massey in Essex, possibly to be near the Catholic Petre family, in whose chapel one of the three Latin Masses, his greatest music, was almost certainly first performed.

In 1997 the record company ASV embarked on a massive project to record all of Byrd's music, much of it for the first time. The choral music alone will take up fifteen CDs, but on the strength of the initial discs (performed by the Cardinall's Musick) this will be a series well worth investigating by those impressed by Byrd's unique blend of musical inventiveness and spiritual intensity.

SACRED MUSIC

Byrd was a prolific composer of church music, and of all the great masters of the sixteenth century only Lassus (see p.216) has a similar range. As well as the *Cantiones Sacrae* of 1575 he published two more collections with the same title in 1598 and 1591, and two sets of *Gradualia* (cycles of music for the Catholic liturgical year) in 1605 and 1607. These last two publications had Byrd's name printed on every page, even though, as Catholic works, they were illegal. In the first volume he wrote of the effect the scriptural texts had upon him: "I have found that there is such a power hidden away and stored up in those words that . . . all the most fitting melodies come as it were of themselves, and freely present themselves when the mind is alert and eager."

⊙ The Great Service and Anthems: Tallis Scholars; Phillips (Gimell 454 911-2).

The *Great Service* is Byrd's finest music for the Anglican Church and his most substantial work, being scored for a ten-part choir divided into two semi-choirs. Byrd uses the size of the choir not so much for volume or declamatory effects, but for a marvellously rich variety of vocal textures and sonorities, which are particularly evident in the *Te Deum*. This is measured and unruffled music, which particularly suits the Tallis Scholars, with their well-balanced voices and emotionally controlled sound.

⊙ The Three Masses: Tallis Scholars; Phillips (Gimell 454 945-2).

It is scarcely surprising that Byrd, a persecuted Catholic, should have produced such concentrated and intense settings of the Mass. Each of the *Three Masses* is written for a different voice combination – for three parts, four parts and five parts – but they share a similar clarity and directness, with the vigorous counterpoint never obscuring the audibility of the words. These works can take a more expressive approach than the Anglican music, and there are times when the Tallis Scholars seem a little too restrained, but the sheer beauty of their sound and the warm acoustic overcome any reservations.

INSTRUMENTAL MUSIC

Byrd is equally important as a composer of secular music – with the exception of lute music, there are surviving examples of virtually every musical form current during his lifetime. He revolutionized the writing of keyboard music, creating complex and inventive pieces which sound surprisingly modern. Mostly contained in two collections, *My Ladye Nevells Virginal Booke* and the *Fitzwilliam Virginal Book*, they include several sets of variations based on popular English airs, like *The Carman's Whistle* – a relatively banal tune which Byrd brilliantly transforms into ever more elaborate figurations.

⊙ Pieces from the Fitzwilliam Virginal Book: Duetschler (Claves CD 50-9001).

Ursula Duetschler plays a seventeenth-century Italian harpsichord which has a warm but assertive tone, well suited to the liveliness of this music. There's a vigorous, no-nonsense quality to these pieces: elaboration never overwhelms the overall shape, with the theme (or "ground") always remaining clear throughout its various transformations – as can be heard even in the two most ambitious pieces, *The Bells* (based on a three-note "peal" motif) and the long *Walsingham Variations*. Duetschler's strong and unfussy playing is well recorded in a spacious acoustic.

JOHN CAGE

(1912–1992)

Guru to some, charlatan to others, John Cage constantly challenged the very idea of music, using randomness as a basis for composition, doctoring instruments to produce new sonorities, and including the widest array of sounds in his works. He wanted to break down the barrier between art and life, "not to bring order out of chaos . . . but simply to wake up to the very life we're living". His most famous work, *4'33"* (1952), requires a pianist to lift the lid of a piano and then not play it for four minutes and thirty-three seconds – the point was to reveal to the audience the impossibility of total silence and to focus their attention on the wealth of sounds that surround them. This blurring of the conventional separation of real life and the concert hall reached its extreme in certain notorious performances in which Cage would sit on stage frying mushrooms – he was a notable expert on fungi, and in 1958 he won $6000 on an Italian TV quiz show answering questions on the subject.

In his twenties Cage studied with the composer Henry Cowell, who had already written pieces for piano in which the performer plucked and beat the strings directly. He also studied with Schoenberg, and their arguments about harmony (Cage thought it unimportant) led Schoenberg to say of him: "He's not a composer, he's an inventor – of genius." Cage's works of the 1930s, mainly for percussion, are based around numerically ordered rhythmic patterns, and are more akin to Eastern than Western music – another aspect of Cowell's influence. In 1938, developing Cowell's ideas, he started inserting objects like screws, wood or paper onto the strings of a piano in order to produce a wide range of percussive sounds. Much of his most expressive music was written for what Cage called the "prepared piano".

In the late 1940s Cage's attitude to music underwent a profound change as a result of his study of Zen Buddhism. In an attempt to rid his music of all vestiges of self-expression and intentionality he started to introduce chance as a guiding principle. In *Music of Changes* (1951) for solo piano, the performer decides what to play and how to play by tossing a coin – a method inspired by the Chinese book of divination, the *I Ching*. Most of his chance

BETTY FREEMAN/LEBRECHT COLLECTION

John Cage (right) with dancer/choreographer Merce Cunningham, at the Lincoln Center in 1978

works were written out, not in conventional notation, but as visually startling and often ambiguous graphic designs. As these became increasingly irrational and anarchic, Cage developed a cult following during the 1960s, though many fellow musicians, such as Pierre Boulez, believed that his emphasis on randomness was a conceptual blind alley. In the last twenty years of his life he returned to more organizational methods of composing.

THE MUSIC

Cage's major contribution to the music of the twentieth century is his "prepared piano", an instrument he invented out of necessity: unable to fit a percussion ensemble onstage to accompany a dance performance, he modified a piano to produce "a percussion ensemble controllable by one player". The potential of this construction is best shown in his *Sonatas and Interludes*, a cycle of pieces written between 1946 and 1948, in which he exploits a wide range of sonorities, some bright and bell-like, others more delicate and subdued. Rhythmic motifs and patterns recur, producing an incantatory and hypnotic quality close to that produced by the gamelan, the percussion orchestras of Java and Bali. Less well-known are Cage's works for the voice, but they are equally inventive in their treatment of the singer as an instrument of endless possibilities.

O Sonatas and Interludes for Prepared Piano: Fremy (Etcetera KTC 2001).

Gerard Fremy's CD is the best introduction to Cage's music – his sympathetic and sensitive playing sustains a hypnotic atmosphere of enraptured contemplation.

O Singing Through: Vocal Compositions by John Cage: La Barbara; Stein; Winant (New Albion NA 035 CD).

Joan La Barbara's selection features vocal music from right across Cage's career, ranging from the lyrical to the difficult and disturbing. *The Wonderful Widow of Eighteen Springs* (1942), Cage's most recorded song, matches the poetic words of James Joyce to a simple folk-like melody, mostly using just three notes over the restless scurrying of a drum. Rather more bizarre is the *Solo for Voice 52,* which employs a fragmentary text of vowels, consonants and words from five languages, all rendered at odd and unpredictable pitches.

JOSEPH CANTELOUBE

(1879–1957)

Around the beginning of the twentieth century, many European musicians began assiduously to explore and study their own indigenous musical traditions. Earlier composers, for instance Dvořák, had already tapped into folk music in order to stimulate their own work and to give it a nationalistic element, but this was something different. The new ethnomusicology aimed to make an accurate record of a vanishing world, either through annotation or through sound recordings. The best known of these researchers were Béla Bartók in eastern Europe, Ralph Vaughan Williams in England and Joseph Canteloube in France.

Canteloube was born at Annonay in the eastern part of the Auvergne, the ancient heart of France's Massif Central – a vast, isolated and proudly independent region. As a young man he studied music at the Schola Cantorum, a Paris music school (more progressive than the Conservatoire) that had been founded by Vincent D'Indy. It was D'Indy's teaching that encouraged Canteloube to continue his investigations into French folk music, an interest that had been kindled by childhood walks in the mountains and which was to become his life's work. Initially, he concentrated on the music of his own native region but he later produced collections of songs from all over France – in particular, the Languedoc and the Basque country.

As with Bartók and Vaughan Williams, Canteloube's fascination with folk song and rural life permeated his own music, including his operas – *Le Mas*, set in a Provençal farm, and *Vercingétorix*, about the Averni chieftain who resisted Julius Caesar's invasion of Gaul. Though both were performed at the Paris Opéra, they have long since disappeared from the repertoire, as has the rest of Canteloube's music with the sole exception of the ever popular *Chants d'Auvergne* (Songs of the Auvergne).

CHANTS D'AUVERGNE

The main body of Canteloube's folk-song collections were published in four volumes between 1923 and 1930, which include a wide range of songs, from poignant romances to boisterous dances. As a composer, Canteloube was decidedly unsympathetic towards the fashions of modernism and, controversially, he decided to arrange this simple peasant music with extremely luscious, and at times overwrought, orchestral accompaniment, full of glittering instrumental detailing that owes something to Debussy. The best-known song, *Baïlèro*, is a case in point. Canteloube purportedly heard it sung across the mountains between a shepherd and a shepherdess, but what you hear in the concert hall is a slow, languid melody, cushioned by a warm body of strings and embellished with an oboe line imitating a shepherd's pipe. Canteloube's aim was to evoke the missing element, the Auvergne landscape, through deft touches of orchestral colour, but the result bears no more relation to folk music than do Mahler's *Knaben Wunderhorn* settings. Dismissed as nostalgic kitsch by some critics, the great strength of these song settings is the way that the vocal line is always paramount and rarely swamped by the orchestral wash. Above all, like the contemporary *Bachianas brasileiras No. 5* of Villa-Lobos (see p.456), these songs have proved a wonderful vehicle for pure and incisive soprano singing.

O Upshaw; Orchestre de l'Opéra de Lyon; Nagano (Erato 4509-96559-2 & 0630-17577-2 [with Emmanuel's *Chansons Bourguignonnes*]).

These two discs contain the complete orchestrated *Chants d'Auvergne*. Some singers, in particular Kiri Te Kanawa on Decca, absolutely wallow in the heavy sensuousness of these songs; others attempt a lighter and more idiomatic approach. Dawn Upshaw is in the latter category: tone is full but never overwhelming and there is a pleasant readiness to her voice which sounds particularly appropriate. She is helped by some stunning orchestral playing, which really succeeds in creating the unobtrusive rustic ambience that Canteloube strived for.

◑ von Stade; Royal Philharmonic Orchestra; de Almeida (Sony 63063).

If you simply want a selection of these songs, then look no further. Frederica von Stade has a more obviously operatic voice than Dawn Upshaw and she dramatizes more with her voice, though without overdoing it. Again there is some exemplary orchestral playing – rich and colourful but never obtrusive.

GIACOMO CARISSIMI

(1605–1674)

The oratorio – the musical setting of a religious text in the form of a dramatic narrative – emerged as a distinct form at the same time as opera, at the end of the sixteenth century. Like opera, it employed solo singers, recitative, a chorus and instrumentalists, but unlike opera it usually employed a narrator and was rarely intended for staging. It developed in Rome, out of an initiative by Filippo Neri to provide a more accessible and emotionally direct form of worship for Catholics in the wake of the Reformation, and was performed at informal gatherings in which readings and a sermon were combined with the musical performance. The venue for these gatherings was not the church itself but a nearby hall called an oratory – hence the name of the new genre.

Giacomo Carissimi, a name now almost forgotten, was the leading oratorio composer of the mid-seventeenth century. Despite several prestigious job offers, including that of successor to Monteverdi at St Mark's in Venice, Carissimi spent almost his entire professional life as *maestro di cappella* at the powerful Jesuit centre, the Collegio Germanico. His numerous oratorios were not composed for the Collegio however, but for the upper-crust confraternity of the Most Holy Crucifix, who every Lent celebrated the miraculous survival of a crucifix from the fire that destroyed the church of San Marcello in Rome.

Carissimi's most celebrated work, *Jepthe*, so impressed Handel that he borrowed its final chorus for his own oratorio *Samson*, and has continued to be performed since it was written. The overt emotionalism of the music, largely conveyed through an aria-like style of recitative that gives a melodic tenderness to the rhythms of speech, makes it the most appealing of his compositions.

JEPTHE

The text of *Jepthe*, taken from the Book of Judges, tells of the dilemma of Jepthah (Jepthe in Italian): having promised to sacrifice the first person to greet him when he returns home, if God will grant him victory over the Ammonites, he is met by his beloved daughter. The story is short and intense, and contains striking contrasts of feeling, as when the daughter's joyous praises to God at her father's homecoming are followed by a touching and intimate dialogue between them as he explains her fate. Most famous of all is her final lament, an extended recitative which achieves its emotional impact largely through dissonances in the accompaniment. Even more beautiful is the ensuing grieving chorus, in which, according to a contemporary, "you would swear that you hear the sobs and moans of the weeping girls".

O Gabrieli Consort and Players; McCreesh (Meridian CDE 84132; with *Judicium Salomonis* and *Jonas*).

There is no shortage of recordings of *Jepthe*, but this one is the best currently available simply because it is the most heartfelt and the most dramatic. Contrasts of mood are pointed up by quite extreme changes of speed – the slowness of the final chorus, for instance, draws out the emotion ever more painfully. The decision to use a light accompaniment – no original details of the scoring have survived – also enhances the immediacy of the characters' predicament, with the lament merely using a marvellously resonant chittarone (a large lute) to offset the declamatory voice. Of the other two oratorios on this CD, *Jonas* (Jonah) is the more dramatically varied and contains one exceptional moment – a marvellously energetic evocation of a storm at sea sung by an eight-part chorus.

ELLIOTT CARTER

(1908–)

If Elliott Carter's music has never completely abandoned European models, it nevertheless belongs to the line of American pioneers whose achievements stress their distance from Europe. His music describes America. Above all, it is urban music, reflecting the density of life in great cities; music which, says the composer, attempts to "make sense of the mess". It may be tough and challenging music, but it is never difficult for difficulty's sake.

Carter came late to composition, despite early encouragement from Charles Ives (see p.203) who sold insurance to Carter's parents until they discovered his subversive influence. Instead Carter was sent to Harvard to study English and mathematics, but from 1930 he devoted himself to music, attending a course given by Gustav Holst at Harvard in 1932 before going to Paris to study with Nadia Boulanger, whose teachings benefited three generations of American composers, from Copland to Glass.

Returning to America, Carter began to compose works combining elements of Boulanger's neo-classicism (a style he later characterized, in the shadow of World War II, as a "masquerade in a bomb shelter") with a more American voice. His first major work was the *Piano Sonata* of 1946, a piece recognizably in the tradition of Ives and Copland, but with its own distinctive rhythmic elasticity: "like jazz improvisation, with the beat left out" is how Wilfrid Mellors has described it.

With the *Cello Sonata* of 1948, Carter's language became more original still, but, soon after its completion, dissatisfied, he retired to the solitude of the Arizona desert where, with no commission, he wrote his *String Quartet No. 1* (1951). Like all Carter's subsequent work, it owes much to cinematic and collage techniques in the way different musical lines move in and out of focus. When it won a quartet competition in Belgium, it established his international reputation. Encouraged, Carter launched a series of increasingly innovative works, the structures of which he likened to Mozart's operatic ensembles; but whereas Mozart's ensembles produce a unified texture, Carter's music stresses disunity, the irreconcilability of opposite forces, strikingly demonstrated in his *String Quartet No. 2* (1959).

During the 1960s, Carter wrote just three works, the *Double Concerto for Piano and Harpsichord* (1961), the *Piano Concerto* (1965) and the *Concerto for Orchestra* (1969). His quartet cycle continued in 1971 with his formidable *String Quartet No. 3*, which, with the *Symphony for Three Orchestras* (1976), marks the outer limits of his strenuous technical experiments; and in 1975 *A Mirror on Which to Dwell* became his first vocal work for almost thirty years. At the age of 70, Carter was mining a new vein of increasingly lyrical creativity still unexhausted two decades later. There have been three further quartets (the most recent premiered in 1995); concertos for oboe (1987), violin (1990) and clarinet (1997); and a constant stream of works both large and small. At the age of 89, he went so far as to undertake his first opera. It has been a remarkable Indian summer.

THE STRING QUARTETS

Complexes of simultaneous musical events constitute the most arresting and challenging feature of Carter's music. While one instrument may accelerate to vanishing point, another slows to immobility; an effusive lyricism may rest on complex metronomic pulses; as many as four independent musical streams can run in parallel. The approach is vividly exemplified in the Pulitzer prize-winning *String Quartet No. 2*, in which each individual instrument works with and against each of the others to produce a dazzlingly inventive rhythmic tapestry. A dozen years later, Carter's next quartet went one step further, dividing the instruments into two contrasting duos, each playing in different tempos: as the composer himself has said, "there are actually two separate pieces from beginning to end". The effect is less disorientating than might be expected: musical maximalism as opposed to minimalism. The *String Quartet No. 4* (1986) withdrew slightly from such complexity, and in so doing perhaps lost some of the composer's individuality.

O Juilliard String Quartet (Sony S2K 47229; 2 CDs; with *Duo*).

The Juilliard premiered the second and third quartets, and the composer himself supervised the recordings, so this set has a unique and palpable authority. The playing sometimes displays a hard edge, but there are many moments of compensating lyricism. The *Duo*, for piano and violin, dates from 1974. Carter compares its opening with a climber's attempt on the Alps, which gives fair warning of the effort and exhilaration it produces in equal measure.

THE CONCERTO FOR ORCHESTRA

One of only three works Carter completed in the 1960s, the *Concerto for Orchestra* was to have the same resounding effect on a generation of composers that Stravinsky's *The Rite of Spring* had fifty years previously. Like *The Rite* it's a work with the titanic impetuosity of a thunderstorm, unleashing elemental forces to devastating effect. After he'd started composing the piece, Carter came across St John Perse's poem *Vents*, with its evocation of mighty winds destroying and then renewing America. This provided a metaphorical focus for the musical drama of a world in which nothing is stable, everything is in a process of constant transformation, until the material of the entire concerto is swept up into the last movement before finally disintegrating into the silence from which it emerged.

O London Sinfonietta; Knussen (Virgin VC 7 91503-2; with *Three Occasions for Orchestra, Violin Concerto*).

There are few conductors whose authority in Carter's music matches that of Oliver Knussen. Carter, who also supervised these sessions, clearly trusts him implicitly. With an ensemble as proficient and committed as the London Sinfonietta, the work gains a transparency that makes its progress inexorable, yet still mysterious. The *Violin Concerto*, here performed by Ole Bohn, who gave its premiere, is one of the most strikingly lyrical of Carter's recent works.

THE CELLO SONATA

Premiered in 1948, the *Cello Sonata* marked a decisive breakthrough for Carter, combining an improvisatory, almost jazzy flexibility, with a rhythmic discipline that was to become the foundation of his music of the following half-century. Carter explores the contrasting personalities of the cello and piano: the first effusively emotional (representing psychological time), the second percussive and admonitory (representing chronometric time). The result is a complex character drama that readily draws the listener in.

O The Group for Contemporary Music (Bridge BCD 9044; with other chamber pieces).

The Group for Contemporary Music was formed in 1962 by Charles Wuorinen, himself a composer of note, who here takes the piano part in the sonata. He and Fred Sherry project the music in a direct, confrontational manner that is wholly persuasive. The works here span a period of 45 years, and include the *Duo* (1993) for violin and piano, another major piece.

EMMANUEL CHABRIER

(1841–1894)

Emmanuel Chabrier was an early collector of Manet and the Impressionists, and like them he made a break with the methods of his immediate predecessors, albeit in a more limited way. In his first significant instrumental work, *Dix pièces pittoresques* (1881), he rejected virtuosity and academicism to produce ten atmospheric piano miniatures of great expressive freedom in which frequently blurred tonality and richly hued harmonies seem to point the way to Debussy. His celebrated *Rhapsody España*, written two years later, is an equally vivid orchestral evocation of Spain (a country he adored), full of flashing colours, whirling skirts and stamping feet.

For the first 39 years of his life, Chabrier's music-making was that of the gifted amateur. As a child his prodigious talent had always been nurtured but his bourgeois father insisted on a broad education, hoping that Emmanuel would follow his own profession – the law. In 1856 the family moved from their home town of Ambert in the Auvergne to Paris, and five years later Emmanuel began work at the Ministry of the Interior. The move to Paris at least brought him into the orbit of successful artists – writers and painters as much as musicians. He was particularly close to the poet Verlaine, whose words he set, and to the painter Manet, who painted his portrait at least twice and who died in Chabrier's arms in 1883. Chabrier's friends admired him for his skill at the piano and loved him for his sense of humour: the composer D'Indy used to call him "the angel of drollery". This potential for comedy led to two operettas: in *L'Étoile* (1877) an overcomplicated and pedestrian plot is set to sparkling and witty music, while the risqué *L'Éducation manquée* (1879) is similarly marred by a vapid spoken text which limited it to just one performance.

The turning point for Chabrier's musical career – and, in one sense, a false step – came in 1879 when he absented himself from the ministry in order to attend a performance of Wagner's *Tristan und Isolde* in Munich. Overwhelmed by the experience, Chabrier quit his job the following year in order to pursue composition full time. The very un-Wagnerian *España* made him an overnight success but it was as an opera composer that he wished to succeed. In *Gwendoline* (1886) he wears his enthusiasm for *Tristan* on his sleeve but it failed to endear him to French audiences. More successful was the comic opera *Le roi malgré lui* (1887), a complex plot redeemed by inventive melodies and unconventional harmony.

Chabrier's final years were painful ones. Racked by depression and terrible headaches (probably brought on by syphilis), composition became more and more difficult for him, and his last work, a Wagnerian lyric drama called *Briséïs*, remained uncompleted at his death.

ORCHESTRAL MUSIC

When Chabrier visited Spain in 1882, he seems to have been equally impressed by the shapeliness of Spanish women as he was by the dance rhythms which he jotted down in his notebook. The result was *España*, an exuberant musical homage which Poulenc, in his short book on Chabrier, saw as "a portrait of Spanish music by a brilliant apprentice" – though several Spanish musicians have dismissed it as a lurid tourist's view of their country. For most listeners it's the sheer energy of the work which sweeps them away, a quality equally in evidence in the driving urgency of the *Gwendoline Overture*, the only part of the opera regularly heard in the concert hall. In fact, Chabrier's orchestral output is disappointingly small. The most popular work after *España* is the *Suite pastorale*, an orchestration of four of the *Pièces pittoresques* which conjures up the sultry and sensuous warmth of a Monet landscape.

⊙ Bourée Fantasque; España; Gwendoline Overture; Suite pastorale: Detroit Symphony Orchestra; Paray (Mercury 434 303-2; with Roussel's *Suite*).

This is one of the best of the Mercury label's legendary recordings from the 1960s. Paul Paray was a scintillating interpreter of French repertoire, extremely sensitive to nuance but quite able to pull out all the stops when needed, as in his hard-driven rendition of the *Gwendoline Overture*. The sound has weathered extremely well and, despite strong competition, this is a clear first choice for *España*.

⊙ Suite pastorale; España: Ulster Orchestra; Tortelier (Chandos 8852; with Dukas' *La Péri* and *L'Apprenti Sorcier*).

Tortelier is marginally less successful with Chabrier than with Dukas on this disc: tone colour and instrumental detail is emphasized, sometimes at the expense of shape and momentum (especially in the *Suite pastorale*) but these are still first-rate accounts.

DIX PIÈCES PITTORESQUES

Chabrier was a brilliant and fiery pianist, who frequently broke the piano strings in his enthusiasm. His piano music rarely reflects this aggressive side but, like his orchestral music, it does express an underlying concern with colour and sonority. *Dix pièces pittoresques* was the breakthrough work – Poulenc thought these pieces "as important for French music as Debussy's *Préludes*". In their ability to pin down a mood or an image, they recall Schumann's more poetic miniatures, like *Kinderszenen*, but with an added humour. The most famous of the set is the exquisite *Idylle*, a lyrical, bittersweet melody given an added urgency by the regular staccato pulse in the left hand. Almost as beautiful is *Sous-bois* (much loved by Ravel), another piece which contrasts a rather dark left-hand presence with a sweet, almost throw-away, nursery tune in the right-hand. The piano-breaking side of Chabrier can be heard in *Tourbillon*, "a typical salon galop" in Poulenc's words, which lets rip some rapid passage work with a characteristically Chabrieresque mixture of delicacy and bravado.

⊙ Dix pièces pittoresques and other piano works: Planès (Harmonia Mundi HMC 901465; with Ravel's *A la manière de Chabrier*).

Alain Planès is an exceptional French pianist but remains largely unknown outside his native France. His repertoire is extremely broad and he brings to everything he plays a probing intelligence and sensitive touch. In Chabrier this means taking the music seriously without being over-serious. There is a wealth of poetic detail in his playing which brings out the melancholy undertow in a piece like *Idylle*.

MARC-ANTOINE CHARPENTIER

(1643–1704)

Neglected for centuries, Charpentier has recently emerged as one of the greatest French composers of sacred music in the seventeenth century, arguably superior to his more successful contemporary, Lully (see p.227). His music shows more diversity than Lully's, ranging – often within the same work – from the stately to the intimate. The key to this achievement was his adoption of a style, based on the new Italian concerto, which employed dramatically telling contrasts between different groupings of voices throughout a work. Moreover, Charpentier softened the predominantly formal and grandiose style of French music, introducing a more Italianate sensuousness and a greater sensitivity to word-setting.

Little is certain about Charpentier's early life. He was born in Paris, and is known to have been in Rome in the mid-1660s, where he studied with the leading oratorio composer Carissimi (see p.99). Back in Paris he served a series of aristocratic patrons, beginning with the Duchess of Guise, noted for her piety and for the excellence of her musical establishment, which Charpentier directed and sang in as a countertenor. He succeeded Lully as the playwright Molière's collaborator, writing the music for his last play, *Le Malade Imaginaire*, in 1673. In the 1680s he was on the fringes of the court, serving the Dauphin as music director and acting as teacher to the Duke of Chartres, but illness intervened when he seemed close to an appointment at the Royal Chapel. It was also in the 1680s that Charpentier gained the position of composer and *maître de musique* of the principal Jesuit church of St Paul, a position he held until 1698, when he moved to the even more prestigious post of *maître de musique* at Sainte-Chapelle du Palais. He wrote just one full-length opera, *Medée* (1693), but the taste for Lully was strong enough to eclipse all rivals, even after his death, and Charpentier's work ran for only ten performances.

SACRED MUSIC

The most striking aspects of Charpentier's choral music are the refined elegance of the melodies, and its rich and expressive harmonies. Though religious sobriety characterizes the overall tone, this is lush music, with subtle underlining of key moments in the text, and marked contrasts between succeeding episodes. Even a large-scale, celebratory work like the D major *Te Deum*, written for the church of St Paul, is broken up into distinct sections with clearly distinguished moods – thus it begins with kettle-drums and trumpets, but contains moments of quiet devotional intensity, like the soprano solo to the words "Te ergo quaesumus" (Therefore we beseech thee). Similarly in the greatest of his Masses, the *Missa Assumpta est Maria*, the prevailing mood is sombre but there are subtle shifts of emphasis achieved by various combinations of the eight soloists.

⊙ Te Deum; Missa Assumpta est Maria; Litanie de la Vierge: Les Arts Florissants; Christie (Harmonia Mundi HMC 901298).

Christie is a Charpentier specialist, and it would be hard to find a better way of getting to know this great composer than through this CD. The balancing and control is exemplary, with the switches from full chorus to small vocal groupings never sounding abrupt. There are many outstanding moments: in the *Te Deum* the magnificently triumphant orchestral prelude and refulgent opening chorus both stand out; in the Mass, an even more beautiful work, the sprightly Sanctus, is followed by a meltingly tender setting of the *Agnus Dei*.

FRÉDÉRIC CHOPIN

(1810–1849)

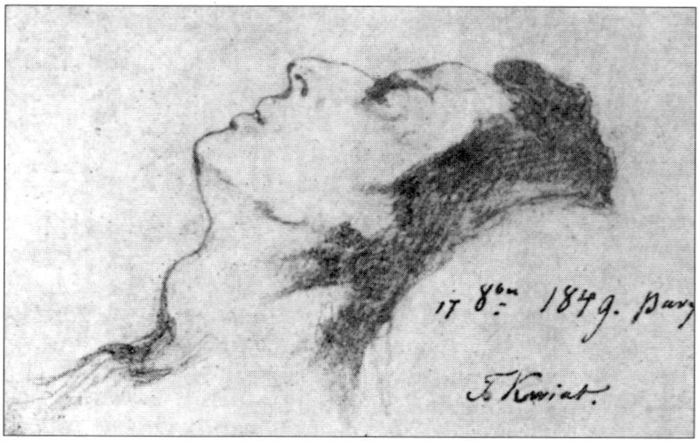

LEBRECHT COLLECTION

Chopin on his deathbed

Frédéric (or Fryderyk) Chopin, the only son of a French father and a Polish mother, was born near Warsaw, and his Polishness always remained immensely important to him, even though most of the latter half of his life was spent in Paris. The music of Poland permeates his compositions, which were written almost exclusively for the piano, an instrument that by then had become the supreme means of Romantic self-expression. But, whereas his great contemporary Liszt used the piano to create heroic self-portraits and vast panoramas, Chopin was an introvert and a miniaturist, infusing conventional forms such as the sonata and the prelude with an intimacy and an emotional intensity which the poet Heine described as the "poetry of feeling".

Chopin was essentially an experimental composer, exploiting the potential of the recent developments in piano construction, like the increase of their range to a full seven octaves and the use of heavily felted hammers which could produce a more refined tone. But although his works are often extremely difficult to play they are rarely – unlike much of Liszt – virtuosic for virtuosity's sake. Another feature that crucially distinguishes Chopin from Liszt, Schumann and most Romantic composers is that he did not write music that carried literary, pictorial or biographical significance – his works are to be understood in purely musical terms. Not that this has stopped people from finding non-musical meanings in his music. And in fact the concentrated and volatile nature of his imagination does invite such speculation. Though Chopin found the process of composition extremely arduous, his solo pieces in particular often sound like spontaneous improvisations that have been forced from the unconscious by overwhelming emotion.

When Chopin arrived in Paris in 1831 he was simply one virtuoso pianist among many. His concert debut early the next year was on a bill which included Kalkbrenner, the most celebrated pianist of the day – who had earlier rather patronizingly offered to give Chopin lessons. Chopin, playing his F minor piano concerto and *Mozart Variations*, was a huge success. Liszt and Mendelssohn were present, and both were greatly impressed by him, despite their own utterly different styles. Chopin's playing was particularly admired for the variety of his touch, and for the singing quality (or cantabile) of his right hand – though later critics were to suggest that many of Chopin's piano works relegated the left hand to a merely accompanying role. He also employed a distinctive interpretative device called rubato (literally "robbed"), whereby rhythm, instead of being applied in strict time, was expressively distorted by shortening some notes and lengthening others, an effect likened by Liszt to the movement of a tree's leaves in the breeze.

However, neither physically nor temperamentally was he suited for a career as a virtuoso, and he only performed on a mere thirty occasions, many of which were private recitals in the salons of the aristocracy.

The dominant influence of Chopin's adult life was the free-thinking novelist Aurore Dudevant, better known as George Sand. Their affair began in the summer of 1838 and they spent the winter of the same year together in Majorca, where, because of Chopin's tuberculosis, they were made to occupy a deserted monastery – a situation that considerably worsened his condition. Back in Paris they lived in nearby apartments and spent each summer at Sand's country house at Nohant, where many of Chopin's greatest works were composed. Their relationship was turbulent, and Sand became increasingly irritated by what she saw as his excessive demands on her affections. In 1847 they finally separated, and Chopin composed very little after that date. After undergoing a purgatorial concert tour of Britain in 1848, he finally succumbed in October of the following year to the tuberculosis which had dogged him for most of his life.

THE PIANO CONCERTOS

Of the several works for piano and orchestra that Chopin wrote, the two concertos are the most significant. Both were written shortly before Chopin finally left Poland, and both show the influence of Hummel and the Irish composer Field in their emphasis on long unbroken lines in the right hand – especially in the two highly poetic slow movements. The orchestra's role is strictly subordinate (for which Chopin has been criticized), either simply accompanying the piano, or providing long introductions that create a sense of expectation before the piano's entrance.

◑ **Vasary; Berlin Philharmonic; Semkow, Kulka** (Deutsche Grammophon 429 515-2).

One of the most poetic of modern recordings is the one made by Tamas Vasary in the mid-1960s. Vasary's playing is understated but his crystalline touch brings out the slightly rarified refinement of the concertos.

○ **Hofmann** (VAI A1002).

Josef Hofmann was one of the supreme interpreters of these works. He possessed an extraordinary touch – delicate and strong at the same time – and used a rubato so spontaneous and unsentimental that it sounds as if he is making the music up as he goes along. These radio performances date from the 1930s (the orchestra is unknown), and the sound is necessarily quite rough, but the intensity of the playing still shines through.

THE PIANO SONATAS

Structure and thematic development have long been held up as the weak areas of Chopin's work, particularly in longer pieces such as the three piano sonatas. One contemporary critic went so far as to dismiss the third sonata because " . . . the entire work is not a consequence of the first idea". But these are Romantic sonatas that should not be straitjacketed by the rigours of sonata form. The best of them, the second in B flat minor (1839) and the third in B minor (1844), are tumultuous displays of sustained energy: the second fast and furious (apart from its famous funeral march), the third more epic in scope and more lyrical, and with a huge sweep of shifting moods and ideas.

◑ **Piano Sonatas Nos. 2 & 3: Argerich** (Deutsche Grammophon 419 055-2).

Marta Argerich is one of the great Chopin interpreters of the last thirty years, famed for the daring and power of her performances. Her playing always stresses the restlessness of Chopin's imagination, nowhere more dramatically than in these two sonatas. The second seems to go at a breakneck pace (even the funeral march is faster than usual), but with a sense of urgency rather than rush; the third has a nobility and grandeur which is largely generated by her brilliant range and control of dynamics.

○ **Piano Sonata No. 3: Kissin** (RCA 09026 62542-2; with twelve *Mazurkas*).

This live performance from a 23-year-old Evgeny Kissin is outstanding for its authority and depth of imagination. It's a less tumultuous reading than Argerich's, but no less passionate and with a greater breadth of conception.

THE PRÉLUDES

The 24 *Préludes* (Op. 2) were written on the island of Majorca during the winter of 1838. They have been

compared to the similarly concise preludes of Bach's *Well-Tempered Clavier*, which work through every major and minor key in the same way. The comparison is reasonable enough, as Chopin took a copy of that score with him to Majorca, but whereas each of the Bach preludes prepares the way for a fugue, there is nothing remotely introductory about Chopin's. These are highly concentrated poetic miniatures, and the most atmospheric works he ever wrote. George Sand's account of their stay at the old monastery tells of Chopin's "morbid anxiety created by his own imagination"; her version of events might be slightly romanticized, but the *Préludes* certainly fluctuate wildly between euphoria and despair.

◑ **26 Préludes: Argerich** (Deutsche Grammophon DG 415 836-2; with *Barcarolle, Polonaise in A Flat Major, Scherzo No. 2*).

This is the most celebrated of all Argerich's recordings, and deservedly so – every note sounds fresh and alive, as if conceived at the moment of its playing. Her richly varied touch perfectly matches the mood of each piece: the restrained melancholy of *No. 6*, the delicate capriciousness of *No. 11*, the passionate drive of *No. 24* – all are conjured with a marvellous sense of elation. The CD also includes two posthumous *Préludes*, a wonderfully warm performance of the *Barcarolle* and scintillating accounts of the sixth *Polonaise* and the second *Scherzo*.

O 24 Préludes: Pires (Deutsche Grammophon 437 817-2; with *Piano Concerto No. 2*).

Not as quite as dazzling as Argerich, but just as effective. Pires is a pianist, like Perahia, whose playing has amazing grace and poise. Her sense of line in the more lyrical *préludes* is particularly beguiling.

THE ÉTUDES

Piano studies were something of a growth industry in the early nineteenth century – practically every virtuoso, from Clementi to Kalkbrenner, was prepared to impart the method behind his prowess via a book of études or studies. Chopin's two collections of twelve études, Op. 10 and Op. 25, are something rather different, however. Although individual pieces are concerned with conventional technical problems, Chopin transforms them into music of real depth and feeling, while at the same time exploring the boundaries of the technically possible and the harmonically acceptable.

O Études Op. 10 & Op. 25: Pollini (Deutsche Grammophon DG 413 794-2).

Like Argerich, Pollini is a former winner of Warsaw's Chopin Piano Competition, but his approach to the composer could hardly be more different. Where she is all quicksilver and passion, he is calm and precise, though not as glacial as some critics have suggested. In the *Études* his more measured style and near-flawless technique produce brilliant results. The abundant rapid cascades of notes, as in the eleventh étude from Op. 25, are managed with an almost imperious ease, but in the quieter and warmer moments, like the gently wistful third from Op. 1, he is no less convincing.

THE POLONAISES

The polonaise is a Polish national dance of a rather stiff and stately nature, written in triple time – it had much the same status in Polish culture as the waltz did in the Austro-Hungarian empire. Chopin's polonaises, as one might expect, greatly transcend the formal restraints of the genre, which in his hands becomes a vehicle for his impassioned feelings about his native land – a land that in his lifetime was partitioned between the great powers of Europe, then invaded by Russia. There is a bold and defiant character to these pieces even when, as in the *C Minor Polonaise*, they are shot through with a melancholy anxiety.

◑ **Polonaises; Polonaise-Fantasie: Pollini** (Deutsche Grammophon 457 711-2).

Chopin wrote a total of sixteen polonaises, of which only the seven later ones are regularly performed. They are all on this CD, along with the *Polonaise-Fantasie*, a remarkable piece that commences with one of Chopin's most arresting ideas then continues into what sounds like an extended improvisation. Again Pollini's unshowy strength makes these accounts utterly compelling. His articulation of the polonaise's martial rhythms is superbly crisp and arrogant, an effect assisted by the way Pollini builds slowly to the climax of each big tune without ever quite reaching it, enabling the tune to retain all its vigour each time it returns. This works as effectively in the sombre *C Minor Polonaise* as it does in the so-called "Heroic" Polonaise, a piece that shows Chopin at his most fiery. Pollini's *Polonaises* are also available in a mid-price box of three CDs, with his recordings of the *Études* (see above) and the *Preludes*.

THE MAZURKAS

The mazurka is another Polish dance form in triple time, but with a dotted rhythm that makes it resemble a kind of lurching waltz; it was usually danced slightly faster than the polonaise but not as fast as the waltz. Chopin clearly did not intend his mazurkas to be danced to, but rather to evoke a more elusive, bitter-sweet image of Poland than was projected by the more forthright *Polonaises*. The moods of the *Mazurkas* are more varied than the *Polonaises*, ranging from the sparklingly energetic first mazurka of Op. 7 to the quiet despair of the fourth from Op. 17.

◉ Complete Mazurkas: Rubinstein (RCA RD 5171; 2 CDs).

Artur Rubinstein is another really great Chopin interpreter, who by his direct and unfussy performances did much to dispel the image of the composer as a sentimental light-weight. The *Mazurkas* reveal him at his best, with a light and subtle touch, completely attuned to the music's quiet charm and the quirky ebb and flow of its rhythms.

◉ Mazurkas 13, 17, 20, 23, 32, 34–41, 49: Kissin (RCA 09026 62542-2; with *Piano Sonata No. 3*).

Breathtaking playing from the prodigy of the 1990s. Evgeny Kissin plays a selection of twelve *Mazurkas* and presents them with a seemingly effortless ease of expression. Not since Rubinstein have they sounded so simple and so profound.

THE WALTZES

The craze for waltzes began in the late eighteenth century and by Chopin's time was in full stride. Though he began writing them himself when he was just 16, a trip to Vienna in 1830 left him markedly unimpressed by the popular waltzes of Lanner and the older Johann Strauss. A greater influence was Weber's *Invitation to the Dance*: a brilliant and sophisticated showpiece that had enjoyed huge popularity since its appearance in 1819. Chopin's *Waltzes* are a similarly personal response to the dance form, an imaginative evocation of the gaiety and abandon, and sometimes the sadness, of the ballroom.

◑ 14 Valses: Lipatti (EMI C 769 802-2; with *Barcarolle, Nocturne Op. 27 No. 2, Mazurka Op. 50 No. 3*).

Dinu Lipatti recorded fourteen of the *Waltzes* in 1950, the year he died aged only 33, and the recording has remained a benchmark for this music ever since. His delicacy of touch and elegance of conception were matchless: the shimmering passage work and his unforced rubato effortlessly convey the music's evanescent brilliance. The mono sound is a little bit boxy, but more than acceptable.

◉ Waltzes: Ohlsson (Arabesque Z6669; with *Waltz in F Sharp Minor*).

Garrick Ohlsson won the Chopin Prize in 1970 and, like Argerich and Pollini, has become something of a Chopin specialist. This disc, part of a Chopin series for Arabesque, doesn't have the vibrancy of Lipatti (no-one on disc does) but it's brilliant playing that sparkles with life.

THE NOCTURNES

John Field invented the piano nocturne as a lyrical and dreamy short piece (not necessarily indicative of night-time), in which an expressive melody in the right hand was gently supported by broken chords in the left hand. Their singing quality was partly derived from the bel canto arias of Bellini's operas. Field's charming but essentially languorous creation was transformed and extended by Chopin into something with a greater emotional range, though a sense of wistfulness generally prevails. These are the pieces that established Chopin's reputation in the aristocratic salons of Paris, and their absolute simplicity and directness of expression has made them the most popular of all his works.

◉ Rubinstein (RCA D 89563; 2 CDs).

The gentle lyricism of the *Nocturnes* is perfectly suited to Rubinstein's unassertive style and limpid tone. But his readings stand out, above all, for the way the long, meandering right-hand phrases, with their finely spun ornamentation, are delicately shaped through subtle shifts of emphasis that bring out every nuance.

◉ Pires (Deutsche Grammophon D 89563; 2 CDs).

Amazingly delicate readings from Maria João Pires, who builds up each nocturne slowly, shaping them with the most subtlely modified of inflections. Of recent recordings, this is definitely the one to go for.

THE SCHERZI

A scherzo was originally a light-hearted piece which had taken over from the minuet and trio as a short animated movement within a symphony or sonata. Beethoven developed it into an even livelier component of a large-scale composition, but in Chopin's hands the form achieved complete independence and, while Chopin retained the mercurial nature of the scherzo, he almost emptied it of any humour. Like the *Ballades* (see p.108), the *Scherzi* are extended pianistic tone poems, into which Chopin pours some of his most tempestuous writing.

◉ Richter (Olympia OC 338; with Schumann, *Bunte Blätter*).

Sviatoslav Richter plays these pieces like a man inspired, with such presence and seriousness that every moment sounds as though it has been carefully weighed up. Yet there's no sense of calculation or strain, and it would be hard to find playing of greater immediacy. High points include his handling, in *Scherzo No. 1*, of the transition from its frantic opening to the lullaby of its middle section, which is played with a rapt tenderness.

◐ Pollini (Deutsche Grammophon 431 623-2; with *Barcarolle* and *Berceuse*).

Pollini, in the four *Scherzi*, is no less convincing than Richter. He's so much in command technically that he can bring an added dimension and a drama to these pieces without needing to posture.

THE BALLADES

The four *Ballades* are among Chopin's most extraordinary and powerful works, abounding in quite startlingly dramatic contrasts, with moments of lyric tenderness being followed by passages of tumultuous energy. The narrative implications of the name "ballade" (here applied to music for the first time) have led many commentators to link these pieces with the longer poems of Chopin's Polish contemporary Adam Mickiewicz, several of whose works Chopin set to music as songs. However, though the poems and the music share a certain volatile and episodic quality, there is no evidence that the composer had any specific programme in mind when writing the *Ballades*.

◐ Perahia (Sony SK 64399; with other Chopin pieces).

This is the best of recent recordings of these pieces. Murray Perahia is a superbly poised and elegant pianist whose tone always sounds perfectly measured and weighted, and yet there is a magical flow to his playing – each *Ballade* unfolds with the most eloquent and unruffled grace.

THE SONATA FOR CELLO AND PIANO

Of the little chamber music that Chopin wrote, the outstanding item is the grave and autumnal *Sonata for Cello and Piano in G Minor*, his last composition of any importance. He had written for the cello before, but the inspiration behind the sonata was his friendship and admiration for the cellist Auguste Franchomme, who helped him with the technical aspects of the work and to whom it is dedicated.

◑ Argerich, Rostropovich (Deutsche Grammophon DG 419 860-2; with *Polonaise brilliante* and Schumann's *Adagio and Allegro for Cello and Piano*).

Chopin's sonata for cello and piano stresses the differences between the two instruments – the piano part full of agitated passage work, the cello calmer, with longer and more subdued phrases. This is a near-perfect pairing of musicians, with Argerich's passion tempered by the insinuating warmth of Rostropovich's tone. Even the rather rambling first movement sounds compelling, but most moving is the third movement, which contains one of Chopin's most poignantly elegiac melodies.

MUZIO CLEMENTI

(1752–1832)

If it were not for the affection with which Vladimir Horowitz regarded his music, Muzio Clementi's prolific contribution to piano literature would by now have faded to the edge of oblivion. As it is, he's known more as a pianist, scholar, theorist, teacher, piano manufacturer, and as Beethoven's friend and publisher, than as a composer. However, as a child Clementi was paraded as a prodigy of Mozartian abilities, and for most of his eighty years he was one of the most famous and highly respected musicans in Europe.

Italian born, Clementi was entrusted by his father to the care of Peter Beckford MP, and in 1767 the 15-year-old was moved to England, where he made his home, with Beckford, in Dorset. In 1774 he was freed of his obligations to his mentor and went to London where, from 1777, he conducted Italian opera. Four years later he began to tour Europe, engaging with rival pianists in public battles of improvisation and sight-reading. Mozart, who was one of his opponents, was not impressed: "He has great facility with his right hand, his star passages are thirds. Apart from this, he has not a farthing's worth of taste or feeling; he is a mere *mechanicus*." In 1810 he made a semi-permanent return to London, where he settled down to composing symphonies, concertos, piano sonatas and the famous *Gradus ad Parnassum*, a series of one hundred keyboard studies which remains a foundation of piano technique. Among his pupils were Hummel (briefly) and the Irishman John Field (the inventor of the nocturne) who toured Europe demonstrating his master's pianos.

After 1810 Clementi made sporadic trips into Europe – two of them extended – with the intention of impressing his symphonic music upon audiences in Paris and Leipzig. These efforts were mostly wasted, for by 1824 his music had all but disappeared from concert programmes, due principally to the increasing fame and popularity of Beethoven's work. Some time after 1830 Clementi retired from professional life and moved to Lichfield and, soon after, to Evesham. Such was his reputation that his funeral was held at Westminster Abbey, and so many people turned up that mourners were obliged to stand; Clementi was then buried in the abbey cloisters, where his tombstone describes him as "The Father of the Pianoforte".

THE PIANO SONATAS

Clementi composed over one hundred piano sonatas, and their influence is hard to overestimate – many of them were highly regarded by Beethoven, for example, and by John Field. The early sonatas are little more than homages to Domenico Scarlatti, but between the Op. 10 and Op. 14 sonatas a distinctive Clementi style comes to the fore. Rejecting the conventional Italianate two-movement form, these sonatas inaugurated the three-movement structure, and in their use of thematic development and generally more abrasive melodic style they anticipated Beethoven's keyboard writing. However, Clementi's music has none of Beethoven's heroics or purposeful self-scrutiny – it's predominantly light in nature, and most of the sonatas up to the end of the century have the feel of harpsichord pieces. Come the advent of the full-grown piano, his style had advanced harmonically to such an extent that some of his late music foreshadows the early work of Field and Chopin. If Clementi never fulfilled the promise of his youth, he nonetheless developed a solid personal style that is instantly recognizable and immediately charming.

◑ **Piano Sonatas Op. 33 No. 3; Op. 34 No. 2; Op. 14 No. 3; Op. 26 No. 2; Op. 47 No. 2: Horowitz** (RCA GD87753).

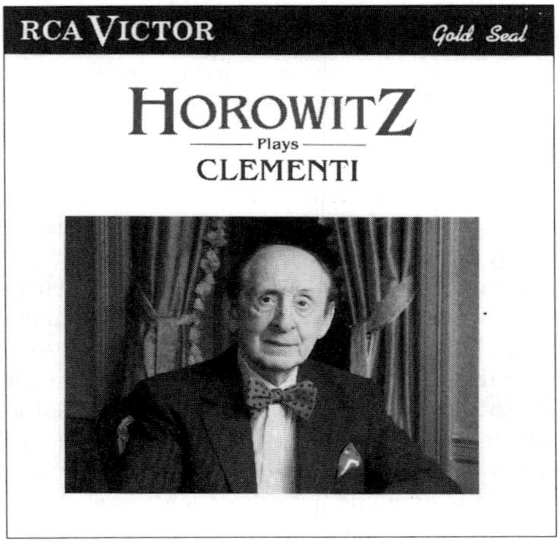

Horowitz's interest in Clementi ensured that his name lived outside the rarefied world of musicology, but there's only one Horowitz CD entirely devoted to Clementi's sonatas. One of his principal reasons for playing them was that they offered scope for personal expression, and Horowitz's interpretations sometimes take liberties. But even if these performances have as much to do with Horowitz as with Clementi, that is all part of their appeal – these are delightful displays of two prodigious musical imaginations at work.

○ **Piano Sonatas Op. 24 No. 2; Op. 25 No. 5; Op. 4 Nos. 2 & 3: Demidenko** (Hyperion CDA 66808).

Demidenko is a more circumspect performer than Horowitz, but still one with an abundance of personality. Though he uses a modern piano, his approach to Clementi is restrained and sensitive – there is little fortissimo playing on this disc. Instead of drama he employs a very refined variety of touch and, when required, some wonderfully clear and quiet playing. It doesn't disguise the fact that Clementi is a derivative composer but it does persuade you that he's a good one.

AARON COPLAND

(1900–1990)

Aaron Copland is best known for his morale-boosting ballets and patriotic pieces of the 1930s and 1940s, and these are certainly among the most remarkable compositions of their time, particularly when you bear in mind that their cowboy hoedowns and jigs were written by a sassy New Yorker of Russian-Jewish background. It would be wrong, however, to view scores like *Billy the Kid*, *Rodeo* and *Appalachian Spring* in isolation. Masterpieces though they undoubtedly are, they are only one side of the work of a highly inquisitive and analytical artist who was always on the lookout for a new challenge.

The seeds of Copland's remarkable independence were sown way back in his student years, a period when American music was squarely provincial. To show just how entrenched things then were, Copland was fond of telling how Rubin Goldmark, his highly conservative music teacher, once caught him looking at the score of Ives' *Concord Sonata* and warned him not to contaminate himself with such things. It is lucky for posterity that he followed the advice of a friend, gathered together his hard-earned savings, and headed for Paris, the haven of every artistic revolutionary from Joyce to Hemingway and Picasso to Stravinsky.

When Copland arrived he set about enrolling at the New School for Americans at Fontainebleau, where he was taught by Nadia Boulanger, the remarkable woman who coached an entire generation of budding American composers between the wars. The four years with Boulanger (1921–25) were the most important musical experience of his life: she opened him up to a huge variety of musical influences and taught him all about the virtues of clarity and restraint, as well as giving him a solid technical grounding and a thorough knowledge of orchestration. Stravinsky's neo-classicism made a particularly strong impact on him, as did the music of Les Six and the exciting new sound of jazz then sweeping Europe. Copland never looked back. On returning to New York in 1925 he resolved to be as distinctively American-sounding as Mussorgsky and Stravinsky were Russian, and now, thanks to Boulanger, he had the courage and the technical means to achieve his ambitions.

In a long and fruitful career Copland went through no fewer than four highly distinct phases: an exuberant jazzy first phase from 1925 to 1929 (as typified by *Music for the Theatre* and the *Piano Concerto*); a severe avant-garde period from 1930 to 1936 (eg the *Piano Variations*); the hugely popular "Americana" phase of 1936–49; and a final return to difficult serial territory (eg the *Piano Fantasy* and *Inscape*). Yet despite these abrupt stylistic shifts there is a distinctive Copland sound, a sound largely determined by his brilliant abilities as an orchestrator. The American composer Virgil Thomson described Copland's orchestration as "plain, clean-coloured, deeply imaginative . . . theatrically functional", and its transparency is the key factor – even in the midst of the busiest textures everything is lucid and opaque. Boulanger had taught him the knack of "keeping instruments out of each other's way", a skill to which he allied a knack of making each part of the orchestra carry its own "expressive idea", bringing a specific emotional connotation to the unfolding drama of a piece.

Copland was also a master of rhythm. The nervous energy of his orchestral music relies heavily on dance and march rhythms, spiced with the displaced accents of jazz, but at the other end of the spectrum he could achieve very complex trance-like effects, as in the slow finale of the *Piano Sonata*. His harmonies were no less expressive and elegant. Time and again Copland found new contexts for conventional intervals and familiar chords, dropping them unexpectedly into very dissonant passages, making them sound fresh and new.

THE BALLETS

The spaciousness of Copland's musical textures has often been compared to America's open landscapes, and nowhere is the comparison more apt than in the ballets of his so-called "Americana" period.

With its sinewy orchestration, jaunty dance rhythms and use of folk tunes, the orchestral piece *El salón México* (1936) was indicative of the ballets to come. *Billy the Kid* (1938) continued the pattern with a vivid depiction of the Wild West, right down to the obligatory shoot-outs. With *Appalachian Spring* (1944), written at the behest of Martha Graham for her dance company, he reached the summit of his achievements in this form. It's a simple story of love and marriage, in which Copland excels himself in music that is by turns poignantly quiet and spiritual one moment, then exultantly joyous the next. *Appalachian Spring* is typical of Copland's ability to wear his sophistication lightly – making ample use of a simple Shaker tune, he evokes emotion in a way that is charmingly straight and accessible, without ever talking down to his audience.

⊙ Appalachian Spring; Billy the Kid; Rodeo; Fanfare for the Common Man; Quiet City: Cincinnati Pops Orchestra; Kunzel (Telarc CD-80339).

This disc has the three major Copland ballets (*Appalachian Spring* and *Billy the Kid* in concert suite versions), plus the famous *Fanfare for the Common Man* and the delightful *Quiet City* for cor anglais, trumpet and strings. It thus presents a good cross-section of the orchestral music in sparkling and idiomatic performances from the Cincinnati Pops.

THE CLARINET CONCERTO

Copland's 1948 *Clarinet Concerto* was commissioned by Benny Goodman – an accomplished player both in swing and classical music – who gave its first performance two years later. It's a work, like *Appalachian Spring*, which makes a simple contrast between quiet, serene music and something more lively and abandoned. The slow, lilting opening movement, in which the clarinet is very much part of the spare orchestral fabric, has been described by one critic as "a perfect fusion of Satie and Mahler". It leads, via a short Cadenza, into the second and last of its movements, marked simply "rather fast". This has been compared to jazz, but though it employs spiky, syncopated rhythms and an abundance of ostinati it's unmistakably Copland in its airiness and feeling of space, and seems to point the way towards the lyrical minimalism of John Adams.

◑ **Goodman; Columbia Symphony Orchestra; Bernstein** (CBS SK 43337; with Stravinsky's *Ebony Concerto*, Bartók's *Contrasts*, Bernstein's *Preludes, Fugues and Riffs*).

This disc collects together the various classical works that Benny Goodman either commissioned or premiered. Copland's concerto was written with Goodman's manner of playing very much in mind, and there's a relaxed air to the performance which seems entirely appropriate.

SONGS

Copland's songs are not numerous, but they have established themselves as permanent fixtures in the recitals of American singers. The outstanding set is the *Twelve Poems of Emily Dickinson*, which Copland completed in 1950 after working on them for six years. Dickinson was a unique voice in nineteenth-century American literature, and it is Copland's achievement to convey her powerful mix of the personal, the quietly resolute and the visionary so convincingly and so sympathetically. This is one of the greatest song cycles written since World War II.

As a relief from the concentrated effort that he'd exerted on the Dickinson settings, Copland decided to make arrangements of some of his favourite American songs. The result was two sets of five songs entitled *Old American Songs I and II*. Originally written for voice and piano, the songs, easy-going charm proved so popular that Copland orchestrated them. The first set is the most lively and contains the Shaker song *Simple Gifts* that was employed in *Appalachian Spring*, and the delightful children's song *I Bought Me a Cat*.

O Old American Songs Sets 1 & 2; Twelve Poems of Emily Dickinson: Hampson; Upshaw; St Paul Chamber Orchestra; Wolff (Teldec 9031-77310-2).

Exemplary performances of the orchestrated versions of these songs. Thomas Hampson sings the *Old American Songs* with immense style and good humour – no other singer on record sounds so thoroughly at home with them. Dawn Upshaw brings a purity and intensity to the Dickinson settings which emphasizes their visionary aspect.

O Twelve Poems of Emily Dickinson: Bonney; Previn (Decca 455 511-2; with songs by Barber, Previn and Argento).

Arguably the Dickinson songs have a more concentrated impact when performed just with a piano – there's more intimacy and greater immediacy. Barbara Bonney, like Dawn Upshaw, has a light clear voice but she manages to convey a greater wealth of detail, and brings out the songs' quirky humour in her performance. She's brilliantly assisted by André Previn.

ARCANGELO CORELLI

(1653–1713)

Though instrumental music was becoming increasingly important by the middle of the seventeenth century, Corelli is still unusual in that he wrote absolutely no music for the voice. Instead he worked exclusively in the three genres which he helped to establish and refine: the concerto grosso, the trio sonata, and the solo sonata. His published output was small but his influence was enormous. All subsequent composers who worked in these genres, up until the last quarter of the eighteenth century, used Corelli's work as a model and some – like Couperin in his *L'Apothéose de Corelli* – paid open homage to him.

Corelli was born in Fusignano, between Bologna and Ravenna, into a family of well-to-do landowners with no history of musical talent. He reputedly studied with a local priest but his main musical education took place at Bologna, then an important centre for instrumentalists. From 1675 he was based in Rome, where he gradually established himself as one of the city's leading violinists, playing in theatres and in church ensembles. As a performer Corelli was renowned for the elegance and pathos of his playing: "I never met with any man", wrote a contemporary, "that suffered his passions to hurry him away so much whilst he was playing on the violin." However, occasionally his technique let him down – indeed, during a visit to Naples in 1701 he had the embarrassing experience, while leading the orchestra in an opera by Alessandro Scarlatti, of being unable to play a high note which the Neapolitans could manage with ease. Among his patrons were Queen Christina, Cardinal Pamphili, whose music master he became in 1687, and Cardinal Ottoboni, in whose palace he lived from 1689 almost until his death. He died a rich man, leaving not just the predictable pile of instruments and manuscripts, but also a fine collection of paintings.

CONCERTI GROSSI

The concerto grosso, a form of orchestral music that appeared towards the end of the seventeenth century, was like most other instrumental music of the time, in that it consisted of a series of contrasting quick/slow movements based on dance forms. What was new about it was the way that the orchestra was organized into two different groups: a small group called the concertino and a larger group called the concerto grosso (later known as the ripieno or tutti). These two groups played in alternation, with the concerto grosso for the most part simply echoing the material of the concertino, creating a contrast between loud and soft passages. Corelli's concerti grossi have a prevailing mood of balance and control: even in their exuberant fast movements these concertos are quite different from Vivaldi's, which are full of unbridled energy and unpredictability.

◑ **Twelve Concerti Grossi: The English Concert; Pinnock** (Archiv 423 626-2; 2 CDs).

This CD contains all the concerti grossi that Corelli published, though he evidently wrote many more. All these pieces are easy-going and graceful, and there's much of great beauty here, particularly in *Concerto No. 8* (Christmas Concerto) with its dramatic opening, its varied and inventive melodies and its grave and sonorous slow movements. (Six of the concerti, as performed on this disc, are also available as a single CD.)

THE TRIO SONATAS

By Corelli's time the term "sonata" – which had originally meant any piece of music that was played rather than sung – normally referred to a piece played by a small ensemble, in four alternately slow and fast movements. A trio sonata – the most important chamber-music genre of the Baroque period – consisted of three parts played by four instruments: two upper parts, usually violins, plus a bass part (called a continuo) played by a keyboard and a low stringed instrument. Generally a distinction was made between the chamber sonata, which employed dance forms, and the more serious church sonata, which usually did not, but in Corelli's hands the difference between the two forms became increasingly blurred. All his trio sonatas are refined and elegant works in which the violin parts, especially in the slower movements, have a lyrical quality akin to the human voice. This is enjoyable but undemanding music, which avoids extremes of register and of emotion.

○ **Pinnock, Standage, Comberti, Pleeth, North** (Archiv 419 614-2).

Of the ten sonatas on this disc, the six from Op. 1 are church sonatas while the four from Op. 2 are chamber sonatas. The playing is consistently warm-toned and graceful in the two violin parts parts but, as if aware of a certain risk of monotony, Pinnock has effectively varied the use of instruments in the continuo part.

SOLO SONATAS

The twelve sonatas that make up Corelli's Op. 5 are called solo sonatas but in fact are for solo violin and continuo – so at least three instruments are heard. Formally they resemble the trio sonatas but include an additional fast movement. Corelli was as influential a performer and teacher of the violin as he was a composer, and these works can be seen as summarizing his understanding of the best qualities of the instrument. Though considerably more virtuosic in the violin part than the trio sonatas, they possess the same classic qualities of tastefulness and easy lyricism. Even in the most technically difficult moments the brilliance of the passage work serves the music rather than the performer.

○ **Sonate a Violino e Violone o Cimbalo Op. 5: Banchini** (Harmonia Mundi HMC 901307).

The enriched continuo part (harpsichord, cello and archlute) make these first six sonatas from Op. 5 seem even more like ensemble works in which the violin has the dominant voice. Chiara Banchini's playing is marvellously full, and she brings a spontaneous and improvisatory quality to the music through small surges of volume and the delicacy of her rapid ornamentation. As in all Corelli's work it is the melting intensity of the slow movements that provide the best movements, notably in the richly ornamented Grave of the sonata that opens the disc.

FRANÇOIS COUPERIN

(1668–1733)

François Couperin, known as Couperin le Grand to distinguish him from his various musical relations, was the outstanding French composer of the period between Lully (see p.227) and Rameau (see p.327). In his music he succeeded in reconciling the graceful lyric qualities of the French style with the energy of the Italian, as exemplified by Corelli – a composer he very much admired. He is mainly known for his four books of harpsichord pieces (*Pièces de Clavecin*): some 220 brilliantly crafted miniatures, whose mysterious titles and delicate wit have frequently been compared to the enigmatic paintings of his contemporary Antoine Watteau.

The Couperins were a musical dynasty to rival that of the Bachs. Indeed François Couperin's first job, as organist at the Paris church of St Gervais, had been held by his father and uncle before him, and was to remain in the family until 1826. At the age of 25 he succeeded his teacher, Jacques Thomelin, as organist to the king, and a few years later consolidated his position at court when he became harpsichord teacher to several of the royal children. Few other details are known about his life. He acquired a coat of arms shortly after arriving at court, and in 1702 was made a Chevalier of the Order of Latran. None of his correspondence with J.S. Bach has survived (it is thought to have finished up as jam-pot covers), but from the tone of his surviving letters and of his famous keyboard treatise *L'Art de toucher le clavecin* (The Art of Playing the Harpsichord) he seems to have possessed a sardonic sense of humour. Perhaps it was this that kept him from any further appointments at court until 1717, when he took over from d'Anglebert as the king's harpsichordist, a position he retained until his death.

VOCAL MUSIC

The wit and inventiveness which is a characteristic of much of Couperin's music gives way in his sacred vocal pieces to something much more simple and direct, though still with an emphasis on melody. These works tend to be small-scale and intimate, following the model of Carissimi and his French pupil Charpentier, and none of them is more beautiful than the *Leçons de ténèbres*, settings of the Lamentations of Jeremiah to be performed on the three days before Easter. The name, which means "lessons of shadows", refers to the fact that during the services held on those three days all the church candles were gradually extinguished to symbolize the sufferings of Christ. Couperin wrote the full quota of nine lessons (three for each day) but only the first three (for Maundy Thursday) have survived. Each lesson opens with a Hebrew letter sung to an exquisitely sensuous and fluid vocal line; thereafter the vocal style is a fusion between the declamatory and the lyrical, providing restrained but eloquent anguish to Jeremiah's lament at the fall of Jerusalem.

Leçons de Ténèbres: Daneman, Petibon; Les Arts Florissants Instrumental Ensemble; Christie (Erato 063017067-2; with *Versets du Motet*).

Perversely Erato have deleted the glorious recording by Guillemette Laurens and Miecke van der Sluis and replaced it with an equally good, but by no means better, version. The *Leçons* were written for a convent, so it's more appropriate to have them sung by two sopranos rather than, as is often the case, two countertenors. The blend of voices is all important and Sophie Daneman and Patricia Petibon make an exquisite combination, and are well supported by French Baroque specialist William Christie and Les Arts Florissants.

INSTRUMENTAL MUSIC

Couperin's four books of harpsichord pieces are organized into 27 suites which he called *Ordres*. Though based on dance forms, most of the individual pieces within these suites have fanciful titles such as *Les Baricades mistérieuses* or *L'arlequine*, some of which are evidently descriptive while others may have had some private significance. The music's expressiveness is enhanced by rich ornamentation, which – unusually for the time – is never left to the discretion of the performer, but always precisely specified. Though lacking the formal fascination of Bach's keyboard works, Couperin's are more personal and idiosyncratic works, with an emphasis on melody and a wide variety of moods, from the light and elegant to the sombre and subdued.

The outstanding item from Couperin's other solo instrumental music is a late work, the *Pièces de violes*. It was written in 1728, the year after the death of Marin Marais, the great viol master of the period (and the subject of the film *Tous les Matins du Monde*), so perhaps Couperin's pieces are a tribute to him – and to an art form that was already in decline. This is certainly some of the finest and most difficult music ever written for the instrument.

⊙ Pièces de Clavecin: Sempé (Deutsche Harmonia Mundi RD77219).

Skip Sempé's personal selection makes the perfect introduction to Couperin's harpsichord music. He includes two complete *Ordres* (the third and eighth), five of the eight preludes written for *L'Art de toucher le clavecin*, while the rest is his own ordering of miscellaneous works, largely by key. The tone of the instrument (a modern copy of the type that Couperin would have played) is exceptionally bright, but it is Sempé's free and expansive playing that brings the music so convincingly to life. Should you want to go on to explore more of Couperin's books of harpsichord pieces, you could go for Christophe Rousset's vigorous recordings of all four books, issued in two-disc sets by Harmonia Mundi, or the budget-price Naxos cycle, which is not yet complete.

⊙ Pièces de violes; Suites from Les Gouts Réunis: Kuijken, Uemura, Kohnen (Accent ACC 9288).

From the opening wistful prelude of the first suite to the scurrying activity of the second suite's concluding movement, the *Pièces de violes* is music of rare inventiveness and charm. It needs technically brilliant playing, and it gets this from Kuijken, although the rather resonant church acoustic puts a little distance on the sound. The bass viol (or viola da gamba) does not have the same incisiveness as the modern cello, but the quality of its string tone gives it a mellowness and a vulnerability that is very appealing. The CD is filled by two suites from *Les Gouts Réunis* (The Styles Reunited), simple and elegant music here played by two viola da gambas.

CLAUDE DEBUSSY

(1862–1918)

Claude Debussy was a radical from the outset. As a student, he continually failed his harmony exams because, like Beethoven over a century before him, he refused to accept the absolute authority of the textbook. A brilliant pianist, he would irritate and shock his contemporaries by inventing harmonies and chords that effectively were reinterpreting tonality – already he was moving towards the creation of musical Impressionism. In 1882 he he failed to win the Prix de Rome, just as the previous great French musical revolutionary, Hector Berlioz, had done, but two years later he took the coveted prize and moved to Rome. He spent the next two years there, meeting Liszt and Verdi, among others, and hearing dozens of contemporary works, including Wagner's *Lohengrin*.

His attendance at the 1888 and 1889 Bayreuth festivals deepened his understanding of Wagner's operas, but although he recognized the importance of *Tristan und Isolde* and *Parsifal* he also saw that these gargantuan, mythic works were something of a dead end. While other French composers such as Chabrier and Chausson responded to Wagnerism by composing their own grand Norse dramas, Debussy looked beyond the mainstream Western traditions as a way of expanding the vocabulary of music. A Javanese gamelan performance at the Paris Exposition of 1889 had a profound effect, overwhelming him with the elemental beauty of its indeterminate harmonies. However, it was within Russian music that Debussy found the clearest guidance as to how he might create a musical aesthetic as distinctly French as the art of the Impressionist painters and Symbolist poets with whom he was so close. For Debussy, Russian music was primarily suggestive and evocative, a corrective to Wagner's sternly philosophical and self-consciously profound dramas.

Debussy began to explore a compositional process that avoided conventional thematic development, instead moving its material through constantly shifting harmonic and orchestral backgrounds – impression mattered more than direction. The first great example of this carefully crafted vagueness was his only opera, *Pelléas et Mélisande* (begun in 1893), followed a year later by his orchestral *Prélude à l'après-midi d'un faune*, an apparently free-floating composition that was attacked for formlessness but turned out to be one of the most influential pieces of music ever written.

His three *Nocturnes*, performed in 1900 and 1901, marked an increasing sophistication of technique, and four years later Debussy produced what many regard as his masterpiece, the symphonic sketches titled *La Mer*. At the same time he wrote one of the finest of his many piano works, the *Images*; evocative music in which he came close to realizing his ideal of the "hammerless piano". His remaining orchestral works, among them the ballet *Jeux*, were received with great enthusiasm in more adventurous circles, but his final years, during which he produced mainly chamber and piano pieces, were clouded by illness and World War I.

By reason of his influence, Debussy could be classed as perhaps the most important composer of the twentieth century – figures as diverse as Stravinsky, Bartók, Ravel, Webern, Messiaen and Boulez all admitted a debt to him. He is also one of the most approachable. However abstract and ambiguous his work may seem, Debussy believed fervently that music should be communicative. As he once wrote: "Love of art does not depend on explanations, or on experience as in the case of those who say 'I need to hear that several times'. Utter rubbish! When we really listen to music, we hear immediately what we need to hear."

PELLÉAS ET MÉLISANDE

Debussy had a clear idea of what he required from opera: "I wanted from music a freedom which it possesses perhaps to a greater degree than any other art, not being tied to a more or less exact reproduction of Nature but to the mysterious correspondences between Nature and Imagination." With Maurice Maeterlinck's play, *Pelléas et Mélisande*, he found his perfect libretto, a misty tale of doomed love that proceeded by hint and implication rather than by dramatic incident. He began setting the play, virtually uncut, in 1893 and revised it obsessively until the first performance at the Opéra Comique on April 30, 1902. It was immediately recognized as a watershed in the history of opera and classical music.

The influence of Wagner's *Parsifal* is clear in Debussy's orchestration, as it is in some of his melodic lines and in his emphasis on the metaphysical dimension of the medieval world in which *Pelléas* is set. Yet this dramatically static work is the very antithesis of Wagnerian heroics. Debussy once remarked that "music in opera is far too predominant", and here he created an opera in which music doesn't so much emphasize the meaning of the text as complement or revise it. In a letter to Chausson he wrote of *Pelléas*: "I have found . . . a technique which strikes me as fairly new, that is silence as a means of expression and perhaps the only way to give the emotion of a phrase its full power." Debussy's conception of silence as a dramatic device is one of his most lasting innovations, while the interaction between his exquisitely delicate music and Maeterlinck's nebulous text produces tensions unimaginable in through-composed operas.

There are no big tunes in *Pelléas*, and it contains few moments of traditional lyricism – on the whole, Debussy writes vocal parts that correspond to the patterns of French speech. Some people find it boring, others regard it as the greatest of all French operas, but there's no disputing its status as a ground-breaker. Moreover, it is one of the few stage works to thrive on record.

LEBRECHT COLLECTION

Claude Debussy in the late 1890s

⊙ Grancher, Michel, Jansen, Roux; Lyric Chorale; RTF National Orchestra; Inghelbrecht (Disques Montaigne TCE8710; 3 CDs).

Désiré Inghelbrecht was a good friend of Debussy, and if any recording of Pélléas can be said to be authentic, it is this 1962 production. The conductor draws out the music smoothly while maintaining tempi that are brisker than most, and his casting is unbeatable. Micheline Grancher is a light, classically Gallic Mélisande, and Jacques Jansen's evenly produced Pelléas is perfectly set against Michael Roux's rougher-sounding Golaud. The sound is less than perfect, but this is a beautifully shaped, elegantly sung performance.

◑ **Shirley, Söderström, McIntyre, Ward, Minton, Britten, Wick; Royal Opera House Chorus & Orchestra; Boulez** (Sony SM3K47265; 3 CDs).

Pierre Boulez's recording of Debussy's opera is a brilliant and rare example of one composer expressing his total sympathy for the work of another. He clarifies the complex orchestral colours and shapes each of the brief scenes as part of the overall structure. Elisabeth Söderström is glowing as Mélisande, while George Shirley conveys Pelléas's confusion without resorting to overemphasis.

PRÉLUDE À L'APRÈS-MIDI D'UN FAUNE

Pierre Boulez once remarked that "just as modern poetry surely took root in certain of Baudelaire's poems, so one is justified in saying that modern music was awakened by *L'Après-midi d'un faune*". Saint-Saëns's took a rather less positive approach – "It's as much a piece of music as the palette a painter has worked from is a painting" – but his dismissal comes close to capturing the essence of this amazing tone poem. Debussy based his composition upon the poem of the same name by Mallarmé and, like the poem, the music works by suggestion rather than statement. A trance-like flute theme opens the work, establishing a uniquely hedonistic and languid atmosphere that is then extended by some marvellously deft and harmonically innovative writing for woodwind.

◑ **Concertgebouw Orchestra; Haitink** (Philips 438 742-2; 2 CDs; with *Images*, *Jeux*, *Nocturnes*, and other orchestral works).

Haitink's outstanding Debussy survey from the late 1970s, now at mid-price, is an irresistible bargain. In *L'Après-midi d'un faune* he marshals his brilliant orchestral forces with the most delicate touch, producing an extraordinary sense of heaviness and other-worldliness.

O Philharmonia; Cantelli (Testament SBT 1001; with *La Mer* and excerpts from *Le Martyre de Saint Sébastian*).

Cantelli's 1954 reading makes the *L'Après-midi* into a less evanescent piece of music, and highlights its structural cohesion. This may not be as close to the composer's spirit as some performances, but it's a memorable and legitimate approach.

NOCTURNES

The three *Nocturnes* feature some of Debussy's most imaginative orchestral writing. Untypically, he provided an explanatory note to the set, providing as fine an introduction as could be wished for. "The title *Nocturnes* is . . . not meant to designate the usual form of a nocturne, but rather all the various impressions and the special effects of light that the word suggests. *Nuages* renders the immutable aspect to the sky and the slow, solemn motion of the clouds, fading away in grey tones lightly tinged with white. *Fêtes* gives us the vibrating atmosphere with sudden flashes of light. The background remains persistently the same: a festival, with its blending of music and luminous dust, participating in the cosmic rhythm. *Sirènes* depicts the sea and its countless rhythms and presently, among the waves silvered by the moonlight, is heard the mysterious song of the sirens as they laugh and pass on."

◑ **Concertgebouw Orchestra: Haitink** (Philips 438 742-2; 2 CDs; with *Images*, *Jeux*, etc).

Haitink excels himself with the *Nocturnes*: only a conductor with a really close bond to an orchestra could produce such utterly specific refinements of mood and colour.

LA MER

In the summer of 1904 Debussy left his wife for another woman, provoking his wife into a suicide attempt. Debussy fled, mistress in hand, to Eastbourne in Sussex, and there he composed his finest orchestral work, *La Mer*. The first performance in 1905 excited hostility in some quarters that seems scarcely credible today, with the critic from *The Times* remarking – "As long as actual sleep can be avoided, the hearer can derive great pleasure from the strange sounds that enter his ears if he will only put away all ideas of definite construction or logical development."

The piece is in three movements titled "From dawn to mid-day on the sea", "Play of the waves" and "Dialogue of the wind and the sea" – at the first rehearsal, Erik Satie facetiously commented that he "particularly liked the bit around half-past ten". While the music is not as programmatic as anything by Strauss, it still conveys clear images of the sea through flickering, fragmentary themes and some of Debussy's finest orchestrations – notable among which is a section in the first movement when the sixteen cellos are divided into four groups of four.

◑ **Concertgebouw Orchestra; Haitink** (Philips 438 742-2; 2 CDs; with *Images*, *Jeux*, etc).

Haitink's *La Mer* is second to none: his delicate command of nuance and texture, his refinement and fluidity of gesture, have been jutifiably praised. But, above all, it is his combination of grace and his majestic sense of architecture that illuminates one of this century's most fastidiously conceived scores.

O Philharmonia; Cantelli (Testament SBT 1011; with *L'Après-midi* and excerpts from *Le Martyre*).

This performance is the highlight of Guido Cantelli's famed "Debussy sessions", recorded in London with what was then one of the world's finest orchestras. Cantelli's worship of his mentor Toscanini is clear from the opening bars – every nuance and colour is achieved with startling immediacy, giving Debussy's instrumental textures a wonderful freshness and vitality.

JEUX

Debussy's last three orchestral works were all ballets. The first and finest of them, *Jeux* (Games), was composed in 1912 and premiered in 1913 by Diaghilev's Ballet Russe. Debussy based the work's construction upon a basic, undulating phrase which is then developed into a wild variety of musical gestures, vaguely corresponding to the strokes of a tennis game. Stravinsky hailed the work as a masterpiece, with the reservation that he found some of the ideas over-kind on the ear – though Stravinsky was probably alone in this reaction to a score which, in its emphasis on percussive orchestration, prefigures much of this century's avant-garde music.

◑ **Concertgebouw Orchestra;** Haitink (Philips 438 742-2; 2 CDs; with *Images*, *Nocturnes* etc).

Jeux is Debussy's most difficult score to bring off, but, once again, Haitink – through a mixture of precision and flexibility – produces a beguiling account, in which individual timbres shine through with amazing clarity.

◑ **London Symphony Orchestra: Baudo** (EMI 62012; with *La Mer* & *Prélude à l'après-midi d'un faune*).

Baudo's account of *Jeux* is considerably brisker than Haitink's, as if he wanted to emphasize the athletic inspiration for the score. It's coupled with fine performances of *La Mer* and *Prélude à l'après-midi d'un faune* and this disc makes a fine way into the orchestral music, should the Haitink seem too much of a good thing.

THE STRING QUARTET

In the early 1880s Debussy was adopted by Tchaikovsky's patron Madame von Meck, for whom he wrote his rarely heard *Piano Trio* and the *Nocturne and Scherzo* for cello and piano. These early forays into chamber music are not particularly successful, but by the time he got round to writing his *String Quartet* in 1893 he had achieved complete mastery of the medium. The first movement's opening theme provides the basic material for all four movements of a work in which rhythm prevails over harmonic and melodic considerations. This quality is particularly remarkable in the Scherzo, where the disruptive combination of plucking and bowing creates a confusion that forces you to concentrate on the textures rather than the linear form.

O Hagen Quartet (Deutsche Grammophon 437 836-2; with quartets by Ravel and Webern).

The Hagen Quartet recording of this wonderful work is beautifully judged – their playing of the opening movement is thrilling, while the Andante has a hallucinatory feel that has never been bettered in the studio.

◑ **Quartetto Italiano** (Philips 420 894-2; with Ravel, *String Quartet*).

This account from the mid-1960s does not have the Hagen Quartet's finesse but it is, nevertheless, a beautiful performance, full of warmth and of brilliantly controlled dynamics that give the works an extra dramatic dimension.

THE VIOLIN SONATA

Written in the year the Great War finally ended, the *Violin Sonata* is a bleak, acerbic score except for its final movement – unable to finish the work to his satisfaction, Debussy tacked on a facile finale that isn't really worthy of the preceding movements. In common with a lot of European chamber music written at this time, the violin writing is indebted to gypsy folk music (or what was perceived as gypsy music), a connection that's unmistakable in the sonata's assertive melodies.

◑ **Little; Lane** (EMI CD-EMX2244; with Ravel's *Tzigane* and *Sonata*, Poulenc's *Sonata*).

Tasmin Little catches every changing nuance of this fickle music and her husky, smouldering tone is calculated to pinpoint its quixotic inspiration. She is brilliantly partnered by Piers Lane in what is a really outstanding performance.

◑ **Heifetz; Bay** (RCA 09026 61775-2; with works by Ravel, Respighi and Martinů).

Jascha Heifetz's account, recorded in 1950, is a remarkably intense performance, though the unrelenting tension does mean that some of the gentler aspects of the piece are bypassed.

SUITE BERGAMESQUE

Composed between 1890 and 1905, the *Suite Bergamesque* shows Debussy hankering after the elegance of an earlier period of French music – as the Baroque dance titles of two of the four pieces indicate. Hovering between major and minor keys, fusing mock-archaisms with Debussy's own freshly minted style, this music is at the same time deeply considered and slightly fey. Debussy always had a fondness for moonlight music, and the third suite, *Clair de lune*, has achieved the status of a classic through its sheer sumptuousness.

Kocsis (Philips 412 118-2PH; with *Pour le piano, Estampes & Images oubliées*).

Crisp understatement and a certain luxurious suavity coincide in this superlative performance, in which Zoltán Kocsis relishes the opulent sonorities of the piano but at the same time keeps them firmly in their place. *Clair de lune* is played without a trace of sentimentality, while *Passepied*, the final piece, glides off into happy oblivion.

CHILDREN'S CORNER

Of all Debussy's piano compositions, the most transparent is the *Children's Corner* suite, written for his daughter in 1906. These are sprightly and good-humoured pieces, some of them satirical – such as *Doctor Gradus ad Parnassum*, a joke at the expense of Clementi's finger exercises (see p.108) – others brilliantly pictorial – such as the delicious *The Snow is Dancing*. Inspired by his daughter's governess, Debussy gave English titles to each of these six miniatures, but his English wasn't quite as perfect as his piano writing, which is how one piece came to be called *Jimbo's Lullaby* – Debussy meant it as a lullaby for a baby elephant.

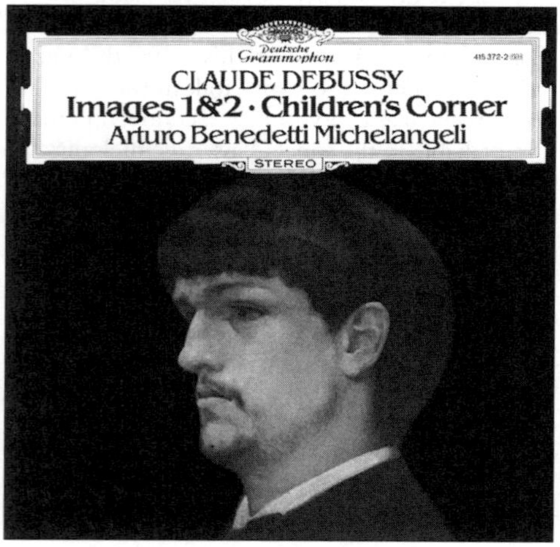

Michelangeli (Deutsche Grammophon 415 372; with *Images*).

Arturo Benedetti Michelangeli has made two dazzling recordings of *Children's Corner*. The DG studio recording is a showcase for his astonishing control of tone and weight, drawing out nuances and establishing layers of sound that few other pianists are equipped even to investigate. This performance is also available as part of a double-CD set, with *Images* and *Préludes I & II*.

Michelangeli (Memories HR4368/9; 2 CDs; with Beethoven, *Piano Concerto No. 5 & Sonata No. 32*; Grieg *Piano Concerto*; Ravel, *Gaspard de la nuit*).

The live performance on Memories' two-CD set is a lighter, more ingenuous and childlike reading. It's coupled with great performances of the *Emperor* and Grieg concertos, and a sensational account of Ravel's *Gaspard de la nuit*.

IMAGES

Debussy's two sets of *Images* (1905 and 1907) are musical homages to pure sensation, conjuring the sound of bells through leaves, sunlight reflected from the scales of goldfish, and a multitude of other transient moments. The opening piece, *Reflets dans l'eau*, straight away establishes Debussy's unique understanding of the keyboard's potential, translating the rhythms of water into hypnotic, refreshing music that's as vividly pictorial as anything Liszt could have created. However, the *Images* require a degree of patience if you're coming to them from the incident-packed music of the nineteenth century, for their dynamic levels are generally very low, and the sense of silence, so mastered in *Pelléas*, is again a central feature of these aural landscapes. Whatever you do, don't reject them on first hearing – these miniatures are among the richest of all piano works.

Michelangeli (Deutsche Grammophon 415 372; with *Children's Corner*).

Michelangeli's performances of these works are astonishing, creating an ever-shifting and constantly fascinating world of sound. This recording, one of the finest Debussy recordings ever made, is also available as part of a double-CD set.

THE PRÉLUDES

Debussy's two books of *Préludes* (1910 and 1913) are the last of his descriptive piano works. Titles such as *La cathédrale engloutie* (The Drowned Cathedral) indicate an affinity with the allusive world of the *Images*, but others, such as *Feux d'artifice* (Fireworks) and *La danse de Puck*, are indicative of a more outgoing element to the *Préludes* – indeed several of the *Préludes* make use of popular musical influences, including Neapolitan songs and music-hall numbers. They might be slightly more accessible than the *Images* (though bear in mind that Debussy did not intend all 24 to be heard in one session), but if anything they are technically even more demanding – only the *Études* require more of the pianist.

O Books 1 & 2: Michelangeli (Deutsche Grammophon 449 438-2; 2 CDs; with *Images* & *Children's Corner*).

For some critics Michelangeli is a cold-hearted musician, preoccupied with the creation of beguiling sonorities at the expense of musical depth, and the playing here is sometimes idiosyncratic. But Michelangeli's epicurean style, with its seemingly infinite gradations of dynamics and timbre, is perfectly suited to Debussy's most macroscopic piano music.

O Books 1 & 2: Gieseking (EMI CDH7 61004-2).

Walter Gieseking's recording of the *Préludes*, made in 1953–54, late in the pianist's life, is a legendary set. The sound is not digital-pure, but this playing transcends any such considerations. No one has evoked the diaphanous quality of Debussy's apparitions quite so well, or summoned the orchestral quality of his piano music with such effortless power.

THE ÉTUDES

The *Études*, Debussy's last major works for piano, were written in 1915 yet they reflect nothing of his depression during the war years. Early in that year, Debussy had edited the complete piano works of Chopin and he duly dedicated his own two books of studies to the memory of his great precursor. Like Chopin's *Études*, these pieces explore different aspects of piano technique, but are far more than mere technical exercises – though extremely difficult, the twelve *Études* are among the most entertaining of all his piano works. The first book is the more traditional, experimenting with problems of overall dexterity, whereas the second is concerned with the very vocabulary of music and displays some typically advanced harmonic and melodic ideas.

O Uchida (Philips 422 412-2PH).

Mitsuko Uchida is on top of even the most demanding studies, playing with a crispness, style and sophistication that mark her out as a brilliant Debussy pianist. On top of this, the recorded sound is of the very highest standard.

LÉO DELIBES

(1836–1891)

Friedrich Nietzsche said he liked Léo Delibes because he made "no pretensions to depth". Like his teacher Adolph Adam, who wrote "my only ambition is to compose music that is transparent, easy to understand and amusing to the public", Delibes was a committed populist, and his music is full of personality – albeit the personality of Meyerbeer, Gounod, Bizet and countless other French composers, rather than his own. He may have possessed no strong musical identity, yet Delibes achieved considerable fame during his lifetime, and is the founder of modern, symphonic ballet music. As a composer of opera he had just one enduring claim to fame, *Lakmé*.

After having worked as a chorister, and later as a chorusmaster (assisting Gounod, Bizet and Berlioz), Delibes composed a string of enormously successful comic operas and operettas, most of which were written in the style of Offenbach. However, he was driven by a desire to compose for the ballet, and in 1866 the success of *La source* (co-written with Louis Minkus) convinced him that his talents were indeed best suited to dance. In 1869 he composed his last operetta and the following year he completed his ballet *Coppélia*, which was a huge hit. Delibes pursued his métier with renewed enthusiasm, but he did not neglect the opera, and in 1883 (a year after the first performance of Wagner's *Parsifal*), *Lakmé* was first performed at the Opéra Comique. It too was an immense success, and his reputation has rested securely upon it – and *Coppélia* – ever since.

LAKMÉ

Lakmé is a particularly egregious example of European exoticism, set in mid-nineteenth-century India. An English lieutenant named Gerald is smitten by Lakmé, the daughter of a Brahmin priest, who eventually stabs Gerald upon discovering his identity. Lakmé tends Gerald's wounds in her forest hut, but he is unable to decide between his love for her and his responsibility to his regiment. Lakmé decides for him by eating a poisonous leaf.

Delibes's deliciously light melodic writing saves the day – the first act's beautiful "Flower Duet" for two sopranos is one of the best-known moments in opera, though that's largely due to the fact that British Airways used it as their theme tune for a while. Lakmé's show-stopping *Bell Song* is the opera's other high spot, but this is not just a virtuoso showpiece for soprano. The male lead role is well drawn and theatrically compulsive, and the music's oriental inflections are consistently entertaining, for all *Lakmé*'s conservatism.

◑ **Sutherland, Vanzo, Bacquier, Sinclair; Orchestre National de l'Opéra de Monte Carlo; Bonynge** (Decca 425 485-2; 2 CDs).

Bonynge's recording stars his wife, Joan Sutherland, as a technically superb heroine – none of the difficulties of the *Bell Song* pose any problems for her. She is admirably partnered by the sweet-toned tenor of Alain Vanzo, and the supporting cast is good too, with a delightful plummy English lady from Monica Sinclair. For those mainly interested in the "Flower Duet", Decca have issued a mid-price single CD of highlights from this performance.

COPPÉLIA

Coppélia prompted Tchaikovsky to remark that he preferred Delibes to Brahms. Admittedly, Tchaikovsky had a special love of ballet and a special hatred of Brahms ("that talentless bastard", as he once called him), but there can be little doubt that, together with Tchaikovsky's dance music, *Coppélia* is one of the seminal nineteenth-century works in this genre. Based upon E.T.A. Hoffmann's short story *The Sandman*, which concerns the toymaker Doctor Coppelius and his dancing doll (a story Offenbach used in his *Tales of Hoffmann*), the music is full of fine melodies, vivid characterization and brilliantly conceived dances. It is not a sophisticated score, but this is one of the few classical ballets that will bear close attention away from the stage.

◑ **Rotterdam Philharmonic Orchestra; Zinman** (Philips 438 763-2; with Chopin, *Les Sylphides*; Gounod, *Faust ballet music*).

David Zinman conducts an excellent version of the complete ballet, with an alert and theatrical sounding Rotterdam Philharmonic. The fine sound, the generous fill-ups and the price all make this a number-one choice.

FREDERICK DELIUS

(1862–1934)

Born in England to a German father, Frederick Delius turned to composing while in Florida, then spent most of his working life in rural France. His music is similarly cosmopolitan and difficult to classify, but it was largely inspired by the composer's deep love of nature, whose beauty and impermanence he tried to evoke in rich, diaphanous orchestral textures, full of shifting chromatic harmonies. A late Romantic composer, he regarded his music as a means of expressing his spiritual values, which were largely an amalgam of the philosophy of Nietzsche and the pantheistic writings of Walt Whitman.

Delius was brought up in Bradford, the son of a prosperous wool-merchant who at first insisted that the boy join the family business. But it had no appeal for him, and in 1884 he left for Florida in order to run an orange plantation. It was here, on hearing the workers' songs wafting across the St John River, that he decided to become a composer. He took some lessons with a local organist named Thomas Ward, a course of instruction he later claimed taught him more than his eighteen months at the Leipzig Conservatorium between 1886 and 1888.

One thing he did gain from Leipzig was the friendship and support of Edvard Grieg, who persuaded Delius's father that Frederick's future was as a composer. Delius came to regard Norway as his spiritual home, and his bohemian spell in Paris, in the early 1890s, was largely spent in the company of Scandinavian artists, including the painter Edvard Munch and the playwright August Strindberg. Paris was also where he met Jelka Rosen, a painter whom he later married. In 1897 the couple moved to the village of Grez-sur-Loing near the forest of Fontainebleau; it was to be their home for the rest of his life, with the exception of the war years, which were spent in England and Norway.

In contrast to roistering years in Paris, Delius's life at Grez was deliberately reclusive, and it was here that he gradually developed his individual impressionistic style. His music gained its initial success in Germany, but its biggest following was in England (a country he claimed to loathe), principally through the advocacy of his greatest interpreter, Sir Thomas Beecham, who organized major Delius festivals in 1929 and 1946. The latter stage of his life, however, was marked by increasing ill-health, which eventually left him blind and paralysed – the result of syphilis contracted in his youth.

CHORAL MUSIC

The orchestral miniatures may be the most popular of Delius's compositions, but it is the orchestral songs for soloists and chorus that are his greatest achievement, and all of them combine, to varying degrees, a sense of the thrilling vitality of life with an underlying sadness at its transience.

Sea Drift (1903–04), a setting of a Whitman poem, tells of a sea bird that has lost its mate and waits faithfully, but in vain, for her return. The *Songs of Sunset* (1906–07) are even more melancholic, setting poems that are permeated by the evanescence of happiness and love. In both works there are no breaks in the music, and Delius employs an idiosyncratic and informal style of vocal writing – part recitative, part arioso – that gives each work a sense of an unfolding awareness.

By contrast, the *Mass of Life* (1904–05) is a rapturous celebration of the life force (though even here there are moments of despair), taken from Nietzsche's *Also Sprach Zarathustra* – also the inspiration for one of Richard Strauss's most popular works (see p.408). Zarathustra is Nietzsche's idea of the Superman, a man disdainful of weakness and conventional morality, and the *Mass of Life* is a fittingly huge and powerful work, full of sinewy and vigorous choral writing, and – especially in the night-time music – some remarkable orchestration. In scope and ambition it stands alongside Mahler's *Symphony No. 2* (see p.237) and Schoenberg's *Gurrelieder* (see p.355).

○ Sea Drift; Songs of Sunset; Songs of Farewell: Terfel; Bournemouth Symphony Chorus & Orchestra; Hickox (Chandos CHAN 9214).

Hickox's second recording of *Sea Drift* is gloriously impassioned and utterly convincing, with no weak links. In Bryn Terfel he has a soloist who knows how to pace a role dramatically – characterization is far more vivid than on rival recordings. And the chorus are superb, utterly responsive to Hickox's sensitive shaping and colouring and, in turn, beautifully served by the wonderfully open and expansive Chandos sound.

◑ A Mass of Life; Requiem: Evans, Rodgers, Rigby, Robson, Coleman-Wright; Waynflete Singers; Bournemouth Symphony Orchestra & Chorus; Hickox (Chandos CHAN 9515; 2 CDs).

The *Mass of Life* has been called a pagan oratorio, and in this 1997 recording Hickox manages to whip up an even greater mood of frenzy and abandonment than Groves did in his EMI recording. This is a marvellous performance which deserves to establish this work, once and for all, as one of the choral masterpieces of the early twentieth century.

ORCHESTRAL MUSIC

Delius's most immediately accessible music is found in short orchestral pieces such as *Brigg Fair* (1907), *Summer Night on the River* (1911) and *On Hearing the First Cuckoo in Spring* (1912) – works whose very titles evoke a benign, pastoralist image of nature. He is not a composer whose strength comes from melodic inventiveness (though he does have some good tunes) or from tightly structured forms; rather it is the orchestration and harmony that make his sound-world unique. Subtle combinations of instruments (including beautifully evocative woodwind writing), gently lilting rhythms, chromaticism that is hazy yet coherent – these are the things that create the overwhelming sense of tranquillity and spaciousness that colours so much of his orchestral work.

○ Brigg Fair; In a Summer Garden; Paris; On Hearing the First Cuckoo; The Walk to the Paradise Garden; Summer Night on the River; BBC Symphony Orchestra; Davis (Teldec 4509-90845-2).

Andrew Davis is yet another skilful Delius advocate (an almost exclusively English band), and he gets the most sumptuous and shimmering sounds from the BBC SO. The selection concentrates on the most popular of the orchestral miniatures, but also includes a scintillating account of *Paris*, a kind of miniature tone poem.

○ Beecham conducts Delius: Royal Philharmonic Orchestra; Beecham (EMI CDS 747 509-8; 2 CDs).

Delius's music is difficult to play well, in such a way that the textures of the scoring are clearly heard. Beecham was the supreme interpreter of Delius, and these recordings of the bulk of Delius's orchestral music are the legacy of his achievement. Despite their age (late 1950s to early 1960s), the sound is remarkably fresh and bright, with the conductor's attention to phrasing and the detailing of dynamics producing spectacular results – nowhere more hauntingly than in *Brigg Fair*, a work which in terms of sumptuousness and delicacy of colouring matches the best of Debussy or Ravel.

THE VIOLIN CONCERTO

Of the four concertos Delius wrote – for piano, violin, cello, and for violin and cello together – it is the *Violin Concerto* (1916) that is the most satisfying work. Though Delius was himself a talented violinist and the work was written for the brilliant English violinist Albert Sammons, it is markedly not a virtuosic showpiece. The solo part might often soar and glide rhapsodically over the orchestral texture, but it is always connected harmonically with the orchestral writing and seems to grow from out of it. The work is in one long movement divided into three clear sections, and abounds in moments of passionate spontaneity, sometimes dreamlike, sometimes fervent.

⊙ Little; Welsh National Opera Orchestra; Mackerras (Argo 433 704-2; with *On Hearing the First Cuckoo in Spring, Summer Night on the River, Dance Rhapsodies*).

Mackerras is an ideal Delius conductor, unerringly judging the music's shape and direction, while Tasmin Little is an inspired soloist, bringing to the work an ardour which is utterly compelling. Balance between soloist and orchestra is perfect, with the musical momentum seeming to pass effortlessly from one to the other.

JOSQUIN DESPREZ

(c.1440–1521)

Josquin Desprez (usually referred to simply as Josquin) dominated western Europe's musical landscape at the end of the fifteenth century in much the same way as Dufay (see p.126) had dominated it at the middle. Like Dufay he came from northern Europe, almost certainly from the Picardy region of France, but worked for much of his life in Italy where he established, if anything, an even greater reputation than Dufay. Contemporaries compared him to Michelangelo, and Luther memorably said of him, "Josquin is master of the notes, which do what he wants, while other composers must do what the notes want." Polyphony came of age with Josquin: he consolidated the achievements of his great predecessors, Dufay and Ockeghem, turning their essentially linear style into something more harmonically complex and expressive. For the first time, real attention was paid to conveying the meaning of words, but it is the sheer beauty of the sound which is most striking. It was Josquin who established the pattern for Renaissance sacred music, creating rich vocal textures made up of long arching phrases, in which consistent imitation between the voices creates a sense both of unity and of progression.

Very little is known about Josquin's early years, but from 1459 he was in Milan, firstly as a singer at the cathedral, next at the Chapel of the Duke of Milan from 1473, then in the service of the duke's brother, Ascanio Sforza, after the duke was assassinated. When Ascanio became a cardinal in 1484, Josquin accompanied him to Rome, where he continued to serve him but also became a member of the papal choir in the new Sistine Chapel. In the early 1500s Josquin briefly returned to France and may have been connected to the court of Louis XII, but by the end of 1502 he had returned south, this time to the court of Duke Ercole of Ferrara. Josquin had been recommended by one of the duke's talent scouts, although another had suggested a different composer, Isaac, on the grounds that Josquin was irascible, composed when he wanted to, and charged too much. The duke chose Josquin and was rewarded with a Mass setting based on his name. When the plague hit Ferrara a year later, Josquin sensibly left the court and returned north (his successor, Obrecht, died of the plague in 1505), where he became provost of the collegiate church of Notre Dame at Condé-sur-l'Escaut, a position he held until his death.

SACRED MUSIC

Though Josquin wrote a substantial number of courtly songs, it is as a composer of motets and Masses that he exerted the widest influence. In much of Josquin's sacred music the technique of imitation, whereby one voice repeats part or more of what another voice has just sung, becomes increasingly apparent. Another device which he exploits is that of suspension, in which a note in one voice is held while the other voices move onto a new chord – the resulting discord sets up a tension which is only resolved when the held note moves onto the correct note. Josquin also makes plentiful use of the old technique of basing music on an already existing tune, called the cantus firmus: he based his Mass *"Ave Maris Stella"* (Hail Star of the Sea) on a plainsong hymn to the Virgin, and wrote Masses that employ a secular cantus firmus, two of them using the popular song *L'homme armé* (The Armed Man).

O Missa "Ave Maris Stella", Motets and Chansons: Taverner Consort and Choir; Parrott (EMI CDC 7 54659 2).

The Taverner Consort's CD is a well-balanced and generous disc, including six chansons and three motets as well as the *"Ave Maris Stella"* Mass. The all-male Taverner choir (nuns were the only women allowed to sing sacred music at this time) might not have such a homogenous and pure style as some of their early music rivals, but their feel for the flexibility of the vocal lines is outstanding. The disc's highlight is the vigorous and joyful motet *Gaude Virgo* (Rejoice Virgin), here given a bright and energetic performance.

O L'homme armé Masses: The Tallis Scholars; Phillips (Gimell 454 919-2).

Though probably written around the same time, the two *L'homme armé* Masses sound very different: the first has a medieval feel, possibly due to the four voices' overlapping in pitch, while the later work spreads the voices wider, creating a more spacious feel. As well as using women to sing the highest part, the Tallis Scholars adopt a different approach to the Taverner Consort, bringing out the long seamless lines of the music and stressing its serenity, despite its frequent rhythmic adventurousness. The clarity of the singing makes the rich and elaborate canonical writing in the *Agnus Dei* particularly memorable. The disc includes the anonymous *chanson* on which both works are based.

GAETANO DONIZETTI

(1797–1848)

It is hard to understand how two adjacent European countries could produce such disparate musical styles as did nineteenth-century Italy and Austria. Gaetano Donizetti and Franz Schubert were born in 1797, the former in Bergamo, the latter in Vienna, and yet there have surely never been two less similar neighbours. Whereas Schubert's music trawled the deepest recesses of the mind, Donizetti's exhibitionistic operas required no one to think too deeply. "Music for the Italians", noted Berlioz, "is a sensual pleasure and nothing more. For this noble expression of the mind they have hardly more respect than for the art of cooking. They want a score that, like a plate of macaroni, can be assimilated immediately without having to think about it." And yet, though it's true that Donizetti's crowd-pleasers won't bear examination by the rigorous standards of contemporaries such as Beethoven, Schubert, Schumann or Chopin, he nonetheless had a genuine artistic vision. Like Bellini – the other master of bel canto opera – he wanted to bring music and drama into a "closer, more direct conjunction", to quote the composer himself.

In all, he wrote some 73 operas, and the majority of them are populated either with historical personalities (eg *Lucrezia Borgia*, *Anna Bolena* and *Maria Stuarda*) or with characters lifted from writers such as Schiller, Hugo and Walter Scott. It was the last of this trio who provided him with the material for his finest opera, *Lucia di Lammermoor* (1835), a daring attempt to reconcile his post-Rossinian devotion to exquisite vocal line with the need for real character development. Like Bellini and Rossini before him, Donizetti was more than happy to accommodate the bravura talents of his star singers (many of whom had worked closely with Bellini), but his career showed an increasing willingness to subordinate display to the needs of the drama. His move away from the strict framework of "aria–recitative–chorus" was gradual, but by the end of his life he was writing through-form operas, in which the action remained constant without interruptions for set-piece singing.

Donizetti undoubtedly wrote too much too quickly, but it should be remembered that the conditions in which he worked were hardly conducive to the creation of profound or sophisticated art. To get further work, the opera composer had to complete his current commission quickly, and when confronted by an impatient, fee-paying impresario, Germanic concepts of self-expression mattered for nothing. For all his "commercialism", Donizetti is, with Bellini, nineteenth-century Italy's most important composer of opera before Verdi, a composer who wrote pastiche Donizetti for his first twenty years – then paid his precursor the compliment of stealing one of his tunes for the Grand Chorus of *Aïda*.

L'ELISIR D'AMORE

In 1832, Donizetti completed his first great comic opera, *L'Elisir d'amore* (The Elixir of Love), a tongue-in-cheek reinterpretation of the Tristan and Isolde myth. A "love potion" is bought from a quack doctor by Nemorino, in the hope of winning the love of Adina. She chooses to marry another man but, before doing so, is forced to realize that she loves Nemorino after all, and they finally marry. The quack then does a roaring trade.

L'Elisir d'amore is a great sentimental-pastoral comedy, and it features some of the composer's finest music, with Nemorino's second-act *Una furtiva lagrima* standing out as one of the most affecting bel canto tenor arias ever written. Adina, the soprano lead, has plenty of beautiful writing, including a first-act duet with Nemorino and a solo in the second act, *Prendi, prendi per me sei libero*.

○ Sutherland, Pavarotti, Cossa, Mala, Casula; Ambrosian Singers; English Chamber Orchestra; Bonynge (Decca 414 461-2DH2; 2 CDs).

Luciano Pavarotti's early recording with Joan Sutherland and Dominic Cossa, conducted by Bonynge, is the most rewarding of the many versions in the current catalogue. Pavarotti's voice might not quite catch Nemorino's naïve innocence, but he and Sutherland establish a genuine relationship, and Cossa is endearingly convincing as the roguish charlatan Dulcamara.

○ Gheorghiu, Alagna, Scaltriti, Alaimo, Dan; Chorus and Orchestra of the Opéra de Lyon; Pidò (Decca 455 691-2; 2 CDs).

The husband and wife team of Angela Gheorghiu and Roberto Alagna make a very impressive double act in this 1997 recording. It's a very theatrical performance, at times a little too much larger than life, with Ghorghiu bringing a toughness of characterization (though not of voice) to Adina. Vocally she is superb, dealing with the most difficult passage work with an almost contemptuous ease. Alagna is equally impressive, although oddly he decides to sing an alternative transposed version of *Una furtiva lagrima* which is slightly less of a show stopper.

LUCIA DI LAMMERMOOR

Sir Walter Scott's *The Bride of Lammermoor* afforded Donizetti with a perfect vehicle for intensely emotional writing. Basically, the tale recounts the long-standing feud between the families of Lammermoor and Ravenswood and the love between Lucia and Edgardo – Lucia being the sister of the head of Lammermoor, and Edgardo the head of Ravenswood. Lucia dies after killing her enforced husband-to-be and, upon seeing her coffin carried towards burial, Edgardo kills himself in desperation.

The superb characterizations of *Lucia di Lammermoor* and its string of glorious melodies – at once fresh and sentimental – make this his most successful opera, and it received frequent productions when bel canto enjoyed a vogue back in the 1950s. The archetypal Romantic Italian opera, *Lucia* is renowned for the extraordinary soprano pyrotechnics of the "Mad Scene" in Act III, but it contains some magnificent tenor passages as well – in fact, the male role attracted more attention from Donizetti's first audiences.

◑ Moffo, Bergonzi, Sereni, Flagello, Vozza, Duval, Pandano; RCA Italian Opera Orchestra & Choir; Prêtre (RCA GD86504; 2 CDs).

The cascading difficulty of Lucia's vocal writing demands fabulous singers and there have been none finer in the two lead roles than Carlo Bergonzi and Anna Moffo. Bergonzi may not have had the ringing "top" of Pavarotti, but his beautiful phrasing is unparalleled, while Moffo's bright, thrilling and absolutely steady voice is perfect for the contrary aspects to Lucia's character. Prêtre's exciting direction serves this amazing partnership well.

○ Callas, di Stefano, Panerai, Zaccaria; La Scala Chorus; Berlin RIAS Orchestra & Choir; Karajan (EMI CMS7 63631-2; 2 CDs).

Callas brought a passion and an immediacy to the role that no other soprano this century has equalled. Her recreation of Lucia's emotional and mental collapse is of such intensity that, to paraphrase one critic, you are not really aware that she is singing. Partnered by the ringing, full-bodied tones of di Stefano, and well supported by Karajan, this is the best of the three official recordings she made, even though the mono sound quality is not brilliant.

LA FILLE DU RÉGIMENT

One of Donizetti's most light-hearted operas, *La Fille du régiment* (1840) was also one of his most successful, receiving 44 performances in its first year in Paris. A tale of love triumphant against the odds, it is famous for two episodes; one for the soprano lead, the other for the tenor. The former, Marie's *Song of the Regiment*, is full of flowing ideas that will stick in your mind for days after you first hear it. However, it is her suitor Tonio's *Ah mes amis* that is the show-stopping *tour de force*, requiring the tenor to sing for upwards of five minutes before a terrifically demanding sequence of nine consecutive high Cs. Few singers have been able to manage such acrobatics, which is why this greatly enjoyable opera rarely reaches the stage.

⊙ Sutherland, Pavarotti, Sinclair, Bruyere, Mala, Garrett, Coates, Jones; Royal Opera House Orchestra & Chorus; Bonynge (Decca 414 520-2DH2; 2 CDs).

In the 1960s, when this record was made, Luciano Pavarotti was unrivalled in bel canto roles, and it was his New York Met appearance as Tonio that made him a superstar. This is a really remarkable performance, powerful, accurate and bursting with character. Joan Sutherland is extremely fine if a bit precious, and Richard Bonynge binds the whole together with his brisk and enthusiastic accompaniment.

DON PASQUALE

In *Don Pasquale* (1843), his late comic masterpiece, Donizetti plundered the classical heritage of Mozart to create a sort of operatic *commedia dell'arte*. Centring on an old man's attempt to find himself a young wife, the opera is remarkable for its free-flowing conversational recitative and the lightness of its orchestration and vocal writing. The small cast, headed by nineteenth-century opera's most perfect soubrette role, make *Don Pasquale* ideally suited to small opera houses, yet it's infrequently performed, perhaps because it doesn't deliver the heart-stopping vocal tricks that people have come to expect from Italian opera. Fortunately, it works extremely well on record, where the quality of its tightly written libretto come to the fore.

◑ Corena, Sciutti, Oncina, Krause, Mercuriali; Vienna State Opera Orchestra & Chorus; Kertesz (Decca 433 036 2DM2; 2 CDs).

The Piccola Scala staged a famous production of *Don Pasquale* in 1959, almost exclusively for the talents of Graziella Sciutti, who was by then one of the world's greatest soubrettes. Decca recorded her in the role of Norina not long after and her perfomance sets the mark against which all others have to be measured – her voice is light, brilliantly flexible and shimmering with personality. Similarly outstanding are Fernando Corena and Tom Krause as the gullible Don and the scheming Doctor Malatesta. István Kertesz, in one of his few operatic recordings, strongly suggests he should have made more.

⊙ Bruson, Mei, Lopardo, Allen, Giaccomotti; Bavarian Radio Chorus; Munich Radio Orchestra; Abbado (RCA 09026 61924-2; 2 CDs).

This recording makes a more than acceptable modern alternative. Renato Bruson is an impressive-sounding Don whose comedic instincts never desert him. Eva Mei manages the difficult coloratura moments with wit and distinction even if she doesn't approach the depth of personality that Sciutti was capable of. Under Roberto Abbado's nimble direction, the whole thing shoots along with infectious brio and panache.

JOHN DOWLAND

(1563–1626)

The lute was the most popular solo instrument in Europe at the end of the sixteenth century and John Dowland was one of its most skilful practitioners. But, despite his prowess, he repeatedly failed to gain the position he so coveted at the English court, a failure he felt strongly in spite of a highly successful career abroad. Perhaps his Catholicism, to which he had converted while resident in France in the 1580s, had hindered him at the English court (though it did not effect his older contemporary William Byrd; see p.95). At any rate Dowland abandoned his new faith in 1597 prior to returning briefly to England from Italy where, as an itinerant performer, he had fallen in with a group of disaffected English Catholics whose treasonable plans had considerably alarmed him. The following year he obtained an extremely lucrative position as lutenist to King Christian IV of Denmark, remaining there until 1606 but making several lengthy trips to London to visit his wife and son – and, almost certainly, to apply again for a post at the English court. Ironically, when he was finally appointed as one of the King's lutenists in 1612, his inspiration – at least as a composer – seems to have deserted him.

Dowland was greatly admired in his lifetime by fellow-musicians as well as by writers: the poet Richard Barnfield, in his sonnet in *Praise of Music and Poetry*, wrote that his "heavenly touch upon the lute doth ravish human sense". Yet despite this esteem he appears to have been a profoundly discontented and melancholic man, a fact reflected in his music, which dwells almost obsessively on sadness and death.

LACHRIMAE

Perhaps Dowland's most famous work is the collection of pieces for viol consort and lute entitled *Lachrimae, or Seaven Teares Figured in Seaven*

Passionate Pavans. This is a series of subtle divisions (variations) on a slow and sombre melody in which the opening motif of a falling fourth recurs throughout the sequence. The melody, which also existed as both a lute solo and as the song *Flow My Tears*, became the most famous in Europe, parodied and imitated by numerous composers. The collection also contained other consort music, including one of Dowland's saddest and most complex pieces entitled, appropriately, *Semper Dowland, semper dolens* (Always Dowland, Always Doleful).

O Hesperion XX (Astree E 8701).

There is no disguising the fact that these are profoundly gloomy pieces, but Hesperion XX combat the prevailing darkness by alternating each pavane with a contrasting galliard, rather than playing these more sprightly pieces at the end, as printed by Dowland. They also employ a warm tone and expressive dynamics which considerably enliven the music, even though their speeds are markedly slower than most rival recordings. Purists have criticized their approach, but the result is the most compelling account of this music currently available.

SONGS

Flow My Tears had originally appeared in 1600 in the second of the four books of songs that Dowland published, most of which consistently reflect the cult of melancholy that was so prevalent in Elizabethan court circles. In fact, though Dowland set the words of several leading poets, many of the most lugubrious texts (*In Darkness Let me Dwell, Go Crystal Tears*) were anonymous. Dowland's greatness as a songwriter lay in his ability to match exactly the music to the feeling of the words, a preoccupation that places him closer to Italian madrigalists, like Monteverdi and Marenzio (who he knew), than to his English colleagues.

O The First Booke of Songs: Muller; Wilson (ASV CD GAU 135).

The First Booke of Songs, the least morose of Dowland's song compilations, has a simplicity and a directness which is well served by Rufus Muller's clear and firm-toned voice. The meaning of the sometimes complex texts is on the whole nicely conveyed, although he sometimes succumbs to the English habit of over-enunciating consonants at the beginning of words. He is at his best in the slower more introsective songs like *Go Crystal Tears* or *Come, Heavy Sleep*, where he allows himself a greater degree of expressiveness and a more intimate tone quality.

SOLO LUTE MUSIC

Dowland wrote more than a hundred lute solos in a wide variety of musical forms, including dance forms like the slow pavane or the sprightly galliard (frequently played as a pair). He was particularly adept at divisions (as variations were then called), and much of his lute music displays a contrapuntal sophistication far in excess of most of his contemporaries. The expressive range of his music is wide, although the self-consciously melancholic nature of much of it is what he is best known for. In fact many lute pieces display a sly wit, not least in their titles: thus we have *The Frogg Galliard, Mrs Winter's Jumpp*, and the mysterious pair *Mrs White's Thing* and *Mrs White's Nothing*.

O Complete Lute Works Volume 1: O'Dette (Harmonia Mundi HMU 907160).

There are many good lutenists around today, but few sound so at ease with the instrument as the American Paul O'Dette, and few have immersed themselves so completely in Dowland's music. His five-disc set of the complete lute music (available individually) is unlikely to be bettered for fluency and spontaneity, and an added bonus is that he plays on three different instruments, including a steel-stringed orpharion. Volume 1 is the logical place to start.

GUILLAUME DUFAY

(c.1400–1474)

Guillaume Dufay is one of an outstanding group of Franco-Flemish composers that emerged from the Dukedom of Burgundy, the most opulent and artistically fertile of the courts of fifteenth-century northern Europe. Dufay was connected to the Burgundian court but never formally attached to it, instead spending much of his working life in Italy, where his reputation grew so high that he was described by Piero de' Medici as "the greatest ornament of our age". Like Machaut, Dufay was a priest and he received a substantial part of his income from largely honorary church appointments, but unlike Machaut much of his music was written for the church. He is a seminal figure in the field of sacred music, helping to establish the Mass as a coherent and unified whole, a development that made it the principal vehicle of elaborate polyphony for the next century and a half.

Dufay was born in or near Cambrai, an important centre of religious music, and he began his career there in 1409 as a chorister at the cathedral. While still a young man he went to Italy to work for the Malatesta family at Pésaro before joining the Papal Chapel in 1428. Apart from two years as *maestro di cappella* to the Duke of Savoy, he remained a member of the papal choir until 1437, based firstly at Rome, then at Bologna and Florence. It was at Florence that he composed a motet, *Nuper Rosarum Flores*, for the consecration of the cathedral after the completion of Brunelleschi's stupendous dome – basing the form of the motet on the mathematical proportions of the cathedral. From 1440 until his death he was back at Cambrai, apart from one more spell with the Duke of Savoy between 1452 and 1458.

SACRED MUSIC

Polyphonic music – which in Dufay's time was reserved for occasions of great importance – was transformed by Dufay into a clearer, richer and more sonorous musical language, with harmonies and carefully placed dissonances that gave the music a feeling of forward progress. In his later Masses, his finest works, he employs the cantus firmus method, in which the musical material is built around an already existing melody, usually a section of plainchant. One of the best of these late Masses is the *Missa Ecce Ancilla Domine* (Behold the handmaid of the Lord), its name taken from the plainsong chant that forms its cantus firmus. It is written for four voices, but at least half the Mass, as a means of contrast, uses just two voices in different combinations. It's a remarkably powerful and attractive piece, in which slow, reverent passages are balanced by more rhythmically lively sections in the two-part writing.

⊙ Missa Ecce Ancilla Domini: Ensemble Gilles Binchois; Vellard (Virgin VC 545 050-2).

The Ensemble Binchois is one of the most exciting early-music groups around, with a wonderfully unforced style. In keeping with increasingly common practice, the *Missa Ecce Ancilla Domine* is here placed within a liturgical context which includes the various chants and hymns appropriate to the service for which it was written (the Feast of the Annunciation), thus helping to create a sense of occasion. The voices, which are all male, have a warmth and a suppleness which brings out the zest of the music without recourse to overt expressiveness. This is a performance which, though solemn, still feels like a celebration.

SECULAR MUSIC

Dufay wrote many secular songs (or *chansons*) and, although he rarely set words as refined as Machaut's, they mostly deal with the same theme of unrequited courtly love. Most of the songs are *rondeaux*, with sections of words and music recurring throughout, and many of them are polyphonic, employing three and sometimes four voices. Although he composed *chansons* throughout his career there is no obviously discernible change of style between the early and the late songs. All are characterized by a refined and lyrical quality, with memorable melodies that are often tinged with a hint of melancholy.

⊙ Ballades, Rondeaus, Lamentation: Ensemble Gilles Binchois; Vellard (Virgin VC7 59043-2).

Eleven of the eighteen works on this disc are by Dufay – the rest are by Binchois, a colleague of Dufay's and his equal as a songwriter. Vellard adopts a flexible approach: some songs are performed by voices, some by instruments, and some by both. As in their recording of *Missa Ecce Ancilla Domine*, there is a delightful lightness and purity to the singing of the Ensemble Gilles Binchois, with the plaintive tones of Brigitte Lesne making an outstanding contribution.

PAUL DUKAS

(1865–1935)

Outside of France Paul Dukas is known for a single work, *L'Apprenti sorcier* (The Sorcerer's Apprentice), which reached its widest audience in the shape of a cartoon. One of the most successful episodes in Walt Disney's *Fantasia* (1940) has a hapless Mickey Mouse confidently conjuring up a broom to carry water for him, only to find, as the house begins to flood, that he's unable to make it stop. Dukas's own problem was almost the reverse: an extremely self-critical and fastidious man, he composed very little and at the end of his life destroyed much of what he had written. What survives reveals a consummate craftsman, but one who found it hard to establish a strong, individual voice.

Dukas career parallels that of his slightly older contemporary, Debussy. Both men studied composition with Guiraud at the Paris Conservatoire (in 1888 Dukas narrowly missed winning the prestigious Prix de Rome which Debussy had won the year before); both of them wrote music criticism; and both wrote an opera based on a play by Maurice Maeterlinck. But, whereas Debussy was a naturally experimental composer, Dukas was a conservative who took a strong lead from others and tended to use established forms.

Before *L'Apprenti sorcier* brought him overnight fame in 1897, Dukas had written two substantial orchestral works. *Polyeucte* (1891), an overture to Corneille's play, reveals a debt to both Franck and Wagner in its rich chromaticism. More impressive is the *Symphony in C Major*, in which a tightening of structure and greater rhythmic incisiveness is combined with skilful atmospheric writing in the slow movement. For some, Dukas's greatest achievement is his opera *Ariane et Barbe-Bleue*, based on Maeterlinck's retelling of the Bluebeard legend. First performed in 1907, five years after the premiere of Debussy's *Pelléas et Mélisande*, it creates a similarly twilit world (with occasional quotes from *Pelléas*), but lacks the depth and intensity of Debussy's masterpiece.

From the time of his last major orchestral work, *La Péri* (1911), until his death in 1935, Dukas composed no more major works that have survived. Instead he spent much of his time as an editor of earlier French composers (including Rameau and Couperin) and as a Conservatoire teacher of future ones – most notably Olivier Messiaen (see p.256).

ORCHESTRAL MUSIC

L'Apprenti sorcier, inspired by a Goethe ballad, is one of the few works by Dukas which is uniquely his own. It's a brilliantly concentrated piece in which a central, jaunty theme is magically transformed from a mood of engaging confidence to one of sinister power through a deft employment of orchestral colour. Brass and wind seem to dominate the changing character of the theme, while shimmering strings are mainly used to establish a "once upon a time" feel at the beginning and end of the work. Tension is maintained, despite a series of false climaxes, through an unnerving dotted ryhthm in the lower instruments which never seems to go away.

La Péri displays a similar gift for theatrical suspense. It was commissioned from Diaghilev's Russian Ballet in 1911, but the company never performed the piece (despite Bakst's beautiful costume designs) because Dukas insisted that the lead should be performed by an outside dancer, Nathalie Trouhanova. The story tells of Prince Iskender's theft of the lotus-flower of immortality which is guarded by a beautiful *péri* or fairy. She dances for him, he falls in love with her and returns the flower, only for her to disappear. Dukas's ballet shares the same exotic sound-world as Rimsky-Korsakov's *Scheherazade* and Stravinsky's *Firebird* (two earlier Russian Ballet successes). As with both those works, there is an emphasis on diaphanous textures, rhapsodic climaxes and striking atmospheric effects, which is both magical and seductive.

⭘ La Péri, L'Apprenti sorcier: Ulster Orchestra; Tortelier (Chandos 8852; with Chabrier's *Suite pastorale* and *España*).

Over the years Yan Pascal Tortelier has built a reputation as one of the finest interpreters of early twentieth-century French repertoire and on this disc you can hear why. In both pieces it is not good enough merely to elicit beautiful and dynamically varied sounds from the orchestra (which certainly happens) – there must also be a keen sense of dramatic pacing, so that the sections grow out of each other naturally. Both conductor and orchestra really triumph in this area, achieving moments of incandescent beauty, especially in *La Péri*.

THE PIANO SONATA

The great French pianist Alfred Cortot called Dukas's *Piano Sonata* "one of the most important efforts ever made to adapt Beethovenian characteristics to the French pianistic style." It's a four-movement work on the grandest possible scale, which daringly juggles many disparate and seemingly contradictory elements into a largely coherent whole. The first movement resembles late Beethoven filtered through the sensibility of Scriabin: there seems to be a permanent and breathless build-up to a climax that never quite happens. The middle two movements evoke the organ loft, first through a radiant and serene religiosity that sounds like an improvisation, then through a fierce and fiery toccata. The final movement, the longest, is a strenously passionate rhapsody paying obvious homage to the last act of *Tristan und Isolde*. This is a work that makes strong demands on both performer and listener alike and should be approached with caution.

⭘ Ogdon (EMI CDM5 65996-2; with Dutilleux's *Piano Sonata*; Schmitt's *Deux mirages*).

Dukas's *Sonata* needs a pianist of skill, daring and vision – in short, a pianist who is more likely to be playing something other than Dukas. Fortunately, John Ogdon was a top-class performer who often investigated the more obscure reaches of the piano repertoire, and here he gives a torrential performance. Passionate without bombast, he conveys a true sense of Dukas's exploratory approach to the piano's possibilities.

JOHN DUNSTABLE

(c.1390–1453)

Very little is known about the English composer John Dunstable (or Dunstaple), but there is no doubt that his music exerted a profound and far-ranging influence throughout fifteenth-century Europe. Even during Dunstable's lifetime, the commentator Martin le Franc was remarking on the debt composers such as Dufay and Binchois owed to their older contemporary. Copied manuscripts of his music are found in libraries in Italy and Germany and even as far afield as Estonia. Dunstable's special impact on European composers can partly be explained by his probable service in the entourage of the powerful Duke of Bedford, regent of France between 1422 and 1437, who had Joan of Arc burnt as a witch. While in France Dunstable may have written music for the coronation of Henry VI in Paris, a possible French connection further strengthened by the fact that he was granted lands in France on the Duke of Bedford's death.

His major patrons in England were the dowager Queen Joan and the Duke of Gloucester (Bedford's brother). Both had links with St Albans Abbey, for which Dunstable wrote at least one motet (*Albanus roseo rutilat*), although he does not seem to have held a position there, nor ever to have taken holy orders – unusually for a composer of this time. It was the abbot of St Albans, John Whethamsteade, who wrote one, if not both, of the two Latin epitaphs commemorating the composer. Each of these refers almost as much to Dunstable's fame as an astronomer as they do to his musicianship, and it seems likely that his later years were devoted to study of the Quadrivium (arithmetic, astronomy, geometry and music). His talents may even have extended to the visual arts: a Dunstable manuscript in Cambridge, concerned with astronomical and astrological speculations, contains a number of fine and imaginative drawings which some scholars have attributed to the composer.

SACRED MUSIC

Dunstable was working at the start of a musical Golden Age in England – indeed some of the music ascribed to him may have been written by his equally talented English contemporary Leonel Power. Both men seem to have written exclusively sacred music and both had fully assimilated the technical innovations of the Ars Nova (see p.231), in particular a more rigorous and numerically ordered approach to rhythm. Dunstable composed several motets for three or four voices, in which the two higher parts were supported by a lower voice moving at a slower speed. Often these motets were isorhythmic, which means that the under part is made up of a repeated rhythmic unit. Most isorhythmic motets were divided into three progressively faster sections and most employed different words in each part. This made for some rich and complex textures, and it was this richness of sonority which made such an impression on Dunstable's continental colleagues. An even greater impact was achieved by the English invention of the cantus firmus Mass, in which a borrowed melody – usually sung in the tenor part – was employed as the structural basis for each movement of the Mass. In an age when the expression of the meaning of the sacred words was of marginal importance, this went a long way towards imposing a stylistic unity on the Mass. Dunstable (or perhaps Power) wrote one such Mass, the *Missa Rex seculorum*, which is based on a plainsong antiphon for St Benedict.

⊙ John Dunstable: The Hilliard Ensemble (Virgin VER 5 61342 2).

This disc first appeared in 1984 and still sounds fresh and exciting, with the usual Hilliard strengths of perfect intonation, meticulous ensemble and rhythmic suppleness well to the fore. The group concentrate on the motets and include two sections of an incomplete Mass. The mood is very much a devotional one, with the group bringing out the beauty of the sonorities by gentle unforced singing, rather than emphasizing the occasionally rather strange harmonies.

⊙ John Dunstaple: Orlando Consort (Metronome MET CD 1009).

The advantages of this disc – despite the higher price – are twenty minutes more music and first ever recordings of the *Missa Rex seculorum* and the extraordinary *Gloria in canon*, which was discovered just as the Orlando Consort went into the studio. It's more of a mixed programme than the Virgin disc and includes five sparkling antiphons. The group's approach is more robust than that of the Hilliards, and the sound is much more forward and not so homogenous – what you lose in solemnity and purity of voice you gain in liveliness.

ANTONÍN DVOŘÁK

(1841–1904)

With the tide of revolutions that swept across the continent during the 1840s, nationalism became a dominating factor in European art. Nowhere was this process more important than in Czechoslovakia, and no composer was more prominently nationalistic than Antonín Dvořák. Of the three great Czech composers – Smetana (see p.395) and Janáček (see p.204) are the others – Dvořák was the one whose influence upon the development of a national voice was the most original and lasting, and it was Dvořák who was most successful in reconciling folk traditions with symphonic music. Few composers of his time could match his flair for infectious melody or his ability to orchestrate with kaleidoscopic colour and nuance.

Born in Bohemia, Dvořák spent his uneventful early life in study and practice, then in 1863 played in a concert of Wagner excerpts, conducted by the composer himself – an experience that had a significant impact on his approach to opera. From 1864 he played viola in the Prague National Theatre Orchestra, where from 1866 the chief conductor was Smetana, the fountainhead of Czech musical nationalism. In 1873 Dvořák left the orchestra to devote himself to composition, and within a year his *Symphony No. 3* had won him an Austrian national prize as well as the respect of

LEBRECHT COLLECTION

Dvořák (far right) and his family in New York, 1892, shortly after their arrival in the US

Brahms, who was on the jury. Two years later, Dvořák's *Moravian Duets* brought him the same prize, and again Brahms was delighted by the young man's progress, going so far as to recommend his music to a publisher.

With the appearance of such distinctively Czech works as the *Slavonic Dances* (1878) Dvořák was soon gaining ever widening recognition: Brahms's friend Joachim commissioned a violin concerto from him (but had to wait years for it); Richter, Elgar's friend, commissioned a symphony; while von Bülow, Wagner's friend, promoted Dvořák's work through concerts and tours. Numerous trips to England, where he was championed for his conducting as much as his composition, extended his fame, brought him money and produced several of his greatest works, including the *Symphony No. 7*.

Dvořák's success reached one of its peaks in 1891, when he was appointed Professor of Composition at the Prague Conservatory, awarded an honorary doctorate by Cambridge University and invited to take up the directorship of the National Conservatory of Music in New York, with an annual salary of $15,000. In October 1892, after a five-month farewell tour of Bohemia and Moravia, Dvořák finally moved to the US, where he remained for three years. This period was not especially happy but it was very fruitful, as Dvořák's discovery of America's folk heritage combined with his aching homesickness to produce a string of masterpieces, including the violin concerto and the *New World Symphony*.

In 1895 he returned to teach at the Prague Conservatory, becoming its director in 1901 – the year of his sixtieth birthday, which was celebrated in Prague by performances of his work. His final years were extremely contented, and most of his time was spent working on tone poems and operas. Unfortunately, though Dvořák produced a total of ten operas, only one of them, *Rusalka*, has achieved any popularity, and that's largely down to one extremely famous soprano aria (*O Silver Moon*). His reputation continues to rest primarily on his orchestral music.

ORCHESTRAL MUSIC

Admiration for the music of Beethoven and Schubert was what first led Dvořák to consider writing symphonic music, and his early symphonies (the first, *Bells of Zlonice*, was completed in 1865) betray these Viennese influences quite strongly, as well as the influence of Brahms. It was not until his wholehearted commitment to Czech nationalism in the mid-1870s that Dvořák's voice began to be heard properly, and though there's a strong Czech element to his fourth symphony (1874) the sequence improves markedly with *Symphony No. 6*. Even stronger expressions of nationalist feeling are to be found in Dvořák's late symphonic poems, a genre in which he could transform the material of Czech folklore freed from the constrictions of classical form.

◑ **Complete Symphonies: London Symphony Orchestra; Kertész** (Decca 430 046-2; 6 CDs; with *In Nature's Realm, My Home, Carnival*).

Istvan Kertész did much to help re-establish Dvořák's earlier symphonies as works to be taken seriously in the complete cycle, which he recorded in the 1960s. These are classic accounts: there's a palpable rapport between orchestra and conductor, and the result is playing of an amazing warmth and enthusiasm, even in the weaker symphonies.

SYMPHONY NO. 6

The marvellous *Symphony No. 6* (1880) owes much to Brahms's second symphony, which is also in D major and in places displays somewhat overweighted orchestration, but at the same time it's unmistakably a Dvořák symphony. Typical of Dvořák's mature style are the frequent, quasi-romantic key modulations within the determinedly classical structure, and the use of the Scherzo for fervently nationalist sentiments. This movement, a *Furiant* (a Czech dance), was the first to establish him as a Slavonic composer, and it clearly distanced him from the plethora of German symphonists (most now forgotten) who were then jostling for attention.

○ **Czech Philharmonic Orchestra; Belohlávek** (Chandos CHAN9170; with *The Wood Dove*).

In the absence of the fine Decca recording of Dohnányi and the Cleveland Orchestra, this is the performance to go for. The Czech Philharmonic could probably give a good performance of this work without a conductor, but under Jiri Belohlávek they really skip along with amazing verve and passion.

SYMPHONY NO. 7

A stark contrast to the well-being of the sixth symphony, the *Symphony No. 7* is overshadowed by intimations of tragedy, and in this respect, as in its sense of retrospection, it is not unlike Brahms's third symphony, of which Dvořák was almost certainly aware – they were written in the same year (1885), and it is surely no accident that this symphony is in the bleak relative minor key to the F major of Brahms's third. The Scherzo and finale contain some of Dvořák's most remarkable musical ideas, and their combination of rhythmic vitality and free-form melody make these movements two of the finest of the late nineteenth century. The emotional gravity of this mighty work gives this symphony a claim to be Dvořák's greatest.

○ Oslo Philharmonic Orchestra; Jansons (EMI CDC7 54663-2; with *Symphony No. 8*).

Driving, almost impulsive zeal from Jansons, whose control over the surging momentum of this music is absolute. There is a polish and all-pervading warmth, which is made to draw together the many fine strands of Dvořák's most disparate orchestral work. There is a better seventh in the catalogue – the Kubelik version – but that's available only as part of his complete symphony set.

○ Scottish National Orchestra; Järvi (Chandos CHAN 8501; with *The Golden Spinning Wheel*).

Neeme Järvi's recording of the seventh is the best of his complete cycle: keen and energetic, with a good sense of scale and revealing attention to detail. The orchestra play with real enthusiasm, and the fill-up performance of one of the late symphonic poems is excellent.

SYMPHONY NO. 8

Dvořák's *Symphony No. 8* (1889) again stands in complete contrast to the preceding symphony. In many ways it harks back to the exuberant cheerfulness and Czech feeling of *No. 6*, and only in the first movement's introduction is there any sign of the seventh's sobriety. Although the main theme from this opening is repeated later in the movement, the bulk of it is dominated by one of Dvořák's most inspired melodies. The Adagio, almost a tone poem of birdsong and country life, is similarly melodic, while the third movement is a rustic dance of infectious good humour. The finale is a set of variations (rare for Dvořák) that builds towards a rousing and suitably conclusive climax.

◑ Berlin Philharmonic Orchestra; Kubelik (Deutsche Grammophon 447 412-2; with *Symphony No. 9*).

Kubelik's is an intense and exciting account – Dvořák seized by the collar and propelled, like one long glowing fanfare. This is a warm and expansive reading, with the BPO in sparkling, virtuosic form.

SYMPHONY NO. 9

The best-known tune in all Dvořák is the main theme from the third movement of the *Symphony No. 9* (1893), a mournfully nostalgic piece of music that has been appropriated by countless TV producers and advertising types – it was the music from the old Hovis ads, with the cloth-capped little lad pushing his bike up the cobblestoned road past the coal pits. The symphony was intended to celebrate the fourth centennial of Columbus's "discovery" of America, and its title, *From the New World*, might lead you to expect a more upbeat tone. Dvořák wrote of it that "the influence of America can be felt by anyone who has a nose", but the symphony's American-influenced rhythmic patterns and tunes are turned into an expression of acute homesickness and thus of Czech identity – similar to his *American Quartet* (see p.134). The music is tirelessly melodic and brilliantly scored for a large orchestra, but be warned that it is very long and in the wrong hands can become tedious.

◑ Berlin Philharmonic Orchestra; Kubelik (Deutsche Grammophon 447 412-2; with *Symphony No. 8*).

Kubelik's *Ninth* is very different in spirit – if not in technique – from the *Eighth*. His *New World* is soul-searching and intensely dramatic. Never has Dvořák's finale hung together so convincingly as it does here; but, throughout, the playing is shatteringly powerful.

◑ Vienna Philharmonic Orchestra; Kondrashin (Decca 430 702-2; with *American Suite*).

Deep affection and high drama also coincide in Kondrashin's interpretation, which is a little less highly wrought than Kubelik's. This time is it the slow movement which is unbeatable for its depth of feeling, although the Scherzo is also a brilliantly vivid realization.

SYMPHONIC POEMS

Dvořák's four symphonic poems – *The Water Goblin*, *The Noonday Witch*, *The Golden Spinning Wheel* and *The Wild Dove* – were written in 1896, and were based upon some gruesome folk ballads by the nationalist writer Erben. Following the examples of Liszt, Smetana and Richard Strauss, Dvořák here uses a single theme for each central character and transforms it as the situation demands, thereby creating musical continuity while projecting a sense of narrative development. If he is less successful than Strauss, it is because he follows the very specific source material too closely but, despite this, Dvořák's masterly orchestration brings considerable life and colour to these Grimm-like creations.

◑ Bavarian Radio Symphony Orchestra; Kubelik (Deutsche Grammophon 435 074-2; 2 CDs; with overtures).

Again, Kubelik is highly sympathetic to Dvořák's rich orchestral style and he allows the music to follow its natural course without straining to score interpretive points. He brings entertaining flair to these pieces, and the Bavarian Radio Symphony Orchestra respond with perfect spontaneity.

THE SLAVONIC DANCES

The *Slavonic Dances* began life as folk-dance rhythms, became piano duets, and ended up not only as Dvořák's introduction to the world beyond Bohemia, but as staples of the orchestral encore repertory. In 1874 the struggling composer had applied for an Austrian State Stipendium, for which one of the judges was Brahms's colleague Eduard Hanslick. In November 1877, Hanslick wrote to Dvořák, "Brahms has taken a lively interest in your splendid talent and was particularly pleased by your two-part Bohemian songs." The upshot was an introduction to Brahms's publisher, Simrock, who immediately commissioned "two volumes of Bohemian and Moravian Dances". The reward for the gaiety and buoyant movement of these eight pieces was, for Dvořák, overnight celebrity. A second set of *Slavonic Dances* followed eight years later.

⊙ Vienna Philharmonic Orchestra; Previn (Philips 442 125-2PH).

Previn's is the most relaxed and good-humoured version. His concern for inner detail behind the surface gloss pays off in a spring-like brightness. A transparent recording lets the VPO's glowing elegance shine through.

THE CONCERTOS

Dvořák wrote four concertos, but the piano concerto is a Beethoven-ish hybrid that never really gets off the ground, while the first of the two cello concertos is a fairly insubstantial work which was only discovered seventy years ago in sketch form, and needed to be orchestrated by a third party. The latter is of interest chiefly as a preparation for the second cello concerto, a piece that ranks alongside the majestic concerto for violin.

CELLO CONCERTO NO. 2

The second cello concerto, the last major composition that Dvořák composed during his stay in America, has become one of the most popular of all his works and perhaps the most popular concerto ever written for the instrument. Dvořák was asked to write the piece by a friend of Wagner, the cellist Hanus Wihan, who gave the first performance of Strauss's cello sonata as well as this concerto. The music that Dvořák composed is richly inventive, full of deep feeling (the final movement was revised after the death of his wife), and perfectly fitted to the cello – Dvořák's experience as an orchestral player enabled him to appreciate the problems of balance and blending that arise when orchestrating for a solo instrument with such a low tonal register. Dvořák's understanding of orchestral sonority and of the cello's distinct textural qualities make this grand and emotionally intense piece one of his finest achievements.

⊙ Rostropovich; Berlin Philharmonic Orchestra; Karajan (Deutsche Grammophon 447 413-2; with Tchaikovsky, *Rococo Variations*).

Modern orchestras tend to distort the concerto's intricately studied proportions, but Karajan was aware of this potential for imbalance and he controls the Berlin Philharmonic with uncommon clarity. Of Rostropovich's many recordings of this score this one, made in 1969, is the best, bursting with energy and fresh ideas. It's coupled with a beautifully paced account of Tchaikovsky's *Rococo Variations*.

THE VIOLIN CONCERTO

Like Brahms's concerto, the *Violin Concerto* was dedicated to and written with the help of Joachim, but unlike the Brahms this is an under-explored work. Certainly it has its weaknesses. The first movement is a truncated affair that finishes before all its thematic ideas have been fully explored, and the finale is an annoyingly irregular movement that never quite grips your attention. The reason for hearing this work is its slow movement, which contains some of Dvořák's most haunting melodies. The central theme, when repeated near the movement's end by the full orchestra, is one of the finest creations in the concerto repertoire.

⊙ Mintz; Berlin Philharmonic Orchestra; Levine (Deutsche Grammophon 419 618-2; with Sibelius, *Violin Concerto*).

Shlomo Mintz's characterful and intensely beautiful sound wins the day in the face of Levine's excessively prominent accompaniment. This is a profoundly lyrical performance that makes much of the sweeping central movement.

CHAMBER MUSIC

Dvořák composed a large amount of chamber music, which is hardly surprising for a viola player who greatly admired the chamber work of the classical masters. His Op. 1 and Op. 2 were both for string quartet, an ensemble for which he wrote some fourteen of his forty chamber pieces, one of which – the *String Quartet No. 12* (known as *The American*) – is one of the most popular quartets ever written. Much of the chamber music has an obvious kinship to that of Brahms, particular in its contrapuntal weight, but Dvořák's style is invariably lighter, more sweetly melodic and more freely inventive.

PIANO TRIOS NOS. 3 & 4

The third piano trio (1883) is the most orchestral and dramatically charged of Dvořák's chamber compositions, containing almost every distinctive feature of his music within its four movements. Characterized by an unprecedented seriousness of purpose, it marked a decisive step forward in his career and foreshadowed the epic expression of the seventh symphony, which came two years later. The Allegretto grazioso contains music of haunting pathos but this tendency towards sadness is restrained by some entrancing, disruptive cross-rhythms.

The last of the trios, known as the *Dumky Trio*, was completed in February 1891. It is one of Dvořák's most bittersweet creations. The *dumka* was a Slavonic folk ballad, predominantly elegiac in mood: Dvořák transformed it into a musical form in which a melancholic slow idea was contrasted with alternating sections of a faster dance-like character. The six movements are intended to be played with the briefest of pauses. The richly eloquent cello part was composed for the virtuoso Hanus Wihan, who premiered the work with the composer and the violinist Ferdiand Lachner.

◑ **Beaux Arts Trio** (Philips 426 095-2).

Brightly energetic playing from the Beaux Arts Trio, who play with all their customary flair and imagination. The performances date from the late 1960s, but the sound is good, if occasionally a little harsh.

STRING QUARTETS NOS. 12–14

The *String Quartet No. 12* (*The American*) was the first of three chamber works composed in 1893 while Dvořák was living in the US, and it was soon established as his best-loved quartet. Although its opening was modelled on the introduction to Smetana's *Quartet No. 1*, there is little of Smetana's raw misery here – frustrated energy and nostalgia are the prevailing moods, the latter element typified by the Lento, with its plaintive, soaring violin melody.

Dvořák's last works, written during a burst of creative activity at the end of 1895, reveal his musical imagination at its most visionary – subtle, complex and harmonically advanced. The last two quartets – *No. 13* in G major and *No. 14* in A flat major – are both characterized by a deeply ambivalent emotionalism. The soulful Adagio variations of *No. 13* are shot through with more joyful moments but ultimately its mood is one of resignation. Similarly, *No. 14* has a slow movement of almost unbearable pathos which is only relieved by the exuberant and folk-inspired finale.

○ **String Quartet No. 12: Hagen Quartet** (Deutsche Grammophon DG 419 601-2; with *Cypresses* & Kodály's *String Quartet No. 2*).

The intonation, style and recorded sound of the Hagen Quartet are faultless, and it's greatly to their credit that they refuse to sentimentalize Dvořák's music. As a bonus, the quartet is coupled with elegant performances of Dvor&ák's lovely transcriptions of his bittersweet songs, *Cypresses*.

○ **String Quartets Nos. 12 & 13: Lindsay Quartet** (ASV CD DCA 797).

The Lindsays' status as one of the most searching interpreters of chamber music is fully deserved, and the Dvořák readings are particularly fresh and revealing. All their hallmarks are in evidence here – the widest range of expressive gestures and, above all, an emphatically spontaneous way of performing.

○ **String Quartet No. 14: Lindsay Quartet** (ASV CD DCA 788; with *Quartet No. 10*).

The Lindsays play with biting incision and spring-like eagerness. This performance is a revelation – a superlative rendering of a rarely acknowledged masterpiece.

STRING QUINTET NO. 2

The second of the three chamber works composed in America, Dvořák's second quintet is scored for unconventional forces – string quartet plus double bass. The music is disarmingly original as well, merging Czech and North American Indian melodies, and, in the Larghetto, following Haydn's example of composing a set of variations with a double theme. It's full of incredibly difficult music, but Dvořák's propensity for instrumental colour and independence makes this one of the most entertaining of all quintets.

◑ **Serenata of London** (Collins COLL 3007-2; with Britten, *Simple Symphony*; Strauss, *Till Eulenspiegl*).

This CD contains some remarkable, spontaneous playing – the Serenata really do seem to be enjoying the melodies and rhythmic élan of the *Quintet*. The sound might be a little too close for some tastes, but it does serve to highlight the vibrant textures of the music.

○ **Panocha Quartet** (Supraphon 11 1461-2 131; with *Intermezzo – Nocturne* and *Sextet*).

The augmented Panocha Quartet is always alive to the Bohemian eagerness of the *Quintet*. The players negotiate every twist and turn in a performance which never loses its spring and metrical wit. Their crisp, deft articulation is a constant pleasure and the fine Czech recording does them full justice.

HANNS EISLER

(1898–1962)

The reason that Hanns Eisler remains confined to the ranks of cult musicians is political – he was one of the few decent composers who took readily to the new political system in postwar East Germany (the national anthem is by him), and his loyalty to that discredited regime is unlikely to make record companies rush to rehabilitate him, though there has been a marked increase in recordings in recent years. Though a convinced communist, Eisler was no socialist-realist hack. He was a pupil of Arnold Schoenberg in the early 1920s, then felt that he had to break with a teacher whose ideals were irreconcilable with Eisler's desire to make serious music a part of the daily lives of ordinary people. This mission to create radically politicized art led him from Vienna to Berlin and into collaboration with Bertolt Brecht, before Nazi persecution forced him into exile – a sequence of events similar to the career of Kurt Weill (see p.476) – though Eisler was much more politically engaged than Weill. Like so many of his generation, he eventually fled to the United States, where he worked in Hollywood and renewed his partnership with Brecht – both men contributed to the Fritz Lang film *Hangmen Also Die*. In 1947 he and Brecht fell victim to Senator McCarthy's witch-hunt of Communists and appeared before the infamous Un-American Activities committee. Despite the intercession of a group of intellectuals, including Einstein and Thomas Mann, Eisler was deported to East Germany in 1950 and remained there for the rest of his life.

DEUTSCHE SINFONIE

Eisler had the idea of writing a large scale antifascist work, provisionally entitled *Concentration Camp Symphony*, in 1935 and had completed the first two movements a few years later. However the Nazis and exile intervened and the work became a work-in-progress, only receiving its first performance in 1959. Again Brecht supplied nearly all of the text, which ranges from the crudely hectoring ("the class struggle alone can liberate the masses in cities and countryside. . . ") to the bitterly ironic ("If God doesn't bother about the rain what does he bother about?"). Eisler puts it all together as a series of cantatas for different soloists and chorus with orchestral interludes, in a style that occasionally recalls others

(Hindemith, Schoenberg and, at times, even Mahler) but which is notable, above all, for its lucidity and lack of bombast. The cumulative effect is surprisingly powerful and by the end very moving.

⊙ Wangemann, Markert, Görne, Lika; Ernst Senff Chor, Berlin; Gewandhausorchester Leipzig; Zagrosek (Decca 448 389-2).

This is the only Eisler (so far) to be included in Decca's Entartete Musik series, dedicated to composers suppressed by the Nazis. It's a marvellous performance that should persuade many people to take Eisler's work more seriously.

FILM MUSIC

Eisler was a highly distinguished film composer, winning Oscars for the Hollywood films *Hangmen Also Die* (1942) and *None but the Lonely Heart* (1944), and collaborating with Alain Resnais on his film *Nuit et Brouillard* (1955). In the 1930s he worked with a number of left-wing documentary-makers and subsequently adapted his own music as orchestral suites. These included *Niemandsland*, an antiwar film by Victor Trivas, which became *Suite No. 2*; *Kuhle Wampe*, a feature film made by Brecht about a worker's holiday camp (*Suite No. 3*); and *Die Jugend hat das Wort*, a documentary by Joris Ivens (*Suite No. 4*) set in the Urals. This is the kind of objective "utility" music that radical German composers like Hindemith and Weill had proposed as an alternative to the subjective emotional wallowing of Expressionism and Romanticism. It's bright, lightly scored music (with wind instruments, as opposed to strings, very much to the fore) with an acerbic and unsentimental edge to it.

⊙ Suites Nos. 2–4: Berlin Radio Symphony Orchestra; Rögner (Berlin Classics 0092 282BC; with *Theme and Variations*).

Originally issued by the East German Nova label, this recording from the 1970s has a rough-edged feel to it which seems entirely appropriate. The performances have real energy, and anyone enamoured of Weill's Berlin music will feel at home here.

SONGS

Eisler wrote little music specifically for the concert hall – he wanted his music to have a social function, and thus devoted much of his energy to composing strongly political songs, many of them to texts by Bertolt Brecht. Brecht frequently used the most scathing irony, not just to point up the exploitation and depredations of the working class but also to denounce political passivity (for instance in the *Ballad on Approving the World*). Eisler perfectly matches the Brechtian tone with music that is clear and direct. Like Weill, he consciously tries to bridge the divide between popular styles and classical music, and many songs are good enough to survive separation from their theatre or cabaret context. The difficulty is finding the right singer to perform them (neither too refined nor too rough), and currently there are no recommendable versions in the catalogue.

EDWARD ELGAR

(1857–1934)

E

The so-called English musical renaissance really got going in the years immediately following World War I, as Vaughan Williams and his contemporaries began to write pieces that reflected their researches into English folk music. Edward Elgar, on the other hand, though he was the progenitor of this renaissance in the sense that he gave international stature to British music, was a more purely European composer, with a musical language derived more from Wagner and Brahms than from anything native. In his own day his older contemporaries Stanford and Parry were equally well respected, but history has established him as the greater original – and arguably the first great English composer since Purcell.

Despite his haughtily aristocratic appearance and later recognition by the Edwardian social establishment, Elgar was always a provincial countryman at heart – although he lived in London during the early years of the twentieth century, he found refuge from city life in the Sussex hills. He was born in a village outside Worcester, where his father served as organist at the Catholic church and ran a music shop and piano-tuning business. Edward never received much in the way of formal musical education. Initially he picked up his skills from the environment in which he lived, helping his father by playing the organ in church and teaching himself the violin in order to play in the local orchestra. His compositional technique was acquired by similar means, trying out his early works with the help of his siblings.

His ambitions grew when in 1889 he married one of his piano pupils, Caroline Alice Roberts, the daughter of a retired army general. The combination of the warmth of this relationship and his acceptance into upper-middle-class circles seems to have inspired him, and the 1890s saw a great increase in his prowess. The *Serenade for Strings* (1892) was his first work to be published, though international fame eluded him until the first performances of the *Enigma Variations* in 1899. His greatest choral work, *The Dream of Gerontius*, was premiered the following year, but to little acclaim at the time, though the succeeding years were to be his most successful. He became a household name following the appearance of his *Pomp and Circumstance March No. 1* in 1901, was knighted in 1904, and in 1911 was awarded the Order of Merit. In the intervening years he composed some of his largest works, among them *The Apostles* (1903), the *Introduction and Allegro for Strings* (1905), *The Kingdom* (1906), *Symphony No. 1* (1908), the *Violin Concerto* (1910), *Symphony No. 2* (1911) and the symphonic study *Falstaff* (1913).

Just a few patriotic works emerged during the war years, but the end of the war brought forth perhaps his greatest work, the *Cello Concerto* (1919). Three major chamber works composed at the same time, a violin sonata, a string quartet and a piano

LEBRECHT COLLECTION

Elgar conducting his first recording session, January 1914

quintet share its valedictory, autumnal mood, as if Elgar were pouring out his disillusionment with the changes the war had brought. The death of his wife in 1920 put a virtual stop to his creativity, and for the fourteen years that remained to him he composed little, concentrating instead on conducting and making recordings of his music.

Elgar was one of this century's consummate masters of orchestral writing – his scores are almost mosaic-like in their selective, ever-changing use of instrumental sounds. Moreover, he was one of the least parochial English composers – Wagner's *Parsifal* pervades the music of *Gerontius*, while the melodic lines and harmonic idiom of Brahms are particularly noticeable in the late chamber works. Yet the grandeur and nostalgia of Elgar, his pastoralism and occasional pomposity, make him the epitome of a particularly Edwardian English style.

CHORAL AND VOCAL MUSIC

Though choral music was a preoccupation of Elgar's early years, nothing of lasting value emerged until *The Light of Life* (1896) and the historical oratorios of the late 1890s, *King Olaf* and *Caractacus*. Most rewarding of his choral compositions is the series of works from the turn of the century, beginning with *The Dream of Gerontius*(1900). From the success of *The Dream of Gerontius* emerged a plan to compose a trilogy of oratorios detailing the founding of the Christian Church, a project abandoned when the first two – *The Apostles* and *The Kingdom* – failed to achieve a positive response from their audiences.

THE DREAM OF GERONTIUS

Elgar had been brought up a Roman Catholic, but his faith had never been particularly strong. *The Dream of Gerontius*, a setting of Cardinal Newman's long poem dealing with the soul's passage from life into death, can be seen as Elgar's attempt to establish his faith more fully – and indeed he followed it up with two biblical oratorios. This is one of his most deeply felt works, a sensitive yet stirring setting of a text that tackles the most fundamental concepts, as Gerontius (tenor) moves through his final illness and is led on his journey to heaven by the figure of an angel (contralto). Elgar's dramatic imagination and the absence of any sentimentality lifts *Gerontius* clear of the morass of forgettable Victorian oratorios. When he had completed it, Elgar wrote on the score "This is the best of me", and arguably *The Dream of Gerontius* is his greatest achievement.

O Palmer, Davies, Howell; London Symphony Chorus and Orchestra; Hickox (Chandos CHAN 8641/2; 2 CDs; with *The Music Makers*).

Hickox is an outstanding choral conductor and creates a particularly bright and vivid impression, without losing sight of the mystical core of the work. His soloists are outstanding, with Arthur Davies an unusually dynamic Gerontius, Felicity Palmer is movingly intense as the angel and Gwynne Howell particularly strong in the double role of Priest and Angel of the Agony.

◑ Wyn-Rogers, Rolfe Johnson, George; Royal Liverpool Philharmonic Orchestra; Handley (EMI CD-EMX 2500; 2 CDs; with *Organ Sonata*).

This recording from Vernon Handley is in the Boult tradition and makes a viable mid-price alternative. All three soloists are excellent, with Anthony Rolfe Johnson a particularly moving Gerontius.

SEA PICTURES

Elgar was not a particularly distinguished songwriter, but he excelled himself in the cycle of five songs that he wrote for contralto and orchestra (premiered by Clara Butt in 1899). The sea evidently inspired him, for his orchestral writing successfully represents its powerful presence through several deft touches – from the heavy chords conveying the swell of the sea in the first song, to the storm-tossed fervour of the last. The choice of verses is typically Edwardian: a mixture of over-wrought religiosity (*Sabbath Morning at Sea*), bombast (*The Swimmer*) and a touch of fairyland (*Sea Slumber Song*). But Elgar manages to raise his material into something genuinely moving, nowhere more so than in the simple directness with which he sets his wife's poem *In Haven*.

O Baker; London Symphony Orchestra; Barbirolli (EMI CDC7 47329-2; with *Cello Concerto*).

It's unfortunate for other contraltos that Janet Baker has made this work so utterly her own. Her reading abounds in fervour and commitment, every word sounds meant, and it's hard not to get swept along by it all. Barbirolli makes sure that the LSO are alive to the score's more subtle detailing.

ORCHESTRAL MUSIC

"Gentlemen, let us now rehearse the greatest symphony of modern times, written by the greatest modern composer, and not only in this country." Thus the conductor Hans Richter greeted the London Symphony Orchestra when preparing Elgar's first symphony for its London premiere. Not unlike his mentor Brahms, Elgar struggled long and hard for many years before embarking on this most exacting of instrumental forms, and he managed to complete only two, both extremely fine works. Compared with the contemporary symphonies of Mahler they are traditional works, but these are arguably the first great British symphonies, revealing often highly original solutions to form and structure. A third symphony, which existed only in sketch form when Elgar died, was "completed" by the composer and musicologist Anthony Payne in 1997. More of a joint work than the completed *Tenth Symphony* of Mahler, it is too soon to tell whether it will achieve the same sort of success, though a recording has already been made.

Some of Elgar's finest music is to be found in his other pieces for full orchestra – the outstanding works being the famous *Enigma Variations* and the rich orchestral tapestry of *Falstaff*.

Just as Elgar only completed two symphonies, so he only turned to the concerto form twice in his life, with a violin concerto and a cello concerto. And in the same way that the two symphonies have quite distinct characters, so these works also show widely different approaches to the form and its traditions.

SYMPHONY NO. 1

As early as 1898 Elgar had contemplated a symphony in memory of General Gordon, the British governor of Sudan who had been killed at Khartoum in 1885. Elgar wrote to a friend that "the thing possesses me, but I can't write it down yet", but when he did come to compose his *Symphony No. 1*, in 1907–08, it seemed to have lost its specific historical reference: as Elgar again wrote, "There is no programme beyond a wide experience of human life with a great charity [love] and a massive hope in the future." It was first performed to great acclaim in Manchester in December 1908, conducted by its dedicatee, Hans Richter. The symphony is dominated by a melody that's given Elgar's characteristic expressive marking of *nobilmente* (nobly); returning at salient points throughout the four movements, this melody encapsulates the mood of this grand, optimistic and distinctly Germanic work.

◑ London Philharmonic Orchestra; Boult (EMI CDM 7 64013-2; with *Serenade for Strings, Chanson de matin, Chanson de nuit*).

For a performance of real majesty and sweep, without interpretative quirks but with plenty of bite and character, Boult's last recording of the work for EMI is unbeatable, with the London Philharmonic Orchestra, which has probably recorded the work more times than any other orchestra, in superb form.

SYMPHONY NO. 2

His confidence boosted by the reception of his *Symphony No. 1*, Elgar soon began a second, completing it in 1911. He dedicated it to the memory of the late King Edward VII, but despite a funereal element in the slow movement Elgar intended no programmatic link to be made. Indeed, its mood is generally cheerful, though its finale is rather understated and its argumentative structure is more complex and subtle than the first symphony, which may well account for the less than overwhelming reception it received in its early years.

⊙ **London Philharmonic Orchestra; Handley** (Classics for Pleasure CD-CFP4544).

The symphony's more enigmatic nature has led to a greater number of failed recordings than other Elgar works have received, though there are still some very fine accounts available. One of the best is Vernon Handley's highly recommendable bargain account. Like Boult, he is a conductor free of mannerisms who lets the music do the persuading.

○ **BBC Symphony Orchestra; Davis** (Teldec 9031-74888-2; with *In the South*).

Andrew Davis and the BBC SO are no less impressive than Handley, and the sound is fractionally better. The Davis account is coupled with a good performance of *In the South (Alassio)*, one of Elgar's most splendid orchestral works (see below).

THE ENIGMA VARIATIONS

The true title of this work is *Variations on an Original Theme*, as the "Enigma" is strictly speaking only the title of the section that introduces the theme. Ever since the work first appeared, musicologists have tried to unravel what this enigma might be: the consensus has long been that the theme was composed as harmony and counterpoint to another theme that is never itself heard, so the crux of the argument is over the identity of that implied theme. The conundrum is irrelevant to the glorious music of the variations themselves, which were all given cryptic titles referring to Elgar's "friends pictured within", as his dedication has it. These friends have long been identified, as Elgar often tagged their initials and nicknames onto the music. Thus the first variation *CAE* is a portrait of his wife Caroline Alice Elgar, while the serene *Nimrod* is a tribute to his publisher friend A.E. Jaeger whose surname is German for "huntsman" – hence the allusion to the Old Testament figure of Nimrod the hunter.

◑ **Philharmonia; Barbirolli** (EMI CDM7 69185 2; with *Falstaff*).

Few conductors have equalled John Barbirolli in the *Enigma Variations*, and his 1962 performance with the Philharmonia is a classic. The recorded sound is admittedly somewhat dated, but the nobility and finesse of the interpretation easily outweigh such a drawback.

◑ **London Philharmonic Orchestra; Boult** (EMI CDM7 64015-2; with *Pomp & Circumstance Marches 1–5*).

Adrian Boult provides a more aristocratic but equally enjoyable reading of the *Enigma*. It comes coupled with lively but earnest accounts of Elgar's celebrated *Pomp and Circumstance* marches – these may not constitute his greatest music, but there is no denying the panache that he brought to the concept of the military march. Incidentally, it was at King Edward VII's suggestion that the trio melody of the best known, *No. 1*, should be set to words – the infamous "Land of Hope and Glory"; Elgar did not approve of its triumphalist sentiments.

THE SERENADE FOR STRINGS & INTRODUCTION AND ALLEGRO

Composed in 1892, the *Serenade for Strings* is the first recognizably Elgarian work – "I like 'em," he later wrote of the *Serenade*'s three movements, "(The first thing I ever did)." But the second of his two major works for strings, the *Introduction and Allegro* was undoubtedly more influential. With its juxtaposition of a string quartet against a full string orchestra, he sparked off a succession of English string works that have their roots in the Baroque concerto grosso idea of "competing" string ensembles, the most notable subsequent examples coming in the works of Vaughan Williams and Tippett.

◑ **London Chamber Orchestra; Warren-Green** (Virgin CUV5 61255-2; with Vaughan Williams, *The Lark Ascending* and *Tallis Fantasia*).

In the tradition of violinist-led string ensembles, the London Chamber Orchestra's performances under Christopher Warren-Green are suitably vigorous yet refined. The *Serenade* is especially excellent – too many performances overindulge in the slow movement – and forms part of a superb programme of Elgar and Vaughan Williams string works.

IN THE SOUTH

In the South, called an overture but more of a tone poem, is Elgar at his most Straussian. Written while he and his wife were holidaying in Italy, it's a kaleidoscopic evocation of the landscape and historical associations of that country and it possesses a sustained exuberance which is almost unique in his output. It opens with a great swirling rush of energy which leads straight into a typically passionate and pulsating Elgarian big tune before subsiding into a quietly poetic passage. There's a homage to Berlioz's *Harold in Italy* by way of a melancholic viola solo, but the work ends with a triumphal blaze of orchestral sound with the brass very much to the fore.

◑ **Bournemouth Symphony Orchestra; Silvestri** (CZS5 69229-2; 2 CDs; with Tchaikovsky, *Symphony No. 5*; Dvořák, *Symphony No. 8*).

It may seem perverse to buy a two-CD set of a twenty-minute piece played by a second division orchestra and a largely forgotten conductor, but nobody has recorded a performance of *In the South* that comes anywhere near this one in terms of sheer ebullience and *joie de vivre*. In Silvestri's hands the piece crackles with energy from beginning to end.

● **BBC Symphony Orchestra; Davis** (Teldec 9031-74888-2; with *Symphony No. 2*).

This performance doesn't have the interpretative chutzpah of Silvestri, but it is still impressively joyous, with the BBC SO clearly enjoying themselves.

FALSTAFF

Elgar's penultimate orchestral work (the *Cello Concerto* came later) is arguably his finest. Unlike Verdi's opera, which concentrates on the womanizing side of Falstaff's character as portrayed in Shakespeare's *Merry Wives of Windsor*, Elgar's "symphonic study" dwells on his relationship with Prince Hal in *Henry IV* and *Henry V*, culminating in the newly crowned king's rejection of his old friend, and Falstaff's death – perhaps symbolic of the passing of the age in which Elgar had grown up and felt secure. The score is marvellously detailed and reveals a sense of humour not heard so openly in any of Elgar's music, though the grandiose and melancholy elements play equally important roles.

⊙ **Handley; London Philharmonic Orchestra** (Classics for Pleasure CD-CFP4617; with *Cockaigne Overture* and *Introduction and Allegro*).

Vernon Handley's recording for the bargain-price Classics for Pleasure label in 1978 first revealed him as the successor to Barbirolli and Boult, combining attention to the symphonic scale and structure of the work with ripe characterization and a superb performance from those experienced Elgarians of the London Philharmonic Orchestra.

THE VIOLIN CONCERTO

"It's good! Awfully emotional, too emotional, but I love it." Elgar's *Violin Concerto* displays all his characteristic trademarks of wistfulness, grandeur and lyricism, but it is immensely virtuosic as well – indeed, some rate it as the most difficult violin concerto in the repertory, and many a fine violinist has been scared off attempting what is a most rewarding piece. This concerto marks a real development from its predecessors in the repertory, most in the notably extended and highly original accompanied cadenza in the last movement, an episode in which the soloist mulls over themes from the whole work.

● **Kennedy; City of Birmingham Symphony Orchestra; Rattle** (EMI CDC5 56413-2; with Vaughan Williams, *The Lark Ascending*).

Kennedy's second recording of the *Violin Concerto* is even more thoughtful and intense than his first. It really sounds like the performance of someone who knows the concerto inside out: no nuance has been missed, no detail left untouched. Some may find the emphasis on the introspective a little self-indulgent, but overall it's a completely convincing account.

◑ **Menuhin; London Symphony Orchestra; Elgar** (EMI CDH7 69786-2; with *Cello Concerto*).

This classic account from the 16-year-old Yehudi Menuhin was made in 1932, with the 75-year-old composer himself conducting. It is one of the most popular versions ever made and there is a palpable rapport between soloist and conductor which is thrilling.

THE CELLO CONCERTO

World War I took its toll on Elgar. Although he was not directly involved in any participatory way, he saw in it the destruction of the world he had known since childhood, and there is a tangible sense of regret and dejection in his last major works. Along with three important chamber works (see p.141), the most famous of these is the *Cello Concerto*, a work that conveys the impression, in the words of the Elgar scholar Michael Kennedy, of "a man wearied with the world . . . finding solace in the beauty of music". The texture has something of the transparency of chamber music, and the form of the concerto reflects a state of emotional flux – it's divided into four movements which further divide into sections with quite contrasting moods, though mournfulness is the dominant tone. Resonant cello chords frame the whole piece, opening the concerto with buttonholing immediacy, and making a poignant comeback towards the end.

O Du Pré; London Symphony Orchestra; Barbirolli (EMI CDC7 47329-2; with *Sea Pictures*).

The *Cello Concerto* was not too well received at first and it could be argued that it was the young Jacqueline du Pré who made the piece popular with her ecstatic performances. Her magnificent recording with John Barbirolli has dominated the catalogue since it was issued in the mid-1960s, even though not a year goes by without the release of a new attempt from the latest star soloist. Few cellists have penetrated the concerto's inner recesses so deeply, or produced a performance of such burning intensity. This is the place to begin any Elgar collection.

CHAMBER MUSIC

Elgar wrote a lot of chamber music in his youth, notably the series of so-called "shed music" he wrote for himself and his young wind-playing friends to play in his garden. But his only works of significance, apart from the various salon pieces for violin, date from the end of World War I, when he rented a quiet cottage in the wooded uplands of Sussex and composed his *Violin Sonata*, *String Quartet* and *Piano Quintet*, works expressing with deep seriousness his disillusionment with postwar life, yet also conveying some of the "wood magic", as Elgar's wife called it, of their surroundings.

The three-movement *Violin Sonata* is Elgar at his most openly, gushingly Romantic, the very antithesis of strait-laced Englishness; the theme of the opening movement is the most arresting idea in all Elgar's chamber music. The *Piano Quintet* is Elgar's most overtly Brahmsian work, but is dominated as much by Elgar's highly personal way of creating a sense of atmosphere with ghostly undertones. The *String Quartet* is more intimate in style: it's a wistful and melancholic piece, but there's plenty of power in it too.

⊙ Piano Quintet; String Quartet: Donohoe, Maggini Quartet (Naxos 8 553737).

This would be a remarkable recording at any price. Both the Maggini Quartet and pianist Peter Donohoe clearly feel a real affinity with this music and they capture its melancholy charm more profoundly than most.

O Violin Sonata: Bean, Parkhouse (EMI CD-CFP4632; with *Violin Concerto*).

For the *Violin Sonata* there's nothing to match the account from Hugh Bean, a pupil of Elgar's great friend Albert Sammons and a musician associated particularly with this work. Suitably sweeping and intense, he generates enormous energy without resorting to crude display.

MANUEL DE FALLA

(1876–1946)

Glimpses of Manuel de Falla's personality, as seen by his contemporaries, are tantalizingly rare, but two images of him are well-known: one is Picasso's melancholy drawing of 1920; the other is Stravinsky's remark that he was "the most unpityingly religious person I have ever known – and the least sensible to manifestations of humour". Yet this austere man, a lifelong bachelor, wrote some of the most sensuous and alluring music to have come out of Spain.

Born into a prosperous family in the seaport of Cadiz, Falla had every encouragement to immerse himself in music, receiving piano lessons first from from his mother and then from an array of eminent teachers. Yet for several years he could not decide between a musical or a literary career. He was about 17 when he finally committed himself to becoming a composer, around the time that he encountered the music of Grieg. Immediately impressed by Grieg's strong national character and his rejection of Teutonic notions of musical structure, Falla conceived "an intense desire to create one day something similar with Spanish music".

After a distinguished spell at the Madrid Conservatory (1898–99), when he took top marks and prizes in all his classes, Falla persuaded Felipe Pedrell, the seminal figure of Spanish musical nationalism, to take him on as a pupil. Pedrell's influence on budding Spanish composers of the day was profound, as important as that which the Russian teacher-composer Rimsky-Korsakov had over the young Stravinsky. Pedrell exhorted Falla, as he had Albéniz and Granados before him, to develop a style based on folk music, and showed him how to achieve this within a wider European framework. Although Falla took many of his teacher's ideas to heart, his own style differed from Pedrell's in two fundamental ways. Firstly, his inclination throughout his life was to write sparely, and he had an abhorrence of music with too many notes – Pedrell's own compositions and those of

LEBRECHT COLLECTION

Manuel de Falla

his other students (eg Albéniz's *Iberia* and Granados's *Goyescas*) are decidedly expansive. Secondly, Falla chose not to quote folk tunes directly as Pedrell would do, but to extract the essence of the music, to build something new from this raw material. As he put it in an essay of 1917, "I think that in popular song the spirit is more important than the letter."

In 1907, two years after winning a prestigious competition for his opera *La Vida Breve*, Falla bought a one-week return train ticket to Paris, and ended up staying seven years. Soon after arriving he was befriended by Debussy, Ravel and Dukas, and got caught up in the anti-Wagnerianism sweeping French musical circles. Even though he was never particularly successful financially, Paris was the making of him as a composer, enabling him to reassess the musical heritage of his homeland in the context of the impressionist masterpieces of the French innovators. The first fruit of this process was *Noches en los jardines de España* (1911–15), a lush composition for piano and orchestra.

At the outbreak of World War I Falla returned to Spain. Many of the compositions of this period, including the two ballet scores *El Amor Brujo* (1915) and *El sombrero de tres picos* (1917–19), derive their character from the *cante jondo*, the highly evocative song style of Andalucía, of which Falla had been making a thorough study. These ballets were highly popular, and suites of dances from *El sombrero* soon became international concert favourites. Falla could have gone on profitably mining the rich orchestral style of his ballets but, inspired by the neo-classicism of his friend Stravinsky, he set off on a new phase, working to condense and distil his style.

In 1919 he moved to Granada, where he gathered around him a circle of intellectuals, the most notable of whom was the writer and poet Lorca. Though each new work took ever longer to write, with Falla poring over every note and phrase, the music of Falla's neo-classical phase attained a lapidary perfection, for example in the small-scale theatre piece *El retablo de maese Pedro* and the *Concerto for harpsichord* (1923–26).

Never a man to repeat himself, Falla then embarked on *Atlantida*, a huge oratorio for soloists, chorus and orchestra. This was the most ambitious work he had ever undertaken and he was to devote the rest of his life to it, but it remained unfinished and was not performed until 1962. Falla's last years were lived out in self-imposed exile in Argentina, where the composer had moved to escape the regime of General Franco.

NIGHTS IN THE GARDENS OF SPAIN

It was the great Spanish pianist Ricardo Viñes who persuaded Falla to transform *Noches en los jardines de España* (Nights in the Gardens of Spain) from a solo work into one for piano and orchestra. The result is one of Falla's most impressionistic and poetic works, full of shimmering and diaphanous textures that recall Debussy but which also possess a hard-edged precision through the presence of the piano. Its three sections are descriptive: the first evokes the Generalife gardens of the Alhambra in Granada; the second – the most animated – is described as a distant dance; and the third was inspired by the gardens of the Sierra de Córdoba. The whole work is shot though with Spanish colour, not through the precise quotation of specific folk songs, but by the subtle utilization of effects – strumming chords, insistently repeated phrases, declamatory unison passages in the piano – which suggest the rhythms and cadences of flamenco song, as filtered through the memory of a dream.

O de Larrocha; London Philharmonic Orchestra; Frühbeck de Burgos (Decca 410 289-2; with Albéniz, *Rapsodia españolas*; Turina, *Rapsodia sinfónica*).

There's a wholely natural feeling to the way the climaxes and sudden changes of direction are so perfectly judged in this performance – a measure of how well the conductor and soloist (both Spanish) know this work. From the perfumed heaviness of the opening to the rapturous piano arabesques of the last movement, a richly mysterious mood is beautifully sustained.

EL AMOR BRUJO

The one-act ballet *El Amor Brujo* (Love the Magician) was finished in the same year as the *Nights in the Gardens of Spain*, and like that work is imbued with the spirit of gypsy music. The story tells how the affair between the beautiful gypsy girl Candelas and her lover Carmelo is thwarted by the interruptions of the jealous ghost of her former lover (indicated by a strident fanfare motif). Only by luring the ghost away – through the charms of another gypsy girl – can Candelas and Carmelo be free of him. Falla conveys all this in ten highly concentrated sections, four of which include song (the work was commissioned by the gypsy dancer and singer Pastora Imperio). The music is vividly atmospheric and creates a genuine sense of supernatural danger, a mood which culminates in the serene but spooky *Magic Circle* and the more famous (an often anthologized) *Ritual Fire Dance*. On a more seductive note comes the delightful *Pantomime*, a luxurious slow tango in 7/8 with which Candelas's friend Lucía successfully captivates the offending ghost. Originally scored for eight instruments, Falla revised it for full orchestra in 1916 and that is how it is commonly heard today.

◑ **Mistral; New Philharmonia Orchestra; Frühbeck de Burgos** (Decca 448 601-2; with Albéniz *Suite española*).

Once again Rafael Frühbeck de Burgos proves himself to be a masterly conductor of Falla. There's an intensely theatrical feel to the proceedings and in Nati Mistral he has an authentic flamenco singer able to do justice to the passionate vocal outpourings that punctuate the score.

THE THREE-CORNERED HAT

Commissioned in 1916 by the impresario Diaghilev for his Russian Ballet company, *El sombrero de tre picos* (The Three-Cornered Hat) was first performed in London in 1919. It boasted an incredible wealth of talent (choreography by Massine, designs by Picasso, Karsavina dancing the role of the Miller's Wife), and was one of the company's greatest successes, putting Falla on the international map as a composer. Based on the novel by Alarcón, it tells of the failed attempt by an elderly local magistrate (whose three-cornered hat is a symbol of authority) to seduce the miller's lovely wife. His failure ends in complete humiliation and his effigy is tossed in a blanket amid general rejoicing. Falla's score offers a strong rebuttal to the charge that he lacked a sense of humour. It abounds in the most sparklingly exuberant array of melodies and the principal characters are all wittily characterized, often through association with a specific Spanish dance rhythm. But there is also greater bite in this score, as if, in writing for the Russian Ballet, Falla felt obliged to acknowledge the rhythmic adventurousness of the company's previous successes, in particular Stravinsky's *Petrushka*.

◑ **de los Angeles; Philharmonia Orchestra; Frühbeck de Burgos** (EMI CMS5 65997-2; 2 CDs; with *Atlántida*).

EMI repackage this 1963 recording of the complete ballet at regular intervals. Currently it is (rather perversely) coupled with Falla's unfinished and somewhat cumbersome choral epic *Atlántida*, but Frühbeck de Burgos delivers again in a sparklingly theatrical account brilliantly played by the Philharmonia.

O Muntada; National Youth Orchestra of Spain; Colomer (Auvidis Valois V4642; with *Harpsichord Concerto*).

For those who only want a single disc, this recording (the only one by a Spanish orchestra) is a good alternative to Frühbeck de Burgos. The National Youth Orchestra of Spain are not a patch on the Philharmonia, but their performance has enormous flair and vitality, and they invest the narrative with more red-bloodied gutsiness than is customary.

GABRIEL FAURÉ

(1845–1924)

Like Delius, Fauré is a composer whose music does not seem to travel well: revered in his native France – above all as a composer of songs – he is known elsewhere almost solely for his hugely popular *Requiem*. Unfortunately this excludes a wealth of highly refined and beautiful music. Fauré's style reveals a Romantic sensibility held in check by a classical sense of form and decorum – it is music of feeling, sometimes of passion, but it never aspires to the epic or the transcendent, preferring a more discreet and intimate means of expression. Some have dismissed him as never aspiring much higher than the salon and, although there are insipid moments in his music, at its best it possesses elegance, harmonic adventurousness, and an understated but intense degree of feeling.

Fauré, the youngest of six children (possibly an unplanned addition to the family), proved to be an extremely precocious talent. When he was 9 he was sent to the École Niedermeyer, a Paris music school with a bias towards ecclesiastical music. In much of Fauré's music, throughout his life, there are hints of the church modes that he would have learned there. In 1861 the 25-year-old Saint-Saëns (see p.346) arrived at the school to teach piano, and proceeded to broaden his students' outlook, introducing them to the music of Lizst and Wagner. The friendship that he formed with Fauré lasted until Saint-Saëns's death in 1921.

Fauré's career began as an organist, firstly at Rennes and then, after serving in the Franco-Prussian war of 1870, at the Paris church of St Honoré d'Eylau. In 1879 he heard the whole of Wagner's *Ring* cycle in Munich, and although he later acknowledged its effect on him ("Such things seep into you just like water seeps through sand") he was not swept up in the Wagner mania that hit Paris a few years later – unlike many other French composers. In 1896 he won two major appointments, as organist at the church of La Madeleine and Professor of Composition at the Paris Conservatoire where he exerted a strong influence on a succession of pupils, including Maurice Ravel and Nadia Boulanger, the twentieth century's most important composition teacher. Even though he gave up the Madeleine job in 1905 when he was appointed Director of the Conservatoire, the time he could set aside for writing music decreased substantially, a problem exacerbated by his growing deafness which left him feeling increasingly alone. This sense of isolation almost certainly contributed to the development of a more introspective style. Fauré's later work is characterized by a paring down of his musical language, an unfashionable restraint that probably accounts for the relative failure of his second opera, *Pénélope* (1913).

CHORAL MUSIC

Of the great Requiems of the nineteenth century, Verdi's sounds as if it was written for the opera house and Brahms's for the concert hall – Fauré's alone has the odour of incense, doubtless thanks to his career as an organist and his familiarity with church music. The Fauré *Requiem* is music to comfort and to reassure the faithful in the face of death, rather than to overwhelm them with the finality of judgement – significantly it omits the full, fearsome text of the Dies Irae (Day of Wrath), allowing only a passing reference to it in the Libera Me (Deliver Me) section. The overwhelming impression is one of peace and serenity which, in the Agnus Dei, is transformed into an almost joyous resignation.

Fauré wrote several other liturgical works, of which the short *Messe Basse* (Low Mass) for high voices is the best known. Originally written in collaboration with Messager, when it was known as the *Messe des Pêcheurs de Villerville*, it was revised by Fauré in 1906 to make it entirely his own, creating a work that's striking for the clarity and simplicity of its religious sentiment.

⊙ Requiem (1894 version); Messe des Pêcheurs de Villerville: Mellon, Kooy, Van Doeselaar; Petits Chanteurs de Saint-Louis, Paris Chapelle Royale; Musique Oblique Ensemble; Herreweghe (Harmonia Mundi HMC 90 1292).

Herreweghe's recording is unusual for giving us the original version of the *Messe Basse* and an earlier and simpler version of the *Requiem*. His decision is fully justified by performances in which the closer balance between orchestra and choir creates a wonderful sense of intimacy.

◑ Requiem (1900 version); Messe Basse: Auger, Luxon, Smy; Choir of King's College Cambridge; English Chamber Orchestra; Ledger (EMI CD-EMX 2166).

For the *Requiem*'s more full-blooded version, the performance by King's College is particularly good value, with an outstanding soprano soloist, Arléen Auger, in the haunting Pie Jesu.

SONGS

Fauré wrote nearly one hundred songs throughout his career, and they show off his lyric gift at its subtle and eloquent best. They include settings of poems by Baudelaire, Gautier and Victor Hugo, but the poet with whom he seems to have the strongest sympathy was Paul Verlaine, who inspired some of his most sensuous and concentrated writing. Both poet and composer are concerned with atmosphere more than description, and the instrumental part in these songs never acts just as accompaniment but rather shapes and directs the vocal line in ways that delicately alter the mood. *La Bonne Chanson* (1892–94), the finest of his song cycles, possesses a fresh and heartfelt ardour that reflects Fauré's feeling towards the work's first performer, his mistress Emma Bardac.

⊙ La Bonne Chanson: Walker; Nash Ensemble (CRD CRD3389; with *Piano Trio*).

The English mezzo Sarah Walker, performing *La Bonne Chanson* in Fauré's arrangement for singer and string quintet, has a darkness and sensuality to her voice that feels absolutely appropriate to this music. This disc also contains a fine account of the spare and enigmatic *Piano Trio*, a late work.

◑ **L'Horizon chimérique and other songs: Souzay, Bonneau** (Philips 438 964-2; 4 CDs; with Ravel and Poulenc songs).

Gerard Souzay is one of the greatest of all interpreters of French song, possessing a warm and sweet-toned baritone which at the same time is always clear and incisive – the perfect combination for Fauré's elusive bittersweet songs. Unfortunately Philips constantly chop and change with how they package their Souzay recordings: *L'Horizon chimérique* was available as a single disc; now it can only be obtained as a four-disc set. But with some marvellous performances of Ravel and Poulenc, it's well worth investigating.

ORCHESTRAL MUSIC

Much of Fauré's orchestral music was written either as commissions for the theatre or transcriptions of existing instrumental pieces. There are no symphonies or concertos, and, perhaps because of this, his orchestral works are rather neglected – a shame, since most of it is of the highest quality and displays his characteristic freshness and clarity. The suite *Masques et bergamasques* started life as a choreographic divertissement inspired by the paintings of Watteau. It's essentially light music, airy and undemanding and, in truth, a little insipid. The incidental music that Fauré wrote for Maeterlinck's play *Pelléas et Mélisande*, also turned into a suite, has considerably more bite, and contains in the third-movement Sicilienne one of the best of those hauntingly melancholic tunes that he seemed to turn out at will. In the one movement, *Elégie for cello orchestra*, this melancholy comes as close as anything Fauré wrote to a genuinely tragic expression of grief. A more wistful tone is found in the *Pavane* for orchestra, a gentle unassuming work that has proved the most popular of his orchestral works.

O Orchestral Works: BBC Philharmonic; Tortelier (Chandos CHAN 9416).

This disc contains a good selection of most of the better-known orchestral works (but not *Pelléas et Mélisande*), which the BBC Philharmonic plays with great sympathy. The emotional range of this music is not wide, and Tortelier finds just the right degree of warmth and elegant charm.

CHAMBER MUSIC

If Fauré was unduly self-critical and nervous about writing orchestral works, then in his chamber music he had no such inhibitions, producing an array of works of a consistently high standard that is unrivalled in French music at that period. Much of it, particularly the two piano quartets, has the breadth and energy that you associate with orchestral music, and nearly all of it includes a piano part. Of his early chamber music, the two most celebrated works are the *Violin Sonata No. 1* and the *Piano Quartet No. 1*, both written in the mid-1870s and both characterized by an underlying melancholy that is offset by sparkling Scherzo-like movements. Both the *Piano Quartet No. 2* (1886) and the *Violin Sonata No. 2* (1917) are darker, less effusive works, in which thematic material from their first movements are skilfully developed in subsequent sections.

O Piano Quartets Nos. 1 & 2: Domus (Hyperion CDA 66166).

Domus have all the qualities required for a perfect chamber group: distinctive instrumental voices that can shine individually when necessary, but above all a strong sense of a common cause. Both piano quartets are held together by some brilliantly nimble piano playing, and there is an emotional depth to the slow movements which is utterly compelling.

◑ **Violin Sonatas Nos. 1 & 2: Grumiaux; Crossley** (Philips 426 384-2; with Franck, *Violin Sonata*).

Grumiaux and Crossley respond warmly and imaginatively to the violin sonatas, treating their rhythmic ebb and flow with a flexibility that brings out their quicksilver charm. Grumiaux's variety of tone and touch is particularly apparent in the slow movements, where his highlighting of details heightens the sense of personal utterance. The addition of Franck's delightful sonata makes this disc exceptionally good value.

PIANO MUSIC

Like his chamber music, Fauré's piano works are extremely personal pieces which are largely introspective in mood. The choice of forms – nocturnes, barcarolles, préludes, impromptus – reveals a debt to an earlier generation: to Chopin for a poetic concentration and clarity of utterance; and to Liszt (who Fauré knew well) for the more mercurial and capricious colouring of his work. Fauré's own unique contribution was a harmonic adventurousness, and a tendency for unexpected modulations which create a restless and elusive quality as if the music is not always quite sure where it is going. In his later piano works, in particular the last three nocturnes, this uneasy dreaminess intensifies, creating music that is curiously enigmatic but strangely moving.

O Piano Music: Rogé (Decca 425 606-2).

All of Fauré's piano music has been well recorded by Kathryn Stott on Hyperion, but for an introductory selection this Decca release would be hard to better. Pascal Rogé's playing is more tempered than that of Stott, but such an understated approach often seems to get closer to the heart of the music than her more tempestuous style.

MORTON FELDMAN

(1926–1987)

As a broad generalization, the music of the American avant-garde differs from its European counterpart in being primarily concerned with the sensual qualities of sounds themselves rather than the shaping and ordering of those sounds. Morton Feldman is typical of this tendency: his sound-world, especially in his later works, consists of small, soft and unhurried musical gestures which emphasize the physical detail of instrumental timbre. With this comes a fondness for repetition and an absence of rhythmic momentum which is, in Feldman's own words, ". . . a conscious attempt at formalizing a disorientation of memory". The cumulative effect is of an hallucinatory stasis, not dissimilar to the large canvases of Mark Rothko, a painter Feldman knew and admired. It is a music where little happens – very beautifully.

Feldman was born in New York and studied composition, unsatisfactorily, with Stefan Wolpe and then Wallingford Riegger. The catalyst for his attempts to liberate sound from structure came when he met John Cage in 1949. *Projections* (1950–51) was a Cage-influenced work, written on squared paper with fairly general instructions, allowing the performer almost limitless freedom of choice over pitch and note duration. This was fairly rapidly replaced as a working method by more precise notation, but with note duration still left relatively free. The effect, in works like *Piece for Four Pianos* (1957) or *The Swallows of Salangan* (1960), is of a kind of anarchic counterpoint in which material disconcertingly overlaps and shifts. In Feldman's later work the emphasis changes again, from a preoccupation with the exploration of timbre to a fascination with time – a fascination exemplified by the *Piano and String Quartet* of 1985.

BETTY FREEMAN/LEBRECHT COLLECTION

Morton Feldman, with John Adams in the background

ROTHKO CHAPEL

In 1971 Feldman attended the opening ceremony of the Rothko Chapel in Houston, Texas. Feldman was asked to write a piece of music specifically for the building and as tribute to Mark Rothko, fourteen of whose large canvases were hung in the chapel, a non-denominational meditative space. The paintings were Feldman's starting point: "Rothko's imagery goes right to the edge of his canvas, and I wanted the same effect with the music – that it should permeate the whole octagonal-shaped room and not be heard form a certain distance." Using very spare forces – viola, celeste, percussion, chorus and soprano solo – in a way that treats them as discrete abstract elements, Feldman creates a musical-spiritual ambience not dissimilar to the later music of Arvo Pärt. The difference is that Feldman's sound-world is cooler, with a greater emphasis on details of timbre as a means of communication. Each of its five sections unfolds with an unruffled glow that seems to heighten the listener's sensitivity as it progresses.

O Abel, Rosenak, Winant; UC Berkeley Chamber Chorus; Brett (New Albion NA039CD; with *Why Patterns?*).

It is sometimes suggested that interpretation is irrelevant in music of such an undemonstrative nature. Suffice it to say that the forces assembled here respond to the music in an appropriately sensitive and self-effacing manner, and the result is extremely powerful.

THE PIANO AND STRING QUARTET

In the *Piano and String Quartet* the piano, with the sustaining pedal held down, plays an arpeggiated chord as the string quartet plays a sustained chord. Notes change, harmonies shift, individual notes are sounded, but the essential pattern of broken chord plus sustained chord continues, to increasingly mesmerizing effect, for the eighty-minute duration of the work. The piece seems to have no beginning or end, no intention or direction, and yet listening to it heightens aural awareness to such a degree that the smallest modification of the chords possess a resonance and an intensity that is startling.

O Kronos Quartet with Aki Takahashi (Elektra Nonesuch 7559-79320-2).

The *Quartet* was written for these specific players, and their performance is characterized by a steady and unruffled calm: Takahashi's piano sound is cool but never hard, while the Kronos Quartet bring an extraordinary precision to their playing, almost as if they were controlled by just one person. This is music that you don't so much listen to as allow to envelop you.

CÉSAR FRANCK

(1822–1890)

Although Belgian, César Franck became the figurehead for a generation of French composers who had little interest in the predominantly operatic fare on offer in France, being instead attracted to Germanic ideas of symphonic form and musical abstraction. Acclaim for his work was meagre in his lifetime, but Franck brought a new seriousness to French music that ultimately would resonate in the compositions of later figures like Debussy and Delibes.

He was born in the Walloon city of Liège to a Flemish family; hence the mixture of French and Flemish in his name. At the age of 11 he made his first tour as a virtuoso pianist and two years later the whole family moved to Paris so he could study there. Mercilessly exploited by his avaricious father, he left home in 1848 in order to marry his pupil Félicité Desmousseaux and shortly after took up the post of organist at Notre Dame de Lorette – the church where he had been married. Franck's earliest compositions were chiefly vehicles for his piano tours, followed by a series of religious works, then by pieces for the organ – at which he showed stunning prowess after the move to Paris – and for full orchestra. For many of his middle years his energies were given over to teaching and disseminating a musical philosophy that wanted to take French music away from its perceived frivolity and mediocrity. Nearly all his finest and best-known works were crammed into his last decade: the *Piano Quintet* (1879), the symphonic poem *Le chasseur maudit* (1882), the *Prelude, Chorale and Fugue* for solo piano (1884), the *Symphonic Variations* for piano and orchestra (1885), the *Violin Sonata* (1886), the *Symphony in D minor* (1888), the *String Quartet* (1889) and the three *Chorales* for organ (1890), as well as two long-forgotten operas, *Hulda*

(1885) and *Ghisèle* (1890) – the last was unfinished when Franck died after being knocked down by a bus.

Franck's first-rate orchestral works amount to just a single symphony, one concertante work for piano and orchestra and a handful of symphonic poems. His reputation rests primarily on his instrumental pieces, the best of which are his *Piano Quintet*, *Violin Sonata* and organ music, most of which comes from the years of his maturity, whereas the piano pieces are mainly the product of his years as a touring virtuoso, when his compositional technique lagged some way behind his dexterity.

THE SYMPHONY IN D MINOR

When Franck began his *Symphony in D minor* in 1886, he had few French examples except Berlioz to follow – his most obvious influences were Liszt's symphonic poems, in which a rigid structure is combined with the inventive transformation of themes that metamorphose as their harmonies and contexts change. Franck's symphony marks a development of the concept of cyclic form, in which music from one movement reappears later on, providing unity and coherence – thus ideas from the symphony's first two movements are recalled in the third. The slow movement is famous for its cor anglais solo, an instrument French critics of the time thought unsuitable for a major role in a serious symphony.

○ Montréal Symphony Orchestra; Dutoit (Decca 430 278-2; with d'Indy, *Symphonie sur un chant montagnard français*).

For all its dynamism and Wagnerian harmonies, the *Symphony* can often sound stolid in performance, due to Franck's conception of orchestral sound, which relies on organ-like blocks of sound. Charles Dutoit and his sleek Montréal Symphony Orchestra avoid such pitfalls, producing a performance of great sweep and majesty.

◑ Chicago Symphony Orchestra; Monteux (RCA GD 86805; with *Pièce heroïque* and d'Indy's *Istar*).

Similarly light-footed is Monteux's 1961 account for RCA, rereleased as part of a splendid fifteen-disc Monteux Edition, but available as a single CD. This clear-sighted and unfussy account does justice to a work that has suffered at the hands of conductors straining for interpretative novelty.

SYMPHONIC VARIATIONS

Often regarded as Franck's masterpiece, the *Symphonic Variations* for piano and orchestra is an engaging showpiece in which Liszt's principle of thematic metamorphosis is once more employed, this time to develop a rather introspective double theme in a miraculous series of transformations, culminating in a breezy final section that is more a full symphonic movement than a mere coda. Unlike Liszt's works for piano and orchestra, there are very few moments of attention seeking virtuosity, the piano part is often closely integrated with the orchestral writing, and there is an emphasis on sonority of which the best example is the strikingly atmospheric reverie of variation six.

◑ Curzon; London Symphony Orchestra; Boult (Decca 424 08-2; with Brahms, *Piano Concerto No. 1*).

Clifford Curzon's romantic account of the *Symphonic Variations* is a wonderfully deft and delicate account. It comes coupled with his blazing performance of the Brahms *Piano Concerto No. 1*, conducted by Georg Szell.

THE PIANO QUINTET

The *Piano Quintet* (1879), written at the beginning of Franck's productive final decade, is his most passionate and personal work (it may well have been inspired by his infatuation for the composer Augusta Holmès) and one of the great chamber works of the nineteenth century. Franck is sometimes accused of having too much of the solemnity of the organ loft to his music, but in the *Piano Quintet* the rawness of the emotion and the vigour with which it is expressed is overwhelming – it has been said to contain more fortissimos and pianissimos than any other chamber work.

◑ Curzon, Vienna Philharmonic Quartet (Decca 421 153-2; with Dvořák, *Piano Quintet*).

The *Quintet* is less popular today than it once was, and for a really fine account of the work you have to go back three decades to Clifford Curzon's passionate version with the Vienna Philharmonic Quartet.

THE VIOLIN SONATA

Franck's other main chamber piece, the melodious *Violin Sonata* (1886), was written as a wedding present for his fellow Liègeois, the great violinist Eugène Ysaÿe. A triumphant example of cyclic form, it has four movements: a languid Allegretto, which was changed from an Adagio after Ysaÿe convinced Franck it worked better at a faster tempo; a fiery Allegro; a recitative-fantasia recalling earlier themes; and a gentle finale which is one of the finest examples of a canon written after Bach. (The first movement, a serenely resplendent dialogue between violin and piano, may have been the inspiration for Marcel Proust's brilliant description of the sonata by the fictitious composer Vinteuil in his novel *Swann's Way*.)

◑ **Chung, Lupu** (Decca 421 154-2; with Debussy, *Violin Sonata & Sonata for Flute, Viola and Harp*; Ravel, *Introduction* and *Allegro*).

Kyung Wha Chung's classic account of the *Violin Sonata*, coupled with some fine Debussy and Ravel, is an essential mid-price CD. Chung has the poise for this music, not swooning over the main theme like some of her competitors, and she has a sympathetic partner in the pianist Radu Lupu.

ORGAN WORKS

Franck's reputation as a composer for the organ rests on the masterful series of about a dozen works written in the early 1860s and during the last ten years of his life, most notably the *Prélude, fugue et variation* (1862) and the three magisterial *Chorales* (1890). Franck was a prodigiously talented organist, and at the church of Sainte Clotilde (where he played from 1858) he had the advantage of a new organ constructed by the most innovative organ builder in France, Cavaillé-Coll. This allowed for more orchestral scope in organ composition, and it was in this medium that Franck felt most at home, even if the organ pieces do not necessarily represent him at his most adventurous and forward-looking.

○ **Prélude, fugue et variation, Chorales Nos. 1–3, and other works: Murray** (Telarc CD80234; 2 CDs).

Michael Murray's two-disc set contains all twelve major works in faithful performances using a Cavaillé-Coll organ that has changed little since Franck's day.

○ **Chorales Nos. 1–3; Pièce héroïque: Dupré** (Mercury 434 311-2; with Widor, excerpts from *Symphonies Nos. 2 & 6*).

Marcel Dupré's more imaginatively played single disc of all of the *Trois Chorales* and one of the *Trois Pièces* is sonically impressive, giving little sign that it was recorded as long ago as 1959.

GIOVANNI GABRIELI

(c.1553–1612)

Towards the end of the sixteenth century many composers were looking for alternatives to the polyphony that had dominated church music for the last 150 years. Among the new styles to appear was one that was peculiar to the state of Venice, a style that had developed out of the lavish ceremonial music performed at the city's magnificent church of St Mark. This Venetian style was called polychoralism because it employed no fewer than two, and sometimes as many as five, separated choirs (*chori spezzati*), which were placed in different locations around the high altar, including the galleries on each side of it.

Much of the most sumptuous music written for St Mark's in the polychoral style was by Andrea Gabrieli and his nephew Giovanni, both of whom served as organists there. The music itself was homophonic; that is, made up of chords rather than the independent lines of polyphony. Great blocks of sound, with an emphasis on sonorous textures and dramatically varied dynamics, acted as the aural equivalent of the sumptuous but hieratic splendour of St Mark's itself, the most Byzantine of all great European churches. In Giovanni's music the textures were further enriched by the use of instrumental music, especially violins, cornetts (an early wooden version of the trumpet) and sackbuts (close to the modern trombone).

Not much is known about Giovanni Gabrieli's life: he studied with his uncle Andrea and, like him, spent some time at the Munich court of Albrecht V, where he would have worked with Lassus (see p.216). He succeeded Merulo as organist at St Mark's in 1585, and when his uncle died the following year he became the church's principal composer of ceremonial music. He was also an organist at the Scuola di San Rocco, a confraternity given to lavish celebration on its patron saint's day. Much of Gabrieli's music was published in 1597 in a collection titled *Sacrae Symphoniae*, and his subsequent fame led to him being sought out as a teacher, especially by pupils from Germany. The greatest of these was Schütz (see p.380), who assimilated Gabrieli's style and perpetuated it in Germany long after it had been forgotten in Venice. He was obviously a favourite pupil of Gabrieli's, since he received a ring from him on his deathbed.

Polychoralism was replaced in Venice by the more eclectic and expressive style of Monteverdi (see p.262), who became *maestro di cappella* at St Mark's a year after Gabrieli's death.

CEREMONIAL MUSIC

Gabrieli's career coincides with one of the most opulent periods of Venetian history, presided over by one of its most lavish doges, Marino Grimani, who spent colossal amounts on state occasions. Obviously such occasions involved the church, but it was Venice rather than God that was being celebrated, and at St Mark's priests could actually be fined if they interrupted the music. Gabrieli clearly revelled in the musical extravagance that was expected of him, and he was one of the first composers to make highly specific instructions about dynamics: one piece is actually entitled *Sonata pian e forte* (loud and soft sonata). Instrumental music was as important as choral for creating the right atmosphere of solemnity, and some of Gabrieli's finest works are his canzoni, in which the instruments are treated with all the sensitivity usually accorded to voices alone.

A Venetian Coronation 1595 – music by Andrea and Giovanni Gabrieli: Gabrieli Consort and Players; McCreesh (Virgin VC 759 006 2).

This disc is a reconstruction of the music that might have been performed at the coronation of Marino Grimani in 1595. Slightly less than half the music is by Giovanni Gabrieli, while the rest is a setting of the Mass by Andrea Gabrieli, plus some fanfares and a small amount of plainsong. Far from being an empty academic exercise, this is a wonderfully exciting and evocative recording which really conveys the splendour and solemnity of the occasion – a fifteen-part canzona sounds all the more splendid if it has been preceded by a minute of plainsong. The performances are wonderfully vigorous, and the engineers have really captured a spatially convincing sound, even though it was recorded in a Northumberland Priory rather than in St Mark's.

GEORGE GERSHWIN

(1898–1937)

Like many other songwriters who held sway over American popular music in the 1920s and 1930s, George Gershwin was a New Yorker of European-Jewish extraction. During his boyhood his family was constantly on the move from one Manhattan tenement to another, and his parents were far too busy trying to support their children to have much time for any cultural pursuits. The young George, however, had a home-grown artistic collaborator in the shape of his older brother Ira, who in later years was to write the lyrics to most of his classic songs. The purchase by the Gershwins of their first piano in 1910 was to change George's life. Originally intended for Ira, the instrument was soon monopolized by George, who quickly went through a variety of neighbourhood piano teachers, rapidly outgrowing what each one had to offer.

By the age of 16 Gershwin had dropped out of business school and was working on Tin Pan Alley as a plugger of other people's songs. In 1919 he had his first hit with *Swannee*, taken from his comedy *La La Lucille*. It was the start of an unending stream of hit shows, peppered with songs that are a roll-call of twentieth-century popular music's high points, including *Fascinatin' Rhythm*, *Someone to Watch Over Me* and *Lady Be Good*.

But despite the money and fame Gershwin was not satisfied. Fascinated since childhood by classical music, he started to entertain the idea of writing extended instrumental works that would use American musical forms, like ragtime, blues and jazz, to convey the vibrant everyday life of the American people. The catalyst for this new departure was provided by the band leader Paul Whiteman, who invited Gershwin to contribute a piece to a concert advertised as "An Experiment in Modern Music". In under a month Gershwin wrote his *Rhapsody in Blue*, and he played the piano part himself at the premiere on February 12, 1924. Attended by the likes of Toscanini, Stravinsky and Rachmaninov, the concert was a sensation, and it made Gershwin famous overnight.

From that time on his reputation was sealed, although he occasionally had periods of insecurity that drove him to snatch lessons wherever he could. On a trip to Paris he even approached Ravel for tuition. Ravel's answer was: "Why do you want to become a second-rate Ravel when you're already a first-class Gershwin?" Legend has it that he also asked Stravinsky for compositional guidance, but that the latter, upon hearing what the young man earned in one year ("About 250,000 dollars"), asked him for lessons instead.

Apart from Stravinsky, the classical composers who most fascinated Gershwin in the mid-1920s were Schoenberg and Berg, yet it was the music

LEBRECHT COLLECTION

George Gershwin hard at work on *Lady Be Good*, 1924

produced by the group of French composers known as Les Six which directly inspired the half-jazzy, half-classical *An American in Paris* (1928). His final "serious" work, the opera *Porgy and Bess* (premiered in Boston on September 30, 1935), was not universally popular at first – some eminent black composers, including Duke Ellington, were less than complimentary – but its array of wonderful songs has ensured its place on the stage ever since.

With *Porgy* he had gone further than ever in fusing popular and classical styles, and at no cost to his mass audience appeal. But at this peak in his career Gershwin was cut down with a brain tumour while working on his third Hollywood film score, *The Goldwyn Follies*. Among those who most keenly felt the loss was his friend Arnold Schoenberg, who said of Gershwin: "Music was what made him feel, and music was the feeling he expressed. Directness of this kind is given only to great men, and there is no doubt that he was a great composer."

PORGY AND BESS

It would have been easy for Gershwin to go on repeating the formula that had made his musical comedies such successes, but in 1926 he came across a novel called *Porgy and Bess* by Dubose Heyward, and the book immediately fired his imagination. He soon determined to turn this story of a South Carolina black community into an opera – "If I am successful," he wrote, "it will resemble a combination of the drama and romance of *Carmen* and the beauty of *Meistersinger*." He succeeded beyond all expectations: just as in *Carmen* there are plenty of beautiful songs, effortlessly woven into the score, and like *Meistersinger* it displays a highly skilful use of leitmotifs and large choral numbers, creating a sense of tight community in Catfish Row similar to that in Wagner's Nuremberg. It didn't please everybody, though: jazz fans were dismissive of his use of African-American music, while opera critics complained that it was just a string of hit tunes. Gershwin responded to this last charge by pointing out that "nearly all of Verdi's operas contain what are known as 'song hits'". He might have added that few twentieth-century composers of any type had written songs as tuneful and powerful as "Summertime", "I Got Plenty o' Nuttin", "Bess You is My Woman" and "It Ain't Necessarily So".

⊙ Carey, Haymon, Blackwell, Evans, White; Glyndebourne Chorus; London Philharmonic Orchestra; Rattle (EMI CDS 749568-2; 3 CDs).

Based closely on the acclaimed Glyndebourne production, this is a highly spontaneous performance with an exhilarating atmosphere. Under Rattle's exuberant direction the LPO inject just the right rhythmic fluidity into their playing, giving a jazzy swing to the proceedings when called for. The characterization on the part of all the singers is of so high a standard that it would be invidious to select anyone for particular praise.

RHAPSODY IN BLUE

Paul Whiteman had achieved enormous success by diluting jazz in order to make it acceptable to white middle-class Americans. In commissioning *Rhapsody in Blue* he wanted to go further and make it acceptable to a classical audience (probably unaware that Milhaud had got there a few months earlier with *La Création du Monde*). His 1924 concert "An Experiment in Modern Music" was a success largely because Gershwin's work (programmed near the end) came as a blast of exuberant and original energy amid the anodyne orchestral arrangements of popular songs that made up the rest of the programme. Made up of one long movement (loosely divided into three sections – fast/slow/fast), the *Rhapsody in Blue* is essentially a collection of inspired show tunes connected by the kind of virtuosic effects that wouldn't be out of place in a Liszt piano concerto. Orchestration was by Whiteman's arranger Ferde Grofé, and the famous wailing glissando on the clarinet which opens the work emerged in rehearsal. None of which alters the fact that it still makes an incredible and immediate impact, especially in Grofé's original orchestration.

⊙ Previn; London Symphony Orchestra (EMI CDC 747161-2; with *Piano Concerto in F, An American in Paris*).

This is not an easy work to pull off: both orchestra and soloist need to shake off their inhibitions without being brash and noisy – in the right hands *Rhapsody in Blue* is extremely sexy music. André Previn makes an ideal interpreter: his own experience as a jazz pianist means that the Gershwin style offers no surprises. This is a fresh, exhilarating and utterly idomatic performance.

THE PIANO CONCERTO IN F

The conductor Walter Damrosch was at the Whiteman concert and as a result Gershwin was commissioned to compose a "proper" piano concerto for the New York Symphony Orchestra. In fact, though there is greater thematic development and the work is divided into clear-cut movements, the mixture is very much as before – a combination of a Romantic-style concerto, Dixieland rhythms, and the melancholy of both the blues and Yiddisher popular music. Gershwin described it thus: "The first movement employs the Charleston rhythm. It is quick and pulsating, representing the young and enthusiastic spirit of American life. . . The second movement has a poetic nocturnal atmosphere. . . The final movement reverts to the style of the first. It is an orgy of rhythms, starting violently and keeping to the same pace throughout."

⊙ Previn; London Symphony Orchestra (EMI CDC 747161-2; with *Rhapsody in Blue, An American in Paris*).

Previn is equally impressive in the concerto: light-touched and spring-heeled, never wallowing in the more sentimental passages, and above all tapping into the humour that seems to elude so many performers.

AN AMERICAN IN PARIS

Gershwin's third orchestral work (again premiered by Damrosch) was clearly inspired by two trips that he made to Paris: "My purpose here is to portray the impressions of an American visitor in Paris as he strolls about the city, listens to the various street noises, and absorbs the French atmosphere." It is thus a kind of easy-going tone poem, unspecific in programme, though Gershwin did purchase some genuinely French car horns to add to its authentically urban feel. There's also a much more assured sense of structure than in his previous orchestral works, with less of a stop-start feel to it. Gershwin thought of it as a "rhapsodic ballet" and its combination of wide-eyed innocence and brash boulevardier spirit were perfectly captured by Gene Kelly's choreography in the 1951 film inspired by the piece.

O Previn; London Symphony Orchestra (EMI CDC 747161-2; with *Piano Concerto in F*, *Rhapsody in Blue*).

Again this is a work that demands complete sympathy and understanding of the idiom for it not to sound heavy-footed and pedestrian. It certainly gets it in this kaleidoscopic performance, which brings out all the jauntiness and sleaze that you could possibly want.

CARLO GESUALDO

(1561–1613)

The music of Gesualdo is some of the strangest ever written. Even in the context of a period when composers were constantly experimenting with ways of enlivening the words they set, his music startles through its bizarre and neurotic sensitivity to meaning – his later madrigals especially make for fascinating but at times uncomfortable listening. The eccentricity of the music is mirrored by the details of Gesualdo's extraordinary life. When, on the death of his elder brother, Gesualdo became Prince of Venosa, it became necessary for him to marry. The choice of bride fell on his twice-widowed cousin Maria d'Avalos and, after special papal permission had been obtained, the two were married in 1586. Four years later Gesualdo discovered that his wife was conducting an affair with a nobleman, the Duke of Andria. One night, having left his palace on the pretext of a hunting trip, he returned home suddenly and found the lovers in bed together, whereupon he had them both instantly murdered – allegedly skewered on a single sword. Gesualdo escaped punishment but unsurprisingly this event seems to have overshadowed the rest of his life. Although he married again, he seems to have become a disturbed and melancholic man, largely cut off from society in the isolation of his palace in southern Italy. In his later years he had himself regularly scourged.

It was not unusual for members of the aristocracy to be musically adept, but it was rare for them to pursue their interest as single-mindedly as Gesualdo did. In 1593 his second marriage, to Eleonora d'Este (who later tried to divorce him for his violent behaviour towards her), brought him briefly into contact with the ducal court of Ferrara, a lively artistic centre with a particularly strong musical tradition. Here he met Luzzasco Luzzaschi, a skilled madrigalist and one of a succession of Ferrara-based composers who were concerned with finding ever more expressive settings for words. A favoured means of achieving this greater intensity was through chromaticism – in other words, composers began exploiting the interval of the semitone, with the result that the progress of the music became less predictable and regularly threw up peculiar harmonies. This was the catalyst that Gesualdo needed: before Ferrara his work is interesting but relatively conventional; after Ferrara it becomes increasingly original and, at moments, extreme.

MADRIGALS

Gesualdo wrote six books of madrigals, the best of them being books three to six, which were written after his return from Ferrara. The texts – usually short and almost exclusively about death and the sufferings of love – are set so that the most highly charged words are always dramatically emphasized, either by dissonance or a change of speed or an unexpected note. Unlike Dowland's similarly morbid songs, where consistency of mood invites the listener's identification, Gesualdo's madrigals are distinguished by disruptive and restless changes of mood, so that the end result is rather like eavesdropping on some unresolvable, private agony.

⊙ Madrigals for Five Voices: Les Arts Florissants; Christie (Harmonia Mundi HMC 901268).

This disc provides a selection of seventeen madrigals taken from books three to six, three of which have been arranged instrumentally. Les Arts Florissants are an ideal group for madrigal singing, as each voice is individually recognizable and yet they all blend well. Their responsiveness to the words is also exemplary: they are always keenly aware of shifts in meaning but convey the meaning – as far as is possible with such spasmodic music – in a subtle and unforced manner. The relatively conventional *Sparge la morte* is treated with a subdued and tragic sobriety, for instance, whereas the stark and angular *Merce grido piangendo* veers from a rapturous opening to increasing enervation.

SACRED MUSIC

Gesualdo appears to have been a devoutly religious man – he greatly admired his uncle Carlo Borromeo (later St Carlo Borromeo), a leading figure behind the Council of Trent and a patron of Palestrina. Church music accounts for about a quarter of Gesualdo's output, and although it is sombre and restrained in comparison with his madrigals, it still carries a far greater sense of the personal and extravagant than that of his contemporaries. Motet settings of gloomy and penitential texts – chosen presumably to reflect his own predicament – comprise the bulk of these works, and stylistically they tend to follow the pattern of Palestrina, but with occasional startling changes of speed that break up the meditative stillness. His greatest religious work, and the closest to his madrigal writing, is the set of responses for Holy Week, published in 1611.

⊙ Sabato Sancto Responsoria; Four Motets: Ensemble Vocal Européen de la Chapelle Royale; Herreweghe (Harmonia Mundi HMC 901320; with Gorli, *Requiem*).

This recording provides Gesualdo's nine responses for Holy Saturday plus four motets. Herreweghe's forces are probably larger than Gesualdo would have employed in his private chapel but they never smooth over the music's constant struggle between serenity and anguish. The fill-up piece is a Requiem by a present-day composer.

⊙ Tenebrae: Hilliard Ensemble (ECM New Series 843867; 2 CDs).

The Hilliard Ensemble's celebrated disc presents all the music that Gesualdo wrote for the Tenebrae services of Holy Week (including the Holy Week music reviewed above). This is the most anguished moment in the Christian calendar and the music perfectly matches the intensity of the mood. The performance is immaculate: heartfelt but not over-demonstrative, and perfectly judged both in terms of phrasing and intonation.

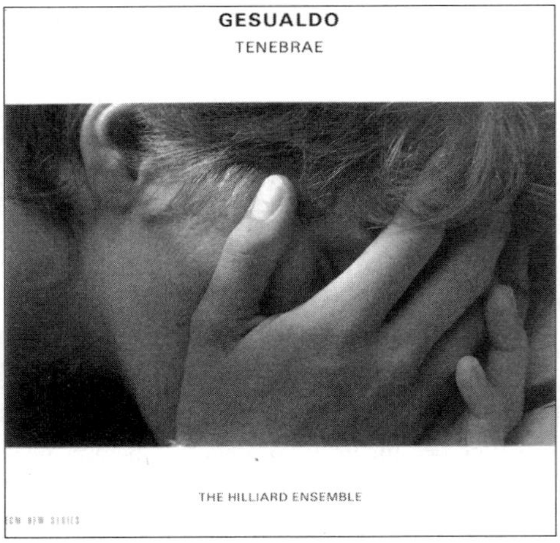

ORLANDO GIBBONS

(1583–1625)

Gibbons was the outstanding composer of English church music in the generation that succeeded William Byrd. He excelled as a writer of anthems (the English equivalent of Latin motets), building on Byrd's richest and most demonstrative Anglican settings to produce his own vigorous and expressive musical language. He was also a renowned composer of keyboard music, notable for its contrapuntal rigour and inventiveness, and as a keyboard player he was described as "the best hand in England".

He was born in Oxford into a musical family: his father William was a player in the city band and his brother Edward was master of the choristers at King's College Cambridge, where Orlando served as a chorister and later studied as an undergraduate.

In 1603 he joined the Chapel Royal in London and became organist there some two years later – a position he held until his death. His success continued with preferment at court: a gift of £150 in 1615, and four years later an appointment as "one of his Majesty's musicians . . . to attend in his highnes privie chamber". In April 1625, as organist of Westminster Abbey, he played at the funeral of King James I, and two months later was summoned to Canterbury as part of the royal household to await the arrival from France of King Charles I's new bride, Queen Henrietta Maria. On Whitsunday, a few days before the Queen's arrival, Gibbons died suddenly from an apoplectic fit and was buried in Canterbury Cathedral.

SACRED MUSIC

By Gibbons' time English was the language of the liturgy in Britain, and the anthem had become the main choral display piece. There were two forms: the full anthem, which was closest to the motet, was a polyphonic piece for full choir, while the more dramatic verse anthem contrasted solo sections with choral sections, both accompanied by either organ or strings. Gibbons' most dramatically appealing music is found in his verse anthems, of which the finest, *This is the Record of John*, is a gentle yet compelling narrative, sung for the most part by an alto soloist with the chorus echoing the closing chords of each section. It is a peculiarly English mixture of solo and choral interplay, pointing the way towards Purcell's more dramatic style.

⊙ Tudor Church Music: Choir of King's College Cambridge; Ledger (ASV CD GAU 123).

There is currently no recording that completely does justice to Gibbons as a composer of sacred music. This 1982 recording is musically very good, with outstanding contributions from alto Michael Chance, who has solos in several of the anthems. The drawback is the notorious King's College acoustic: the engineers have tried to retain the resonance without losing the clarity of the voices, and the result creates a curious inbalance between the soloists and the full choir. It's a well-selected programme, though, covering the whole range of Gibbons' liturgical music: from the simplicity of the four-part setting of the *Magnificat* and *Nunc Dimittis*, through *This is the Record of John* to the lush exuberance of the full anthem *Hosanna to the Son of David*.

SECULAR MUSIC

Gibbons was a versatile and wide-ranging composer. Along with Byrd and John Bull he

contributed to *Parthenia* (1613), the first collection of keyboard music to be published in England, and also wrote a set of madrigals on rather sombre texts, the most famous of which is the poignant *O Silver Swan*. His thirty or so pieces for viols are mainly fantasias, which were freely composed works in several sections that often developed contrapuntally from a particular theme. These were the most common form of chamber music in seventeenth-century England.

◑ Fantaisies Royales: Savall, Coin, Casademunt, Sonnleitner (Auvidis Astrée E 7747).

The three-part and four-part compositions gathered on the *Fantaisies Royales* are exceptionally rich and inventive, less melancholic than Dowland's viol pavans and less cerebral than Byrd's viol fantasias. Here they are performed by musicians who are especially responsive to the sensuality of the music, favouring a full but not a heavy tone, and treating Gibbons' lilting rhythms with a stylish and easy charm.

◑ Consort of Musicke by William Byrd and Orlando Gibbons: Gould (Sony SMK 52 589).

Though he publicly performed just one work by him – the *Lord of Salisbury Pavan and Galliard* – Glenn Gould claimed on several occasions that Gibbons was his favourite composer. He saw the early English keyboard masters as anticipating the elaborate counterpoint of Bach that was his major preoccupation as a pianist, a prophetic quality most apparent in Gibbons' brilliant C major *Fantasy*. Interestingly, though, he treats several other works more as poetic miniatures than as formal studies, with a hushed rapture that is particularly evident in the ordered and stately calm of the pavans on the disc (one by Gibbons and two by Byrd).

UMBERTO GIORDANO

(1867–1948)

As with so many *verismo* composers, such as Leoncavallo and Mascagni, Umberto Giordano's name has survived on the strength of a single opera. Typically for an Italian composer of his time, Giordano was drawn to opera almost from the start, and his early life was spent battling with parents who strongly objected to his pursuing a life in music. It was not until 1890 that he graduated from the Naples Conservatory, but by then he had already completed his first opera, the one-act *Marina*, which he had submitted as an entry in the 1889 Sonzogno opera competition. *Marina* fared no better than sixth place, but it secured him a commission for a full-length work, the result of which, *Mala vita*, was one of the most sensational of all *verismo* operas, with a plot that contrived to bring together a prostitute and the Virgin Mary. It was violent, crude and, for a short time, extremely popular.

His next opera, *Regina Diaz*, was ditched after only two performances, but in 1896, having moved to the warmer audiences in Milan, Giordano composed his masterpiece, *Andrea Chénier*. Unfortunately its premiere came less than two months after the first staging, also in Milan, of Puccini's *La Bohème*, and *Chénier* was inevitably overshadowed to a large extent. Nonetheless, *Chénier* brought its composer considerable acclaim, and two years later he produced another extremely popular opera, *Fedora* – a work which gave rise to the witticism "Fedora fè d'oro" (Fedora made money). Its success was guaranteed when Caruso, who sang on the first night, gave a thrilling performance of the opera's only tenor aria *Amor ti vieta*, which was so well received that he was obliged to sing it twice.

Of his other operas, only *Madame Sans-Gêne* achieved anything like the success of *Andrea Chénier* or *Fedora*, and he composed his last, *Il re*, in 1929. For the remaining nineteen years of his life he composed nothing but songs and a few light salon pieces.

ANDREA CHÉNIER

Like Puccini, Giordano was heavily influenced by the lyricism of Massenet but he is on the whole less subtle than both – he was generally at his best when writing fervent music for fervent situations. Yet with *Andrea Chénier* he created a group of three-dimensional personalities, a string of memorable tunes, and some of the most dramatic scenes in all opera.

The eponymous hero is based upon the real-life Andrea Chénier, an eminent poet in Revolutionary France, but the events are a romanticized tale of love across the social classes, political intrigue, injustice and tragic death. There are some remarkable moments in the course of the four acts – notably Chénier's improvised poem *Un di all'azzuro spazio* in Act One, his beloved's Act Three aria *La mamma morta* (recently used to great effect in the film *Philadelphia*), and Chénier's reflection on his imminent death, *Come un bel di di Maggio* – but the overall orchestration and pacing are just right as well. The eighteenth-century pastiche shows a masterly understanding of the orchestra and Giordano's word-setting must have been the envy of all his contemporaries, excepting Puccini. *Andrea Chénier*'s absence from the opera-house stage has more to do with a dearth of genuine heroic tenors than with any intrinsic weaknesses in the music.

◑ **Corelli, Stella, Sereni, De Palma; Rome Opera Chorus and Orchestra; Santini** (EMI CMS565287-2; 2 CDs).

This is one of the greatest Italian opera recordings ever made. Andrea Chénier is the part Franco Corelli was born to play, and here he plays it at the peak of his form. Full and baritonal, his voice is nonetheless capable of glass-breaking heights. His two big solos are sung with all the self-indulgent mannerisms for which his performances were so memorable, while the the final *Vicino a te* is uniquely moving, even if Antonietta Stella is so outweighed that the final duet is more like a tenor solo with soprano accompaniment.

PHILIP GLASS

(1937–)

Philip Glass is the most famous and financially successful serious composer alive, thanks mainly to the instant accessibility of his brand of Minimalism. Whether he's writing for ballet, opera, theatre, film or even for a TV jingle, Glass's style is unmistakable, with its repetitions of cell-like phrases built usually from brightly coloured keyboard sounds enhanced by soothing vocals and hot horns. Though often criticized as shallow and uneventful, Glass's music is insidiously effective – hear a Glass piece and you won't be able to get it out of your head for the rest of the day.

Of immigrant Jewish parentage, Glass grew up in Baltimore and got a taste for commercial music when he sold Elvis Presley records in his father's music store. He was an accomplished flautist and violinist by the age of 15, when he attended Chicago University to major in maths and philosophy. By the late 1950s he was in New York studying with Steve Reich (see p.336) at the Juilliard School, and went on to study with Darius Milhaud (see p.261) at Aspen and Nadia Boulanger in Paris.

While in Paris Glass assisted the renowned sitarist Ravi Shankar with the soundtrack for Conrad Rooks' film *Chappaqua*. Received wisdom says that Minimalism was a reaction against the dry, elitist Modernist schools, particularly the serialist establishment of the 1960s, but Glass explains it somewhat differently: "There was a generation about ten years older than me who were so damn good at what they did that there was no need to write any more of that kind of music. Working with Ravi, I saw there was another way music could be organized, around rhythmic ideas instead of around structure. Rhythm could be the structural basis of the music instead of just an ornament."

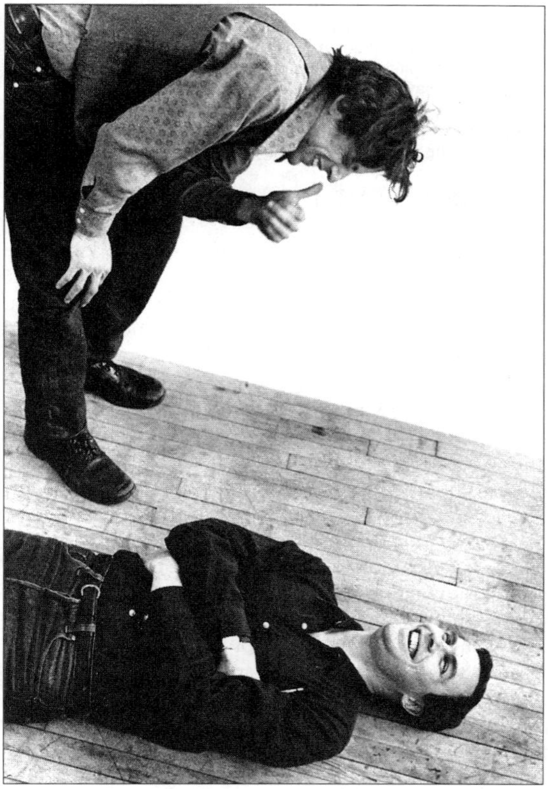

BETTY FREEMAN/LEBRECHT COLLECTION

Glass shares a joke with the recumbent Robert Wilson

Returning to New York in 1967, Glass threw himself into the bohemian art scene of lower Manhattan, giving loft concerts with Terry Riley and Steve Reich, and forming the Philip Glass Ensemble. From this period came *Music in Similar Motion* (1969) and *Music in Changing Parts* (1970), both written for organs, flute, trumpet and saxes, and combining rock-type grooves with perpetual drones, all played at incredible volume. In 1974 Glass declared: "Music no longer has a mediative function, referring to something outside itself . . . it must be listened to as a pure sound-event, an act without any dramatic structure." He did not stay long in such abstract territory, and for many years has been an indisputably theatrical composer. In the early 1990s he explained: "the most important thing is that music provides an emotional framework or context. It tells you what to feel about what you're seeing."

The real breakthrough came when he met theatre conceptualist Robert Wilson, with whom he produced the hallucinogenic four-hour opera *Einstein on the Beach* (1976) – a sellout at the Met, this was the work that pushed Minimalism into the mainstream. Assisted by engineer Kurt Munkacsi, Glass built up a reputation for technical brilliance in the studio, and his first digital album *Glassworks* (1982) was a hit across the whole spectrum of musical taste. On a larger scale, the operas *Satyagraha* (1980) and *Akhnaten* (1984), drawing on the lives of Gandhi, Tolstoy, Martin Luther King and a sun-worshipping Egyptian pharaoh, completed the trilogy begun with *Einstein*, and thrillingly combined his trademark repetitions and overlappings with the ceremonial grandeur of the stage.

Glass maintains a formidable rate of output – he was the first composer to develop a production-line system, using sampling techniques so that every musical sketch could be speedily turned into finished product. He currently lives in the East Village, where he spends each morning composing before taking the short walk to his hi-tech Living Room Studios, to oversee record production and the rehearsal of opera and ensemble pieces. One of the most stimulating projects of recent years was his 1990 reunion with Ravi Shankar, *Passages*, a true collaboration in which each gave the other basic material to expand into full compositions. In 1998 Glass and Robert Wilson premiered their latest collaboration – *Monsters of Grace*, an audiovisual extravaganza based on the writings of the thirteenth-century dervish Rumi, mixing live action with illusionistic 3-D movie projections.

AKHNATEN

Glass is interested in visionaries, in people who have changed the world by the sheer force of their ideas. Having written about Einstein and Gandhi (*Satyagraha*) he looked for another inspirational figure. The catalyst for the third opera in his epic trilogy was Velikovsky's book *Oedipus and Akhnaten*, and the original idea was to have two operas on stage simultaneously, one telling the story of Oedipus and the other that of Akhnaten. In the end Glass decided to concentrate on Akhnaten and his ultimately unsuccessful attempt to introduce the world's first known monotheistic religion to Egypt.

Glass's decison to omit violins from his score creates a number of dramatic advantages: the dark, warm sound which results from the loss of many of the higher registers and timbres (and from some stunning music for brass) perfectly evokes the mysterious and the exotic. It also contrasts with the solo voices and emphasizes the other-worldly quality of the music for Akhnaten himself – sung by a countertenor. Akhnaten is also set apart when he sings the *Hymn to the Sun* (believed to have been written by the pharaoh himself) in the language of the audience – most of the rest of the opera is in Egyptian, Akkadian and Hebrew. *Akhnaten* is one of Glass's most majestic, lyrical works, with several long-limbed, graceful arias

leavening the familiar restless, staccato instrumental music, and even without the visual spectacle it's a compelling experience.

○ Esswood, Vargas, Liebermann, Hannula; Stuttgart Opera Chorus and Orchestra; Davies (Sony M2K 42547; 2 CDs).

Russell Davies here conducts many of the original cast from the Stuttgart premiere of *Akhnaten*. Paul Esswood makes the pharaoh a convincing and touching figure, and the remaining players are all well cast – though anyone who saw the rather more dynamic London production will regret that it was never recorded. However, *Akhnaten* is an opera in which the orchestra is the leading voice and the Stuttgart players really rise to the occasion.

KOYAANISQATSI

In his work for film Glass insists on working on a project from the beginning, so that "the music has a totally functional relation to the image. It's not something that's carved out and stuck on a film, they're made together." Glass has worked with Schrader (*Mishima*) and Scorsese (*Kundun*), but the best known of his soundtracks were written for Godfrey Reggio's non-narrative documentaries *Koyaanisqatsi* and *Powaaqatsi*. *Koyaanisqatsi*, filmed entirely in North America, was a portrait of the US seen in terms of an imbalance of technology (the title is a Hopi word meaning "life out of balance"). It used filmic devices like freeze-frame and slow motion, to create a mesmeric visual impression, which is perfectly matched by Glass's hypnotic score. Much of the music is filled with Glass's typically restless and rippling surfaces but it is the slower, more reflective moments that stay in the memory, in particular the title track – a slow portentous organ and deep chanting voices – which is reprised at the end of the film over a haunting image of rocket remains slowly tumbling to earth.

◑ **Glass, Western Wind Vocal Ensemble etc** (Island IMCD 98).

The CD includes a selection of six sequences from the original soundtrack. Glass's band is augmented by brass, strings and the Western Wind Vocal Ensemble into a large orchestra, but the music still retains its energy. A new recording, made under Glass's supervision, is currently being prepared, and may well supersede this one.

MUSIC IN TWELVE PARTS

Music in Twelve Parts, written between 1971 and 1974, represents a beginning and an end. Stretching a point, it might be seen as Glass's equivalent to Bach's *The Art of Fugue* in that it summed up his work and acted as an encyclopedia of its theoretical basis. In so far as Glass ever accepted the tag, he regarded *Music in Twelve Parts* as the conclusion of his Minimalist period: "Although *Music in Twelve Parts* would be classified as a minimal work, it was a breakthrough for me and contains many of the structural and harmonic ideas that would be fleshed out in later works." In fact, although the processes employed are varied, the music still has all the restrictions and characteristics of stereotypical minimalism: short, repetitive motifs rather than legato melodies, little harmonic variety, relentless rhythms and hard, glittering textures. Part One, written in 1971, was originally intended to stand alone. The most meditative of the twelve pieces, the strands of its twelve-voice counterpoint create an acoustical phenomenon that especially fascinated Glass – overlapping figures suggest a drone of a fifth that is not actually written into the music. Glass continued with the series and by the time he reached Part Eight had completed what he had set out to do. The final four parts pursue a slightly different direction.

○ **Philip Glass Ensemble; Riesman** (Elektra Nonesuch 7559-79324-2; 3 CDs).

Music in Twelve Parts is modular – its separate parts can be played in any sequence or combination. From beginning to end it lasts about three and a half hours, but it's a crucial part of the Glass canon and should be heard. This set, recorded in 1993, is markedly more human than the original Virgin recordings in which the performances had the precision and, in many passages, the coldness of machines. The sound is softer and the effect is more hypnotic and less forbidding than the earlier version.

ALEXANDER GLAZUNOV

(1865–1936)

Glazunov is best known for things other than his own compositions: for helping complete some of Borodin's music, for example, or for teaching Shostakovich, or for conducting the premiere of Rachmaninov's first symphony while drunk and thereby triggering the young composer's nervous breakdown. With its undisguised assimilations of Tchaikovsky, Rimsky-Korsakov and Scriabin, Glazunov's music might not have the individuality of the music of some of his compatriots, yet it is often attractive and colourful, and it brought him worldwide acclaim in his day.

Glazunov's main problem is his conservatism. This was the charge laid against him long ago by both Prokofiev and Shostakovich, and there is no denying that by the standards of his friend Scriabin, for example, his music showed little advance on that of the nationalist circle surrounding Mily Balakirev, though he did manage to fuse their general techniques with the European-oriented style of Tchaikovsky.

His musical talents were nonetheless prodigious and he soon outgrew Rimsky-Korsakov's tutelage. His first mature works date from the 1880s, when he produced the first two of his eight symphonies (a ninth got no further than a single movement). Three more date from the 1890s, as do the two ballets which brought him more acclaim than anything else he wrote, *Raymunda* (1897) and *The Seasons* (1899). In the year of the latter work he was appointed professor at the St Petersburg conservatory, where he remained until 1930, having become its director in 1905. In the early years of the century he produced the *Violin Concerto* (1904) and the *Symphony No. 8* (1906), and from then on he composed little of any consequence, concentrating instead on his academic responsibilities, thereby managing to stay in favour with the regimes both before and after the Revolution. He settled in Paris in 1932, where he died four years later.

BALLET MUSIC

When Tchaikovsky died in 1893, the Director of the Imperial Theatres, Vsevolozhky, needed a composer in a similar vein to maintain the standards set by Tchaikovsky's three great ballet scores. Glazunov's reputation was already fairly high when, in 1897, he was invited to compose a full-length ballet, *Raymunda*, to be choreographed by the legendary Marius Petipa. The result was such a success that Glazunov wrote two more ballets for St Petersburg, *Les Ruses d'amour* and *The Seasons*, before turning his back on the theatre. Of these three, *The Seasons* is the finest: its debt to Tchaikovsky is always apparent, but it is not the pale imitation that some have suggested, and its fifteen short sections (none longer than four minutes) sparkle with brilliantly conceived, and highly danceable, ideas. Each of the seasons is vividly but lightly characterized: best of all is winter, which consists of a shimmeringly delicate theme followed by four witty variations representing frost, ice, hail and snow.

O Scottish National Orchestra; Järvi (Chandos CHAN 8596; with *Violin Concerto*).

Neeme Järvi is something of a Glazunov specialist (he has recorded all the symphonies) and his enthusiasm for this music is apparent in every bar. *The Seasons* is more lightly textured than Tchaikovsky's great ballets, and Glazunov's delicate instrumental colouring is exquisitely presented by the Scottish National Orchestra.

THE VIOLIN CONCERTO

Glazunov's *Violin Concerto* was written in 1904 for the virtuoso Leopold Auer (a future colleague at the St Petersburg Conservatoire). It's very much a Romantic showpiece in the manner of Mendelssohn or Tchaikovsky, but with the violin's melodic material more closely related to its orchestral background than in their concertos. There are two sections (bridged by a cadenza): the first is dominated by a gently lyrical melody with a hint of Slavic melancholy; the second is heralded by a jaunty fanfare-like motif in the trumpets which is then developed by the soloist into an ever more spectacular display of technical bravura. This is the one work by Glazunov to have established itself as a repertoire standard outside of Russia, not least because of the advocacy of Auer's most brilliant pupil, Jascha Heifetz.

O Vengerov; Berlin Philharmonic Orchestra; Abbado (Teldec 4509-90881-2; with Tchaikovsky's *Violin Concerto*).

Heifetz's stunning recording of the *Violin Concerto*, from the 1960s, is not currently available as a single CD. Of recent alternatives, this by Maxim Vengerov is by far the most spectacular. It's a more subtle reading than most, with Vengerov bringing some exquisite shifts of tone to each unfolding melody.

O Shumsky; Scottish National Orchestra; Järvi (Chandos CHAN 8596; with *The Seasons*).

Veteran violinist Oscar Shumsky may not have the range or the brio of Vengerov, but his old-fashioned approach has a delicacy of touch and a warmth that is extremely satisfying.

MIKHAIL GLINKA

(1804–1857)

Glinka was the father of Russian musical nationalism, the first Russian master of operatic writing, and the first Russian composer to find acceptance in the rest of Europe. He was born into a wealthy landowning family, and as a 13-year-old took piano lessons with John Field, the creator of the nocturne (see p.107). But in 1824 he abandoned his musical studies in favour of a post at the Ministry of Communication, and even though he gave recitals as an amateur singer he did not fully devote himself to music until 1828, when he began full-time composition lessons.

Two years later he moved to Milan, where his exposure to Italian music forced him to acknowledge the weakness of his native national tradition – every aspect of Russian music at this time, even its folk songs, was contaminated by the overbearing influence of Western European culture. In 1833 he moved on to Vienna, but homesickness and the death of his father forced him to return to St Petersburg where, in 1835, he set about writing his first opera – *A Life for the Tsar*, the first serious attempt at creating classical music with a genuine Russian character, though Italian lyricism is an important element of its style. *A Life for the Tsar* is always being brought out for the openings of operatic seasons in Russia, but it's not the subtlest opera ever written, and its interest remains chiefly historical.

The opera's successful production in 1836 proved that Glinka had struck a chord, and his subsequent appointment in 1837 as Imperial

GUUS ONG

Kapellmeister cemented his position as Russia's most important composer. Midway through that year, Glinka began to plan an opera based upon Pushkin's poem *Ruslan and Lyudmila* and, even though the poet's death prevented their collaboration, a libretto was patched together. Glinka's second opera was produced in 1842 and its massive success finally secured his fame outside Russia. Numerous aspects of *Ruslan and Lyudmila* marked it out as essentially Russian: its use of Russian folk polyphony and melodic themes; the recitatives based upon the rhythms of the Russian language; the texture of its sounds, in which instruments such as the balalaika played a significant part. It was a declaration of musical independence, and at Glinka's death in 1857 a generation of composers was ready to continue writing music that was Russian in style, flavour and inspiration – the first such generation in Russia's history.

RUSLAN AND LYUDMILA

From the famous, toe-tapping overture to the tuneful, boisterous finale, Glinka's second opera is a thoroughly entertaining piece. Based upon Pushkin's poem, Glinka's magical tale can be seen as anticipating the fantastic and grotesque elements of the operas of Rimsky-Korsakov and Stravinsky. Basically, Lyudmila vanishes from a feast organized for her three suitors. Her father promises her hand to the one who finds her first. Ruslan, the heroic knight, learns that she has been stolen by an evil dwarf, and then battles with a giant decapitated head to win a magic sword with which to defeat the dwarf and rescue Lyudmila. The tale may have its dramatic weaknesses, but the music's overall stylistic cohesion, melodic invention and idiomatic Russian harmonies more than compensate.

O Ognovienko, Netrebko, Diadkova, Bezzubenkov, Gorchakova; Kirov Opera; Gergiev (Philips 446 746-2; 2 CDs).

This 1996 live recording is one of only two versions of *Ruslan* in the catalogue, and it's so good that it's unlikely anyone will try to challenge it. The intensity of the orchestral playing is white-hot and all the soloists are outstanding. There's a fair amount of audience noise but it's a minor price to pay in the context of such a fine performance.

CHRISTOPH WILLIBALD GLUCK

(1714–1787)

It was Gluck who put into practice the principle defined by his near-contemporary Pietro Metastasio – "when the music in union with drama takes precedence, then the drama and music itself suffers in consequence". Gluck was the first composer to deny his singers any opportunity to indulge mere display, for in Gluck's operas the role of the music is to transmit the meaning of the libretto. Technically he may not have been the most accomplished of eighteenth-century composers, but he was the first to write operas in which music and drama achieved a state of complete balance.

German-born, Gluck was educated in Prague then moved to Vienna in 1736, where he played cello in a nobleman's private orchestra. In 1737 the orchestra travelled to Milan where Gluck took lessons with Sammartini (a pioneer of sonata form), under whose guidance he composed his first opera *Artaserse*. Its success led to the completion of a further seven operas before he left for London in 1745 and, although his two London operas failed, his friendship with Handel was to prove of inestimable musical benefit.

Upon leaving London in 1746, Gluck spent the next four years in travel, during which his operas

Semiramide riconosciuta and *La Clemenza di Tito* were well received, and then settled in Vienna. At the end of 1752 he was appointed Kapellmeister to the Prince of Saxe-Hildburghausen, a position that cemented his dominance of Vienna's musical life. Giacomo Durazzo, the manager of Vienna's state theatres, saw in Gluck's talent an opportunity to capitalize on the popularity of the lively and flexible French *opéra-comique*, and he engaged Gluck to adapt various existing works in the genre. Gluck responded by producing his own series of "French" comic masterpieces, following the successful premiere of *La fausse esclave* in 1758.

Inundated with requests for operas, it was not long before Gluck was working directly with his librettists, rather than accepting completed texts as part of a commission. His collaboration with the poet Raniero de' Calzabigi brought about radical reforms in the composition and production of opera, as typified by *Orfeo ed Euridice* (1762), a work whose dramatic use of orchestration and overall sense of direction were enthrallingly original. *Alceste*, composed in 1767 to a libretto by Calzabigi, furthered the development of Gluck's mission to "restrict music to its true office by serving poetry by means of expression and by following the situation of the story" and "to strive for a beautiful simplicity".

Alceste was not immediately the success it would later become, and in 1770 Gluck left his Vienna position, settling three years later in Paris, in order to fulfil the Opéra's commission for *Iphigenie en Aulide*. Its production was a sensation, as were his revisions of *Orfeo* and *Alceste*. However, his fame resulted in jealousy and, in an episode worthy of a Feydeau farce, a quarrel was engineered between Gluck and his bitter rival Piccini by asking the latter to set *Iphigénie en Tauride*, a libretto on which Gluck was working at the time. Piccini's version was moderately successful, Gluck's was his masterpiece: boasting an astonishingly integrated fusion of dance, drama, chorus and song, it rapidly eclipsed the competition. In 1779, Gluck retired to Vienna where, living in regal splendour, he died after refusing his doctor's orders that he drink no alcohol after dinner.

ORFEO ED EURIDICE

Gluck composed *Orfeo* twice: in 1762 for Vienna (in Italian), and again in 1774 for Paris (in French, as *Orphée et Euridice*). The Viennese version lasted an hour and forty minutes, the title role was scored for castrato, and dramatic fluency was its main aim and achievement. The Paris version was longer, the title role was written for a soprano, and it included two new ballets, the *Dance of Furies* and the *Dance of the Blessed Spirit*. These concessions to Parisian taste dissipated the emotional gravity and dramatic cohesion of the original score, and it's the first *Orfeo* that became the starting block for subsequent composers, most notably Mozart.

Ironically, Gluck's reformist opera is based upon the myth that had served as the foundation for the first Florentine operas, way back in 1600. Orfeo (Orpheus) is mourning the death of his wife Euridice. Zeus is so struck by his grief that he allows him to attempt to reclaim her from Hades. If, through his playing, he can persuade Pluto to release her, he may guide her back to earth, but he must not look upon her until they have crossed the River Styx. Orfeo succeeds in his task until Euridice, unable to understand his strange behaviour, claims she would rather be dead then be so spurned by him. He turns to look at her, and she is lost – but then touched by his lament, Amor restores Euridice to life, an artificially happy ending typical of the eighteenth-century stage.

The eruptions of emotion that occur throughout *Orfeo* gain potency from the poise with which they are expressed. Stripped of all ornament, Gluck's vocal writing possesses a simple beauty that reaches its highest pitch in Orfeo's "Che faro senza Euridice?" (What shall I do without Euridice?). Gluck's recitative is far more fluid use of a convention that had too often dragged the action to a standstill. Choruses are sumptuous and are allocated sparingly throughout the whole. *Orfeo* may not be Gluck and Calzabigi's greatest work but it is probably their most exhilarating. As the composer wrote many years later: "However much talent a composer may have, he will never produce any but mediocre music if the poet does not awaken in him that enthusiasm without which the productions of all the arts are but feeble and drooping."

○ Ragin, McNair, Sieden; Monteverdi Choir; English Baroque Soloists; Gardiner (Philips 434 093-2PH2; 2 CDs).

John Eliot Gardiner has conducted two recordings of different texts of *Orfeo*, and both are superb. This digital set of the Viennese version features Derek Lee Ragin's countertenor and Silvia McNair's soprano, an ideal partnership. McNair, one of the outstanding lyric talents of our time, is especially impressive, giving an effortless portrayal of Euridice. Under Gardiner's flexible direction this performance is wonderfully fresh, and benefits from well-spaced recording and full documentation.

○ von Otter, Hendricks, Fournier; Monteverdi Choir; Lyon Opera Orchestra; Gardiner (EMI CDS7 49834-2; 2 CDs).

For his stab at the French *Orfeo* Gardiner turned to Berlioz's edition of the score, which is a sort of hybrid of the two versions, with a chorus from *Echo et Narcisse* tacked onto the finale. (Berlioz also cut the *Dance of the Furies*, which Gardiner reinstates.) Gluck's proto-Romantic gestures, emphasized by Berlioz's rehashed instrumentation, are nicely brought out by Gardiner, whose orchestra plays with varying degrees of urgency and repose. However, the recording's prime attraction is Anne Sofie von Otter's beguiling mezzo-soprano, here at its most youthful; she brings a disciplined suffering to her portrayal of Orphée. Barbara Hendricks' high-lying soprano works well with von Otter, and Fournier makes an attractive if rather too sexy Amour.

IPHIGÉNIE EN TAURIDE

First performed in Paris on May 18, 1779, *Iphigénie en Tauride* was Gluck's last important work. Its libretto, by Nicholas-François Guillard, is the finest poem set by Gluck, and the opera as a whole comes as close as possible to the composer's ideal of a modern revival of the spirit of Greek tragedy. Listen to this opera and you'll hear the inspiration for the classical scenes composed by Bellini, Berlioz and Strauss.

Ultimately derived from the plays of Euripides (the twists and turns of the plot are too complicated to detail here), *Iphigénie en Tauride* contains some extraordinary moments of great drama, not least the introductory storm (there is no overture) and the chorus of the Furies in Act II, when Orestes' terrible, haunting conscience (he has murdered his mother) is portrayed as if in a dream. The arias throughout are innovatively plain and eloquent, while the finely realized orchestration lifts the ensemble high above the status of mere accompaniment. *Iphigénie en Tauride* is an extraordinarily colourful but plaintive work, which, for all its heroic subject matter, set opera squarely on the path to realism.

○ Montague, Aler, Allen, Argenta, Boulton, Alliot-Lugaz, Massis; Monteverdi Choir; Lyon Opera Orchestra; Gardiner (Philips 416 148-2PH2; 2 CDs).

This recording is a masterly account that buzzes with a sense of purpose and engagement. In the title role, Diana Montague produces an extraordinary, glowing performance. Gardiner rushes some of the ensembles, but his control of the choruses and his attention to clarity are superb.

HENRYK GÓRECKI

(1933–)

Henryk Górecki's third symphony, the *Symphony of Sorrowful Songs*, is one of the most remarkable music success stories of the past decade. Written in 1976, this cathartic vision of post-Holocaust, post-industrial humanity was recorded several times in Górecki's native Poland, and was begining to develop a small cult following in the rest of Europe (a small section features at the end of Maurice Pialat's 1990 film *Police*). Then in 1992 a version was recorded featuring soprano Dawn Upshaw with the London Sinfonietta, which within a few weeks of its release hit the top of the classical charts in both Britain and the United States. To date it has sold over a million copies, transforming its previously obscure creator into a major international figure.

Born near the bleak industrial town of Katowice, Górecki studied at its academy of music in the late 1950s, quickly establishing a reputation for his fierce individualism. He utilized a frenzied form of serialism in his *Symphony No. 1* (1959), which duly outraged the communist officials, as did the subsequent *Scontri* (Collisions) for orchestra, an even more scorching work. After the short-lived post-Stalinist thaw in Poland, the disillusioned composer sought solace in his country's folk songs and in religion, as exemplified by his *Symphony No. 2* (1972), with its setting of texts from the Psalms. Spending much of his time walking in the Tatra mountains, an agricultural area rich in ancient cultural traditions but close to the site of Auschwitz, he then began to conceive of unifying the emotional history of Poland in one great work. The result was the awesome *Symphony No. 3*, for which he took words from the Holy Cross lament and an inscription left by a girl imprisoned by the Nazis at Zakopane, in the Tatras.

Three years later Górecki's frail health forced him to withdraw from teaching, but since then he has written a harpsichord concerto, *O Domina Nostra* for soprano and organ, and *Lerchenmusik* for cello, piano and clarinet, while the Kronos Quartet have recorded his difficult string quartet *Already it is Dusk*. Sales of the *Symphony No. 3* CD have now allowed him to buy a house in his beloved Tatra mountains and enjoy his worldwide celebrity for a work which he views as an "intensely felt revelation of the human condition".

SYMPHONY NO. 3

For his "Symphony of Sorrowful Songs", written in 1976, Górecki evidently took inspiration from Ives and Szymanowski, particularly in the use of overlapping melodies drawn from folk song and church music. The opening wells up from deep bass melodies, developing the first half of a canon for strings until, eventually, a bell-like figure from a muffled piano ushers in the soprano singing a fifteenth-century hymn. In the second movement – the emotional heart of the work – yearning, radiant orchestral writing frames an exceptionally lovely song for the soprano. The contrast between the beauty of the sounds and the horror of their origins (they were scratched onto the wall of a Gestapo cell by an 18-year-old girl) intensifies the effect of the song – the listener clings for comfort to the tenderness of the music as a way of softening the nightmare vision of the circumstances in which they were written (a markedly different approach to that of Nono in his response to Nazi brutality, *Il Canto Sospeso* – see p.286). The final movement sets a folk song mourning a lost son who may have been killed in combat, ending in a soft, extended and rather inconclusive cadence.

Upshaw; London Sinfonietta; Zinman (Elektra Nonesuch 7559-79282-2).

Dawn Upshaw's pure and incisive tones are certainly breathtaking, but what sets this recording apart from other recordings is the incredibly wide panoramic sound (mastered by rock engineer Bob Ludwig) which gives an extraordinarily embracing resonance to the performance.

CHORAL MUSIC

The 1981 *Miserere* is, unusually for Górecki, overtly political. In March of that year a sit-in by members of Rural Solidarity was violently ended by the militia. The unaccompanied *Miserere* was Górecki's immediate response, though censorship prevented its public performance until 1987. Employing an outwardly calm manner, couching his anger in rich solemn sonoroties, Górecki contrasts secure religious faith with the perilous unpredictability of political repression. After about twenty minutes, a sudden outburst of volume seems more like an outburst of pent-up grief than a threat of retribution. Less than five minutes later, at the insistent repetition of the word "Domine", it is as if the choir is hyperventilating and the music finally allowing itself to sob.

Like Henze's *Requies*, *Good Night* (1990) was written in memory of Michael Vyner of the London Sinfonietta, who did much to promote Górecki's music in the West. Scored for soprano, alto flute, three tam-tams and piano, *Good Night* is an austere, heartfelt work constructed in three movements from the simplest of materials. Tiny melodic fragments evoke the difficulty of resolving grief, symbolizing things left unfinished and the forlorn attempts of mourners to find meaning in the sudden absence of someone close.

Miserere: Chicago Symphony Chorus, Chicago Lyric Opera Chorus; Nelson (Elektra Nonesuch 7559-79348-2 CD-80417; with *Three Pieces in Old Style* & *Kleines Requiem für eine Polka*).

An outstanding performance of this emotionally compelling and powerful work. John Nelson controls his combined choirs with a sure grasp, building the work gradually to its shattering climax. One small, but unimportant drawback is the occasional presence of background noise.

Good Night: Szmytka, Edmund-Davies, Gleizes, Righarts (Telarc CD-80417; with *Three Pieces in Old Style* & *Kleines Requiem für eine Polka*).

A reverential and moving account of *Good Night*, in which the performers communicate a powerful atmosphere of quietly shared pain.

CHAMBER MUSIC

After annoying Polish officialdom with his serial style in the early 1960s, Górecki spent some time in Paris before returning to Katowice and writing *Three Pieces in Old Style* in 1963. These miniatures for string orchestra (the longest is three and a half minutes) are significant examples of Górecki's developing individual voice. The first sets a wistfully lyrical modal melody against a diatonic background, the second suggests a folk dance, while the last moves the grave chorale-like tune from serene harmonies through dissonance to a final tussle out of which a consonant sound (like a final "amen") emerges triumphant.

The flavour of Górecki's chamber music is typified by *Kleines Requiem für eine Polka* for piano and thirteen intruments (1993). Fast and slow tempi interact during four movements, where episodes of boisterousness contrast with funereal bells and horn solo. Although the opening Tranquillo is soft, simple and pensive, the succeeding Allegro reminds the listener that Górecki's music often contains echoes of Bartókian dances, Stravinskian fanfares or implacable Messiaen-like chords, illustrating that he is quite capable of running amok in outbursts of parody, anguish or defiance. The work is usually translated as "Requiem for a Polka" but it can also mean "Requiem for a Polish Woman". Górecki refuses to elucidate, and the music continues to tantalize, suggesting an underlying story whose plot we cannot deduce.

⭘ Three Pieces in Old Style; Kleines Requiem für eine Polka: I Fiamminghini; Werthen (Telarc CD-80417; with *Good Night*).

The excellent Flemish orchestra I Fiamminghini gives moving performances of these intensely personal yet accessible works. Under their founder and director, Rudolf Werthen, they give full value to Górecki's characteristically high, shimmering, patiently sustained chords as well as to the hollow, bell-like ones which mirror the intervals of his confined, tentative melodic cells.

CHARLES FRANÇOIS GOUNOD

(1818–1893)

For most of the first seventy years of the nineteenth century, Paris was the great centre of musical Romanticism, but this situation arose more from the city's ability to attract foreign talent – Chopin, Liszt, Meyerbeer, et cetera – than from the recognition of its native talent (such as Berlioz). Between 1852 and 1870 only five new French works were added to the Paris Opera's repertory, and it was thanks only to the Théâtre Lyrique that any new French music was heard in the capital at all. Charles François Gounod was the first home-grown composer to break the trend. Although his debt to German music is undeniable (he had a fondness for Beethoven's late quartets), Gounod is the most thoroughly representative French composer of the mid-nineteenth century, and is the man chiefly responsible for leading French opera away from the elephantine spectaculars of Meyerbeer (see p.260), France's most popular operatic composer at the time.

LEBRECHT COLLECTION

Gounod at home in his library

His first operatic attempts were far from successful, being pastiche Gluck with thin plots and weak texts, and it was not until 1859 that he hit upon an operatic subject that really stimulated him – Goethe's *Faust*. Deeply religious but with a great weakness for women, Gounod concentrated on that aspect of the poem that spoke to him most directly – he and his librettists duly pulled *Faust* to pieces in order to emphasize the love story of Faust and Marguerite rather than Goethe's wider metaphysical considerations (which is why German writers call the work *Margarethe* rather than honouring it with the same title as their national poet's masterpiece). Reductive though it may be, Gounod's *Faust* is an inspired mixture of melodic invention, religious solemnity and vivid characterization, and gave the country's composers a new sense of direction and identity. It also became the most successful French opera in history. As early as 1863, an English critic was complaining – "Faust, Faust, Faust, nothing but Faust. Faust on Saturday, Wednesday and Thursday; to be repeated tonight, and on every night until further notice." To date, *Faust* has been performed in over fifty countries and translated into 25 different languages.

Faust's huge international success did not inhibit Gounod, as did the similar triumphs of Mascagni and Leoncavallo (see p.247 and p.218), but despite the quality of what he wrote post-*Faust*, he never again experienced a similar degree of success. Even so, it was Gounod who maintained and promoted characteristic French qualities in serious dramatic music, inspiring the likes of Bizet, Fauré, Massenet (who was known as "the son of Gounod") and Ravel.

FAUST

Gounod's *Faust* is but a distant relative of Goethe's, but the libretto has a directness and lack of pretension that's perfect for the operatic stage, and the score is so stuffed with memorable tunes that it has served as the basis for more instrumental transcriptions, fantasies and variations than almost any other opera. The tenor lead is especially memorable, with the third act's *Salut! demeure chaste et pure* standing out as a sublime example of Gounod's lyric style. Similarly, the duets in Act One for Faust and Mephistopheles, and in Acts Three and Five for Faust and Marguerite, are irresistibly appealing. In short, *Faust*'s seemingly endless stream of hummable melodies make this one of the most completely enjoyable operas ever written.

◑ **Gedda, de los Angeles, Christoff, Blanc; Paris Opera Chorus and Orchestra; Cluytens** (EMI CMS7 69983-2; 3 CDs).

This 1958 recording has an authentically theatrical atmosphere. Gedda's Faust is beautifully stylish and Gallic, with a range of expression available on no other recording. Victoria de los Angeles's Marguerite projects an appropriate purity, while the demonic Boris Christoff gives the most over-the-top performance of his life, roaring and bawling his way through the score. The French forces play with great enthusiasm. If you want to test the water, excerpts form this performance are available on a single disc at mid-price.

◑ **Corelli, Sutherland, Ghiaurov, Massard, Elkins, Sinclair, Meyers; Ambrosian Opera Chorus; London Symphony Orchestra; Bonynge** (Decca 421 240-2DM3; 3 CDs).

Sutherland does well with the character of Marguerite, while Ghiaurov's powerful and colourful voice brings ominous dimensions to Gounod's potentially spineless Mephistopheles. However, it is the Italian tenor Franco Corelli who dominates in the title role – he might struggle with the French, but he is utterly immersed in the character's emotional turmoil. Bonynge's conducting is thrilling from start to finish, and the recorded sound is exemplary.

PERCY GRAINGER

(1882–1961)

Percy Grainger is one of twentieth-century music's strangest figures, a man whose eccentricity, both in his music and in his life, teetered on the brink of insanity. Possessing enormous energy and a restless, inquisitive mind, he produced compositions that frequently employ weird instrumental combinations in unconventional musical forms. Yet he is best known for a handful of unremittingly jolly folk-song arrangements like *English Country Gardens* or *Molly on the Shore*. To explore his output a little more deeply is to discover much that is dark and disturbing, though rarely in a way comparable to any of his *fin de siècle* contemporaries. Only the music of Charles Ives (see p.203) emits a similar uneasy tension between the desire to be both experimental and easily expressive.

Grainger's early years were deeply distressing. Born in Melbourne, the only child of a drunken architect father, he was regularly beaten by his dominating mother, who also instilled in him some bizarre ideas about racial purity. In 1895 mother and son went to Frankfurt in order to improve Percy's youthful piano skills and it was here that he first began composing under the tutelage of an inspired amateur musician, Karl Klimsch, who introduced him to the central inspiration of his career, folk song. Forced by his mother's ill-health to pursue a career as a concert pianist, Grainger moved to London in 1901. When not performing, he was a diligent and pioneering collector of folk song and established some vital musical friendships, notably with Grieg, to whom he dedicated his British folk-song arrangements, and with Delius, who encouraged him to have his works performed.

With the onset of World War I, Grainger and his mother moved to the United States, where they took up citizenship at the war's end. His mother's suicide four years later was both deeply traumatic and a liberation. In 1926 he married the Swedish-born Ella Ström. The wedding took place in front of 20,000 people at the end of one of Grainger's concerts at the Hollywood Bowl, and a choral work, *To a Nordic Princess*, composed especially for the occasion, was performed.

In later years Grainger's interests continued to range widely: he particularly admired Duke Ellington and invited him and his band to illustrate one of his lectures at New York University. He also began to design and build his own "free music machines", strange contraptions with which he aimed to develop a beatless music capable of a vast range of different pitches. By this time, however, few people took him seriously and at his death Grainger was regarded as a completely marginal figure, despite the enthusiasm of such figures as Benjamin Britten. Today, with the Chandos record company committed to recording everything he ever wrote, a more reasoned assessment of Grainger's value is becoming possible.

LEBRECHT COLLECTION

Rose and Percy Grainger at White Plains, 1921

CHORAL MUSIC

Grainger's passion for folk song is reflected in the highly imaginative arrangements that he made of them. It's as if, through quirky harmonies or by vivid orchestral colouring, he was trying to distil not just the essential mood of a song but also to recreate the emotion of its original singer. The haunting *Brigg Fair* pits a lone tenor soloist against a hushed but fervent choral backgound; *The Lost Lady Found* contrasts, with increasing urgency, a vigorous unison line of women's voices against a crisply accented orchestral part. Best of all is the sea shanty *Shallow Brown*, in which a desperate woman bemoans the loss of her lover, her words echoed by an indifferent chorus against the furious tremolando rise and fall of guitars, mandolins and ukuleles.

O Salute to Percy Grainger: Pears, Shirley-Quirk; Ambrosian Singers, Linden Singers, English Chamber Orchestra; Britten, Bedford (London 425 159-2).

There have been several Grainger choral discs since this first appeared in the early 1970s but this affectionate tribute more than holds its own, largely because of the quality and committment of the soloists. John Shirley-Quirk's moving account of *Shallow Brown* has never been bettered (and conductor Britten doesn't exaggerate the tremolando crescendos as John Eliot Gardiner does in a more recent recording), while Peter Pears, despite his age, gives a wonderfully intense rendition of *Brigg Fair*.

ORCHESTRAL MUSIC

Grainger avoided conventional forms, preferring to write orchestral miniatures, which he sometimes gathered together in the form of a suite. Refusing to acknowledge any distinction between light and serious music, he had no qualms about bringing widely disparate types of music together. The first two movements of *In a Nutshell* (1916) are typically high-spirited: an energetic romp of a tune – the sort, Grainger stated, that you might hum on a railway platform while waiting for your lover – is followed by a pastiche music-hall song which is all sauntering, easy-going charm. After this comes the extraordinary *Pastoral*, which begins as a lilting

Delius-like nature picture then gradually disintegrates into something dark and disturbing.

In the same year Grainger wrote one of his longest and strangest pieces, *The Warriors*. Originally planned for the Russian Ballet (though never performed by the company), it's a wild and passionate work in which seemingly incongruous styles seem to fight it out. Scored for orchestra, three pianos and an endless array of percussion, it has been described by Simon Rattle as being like Holst's *The Planets* with Stravinsky's *Les Noces* laid on top of it. For Grainger, rich and striking sonorities were half the battle.

O In a Nutshell; The Warriors; Country Gardens; A Lincolnshire Posy: City of Birmingham Symphony Orchestra; Rattle (EMI CDC5 56412-2).

There's some really sparkling and energized playing on this disc, with Rattle (a former percussionist) clearly relishing the spectrum of percussive sonorities at his disposal. *The Warriors* is particularly exciting, though it still sounds perverse. Even better, from a percussive point of view, are Grainger's transcriptions of Ravel's *La Vallée des Cloches* and Debussy's *Pagodes*, in which each work's oriental inspiration is made startlingly manifest. If this disc doesn't convert you to Grainger, nothing will.

PIANO MUSIC

Despite his international reputation as a concert pianist, Grainger claimed to loathe the instrument: "I consider it an affront to destroy a melodiously conceived idea by trying to fit it into the limitations of two hands and a box full of hammers and strings." He managed, however, to "dish up", as he called it, a substantial body of pieces for the piano, although most were arrangements of his own and other composers' works. All are marked with detailed instructions in pointedly Anglo-Saxon English (Grainger wished to "free" the language of its Latin and Greek "impurities"), for example "louden hugely", "heavily but clingingly", "harped all the way", etc. Many of these piano pieces are extremely difficult, despite their insouciant air, frequently combining traditional dance forms with elaborate counterpoint. *Handel in the Strand* mixes Handelian vigour with musical-comedy swagger; *In Dahomey* is Grainger's stupendously virtuosic tribute to black American music, while a more contemplative mood is found in *Harvest Hymn* and his marvellously sentimental homage to Australia, *Colonial Song*.

O Piano Music: Hamelin (Hyperion CDA66884-2).

Hamelin is one of a small group of internationally acclaimed pianists prepared to expend their energies and talent on non-mainstream repertoire. The result, as here, is often revelatory: Hamelin brings out all Grainger's technical wizardry – like his capacity to juggle more than one melody simultaneously – without it sounding merely flash, and his own technical ability allows the more emotional pieces, such as *Colonial Song*, room to speak for themselves.

ENRIQUE GRANADOS

(1867–1916)

It is with good reason that Enrique Granados is banded together with his compatriots Isaac Albéniz and Manuel de Falla in most histories of music. Like them he was taught by the eminent musicologist Felipe Pedrell, who inspired all three to forge an individual style based on indigenous folk music; and, just as Albéniz and Falla had, Granados made the *de rigueur* student trip to Paris, hotbed of the European avant-garde. All three became masters at taking native folk melodies and overlaying them with a highly spiced chromatic idiom, more often than not French in derivation. When it came to character, however, it was a different matter. The spontaneously warm Granados was closer in temperament to his friend Albéniz than to the drier Falla, and the similarities did not end there. Both Granados and Albéniz were concert pianists of international repute who chose to write primarily for the piano, and their reputations rest primarily on just one concert suite – though the quality of Granados's *Goyescas* and Albéniz's *Iberia* is of the highest order.

Granados started off by composing pretty, salon-type pieces in a post-Lisztian manner. However, with the 1892 premiere of an orchestral version of three of his *Danzas españolas* for piano, it was clear that a new direction in Spanish music was opening up. The *Danzas españolas* were much admired by Massenet, Saint-Saëns and above all Grieg, an endorsement which must have given Granados much satisfaction, as the nationalism of Grieg's music was much appreciated by Spanish audiences and young composers alike. Granados, well aware of prevailing fashions, knew that the best way to get noticed in Spain was to write a zarzuela (a distinctly Spanish type of operetta), and a few years later he composed the highly successful *Maria del Carmen* (1898), which gained him a commendation from the king. Although he cashed in on his success with a string of other zarzuelas, over the next decade or so he devoted himself as much to teaching and performing as to composition. From time to time Granados's talents took him away from music altogether – he once said of himself, "I am not a musician but an artist", and by all accounts he was a fine writer and excellent painter. But despite these creative diversions Granados remained first and foremost a musician, and was in great demand as an accompanist by such virtuosos as the cellist Pablo Casals and the violinist Jacques Thibaud.

During the early 1900s Granados composed a variety of works, most of which are now unknown, but all the while he was contemplating the music of what was to be his most ambitious work to date, *Goyescas*. It was *Goyescas* that made Granados a name to be reckoned with. After its French premiere in 1914, at the Salle Pleyel in Paris, all sorts of honours came his way, including election to the *Légion d'Honneur* and a commission from the Opéra to compose a piece of music theatre derived from *Goyescas*. The outbreak of World War I soon scotched the idea of a production, but interest then unexpectedly came from New York's Metropolitan Opera.

The composer travelled over with his wife to be present at the resoundingly successful premiere on January 26, 1916, then prolonged his stay to play at the White House at the invitation of President Wilson. Consequently they missed a direct boat back to Spain, so decided to travel back to Europe via England. The *Sussex*, the boat they took from Liverpool to Dieppe, was torpedoed by a German submarine with the loss of many lives, including that of Granados and his wife. Just two months before his death, Granados had written to a friend: "I have a whole world of ideas . . . I am only now starting my work."

GOYESCAS

The *Goyescas* were inspired by the paintings of Goya, and rarely has a composer captured the underlying mood of the work of another artist with such clarity as Granados did with this series of piano pieces. Eighteenth-century Spanish music plays an important part in the sound-world of *Goyescas*, but, as the critic Harold Schonberg wrote, it's the general "scent of Spanish rhythms, Spanish melodies, and Spanish life" which makes the suite so memorable. The Andalusian flamenco elements sometimes have a tendency to be a touch over-repetitive, but in the most famous piece, *Quejas, o la maja y el ruiseñor* (known in English as *The Maiden and the Nightingale*), every statement of the plaintive melody and its concluding arabesque is beautifully constructed, with nothing overstated.

⊙ de Larrocha (Decca 411 958-2).

The music of *Goyescas* can sound flat if the pianist can't muster a supercharged rhythmic vitality, but Alicia de Larrocha rises to the occasion – this account of the complete *Goyescas* is beautifully fashioned. She brings an equally evocative flair to the two exhilarating companion sets, the *Escenas románticas* and *6 Piezas sobre cantos populares*.

EDVARD GRIEG

(1843–1907)

Grieg may have been the only internationally successful composer to have come out of Norway, but it would be a mistake to regard him as a peripheral figure. He ranks with names such as Sibelius and Dvořák in the late nineteenth century's upsurge of musical nationalism, inspiring musicians across Europe to follow his example in looking to his country's folk heritage for source material. In Spain, for example, the impact of Grieg's music on the likes of Manuel de Falla (see p.141) was instrumental in the formation of an essentially national school of music. The depth of Grieg's influence is all the more remarkable when you compare his output to that of Sibelius and Dvořák, for, whereas they were devoted to mighty large-scale compositions, Grieg was a committed miniaturist. His *Piano Concerto* might be his best-known creation, but it's not at all typical.

His first lessons came from his mother. Then in 1858 the Norwegian violinist and folk enthusiast Ole Bull heard Grieg play the piano and persuaded his reluctant parents to send the boy to the Leipzig

Conservatory. Bull was delighted, Grieg was not. He hated his time there, but had the good fortune to attend concerts at which the likes of Clara Schumann and Richard Wagner were regular artists.

In the spring of 1862 his Opus 1 was published, and in May of the following year he settled in Copenhagen, where he was taken under the wing of Niels Gade, Denmark's leading Romantic composer and a close friend of Schumann and Mendelssohn. Gade was enthusiastic about the young composer's potential but his optimism was tempered by misgivings about his lack of large-scale work, and so he set Grieg the task of writing his first and only symphony, something for which he was neither technically equipped nor temperamentally suited.

Soon afterwards he met his cousin, the singer Nina Hagerup; a year later, the two were engaged to be married and Grieg was back in Norway, living in the house of Ole Bull. From this point, his artistic personality began to change as he started taking a studious interest in his country's musical heritage, having previously spent a long time away from home or immersed in a middle-class milieu that had been dominated by Danish culture. His commitment to Norwegian nationalism was confirmed by his encounters with Rikard Nordraak, Norway's great hope for the formation of a national school (Rikard died in 1866 aged just 24, having written what is now Norway's national anthem), and by a meeting with Henrik Ibsen in Rome in 1865.

He returned to Norway confident of his mission, and after promoting concerts of his own music he was quickly recognized as one of his country's foremost composers. In 1867 he married Nina and settled in Oslo, where he became a teacher and conductor of international renown. A year later he and his family moved back to Denmark where he composed his *Piano Concerto*; in Italy the following year he presented Liszt with his very badly handwritten draft of the piece and, to his amazement, Liszt played the whole concerto right through. "Go on, you have the stuff," Liszt is said to have encouraged him.

By 1874 Grieg was so famous and so highly valued that the Norwegian government voted to grant him an annuity, and Ibsen similarly paid his respects by asking him to provide incidental music for his play *Peer Gynt*. His popularity took him to England, where he and his wife gave numerous recitals and, in an extraordinary display of affection, both Oxford and Cambridge granted him honorary degrees. The last twenty years of his life followed a rarely changing pattern of holidays, composition and concert tours and he became one of the elder statesmen of European music.

One year after Grieg's death, Schoenberg composed his first atonal works and within five years Grieg's name had become synonymous with everything outdated in music. There is indeed nothing too challenging in Grieg. His music is on the whole a sweetly harmonic synthesis of folk song and German-based Romanticism – the Romanticism of Schumann, not of Wagner, for whose lofty ambitions Grieg felt no affection. Within these limits, however, he is one of the most distinctive and enjoyable composers of his time, a master of small-scale form whose greatest music is, in a sense, his slightest.

THE PIANO CONCERTO

Grieg was a fine pianist and hardly a year passed when he did not give concerts either as a soloist or with his wife. He wrote his *Piano Concerto* as a vehicle for his own talents, and its youthful exuberance – reminiscent of Schumann's only concerto, also in A minor – has ensured its place on the CVs of most concert pianists. Composed in 1868 while Grieg was holidaying with his wife and young child in Denmark (although revised to the version played today in 1907), it's replete with a sense of tenderness and wellbeing, expressed in a proliferation of enchanting thematic ideas. The opening motif – an idea as well-known as the opening of that other virtuoso warhorse, Tchaikovsky's first concerto – is built upon a descending second followed by a descending third, intervals typical in Norwegian folk music.

◑ **Kovacevich; BBC Symphony Orchestra; Davis** (Philips 446 192-2; with *Piano Sonata No. 7* & Schumann's *Piano Concerto*).

Stephen Kovacevich's mid-1970s recording still holds up extremely well. His playing is clear, unaffected and lyrical, showing a great overall awareness of shape and colour.

◑ **Perahia; Bavarian Radio Symphony Orchestra; Davis** (Sony SK44899; with Schumann's *Piano Concerto*).

Murray Perahia's more recent account (again with Davis) is also excellent. His touch is more sinewy and less forceful than that of Kovacevich, but his playing is equally persuasive, especially in the more lyrical passages.

PEER GYNT

In 1874 Henrik Ibsen decided to adapt his verse play *Peer Gynt* for a performance at the theatre in Christiania (now Oslo). Norway's theatrical tradition at the time was based upon operettas and musical plays, and Ibsen recognized that his sprawling play needed a soothing soundtrack in

order to succeed – and accordingly asked Grieg to supply incidental music. The new production was first staged in February 1876 and was hugely successful, playing for several nights until a fire destroyed the sets and costumes.

To give his music an existence apart from Ibsen's drama, Grieg extracted two suites for concert performance, and these two spin-offs – Op. 46 and Op. 54 – contain his most striking orchestral music, showing a directness and freshness that generally eluded him when he came to write for large forces. Its best-known section is the flute's principal theme from *Morning*, but this is one of many examples of a piece of music being identified with a sound bite from one of its less remarkable moments. Most of the other self-contained episodes make *Morning* sound banal, none more so than *Solvejg's Song*, a piece of wonderfully fragile lyricism.

⊙ Peer Gynt (complete): Bonney, Eklöf, Sandve, Malmberg; Gothenburg Symphony Orchestra; Järvi (Deutsche Grammophon 423 079-2; 2 CDs; with *Sigurd Jorsalfar*).

Neeme Järvi conducts the whole of the musical score of *Peer Gynt* but includes just the bare bones of Ibsen's text to keep the action clear (the full play can go on for four hours). The Gothenburg Symphony Orchestra respond with delightful enthusiasm to Järvi's sensitive but direct conducting. Järvi and the Gothenburg Orchestra have also recorded the two suites for Deutsche Grammophon.

◑ Peer Gynt (excerpts): Hollweg; Royal Philharmonic Orchestra; Beecham (EMI CDM7 64751-2; with orchestral pieces).

For those who prefer the purely musical highlights, this classic recording from 1956–57 presents Beecham's own selection of *Peer Gynt* (which includes all the music from the suites) in a fine performance which is by turns radiant and waspish.

SONGS

"I loved a young girl who had a wonderful voice and an equally wonderful gift for interpretation. That girl became my wife and my lifelong companion to this very day. For me, she has been – I dare admit it – the only genuine interpreter of my songs." So Grieg wrote to his American biographer Henry Fincke in 1900. Grieg's adoration of his wife was the wellspring of his songs, his greatest body of music and, though she could not be regarded as the the sole inspiration for all 140, there is little doubt that, from Op. 5 onwards, she had a defining influence on their evolution.

Grieg had a rare understanding of the expressive potential of the human voice, allied with a gift for piano writing that gives many of his songs – the later ones in particular – the sort of balance between accompanist and singer that you find in the songs of Schubert. As with Schubert, Grieg's emotional range is vast, and the melodic directness and limpidity of his music allows anyone to grasp immediately the nature of each song – but on the other hand, you'll need a translation to hand in order to appreciate the delicacy with which Grieg augments the content of each text. In contrast to Schubert, most of Grieg's songs are strophic (whereby the same music is repeated with each successive stanza), in honour of their folk inspiration.

⊙ von Otter; Forsberg (Deutsche Grammophon 437 521-2).

Anne Sofie von Otter gives marvellously characterful interpretations, beguilingly frank in the folksy pieces, deeply moving in the more intimate songs such as *I Love You* and *Last Spring* – the latter song possessing a melody so perfect that Grieg couldn't resist recycling it for a couple of other compositions. Her regular pianist, Bengt Forsberg, provides exemplary accompaniment throughout.

⊙ Bonney, Hagegård, Steene, Telefsen; Gothenburg Symphony Orchestra; Järvi (Deutsche Grammophon 437 519-2).

Grieg's orchestrations of some of his finest songs turn up on the recital from Barbara Bonney and Håkan Hagegård; the orchestra doesn't add anything to the meaning of the songs, but the thicker sonorities certainly give a sense of swoony luxuriance.

LYRIC PIECES

Grieg's talent for uncomplicated, sincere and brief musical ideas is well displayed in his *Lyric Pieces*, ten sets of piano pieces spanning his career from 1867 to 1901. Ranging from forty seconds to four minutes in length, they are extraordinarily crafted compositions, defining a mood in the space of a bar or two, giving it enough time to completely infiltrate the listener's mind, then letting it go. At their best the *Lyric Pieces* are as touching as some of Chopin's miniatures, and even when they amount to little more than whimsical musings they are never less than tunefully pleasant.

◑ Lyric Pieces (selected): Gilels (Deutsche Grammophon 449 721-2).

Emil Gilels' 1974 recording of selections from the *Lyric Pieces* is justifiably regarded as a classic. It's a performance of sublime, fluid romanticism with Gilels perfectly attuned to the mood of each piece.

SOFIA GUBAIDULINA

(1931–)

Sofia Gubaidulina has said of herself, "I am the place where East meets West", which is as good a categorization as any. One of the leading innovative composers in the former Soviet Union, she comes from a mixed Tartar and Slavic background, and the influence of Eastern philosophies is clear in many of her attitudes towards spirituality and its expression – whether writing for huge orchestral forces or a few solo instruments, she tends to explore a wide range of sonorities in order to create music that is extraordinarily still and serene, leaving the listener with a sense of timelessness rare in Western music.

She started writing music at an early age and then studied in Kazan (in the present-day Tatar Republic) before moving to Moscow, where she attended the conservatory until 1963. Until around that time the Soviet regime had been diligent in keeping Russian composers isolated from the corrupting influence of modern Western music, but as the 1960s wore on there was a gradual thawing of official attitudes, marked by visits from avant-garde composers such as Luigi Nono and Pierre Boulez. Having started her career writing in straightforward tonal idioms, Gubaidulina took every possible chance to explore the new languages and techniques, such as serialism, electronics and the use of numerical patterns in composition. Soon she had emerged as one of the country's most interesting contemporary composers, along with the more turbulent Alfred Schnittke (see p.352).

For most of her life Gubaidulina has supported herself by writing music for films and the theatre, disciplines that have enabled her to experiment with a wide variety of sounds and procedures. Another crucial contribution to her work has come from the traditional music of the Soviet Union – in 1975 she founded an improvisation group called Astreya, which made wide use of folk instruments and forms, and had a great influence on her concert-hall pieces. If there is one common denominator to her output, it is her belief in the transforming power of art. Much of her music is rooted in religious imagery, and she believes passionately in the ability of music to establish a sense of connection with the transcendent – a belief that allies her with the likes of Pärt (see p.298) and Tavener (see p.423).

OFFERTORIUM

Gubaidulina's violin concerto, *Offertorium* (1980, revised 1982 & 1986), was one of her first works to become known outside the Soviet Union. It's a moving and virtuosic piece, built entirely around the theme from J.S. Bach's *Musical Offering*. In the first part of the work's single movement the theme is heard several times, but on each hearing it gradually disintegrates; by the end of *Offertorium* the theme has been transfigured and is played in retrograde by the soloist – a moment of calm beauty and resolution.

◆ Kremer; Boston Symphony Orchestra; Dutoit (Deutsche Grammophon 427 336-2GH; with *Hommage à T.S. Eliot*).

The best performance comes from Gidon Kremer, for whom the work was written; his passionate account is coupled with *Hommage à T.S. Eliot* (1987) for soprano and octet, a setting of lines from *The Four Quartets* in which Gubaidulina explores Eliot's concept of the transformation of time.

STIMMEN . . . VERSTUMMEN . . .

The twelve-movement *Stimmen . . . Verstummen . . .* (Voices . . . Fall Dumb . . .), written in 1986, opens with one of Gubaidulina's most original flourishes – an ecstatic D major triad in the wind instruments, over strange scurrying sounds from the strings. The triad is disrupted at the end of the first movement by a menacing D flat from the brass instruments, and throughout this massive and entrancing work movements of static tonal calm are broken by uneasily chromatic episodes. The work reaches an extraordinary climax in the minute-long ninth movement, which is almost completely silent – rhythmic gestures for the conductor are notated in the score at this point, but even without this visual contribution it's a powerful and strange moment.

◆ Royal Stockholm Philharmonic Orchestra; Rozhdestvensky (Chandos CHAN 9183; with *Stufen*).

These excellent performances are conducted by Gennady Rozhdestvensky, the champion of so much new Russian music. The intensity of *Stimmen . . . Verstummen . . .* carries the listener through the almost silent ninth movement, when the pulse of the rhythmic patterns that Gubaidulina has established can still be felt.

CHORAL AND VOCAL WORKS

Gubaidulina has set a wide range of texts demonstrating the breadth of her philosophical, spiritual and artistic concerns – from ancient Egyptian and Persian texts through the writings of St Francis of Assisi to the works of poets such as Maria Tsvetayeva and Rainer Maria Rilke. *Perception* (1983), for soprano, baritone and seven strings, sets writings by Francisco Tanzer and uses a variety of different vocal techniques including sprechstimme. Rather more striking is the recent *Jetzt immer Schnee* (Now Always Snow, 1993) a hauntingly beautiful setting of Gennady Aigi's mystical and impressionistic verses. A vast landscape, both serene and threatening, is evoked through spare orchestral writing over which the voices sound intimate and vulnerable. The opening is especially memorable: an incantatory phrase is repeated between the voices with a whispered intensity, while scuttering strings animate the background.

◆ Jetzt immer Schnee; Perception: Kliendienst, Lorenz; Netherlands Chamber Choir; Schönberg Ensemble; De Leeuw (Philips 442 531-2).

Striking performances from all concerned on this CD, particularly in *Jezt immer Schnee* (sung in Russian). The devotional qualities of the music are conveyed with an hallucinatory vividness by the Netherlands Chamber Choir.

CHAMBER WORKS

One of Gubaidulina's most frequently performed chamber works is the radiantly contemplative *Garten von Freuden und Traurigkeiten* (Garden of Joys and Sorrows). Written in 1980, this piece creates an enthrallingly beautiful sound-world using all the resources of just three instruments – flute, viola and harp. In *Seven Last Words*, written in 1982, Gubaidulina creates an equally unusual but quite different texture. Here two solo instruments – a cello and a traditional Russian *bayan* or button accordion – play beautiful lamenting melodies and strange, agitated scratching sounds over chant-like passages from the string orchestra. *In croce*, for cello and organ, is another work in which the exploration of unusual sonorities produces an extraordinary atmosphere of spiritual struggle and resolution. The *String Trio* (1988) is a demanding work for the more conventional line-up of violin, viola and cello – "three characters who reveal their individual wills", to quote the composer's description. The first movement moves from a violently sparse opening through to full rich harmonies, and is followed by a second movement of floating pizzicato and ethereal harmonics. The often disturbingly agitated final movement ends with a feeling of uneasy peace.

◆ Seven Last Words; In croce; Five Pieces "Silenzio": Rabus, Kliegel, Moser; Camerata Transylvanica; Selmeczi (Naxos 8.553557).

With Gidon Kremer's live recording of *Garten von Freuden und Traurigkeiten* and the *String Trio* currently out of the catalogue, this CD becomes the first choice as an introduction to Gubaidulina's chamber music – outstanding performances of three of her most mysterious works.

GEORGE FRIDERIC HANDEL

(1685–1759)

The death of Henry Purcell in 1695 (see p.318) ended two remarkable centuries of achievement in English music. But Purcell had no obvious successor, and by 1700 English music was in the doldrums – though London continued to be a major centre of musical excellence. Salvation came in the form of George Frideric Handel, whose arrival in 1710 injected a new vitality into English musical life. Handel's melodic flair and his cosmopolitanism – he had successfully assimilated the Italian and French styles – made an immediate impact. If his attempt to establish opera in England was ultimately a failure, then his transformation of oratorio into a quasi-operatic form had a deep-rooted effect on English taste that was to last until Elgar. Of his contemporaries, only J. S. Bach produced work in which the qualities of robustness, lucidity and passion were so finely balanced.

Handel was born in the north German town of Halle in 1685, son of a surgeon who was convinced that the law was the proper calling for his son. Yet the musicians at the Court of Saxe Weissenfels, where his father worked, soon introduced Georg Frideric Händel (as he was then) to their profession, and recognized his remarkable potential. His teacher, F.W. Zachow, gave him a grounding in counterpoint and instrumentation as well as a bravura keyboard technique, and by 1702 Georg was a major figure in the region – cathedral organist, composer and friend of Telemann (see p.434).

In 1705 he presented several operas in Hamburg. Their mixed fortunes convinced him he should learn his operatic trade in Italy: he duly went to Florence, where he came to know both Alessandro and Domenico Scarlatti; and to Venice, where his opera *Agrippina* was a huge success and where he met Prince Ernst of Hanover. At the prince's recommendation, Handel was appointed court conductor to the Elector of Hanover, Georg Ludwig. But, aware of the limitations of his new position, Handel took official leave of absence and

LEBRECHT COLLECTION

Handel presenting his *Water Music* to his patron, George I

set out for England in search of a more lucrative marketplace for his operatic skills. Shortly after his arrival, Handel persuaded the management of the Haymarket Theatre to stage an opera by him. The result was *Rinaldo*, written in fifteen days flat. The furore it produced – not least when Handel released a flock of sparrows for one aria – made him an overnight success.

Despite his poor English, Handel seems to have been adept at making good contacts: the influential Earl of Burlington was an important early patron, while the composition of a magnificent *Te Deum* in celebration of the Peace of Utrecht secured him a state pension from Queen Anne. There was a brief moment of embarrassment in 1714 when his Hanoverian employer succeeded to the English throne as George I, but the success of another opera, *Amadigi* (1715), quickly restored his fortunes. In 1716 Handel accompanied George I on a return visit to Hanover, where he persuaded an old friend, Johann Christoph Schmidt, to return to England with him as his amenuensis. Shortly after his return, Handel was employed by the rich Duke of Chandos in the unusual position of composer-in-residence.

In 1719 a society of wealthy amateurs founded the Royal Academy of Music. Handel was appointed music director and composed operas alongside his chief rival Giovanni Bononcini. Its nine seasons drew from him a stream of masterpieces (including *Giulio Cesare*) but the squabbles and enormous fees of competing prima donnas crippled the Academy, as did the long-running popular success of John Gay's satirical *Beggar's Opera* (1728), a work which lampooned the contrivances and downright idiocies of opera seria. Handel himself remained solvent, however, and a patriotic potboiler, *Riccardo I, Re d'Inghilterra* (1727), ensured that he stayed in grace with the newly crowned George II. In 1729 he formed another company, but his new works were not so well recieved as before. Four years later a rival group, the Opera of the Nobility, was set up with many of the stars of Handel's old company and with the backing of the Prince of Wales. Handel retaliated with a new style of opera in which singing was interspersed with ballet, but a revival of one of his early oratorios, *Esther*, suggested a new direction, a notion confirmed by the reception of another oratorio, *Deborah*, in 1733.

Yet by 1741, again a victim of fickle public taste, his finances were ailing once more, and Handel was thrown into despair when his *Messiah* failed to enthral its first audiences. He was reported "disordered in mind", but the late 1740s saw his reputation revive through oratorios of operatic power and splendour – *Samson*, *Judas Maccabaeus* and then *Solomon*, written in the same year that the *Music for the Royal Fireworks* was produced to celebrate the peace treaty of Aix-la-Chapelle.

In April 1759 Handel fainted during a performance of *Messiah*, and died soon after. He was buried in Westminster Abbey, the only possible resting place for the figure who had become in effect the composer to the nation.

THE OPERAS

Handel was the greatest of all composers of opera seria, the dominant operatic genre of the eighteenth century. Opera seria had been formulated by the Italian poet Pietro Metastasio in an attempt to get rid of opera's more absurd aspects. A typical Metastasian libretto revolved around a conflict between love and duty: there were three acts in which recitative and aria were alternated – recitative usually expressing dialogue, arias being reserved for soliloquy. Handel's achievement was not so much to transform the conventions of the genre as invest them – especially the da capo arias – with a new emotional conviction and psychological insight. His operas possess both tenderness and vigour, which perhaps explains why they alone, out of all the thousands of Baroque operas, have been regularly and effectively staged over the last fifty years – despite their often static quality and implausible plots. Though all of them contain music of rare beauty, their length often puts potential listeners off. With this in mind, we have selected a recital disc of some of the most celebrated arias and recommended the most famous, and frequently performed, of all Handel's operas – *Giulio Cesare in Egitto*.

O Great Handel Arias: Murray; Orchestra of the Age of Enlightenment; Mackerras (Forlane UCD16738).

The mezzo-soprano Anne Murray is something of a Handel opera specialist, having played several important roles in the opera house mainly for English National Opera. With the lively support of Charles Mackerras and the OAE, she sings a selection of beautiful arias from four of the most-performed Handel operas – *Ariodante*, *Alcina*, *Giulio Cesare* and *Serse*.

GIULIO CESARE IN EGITTO

Giulio Cesare in Egitto, written for the Royal Academy of Music in 1724, is perhaps Handel's most fully wrought example of the heroic ideal. Voluptuous and exotic, introducing a new orchestral brilliance and magnificence of spectacle, it was a success from its first appearance – "the house was just as full at the seventh performance as at the first", noted a courtier, Monsieur de Fabrice. The story tells of Julius Caesar's Egyptian campaign, the machinations of the Egyptian ruler Ptolemy, and the love of his sister Cleopatra for the Roman emperor. The role of Cleopatra is one of Handel's greatest creations for the female voice, and her Act II recitative and aria "Se pietà di me non sento", in which she laments her fate, yearns for revenge and longs for the love of Caesar, is especially wonderful – with a melody of effortless conviction, this is the opera's most emotional episode. The title role is the weak link in Nicola Haym's libretto, and it is Handel's music alone which brings Caesar's idealized nobility and courage to life.

O Larmore, Schlick, Fink, Rorholm, Ragin, Zanasi, Visse; Concerto Köln; Jacobs (Harmonia Mundi HMC 901385/7; 3 CDs).

Where the recording triumphs is in the richness of characterization. Jennifer Larmore has real brio as Caesar (originally a castrato role) but the crucial role is Cleopatra. Handel matches Shakespeare in the infinite variety he reveals in Cleopatra's eight arias, and Barbara Schlick rises marvellously to the occasion, moving from frothy innocence through pathos to seductive insinuation. René Jacobs' genial direction sometimes loses dramatic potency, but he brings out the design of the opera's balanced progression of symphonic movements and gorgeous set pieces.

THE ORATORIOS

Oratorio had emerged in Italy at the end of the sixteenth century (see p.99), at about the same time as opera, to which it provided a religious counterpart. Composers who wrote for one genre almost inevitably wrote for the other. Handel was no exception: during his stay in Italy he wrote an oratorio, *La Resurrezione*, for Rome (which was probably staged), and an opera, *Agrippina*, for Venice. In England, where oratorio was largely unknown, Handel fashioned his own version of the genre in a manner calculated to appeal to middle-class Protestant taste. Most of the stories were taken from the Bible (though classical and allegorical subjects were also used); they were sung in English; and they had substantial choruses, which drew on the varied tradition of the English anthem. They were not church music – most were performed in the concert hall or in the theatre – but neither were they opera, although the narrative of many makes effective staging perfectly feasible. *Messiah*, far and away the most celebrated of the oratorios, is actually the least typical because it doesn't tell a story.

MESSIAH

By 1740 Handel realized that his operatic career was finished and, facing an indifferent audience, he contemplated retirement. But in the summer of 1741 came an invitation from the Lord Lieutenant of Dublin to write a sacred oratorio to be performed in the city. Handel collaborated with his friend Charles Jennens, who fashioned a skilful libretto combining both Old and New Testament texts – the subject being a non-dramatic presentation of Christ as the world's saviour. The essential mood that Jennens established is one of contemplation: characters are not named, though there is a slight suggestion of narrative in the Nativity sections. The first performance took place at the New Music Hall on April 13, 1742, with the profits from the concert being distributed between two hospitals and a debtors' prison.

George Bernard Shaw has commented on the near impossibility of recapturing the novelty of *Messiah*: "We have all had our Handelian training in church . . . thus we get broken into the custom of singing Handel as if he meant nothing." Yet this music bears intense meaning in every bar, and has a visionary quality in its evolution from darkness to light. In his deployment of soloists and choruses, Handel's sense of timing and proportion is matchless, and the sheer physical pleasure of the sound is remarkable too. There's a plethora of beautiful arias (recitative is minimal), which vary greatly in both type and mood: from the grandiose da capo aria of "He was despised" to the more simple lyricism of "How beautiful are the feet". Equally memorable are the magnificent choruses in which grand ceremonial music is frequently combined with elaborate, often fugal, counterpoint, thus emphasizing how the religious experience is as joyful as it is reverential.

O Marshall, Robbin, Rolfe-Johnson, Hale, Brett, Quirck; Monteverdi Choir, English Baroque Soloists; Gardiner (Philips 434 297-2; 2 CDs).

Gardiner's version stands out for its sheer transparency of sound and the way the music's development from gravitas to celebration is so sensitively captured. Dramatic impact and a sense of joy are strong – the Monteverdi Choir bring a lightness of touch and rhythmic spring to the choruses – and there is a real sense of the work being approached as if for the first time.

O Auger, von Otter, Chance, Crook, Tomlinson; The English Concert & Concert Choir; Pinnock (Deutsche Grammophon Archiv 423 630-2; 2 CDs).

There's not much between these two versions. Pinnock's smooth phrasing, his ear for orchestral timbre and his concern for the meaning of what's being sung is what makes his account so remarkable. It's not so spontaneous-sounding as the Gardiner account, but some will prefer the glossier sound quality.

JUDAS MACCABAEUS

Ever the consummate opportunist, Handel dashed out *Judas Maccabaeus* by way of a compliment to the Duke of Cumberland, who in April 1746 had defeated the Jacobite rebels at the Battle of Culloden. In his haste Handel lifted sections from his existing oratorios *Joshua* and *Belshazzar*, the rest of the libretto being patched together by the congenial Reverend Thomas Morell, who could match something of the composer's breakneck speed. In the event the premiere had to wait until April 1747.

Perhaps out of fear that his dedicatee might find something offensive in the portrayal of the oratorio's military hero, Handel here avoided the intense personal drama that had characterized *Belshazzar* – which in any case seemed to have baffled a public used to milder fare. *Judas* deals with the anticipation of events and of reactions to them, rather than with events themselves, yet its contrasts of mood and tempo sustain it well over three acts, and it has endured as one of the finest of all celebratory compositions.

O De Mey, Saffer, Spence, Thomas, Asawa, Kromm; Berkeley Chorus; Philharmonia Baroque Orchestra; McGegan (Harmonia Mundi HMU 9077077.78; 2 CDs).

Nicholas McGegan's small forces add crisp refinement to music which, on the whole, is more contemplative than theatrical; resiliently phrased, this performance rarely sounds undernourished, as it so easily could.

SOLOMON

Opening on March 17, 1749, Handel's most sumptuous and musically thrilling oratorio was unveiled to a nation in the midst of exuberant mass celebration – the War of the Austrian Succession was over, and in Green Park stood a wooden structure over a hundred feet high, depicting the King amid the Greek gods. "Record him, ye bards, as the pride of our days . . . E'vry object swells with state, All is pious, all is great" – this is the heart of *Solomon*, a piece that idealizes Georgian England through implicit historical comparison. Pantheistic rather than narrowly Christian, *Solomon* is more a pastoral idyll and pageant than a dramatic narrative (the dispute of the two harlots being the only moment of excitement), combining episodes of ceremonial with an enraptured lyricism. This is especially true of the glorious Act I in which, after a grand opening, Solomon and his Queen seem to do very little but exchange increasingly sensuous blandishments. Handel anticipated "above one hundred voices and performers" – huge forces for those days.

O Watkinson, Argenta, Hendricks, Rodgers, Rolfe Johnson, Varcoe; Monteverdi Choir & English Baroque Soloists; Gardiner (Philips 412 612-2; 2 CDs).

John Eliot Gardiner's performance has won many awards for its ebullient pace and lyrical sensitivity. With Joan Rodgers' Queen and Barbara Hendricks's Queen of Sheba in especially luscious voice, and with the Monteverdi Choir superlatively clear and precise, this is a landmark not only in authentic performance but in modern Handel interpretation.

SACRED MUSIC

Handel's operas and oratorios have tended to eclipse his achievements in the less ambitious areas of choral music. In fact he wrote a great deal of excellent music for the church, though this does tend to lean towards the grandiose and the ceremonial. His travels had given him a highly detailed knowledge of different styles and, by the time he settled in England, Handel had appraised what was needed and then enhanced it with a fusion of Italian harmonic intensity, German polyphony, elements of French music and Purcellian grandeur.

DIXIT DOMINUS

Handel reached maturity as composer while in Italy, and of all his Italianate works the best known, and the most exuberant, is the psalm setting *Dixit Dominus*. The influence of Vivaldi is evident in the vivid harmonies – in particular the spine-tingling soprano duet of the last verse – and of Corelli in the way solo and tutti passages are frequently contrasted. But the sheer energetic vigour of the contrapuntal writing, in particular the toe-tapping and exuberant Gloria, is unmistakably Handelian.

O Auger, Dawson, Montague, Nixon, Birchall; Choir and Orchestra of Westminster Abbey; Preston (Archiv 423 594-2; with *Nisi Dominus* and *Salve Regina*).

Of the several available recordings of *Dixit Dominus*, this is the most thrilling (though Gardiner on Erato runs it a close second). The choral singing is crisp and precise, the ad hoc orchestra plays with real verve and the soloists are outstanding. The two other works included also date from Handel's time in Rome.

ANTHEMS

In England the anthem was a more sobre and ceremonious affair than the continental motet. The eleven so-called *Chandos Anthems*, written in 1717–20 for the First Duke of Chandos, are typical examples of Handel's prowess in the genre. By turns stately, penitential and joyful, these early works were significant in laying the foundations of Handel's career as a composer of oratorios. The sixth of the group, *As Pants the Hart*, is an absolute *tour de force* of choral writing. But in terms of dramatic impact nothing can quite match *Zadok the Priest* – one of the anthems written for the coronation of George II in 1727. Its opening is a masterpiece of mounting tension, with a long orchestral introduction of arpeggiated strings gradually building to an explosive choral entry. It's an ecstatic moment and, perhaps unsurprisingly, has been played at every subsequent coronation.

⭘ Chandos Anthems Nos. 4–6: Dawson, Partridge; The Sixteen Choir and Orchestra; Christophers (Chandos CHAN 0504).

The Sixteen are the only choir to have recorded all eleven of the Chandos anthems. These are available as a four-CD set at a special price or as four full-price individual CDs. This disc includes the outstanding *As Pants the Hart* and serves as a good introduction to the set. The sound quality is full-bodied but the clarity and intimate scale of the Sixteen's singing is never compromised. The soloists are at the heart of these performances, lustrous in tone yet capturing the essential directness of the music.

⭘ Coronation Anthems: Choir of Westminster Abbey; The English Concert; Preston (Deutsche Grammophon Archiv 410 030-2).

This outstanding disc presents radiant interpretations of this often jubilant music. *Zadok* is the best-known and the briefest item here, but best of all is *My Heart is Inditing*, with the Westminster Choir as smoothly assured in the lyrical inner sections as in the cumulative grandeur of the conclusion.

THE ODES

The duty of writing a celebratory ode in honour of the monarch's birthday was one of the tasks of the Master of the Queen's Musick. It's a measure of both Handel's impact in England and his opportunism that he managed to appropriate this task soon after his second stay. Another annual celebration was the festival in honour of St Cecilia (the patron saint of music). Since 1683, this was an occasion when London musicians gathered together to honour both the saint and their profession in the form of a church service and a banquet at which an ode was performed.

ODE FOR THE BIRTHDAY OF QUEEN ANNE

The *Ode for the Birthday of Queen Anne* was written around the same time as the *Utrecht Te Deum* during Handel's second visit to London. It celebrates the Queen as a peace maker (The Peace of Utrecht had ended the eleven-year War of the Spanish Succession) but its imagery is predominantly pastoral. It opens with a stunning masterstroke: a slow, sinewy phrase sung by the alto soloist is repeated by a solo trumpet before the two voices interweave themselves in elegant combination. It's a brilliant fusion of the stately and the sonorous, a pattern that recurs throughout the work.

⭘ Nelson, Kirkby, Minty, Bowman, Hill, Thomas; Christ Church Cathedral Choir and the Academy of Ancient Music; Preston (L'Oiseau Lyre 421 654-2; with *Anthem for the Foundling Hospital*).

Another scintillating Handel performance under the direction of Simon Preston. The Christ Church Choir are in absolute peak form, as is countertenor James Bowman, who gives a beautifully poised account of the Odes' opening lines. It's coupled with a late work which Handel wrote for a fund-raising concert for the Foundling Hospital.

ODE FOR ST CECILIA'S DAY

Handel's *Ode for St Cecilia's Day*, written in 1739, sets words by John Dryden (who also wrote a longer work honouring the saint, *Alexander's Feast*, that Handel had set three years earlier). Dryden's poem is a work rich in classical allusion: in its outer sections it ascribes to music a role in both the creation and the end of the world, while its central verses – divided between tenor and soprano arias – celebrate the qualities of individual instruments. Handel's music consistently matches the verve of Dryden's text with some highly colourful word-setting. The *Ode* culminates in a marvellously stirring climax evoking the final trump: a chorale-like melody is sung accompanied by the soprano and echoed by the chorus before a trumpet heralds a final joyous chorus – "The dead shall live, the living die, And Music shall uptune the sky".

◑ Palmer, Rolfe Johnson; Bachchor Stockholm, Concentus musicus Wien; Harnoncourt (Teldec 0630-12310-2).

Recorded in 1977, this performance still holds its own. It's very much a work that relies heavily on its two soloists, especially the soprano. Felicity Palmer's incisive and slightly hard tone may not appeal to everyone, but the very instrumental quality of her voice comes into its own in the final section. That she is also capable of the most delicate singing can be heard in her tender account of the long-phrased opening solo.

ORCHESTRAL SUITES

The orchestral suite was developed in Germany, where the formal elegance of French court music had been introduced by German followers of Lully. The suite consisted of a set of contrasting dances modelled on the type found in Lully's operas and ballets. They were also known as overtures because of the two-movement overture which always preceded the dances. The form became highly popular in German aristocratic circles (Bach and Telemann both wrote them for princely patrons). Handel had no qualms about plundering previously written works for his two famous sets, the *Water Music* and *Music for the Royal Fireworks*. With bright clear sonrities of woodwind and brass (ie sounds that were meant to carry), these are both very clearly music for outdoors.

THE WATER MUSIC

On July 17, 1717, an event occurred of which the *Daily Courant* reported: "Many barges with Persons of Quality attended, and so great a Number of Boats, that the whole River in a manner was cover'd; a City Company's Barge was employ'd for the Musick, wherein were 50 Instruments of all sorts, who play'd all the Way from Lambeth . . . the finest Symphonies, compos'd express for this Occasion, by Mr Hendel; which his Majesty liked so well, that he caus'd it to be plaid three times in going and returning."

The occasion was prompted by George I having taken a fancy to the idea of a water-party – a reasonably common occurrence, as is indicated by the fact that Handel wrote at least three *Water Music* suites (there may have been others). Those with horns or trumpets were most suitable for the outdoors, whereas the softer G major suite (with flutes) was apt for the "choice supper at Lord Ranelagh's villa at Chelsea, where there was another fine Consort of Musick, which lasted until two".

Each of the suites is as sophisticated as it is instantly engaging. Handel had saturated himself in the musical traditions of his adopted country, not least its naval and country dances, but brought to them (in the words of the Handel expert, H.C. Robbins Landon) "far more than the usual international flair: a remarkable fusion of solid German upbringing, Italian training and a thorough acquaintance with French taste". The result is, alongside Vivaldi's *Four Seasons*, the most popular instrumental music before Mozart.

English Baroque Soloists; Gardiner (Philips 434 122-2).

John Eliot Gardiner, characteristically vital, creates an object lesson in the articulation of textures and accenting. His sense of the natural growth and fluctuating tension of the music is the key to this recording's spontaneity – the slow movements have a dying fall to them, and rarely have Allegros or Prestos been so effervescent yet without sounding frenetic.

The English Concert; Pinnock (Deutsche Grammophon Archiv 410 525-2).

Pinnock, a little less high-spirited, brings out the stateliness of it all, giving his players the space to find the widest range of characterization. If the dynamic range of Pinnock's recording is a little less than Gardiner's, the results are sometimes more poignant.

THE FIREWORKS MUSIC

Within a few weeks of *Solomon*'s first performance, another spectacular Handel premiere took place. As part of the celebrations for the ending of the war, a pavilion over four hundred feet long was erected in Green Park, and Handel – having composed fire music for his opera *Atalanta* – was asked by George II to create a suite for an immense pyrotechnic display to be held there on April 27, 1749.

There were ructions about orchestration: Handel wanted strings, the king insisted on "martial instruments". The final forces used for the *Music for the Royal Fireworks* are unclear, but included nine trumpets, nine horns, twenty-four oboes, twelve bassoons and three pairs of kettledrums. A rehearsal on April 21 went well, with a hundred musicians playing to a crowd of over twelve thousand, and bringing the centre of London to a standstill. The same could not be said of the big night: "The rockets succeeded mighty well; but the wheels, and all that to compose the principal part, were pitiful and ill-conducted . . . and then, what contributed to the awkwardness of the whole, was the right pavilion catching fire, and being burnt down in the middle of the show." In the end Servandoni – designer of the pavilion – drew his sword on the Comptroller of Fireworks.

The overture is one of Handel's most exhilarating, brilliant creations, and if the remaining numbers are slighter, there is no finer demonstration of Beethoven's comment that Handel knew best how to achieve grand effects with simple means.

The English Concert; Pinnock (Deutsche Grammophon Archiv 431 707-2; with *Alexander's Feast* and *Concerto Grosso Op. 6 No. 6*).

The opening here, all slicing upbeats, has a marvellous bite and sense of pride. The rest is a demonstration of the fine textures and phrasing that authentic Baroque practice can create. Pinnock rerecorded *The Fireworks Music* in 1997 but this version is still a safe bet.

THE CONCERTOS

The concerto grosso, in which the main body of an orchestra (called the ripieno or concerto grosso) is in dialogue with a small group of instruments (the concertino), achieved its definitive form in the concertos of Corelli written at the end of the seventeenth century. Handel was prompted to turn to the genre after the great success of two sets by a rival in London, Francesco Geminiani. Handel's Opus 3, published in 1734, and his Opus 6, of six years later, constitute the concerto grosso's final grand flourish. Thereafter concertos were largely a dialogue between the orchestra and an individual soloist. Handel's own main contribution to the solo concerto were the two sets of organ concertos, Opus 4 and Opus 7. Organ concertos were, more or less, a form invented by Handel, who wrote them to be performed as interludes between the acts of his oratorios.

THE CONCERTI GROSSI

Handel's first great contributions to the genre, the Opus 3 of 1734, are six concerti grossi with woodwind, featuring a mix of new writing and pieces reworked from existing compositions by Handel and others. These are robust and clearly articulated pieces which make the most of the form's dramatic contrasts of solemn grandeur and vitality. Outstanding among them is the second in B flat, which displays Handel's fascination with combining sweet melodies with unusual sonorities – especially beautiful is the Largo in which a mournful oboe tune hovers above an apreggiated line played by two cellos.

Handel's orchestral masterpiece appeared five years later – the Opus 6 concerti grossi, published as *Twelve Grand Concertos*. Amongst the most powerful works of the Baroque era, these concertos form part of a family tree that begins with Corelli, but Handel brings a new vibrancy and motion – his dances are fresh and flexible, his instrumentation lyrically ripe, his polyphony adventurous and tantalizing. "No great music has been more derivative," wrote the musicologist Basil Lam, "yet none bears more firmly the impression of personality." The very last concerto, *No. 12 in B Minor*, forms a suitable climax: bristling with restless energy and yet full of mystery, its has in its central movement a quintessentially serene Handelian melody (hard not to imagine it being sung) that is twice repeated in variation form.

⊙ Concerti Grossi Opus 3: The English Concert; Pinnock (Deutsche Grammophon Archiv 413 727-2).

The Pinnock CD of the Opus 3 concerti is a performance of great charm – fragile where necessary, but very dignified in the slow movements.

⊙ Concerti Grossi Opus 6: The English Concert; Pinnock (Deutsche Grammophon Archiv 410 897-2, 410 898-2 and 410 899-2).

Pinnock's recording of the Opus 6 concerti is equally rewarding. Both sets of *Concerti Grossi*, conducted by Pinnock, are available on a mid-price six-CD box (423 149-2), which also contains the *Water Music*, the *Fireworks Music* and the concerto grosso *Alexander's Feast*.

ORGAN CONCERTOS

Sir John Hawkins, Handel's contemporary, leaves a description of him at the organ: "His amazing command of the instrument, the grandeur and dignity of his style, the copiousness of his imagination, and the fertility of his invention were qualities that . . . no one ever pretended to equal." Handel's delight in improvisation is crucial to his finest works for this instrument, his organ concertos – the form of keyboard music to which he devoted himself after 1730. These works were written to be played on the organ or harpsichord, since English organs normally lacked the pedal-boards and multiple manuals fitted to their hefty continental counterparts, and the consequence is that the texture of these pieces is extremely transparent. Many passages were left as skeletons to be fleshed out with improvisation, which is why they demand a performer with both knowledge and flair to bring them to life.

⊙ Organ Concertos Op. 4 & Op. 7: Amsterdam Baroque Orchestra; Koopman (Erato 4509 91932-2; 2 CDs).

Koopman's playing of both sets is elegant, springy and suave, catching the festive sparkle and pastoral homeliness of the music. The interplay between the instrumentalists is lively, and the recorded sound excellent.

KEYBOARD MUSIC

Handel was a brilliant keyboard player and during his stay in Italy he took part in one of those keyboard duels between competing virtuosos that aristocratic patrons so loved to set up. This one was at the palace of Cardinal Ottoboni in Rome, and pitted Handel against his Neapolitan contemporary Domenico Scarlatti (see p.350). According to Handel's first biographer, ". . . there was a total difference in their manner. The characteristic excellence of Scarlatti seems to have consisted in a certain elegance and delicacy of expression. Handel had an uncommon brilliancy and command of finger: but what distinguishes him from all other players. . . was that amazing fullness, force, and energy, which he joined with them." Handel wrote more than twenty keyboard suites, of which the most distinguished are the first published set, sometimes known as the eight *Great Suites*.

EIGHT SUITES FOR KEYBOARD

As had happened before with his music, Handel was prompted into revising and publishing his keyboard suites in an attempt to undermine the sale of pirated versions that had appeared. The first set of eight were published in 1720 but were probably written quite a bit earlier. They incorporate a wide range of styles – French, Italian, German – sometimes within the same suite. Thus the glorious second suite has as its first movement an aria-like Adagio but culminates in a fugue of enormous wit and invention. The fifth suite is the most frequently recorded, popular above all for its last movement air and variations in which can be heard, according to legend, the clear sound of the blacksmith's hammer against an anvil – hence its nickname *The Harmonious Blacksmith.*

o Keyboard Suites Set 1, Nos. 2, 3 and 5: Perahia (Sony SK 62785; with *Chaconne in G Major* and Scarlatti *Seven Sonatas*).

Handel's suites lend themselves to being played on the piano as well as any keyboard music of the Baroque period. When the playing is this good it is hard to imagine them on any other instrument. This is one of the most refreshing and buoyant piano discs of recent years. Murray Perahia brings a sound and touch to this music which is both mellow and incisive, and above all his playing emphasizes the brilliance of the music rather than the brilliance of his own playing.

o Keyboard Suites Set 1, Nos. 1–5: Souter (ISIS CD003).

If you feel that this music is best served by being played on the kind of instrument for which it was written, then you won't find anything more authentic than this. Martin Souter plays an instrument from the Bate collection at Oxford University that almost certainly belonged to Handel himself. It's a one-manual instrument, surprisingly warm in tone and well recorded, which Souter plays with real flair and energy. It's a disc to be dipped into rather than listened to in its entirety: too much of it and the sound begins to seem a little relentless.

JONATHAN HARVEY

(1939–)

Almost uniquely among contemporary composers, Jonathan Harvey strives to make music of a consciously spiritual nature without rejecting the methods and strategies of modernism. While his contemporaries Arvo Pärt and John Tavener – inspired by the simple harmonies of pre-Renaissance polyphony – have sought the numinous by paring down their musical language, Harvey embraces complexity, revelling in the infinite sonic possibilities afforded by modern electronics. One of his most celebrated works, *Mortuos Plango, vivos voco* (1980), mixes the sounds of his young son's treble voice with the tolling of the great bell of Winchester Cathedral. The result is both poignant and reassuring in the way recognizable sounds are atomized via electronics into something timeless and ethereal.

Born at Sutton Coldfield in England, Harvey began his musical career as a chorister at St Michael's, Tenbury. While at Cambridge University he had private lessons in composition with Erwin Stein and in analysis with Hans Keller. His early works reveal the influence of Britten as well as interest in Schoenbergian serialism and the modalism of Messiaen. In 1969 a scholarship to Princeton brought him briefly within the orbit of Milton Babbitt, whose total serialism taught him the value of disciplined structural procedures. A more liberating influence was Stockhausen (the subject of a book by Harvey), whose experiments in rhythmic duration, the use of silence and the division of the orchestra into separate groups helped Harvey to develop a more personal and individual musical voice. Stockhausen's interest in Eastern ideas – both musical and mystical – has clear parallels with Harvey's own spiritual preoccupations.

Harvey's Christianity, coloured by both Buddhism and the ideas of Rudolf Steiner, is at the heart of his music. Much of what he writes for the voice – be it liturgical music or opera – is deeply contemplative and informed by a strong sense of ritual. But in all his music there is an extraordinarily ecstatic quality, a sensual enjoyment of the purely physical qualities of the sounds, sometimes violent, that he conjures up. This quality or the way that, as Harvey puts it, "music perpetually plays between the physical sound and our subjectivisation of it", is graphically realized in *Bhakti* (1982) – the most thrilling and visionary of all his works to date.

BHAKTI

In the early 1980s, at the invitation of Pierre Boulez, Harvey worked at IRCAM, where he created *Bhakti*, a work for chamber orchestra with quadrophonic tape. Bhakti, a Sanskrit word meaning "to revere", is a Hindu movement emphasizing deep devotion to an individual god. Each of the work's twelve movements has a quotation from one of the ancient *Rig Veda* hymns, which encompass a range of moods, feelings and images and act as a stimulus to the musical ideas. *Bhakti* begins with a powerful representation of nothingness and the first stirrings of thought: it focuses on a single note, played by different instruments, which quietly builds and expands before a sudden flurry of more complex musical material. The tape (which is mostly composed of the electronically transformed sounds of the ensemble) acts as a contrasting voice in a dialogue with the acoustic material, and as a means of conveying a tangible sensation of space, both outer and inner. In the first half of the work a sense of restless and questing energy predominates, then from section seven – brimming with bells and bell-like sounds – a more celebratory mood begins to take over. The last section, which manages to be both clamorous and serene, almost fulfils Harvey's desire to reach "beyond the instrumental scale to a more universal dimension".

○ Bhakti: Nouvel Ensemble Moderne; Vaillancourt (Auvidis Montaigne MO 782086).

This disc, the second recording of *Bhakti*, illustrates how a "difficult" contemporary work will become clearer and more coherent the more often it is performed. There is a much stronger sense of the development of ideas in this performance, as if the performers themselves were thinking in terms of a journey – spiritual or otherwise. It's a quality enhanced by the stunning sound, which is wonderfully atmospheric in both depth and detail.

MUSIC FOR CELLO

Harvey was a professional cellist for a brief time and the cello is the instrument with which he has made some of his most personal utterances. He regards it as the most human of instruments, ". . . it speaks with every aspect of the human voice, masculine, feminine, powerful, tender, poetic, exclamatory, dreamy". The 1990 *Cello Concerto* was inspired, like *Bhakti*, by Hindu text (a quotation from *The Mahabharata*) and it too unfolds as a journey – in this case the individual's journey towards a state of bliss. The soloist is, for the most part, surrounded by a web of bright percussive sounds (vibraphone, celeste, glockenspiel) which suggests an aura of protective light carrying it across the more earthbound sounds of the rest of the orchestra. The concerto was created in collaboration with its first performer, Frances-Marie Uitti, with whom Harvey has developed several subsequent pieces. In 1995 the pair spent two days improvising in Harvey's studio – Uitti exploring the full gamut of her avant-garde technique, Harvey responding on two synthesizers programmed with the same sound sources that were used in his opera *Inquest of Love*. The resulting CD, *Imaginings*, ranges from the rhapsodic to the explosive and possesses a directness and a spontaneity which is all too rare in contemporary classical music.

○ Imaginings: Harvey, Uitti (Chill Out CHILLCD 007).

On the whole it is Uitti who occupies the driving seat, generating melodic ideas which Harvey helps to develop discreetly and sensitively. The predominant mood is one of contemplation, but this is not New Age background music, and the shifts and feints of the performers are, for the most part, unpredictable. The performers are greatly assisted by sound engineer John Whiting, who has created an intimate ambience with minimal editing (the contributions of the family dog have been excised).

JOSEPH HAYDN

(1732–1809)

Until recently, Joseph Haydn was commonly regarded as John the Baptist to Mozart's Jesus Christ; a great man, certainly, but a secondary figure nonetheless. Haydn did the spadework, entrenching the symphony and the string quartet in the cultural landscape, and then dazzling Mozart came along, refining and perfecting what Haydn had doggedly constructed. This misjudgement of Haydn's music was supported by the image of "Papa Joe", a nickname bestowed on him many years before his death. Apart from his occasionally brutish treatment of Frau Haydn, he does seem to have been an agreeable person, well-respected by all, concerned about the wellbeing of others, and – when compared to someone like Beethoven – generous to a fault. But this genial portrait obscures the truth, for Joseph Haydn was one of the great revolutionaries of classical music, making huge advances in structure, harmony and melody, investing every form with inexhaustible potential for expression. He was born into the Baroque age, and went on to write music which prefigures the stormy creations of Beethoven.

LEBRECHT COLLECTION

George Dance's 1794 portrait of Haydn

Haydn was born in the Austrian town of Rohrau, and in 1761, after a conspicuously ordinary early life, was engaged as vice-Kapellmeister by Prince Paul Esterházy, a Hungarian nobleman. He remained exclusively in that family's employment for the next thirty years, working for Prince Paul and then for his son Nikolaus, at their palaces of Eisenstadt and Esterháza. Unlike Mozart, whose relationships with his patrons was neither easy nor consistent, Haydn lived happily within the confines of his master's world and benefited enormously from the seclusion and from having a permanent orchestra with which to work. As he later remarked, "there was no-one there to confuse me, so I was forced to become original". His duties demanded that he compose almost constantly, but as he travelled rarely and was overawed at the prospect of having to perform as a pianist, violinist or conductor outside the palaces, his fame as a composer was spread almost solely through publishing.

In 1790 Nikolaus Esterházy died and the court musicians were dismissed by his successor. Haydn was also deemed surplus to requirements but, as a sign of the family's respect for his loyalty, they continued paying his salary and allowed him to keep his Kapellmeister title. He moved to Vienna, but shortly afterwards he received an invitation from the impresario J.P. Salomon to visit England. Fêted by the music world and entertained by royalty, his first stay in England (1791–92) was a remarkable success and his life in London remains the most fascinating episode in what was a fairly uneventful life. He remained in England for some eighteen months, and took enormous satisfaction in receiving an honorary degree from Oxford University.

Having returned from London, he bought a house in Vienna where he taught Beethoven, among others, but in 1794 he was commissioned by Salomon to write six new symphonies and so made the journey back to England. This second visit lasted from February 1794 to August 1795 and brought him even greater fame and success. After his return, he moved back into employment with the Esterházys, but he worked for their household only on special occasions, devoting most of his time to composing. Between 1796 and 1802 Haydn produced some of his greatest music (in particular, the oratorio *Die Schöpfung*), but from 1802 his health began to fail, leading towards an illness from which he died in 1807.

Haydn's life may have been unenthralling, but his music is not. In some ways he was more radical than Mozart: whereas Mozart was obsessed with symmetrical perfection, in which the four- and eight-bar phrase reigned unchallenged, Haydn experimented with phrases lasting three, five, seven, and even nine bars; and while Mozart almost never veered from the sonata convention of first and second subjects, Haydn sometimes built movements on single themes, a procedure that didn't become a convention until the nineteenth century. As with any prolific composer, his output has its pedestrian moments, but his best music is outstandingly fresh and sprightly. Above all, Haydn is the most humane and comforting of composers. In his own words, he wrote music so that "the weary and worn, or the man burdened with affairs, may enjoy a few moments of solace and refreshment".

OPERA

Opera is the one field of musical activity in which history has judged Haydn a failure, yet opera consumed an enormous amount of his time and in his day he was regarded as one of the most important composers for the stage – greater even than Mozart. Nowadays the judgement has been reversed, and Haydn's fifteen surviving operas (out of twenty) are rarely seen except in productions by small-scale companies. The neglect isn't altogether unjustified, but a handful of the fifteen show a real flair for dramatic orchestration, characterization and use of ensemble – nothing to stand comparison with Mozart's masterpieces, but certainly more sophisticated than contemporaneous Italian opera. Particularly notable is Haydn's penchant for mixing tragic and comic elements, an ability used to the full in his delightful "drama giocoso", *Il mondo della luna.*

IL MONDO DELLA LUNA

A number of Haydn's comic operas were written for the entertainment of guests at Esterháza – weddings, birthdays and social gatherings. Supreme among these is *Il mondo della luna* (The World on the Moon). Written in 1777 to celebrate the marriage of Prince Paul's second son, this three-act opera was described by Count Zinzendorf as "une farce pour la populace et pour les enfants" – and it is indeed a work for everyone.

Carlo Goldoni's libretto and the overall premise are endearingly preposterous. Bonafede has two daughters, whose proposed marriages to Ecclitico and Ernesto he strongly opposes. Ecclitico tells Bonafede that he has received an invitation to the moon and Bonafede begs that he may travel with him. The two fiancées transform a garden into a lunar landscape and, waking from a sleeping potion, Bonafede believes he is on the moon. Both couples join in the charade and marry "on the moon". When Bonafede discovers the trickery he is unsurprisingly hostile but, eventually, he is reconciled to the marriages.

This farrago clearly engaged Haydn's highly tuned sense of the ridiculous, and his witty music and multifaceted portrayal of his characters are highly enjoyable throughout. The ensemble writing in the garden scene is outstanding and Haydn's interweaving of the characters' individuated musical styles must surely have influenced the young Mozart.

○ Auger, Mathis, von Stade, Rolfe Johnson, Alva; Orchestre de Chambre de Lausanne; Dorati (Philips 432 420-2; 3 CDs).

Antal Dorati recorded eight of Haydn's operas in the 1970s, all of which are available on CD. Only the most devout Haydn fan would embark on the whole series, but this recording of *Il mondo della luna* is a delight, made with young and highly talented singers (now all major stars) who evidently shared Dorati's enthusiasm for the music. The individuality of each of the voices (especially Auger and von Stade) and the first-rate ensemble work brings wonderful clarity to Haydn's complicated counterpoint.

CHORAL MUSIC

Haydn was a deeply religious man and much of his most heartfelt and passionate music can be found in his sacred choral works. In his early Masses and in works like the *Stabat Mater* (1767) there is a freshness and vigour to the writing which suggests that his faith was an essentially joyful aspect of his life. Unfortunately his activities as a composer for the church were curtailed by an imperial edict of 1783 restricting the use of orchestral music in the Catholic liturgy. The advantage of this was that when he returned to writing sacred music in 1796 he had a new-found confidence as a composer which enabled him to produce choral works of a hitherto unknown power and profundity. Supreme among these were the six final Masses that he wrote, commissioned on a yearly basis by Prince Nikolaus Esterházy for his wife's name day, and his greatest oratorio *Die Schöpfung* (The Creation), a work largely inspired by hearing several of Handel's oratorios while in London.

MASSES NOS. 11 & 12 – THE NELSON AND THERESA MASSES

Haydn wrote the third of his last set of Masses in the summer of 1798, naming it *Missa in angustiis* – "Mass in anxious times". The anxiety was caused by Napoleon Bonaparte who had shelled Vienna the year before and was now in Egypt. It is more commonly known as the *Nelson Mass* in honour of the British admiral who destroyed the French fleet in August 1798 and for whom it was performed two years later. Scored for three trumpets, timpani, strings and organ, it begins in the most thrilling fashion with a restless Kyrie in which the soprano soloist has some brilliant soaring runs. This and the unsusually sombre Benedictus are in D minor; the rest of the Mass is more celebratory but with the nervous energy of its opening never far from the surface. The so-called *Theresa Mass* (named after the empress Maria Theresia but not, in fact, dedicated to her) is a less hard-driven work, more ample and confident and full of the most glorious melodies, in particular a beautiful alto solo in the Gloria. Both Masses divide the Gloria and Credo into sections which are distributed between solo voices and the chorus, thus increasing the impact of the words and creating some telling contrasts in mood. There is also a new prominence given to the orchestra, which adds an even greater element of grand drama to these works.

◑ **Leipzig Radio Choir and Staatskapelle Dresden; Marriner** (CZS5 68592; 2 CDs; with *Masses 7 & 9*).

Marriner's strength as a conductor of Haydn's choral works is the way he incorporates moments of individual beauty within a view of the work as a symphonic whole. He also never loses sight of the sheer drama of the late Masses, and there's plenty of atmosphere in both these performances. He's helped by some excellent soloists – in particular some powerful and incisive singing from soprano Margaret Marshall in the *Nelson Mass* and the warm tone of mezzo Doris Soffel in the *Theresa Mass*.

DIE SCHÖPFUNG

Handel remained an extremely popular composer with the English, and Haydn (like Mozart) had a great deal of respect for his music – especially the oratorios. The original English text for *The Creation* – a fusion of the early chapters of Genesis with sections of *Paradise Lost* – was put together with Handel in mind, but for reasons unknown he never set it. When Haydn saw the text, he immediately recognized its potential and asked his friend Baron van Swieten to revise it and translate it into German. Like a Handel oratorio, *Die Schöpfung* is full of fresh and vivid imagery, depicting all the manifold glories of the Creation with a pictorialism that's nothing short of startling. You can hear the worm crawling, the lion leaping, the wind blowing and – in the prelude leading toward the rising of the sun – you can almost feel heat coming off the music.

The overture, depicting Chaos before the first day, is a bleak, formless and dissonant introduction to the arrival of the Archangel Raphael, who shares with the other archangels the narration of subsequent events – the first being the creation of light. With a lapidary simplicity typical of Haydn, the dawning of light is achieved by modulating from the darkness of C minor into a stupendous C major fortissimo chord that foreshadows the similar device in Bartók's *Bluebeard's Castle* (see p.25). The subsequent arias achieve a transcendant simplicity that, perhaps, only Haydn could have brought to such a demanding subject. The choruses are similarly clear in their expression and, notably in *The Heavens are Telling the Glory of God*, Haydn shows his genius for multiple voice part-writing.

○ **McNair, Brown, Schade, Gilfry, Finley; Monteverdi Choir; English Baroque Soloists; Gardiner** (Archiv 449 217-2; 2 CDs).

If you want to hear really superb choral singing and an interpretation that is both invigorating and uplifting, then this is the recording to get. Gardiner marshals his forces with superb discipline producing a wonderfully fresh sound which still manages to possess the requisite amount of mystery that is so essential for this work. His soloists are nicely contrasted and uniformly excellent – the baritone Gerald Finley in particular brings a wonderful combination of the noble and the sympathetic to the role of Raphael.

◑ **Janowitz, Ludwig, Wunderlich, Krenn, Fischer-Dieskau, Berry; Vienna Singers; Berlin Philharmonic Orchestra; Karajan** (Deutsche Grammophon DG 435 077-2; 2 CDs).

Like his *Missa Solemnis* recording (see p.32), Karajan's *Die Schöpfung* boasts an incredible cast – though tragically Fritz Wunderlich died before completing the sessions and was replaced by Werner Krenn. Apart from this, Karajan (like Gardiner) employed two singers for the roles of Raphael and Adam and brought in Christa Ludwig for the final movement's *Let Every Voice Sing unto the Lord*. This might suggest a fragmentary performance, but in fact this is one of the most most brilliantly realized and cohesive of all Karajan's interpretations.

THE SYMPHONIES

Between 1757 and 1795 Haydn composed some 104 symphonies, refining the form from the relatively simple early works – based on the Italian sinfonia of three movements (fast–slow–fast) – to the highly sophisticated symphonies of his maturity which served as a model for practically every composer of the nineteenth century. All the symphonies after *No. 31* are in four movements (usually arranged fast–slow–fast–fast), each with a second- or third-movement Minuet and a finale that functioned as a fast-moving and dramatic climax to the whole work. All but one of the last fourteen symphonies opens with a slow introduction. However, these similarities are largely superficial, for each of these symphonies is a markedly original blend of deep feeling and elegance, with the final twelve manifesting a perfect, Mozartian synthesis of form and substance. To discuss them all would require a book in itself, so we've picked out a few exceptional works.

◑ **Complete Symphonies: Philharmonia Hungarica; Dorati** (Decca 430 1002DM32; 33 CDs).

Dorati's complete edition of the symphonies (recorded in the early 1970s) continues to hold up well but it now has some serious challengers, the most impressive of which are the Tafelmusik recordings for Sony (see below). Dorati's is old-fashioned, big ensemble conducting but his approach is human and flexible – communication is clearly the main priority. The cycle is currently only available as a box of 33 CDs and we suggest you check out the alternatives first.

SYMPHONY NO. 44 – THE TRAUER

Almost a third of Haydn's symphonies have acquired nicknames, most of which fit the music well. *Symphony No. 44*, known as the *Trauer* or "Mourning" symphony, dates from the early 1770s when Haydn's symphonic writing took on a more emotional and dramatic character. Critics have dubbed such works *Sturm und Drang* (Storm and Stress) after an eighteenth-century German literary movement. The musical precedent for this darker more restless style can be found in the work of C.P.E. Bach (see p.10). Haydn applied it to certain of his minor key symphonies and to various choral works. From the very beginning the *Trauer* symphony is full of startling contrasts: in the first movement a strong unison statement is immediately followed by a restless scurrying figure, and there are frequent dynamic extremes and the repetition of major key phrases in the minor. It is one of Haydn's most brilliantly inventive works, which apparently gained its nickname from Haydn's desire that the stately Handelian slow movement be played at his funeral.

○ **Tafelmusik; Weil** (Sony SK 48371; with *Symphonies Nos. 51 & 52*).

If Tafelmusik's recordings turn out to be a complete cycle, then they are certainly the ones to collect. There's something effortlessly idiomatic about these performances, which are crisp and energetic but without ever any sense of strain.

SYMPHONY NO. 45 – THE FAREWELL

Symphony No. 45 – The Farewell – culminates in a piece of musical industrial action organized by Haydn on behalf of his disgruntled musicians. Near the end of the last movement an Adagio coda commences, during which the musicians stop playing one by one and leave the stage until only two violins are left. This was a hint to Prince Nikolaus Esterházy that the stay at his summer residence had gone on too long and that the musicians missed their wives. This is not Haydn's most tuneful symphony but it is one of his most highly charged and one of the finest of the *Sturm und Drang* symphonies.

○ **Tafelmusik; Weil** (Sony SK 53986; with *Symphonies Nos. 46 & 47*).

Bruno Weil's direction is particularly effective in the so-called *Sturm und Drang* symphonies. He really manages to get under the skin of this music, finding just the right balance between fury and finesse.

SYMPHONIES NOS. 48 & 49

The empress Maria Theresia visited Esterháza in the autumn of 1773 and for a long time the *Symphony No. 48* was thought to have been written to celebrate the event – hence its nickname *Maria Theresia*. Despite the fact that it is now known to have been written several years earlier, the symphony certainly has a festive quality and opens with a grand flourish – a lively fanfare in which two high horns are strikingly prominent. It's a C major work (traditionally a key of celebration) but the general sense of bustle in the outer movements is offset by the long, tranquil slow movement in which there are some marvellous moments for the horns and oboes. The *Symphony No. 49*, nicknamed *La Passione*, could not be more different. It begins slowly in a mood of almost funereal solemnity, a feeling that never entirely deserts it even during the frenetic second-movement Allegro. A decidely sombre Minuet and a Presto that fizzles with nervous energy make this one of the most darkly coloured of all Haydn's symphonies.

○ **Hanover Band; Goodman** (Hyperion CDA66531; with *Symphony No. 50*).

Roy Goodman's excellent cycle with the period instrument Hanover Band looked all set to finish, but was axed well over halfway through. They are the nearest in style to Tafelmusik, powerful and direct (with a prominent harpsichord continuo), more concerned with momentum and inner drama than with refinement.

SYMPHONIES NOS. 82–87 – THE PARIS SYMPHONIES

In 1779 Haydn signed a new contract with Nikolaus Esterházy whereby his music was no longer the exclusive property of the prince. The result was a wealth of commissions from publishers and, eventually, from impresarios throughout Europe. One such – for six symphonies – arrived from the Comte d'Ogny, one of the financial backers of a Parisian concert society called "Concerts de la Loge Olympique".

Written during 1785 and 1786, symphonies nos. 82–87 display an extremely wide-ranging imagination both formally and in terms of orchestral virtuosity and colouring. Haydn was clearly aware of the prowess of the Paris orchestra, which was one of the biggest and best in Europe, and there are extensive wind parts in all six works. The Paris symphonies are among Haydn's most scintillating; all are worth hearing but three have proved especially popular.

Symphony No. 82 – The Bear – is a C major work, predominantly jovial but with a melancholy tinge running through it. It gets its name from the last-movement Vivace in which a rollicking "Bear dance" over a drone of fifths recurs throughout the movement.

The animal association of *Symphony No. 83 – The Hen* – derives from the "clucking" second subject of its first movement. It's the only minor-key symphony in the Paris set and its opening subject and cantabile slow movement seem like a return to the angst-laden feel of the *Sturm und Drang* symphonies.

Symphony No. 85 was a favourite of the French Queen Marie Antoinette and was therefore nicknamed *La Reine* (The Queen). It has something of the elegant fake rusticity which the queen so much enjoyed, especially in its second movement – a set of variations on the French folk song *La gentille et jeune Lisette*.

Tafelmusik; Weil (Sony SK 66295 & 66251).

More ambitious in terms of orchestration, the "Paris" Symphonies really allow an ensemble to show off, and on these two discs Tafelmusik reveal just why they have a reputation as one of the very best period-instrument groups around. The extra colouring provided by the wind parts is pointed up in a way that makes these works sound strikingly original.

SYMPHONY NO. 88 – LETTER V

Symphony No. 88 continues the rich orchestration of the later Paris symphonies and has a large wind and brass section. Throughout the first movement (Adagio-Allegro) Haydn contrasts different sections of the orchestra, a tactic he employs to even more telling effect in the Largo – a movement greatly admired by Brahms. This is essentially a set of variations on a simple chorale-like theme first heard in the wind section, then by the strings, before being repeated in various permutations (with periodic sinister interruptions from the whole orchestra playing fortissimo). There is also a very striking rustic Trio complete with simulated hurdy-gurdy sounds.

Tafelmusik; Weil (Sony SK66253; with *Symphonies Nos. 89 & 90*).

Here it's the elegance and panache of the playing that shines through. Instead of wallowing in the slow movements as some conductors do, Weil reveals them to have as much character as any other movement. His treatment of the Largo of No. 88 is magically revealing.

SYMPHONY NO. 92 – THE OXFORD

In 1791 Oxford University conferred an honorary doctorate on Haydn who conducted his *Symphony No. 92 – The Oxford* – at the celebrations (though it was actually composed two years earlier and dedicated to Comte d'Ogny). It's one of the most warm and serene of all Haydn's later symphonies, full of cantabile melodies reminiscent of Mozart. Its broad and sunny slow movement is occasionally startled by dark minor-key outbursts, and the fizzing finale injects an element of almost neurotic fussiness into the otherwise untroubled proceedings.

Hanover Band; Goodman (Hyperion CDA66521; with *Symphonies Nos. 90 & 91*).

In the final analysis, the Hanover Band do not find quite the range and colour of their Candian counterparts Tafelmusik. Nevertheless, despite some rough edges, this is a highly entertaining and spirited account of the *Oxford*.

THE LONDON SYMPHONIES – NOS. 93–104

London was a demanding and sophisticated musical centre, and to satisfy demand the impresario J.P. Salomon tried to secure the services of both Haydn and Mozart for his concerts in the Hanover Square Rooms. Only Haydn arrived, composing the first six symphonies for seasons in 1791 and 1792, and the second six for the season of 1794. These last twelve symphonies are arguably Haydn's greatest achievement in the genre. The orchestra is even larger than for the Paris symphonies, and the harmonies more daring, with frequent unexpected moves to different keys. The slow introductions are as grand as before but with an added tension which sets you up for the splendours which follow. All twelve are inventive and infinitely rewarding works, but we have singled out three of the most celebrated.

Symphony No. 94 – The Surprise – was written in Hertfordshire, in the course of Haydn's first visit to England in 1791. The "surprise" of the nickname comes in the second movement when, halfway through a light and seemingly insignificant Andante, there comes a fortissimo bang from the timpani. It was suggested that Haydn had placed the explosion there in order to wake up any dozing members of the audience, but he insisted that he had merely wanted to surprise the listener with something new.

Symphony No. 100 – The Military – was performed at the eighth concert on March 31, when it was introduced as a "Grand Military Overture", a reference to the use of a military battery of kettledrums, triangle, cymbals and bass drum in its second movement. The work became especially famous for the final movement, a rondo whose main theme managed to find its way into England's ballrooms. The military flavour returns near the end of the symphony with great grandeur, but the parade-ground pomp is ultimately absorbed into the atmosphere of the salon.

The very first bar of *Symphony No. 103* – an unannounced drum-roll – is a marvellous, unprecedented coup, which inevitably led to the symphony's becoming known as the *Drum Roll*. This dramatic flourish announces one of Haydn's most original works, leading into a quiet, sustained phrase for bassoons, cellos and basses which has a mystery comparable to the opening of Schubert's *Unfinished Symphony*. Later in the symphony you get a masterful set of double variations on two themes derived from folk tunes, a Trio that makes intriguing use of the clarinets, and a finale that is ingeniously based upon a single theme.

◑ **Symphonies Nos. 95, 96, 98, 102, 103 & 104: Concertgebouw Orchestra; Davis** (Philips 442 611-2; 2 CDs).

Recorded in the late 1970s and early 1980s, this set hold up remarkably well – due, in no small measure, to Davis's energetic conducting, which makes even as experienced an orchestra as the Concertgebouw sound as though they are really enjoying themselves. An exhilarating and uplifting experience.

◑ **Symphonies 99–104: Royal Philharmonic Orchestra; Beecham** (EMI CMS7 64066-2; 2 CDs).

This set is a marvel of interpretative freshness: Beecham was in astonishing form when he made these recordings, generating a sense of the unexpected and a joyfulness that makes you oblivious of the dated sound quality. Few conductors have shaped Haydn's thematic lines with such care and understanding or made the climactic moments so shattering.

THE CONCERTOS

Haydn composed numerous concertos for violin, cello, flute, oboe, trumpet, horn, bassoon, piano and organ. The problem is that not all of them were published during his lifetime and many known works are lost (some presumably in the fires that destroyed Haydn's home in 1768 and again in 1776). The good news is that several works in manuscript have reappeared relatively recently: the *Cello Concerto in C*, for instance, was accidently discovered in 1961 in the Prague National Library and, for all anyone knows, there may more such gems scattered across Europe. None of Haydn's concertos reach the same level of profundity as the best of Mozart's, but there is much to enjoy here, in particular the brilliant *Trumpet Concerto* – the most important ever written for the instrument.

THE TRUMPET CONCERTO

In the late eighteenth century the trumpet attained great prominence as a solo instrument, its natural limitations gradually being overcome by developments which culminated in a fully chromatic instrument – but with keys, like a keyboard intrument. It was for this keyed trumpet – later superseded by the valved instrument – that Haydn wrote his *Trumpet Concerto* in 1796, for the Viennese trumpet player Anton Weidlinger. It was Haydn's last fully orchestral work, and strangely it found little popularity at first, probably due to the unusual sound of the keyed trumpet. Nowadays it's a favourite vehicle for trumpet virtuosos, who get plenty of opportunity to show off in the first movement's thrilling cadenza. The slow movement is extremely lyrical (making it as demanding for a trumpet player as the fireworks of the cadenza), while the last movement is typical of the restrained exuberance of all Haydn's concerto finales.

⊙ **Steele-Perkins; English Chamber Orchestra; Halstead** (Carlton 30366 00662; with concertos by M. Haydn, Torelli, Telemann, Neruda and Humphries).

Crispian Steele-Perkins, one of England's finest players, is also a renowned expert on the history and playing styles of the natural, keyed and valved instruments. For this recording he prepared all his phrasing, articulation and cadenzas on a keyed trumpet, though his actual performances are on a modern instrument. He makes a clear and vibrato-less sound with a bright and ringing top which, in the extremely high passages, is exceptionally beautiful.

THE CELLO CONCERTOS

The two cello concertos widely attributed to Haydn (the first is still regarded as spurious in some quarters) were almost certainly written for Joseph Weigl, a cellist in the Esterházy court orchestra – which suggests that their standard of ensemble playing must have been high, as the technical demands of both works are extreme. The first concerto, in C major, was probably written between 1761 and 1765, and opens with a movement that is really nothing more than a virtuoso display; a cheery mood generally prevails throughout the concerto, and the Adagio boasts an extremely affecting and well-extended melody. The second concerto, in D major, is notable for the exquisite beauty of its Adagio, but the first movement is far too long for the material upon which it is based. Though written in 1784, when Haydn was at the height of his powers, the second concerto is less involving than its predecessor.

⭘ Rostropovich; Academy of St Martin-in-the-Fields; Brown (EMI CDC7 493052-2).

Rostropovich is well-suited to the vivacity of these concertos, and the orchestra is perfectly attuned to his endearing ebullience. He favours quick tempi and a big gruff sound, foregoing the twee delicacy of some other cellists, and the enthusiasm with which he attacks the works' outer movements is highly engaging. His playing of the central Adagios is exquisite – in the C major concerto he produces an ethereal sense of stillness that is breathtaking.

THE KEYBOARD CONCERTOS

Haydn wrote several relatively simple organ concertos, plus some for the harpsichord or fortepiano (an early version of the piano). Of these, one in particular stands out. The *Keyboard Concerto No. 11* in D major, written around 1780, is full of the strikingly dramatic contrasts that Haydn so much enjoyed. In the opening Vivace the rather skittish main theme – delicate filigree right hand over thumpingly insistent left – is systematically transformed and undermined by quixotic major–minor contrasts. The highlight is the slow movement, which is dominated by the soloist's marvellously long-breathed and expressive cantabile melody. The concerto ends with a spirited Rondo all'Ungherese in which the piano quotes a frenetic Balkan dance, the "Siri Kolo", with the orchestra in very much a supporting role.

◑ Keyboard Concerto No. 11: Argerich; London Sinfonietta (EMI CDM7 63575-2; with Beethoven *Piano Concerto No. 2*).

Martha Argerich is a great champion of this concerto and has recorded it twice. The earlier version, in which she directs from the keyboard, is the better of the two despite some overly romantic playing in the slow-movement cadenza. Apart from that, this is an exemplary account, notable, above all, for the way she combines a vigorously incisive touch with expressive delicacy. A performance of the quality that this concerto deserves but rarely gets.

THE STRING QUARTETS

Like Mozart, Haydn wrote a large amount of chamber music, including more than 120 trios and more than thirty duos for the baryton, a stringed instrument resembling the cello that was played by Prince Nikolaus Esterházy. The core of Haydn's legacy as a chamber composer, though, is his work for string quartet. Whereas Mozart composed a mere 23 string quartets, Haydn completed around ninety – the exact number remains unknown.

Not a single quartet written before Haydn's has survived to modern times, but Haydn wrote within the context of a suffocating Viennese tradition whereby every work ended with a fugal finale. By the time he came to write his *Opus 20* quartets, around the age of 40, Haydn had taken the quartet so far from the formulaic sterility of his predecessors that he could allow himself to end his works with fugues once again – but fugues of such inventiveness as to further widen the gap between himself and the past. Musicologist Hans Keller wrote of Haydn's quartets: "On a conservative count, he composed 45 profound and profoundly different, absolutely flawless, consistently original master quartets, each a violent, multi-dimensional contrast to any of the others." Indeed Haydn seems to have given his quartets more intense attention than his symphonies, for they display a greater thematic, structural and textural richness than any of his orchestral music. No other composer has so completely understood the expressive capabilities of the quartet's four parts, and this body of work represents the apogee of Haydn's genius for outward simplicity and inward complexity.

⊙ Complete String Quartets: Kodály Quartet (Naxos).

The Kodály Quartet's cycle of Haydn's quartets, a long-term project that's now almost complete, features some excellent quartet playing which, at budget price, is superb value. As is essential with Haydn's music, the leader directs the performances with absolute clarity of intention, and the result is at once extremely lyrical, dramatic and spontaneous. Naxos have released the quartets on single CDs, each containing three or four pieces, but they are also available in five-disc sets.

STRING QUARTETS OP. 1

It's emblematic of the importance of the string quartet to Haydn that his Opus 1 should be a group of six string quartets. Published in 1764 (it's not exactly when they were completed), they follow a standard pattern of five short movements – Presto/Allegro, Minuet, Adagio, Minuet, Presto/Allegro – with the central Adagio nearly always the longest. It is the Adagio of the E flat quartet, the first of the set, that singles it out as the finest of them – the Italianate beauty of the very long principal melodic line is unparalleled in his writing for quartet. Accompanied by simple harmony, this seamless music melts off the page. Of the other Opus 1 quartets, *No. 6* is also outstanding for its Adagio, less liquid in form than that of *No. 1*, but almost as moving.

⊙ **Kodály Quartet** (Naxos 8550399 & 8550398; with *Op. 2 No. 1 & Op. 2 No. 2*).

The Kodály Quartet's playing of these very simple works is nothing short of spiritual, especially in the Adagios, where their sonority becomes a single voice. Tempi are always quick and the players avoid anything akin to sentimentality. In short, as an introduction to Haydn's quartets, this cannot be beaten.

STRING QUARTETS OP. 20

With the six quartets of Op. 20, written in 1772, Haydn brought the form to a state of maturity: all four instruments are employed as equal voices (with the cello used as a solo instrument on occasions) and the musical material is much more complex – both rhythmically and harmonically, and in the way ideas are developed. These are probably the darkest and most intellectual of all Haydn's quartets, there is strong emphasis on counterpoint, and several of the final movements are written as fugues. But they are also extremely varied in mood: *Quartet No. 2* has a fulsome ripeness, especially in its slow movement; *No. 4* abounds in a kind of radiant joyfulness; while *No. 5* is the most subdued and melancholy of the whole set.

⊙ **Kodály Quartet** (Naxos 8550701 & 8550702).

The more introspective the work, the more the Kodály Quartet seem to invest themselves into the music. There's some marvelously rapt and concentrated playing and the closeness of the ensemble is exemplary.

O Quator Mosaïques (Astrée Auvidis E8784; 2 CDs).

The Quator Mosaïques provide an interesting alternative to the Kodály Quartet. They are unquestionably the most consistently fine period-instrument quartet around, and possess immense flair and style. If anything the individuality of the four voices comes across more strongly, and the gut strings of their instruments produce a sound which is thicker and more sinewy.

STRING QUARTETS OP. 33

The six quartets of Op. 33, composed in 1781, are no less complex than those of Op. 20 but they are cast in a very much lighter vein. Dedicated to the future Tsar Paul II (which is why they're sometimes known as the "Russian" Quartets), these works reveal Haydn at his most playful and light-hearted – a fact that some have attributed to Haydn's love affair with the Italian singer Luigia Polzelli. The arioso-like slow movements of several of them may also be a kind of homage to Luigia. Nicknames reflecting their whimsicality have accrued to the three most popular quartets in the set. *No. 2 – The Joke* has an easy-going last movement with a coda whose sudden unexpected silences give you no idea when the work has finished. *No. 3* in C major, the most enchanting of the set, is called *The Bird* because of the grace notes that adorn the principal theme of the first movement and the trills in the second-movement trio. *No. 5* goes by the unlikely name of *How Do You Do?* on account of its opening phrase. It's rather more notable for the yearning nature of its cantabile slow movement.

⊙ **Kodály Quartet** (Naxos 8550788 & 8550789).

More beautiful playing from the Kodály Quartet. Their slow movements are considerably slower than the Mosaïques but there is never any sense of indulgence; rather there's a feeling that they want to present the music in as pristinely classical a manner as possible. The slightly recessed sound contributes to this sense of distance.

O Quator Mosaïques (Astrée Auvidis E8784; 2 CDs).

The Quator Mosaïques are much more on top of the listener and, like Tafelmusik in the symphonies, there's a sense that it's the character and colour of these quartets which they find attractive, and their dynamic shading is much more pointed than with the Kodály Quartet.

STRING QUARTETS OP. 76

The six Op. 76 quartets are, understandably, Haydn's most famous, for they mark the culmination of his quest for expressive perfection. Commissioned by a Viennese nobleman named Count Joseph Erdödy, who retained their exclusive use for two years, they were completed in 1797, when Haydn had turned 65. He must have felt some satisfaction with the outcome, for they are the strongest and most finely wrought of all his chamber compositions and clearly inspired Beethoven's first attempts at quartet writing – even if he was reluctant to admit the influence.

In the Op. 76 set you can find everything with which Haydn's style is synonymous – ingenious variation, complex fugal writing, folk-influenced melodies, perfect ensemble writing and general transparency. The range of expression is astonishingly wide: the slow movement of *No. 3, The Emperor*, is a deeply moving, hymn-like theme composed in response to England's national anthem (it was adopted as the Austrian national anthem and is now the German); the slow movement of *No. 5*, marked *mesto* (sadly) is proto-Romantic in its supple beauty; the forcefulness of Beethoven is prefigured by the first movement of *No. 1*, with its sudden fortissimo outbursts; and the so-called *Witches' Minuet* of *No. 2* is a fine example of Haydn letting his hair down.

⊙ **Kodály Quartet** (Naxos 8550314 & 8550315).

The Kodály Quartet's performances of Op. 76 possess a steady, reliable elegance that's typical of their entire Haydn cycle. They are expressive without sentimentalizing the often lush writing, and their sense of experimentation makes this sound like music freshly minted.

THE SEVEN LAST WORDS

The *Seven Last Words* occupies a unique place within Haydn's output. It was commissioned in 1785 by the administrators of Cadiz Cathedral, who asked him to provide instrumental music for a special Good Friday service, to be performed between meditations on Christ's seven last words on the Cross. As Haydn wrote: "Each time, at the end of the sermon, the orchestra would begin again and my composition had to be in keeping with the presentation." To compose seven consecutive Adagios, each lasting ten minutes, was a taxing proposition, and Haydn missed his deadline – the first Cadiz performances took place in Holy Week of 1787, though there were performances in Vienna and Bonn the month before.

Haydn's achievement was extraordinary. Not only did he avoid monotony, he produced some of his most innovative and expressive work in the *Seven Last Words*, building music of almost symphonic density around the weighty, declamatory melodic lines that represent the words of Christ. The fact that he reworked the orchestral score into a string quartet (among other formats) shows he was justly proud of this remarkable work.

O Lindsay Quartet (ASV DCA853).

This splendid recording demonstrates that this piece works best in its reduction for string quartet, as the four voices define the harmonic and thematic material more clearly than a full orchestra. The Lindsays give full scope to the pathos and reverence of the music, while losing nothing of its momentum. As usual with this group, the ensemble playing isn't as tight as it might be, but for spontaneity and deep feeling they are without equal.

KEYBOARD MUSIC

Haydn's keyboard music owes most to the instrumental traditions of North Germany, in particular C.P.E. Bach (see p.10), which means that it possesses an expressiveness and an occasional whimsicality that contrasts with the more lyrical spirit of Mozart's work in the same medium. But even among those concert pianists who specialize in the core classical repertoire (Mozart, Beethoven and Schubert) there is disagreement over the merits of most of Haydn's keyboard sonatas – Glenn Gould played the late ones and was rumoured to have planned to record them all, Sviatoslav Richter played just a few of them, Stephen Kovacevich steers clear of all of them – but the *Sonata in C Minor* is an unqualified masterpiece, as is the astonishingly inventive *Variations in F Minor*. In recent years Alfred Brendel has been the most consistent advocate of this music and it is his recordings that we recommend you hear first.

PHILIPS/ISOLDE OHLBAUM

Alfred Brendel

SONATA IN C MINOR

The *Sonata in C Minor* (No. 20) dates from 1771 and is something of a watershed, marking a decisive move away from dance-music style and towards the storm and stress of early Romanticism. It is also Haydn's first sonata to carry specific dynamic markings, suggesting that the work was intended for a fortepiano and not a harpsichord, as were all works previous to this. The work's emotional contrasts and overall pacing make it a stylistic companion to the *Farewell Symphony* and the Op. 20 string quartets, and the combination of outright drama and reflective melody – especially in the outer movements – marks the inauguration of the Viennese Classical style, the style which Beethoven was eventually to bring to the point of dissolution.

O Brendel (Philips 426 815-2; with *Sonatas in E Flat No. 49*).

Brendel plays this sonata with just the right blend of wit and meticulousness. He's a gentle advocate, never pushing too hard: his reading of the Andante brings out all its quirky charm and points up its odd resemblance to the slow movement of Bach's *Italian Concerto* (see p.19).

VARIATIONS IN F MINOR

Described by Haydn as "Un piccolo divertimento" the *Variations in F Minor* stand as one of the pinnacles of the keyboard repertoire. The theme is brilliantly conceived for variation form and the variations themselves are notably innovative, but it is the finale, with its sixty bars of Beethoven-like fury, that is the most striking aspect of this piece. The intensely personal nature of this music has prompted various theories as to the identity of the person to whom Haydn was so openly baring his soul. In all probability there was no such person – in 1773 Haydn had simply written a piece of music so expressive as to have generations of Romantics looking for an answer to a question that had never been posed.

O Brendel (Philips 416 315-2; with *Sonatas Nos. 52, 37* and *40*).

Again Brendel is reticent in this, the most profoundly emotional of Haydn's keyboard works, simply letting the music do its own persuading without any forced bravura. The result is extremely touching and eloquent. The disc also includes another masterpiece, the delightful *Sonata in E Flat*.

HANS WERNER HENZE

(1926–)

Henze is one of the most significant, most approachable and most political of postwar European composers. His social commitment, which grew out of disgust with the Nazi Germany of his youth and his disappointment with the society of postwar Germany, eventually led him into the espousal of communism, an infatuation with the idea of world revolution, and a lengthy sojourn in Cuba. In a whole series of works, concentrated between 1968 and 1980, Henze gave vent to his disaffection with Western capitalism, but he is far from being a straightforward propagandist – on the contrary, Henze is a subtle and complex composer.

His early works show the influence of Stravinsky, Hindemith, Bartók and Schoenberg, yet Henze has always retained a loyalty to classical forms – he has, after all, written nine symphonies. He has always been a profoundly theatrical composer as well: he has stated that all his work ultimately derives from the theatre, and has referred to his hearing *The Marriage of Figaro* as a formative childhood experience. The directness and lucidity of his writing can largely be attributed to his development of a hard-hitting style for the political works he created for small ensembles in the 1960s and 1970s, such as *The Raft of the Medusa*, *La Cubana* and *El Cimarrón*.

One last essential component in Henze's work is its sensuousness, a quality that came to the fore after he left his native country at the age of 27 to live in Italy, which is still his home. Italy has stimulated his work in innumerable ways: through its light and colour; through its freer attitude towards his homosexuality; and, perhaps above all, through its emphasis on community. Of the various popular projects with which Henze has been involved, none has been more important than the festival he created at the Tuscan town of Montepulciano. Here, working with professional musicians and local people, Henze established a forum for the performance of a range of projects, from new works to little-known Italian operas, most of them staged in the town square. Innovative and highly popular, the festival in

Montepulciano epitomizes the best qualities of this prolific composer.

◑ **The Henze Collection** (Deutsche Grammophon 449 860-2; 14 CDs).

Containing the first six symphonies, *Der junge Lord*, *The Raft of the Medusa*, *El Cimmarón*, a sequence of concertos and numerous other works, this survey of Henze's career is as comprehensive and illuminating an overview as any major label has given to a living composer. It has its longueurs, but there's much to relish here. The set is also available in one-disc and two-disc instalments.

THE BASSARIDS

The Bassarids (1965) is Henze's greatest opera. Taking a reworked version of Euripides' *The Bacchae* by W.H. Auden and Chester Kallmann, Henze creates a highly complicated structure which is in effect a single-spanned two-hour symphony with voices. The formal aspects of the opera are demonstrations of a remarkable technical proficiency, but what matters most is Henze's ability to portray the conflicts of sense and sensuality in music that is immediately effective. Praising the libretto he had been given, Henze wrote that Auden ". . . understood the ability of music to forget itself. . . the crude shamelessness of musical expression", and *The Bassarids* abounds with correspondingly rich and expressive music. Agave's haunting description of her first exposure to the cult, the wild hunt of the Bassarids, and the appearance of Agave carrying her son's head are all extremely intense episodes, and throughout the opera the conflict between rationality and sensuality is mirrored in clashes between harmony and cacophony. The cumulative impact is extraordinary. The most original moment comes right at the end when, with disorder triumphant, Pentheus dead, Cadmus and his court banished, and Dionysus in total command, the music becomes subdued – a moment more dreadful in its calm acceptance of the new order than any Dionysian orgy.

O Riegel, Schmidt, Tear, Armstrong, Lindsey; Berlin Radio Symphony Orchestra; Albrecht (Schwann 314 006-2; 2 CDs).

Gerd Albrecht is a noted champion of Henze's music, and this 1986 performance of the German-language version of *The Bassarids* is full of conviction and confidence. The casting is exceptional, with the baritone Kenneth Riegel and Andreas Schmidt outstanding as Dionysus and Pentheus. The sound is full, capturing the sumptuous Berlin forces with clarity and warmth.

THE SYMPHONIES

The nine symphonies that Henze has composed since 1947 cover an even wider ground than the operas, from the classical forms of the first and the sumptuous late Romantic textures of the second, to the agitprop of the sixth and the grief-stricken bombast of the ninth (choral) symphony. They form the best introduction to a prolific output that is stylistically very diverse – often bewilderingly so. *Symphony No. 7* (1984), the finest of them all, has been explained by Henze in the following terms: "Again and again I have felt drawn towards the Beethovenian tradition. . . My seventh symphony is a German symphony and it deals with matters German." If this is the case, then his view of his native land is a profoundly ambiguous one. Only the first of the four movements, an energetic almost bullish Allemande, exudes optimism; the other three are predominantly melancholy, with the Scherzo and the finale both inspired by the tragic figure of the Romantic poet Friedrich Hölderlin. Most elegiac of all is the grandiose second movement, which exudes an almost funereal sense of darkness and resignation.

◑ **Symphonies Nos. 1–6: Berlin Philharmonic & London Symphony Orchestra; Henze** (Deutsche Grammophon 449 861-2; 2 CDs).

This mid-price symphony set, conducted by the composer, gives you a fair slice of his best music. The sixth symphony is the problem piece, tending towards a rather stale political attitudinizing, but the set is well worth having for a concise history of Henze's musical development up until the Cuban years.

O Symphony No. 7: City of Birmingham Symphony Orchestra; Rattle (EMI CDC754 762-2; with *Barcarola Per Grande Orchestra*).

The finest single Henze recording is Simon Rattle's amazing performance of the *Symphony No. 7* and the *Barcarola*, recorded live in Birmingham. These are perfect interpretations of frequently complex and always rich music – Rattle brings total conviction to the four contrasting dance move-

ments that make up the symphony, and manages the sweep of the *Barcarola* with real panache.

THE STRING QUARTETS

Henze once remarked that the string quartet "should at least lean towards a reflection of the demands of classical music", and his own quartets are some of Henze's most obviously coherent works. The first two, from 1947 and 1952, are rather hard-boiled – neo-classical and serial works respectively. The series picks up considerably with the sudden rush of three quartets in 1975–77 commissioned by the Schwetzingen festival. Much of their musical material derives from Henze's opera *We come to the River*, and all three were written in memoriam: the third, a single-movement work of a burnished intensity, was dedicated to Henze's mother; the fourth, a more densely argued work with a heart-rending slow movement, to the left-wing Chilean musician Victor Jara; while the fifth, the most episodic and pithy of the three, commemorates Benjamin Britten.

⊙ String Quartets Nos. 1–5: Arditti Quartet (Wergo WER 60114/5-50; 2 CDs).

It's a mark of fashion, or maybe of the composer's prolific output, that there's only one available recording of these rewarding works. The Ardittis are on predictably good form: in particular, they eloquently express the intensely elegiac mood of the fourth quartet, with its long and beautiful slow movement. The recording is, as is usual with Wergo, rather dry but well projected.

HILDEGARD OF BINGEN

(1098–1179)

The tenth child of a noble family, Hildegard of Bingen was sent, at the age of 8, to live in an enclosed cell with the anchoress Jutta at the Benedictine monastery of Disibodenberg in southern Germany. Jutta died in 1136 and Hildegard became the leader of the small group of nuns attached to the monastery. Between 1147 and 1150, against the wishes of her abbot, she left with her eighteen nuns and her secretary – the monk Volmar – to found an independent convent on the Rupertsberg near Bingen and remained there for the rest of her life.

Hildegard was an ecstatic mystic, and from 1141 she had a series of 26 visions which were dictated to Volmar and recorded in a book, *Scivias* (Know the Ways). The language of these visions, and of the religious poetry that she set to music, is highly personal and full of startling images, both apocalyptic and sensual – "When I was forty-two years and seven months old, the heavens were opened and a blinding light of exceptional brilliance flowed through my entire brain. And so it kindled my whole heart and breast like a flame, not burning but warming." The widespread fame Hildegard achieved during her lifetime – she was known as the "Sybil of the Rhine" – was due not so much to her music as to her intellect and influence. She led four preaching missions throughout Germany and her many correspondents included two popes, the Holy Roman Emperor Frederick Barbarossa (whom she berated for failing to reply promptly) and the powerful head of the Cistercian order, St Bernard of Clairvaux. As well as two more books of mystical writings she produced important works on natural history (*Physica*) and medicine (*Causae et Curae*) and a secret language (probably used by her nuns). Much of her work centres on a notably feminine theology, celebrating the female figures of the Virgin Mary, Ecclesia (the community of the church) and Sapientia (holy wisdom). After her death she was considered for, but never achieved, canonization.

SYMPHONIA HARMONIAE

In the 1150s Hildegard gathered together her 77 liturgical songs (antiphons, responsories, sequences and hymns) into a collection which she called *Symphonia harmoniae, caelestium revelationum* (Symphony of the Harmony of Heavenly Revelations) and which were used for worship at the convent. The word "Symphonia" signified for her not just the harmonious combination of different musical sounds but also the divine harmony of the cosmos, and she saw the act of making music as a union between the physical and the spiritual that brought the participant closer to the divine: "Words symbolize the humanity of the son of God but music symbolizes his divinity." Hildegard's musical language has the same inspired quality as her poetry. It is not based on the traditional for-

mulas of plainchant but consists of freely composed single melodic lines using frequent embellishments and a wide melodic range to convey a lyrical and sensual quality.

⊙ A Feather on the Breath of God: Gothic Voices; Page (Hyperion CDA 66039).

This pioneering recording first appeared in 1984 and remains one of the best introductions to Hildegard's music, with all the singers conveying a powerful sense of joy and spontaneity. Page varies male and female voices, solo and ensemble singing, to produce an absorbing collection of hymns and sequences from the *Symphonia*. That there is so much interest in Hildegard's music today is largely due to this recording.

⊙ Canticles of Ecstasy: Sequentia; Thornton (Deutsche Harmonia Mundi 05472 77320).

Under the direction of Barbara Thornton, Sequentia are in the process of recording all Hildegard's music. This CD, the third of the five released to date, consists of antiphons, responsories and sequences dedicated to the Virgin Mary and the Holy Spirit. Thornton's all-female singers bring a passionate, soaring intensity to the music, accompanied in places by fiddles and harps.

⊙ 11,000 Virgins – Chants for the Feast of St Ursula: Anonymous 4 (Harmonia Mundi HMU 907200).

St Ursula, who was said to have been martyred with 11,000 companions in Cologne, seems to have had a special significance for Hildegard, who wrote several works for her feast day. Anonymous 4's recording is based on those works, which they have interspersed with chants from other sources to recreate something of their liturgical context. The singing is characteristically resonant yet always retains an exquisite purity.

PAUL HINDEMITH

(1895–1963)

Paul Hindemith was one of the twentieth century's greatest musical polymaths, equally adept as a string player, conductor, theorist and composer. His style was similarly varied, ranging from the dense Expressionism of his early one-act operas to the sinewy contrapuntalism of his neo-Baroque maturity. Like several German composers during the interwar period, Hindemith saw himself as an opponent of bourgeois culture, with a political commitment to the idea of making "useful" music (*Gebrauchsmusik*) that was direct and accessible ("for people with ears my stuff is really easy to grasp"), and throughout his life he wrote regularly and extensively for amateurs. His standing as one of the seminal figures of modern music was partly undermined by his extraordinary facility (it took him less than six hours to write *Trauermusik* to commemorate George V's death) and by his stylistic diversity, but if his reputation sharply declined at his death it has undergone a steady reappraisal since the late 1980s.

Hindemith came from a poor, working-class background but his father, recognizing his children's talent, had them coached in music. Between 1909 and 1914 Paul studied at the Hoch Conservatory in Frankfurt and then, at the start of the war, got a job at the Frankfurt Opera orchestra and the position of second violinist in the string quartet of his teacher, Adolf Rebner. It was while at the Frankfurt Opera that Hindemith came to the attention of the conductor Fritz Busch, who was looking for new operas by up-and-coming composers. Busch gave the premieres of Hindemith's first two operas, *Mörder, Hoffnung der Frauen* (Murder, Hope of Women) and *Das Nusch-Nuschi* at Stuttgart in 1921. Both were extreme works: the first a setting of a violent play by the Expressionist painter Oscar Kokoschka, the second containing a castration scene. Busch drew the line at conducting Hindemith's third one-act opera, *Sancta Susanna*, which centred on the sexual fantasies of a young nun.

Such shock tactics made Hindemith's name but in the 1920s he began to review his musical language, gradually developing a more disciplined style based on Baroque composers like J.S. Bach, which first appeared in *Kammermusik No.1* of 1921 and can be heard in his fourth opera *Cardillac.* His ability to startle, however, had not deserted him: *Neues vom Tage* (News of the Day, 1929) had a scene featuring a woman in bath (which upset Hitler) as well as a fashionable jazz element to the score. Hindemith then undertook another change of direction, writing a series of staged cantatas (including *Lehrstück*, with a polemical text by Brecht) in which thinly disguised political messages were set to archly neo-Baroque music. In 1929 he visited London for the first time, where his friend William Walton (see p.469) engaged him as soloist at the first performance of Walton's *Viola Concerto*; in 1930 he returned to give the premiere of his own *Viola Concerto.*

In 1933, with Hitler's rise to power, Hindemith began work on *Mathis der Maler* (Mathis the Painter), an opera based upon the life of the painter Matthias Grünewald (c.1460–1528) during a time of bitter and violent struggles between Catholics and Lutherans. It had to wait a long time to reach the stage, but in March 1934 Wilhelm Furtwängler – a champion of Hindemith's music – conducted the first performance of the *Mathis der Maler Symphony*, three interludes extracted from the full score. Its success was immediate but the authorities – in particular Hitler – expressed their anger at the subject matter. In November, Furtwängler defended the music and its composer in an open letter, but the controversy resulted in the banning of the symphony and the opera, and, ultimately, to Hindemith's departure for Turkey, where he helped establish a music school. Upon his return, the Nazis were better disposed towards him, but worryingly "demonstrative" applause at the first performance of his new *Violin Sonata* in 1936 led to a ban on all Hindemith's work.

After another brief spell in Turkey, Hindemith returned to Germany to resign from his post, and left for America. In 1938 *Mathis* was staged in Zurich, but its production was never reported in the German press. In 1940 he was appointed visiting professor at Yale and head of advanced composition at Tanglewood, where he taught Leonard Bernstein (see p.60). After the war his music again began to circulate in Germany, and his fiftieth birthday was marked by numerous performances. The majority of his remaining years were spent teaching in America and Switzerland, devoting ever less time to composition.

MATHIS DER MALER SYMPHONY

Mathias Grünewald was a German painter whose work – most famously the *Isenheim Altarpiece* – is characterized by intensely heightened colour and graphic depictions of physical suffering. In the early years of the twentieth century he had become something of a talismanic figure for, in particular, Expressionist artists. In his opera about the painter, Hindemith clearly intended his audience to draw parallels with their own time, describing Mathis as a man "plagued by the devilish torments of a doubting, seeking soul, who experiences. . . the breakdown of a new era". *Mathis der Maler* is a powerful, if somewhat prolix, work and, though two complete recordings exist, you're best advised to listen first to the *Mathis der Maler Symphony* – arguably the composer's masterpiece. Completed before the opera, in order to give something for Furtwängler to take on a planned tour with the Berlin Philharmonic, the symphony was banned by the Nazis as degenerate. This might seem odd, in view of the fact that the music represents a distinct move back towards traditional melody rather than away from it, but the symphony was incriminated by the antiwar message of the opera, and its depiction of the corruption of power. Each of the symphony's three movements – *The Angelic Concert*, *The Entombment* and *The Temptation of St Anthony* – represents a panel from the *Isenheim Altarpiece*, a work which in the opera is presented as the distillation of the peasants' hatred of their lords. The final movement, and in particular its brass chorale, is one of Hindemith's most sensational achievements.

O San Francisco Symphony Orchestra; Blomstedt
(Decca 421 523-2; with *Symphonic Metamorphosis; Trauermusik*).

This recording is something of a bench mark. Blomstedt has an unmatched empathy for Hindemith's inner torment, and the San Francisco Orchestra respond with amazing sensitivity, revealing layers of inner voices that are commonly ignored. The accompanying pieces are equally fine. *Symphonic Metamorphosis of Themes by Weber* is one of Hindemith's most inventive and entertaining orchestral scores. It arose from a commission, in 1940, to compose a ballet based on the music of Weber. Hindemith began, then pulled out of the project, but returned to the idea three years later, producing a set of transformations that are considerably more rewarding than the originals.

REQUIEM FOR THOSE WE LOVE

Hindemith's *Requiem* was composed in 1946 as a lament for President Roosevelt and the victims of World War II. In tribute to his adoptive country during the war years, Hindemith took the text not from the Latin Mass but from Walt Whitman's great elegy for the dead of the American Civil War, *When Lilacs Last in the Door-yard Bloom'd*. The *Requiem* displays Hindemith's great technical expertise as a composer (there are fugues, marches and even a passacaglia), but is far from being a didactic display of classical orthodoxy (there's enough of that in the chamber music) – everything here is subjugated to deeply felt personal expression. The sonorous opening prelude, in which heavy brass chords suggest the tolling of bells, is occasionally performed separately, but you should hear the work complete – it's one of those rare twentieth-century scores that can invoke the unqualified spiritual devotion of earlier centuries without seeming phoney.

O De Gaetani, Stone; Atlanta Symphony Orchestra; Shaw (Telarc CD 80132).

Hindemith's own fine recording of the *Requiem* is not currently available on CD but this is the sort of music that demands the clarity of digital sound anyway. Robert Shaw, the conductor of this performance, commissioned the *Requiem* for the Collegiate Chorale of New York and his detailed knowledge and deep sympathy for the work is apparent in every bar.

KAMMERMUSIK

Kammermusik literally means "chamber music", which the seven works of that name written by Hindemith in the 1920s clearly are not. The first is a suite for twelve solo instruments, the other six are concertos – all with different solo instruments. They were written for a festival of contemporary chamber music, and mark the start of a new phase in Hindemith's development in which he strove to translate some of the dynamism, clarity and contrapuntal vigour of Baroque orchestral music into modern form. Hindemith's youthful delight in shocking bourgeois taste is still to the fore in *Kammermusik No. 1*, the scoring of which includes parts for siren, accordion and a canister of sand. The first two movements are dominated by edgy motor rhythms, which are followed by a haunting slow movement whose spare scoring recalls the Stravinsky of *The Soldier's Tale*. The last movement, the longest, is a swirling rush of energy, culminating in the quotation of a contemporary foxtrot by the trumpet and an ensuing wail from the siren.

O Kammermusik Nos. 1, 4 & 5: Blacher; Christ; Berlin Philharmonic Orchestra; Abbado (EMI CDC5 56160-2; with violin and viola concertos).

Scintillating and spirited performances from the BPO under Abbado are given an added dimension by the EMI engineers, who provide a wonderfully clear and open sound. Abbado points up the quicksilver wit of *Kammermusik No. 1* rather than making it sound strident as do many conductors. The rest of the disc contains two rather mellow concertos: *No. 4* for violin, and *No. 5* for what was by then (1927) Hindemith's own instrument, the viola. If you want to go on to explore the complete *Kammermusik*, go for the Decca set, conducted by Riccardo Chailly.

THE VIOLA SONATAS

Hindemith trained as a violinist but by 1919 the viola was his instrument of choice. Two years later he was the viola player of the Amar-Hindemith Quartet (later the Amar Quartet) which had been founded to give the first performance of his *String Quartet No. 2*. Hindemith raised the profile of an instrument with a lowly reputation, and was much in demand as a soloist for other composers' works as well as his own. His eight viola sonatas (four for viola alone and four accompanied by the piano) contain his most personal voice, and two, in particular, are among his finest works. The *Sonata for Viola and Piano Op. 11/4*, written in 1919 (ostensibly during Hindemith's expressionist phase), has a quiet intensity and an elegiac warmth reminiscent of Vaughan Williams, above all in its opening rhapsodic Phantasie. Three years later came the Second Sonata for solo viola (Op. 25/1) and a striking change of tone. Where before the instrument's mellow sonority had been emphasized, now there is a concentration on line and contrapuntal energy, which reaches extremes in the infamous fourth movement, marked by Hindemith: "Raging tempo. Wild. Beauty of tone of secondary importance".

O Kashkashian; Levin (ECM New Series 1330/32; 2 CDs).

Kim Kashkashian, one of the finest viola virtuosos around, really has the measure of these works. There is an electricity to her playing (coupled with a ripe tone) which eclipses all other recordings. In particular, the solo sonatas have a rigour and an intensity that is truly compelling.

LUDUS TONALIS

Ludus tonalis (Tone Games, 1942) is Hindemith's finest work for the piano. Written when he was Visiting Professor of the Theory of Music at Yale University and subtitled "Studies in Counterpoint, Tonal Organisation and Piano Playing", it consists of a sequence of alternating fugues and interludes with an opening prelude mirrored by a closing postlude. The inspiration is clearly the didactic keyboard works of J.S. Bach – the *Well-tempered Clavier* and *The Art of Fugue* – and several of the twelve fugues employ traditional contrapuntal devices like inversion or stretto. But these pieces are no more dry academic excercises than are the keyboard works of Bach, and throughout there is a palpable sense of excitement at the scope for imaginative solutions which the fugue permits. There is no other twentieth-century keyboard work – with the possible exception of Shostakovich's *Preludes and Fugues* – that re-invents an archaic form with such a spirit of adventure.

⭘ Mustonen (Decca 444 803-2; with Prokofiev *Visions fugitives*).

It is unusual for a major pianist and a major record company to invest such relatively neglected music with such care and attention as Oli Mustonen and Decca do here. Mustonen approaches every piece on its own terms. His touch is remarkably varied but never heavy or percussive, and the prevailing mood is sunny with many instances of a sly puckish humour at work.

GUSTAV HOLST

(1874–1934)

Gustav Holst – an Englishman with a Swedish name – was to a large extent hampered by the period into which he was born, a period in which there was no English musical tradition from which to draw and little chance of a favourable reception for new English music. He composed only as and when he felt the urge, was rarely performed in his lifetime, and relied on classroom work for his income. Holst is one of the many composers for whom popularity was posthumous.

As a young man he was prodigiously talented, having his first opera – *Lansdown Castle* – performed in 1893. However, recognizing that the 19-year-old needed further tuition, his father then sent him to the Royal College of Music. It was while at the college that he met and became friends with Ralph Vaughan Williams, who introduced him to English folk music, a passion they shared until Holst's death in 1934 (the same year as Elgar's). Yet Holst did not respond to these folk influences as readily as his mentor, for the presence of Wagner loomed too powerfully, and a large proportion of his early music veered towards the grandeur of Wagner's operas.

Eventually he rid himself of Wagner's influence and produced a steady stream of notably original music, including the *The Planets*, an orchestral suite that gave him his only taste of acclaim. This work, and the late, grim *Egdon Heath*, show what Holst was capable of when he allowed himself to think on a large scale. Much of his music, though, was written in the certainty that professional performances would never come his way, which is one reason why so much of his output was composed for amateur and children's groups, such as those at the schools of Dulwich and St Paul's, where he spent most of his life teaching.

THE PLANETS

The Planets, Holst's most brilliantly inventive and famous score, was one of many pieces inspired by the composer's extra-musical interests. In 1913 a friend introduced him to astrology, thus sparking the idea of creating a seven-part tone poem in which the characters of each of the planets would be evoked. This often turbulent and melancholic music was first performed on September 29, 1918, and it was inevitable that *The Planets* would be perceived as an expression of the nation's collective emotions during the war years. Listening to *Mars* they heard the fury of the Somme and Paschendale, yet Holst declared that there was no programme to his orchestral suite, and in the case of this particular episode such a programme was impossible – Holst had finished the movement before August 1914.

Jupiter – source of the patriotic hymn *I Vow to Thee my Country* – is perhaps the best-known episode, but listening to *The Planets* for the first time is bound to produce several moments of strange familiarity, as this is one of the most often quoted and plagiarized scores of the twentieth century.

◑ Mitchell Choir; London Philharmonic Orchestra; Boult (EMI CDM7 64748-2).

Sir Adrian Boult gave the first performance of *The Planets* in 1918 and, sixty years later – shortly before his ninetieth year – he entered the studio to record it for the third and last time. His interpretation is coloured by intense passion but also suggests the deep reflectiveness of advancing years. Well recorded, this is a fine and moving introduction to Holst.

⭘ BBC Symphony Orchestra; Davis (Teldec 4509 94541-2; with *Egdon Heath*).

If you want a single disc of Holst's two finest orchestral works, look no further than this recording. Davis falls short of Boult's incisive interpretation, but is nonetheless highly recommendable.

EGDON HEATH

The tone poem *Egdon Heath*, composed in 1927 in homage to Thomas Hardy, was Holst's first full-scale orchestral work after *The Planets*. The music is based upon a passage from *The Return of the Native* in which the heath (a fictionalized Salisbury Plain) is described as "a place perfectly accordant with man's nature – neither ghastly, hateful, nor ugly; neither commonplace, unmeaning, nor tame; but like man, slighted and enduring; and withal singularly colossal and mysterious in its swarthy monotony". Witheringly bleak at times, this music is the polar opposite of sunny English bucolicism and Holst believed it to be his finest orchestral work.

◑ **London Philharmonic Orchestra; Boult** (Decca 444 549-2; 2 CDs; with *The Planets, The Perfect Fool – Ballet Music, St Paul's Suite, Hymn of Jesus*).

Boult excels himself in *Egdon Heath*, getting as close to the soul of the composer as one is likely to hear on record. This two-for-the-price-of-one CD set (called *The Essential Holst*) includes fine performances by Boult of *The Perfect Fool* and *The Hymn of Jesus*, a hard-driven *Planets* from Solti, and a lively account of the *St Paul's Suite* from Christopher Hogwood.

⊙ BBC Symphony Orchestra; Davis (Teldec 4509 94541-2; with *The Planets*).

In recent years Andrew Davis has become an outstanding exponent of English twentieth-century music, and this performance does full justice to the score.

ST PAUL'S SUITE

St Paul's Suite, Holst's most famous score for amateurs, was written for the orchestra of St Paul's girls' school in 1912–13. Famous for a final movement that quotes and builds upon the perennial English folk tune *Greensleeves*, it's a good-natured piece of music, with none of the depths of *The Planets* or *Egdon Heath*, but essential listening if you want an idea of Holst's range.

⊙ Academy of St Martin-in-the-Fields; Sillito (Collins COLL 1234-2; with works by Tippett, Walton and Berkeley).

The *St Paul's Suite* is simple music that demands crisp, attentive playing, and this performance under the leadership of Kenneth Sillito bristles with enthusiasm. Excellently recorded, this disc features a good selection of twentieth-century English music for strings.

ARTHUR HONEGGER

(1892–1955)

Though Honegger spent much of his life in Paris, he retained close links with the German-speaking heritage of his native Switzerland, hence the hybrid Franco-Teutonic character of much of his music. Honegger's earliest significant compositions, such as his violin sonata of 1918, were written around the time that he became one of the chic group of French composers known as Les Six (which included Milhaud and Poulenc), but his relationship with the other five was always ambiguous, chiefly because of the distinct lack of humour in his outlook – manifested particularly by Honegger's antipathy to the quirky Erik Satie, spiritual guru of Les Six. Honegger wrote at the time: "I have no taste for the fairground, nor for the music-hall, but, on the contrary, a taste for chamber music and symphonic music in its most austere form." When it came to modern French music, Honegger's preference was for Debussy, whom most of Les Six considered decidedly passé, but he was just as likely to draw upon German, Central European and Russian music for inspiration.

Honegger's opera *Antigone*, a collaborative venture with Jean Cocteau, was a disaster on stage, but early success came with the semi-dramatic biblical oratorio *Le Roi David* (1921) and a series of orchestral works including *Pacific 231*, the piece with which he's associated as strongly and unfairly as Ravel is associated with *Boléro*. From the mid-1920s he entered a very productive period, composing several dramatic works, a cello sonata and his first symphony, as well as pursuing the parallel careers of lecturer, writer, music critic and accompanist – he often appeared with his wife, the pianist Andrée Vauraborg, on international and transatlantic tours. Even though Honegger

GUUS ONG

was based in Paris, he maintained firm ties with Switzerland through his close connection with Paul Sacher, the founder and conductor of the Basle Chamber Orchestra. Sacher premiered a significant number of his works and even commissioned two symphonies, the best known being the *Symphony No. 2* (1941).

Honegger held that music required not a change in the rules but "a new player in the same game". This he duly became, producing works that were essentially a natural outgrowth from the tradition of Bach, Beethoven and Richard Strauss. Stravinsky's neo-classicism was also an important influence, and in general Honegger was a surprisingly cosmopolitan composer – his extensive output shows that he was happy to experiment with all sorts of forms, including populist ones such as jazz, which he used to great effect in the 1925 *Piano Concertino*. Characterizing himself as "an honest workman", he even tried his hand composing for the film and radio industries, most notably for two Abel Gance films, *Napoléon* (1927) and *Les Misérables* (1934).

World War II profoundly affected Honegger, whose troubled state found expression in works such as *Cris du Monde*, *Jeanne d'Arc* and the *Symphony No. 3*. After the war he could never quite shake off the depression that that conflict had brought him, and although he continued to create he frequently made it plain that he had become disillusioned with his life – "the profession of a composer is peculiar", he once wrote, "in that it is the principal activity and occupation of a man who exerts himself to produce wares for which no-one has any use". As if continuous depression were not bad enough, Honegger contracted angina on a tour of the USA in 1947, a debilitating condition from which he was never to recover.

SYMPHONIES NOS. 2 & 3

Symphony No. 2 was commissioned in 1936, but by the time Honegger had completed it World War II had begun and his mental state had completely altered. This is the work of a deeply unhappy man, full of a troubled energy that suggests the frustration of someone unable to stop (or to come to terms with) the madness that surrounds him. It is scored for strings and a trumpet, which only enters in the last movement to reinforce the chorale tune played by the first violins – a supremely moving moment.

Five years later, with the war ended, Honegger's mood was still one of despair. *Symphony No. 3* (1946) was subtitled "Liturgique", as each of its three movements is headed by a quotation from the Requiem Mass. It's the most programmatic of all his works: "I wanted to portray man's terror in the face of Divine anger – to depict the brutal, eternal feelings of persecuted tribes which are subjected to the whims of fate. . ." A clamorous and angry first movement of endless chugging strings and strident brass is followed by an Adagio (De profundis) in which a lyrical melody seems always on the point of disintegration. The finale begins even more darkly: an ominous march ("the rise of collective stupidity") builds inexorably before subsiding into a warm Mahlerian Adagio, which ends in a solo piccolo rising, bird-like, above the rest of the orchestra – a symbol of peace after the preceding gloom.

◑ **Berlin Philharmonic Orchestra; Karajan** (Deutsche Grammophon 447 435-2).

Stunning accounts of both symphonies from Karajan and the BPO, who resist the temptation to soften the rugged contours of the *Symphony No. 3* by being overly expressive. Instead, both symphonies are beautifully served by the orchestra's immaculate technical finesse – the end of the third is like emerging out of a terrible storm.

THREE SYMPHONIC MOVEMENTS

Honegger's *Three Symphonic Movements* was actually written as three separate works and that is the way it is usually performed. The first and best known, *Pacific 231* (1923), was seen at the time as the height of modernity (largely because of its subject matter). In fact it's a kind of miniature tone poem that aimed to conjure up a visual impression of ". . . the quiet turning-over of the machine at rest, the sense of exertion as it starts up, the increase in speed and then finally the emotion, the sense of passion inspired by a 300-ton train racing through the night". *Rugby* (1928) also attempted to translate extreme physical exertion ("the attacks and counters of the game"), this time through a delightful freewheeling rondo of sinewy, contrapuntal energy. The last of the three, finished in 1933, is purely abstract: a restless Allegro in which strings and brass awkwardly co-exist as two distinct battling elements, and an Adagio whose lugubrious saxophone opening and spare orchestration is reminiscent of Hindemith and Weill.

⊙ Bavarian Radio Symphony Orchestra; Dutoit (Erato 2292 45242-2; with *Symphony No. 1* and *Pastorale d'été*).

An excellent cross-section of Honegger's work is featured on this recording from the Bavarian Radio Symphony Orchestra directed by Charles Dutoit. As a counterpoint to the vividly interpreted and rumbustious *Pacific 231*, there's the highly accomplished *Symphony No. 1*, whose second movement has rarely sounded so elegantly poised as it does here, and the delightful *Pastorale d'été* – an early work of a surprisingly sensuous lyricism.

JOHANN NEPOMUCK HUMMEL

(1778–1837)

Hummel's career has many parallels with his older contemporary Beethoven. Both studied with several of the same teachers (including Salieri and Haydn), and both developed careers as virtuoso pianists. But, whereas Beethoven was a daring innovator, both as a composer and as a pianist, Hummel was essentially a conservative – which is why his relationship with Beethoven was rather uneasy, and why his music has been largely ignored since his death. This is unfortunate since at his best, particularly when writing for the piano, he is a composer of elegance and charm, with a special facility for producing ornate and lyrical melodies spun out over light and delicate accompaniments.

Hummel began his career as an infant prodigy, impressive enough to be given free lessons by Mozart. Like Mozart he was touted around Europe by an ambitious father, and it was during a trip to England in 1790 that he got to know Haydn, through whom he later obtained the position of Konzertmeister at the court of Prince Nikolaus Esterházy (Haydn was still the prince's Kapellmeister, in title if not in practice). Hummel's time there was not especially successful, but he remained at the court, on and off, until 1811 when he returned to Vienna. Thereafter his career alternates between that of a jobbing composer (Kapellmeister to the Grand-Duchy of Weimar from 1819 until his death) and a concert pianist. His piano playing epitomized the classic Viennese style, and was described by Czerny, Beethoven's most successful piano pupil, as "a modern cleanness, clarity and of the most graceful elegance and tenderness". It was a style that made Hummel, during the 1820s, one of the most celebrated performers in Europe, but the following decade he had been superseded by the more expressive and passionate playing of Romantic pianists such as Chopin and Liszt.

THE CONCERTOS

The *Trumpet Concerto* is Hummel's most-recorded work, largely because trumpet players have so limited a repertoire that they gratefully accept any halfway decent piece that comes their way. That said, it is one of the liveliest concertos for the instrument, with a lyrically wistful slow movement and a virtuosic last movement. Even better are the concertos Hummel wrote for his own instrument, the piano. These are bravura works, written to show off Hummel's pianistic skills, especially his ability to play long highly ornamented melodies. They may not be as poetic as Chopin's two concertos (on which they exerted a very powerful influence) but they are better orchestrated and far more extrovert works, whose neglect over the years is hard to understand.

⊙ Trumpet Concerto: Hardenberger; Academy of St Martin-in-the-Fields; Marriner (Philips 420 203-2; with concertos by Haydn, Hertel and Stamitz).

Håkan Hardenberger plays all four concertos on this CD with astonishing technical expertise and an enormous amount of flair – you would never have believed a trumpet could be made to sound so light. His articulation is always exceptionally clear and bright, and there is wit and warmth in his playing of the Hummel, particularly in the way he rattles through the ebullient last-movement rondo.

⊙ Piano Concertos in A Minor and B Minor: Hough; English Chamber Orchestra; Thomson (Chandos CHAN 8507).

The success of Stephen Hough's recording of the two piano concertos has done much to re-establish Hummel's reputation. He tackles the amazingly difficult solo parts not just with ease but with a great deal of artistry, shaping the music's sometimes abrupt transitions from boldness to lyricism with delicacy and style. The A minor concerto is marginally the better work, energetic and exciting, with a breathtaking last-movement coda.

ENGELBERT HUMPERDINCK

(1854–1921)

Humperdinck's masterpiece, *Hänsel und Gretel*, is a fairy-tale opera that's emphatically not for children. Operas with supernatural themes had dominated German opera since the days of Weber (see p.471), but Humperdinck gave these subjects a new gravity by turning the harmony, orchestration and mythic power of Wagner's operas to the service of the fairy-tale. Lightening the ponderousness of his master's music with the use of folk-style music, he perpetuated the Wagner line while taking it to a more populist level.

Humperdinck was a highly gifted child and began composing operas before formal studies at Cologne University, where he won dozens of prizes. It was there that he fell under the spell of Wagner's music, joining a Wagnerite student society in Munich called The Order of the Grail. He met the man himself in Naples in 1880 and was invited to Bayreuth to help with preparations for the first performance of *Parsifal* in 1881–82. After Wagner's death in the following year, Humperdinck returned to Cologne, worked for the music publishers Schott, then tried his hand at teaching and music criticism. In 1890 he returned to composition and three years later Humperdinck's friend and champion Richard Strauss – then the *enfant terrible* of German music – conducted the first performance of *Hänsel und Gretel* in Weimar. The opera's popularity was enormous, and it made the composer a house-hold name in Germany almost overnight. (The reception abroad was initially less rapturous; the English impresario Augustus Harris hardly helped when he introduced the opera to an American audience as "the wonderful work of this great composer Pumpernickel".) The royalties from *Hänsel und Gretel* allowed Humperdinck to devote the remaining years of his life to composition, his major later achievement being *Königskinder* (Royal Children), first performed at the New York Met in 1910. At his death he was acknowledged as one of the last great Romantic composers, through whom the line of Beethoven could be traced through Wagner and on to Richard Strauss.

◑ **Music from Hänsel und Gretel; Königskinder; Dornröschen and The Blue Bird: Bamberg Symphony Orchestra; Rickenbacher** (CUV 5 61257-2).

This CD is the best introduction to Humperdinck if you don't feel ready to jump into one of the full-length operas. It contains the best-known orchestral passages from *Hänsel*, as well as excerpts from *Dornröschen* (Sleeping Beauty), his ballet *The Blue Bird*, and *Königskinder.*

HÄNSEL UND GRETEL

Humperdinck's first opera began as a commission from his sister – she asked him to write music for a children's play that she'd adapted from the famous story by the Brothers Grimm. The resulting three-act opera has been a mainstay of the Christmas operatic season since its first performance. Described by Richard Strauss as "a masterpiece of the highest quality", it was translated into some twenty languages within a couple of decades of its premiere, and in 1923 became the first opera ever to be broadcast live on radio. Combining the artless charm of German folk songs with a Wagnerian orchestral magnificence, it brings the natural and supernatural worlds vividly to life, particularly in the interludes of the *Witch's Ride* (shades of the *Ride of the Valkyries*) and *Dream Pantomime*.

O Larmore, Ziesak, Behrens, Weikl, Schwarz; Tolz Boys' Choir; Bavarian Radio Symphony Orchestra; Runnicles (Teldec 4509-945492; 2 CDs).

There are several fine recordings currently available from which to choose, and yet many are let down by the two main singers failing to sound anything but operatic. You must be convinced that Hänsel and Gretel are children or the opera doesn't work. This is where Jennifer Larmore and Ruth Ziesak excel: they may not give the most polished performances, but they convince. They receive fine and sumptuous support from Donald Runnicles.

⊙ Grümmer, Schwarzkopf, Metternich, Schürhoff; Bancroft's School Choir; Philharmonia; Karajan (EMI CMS7 69293-2; 2 CDs).

It would be perverse not to recommend Karajan's 1953 *Hänsel und Gretel*, a performance famed for his insight into the symphonic texture of the orchestral score. Elizabeth Grümmer's Hänsel is an equally remarkable achievement, and remains one of the most beautiful vocal performances ever recorded, rather overshadowing the wispily self-conscious Gretel of Elisabeth Schwarzkopf.

CHARLES IVES

(1874–1954)

Charles Ives was one of the most extraordinary innovators Western music has produced, and an equally fascinating man – for years he led a double life, working as a highly successful insurance agent by day, and as a composer by night. His music uses collage, atonality, polytonality, dissonance, quarter tones, asymmetrical rhythms and elements of jazz and ragtime – a panoply of devices that anticipated many of the experiments of Stravinsky, Debussy, Schoenberg, Berg and Webern, before some of them had written their first note. Apart from his wife and a handful of friends and contemporaries, no one understood what he was up to for years, but Ives could not care less. Composing in virtual seclusion, he went on following his instincts until he stopped writing in his fifties.

GUUS ONG

Almost every work he wrote contains quotes from the tunes, patriotic songs, hymns and marches he heard while growing up in Danbury, where he received a highly unorthodox musical education from his army bandleader father. He became an intensely patriotic man, whose adoration of his country was often expressed by referring back to his happy Connecticut childhood. Ives had a virtually photographic memory and everything he heard and saw as a child made a lasting impression on him – nothing more so than a baseball rally he once attended, where two marching bands met head on, each playing totally different music. Ives was so entranced by the sound that in adulthood the juxtaposition of different musics became a favourite compositional ploy.

Despite moments of wistfulness and tenderness in works like the *Symphony No. 3*, *The Unanswered Question* and *Three Places in New England*, Ives did not write pretty music, the sort admired by the conventional public. His hardy background gave him an aversion to "cissy sounds", and his opinions on many revered figures were not flattering – Chopin he considered to be "soft . . . with a skirt on", while Mozart was "effeminate". He was a musical Ernest Hemingway – where he came from people "got up and said what they thought regardless of the consequences". Allied to this forthrightness was an earthy idealism, central to which was the belief that art should become part of the fabric of humanity; he looked forward to the day when "every man, while digging his potatoes, will breathe his own Epics, his own Symphonies (Operas if he likes)". It's no wonder that he became a hero to America's twentieth-century musicians. Every marginalized composer has at some time or another taken courage from his bold and stoically independent stance, epitomized in his declaration that "the impossibilities of today are the possibilities of tomorrow".

ORCHESTRAL MUSIC

If Gustav Mahler had lived a little longer he might well have put Ives on the musical map decades before the old man received his long overdue recognition. Evidently Mahler had come across a score of Ives's *Symphony No. 3* (1901–04) towards the end of his tenure as conductor of the Metropolitan Opera and the New York Philharmonic, and had copied it out ready to perform when he returned to Vienna. It was not to be. The third was indeed to be the first of Ives's symphonies to receive a complete performance, but that was not until April 5, 1946 in New York. To Ives's immense surprise and satisfaction it took the Pulitzer prize. One of his most popular symphonic works, it is based on music he had played as a young organist at the Central Presbyterian Church in New York, using favourite hymns like *What a friend we have in Jesus* to build the outer movements' melodic and harmonic structures. The end result is a highly ingratiating piece, which is by turns gentle, jaunty and devotional in mood.

In 1906 Ives wrote what has a claim to be his watershed piece, *The Unanswered Question*, the first composition in which he juxtaposed contrasting groups of instruments, each having its own distinctive style. Described as a "Cosmic Landscape", *The Unanswered Question* is a symbolic drama in which the "Perennial Question of Existence" is asked seven times by a solo trumpet against a background of muted offstage strings that represent "the Silences of the Druids – Who Know, See and Hear Nothing". Four woodwinds are unleashed to seek "the Invisible Answer", but to no avail, and they leave the scene before the trumpet reiterates the question for the last time.

The ten years following *The Unanswered Question* were marked by feverish activity. One of the classic works produced in this decade was *Three Places in New England* (1903–14), the second part of which – *Putnam's Camp* – is one of the most celebrated instances of Ives's love of clashing sounds, with a wild march full of duff notes and players missing the beat. This section is preceded by a piece subtitled *Col. Shaw and His Coloured Regiment*, a memorial to America's first black army company, taking the form of a highly effective dreamlike blues, spiced with dissonant harmonies. The final part, *The Housatonic at Stockbridge*, was inspired by Ives's memory of an autumn walk he and his wife took soon after they were married; it's a stunning piece, memorable for the way it sets a simple folk tune against a turbulent orchestral texture and then, at the end, fades into silence.

○ Symphony No. 3; The Unanswered Question; Three Places in New England: Saint Louis Symphony Orchestra; Slatkin (RCA 09026-61222-2; with other Ives pieces).

When it comes to the interpretation of robust American music there are few American conductors to match what Leonard Slatkin brings to a performance. He takes hold of Ives's more wildly extravagant moments in the *Three Places in New England* and, rather than taming them, actually heightens the electric charge. By the same token the poetry of *The Unanswered Question* and the folksy imagery of *Symphony No. 3* are brought out with remarkable warmth and finesse.

LEOŠ JANÁČEK

(1854–1928)

Although he was born halfway through the nineteenth century, Janáček's best music belongs decisively to the twentieth. His finest works – the last four operas, the *Sinfonietta*, *Glagolitic Mass*, *The Diary of One Who Disappeared* and the two string quartets – were composed in an astonishing burst of creativity in his last decade, and they are among the most impressive and accessible pieces of the last hundred years, distinguished by terse dramatic power, emotional lyricism, eccentric orchestration and rhythmic bite.

Janáček was the fifth of nine children born into a poor teacher's family in Hukvaldy, northern Moravia. He was educated in Brno, the Moravian capital, and spent most of his life there – the National Theatre in Brno premiered the operas that are the basis of his reputation, and the Czechs' reluctance to place him alongside their beloved Smetana and Dvořák is perhaps due to his being perceived as too Moravian.

As with so many central European composers, folk music was the liberating ingredient in his career. In 1888 he set off on a tour of northern Moravia with the ethnographer Frantisek Bartos, and this intense encounter with the indigenous culture led to a decisive change in his compositional style. Certain folk tunes made their way into his orchestral and choral compositions, but more generally the short, irregular melodic phrases of Moravian music became integral to Janáček's idiosyncratic constructions, while echoes of folk ensembles influenced his distinctive orchestral sound.

Janáček's work can be seen as a fight against the German domination of his country, and the foundation of the Czechoslovak republic in 1918 was a factor behind the amazing creativity of his last years. But as well as being a Czech patriot, he was also an ardent believer in a pan-Slavic culture – he learned Russian, visited that country twice, sent his daughter to study in St Petersburg and founded a Russian club in Brno. In 1900 he conducted a concert featuring dances from the various Slav nations, for which he wrote a *Serbian Kolo* and *Russian Cossack Dance*. The Russian writers Gogol, Ostrovsky, Tolstoy and Dostoevsky inspired some of his greatest works (the libretto of *From the House of the Dead* was translated by Janáček from Dostoevsky), and the monumental *Glagolitic Mass*, with its text in Old Church Slavonic, can be heard as a sort of manifesto for a pan-Slavism.

LEBRECHT COLLECTION

Janáček and his wife, in the early days of their ill-fated marriage

The other dominating feature of much of Janáček's work is its erotic charge. His marriage, to a pupil ten years his junior, was never very successful – they were formally separated in 1917, when Janáček had an affair with Gabriela Horvátová, singer in the Prague production of *Jenůfa*. Soon afterwards he began the crucial relationship of his last decade when at the Moravian spa town of Luhačovice he met Kamila Stösslová, a married woman half his age. Janáček conceived an all-consuming but unreciprocated passion for Kamila, to whom he wrote over 700 letters, the most passionate ones being written almost daily in the last sixteen months of his life. (They have recently been published in English, edited and translated by John Tyrrell.) *The Diary of One Who Disappeared* was the first work to be inspired by Kamila, who was then transformed into the heroines of three of his finest operas, *Kát'a Kabanová*, *The Cunning Little Vixen* and *The Makropulos Case*. However, the most direct expression of their relationship is his *String Quartet No. 2 "Intimate Letters"*, one of the most intimate pieces of music ever written. Less than six months after it was composed, Janáček died of pneumonia from a chill he caught while the aloof Kamila was staying with him in Hukvaldy.

JENŮFA

The creation of *Jenůfa* lasted nine years (1894–1903), a period in which his whole musical style was undergoing major changes. In addition to finding a way to fully integrate folk music into large-scale pieces, Janáček was abandoning the idea of opera divided into individual set pieces in favour of through-composed dramatic form. He had also become passionately interested in the melodies of everyday speech, and kept a diary in which he noted down the way people spoke in musical notation. None of these "speech melodies" were actually incorporated directly into his music, but they honed his dramatic vocal writing so that it approached the ideal that he had defined – "to compose a melodic curve which will, as if by magic, reveal immediately a human being in one definite phase of his existence".

Jenůfa was performed in Brno in 1904 and revived several times, but, had Janáček died before 1916, when the opera finally made it to Prague, he would be no more than a footnote in the history of Czech music. When *Jenůfa* was accepted in Prague in 1916 it was on condition that it was revised and re-scored by the artistic director of the National Theatre, Karel Kovařovic. Ironically, it was this watered-down version, with its late-Romantic gloss, that launched Janáček's spectacular international career and his climactic creative surge.

The play on which the opera is based, *Její pastorkyna* (Her Foster-Daughter) by Gabriela Preissová, is a slice-of-life drama set in a Moravian village, a world Janáček had come to know deeply through his folk-song collecting. The plot has a brutal simplicity that places it poles apart from the cheery bucolicism of Smetana's *Bartered Bride* (see p.395): two men, Steva and Laca, are rivals for Jenůfa's affection; she gets pregnant by the former, the unreliable one, but is truly loved by the latter; Steva moves on to another girl, whereupon Jenůfa's stepmother drowns the baby; finally Jenůfa and Laca are reconciled, in one of the great moments of opera.

Janáček's absorption of Moravian folk music underpins the entire score, which has a rough-edged veracity that's typical of his mature work, while the use of widely spaced instrumental writing prefigures the more extreme contrasts of his later works. Janáček very often writes for only the high and low strings, leaving out the middle registers for a more unsettling effect – there's a series of incisive chords like this in the prelude to the second act, which were smoothed out in the Kovařovic version. Where a shade more emotional warmth is required, however, he fills out the string texture to cover the full spectrum.

⊙ Söderström, Ochman, Dvorsky, Randová, Popp; Vienna Philharmonic; Mackerras (Decca 414 483-2; 2 CDs).

Mackerras's Decca series of Janáček's operas is unsurpassed, and this premiere recording of Janáček's original score is magnificent in every way. In many ways it's the stepmother that dominates the drama, and Eva Randová brings out every nuance of this tyrannical yet well-meaning character. Elizabeth Söderstrom and the two male leads are also finely cast, while the orchestral playing is superb.

KÁT'A KABANOVÁ

Kát'a Kabanová, a story of adultery in a tyrannical family setting, was written in 1919–21 and is based on *The Storm* by the Russian playwright Ostrovsky – one of several works Janáček based on Russian literature. His love for Kamila Stösslová is crucial to the psychological portrait of Kát'a, whose love for another man can be read as Janáček's wish-fulfilment. The action is concise and dramatic: Kát'a is reluctantly attracted to Boris, with whom she has an affair while her husband is away, then confesses to her mother-in-law (another strong female character) and is driven to commit suicide in the river. This is probably Janáček's best-constructed work, and it contains some quite extraordinary love music. The opening is especially fine – a brooding orchestral prelude in which the melodic line keeps turning in on itself before reaching the glorious melody that is associated with Kát'a throughout the opera. The timpani then burst in ominously, to return at decisive moments later in the opera.

⊙ Benackova, Straka, Randova, Pecková, Knopp; Czech Philharmonic Orchestra; Mackerras (Supraphon SU 3291-2632; 2 CDs).

This is Mackerras's second recording of *Kát'a*, made in 1987, more than twenty years after the first. This time it's an exclusively Czech affair with a rawer more urgent sound from the orchestra and in Gabriela Benackova's Kát'a a more febrile performance than Söderström's.

⊙ Söderström, Dvorský, Kniplová, Márová, Krejcík, Vienna Philharmonic Orchestra; Mackerras (Decca 421 852-2; 2 CDs; with *Capriccio* and *Concertino*).

Made in 1976, this was the first of Mackerras's Janáček opera recordings, and it perfectly evokes the claustrophobic world of this piece. Söderström is a more passively tragic figure than Benackova, and the warm string sound of the VPO slightly blunts the terrible impact. Apart from that there's little to choose between these two fine recordings.

THE CUNNING LITTLE VIXEN

Kamila Stösslová was again an inspiration for *The Cunning Little Vixen*, this time as self-sacrificing wife and mother – but an equally crucial inspiration was the countryside around his native village of Hukvaldy, where Janáček bought a house in 1921, shortly before starting work on this opera. Derived from a regular cartoon strip that appeared in a Brno newspaper, *The Cunning Little Vixen* is the beguiling anthropomorphic tale of a young vixen called Bystrouška, who is caught and raised by a gamekeeper. She kills his chickens, escapes, finds a mate, and is finally shot by a poultry dealer; at the end of the opera the gamekeeper is found back in the forest, surrounded by a troop of animals including a young vixen, Bystrouška's cub. Conjuring a broad vision of life's richness and transience, and nature's capacity for renewal, *The Cunning Little Vixen* shows Janáček at his most sumptuous and lyrical.

⊙ Popp, Jedlička, Randová; Vienna Philharmonic Orchestra; Mackerras (Decca 417 129-2; 2 CDs).

Full of luscious orchestral interludes, this is probably the most entrancing Janáček opera, and this recording of it is another triumph from Mackerras. Lucia Popp is immensely lively and characterful in the title role, and the Czech supporting cast is very fine indeed.

THE MAKROPULOS CASE

After the erotic passion of *Kát'a* and the fresh vitality of the *Vixen*, Janáček completed his trilogy on different aspects of women with the creation of the captivating, beautiful and cold Emilia Marty, protagonist of *The Makropulos Case* (1925). The opera is based on a dark comedy by Karel Čapek about a woman who has lived three hundred years thanks to an alchemical potion. She makes an uncanny intervention in a long-running court and property dispute, having been the mistress of one of the dispute's protagonists a century back, and the plot gets even more complicated as she begins to exert a powerful fascination on the men now involved. Of course, this portrait of a woman insensitive to the desires of those around her is to an extent a portrait of Kamila.

Lacking much in the way of conventional dramatic excitement, the opera gains its momentum almost purely from its music, which propels the action through the subtle development of a mosaic of motifs and ideas. *The Makropulos Case* is a very powerful piece, but one that reveals itself slowly, by an almost organic process.

⊙ Söderström, Dvorský, Zítek; Vienna Philharmonic Orchestra; Mackerras (Decca 430 372-2; 2 CDs; with *Lachian Dances*).

The success of another recording of *The Makropulos Case* depends of course on the casting of Emilia Marty, and Elisabeth Söderström is perfect, managing to convey the vulnerability underneath the chilly exterior. This might not be first-buy Janáček, but it's another masterful set from Mackerras, and has the early orchestral *Lachian Dances* as a fill-up.

THE GLAGOLITIC MASS

For several years Janáček conducted a male choir in Brno, and choral music actually comprises the largest element of his output. His masterpiece of the genre is the *Glagolitic Mass*, a piece bursting with brassy fanfares and rhythmic energy, though it has some quieter moments of rapt contemplation. It was written at white heat in a single month in 1926, after an inspirational walk in the woods at Luhačovice, the spa where he had met Kamila. "I felt a cathedral grow out of the giant expanse of the woods," he wrote. "A flock of sheep were ringing their bells. Now I hear the voice of an arch priest in the tenor solo, a maiden angel in the soprano and in the choir – the people. The tall firs, their tips lit up by the stars, are the candles and during the ceremony I see the vision of St Wenceslas and I hear the language of the missionaries Cyril and Methodius."

The text of the *Glagolitic Mass* is written in Old Church Slavonic, and the piece is a patriotic hymn to the greatness of the Czech nation and Slavic culture. Judging by his letters to Kamila, he also imagined the piece as a celebratory wedding Mass for the two of them.

⊙ Söderström, Drobková, Livora, Novák; Czech Philharmonic; Mackerras (Supraphon 10 3575-2).

Janáček's fiendishly high solo writing means that a lot of otherwise excellent recordings of the *Glagolitic Mass* suffer from wobbly and shrieking sopranos. Elisabeth Söderström on the Charles Mackerras recording is very good indeed, and the sheer passion and idiomatic panache of the rest of the performers make this the recording to go for.

SINFONIETTA AND TARAS BULBA

Janáček's orchestral *tour de force*, and justifiably his most popular work, is the *Sinfonietta*, which was written at the same time as the *Glagolitic Mass* and is comparable in its exuberance and overall tone. Encapsulating Janáček's patriotic pride in the newly formed Czechoslovakia, it also – inevitably – has its connection with Kamila. A military band that she and Janáček heard playing in her hometown of Písek gave him the idea of the massive brass fanfares that open and close the piece. The five movements are dramatically scored and highly contrasted, but it's a remarkably coherent piece, thanks mainly to a melodic motif that underpins each part.

Taras Bulba is an exceptionally vivid and rather gory "Rhapsody for Orchestra" which tells of the death of the Ukrainian Cossack leader Taras Bulba and his two sons in the 1628 war against the Poles. Based on the story as told by Gogol, it's in three sections: the first two evoke the battle at Dubno and the death of the two sons; the third tells of the capture of Taras and his subsequent excecution.

◑ **Vienna Philharmonic; Mackerras** (Decca 430 727-2).

Mackerras's recording of the *Sinfonietta* is rugged and highly charged, and is coupled with an equally powerful rendition of *Taras Bulba*.

THE DIARY OF ONE WHO DISAPPEARED

The first composition to emerge from Janáček's infatuation with Kamila Stösslová was the song cycle *The Diary of One Who Disappeared*, a piece which, like *The Cunning Little Vixen*, was spurred by something printed in the Brno paper *Lidové noviny* – in this instance some poems about a young man becoming infatuated with a gypsy girl and forsaking his family. The form of the work is unprecedented: it's a cycle of 22 numbers for tenor and piano, a combination joined in the middle three songs by a female chorus plus a mezzo-soprano to personify the gypsy girl, Zefka. "While writing the *Diary*," Janáček wrote to Kamila, "I thought only of you. You were Zefka!"; unsurprisingly, in view of its heavily autobiographical burden, the story is told principally through the thoughts of the young man, while the gypsy's true feelings remain ambiguous – despite an episode of lovemaking, discreetly masked by a piano solo.

○ **Keller, Wirz; Venzago** (Accord 22031-2).

The *Diary* can sound thin in comparison to the operas, but Peter Keller and the Clara Wirz make a good case for this awkwardly self-conscious work. The dusky tone of Wirz's voice is especially attractive.

STRING QUARTETS

Janáček's two string quartets are amongst the greatest ever written, containing extraordinary textures and sudden juxtapositions of contrasting ideas. The first, written in a week in 1921, is based on Tolstoy's novella *The Kreutzer Sonata*, a portrait of jealousy in a loveless marriage. It's possible to find musical correspondences to the incidents in the story, but it's better to ignore these programmatic elements and simply enjoy the outstanding lyrical and dramatic invention of the score. The same goes for the second quartet, which was written in about three weeks in 1928 and to which Janáček gave the unambiguous subtitle *Intimate Letters*. Judging by Janáček's letters to Kamila, the quartet contains depictions of specific characters and events – the stormy opening theme must represent the composer and the chilling viola reply introduces us to Kamila – but it's futile to speculate on the extra-musical meanings. The passion is what matters, and that's evident in each phrase – in Janáček's own words, "This piece was written in fire." After hearing it played he wrote: "It's a work as if carved out of living flesh. I think that I won't write a more profound and a truer one." Little more than a month later he was dead.

○ **Talich Quartet** (Supraphon 11 1354-2; with *Mládí*).

There are many fine recordings of the quartets and the Talich on Supraphon tops the bunch – the performances are exemplary and the acoustic gives a warm glow to the fantastic musical textures. This CD also contains Janáček's vivacious and exuberant wind sextet *Mládí*, composed shortly after his seventieth birthday.

PIANO MUSIC

The solo piano works of Janáček contain his most intimate and spontaneous music and, in the *Sonata 1. X. 1905 "From the Street"*, some of his greatest. The sonata's unusual title refers to the death of a Czech worker during a demonstration demanding a Czech University in the predominantly German town of Brno. The response to this tragedy is heartfelt and unmistakably Janáčekian; simple thematic material is developed improvisatorily; unexpected harmonies and changes of mood abound; scurrying sub-textural figurations suggest inner turmoil and unease. There are just two movements (a third was destroyed by just before the first performance): the first entitled "Presentiment", the second "Death". Both are extremely atmospheric: in the second a repeated dotted motif evokes a funeral procession where anger slowly mounts and then recedes.

The collection of ten short pieces, *On the Overgrown Path*, was written between 1901 and 1908. As a group they resemble Schumann's *Kinderszenen* and were partly written as a response to the death of Janáček's daughter Olga. The individual titles were added just before publication but they reinforce the themes of sadness and reminiscence. These are incredibly intense poetic miniatures, which pinpoint a mood or an image with a laconic ease. The most striking of them all is the dramatic *The Barn Owl Has Not Flown Away*, where clamorous arpeggios represent the cry of the owl – a portent of death in Czech folklore.

◑ **Sonata 1.X.1905; On an Overgrown Path; In the Mists: Firkusny** (Deutsche Grammophon 429 857-2).

Czech pianist Rudolf Firkusny plays with the authority of somebody with a deep knowledge of this music and he gets right to its heart. There is no straining after poetic effects in his playing, which is straightforward and restrained and gives a clear sense of the shape of each of the sonata's movements with no loss of intensity. Again in the miniatures a compelling urgency is achieved through the clarity of his phrasing.

ARAM KHACHATURIAN

(1903–1978)

In 1948, at the infamous conference of the Composers' Union in Moscow, Khachaturian (like his colleagues Shostakovich and Prokofiev) was denounced for the "formalist" tendencies in his music; that is, for deviating from the melodious, flag-waving jollity as prescribed by Stalin. In retrospect it's extremely difficult to see how this happened, for, with the exception of the more experimental *Symphony No. 3* (1947), his unashamedly Romantic and folk-inflected works, in which he gave international voice to the distinctive melodies and harmonies of his native Armenia, seem the ideal Soviet mixture of conservatism and nationalism. It is precisely these qualities that have seen him looked down on by Western critics (despite the popularity of several of his works), and it is true that his music, while always strong on melody, is frequently rather weak in structure and the development of ideas.

Khachaturian had shown little musical talent until his brother persuaded him to go to Moscow in 1921, where he somehow managed to gain a place at the Gnesin Music Academy to study the cello, an instrument he had never played before. By 1925 he was studying composition with Myaskovsky and making rapid progress; his first work – a dance for violin and piano – was published only a year later. His international reputation was established by his *Piano Concerto*, written in 1936, followed four years later by the *Violin Concerto*. By the close of the 1940s he had completed three symphonies, but it was two full-length ballet scores – *Gayaneh* and *Spartacus* – that brought him the most widespread attention.

Khachaturian's three symphonies lack the immediate impact of his concertos and ballets, but they all have an individual stamp. The three-movement *No. 1*, first performed in 1934, introduced a new, personal way of combining his native folk music with symphonic processes. Although having no specific programme, *No. 2* (1943) undoubtedly reflects the wartime circumstances of its composition, with its ominous bells and musical calls-to-arms suggesting the darkness, sacrifice and heroism of the USSR's "Great Patriotic War".

THE VIOLIN CONCERTO

Khachaturian's *Violin Concerto*, written in 1940 for the great Russian violinist David Oistrakh, is a brash and exuberant work completely lacking in any subtlety. The overblown orchestral writing frequently teeters on the banal and ideas often outstay their welcome. The work's saving grace is the violin part, whose insinuating and pushy charm can overcome nearly all critical resistance when in the hands of an outstanding performer. It's an exceptionally vocalized solo line, coloured by the Eastern inflections and ornamentation of Armenian folk music, and dominated by a yearning, rhapsodic quality. This is given a nocturnal sultriness in the second movement and an almost rowdy air of abandon in the third. For those who are won over by its naive energy, there will be as many who dismiss it as shameless kitsch. It won a coveted Stalin Prize in 1941.

○ **Mordkovitch; Scottish National Orchestra; Järvi** (Chandos CHAN 8918; with Kabalevsky, *Violin Concerto*).

Chandos have gone for broke with this disc: an extremely rich and detailed sound with the soloist placed well forward. Lydia Mordkovitch, a David Oistrakh pupil, is just the kind of violinist to revel in all its sensual overloads and she plays it as if it were a masterpiece.

BALLET MUSIC

Khachaturian's particular gift for brightly memorable melodies and boisterous orchestral writing is far better suited to the frequently episodic nature of ballet music, and his ballets *Gayaneh* and *Spartacus* are the works that have maintained his international reputation. *Gayaneh* is a classic example of Socialist Realism in which the epony-

K

omus heroine is a worker on a collective farm who wins the love of a Red Army commander. Filled with a sparkling array of folk-inspired tunes, its most famous episode, the manic *Sabre Dance*, has had a life of its own, even materializing as a pop single. *Spartacus*, which tells of the famous slave revolt against the Romans, though equally propagandist, has survived the collapse of communism and is still performed as a ballet. The music is very much geered to the energetic leaps of the Bolshoi's male dancers, but like *Gayaneh* it's famous for one hit tune – the surging Adagio, danced by Spartacus and his wife Phrygia, which was used as the theme music for the BBC television series *The Onedin Line*.

O Suites from Gayaneh and Spartacus: Armenian Philharmonic Orchestra; Tjeknavorian (ASV DCA 773; with *Masquerade* and Ippolitov-Ivanov's *Caucasian Sketches*).

Armenians are extremely proud of Khachaturian and this recording by Loris Tjeknavorian and an Armenian orchestra is both lively and passionately committed. Rather than play either of Khachaturian's own suites from *Spartacus*, Tjeknavorian has made his own selection in both ballets, with more of the same in the shape of five pieces from the incidental music to *Masquerade*.

ZOLTÁN KODÁLY

(1882–1967)

K

Zoltán Kodály's career was unremarkable until after his graduation from Budapest University in 1905. It was then that he encountered Béla Bartók, with whom he was to change the direction of Hungarian music. Shortly after meeting, they embarked upon a pilgrimage to collect folk songs, the first of several expeditions which helped formulate their musical identities and cement their lifelong friendship. Kodály later recalled the inspiration behind their studies: "This vision of an educated Hungary, reborn from the people, rose before us. We decided to devote our lives to its realisation." This devotion resulted in a book of Hungarian folk songs with a preface by Kodály, published in 1906, and, later that year, the premiere of his symphonic poem *Summer Evening*.

In 1908 Kodály took over the composition classes at Budapest's Liszt Academy from his own teacher, Franz Koessler, and from then on became closely involved with the formation of the musical curriculum in Hungary's schools. With Bartók, he formed a society for the promotion and performance of contemporary music, a scheme that met with official hostility and public indifference, and their attempts to promote folk song were no more successful, although the pair continued compiling information until the outbreak of war.

In 1923, however, Kodály's fortunes changed with the widespread success of his *Psalmus Hungaricus*, written for the fiftieth anniversary of the unification of Buda and Pest. Soon afterwards a contract with Universal Edition resulted in the publication of a large amount of his music. In 1926 he composed his folk-opera *Háry János*, which was followed by *The Spinning Room* (1932), a work steeped in the folklore of Transylvania. In 1933 Kodály and Bartók were requested by the Hungarian Academy of Sciences to compile a compendium of the country's folk music; with Bartók's departure for America, Kodály assumed editorial control of a project that finally reached the presses in 1951.

Kodály remained in Hungary during World War II, and after Bartók's death in 1945 was hailed as Hungary's greatest living composer, being inundated with invitations to head colleges, universities and artistic institutions, and receiving dozens of governmental decorations. Most of his remaining years were devoted to the composition of choral music and to tours as a conductor, musician and lecturer. He died happy in the knowledge that his two greatest ambitions – the publication of his books of Hungarian folk music and the introduction of daily music lessons into Hungarian schools – had been fulfilled.

Kodály remained a conservative composer throughout his life, in that he had no interest in subverting the established classical forms, and was devoted primarily to melody. Yet his music has a distinctive voice, thanks in large part to the rich mix that went into it – in addition to the folk songs of his native land, he was fascinated with Debussy, and Bach, Palestrina and Gregorian chant all became components of Kodály's sound. Kodály might lack cosmopolitan flair, but his music is an instantly enjoyable and consistently rewarding alternative to the more demanding idiom of his friend and colleague Bartók.

PSALMUS HUNGARICUS

The *Psalmus Hungaricus* represents the climactic fusion of two fundamental elements in Kodály's musical philosophy – his belief in the supremacy of the human voice, and his belief that any musical culture was dependent upon the nurture of amateur performance. He wrote a large amount of choral music for amateur societies, and *Psalmus Hungaricus* is by far the finest. It's a piece that's redolent of the spirit of Hungarian music, yet surprisingly it contains no direct folk quotations: stylistically, the chief influences are Gregorian melody, Bachian polyphony and Renaissance harmony. For all these decorous influences, *Psalmus Hungaricus* is an urgent and often barbaric composition, showing Kodály at his most thrilling.

◑ **Kozma; London Symphony Orchestra; Brighton Festival Chorus; Kertész** (Decca 433 080-2; with *Missa Brevis, Pange Lingua, Psalm 114*).

Kertész's pulsating performance is a marvellous tribute to Kodály, his friend and teacher. This is a controlled but beautifully coloured and passionate account, and the tenor Lajos Kozma gives a finely considered performance, singing with ample weight. It comes coupled with a representative array of other choral pieces.

THE CONCERTO FOR ORCHESTRA

Kodály's *Concerto for Orchestra* was composed for the Chicago Symphony Orchestra, who first performed it in 1941 – two years before they gave the premiere of Bartók's *Concerto for Orchestra*. Unlike Bartók's five-movement virtuosic score, Kodály's concerto is a one-movement, twenty-minute piece that rejects what he characterized as "false brilliance" in favour of "melancholy and uncertainty". Again, unlike Bartók's massive score, Kodály's heavily contrapuntal piece is scored for an ordinary orchestra, the only addition to standard forces being the appearance of a triangle. A tension between modernity and more folkloric rhythms and harmonies runs through the concerto, producing music of wonderful emotional intensity.

◑ **Philharmonia Hungarica; Dorati** (Decca 443 006-2; 2 CDs; with *Háry János Suite*, *Dances of Galánta*, *Dances of Marosszék*, *Peacock Variations*, *Summer Evening*, *Symphony in C*).

Antal Dorati was a great advocate of Kodály's music, recording it on several occasions. This recording of the *Concerto for Orchestra* dates from the early 1970s and is currently the only one in the catalogue. Fortunately, the performance is a very eloquent one and these two discs make a splendid introduction to Kodály's range as an orchestral composer.

THE HÁRY JÁNOS SUITE

Háry János is a Baron Münchhausen-type tale of a soldier whose fantastic adventures are, to quote the composer, "the personification of the Hungarian story-telling imagination". First produced in October 1926, it's a delightful comic opera (or, rather, a play with music), but because of the language barrier and its uneven construction it is rarely staged outside Hungary. The Kertész recording of the complete work is currently available, but it is far better to approach it through the orchestral suite that Kodály created from the opera's main ideas, a translation that secured the opera's fame. You know what you're in for right from the start, when the full orchestra explodes in a huge musical "sneeze", signifying that what follows is not to be taken too seriously. Among the ensuing episodes are a battle scene in which János single-handedly defeats Napoleon, and the representaion of a Viennese musical clock. Beautifully orchestrated and superbly constructed, the *Háry János Suite* is Kodaly's most entertaining score, the perfect follow-up for the child who has enjoyed Prokofiev's *Peter and the Wolf* or *Lt Kijé*.

◑ **Philharmonia Hungarica; Dorati** (Decca 443 006-2; 2 CDs; with *Concerto for Orchestra*, etc).

Dorati's is the kind of performance that makes it almost impossible to keep still when listening to it. The *Dances of Galánta* is no less vivid a work in its rich profusion of orchestral colour and sweeping melodies, even if there is just a hint of the tourist board in its folksiness. Similarly the *Peacock Variations* occasionally conjure up Hollywood in the way it so blatantly wears its heart on its sleeve.

THE SONATA FOR UNACCOMPANIED CELLO

The prodigious *Sonata for Unaccompanied Cello*, written in 1915, is one of the peaks of twentieth-century music for that instrument. Anyone thinking Kodály too safe a composer should listen to this. It's a *tour de force* that takes the folk tradition, in which Kodály had immersed himself so thoroughly, and gives it the kind of acerbic modern spin that you normally associate with Bartók. Every technical skill is employed – double-stopping, playing with the bow and plucking the strings at the same time, harmonics – to create a wild, improvisatory fantasy (albeit constructed as a sonata) which one moment suggests a mournful Transylvanian dance and, the next moment, Bach.

O Haimovitz (Deutsche Grammophon 445 834-2; with Britten, *Suite No. 3*; Henze, *Capriccio*; Berio, *Les Mots sont allés*).

Astonishingly enough there are sixteen performances currently listed in the catalogue, making this one of the most recorded of all Kodály's works. Some cellists play it rather formally; others as if they were a demented one-man folk band. Matt Haimovitz steers a middle course: there's a tough spontaneity to his playing and yet his technical ability is such that this never descends into wildness or imprecision.

ERICH WOLFGANG KORNGOLD

(1897–1957)

Erich Wolfgang Korngold, the son of the leading Viennese music critic, Julius Korngold, was one of the most astonishing musical prodigies of the century. At the age of 9 he wrote a cantata, *Gold*, which so impressed Gustav Mahler that he proclaimed the boy a genius and arranged for him to study with Zemlinsky (see p.484). His ballet-pantomime *Der Schneemann*, written in his thirteenth year, was premiered under Zemlinsky's baton and subsequently performed all over Austria and Germany. Both Puccini and Strauss – the dominant influences on his style – were admirers, the latter remarking that "this firmness of style, this sovereignty of form, this individual expression, this harmonic structure – one shudders with awe to realize these compositions were written by a boy."

Korngold's first two operas, *Der Ring des Polykrates* and *Violanta*, were produced in 1916 as a double bill at the Munich Staatsoper, conducted by Bruno Walter. Both were emotionally charged works employing a rich post-Wagnerian chromaticism that became even more intense for his next opera, *Die tote Stadt* (The Dead City), which is generally considered his masterpiece in the genre. *Die tote Stadt* was staged simultaneously at Cologne and at Hamburg (where Korngold was musical director) to huge acclaim.

Throughout the 1920s Korngold was involved with the renowned producer Max Reinhardt, making arrangements of operettas for him. He also wrote another opera, *Das Wunder der Heliane* (1924–26), which he considered his finest work but which was overshadowed by the extraordinary success of Ernst Krenek's jazz opera *Jonny spielt auf*. But his success in Germany was not to last. By the early 1930s the growing intensity of anti-Semitism in Germany led his publishers, Schott, to warn him that future performances of his music would be extremely difficult. In 1934 Max Reinhardt invited him to accompany him to Hollywood to work on a film version of *A Midsummer Night's Dream,* for which Korngold rescored Mendelssohn's incidental music. He returned briefly to Vienna to work on his final opera, *Die Kathrin,* before returning to Hollywood, where over the next twelve years he was to write eighteen outstandingly imaginative and atmospheric film scores, mainly for Warner Brothers, two of which –*Robin Hood* and *Anthony Adverse* – were to win him Oscars.

Arguably his American years ruined his career. Leaving Hollywood for Vienna in 1949, he was now disparaged as much for having worked in the cinema as for the old-fashioned style of his music. After the critics panned the belated Viennese performance of *Die Kathrin* (the Nazis had cancelled the 1937 production), he gave up the idea of a sixth opera and he devoted the remaining years of his life to orchestral music, including a violin concerto which was performed and recorded by Jascha Heifetz. Many of these later works employed material previously used in his film scores.

Korngold is one of several candidates for the title of "last of the great Romantics", for as a boy he brilliantly assimilated a late Romantic style from which he never later deviated. His work is full of warm and expansive melodies and the lushest of harmonies while lacking the contrapuntal adventurousness of Strauss or Pfitzner. But in the last twenty years there has been a major revival of interest in his work: *Die tote Stadt* is now staged fairly regularly and several young virtuosos have added the *Violin Concerto* to their repertoire. The hothouse emotionalism of his work will not appeal to everyone, but those unafraid to wallow will not be disappointed.

DIE TOTE STADT

Puccini declared *Die tote Stadt* to be "among the most beautiful and the strongest hope of new German music", but Korngold's masterpiece never achieved the worldwide popularity of Strauss's operas, even though the musical line dividing them is extremely thin. Perhaps it was the rather morbid subject matter, closer in spirit to Schreker, that has put people off. The story tells how the recently widowed Paul meets a dancer who resmbles his wife, but when she mocks him he eventually strangles her. Julius and Erich Korngold's adaptation of George Rodenbuch's symbolist novel *Bruges-la-Morte* retains the dreamy atmosphere of the original but relegates the brooding presence of the city to the background, making the psychological vulnerability and anguish of the protagonist its main concern. The trauma of World War I lies just beneath the surface.

The score veers between a quasi-religious profundity and a honeyed sweetness which to many ears comes dangerously close to kitsch, but Korngold marshals his huge orchestral forces with great precision, and the opera also contains some powerful melodic writing – as in the Act I aria "Gluck, das mir verblieb" (Joy sent from above), sung first by Marietta and then by Paul. This inspired episode, made famous by Lotte Lehmann and Richard Tauber, illuminates Paul's despair with wonderful clarity and is the opera's finest vocal moment.

◑ **Kollo, Neblett, Luxon, Wageman, Prey; Bavarian Radio Chorus; Munich Radio Orchestra; Leinsdorf** (RCA GD87767; 2 CDs).

This recording has never left the catalogue and, for many, it is the finest achievement of both René Kollo and Erich Leinsdorf. The tenor's voice is never under any strain, and is both smoother and darker than on almost everything else he recorded. Carole Neblett is in similarly glowing form, tapping into the sentimentality with shameless abandon. Leinsdorf is clearly in love with Korngold's sweet orchestrations – holding suspensions beyond their natural length – and he revels in the chromatic wash.

THE VIOLIN CONCERTO

Written in 1945 for Bronislav Hubermann, the *Violin Concerto* was actually premiered in 1947 by Jascha Heifetz, who became its greatest champion. It's a good example of how Korngold plundered parts of his film scores in order to create a concert work, and the insinuating, heart-tugging opening theme is indeed pure Hollywood (lifted from *Another Dawn*, in which Leslie Howard played a concert violinist). The second movement is, if anything, even more lachrymose, with a lyrical melody (from *Anthony Adverse*) and a shimmering vibraphone creating a suitably febrile atmosphere. The Rondo finale is the most distinctly American-sounding (as opposed to Hollywood) movement: a rhythmically lively opening suggests a hoedown though in fact the movement's main melody was taken from the costume drama *The Prince and the Pauper*. The critic of the *New York Sun* famously called the work "more corn than gold": it's an unfair dismissal though it is true that Korngold plays around with each of the big tunes rather than seriously developing them. It does not stop it from being a hugely enjoyable, if essentially superficial, piece.

○ **Shaham; London Symphony Orchestra; Previn** (Deutsche Grammophon 439 886-2; with Barber's *Violin Concerto*).

This is a performance that takes this concerto completely seriously as an orchestral work, rather than merely treating it as a collection of radiant moments. Balance between orchestra and soloist sounds more realistic than is usually the case, and Shaham's warm tone is held in check – he only pulls out all the stops for the really syrupy moments.

◑ **Heifetz; Los Angeles Philharmonic Orchestra; Wallenstein** (RCA 09026 61752-2; with Rozsa, *Violin Concerto*; Waxman, *Carmen Fantasia*).

Heifetz's classic recording of the *Violin Concerto* from 1953 is still one of the best available. The violin sound is recorded well forward of the orchestra, and Heifetz treats the concerto entirely as a showpiece for his talents. It's an extremely old-fashioned, vocalized reading – all throaty tone colour and delicate swoops, which tends to point up its Hollywood origins.

SYMPHONY

Korngold's *Symphony* (1952) is the most uncompromisingly modern of all his works, more angular than his earlier compositions, yet no less enjoyable. Written five years before his death, it sounds like a final bid for respectability, with all the thick luscious orchestration that one associates with him cut away to a leaner and more eloquent mix. It's an epic work in four long movements, with an underlying tension between major and minor, tragedy and resolution. Its startling opening, in which a battery of percussion creates a mood of foreboding, gives way to a long mysterious clarinet tune. A bold and brassy Scherzo precedes a rich, deeply felt Mahlerian Adagio of unrelieved sombreness, while the seemingly playful finale is interspersed with moments of an almost bitter edginess.

○ **London Symphony Orchestra; Previn** (Deutsche Grammophon 453 436-2; with *Much Ado About Nothing Suite*).

Since Rudolf Kempe's trailblazing account in 1972, this symphony has been recorded no fewer than four times. André Previn's is the latest and the best, with the conductor judging the work's ambiguity and subtle changes of mood with great precision.

GYÖRGY KURTÁG

(1926–)

Shortly after World War II, György Kurtág and György Ligeti (see p.219) were fellow composition students at the Franz Liszt Academy in Budapest. Artistic freedoms were severely limited in Hungary at that time, and it was not until the 1950s that the two men had any direct contact with the European avant-garde. Both were completely transformed by the experience, but whereas Ligeti stayed away from his homeland and completely embraced new ways of organizing sound, Kurtág returned to Hungary where his newly acquired experimental techniques became another element of an extremely idiosyncratic musical personality. Kurtág's mature musical language, in which a sense of alienation and human frailty is never far from the surface, shows an awareness of the concentrated and concise forms of Webern in combination with a highly charged expressiveness that has much in common with Bartók.

In Paris, where he studied with both Darius Milhaud and Olivier Messiaen, Kurtág also came into contact with the Hungarian psychologist Marianne Stein, who encouraged him to go back to first principles as a composer. Performances of Stockhausen's *Gruppen* for three divided orchestras and Ligeti's electronic *Artikulation* were further formative influences, as were the Domaine Musical concerts organized by Pierre Boulez. In 1959, shortly after returning to Budapest, Kurtág composed a string quartet (*Quartetto per archi*) in six short and densely argued sections – designated his Opus 1 (and dedicated to Marianne Stein), it marked a new beginning.

Kurtág's strong tendency to self-criticism meant new works came slowly throughout the 1960s and 1970s – between 1959 and 1973 his total output amounted to less than ninety minutes of music. A set of whimsical semi-pedagogical piano pieces, *Játékok* (Games, 1973–76), grew from his work as professor of piano at the Franz Liszt Academy, and a song cycle, *Messages of the Late Miss R.V. Troussova* (1976–80), helped to establish his wider reputation when it was performed at IRCAM in

LEBRECHT COLLECTION

Kurtág (left) with György Ligeti, 1993

Paris. *Messages* was the first of several settings of the work of a Russian poet Rimma Dalos, resident in Budapest, and it marked the start of Kurtág's fascination with Russian language and literature, in particular the novels of Dostoevsky.

More recently Kurtág has begun to write for larger forces, although his utterances are no less pithy and gesture-packed than before. If anything, in pieces such as *Grabstein für Stephan* and *Stele,* his preoccupation with mortality has generated an even more personal musical language, one in which the characteristically vulnerable voices of small instrumental groups are made all the more acute through a background setting of grand statements and rich sonorities.

MESSAGES OF THE LATE MISS R.V. TROUSSOVA

The success of the Paris performance of *Troussova* has helped to make it the best known of all Kurtág's works. Written from the viewpoint of a woman looking back on a life of love, frustration and despair, it comprises 21 songs divided into three sections entitled *Loneliness*, *A Little Erotic* and *Bitter Experience – Delight and Grief.* Dalos's stark imagery and the cycle's fragmentary nature allows Kurtág to give full rein to his brilliance in depicting sudden shifts of mood and tone through unpredictable instrumental combinations and virtuosic vocal effects. *Troussova* is suffused with a restless energy and is the most obviously expressionist of all Kurtág's works, but there also moments of great lyricism, like the haunting seventh song, *You Took my Heart.* There's also an obvious kinship with Bartók's opera *Bluebeard's Castle* – in the overriding sense of loneliness, and in the way the non-vocal music seems like a projection of the central character's troubled psyche.

⭘ Messages of the Late Miss R.V. Troussova; Quasi una fantasia; Scenes from a Novel: Hardy; Ensemble Modern; Eotvos (Sony SK53290).

This performance of *Troussova* wins out over the rival Erato recording on account of its clear sound quality, which allows the precise, painterly qualities of Kurtag's soundworld to emerge with great vividness. Soprano Rosemary Hardy manages her fearfully difficult part not just with ease but also with great expressiveness and musicality. The two other works, another song cycle and the powerful *Quasi una fantasia* for piano and various instruments, are equally well performed.

GRABSTEIN FÜR STEPHAN & STELE

Grabstein für Stephan (Gravestone for Stephan) was written in 1989 as a memorial to the husband of Marianne Stein. At its centre a solo guitar seems to represent a static, human presence around which groups of instruments are placed like mourners. It opens with the soloist's gentle plucking of open strings – the work's central motif – over which a shifting array of grief-suggesting sounds (low strings, assorted percussion, wailing alarm signals) are layered. *Stele* (1994), essentially a three-movement symphony, employs the orchestra in a more conventional manner, though with a large tuned percussion section which includes pianos, celesta and cimbalom. At times the sensuousness of its richly clotted textures sounds almost Mahlerian. This is intensely sad music: a tentative, ghostly opening movement moves, without a break, into a clamourous, angry lament before culminating in a finale of immense and terrible gravity in which, once again, the shadow of Bartók's *Bluebeard* is never far away.

⭘ Grabstein für Stephan; Stele: Berlin Philharmonic Orchestra; Abbado (Deutsche Grammophon 447 761-2; with Stockhausen's *Gruppen*).

The Berlin Philharmonic respond brilliantly to this music. There's a strong sense, in both works, of the different sections of the orchestra functioning like actors in some powerful tragedy; by that analogy the Berlin players are strong on ensemble and free of any attention-seeking bravura. Abbado controls his forces with an unfailing sense of the right emphasis at the right moment to deliver performances of affecting power and simplicity.

MUSIC FOR STRINGS

The small-scale string ensemble has been central to Kurtág's work, ever since he chose to mark his first string quartet as his first composition worthy of an opus number. His music for strings exemplifies the creative processes of a composer who combines an uncompromisingly questing intelligence with a profound consciousness of his place within a tradition – his output includes homages to forerunners as diverse as Mussorgsky, J.S. Bach, Schubert, Verdi and Schumann.

Bartók ("my mother tongue") and Webern occupy the foreground of Kurtág's mental landscape, as is clear from the Opus no. 1, a fifteen-minute assemblage of splintered, scurrying episodes and charged silences. It's clearly the creation of a major composer, but a greater cohesion (and lyricism) is evident in the *Hommage à András Mihály* (1977). Subtitled "12 microludes for string quartet", it was germinated by "a few notes" in the cello concerto of András Mihály, one of Hungary's most energetic proponents of modern music. Compression and expressivity are equally manifest in the third quartet, *Officium breve in memoriam Andreae Szervánsky* (1989), a typically allusive work (referring notably to Webern, Beethoven, Bach and Szervánsky) that condenses fifteen movements into a span of just thirteen minutes. These delicate melodic fragments were composed in the same year as *Ligatura – Message to Frances-Marie*, Kurtág's response to the musical interrogation of Charles Ives's *Unanswered Question* (see p.204). Written for Frances-Marie Uitti, a cellist who has developed a technique of using of two bows simultaneously, *Ligatura* is an aphoristic yet texturally rich piece, as is *Aus der Ferne III* (1991), an elegiac quartet which is constructed around a slowly pulsing low C on the cello and finally fades "into the distance", as its title suggests.

○ Musik für Streichinstrumente: Keller Quartett (ECM 78118-21598-2).

This disc in effect offers a panoramic survey of Kurtág's career, as it contains all the works discussed in the previous section – plus a second version of *Ligatura*, scored for two cellos in addition to two violins and celesta (played by Kurtág himself). The performances by the Keller quartet are technically precise and deeply committed, as you might expect from a group that studied with the composer. This is the second in an excellent Kurtág series from ECM – it was followed by an outstanding selection from *Játékok*, played by the composer and his wife.

ROLAND DE LASSUS

(1532–1594)

Roland de Lassus (or Orlando di Lasso as he was known in Italy) was a contemporary of Palestrina and, like him, was one of the truly outstanding composers of the sixteenth century. They almost certainly knew each other, since in 1555 Palestrina succeeded Lassus as *maestro di cappella* at the church of St John Lateran in Rome, and their respective careers make an interesting comparison. Lassus travelled throughout Europe, while Palestrina was firmly based in the region of Rome. Both men wrote polyphonic music but, whereas Palestrina evolved a style that was notable for its calmness and serenity, Lassus wrote pieces that were altogether more individual and quirky. He was also far more versatile than Palestrina, and his works encompass every major musical genre of the time.

Lassus was born at Mons, in the Franco-Flemish province of Hainaut. He may have been a chorister at the church of St Nicholas, but there is nothing to substantiate the legend that he was kidnapped by talent scouts, on account of the beauty of his voice. However, he was in Italy by the age of 12, in the service of Ferdinand Gonzaga, the viceroy of Sicily. His prestigious appointment at St John Lateran at the age of 21 is a tribute to his remarkable talent, but he was there for only eighteen months before returning north to Antwerp. Shortly after his return, Lassus was summoned to Munich to join the ducal court of Bavaria, firstly as a singer and then in 1562 as Kapellmeister. He was to remain there for the rest of his life, enjoying a unique familiarity with the duke, Albrecht V, and with his son and successor Wilhelm. Lassus's correspondence with Wilhelm has been preserved: written in a mishmash of languages and full of puns and bad jokes, it shows him as a remarkably spirited and affectionate person. He also had a dark side, however, and in his last years suffered from such extreme depression that his music almost dried up.

CHORAL MUSIC

From the middle of the sixteenth century the term *musica reservata* (reserved music) was applied to those composers who were concerned with trying to convey the meaning of the words they set. Of Lassus a contemporary wrote that he could make ". . . the things of the text so vivid that they seem to stand actually before our eyes". Devices such as chromaticism, whereby the melody was made more expressive by employing notes apart from those from the key it was written in, became increasingly common at this time, and in his early work – especially in his songs and madrigals – Lassus employs quite extreme chromaticism, as well as frequent declamatory passages. But as his career progressed his writing became more subtle and economic in its expressiveness. The eight-part *Missa Bell' Amfitrit'altera* has an ineffably radiant but simple opening and its shifts of mood are achieved mostly by varying the musical texture and the rhythm. His final work, *Lagrime di San Pietro* (Tears of St Peter), is an extraordinarily powerful cycle of sacred madrigals in which the music's austerity and intensity of feeling perfectly match the clarity of the poetic imagery.

⊙ **Missa Bell' Amfitrit'altera: Schola Cantorum of Oxford; Summerly** (Naxos 8.550836; with Palestrina, *Missa Hodie Christus natus est, Stabat Mater*).

Schola Cantorum perform the Lassus and Palestrina works in ways that bring out the similarities between them rather than any differences. They are performances very much in the English style, with clear diction, well-blended voices and carefully controlled phrasing. The result is remarkably beautiful, if at times a little cool.

O Lagrime di San Pietro: Ensemble Vocal Européen; Herreweghe (Harmonia Mundi HMC 901 483).

The Ensemble Vocal Européen have a rather more vivid approach, in music where it is certainly more necessary. Their seven voices combine perfectly but are strong and individual, with some wonderfully judged contrasts in dynamics. They are helped by a more sympathetic recording, which brings out the immediacy of the voices yet also suggests the space that surrounds them.

FRANZ LEHÁR

(1870–1948)

Franz Lehár was the Andrew Lloyd Webber of his day: within two years of the premiere of *Die lustige Witwe* (The Merry Widow) he was a dollar millionaire, and the show ran for a record 778 performances in London – King Edward VII saw it four times. *The Merry Widow* pioneered the concept of merchandizing, with "Merry Widow" hats, corsets, cigarettes and cocktails going on sale in New York. Several other operettas virtually repeated the success of his best-known work, and *Der Graf von Luxemburg* (The Count of Luxembourg), *Zigeunerliebe* (Gypsy Love) and *Das Land des Lächelns* (The Land of Smiles) were exported to theatres right around the world.

The son of a military bandmaster, Lehár spent his childhood stationed with his father's regiment in various towns across the Austro-Hungarian empire, and for a short while he studied with Dvořák at the Prague Conservatory– "Hang up your fiddle and start composing", he is reputed to have been advised. He had already composed a couple of fairly successful operettas by the time he was given the libretto of *Die lustige Witwe* by Oscar Léon and Leo Stein, the authors of Strauss's hugely popular *Wiener Blut*. In fact Lehár was the second choice as composer – he got the job after being set a trial song, which he composed in a single day and played down the telephone to Léon.

By the time the show was in rehearsal, the Theater an der Wien (Vienna's main operetta theatre) had little faith in the piece, and at one point offered Lehár five thousand crowns to withdraw it. The premiere on December 30, 1905 went well enough, but business was slow and free tickets were handed out to fill the house. But eventually word got round, and *Die lustige Witwe* is still a regular fixture at the Theater an der Wien, even displacing *Cats* from the summer season's programme. After a couple of flops, Lehár hit a winning streak with *Der Graf von Luxemburg* (1909) and *Zigeunerliebe* (1910), both of which had highly successful worldwide runs and are still regularly performed in Central Europe.

Lehár's career then took another downturn until it was revitalized by the tenor Richard Tauber, who became the most celebrated performer of Lehár's music and gave his name to *Tauberlied* – songs that have become far more popular than the operettas that spawned them. The most famous of these *Dein ist mein ganzes Herz* (You Are my Heart's Delight) comes from Lehár's last international triumph, *Das Land des Lächelns* (The Land of Smiles), premiered in Berlin in 1929. At Christmas 1930, Lehár's sixtieth birthday year, some two hundred productions of *Das Land des Lächelns* were in progress in Europe, and five hundred different Lehár productions in total. His last major work, *Giuditta*, was premiered at the Vienna State Opera in 1934, the only operetta to have been given that honour, and the show was relayed internationally by 120 radio stations.

Many operetta composers and performers of Jewish extraction were forced to emigrate when Hitler came to power, but – although his wife was Jewish – Lehár stayed in Vienna. He is said to have been the favourite composer of Hitler, who as a young man was a regular visitor to the Theater an der Wien's production of *Die lustige Witwe*. After the Anschluss Lehár composed a new overture to *Die lustige Witwe*, which he dedicated to Hitler to protect himself and his wife. This didn't help Lehár's Jewish colleagues, however, and Fritz Löhner-Beda, one of the librettists of *Das Land des Lächelns* and *Giuditta*, was murdered in a concentration camp while his work was playing in Vienna. After moving to Switzerland for a few years Lehár returned to his villa in Bad Ischl, where he died in 1948.

◑ Composers in Person – Lehár: Lehár; Tauber; Schwarz; Novotná (EMI CDC 754838-2).

This compilation, with Lehár himself conducting, is as close as you can get to original-cast recordings. Prominently featuring Richard Tauber – who's essential to any operetta buff's collection – the disc has substantial selections from *Das Land des Lächelns* (recorded in 1929) and *Giuditta* (in 1934), plus the second *Die lustige Witwe* overture.

○ Marilyn Hill Smith Sings Kálmán and Lehár: Marilyn Hill Smith; Chandos Concert Orchestra; Barry (Chandos CHAN 8978).

This CD is by far the best compilation of Lehár (and Kálmán) arias, partly because Marilyn Hill Smith steers away from the popular favourites and comes up with some little-known but high-quality numbers from *Giuditta*, *Zigeunerliebe* and others. Hill Smith's tone is usually just right, while Stuart Barry brings out the fine orchestration and transparency of the scores.

DIE LUSTIGE WITWE

The story of *Die lustige Witwe* is one of absurd aristocratic intrigue to prevent a wealthy widow, Hanna Glawari, marrying a Frenchman and thereby depriving the fictional Balkan kingdom of Pontevedrino of her fortune. In typical operetta style, Danilo, the man chosen to lure Hanna from the Frenchman, turns out to be her former heart-throb, although there are plenty of diversions on the way. Lehár throws Balkan spice into the score with some folk dances and Hanna's famous *Vilja-Lied* – the *vilja* is a wood spirit from Montenegrin folklore. (Furthermore, Danilo's costume for the premiere was closely modelled on that of the Crown Prince of Montenegro). The celebrated *Merry Widow Waltz* and some splashes of French nightclub music further enrich the mix.

○ Schwarzkopf, Waechter, Gedda, Steffek; Philharmonia Chorus and Orchestra; Matačic (EMI CDS7 47178-8; 2 CDs).

This classic recording, made back in 1962, has never been bettered. Elisabeth Schwarzkopf has all the alluring mystery that Hanna Glawari requires, and her seductive performance of the *Vilja-Lied* has just the right delicacy and poise. Eberhard Waechter and Nikolai Gedda are suitable foils as Danilo and the Frenchman, Camille. The more rumbustious parts of the score are also dashed off with splendid abandon.

○ Studer, Skovhus, Bonney, Trost, Terfel; Vienna Philharmonic; Gardiner (Deutsche Grammophon 439 911-2).

The Vienna Philharmonic sound as if they have this music in their blood, but amazingly they hadn't touched it for forty years prior to this vivid and seductive set. All the singers bring a quality of unforced clarity and ease to the vocal lines, although only Boje Skovhus (Danilo) is a regular performer of operetta. The other great pluses of this recording are that it is contained on one CD, includes all the music, and cuts the spoken dialogue down to a minimum.

RUGGERO LEONCAVALLO
(1857–1919)

Just as Italians in the eighteenth century would have nothing to do with Gluck, so in the nineteenth century they were extremely uncomfortable with Wagner, an attitude typified by the career of Ruggero Leoncavallo. Enamoured of Wagner's music as a young man, he came to write one of the two great examples of operatic verismo, the low-life counterblast to Wagnerian epic music-drama.

He first experienced Wagner's music in 1878 and was deeply affected by it – or rather, by its literary and dramatic scope. He set about writing *Crespuculum*, a quasi-Wagnerian Renaissance trilogy, but was soon sidetracked into completing a project that had occupied him since his student days, an opera called *Chatterton*, about the young English poet who killed himself by taking strychnine. When the promoter of the premiere disappeared with all the money before the first night, Leoncavallo approached a publisher with a view to issuing *Chatterton* in print. However, the publisher felt Leoncavallo to be a better librettist than composer, and commissioned him to write the text for Puccini's *Manon Lescaut*. Puccini had him removed from the project.

After two years' further dissatisfaction, the ever-ambitious Leoncavallo found his inspiration in the success of Mascagni's *Cavalleria rusticana* (see p.247), the work that launched verismo opera in 1890, and promptly dominated the limelight in Italy. As he later wrote – "I shut myself in my house . . . and in five months I wrote the poem and music of *Pagliacci*." Toscanini gave the first performance of *I Pagliacci* (The Clowns) on May 21, 1892, and overnight Leoncavallo found his fame and made his fortune.

On the back of this success he arranged for the first part of his *Crespuculum* to be performed and, after a blaze of pre-publicity, *I Medici* was duly premiered on November 9, 1893. The evening was a disaster, and from then on he was embroiled in a losing battle with Puccini for the affections of the Italian people. Leoncavallo's *La Bohème* was performed almost a year after Puccini's and, even though it met with some success, he never came to terms with its inevitable disappearance from the stage. He was one of the first composers to take a serious interest in the gramophone, composing the song *Mattinata* expressly for the G&T record company (Caruso recorded it in April 1904), but life went steadily downhill after *Pagliacci*. The man who had once proposed writing a music drama to rival Wagner's, spent his dying months composing an operetta entitled *A chi la giarettiera?* – or *Whose Garter is This?*

I PAGLIACCI

The central idea of *I Pagliacci* – a travelling actor discovers that his younger wife has been having an affair with a friend and colleague, and wreaks a dreadful revenge – was taken from a case that Leoncavallo's magistrate father had judged, and it typified the verismo ideal. From this sordid tale he made one of the finest dramatic operas ever written, showing a command of proportion, timing and characterization that is absent from the rest of his output. The cheated husband (Canio) is one of the greatest dramatic tenor roles in all opera; Nedda, the cheating wife, is a less involved part than that of the adulterer Tonio, but their set pieces and exchanges are riveting in their energy and conviction. The last ten minutes, during which Leoncavallo's play within a play reaches its shocking conclusion, are the ultimate in verismo.

◑ **Corelli, Amara, Gobbi, Zanasi, Spina; La Scala Orchestra & Chorus; von Matačic** (EMI CMS7 63967-2; 2 CDs; with Mascagni, *Cavalleria Rusticana*).

Matačic's 1960 recording, with Franco Corelli as Canio, Titto Gobbi as Tonio and Lucine Amara as Nedda, is a masterpiece of base emotion and divine inspiration. Corelli's awesome singing is unmatched by any Canio before or since, and his massive, ringing sound produces the sort of electric thrill rarely heard from studio recordings. Gobbi's performance is similarly impressive, with all Tonio's contradictory qualities brought to the surface. Amara has a light and unstable voice that produces little of the malice demanded of her role but, ultimately, Matačic's driving direction overcomes these vocal limitations. Unfortunately, the accompanying *Cavalleria Rusticana* is not in the same league.

◑ **Bergonzi, Carlyle, Taddei, Panerai; La Scala Orchestra & Chorus; Karajan** (Deutsche Grammophon 449 727-2GOR).

Karajan's 1965 recording of *Pagliacci* is fabulously lush, a fine testament to his transformation of the Scala forces from a second-rate band into the most expressive opera orchestra ever to record the work. Carlo Bergonzi's voice might have lacked some steel, but this is a menacing portrayal of Canio, and the weight and fluency of his phrasing are intoxicating. Joan Carlyle's light soprano is vital and beautifully produced and Giuseppe Taddei is a feverish Tonio, but the overwhelming influence is Karajan's.

GYÖRGY LIGETI

(1923–)

Ligeti once remarked: "I am permanently scarred; I will be overcome by revenge fantasies to the end of my days." His outlook has been formed by his experiences under two dictatorships – those of Hitler and Stalin. A Jew born in Transylvania just as Hungary was losing that region to Romania, he survived World War II in a labour camp. He studied and taught at the Budapest Academy, but fled after the crushing of the anti-Soviet uprising in 1956. Arriving in Cologne he became an associate of Stockhausen at the WDR electronic music studio, where he rapidly caught up on musical developments from which he had been cut off in Hungary. In the 1960s he emerged as a leading member of the avant-garde. Since then he has lived mostly in Hamburg and Vienna, becoming an Austrian citizen in 1967. Political repression and exile have resulted in a proclivity for the macabre and the absurd – most obviously in his opera *Le Grand Macabre*.

And yet he is the most approachable, as well as one of the most fascinating and compelling, of postwar composers. A feeling of loss and nostalgia characterizes much of his output, often evoked by the haunting modalities of East European folk music – most obviously in the early Hungarian period directly influenced by Bartók, from which come the delightful *Six Bagatelles for Wind Quintet* of 1953. But pathos is balanced by absurdist humour, most notoriously in the twenty-minute *Poème symphonique for 100 Metronomes* (1962), a piece of "mechanical music" which lasts until the last device finally stops beating.

The mechanical is one aspect of the "clocks and clouds" ethos that made Ligeti's name in the early 1960s – a piece with that title appeared in 1973. In *Atmosphères* (1961) and other "cloud" pieces, Ligeti abandoned Stockhausen's serialism in favour of a "micropolyphony" which suspends pulse and harmony – part of a tendency towards "texture music" represented in other ways by Lutosławski and Penderecki. Clusters of adjacent sounds were used to achieve slow, seamless change, most famously in *Lux Aeterna* for unaccompanied voices, in which fine gradations of pitch create a kind of warped polyphony. (It was used in Stanley Kubrick's film *2001*.) Both "clock" and "cloud" styles reflect the composer's characteristic concern with acoustic illusions or puzzles, influenced by Escher's paradoxical drawings. This is shown especially in *Monument-Selbsportrait-Bewegung* for two pianos (1976), a kind of tribute to American minimalism. Here a pulse is "created" for the listener from individually pulseless parts.

Ligeti's late period, from 1982, followed a period of illness and compositional crisis. He rediscovered a kind of tonality and metre, but one which was dislocated or lopsided to disturbing or comic effect. The *Piano Etudes* and the piano and violin concertos are all from this period, as is the *Trio for Violin, Horn and Piano*, a work which he has described as "half ironic, half deeply serious, conservative/postmodern". Ligeti is beyond tonality and atonality, and, he believes, beyond postmodernism – "the ironic theatricalizing of the past is quite foreign to me". Ligeti is utterly unique, but until recently he has been sparsely served on disc; Sony are now rectifying this with a Complete Ligeti Edition, a commendably adventurous series that so far has set itself high standards.

LE GRAND MACABRE

Perhaps Ligeti's finest work is *Le Grand Macabre*, a savage burlesque written for Stockholm Opera between 1974 and 1977. Set in "Breughelland", a world derived from the visionary paintings of Breughel and Bosch, the opera depicts the end of the world, as experienced by a gang of grotesques – among them the infantile Prince Go-Go, the permanently intoxicated Piet the Pot, the lovestruck Amando and Amanda, and the sluttish Mescalina, who at one point gets ravaged by the opera's master of ceremonies, Nekrotzar. It's a two-hour musical helter-skelter, as raucously enjoyable as anything written since the war.

○ Davis, Walmsley-Clark, Smith, Weller, Krekow; Austrian Radio Symphony Orchestra; Howarth
(Wergo WER 6170-2; 2 CDs).

The Wergo recording of *Le Grand Macabre* reinforces the argument that this is likely to prove one of the most durable of modern operas; the singers vividly characterize Ligeti's nightmarish creations, and the sound is superb.

ORCHESTRAL WORKS AND CONCERTOS

Apparitions was the first of Ligeti's "texture" pieces, and its first performance in 1960 offered a challenge to the serialist complexity of Stockhausen and Boulez. His new technique was expressed more masterfully in *Atmosphères* (1961), in which he aimed to avoid all sense of pulse and suspend harmonic movement by the use of tone-clusters. These "cloud" pieces, and the mechanical "clocks" which complemented them, were distinctive products of Ligeti's work in the 1960s and 1970s, whose influence endures in his late work. Other important works from this period include *Ramifications* (for two string ensembles tuned a quarter-tone apart), the texturally complex *Chamber Concerto*, and the concerto for cello (1966), a minimalist piece which subverts the traditional concerto, in that the soloist is given the initial dynamic marking of *ppppppp*, and never rises to any prominence. Ligeti's later output includes the *Piano Concerto* (1985–88) and *Violin Concerto* (1989–93), the latter a magnificent piece, conjuring a volatile aural world that relects the composer's abiding fascination with Shakespeare's *Tempest*. A remarkable product of Ligeti's later style, it offers perhaps the

most extreme example of his concern with "wayward intonation" – some instruments in the small orchestra are retuned to natural harmonics, and ocarinas and recorders are introduced. The resulting "haze of intonation" is a beguiling combination of clarity and weirdness.

◑ **Chamber Concerto; Ramifications; Aventures; Lux Aeterna: Manning, Thomas, Pearson; Ensemble Intercontemporain, La Salle Quartet; Boulez** (Deutsche Grammophon 423 244-2).

This CD of selected chamber, vocal and choral works is simply the best introduction to the multitudinous styles of this fascinating composer.

◑ **Chamber Concerto; Ramifications; Lux Aeterna; Atmosphères: South West German RSO; Bour** (Wergo 60162-50).

This disc features an "historic" interpretation of the *Chamber Concerto* under Friedrich Cerha, who premiered the work, and similarly contemporary recordings of the other pieces. As a whole it takes second billing to the Boulez recording, but unlike its rival it does include *Atmosphères*.

○ **Cello, Violin and Piano Concertos: Queyras; Gawriloff; Aimard; Ensemble Intercontemporain; Boulez** (Deutsche Grammophon 439 808-2).

The DG recording comes out just ahead of a comparable set on Sony: Pierre-Laurent Aimard is more incisive than Ueli Wiget on the *Piano Concerto*, and the sound is brighter with the piano well projected from the ensemble. Both are fine recordings, however, and the choice may come down to the couplings – DG offers the only recording to date of the *Violin Concerto*, while Sony has the *Chamber Concerto* instead. Saschko Gawriloff was the dedicatee and first performer of the *Violin Concerto*, and gives a vibrant and compelling performance.

THE PIANO ETUDES

Ligeti completed his first book of piano studies in 1985, the second in 1993, and he is working on a third set. They originated as teaching aids, but – in the manner of Chopin – poetry and technique have been allied. Much of the music here is as rhythmically complex as a non-machine can handle – the influence of Conlon Nancarrow's player-piano studies is clear. Sub-Saharan rhythms, Javanese gamelan and American minimalism are other influences. Most of the studies are uptempo but there are some slow pieces, including *Arc en-ciel,* a transcendentally beautiful meditation.

○ **Works for Piano – Etudes, Musica Ricercata: Aimard** (Sony SK 62308).

This is the third instalment in the excellent Sony Ligeti Edition, and is perhaps the finest to date. Pierre-Laurent Aimard masters the prodigious demands Ligeti makes on the pianist, bringing out each of the tangle of lines in different metres. On slow pieces Aimard offers sensitive rubato, although the clarity of his playing would have been better served by a less reverberant acoustic.

MAGNUS LINDBERG

(1958–)

Magnus Lindberg began his compositional career committed to the idea of pushing the language of music into uncharted territory: "Only the extreme is interesting. Striving for a balanced totality is nowadays an impossibility." The music he wrote in the 1980s reflects this dictum – it is dense, monolithic and gritty, often evoking images of a harsh and unyielding landscape. More recently, however, there has been a pronounced mellowing in style. Whereas his earlier music had conveyed a sense of static verticality, his more recent works are far more linear, with an emphasis on brighter and more sonorous textures. As he describes it himself: "Earlier I used to hack away at stone; these days my approach has been softer, gentler, as if I were moulding in clay."

Born in Helsinki, Lindberg studied composition at that city's Sibelius Academy with Rautavaara (see p.329) and Paavo Heininen, who introduced him to a wide range of contemporary music. With fellow-student Essa-Pekka Salonen (then a horn player, now a conductor) he founded the instrumental ensemble Toimii as a means of working out and performing his compositions. After graduating, he travelled widely in Europe and studied in Paris with Vinko Globokar and Gérard Grisey. His early works were strongly influenced by serialism but he was also interested in computers, and in *Kraft* (1985) he used a computer to calculate the highly complicated rhythmic transformations that occur in the work. *Kraft's* percussive impact – it uses objects from a scrap-metal yard – and punk-inspired sounds summarize Lindberg's rather brutal preoccupations at this period.

His post-*Kraft* works show a gradual change of direction to a sound-world in which there is greater sense of momentum and details of instrumental timbre are far more apparent. By the 1990s Lindberg was reinventing himself with bewildering regularity, first employing the chaconne as an organizational method, then abandoning it in favour of pulsating ostinatos that seem to derive from Stravinsky, with a sideways glance towards minimalism.

WORKS FOR CHAMBER ORCHESTRA

Lindberg's compositions of the 1990s are much more listener-friendly than his earlier works and are a good place to start for someone new to his music. *Corrente* (1992) takes a look at a Baroque dance form and transforms its rapid, flowing character into a kaleidoscopic melee of scurrying voices which are built up layer by layer. There's an ominous undertow to the piece running through to the three darkly dramatic chords with which it ends. *Coyote Blues* (1993) started life as a commission for a vocal work, but Lindberg's interest in rhythmic complexity meant that it soon developed into another orchestral piece, albeit one with a more pronounced lyrical strain than usual. Its brilliant opening fanfare and obsessively repeated ostinati suggest a clear debt to Stravinsky's *Les Noces* and *Octet* but there's also a distinctly American feel to it, not least in the bright open sonorities of its closing moments. His move to a more vividly hued instrumental palette climaxes in *Arena* (1995), a commission for a conducting competition which is his richest score to date, even in its pared-down version *Arena II*. Its use of repeated motifs, vivid colours and the edgy anxiety of its first half suggest a *hommage* to the more experimental Hollywood film scores – in particular, the work of Bernard Herrmann.

O Arena 2; Coyote Blues; Tendenza; Corrente; Avanti!: Chamber Orchestra; Oramo (Ondine ODE 882-2).

This is a remarkaby well-recorded and -performed disc, with Lindberg's vivid orchestral colours coming across in all their brilliance, thanks to the individual virtuosity of many of the players. The strong dramatic, and at times restless, element that underlies Lindberg's more recent work is pushed to the fore by Sakari Oramo, and it even comes across in such a solid and ungainly work as the early *Tendenza*.

FRANZ LISZT

(1811–1886)

In certain circles Franz Liszt is still not taken seriously, and the reason for this lies in his brilliance as a performer – Liszt, the argument goes, was all self-promotion and no substance. The accusation is nothing new. In 1874 the critic Eduard Hanslick wrote: "The main objection against Liszt is that he imposes a much bigger – an abusive – mission on the subject of his work: namely either to fill the gap left by the absence of musical content or to justify the atrociousness of such content as there is."

Certainly Liszt was a large-scale character. Born Ferenc Liszt, the son of a minor Hungarian court functionary, he became the greatest pianist of his age – indeed, possibly of any age. Like Paganini (see p.294), he developed his technique to the point at which he had to create his own style of music to do justice to his capabilities, and much of that music did little more than show off his technique. Instead of working from his own ideas, he quarried all available musical sources and reworked the material into show stoppers that would demonstrate that he could play octaves faster than anyone else, and hit the keys harder (he used to break his wooden-framed pianos). His offstage character hardly suggested serious devotion to music. Liszt was the ultimate Romantic blend of immorality and piety, an infamous womanizer who had the face of St Francis carved on his walking stick – alongside Mephistopheles and Gretchen, heroine of Goethe's *Faust*.

There was indubitably more than a dash of the showman in Liszt, but his contribution to the development of nineteenth-century music was immense. On a practical level, he was an uncommonly generous man who gave freely of his time and money to champion the music of other composers. As for his own compositions, the fireworks represent just the surface, for in his symphonic music he anticipated the tone poems of Strauss and the vast fluid structures of Wagner (his son-in-law), while in his austere late piano music he created perhaps the most prophetic work of his time. As Schoenberg once wrote – "one must not overlook

LEBRECHT COLLECTION

Liszt surrounded by his students at Bayreuth, home of his son-in-law, Richard Wagner

how much there is in his music that is new, musically, and discovered by genuine intuition. Was he not after all one of those that started the battle against tonality?"

Liszt invented the piano recital and the career of travelling virtuoso, but his first major works were created after making a break with his self-established tradition. In 1847, after nearly thirty years as Europe's most revered pianist, Liszt met and fell in love with the Princess Carolyne von Sayn-Wittgenstein, who convinced him that, having sown more oats than most could imagine, he should settle down. Somewhat in awe of the princess, Liszt renounced his career as a roaming virtuoso and in 1848 accepted an invitation to become Kapellmeister to the Grand Duke of Weimar. During his ten years at Weimar he wrote or revised most of the pieces for which he is now best known, and made the city a pre-eminent musical centre by conducting a vast number of new works, including music by Schumann, Berlioz, Verdi, Donizetti and Wagner. Weimar became the centre of the progressive faction of which Wagner was the figurehead, a group opposed by Brahms, Hanslick and the traditionalists of Vienna.

In 1860 he moved to Rome, where five years later he took minor orders. His music from this time was soaked in religious sentiment, but his heart was never really in it and in 1869 he began to divide his time between Rome, Weimar and Budapest. The more he travelled, the more he reverted to his old ways, and his amorous adventures once again became the talk of Europe. As his increasing years began to take effect, however, he devoted ever larger amounts of time to teaching and, together with Clara Schumann, he helped produce some of the early twentieth century's greatest pianists. In the 1870s his music entered its final and most radical phase, and he remained active as a composer and performer right to the end of his life – his Jubilee tour, marking his 75th birthday, was reported across the world. He died soon after. His career had bridged a whole era in the cultural development of Europe: had he been born two years earlier, his life span would have overlapped with both Haydn and Stravinsky.

THE FAUST SYMPHONY

In 1846 Berlioz dedicated his dramatic cantata *La Damnation de Faust* to Liszt. It was to be nearly ten years before Liszt repaid the compliment by dedicating his own interpretation of Goethe's two-part poem to Berlioz. The *Faust Symphony* was one of the major works to emerge from the years in Weimar (along with Liszt's only other symphony, the weaker *Dante Symphony*), but was constantly revised – nineteen years after the first performance in 1861, he was still revising the slow movement.

There are three movements – *Faust*, *Gretchen* and *Mephistopheles* – and each is, essentially, a character study. The grand and sweeping first movement is an extraordinary example of Liszt's technique of transforming his basic themes: lasting nearly half an hour, it is built on just five short phrases. After a second movement of almost chamber-music delicacy, which looks towards the anti-Wagnerian simplicity of his final decade, the finale represents Goethe's "spirit of negation" by grotesque parody of the themes heard in the opening movement. The latter half of *Mephistopheles* depicts "the great struggle" and concludes with his defeat, in which the *Chorus mysticus* (end of Part Two of Goethe's *Faust*) is strikingly set for tenor, male chorus and full orchestra.

O Cole; Dresden State Opera Chorus; Staatskapelle Dresden; Sinopoli (Deutsche Grammophon 449 137-2).

There are three outstanding recordings of this work by Beecham, Bernstein and this live version by Giuseppe Sinopoli. Sometimes accused of favouring rather ponderous speeds, Sinopoli sets an electrifying pace here, but keeps the whole thing perfectly under control. Vinson Cole's fervently dramatic tenor is the icing on the cake of this riveting performance.

LES PRÉLUDES

Liszt can be credited with inventing the genre of the symphonic poem, an extended orchestral piece presented as the interpretation of a non-musical subject. He completed thirteen of them, illustrating subjects taken from classical mythology, Romantic literature, recent history or imaginative fantasy and, while not all of them are successful, *Les Préludes* (another product of the Weimar years) is a masterpiece. Liszt actually composed the twenty-minute piece before deciding that the music was a paraphrase of a poem by Lamartine, in which life is presented as a series of preludes to the afterlife. As with the *Faust Symphony*, the opening theme appears in many guises throughout the work and, more than almost any other of his orchestral compositions, *Les Préludes* is a brilliantly organic, well-structured creation.

◑ Berlin Philharmonic Orchestra; Karajan (Deutsche Grammophon 447 415-2; 2 CDs; with *Mazeppa, Hungarian Rhapsodies*).

Liszt's grand and spectacular music brings out the best in Karajan and his orchestra – this is one of his most exciting recordings, and in the closing measures the music simply tears off the page. This two-disc set is an excellent introduction to Liszt's large-scale work.

PIANO CONCERTO NO. 1

The more famous and certainly more enjoyable of Liszt's two piano concertos is the first, in E flat. It was begun in 1830 then revised for years until, in what must have been one of the concerts of the century, Berlioz conducted the first performance with Liszt himself at the piano in 1855. With its unison opening theme, leading into a series of startling octave leaps, the concerto's opening is one of the most dramatic of any Romantic piano concerto. This introduction is followed by a fiery cadenza which, in turn, leads to a series of calmer, more reflective passages, and the concerto carries on in this exchange of moods, keeping you on the edge of your seat in anticipation of the next burst of pyrotechnics. Moments of incredible banality are dotted through the score, but there are enough Romantic gestures to distract your attention.

◑ Richter; London Symphony Orchestra; Kondrashin (Philips 446 200-2; with *Piano Concerto No. 2* and *Piano Sonata in B Minor*).

Richter gives overwhelmingly powerful and authoritative readings of both concertos. He was at his technical peak when he recorded them in the 1960s, and his finger-work has a steely energy to it which is remarkable. He is well supported by Kondrashin, one of the most sympathetic of concerto conductors, and the LSO.

O Barere; unknown orchestra; Brockman (Appian CDAPR 7007; various works by Liszt).

Simon Barere, now almost forgotten, was one of the great pianists of the century – as mercurial as Horowitz but equipped with unfailing good taste. This performance, recorded in 1946 at Carnegie Hall, comes with a selection of other Liszt performances from the same venue but on different occasions. There is no more exciting Liszt recital on disc.

OPERATIC TRANSCRIPTIONS

Liszt's operatic transcriptions served a double function: on the one hand they enabled Liszt to create a fund of bravura piano music without the sweat of arduous creative thought; and on the other they assisted his colleagues by publicizing contemporary operas – before the age of the gramophone, piano transcriptions were the way most people got to hear the operas of Wagner, Berlioz, Verdi, Tchaikovsky, Bellini, Donizetti, Gounod and Meyerbeer. Sometimes Liszt made a straightforward bar-for-bar transcription, as in the works of Rossini and Wagner (whose music he felt was perfect to begin with), but of his sixty works in this genre a number are a good deal better than the originals upon which they were based. He composed an opera as a child of 13, and you can only regret that his interest in opera was stifled by his enthusiasm for the work of others.

◉ Howard (Hyperion CDA 66371-2; 2 CDs).

As an introduction to Liszt's operatic transcriptions, there is nothing finer than Leslie Howard's two-disc survey, which encompasses *Faust*, *Norma*, *Don Giovanni*, *Aida*, *Eugene Onegin*, *Tristan und Isolde* and *Lucia di Lammermoor*, to name just a few. Howard's playing is at times splashy and thumping, but he's an excellent, dramatic pianist and his continuing project to record all Liszt's solo piano music for Hyperion (now reaching volume 50) is one of the great recording feats of the century.

ÉTUDES D'EXÉCUTION TRANSCENDANTE

Listzt's eight *Études d'exécution transcendante* (or *Transcendental Studies*) comprise one of the great documents of musical Romanticism and a landmark in the history of the piano, amounting to nothing less than the creation of modern piano technique. These studies teem with such outrageous difficulties that, in their day (1831), they were the most difficult works ever written for the piano; even now, there's but a handful of pianists able to play them authoritatively. The versions most commonly performed today are Liszt's revisions of 1851, which cut back on the pyrotechnics but, even so, are as fiendish as anything written since. If played well, this music rises above mere display to reach a plateau of intense emotional conviction – especially the first four.

◉ Berezovsky (Teldec 4509-98415-2).

To play these works at all requires a formidable technique; to play them so that the poetry (rather than the effort) is what shines through is a gift accorded very few. Most of the great interpreters of the *Études* – Berman, Richter, Ovchinikov – are Russian, as is one of the latest players to record them. Boris Berezovsky has the technique to deal with the pyrotechnics but he also enters the introspective core of such pieces as the beautiful *Harmonies du soir* and *Ricordanza*.

THE HUNGARIAN RHAPSODIES

A lot of Liszt's music bears the stamp of his Hungarian heritage, and of all his quasi-gypsy compositions the most inventive and popular are the nineteen *Hungarian Rhapsodies*. Growing out of Liszt's renewed interest in the folk music of his native country, the first fifteen were written between 1840 and 1847, whereas the last three were not added until the 1870s. This is not his greatest work, often being contrived and superficial, but his rhythms and melodies are immediately infectious, and his transcriptions of the sounds of a gypsy orchestra (solo violin, clarinet, cimbalom and strings) are breathtaking. You'll recognize the second rhapsody – Tom and Jerry, and Daffy and Donald, all skittered around to it.

◑ Cziffra (EMI CMS 764882-2; with *Années de pèlerinage* Books 1 & 2; 4 CDs).

Remembered as one of the greatest Lisztians in history, the Hungarian pianist György Cziffra died at the end of 1993, aged 72. In his memory, EMI have released this mid-price box set of what are probably his finest recordings, the complete *Hungarian Rhapsodies* and the first two books of *Années de pèlerinage*. Unpredictable and risk-taking, Cziffra produces just about the most hair-raising playing on record. Marvellous entertainment, this set is a worthy tribute and a superb introduction to the very best and the very worst of Liszt's piano music. If, however, you want to test the water first, there is also a single CD (from this set) of Cziffra playing seven of the best-known *Rhapsodies*.

THE SONATA IN B MINOR

As you'd expect, works for solo piano make up the largest part of Liszt's output, and the greatest of these is the *Sonata in B Minor*, a monumental construction that stands apart from almost everything else he wrote. Liszt purged his language of all unnecessary virtuosity, creating a piece in which the dramatic changes of mood are subsumed into the overall construction – and here the construction is purely musical, as Liszt attached no programme to the sonata.

Composed between 1851 and 1853, and dedicated to Schumann (who died the year before its 1857 premiere), it is cast as three movements to be played without a pause, the whole musical span being underlaid by a series of themes and motifs that grow, fuse and eventually expire. It's a piece that traverses enormous distances: the music at the start and at the close of the sonata gives a foretaste of the sparse angularity of Liszt's late style; in between lie passages of fulminating emotion, as thrilling as anything Liszt ever wrote.

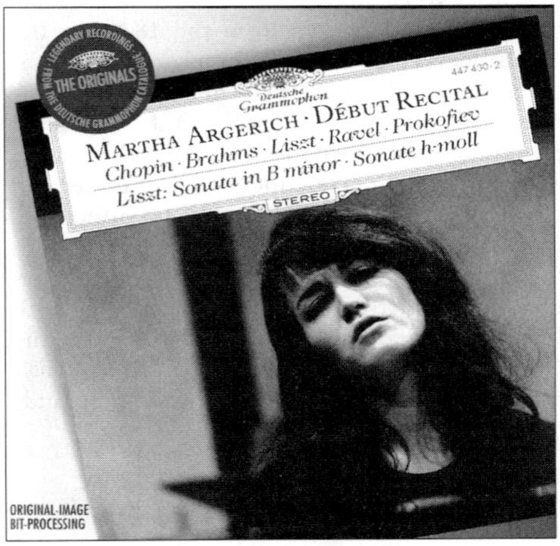

◑ **Argerich** (Deutsche Grammophon 437 252-2; with Schumann, *Piano Sonata No. 2*; Brahms, *Rhapsodies*).

Martha Argerich's recording of the sonata is a magnificent high-voltage account, pulsating with the most astonishing energy but always remaining utterly coherent. In the opinion of many it is the finest thing she has ever recorded.

◑ **Richter** (Philips 446 200-2; with *Piano Concerto Nos. 1 & 2*).

This live recording was made in 1994, right at the end of Richter's career, when his performances were often characterized by an almost ruthless objectivity and concentration. This performance has a grandiosity and a sense of occasion coupled with an intense vibrancy that is truly mesmerizing.

MEPHISTO WALTZ NO. 1

The first of Liszt's three *Mephisto* waltzes – an orchestral piece transcribed for piano in 1881 – is a virtuoso's delight and one of his most popular works for piano. Lasting only ten minutes, it is full to bursting with Romantic imagery, including evocations of violins, nightingales, the play of starlight and village dances. When it first emerged, *Mephisto No. 1* caused a sensation, provoking the *Boston Gazette* into suggesting that "it has about as much propriety on a programme after Schumann and Handel as a wild boar in a drawing room".

○ **Ashkenazy** (Saga EC3362; with performances by Richter of Chopin, Liszt and Haydn).

Vladimir Ashkenazy was just 18 years old when this live recording was made in 1955. Although he has never been particularly associated with Liszt's music, this is a blistering performance, adopting dangerous tempi which no other recorded pianist has been able to pull off.

ANNÉES DE PÈLERINAGE

The first two volumes of Liszt's *Années de pèlerinage* (composed and revised from the 1830s to the 1870s) are perhaps the most complete overview of his talents as a composer. (The third volume, compiled against Liszt's will and published posthumously, is inferior to the other two.) Standing in complete contrast to the glitter and dazzle of the studies, these pieces are principally lyrical miniatures, and are more concerned with the creation of atmosphere than the construction of a literal narrative. The first book, dealing with his travels through Switzerland, includes the exquisite *Au bord d'une source* and *Vallée d'Obermann*, both of which are as fresh as the landscapes they portray. In the second volume, the so-called "Italian book", art and literature are the subjects, and here the music is, if anything, even more beautiful. *Sposalizio* and *Petrach Sonnet 104* are two of the most translucent, unaffected piano pieces he ever wrote, and if *Après une lecture du Dante – Fantasia quasi Sonata* looks back to the virtuosic indulgence of his youth, it does so in the spirit of re-evaluation.

◑ **Années de Pèlerinage vols. 1–3: Berman** (Deutsche Grammophon 437 206-2; with *Venezia e Napoli*; 3 CDs).

Radiant, incandescent performances of all three *Années* from one of the greatest Liszt pianists of the postwar period. Lazar Berman is the complete Lisztian, able to make what in other hands sounds merely exhibitionistic into a discursive stream-of-consciousness of the highest poetic quality.

◑ **Années de Pèlerinage vols. 1 & 2: Cziffra** (EMI CMS 764882-2; 4 CDs; with *Hungarian Rhapsodies*).

Part of EMI's Cziffra retrospective, these performances perfectly capture the essence of Liszt's deeply considered poetry – a stark contrast to the circus act of the *Hungarian Rhapsodies*.

THE LATE PIANO PIECES

While his contemporaries were piling more and more notes into their scores and trying desperately to out-Wagner Wagner, Liszt pushed music to the opposite edge in his late piano works. With their raw dissonances and attentuated textures, their use of silence as a dramatic means, their denial of absolute tonality and their lack of any audible themes, these terse utterances are prophetic of the world of Schoenberg and Webern. Many of them speak of an obsession with death and repentance, as typified by the two pieces entitled *La lugubre gondola*, which were inspired by Liszt's premonition of Wagner's death two months before it occurred, in Venice in 1883. Clashing chords and ideas that offer no centre or direction suggest an emptiness and despondency that is nothing short of desolate.

○ **Howard** (Hyperion CDA 66445).

Leslie Howard gives superb accounts of thirty of Liszt's final works for piano, five of which have never been recorded before. His playing is always deeply infused with emotion, and in the four pieces associated with Wagner's death the sense of loss and desperation is movingly portrayed without any recourse to sentimentality. A brilliantly programmed recording boasting equally memorable performances.

JEAN-BAPTISTE LULLY

(1632–1687)

Rarely has a composer so dominated a cultural environment as Lully dominated the French court in the reign of Louis XIV. Through his friendship with the king, and some unscrupulous wheeler-dealing, he managed to achieve almost complete control of the musical life of Paris and Versailles. He was also extremely talented: he wrote sprightly and energetic dance music which, collected together as suites, exerted a strong influence on European orchestral music until the middle of the eighteenth century; and much of his more serious music, including his operas, possesses a powerful stateliness, though it can, on occasions, subside into pomposity.

Lully was born an Italian but went to France at the age of 14 as a servant to a cousin of Louis XIV. Though an outstanding violinist, he first attracted attention as a dancer and a mime, performing alongside the young king in a court ballet in 1653. In the same year he joined the royal household as Composer of the King's Instrumental Music, and composed a number of ballets that were performed by his own orchestra, La Petite Bande – an ensemble that he moulded into one of the finest of the age. During the 1660s he produced a series of *comédies-ballets* in collaboration with the playwright Molière, the most famous of which was *Le Bourgeois Gentilhomme* (1670).

Lully's increasing control of French theatre music was consolidated in 1672 by his purchase of the exclusive right to produce opera. His first theatre was a converted tennis court, but with Molière's death he moved, rent-free, into the theatre of the Palais Royal. For the next fifteen years he produced an opera per year, mostly to librettos by the tragedian Philippe Quinault. His unrivalled power – he even forbade music in the marionette theatre – made him many enemies. One resentful entrepreneur, Henri Guichard, allegedly tried to have him poisoned by putting arsenic into his snuff. More damaging were reports of Lully's homosexuality, which reached the ears of the king, who threatened to make an example of him. His death was a strange mixture of grandeur and farce: while conducting his *Te Deum*, in celebration of the king's recovery from illness, he jabbed one of his toes with the stick he was using to beat time. A gangrenous abscess developed but he refused

GUUS ONG

amputation, and died – an immensely wealthy man – some two months later.

ARMIDE

Lully virtually created French opera, or *tragédie lyrique* as it was known, by fusing the courtly ballet with the conventions of classical French tragedy into one enormous and lavish spectacle in which the setting, the scenic effects and the choreography were all as important as the music. The elaborate, often fantastical, plots – usually taken from Greek myths or from the epics of chivalry – were combined with the examination of moral issues in such a way as to pay flattering tribute to the sagacity of the king for whom they were written. One highly influential innovation was the introduction of an overture in two sections: the first slow and stately, the second more animated and usually fugal. Lully also developed a type of recitative which was less florid than the Italian model and supposedly based on the declamatory style of the French tragedians like Racine and Corneille. To a modern audience much of the proceedings, if not the music, can seem cumbersome and laboured, and today Lully's operas are rarely staged outside France.

Armide, a late work, is his masterpiece. The libretto, by Quinault, is based on a story from Torquato Tasso's *Gerusalemme Liberata*, the great chivalric poem of Renaissance Italy. Armide (Armida in the original) is a sorceress obsessed by the Christian knight Renaud (Rinaldo), who seems impervious to her beauty. She captures and plans to kill him, but instead falls in love with him. Renaud is bewitched into loving Armide but he is rescued by two of his fellow knights and she flies away as her palace is destroyed by demons. It is a plot with a similar outline to Purcell's *Dido and Aeneas*: a noble warrior is unmanned by love until duty prevails and the joys of the flesh are abandoned. That Lully turns this into such a compelling drama is a tribute to his flexible vocal writing, which generates a powerful dramatic momentum. His recitatives are never far away from the rhythms of normal speech and even the more elaborate airs do not stop the action in the manner of an Italian operatic aria.

O Laurens, Crook, Gens, Rime, Deletré, Ragon; Collegium Vocale, La Chapelle Royale; Herreweghe (Harmonia Mundi HMC 90 1456/57; 2 CDs).

No recording of a Lully opera can represent anything like the totality of the proceedings, but this forceful and persuasive performance goes a long way to making Lully's music seem dramatically feasible on its own. There is a great deal of contrast and variety here, ranging from the sprightly rhythms of the ever-present dance music to the meltingly beautiful prelude at the beginning of the third scene of Act Two. Herreweghe is well served by his soloists, with Guillemette Laurens brilliant at conveying the ambivalent emotions of Armide, nowhere more powerfully than in her final air, which wavers between rage and despair. Howard Crook's Renaud is necessarily a rather bloodless characterization, but he has an unerringly elegant sense of the music's line.

WITOLD LUTOSŁAWSKI

(1913–1994)

Lutosławski is Poland's greatest composer between Szymanowski and Penderecki, and his work distils key influences in twentieth-century music: Bartók in the early *Concerto for Orchestra*, Cage's chance techniques in the post-1960 music, and a French fastidiousness and delight in colour throughout.

Lutosławski matured late as a composer, and then suffered from the restrictions imposed by the postwar Communist government in Poland. Lutosławski was a non-political figure, as far as that is possible for a Polish composer of that time, and forty years later he claimed – probably disingenuously – he "never felt any pressure to write a certain way". But his *Symphony No. 1* (1947) was banned for being "formalist", and he then turned to Polish folk material, producing his remarkable *Concerto for Orchestra* (1954), in which he used folk themes as "raw material to build a large musical form". The *Concerto* is one of his most popular works, and the best place to begin for those new to his music. The often searingly intense *Funeral Music* for string orchestra (1958) is dedicated to the memory of Bartók, whose influence on Lutosławski was pervasive.

After the post-Stalin thaw, Poland became the most liberal artistic environment in the Soviet bloc. In 1958 Lutosławski heard on radio the chance-based *Concert for Piano and Orchestra* by John Cage, and he "suddenly realised I could compose music differently from that of my past". In response, Lutosławski composed his seminal work *Venetian Games*, which began his true modernist period. His individual use of chance has been termed "aleatory counterpoint" – the precise coincidence of voices is left open. However, unlike Cage, Lutosławski insisted on "a clear delineation of duties between composer and performers. . . I have no wish to surrender even the smallest part of my claim to authorship of even the shortest passage". Chance under tight compositional constraints and "experimenting within tradition" governed Lutosławski's way of working for the rest of his career.

For Lutosławski, sound in itself is the primary element of his music, an approach that many find difficult, as he himself acknowledged in writing that some listeners "feel alien in the world of sound; their thoughts escape to a realm of images or feelings that do not exist in a piece of music". But his music is not impressionist either; it always shows a deep concern with form. The symphonies are central to his later output, together with the three orchestral pieces entitled *Chain*, in which the composer diluted his aleatoric approach with more straightforwardly melodic elements.

CONCERTO FOR ORCHESTRA

"I do not like this work of mine very much, but apparently it has preserved some freshness", said Lutosławski in 1973. Maybe its effects became too obvious for his refined sensibilities, but audiences and critics beg to differ – the *Concerto for Orchestra* is of the few great postwar works with immediate audience appeal. The *Concerto* was, he said, "the only serious piece among the folk-inspired works" which he wrote in response to official criticism. The stamping chords of the *Intrada* grab attention immediately, and the writing uses bold and vivid colours.

⭘ BBC Philharmonic Orchestra; Tortelier (Chandos CHAN 9421; with *Mi-parti* & *Musique Funèbre*).

A gripping interpretation. From the opening chords the effect is thrilling, and the recording has superb presence and clarity. The masterly *Mi-parti* is one of the later aleatoric works: its sonorities here are shimmering and subtly shifting, the effect less direct but beautifully captured.

⭘ Chicago Symphony Orchestra; Barenboim (Erato 4509-91711-2; with *Symphony No. 3*).

This too is a fine performance, resonantly recorded, and it is coupled with an impassioned account of the third symphony.

THE SYMPHONIES

The first symphony is a fairly conventional piece, full of easily recognizable tunes, but with the *Symphony No. 2* Lutosławski employed aleatory techniques to a large-scale work for the first time. It's a two-movement structure, the first preparatory to the second: the shimmering, tremulous textures and motifs of the episodic opening movement *Hésitant*, are put forward tentatively then taken up in the second movement, *Direct*, with firmer purpose. Within each section there is a "rhythmically elastic counterpoint", a kind of "collective ad lib" in which each musician plays, in effect, as a soloist. When the sign for the end of the section is given, the performers stop immediately. If before this time a player has played their part to the end, they repeat it from the beginning. The *Symphony No. 3* is also in two connected movements, integrated by an insistent four-note motto which dramatically opens the work – as in the "fate" motif of Beethoven's *Symphony No. 5* – and also closes it. The fourth symphony, completed in 1992, two years before his death, reintroduces a melodic aspect that Lutosławski had previously downplayed.

⭘ Symphony No. 2: Los Angeles Philharmonic; Salonen (Sony 01-067189-10; with *Piano Concerto* & *Chantefleurs et Chantfables*).

Symphony No. 2 receives a performance of great drive and intensity from Salonen, and the recording has excellent clarity. The *Piano Concerto*, a late work, is given persuasive advocacy by Paul Crossley, while Dawn Upshaw offers magical interpretations of Lutosławski's settings of the surrealist poetry of Robert Desnos.

⭘ Symphony No. 3: Chicago Symphony Orchestra; Barenboim (Erato 4509-91711-2; with *Concerto for Orchestra*).

Barenboim brings out the drama and passion of this music in a single sweep – and it's combined with a superb reading of the *Concerto for Orchestra*.

⊙ Symphony No. 4: Bakowski; Polish National Radio Symphony Orchestra; Wit (Naxos 8.553202; with *Chain II*, *Partita for Violin and Orchestra*, *Funeral Music* & *Interlude*).

The Naxos disc features some accessible and compelling late works, notably a first-rate interpretation of the *Symphony No. 4*.

CHAIN

The three orchestral pieces known as *Chain* were composed in the mid-1980s in the wake of the third symphony and share that work's intense musical language. Constructed so that each forms a self-contained unit that nonetheless connects with the other two, like links in a chain, they incorporate fully written sections and episodes in which the instrumentalists are given some leeway to improvise. Of the three, the best is the second, which was written specifically for the violinist Anne-Sophie Mutter.

⭘ Chains II & III: Mutter; BBC Symphony Orchestra; Lutoslawski (Deutsche Grammophon 455 576-2; with *Partita* & *Novelette*).

There is something really special about Mutter's performance of *Chain II*; boasting committed accompaniment and fine recorded sound, as well as a splendid performance of other Lutosławski orchestral pieces, this DG disc is the obvious place to begin exploring the composer's work.

⊙ Chain II: Bakowski; Polish National Radio Symphony Orchestra; Wit (Naxos 8.553202; with *Symphony No. 4*, *Partita for Violin and Orchestra*, *Funeral Music* & *Interlude*).

Krzysztof Bakowski's offers an interpretation less precise in its effects than Mutter's but with more emotional appeal.

THE STRING QUARTET

As with the second and third symphonies, Lutosławski's only string quartet (1965) is in two movements, the first introductory, and it is aleatory in the same way as those orchestral works. The composer wrote: "Each of the interpreters is to play his part as if he alone existed. . . When playing as a soloist. . . his playing [can be] flexible, free and individual." Distinctly characterized short segments are played by the musicians together, who then diverge, thus subverting the traditional conversational dynamic of the quartet medium – as with some of Elliott Carter's quartets. The paradoxical result is that in different performances the overall effect is quite similar – texture becomes more important than individual lines.

⊙ Arditti Quartet (Auvidis Montaigne MO789007; with string quartets by Kurtág and Gubaidulina).

As one would expect from the leading exponents of contemporary music for string quartet, the Ardittis are compelling – this is a taut, dramatic performance whose violent impact is enhanced by a dry acoustic.

ELISABETH LUTYENS

(1906–1983)

Nicknamed "twelve-tone Lizzie", Elisabeth Lutyens was one of the most radical British composers of her generation. Although music by the Viennese serialists Schoenberg and Webern was being played in London while she was a young woman, Lutyens always claimed that she had developed her twelve-note technique independently of them, and certainly she was to display a staunch self-reliance throughout her career. Her style was constantly changing and developing, and her complex but ultimately rewarding music has gone in and out of fashion, although the best of it has never received the attention it deserves.

She was born into a well-to-do artistic family: her father was the architect Edwin Lutyens and her mother, Lady Emily Lytton, became a devoted follower of Krishnamurti and theosophy. Determined from an early age to become a composer, Lutyens studied briefly at the École Normale in Paris in her late teens and then at the Royal College of Music. It took her some years to find a musical language with which she was satisfied, and she later withdrew most of her works before the ground-breaking *Chamber Concerto No. 1* (1939–40).

The early 1940s were a period of experimentation, culminating in her glorious cantata *O Saisons, O Châteaux!* (1946), to words by Rimbaud. By this time she had left her husband for Edward Clarke, a former pupil of Schoenberg and a leading figure in contemporary music circles. He was also frequently unemployed, leaving Lutyens with the responsibility of providing for Clarke and her four children, which she did by writing countless scores for film and radio. She became a well-known figure amongst the writers and artists who frequented the pubs of London's Fitzrovia, hanging out with such luminaries as Dylan Thomas, Louis MacNeice and Francis Bacon.

After overcoming a nervous breakdown and alcoholism at the beginning of the 1950s, Lutyens started to produce some of her most striking works. Yet compositions such as the *String Quartet No. 6* (1952), and her Wittgenstein-inspired *Excerpta tractatus-logico philosophici* (1952), were simply too advanced for the British musical establishment, and she was rarely performed. The successful first performance in 1962 of the powerful *Quincunx* for baritone, soprano and orchestra saw the beginning of a change in the reception of her music. The more adventurous musical climate of the 1960s and 1970s was more open to her uncompromising ways, and she produced a stream of important works, such as *And Suddenly It's Evening* (1966), a setting of four poems by Salvatore Quasimodo for tenor and instrumental ensemble, and *Essence of Our Happiness* (1968), which used Islamic texts and words by John Donne.

During this late period her music became less dry and more immediately lyrical, but by the time of her death Lutyens had become as well-known for her caustic wit and outspoken opinions on the British musical establishment as for her music.

CHAMBER MUSIC

Luytens' large-scale works are absent from the CD catalogue, but there is a wealth of dramatic and expressive music to be found among the chamber works that have been recorded. One of the earliest pieces she was later prepared to acknowledge was her *Chamber Concerto No. 1*, the first of six chamber concertos composed during the 1940s. Its bare textures and serial language must have seemed unrelentingly austere to its first audience in 1943. By 1957, when she wrote *6 Tempi for 10 Instruments*, Lutyens was experimenting with different ways of using rhythm: this work, admired by Stravinsky, comprises six short movements which are all of the same duration but use that time in very different ways.

⊙ Chamber Concerto No. 1; 6 Tempi For 10 Instruments; Triolet I and Triolet II: Jane's Minstrels; Manning (NMC DO11; with *The Valley of Hatsu-Se* etc).

All credit to NMC for issuing the only currently available CD to consist entirely of music by Lutyens. It presents a wide-ranging selection of her chamber music in excellent and incisive performances.

VOCAL MUSIC

O Saisons, O Châteaux!, a setting of Rimbaud's short poem for soprano and string orchestra, guitar, mandolin and harp, is one of Lutyens's better-known works. First performed in 1947, it is an immediately appealing piece with the soprano soaring over the accompanying ensemble, which Lutyens described as like "an enlarged amplified guitar".

Much of Lutyens' work in the 1960s was vocal, and her music from this decade includes *The Valley of Hatsu-Se* (1965), settings of eight ancient Japanese poems for soprano, flute, clarinet, cello and piano, and *Lament of Isis on the Death of Osiris* (1969), which was extracted from Lutyens' unsuccessful opera *Isis and Osiris*. Using writings by Plutarch and from the Egyptian Book of the Dead, the *Lament* makes strenuous use of the soprano soloist's full emotional and technical range. Her later, more lyrical writing can be heard in two works dating from 1971: *Requiescat* for soprano and string trio, and *Driving out the Death* for oboe, violin, viola and cello. Brief yet deeply moving, *Requiescat* was commissioned by the music magazine *Tempo* in memory of Stravinsky and uses as its text a passage from *The Couch of Death* by William Blake. *Driving out the Death*, probably the most frequently performed of all Lutyens' work, was inspired by ancient rituals marking the changing seasons; in six sections, it opens with an oboe call, and it is the expressive voice of the oboe that dominates the whole work.

⊙ O Saisons, O Châteaux!: Cahill; Brunel Ensemble; Austin (CALA CACD 77005; with *Six Bagatelles* and works by McCabe, Saxton and Williamson).

Soprano Teresa Cahill is utterly convincing on this recording of *O Saisons, O Châteaux!*, her strong tones ringing out over the rich string colour. On the same disc the Brunel Ensemble give a convincing and well-judged account of the complex *Six Bagatelles*, a work of which they gave the first performance in 1996, twenty years after it was written.

⊙ The Valley of Hatsu-Se; Lament of Isis on the Death of Osiris; Requiescat: Jane's Minstrels; Manning (NMC DO11; with *Chamber Concerto No. 1, 6 Tempi for 10 Instruments, Triolet I & Triolet II*).

Jane Manning, for whom both *The Valley of Hatsu-Se* and *Lament of Isis on the Death of Osiris* were written, gives finely characterized and expressive readings of the vocal works on this disc.

GUILLAUME DE MACHAUT

(c.1300–1377)

Round about the year 1320 the French composer and theoretician Philippe de Vitry wrote a treatise entitled *Ars Nova* (New Art) in which he claimed that the recent technical innovations in music amounted to a major break with the music of the immediate past. Musicologists later employed the term Ars Nova for the developments that took place in French and Italian music in the fourteenth century, designating the previous period – the period of early polyphony (c.900–1250) – Ars Antiqua.

Guillaume de Machaut was the outstanding Ars Nova composer, exploiting new musical techniques that make much of his work sound startlingly modern. One of the most significant innovations was that of isorhythm, whereby a fixed rhythm was applied to the cantus firmus, the borrowed melody that often underpinned a new composition. This fixed rhythm might have a different number of notes from the main melody, so that each time it was repeated it would begin at a different point along that melody – a numerical system of composing that has led to Machaut being bracketed with Schoenberg as an essentially intellectual composer. In addition, Machaut also employed musical forms that were in decline, and many of his most moving songs are monophonic.

Machaut was almost certainly born in Rheims, a city where he spent most of his later years. Around

1323 he joined the household of John of Luxembourg, the King of Bohemia, serving as his secretary on many military and diplomatic expeditions. When King John died at the Battle of Crécy in 1346, Machaut went on to serve a succession of aristocratic patrons including the king's daughter Bonne, King Charles the Bad of Navarre, the king of Cyprus and the dukes John of Berry and Amadeus of Savoy. As a priest much of his income came from a number of largely honorary positions awarded him by various churches throughout France.

Machaut's fame during his lifetime was gained as much by his skills as a poet as by his musicianship, and he was admired as such by his great English contemporary Geoffrey Chaucer. In his later years, he fell in love with a woman much younger than himself and he tells their story – the source of much biographical detail – in a long poem, *Voir Dit* (The Tale of Truth). "All my works", wrote Machaut to his beloved, "were made from your feelings, and are for you especially."

SONGS

Machaut exemplifies the poetic and courtly conventions of his day. Despite his income from the church, nearly all of his compositions are secular songs about love, the courtly, spiritual love of the Middle Ages which requires the love object to be an unattainable woman of unrivalled beauty. Her devoted admirer pays extravagant tribute to her, and swears undying devotion, even though she is the cause of as much pain as pleasure. Machaut's language is in the tradition of the troubadours of northern France, poet-musicians who performed their work at the chateaux of the nobility. One of his favoured song forms is the *virelais*, in which a refrain alternates with three stanzas, and these compositions have all the simple directness of folk song. His polyphonic songs, on the other hand, are more adventurous and possess greater rhythmic variety, often using a form of syncopation called the hocket (from the Latin for "hiccup"), which breaks up the line of a melody in one voice by inserting sudden gaps which are then filled by the other voices, thus creating a gentle undulating quality.

⊙ The Mirror of Narcissus – Songs of Guillaume de Machaut: Kirkby, Philpot, Covey-Crump; Gothic Voices; Page (Hyperion CDA 66087).

Gothic Voices' decision to perform the songs with voices only – a valid alternative would have been to have instruments in the lower parts – is fully justified by the textual clarity that results. Unaccompanied performances of these three- and four-part songs show off their complexity and energy in a much more immediate way. This is especially true of the one sacred work on the disc, the motet *Inviolata genitrix*, where it really does sound, at moments, as if three people were singing completely different songs simultaneously. The way it all fits together, and the haunting harmonies that are thrown up, are what makes this such a powerful and pleasurable work.

MESSE DE NOTRE DAME

Machaut's most important work for the church was the four-part *Messe de Notre Dame*, the first polyphonic setting of the Ordinary of the Mass which shows some kind of stylistic unity between the sections. The Ordinary of the Mass is those parts of it which are constant – ie the Kyrie, Gloria, Credo, Sanctus and Agnus Dei – as opposed to those sections whose texts vary according to the occasion, and which are called the Proper of the Mass. Austerity is the chief characteristic of the *Messe de Notre Dame*, in which the general simplicity of the word-setting places the few dramatic moments in particularly sharp relief.

⊙ The Hilliard Ensemble; Hillier (Hyperion CDA 66358; with *Le Lai de la Fonteinne & Ma fin est mon commencement*).

The Hilliard Ensemble's approach to this music is to avoid the obviously expressive and to concentrate on making the music's constant rhythmic ebb and flow sound coherent. The result creates an atmosphere of extraordinary devotional intensity.

JAMES MACMILLAN

(1959–)

James MacMillan is one of the rare contemporary composers whose works readily find an audience, not least in his native Scotland: the 1993 Edinburgh Festival, for example, featured no fewer than eighteen of his compositions. Yet, although it is impossible to separate his music from his socialism, his Catholicism and, not least, his Scottish patriotism, his work is far from didactic, its appeal far from parochial. In the five years after its 1992 BBC Proms premiere, his percussion concerto *Veni, Veni, Emmanuel* received more than 100 performances around the world, and his 1996 *Cello Concerto* was first performed by no less illustrious an advocate than Mstislav Rostropovich.

His work is often placed alongside that of other deeply religious composers, notably Arvo Pärt (see p.298) and John Tavener (see p.423); and, like theirs, it is frequently derided as "Holy minimalism", but his music is more raw and turbulent than that implies. As MacMillan himself has remarked of his kinship with Tavener: "Tavener has always said that for him the most important image is that of the Risen Christ. For me, it's Christ Crucified. It shows in our music: in Tavener's, it's as if Heaven is already attained. In mine, it's still to be fought for."

Profoundly influenced by the ideas of liberation theology, MacMillan insists that "you cannot divorce the religious and political". One of his first works to evince this belief was the movingly disturbing music theatre piece *Busqueda* (1988; the title means "search"), written as a companion piece to Luciano Berio's *Laborintus II*. The text derives from poems written by the mothers of those who "disappeared" during the Argentinian junta, brilliantly interwoven with fragments of the Latin Mass. MacMillan has said that the work allowed him to become "a serious composer who was also a folk musician".

For polemical as well as practical purposes, MacMillan has often stood against "the old guard of the avant-garde" who "are deeply suspicious of any significant move towards tonality, any hint of pulse that is actually discernible, and any music which communicates successfully with a non-specialist audience". Nevertheless his early music grew from an engagement with Polish modernism, and with the then avant-garde Peter Maxwell Davies (see p.250), and more recently he might be said to have reached a rapprochement with some of the ideas of Harrison Birtwistle (see p.63), as well as the distinctly Russian styles of Sofia Gubaidulina and Galina Ustvolskaya.

Yet everything that MacMillan does aims at direct emotional and dramatic communication, an enterprise in which Scottish traditional music is an important source of inspiration. His largest work to date is the opera *Inès de Castro* (1996), a work which divided the critics more deeply than most. One described it as "pornography" because it "tempts us with the thrill of transgression without the slightest challenge to our values or experience". Others applauded its vision of a woman who pays the highest price for allowing love to intrude on realpolitik. Significantly, the opera was well received by audiences, no doubt grateful for a work that, in the tradition of Verdi and Mussorgsky, engaged heart and mind in its musical drama. In that sense it could be said to be a companion piece to the purely orchestral *The Confession of Isobel Gowdie* (1990), the Proms debut of which marked a turning point in MacMillan's professional life.

THE CONFESSION OF ISOBEL GOWDIE

It's not difficult to see why this large orchestral work became such a firm favourite in the wake of its ecstatic reception at its premiere. With its references to the Scottish ballad tradition and to Gregorian chant, not to mention its occasional echoes of Stravinsky, Messiaen, Berg, Vaughan Williams and Purcell, this is a composition in which resonant textures and violent dynamics achieve a transformative immediacy, the effect of which more than one critic has likened to listening to a Mahler symphony. The title refers to a woman who, in 1662, was tortured into confessing herself a witch, an incident that serves as a metaphor for MacMillan's "fears about the new rise of fascism" in Europe.

⭘ BBC Scottish Symphony Orchestra; Maksymiuk
(Koch Schwann 3-1050-2; with *Tryst*)

Jerzy Maksymiuk and the BBC SSO gave the premiere of *Isobel Gowdie*, and here present a performance that sensitively moulds every phrase of MacMillan's slow-moving lament, handling the abrupt and shocking change of gear in the work's *Rite of Spring*-like middle section with easy virtuosity. Written for chamber orchestra, *Tryst* is another single-movement work of great cumulative power, its fundamental melody deriving from an earlier MacMillan setting of *The Tryst*, a love poem by William Soutar.

VENI, VENI, EMMANUEL

In a series of works written in the 1990s, MacMillan has harnessed the implicit drama of concerto form in a way that considerably enriches his musical vocabulary. This is nowhere more apparent than in the one-movement percussion concerto *Veni, Veni, Emmanuel*, which fully exploits the vast battery of instruments available to the modern percussionist. The musical material, drawn from fifteenth-century French Advent plainchant, represents, the composer says, "a musical exploration of the theology behind the Advent message", and what is most striking about the work is its balance of exuberance and contemplative calm. MacMillan makes the utmost demands of his soloist, who is rewarded with not only a showpiece but a work of immense communicative force.

⭘ Glennie; Scottish Chamber Orchestra; Saraste
(RCA 09026 61916 2; with "*. . . as others see us . . .*" and *Three Dawn Rituals*).

Evelyn Glennie premiered *Veni, Veni, Emmanuel* at the 1992 BBC Proms, a performance that repeated the earlier Proms impact of *Isobel Gowdie*. Glennie is a tireless champion of new music for percussion, but few of the pieces she has ushered into the world have the integrity and power of this, here given a performance of commanding authority. The most substantial of the accompanying works is "*. . . as other see us . . .*" (1990), a set of musical portraits of seven English men and women, from Henry VIII to the Nobel prizewinning biochemist Dorothy Hodgkin.

ELIZABETH MACONCHY

(1907–)

Elizabeth Maconchy has described her work as "an impassioned argument", and indeed her compositions are characterized by the combination of heartfelt lyricism and clear logical structures. Her vigorous music, which has remained rooted in tonality except for an experiment with twelve-note techniques during the 1940s, is among the most dynamic to have been produced in twentieth-century Britain, and deserves to be far more widely heard than it is at present.

Maconchy spent most of her childhood in the countryside of England and Ireland, with little exposure to any music other than what she played on the piano or made up for herself. At 16 she went to the Royal College of Music in London, where she studied with Ralph Vaughan Williams and explored new music by composers like Bartók, while developing her own highly personal musical language. She first sprang to public attention at the age of 23 when her powerful orchestral work *The Land*, based on a poem by Vita Sackville-West, was premiered at the Proms in August 1930, to enthusiastic reviews.

In 1932 Maconchy developed tuberculosis, the disease which had killed her father ten years previously. She cured herself by moving out of London and living in a shed at the bottom of the garden of her house in Kent. In spite of this enforced isolation, her music continued to be performed all over Europe throughout the 1930s, although some British critics found the modernity and intellectual power of her music hard to accept in a woman. Having married in 1930, Maconchy had two children in 1939 and 1947, and had to spend much of her time looking after her family. Nonetheless, in the face of resistance from the male-dominated establishment, she continued to develop her musical voice, composing a powerful collection of works in many diffrent genres, from chamber music to opera. An increasing volume of commissions from performers, institutions and festivals came her way in the 1970s and 1980s, but her innovative edge was not blunted by her increasing success. In 1987 her contribution to British music was fully recognized when she was made a Dame of the British Empire.

ORCHESTRAL MUSIC

The success of *The Land* was followed by various smaller works for orchestra, including the prizewinning overture *Proud Thomas* and her *Symphony for Double String Orchestra* – both from 1953. The string orchestra was to remain a favoured medium, as is shown by later works such as the exuberant *Music for Strings*, first performed at the Proms in 1983. Maconchy's two works for clarinet and orchestra show clearly the changes in her style over the years. The *Concertino No. 1* (1945) is a richly ominous work in three movements with exciting, driving rhythms and dramatic brooding passages. *Concertino No. 2* (1984) is a shorter, more exposed work, in which the clarinet is accompanied by an orchestra which includes wind, brass and timpani creating an enthralling soundworld where stark harmonies and textures are reconciled with lyrical warmth.

⊙ Clarinet Concertinos: King; English Chamber Orchestra; Wordsworth (Hyperion CDA66634; with works for clarinet and orchestra by Arnold and Britten).

This Hyperion recording of the *Clarinet Concertinos* is still the only available CD to contain any of Maconchy's orchestral writing. Clarinettist Thea King, who has recorded many little-known works by British composers, gives gloriously persuasive performances with sensitive accompaniment from the English Chamber Orchestra.

THE STRING QUARTETS

Maconchy wrote string quartets throughout her life, and her fourteen works in the genre make up a sequence as rewarding as those by Bartók or

Shostakovich. The string quartet was the perfect medium for her closely argued musical language, clearly demonstrating her fascination with melodic and rhythmic counterpoint.

Maconchy described her *Quartet No. 1,* written when she was 25, as "extrovert, direct and rhythmical"; its high-spirited energy is apparent from the characteristic driving rhythms of the opening bars. The dramatic and darkly brooding *Quartet No. 4*, written during World War II, demonstrates her technique of building the material of a work from one cell, in this instance an idea first heard in the opening cello pizzicato. The prizewinning *Quartet No. 5* – her own favourite – contains an achingly beautiful slow movement, while *Quartet No. 8* (1966) is the most dissonant. *Quartet No. 9*, with its deeply moving, elegiac slow movement, was written in August 1968 at the time of the Soviet occupation of Prague.

The viola was Maconchy's favourite instrument and this can be clearly seen by its central role in the two single-movement quartets of the 1970s, *Quartet No. 10* and *Quartet No. 11,* both characteristic of Maconchy's later, more condensed style. The latter she described as like "a piece of woven material, with contrasting colours and patterns running through it".

⭘ String Quartets Nos. 5–8: Bingham Quartet (Unicorn Kanchana DKPCD9081).

This central volume of the Unicorn Kanchana series of Maconchy's complete quartets (performed by young British ensembles) makes a good introduction to her work in this genre. The Bingham play the four quartets (written between 1948 and 1966) with great passion and sincerity. Each of the volumes contains valuable notes on the individual works as well as an interesting essay on composing string quartets, all written by Maconchy herself.

VOCAL MUSIC

Maconchy's vocal music ranges from early solo songs to the haunting *My Dark Heart* (1981), a setting of three of the Irish writer J.M. Synge's prose translations of Petrarch's sonnets, in which the singer laments lost love while recalling moments of past happiness. Synge's words have a particularly Irish cadence, which is echoed in Maconchy's finely judged lyrical writing.

⭘ My Dark Heart: Manning; Lontano; de la Martinez (Lorelt LNT 101; with LeFanu, *The Old Woman of Beare*).

This strong performance of *My Dark Heart*, sung by the versatile, modern music specialist Jane Manning and the contemporary music group Lontano, comes with an equally impressive version of *The Old Woman of Beare* by Maconchy's daughter Nicola LeFanu.

GUSTAV MAHLER

(1860–1911)

Until little more than thirty years ago, Mahler's heady, epic compositions were regarded with a degree of suspicion similar to that which still dogs many of his contemporaries, such as Zemlinsky and Schreker. In his own time he was known far more for his conducting than for his music and it took many decades of proselytizing by conductors such as Bruno Walter, Wilhelm Mengelberg and, later, Leonard Bernstein, before the symphonies became the audience-pullers they are today – though there were always pockets of support, notably in the Netherlands and New York, both places where Mahler frequently conducted. That the symphonies finally caught on in a big way after World War II is doubtless due to an affinity between their unstable, angst-ridden content and the complex world of the late twentieth century.

Sigmund Freud, to whom Mahler turned for analysis in later life, found the roots of the composer's neuroticism in his childhood, which was spent in a somewhat tense family atmosphere. One memorable event occurred when the young Gustav rushed out into the street to escape a particularly heated parental argument, to be confronted with the playing of a military band (they lived next to a barracks) – an incident often seen as prophetic of Mahler's later juxtaposition of widely contrasting moods in his music. In a Mahler symphony one passes from the tragic to the commonplace, from the ingenuous to the ironic, from rustic folk song to spiritual ecstasy, in the space of a moment.

Mahler was born into a Jewish-Bohemian family at a time when official attitudes to Jews in the Austro-Hungarian Empire were relaxing after years of residence restrictions. Thus he was able to benefit

LEBRECHT COLLECTION

The last studio portrait of Mahler – Munich, September 1910

from a decent education in Prague and later at the Vienna Conservatory, where his fellow pupils included Hugo Wolf (see p.480) and Hans Rott. A recently rediscovered symphony by Rott (available on Hyperion CDA 66366) gives an intriguing insight into Mahler's early work: it predates Mahler's own symphonies yet prefigures many of their musical themes, suggesting that Rott, who died insane at the age of 26, was a significant influence. Among the many other influences on Mahler in Vienna was the music of Bruckner who, though only beginning to receive the recognition he deserved, was idolized by Mahler and his fellow students.

Just as he was beginning to find his voice as a composer in the dramatic cantata *Das klagende Lied* (1880) and other early songs, Mahler discovered his talents as a conductor and soon won renown for his performances of the operas of Mozart, Beethoven and Wagner. By 1888 he was chief conductor at the Budapest Opera and within a few years was in charge at the more prestigious house in Hamburg, where his thoroughly prepared performances – at a time when rehearsal was often seen as an encumbrance – gained him more plaudits. It was also during this period that he established the pattern of composing that would last until his death: with concert and opera seasons taking up most of the year from autumn to spring, he had to confine his writing to the summer months, usually retiring to the idyllic surroundings of the Carinthian lakes in southern Austria. To Mahler, it was a life of great continuity, for he saw little distinction between bringing masterpieces to life in the concert hall and opera house, and expressing his innermost thoughts in his own music. Refusing to separate life from art, Mahler embodied the apotheosis of Romanticism.

As Mahler became disenchanted with musical life in Hamburg he set his sights on Vienna and went to the lengths of converting to Roman Catholicism to make himself acceptable to the anti-Semitic Viennese court that ran the opera house. He was duly appointed principal conductor in 1897 and survived ten acrimonious years at the head of one of Europe's top musical establishments, where he raised musical and dramatic standards to unforeseen heights, but at the expense of never-ending battles with orchestral players, singers and critics. (The top job at Vienna is still one of the most antagonistic posts in the music world.) Mahler rarely conducted his own music in Vienna, not wanting to be seen taking advantage of his position, but toured widely through northern Europe with his symphonies and song cycles.

In 1907 he resigned from his Viennese post and accepted the offer of a contract at the Metropolitan Opera in New York, but ended up becoming more involved in the regeneration of the New York Philharmonic. At the same time a serious heart disease began to manifest itself, a bacterial infestation brought on by the throat infections that had plagued him throughout his life. His last compositions, the ninth and tenth symphonies and the song cycle *Das Lied von der Erde*, are overwhelmingly imbued with premonitions of his death, which finally occurred on May 18, 1911, after a fruitless visit to a bacteriologist in Paris on the way back from his final American trip.

THE SYMPHONIES

"The symphony is a world", proclaimed Mahler to Sibelius, and indeed few if any composers have crammed so much into their symphonies, from funeral marches to vast images of nature, from ironically quoted popular tunes and dances to great apostrophes to love. These are not purely abstract works in the tradition of Brahms and Bruckner: all have strong extra-musical elements, incorporating poems or religious texts, or possessing an ambitious philosophical "programme". On the other hand, these programmes are not the detailed paraphrases that you'll find in symphonic poems of Berlioz or Strauss, and it's not necessary to know the "meaning" of the piece before listening to it – Mahler himself regarded his explanatory subtitles as mere crutches, and often deleted them from his revisions. Most of the symphonies describe a dramatic progression of some sort, and accordingly demonstrate "progressive tonality", where the symphony ends in a different key from that in which it began.

The first four were influenced by the folk-like verses of *Des Knaben Wunderhorn* and his own settings of them (see p.241), and three of them incorporate solo singers and/or choirs. There followed three purely instrumental works of enormous power and range, but he returned to the vocal symphony with *Symphony No. 8* – in terms of number of performers required, his most massive work. After that came the incomparable, valedictory *No. 9* and an attempt at completing a tenth (since reworked into a performable version). Of the ten, the first and fifth are probably the best places to start.

◑ **Symphonies Nos. 1–9; Adagio of Symphony No. 10: Kubelík; Bavarian Radio Symphony Orchestra**
(Deutsche Grammophon 429 042-2; 10 CDs).

If Simon Rattle gets around to recording the whole set (he has spoken of having reservations about *No. 8*), his could well prove to be the first choice for a complete symphonic cycle. In the meantime the choice lies between the cycles from Abbado, Bernstein, Haitink, Kubelík, Maazel, Solti and Tennstedt, all of which are available at mid- or bargain price. Inevitably in a body of work with such a range of challenges it would be a miracle if a single conductor were to produce the ideal performance of each and every symphony, but the most consistently satisfying attempt is Rafael Kubelík's. Though none of the symphonies merits an outright first choice individually, this is a low-cost way of getting hold of the lot in consistenty excellent performances.

SYMPHONY NO. 1

Mahler's *Symphony No. 1* (1885–88) began life as a symphonic poem, and a vestige of this early draft survives in the subtitle that is occasionally attached to it, *Titan*, and in the appearance on some recordings of a subsequently discarded movement entitled *Blumine*. The flower imagery of this movement provided an interlude in the rather confused narrative of the original, which was based on a novel by Jean-Paul, in which the hero figure's contemplation of nature leads to a fatal self-absorption. Suggestions of this extra-musical programme remain in the work's evocative, primordial opening, the slow movement's funeral march (based upon *Frère Jacques*) and the presence of song tunes from Mahler's own *Lieder eines fahrenden Gesellen* (see p.241). It is remarkably original for a first symphony and its direct influences are hard to define, beyond a melodiousness recalling Schubert and a sense of scale derived from Bruckner.

○ City of Birmingham Symphony Orchestra; Rattle
(EMI CDC 7 54647 2; with *Blumine*).

Simon Rattle's live recording with CBSO best captures the music's scale, with the twilight opening played at an extreme pianissimo and evolving into a most magical evocation of awakening nature. The rustic Scherzo has a real Austrian rumbustiousness, with the horns playing at full tilt, while the sense of irony in the funeral march is never far from the surface, and the climax of the finale is truly breathtaking.

◑ **Bavarian Radio Symphony Orchestra; Kubelík**
(Deutsche Grammophon 449 735-2; with *Lieder eines fahrenden Gesellen*).

Rafael Kubelík's account is somewhat undercharged when compared to that of Rattle, but it's an approach that is utterly convincing, emphasizing the work's delicacy and poetry. Speeds tend towards the brisk, but the lightness of Kubelík's touch and his complete control of the orchestra means that an idiomatic lilt is always guaranteed.

SYMPHONY NO. 2 – THE RESURRECTION

The first movement of the *Symphony No. 2* (1888–94) also began life as a symphonic poem, *Totenfeier*, or "Funeral Rites", in which Mahler claimed to show the "hero" of his first symphony being "borne to his grave". He later reworked this as the first movement of a symphony broadly expressing the concept of the life force's ability to rise again from the ashes of fate through faith in God – hence the symphony's subtitle.

The first three movements are purely instrumental, the self-explanatory funeral march being followed by two interludes looking back on the happy and bitter times of life; in the fourth movement, the "hero" hears the call of God in an evocative alto solo, *Urlicht* (Primeval Light); and in the finale he has to face the Day of Judgment before being granted immortality. Such a grand theme called for grand treatment and Mahler uses a vast orchestra (including ten horns and eight trumpets), together with two solo singers and a choir, in a work that lasts some ninety minutes.

○ Augér, Baker; City of Birmingham Symphony Orchestra & Chorus; Rattle (EMI CDS 7 47962 8; 2 CDs).

Simon Rattle is again the first recommendation here. He shapes phrases with attention paid to every nuance of the score, while the grand sweep remains paramount; his performers play and sing magnificently and the recording is often overwhelming.

◑ Cotrubas, Ludwig; Vienna State Opera Chorus, Vienna Philharmonic Orchestra; Mehta (Decca 440 615-2; 2 CDs; with Schmidt, *Symphony No. 4*).

Zubin Mehta is now a rather unfashionable conductor, but he has made some marvellous recordings and this is among the best of them. The Vienna Philharmonic Orchestra plays with an incandescent fervour, but what is more impressive is Mehta's control of the overall shape of the symphony, so that by the time you reach the finale there is an extraordinary sense of culmination and resolution. Coupled with a powerful performance of the *Symphony No. 4* by Franz Schmidt (a Viennese contemporary of Mahler), this is an exceptional bargain.

SYMPHONY NO. 3

Whereas *Symphony No. 2* is a hymn to humanity's salvation through spirituality, *Symphony No. 3* (1895–96) is a hymn to the natural world. Conceived as a seven-movement paean entitled *The Joyful Knowledge* or *A Summer Morning's Dream*, it originally bore movement headings such as *Summer Marches in*, *What the Meadow Flowers Tell Me* and *What Love Tells Me*, and ended in a child's view of heaven. In the event, Mahler turned this last movement into the finale of *Symphony No. 4* and, as with *No. 1*, he suppressed the somewhat twee details of the programme.

Although written for a slightly smaller orchestra than *No. 2*, it uses extravagant vocal forces (soprano, boys' chorus, women's chorus) for two brief movements. This was to be Mahler's broadest work in terms of scale, with a vast first movement suggesting the awakening of primeval life from the depths of winter, four contrasting middle movements (one a setting of Nietzsche's *Midnight Song*, another of a naive *Wunderhorn* poem), and an extended, slow-building Adagio finale culminating in an apotheosis in which, in Mahler's words, "Nature in its totality may ring and resound".

◑ Procter; London Symphony Orchestra, Wandsworth School Boys' Choir, Ambrosian Singers; Horenstein (Unicorn-Kanchana UKCD2006/7; 2 CDs).

For the best recording of this symphony you have to go back to Jascha Horenstein's classic recording with the LSO in the 1960s: no one has delved deeper into this majestic work. The sound quality might leave something to be desired by modern standards, but this is one of those cases where the music has to come before technology.

○ Ludwig; New York Choral Artists, Brooklyn Boy's Chorus, New York Philharmonic Orchestra; Bernstein (Deutsche Grammophon 427328-2; 2 CDs).

Leonard Bernstein was a renowned interpreter of Mahler, but his epic readings will not appeal to everyone. Bernstein's Mahler is, above all, a creature of emotional extremes, and there are times when he wallows in the angst to excessive lengths. This is not the case here: rather there is a sense of grandeur without bombast, and depth of feeling without sentimentality.

SYMPHONY NO. 4

The projected finale of *Symphony No. 3*, a soprano setting of the *Wunderhorn* song *Das himmlisches Leben* (The Heavenly Life), became the climax of *Symphony No. 4* (1899–1901), a much more restrained work than its predecessors. The orchestra is of a normal size, there are only four movements and the childlike sentiments of the finale's text affect the whole work. It is not devoid of weightier moments, however – its Scherzo requires the lead violinist to tune the violin up a tone to add a sinister touch to proceedings.

◑ Lott; London Philharmonic Orchestra; Welser-Möst (EMI CD-EMX2139).

Although Franz Welser-Möst had a rough critical ride when he was music director of the LPO, his performance of this symphony is completely successful, with a perfect balance between the music's naivety and irony, and Felicity Lott singing radiantly in the last movement.

⊙ Raskin; Cleveland Orchestra; Szell (Sony SBK 46535; with *Lieder eines fahrenden Gesellen*).

Mahler's sunniest symphony is handled with a perfect touch by Georg Szell in this 1964 recording. The Cleveland Orchestra was at a high point at this period and there is great subtlety and colouristic variety throughout. In Judith Raskin (as has often been pointed out) Szell had the ideal soloist for the last movement's ingenuous charm.

SYMPHONY NO. 5

With his *Symphony No. 5* (1901–02), Mahler abandoned the use of vocal forces for a five-movement symphony that for once has no preconceived programme, though it follows the dark-to-light pattern of the earlier symphonies, beginning with a funeral march and ending with a triumphant, exuberant finale. The intervening episodes are a ferocious Allegro, whose mood is then completely banished by the ensuing, uninhibitedly jolly

Scherzo and the ineffably tender Adagietto for harp and strings, a piece of music made famous by Visconti's film of *Death in Venice*.

O Vienna Philharmonic Orchestra; Bernstein (Deutsche Grammophon 423 608-2).

Only the first symphony is more often recorded than the *Symphony No. 5*. The most invigorating account is Leonard Bernstein's live recording with the Vienna Philharmonic: his self-indulgent way with Mahler has always had its detractors, but here his empathy with the composer's intentions is unsurpassed. The playing conveys the excitement of a live event and the recording is unusually spacious.

◑ New Philharmonia Orchestra; Barbirolli (EMI CDM 7 64749 2; with *Blumine*).

This is a justly famous account. In particular it is the warmth and geniality of Barbirolli's reading that sticks in the memory – this is Mahler with a very human face. It doesn't have the detail or incisiveness of Bernstein's reading, and there are a few moments when the music seems to lose its way, but nevertheless this is well worth investigating.

SYMPHONY NO. 6

The *Symphony No. 6* (1903–04) was Mahler's only symphony to follow the conventional four-movement pattern and to be centred on a single key, A minor. He at first toyed with the idea of naming it the *Tragic* and, while there may be no specific text attached to the work, it's a powerful, pessimistic composition. In its first version, the last movement contained three crashing blows, marked to be played with a sledgehammer on a resonant surface; intended to represent the hammer-blows of fate, they were to prove prophetic when a year after the first performance in 1906 he lost his position at the Vienna Opera, his daughter died and his heart condition was diagnosed. Mahler was highly superstitious and later excised the third of the blows from the score as if to ward off his death, yet the bleakness of the work's ending is matched only by Tchaikovsky's sixth symphony and Mahler's own ninth.

O Vienna Philharmonic Orchestra; Boulez (Deutsche Grammophon 445 835-2).

Pierre Boulez is perhaps not an obvious choice as a Mahler interpreter but in this, the bleakest of all his symphonies, he excels himself in a performance of unrivalled cumulative impact. It's a highly controlled performance but by no means unemotional and the Vienna Philharmonic's sumptuous sound really benefits from having such a firm hand at the tiller.

O Israel Philharmonic Orchestra; Mehta (Teldec 4509 98423-2).

Zubin Mehta's approach is more expansive and luxuriant than that of Boulez but he never becomes self-indulgent (a big risk in this symphony). The Israel Philharmonic has a reputation for being an orchestra of individuals, but the response to Mehta's direction is electrifying in its level of commitment and this is a tremendously exciting performance.

SYMPHONY NO. 7

As if trying to exorsize the gloom of *No. 6*, Mahler's *Symphony No. 7* (1904–05) ends with his most uninhibited attempt at being cheerful, in a finale that combines allusions to Offenbach's *Can-Can* and Wagner's *Die Meistersinger* in a general melange of C major joyfulness that can seem merely gaudy in the wrong hands. It is probably this movement that has led to the work's relative neglect until recent years, when the glories of its other movements have at last been recognized. The funereal first movement may not be one of his most profound symphonic essays, but is made up for by the three movements that follow. The outer pair are entitled *Nachtmusik* (Night Music) and combine the moods of the nocturne with those of a serenade (the song-like second includes important parts for mandolin and guitar), while the central movement is one of Mahler's most miraculous creations – a ghostly Scherzo revealing his mastery of orchestral colour.

O Cleveland Orchestra; Boulez (Deutsche Grammophon 447 756-2).

In what is arguably Mahler's most problematic symphony, Boulez gives a vigorously assured performance that brings out the work's richly various sonorities and rhythmic energy. Boulez is one of the few conductors who manages to bring real coherence to the last movement.

⊙ City of Birmingham Symphony Orchestra; Rattle (EMI CDC 7 54344 2).

Simon Rattle brings this music vividly to life. The symphony has been in the CBSO's repertoire for many seasons and this live recording combines the advantages of familiarity with the risks inherent in live performance. The acoustic is perhaps a little dense for the large forces used, but the whole enterprise is thrillingly executed, with every detail in the score given its proper weight.

SYMPHONY NO. 8 – THE SYMPHONY OF A THOUSAND

If *Symphony No. 6* descends to Hell, *Symphony No. 8* (1906) rises heavenward. It is in two parts – the first a setting of the Pentecostal Latin hymn *Veni Creator Spiritus*, the second a setting of the closing scene from Goethe's *Faust*. Thus Mahler returned to the use of vocal forces, and not simply for the odd movement, as in the second, third and fourth symphonies: here he calls for eight soloists, a boys' chorus and large mixed chorus, hence the nickname of the *Symphony of a Thousand*. The result is a wide-ranging work, the rigorous counterpoint and earnestness of the opening hymn contrasting with the lush treatment of the Goethe; but the two parts are linked by certain musical themes and by their conceptual similarity – the first is a humanist interpretation of a Christian text concerning the search for enlightenment, the second a portrayal of Faust's redemption through wisdom and love.

⊙ Harper, Augér, Popp, Minton, Watts, Kollo, Shirley-Quirk, Talvela; Chicago Symphony Orchestra; Solti (Decca 448 293-2; 2 CDs).

The choice of recordings rests between Solti and Tennstedt, both superb but quite different in approach. Solti's is an operatic reading, stunningly recorded and with a first-class roster of singers; the engineers capture the scale of the work like no others, from the pungent organ at the opening and close to the tintinnabulating pianos and harps in the second movement.

⊙ Connell, Wiens, Lott, Schmidt, Denize, Versalle, Hynninen, Sotin; London Philharmonic Orchestra & Choir, Tiffin School Boys' Choir; Tennstedt (EMI CDS 7 47625 8; 2 CDs).

Klaus Tennstedt's recording, on the other hand, while no less massive in overall concept, is a more personable account, with greater care taken over orchestral detail and more air around the notes. A difficult choice, then: Solti for greater physical impact, Tennstedt for greater musical qualities.

SYMPHONY NO. 9

Mahler was a very ill man by the time he wrote his *Symphony No. 9* (1908–11). Ever superstitious, he attempted to trick fate out of its habit of terminating composer's lives after their ninth symphonies (as in the cases of Beethoven, Bruckner and Dvořák) by pretending that this was really his tenth, with his intervening symphonic song cycle *Das Lied von der Erde* (see p.242) as the true *No. 9*. This sleight of hand did nothing to lighten the tone of the music, for this symphony is the most desperately death-ridden piece Mahler ever wrote. The opening movement, in which you can hear ominously tolling bells, the tread of a funeral march and a faltering heartbeat, gives way to a deliberately charmless rustic Ländler with a vulgar, distorted waltz at its centre. The Rondo-Burlesque third movement is, in the words of Mahler scholar Deryck Cooke, a "contrived chaos . . . a ferocious outburst of fiendish laughter at the futility of everything". From this emerges the Adagio finale, in which death is stoically accepted and the music fades into tranquillity.

◑ Berlin Philharmonic Orchestra; Karajan (Deutsche Grammophon DG 410 726-2; 2 CDs).

The ninth is the most difficult of Mahler's symphonies to bring off in performance – its colossal structures, drastic changes of tone and profound solemnity require the greatest conductors and orchestras to do it justice. Herbert von Karajan and the Berlin Philharmonic are such a partnership. Their live concert performance, recorded in 1982, is immaculate, displaying an intensity rarely found in other performances of the work, with the orchestra playing as if their lives depended on it.

◑ Vienna Philharmonic Orchestra; Walter (Dutton Labs CDEA 5005; 2 CDs).

Bruno Walter, Mahler's friend and chief acolyte, conducted the first performance of the ninth in 1912. Twenty-six years later Walter gave another performance in Vienna, just a few weeks before the Nazis invaded Austria. Dutton Labs have now improved the previously rather constricted sound to something much more than merely acceptable, and the result is unmissable – here is a highly charged and intensely dynamic reading which makes a uniquely powerful impact, irrespective of its profound historical significance.

SYMPHONY NO. 10

In the summer of 1910 Mahler made a sketch of a new symphony, but left it in an unfinished state when he died the following spring. All five movements of the *Symphony No. 10* had a continuous line of music and three of them were filled out in more detail and partially scored for orchestra. Two movements were edited for performance in 1924, but it wasn't until the early 1960s that Deryck Cooke produced a performing version of the whole work, judiciously filling out passages that Mahler had not had time to expand beyond a single melodic line. This version took a while to be accepted by the musical establishment and there are still many eminent conductors who refuse to touch it on the grounds that it never can be a true representation of Mahler's intended completion. Yet those who do ignore it ignore a valuable insight into Mahler's state of mind a year after completing the doom-laden ninth. Here, death is again very much a subject of the work, but the overall impression is one of achieved peace, as if Mahler had at last exorcized his terrors.

O Bournemouth Symphony Orchestra; Rattle (EMI CDC 7 54406-2).

One conductor who has never had any doubts about the completion of the work, and indeed has included his own editorial additions in performance, is Simon Rattle. His recording with the Bournemouth Symphony Orchestra precedes his partnership with the CBSO, but is as assured a performance as his later ones in Birmingham.

VOCAL MUSIC

A smaller but no less important part of Mahler's heritage is his contribution to German song, as significant in its own way as that of Schubert, Wolf and Strauss. Like Schubert, he had a supreme melodic gift, with a vocal style that was honed by setting various folk texts in his early songs – and indeed the folkloric element remained central to all his vocal work, including the solo and choral sections of his symphonies. Virtually all his songs exist in versions accompanied by piano or orchestra (even the symphonic *Das Lied von der Erde* has an authentic piano version), but, given Mahler's skills in orchestration, the fuller alternatives are invariably more effective.

DAS KLAGENDE LIED

Das klagende Lied, a cantata for four soloists, chorus and orchestra, setting Mahler's own poem relating a folk tale about a fratricide, sounds too accomplished to be the work of a 20-year-old. This immensely accomplished piece is the composition in which he "found himself as Mahler", as he once said, and apart from a few songs and a movement for piano quartet he destroyed everything that had preceded it. In the 1890s he revised the cycle and discarded its first movement, which he felt to be superfluous to the storytelling, but fortunately this inspired if sprawling movement has now returned to circulation – though beware that some older recordings still omit it.

O Dunn, Baur, Fassbaender, Hollweg, Schmidt; Berlin Radio Symphony Orchestra, Düsseldorf City Music Society; Chailly (Decca 425 719-2).

Riccardo Chailly's recording of the complete work is magnificent in every way. He has a superb orchestra and a fine quintet of soloists – a quintet, since the imaginative decision has been taken to have a boy treble sing the murdered brother's lament, rather than the marked mezzo-soprano, an evocative and eerie touch. The recording is up to Decca's best standards, with the offstage band in the finale (representing the behind-the-scenes revelry of the wedding feast) at just the right distance, and the main orchestra and chorus caught to thrilling effect.

THE SONGS

The text of Mahler's first song cycle, *Lieder eines fahrenden Gesellen* (Songs of a Wayfarer; 1883–85) is again his own, and is again in the style of the poetry from the immensely popular collection of folk texts titled *Des Knaben Wunderhorn* (The Boy's Magic Horn). There are four songs, all dealing with a rejected lover's attempts to find solace in nature and, ultimately, in death – the second song became the main theme in the first movement of *Symphony No. 1*, the composition of which followed immediately on from these songs.

Mahler's settings from *Des Knaben Wunderhorn* itself do not form a cycle as such, but are a collection of individual songs composed between 1892 and 1901. The range of these songs – some of which percolated into the symphonies written during this period – is impressively wide, from the mournful *Das irdische Leben* (Earthly Life) to the witty *Lob des hohen Verstandes* (Praise of Lofty Intellect), and they are usually shared between a female and a male singer.

After such folksiness, the *Kindertotenlieder* (Songs on the Deaths of Children; 1901–04) are made of sterner stuff. Although these settings of five poems by Friedrich Rückert predate the tragic death of one of Mahler's children, they seem an expression of an overwhelming fear for their wellbeing. While working on these songs, Mahler composed five more settings of poems by Rückert; these

Rückert-Lieder are no more a cycle than is the *Wunderhorn* series, instead dwelling on a variety of Mahlerian themes, from love and life to loneliness and death.

⊙ Lieder eines fahrenden Gesellen; Kindertotenlieder; Rückert-Lieder; Des Knaben Wunderhorn (three songs): Fassbaender; German Radio Symphony Orchestra; Chailly (Decca 425 790-2).

The mezzo-soprano Brigitte Fassbaender has no equal in the early cycles, and her disc with Chailly is nothing short of stunning, giving each song a character and personality of its own. In terms of tone quality, her voice is perhaps coarser than many of her rivals (both male and female), but its innate expressiveness is totally involving.

⊙ Des Knaben Wunderhorn: Schwarzkopf, Fischer-Dieskau; London Symphony Orchestra; Szell (EMI CDC 7 47277 2).

For the *Wunderhorn* songs, Elisabeth Schwarzkopf and Dietrich Fischer-Dieskau are the most effective pairing in their classic 1968 recording with Georg Szell conducting the London Symphony Orchestra. Both singers are renowned for the way they stress the meaning of the words, and the result here is particularly characterful and communicative.

⊙ Des Knaben Wunderhorn: Hampson, Parsons (Teldec 9031-74726-2).

Thomas Hampson and Geoffrey Parsons have resurrected Mahler's original piano versions of the *Wunderhorn* songs on a splendidly sung and played recording. Most other piano-accompanied recordings use an edition made from piano reductions of the orchestral score, whereas this version uses a piano score which preceded the orchestration.

DAS LIED VON DER ERDE

The valedictory song cycle *Das Lied von der Erde* is one of Mahler's most personal works and is perhaps his most beautiful, combining symphonic scale and structure with the narrative clarity of a song cycle. The six songs are settings of translated Chinese poems conveying the relationships between death and nature, with human life presented as a transient stage in the ever-renewing processes of the earth. Mahler emphasized the message with some words of his own at the end of the last song, as the music fades away: "The dear earth everywhere/Blossoms in spring and grows green again!/Everywhere and eternally the distance shines with a blue light!/Eternally . . . eternally . . .". The cycle calls for a tenor and mezzo-soprano, who alternate between songs of defiance and resignation, but the dominant performer is the mezzo, who has the final thirty-minute movement to herself.

◑ Ludwig, Wunderlich; New Philharmonia Orchestra; Klemperer (EMI CDC 7 47231-2).

In terms of the vocal quality of both soloists, this 1964 recording has never been bettered. Fritz Wunderlich's golden tenor deals effortlessly with the relatively unrewarding tenor part, and Christa Ludwig similarly brings an ease of delivery and a warmth to the role that seems absolutely right. Klemperer was an assured and unmannered Mahlerian and he draws a rhapsodic performance from the New Philharmonia.

⊙ Fassbaender, Araiza; Berlin Philharmonic Orchestra; Giulini (Deutsche Grammophon 413 459-2).

For those wanting a more vivid sound, this is the modern recording to go for. Few mezzos have penetrated more deeply into this profound music than Brigitte Fassbaender, whose voice takes on a truly gut-wrenching quality at the moment of death towards the end of the last poem. Her tenor is Francisco Araiza, forthright and assured, but also more lyrical than some of his rivals. Giulini conducts the Berlin Philharmonic in a slow but passionate and heart-rending account of the score.

⊙ Donose, Harper; National Symphony Orchestra of Ireland; Halász (Naxos 8.550933).

Naxos's recordings of Mahler's symphonies have been decidedly patchy; this, however, is an unqualified success. It stands at the other end of the spectrum to Giulini's recording, being both sprightly in pace and relatively reticent in interpretation. If this makes it sound insipid, it isn't. Ruxandra Donose, who has a rich but incisive voice of an eastern European tint, is completely in control of Mahler's long phrases and her undramatic approach lets the music provide the poignancy.

⊙ Ferrier, Patzak; Vienna Philharmonic Orchestra; Walter (Decca 414 194-2).

Kathleen Ferrier became a noted exponent of this work, and that is the principal reason for getting this 1952 mono recording (Julius Patzak's voice was by this time a little frayed at the edges). Ferrier's voice has a poignant vulnerability which is deeply moving (especially in the final song), but be warned – the transfer to CD has not improved the sound.

FRANK MARTIN

(1890–1974)

Swiss culture has always been a bridge between the Germanic and Latin worlds, a situation embodied in the person and music of Frank Martin, who was born into a Geneva-based family of French Protestant descent but was more inclined towards the German approach to art. Martin composed from the age of 8 (Bach's *St Matthew Passion* was an early inspiration), and was taught harmony and counterpoint but never underwent any formal conservatory-level training – he actually began, but never completed, a course in mathematics and physics. Initially he was more interested in music theory and education than in composition (he became a renowned teacher and lecturer), and the now more or less forgotten works from the 1920s were let down by their excessively theoretical basis – the exception is the remarkable *Mass for Double Choir* (1926). During the 1930s his work gained more focus with the development of a personal language, albeit one which drew on various aspects of modernism including Schoenberg's serialism and the neo-classicism of Stravinsky. Martin was essentially a craftsman, and though analogies with watch-making are a little far-fetched, there is a consistently meticulous and ordered quality to much of his work.

His best-known orchestral works date from the 1940s, in particular the ingeniously neo-classical *Petite Symphonie Concertante* (1945) and the *Concerto for Seven Wind Instruments* (1949). But it is as a setter of words that Martin comes into his own: his choice of, usually mythic, texts is always intensely personal and often highly original, and his settings exude a sincerity and a respect for the words that reminds one of Britten. These include the oratorios *Le Vin herbé* (1941) and *In terra pax* (1944), and the song cycles *Der Cornet* (1943) and *Sechs Monologe aus "Jedermann"* (1943). Martin later wrote a pair of operas, *Der Sturm* (1955), based on Shakespeare's *The Tempest*, and *Monsieur de Pourceaugnac* (1962), based on Molière, and there are numerous chamber and vocal works sprinkled throughout his career, as well as a series of concertos. Only a small portion of his output is performed with any regularity outside of Switzerland, but an increasing number is now available on CD.

◑ **Petite Symphonie Concertante; Concerto for Seven Wind Instruments; Violin Concerto; Passacaglia; In terra pax: Lausanne Choral Union; Suisse Romande Orchestra; Ansermet** (Decca 448 264-2; 2 CDs).

Decca have gathered together all Ansermet's pioneering recordings of Martin (made in the 1950s and 1960s) in their two-for-the-price-of-one series. The sound does occasionally show its age, but these are fresh and incisive performances, and an inexpensive and effective way of getting to know this composer in depth.

ORCHESTRAL WORKS

The *Petite Symphonie Concertante*, arguably Martin's masterpiece, was written as a commission from the Basle-based conductor and impresario Paul Sacher, who asked Martin to compose something that gathered together all the common stringed instruments – harp, harpsichord, piano and string orchestra. Martin came up with a piece that used the eighteenth-century concerto grosso as its model, but reversed the priorities of that form by giving prominence to the harp and harpsichord, the parts conventionally associated with the accompanying role. Martin's deployment of this unique combination of instruments is highly resourceful, and like many of his works it is constructed from themes using all twelve tones of the chromatic scale, but clothed in a harmonic style that makes the music sound almost tonal.

The most intriguing of Martin's other orchestral works is the *Concerto for Seven Wind Instruments*, an instantly appealing and occasionally astringent piece, spiced with musical allusions – a jibe at a Ravel-like waltz in the first movement, and references to Haydn's *Clock* symphony in the steady tread of the slow movement.

○ **Petite Symphonie Concertante; Concerto for Seven Wind Instruments; Passacaglia: Chevallier, Cybulska, Caillat; Chamber Orchestra of Geneva; Fischer** (Dinemec Classics DCCD012).

Thierry Fischer is an outstanding advocate of Martin's music and these are fine performances of the two most important orchestral works (but not quite up to the standard of his superb Deutsche Grammophon recording of the *Wind Concerto*, which is currently unavailable). The Chamber Orchestra of Geneva clearly knows these works well and brings just the right combination of virtuosity and delicacy to them.

SECHS MONOLOGE AUS "JEDERMANN"

The *Sechs Monologe aus "Jedermann"* (Six Monologues from "Everyman") is a song cycle extracted from the play *Jedermann* by Hugo von Hoffmannstahl (Richard Strauss's librettist), which is in turn based on the English medieval morality play *Everyman*. Its theme is the destructive power of excessive wealth. No knowledge of the play is necessary, and in fact dropping the listener straight into these contextless but connected monologues only heightens the sense of the mythic and the mysterious. The prevailing mood of intense foreboding is created by some powerfully atmospheric orchestral writing which has a distinctly *fin-de-siècle* feel to it. Indeed, in its overriding sense of an unnamed horror being faced by a lone, morally lost figure, it has a strong emotional kinship with Bartók's *Bluebeard's Castle*, though it is more lightly scored. For a dramatic and characterful baritone it is among the most rewarding of modern song cycles, a fact that has not escaped Dietrich Fischer-Dieskau who has recorded it at least twice.

⊙ Wilson-Johnson; London Philharmonic Orchestra; Bamert (Chandos CHAN 9411; with *Maria-Triptychon* and suite from *Der Sturm*).

This is the most readily available of current recordings (the better of the Fischer-Dieskau versions has been deleted) and boasts some beautifully controlled orchestral playing from the LPO and a searingly dramatic interpretation from David Wilson-Johnson. It comes with the equally intense but more acerbic *Maria-Triptychon*, settings of three famous Marian texts for soprano, violin and orchestra, and a tantalizing selection from the opera *Der Sturm*, which suggests a work of the highest quality.

MASS FOR DOUBLE CHOIR

The glorious a cappella *Mass for Double Choir* was completed in 1926 but not performed until 1963 – Martin apparently regarded it as a purely personal offering to God. It is one of the greatest of twentieth-century liturgical works, very much rooted in the tradition of early Christian music (chant-like passages are a major feature) but with an unmistakable modernity – above all in its imprecise tonality. There is something similar to the music of Arvo Pärt (see p.298) in the startling simplicity of its opening Kyrie, in which an undulating line in the altos is passed back and forth between the voices, building and overlapping with a supplicatory eloquence. Martin's sensitivity to words is everywhere apparent, but what is so effective is the way he applies a variety of devices – chant-like repetitions, melismatic passages, declamatory writing – and manages to weave them all together into a seamless and perfectly unified whole. The most exuberant writing occurs in the Gloria and Credo (the "Et Resurrexit" has all the eagerness of a nursery rhyme) but the work ends with a mood of stillness and peace in the Agnus Dei.

⊙ Christ Church Cathedral Choir; Darlington (Nimbus NI 5197; with Poulenc, *Mass in G* and *Salve Regina*).

There are now nine recordings of this work in the catalogue. This is one of the best, largely because it treats the Mass with the energy and a joyousness with which it was so clearly conceived. There are a few rough moments (the altos are a little hooty), but this is a very good choir whose sense of commitment makes this performance much more preferable to more meticulous but sedate renditions.

BOHUSLAV MARTINŮ

(1890–1959)

After Janáček, Martinů is the leading Czech composer this century, but – like Milhaud and Villa-Lobos – his reputation has suffered because he was both prolific and inconsistent. He often wrote at high speed, almost never revised his scores and was curiously indifferent to performance or acclaim. There's always a lyrical ingredient in his work, a strong rhythmic drive and, often, a sense of ebullience and fun.

Martinů was born in the little town of Polička in the Bohemian-Moravian highlands, an area remarkable for the richness of its musical traditions (Smetana and Mahler came from this region too). His family lived in a tiny room at the top of a church tower, where his father – a cobbler by trade – earned money by keeping an eye open for fires in the town below. For the rest of his life Martinů carried a postcard of the view from the tower, and his home town was to remain an inspiration for him even after World War II had forced him permanently into exile. A sickly child, he spent most of his time closeted in the tower until the age of 6, when school brought his first real confrontation with the outside world – a disorienting experience later echoed when he uprooted himself to live in Prague, Paris and the USA.

Martinů learned the violin, started composing aged 10, and in 1907, thanks to local donations, was sent to the conservatory in Prague, where he was not a very successful student. Though his *Czech Rhapsody*, written to celebrate the founding of the new republic in 1918, was played in the presence of President Masaryk, Martinů was a late developer as a composer – it wasn't until he was regularly playing the violin in the Czech Philharmonic in the early 1920s that his musical education really began. In 1923 he took advantage of a small grant from the ministry of education and went to Paris, intending to stay just a few months. He remained there for over seventeen years.

Paris was then the artistic capital of Europe, and Martinů – despite his shyness and inability to speak French – threw himself into the maelstrom. He went to the composer Albert Roussel for lessons and, fascinated by Stravinsky, popular music and jazz, dashed off a couple of noisy orchestral pieces and some experimental ballet scores, culminating in *La revue de cuisine* (1927), in which various kitchen utensils dance the charleston, tango and foxtrot. Later Parisian works included his most interesting opera, *Julietta*, a number of works on Czech folk themes – notably the ballet *Špalíček* (a huge success in Prague in 1933) and the beautiful cantata *Kytice* – and several concertos and concertante pieces in a sort of neo-Baroque style. In 1940, soon after the premiere of the magnificent *Double Concerto* (his best work), Martinů was blacklisted by the Nazis and his music was banned in Czechoslovakia. He and his wife fled Paris with no more than a suitcase and went to start a new life in America.

Like Bartók, Martinů didn't feel at home in the USA, although he was highly regarded by influential conductors such as Serge Koussevitsky and Eugene Ormandy, and received plenty of commissions. After the war ill-health prevented Martinů returning to Czechoslovakia, and with the arrival of the communist regime in 1948 he decided reluctantly to stay in America.

The most important works from this period of exile were the six symphonies composed between 1942 and 1951, but some of Martinů's best and most deeply Czech music was written after his return to France in 1953. There he composed a series of four cantatas inspired by the poems of Miloslav Bureš, a poet from his home town, and an opera, *The Greek Passion*, based on a story by Nikos Kazantzakis of *Zorba the Greek* fame. Martinů died in a Swiss hospital before the first performance; twenty years later his body was transferred to the family grave in Polička, in sight of his beloved tower.

JULIETTA

Martinů wrote fourteen operas and even more ballets in a wide variety of styles, but his greatest stage work, and his personal favourite, was the opera *Julietta* (1936–37). Based on a surreal play by the French writer Georges Neveux, it doesn't have a plot as such, being more an exploration of dreams and reality in a world where everyone has lost his or her memory. A young man named Michel comes into this strange world in search of Julietta, a young girl with whom he's been obsessed since his previous visit to the harbour town in which the opera is set, but he never manages to find anything tangible to grasp. Martinů kept the score of *Julietta* beside him on his deathbed, and it's easy to see why the work held a particular personal significance for a man who was a traveller and exile for much of his life. He associated the figure of Julietta not only with his wife, Charlotte, but also with a young composition student named Vítězslava Kaprálová with whom he had become infatuated. When she died, aged only 25, her last words were "Julietta, Julietta", and the musical motif associated with her crops up in subsequent works.

○ Tauberová, Zídek; Prague National Theatre Chorus and Orchestra; Krombholc (Supraphon 10 8176-2; 3 CDs).

On stage *Julietta* is a fascinating work, but is inevitably less captivating on disc. That said, the splendid recording from the Prague National Theatre captures as much of its haunting beauty as any CD could. There are no weak links in the substantial cast, which is led by Maria Tauberová as the intangible Julietta and Ivo Zídek as the troubled dreamer Michel.

CHORAL MUSIC

All of Martinů's finest choral music was written to folk texts, and perhaps the most beguiling examples of the genre are the four chamber cantatas composed as an act of homage to his home town at the end of his life. Setting texts by local writer Miroslav Bureš, the cycle follows a seasonal sequence beginning with *Otvírání studánek* (The Opening of the Wells), celebrating a May-time custom in the Moravian countryside when processions go into the hills to cleanse the wells and springs. Written for soloists, female chorus and a chamber group of two violins, viola and piano, this piece is fresh and naive, whereas there's a greater intimacy and softness to *Romance z pampelišek* (Romance of the Dandelions), for unaccompanied mixed chorus and soprano solo. *Legenda z dymu bramborové nati* (The Legend of the Smoke from Potato Fires) recounts the harvest-time legend of how the Virgin Mary steps down from a stained-glass window to work in the fields as a peasant; the soloists and chorus are accompanied by an ensemble of piano, recorder, clarinet, horn and accordion, which creates a sound rather like a band of village folk musicians. *Mikeš z hor* (Mikeš of the Mountains), for the same ensemble as the first cantata, tells how a shepherd boy settles his flock on a mountain so that the frost mistakes their white coats for snow and moves elsewhere, leaving them to enjoy a mild winter.

○ Chamber Cantatas: Kühn Mixed Chorus and soloists; Kühn (Supraphon 11 0767-2).

The cantatas are amongst Martinů's most profound celebrations of his homeland, and three of them are on this disc (*The Romance of the Dandelions* is coupled with the *Špalíček* CD listed below). *The Opening of the Wells* is sung with unsentimental freshness and is given a spirited instrumental accompaniment, though it's a little spoiled by an overintrusive narrator – thankfully, he's absent from the other two cantatas. The recording of all three is crystal clear.

BALLETS

Martinů wrote a series of ballets in Paris, several of which were experiments involving film, puppets, projections and impossible sets. Typical of this period is *Vzpoura* (Revolt), a ballet-fantasy in which bedlam breaks out among the musicians and sounds: black notes fight against white notes, high notes against low ones; the gramophone mutinies against ragtime and jazz; critics commit collective suicide and Stravinsky emigrates to a desert island. From the chaos a Moravian girl in national costume emerges singing a folk song, and a lyrical order is restored. *Špalíček*, written in the early 1930s, was Martinů's first large-scale work drawing primarily on Czech folk material – he called it a ballet of "popular plays, customs and fairy-tales". It's a piece that also bears the influence of Stravinsky's *Les Noces*, in that the texts sung by the soloists and chorus are integral to the score.

○ Vzpoura; Échec au Roi: Prague Symphony Orchestra; Bělohlávek (Supraphon 11 1415-2).

This CD is the premiere recording of *Vzpoura* and the chess ballet *Échec au Roi*. Bělohlávek's lively direction really underlines the cartoon-like high-spirits of Martinů's music in the 1920s.

○ Spalíček; Romance z pampelišek: Brno Philharmonic Orchestra; Jílek (Supraphon 11 0752-2; 2 CDs).

This colourful and fresh recording of *Špalíček* also includes *Romance z pampelišek*, one of the four cantatas to verses by Miroslav Bureš composed in the 1950s (see p.245).

SYMPHONIES AND CONCERTOS

Martinů's orchestral sound is very recognizable, with its driving momentum tempered by Czech lyricism, and the texture of the orchestra almost always given extra bite by a piano part. The remarkably varied six symphonies, all of which were written in America, are the most impressive of his orchestral pieces. *Symphony No. 1*, written in only fifteen weeks, is very lyrical and epic in scale; *No. 2* is pastoral and distinctly Czech-sounding; *No. 3* has an undertow of tragedy, reflecting its creation in wartime; *No. 4* is closer in spirit to the first symphony, and is reminiscent of Dvořák; *No. 5*, written at the end of the war, is more gentle and understated; and *No. 6*, subtitled "Fantaisies Symphoniques", is full of changing moods and intriguing textures, and includes a quotation from his fantasy opera *Julietta*.

Many of Martinů's huge number of concertos and concertante works settle into a note-spinning neo-Baroque groove which can be long-winded and tedious, but his *Double Concerto* – for two string orchestras, piano and timpani – is one of the masterpieces of twentieth-century music. Written in 1938 for Paul Sacher and his Basle Chamber Orchestra, this taut and powerful work was composed as a direct response to the imminent Nazi invasion of Czechoslovakia, and marks a turning point in his life. After 1938 Martinů was never to see his family or homeland again.

○ Symphonies 1–6: Bamberg Symphony Orchestra; Järvi (BIS CD 362, 363 & 402).

Several versions of Martinů's symphonies are now available, but Neeme Järvi's performances have the edge: the playing is both lyrical and dynamic, with a splendid sinewy quality in the syncopated rhythmic passages, and the recordings are very clear with a great dynamic range. If you want to sample just one disc from the series of three, begin with the CD of the third and fourth symphonies, as the two works are very contrasted and the fourth is one of Martinů's most immediately appealing works.

○ Double Concerto; Rhapsody-Concerto for viola and orchestra; Fresques de Piero della Francesca: Malmö Symphony Orchestra; DePriest (BIS-CD 501).

The *Double Concerto* is one of Martinů's most widely recorded works, and there are several fine versions available. We have selected this rugged performance by the Malmö Symphony Orchestra, not least because of the other delightful works on the CD – the unashamedly romantic *Rhapsody-Concerto* and the powerfully atmospheric *Fresques de Piero della Francesca*. This would be the ideal disc with which to start a Martinů collection.

PIETRO MASCAGNI

(1863–1945)

Verismo opera, which flared onto the musical landscape of Italy during the last ten years of the nineteenth century, was largely inspired by the literary realism of writers like Zola and the Sicilian Giovanni Verga, and it, in turn, foreshadowed the world of soap opera. In verismo operas emotions are extreme, characters are one-dimensional, the tension is high, the pace is fast, and the attention span is short – the two most successful verismo operas, Mascagni's *Cavalleria rusticana* and Leoncavallo's *I Pagliacci* (see p.218), last only an hour.

Pietro Mascagni, the father of "realistic" opera, shot to prominence on May 17, 1890, with the Rome premiere of *Cavalleria rusticana*, or "Rustic Chivalry". Things might have turned out very differently. Reading, by chance, of a competition for one-act operas, he prepared to send in the fourth act of his full-length opera *Ratcliff* but, unknown to him, his wife had already submitted the recently completed *Cavalleria* on his behalf. It was one of three winners, and received its first performance in front of a half-empy but wildly enthusiastic house.

The rapid international vogue for *Cavalleria* was unprecedented and its popularity remains undimmed – every opera house plays it once every few years, invariably on a double bill with *I Pagliacci* (*Cav & Pag*, as it's known in the trade). However, unlike Leoncavallo, Mascagni found success beyond his name-maker, and went on to produce some extremely fine music, most notably the three-act opera *L'amico Fritz*. He was also a respected conductor and assumed some of Toscanini's duties at La Scala when the maestro resigned in protest over the fascist regime. Mascagni had no such qualms and blithely launched each performance with the fascist hymn - indeed he was swiftly adopted by Mussolini's government as their official composer. Though this move earned him the obloquy of the victorious allies, by the 1950s he was back in the ranks of the one-hit wonders.

CAVALLERIA RUSTICANA

Set in Sicily, the plot of *Cavalleria rusticana* revolves around the relationship between Santuzza and Turiddu. Before the action starts, the latter has seduced the former, then deserted her for Lola, a former lover, now the wife of Alfio. In revenge, Santuzza reveals all to Alfio, who takes it rather badly and ends up killing Turiddu in a duel behind the church (to heighten the pathos, this all takes place on Easter Sunday). It's a cheap and cynical tale, similar to that of *I Pagliacci*, but *Cavalleria rusticana* is musically the superior – melodically, it stands up to comparison with the bulk of Puccini. The Intermezzo has been used time and time again in advertising campaigns, but the best part of the opera is the final fifteen minutes, during which Turiddu, the tenor lead, sings his marvellous testament to the wonders of wine, *Viva il vino*, and his concluding lament, *Mama, quel vino e generoso* – the latter is an extraordinary, highly moving bit of music. Alfio's involvement is one part bluster and one part ballast, but Santuzza gets some excellent writing, not least *Voi lo sapete*, in which she sings of her betrayal.

⊙ **Arragal, Evstatieva; Bratislava Radio Symphony Orchestra; Slovak Philharmonic Chorus; Rahbari** (Naxos 8 660022).

Though you can buy versions with flashier singing and finer sound quality, Naxos's account with the splendid Giacomo Arragal as Turiddu and Stefka Evstatieva as Santuzza wins hands down on purely musical terms. Rahbari's conducting has a few moments of indiscipline, but for the most part he's worthily solid and he avoids the self-consciousness and sentimentality so common amongst his better-known colleagues. The Slovak Philharmonic's playing does not stand comparison with that of Karajan's Berlin Philharmonic on DG, but the performance is blessed with an integrity and a sense of occasion sorely missing from that full-price "bench mark" (which is available only on a three-CD set).

JULES MASSENET

(1842–1912)

With the advent of Wagner, French composers such as d'Indy, Chausson and Chabrier reacted by creating their own vast Gothic operas, which usually amounted to little more than Teutonic heroics in French fancy dress. Jules Massenet, nineteenth-century France's finest prolific composer of opera, offered an alternative by redefining the lyrical French tradition – the tradition of Gounod (see p.165) – in the light of Wagner's advances in dramatic structure. Massenet was uninterested in profundity of any sort, but few composers have ever created such attractive surfaces.

After studies with Ambroise Thomas, Massenet won the Prix de Rome in 1863, then spent three years in Italy, where he visited Liszt, and got married. He had his first opera performed in 1867 and, after interruptions from the Franco-Prussian war, achieved his first major success in 1872 with *César de Bazan*. This was followed a few months later by the yet more popular *Marie-Magdeleine*, a work of "discreet and pseudo-religious eroticism", to use d'Indy's words. This eroticism, together with an affection for orientalism, coloured most of Massenet's subsequent work, and he was openly cynical about pandering to the French taste for religiose themes, declaring "I don't believe in all that creeping Jesus stuff, but the public likes it and we must always agree with the public."

In 1881, after a string of finely constructed oratorios, he produced *Herodiade*, a work whose free and semi-declamatory melodies can be seen as anticipating Debussy's *Pelléas* (see p.115). His next success, *Manon* (1884), used leitmotifs and weightier brass, a development that led to the composer's being labelled "Mademoiselle Wagner", a jibe produced partly by envy, for by now Massenet was the country's most popular opera composer. After *Manon*, Massenet produced three notable failures – *Le Cid*, *Le Mage* and *Esclarmonde* – but in 1892 he came up with his masterpiece, *Werther*. Taking his inspiration from Wagner's *Parsifal* and Goethe's *Sorrows of Young Werther*, Massenet here achieved a genuinely moving work which contrasts the Germanic sobriety of Charlotte, Werther's love, with the Gallic charm of Sophie – and in the characater of Werther himself he created his finest tenor role.

For a while Massenet produced verismo operas (after all, the French opera *Carmen* was the progenitor of verismo), but he finally settled back into his natural style of light, lyrical and saccharine music. His younger contemporaries were, however, unimpressed by his crowd-pleasing rhetoric. Indeed, it was Debussy's hatred of Massenet and his easily won success that drove him to complete *Pelléas et Mélisande*, a work which set the seal on Massenet's fall from grace. After *Sapho* (1897), only *Don Quichotte*, produced in 1910, brought Massenet any reminder of past glories, and he died bitter at the direction in which, in Debussy's hands, French music was now heading.

MANON

The source for Massenet's *Manon* is the same as that to which Puccini turned for his third opera – *Manon Lescaut*, by Abbé Prevost. As with *Werther*, the tale offers plenty of opportunities for lavish emotionalism – humble Manon elopes with the young nobleman Des Grieux, abandons him, returns to him after he has joined the priesthood in despair, is accused of prostitution and finally dies in a prison cell, in the arms of her lover. Though Massenet doesn't go for the extreme passions that Puccini wrung out of his source, his most affecting music is to be found in the five acts of this melodious tragedy – not least in the seminary scene, where Manon begs Des Grieux to leave the priesthood, and in Manon's death scene. Less dramatic but more emotional than *Werther*, this is a beautifully written opera and, of all his heroines, Manon is the most alive.

O Cotrubas, Kraus, Quilico, van Dam; Chorus and Orchestra of the Capitole de Toulouse; Plasson (EMI CDS7 49610-2; 3 CDs).

EMI's outstanding 1955 set, conducted by Pierre Monteux and with Victoria de los Angeles in glowing voice, is not currently available. Until it reappears, Michel Plasson's 1982 set is the best bet. Ileana Cotrubas is a lyrical, beautifully paced but nicely theatrical Manon, even if she lacks the darker qualities needed for the last two acts. Alfredo Kraus is as stylish as ever, and Gino Quilico is a huge success as Lescaut, making much of Massenet's rather one-dimensional material. The supporting cast are all excellent and the recorded sound is fresh and flexible.

WERTHER

Like Puccini, Massenet was obsessed with melody. Tender, sweetly sensuous, never violent or uncomfortably dramatic, his melodies determine the texture of the music as a whole, and there are instances in which Massenet produced strings of tunes that have little or nothing to do with what's happening on stage. With *Werther*, though, he achieved a perfect balance between drama, characterization and beauty of sound.

Based upon Goethe's novel, the tragedy principally concerns the affections of Werther, Charlotte and Albert. The poet Werther loves Charlotte, who loves Werther but is engaged to marry Albert. Werther leaves, returning to find Charlotte married. She begs him to leave her alone but upon finding that her husband has loaned him his pistols she rushes through a blizzard to find him dead. As you might imagine, the opera is remarkable for the pathos of much of the music, and it boasts moments of thrilling atmosphere. It also shows Massenet's fascination with the psychology of women, again like Puccini, and if Charlotte lacks the insight of some of Puccini's heroines, Massenet nonetheless gives her a highly convincing and sympathetic gravity. The first act contains the majority of *Werther*'s finest writing, but the Act Three reconciliation scene is perhaps the most impressive demonstration of Massenet's understanding of the human voice, while the finely constructed development towards the tragedy of Werther's death is unforgettable.

◑ **Kraus, Troyanos, Manuguerra, Barbaux; London Philharmonic Orchestra; Plasson** (EMI CMS 5 66516-2; 2 CDs).

Plasson does his best to get the LPO to adopt French tone and phrasing, allowing the heavy orchestrations their due without letting them overwhelm things. His stylistic inclinations are well served by the mellifluous Alfredo Kraus (although the Spanish tenor's pronunciation is frequently odd), and he and Tatiana Troyanos make a perfect couple, with the latter's naturally rapid vibrato and dark tone are nicely placed against Kraus's lighter voice. Manuguerra does well to hold back his formidable baritone as Albert, and he conveys just the right level of arrogance and cruelty. The sound is excellent and the price fair.

O Thill, Vallin, Roque, Féraldy; Opéra-Comique Orchestra; Cohen (EMI CHS 7 63195-2; 2 CDs).

This is one of the greatest of all French operatic recordings, notable for its old-fashioned style and glorious singing. Georges Thill maintains a powerful sense of line and heroic timbre whilst remaining alive to the sensuality of the language. Ninon Vallin's soprano has an urgency that perfectly complements Thill's regal sophistication. The sound is fine for 1931, but the full price is outrageous nearly seventy years after it was first released.

NICHOLAS MAW

(1935–)

Like his contemporaries Peter Maxwell Davies (see p.250) and Harrison Birtwistle (see p.63), Nicholas Maw has absorbed the legacy of serialism, yet his strongest affinities are with the luxuriant opulence of the late Romantic movement. The reconciliation of these influences has taken years to achieve, but has produced at least one work of major status.

Maw studied at the Royal Academy of Music in the mid-1950s, and in 1958 produced his first signicant piece, *Nocturne*. Written under the tutelage of the neo-classicist Lennox Berkeley, and owing much to Bartók, *Nocturne* won him a French government scholarship which allowed him to study in Paris with two of the most eminent teachers of his day, Max Deutsch (a pupil of Schoenberg) and Nadia Boulanger. A period of creative sterility followed, in which Maw eked out a living as a writer and teacher. His breakthrough came with the *Scenes and Arias* of 1962, a setting of twelfth-century texts for three sopranos and orchestra, in which the hedonism of Richard Strauss – and something of the attack of the Second Viennese School – found fresh chromatic richness. Developing this new idiom took the next eight years, an evolutionary process which Maw referred to as "my second apprenticeship". His series of operas from the mid- and late 1960s – *One Man Show*, *The Voice of Love* and *The Rising of the Moon* – are full of lyrical music, as deeply argued as before, yet more clear cut in its effects and now revealing the influence of Alban Berg alongside Strauss, Britten, Wolf and Brahms. Yet Maw's operas enjoyed limited success, which some have attributed to the crassness of some of the librettos – they include, for example, the sexual initiation rites of British soldiers in nineteenth-century Ireland.

In the 1970s Maw further developed his finesse in orchestration, blending colours and timbres in a way that gave clarity to music in which melodic motifs were elaborated with increasing drama, and at ever greater length. This is the period to which *Odyssey*, his major work, belongs.

LIFE STUDIES

Life Studies (1976), an eight-movement work for fifteen solo strings, clearly has strong affinities with some of the classics of twentieth-century string writing – Schoenberg's *Verklärte Nacht* and Tippett's *Concerto for Double String Orchestra* spring to mind – and yet has a unique and powerful energy of its own. Maw is obviously fascinated by the wide range of sonorities that can be obtained from limited forces, and the work abounds in mysterious contrasts of timbre: in the third study (*poco agitato*) a restless scurrying is countered by a slower, smeary string sound, while the next movement is dominated by jazzy pizzicato cadenzas on the double bass. Maw divides his forces into two groups and there is a constant sense of antiphonal argument in each of the studies, a tension that is finally dissipated only on the last note of the final study where all the instruments come together.

⊙ Life Studies; Sonata Notturna: English String Orchestra; Boughton (Nimbus NI 5471).

This is the second time that *Life Studies* has been recorded, but William Boughton's reading has a depth and an understanding of the music, not to say a marvellously thick sound, which makes it a clear first choice. It is coupled with the intensely lyrical *Sonata Notturna* for cello and strings, in which the soloist is Raphael Wallfisch.

ODYSSEY

Written between 1973 and 1979, then revised until 1985, *Odyssey* is the summation of Maw's expressive progress over the years, and is a journey in itself. It was composed in its playing order, and during its development Maw's style became less ambiguous, his debt to tonal music more blatant. Lasting ninety minutes, the whole gigantic structure is spun out of a 44-bar melody and owes something to Bruckner's sense of epic symphonic form. It begins with an Introduction which the composer has summarized as "a gigantic upbeat groping towards articulation", and moves through four contrasting movements before reaching an Epilogue which closes the music serenely.

⊙ City of Birmingham Symphony Orchestra; Rattle (EMI CDS 7 54277 2; 2 CDs).

Simon Rattle, the conductor in this premiere recording, rates Maw as the spiritual heir to William Walton, and comments, "I am convinced that *Odyssey* is a masterpiece, a whole world of ideas miraculously welded together: new, alert and alive." Rattle's interpretation, transparent and unforced, makes a case for *Odyssey* as a solid contribution to the English lyric tradition.

PETER MAXWELL DAVIES

(1934–)

With the English pastoral tradition flogged almost to death, and with serialism a battle won long ago, Peter Maxwell Davies has found a fresh source of inspiration in quotation from past ages and styles – but quotation lifted beyond pastiche onto an entirely individual level. His preoccupations are not merely stylistic. He presents himself as a composer "torn by the fundamental question of good and evil", writing in the face of a modern world which seems to look upon past atrocities and pronounce "They couldn't happen now."

Born in Manchester, he studied at the Royal Northern College of Music with Harrison Birtwistle, John Ogdon and Alexander Goehr, and soon became identified with the "Manchester Group" and its commitment to the serialist avant-garde. At the same time he developed an affection for medieval music – not just for its rhythmic devices but also for its notions of damnation. The stamp of medievalism would be audible in Maxwell Davies's work for years to come.

In 1957 Maxwell Davies won a scholarship to study composition in Rome, and two years later his orchestral piece *Prolations* won the Olivetti Prize. He returned to England and took up the post of Music Director at Cirencester Grammar School, at first just to make ends meet. The experience proved invigorating, and made his music clearer and simpler. His pleasure in writing for young people, evident in the 1960 carol sonatas *O Magnum Mysterium*, has remained with him.

Peter Maxwell Davies

Maxwell Davies's fascination with the life and music of John Taverner (see p.425) gave rise to two orchestral fantasias, the opera *Taverner* (1962–70) and other works developed from plainsong fragments. His methods were similar to those used in "parody" Masses in the fifteenth and sixteenth centuries, where the material of one composition is used to create another, but they also allowed parody in our modern sense – parody as critique. Thus *St Thomas Wake* is a "foxtrot for orchestra" based on a pavane by John Bull.

In 1968 – after periods at Princeton and at Adelaide University – Maxwell Davies returned to Britain and founded, with Harrison Birtwistle, the Pierrot Players, later renamed the Fires of London. Before long Maxwell Davies was writing most of his music for them: for instance, *Eight Songs for a Mad King* (1969), one of several music-theatre spectacles exploring extremes of delusion and hysteria. In chamber pieces composed for the group Maxwell Davies refined his elaborations of the rhythmic involutions of medieval scores, while the sonorities of certain instruments began to spark a new sharpness and clarity of ideas. The astringent tones of out-of-tune instruments connected with Maxwell Davies's fascination for "music of the absurd".

In 1971 he moved to Orkney. The sounds, landscapes, literature and history of the place have inspired many works since, including the first and second symphonies (1976 and 1980). His religious thought has become more mystical than it used to be, as exemplified by his *Hymn to St Magnus*, based on a twelfth-century psalm to the Orcadian saint. Crucial too has been the work of local writer George Mackay Brown, whose texts Maxwell Davies used for *St Magnus* (set in a concentration camp) and *Black Pentecost*.

These more recent works are the most immediately appealing, demonstrating his success in creating a harmonic language within a non-tonal idiom. Craggy and uncompromised, sometimes with a gruelling obsession for working through the formal implications of the music (first hearing can be exhausting work), Maxwell Davies is one of Europe's most challenging and theatrical composers.

WORLDES BLIS

Worldes Blis (1969) took three years to create, and painstaking craft is evident in every section of this granitic work. In the composer's own words, *Worldes Blis* develops "slowly in extremely articulated time-spans . . with a minimal presentation of the material in such a way as to make the structural bones as clear as possible". The title is taken from a thirteenth-century monody ("worldes blis lasts no time at all"), and the piece flows from isolated musical cells towards the theme of this source material through ever-changing melodic, rhythmic and harmonic contours, moving from serenity through tension to an explosive climax. It's as if traditional symphonic development, which sets out with the exposition of the subject, has here been thrown into reverse.

⊙ Manchester Cathedral Choir; Royal Philharmonic Orchestra, BBC Philharmonic Orchestra; Maxwell Davies (Collins 13902; with *The Turn of the Tide*).

Maxwell Davies paces this performance immaculately, maintaining the flow through each successive part. Its coupling, *The Turn of the Tide* (1992), depicts the creation of life on earth and the threat humanity poses to the rest of nature; intended to be played by professionals, with interludes in which schoolchildren can improvise, it shows Maxwell Davies at his most accessible.

BLACK PENTECOST

Written in 1979, the polemical *Black Pentecost* is a four-movement symphony with voices. Its title is taken from George Mackay Brown's poem *Dark Angels* ("Now, cold angels, keep the valley from the bedlam and cinders of a Black Pentecost") and the text is from his novel *Greenvoe*, set on the imaginary island of Hellya as it is ripped to bits by commercial exploitation. What set Maxwell Davies working was the threat of uranium mining in Orkney. "But it could be anything," he has said. "The pollution is there, and the kicking of people out of their houses is there, and the destruction of a way of life is there. The LSO commissioned it," he added, "but when they found out what it was, they didn't want to touch it."

The piece plays out a dramatic encounter between a baritone, in the role of Operation Black Star, and a mezzo-soprano who takes on the personae of both narrator and of Bella Budge, one of Black Star's innocent victims. An orchestral introduction, which hovers between menace and meditative stasis, sets the scene before the singers explore the moral consequences of "the catastrophe of nations" as "piecemeal a village died, shrivelled slowly with the radiance of Black Star." Relentlessly slow-paced, with episodes of savage parody and near-chaos, vocal interludes that vacillate between lament and hysteria, cavernous resonances and abrasive outbursts, *Black Pentecost* is an arduous masterpiece, comparable in its fatalism and ambition to Mahler's *Das Lied von der Erde*.

⊙ Jones, Wilson-Johnson; BBC Philharmonic Orchestra; Maxwell Davies (Collins 13662; with *Stone Litany*).

The composer's insight is invaluable in teasing out the densely unfolding musical rhetoric of *Black Pentecost*, and the performance is excellently recorded. The coupling, *Stone Litany* (1973), again features a haunted orchestral landscape which is shattered by vocal interpolation, here symbolizing the birth of speech. Della Jones handles with aplomb the pyrotechnics which Maxwell Davies imposes on the sparse Old Norse text.

SYMPHONY NO. 5

Completed in 1994, the *Symphony No. 5* is the most impressive of Maxwell Davies's recent compositions, a single-movement symphony which in its elemental starkness recalls Sibelius's seventh (which Maxwell Davies had conducted just prior to starting work). The tone is austere but eloquent and, rather like the work of another Finnish symphonist Rautavaara, it conjures up images of unyielding northern landscapes – there is even a suggestion of bird cries towards the end of the work. Maxwell Davies employs his customary device of using plainchant to underpin the thematic material, which gives the work its unity, but there is also a developing sense of tension within the symphony as nervous, scherzo-like music is set against long-drawn-out music of translucent expansiveness.

⊙ Philharmonia Orchestra, BBC Philharmonic Orchestra; Maxwell Davies (Collins 14602; with *Chat Moss, Cross Lane Fair* & *Five Klee Pictures*).

The Philharmonia give an enthrallingly and highly concentrated performance of the *Symphony No. 5*, one that really communicates its monumentality and its charged atmosphere. The symphony developed material from *Chat Moss*, a short work inspired by the barren marshes near Maxwell Davies's childhood home.

FELIX MENDELSSOHN

(1809–1847)

The conductor Hans von Bülow said of Mendelssohn that he began as a genius and ended as a talent, and Mendelssohn was indeed a terrifyingly gifted child. He painted with skill, wrote fine poetry, was an excellent athlete, spoke several languages, played many instruments and, in 1825, aged only 16, he composed one of the greatest pieces of chamber music – his *Octet for strings*. With this work he set himself impossible standards, and though he went on to produce much excellent music, he never again came so close to perfection.

He was born into a wealthy Jewish-German family, and his talents were encouraged by his mother and elder sister, Fanny, who was almost as gifted a pianist as her brother. He made his concert debut in 1818 and had some of his music performed the following year. In 1821, aged 12, he was taken to meet the 72-year-old Goethe in Weimar, and the two became strong friends. In 1826, a year after the composition of the *Octet*, he wrote his overture to *A Midsummer Night's Dream*, a work that established his name internationally, yet remarkably it was not until he had completed three years' study at Berlin University that he finally decided upon a career in music. In March 1829 he gave the first performance of Bach's *St Matthew Passion* since the composer's death in 1750, and he was to be one of the principal influences behind the European revival of Bach's music. Near the end of that year he made his first visit to England where, apart from conducting concerts of his own work, he played the piano in the first English performance of Beethoven's *Emperor Concerto*. The English loved him and for many years he was the country's most popular foreigner.

After touring Scotland (where he met Sir Walter Scott) he returned to mainland Europe, to spend two years touring Germany, Austria and Italy. Further visits to England in 1832 and 1833 cemented his position within that country's musical life and he became a frequent guest artist with the Philharmonic Society Orchestra. In 1835 he became conductor of the Leipzig Gewandhaus Orchestra, and in 1837 he married. The next few years saw him produce a wide range of superb music, including his *Violin Concerto*. In 1843 he established a new conservatory of music in Leipzig, where he was assisted by Robert Schumann, and in 1847 he made his tenth and last visit to England, when he became friends with Queen Victoria and Prince Albert, teaching the latter at the piano. In May of that year his beloved sister Fanny died and the shock of this loss, together with the pressure of severe overwork, led to his own death six months later.

It had been a brilliant career and yet also something of an anticlimax. Mendelssohn was described by von Bülow as the most complete master of musical form after Mozart, and this very mastery is perhaps the chief reason for his relapse into self-conscious politesse – the creation of pleasing, impeccably structured music came easily to him. His music is as bereft of struggle as was his life. Never did he lack money, praise or support, and not until the death of his sister did he experience genuine misery – and by then it was too late. No other great composer experienced such complete insulation from hardship, and there is little question that his cushioned existence impaired his creative development. His emotional range never really broadened, so is it surprising that his music remained consistent? One example tells the whole story – his *A Midsummer Night's Dream*. He wrote the overture in 1826 and, seventeen years later, added the incidental music. As if but seventeen days divided its composition from that of the overture, the additional music is identical in style, showing not the slightest evidence of creative evolution in its hugely enjoyable, supremely elegant and completely untroubling pages.

ELIJAH

Mendelssohn's extraordinary popularity in England was due mostly to his oratorios and other religious works, in which he satisfied the Victorians' craving for pious tunes and grand choruses. Of the pious tunes the finest is his beautiful hymn *Hear my Prayer*, which contains *O for the Wings of a Dove*. Of the more grandiose sacred compositions, the most rewarding is his oratorio *Elijah*, written in the summer of 1844, some eight years after Mendelssohn had first approached his librettist, Julius Schubring, about a possible collaboration on a work celebrating the prophet. Dominated by the bass role of Elijah and the chorus, the oratorio is very dramatic in a civilized sort of way, combining vivid sound-pictures of oceans, earthquakes and fires with more urbane passages of orchestral music. As you'd expect from someone who spent so much time in England, Mendelssohn pays homage to Handel in his choral writing, and he also shows his proficiency in Bach-like counterpoint. *Elijah* is an engaging piece, but it is long and potentially demanding.

O Terfel, Fleming, Bardon, Ainsley; Edinburgh Festival Chorus; Orchestra of the Age of Enlightenment; Daniel (Decca 455 688-2; 2 CDs).

Elijah comes in English and German versions (both sanctioned by the composer), and arguably packs more of a punch if you know what is going on. This performance, directed by the young opera conductor Paul Daniel, has real narrative drive and boasts the most powerful Elijah on disc in the shape of Bryn Terfel (his cover photo as Elijah shows he has a sense of humour). Just occasionally one feels that more drama is being squeezed out of the work than is, in fact, there, but if this performance doesn't convince you of the work's merits, nothing will.

O Donath, Klein, van Nes, George, Miles; Leipzig Radio Choir; Israel Philharmonic Orchestra; Masur (Teldec 9031 73131; 2 CDs).

Kurt Masur is often a leaden conductor, which makes it strange that he should be tackling so much Mendelssohn as part of his Teldec contract. His direction of the German-language version is a touch stolid in places, and he plays down the excitement wherever possible, but this set is lifted to another plane by the singing: Alastair Miles is in particularly forceful voice in the title role, and Helen Donath gives a finely considered performance.

SYMPHONY NO. 3 – THE SCOTTISH

At twilight on August 30, 1829, during a holiday to recover from a gruelling concert series in

London, Mendelssohn visited Holyrood Palace. He knew from Schiller of the tragic Mary Queen of Scots, and of the murder of her secretary Rizzio at Holyrood. Steeped in the gloom, he jotted down the first sixteen bars of a new symphony, an unbroken stream of melody later to be christened the *Scottish*. A week later, on a trip to Fingal's Cave on the island of Staffa, the opening of *The Hebrides* overture also came to him, but years passed before either work reached its final form. Mendelssohn returned to the symphony in 1841, and the following year introduced it to England, dedicating it to two new friends: Queen Victoria and her consort Albert. The third symphony opens with an impassioned recitative, and rises from a warlike Allegro to a noble closing hymn. Schumann pinpointed the relationship of these two movements when he wrote, "We consider it most poetic – like an evening corresponding to a lovely morning."

⊙ San Francisco Symphony Orchestra; Blomstedt (Decca 433 811-2; with *Symphony No. 4*).

Herbert Blomstedt's version offers a unique balance of qualities. The second movement may not be as crisply pointed as some, but Blomstedt's finale bursts in like a firework. The sense of liberation is palpable here, and the slow movement has a wistfully affectionate quality which degenerates into sentimentality. A radiant performance of the *Italian* completes an outstanding CD.

SYMPHONY NO. 4 – THE ITALIAN

Of Mendelssohn's five mature symphonies (he wrote a group of string symphonies as a child), the fourth, the *Italian*, is the one that shows the composer at his most winning. Written in Berlin in the winter of 1832, a few weeks after his return from Italy, the symphony's ebullient mood reflects the wealth of pleasures he found there, in the country's landscapes, art and people. Apart from the brilliant and lively Neapolitan tune that forms the basis to the last movement, there's nothing that's specifically Italian about the music – indeed, one of Mendelssohn's contemporaries insisted that the Andante was based upon a Czech pilgrim folk song, while the boisterous Scherzo that follows it was inspired by Goethe's poem, *Lilis Park*. The overall ambience, however, is one of Mediterranean spontaneity and expansiveness, and its life-affirming attitude is established right at the outset with the opening movement's skipping main theme, prelude to one of the composer's most delightful movements.

⊙ London Symphony Orchestra; Abbado (Deutsche Grammophon 415 974—2; with *Symphony No. 5*).

There's an adroitness, a boundless impression of urgency and power, underpinning Claudio Abbado's reading which puts him in a different league from most of his recent competitors. Wonderfully judged and sprung, this is one of those performances that makes the inevitable into a surprise.

A MIDSUMMER NIGHT'S DREAM

Mendelssohn's most popular work is now the *Violin Concerto* but it hasn't always held that place in the public's affection – previously his best-loved piece was the overture to his *A Midsummer Night's Dream*, source of the famous *Wedding March*. Deeply impressed by Schlegel's translations of Shakespeare, Mendelssohn composed the overture when he was only 17, and it beautifully captures the elfin atmosphere of the original. The incidental music, composed in 1843, is rarely performed complete, which is a pity, for as Schumann rightly commented, it glows with "the bloom of youth". Innovatively constructed from motifs heard in the overture – thus, for example, the opening chords are used as the basis for the entry of Oberon and Titania in the finale – it's a wonderfully evocative series of musical tableaux.

◑ Watson, Wallis; Finchley Children's Music Group; London Symphony Orchestra; Previn (EMI CDC 7 47163-2).

This is currently the best of the complete versions of the incidental music. Previn is not a theatre conductor, but there's a strong dramatic element to this reading and some suitably spirited singing from the Finchley Children's Music Group.

OTHER ORCHESTRAL MUSIC

His overtures combine two of Mendelssohn's earliest passions: for travel and for the stage. By the age of 20 he had written seven operas, which the Berliners resolutely ignored; but nowhere else would Mendelssohn continue to fuse form and dramatic tension as effectively as he does in his overtures. His youthful discovery of *A Midsummer Night's Dream* had been made with his sister Fanny, and his response was originally scored for two pianos, so that they could play it together before family and friends. The memory of a buffeting at sea would in Rome be worked into *The Hebrides* overture; this was in 1830. Goethe's paired poems *A Calm Sea* and *A Prosperous Voyage* had drawn a choral-orchestral setting from Beethoven before Mendelssohn wrote his concert piece in 1829; and Mendelssohn echoes his predecessor in theatrical sense and structural rigour. Yet even the slightest of Mendelssohn's stage music keeps evergreen freshness, and its place in the staple orchestral repertoire is deserved.

❍ The Marriage of Camacho; Overture to a Midsummer Night's Dream; Calm Sea and Prosperous Voyage; Ruy Blas; Athalia; The Hebrides: Bamberg Symphony Orchestra; Flor (RCA 07863 57905-2).

Flor never rushes a fence or miscalculates a gesture. Always animated, these are actually rather dark performances which leave the big-band approach far behind. The result has no false gloss, but a lightness of touch which brings one far closer than usual to Mendelssohn's spring-like intimacy.

THE VIOLIN CONCERTO IN E MINOR

As a young boy Mendelssohn wrote two concertos for violin, both of them immensely accomplished works, but scarcely anticipating the breathtaking originality of his *Violin Concerto in E Minor*, which he composed in 1844. One of the summits of his output, it is stuffed full of tunes, all of them instantly memorable. The passionate and forceful first movement is linked by a solo bassoon note to an Andante whose mood can perhaps best be described as rapturous melancholy (you may recognize the source of a Lloyd-Webber tune here); in the final movement, Mendelssohn's complete understanding of the instrument is realized in a superb display of virtuoso writing that demands as much of the orchestra as of the soloist. No concerto ends with such brilliant éclat.

◑ Lin; Philharmonia Orchestra; Tilson Thomas (Sony SMK 64250; with Bruch *Violin Concerto No. 1*, Vieuxtemps *Concerto No. 5*).

Lin's vibrant reading is an ideal mix of fire and tenderness. He regularly wrong-foots clichéd expectations – as good performances are apt to do – with delicate dynamic shading and finely tapered phrases. Both soloist and conductor play this so-familiar music with poise, delicacy and an unfailing sense of newness. A marvellous bargain.

◑ Menuhin; Berlin Philharmonic Orchestra; Furtwängler (RCA RD85933; with Tchaikovsky, *Violin Concerto*).

Heifetz's RCA recording with Munch, recommended in the first edition, is currently only available in a five-disc box set. This is another "classic" account in a rather different vein. Menuhin was very much at his peak in the early 1950s, and the rare sweetness of his tone and his impeccable phrasing are at their most beguiling in the slow movement.

THE PIANO CONCERTOS

"He played the piano as a lark soars," Ferdinand Hiller recalled of Mendelssohn the performer. The corollary might be that he had little notion of conflict or any propulsive inner need; and the piano concertos, heard in a weak performance, seem to sum up Mendelssohn's idiom at its most garrulously trite. But in the right hands they reveal a genuine dramatic clout and irresistible flow of melody.

The *Concerto No. 1* in G minor was "thrown off", as Mendelssohn himself put it, in Rome during November 1831. The premiere came in Munich a year later: "I was received", the composer recalled, "with loud and long applause. . . but I was modest and would not appear." The second concerto, in D minor, was composed in 1837 for the Birmingham Festival. "The people made such a fuss over me that I was quite dumbfounded." Its second movement is as restful as any *Song Without Words* (see p.256), but there are innovations too: the way in which soloist and orchestra weave together from the outset, the unity of three seamless movements connected by fanfares.

❍ Shelley; London Mozart Players (Chandos CHAN 9215; with *Capriccio Brillant*).

Howard Shelley's bravura is combined with an acute sensitivity over matters of pacing and of light and shade. Within the overall fleetness of tempo and touch there are interludes of lush intimacy in which sentimentality is kept firmly at bay.

◑ Perahia; Academy of St Martin in the Fields; Marriner (Sony SMK 42401; with *Prelude and Fugue, Variations Serieuses, Rondo Capriccio*).

Incisive playing too from Murray Perahia, and at a more competitive price. Perhaps his conception of the music is not quite as organic or as variegated as Shelley's, but this is persuasive and beautiful playing nevertheless. The three famous solo encores are excellent.

THE OCTET

No one, not even Mozart, created anything as profound as the Mendelssohn *Octet* at so young an age. In its structure the *Octet* is purely conventional, but it possesses an intensity and dynamic thrust that none of the composer's later works recaptured. The wisp-like Scherzo is best known for its use as an orchestral showpiece, but it is the final movement that marks the work out for greatness – its jubilant energy and tight fugal construction give it a power that is equalled by few other finales in chamber music, and the final three minutes are the most exciting thing Mendelssohn composed. A towering achievement, the *Octet* makes the best introduction to its composer.

◑ Academy of St Martin's Chamber Ensemble (Chandos CHAN8790; with Raff, *Octet*).

The Academy Ensemble have recorded this extraordinary work more than once but their performance for Chandos, led superbly by Ken Sillito, is the finest in every respect. The eight players employ tempi quick enough to maintain the tension but they do not rush the outer movements; conversely, they do not wallow in the gloriously tender central Adagio. The Scherzo is almost brushed off the strings, so delicate is the delivery, but the final movement is the performance's glory, leading towards a conclusion that is at once inevitable and revelatory.

STRING QUINTET NO. 2

Mendelssohn completed his second quintet in 1845, more than twenty years after his first essay in the genre and nearly twenty after the *Octet*, a work with which it has some similarities. As with the *Octet*, each of the instrumental parts is given almost equal weight, and any good performance will clearly reveal Mendelssohn's genius for counterpoint. The first-movement Allegro is a perfect example of multi-thematic writing, showing his consummate ability to juggle more than four voices at once. Full of elegiac tunes, especially in the haunting Adagio, the *String Quintet No. 2* looks forward to the world of Brahms's mature chamber music, and is Mendelssohn's most rewarding chamber piece after the *Octet*.

◑ **Laredo, Kavafian, Ohyama, Kashkashian, Robinson** (Sony MPK45883; with *String Quintet No. 1*).

Recorded at the Malboro Festival, this group of young musicians gives a refreshing performance of Mendelssohn's late quintet. The recording is less than perfect and the aggressive tone occasionally frustrates the music's lyricism, but this hardly matters in the face of such joyful commitment. Especially fine is the cello playing in the Adagio, an extremely difficult part which is carried off with seemingly no effort at all.

SONGS WITHOUT WORDS

Mendelssohn wrote three large-scale piano sonatas, a fantasia and a major set of variations, but his reputation as a composer for the piano is dominated by the *Lieder ohne Worte* or *Songs Without Words*. Composed from 1830 onwards, these 48 miniatures were published in six cycles of six during his lifetime, with two other sets issued posthumously. Combining surface virtuosity with a lyrical sense of line, they are exquisitely constructed and intimate little pieces, but some of them have proved too tuneful for their own good: numbers such as the *Bee's Wedding*, *Andante and Rondo Capriccioso*, *Funeral March* and *Spring Song* have been repeatedly quarried by jingle-writers and other hacks.

◑ **Barenboim** (Deutsche Grammophon 415 118-2; 2 CDs).

Barenboim's account of the complete set is suitably light and unfussed, with none of the didactic ponderousness that sometimes creeps into his playing. He gives relaxed and engaging performances, which are ideally captured on a well-engineered recording. The *Songs Without Words* were not intended to be heard in a continuous stream and, for those who think a two-CD set sounds like too much of a good thing, Deutsche Grammophon have also issued a selection of the Barenboim set on a single disc coupled with some Schubert and Liszt.

OLIVIER MESSIAEN

(1908–1992)

The greatest twentieth-century French composer after Debussy, Olivier Messiaen was an intriguing mixture of the ascetic and hedonistic. On the one hand he was a devout Catholic who found inspiration in medieval chant, wrote a vast opera on the life of St Francis of Assisi, and had the Trinité church in Paris as his postal address. Yet his music is also an ecstatic celebration of earthly life, deriving much of its material from the natural world – when Messiaen went on a pilgrimage to the Holy Land in the last decade of his life, he spent the time between prayer transposing the songs of the local birds. The inventor of a thrillingly sensuous music of bright acoustic colours and resonant fades, he single-handedly created a vocabulary that was eagerly seized on by Xenakis, Boulez and most importantly Stockhausen, who applied Messiaen's detailed work on note durations, attack and intensities to electronic music. Furthermore, Minimalists such as Steve Reich and Philip Glass owe their interest in non-Western musics to Messiaen's wide-ranging precedent.

Born in Avignon, Messiaen was a self-taught musician, and he was composing by the age of 7. After World War I he attended the Paris Conservatoire, where his brilliant piano playing

LEBRECHT COLLECTION

Olivier Messiaen at the Royal College of Music, 1987

won all available prizes, while he began privately studying Eastern musical scales and rhythms. His first major composition, *Préludes* (1929), owed much to Debussy but shimmered with the exotic sound of what he termed his "modes of limited transposition", special scales which lent his music a strange harmonic richness. It was during this period that he was appointed organist at the church of La Trinité, where he was to play for over five decades.

From 1936 to 1940 he was professor of music at the École Normale in Paris, where he demonstrated his fierce nationalism by founding La Jeune France, a group devoted to the propagation of a French music aesthetic to counter the influence of the Germanic tradition. The outbreak of war saw Messiaen conscripted as a medical auxiliary but he was then interned by the Germans in Stalag VIIIA at Görlitz. Finding himself in the company of three other French musicians, a clarinettist, a violinist and cellist, Messiaen strove to overcome the hunger, squalor and bitter cold by writing an eight-part quartet to "bring the listener closer to eternity in space, to infinity". Based on the Book of Revelation, it was titled *Quatuor pour la fin du temps* (Quartet for the end of time), was premiered with a banged-up piano and a broken cello in front of 5000 prisoners on January 15, 1941, and was to prove one of the seminal works of the twentieth century.

After his repatriation he was made professor at the Paris Conservatoire, a post he held until 1978 and which was to provide a platform for the dissemination of his immensely influential ideas. In 1944, during the liberation of Paris, he wrote *Vingt Regards sur l'enfant Jésus*, a twenty-part meditation on the nativity for solo piano. Then in 1945, entranced by the pianist Yvonne Loriod, Messiaen wrote *Harawi*, a song cycle full of birdsong, Peruvian lore and echoes of the Tristan myth. He subsequently visited the USA, where he conceived the monumental *Turangalîla-symphonie* (1948), an epic celebration of America's vistas and of his passion for Loriod. Featuring the unique tones of the ondes Martenot (an early electro-acoustic instrument with a distinctive quivering sound), and shot through with the bell-like sounds of the Javanese gamelan, it was an instant classic.

From 1953 he committed himself wholly to notating the sounds of birds, roaming rural France with pen and paper in hand to transpose every song. The project bore fruit with the massive piano piece *Catalogue d'oiseaux* (1956–58), in which Messiaen utilized Greek and Indian rhythms to convey the cries of the alpine chough, tawny owl and numerous other species. His love of nature reached overflow with *Chronochromie* (1960) – meaning "the colour of time", it was a ten-part homage to the Alps, full of luminous percussion and shifting dense string parts. In 1962 Messiaen finally married Loriod, his first wife – the violinist Claire Delbos – having died in 1959 after a long illness.

A visit to Japan left an Eastern imprint on *Et Exspecto Resurrectionem Mortuorum* (1964), written for woodwind and percussion, and intended for "vast spaces, churches, cathedrals and the open air of the mountainside". Returning to America in the early 1970s, he was amazed by the landscapes of Utah, which resulted in the intoxicating *Des canyons aux étoiles* (1971–74) for piano and orchestra, a ninety-minute merging of natural sounds, Christian contemplation and the grander themes of American symphonic music. In a search for a "music that touches everything and at the same time touches God", Messiaen then spent nearly a decade on the most ambitious of all his works, *Saint François d'Assise* (1975–83), a four-hour opera which assailed audiences with blocks of almost static sound. The culminating statement of his religious dedication was the *Livre du Saint-Sacrement* (1984), a brilliantly innovative organ cycle in eighteen movements, incorporating scenes from the Gospels and the liturgy of the Eucharist.

If you just want a taste of Messiaen's music before committing yourself to an entire piece, get hold of *To the Edge of Dream* (Sony SMK 53473), a mid-price disc which features two movements from *Turangalîla* as well as the vaporous "Song of the Star" section of *Des canyons aux étoiles*. It's an excellent sampler, brilliantly marshalled by Esa-Pekka Salonen, and should whet your appetite for more ambitious listening.

QUATUOR POUR LA FIN DU TEMPS

The symmetry and quiet beauty of Messiaen's great quartet belies the terrible circumstances under which it was created – this 45-minute free-flowing masterpiece is one of the century's supreme examples of transcendent art. The score is prefaced by a quotation from the Revelation of St John, in which the angel of the apocalypse shouts, "There shall be time no longer", yet the music is hauntingly beautiful, its labyrinthine sounds replete with the shimmering harmonies and archaic tones that Messiaen codified in his *Techniques of My Musical Language*, published in 1944. The piano, "enveloped in pedal", insistently keeps time through most of the piece, while the clarinet – especially in the solo *L'abîme des oiseaux* (Abyss of the Birds) – follows a path like a bird's song. It's a work of delightful contrasts too, as when a surprisingly light, dancy interlude gives way to the seductive slow cello phrases of *Louange à l'éternité de Jésus* (Praise to the Eternity of Jesus). This fervently devotional work reaches its climax with the last movement's *Louange à l'immortalité de Jésus*, an extensive violin meditation in which the instrument is slowly extended to its highest register, expressing Messiaen's spirituality at its most direct.

O Chamber Music Northwest (Delos CD 3043; with Bartók, *Contrasts*).

This is a superlative recording of a joyful performance, with especially fine interplay between piano and violin. Interesting sleevenotes by pianist Williams Doppmann provide an added bonus.

O Isserlis, Collins, Bell, Mustonen (Decca 452 899-2; with Shostakovich, *Piano Trio No. 2*).

An extremely lucid interpretation: Michael Collins' clarinet really draws out the notes and he is well supported by some sweet-toned string playing and Oli Mustonen's superb piano. But it just lacks the cohesiveness of the Delos disc.

TURANGALÎLA-SYMPHONIE

The title of the *Turangalîla-symphonie*, derived from Sanskrit, can be translated as the "speed of life", and the sound explosions of this colossal work certainly live up to the name. Messiaen imparts a certain amount of subtlety to the loud sonorities by use of glockenspiel, vibraphone and above all the ondes Martenot, an instrument whose ethereal tones are perhaps the most distinctive feature of *Turangalîla*. It creates a kind of Hollywood horror effect in the third movement, but it's in the pivotal sixth movement – the exquisite slow *Jardin de sommeil d'amour* (Garden of Sleeping Love) – that the metallic timbre and delicate harmonies of the instrument come into their own. Set against rhythmic piano and floating strings, the ondes Martenot make parts of *Turangalîla* sound ambient and Minimalist, years before those styles had been invented.

O Crossley, Murail; Philharmonia Orchestra; Salonen (Sony SK 66281).

Finnish conductor Esa-Pekka Salonen and the Philharmonia are in sprightly form on this recording, giving Messiaen's sprawling magnum opus the whirlwind treatment. This is a performance that stresses the angular, jazzy aspects of the symphony.

O Loriod, Loriod; Orchestre de la Bastille; Chung (Deutsche Grammophon 431 781-2).

A recording that comes with the imprimatur of Messiaen himself, and you can hear why. Chung takes a more luxuriant view of the score, underlining Messiaen's own view of it as a "love song" and lingering over its more ingratiatingly sensual side.

ET EXSPECTO RESURRECTIONEM MORTUORUM

Written to commemorate the dead of two world wars, Messiaen's *Et Exspecto Resurrectionem*

Mortuorum (And I await the Resurrection of the Dead) was commissioned in 1964 by the writer André Malraux in his capacity as Minister of Culture. Written for wind, brass and percussion, it was "conceived", as he put it, "to be played in a church, taking resonance for granted, also the ambience and even the echoing of sounds . . . I even wanted it to be played in the open air and on a mountain height." This, then, is one of Messiaen's most monumental works: its five sections, each headed by a biblical quotation, move gradually from a state of despair to one of joyous exultation by way of a range of extraordinarily rich and varied sonorities. There's an overriding feeling of mystery to this work with its dramatic bursts of sound and silence being applied in abstract blocks or delicate touches of colour. The fourth-section climax alternates the sombre plainsong of the brass with the animated chirruping of the woodwind, the latter representing the song of the Calandra lark – a symbol of heavenly joy for the composer.

O Cleveland Orchestra; Boulez (Deutsche Grammophon 445 827-2; with *Chronochromie* and *La Ville d'en haut*).

Boulez's second recording of this work is more meditative and spiritual than his earlier version. There's a fantastic spatial dimension in evidence and some beautifully controlled brass playing from the Cleveland Orchestra.

◑ Groupe Instrumental à Percussion de Strasbourg; Orchestre du Domaine Musical; New York Philharmonic; Boulez (Sony SK 66281; with *Couleurs de la Cité Celeste* and Stravinsky's *Symphonies of Wind Instruments*).

For those seeking a cheaper alternative, go for this 1966 recording, supervised by Messiaen himself; Sony's subsequent digital remastering has made what was already a fine performance sound even better.

VINGT REGARDS SUR L'ENFANT JÉSUS

Vingt Regards sur l'enfant Jésus is a two-hour work for solo piano which seeks to convey, in Messiaen's words, "the various contemplations of the child Jesus in the crib and the Adorations which are bestowed upon him". Written in 1944, the background behind the creation of this masterwork, was highly charged. Messiaen's wartime experiences had given him a completely new understanding of musical colour and he was currently fascinated by the music of the East and by the striking sound of the ondes Martenot. On top of this, he had recently become infatuated with a young pupil at the Conservatoire, the pianist Yvonne Loriod. In *Vingt Regards* you can hear all of this, for spread over its intense trance-like passages is every aspect of Messiaen's musical knowledge up to 1944 – extended to its limits by Loriod's extraordinary pianistic capabilities. The faster, more compressed passages are utterly dazzling (and notoriously difficult for the performer) while the slower sections, like *Regard du Fils sur Fils*, hover in the air like gossamer, enticing one around their delicate filigree of sound. Messiaen's love of the piano music of Debussy and Ravel is frequently revealed, but his repeated chords and recurring themes reveal a mind that had just glimpsed a vast new world of sonic possibilities at his disposal.

O MacGregor (Collins 70332; 2 CDs).

Joanna MacGregor's 1995 account of *Vingt Regards* on a sonorous Steinway is passionately engaged in the more elaborate areas while achieving a refined glow in the delicate passages. The opening of the *Regard du Père* is particularly mesmerizing.

⊙ Austbo (Naxos 8.550829-30; 2 CDs).

Austbo's approach makes a startling contrast to MacGregor: drier and more understated, he lets the music, rather than his own brilliant technique, do all the persuading. The result is completely convincing.

LIVRE DU SAINT-SACREMENT

The sprawling *Livre du Saint-Sacrement* is the most extensive of Messiaen's explorations of the capabilities of the solo organ. Throughout its eighteen sections, which celebrate the transubstantiation of Christ during Holy Communion, Messiaen demonstrates a total control over the dynamics and harmonic possibilities of his favourite instrument. Though initially austere, *Livre du Saint-Sacrement* gradually transforms itself through the incorporation of birdsong, Indian melody and a host of other musical devices into a stunningly inventive display, where silences and lengthily sustained notes create a soundworld never previously envisaged for the organ.

O Ericsson (Bis CD-491/492; 2 CDs).

This brilliant recording is the sixth instalment in Hans Ericsson's cycle of Messiaen's complete organ works, and comes with exemplary notes by Anders Ekenberg on Messiaen's birdsong transcriptions, explaining how their elements are transformed in the organ music.

GIACOMO MEYERBEER

(1791–1864)

During the first half of the nineteenth century, French opera was dominated by outstanding but decidedly non-French talent. Berlioz, in particular, was forthright in his condemnation of his country's "occupation", directing his frustrations at the composer who, he believed, was most responsible for the neglect that Berlioz suffered. For him, Giacomo Meyerbeer's influence upon managers, artists, critics and public had put a stranglehold on the Paris Opéra, an institution he accused of being "madly in love with mediocrity". Posterity has tended to side with Berlioz, and the very qualities that ensured Meyerbeer's success in his lifetime are those for which he is now condemned. The public demanded grand Romanticism and Meyerbeer gave it to them, in huge melodramas that required armies of musicians and extraordinary stagings – so extraordinary that eventually what the audience saw was more important than what they heard.

Born in Germany, of Jewish descent, Meyerbeer began as a piano virtuoso but, nursing an ambition to write opera, attempted a number of oratorio-like dramas, each of which proved as disastrous as the last. Salieri advised him to study in Italy, and within a few months of arriving he had composed six "Italian" operas and was being compared to Rossini. However, this change of direction did him no favours in Germany and, though Weber produced Meyerbeer's operas, he did so while complaining of his Italian "aberration".

The massive success of *Il crociato in Egitto* in Venice 1824 encouraged Meyerbeer to take the work to Paris, which he did the following year. The first night inspired the sort of lunatic fuss that would not be seen again until the appearance of Paganini six years later. With this single piece Meyerbeer was established as the dominating influence in French grand opera, a position strengthened by the success of *Robert le Diable*, *Les Huguenots* and a whole series of unfailingly popular operas.

His influence was not maintained entirely by his music. Meyerbeer possessed enormous inherited wealth, and many of France's critics, managers and musicians came to him for loans, a situation that assured him of praise. In one instance, however, Meyerbeer's largesse produced the opposite result. He helped Wagner produce his first two operas by lending him a regular monthly retainer, but after Meyerbeer heard of Wagner's resentment of this patronage he removed his support, provoking Wagner to turn upon Meyerbeer as the principal target of his outrageous anti-Semitism. And yet Wagner's early music attests to the influence of Meyerbeer, for Wagner's *Rienzi* is but a grand imitation of Meyerbeer's style, trumping his massive choruses, set pieces and Gothic settings. Meyerbeer's ideal of Grand Opera is equally evident as an influence on Verdi's *Don Carlos* and *Aida* as well as on countless other nineteenth-century works. His operas might contain lots of empty eclecticism and bombast, but there remains much of real quality – most notably in *Les Huguenots*, in which his effulgent orchestration, incisive dramatic pacing and glorious vocal melody combine to produce one of the most entertaining operatic spectacles of its time.

LES HUGUENOTS

Meyerbeer's extravagance keeps his work off the stage, and only three of his sixteen operas are presently available on CD – fortunately, *Les Huguenots* is one of them.

Les Huguenots is set during France's Wars of Religion, a subject that had never been set to music before. It's doubly unique in that Meyerbeer, when approaching this work, became the first major opera composer to carry out research into musical history as part of the composition process: to establish the appropriate historical tone, he spent a long time studying sixteenth-century manuscripts in the national library, and also incorporated traditional Jewish music into the score. The opera is probably his finest for voices, and the roles of Raoul and Marguerite, in particular, are marvellous examples of Meyerbeer's melodic talents – Raoul's *Romance*, in Act One, is an extraordinary piece of tenor writing, as is the seventeen-minute tenor and soprano duet that ends the second act. Marguerite's role might be less exciting, but her Act Two aria *O beau pays de la Touraine* perfectly complies with Richard Strauss's dictum, "Give the aria its due by keeping the orchestra quiet."

⊙ Sutherland, Arroyo, Tourangeau, Vrenios; Ambrosian Opera Chorus; New Philharmonia; Bonynge (Decca 430 549-2; 4 CDs).

Franco Corelli's astounding live performance from La Scala in 1962 is at the moment unavailable, which leaves Decca's recording, made seven years later, as the only option. It features a fine cast, including Arleen Augér, Martina Arroyo, a very young Kiri Te Kanawa and Joan Sutherland as Marguerite – the only real vocal weakness is tenor Anastasios Vrenios as Raoul, who lacks both weight and colour. Richard Bonynge offers fine and sensitive support, and if he sometimes allows Sutherland too much room to manoeuvre then the beauty of her singing more than compensates for his vague grasp of the work's overall shape. A well-recorded and exciting performance, and a perfect introduction to Meyerbeer.

DARIUS MILHAUD

(1892–1974)

The key to Milhaud's musical personality lies in the very first words of his autobiography: "I am a Frenchman from Provence". He was born into a wealthy Jewish family in Aix-en-Provence, and his musical style is underpinned by his enduring affection for his native region. His unselfconscious ability to soak up folk materials can be traced to the earthy culture of Provence, while his characteristic polytonality (the simultaneous use of more than one key), was not a mere trendy musical excursion on Milhaud's part, but – at least in part – a further legacy of the Provençal landscape, as refracted by the painter Cézanne.

Showing prodigious musical talent, Milhaud started to learn the violin at the age of 7 and made brilliant progress. Although he entered the Paris Conservatoire as a violin student he soon became convinced that composing was his true vocation, and he began to take lessons from such illustrious teachers as Paul Dukas and Charles-Marie Widor. In the late 1910s Milhaud became a central figure in Les Six, an iconoclastic group of young composers (that included Poulenc and Honegger) who rejected not only the inflated Romanticism of Wagner but also what they regarded as the imprecision of Debussy and Ravel. The voice-piece for the group was the writer Cocteau, a charmingly unscrupulous man who used people very much to his own ends. At the instigation of Cocteau, Milhaud found himself composing a self-conscious ballet called *Le Boeuf sur le Toit* (1920), and overnight he became the talk of Paris – not as a serious musician but rather as a joker who had jumped on the bandwagon of high fashion. It was to take him a good few years to shake off the tag.

Milhaud was already highly receptive to the folk music of the Americas, having accompanied the poet and diplomat Paul Claudel to Brazil, an episode that was the inspiration for the nostalgic piano pieces titled *Saudades do Brasil*. Then in 1920 he visited London and got his first taste of jazz, which prompted him to set off to New York in order to explore this new musical language at first hand. After that he developed strong sympathies with Viennese expressionism, doing much to help the success in Paris of Schoenberg's *Pierrot Lunaire*. Throughout this decade and the 1930s Milhaud broadened his composing activities to include writing for the cinema (including the score for Renoir's *Madame*

GUUS ONG

Bovary, 1933), for children's and amateur groups, and for the stage (most notably *L'annonce faite à Marie*, 1932, and *Le trompeur de Seville*, 1937).

Fleeing France in 1940, he took refuge in the USA, where he started teaching at Mills College in Oakland, California, a post he was to hold in tandem with the professorship of composition at the Paris Conservatoire after 1947. Much of the vitality went out of Milhaud's work now that he was distanced from his rural roots, but he found some compensation for his dislocation through his growing awareness of his Jewish heritage – the stimulus for fine pieces such as the ballet *Moïsé* (1940) and the *Service sacré* (1947). Crippling rheumatoid arthritis finally forced him to quit Mills College, and he retired with his wife to Geneva in 1971. Tenacious and optimistic as ever he went on composing into his 81st year – his last work was a cantata written for the 1973 Festival of Israel.

STAGE WORKS

Despite his large output as an orchestral composer (including twelve symphonies), Milhaud's most durable pieces have proved to be the two stage works, written in the early 1920s, which established him as French music's *enfant terrible*. *Le Boeuf sur le Toit* (The Ox on the Roof) is one of several homages by Milhaud to Brazilian music: "I assembled a few popular melodies, tangos, maxixes, sambas, even a Portuguese fado, and transcribed them with a rondo-like theme recurring between each two." The work was named after a Brazilian popular song and Milhaud originally envisioned it being used as music for a Charlie Chaplin film. When Cocteau got his hands on it, he devised a scenario set in an American bar involving a number of bizarre characters (played by a troupe of clowns) including a policeman who gets beheaded by the overhead fan. Musically it's a highly exhilarating romp to which Mihaud's distinctive polytonality adds a certain acidity.

While in London for a production of *Le Boeuf* Milhaud heard jazz for the first time: such was his enthusiasm that two years later he went to New York in search of the real thing. Entranced by the melodic lines, rhythms and percussion playing he heard in the jazz clubs of Harlem, on his return to Paris he composed *La Création du Monde* (1923), the first major jazz-inspired piece by a classical composer (predating Gershwin's *Rhapsody in Blue* by a few months). This seminal ballet (scenario by Blaise Cendrars and designs by Léger) portrays the creation of the world as told in African legend, and is scored for a small ensemble modelled on those Milhaud had seen in New York. It's a near-perfect synthesis of syncopated jazz elements with classic Western procedures, including an overtly Bachian opening (recalling the opening of the *St John Passion*) given a sultry twist by the presence of an alto saxophone.

O Le Boeuf sur le Toit; La Création du Monde: Lyon Opéra Orchestra; Nagano (Erato 2292 45820-2; with *Harp Concerto*).

Bright and effervescent playing from the Lyon Opéra Orchestra under Nagano, who bring out all the fresh-faced humour and *joie de vivre* of *Le Boeuf* and a genuine sense of exotic mystery for Milhaud's masterpiece *La Création du Monde*. In addition there is a good performance of the 1953 *Harp Concerto*, a fluent enough work but not especially memorable.

O Milhaud Plays and Conducts Milhaud: Milhaud, Meyer; Champs Élysées & Concert Arts Orchestras (EMI CDC 754604-2).

The sound quality is a bit dodgy in places (most of the sessions are from the 1950s, and the oldest was cut in 1932), but this is a fascinating document, with the composer in charge of what is in effect a "greatest hits" programme, comprising *Le Boeuf*, *La Création*, *Suite provençale*, *Saudades do Brasil* and the two-piano version of *Scaramouche*.

CLAUDIO MONTEVERDI

(1567–1643)

Monteverdi's career coincides with a period of profound change in European music. From the time of Josquin (see p.122), composers had become increasingly concerned with how best to communicate the meaning of the words that they set to music. By the end of the sixteenth century progressive composers were beginning to reject polyphony for a new form of music, called monody, in which the melody was confined to just one part – any additional parts provided a supportive role, filling in the harmony underneath the melody, usually in the form of chords. The increased verbal clarity of this new method gave composers greater scope for expressing ideas and emotions, and no composer was more concerned with affecting the emotions than Monteverdi.

LEBRECHT COLLECTION

Bernardo Strozzi's 1630 portrait of Monteverdi

In 1599 Monteverdi married one of the court singers, Claudia de Cattaneis, and by 1601 had become *maestro di cappella* at the ducal chapel of Santa Barbara. His first opera, *Orfeo*, was performed in 1607, at the instigation of the duke's eldest son Francesco. In the same year, the death of his wife sent Monteverdi into a deep depression. He returned to his father in Cremona but was summoned back to court in 1608 to write a new opera, *Arianna*, for the wedding of Francesco Gonzaga. The work was an enormous success but, unlike *Orfeo*, it was never published and only a fragment of it, the lament of Arianna, has survived.

Monteverdi's final years in Mantua seemed to have been frustrating, and his famous *Vespers* of 1610 was published with a dedication to the pope in an attempt to find employment in Rome. Nothing came of it, and when Francesco Gonzaga succeeded to the dukedom

However, he did so not by concentrating on one style alone but by using choosing a particular style whenever it seemed most appropriate. His greatest works, the operas and the *Vespers*, combine a range of musical methods – from monody to madrigalian choruses – which succeed in creating an exuberantly varied and, above all, dramatic whole.

Monteverdi was born in Cremona in northern Italy, the son of a pharmacist-cum-barber-surgeon. After studying with Marc'Antonio Ingegneri, the *maestro di cappella* at Cremona Cathedral, he joined the ducal court of the Gonzaga family at Mantua, where he was employed for over twenty years. This was a highly cultivated if somewhat claustrophobic working environment: Duke Vincenzo I was tyrannical and demanding, and Monteverdi frequently felt underappreciated. The Gonzagas were not one of Italy's most politically powerful families but they lived in great style, employing several important artists including the painter Rubens and, as their *maestro di cappella*, Giaches de Wert – an important influence on his younger colleague.

in 1612, Monteverdi found himself out of a job. Once again he returned to Cremona before unexpectedly being offered the post of *maestro di cappella* at St Mark's in Venice. He greatly improved musical standards at St Mark's, and in turn he was better appreciated, enjoying a substantial and regular salary.

Following the terrible plague that hit Venice in 1630 he became a priest and his final years might have passed quietly but for the opening of the first public opera house in Venice, the San Cassiano, in 1637. For the remaining years of his life he wrote regularly for the opera but unfortunately only two works have survived: *Il ritorno d'Ulisse* (1640) and, one of his greatest works, *L'Incoronazione di Poppea* (1642).

ORFEO

Monteverdi did not invent opera but he produced its first masterpieces, works that – though neglected between his death and the twentieth century – are now firmly established in the operatic canon. Opera had emerged in the last decade of the sixteenth century partly from theoretical discussions about the nature of Greek theatre. A scholar named Girolamo Mei proclaimed that all the words in Greek tragedy had been sung, not polyphonically but to a single line of music, an idea taken up by a group of Florentine intellectuals known as the Camerata. One of their number, Vincenzo Galilei (father of the astronomer), agreed that polyphony was hopelessly complex for conveying the meaning of poetry, and he advocated the single-line approach, monody, to contemporary composers.

The earliest composers to adopt monody were Caccini, Cavilieri – who wrote the first oratorio – and Jacopo Peri, who wrote the first opera, *Dafne* (now lost). It was Peri who developed a form of rhythmically free, declamatory singing called *recitativo*, which was used for dialogue and narration. It was Monteverdi who showed how this new genre could be used for the creation of a dramatic narrative, by combining a wonderfully varied and flexible *recitativo* with a wide range of musical styles to provide contrast and depth.

Orfeo, Monteverdi's first opera, took as its subject the classical myth of Orpheus, a theme treated by Peri in his second opera, *Euridice*. Both operas tell of the death of Euridice, and how her betrothed, the poet and singer Orpheus, journeys to the underworld in an attempt to bring her back from the dead. The power of his music persuades Pluto into letting her return, on condition that Orpheus should not look back as he leads her to the upper world. At the last moment he does so and loses her once more. In the original versions of the story Orpheus despises all women after his loss, and is torn to pieces by the frenzied female followers of Bacchus. This ending was changed after the first performance of the opera, to one in which the god Apollo, Orpheus's father, conveys Orpheus to the heavens, where he is able to view the likeness of Euridice in the stars.

O Ainsley, Gooding, Bott; New London Consort; Pickett (L'Oiseau-Lyre 433 545-2; 2 CDs).

From the sparkling attack of the opening toccata it is clear that this is going to be a spirited account. Pickett's sleevenotes give detailed reasoning about his choice of instrumental combinations, and the result brilliantly communicates the freshness and the intimacy of the drama. The dilemmas and emotions of the protagonists seem real and immediate, not simply because of the consistently convincing characterization but also because the instrumental colouring does so much to create a context for the action. Orfeo himself is a complex and self-centred character, qualities strongly conveyed by John Mark Ainsley's well-judged performance. Also excellent are Julia Gooding's poignant Euridice and Catherine Bott in the multiple roles of Prosperina, the messenger who brings news of Euridice's death (a particularly moving moment), and as Music, who presents the prologue to the main action.

IL RITORNO D'ULISSE IN PATRIA

A gap of over thirty years separates *Orfeo* from Monteverdi's second surviving opera, *Il ritorno d'Ulisse*, which was first staged at the San Cassiano theatre in 1640. Its libretto, by Giacomo Badoaro, is based on Homer's *Odyssey*. While Ulysses has been away for twenty years (fighting at Troy and then attempting to return home to Ithaca), his wife Penelope has remained faithful to him, despite the attentions of several suitors. At the opera's conclusion Penelope holds a contest: whoever can draw the bow of Ulysses will win her hand. They all fail with the exception of Ulysses who, disguised as a beggar, not only draws the bow but kills all of the suitors. Penelope, fearing a trick, refuses to acknowledge that it is indeed her husband until he describes the embroidered cover of their wedding bed.

Il ritorno d'Ulisse is the most neglected of Monteverdi's surviving operas, perhaps because it is the most courtly, yet its fabric is more varied than that of *Orfeo*. *Recitativo* is still the major vehicle for expression here, but arias occur regularly to intensify the drama – most notable being Penelope's moving *Illustratevi, o cieli* in Act Three.

O Pregardien, Fink, Hogman, Hunt; Concerto Vocale; Jacobs (Harmonia Mundi HMC 901427.29; 3 CDs).

This is a rather more epic work than *Orfeo* and here receives a correspondingly larger and more obviously operatic performance. The instrumental combinations are darker than in *Orfeo*, and Jacobs' choice of singers also tends towards the overtly expressive, particularly in the near-neurotic Penelope of Bernarda Fink. The recording's one drawback is that it occasionally lacks the energy and spontaneity of Pickett's *Orfeo*.

L'INCORONAZIONE DI POPPEA

Monteverdi selected another classical theme for his last and greatest opera, but this time from history rather than mythology – the first known example of an opera based on fact. The choice of subject for *L'Incoronazione di Poppea* might seem strange, since it concludes with the complete triumph of immorality. The Roman emperor Nero decides to cast aside his wife Ottavia and to marry his new mistress, Poppea. When his tutor, the philosopher Seneca, is critical of his decision, Nero – goaded on by Poppea – orders his execution. Ottone, Poppea's former lover, is blackmailed by Ottavia into making an attempt on Poppea's life. He does so disguised as Ottavia's maid Drusilla, who is in love with him. His failure duly brings him capture and exile. Nero then divorces and exiles his wife, and the opera ends with Nero and Poppea luxuriating in their success and their love for each other in a highly sensual and disturbingly moving duet.

There are several features that distinguish *L'Incoronazione* from its predecessors, apart from the likelihood that it contains music by more than one composer. Its orchestration is pared down from that used in *Il ritorno*, and the music is characterized by more marked contrasts between juxtaposed sections, as when Seneca's preparations for suicide are followed by the badinage of Nero's decadent flunkies. The arias here are longer and more prominent as well, and the characterization is more complex than anything Monteverdi had attempted before – Nero is the most rounded of his creations.

McNair, von Otter, Hanchard, Chance; English Baroque Soloists; Gardiner (Archiv 447 088-2; 3 CDs).

If theatricality is what you want, then look no further than this 1993 live recording which has an unsurpassed vitality and immediacy. Gardiner conducts an orchestra that's smaller than on the rival sets, pushing the voices into sharp relief. Sylvia McNair is a very sexy Poppea and Diana Hanchard is an imperiously hard Nero, but Octavia and Otho practically steal the show – as is so often the case. Anne Sofie von Otter's Octavia is especially moving in her long farewell to the city and her friends.

THE VESPERS

The Gonzagas employed Monteverdi primarily as a composer of secular music and, despite becoming *maestro di cappella* in 1601, his religious output was fairly small before his appointment to St Mark's in Venice. Undoubtedly his greatest achievement in the field of religious music was the *Vespro della Beata Vergine*, a collection of music for the service of Vespers, published in 1610. For what occasion this music was written has proved difficult to establish, but it is fairly certain that Monteverdi intended its publication as a showcase for his skills, above all for his ability to write effectively in a variety of styles both old and new. The Vespers provides an extraordinarily theatrical approach to church music, with a range of startling effects throughout the service, from the opening fanfare to the use of an echo in the motet *Audi coelum*, or the dramatic ornamentation of the part for three tenors at the end of *Duo Seraphim* – not to mention the consistently sumptuous instrumental writing.

Kirkby, Rogers; Taverner Consort and Choir; Parrott (Virgin VMD5 61347 2; 2 CDs).

Parrott's was a trailblazing recording when it appeared in 1984, being the first to place Monteverdi's music in a complete liturgical context through the addition of chants and material by Monteverdi's contemporaries. The approach is largely soloistic rather than choral, and Nigel Rogers, an expert in Monteverdian ornamentation, gives an outstanding performance of the *Audi coelum*.

Figueras, Kiehr; La Capella Reial; Coro del Centro Musica Antica di Padova; Savall (Astrée E 8719; 2 CDs).

Savall's performance, though not in a liturgical context, has the advantage of being more atmospheric: the recording was made in the ducal chapel of Santa Barbara in Mantua – possibly the site of its original performance – and the warm and resonant acoustic has been beautifully captured. Its other main attraction is the use of European singers with consistently rich vocal timbres. This is at its most marked in the darkly expressive tones of soprano Montserrat Figueras, a penetrating voice but one that combines well with others, most beguilingly with the more reticent Maria Kiehr in an intense performance of *Pulchra es*. There is also some thrillingly lively instrumental playing, especially in the *Sonata sopra Sancta Maria*, essentially an instrumental piece over which the words "Holy Mary pray for us" are repeatedly intoned by the chorus.

MADRIGALS

Secular songs for a number of different voices, called madrigals, developed in Italy in the sixteenth century and reached its peak with Monteverdi. Texts were usually of an amorous nature, either taken from the sonnets of Petrarch or written in imitation of him. Monteverdi had already published two collections of madrigals by the time he reached Mantua in 1592. These were in the standard five-part polyphonic fashion and show great charm and imaginative word-setting. At Mantua, under the influence of de Wert, his madrigals became much bolder, especially in their use of dissonance and in a tendency towards a more declamatory mode of expression. This prompted a conservative theorist named Artusi to launch a biting attack on him. Monteverdi's defence, later amplified by his brother Guilio Cesare, appeared in the preface to the fifth book of madrigals (1605), where he makes a distinction between the old style of composing (the *prima prattica*), where the music governed the words, and his new style (the *seconda prattica*), where the words governed the music.

From his fifth book of madrigals onwards Monteverdi becomes increasingly radical: instruments are introduced, the harmony becomes increasingly expressive, and the vocalists are divided into contrasting groups. In the eighth book, subtitled "Madrigals of War and Love", he outlines his aesthetic agenda in a foreword. Harking back to classical ideas, he argued that music should be able to evoke in the listener the contrasting states of calmness, love and war. This is exemplified by one of his finest Petrarch settings, *Hor ch'el ciel a la terra*, a startlingly dramatic example of word-setting in

which changes of mood are reflected in changes of speed and sonority, and which culminates in one of the most serene and poignant closing lines in all Monteverdi's output.

O Il Quarto Libro dei Madrigali: Concerto Italiano; Alessandrini (Opus 111 OPS 30-81).

The fourth book of madrigals was published in 1603 but contains several works written considerably earlier. The music is still unaccompanied five-part polyphony, but the harmonies are more adventurous than in earlier books and there is an increased emphasis on declamation (making the words follow the pattern of speech), notably at the beginning of *Sfogava con le stelle*, where the dominance of a single chord gives the impression of chanting. Concerto Italiano, a group of young Italian singers, are the best performers of this type of repertoire: sensitive, passionate, theatrical when necessary, but always making the often extreme harmonies seem natural and unforced.

O Il Ottavo Libro dei Madrigali: Concerto Italiano; Alessandrini (Opus 111 OPS 30-187).

Another outstanding release from Concerto Italiano, every one of whose Monteverdi recordings (all on Opus 111) are worth investigating. The eighth book of madrigals really shows off the individual vocal quality within the group, since Monteverdi continuously varies the combination of voices – there are songs for solo and duet as well as three-, four-, five-, and even eight-part settings.

IL COMBATTIMENTO DI TANCREDI E CLORINDA

Monteverdi's move towards a more graphic form of musical realism (called *stile concitato* or "excited style") can be seen most clearly in the dramatic piece included in the eighth book of madrigals, *Il Combattimento di Tancredi e Clorinda* (The Combat of Tancred and Clorinda), an oddly unclassifiable work that's not quite an opera but more than a madrigal. First performed in 1624 at the home of the Venetian nobleman Girolamo Mocenigo, it takes its story from Tasso's chivalric epic *Gerusalemme liberata* and tells, mainly through a narrator, of a duel between a disguised Saracen woman, Clorinda, and a Crusader knight, Tancredi. Monteverdi employs several startling imitative effects, including the trotting of the horse and the clashing of swords, but the essence of *Il Combattimento* is its expressive vocabulary. He selected Tasso because of the wide range of emotions in his work, and the success of Monteverdi's setting rests in the extent to which he convincingly conveys these emotions through music. The original performance is said to have reduced its audience to tears.

◑ Les Arts Florissants; Christie (Harmonia Mundi HMT 7901273).

The performance of *Il Combattimento* from Les Arts Florissants works almost perfectly because the details and the spirit of the piece are so closely adhered to. Nicolas Rivenq makes an outstanding narrator and the instrumentalists bring the work to life through the variety and refinement of their tone colour.

WOLFGANG AMADEUS MOZART

(1756–1791)

"It is a mistake to think that the practice of my art has become easy to me – no one has given so much care to the study of composition as I have. There is scarcely a famous master in music whose works I have not frequently and diligently studied." Thus wrote Wolfgang Amadeus Mozart to his father, Leopold. The idea that Mozart had to work at anything doesn't quite match the received image. We know Mozart as the artless child of nature, producing music in unconscious, effortless profusion, untrammelled by knowledge of the heights and depths of human experience. It's an immensely alluring image, as attested by the success of the film *Amadeus*, which marketed a caricature of the com-

LEBRECHT COLLECTION

Lange's Mozart portrait, said by Mozart's wife to be the truest likeness of him

Mozart started working earlier than most, of course. He learned how to play the keyboard at the age of 3 and was composing from 5. From 1762, his father toured Wolfgang and his gifted older sister, Maria Anna, throughout Europe, during which the 6-year-old learned to play the violin with a minimum of formal teaching. During these tours, he met and played for some of the world's most powerful figures, including Louis XV at Versailles and George III in London. Not until 1766, when he was 10, did he return home to Salzburg. Two years later he completed two operas and journeyed to Italy, where he was acclaimed as the "greatest genius in all music". While he was in Rome, he heard a performance of Allegri's *Miserere* (see p.5) and wrote it down from memory to spite the authorities, who had refused him access to a copy of the score. After returning to Austria then making further trips to Italy, he came home to work for the new Archbishop of Salzburg, Hieronymus Colleredo. Neither of them liked the other, however, and after five frustrating years Mozart once again left on tour, this time with his mother.

poser as a prodigious and foul-mouthed superbrat. Like any caricature, it necessarily bears a recognizable relationship to reality – there are numerous stories of Mozart completing an entire symphony in the course of a coach journey, and many of his manuscripts are entirely free of second thoughts, as if he had been taking dictation from the Almighty. But to categorize Mozart as a brilliant freak who exhaled music as others exhale air is to diminish him. Mozart possessed a profound and profoundly self-aware mind, and his unequalled facility was founded upon a comprehensive knowledge of the traditions within which he was working. He crammed more work into a couple of decades than many composers managed in a lifetime. An attempt to catalogue his vast output, published in 1862 by Ludwig von Köchel, ran to more than 600 works and began a chronological numbering system (Köchel numbers) which is still favoured by musicologists.

In 1778, while they were in Paris, Mozart's mother died, leaving the 22-year-old in a state of deep distress. Unable to find a court position such as Haydn had procured, Mozart again returned to Salzburg, where he spent the next two years as court and cathedral organist to the archbishop. Unfortunately their relationship deteriorated to such a degree that in 1781, having been granted his request to leave, Mozart was ignominiously booted out of the room by the archbishop's chamberlain. The following year he moved to Vienna, where he married the singer Constanze Weber (he had previously fancied her older sister). There he gave many concerts as conductor and pianist, and spent a great deal of energy on composing opera, an area in which he excelled even his own standards by writing *Don Giovanni* in only a few months in 1787 – shortly after his father's death. But despite his success as an opera composer,

Mozart's finances were constantly in bad shape and he was forced to use his contacts as a freemason to borrow money, in particular from the ever-loyal Michael Puchberg. His last three years were ones of hectic activity and increasing financial difficulty. *Così fan tutte* was successfully premiered in 1790, while the old-fashioned *La Clemenza di Tito* and the populist *Die Zauberflöte* were written more or less simultaneously in the summer of 1791. Fatigued by overwork and with a sick wife, it is hardly surprising that Mozart began to imagine that the *Requiem*, commissioned by an anonymous patron, was being written for himself. He died – without completing it – on December 5 of that year. Constanze was too distressed to attend the funeral and Mozart was buried in a communal grave which has never been identified. The popular theory (central to the film *Amadeus*) that he was poisoned by his colleague, Antonio Salieri, has some evidence to support it, but is not widely accepted.

These brief facts give no idea of the complexity of his short life, but his music is easier to break down. As with most composers, his early music is very much of its time and there is little that's remarkable about his first works except that they were composed by a boy. His "middle period" begins in his sixteenth year, a curious passage of nine years during which much of Mozart's composition reflected his general unhappiness with life, ruled as it was by his strict patron, the Archbishop of Salzburg. As he wrote to his father in 1778: "Frequently I fall into a mood of complete listlessness and indifference; nothing gives me any pleasure."

In his 25th year he broke free from the archbishop, and what followed was one of the most remarkable decades in musical history. The list of pieces composed between 1781 and 1791 takes in almost everything for which Mozart is best known – music which has no parallel in its achievement of depth without pomposity, clarity without banality and simplicity without shallowness. This music is a synthesis of many different elements, each adopted, modified and then outgrown. As a travelling virtuoso he absorbed an enormous variety of European music – England, Germany, France and, most importantly, Italy (especially Italian opera) all left indelible marks on his musical character. Except in the world of opera, Mozart broke no new ground, but – unlike Haydn and Beethoven, who did – he excelled in every genre current in his time. To his contemporaries Mozart's skill was almost too dazzling: the composer Dittersdorf felt that he left ". . . his hearer out of breath: for scarcely has one thought through one idea, than stands there already in its place another which drives out the first, and this goes on. . . " Today, having become accustomed to this profusion of ideas, we admire Mozart for the way he breaks through the Rococo artifice of eighteenth-century forms to produce music which both seduces by its brilliant melodic facility but which also frequently reaches the very depths of human emotion.

THE OPERAS

The most obvious distinction between Mozart and the majority of opera composers is that he was the master of all other branches of composition. Almost every great composer of opera after Handel specialized in writing operas and left it at that. Mozart's operas are the product of a mind that thought symphonically – so even if you haven't got a clue what's going on, you can tell that you're listening to an extended piece of music in which the dramatic incidents form part of a perfectly coherent whole. Mozart set some excellent libretti (those of Lorenzo Da Ponte are just about the best texts a composer ever had to work with), yet the music is always the dominant element, giving the action inflections of meaning that the words alone wouldn't bear. Furthermore, until Mozart's emergence operatic characters were generalized and typical, often superhuman or supernatural. As they were at the beginning of an opera, so they were at the end. Mozart was the first to succed in putting real people on the stage, individuals whose emotions were inconsistent and whose personalities were evolutionary. In short, Mozart combines the playwright's psychology with the musician's sense of form.

In all, Mozart wrote 22 operas, half a dozen of which are performed regularly in all the world's major opera houses, with another half-dozen receiving attention from smaller companies. To discuss all of them in any detail would obviously take up an entire book – we've singled out what we think are the four finest.

LE NOZZE DI FIGARO

Le Nozze di Figaro (The Marriage of Figaro) was first performed in Vienna on May 1, 1786. In keeping with that decade's vogue for Italian rather than German opera, Mozart chose to set a text by Vienna's most gifted librettist, Lorenzo Da Ponte. Da Ponte's text was based upon Beaumarchais's recently banned comedy *La Folle Journée, ou le Mariage de Figaro*, in which a libidinous count attempts to seduce the fiancée of his servant, but is outwitted by an alliance between the serving classes and his own long-suffering wife. The plot is bursting with intrigue and misunderstanding, and Mozart responded to it by creating an extraordinarily witty piece of music, in which even the most minor characters are precisely characterized. But the magic of *Figaro* lies not in the panache with which Mozart handles the logistics of farce, but rather in the profundity of emotion that he reveals, through some of his most moving arias and perhaps the greatest ensembles ever written. There is no more potent demonstration of Mozart's economy of means than the opening of the second act: virtually everything up to that point has been knockabout humour; within the space of a single two-minute aria from the heartbroken Countess, Mozart changes the mood of the opera completely.

◑ **Siepi, Gueden, Poell, Della Casa, Danco, Rossl-Majdan, Corena; Vienna State Opera Chorus; Vienna Philharmonic Orchestra; Kleiber** (Decca 417 315-2DM3; 3 CDs).

There are over twenty studio recordings of *Figaro* and around twice that number of live recordings in the catalogue, and many of these are superb. None, however, is better than Eric Kleiber's 1955 recording, made with what must be one of the greatest Mozart casts ever assembled. The characterization and dramatic direction are impeccable from first to last, and the singing is a testament to one of opera's golden ages – this set would be worth the money just for the vitality and freshness of Hilda Gueden's Susanna and Lisa Della Casa's Countess Almaviva.

O Ramey, Popp, Allen, Te Kanawa, von Stade, Moll, Tear, Langridge; London Opera Chorus; London Philharmonic Orchestra; Solti (Decca 410 150-2DH3; 3 CDs).

Recorded in 1981, this was the first digital *Figaro*. It was also Solti's finest operatic recording – graceful, refined and tender (not qualities readily associated with the Hungarian dynamo). Frederica von Stade indulges her lyrical gifts to the full in the role of Cherubino, but the highlight is Kiri Te Kanawa's Countess. Her voice was especially rich in 1981, but there's more to her performance than just radiant sound – there is a freshness and spontaneity to this portrayal that has scarcely ever been matched.

DON GIOVANNI

Mozart's next opera was commissioned from the Prague opera house as a result of Figaro's success there, and again he turned to Da Ponte for his libretto. The plot of *Don Giovanni* is the familiar morality play concerning the philandering Don Juan and his eventual damnation, but Mozart transforms this cautionary tale into an enthralling assembly of character studies. The Don himself is a monster, but he is an irresistible monster: the seductive beauty of his famous serenade (sung to the servant of one of his thousands of deceived lovers), the superhuman energy of the "champagne aria",

and the ambiguous passions he inspires in the women he encounters, all prompt the suspicion that Mozart was, as Blake said of Milton, "of the Devil's party without knowing it." The action of *Don Giovanni* oscillates between high farce and deep tragedy, culminating in an extraordinary banquet scene, during which Giovanni refuses to repent and is dragged to hell by the ghost of the man whom he had murdered in the first scene. Two hundred years later, it is still one of the most terrifying scenes in opera.

O Waechter, Sutherland, Schwarzkopf, Sciutti, Alva, Taddei, Capuccilli; Philharmonia Chorus and Orchestra; Giulini (EMI CDS7 47260-8; 3 CDs).

Don Giovanni is Mozart's most melodramatic opera and Giulini's is the most melodramatic recording, full of exaggerated colour and generally fast-paced. Waechter's Don is the nastiest on record – he employs his large voice with ringing clarity. Taddei's Leporello can appear both repulsive and lovable within the space of ten bars, while the women are magnificent. This kaleidoscopic and visceral performance is an obvious first choice if you're coming fresh to this opera.

O Gilfry, Silvestrelli, Orgonasova, Prégardien, d'Arcangelo; Monteverdi Choir; English Baroque Soloists; Gardiner (Archiv 445 870-2; 3 CDs).

This 1994 live period-instrument performance is astoundingly dramatic: the tempi are fast but flexible, with minute fluctuations causing an unnerving feeling of tension. The two final scenes are taken very quickly but everything fits as if there could be no other way. The cast work brilliantly together: d'Arcangelo is a scene-stealing Leporello, Silvestrelli is a Commendatore you wouldn't pick an argument with, while Prégardien's Ottavio is the most beautiful on record. The sound is clear and bass-rich, making this the best recent *Don* by a long way.

COSÌ FAN TUTTE

After *Don Giovanni*, Mozart and Da Ponte produced their last opera together, *Così fan tutte* – or, in full, *Così fan tutte, ossia la scuola degli amanti* (Thus Do They All, or The School for Lovers). Though repeated ten times in 1790, the year of its premiere, *Così* did not achieve the popularity of the other Mozart–Da Ponte operas, and by the 1830s it had disappeared from the repertoire, resurfacing only when the likes of Mahler and Strauss began to promote its cause. Beethoven attacked the "immorality" of *Così*, and squeamishness about its apparent cynicism probably goes a long way to explaining its neglect. The plot has the dovetailed perfection of farce: two young men, riled by a friend's insinuations about the trustworthiness of their girlfriends, disguise themselves in order to attempt to seduce them. They expect to fail but in fact succeed; a reconciliation is finally achieved. Mozart takes this formulaic plot and makes it the vehicle for some uncomfortable irony, writing superlatively melodious music whose cheerfulness often has an undertow of melancholy and disillusionment. It's an opera with no hero, not even in the sense of a main character – the six lead roles are all equally important, and more than any other opera this one is carried by its ensembles.

O Schwarzkopf, Ludwig, Steffek, Kraus, Taddei, Berry; Philharmonia Chorus and Orchestra; Böhm (EMI CMS7 69330-2; 3 CDs).

This 1962 performance of *Così* has no equal. Schwarzkopf, as Fiordiligi, gives a fine display of character singing, and her silvery voice makes an ideal contrast with Christa Ludwig's darker, more mature sound. None of the men had sung their roles before, but all three give inimitable portrayals, with Kraus especially delightful as Ferrando. There is only one possible weakness – that the orchestra plays with too much English reserve.

◑ Della Casa, Ludwig, Loose, Dermota, Schöffler; Vienna State Opera Chorus; Vienna Philharmonic Orchestra; Böhm (Decca 417 185-2DM02; 2 CDs).

Böhm's first *Così* is more heavily cut than the above version, but this 1955 recording is still a landmark achievement. The tempi are generally spacious and the orchestral phrasing is wonderfully vocal, but above all else this recording transmits an unrivalled feeling of intimacy, for Böhm was working with an orchestra and a cast that had worked on this opera together for some time. The voices are radiant, warm and neatly articulated, and the early stereo is sweet.

DIE ZAUBERFLÖTE

After the comparative failure of *Così*, Mozart made an unexpected return to the fantasy and magic of Gluckian opera. Mozart was a Freemason for most of his adult life and the masonic subplot of *Die Zauberflöte* (The Magic Flute) has provoked reams of academic commentary since the opera's first performance in 1791. The ritualistic element of *Die Zauberflöte* is undeniable, but you do not need to know anything of masonic esoteric teaching to enjoy this opera, for it can heard simply as an incident-packed tale of love tested and found true. *Die Zauberflöte* ranges from buffoonery to hieratic solemnity, and features some of the most unusual and vivid characters in all opera – such as Papageno the guileless bird-catcher, the flamboyantly evil Queen of the Night (who gets two of the most startling arias you'll ever hear), and the comically thuggish Monostatos. In short, *The Magic Flute* is a sort of cerebral pantomime for grown-ups.

O Lear, Peters, Wunderlich, Fischer-Dieskau, Crass, Hotter, Otto, King, Talvela; Berlin RIAS Chamber Choir, Berlin Philharmonic Orchestra; Böhm (Deutsche Grammophon 3371 002; 3 CDs).

Böhm's later *Zauberflöte* has some distinct advantages of his earlier Decca set – it includes much of the dialogue and the stereo is fresher and better balanced. Above all, it boasts a one-in-a-million cast: Wunderlich's Tamino is honey-toned and uniquely beguiling; Fischer-Dieskau recreates one of his greatest successes as Papageno; Franz Crass makes the most convincing Monostatos on record and Roberta Peter's is an electrifying Queen of the Night – indeed, Evelyn Lear's somewhat workaday Pamina is the only real weakness.

O Mannion, Kitchen, Blochwitz, Scharinger; Les Arts Florissants; Christie (Erato 0630-12705-2; 2 CDs).

This 1996 recording is an absolute triumph. Christie's identification with the opera's mercurial character is absolute, and his period-instrument orchestra brings unusual warmth and colour to their playing. None of the principals is outstanding, but the way they enter into the spirit of this performance more than compensates and, with even the smaller parts well cast, this is a high point among recent Mozart recordings.

SACRED MUSIC

Ever since Mozart's day it has been suggested that the bulk of his sacred music was written as a means of remaining in favour with his patrons. This is unlikely, but even if it is true it makes no difference to the meaning of the music, for even the earliest of his Masses (he wrote nearly twenty) express a deep, childlike and unquestioning faith. Following the appointment of Hieronymus Colleredo as Archbishop of Salzburg, Mozart's liturgical music takes on a greater concision in line with the archbishop's reformist views that music should not obscure the audibility of the words. It is possible that this was a contributing factor to Mozart's frustration with his life as Colleredo's employee. But, of his three finest masses, only one, the so-called *Coronation Mass*, was written for Salzburg. The unfinished *Mass in C Minor* was probably written for personal reasons, while the unfinished *Requiem* was comissioned by an aristocrat in the last months of Mozart's life.

MASS IN C – THE CORONATION MASS

The *Mass in C*, the penultimate mass for Salzburg, derives its nickname either from the annual coronation of a local miracle-working statue of the Virgin Mary or, as is more likely, from the fact that it was performed (under the direction of Salieri) at the coronation of Leopold II in Prague in 1791 – twelve years after it was written. It's a short work but it manages to sound extraordinarily grand – especially the opening Kyrie – partly because of the ample brass section of two horns, two trumpets and three trombones. Much of the choral writing is homophonic; that is, the words are sung in each part to the same rhythmic values, and the effect, in movements like the joyous Gloria, has a thrilling directness and simplicity. The solo writing is marginally more complex and operatic, culminating in the soprano's Agnus Dei, which has all the intense fervour of a love song.

⊙ Kirkby, Robbin, Ainsley, George; Winchester Cathedral Choir & Quiristers, Academy of Ancient Music; Hogwood (L'Oiseau Lyre 436 585-2; with *Vesperae solennes de confessore, Epistle Sonata in C Major).*

There are some very good recordings of this imposing work in the catalogue. Hogwood's impresses in particular because he manages to convey a sense of ceremony and occasion without recourse to sluggish tempi. Emma Kirkby makes the most of her glorious solos.

MASS IN C MINOR

The *Mass in C Minor*, Mozart's first non-commissioned Mass, was probably written in celebration of his marriage to Constanze, which may well explain the music's breathtaking sense of personal utterance. What remains unexplained is why he chose to leave the score incomplete (the Credo ends after the beautiful *et incarnatus est* and there is no Agnus Dei). A number of suggestions have been made – the most watery-eyed being that he did not know how to finish a score already beyond perfection – but nothing convincing has yet emerged and, in fact, Mozart reused much of the music for his cantata *Davidde Penitente*. Whatever the truth, movements such as the Qui tollis, with its soul-shuddering *subito piani* (sudden quiet), eclipse anything in the *Requiem*, and only the latter half of Beethoven's *Missa Solemnis* stands comparison with this extraordinarily solemn and God-fearing work. Much of its solemnity derives from the work's deliberately "antique" style – the start of the Credo, for instance, reveals Mozart's interest in the music of Handel.

⊙ McNair, Montague, Rolfe Johnson, Hauptman; Monteverdi Choir, English Baroque Soloists; Gardiner (Philips 420 210-2PH).

John Eliot Gardiner's semi-academic methods sometimes result in performances that inspire admiration rather than affection. However, for his recordings of the *Mass in C Minor* and *Requiem* he struck gold. The depth and range of expression is overwhelming, and in Sylvia McNair (then largely unknown) he found the perfect soprano – in particular, her performance of Et incarnatus est has a wondrous, unaffected purity.

REQUIEM MASS IN D MINOR

The anonymous commission for the *Requiem* is now known to have come from Count von Walsegg, who wished to pass the composition off as his own. Walsegg did not kill Mozart but he might as well have placed a pistol in the sick man's hand, so disastrous was the commission's effect on Mozart's health. Other than a small funeral motet *Ave verum corpus*, it was his first sacred composition since the abandoned *Mass in C Minor* and it too was to remain incomplete – Mozart died while working on it, and it was left to one of his pupils, Sussmayr, to finish it. If Sussmayr was telling the truth (and many people think he aggrandized his contribution), then he composed a substantial amount of the *Requiem*, using Mozart's sketched bass parts as a guide to harmonic and melodic direction. Whatever Sussmayr's role, much of the *Requiem* bears Mozart's unmistakable stamp, and its strong contrapuntal element reflects Mozart's immersion in the music of Bach and Handel towards the end of his life. It's impossible to hear the *Requiem* as anything other than Mozart's acceptance of fragile mortality, the last testimony of the man who wrote: "I never lie down in my bed without reflecting that perhaps I, young as I am, may not live to see another day."

⊙ Bonney, von Otter, Blochwitz, White; Monteverdi Choir, English Baroque Soloists; Gardiner (Philips 420 21-2PH).

Gardiner's performance boasts some superb vocal talent, and as with the *Mass in C Minor* he achieves a sense of occasion that is palpable from start to finish. The rock-steady voices of Barbara Bonney and Anne Sofie von Otter are perfectly suited to the plainer and more linear style of the *Requiem*, and the small orchestra and choir contribute greatly towards the intimacy of expression.

THE SYMPHONIES

Mozart's 41 symphonies represent but a fraction of his enormous output of orchestral music. It's an amazing volume of work, especially when you consider that, unlike Haydn, Mozart was not working in circumstances that guaranteed performance of whatever he wrote. But, also unlike Haydn, Mozart's symphonies do not constitute a great body of work – the first dozen or so are the weightless creations of a prodigiously adept boy, and even in the "middle period" symphonies there are traces of hackwork. There is thus no point, unless you have a mania for completeness, in buying a colossal set of the Mozart symphonies. With the later works, however, it's a different story – the last three in particular represent one of the most remarkable feats of composition ever accomplished. All three – nearly an hour and a half's music – were uncommissioned and were completed in less than six weeks, a period in which Mozart was busy writing other (money-earning) music. These three masterpieces are the expression of an inner compulsion that demanded satisfaction.

SYMPHONIES NOS. 29 & 35

Written in Salzburg when he was a mere 19 years old, the *Symphony No. 29* is justifiably one of Mozart's most popular orchestral works. Its brilliant opening is instantly engaging: restless upper strings over a smooth steady line in the lower strings establish a tension which increases throughout the movement. The elegant Andante and Minuet seem to look back to earlier statelier times while the energetic finale veers between wit and urgency. Eight years later Mozart wrote a serenade in celebration of the ennoblement of Sigmund Haffner – a friend of the family – hence its nickname, the "Haffner", when he worked it up into a symphony. This is another light but powerful work with a dramatic opening, this time an upwardly leaping octave which fixes the celebratory mood of the whole movement. The other movements seem to disclose its serenade origins – lyrical slow movement, lively minuet, and opera buffa finale to be played "as fast as possible".

◑ **Academy of St Martin-in-the-Fields; Marriner** (Philips 446 225-2; with *Symphony No. 41*).

Marriner is an extremely distinguished Mozartian who, in combination with the light but sinewy sound of the Academy, delivers near-perfect accounts of these two symphonies. These are modern instrument accounts, notable for the suavity and finesse of the playing which at the same time conveys a real sense of passion.

SYMPHONIES NOS. 36 & 38

In October 1783 Mozart and his wife were returning to Vienna from Salzburg (where he had introduced Constanze to his disapproving father) when they stopped at the small town of Linz – home of the music-loving Count Thun. Needing

Bruno Walter

a symphony for an unscheduled concert, Mozart simply wrote one on the spot ". . . at breakneck speed". The "Linz" symphony, as it is known, is a richly scored ceremonial work that even retains its trumpets and drums during the slow movement. Its sophisticated mixture of the intimate and the grandiose made a great impression at its Vienna premiere and it remained one of Mozart's own favourite works. Three year passed before Mozart wrote *Symphony No. 38*, this time with the idea of capitalizing on his great popularity at Prague where *The Marriage of Figaro* was about to be staged. The "Prague" symphony is a temporary return to the three-movement Italian-style symphony, but it is also suffused with the mood of *Figaro* in its sparkling finale, and seems to prefigure *Don Giovanni* in its brooding introduction and sombre slow movement. It makes a fitting prelude to his three greatest symphonies.

◑ **Prague Chamber Orchestra; Mackerras** (Telarc CD80148).

Mackerras's approach is a little more gutsy than Marriner, with a more emphatic string sound and some characterful wind playing. It works well in the "Linz" and even more so in the "Prague" symphony, a grander work which benefits from a more dynamic sound.

◑ **Columbia Symphony Orchestra; Walter** (Sony SM3K 46511; with *Symphonies Nos. 35, 39, 40* & *41*; 3 CDs).

Bruno Walter is renowned for his Mahler, but critics have tended to ignore his refreshingly imaginative approach to Mozart. His recordings of the late symphonies is outstanding. Completely devoid of pomposity, he leads the purposeful Columbia Symphony Orchestra through performances that give the music a bracing sense of freedom (where many have imposed metronomic regularity).

SYMPHONIES NOS. 39–41

The *Symphony No. 39* seems a smiling work, full of sunlight and mellow, flowing lines. But it begins with a harsh and angry introduction and the autumnal glow of its slow movement is broken up by dark minor-jkey interruptions. Much of the ambivalence of mood comes from the way Mozart exploits the rich colours of the woodwind – two clarinets, two bassoons and a flute. The *Symphony No. 40* is a more obviously tragic utterance quite unlike anything previously written by Mozart. The tone is set by its remarkable first movement, a brilliant conception which, like the opening of Beethoven's fifth symphony, is built upon a single urgent idea whose interest is primarily rhythmical. The slow movement is as profoundly spiritual a moment as anything in the symphonic repertoire although commentators are divided as to whether the prevailing mood is one of gloom or optimism. It was the haughty and imperial nature of the first movement of the *Symphony No. 41* that earned it the title "Jupiter" early in the nineteenth century – when you hear the opening's march-like progress and forceful trumpets and drums, you'll know why the association caught on. Haydn echoed the wonderful middle movement in the slow movement of his *Symphony No. 98*, as a tribute to his friend and one-time pupil. For complexity and sheer excitement, there is nothing comparable to the finale: there are no fewer than six distinct themes here, and Mozart juggles each throughout the movement until, in the coda, he unites them all in a dazzlingly inventive display.

◑ **Columbia Symphony Orchestra; Walter** (Sony SM3K 46511; with *Symphonies Nos. 35, 36* & *38*; 3 CDs).

Walter comes into his own with the last three symphonies. This is broad and expansive conducting which could be called old-fashioned were it not for sheer grandeur and sense of energy which Walter gets from his players. There's a particularly invigorating "pause for breath" halfway through the first movement of *Symphony No. 40* which is completely thrilling, and the "Jupiter" symphony can rarely have had such a powerful and coherent reading.

○ **English Baroque Soloists; Gardiner** (Philips 426 315-2).

Gardiner, with his period-instrument band, should be at the other end of the spectrum from Walter but in fact the approach is not so very different. As in his choral conducting, he takes full advantage of the dramatic moments with some splendidly vigorous fast movements which, however, never undermine the dignity and architectural splendour of these works.

THE CONCERTOS

Mozart's 27 piano concertos dominate his concerto output, and they are remarkably consistent in form. Eighteenth-century pianos were incapable of offering any dynamic challenge to the orchestra – small though it was – and so much of the writing follows the simple system of exchange, whereby the orchestra plays a theme which is then repeated or developed by the pianist and vice versa. All but one of the concertos opens with a straightforward orchestral statement, presenting the main-movement subject as well as any other relevant themes, and then the piano takes over. But if the structure remains essentially the same, the inventiveness within that structure is astonishing. The music can seem brittle at first, with decoration after decoration poured onto simple melodic lines, but beneath the elegant facade is a spirit of immense strength and imagination. Mozart didn't write a proper piano concerto until he was 17 (the first four concertos are arrangements of other people's music), and so – unlike the symphonies – they comprise a body of work that's of consistently high quality. If you don't want to commit yourself to the lot straightaway, sample the seven we've selected below – the first will give you a taste of middle-period Mozart, the others reveal him at his peak.

At the age of 19 Mozart wrote five violin concertos at the instigation of his father (a noted violin teacher), who believed that they would make his name abroad. Composed within a matter of months, for performance by the Italian violinist Brunetti and his court orchestra in Salzburg, they are all extremely pretty, but the fifth is superior to the rest. Of his other concertos, the *Clarinet Concerto* is the finest of his numerous works for wind instruments (he also wrote two for flute, one for flute and harp, and four for horn).

◑ **Complete Piano Concertos: Anda; Salzburg Mozarteum Camerata Academica** (Deutsche Grammophon 429 001-2; 10 CDs).

Geza Anda's concerto cycle established a bench mark back in the 1960s and, though it now has several excellent rivals, none has surpassed it. Anda's style is intimate, romantic and unfussy, the sound is good for the time, and the set is excellent value for money.

◑ **Complete Piano Concertos: Perahia; English Chamber Orchestra** (Sony SX12K 46441; 12 CDs).

Murray Perahia's more recent set is the obvious alternative. Perahia is a consummate Mozartian with an unerring sense of line and a wonderfully precise and pellucid tone. There's a joyous celebratory quality to this set which makes it hard to resist. All of the twelve discs are available individually.

◑ **Piano Concertos Nos. 19, 20, 21, 23 & 24: Brendel; Academy of St-Martin-in-the-Fields** (Philips 442 269-2; 2 CDs).

◑ Piano Concertos Nos. 9, 15, 22, 25 & 27: Brendel; Academy of St-Martin-in-the-Fields (Philips 442 571-2; 2 CDs).

If you want to concentrate on the most famous concertos, then a near-ideal way is to purchase these four CDs in the Philips Duo series (two for the price of one). Brendel has a rather more robust approach to Mozart than either Anda or Perahia, but he is always supremely elegant and he's supported by some superbly refined playing from the Academy of St-Martin-in-the-Fields.

PIANO CONCERTO NO. 12

The delightful *Piano Concerto No. 12* was written in 1782, soon after Mozart had resigned from the service of the Archbishop of Salzburg. Perhaps the plethora of melodic invention in the first movement are signs of Mozart's relief. Only the solemn slow movement, which opens with a theme by the recently deceased J.C. Bach, subdues the concerto's predominant cheerfulness. It was one of a set of three concertos, of which Mozart wrote to his father: "These concertos are a happy medium between what is too easy and too difficult; they are very brilliant, pleasing to the ear, and natural without being vapid. There are passages here and there from which connoisseurs alone can derive satisfaction; but these passages are written in such a way that the less learned cannot fail to be pleased, though without knowing why."

○ Schiff; Salzburg Mozarteum Camerata Academica; Vegh (Decca 417 886-2; with *Concerto No. 14*).

Although he plays on a massive nine-foot Bösendorfer, Andras Schiff (who has recorded all the concertos) is able to produce a delicate and highly varied tone which is perfectly suited to this uncomplicated, light and colourful concerto.

PIANO CONCERTO NO. 15

This concerto marks a turning point in Mozart's development of the form into something more expressive and sophisticated. Taking his lead from the Mannheim school of composers, who enriched orchestral sonority by employing a wide range of instruments, Mozart introduced a clearly defined wind section in this concerto, which he uses to telling effect, mainly through conversational exchanges between wind and strings in the outer movements. The meditative slow movement is the first time that the variation form is employed by Mozart in a concerto: it's a movement of great subtlety, which reaches a peak of textural elegance midway when the wind section plays the theme against a background of pizzicato strings and undulating arpeggios in the piano part. The concerto closes with a typically invigorating Mozartian rondo.

○ Perahia; English Chamber Orchestra (Sony SK37824; with *Concerto No. 16*).

This makes the perfect sampler with which to judge Perahia's graceful and tender style. There's a marvellous rapport between him and the orchestra (which he directs from the keyboard as Mozart would have) and the sense of these works as a dialogue has never come across so freshly.

PIANO CONCERTO NO. 20

The concertos initiated in 1785 by *No. 20* mark a broadening of the emotional content of the genre, in particular – in this work – a marked darkening of mood. The menacing opening of the first movement, in which insistent syncopation contributes to a brooding tension, seems to anticipate the harsh and shadowy world of *Don Giovanni*, written about two years later. This mood is alleviated by the calm and sunny Romanze, a movement which has been criticized for being rather too placid. Almost certainly Mozart would have expected that the repeated main theme would have been ornamented by the soloist each time it returned. The finale is a breathtaking helter-skelter of a movement which opens with a dramatic upward-moving arpeggio known as a "Mannheim rocket"! This movement also has shades of the last act of *Don Giovanni* in the way it contrasts furious energy with moments of opera buffa comicality.

○ Curzon; English Chamber Orchestra; Britten (Decca 417 288-2; with *Concerto No. 27*).

This is an absolutely classic performance from Clifford Curzon, an immaculate stylist whose Mozart-playing often takes on a Beethoven-like grandeur, as is the case here. The ECO, under the direction of Benjamin Britten, provide nimble and fluent support.

PIANO CONCERTO NO. 21

Like the preceding concerto, *No. 21* seems to inhabit the same harmonic world as Mozart's late operas, though here it's more *Così* than *Don Giovanni*. The march-like and jaunty opening soon gives way to piano writing that is especially song-like. Many people know the dreamy slow movement of this concerto in which a glorious rising piano line is set over throbbing orchestral triplets. It was used for the soundtrack of the rather soppy film *Elvira Madigan* and, indeed, it now appears as "The Elvira Madigan" on concert programmes, as if Mozart had thought up the title. The association does the concerto a disservice, for this is a serene rather than a sentimental work full of exquisite melodies and limpid textures, only giving rein to the virtuosity expected by Viennese audiences in the brilliant passage work of the last movement.

◑ **Anda; Salzburg Mozarteum Camerata Academica** (Deutsche Grammophon 429 522-2GR (with *Concerto No. 17*).

Geza Anda's lyrical performance is beautifully constructed, and the recording is bright and well focused. This was the recording used in the film *Elvira Madigan*, and Anda's reading of the slow movement might be thought, by some, to be a little too romantic. For a more forthright approach try Brendel (see above).

PIANO CONCERTOS NOS. 23 & 24

No. 23 is one of the most popular of all Mozart's piano concertos, largely because of the sunny and easy-going disposition of its first theme. Near the end of the movement this is replaced by a rather more wistful second subject played by the orchestra, around which the piano weaves a delicate filigree variation. The slow-movement Adagio, in the rarely used key of F sharp minor, is one of the most beautiful of all. It makes its impact largely through the simplicity of its tender theme which is strongly reminiscent of the slow movement of the earlier *Piano Sonata in F*, K280. Another exhilarating finale, with woodwind very much to the fore, brings the concerto to a close.

Though Mozart wrote *No. 24* in 1786 shortly after *No. 23*, it couldn't be more dissimilar. It marks a return to the dark style of *No. 20* and is the grandest in scale of all the concertos, augmenting the already sizable wind section with trumpets and drums. These are used to create the kind of threatening atmosphere which, again, recalls the more ominous moments of *Don Giovanni*. The long first movement is dominated by the stirring opening theme, which establishes a feeling of defiance. A subdued slow movement is followed by an Allegretto in variation form – one of Mozart's most brilliant – which re-establishes the concerto's original tragic mood. The finale's fiery coda was particularly admired by Beethoven and was an influence on his *Appassionata Sonata*.

◑ **Curzon; London Symphony Orchestra; Kertész** (Decca 452 888-2).

Curzon's pianistic range is very much on show here: there's a delicacy and a grace to his reading of *No. 23* which is utterly infectious, whereas in *No. 24* he stresses the proto-Romantic aspects of the work in a performance of controlled power. Orchestral support isn't quite as good as on the other Curzon disc (see p.274), but it is more than adequate.

PIANO CONCERTO NO. 27

The *Piano Concerto No. 27* was Mozart's last: he completed it on January 5, 1791, eleven months before his death. It followed two years of extreme hardship, in which his financial situation had become critical and his relationship with Constanze placed under great strain. The least virtuosic of all his concertos, it is characterized by an autumnal mood of introspection and resignation that is typical of his late work. Some critics have rather fancifully perceived a consciously valedictory tone in this concerto.

○ **Gulda; Vienna Philharmonic Orchestra; Abbado** (Deutsche Grammophon 419 479-2; with *Concerto No. 20*).

Frederic Gulda now spends most of his time performing and writing jazz music, and an improvisatory approach infuses this immensely flexible performance. An illuminating sense of the unexpected is also to be found in the coupled performance of *Piano Concerto No. 20*.

THE VIOLIN CONCERTOS

The five violin concertos, all written at Salzburg in 1775, may also have been intended for a specific performer (though Mozart is known to have played some of them himself). The way that they rapidly progress in sophistication is truly astonishing. What distinguishes the fifth violin concerto from the rest of the set is the greater responsibility given to the orchestra – in the other four, the orchestra does little more than merely accompany the soloist. The melodies are engaging and instantly memorable: virtuosic in the first movement, tender in the second, and wild in the third. The finale is especially memorable for its "Turkish" episode, a piece of music which reflects the then craze for all things Ottoman.

○ **Violin Concerto No. 1: Zukerman; St. Paul Chamber Orchestra** (Sony SBK46540; with *Concerto No. 4, Rondo and Adagio*).

Zukerman gives a witty performance and milks the music for every drop of emotion, especially in the slow movement. The small size of his chamber orchestra ensures that the countrapuntal writing is not lost beneath washes of thickly vibrating strings, as happens on many recordings.

◑ **Concertos Nos. 1–5: Grumiaux; London Symphony Orchestra; Davis** (Philips 438 323-2; 2 CDs; with *Sinfonia concertante for violin, viola and orchestra*).

If you want to explore all the concertos, then, once again, Philips offer outstanding value for money. Grumiaux's 1960s performances are models of their kind: poised, elegant and with a tone that was both incisive and sweet.

SINFONIA CONCERTANTE FOR VIOLIN AND VIOLA

Four years after the five concertos for violin, Mozart wrote the finest of all his concertos for strings. Calling it a sinfonia concertante – rather than a concerto – aligns it with the Baroque concerto grosso in which the solo players were more closely integrated with the full orchestra than in the classical concerto. The magical first entry of the violin is a case in point: it simply emerges on a long sustained note as the orchestra falls away. From there ensues a marvellous series of conversational interchanges between the two instruments, the viola sounding less gravelly than usual since Mozart specified that it be tuned a semi-tone higher than usual. The high point is the slow movement, an operatic lament of great feeling in which the two instruments have long solo passages before weaving a delicate canonical phrase around each other. Both this and the boisterous final movement contain quotations from works by Michael Haydn (brother of Joseph), who may well have played the viola part in the original performance.

◑ **Grumiaux; London Symphony Orchestra; Davis** (Philips 438 323-2; 2 CDs; with *Concertos Nos. 1-5*).

The complete violin concertos set (reviewed on p.275) also contains a near-perfect account of the *Sinfonia concertante* in which Grumiaux is partnered by the viola player Arigo Pelliccia. This is magical music-making, with the soloists weaving a web of the most exquisite sounds around each other in what is one of Mozart's most beautiful works.

THE CLARINET CONCERTO

Mozart's *Clarinet Concerto* has for many years been the subject of controversy. While it is quite clearly the finest ever written for the instrument (and almost certainly by Mozart), no one really knows how much of it is actually Mozart's – but for 199 bars of the first movement, there is no complete manuscript in the composer's hand. Written in Mozart's last year (so, like much of his last works, seen as valedictory) the music has a consistently melancholy beauty, reserving its deepest emotion for the elegiac slow movement. It was written for Mozart's friend and fellow Mason Anton Stadler, a performer in the Vienna court orchestra, who devised a downward extension to the instrument and was admired for his playing in the lower register. Mozart exploited this ability and there are several passages which seem to wallow in the instrument's chocolatey lower notes.

○ **King; English Chamber Orchestra; Tate** (Hyperion CDA 66199; with *Clarinet Quintet*).

Thea King plays this concerto on the instrument for which it was written, the basset clarinet, and the result is a darkly refined sound which is extremely beguiling. There is a natural directness to her playing which is well matched by Tate and the ECO.

◑ **Goodman; Boston Symphony Orchestra; Munch** (RCA RD85275; with *Clarinet Quintet*).

Benny Goodman was the dedicatee of works by Bartók, Hindemith and Copland, but the bulk of his recordings were made as a jazz clarinettist and swing-band leader. His recording of Mozart's concerto, however, is probably the most famous ever made: the recording is old but its age is more than compensated for by Goodman's shimmering beauty of tone.

HORN CONCERTOS NOS. 1–4

One of Mozart's longest friendships was with another member of the Salzburg court orchestra, the horn player Joseph Leutgeb – a regular butt of Mozart's heavy-handed humour. In 1777 Leutgeb moved to Vienna to continue his musical career but also to set himself up as a cheesemonger. He requested a concerto from Mozart, but in the end he got four, plus a horn quintet. Rather confusingly, *No. 1* is now known to have been the last and was incomplete at the time of Mozart's death. Though not Mozart's most profound works, each of these concertos is great fun and *Nos. 3* and *4* are especially enjoyable: both have serene slow movements which show off the purity of the instrument's tone, and both finish with rollicking "hunting"-style finales. In Mozart's day the soloist would have used a horn without valves – an extraordinarily difficult instrument to play well.

⊙ **Briggs; Royal Liverpool Philharmonic Orchestra; Kovacevich** (Classics for Pleasure CD-CFP 4589; with Haydn, *Trumpet Concerto*).

This is a remarkable bargain: the former principal horn player of the RLPO, Claire Briggs, gives an absolutely scintillating performance: spirited, vivacious but always magnificently controlled.

THE SERENADES

In addition to writing a lot of the large-scale music – operas, symphonies and the like – Mozart was a jobbing composer who also produced a large quantity of lighter music for special occasions of varying degrees of formality, often held out of doors. Such music was usually called a serenade or a divertimento, the two names being virtually interchangeable, although a serenade carried the connotation of an evening entertainment and was often referred to by its German name, *Nachtmusik*. This was essentially background music, against which you could eat, talk or party as the occasion demanded, but such restrictions did not prevent Mozart from writing works of great style and sophistication. A serenade did not conform to any particular form, although they often had several movements: thus *Serenade No. 7*, the "Haffner", is a kind of scaled-down sinfonia-concertante, *No. 10* is mainly for wind instruments, and *No. 13* – the most famous of all – was originally written for string quartet and double bass.

SERENADE NO. 10 – GRAN PARTITA

Wind bands were highly fashionable in Vienna in the early 1780s – even the emperor had one – and several arrangements of Mozart's operas were made for such ensembles. Mozart's wind-band masterpiece is known as the *Serenade for 13 Wind Instruments*, although it is actually for twelve plus one double bass. There is some doubt as to whether it was written for Mozart's own wedding celebrations or, as seems more likely, for a benefit concert for his old friend the clarinettist Anton Stadler. Clarinets and basset horns (a lower-pitched version of the instrument) make up four of the instruments, but the great glory of this work is the way the various instuments move in and out of the limelight dictating the mood of its seven movements. The core of the work is the third-movement Adagio which begins with a rather unassuming, lilting introduction from which a long sustained note on the oboe suddenly appears. It's a moment of heart-melting magic.

◑ **Chamber Orchestra of Europe Wind Soloists; Schneider** (ASV CDCOE804; with *Serenade for Wind Octet*).

There's no shortage of fine recordings of this great work, but this has a panache and a sense of common cause that is exceptional. The individual players are all outstanding but it's the way they coalesce, with some finely judged dynamics, that is so impressive.

SERENADE NO. 13 – EINE KLEINE NACHTMUSIK

This is the piece which practically everybody who has had any contact with classical music can recognize and even hum the beginning of – though they might not be able to put a name to it. Notwithstanding its popularity, it remains a bit of a mystery. It was composed in 1787, at the same time as the second act of *Don Giovanni*, but for what occasion is not known. The scoring, for string quartet and a double bass, is quite specific, although nowadays it is more commonly played by a small string orchestra. It is undoubtedly one of Mozart's most effortlessly sunny works, from its attention-grabbing opening to its sparking finale. Only in the languid second movement is there any hint of disquiet – a momentary flutter of agitation – otherwise, all is serene and easy-going.

O Orpheus Chamber Orchestra (Deutsche Grammophon 419 192-2; with *Divertimentos in E Flat Major* and *D Major*).

One of the most over-recorded pieces of music here gets the kind of fresh-faced performance you might expect from a group discovering this music for the first time. The Orpheus Chamber Orchestra can sometimes produce a somewhat homogenized sound, but here the sheer energy and sweetness of their playing seems totally appropriate.

CHAMBER MUSIC

By the middle of the eighteenth century various instrumental combinations, had become established as permanent ensembles, with a corresponding demand for music. Such music was usually commissioned by aristocratic patrons or written with a view to publication – middle-class, amateur music-making being then very much on the increase. Mozart produced a vast body of chamber music beginning at the age of 12 and continuing right up to his death. He was no innovator; rather he assimilated, with remarkable insight, the developments and innovations made by others. Above all he built on the great achievements of Haydn in making chamber music, especially the string quartet, a vehicle for complex musical argument and personal vision. In Mozart's greatest chamber music – the last ten quartets, the middle two string quintets and the clarinet quintet – thematic development and the most intensely personal expression achieve a perfect equilibrium.

THE STRING QUARTETS

Mozart wrote a total of 23 string quartets, though it was not a genre that came particularly easily to him. Haydn was regarded as the absolute master of the form and it was the publication of his Op. 33 set of quartets in 1781 which pushed Mozart to new levels of achievement. Between 1782 and 1785 he wrote six quartets ("the fruits of a long and laborious effort") which he dedicated to his older colleague. The *"Haydn" Quartets* (*Nos. 14–19*) were begun soon after Mozart first made Haydn's acquaintance. How they met is unknown, but their friendship was probably cemented at "quartet" parties, at which Haydn played second violin to Mozart's viola – as they did for the first performances of the *"Haydn" Quartets*. All six bear repeated listening. The second of the set is a particularly strong and determined work: according to Constanza, the trio of the second movement was her husband's response to her difficult labour prior to the birth of their first son. The third (*No. 16*) is remarkable for the rich sonorities and unpredictable harmonies of its mysterious slow movement.

The two best-known of the group, *Nos. 17* and *19* (known as the "Hunt" and the "Dissonance") have proved the most popular of all the Mozart quartets and are good places to start. The "Hunt", named after its galloping opening with its hunting-horn motif, is a clear attempt by Mozart at mastering not just four-part harmony but four-part "discourse". The Adagio boasts some richly organized textures that could easily have been composed early in the nineteenth century, while the Minuet is a brilliant and suitably brief study of sophisticated invention. The startling discords that open the last of the *"Haydn" Quartets* earned it the subtitle the "Dissonance" after Mozart's death. It is an astonishingly complex piece of music and plunges to depths that remained beyond Haydn's grasp. The dissonant opening turns out to be a ruse, misleading the listener into believing that the remainder of the work will be of a similarly haunting sobriety. Nothing of the sort happens, although the second movement does hark back to the gravity of the first. Mozart may have been no innovator, but the chromaticism of this quartet is an instance of him employing musical language that would not really become acceptable until the following century.

Mozart immediately followed the six *"Haydn" Quartets* with *Quartet No. 20* (known as the "Hoffmeister"), a classically elegant and rather demure work which forms a bridge between the *"Haydn" Quartets* and the last three. These, the *"Prussian" Quartets*, were begun in 1789 following a trip to Berlin where Mozart had been introduced to (and offered a job by) the King of Prussia, Friedrich Wilhelm II. Intending to dedicate them to the cello-playing king, Mozart found them particularly difficult to write, perhaps through trying to make the cello part more interesting than was customary. Certainly they are markedly different from the earlier set – more concentrated, with the weight of each work shifted from the first movement to the last, and with several passges in which the cello does, indeed, dominate. Though written at a time of great crisis for Mozart, their overall mood – in particular in the slow movements – is less melancholy and more wistful than the *"Haydn" Quartets*. The original idea was to write a set of six but Mozart died after the first three and the King of Prussia, almost certainly, never got to play them.

O Quartets Nos. 14–23: Alban Berg Quartet (Teldec 4509-95495-2; 4 CDs).

For an overview of the finest of Mozart's quartets, this set (recorded in the 1970s) is hard to beat. Indeed these performances are among the finest that this distinguished quartet has made. There's a vigour and a gutsiness to their approach which really pays off in the darker-hued works.

O The "Haydn" Quartets: Quator Mosaïques (Auvidis Astrée E 8596; 3 CDs).

Acclaimed for their performances of the quartets of Haydn, the Quator Mosaïques are equally strong in Mozart – their strong, burnished tone (they play on period instruments) is especially suited to the rich sonorities of the Haydn set. All three discs are available individually.

◑ Quartets Nos. 17 & 19: Alban Berg Quartet (Teldec 2292-43037-2).

Briskly driven performances from the Alban Berg Quartet in the Hunt, but equally ruminative when the music demands it, as in the opening of the Dissonance. This makes the perfect sampler of their four-CD set recommended above.

⊙ Quartets Nos. 17 & 19: Moyzes Quartet (Naxos 8.550105).

Accomplished performances from the Moyzes Quartet of Bratislava. They do not have the range or the subtlety of the Alban Bergs but there is a unity of vision, even if occasionally it feels a little on the safe side.

STRING QUINTETS NOS. 3 & 4

In Mozart's day a string quintet constituted a string quartet augmented by an extra viola – the enriched inner voices allowing for greater contrapuntal elaboration. In the spring of 1787, shortly after the success of the *Le Nozze di Figaro* in Prague, Mozart composed two such quintets – one in C and one in G minor. Written at a time when he had become resigned to the indifference of the audiences in his home city of Vienna, both works seem to have been composed solely to satisfy his own requirements and both are highly personal. C major is not a key that is normally associated with complex feelings, but *No. 3* is a work of almost disturbing mood swings, in particular in its long first movement. The G minor quintet seems even more deeply felt: it speaks of resolution and self-reliance in the face of mounting despair. Its dreadfully bleak third movement (some have seen it as a premonition of death) is almost certainly the most powerful thing Mozart ever wrote for a chamber ensemble.

O Alban Berg Quartet; Wolf (RCA 09026 61757-2; with *Violin Concerto No. 5, Violin Sonata No. 26*).

There are only four recordings that couple these two quintets on a single disc and it's this one, on which the Alban Berg Quartet are joined by violist Markus Wolf, that best convey the extraordinarily variegated nature of these profound works.

◑ Heifetz, Baker, Primrose, Majewski, Piatigorsky (RCA 09026 61757-2; with *Violin Concerto No. 5, Violin Sonata No. 26*).

This historical recording of *Quintet No. 4* is something special. Recorded in 1961, with Heifetz joined by Gregor Piatigorsky, William Primrose and two of the finest session musicians of the day, this is a highly charged and profound interpretation. Heifetz is the dominant voice, but this performance radiates a sense of complete accord.

THE CLARINET QUINTET

Mozart first met the clarinettist Anton Stadler in 1782, and the two men – both Freemasons – quickly became close friends, with Stadler frequently taking financial advantage of the far from wealthy composer. This never dented Mozart's admiration for the way Stadler played the clarinet, an admiration that resulted in a concerto, a quintet and a trio. The first two are masterpieces, showing a complete mastery of the instrument's particular tone and blending capabilities. The quintet was composed in 1789 and received its first performance late that year, with both Stadler and Mozart taking part. Mozart included plenty of opportunities for Stadler to show off his and the instrument's dexterity, but this is not merely an exercise in great technique – the second movement is intensely romantic, for example, and the final movement has moments of almost unbearable yearning. With its wide palette of colour, extreme emotional contrasts, wonderful melodies and innovative exploration of the clarinet's range, "Stadler's Quintet" (as Mozart titled it) is one of the composer's most brilliant and characterful creations.

O King; Gabrieli String Quartet (Hyperion CDA 66199; with *Clarinet Concerto*).

On the same disc as the *Clarinet Concerto* (see p.276) is Thea King's equally refined and sensitive performance of the *Quintet*. Its restrained and intimate character is well served by the excellent Hyperion sound.

◑ Goodman; Boston Quartet (RCA RD85275; with *Clarinet Concerto*).

Goodman first recorded the *Clarinet Quintet* in 1938 with the great Budapest Quartet; this second version, with the Boston Quartet, was made at the same time as his recording of the concerto (see p.276) and, while the American quartet are not as good as the Hungarians, Goodman is in fine form and the sound quality is vastly improved.

SOLO PIANO MUSIC

Mozart was, for the first half of his career, primarily a performer rather than a composer. In fact he was the first great exponent of the then relatively new pianoforte. As a performer and teacher he encouraged clarity above keyboard wizardry – he loathed the playing of Clementi (see p.108) – and this attitude is largely reflected in the relative simplicity of his solo piano works. His first piano compositions were variations and sonatas for four hands written for himself and his sister. He did not begin writing sonatas until 1774, but within six months he had composed six, all of which reveal the influence of Haydn. The later sonatas display a far greater harmonic ingenuity and melodic richness than the earlier ones, though they are no more technically demanding. Virtually all eighteen of Mozart's piano sonatas are neglected by pianists and record buyers alike, almost certainly because they have little of the colour, emotional range or virtuosity of a nineteenth-century piano work. What they do have is spareness, charm and elegance and an almost endless supply of sparkling melodies.

PIANO SONATAS NOS. 11 & 14, AND THE FANTASIA IN C MINOR

Alone among Mozart's solo piano music, these three works are regularly performed and recorded. *Sonata No. 11* is very much a showpiece work written to show off Mozart's wide-ranging skills at the piano. It begins not with the customary fast movement but with a gentle, almost folk-song-like lullaby which goes through a series of sprightly, if conventional variations. The ensuing Minuet and Trio leads without a break into the infectiously animated Rondo "Alla Turca" – a whirling dance which, like the fifth violin concerto, reflects the fashion for all things Turkish. The *Sonata No. 14* in C minor, written in 1784, could hardly be more different. It is Mozart's grandest solo work: terse, pithy and inward-looking in a way that seems to anticipate Beethoven. Seven months after completing it, Mozart wrote an introduction to the sonata in the form of a Fantasia. A studious and intense work, with a startling range of moods, it provides the most vivid portrait of Mozart the brilliant keyboard improviser.

⊙ Pires (Deutsche Grammophon 429 739-2; with *Fantasia in D Minor*).

Maria-João Pires has recorded nearly all of Mozart's keyboard works (available as a six-CD set), for which her steely but lyrical style is perfectly suited. Some pianists treat the solo piano music as essentially decorative, but in Pires's readings there is always a degree of grit beneath the filigree surface.

MODEST MUSSORGSKY

(1839–1881)

Of all the composers in the Russian nationalist school known as "The Five" or "The Mighty Handful", Mussorgsky is arguably the greatest. True, Rimsky-Korsakov's highly colourful style left its mark on the likes of Glazunov and Stravinsky, but Mussorgsky's works were invariably groundbreaking, though few in number. Indeed, Mussorgsky's music was too innovative. Rimsky-Korsakov, while recognizing that Mussorgsky was "talented, original, full of so much that was new and vital", asserted that his manuscripts also revealed "absurd, disconnected harmony, ugly part-writing, sometimes strikingly illogical modulation . . . unsuccessful orchestration . . . " and began a dedicated project to make his music more performable, either by completing works Mussorgsky had failed to finish or by the wholesale rewriting of complete compositions. Yet these are the very elements – power, earthiness and sheer invention – that gave Mussorgsky his unique musical personality.

Mussorgsky was born into a land-owning family and led a rather dilettantish early life. He found his way into Balakirev's circle in the late 1850s and began composing in earnest, under Balakirev's guidance. After the emancipation of the serfs in 1861, his family lost much of its wealth and he had to find work with the engineering department of the Ministry of Communications, and later with the forestry department of the Ministry for State Property. (As with many of his contemporaries, composition was always a spare-time activity, though his dipsomania probably had a more deleterious effect on his writing than did his lack of time.)

In the meantime, he had been gaining a growing reputation for his songwriting abilities, bringing a new sense of realism and integration to the form. He also worked on a couple of operas that he never got round to completing, *Salammbô* (1863–66) and *The Marriage* (1868) – from the former emerged one of his best-known works, *St John's Night on the Bare Mountain* (1867). He then embarked on an operatic adaptation of Pushkin's play *Boris Godunov*, which went through two versions in his own lifetime (1869 and 1872), and found lasting success in the second. In 1874 he wrote his best-known work, *Pictures at an Exhibition*, a piano suite more often heard today in orchestral guise. His last great projects, which vied for his attention and thus were never finished, were another historical opera, *Khovanshchina* (1872–80, completed by Rimsky-Korsakov and revised by Shostakovich) and the Gogol-based comedy *Sorochintsy Fair* (1874–80, completed by Liadov).

GUS ONG

BORIS GODUNOV

Boris Godunov is roughly based on the life of the man who became tsar in 1598, having murdered his rival, and the plot depicts the attempt of a pretender to the throne, who knows of the murder, to usurp him. Mussorgsky exploits the dramatic potential of this scenario to the full, creating a powerful contrast between the spectacle of the Coronation Scene and Boris's inner torment as he tries and fails to come to terms with his guilt. His greatest achievement, however, is his musical characterization, in which the words, thoughts and moods of the protagonists are mirrored in the orchestral accompaniment. Composers as diverse as Debussy and Janáček were undoubtedly influenced by Mussorgsky's skill in word-setting, in particular his way of setting dramatic prose so that the music reflects the inflections of the spoken text.

The work exists in three versions: Mussorgsky wrote two (in 1872 he added two scenes set in Poland, but cut a scene in the last act), and Rimsky-Korsakov produced one soon after the composer's death with the intention that it should help the reception of the opera, while admitting that a time might come when it was superseded by a reappraisal of Mussorgsky's original. This has now happened and, while Rimsky's version is undoubtedly colourful, it misses the profundity and dark hues of the original orchestration.

O Raimondi, Polozov, Vishnevskaya, Plishka; Washington Choral Arts Society; Washington National Symphony Orchestra; Rostropovich (Erato 2292-45418-2; 3 CDs).

This 1987 performance remains the most authentic yet produced, thanks to Rostropovich's fanatical attention to detail, shape and expression. Ruggiero Raimondi's baritonal Boris lacks physical weight and his approach is too lyrical, but the intensity with which he portrays Boris's vertiginous fall is unforgettably haunting. Vyacheslav Polozov hurls himself into the tenor role of Dimitri and Galina Vishnevskaya sings her second Marina with an often brutal passion.

O Kotscherga, Larin, Lipovšek, Ramey, Nikolsky, Langridge; Slovak Philharmonic Choir; Berlin Philharmonic Orchestra; Abbado (Sony S3K58977; 3 CDs).

It is a testament to Abbado's affinity for Mussorgsky's music that he managed to mould his "celebrity cast" into a convincingly theatrical unit. Anatoly Kotscherga is a formidable Boris, although he sometimes delivers the words with excessive force. Marjana Lipovšek is a little mature as Marina and Sam Ramey struggles with the language as Pimen, but both give lyrical performances that contrast with Kotscherga's declamatory approach. The rest of the cast are splendid, but the show really belongs to Abbado and the sonorous BPO.

PICTURES AT AN EXHIBITION

When Mussorgsky's close friend, the architect-painter Victor Hartmann, died in 1873, a mutual friend named Vladimir Stasov arranged a memorial exhibition of the artist's work in St Petersburg. Visiting the exhibition, Mussorgsky conceived his own tribute in the form of a suite of piano pieces depicting a selection of the works on show, with a recurring theme (the *Promenade*) representing the viewer walking between the pictures. Although completed in 1874, the suite wasn't published until after Mussorgsky's death, and the pictorial quality of these pieces inevitably drew the attention of other composers and arrangers – it's only surprising that Rimsky didn't attempt an orchestral arrangement himself. Of the many subsequent orchestrations, the most successful, if hardly the most Russian, is that made by Ravel in 1922.

O Piano version: Pletnev (Virgin VC 7 59611-2; with Tchaikovsky/Pletnev, *Sleeping Beauty*).

Mikhail Pletnev gives a strong reading of the original piano suite, with bold and dramatic playing that makes one think that orchestration didn't really add anything really substantial to this work.

O Ravel orchestration: London Symphony Orchestra; Abbado (Deutsche Grammophon 423 901-2; with Stravinsky, *Petrushka*).

Abbado's excellent LSO performance of Ravel's version can't prevent the piece sounding less like Mussorgsky than like Ravel, but there is still plenty of character and excitement here.

ST JOHN'S NIGHT ON THE BARE MOUNTAIN

Mussorgsky's only major orchestral work – *St John's Night on the Bare Mountain* – is another work that Rimsky wouldn't leave to fend for itself. It exists in two versions, Mussorgsky's original (intended as an episode in his opera *Sorochintsy Fair*) and Rimsky's beefed-up recomposition, incorporating other Mussorgsky fragments. The work is a portrait of midsummer night when, according to Russian folklore, a witches' Sabbath is held on the Bare Mountain near Kiev; the musical whirlwind at the heart of the piece is one of those bits of music that hi-fi shops use to impress customers.

◑ Original version: London Symphony Orchestra; Abbado (RCA 09026 61354-2; with other orchestral and choral works).

Although not nearly as well-known as Rimsky's reworking, the original is arguably a more effective portrait of the midsummer mayhem, and Abbado's fine recording of it comes coupled with an invaluable collection of rarely heard choral and orchestral works.

⊙ Rimsky-Korsakov version: Royal Liverpool Philharmonic Orchestra; Mackerras (Virgin CUV 5 61135 2; with *Pictures at an Exhibition* & Borodin's *Prince Igor* – excerpts).

The most recommendable account of the bastardized version is Mackerras's spirited performance with the Royal Liverpool Philharmonic – it's a potent enough piece, but make sure you hear the Mussorgsky version as well.

SONGS

Mussorgsky is arguably the greatest nineteenth-century songwriter after Schubert and Schumann, though this aspect of his music is not well enough known outside of Russia. In his songwriting, as in his operas, he was especially concerned with realism and attempted, wherever possible, to follow the rhythms of natural speech. He also, more than any other composer of the period, had no qualms about introducing the modality of folk song into his vocal music, though actual quotation from folk music is relatively rare in his output. As well as many fine individual songs, he wrote two outstanding cycles: *The Nursery* (1872) deals with childhood fears and imaginings on going to bed, while *Sunless* (1874) is striking for its simple and highly original harmony. The *Songs and Dances of Death* (1877) were originally intended as a set of twelve songs, but finished up as four amazingly intense and startling depictions of death.

⭘ Leiferkus; Skigin (Conifer CDCF229).

The Russian baritone Sergei Leiferkus has become well-known on the international opera circuit with his rich colourful voice and strong presence. If anything he is even more effective as a singer of songs, and in Mussorgsky he is unmatched. In this, the first of two volumes of Mussorgsky songs, he performs the best-known pieces (including the *Songs and Dances of Death* and *The Nursery*) with a tonal control and a dramatic flair worthy of Fischer-Dieskau.

CARL NIELSEN

(1865–1931)

N

Of all Scandinavian composers, one of the most accomplished and original is Carl Nielsen, who was born into the peasant island community of Funen in eastern Denmark (birthplace of Hans Christian Andersen), and went on to become his country's musical figurehead. The first step in his career came at the age of 14, when he joined a military band in Odense. Ten years later he joined the violins of the Royal Theatre Orchestra in Copenhagen and in 1890 he won a scholarship that enabled him to travel to Dresden and Berlin. Performances of Wagner's *Ring* and *Die Meistersinger* greatly impressed him, but Brahms was a more important influence, particularly on his early symphonies, and he also recieved guidance from the music director at the Royal Theatre, the composer Johan Svendsen. His first symphony was premiered by the orchestra in 1894 and from then on his rise was rapid. His two operas, *Saul and David* (1902) and *Maskarade* (1905), were both performed under his direction; he then left the orchestra to concentrate on composing but returned three years later as principal conductor, a post he held for six years.

The rest of his life was taken up with composition – he once wrote that his life was lived through music rather than out in the everyday world. Arguably his unique combination of the lyrical and the dynamic is derived largely from his memories of childhood – the songs his mother sang to him and his father's village dance band in which, as a boy, he played the violin. He wrote concertos for flute, clarinet and violin, and some fine tone poems, including *Helios* (1903), a short evocation of sunrise, and *Pan and Syrinx* (1918), an impressionistic depiction of characters from Ovid. But his fame rests solidly on his symphonies, works which are characterized by an emotional directness devoid of sentimentality, and by a constant search for clarity in line and orchestral texture, spinning out long lines of melody that build into complex yet clearly defined contrapuntal melees. His orchestration can often be stark in its sustained concentration on just a few instruments, yet come the climax of a movement or work Nielsen can unleash the orchestra's full force in a blaze of energy.

THE SYMPHONIES

Nielsen's six symphonies are almost contemporary with the seven of Sibelius, yet they could hardly be more different in style, form and intent: where Sibelius seemed to be aiming for ever greater concision, Nielsen's symphonies get more adventurous and wide-ranging as the cycle progresses. The ones to explore first are numbers 3, 4 and 5, the first of these being the most immediately appealing.

The last decade has seen a real boom of Nielsen symphony recordings, with the result that there are now several good complete sets, of which the most outstanding are by Bryden Thomson, Herbert Blomstedt, Neeme Järvi and Paavo Berglund. These are all full price, but only Blomstedt on

Decca and Thomson on Chandos are available as individual discs. (The budget recordings on Naxos have plenty of energy but are lacking in sufficient depth to be completely recommendable.)

SYMPHONY NO. 1

Even in his first symphony (1890–94) Nielsen was striking out in new directions. While his model was undoubtedly the Romantic classicism of Brahms (whom he met in the year of its composition), there is plenty to mark it out as the work of a fresh talent, including the concept of "progressive tonality", a Nielsen hallmark whereby the work ends in a different key from the one in which it began.

⭘ San Francisco Symphony Orchestra; Blomstedt (Decca 425 607-2; with *Symphony No. 6*).

This disc couples Nielsen's first and last symphonies, showing how far he travelled in the thirty years that separate them. Blomstedt brings a sense of spontaneity to the exuberant early work and the recording quality is superlative.

SYMPHONY NO. 2 – THE FOUR TEMPERAMENTS

Nielsen's second symphony emerged nearly a decade later, in 1902. It was inspired by a chance sighting in a village pub of a painting representing the four temperaments that were thought in medieval times to make up the human personality: choleric, phlegmatic, melancholic and sanguine. Here he found the "characters" for the four movements of his symphony, where the temperaments are suggested both by the tone of the music and the degree of sloth or energy with which it progresses.

⭘ San Francisco Symphony Orchestra; Blomstedt (Decca 430 280-2; with *Symphony No. 3*).

Blomstedt's superb Decca recording is again the top choice, his San Francisco orchestra characterfully portraying the great mood swings from movement to movement.

SYMPHONY NO. 3 – SINFONIA ESPANSIVA

Another "theme" dominates Nielsen's third symphony (1910–11) – expansiveness – and again it works at every level, with the musical material seeming to be pushing inexorably further beyond its rightful bounds through repetitive rhythms, onward-forcing harmonic progressions and endless melodies. Another dimension of spaciousness is achieved in the marvellous slow movement, in which distant wordless voices join the melodic melange.

⭘ Fromm, McMillan; San Francisco Symphony Orchestra; Blomstedt (Decca 430 280-2; with *Symphony No. 2*).

The third gets an even more scintillating reading from Blomstedt than the second with which it is coupled. He seems to have an almost instinctive feel for the organic flow of this work and it rides along with all the powerful energy of a wave.

◑ Guldbaek, Møller; Royal Danish Orchestra; Bernstein (Sony SMK47598; with *Symphony No. 5*).

This is a classic reading from Bernstein and the Royal Danish Orchestra, with a really majestic flow to the opening movement. Coupled with a brilliant version of the fifth (see p.284), this disc would be a good starting point for those new to these symphonies.

SYMPHONY NO. 4 – THE INEXTINGUISHABLE

The life spirit is at the heart of the third symphony, and the same goes for *Symphony No. 4 – The Inextinguishable* (1914–16). As Nielsen wrote in the foreword to the published score: "The composer has sought to indicate in one word what only music has the power to express in full: the elemental Will of Life. Music is Life and, like it, inextinguishable." It was written at a difficult time: World War I was raging (though Denmark remained neutral); his marriage was on the rocks; and he had resigned from his conducting post at the Copenhagen Opera. This symphony is patently a kind of emotional exorcism, culminating in a musical battle between two sets of timpani, a conflict resolved in the recall of a lyrical melody from the first movement.

◑ Berlin Philharmonic Orchestra; Karajan (Deutsche Grammophon 445 518-2; with Sibelius, *Tapiola*).

This is a thrilling account, restless and driven but always kept fully under control by Karajan's superb direction. The orchestra attack this symphony with titanic force but also with its customary richness of tone.

⭘ San Francisco Symphony Orchestra; Blomstedt (Decca 421 524-2; with *Symphony No. 5*).

Karajan's dramatic account just edges Blomstedt into second place for this symphony, but this is nonetheless one of the most exciting performances currently available, and recorded with splendid presence and bite.

SYMPHONY NO. 5

This sense of conflict resurfaced in Nielsen's *Symphony No. 5* (1921–22). Here a tense, sparely scored opening gradually breaks out into a battle for supremacy between a solo side drum and the rest of the orchestra – depicting, according to the composer, a fight between good and evil. The orchestra triumphantly subsumes the side drum's martial improvisations and, after a warmly scored Adagio, the first movement ends quietly with the side drum heard again in the distance over a plangent clarinet solo. As this movement had contained both the traditional opening and slow movements, so the second exuberantly combines Scherzo and finale.

⊙ San Francisco Symphony Orchestra; Blomstedt (Decca 421 524-2; with *Symphony No. 4*).

Performances and recordings of this symphony often disappoint in the most vital place – the side-drum battle, which can often sound too easily won. Not so in Blomstedt's account, which makes a worthy partner to his recording of *Symphony No. 4*.

◑ New York Philharmonic Orchestra; Bernstein (Sony SMK47598; with *Symphony No. 3*).

Bernstein and the New York Phil really get under the skin of this great symphony, generating a tension which is nothing short of electrifying.

SYMPHONY NO. 6 – SINFONIA SEMPLICE

Nielsen's last symphony (1924–25) seems to convey his uncertainties about the way music was going in the 1920s. At once good-humoured, ironic (as is the title, "Simple Symphony") and intensely moving, it alternates passages that seem to be poking fun at atonal modernity with others that suggest deeper soul-searching. The whole enigmatic work ends with an unmistakable bassoon "fart". It is often unclear whether Nielsen meant his audience to laugh or scream at this music, but this is one of his most fascinating and phantasmagorical works, looking forward to the irony of Shostakovich and nostalgically back at his own achievements.

⊙ San Francisco Symphony Orchestra; Blomstedt (Decca 425 607-2; with *Symphony No. 1*).

Blomstedt is more restrained than some in this, the most chilling of Nielsen's symphonies, but the requisite nightmare quality is certainly in evidence and, as in the whole of this series, the sound quality is outstanding.

THE CONCERTOS

Nielsen wrote three concertos – for violin (1911), for flute (1926) and for clarinet (1928). The violin was, of course, his own instrument and there is a warmth and a geniality to this work which perhaps reflects his affection for it and the fact that it was written for his son-in-law Emil Telmányi. The two later concertos are rather more austere in character. After Nielsen had composed his *Wind Quintet* (1922) he planned to write concertos for each of the players who had first performed it, but only completed two before he died. The *Flute Concerto* is a predominantly high-spirited work, while the *Clarinet Concerto* sees Nielsen embracing (or parodying) the unsentimental angularity of modernists like Stravinsky.

THE VIOLIN CONCERTO

Nielsen's *Violin Concerto* is a buoyant and expansive work which deserves to be better known. Constructed in two sections, it pitches soloist (and listener) straight into the action with an extended cadenza which leads into a first movement proper of gentle poetry and quixotic charm (marked "Allegro cavalleresco"). It's a movement of great variety, mainly optimistic but with moments of an almost Elgarian wistfulness. This mood is developed in the second section, where a ruminative and subdued theme is exchanged, at first between soloist and woodwind and then with the whole orchestra. The work ends with a rather quirky Rondo which just occasionally hints at the village band music that Nielsen had once played himself.

⊙ Lin; Swedish Radio Symphony Orchestra; Salonen (Sony SK 44 548; with Sibelius, *Violin Concerto*).

Cho-Liang Lin, one of the most underrated of top violinists, gives a brilliant account of this concerto. His articulation and phrasing are immaculate, but what is especially impressive is the way he avoids a vibrato-thick tone in favour of an emphasis on a good clear line. He's helped by the natural-sounding balance which does over-favour the soloist. In short this is no flashy attention-seeking reading but one that does full justice to the music's subtle and numerous charms.

SIBELIUS · NIELSEN
VIOLIN CONCERTOS
CHO-LIANG LIN
ESA-PEKKA SALONEN
SONY CLASSICAL
Philharmonia Orchestra · Swedish Radio Symphony Orchestra

LUIGI NONO

(1924–1990)

Of the three major composers – Boulez, Stockhausen and Nono – who dominated the European avant-garde in the 1950s, Luigi Nono alone believed that the new revolutionary language of total serialism was compatible with revolutionary politics. Even in Nono's earliest works, such as the *Variazioni canoniche* (1950), his Marxist/humanist ideology is allied to the formality of serialist technique, albeit a technique tempered slightly by a characteristically Italian lyricism. There's also a strong dramatic element in much of his music, so it's not surprising that he was the first truly experimental postwar composer to tackle opera, a genre that many of his modernist colleagues affected to despise.

LEBRECHT COLLECTION

Nono lecturing at Darmstadt, 1957

Nono was born in Venice and went on to study law at Padua University as well as taking composition lessons with Malipiero in Venice. An early champion of his work was the conductor Hermann Scherchen, who introduced Nono's work to Darmstadt – at that time the forcing-house of postwar modernism. Nono adopted Schoenberg's serialism (and married his daughter Nuria), but he always regarded technique as the servant of political radicalism, to which ends he also deployed chance methods, *musique concrète* and electronics. His first major composition with an overt political message was the cantata *Il Canto Sospeso* (1956), in which he set the letters of various condemned anti-Fascists. His first opera, *Intolleranza 1960*, is an attack on racism, capitalism and colonialism presented as a montage of fragmentary images and ideas loosely centred on the story of an immigrant worker. Its premiere in Venice caused a riot.

The 1960s saw him turn to electronics, in particular the use of taped sounds, to produce a music that was more brashly political and more rooted in the raw material of working life. At the same time, Nono reacted against what he saw as the middle-class elitism of conventional performing venues, and had his work performed in factories and workers' canteens. Finally, in the mid-1970s, Nono's music underwent an astonishing stylistic change of direction: the bold, strident gestures of his most radical statements were replaced by an introspective language of poetic meditation in which complex literary allusions were frequently woven into the fabric of the music. This late style is exemplified by *Fragmente-Stille* (1980), a string quartet of tremulous delicacy which calls on its players silently to read and project into their playing quotations from the poetry of Holderlin.

IL CANTO SOSPESO

Il Canto Sospeso is one of the masterpieces of postwar serialism. Scored for chorus, soloists and orchestra, it's a work in which the harsh, pointillist style (the music presented in dots rather than as melodic phrases) is perfectly matched to the unbearable poignancy of the words – the final messages of Resistance fighters before their execution. The mysterious title – "The Song Suspended" – makes sense when you hear it: Nono creates an extraordinary feeling of time having stood still, a frozen moment of both terrible pain and enormous dignity. In the chorus sections this is achieved in a remarkably effective way by spreading the text out (dividing words and sometimes syllables) across the different voices so that the words seem to flit, like a troubled spirit, between one vocal register and another. There are also several less dislocated moments, in particular the penultimate vocal section in which the soprano solo carries a sustained line of lyrical intensity over a ghostly chorus of women's voices. This is a disturbing and difficult work, but ultimately an extremely rewarding one.

⊙ Bonney, Otto, Torzewski; Rundfunkchor Berlin; Berlin Philharmonic Orchestra; Abbado (Sony SK 53360; with Mahler's *Kindertotenlieder*).

This live performance, recorded in the Philharmonic Hall in 1992, gets a wonderfully rapt and concentrated performance, particularly from the Rundfunkchor and an ethereal-sounding Barbara Bonney. A minor drawback (which can be programmed out if required) is the recitation by two actors of the original letters at the beginning and middle of the performance – well intentioned, but a distraction. On its own *Il Canto Sospeso* comes across as a work of searing emotional honesty and compassion.

FRAGMENTE-STILLE, AN DIOTIMA

Nono's only work for string quartet, *Fragmente-Stille, An Diotima* (Fragments-Silence, To Diotima), was completed in 1980. It's a strangely conceived and oddly affecting work. Nono places a series of enigmatic quotations from the poetry of Holderlin over the notes as a way of helping the musicians inhabit the music more deeply. The music acts as a meditation on the text, and if a string quartet traditionally represents a varying conversation between four equal voices, then this is more like a collective effort at articulation in the face of an overwhelming silence. There's a real vulnerability in the way the instruments speak: sometimes tentatively, sometimes with a startling rush of energy, but always as if every statement was one that had to be made. *Fragmente-Stille* is a spiritual work, but demands a high level of concentration from the listener – only then will its seemingly arbitrary gestures and nervous fervour begin to make sense.

⊙ Arditti String Quartet (Auvidis Montaigne MO 789005; with *"Hay que caminar", soñando*).

Few musicians have the same level of experience and commitment in playing contemporary music as the Arditti String Quartet. Their playing combines virtuosity and intensity in equal proportions, qualities which bring to their performance of *Fragmente-Stille* a touchingly raw fragility. The disc also contains Nono's last work, *"Hay que caminar", soñando*, another introspective piece, written for two violins who take up different positions within the performing space.

MICHAEL NYMAN

(1944–)

One of the most successful British composers of recent times, Michael Nyman has often courted controversy through the sheer eclecticism of his music. Initially he was part of a group of British experimental musicians who, influenced by Cage, wanted to escape the straitjacket of serialism and embrace a more pluralistic – even anarchic – approach. It has taken him nearly a quarter of a century to move from avant-garde film composer to somewhere near the mainstream, but although he is championed by major companies like Decca and EMI the more entrenched section of the British classical musical establishment still find him beyond the pale.

Nyman attended the Royal Academy of Music in the early 1960s, and his earliest compositions reflect an unlikely enthusiasm for Shostakovich and for the post-serialist works of Harrison Birtwistle. Further studies at King's College London, however, were as a musicologist specializing in seventeenth-century music, and around this time he travelled to Bucharest to study Romanian folk music. By the late 1960s Nyman had become a critic, notably for the *Spectator*, where he supported Stockhausen and the Beatles in equal measure. He also began to develop an enthusiasm for the more melodic strain of pattern music emerging from the USA, and in his book *Experimental Music* (1974) he became the first person to apply the term "Minimalism" (borrowed from the visual arts) to the music of Steve Reich and Philip Glass.

Michael Nyman

Nyman's break as a composer came by way of Harrison Birtwistle: Nyman had already provided the libretto for Birtwistle's opera *Down by the Greenwood Side* (1968), when in 1977 as musical director of the National Theatre, Birtwhistle asked Nyman to provide music for a production of Goldoni's play *Il Campiello*. Nyman put together the loudest band he could think of: banjo and soprano saxophone alongside rebecs, sackbuts, shawms and Nyman's own pumping piano. Nyman liked the sound so much that he kept the band together, first as the Campiello Band, then as the Michael Nyman Band. The outfit needed repertoire, Nyman had to provide it, and so began his full-time career as a composer.

At about this time he also wrote *1-100* for a film by Peter Greenaway, with whom he became a regular collaborator, providing music that the director would edit to suit his own cinematic priorities. So successfully did his music marry up with Greenaway's esoteric and self-referential imagery that it now seems impossible to imagine films like *The Draughtsman's Contract* and *The Cook, The Thief, His Wife and Her Lover* without hearing Nyman's music (one H. Purcell is credited as "music consultant" for the former). In the end, the collaboration was terminated by mutual disagreement. Nyman has continued to write film scores, notably for Jane Campion's *The Piano* (from which he has extrapolated a *Suite* and a *Piano Concerto*) and for Volker Schlöndorff's *The Ogre*.

Success with film has not interrupted Nyman's other musical activities. He is a prolific composer, whether writing for his band or for more conventional concert-hall ensembles and soloists. He has written several operas, the best known of which, *The Man Who Mistook His Wife for a Hat* (1986), was based on an Oliver Sacks neurological case-study. Controversy surfaced again in 1997 when the car manafacturer Mazda commissioned a concerto that would reflect its business philosophy. In the end the *Concerto for Saxophone, Cello and Orchestra* was no corporate puff, but a darkly rhapsodic piece inspired by the image of the permanent "shadow" of a Hiroshima victim.

THE DRAUGHTSMAN'S CONTRACT

When Peter Greenaway called on Nyman in 1981, all he had was an idea for the outline of a plot: a seventeenth-century draughtsman is employed to create twelve drawings of an English country house. Nyman would write the music and Greenaway would shoot the film around it. The resulting drama was as hard, glittering, formally intricate, amoral and heartless as the society it depicted. Nyman's music was among his spikiest and cleverest scores, threaded through with ground basses and chaconnes borrowed from Purcell and with the cyclical harmonies of Minimalism. "Chasing Sheep is Best Left to Shepherds" is a dynamic combination of piercing fanfares, pulsing bass and climbing reed and woodwind lines, while in "The Disposition of the Linen" simple repetitive motifs are layered and interwoven against staccato wind figures to produce dense, shifting designs.

◑ Michael Nyman Band (Virgin Venture CDV2774).

With a band including longtime associates Alexander Balanescu (violin), John Harle (soprano sax) and Malcolm Bennett (bass guitar), Nyman is aided by David Cunningham's accomplished production. Although the music fits the action so perfectly, it survives its separation from the on-screen complexities. Listened to purely as music, this comes across as a well-balanced programme.

THE STRING QUARTETS

In 1989 Nyman provided music for Angnieszka Potrowski's documentary on the aftermath of the Armenian earthquake – a very different kind of film-making from Greenaway's cool cerebralism, and one that resulted in a beautiful choral work, *Out of the Ruins*. Later that year, following the Romanian revolution, Nyman decided to turn this piece into his third string quartet, weaving folk tunes around a framework derived from the choral piece. This new work deploys Nyman's trademark repetitions and strong rhythms, but is unusually elegiac, displaying an emotional dimension that is rarely evident in his music. The *String Quartet No. 2*, written in 1988 for Shobana Jeyasingh's dance piece *Miniatures*, succeeded in being unmistakably Nymanesque while evoking and appropriately complementing the essence of South Indian dance. His first quartet, commissioned by the Arditti Quartet in 1985, creates a compelling fusion out of borrowings from Schoenberg's *String Quartet No. 2* and from the seventeenth-century composer John Bull's variations on the popular song *Walsingham*.

○ String Quartets Nos. 1–3: Balanescu Quartet (Argo 433 093-2).

The textural and rhythmic tightness of Nyman's writing and the intensity of the Balanescu Quartet's playing give this record a compressed timbre which, despite digital technology, make it sound like something by the Busch Quartet. As the Busch Quartet set a standard that has seldom been emulated, that is as good a recommendation as you could wish for.

THE UPSIDE-DOWN VIOLIN

The Upside-Down Violin refreshed Nyman's work with an injection of practices from a non-European musical tradition. It was commissioned for Expo '92 in Seville, and teamed Nyman's band with the distinguished Moroccan ensemble, the Orquestra Andaluzi de Telouan. Nyman described the work as a departure from the "knitting pattern" techniques of the early Minimalist pieces, and he developed its final form after listening to what the Moroccan musicians did with his melodies during rehearsals. He neither required them to adopt his style nor tried to imitate their music. Instead, he wrote melodies which he hoped they would find congenial, then added material for his own band before bringing the two groups together. The first movement ("Slow") unfolds an undulating melody in the strings and reeds against the flowing rhythms of the tambourine and derboliga (drums), with the laud (lute) moving from rhythm to melody at the end. At the end of this middle movement ("Faster") the music was devised by the Orquestra Andaluzi in response to Nyman's Stockhausen-like admonition, "make music suggested by what you have just played". The final movement ("Faster Still") is a glorious, headlong celebration of instrumental virtuosity.

O Michael Nyman Live: The Nyman Band; Orquestra Andaluzi de Telouan (Virgin Venture CDVE924).

Recorded in concert in Albecete and Madrid in 1994, this disc includes a fine performance of *The Upside-Down Violin* alongside *Water Dances, Queen of the Night, Bird List, In Re Don Giovanni* and *The Piano* concert suite. Despite an annoying amount of applause, this is an excellent CD, not only for the immediacy of the performances and the exhilarating interplay between the two sets of musicians on *Violin,* but for the useful survey of more than a decade of Nyman's music.

JOHANNES OCKEGHEM

(c.1420–1497)

When Ockeghem died, Josquin Desprez – who may have studied with him – wrote a lament describing him as "Music's very treasure and true master", a fair reflection of the esteem in which he was held during his lifetime. This esteem virtually vanished with his death and, when musical scholarship finally caught up with him in the nineteenth century, he suffered the indignity of being dismissed as too clever by half, a purveyor of over-elaborate formal tricks. This is not a conclusion you reach once you have heard his music, for in works like the motet *Intemerata Dei Mater* Ockeghem displays a pellucid and ethereal beauty.

Unlike his two great Franco-Flemish contemporaries, Dufay (see p.126) and Josquin (see p.122), very little documentary information about Ockeghem's life has survived. He may have been born at the village of Ockeghem in eastern Flanders and may have studied with Binchois (he wrote a lament on Binchois's death), but there is no real evidence to support either theory. It is known that in the mid-1440s he served at the court of the Duke of Bourbon at Moulins, and that by 1453 he was in the service of the king of France, Charles VII. He remained a favoured member of the royal chapel until his death, serving Charles VII, Louis XI and Charles VIII as their premier chaplain, and was awarded the honorific and highly lucrative position of treasurer at the abbey of St Martin-de-Tours. His contemporaries admired him not just for his music but also for the remarkable sweetness of his singing voice. Several accounts suggest an exceptionally attractive character; one, by Francesco Florio, states – "you could not dislike this man, so pleasing is the beauty of his person, so noteworthy the sobriety of his speech and of his morals and his grace".

CHANSONS

Considering that he lived so long and was so revered, Ockeghem was a curiously unprolific composer. About twenty secular songs have survived, just four motets that can be confidently ascribed to him, and some fifteen Masses, including the earliest surviving polyphonic setting of the Requiem. As a songwriter Ockeghem continued the manner of Machaut (see p.231) and Dufay, employing the traditional forms of ballade, rondeau and virelai (all of which employed textual refrains). Each form was thought appropriate for different moods. Thus we have *Fors Seulement*, a rondeau of unrequited love, the virelai *Tant fuz gentement*, which again deals with love but in a more ambivalent fashion, and the solemn ballade (favoured for serious themes) which Ockeghem employs for his moving lament on the death of Binchois, *Mort tu as navré*.

O Orlando Consort (Archiv 453 419-2; with *Missa De plus en plus*).

The Orlando Consort (a group of four male voices) combine seven of Ockeghem's *chansons* with a Mass based on a song by Binchois. They present the songs unnacompanied and with a more intensely expressive quality than most, employing an almost tremulous quality for *Mort tu as navré*.

SACRED MUSIC

Ockeghem's reputation for complexity derives from his four-part *Missa Prolationum*, in which two separate canons are sung simultaneously. In contrast, the middle-period three-part *Missa Ecce Ancilla Domine*, the only Mass by Ockeghem based on a plainsong cantus firmus, is on the whole a model of simplicity, though its later sections contain some fairly florid and thick writing. On the whole, Ockeghem's later works achieve an amazingly economic expressivity. Masterpieces like the *Missa Fors Seulement* (based on a rondeau of that name) and the motet *Intemerata Dei Mater* have a fluidity and directness which is inspiring.

The *Requiem* is a more problematic work. It may have been composed for the funeral of Charles VII in 1461, but each of its movements are so varied in style that it may have been cobbled together from a number of different works. It incorporates the plainsong chants traditionally used for the Requiem into the texture of the polyphony, usually placing it with some ornamentation in the highest voice.

⊙ Missa Ecce Ancilla Domine; Ave Maria; Intemerata Dei Mater: The Clerks' Group; Wickham (Proudsound PROU CD 133; with motets by Obrecht and Josquin).

The Clerks' Group is a young choir with a fresh and clear sound that effectively brings out the elasticity of Ockeghem's vocal lines, notably in the bright performance of the motet *Intemerata Dei* (Inviolate Mother of God) in which they employ women's voices on the top line. All the other Ockeghem works on the disc are sung by the men alone, but still with a strong sense of the music's rhythmic flow and an emphasis on clarity.

⊙ Requiem; Missa Fors Seulement: The Clerks' Group; Wickham (ASV CD GAU 168; with works by Brumel and de la Rue).

Since the quincentenary of his death, there has been a veritable spate of Ockeghem recordings, with The Clerk's Group making a major contribution. This disc includes the song *Fors Seulement*, the Mass based on it, and two arrangements by slightly later composers. The performance of the Mass is beautifully sung and the most persuasive version now available.

JACQUES OFFENBACH

(1819–1880)

Jacques Offenbach, "the Mozart of the Champs-Élysées", was the composer who made operetta an international art form, and so paved the way for Lehár (see p.217), Sullivan (see p.418) and the musicals of this century. Fusing dialogue and show-stopping set pieces in productions of unrivalled musical verve and satirical bite, he deflated the morals and manners of the Second Empire in its prime – and they paid him for it.

Jacob, as he was named, was born in Cologne in 1819, seventh of ten children. He was taught music in his native city, then in 1833 the family resettled in Paris, allowing him to study at the Conservatoire. Joining the orchestra of the Opéra-Comique, he published waltzes and concert pieces for his own instrument, the cello. Throughout the 1840s he survived as a virtuoso performer, failing to get his stage works performed except when he paid for the privilege, but his luck changed in the following decade. In 1850 he was made conductor of the Théâtre Français, which in 1855 accepted his *Oyayaie, ou La reine des iles*. Its success gave him the cash and the credibility to set up as composer and stager of his own music, despite the disdain of Paris's "respectable" cognoscenti.

GUS ONG

His two-act *Orphée aux enfers* (Orpheus in the Underworld), unleashed the cancan on the world in 1858, and typified Offenbach's irreverence – the opera's starting point is that Orpheus is bored with Eurydice and she is being driven to distraction by his violin playing. His big hit of 1864, *La belle Hélène*, was concerned with the infidelities of Helen of Troy, lampooning Donizetti and Wagner in the process. Two years later came *Barbe-Bleu*, in which Bluebeard searches for his sixth wife, and *La vie parisienne*, a glittering portrait of contemporary Paris society. In 1867 his mordantly satirical *La Grande-Duchesse de Gérolstein* (1867) was described by George Bernard Shaw as "an original and complete work of art which places its composer heavens-high", and was a colossal box-office success. The risqué *La Périchole* (1868), which concerns the adventures in Lima of a pair of down-at-heel street singers, marked the end of Offenbach's heyday, a period during which he had composed some ninety operettas.

He had made his name amid the frivolous decadence of the Second Empire. Public taste changed after the Franco-Prussian War of 1870–71, and Offenbach, once made a Chevalier of the Legion of Honour, was now branded "the great corrupter" of decorous taste. He fled to the admiring audiences of England and the USA, and from 1877 was occupied with the work that would become his masterpiece, *Les contes d'Hoffmann*. He died leaving much of it still in piano-score.

LES CONTES D'HOFFMANN

Produced in 1881, *Les contes d'Hoffmann* (Tales of Hoffmann) is Offenbach's most sober piece, his attempt to show himself worthy of the great German tradition. If it doesn't merit inclusion in the exalted ranks of Gluck and Mozart, it's nonetheless a highly accomplished and melodic fantasy. It takes its text from three tales by the German Romantic writer E.T.A. Hoffmann, presenting them as the disillusioned reminiscences of the writer himself. Hoffmann entertains the customers of a Nuremberg beer cellar with a recital of his three great loves, then is told by his Muse that all three were personifications of his latest love, Stella. Miserably self-absorbed, Hoffmann allows Stella to be drawn away by his rival, whereupon his Muse consoles him with the thought that his writing will be enriched by his woe. The great strength of *Les contes d'Hoffmann* is its vocal writing: some wonderful ensembles punctuate the action, the multi-faceted female lead is a consistent delight, and there is at least one fabulous duet – the Act Four barcarolle, *Belle nuit, o nuit d'amour.*

O Domingo, Sutherland, Tourangeau, Bacquier, Cuénod; L'Orchestre de la Suisse Romande, Radio Suisse Romande Chorus; Bonynge (Decca 417 363-2; 2 CDs).

The sweep and wit of Offenbach's score is supremely caught by Bonynge in a reading which tingles with frenetic urgency while bringing out the lushness of Guiraud's orchestration. Domingo is in his richest voice, summoning the impetuous ardour of Hoffmann, and Sutherland excels in one bravura aria after another.

◑ Jobin, Doria, Bovy, Musy; Paris Opéra-Comique Chorus and Orchestra; Cluytens (EMI CMS5 65260-2; 2 CDs).

This 1948 recording really captures the opera's native style: nothing is exaggerated and no one tries to outdo anyone else. There's a tightness that stems from André Cluytens' quick and spontaneous direction which creates an ideal atmosphere for the near-perfect cast. The mono sound is bright and well focused.

CARL ORFF

(1895–1982)

Carl Orff is generally known as the creator of the hedonistic *Carmina Burana*, one of the most popular of all twentieth-century choral works, but he was both more prolific and more versatile than his reputation suggests. As well as composing nearly twenty music-theatre works, he was a highly influential educationalist, whose teaching methods are still in use all over the world.

Scion of an old Bavarian military family, Orff showed precocious musical gifts and quickly learned to play the piano, cello and organ. He graduated from the Munich Academy of Music in 1914, and the outbreak of World War I did not particularly hinder his advancement: he held the position of Kapellmeister at the Munich Kammerspiele from 1915 to 1917, going on to work at Mannheim's Nationaltheater and the Landstheater in Darmstadt. By this time Orff had several works behind him, the earliest of them bearing the mark of Debussy, whose influence soon gave way to that of Austro-German masters such as Schoenberg and Strauss.

However, he was later to disown all the compositions written before 1924, the year he and Dorothy Günther founded the Güntherschule in Munich. Working from the belief that everyone has inherent musical understanding and that movement and music cannot be separated, this innovative institution took its young adult students through a coordinated course of music, gymnastics and dance. In the early 1930s the Ministry of Culture recommended that a simplified version of the Güntherschule curriculum be adopted in elementary schools, but the project was thwarted by the rise of the Nazis, who were inimical to the radicalism of the school, with its emphasis on improvisation and percussion-based music.

LEBRECHT COLLECTION

Orff at work, 1939

In 1930 Orff found time to take up the post of conductor of the Munich Bach Society, and during his three-year tenure he became steeped in the compositions of the seventeenth and eighteenth centuries, especially Bach and Monteverdi. Augmented by his fascination with classical tragedy, Bavarian peasant life, primitive musical forms and Christian mysticism, this immersion in early music led to the creation of *Carmina Burana*, which was premiered at Frankfurt am Main in 1937.

After World War II Orff continued to refine his ideas about a "total theatre" in which music, speech and movement would combine to produce a spectacle both mentally stimulating and visually exciting. This conception of music as an essentially dramatic art form bears similarities with Wagner and his notion of the *Gesamtkunstwerk*, but Orff's methods were fundamentally simpler than those of his predecessor, employing punchy harmonic effects to create music of immediate sensuality. The compositions with which he consolidated his reputation as a dramatic composer drew on the classic stage repertoire for their raw material: *Antigonae* (1949) and *Oedipus der Tyrann* (1959) were derived from Sophocles, *Ein Sommernachtstraum* (1966) from Shakespeare.

Although Orff continued composing into old age (for example, writing a piece for the opening of the Munich Olympics in 1972), it was as a teacher that he was most influential. His educational activities were given fresh impetus when, in 1948, the German radio authorities commissioned him to adapt the Güntherschule's exercises as a series of broadcasts for children. Running for five years, these programmes were so successful that the transcripts were translated into languages as diverse as English, Welsh, Japanese and Greek, and in 1961 Orff was invited to set up the Orff Institute in Salzburg, in order that his methods could be taught at first hand. In the final analysis, those methods, and the *Carmina Burana*, are his chief legacy.

CARMINA BURANA

Though nowadays performed as a choral concert item, *Carmina Burana* was conceived as a "scenic cantata" for the stage. Orff took the libretto from a sequence of medieval Latin lyrics that mix Christian piety with a celebration of the world's delights, but the latter element sets the dominant tone here, as you can tell from the titles of the work's three parts: *Spring*, *In the Tavern* and *Love*. The musical style of *Carmina Burana* owes a considerable debt to Stravinsky's *Les Noces* and *Oedipus Rex*, a connection most evident in Orff's use of the chorus and his use of rich percussive orchestration. Unlike Stravinsky, however, Orff makes little use of extended melodic writing, thematic development or polyphony – with him the rhythm is paramount. Allied to explicit harmonies, this rhythmic drive gives *Carmina Burana* a sense of wild abandonment.

◑ **Haranyi, Petrak, Presnall; Rutgers University Choir; Philadelphia Orchestra; Ormandy** (Sony SBK 47668).

Of the many excellent versions on CD, the cream of the crop is the 1960 version from Eugene Ormandy and Philadelphia Orchestra, a performance in which it's abundantly clear that everyone had a roisterous good time. The soloists hit a perfect balance between vivid characterization and vocal accuracy, the Rutgers University choristers bring an appealing roughness, swagger and wit to their singing, and Ormandy's orchestra projects an ideal combination of rugged power and warmth.

◑ **Janowitz, Stolze, Fischer-Dieskau; Berlin German Opera Orchestra & Chorus, Schöneberger Sängerknaben; Jochum** (Deutsche Grammophon 447 437-2).

Bearing the imprimatur of Orff himself, this recording has been a bench mark since its release in 1968. The aristocratic Dietrich Fischer-Dieskau hams it up convincingly, Gundula Janowitz's creamy voice is as seductive as ever, and the CD remastering has augmented the dynamism of Jochum's orchestra.

⊙ **Walmsley-Clark, Graham-Hall, Maxwell; Southend Boy's Choir; London Symphony Orchestra & Chorus; Hickox** (Carlton Classics 30369 0030-2).

Richard Hickox's budget-price recording also offers a thrilling ride, with the orchestra and chorus giving it all they have got, while the soloists are full of sexual knowingness. The only real reservation is that there is no line-by-line translation of the Latin, though a synopsis is provided.

JOHANN PACHELBEL

(1653–1706)

Along with Albinoni's *Adagio* (see p.4), Pachelbel's *Canon and Gigue* has, in modern times, become a Baroque popular hit to rival Vivaldi's *Four Seasons*. Ironically, however, its very popularity has tended to obscure rather than enhance Pachelbel's reputation as one of the leading European composers of his time. As an organist (which also meant a composer for the organ), his contemporaries valued him more highly than anyone else, with the possible exception of Dietrich Buxtehude. He was intimate with the Bach family and among his many pupils was Johann Christoph Bach, the elder brother and teacher of Johann Sebastian. His music even reached America via his second son Charles Theodore, an organist who settled there around 1730. Though primarily a composer for the organ, Pachelbel wrote a substantial body of choral music (mostly at Nuremberg) and some chamber music, little of which seems to have survived.

Johann Pachelbel's outstanding ability – both intellectual and musical – was apparent from an early age. A native of Nuremberg, at 17 he was awarded a scholarship to the Gymnasium Poeticum at Regensburg where, outside of school hours, he studied music with Kaspar Prenz. In 1673 Pachelbel, who was a Lutheran, was appointed deputy organist of the Catholic cathedral of St Stephen in Vienna, where he remained for four years, possibly taking lessons with J.K. Kerll, one of the leading composers of the day. A series of prestigious appointments followed, the first at Eisenach where he was briefly court organist to the Duke of Saxe-Eisenach and then, in 1678, at nearby Erfurt as organist of the Predigerkirche. Erfurt is where he established his reputation, started a family and consolidated his friendship with the Bach family. But after twelve years he moved on, initially to Stuttgart, then on to Gotha before returning to his home town in 1695, having been specifically invited by the authorities to fill the position of organist at St Sebald's church, the most important in the town.

THE CANON AND GIGUE

The simple, short but extremely effective *Canon and Gigue in D Major*, for three violins and continuo, is of course the best known of all Pachelbel's creations. The *Canon*, which is often performed on its own, takes the form of 28 variations over an eight-note ostinato pattern in the bass and continuo. The piece has proved so appealing partly because the strictness of the form (ground bass plus canon) gives it a predictable and solid underpinning which the freedom of the variation form works against in a rather playful fashion. Perhaps its sunny and unemotional disposition serves also as a foil to the rather lugubrious solemnity of Albinoni's *Adagio* with which it is inevitably coupled on recordings. The *Canon and Gigue* was only published in 1920 and didn't achieve its modern status until the early 1970s when a number of recordings – in particular one by the Stuttgart Chamber Orchestra – plus films and television commercials began to fix it in the popular consciousness.

O Canon and Gigue; Partie in G; Partie in E Minor; Aria con variazioni in A: Cologne Musica Antiqua; Goebel (Archiv 427 118-2; with Buxtehude, *Three Trio Sonatas*).

Here is a rarity – a Pachelbel chamber disc with more than just the *Canon and Gigue* on it. The performance of that work is excellent, though some may find Goebel's fresh approach a little raw and hard-driven. The other works are even more exciting partly because of their novelty, but also because the lively performances – especially of the delightful *Partie in G* – suggest a chamber composer almost as inventive as his more celebrated contemporary Biber.

◑ Canon and Gigue: I Musici (Philips 442 396-2; with Albinoni's *Adagio* and other pieces).

If you want the *Canon and Gigue* on a menu of Baroque "greatest hits", then this is the CD to buy. I Musici produce a full string sound that is characteristically warm and rich, and manage to generate a real sense of momentum from variation to variation in the Pachelbel.

ORGAN MUSIC

The chorale or metrical hymn formed the heart of the Lutheran liturgy, and an organist had to be able to compose pieces of music – chorale preludes – that took the chorale's melody as a starting point and transformed it into a single variation. How this was achieved varied from organist to organist and gradually became increasingly sophisticated. Several of Pachelbel's chorale preludes involve a fugal treatment of the chorale's first phrase while the ensuing phrases are voiced in extended note values. This rather intellectual approach (in contrast to Buxtehude's more poetic one) is also evident in Pachelbel's keyboard variations, of which the most distinguished examples are the six arias with variations collected under the title *Hexachordum Apollinis* (1699). Here Pachelbel follows a strict numerical system for determining keys, which possibly had some kind of arcane symbolism. All the airs have a stately elegance and easy grace and the variations are brilliantly inventive. The grandiose *No. 6* seems to have had some special significance: named after the church of St Sebald, it breaks the rule of the collection's key system and is the only one in triple time.

O Hexachordum Apollinis: Butt (Harmonia Mundi HMU 907029).

The English organist John Butt plays on a modern organ at Berkeley, California, modelled on the type of German instrument available to Pachelbel in his heyday. The organ may lack that final ounce of character that you associate with an older instrument, but in the choice of registration and generally flexible approach Butt brings out the composer's playfulness and his formality. The airs and variations are framed by two chaconnes, the first of which, in D major, is very clearly from the same hand as the *Canon and Gigue*.

NICOLÒ PAGANINI

(1782–1840)

Nobody had ever played the violin like Nicolò Paganini. The first musician to employ an agent, he was part Jascha Heifetz, part P.J. Barnum. People flocked to hear him play, not just for the promise of astonishing technical virtuosity but also because of the whiff of scandal that surrounded him. One persistent rumour suggested that his extraordinary talent was a result of a pact with the devil. Certainly there was something demonic about him: as a boy he mutilated his left hand in order to increase the spread of his fingers, and most contemporary portraits of the adult Paganini present an almost demented figure: gaunt, long-haired and with an intense, piercing gaze. Like all virtuosos of the time he mostly performed his own compositions, works which were designed to show off the whole range of his skills, from the lyrical to the acrobatic – his party piece was to break three strings on his violin and still keep playing. His music is rarely if ever profound, but its combination of easy-going charm and flagrant exhibitionism exerts a fascination above that of mere curiosity.

Paganini's worldwide reputation as the greatest violinist of the age followed a series of recitals that he gave in Vienna in 1828, and his triumphant progress throughout Europe continued for the next six years. Some musicians, like Spohr, denigrated him for the superficiality and trickery of his playing, but his many admirers included Chopin and Schumann – both of whom wrote musical tributes to him – and above all Liszt, who successfully transformed himself into the Paganini of the piano. By 1834 Paganini was pretty well burnt out, worn down by exhaustion, illness, and persistent press rumours of his miserliness and immorality. He retired to Parma and performances became increasingly infrequent. A venture in 1837 to start a casino in Paris bearing his name lost him large sums of money, and three years later he died in Nice from a disease of the larynx, resolutely refusing to see a priest.

VIOLIN CONCERTO NO. 1

Of Paganini's six violin concertos only the first two are now performed with any regularity. The first, the most uninhibited and most enjoyable, was written in 1817–18, when Paganini's fame was still confined to Italy. Like many virtuoso concertos of the period, including the piano concertos of Hummel (see p.201), the influence of Italian opera, particularly of Rossini, looms large. The work begins with a long and extremely bouncy orchestral introduction (with a lot of cymbal crashing) before the soloist enters with a theme full of leaps and runs which eventually leads into a sweet if rather simpering melody. The short slow movement is darker and more thoughtful, and it's not until the last movement that the technical stops are pulled out, with high chords, brilliant runs and "ricochet" bowing, a Paganini speciality in which several bouncing notes are played on one stroke of the bow.

O Perlman; Royal Philharmonic Orchestra; Foster (EMI CDC 7 47101 2; with Sarasate, *Carmen Fantasy*).

Many violinists are now technically capable of playing Paganini's music, but few bring to it the finesse and the panache of which Perlman is capable. As usual with Perlman, the warmth and sweetness of tone is beguiling, but on top of this is the fact that he enters so fully into the spirit of the music, treating the insinuating first-movement melody completely seriously, but injecting a witty playfulness into the music when it demands it. The concerto is coupled with another show stopper, the *Fantasy on Themes from Bizet's Carmen* by Sarasate, a great violin virtuoso of the second half of the nineteenth century.

24 CAPRICES

Paganini's *24 Caprices*, published in 1820, are the most famous of all his compositions. Like Chopin's *Études* (which they directly inspired), the *Caprices* are technical exercises that transcend the pedagogic limitations of the genre to become virtuosic miniatures – not as wide-ranging in mood as Chopin's pieces but no less brilliant. Paganini dedicated them "Agli Artisti" (To the Artists), but there could have been few artists capable of performing them, apart from himself. Each one explores a different aspect of violin technique: fast passages of double stopping, trills, harmonics, the combination of pizzicato and bowing, are just some of the more spectacular examples. *Caprice No. 24* is the best known, having been used by a wide number of composers (Brahms, Rachmaninov, Lutoławski, Andrew Lloyd-Webber) as the theme for sets of variations.

O Perlman (EMI CDC 7 47171 2).

As with the concertos, many violinists can now play the *Caprices* (selections are often employed as encore pieces), but few can make their pyrotechnical bravura and quirkiness seem really musical. Perlman manages it with ease: whether in the Bach-like opening of *No. 2*, the mysterious trilling of *No. 6*, or the sheer chutzpah of *No. 24*, his response always suggests something more than mere showmanship.

GIOVANNI DA PALESTRINA

(c.1525–1594)

Giovanni Pierluigi da Palestrina wrote music for the Catholic Church during one of the most traumatic periods of its history, a period during which its leaders were looking for ways to reverse the damage caused by the Reformation and the rising popularity of Protestantism. The function of church music was one of the many subjects under discussion. To its critics polyphony had become an overelaborate web of sound that obscured rather than enhanced the meaning of the sacred words. Some, like the Bishop of Modena, even advocated an exclusive diet of plainsong for church services.

Palestrina is often credited as the composer who single-handedly saved polyphony: with the Church on the brink of abolishing it, he was requested to compose a Mass which would show decisively that the polyphonic style was not irreconcilable with clarity of meaning or a truly devotional spirit. The result, the *Missa Papae Marcelli* (Mass of Pope Marcellus), swayed the critics and saved the day, at least till the end of the century. This story forms the basis of Pfitzner's opera *Palestrina* (see p.304), and although it is now regarded as more legend than fact there is an important element of truth in it. Palestrina had indeed begun his career by learning and assimilating the techniques of the great Franco-Flemish composers, such as Josquin Desprez (see p.122), but had gone on to forge his own more simple and direct style, one which combined polyphony with sections of more simple homophony – music in which the individual parts are melodically different, but are rhythmically in step with each other.

Palestrina's name derives from the hill town near Rome where he was born. After serving as a chorister at the church of Santa Maria Maggiore in Rome he returned to Palestrina in 1544 to be the organist at the cathedral of Sant'Agapito. He might well have remained in provincial obscurity had not the Bishop of Palestrina been elected Pope Julius III and in 1551 appointed him *maestro da cappella* at the Cappella Giulia, one of the choirs at St Peter's. Palestrina also sang in the Sistine Chapel choir, and almost certainly composed his *Missa Papae Marcelli* on the accession of Pope Marcellus II, possibly in response to the new pope's directive to his singers that the music for his enthronement "must be sung in a proper manner".

Dismissed in the same year from the Sistine Chapel for being married (it was meant to be a choir of celibates), Palestrina spent five fruitless years at the underfunded church of St John Lateran before being appointed to the rather more affluent Santa Maria Maggiore. By the 1560s his fame was such that several aristocratic patrons sought him out. In 1571 he was re-appointed *maestro* to the Cappella Giulia, a post he kept until his death. The deaths of both his sons in the 1570s and of his wife in 1580 led him to consider joining the priesthood but instead he got married again, to a wealthy widow with a thriving business in the fur trade, thus enabling him to spend his final years in relative financial security.

SACRED MUSIC

Although Palestrina wrote many madrigals (a source of pious embarrassment to him in later years), the main body of his work is made up of sacred music. As well as the 104 Masses, there are at least 250 motets and 7 settings of the Magnificat. Obviously such a long and prolific career is bound to contain a great deal of variety; nevertheless Palestrina's name, especially after his death, came to be synonymous with the classic style of Catholic church music, a style characterized by clarity, sweetness of sound and a serenely optimistic mood. He avoids the startling dissonances then in vogue with avant-garde composers like Gesualdo (see p.139), and makes the music unfold in slow, steady steps – there are rarely any great interval leaps in his work. Comparisons are sometimes made with the Renaissance painter Raphael, another artist striving to create an ideal world of balance and harmony. Some have found this ordered and reverential approach unrewarding and even boring, but at its best Palestrina's music creates a powerful impression of spiritual joy, unencumbered by doubt.

⊙ Missa Papae Marcelli; Missa Brevis: Westminster Cathedral Choir; Hill (Hyperion CDA 66266).

The ethereal purity of the *Missa Papae Marcelli* is well served here by a great choir. The trebles have a bright, strong sound that is especially appropriate for the sense of line and momentum in Palestrina's melodies. Particular moments are given a restrained emphasis: for instance, in the traditional slowing down of the words *et incarnatus est* (and was incarnate) in the Creed, or when the solemn treatment of the Benedictus is followed by the exuberant joyousness of the Hosanna. Such moments are brought into relief by a flexible but subtle attitude to dynamics and tempi. The performance of the *Missa Brevis*, one of Palestrina's best-loved and most often performed works, is equally effective; this is a rather more lively and less rarefied Mass than the other but no less radiant.

⊙ Missa Hodie Christus Natus Est; Stabat Mater: Schola Cantorum of Oxford; Summerly (Naxos 8.550836; with Lassus, *Missa Bell' Amfitrit' altera*).

Written for Christmas Day, the *Missa Hodie Christus Natus Est* (Today Christ is Born) is one of Palestrina's most buoyant and energetic Masses. A Mass for double choir, it is based on the motet of the same name, which is also included on the disc and is given an equally exuberant performance by the Schola Cantorum. Palestrina's *Stabat Mater* is one of his most celebrated and glorious works. Its static and supremely tranquil music makes a startling contrast to the Mass, and the separation of the two choirs at its opening creates a wonderfully mysterious effect. The Naxos disc has a slightly dry and ungiving acoustic, but that is its only failing.

HUBERT PARRY

(1848–1918)

Hubert Parry seems doomed to be known solely as the composer of *Jerusalem*, a piece of music written in the depths of World War I which, like Elgar's *Land of Hope and Glory*, has become a sort of alternative national anthem. However, Vaughan Williams was acutely aware of the magnitude of Parry's contribution: "We pupils of Parry have . . . inherited from him the great English choral tradition which Tallis passed on to Byrd, Byrd to Gibbons, Gibbons to Purcell, Purcell to Battishall and Greene and they in turn through the Wesleys to Parry. He has passed the torch to us, and it is our duty to keep it alight." As composer, scholar and teacher (he became director of the Royal College of Music), Parry exercised a revitalizing influence upon British musical life at a time when it desperately needed it.

At Oxford, he studied with Schumann's friend Sterndale-Bennett, but in 1871 he gave up music to pursue business interests. Within three years, he returned to his musical studies, and after piano lessons with Dannreuther (a friend to both Tchaikovsky and Wagner), he had his first piano concerto performed in 1880. However, it was the premiere, seven years later, of his cantata *Blest Pair of Sirens* that established him as one of England's leading composers. His deep affection for Wagner's music and his immersion in the British sacred traditions nurtured a distinctively Romantic voice that found clearest expression in his work for the voice – and, in particular, choral music, much of it written for English choral music festivals. Hymns and anthems comprise but part of an output that was perhaps too vast for the good of Parry's reputation. At its best, however, Parry's music is a tuneful and enjoyable alliance of Edwardian grandiosity and highly original polyphony.

CHORAL MUSIC

Parry was an avowed agnostic yet he produced some of Britain's finest sacred choral music. Apart from the hymn *Jerusalem* and the coronation anthem *I Was Glad*, his best-known choral work is the cantata *Blest Pair of Sirens* (1887), a somewhat bombastic setting for eight-part chorus and orchestra of Milton's *At a Solemn Music* which nevertheless contains some genuinely poignant melodies. Of much greater interest is the intensely dramatic cantata *The Soul's Ransom (A Psalm for the Poor)*, first performed at the Three Choirs Festival of 1906 and then not heard again until its revival in 1981. The text was created by Parry from carefully chosen biblical passages, ending with one of Parry's own poems and offering divine harmony to suffering humans. Parry also composed many secular choral works, including *The Lotos Eaters* (1892), his ravishingly lyrical setting for soprano, chorus and orchestra of the Choric Song from Tennyson's poem of the same name.

O The Soul's Ransom; The Lotos Eaters: Jones, Wilson Johnson; London Philharmonic Choir and Orchestra; Bamert (Chandos CHAN 8990).

A fascinating recording of a pair of choral works which challenge the stereotyped image of Parry as stuffy late Victorian. Matthias Bamert has also recorded all Parry's symphonies (as well as other works) for Chandos and is deeply committed to upgrading the status of this neglected composer.

◑ Blest Pair of Sirens: London Philharmonic Choir and Orchestra; Boult (EMI 7243 5 6510722; with *Symphony No. 5, Symphonic Variations* & *Elegy for Brahms*).

An appropriately rich, if rather old-fashioned, performance of the cantata, recorded in 1966, fills up what is this disc of mostly orchestral works. Overall this provides an excellent introduction to Parry's music.

ORCHESTRAL MUSIC

When Elgar's *Symphony No. 1* was premiered in 1908, it was hailed as a "first" by an English composer; the distinction really belongs to Parry's *Symphony No. 1* of 1882. An extraordinary achievement, it's a work bursting with youthful enthusiasm, and is full of beguilingly simple tunes that at times recall Mendelssohn. Parry wrote four more symphonies, the best of which is the cyclic *Symphony No. 5*, first performed in 1912, and an especially fine example of an ardent Romanticism very much influenced by Brahms. The subtitles of the four linked movements ("Stress", "Love", "Play" and "Now") suggest a musical exploration of the human condition. As a group, Parry's symphonies may not reach the exultant heights of Elgar's two, and they lack the humanist gravity of Vaughan Williams's symphonies, but there is much to enjoy here. His other orchestral works include the dramatic *Symphonic Variations,* first performed in 1897, and the moving *Elegy for Brahms,* written in the same year and given a posthumous premiere, conducted by Stanford, in 1918.

◑ **Symphony No. 5; Symphonic Variations; Elegy for Brahms: London Philharmonic Orchestra; Boult** (EMI 7243 5 6510722; with *Blest Pair of Sirens etc*).

Recorded in 1978 when Sir Adrian Boult was 89, this was the last recording he ever made – a clear indication of the high regard he had for Parry ("I do hope this will help put him where I feel he ought to be in our history," he wrote). His conviction about the quality of Parry's music shines through in performances that are heartfelt and uplifting.

ARVO PÄRT

(1935–)

If any one composer can be said to be responsible for creating a public receptive to the "sacred minimalism" of John Tavener and Górecki's third symphony, it's the monkish Estonian composer Arvo Pärt. Trained at Tallinn's conservatory while working as technician in the music department of Estonian Radio, Pärt began – like Górecki – as a recalcitrant serialist, using the dissonances of atonal music to kick against the Soviet system. Towards the end of the 1960s, having composed a depressing *Second Symphony* (1966) in a more polystylistic vein, he temporarily abandoned composition and embarked on a study of medieval Franco-Flemish choral music. This resulted in his first religious piece – *Credo*, which was duly banned by the secularist state. The more serene *Third Symphony* (1971), mixing seventeenth-century elements with Orthodox chant, indicated the way Pärt's music was to move forward by looking back.

ECM RECORDS

Arvo Pärt

Years of meditation and religious consultation yielded three stunning instrumental compositions in 1976–77 – *Tabula Rasa*, *Fratres* and *Cantus in Memory of Benjamin Britten*, the first examples of Pärt's unique species of highly charged minimalism. His music continued to annoy the authorities, however, and a year later Pärt and his Jewish wife and two children were granted permission to go to Israel; instead he fled to Vienna, where he lived for eighteen months before settling in Berlin. Since the late 1970s he has unwaveringly followed a spiritual path, producing a succession of small-scale vocal works such as *Summa* (1978) and *De Profundis* (1980) as well as lengthy choral pieces such as the eighty-minute *Passio* (1982), the *Te Deum* of 1986, and most recently the *Kanon Pokajanen* (1998).

In describing his work Pärt frequently invokes the term "tintinnabulation" (the sound or music of bells): "I have discovered that it is enough when a single note is beautifully played. This one note, or a silent beat, or a moment of silence, comforts me. I work with very few elements – with one voice, with two voices. I build with the most primitive materials – with the triad, with one specific tonality. The three notes of a triad are like bells. And that is why I call it tintinnabulation." Pärt's spirituality is rooted in the Eastern Orthodox church, whose musical tradition has remained largely consistent throughout its history, but he also writes music for the Catholic liturgy, though here his inspiration comes from Catholic music of the early Renaissance and before. Much of the timeless quality of his work derives not just from its apparent simplicity, but from the fact that their harmony does not modulate (change key) and so there is none of that sense of movement towards a climax that exists in nearly all post-Renaissance music. That is not to say that the music is entirely static – rather that its energy seems permanently rooted in the present.

INSTRUMENTAL MUSIC

When Manfred Eicher founded the ECM label in 1969 he announced his intention of recording "the most beautiful sound next to silence", and when he first heard Pärt's short but powerful homage to the recently deceased Benjamin Britten he knew that he'd found a composer who conformed to his ideal. Scored for string orchestra and tubular bells, the *Cantus in Memory of Benjamin Britten* (1976) has an amazingly pared-down simplicity: a slow descending minor scale (recalling Britten's ballad *Old Abram Brown is Dead and Gone*) is interspersed with the tolling of bells. As the music gradually slows down, it intensifies in volume before the strings cease, leaving the thin but resonant echo of a lone bell.

Fratres, written the following year, is an equally sombre work in which a chorale-like melody is repeated over a drone of a fifth. The occasional beat of a drum underlines the processional quality of the work and its title surely hints at a monastic inspiration. It was originally written for the Estonian early music ensemble Hortus Musicus, but Pärt has subsequently made a number of arrangements of it. *Tabula Rasa*, also written in the late 1970s, is another work based on a hypnotic series of repetitions. An animated flurry of strings – like a group of people moving towards you – is punctuated by static and subdued moments for violin and prepared piano. The second half is more contemplative: slow-moving and ethereal strings answered by the bell-like middle register of the prepared piano.

Tabula Rasa; Fratres; Cantus: Russell Davies; Lithuanian Chamber Orchestra, Berlin Philharmonic cello section, Stuttgart State Orchestra; Kremer, Jarrett, Schnittke, Sondeckis (ECM New Series 817 764-2).

This ECM disc was largely responsible for Pärt's breakthrough in the West. Manfred Eicher's production creates a wonderfully rich sound that seems to register a profound sense of concentration – above all in the *Cantus*. *Tabula Rasa* is given a fittingly intense performance by Alfred Schnittke (on prepared piano) and the violinist Gidon Kremer – a frequent collaborator with the composer. *Fratres* is performed here in two versions, a dramatic one for violin and piano and a more solemn one for twelve cellists.

⊙ **Fratres; Cantus: Hungarian State Orchestra; Benedek** (Naxos 8.553750).

For those who find the intense ambience of the ECM recording a little too precious, this recording provides a more meaty alternative. Recorded in Budapest, it contains several different versions of *Fratres* and a more elemental but less spiritual version of *Cantus* which is a full two and a half minutes longer than the ECM performance.

CHORAL AND VOCAL MUSIC

As with the orchestral works, variety in Pärt's choral music is achieved largely though a build-up of dynamics and by contrasting sonorities, but if this makes for any sense of progression in the music it is a strictly of a circular nature. In longer works, like the *Stabat Mater* (1985), there is still that sense of a unifying image pervading the whole work. The verses, concerning the emotions of the Virgin Mary as she stands at the foot of the cross, are among the most poignant of all Christian writings. But Pärt does not wallow in the pain (though there are several loud declamatory passages from both voices and strings); rather he imbues the sadness with a ritualistic element by way of the gentle rocking motion that forms the basis of the work.

Pärt's longest work is the *Kanon Pokajanen* (Canon of Repentance, 1998), a setting of an eighth-century text by St Andrew of Crete which is particularly dear to him. It deals with the symbolism of transformation: night into day, prophecy and fulfilment, sin and redemption. Pärt sets it as a series of odes in which subdued supplicatory music is contrasted with more refulgent songs of praise. There is both an element of communal worship and something intensely personal in the mesmerizing repetitions and subtly varied voice combinations. Much of the spare harmony is redolent of Orthodox music but, for all its archaisms, this is clearly a modern work, with spicier harmonies for the higher voices which calls to mind Britten's *Ceremony of Carols*.

⭘ Arbos; Pari Intervallo; An den Wassern zu Babel; De Profundis; Es sang vor langen Jahren; Summa; Stabat Mater: Kremer, Dawson, Bowers-Broadbent; Stuttgart State Orchestra; Hilliard Ensemble; Russell Davies (ECM New Series 831 959-2).

Arbos, the second ECM recording of Pärt's music, was released in 1987. The title piece – a clamorous orchestral work meant to suggest the image of a tree – is the odd one out, since the rest of the disc consists of still and contemplative choral works. These are all exquisitely performed by the Hilliard Ensemble whose then director, Paul Hillier, was and still is very much a Pärt expert. Phrases are beautifully moulded, not least in the *Stabat Mater* and the exquisite *An den Wassern zu Babel* (By the Waters of Babylon). The one irritation is ECM's decision not to supply the texts and their translations with the disc.

⭘ Kanon Pokajanen: Estonian Philharmonic Chamber Choir; Kaljuste (ECM New Series 1654/55 457 834-2; 2 CDs).

Written to commemorate the 750th anniversary of Cologne Cathedral, the *Kanon Pokajanen* was first performed there in March 1998 and recorded shortly afterwards. It's hard to imagine a more radiant and enraptured performance than the one it gets from the Estonian Philharmonic Chamber Choir. They are a much bigger group than the Hilliard Ensemble but there is a similar attention to detail, while the atmospheric acoustic is captured by the ECM engineers with astonishing immediacy.

KRZYSZTOF PENDERECKI

(1933–)

Penderecki is a problematic presence in contemporary music. Until his contemporary Henryk Górecki (see p.163) became an unlikely New Age icon in the 1990s, he was the most-performed living Polish composer, more so than his distinguished older compatriot Witold Lutosławski (see p.228). He studied then taught at the Krakow Conservatory, and burst on the scene in 1960 with *Threnody for the Victims of Hiroshima*, an anguished piece of expressionism tolerated by the Communist authorities perhaps because of its subject matter. Penderecki's use of note-clusters, extreme registers and other effects constituted one form of 1960s "texture music", of which less violent manifestations are found in Lutosławski and Ligeti.

The Polish regime of the 1960s and 1970s was liberal in comparison to others in Eastern Europe, and its relative tolerance of contemporary music was manifested in the Warsaw Autumn Festival, which enabled some of Europe's leading avant-gardists to pursue a thriving career on the "wrong" side of the Iron Curtain. The politically quiescent Penderecki was given a certain latitude and so prospered, while Górecki, less diplomatic in attending to the regime's sensitivities, languished in obscurity.

The *St Luke's Passion* of 1966 marked Penderecki's arrival as a composer of international status. His first opera, *The Devils of Loudon*, followed in 1969. Then suddenly, during the 1970s, he turned conservative. His lurch to neo-Romantic symphonism, apparently without a hint of irony, was much criticized, but Penderecki commented later: "Now is the time of synthesis. What we should do now is to find a sort of universal language, which we don't have in our century." During the 1980s Penderecki developed a blend of Romanticism and modernism. His penchant for the big theme and the grand gesture is epitomized by the *Polish Requiem* (1980–84), which was linked with the political programme of the Solidarity trade union – the Lachrymosa, composed for Solidarity leader Lech Walesa, is dedicated to the victims of the 1970 Gdansk rising.

Like his English contemporary Peter Maxwell Davies, Penderecki now comes across as an advocate of modernity rather than thoroughgoing modernism. Critical characterization of him as a merchant of hollow rhetoric and incoherent expressionism has some force, as has the charge that he is a stylistic chameleon. But, though he is an uneven composer, Penderecki is capable of powerful utterances, and the "neo-Romantic" symphonies and concertos are impressive achievements.

ST LUKE'S PASSION

The *St Luke's Passion*, for three solo voices, narrator, three mixed choirs, boys' choir and orchestra, was Penderecki's most ambitious concert work up to the time of its composition (1962–66). The earliest and most concentrated section was the a cappella *Stabat Mater*, which is often performed as a separate work. Following the extreme expressionism of the early 1960s, the *Passion* marks a synthesis of avant-garde techniques with the great traditions of Western choral music – Bach, Palestrina and Gregorian chant. The *Passion* employs angular dissonances and some unconventional but dramatic effects (such as crowd noises), but communicates a genuinely devotional mood and tells its story with undeniable authority and intensity. It was commissioned to commemorate the 700th anniversary of Münster Cathedral.

○ **Cracow Boy's Choir & Warsaw National Philharmonic Chorus; Polish National Radio Symphony Orchestra; Penderecki** (Argo 430 328-2).

This is Penderecki at his most impressive, both as composer and conductor. The majestic solo voices are well projected and the recording has great presence; but also, perhaps due to a combination of close and distant miking, there's a exceptional amount of reverberation, producing a very immediate effect.

THE SYMPHONIES

Penderecki maintains that he is a symphonist first and foremost. The appearance of his *Symphony No. 1* in 1973 (commissioned somewhat incongruously by Perkins Motors of Peterborough) caused surprise, although the appropriately mechanistic and often expressionist sound-world was recognizably continuous with Penderecki's famous earlier pieces, despite a sonata-form structure. It was the *Symphony No. 2* of 1980 that occasioned real astonishment – "the most Romantic piece I ever wrote," Penderecki says. "Pages from the Symphony Writer's Handbook, chapters on Bruckner and Mahler" was how one ill-tempered critic responded. The work certainly does achieve a kind of Brucknerian dignity and pace by using simple motivic material, including the carol *Silent Night* – hence its subtitle "Christmas Symphony". The *Symphony No. 4* (1989) began as an Adagio movement but, at over thirty minutes in length, the composer decided it should stand as a symphony in its own right. It's an unreservedly Romantic work with distinctly Tristanesque touches to the harmony.

○ **Symphonies Nos. 2 & 4; NDR-Sinfonieorchester; Penderecki** (Wergo 6270-2).

The two symphonies are given expansive, measured interpretations by the composer. The orchestral sound is sumptuous in a state-of-the-art live recording in which audience noise is minimal.

OTHER ORCHESTRAL WORKS

At a time when the avant-garde was a ghetto within the wider ghetto of modern music, Penderecki popularized the gestures of

Stockhausen and Xenakis by making them even more brutally expressive. Works such as the *Threnody for the Victims of Hiroshima*, in which tone-clusters eradicate the boundary between noise and pitch, are the last word in textural music. With its sickening glissandos, piercing high-note passages and sepulchral pizzicato and knocking effects, it's a shattering musical evocation of the effects of nuclear destruction. *Anaklasis* (1960) is no less visceral in its impact: this time a dialogue is set up between 42 strings and an armoury of assorted percussion. These works of the 1960s seem to hang together by emotional effect alone, and it's not clear how far Penderecki could have gone in this direction. It has become fashionable to deride the result as dated 1960s avant-gardism, but this is music that still creates a powerful impression, and the shorter works from the 1980s and 1990s seem paler efforts in comparison.

◑ **Anaklasis; Threnody for the Victims of Hiroshima; Canticum Canticorum Salomonis; Fonogrammi; De natura sonoris I & II; Capriccio; Dream of Jacob; Polish Radio National Symphony Orchestra; Penderecki** (EMI CDM5 65077).

There are some searing performances in this admirable collection of Penderecki's orchestral pieces of the 1960s and early 1970s, though the rather boxy sound is disappointing. The *Threnody* for 52 string instruments, lasting only ten minutes, is the high point. The rest is unremittingly dense and anguished, and is best listened to in small doses.

CHAMBER MUSIC

Penderecki's two string quartets, from 1960 and 1968, find him at his most expressionistic and direct. Both works are concentrated (under ten minutes each) and replete with the composer's trademark avant-gardisms: quarter-tone vibrato, the bow drawn across the tailpiece, knocking on the body of the instruments, guitar-like strummings – these all make a dramatic and immediate impact. The neo-Romantic and neo-Bartókian chamber pieces Penderecki wrote in the 1980s and 1990s are less effective, though pleasing enough.

⊙ String Quartets Nos. 1 & 2; Prelude for clarinet solo; String Trio; Quartet for Clarinet and String Trio: Tale Quartet; Fröst (BIS CD-652).

Fine performances by a young Scandinavian quartet. There is both fervour and sensitivity in their accounts of the two string quartets, and the later works are given persuasive interpretation.

GIOVANNI PERGOLESI

(1710–1736)

Though only a moderately successful composer during his short life, Pergolesi managed to write two works that not only brought him posthumous fame but significantly influenced the direction of vocal music in the eighteenth century.

The first, *La Serva Padrona* (The Maid as Mistress), was an early example of comic opera, or opera buffa, in which the characters were drawn from everyday life. Pergolesi worked mainly in Naples, where an operatic style had developed which emphasized the beauty and virtuosity of the solo voice, often at the expense of dramatic unity. *La Serva Padrona*, a short intermezzo performed between the acts of Pergolesi's opera seria *Le prigionier superbo*, introduced a more naturalistic tone, but its notoriety came about after the composer's death, when a performance in Paris in 1752 instigated a furious theoretical debate about the respective merits of Pergolesi's opera buffa as opposed to the more formal and serious French opera.

The second, a setting of the Stabat Mater for two solo voices and strings, pioneered a style of church music which combined emotional directness with an elegant and graceful expressiveness. Here, as in his operatic work, Pergolesi epitomized a progressive tendency which was championed by the philosopher Jean-Jacques Rousseau, who described the opening of the *Stabat Mater* as "the most perfect and most touching to have come from the pen of any musician".

LA SERVA PADRONA

La Serva Padrona should be approached with a certain amount of caution. Several of the arias are charming and inventive (and sound surprisingly Mozartian) but over a third of the opera takes the form of long recitatives which, though tolerable with accompanying stage business, can be wearisome on record. The plot tells of how a tyrannical maid-servant (Serpina) tricks her elderly master (Umberto) into marrying her by disguising a fellow servant (Vespone) as a prospective suitor. Much of the comedy derives from the fact that the role of Vespone is mute, thus providing scope for several comic misunderstandings. The characterization is simple but vivid and the players' primary emotions are neatly established through direct and tuneful writing. Serpina's "Stizzoso, mio Stizzoso" establishes her as a demanding shrew, and neatly sets the scene for her Part II aria "A Serpina penserete" in which she proves, through music of almost introverted beauty, that she is not so bad after all. The opera ends with a wonderful ensemble in which Umberto finally confesses his love and Serpina celebrates her victory.

⊙ Poulenard, Cantor; Ensemble Baroque de Nice; Bezzina (Pierre Verany PV 795111).

This is not a perfect recording but it is certainly a very engaging one. The recitatives are delivered with a panache that prevents them from clogging up the momentum, and throughout the well-cast soloists work effectively and dramatically together. Bezzina's busy but unfussy direction keeps the whole thing scampering along with considerable élan.

STABAT MATER

The *Stabat Mater* is Pergolesi's masterpiece: the great medieval text, detailing the Virgin's suffering at the foot of the Cross, drew an enormously intense response from him, in which the expressive use of pauses and of dissonances is much in evidence. If it sounds rather operatic for a religious work, it is largely because Pergolesi dispenses with a chorus in order to present the text through the immediacy of the solo voice – each of the twelve sections is allocated either to the soprano or the alto or to both in duet. The music is astonishingly varied given that the prevailing mood is one of pain and supplication, though there are a couple of sections of relative liveliness. According to legend it was the last work Pergolesi wrote before his death, probably from consumption, at the Franciscan monastery in Pozzuoli near Naples. What is certainly true is that it became one of the most popular and enduring works of the entire eighteenth century.

⊙ Stabat Mater; Salve Regina in F Minor; Sinfonia a tre: Gens, Lesne; Il Seminario Musicale (Virgin VC5 45291-2).

Earlier recordings of the *Stabat Mater* tended to sentimentalize the work by using a lush orchestral sound and two female operatic voices. More recently, in the name of greater authenticity, there has been a tendency to pare down the accompaniment and use a male alto with a female soprano. With Véronique Gens and Gérard Lesne (who also directs) you get a near-perfect balance of well-rounded voices that emphasize the almost sensual quality of the music. In addition to the *Stabat Mater*, Lesne gives a beautifully judged account of the *Salve Regina in F Minor*.

PÉROTIN

(c.1170–c.1236)

The earliest composers of polyphonic music whose names have come down to us are Léonin (c.1159–1201) and Pérotin, both of whom were part of an extraordinary flowering of culture that took place in Paris in the late twelfth century. Almost nothing is known of their lives. They probably had some connection with the new cathedral of Notre Dame, but the theory that Pérotin was taught by Léonin and succeeded him as choirmaster of Notre Dame is now generally discredited. Léonin's music is relatively simple two-part writing, whereas Pérotin wrote in three and sometimes four parts – strange but utterly compulsive music, in which harmonic plainness is carried joyously along by rhythmic suppleness.

Up to the time of Pérotin, the dominant musical form of the Christian church had been monophonic chanting – that is the singing of a single line of music, either by one voice or by several voices. This became known as plainsong (or plainchant), and several different versions of it existed, the best known of which, Gregorian chant, seems to have developed in France between the eighth and tenth centuries. Sometime in the ninth century the addition of another voice with its own independent line of music marks the beginnings of polyphony. At first it was very simple: the added line moved in parallel to the plainsong melody, usually beneath it, at a fixed interval. The plainsong melody was known as the cantus firmus (fixed song), the voice that sang it was the vox principalis, and the added voice the vox organalis. This simple form of polyphony was called organum and it was employed as an occasional, ornate addition to liturgical plainsong rather than as a replacement for it.

This parallel duplication of the melody had obvious musical limitations, and freer developments soon began to appear, such as the use of more than two voices. One especially important progression was that vox organalis, instead of moving note-on-note with the cantus firmus, was placed on top of the cantus firmus and was made rhythmically independent and melodically dominant, employing as many as twenty notes to one in the lower part. The voice singing the cantus firmus became known as the tenor (from the Latin "to hold") since the plainsong was drawn out to accommodate the ornate phrases above it. This style was called florid or melismatic organum and it existed alongside the older note-on-note style, which became known as discant.

In Pérotin's hands organum became increasingly lively and exciting – two of his most moving contributions to the genre, the extraordinary *Viderunt omnes* and *Sederunt principes*, are the earliest examples of Western music written in four parts. Both contain startlingly dance-like rhythms in the higher voices, which lilt and weave their way around the drawn-out line of the cantus firmus, echoing each other's material in a way that dissolves the dominant melodic line to create, in Paul Hillier's words, "a kaleidoscope of constantly shifting textures".

⊙ Pérotin: The Hilliard Ensemble; Hillier (ECM 837 751-2).

This CD of music attributed to Pérotin and his contemporaries is no archeological curiosity – on the contrary, the Hilliard Ensemble's performances are direct and deeply moving, their wonderfully flexible approach creating an image of the Gothic as something delicate and light-filled. Of the nine pieces on this disc, four (all by Pérotin) are organum while the other five (two by Pérotin) are conductus, a simple form of music which was employed for ceremonial or processional occasions within the church. The one minor irritation is that the sleevenotes include the Latin texts but no translation of them.

HANS PFITZNER

(1869–1949)

The Third Reich effectively wrecked the reputation of Hans Pfitzner. Though he may have liked to regard himself as apolitical, he held strongly expressed anti-Semitic nationalist views and complied with what the Reich demanded of him, allowing them to use his name as and when they chose. Pfitzner's self-consciously Wagnerian music was lauded for upholding the best in the German tradition, and he was used by the Nazis as a stick with which to beat the "degenerate" Richard Strauss when the latter fell from favour. Choral works such as *Von deutscher Seele* and *Das dunkle Reich* were used as musical propaganda, paraded as examples of all that was best about the Germanic (ie the Aryan) tradition. It is scarcely surprising that after the war his music was seen as nothing more than a reflection of Germanic megalomania, despite support from such figures as the great (Jewish) conductor Bruno Walter.

It's ironic that such a proudly German composer was born in Moscow, where his father was working as a violinist. Moving to Frankfurt as a child, he studied at the conservatory until 1890, then he began teaching in Koblenz from 1892. Teaching and conducting dominated the next twenty years of his life, although Mahler conducted two of his operas in Vienna, and his songs, chamber music and early symphonies all found champions. His status as a composer was sealed in 1917 with the premiere of his music-drama *Palestrina* (conducted by Walter), a composition that defined his Romantic-conservative stance against the radicalism of Schoenberg and Busoni, whom he later attacked in a reactionary essay "The New Aesthetic of Musical Impotence". His career prospered under the Nazis but ended pathetically. At the end of the war his house in Munich was destroyed by Allied bombing, and in 1946 the president of the Vienna Philharmonic Orchestra found him living in a home for the aged in Salzburg. Supported by the orchestra, he lived out the rest of his days in Vienna.

PALESTRINA

Composed between 1912 and 1915, while Pfitzner was director of the Strasbourg Opera, *Palestrina* was his most successful and finest work. Set in 1563, it concerns the legendary incident in the life of the eponymous composer, when, at the instigation of Cardinal Borromeo, he saved the polyphonic tradition by composing the brilliant *Missa Papae Marcelli*, a piece that demonstrated to the Council of Trent that the Catholic Church could repel the Protestant onslaught through beautiful polyphonic music (see p.296 for more). It's a long, doggedly serious work, but Pfitzner sustains concentration throughout the three acts by a skilled deployment of devices learned from Wagner. The orchestration of *Palestrina* is decidedly Wagnerian, as are Pfitzner's extended mystical moods, dissonant contrapuntal textures and long-breathed melodic lines – and as a true Wagnerian he also wrote his own libretto, after spending two years researching the history of the Council of Trent. Musical motifs from the *Missa Papae Marcelli* are incorporated into the score, underlining the point that this is, in essence, Pfitzner's aesthetic manifesto as defender of the faith against the philistines and modernists.

◑ **Palestrina – complete: Ridderbusch, Wiekl, Steinbach, Fischer-Dieskau, Prey, Gedda, Donath, Fassbaender; Tolz Boys Choir, Bavarian Radio Chorus; Bavarian Radio Orchestra; Kubelik** (Deutsche Grammophon 427 417-2GC3; 3 CDs).

Kubelik's monumental and widely acclaimed account has an incredible cast, including Fischer-Dieskau as Borromeo, the superb Karl Ridderbusch as Pope Pius IV, and Nicolai Gedda as Palestrina – a wonderful performance, creating a sense of fragility well suited to this semi-autobiographical role. As with most of Kubelik's work, he maintains brisk tempi throughout, and he achieves a clear orchestral sonority that serves Pfitzner's orchestrations well.

⊙ **Preludes to Acts 1–3: Orchester der Deutschen Oper Berlin; Thielemann** (Deutsche Grammophon 449 571-2; with other preludes and overtures by Pfitzner and Strauss).

This is very much a labour of love: Christian Thielemann chose to make his recording debut with Pfitzner because it is music he greatly admires, and that admiration is strongly communicated. From the opening bars of the rapt and ethereal first prelude from *Palestrina* it becomes clear that this is music of the highest quality. For those daunted at the prospect of the entire opera, this is the perfect way of testing the water.

FRANCIS POULENC

(1899–1963)

For years Francis Poulenc was pigeonholed as the playboy of French music, and superficially there's some justice to the charge. He was born into money and had a privileged social position. Through his piano teacher Ricardo Viñes he gained access to the fashionable Parisian artistic scene, and became a key member of a group of iconoclastic young composers called Les Six, who, spearheaded by the writer Jean Cocteau, rejected not only the inflated Romanticism of Wagner but also what they regarded as the imprecision of Debussy and Ravel. Of all the group, Poulenc seemed the most facile and clownish, the man with the permanent grin on his face. But he was also a serious craftsman, who had made a careful study of counterpoint and was the only one of Les Six to develop in new directions. By no stretch of the imagination could Poulenc be described as a modernist, yet he always had a keen interest in the international scene, and in 1921 travelled to Vienna with Milhaud (another member of Les Six) in order to meet Schoenberg and his pupils.

Like many young French composers of the interwar years, he was immensely taken by the wit of Erik Satie (see p.348) and by the taut discipline of Stravinsky's early neo-classical works. His masterstroke was to take the irony, implicit in both men's work, and turn it into something beguilingly French. In this project, the influence of his friend Jean Cocteau was never far away, and the rather brittle, jewel-like works of these years show Poulenc taking to heart Cocteau's principle that artists must aim for a coolly elegant modernity, braced with a classical sense of proportion. There is artifice aplenty in the *Aubade* for small orchestra, the ballet *Les Biches* (written for Diaghilev's Ballet Russe), but there was also much ingenuity in the way he achieved fresh sounds with conventional materials.

But there was also a dark side to Poulenc's personality, and in the 1930s a series of disastrous love affairs (mostly with younger men) and the death of a friend, the composer-critic Pierre Octave-Ferroud, precipitated a return to the Catholic Church and a spate of powerful religious works which begin with the *Litanies à la vièrge noire* (1936). Poulenc also began a long association with the baritone Pierre Bernac, who became the greatest interpreter of his songs and introduced him to the surrealist poet Paul Éluard, many of whose poems he later set. Éluard, whose surrealism was of a decidedly emotional and sensual strain, encouraged Poulenc to modify his rather detached Stravinskian style and embrace the spicier sound-world of Chabrier and Ravel.

Arguably Poulenc's greatest strength was as a lyrical melodist and a writer for the voice: few could match the exquisite delicacy of his word-setting, which was capable of revealing every nuance of his native tongue. But, despite a childhood wish to be an opera singer, he turned to opera relatively late in his career. *Les mamelles de Tirésias*(1944), a setting of Apollinaire's surrealist comedy, epitomized Poulenc at his most ebullient and light-hearted. It was followed, nine years later, by a work utterly different in tone and mood. *Les dialogues des Carmélites*, based on the true story of a group of persecuted nuns during the French Revolution, confirmed Poulenc's transformation from young turk to arch conservative. His final opera, *La voix humaine*, chronicles the psychological disintegration of a desperate woman as she converses on the telephone with her apparently indifferent lover. It is Poulenc's rawest and most extreme work, in which he revealed the vulnerability and pain of his own emotional life.

The best summary of Poulenc's place in the history of modern music is contained in a letter he wrote in 1942: "I know perfectly well that I'm not one of those composers who have made harmonic innovations like Igor [Stravinsky], Ravel or Debussy, but I think there's room for new music which doesn't mind using other people's chords. Wasn't that the case with Mozart-Schubert?" For all his chic use of spicy dissonances and his flirtation with advanced techniques such as polytonality, Poulenc was quite happy to be seen as part of a

French tradition stretching back through Chabrier deep into the nineteenth century and beyond.

THE CONCERTOS

Poulenc was a very gifted pianist and all of the four concertos that he composed were for keyboard instruments, beginning with the *Harpsichord Concerto*, known as the *Concert champêtre*, which he wrote for Wanda Landowska in 1928. Though inspired by the example of Stravinsky's *Concerto for Piano and Wind Instruments*, Poulenc's own brand of neo-classicism is, by contrast, a rather superficial affair more concerned with eighteenth-century flavouring than with structural cohesion. Rather more successful is the delightful *Concerto for Two Pianos* (1932), in which Poulenc's uanshamed eclecticism is given full rein. Plenty of affectionate homage is paid to his classical forebears (including a substantial chunk of Mozart in the slow movement) but this is constantly undermined by a wonderful mixture of madcap buffoonery, mock heroics, and Ravelian exoticism – all three occurring in the work's scintillating first movement. Six years later, after his return to the church, Poulenc wrote an organ concerto which he described as existing "on the fringe of my religious music". It's a grandiose and serious work that ranges far and wide in its exploitation of the organ's endlessly rich sonorities. The spirit of Bach presides (specifically his *G Minor Fantasia*) but, once again, there is a profusion of near-incongruous mood swings – meditative, melodramatic and even playful – in its single-movement span. Poulenc's last concerto, for solo piano, was written in 1949 for the Boston Symphony Orchestra. It's not as focused as the *Concerto for Two Pianos*, and the familiar element of pastiche (a Mahlerian slow movement) had rather lost its bite.

⊙ Piano Concerto; Concerto for Two Pianos; Organ Concerto: Rogé, Deferne, Hurford; Philharmonia Orchestra; Dutoit (Decca 436 546-2).

Pascal Rogé is very much at home with this repertoire and his witty playing makes a convincing case for the uneven *Piano Concerto*. He is partnered by Sylviane Deferne in a boisterous and hugely enjoyable performance of the double concerto, in which the Philharmonia are the lightest of accompanists. All the stops are pulled out, literally, for the *Organ Concerto*. Recorded at St Albans Abbey, where he is resident organist, Peter Hurford really does justice to the kaleidoscopic nature of this work.

CHORAL WORKS

Poulenc had no doubts as to which of his works gave him most satisfaction: "I think I put the best and most authentic side of myself into my choral music." Certainly it reveals a more emotional side to his personality, although he was not one to differentiate between what was musically appropriate for sacred texts and what was fitting for more earthly subjects. Indeed, when the words required it, Poulenc's religious choral music could be as warm and humane as his secular songs. That said, he often chose to set quite sombre texts: in the *Litanies à la vièrge noire* (Litanies of the Black Madonna), for female chorus and organ, monophony, simple harmony and startling dissonance all reinforce the text's supplicatory intensity. Similarly, in the *Stabat Mater* (1950), for soprano, divided chorus and orchestra, the prevailing darkness of mood is achieved through a kind of Baroque solemnity in which there is a lot of unison singing and repetition. There are even echoes of Mozart's *Requiem* in the animated *Cujus animam gementem*, but the eclecticism of the *Stabat Mater* doesn't leap out at you as in so much of Poulenc's work, because the overall emotion seems so heartfelt. It's certainly the masterpiece among his sacred works, though the more extrovert *Gloria* (1959), written for similar forces, is often rated more highly. From its magnificently ceremonial opening, this is a work that exudes confidence and energy and some momentary glimpses back to the Poulenc of the 1920s. Between its two most tender moments – both for soprano solo – are sandwiched some mischievously insouciant orchestral writing which scandalized some members of the original audience.

⊙ Gloria; Stabat Mater: Watson; BBC Singers & Philharmonic; Tortelier (Chandos CHAN 9341).

Radiant and refined singing plus sensitive orchestral playing make this an obvious first choice. Jan Pascal Tortelier, a specialist in French music, treats singers and players as one force and maximizes the dramatic impact. Janice Watson makes the most of her passionate and intense solos.

SOLO PIANO MUSIC

At the age of 17 Poulenc began studying with the brilliant Spanish pianist Ricardo Viñes. As a performer Viñes specialized in contemporary music (he premiered works by Debussy and Ravel) so that, according to Poulenc, "... if the classics were at the basis of Viñes' teaching, it didn't mean Schumann excluded Satie from my lessons". Satie was the major influence on Poulenc's piano music – both his irreverent humour (evident in the quirky titles of his pieces) and his textural clarity made a lasting impact. Odd, then, that Poulenc's first published piece, the mysterious *Pastorale*, shows the equal influence of Satie and Ravel, the latter a composer whose music Poulenc claimed to dislike. A greater impact was made with the *Trois mouvements perpétuels* (1918), three short pieces whose Stravinskian rhythmic drive is modified by an insinuating charm. Charm is a quality that dominates much of Poulenc's piano music, especially that written during the 1930s. Both *Les Soirées de Nazelles* and *Improvisations* are sets of poetic mood pieces that evoke a milieu of easy-going friendships and relaxed evenings in the country. These unassuming, light-hearted vignettes are occasionally, as in the last two *Improvisations*, coloured by feelings of melancholy and regret.

○ Piano Works: Rogé (Decca 417 438-2).

Such hedonistic music needs delicacy and sensitivity in equal measure, and it certainly gets them from Pascal Rogé. His crystalline touch and subtle pedalling reveal aspects of these pieces that other pianists only hint at, revealing them as multifaceted jewels that may be undemanding but are never bland.

SERGEY PROKOFIEV

(1891–1953)

Though he was regarded as impossibly avant-garde in his youth, Sergey Prokofiev in fact belongs squarely to the same great tradition of Russian music as Tchaikovsky and Mussorgsky, a tradition resonant with a sense of the country's history. Writing in an immediately recognizable style which reconciles progressive technique with melodic traditionalism, he produced some of the most enjoyable of all twentieth-century compositions, and contributed to almost every musical genre. It's an achievement all the more remarkable in view of the fact that much of it was achieved in the face of the dogmatic repression of Stalinism, and in the midst of Russia's suffering in World War II.

Born in the Ukraine, he soon displayed prodigious talent as a composer and as a pianist, as well as a somewhat overdeveloped sense of his own importance. At the St Petersburg academy he proved rebellious, disruptive and totally unsuited to the disciplines of academic study, earning the hostility of, among many others, Glazunov (see p.159). Stifled by conservative Russia, he packed his bags after graduation in 1914, and left for a spell in London, where he met Diaghilev and Stravinsky.

Stravinsky's music had a deep and lasting impact on the young man – although it was one that Prokofiev, curiously, always failed to acknowledge – and his relationship with Diaghilev was equally productive. The great impresario of the Ballet Russe set Prokofiev to work on three different ballets and also encouraged him to remain away from Russia. This resolve, though weakened by intermittent concert tours and visits to his homeland, held out until 1926, when he began a correspondence with the concert authorities in the USSR. Cautiously, he accepted their invitation to make an extensive tour of western Russia, his first visit for nine years. To his surprise, Prokofiev was treated as a celebrity and a hero of Russian music, and the great success of the series of 21 concerts, coupled with his joy in renewing old friendships, must have made the prospect of a permanent return seem very attractive. He managed to avoid the inevitable for another seven years until 1933, when Prokofiev and his wife left Paris and went home to Russia for good. It was the worst decision of his life.

He could have stayed in the West – as had Rachmaninov and Stravinsky – but he saw himself as an apolitical artist and disregarded the political implications of his return, believing that the Soviet authorities would grant him immunity as a famous composer. Prokofiev genuinely felt that the pressures being brought to bear on other composers, such as Shostakovich, would somehow not apply

LEBRECHT COLLECTION

Prokofiev in the 1930s

to him. His timing could not have been worse. By 1936 the musical establishment was run by politicians and, when he arrived in Moscow, Prokofiev effectively threw himself upon the mercy of a system that now expected composers – without exception – to write music for "the people", extolling the brave new world of Soviet socialism. The ensuing years were hard. His relationship with the authorities, though stable to begin with, rapidly disintegrated and he suffered frequent humiliation, often having to thank the authorities for belittling him and his music in the press. When war broke out, ill-health and deep-seated resentment towards his country prevented him from taking any involvement and in 1941 his relationship with a 25-year-old student, Mira Mendelson, ended his marriage.

For all that he suffered, Prokofiev wrote some superb music during the war years, including the opera *War and Peace*, the violin sonatas, the film score to *Ivan the Terrible* and the ballet *Cinderella*. Through works such as these he attained a dominant position within the Russian musical world, and for the first few years after the war it seemed that he was above persecution. In 1948, however, it became clear that Prokofiev's position was not as secure as he had imagined. The Central Committee of the Communist Party held a meeting at which Prokofiev, Shostakovich and many others were accused of "formalism", a catch-all term applied to any music that had no immediately utilitarian function. The errant composers were charged with "anti-democratic tendencies that are alien to the Soviet people and its artistic tastes" and condemned for writing music "strongly reminiscent of the spirit of contemporary modernistic bourgeois music of Europe and America". Unequivocal apologies were wrung out of all the "defendants".

After this idiotic and brutal farce, all sense of purpose was knocked from Russia's composers and Prokofiev was reduced to turning out pallid and predictable scores, almost entirely derived from Russian folk music. The opera *War and Peace* is the only work that stands out from the morass – the rest is the musical equivalent of the paintings of agricultural labour that the country's artists were obliged to churn out. Prokofiev died on March 3, 1953 – only a few hours before Stalin. The irony would have appealed to him.

THE LOVE FOR THREE ORANGES

Prokofiev's relationship with the theatre was lifelong but never particularly happy. Before the end of his student days he had already written over half a dozen complete operas. His first work after graduation remained incomplete, while his second, based upon Dostoevsky's *The Gambler*, was beset by so many problems – orchestra and singers who hated the violent music, a director who resigned – that it wasn't performed until 1929, and even then the music was substantially revised from the original of 1917.

The Love for Three Oranges, Prokofiev's first successful opera, was written between 1919 and 1921 while he was living in America. Reworking the *commedia dell'arte* traditions of Gozzi's eighteenth-century play *Fiaba dell'amore delle tre melarancie*, *Three Oranges* is whimsical, melancholy and very strange, as you can tell from a glance at the cast list, which features ten "ridiculous people", a chorus of "little devils", a "Gigantic Cook" and a smattering of princesses. Prokofiev was deeply impressed by Meyerhold's theories on drama, which included "the diminution of the role of the actor and a challenge to conventional audience relationships", and in Gozzi's lunatic plot he found the perfect vehicle for such a challenge. Displaying Prokofiev's talent for musical grotesquerie, *Three Oranges* places mock neo-classicism against barbarically rhythmic modernism, and interweaves bizarre choruses with tortuous solo parts. The orchestration is sparse yet colourful, but the only real tunes materialize in the well-known March and Scherzo.

⊙ Love for Three Oranges – complete: Bacquier, Viala, Perraguin, Le Texier, Gautier, Henry, Reinhart; Lyon Opera Chorus & Orchestra; Nagano (Virgin VCD7 59566-2; 2 CDs).

The Virgin recording won the 1989 *Gramophone* award for Best Opera and it is easy to see why. Nagano's handling of the dramatically anti-Romantic score is intelligent and exciting (if sometimes overaggressive), and the cast revel in the surreal quality of the characterization.

⊙ Love for Three Oranges – excerpts: Scottish National Orchestra; Järvi (Chandos CHAN 8729; with *Chout* and *Le Pas d'acier*).

It has to be said that *The Love for Three Oranges* relies so much on the visual element that much of its dramatic motion is lost on disc. With that in mind, you might prefer to go for the March and Scherzo, as arranged by Prokofiev for concert performance – it's entertainingly thrashed out by Järvi on this CD, which also includes two ballet suites.

THE SYMPHONIES

Prokofiev's seven symphonies span the years 1917 to 1952. They are, in general, tremendously exciting works, but all except two of them are marked by sharply antagonistic harmonies, rhythmic percussiveness and a paucity of melodies, so they may take some getting used to.

Prokofiev's most accessible orchestral work is the twenty-minute *Symphony No. 1*, a tuneful homage to Haydn and Mozart that is sometimes linked to the neo-classicism of Stravinsky, although in fact Prokofiev got there first. The young Prokofiev revelled in his status as *enfant terrible:* ostracized by Glazunov, and hammering out his avant-garde piano pieces within months of Rimsky-Korsakov's death. It was with ironic delight that he announced that his first major work after graduation from the St Petersburg Conservatoire was to be "a symphony in the style of Haydn. . . if Haydn were writing today, I thought, he would keep to his way of writing, whilst at the same time incorporating newer ideas. I wanted to compose just such a symphony. I gave it the name *Symphonie Classique* – firstly because it was so simple; also in the hope of annoying the philistines, and in the secret desire to win in the end, if the symphony should prove itself to be a genuine 'Classic.'" The symphony was sketched in 1916, and its 1918 world premiere in St Petersburg brought overwhelming applause. Seldom has twentieth-century music sounded so transparent or so free from care: and it was welcomed keenly into the mainstream Western repertoire, thanks above all to the advocacy of his friend, the conductor Serge Koussevitsky.

After the *Symphony No. 1*, the loftily heroic *Symphony No. 5* is the most popular. Begun in 1944, as the imminent ending of hostilities was becoming self-evident, it was conceived by Prokofiev "as a symphony of the greatness of the human spirit, a song of praise of free and happy mankind". His first symphony for sixteen years, it was premiered in Moscow on January 13, 1945, and was immediately acclaimed at home and abroad, having been introduced to the West by Koussevitzky.

Yet, while the *Symphony No. 5* is Prokofiev's most popular symphony, its successor is arguably his greatest. Though written in 1948, the *Symphony No. 6* is largely a response to the war years and a commemoration of those who died. It's a remarkably daring work for a composer who, through necessity, was much exercised with producing music that would be acceptable to the authorities. Here Prokofiev writes a deeply heartfelt work which seems to function, like the contemporary symphonic writing of Shostakovich, on several levels of meaning. The central Largo has a particularly grief-stricken opening which then opens out into something more lyrical. After this the finale, with its boisterous toe-tapping energy, comes as a startling surprise. But the mood is not sustained and by the end of the movement the energy seems merely mechanical, not to say desperate. The symphony was not approved of by the authorities.

○ Symphonies 1–7; Scottish National Orchestra; Järvi (Chandos CHAN 8931–4; 4 CDs).

The most reliable of the three complete cycles currently available is Chandos's with Järvi, available as four separate CDs. He has a solid grasp of Prokofiev's irregular architecture and is keen to move the music on, without resorting to the histrionic savagery that some conductors indulge in. The recorded sound is excellent on each of the CDs.

◑ Symphonies Nos. 1 & 5: Berlin Philharmonic Orchestra; Karajan (Deutsche Grammophon 437 253-2).

Karajan plays the first symphony with an elegance and poise that reminds one of chamber music, with an emphasis on lightness and sparkle. There is little sense of Koussevitzky's fast-flowing stream, but instead a compensating clarity, crispness and polish. His account of *No. 5* is a straightforward, opulent performance with some of the inner demons absent, but with plenty of elegance and pace.

○ Symphonies Nos. 1 & 5: Boston Symphony Orchestra; Koussevitsky (RCA 09026 61657-2).

Dazzling speed from Koussevitzky in *No. 1*, who commands this music as if it had been written for him. The second movement is made a true Larghetto, and most modern performances sound lugubrious in comparison. With *No. 5* he manages to clarify Prokofiev's orchestral writing so as to make the development really flow. On top of this, he seems to revel in conveying an impression of granitic strength, while at the same time suggesting a sardonic undercurrent. The mono recording, taken from 78s, sounds surprisingly good.

○ Symphony No. 5: Philadelphia Orchestra; Szell (Orfeo 87689-2; with Haydn, *Symphony No. 93*).

An equally fine account of Prokofiev's greatest symphony is this thrilling, uninhibited performance from George Szell – a live recording in every sense of the word. Szell's conducting was at its most athletic in the heavy Slavic music, where rhythmic considerations predominate over melodic, and his performances of Prokofiev's symphonies were renowned. This 1954 recording shows him at his zenith.

◑ Symphony No. 6: Royal Scottish National Orchestra; Järvi (Chandos CHAN 8359; with *Waltz Suite*).

This is the most successful of the Järvi cycle with an intensity and a commitment which is electrifying. The work's somewhat baggy structure is given a greater sense of shape than usual and and the sound quality is exceptionally good.

ROMEO AND JULIET

The ballet music for *Romeo and Juliet* (1936) is one of Prokofiev's greatest achievements. The emotional scope and scale of this piece has no rival in ballet music and no other composer has so perfectly interpreted this play – indeed, only Verdi's late Shakespearean operas, *Falstaff* and *Otello* (see p.454), can compare with it as a translation of Shakespeare into music. Prokofiev was long troubled by the ending of the ballet for, as he said, "living people can dance, the dying cannot". As did Rossini with his *Otello*, Prokofiev rewrote the ending so that Romeo arrives just in time to prevent disaster, thus ending the ballet happily. However, he had his mind changed for him by the choreographers, who assisted the composer in following the play almost to the letter – Juliet gets rather longer to expire than Shakespeare allowed her.

○ Romeo and Juliet – Three Suites: Scottish National Orchestra; Järvi (Chandos CHAN 8940).

Romeo and Juliet is a long ballet which works marvellously well in the theatre. When lisening to it on CD the best option is to listen to one or all of the three suites (1936, 1937 & 1944) into which Prokofiev divided the work's main numbers. Järvi's is a wonderful account, principally because he adopts some undanceably slow tempi – they would incite backstage revolt, but on CD his approach is inventive, original and entirely successful.

LIEUTENANT KIJÉ

Prokofiev's first commission to write film music came from the Director Feinzimmer in the spring of 1933. A satirical tale of the soldier who never was, it matched Prokofiev's quirky sense of humour; and he spent a blissful Parisian summer working on what was to become his frothiest and most popular score. The symphonic suite begins with Kijé's "birth", followed by a Romance, and two movements more quoted today than when they were first conceived: the *Wedding* and famous *Troika*. The tale ends as mock-mournfully as it began, with the little man's interment.

◑ Chicago Symphony Orchestra; Abbado (Deutsche Grammophon 447 419-2; with *Alexander Nevsky* and the *Scythian Suite*).

Abbado resists any temptation to make *Kijé* an exercise in gallumping jollity. The melodic lines are accented to the point of jauntiness, but their snap is used to emphasize the genuine pathos as well as the exuberance of Prokofiev's dazzling invention. Not a bar here is cloying or inert, and the effect is magical. This recording is available in various couplings, all equally good, but the digital remastering is best on this release.

ALEXANDER NEVSKY

In the course of a 1938 trip to the USA, Prokofiev was able to visit Hollywood and study the techniques of composing for film. The first fruit of these labours was a commission from the Soviet director Sergei Eisenstein, for a score which depicted the struggle on the River Neva between Alexander

Nevsky's Russian army and Swedish invaders. It was a collaboration made in heaven: two virtuosos came together from separate spheres and from the start were able to deal, almost intuitively, with each other's art. The climax of Eisenstein's film is the famous battle on the ice for which Prokofiev wrote music from Eisenstein's storyboard, and the sequence was then filmed to fit in with the idea of the music. The result is the most thrilling synthesis of sound and vision, in which a gradual momentum builds to a brilliant climax as the ice breaks and the Teutonic knights are drowned. For the concert hall Prokofiev rearranged his soundtrack as a dramatic cantata ("Arise you people free and brave, defend our fair native land!"), culminating with Nevsky's triumphant entry into the city of Psov.

◑ **Chicago Symphony Orchestra; Abbado** (Deutsche Grammophon 447 419-2; with *Lieutenant Kijé* and the *Scythian Suite*).

Claudio Abbado is a thrilling conductor of Prokofiev: here he creates an atmosphere of desperate, stabbing intensity. A mood of harrowing despair pervades his interpretation – due, in part, to Abbado hanging back almost to the point of stasis, so that explosive climaxes can be unleashed with real ferocity.

PETER AND THE WOLF

January 1936 brought the beginning of an official crackdown on avant-garde composers in the Soviet Union, prompted by Stalin's horrified reaction to Shostakovich's *Lady Macbeth of Mtsensk* (see p.385). Prokofiev was smarting with disappointment over the belittlement he had received for *Romeo and Juliet,* and already he had felt the effects of censorship with *The Gambler* and *The Steel Step*. Perhaps in despair, seeming to lose his way, he turned to writing little pieces for children.

But *Peter and the Wolf* is one of the few masterpieces of music written specifically with children in mind. A simple story, written by Prokofiev himself, it tells of the capture by a boy of a dangerous wolf. All the principal characters – which also include a duck, a cat and Peter's various querulous relatives – are represented by their own theme and a different instrument of the orchestra. The result is immensely charming; for this is a suite which has proved magical for a young audience, and wittily mock-innocent for everyone else.

○ **Sting; Chamber Orchestra of Europe; Abbado** (Deutsche Grammophon 429 396-2; with *"Classical" Symphony, Overture on Hebrew Themes* and *March in B Flat*).

Sting has rewritten the narration a little, but his changes are just right. His laconically stylish and no-nonsense manner is ideal above all for children, while Abbado's sly and bouncy accompaniment is perfect for anyone. Recording quality is exceptional, and there's an outstanding performance of the *"Classical" Symphony* as well.

◑ **Gielgud; Academy of London; Stamp** (Virgin CU5 61137-2; with Saint-Saëns, *Carnival of the Animals*).

Sir John Gielgud's storytelling is avuncular – more strait-laced than Sting's, but with compensating charm and gentle humour. Richard Stamp's direction is suitably spirited and only slightly less vital than Abbado's.

THE PIANO CONCERTOS

It's baffling that Prokofiev's piano concertos are so infrequently performed, as they are among the most inventive ever written. The first was written in 1912; two years later Prokofiev used it to get back at his piano teachers when he graduated not with the standard performance of a classical composition, but with a piece of his own. He won first prize and widespread resentment. The second is notable for the terrifying difficulty of the piano part and, especially, for the maniacal demands of the opening movement's cadenza. The third, the most popular, was composed as a virtuoso vehicle for himself and, though its stylistic diversity lends a sense of detatchment to the music, much of it is demonically exciting.

The fourth, composed ten years later, was commissioned by Ludwig Wittgenstein's brother Paul, a brilliant pianist who lost his right arm in World War I (he also commissioned a one-handed concerto from Ravel). It dominated Prokofiev's attention over the summer of 1931, and emerged modest in scale but awesomely demanding; Wittgenstein didn't understand it and never played it, but held onto the score until 1956, when it finally had its premiere. Prokofiev's last concerto began as a slight, almost backward-looking composition, but the performer in him took over and the concerto evolved as yet another barnstorming test of digital prowess. Its five movements are more like a suite than a concerto, and its consequent lack of cohesion has contributed to its lack of popularity.

◑ **Piano Concertos Nos. 1–5: Ashkenazy; London Symphony Orchestra; Previn** (Decca 425 570-2; 2 CDs).

This was a landmark in Ashkenazy's recording career: lyrical, audacious, and as cheeky as Prokofiev's self-avowedly "laconic" idiom demands – and the cool reflection of the last works is probed just as memorably.

○ **Piano Concertos Nos. 1–5: Gutierrez; Concertgebouw Orchestra; Järvi** (Chandos CHAN 8938; 2 CDs).

These thumping, thrashing performances take some of the risks that Prokofiev obviously wanted the soloist to take, and Järvi's conducting is suitably characterful, though the recorded sound is not quite up to Chandos's normal high standards.

◑ **Piano Concerto No. 3: Argerich; Berlin Philharmonic Orchestra; Abbado** (Deutsche Grammophon 439 413-2; with *Violin Concerto No. 1* and *Lieutenant Kijé*).

Argerich is rightly famous for her playing of the third concerto. Its explosive energy and sharply contrasted character suit her mercurial temperament perfectly and, though the studio removes some of the fire from her playing, this recording is required listening.

THE VIOLIN CONCERTOS

Together with those by Bartók and Shostakovich, Prokofiev's two violin concertos are the finest written this century. The first was composed in 1917, shortly before he left Russia for his long sojourn in Europe, and was premiered by the leader of a Paris orchestra, Marcel Darrieux, after a string of much grander names had declined to learn the very difficult score. Though it ends in a dreamy, lyrical mood, this concerto is far more prickly than the later one, being pivoted on a fierce and angular central Scherzo. It was Prokofiev's intention that the second concerto be "altogether different", and so it is. Composed after his return to Russia in 1935, it has a quality of emotional transparency similar to *Romeo and Juliet*, on which he was working at the same time. The soloist dominates far more than in its predecessor, and the only real harmonic irregularities occur in the first movement. The second movement is one of Prokofiev's most inspired creations, a huge and plaintive melody coloured by rapturous modulations and a jaunty accompaniment. A sprightly dance-like finale rounds off the concerto.

○ **Shaham; London Symphony Orchestra; Previn** (Deutsche Grammophon 447 758-2).

This is currently the best modern performance in which both concertos are coupled on a single CD. Shaham possesses a rich tone and a marvellous sense of line and, like Repin in the violin sonatas (see below), he's not afraid to bring out the expressivity of these works. The recorded sound is bright and natural, and Previn and the LSO provide exemplary support.

THE STRING QUARTETS

Prokofiev's two string quartets epitomize his stylistic schizophrenia. The first quartet was commissioned during a visit to America in 1929–30 and received its first performance in 1931 at the Library of Congress in Washington. At that time, Prokofiev had recently immersed himself in the quartets of Beethoven, so it is no surprise that the opening movement is classical in feel, though this classicism is tempered by pungent dance-like rhythms that colour a string of memorable tunes. This energetic movement leads to an Andante of deceptive tranquillity – almost immediately the quartet breaks into a forceful Scherzo, which leads into a disturbing section where the players are directed to use the heel of their bows, a technique that puts violent pressure on the strings. The finale is the work's slow movement, which by classical rules should have preceded the Scherzo; profoundly expressive, and detailed with moments of sweet lyricism, it closes with a mournful recapitulation of the movement's opening theme.

The second quartet was completed a decade later, "for the people", and is too much a product of its environment; evidently the work of a composer working under constraint, it contains none of the idiosyncratic wit of the first.

○ **Emerson Quartet** (Deutsch Grammophon 431 772-2GH).

This CD has no serious rival. The Emersons are one of the best quartets in the world and have matured in recent years to produce performances of unfailing clarity and freshness. On occasion their staggering technique might create a slightly sterile atmosphere, but with these two quartets they are at their finest, giving performances full of wit and genuine emotion.

THE VIOLIN SONATAS

The first violin sonata, begun in 1938 and completed eight years later, is a bleak and sombre work. The second, on the other hand, though completed in 1944, is a positive composition that conveys no sense of the strain the composer was under. It was written as a flute sonata (and has been recorded in this original state many times) and was only later transcribed for the violin, at the insistence of David Oistrakh. Although flautists would argue, it works better in the hands of a good violinist, taking on a life that the colourless flute can't give it.

○ **Repin; Berezovsky** (Erato 0630-10698-2; with *Five Melodies*).

Vladimir Repin and Boris Berezovsky judge the style needed for this music perfectly: there's plenty of hardness and drive, but there's also no embarrassment about being lyrical and warm-toned when it's needed. This is a much more engaged performance than these works often receive.

THE PIANO SONATAS

As can be heard on his own recordings (on the Pearl label) Prokofiev possessed an awesome piano technique, and as a young man his muscular approach confused and shocked his contemporaries, who were then revelling in the meanderings of the Scriabin and post-Debussy schools of performance.

The tempestuous music of his nine piano sonatas demands a flawless technical command, but many pianists allow them to sink into empty ostentation – this is sharply characterized music that demands a sense of structure and momentum, as well as fingers of flexible steel. Prokofiev's two greatest (and most extreme) works for solo piano are the sixth and the seventh sonatas. Both have an almost violent energy: the sixth contains what Richter called "the shattering pulse of the twentieth century", while the seventh is a titanic construction with a piston-driven last movement that distils the fury and violence of World War II – it's a fierce, draining experience, making terrible demands on the pianist.

Piano Sonatas Nos. 1–9: Nissman (Newport NCD60092, NCD60093 & NCD60094).

The under-recorded American pianist Barbara Nissman plays all nine sonatas (plus the incomplete fragment of the tenth) with a wide tonal range and sharply drawn contrasts that single her out as someone fully in command of the music's intricate detail. The energy and sense of occasion make this the best complete sonata cycle.

Sonata No. 6: Pogorelich (Deutsche Grammophon 413 363-2GH; with Ravel, *Gaspard de la Nuit*).

This is a fantastically virtuosic performance of one of Prokofiev's greatest sonatas. Pogorelich plays like a man possessed, but the breathtaking variety of his touch means that the less hard-driven passages have an unparalleled degree of subtlety and nuance.

Sonata No. 7: Pollini (Deutsche Grammophon 447 431; with pieces by Stravinsky, Boulez & Webern).

Maurizio Pollini's recording of the seventh sonata is a performance that has acquired legendary status since its release in 1977. Pollini commands unrivalled power, concentration and dynamic range, assaulting the listener in a scorching performance that becomes almost diabolical in the last movement. The performances of the other pieces on this CD are of comparable brilliance.

VISIONS FUGITIVES

These twenty miniatures, snapshots of Prokofiev's idiosyncratic moods, were assembled between 1915 and 1917. Like most miniatures, they are meant to be accessible – a touring virtuoso's calling cards, his intimate confessions, splinters from grander experiments. The title quotes the poem "I do not Know Wisdom" by Konstantin Balmont: "In every fugitive vision I see whole worlds. They change endlessly, flashing in playful rainbow colours."

The *Visions Fugitives* are Prokofiev's most popular piano work. They are, as David Fanning has put it, "sometimes grotesque, sometimes incantatory and mystical, sometimes simply poetic, sometimes aggressively assertive, sometimes so poised as to allow the performer and the listener leeway to make up their own minds." The composer himself claimed that *No. 19* reflects the excitement of crowds at the time of the February Revolution.

Berman (Chandos CHAN 8881; with *Sarcasms*, *Sonata No. 7*, *Tales of an Old Grandmother*).

Berman lacks a little of both Richter's audacity and insight, yet he offers an affectionate (and complete) account which never descends into the routine. A feeling for the composer's playful streak is always apparent, as is an awareness that much of this music draws its inspiration from an older vein of impressionism.

Richter (Philips 438 627-2; 2 CDs; with pieces by Scriabin, Prokofiev, Shostakovich).

Richter's concert selection extends the emotional and pianistic ranges of Prokofiev's soft-centred modernism. His wit is indefatigable, but there are also moments of dreamy repose and strident caricature. This is playing which is light of touch and has an effortless freshness.

GIACOMO PUCCINI

(1858–1924)

It has been said that Wagner's music is better than it sounds. Conversely, Puccini's often sounds better than it is. Puccini had a taste for melodrama, and possessed in abundance the talents necessary to achieve his ends, principally a highly developed sense of theatre and an uncanny facility for memorable melodies. His genius for emotional blackmail soon settled upon the most effective techniques and then stuck to them – from his third opera, *Manon Lescaut*, to his twelfth and last, *Turandot*, his style evolved only slightly. He was frequently accused of decadence, as he still is, but judged by box-office receipts Puccini is the most successful of twentieth-century composers.

He was born into a long line of Italian church musicians and, as was expected, first became a church organist. Then in 1880 he entered the Milan Conservatory, where he took lessons with Amilcare Ponchielli, who steered Puccini towards opera. With Ponchielli's encouragement he entered the Sonzogno opera competition in 1883, submitting the one-act *Le Villi*; it was not a success, but it did indirectly lead to a commission, five years later, for a second opera, *Edgar*. Premiered the following year, it too was a failure, but in 1893 Puccini produced his first masterpiece, *Manon Lescaut*, a verismo opera to rank with those of Mascagni and Leoncavallo. In part inspired by Massenet's similarly ardent interpretation of Prevost's play, *Manon Lescaut* made use of five librettists (including Leoncavallo) and inspired George Bernard Shaw to proclaim Puccini the rightful heir to Verdi.

Remarkably, his next opera didn't get the same acclaim as *Manon* when it was first produced in 1896, but within a year *La Bohème* had become what it remains today – the most popular opera ever written. It established Puccini as Italy's supreme master of the human voice, a reputation further enhanced by the similarly effulgent *Tosca*, premiered in 1900. His career suffered a slight hiccup with the disastrous opening of *Madama Butterfly* at La Scala in 1904; he withdrew the work, rescored it in three acts, and gave it a second premiere three months later, when it was duly acclaimed as a triumph. Puccini turned to the author of *Butterfly*, Belasco, for his next opera, *La fanciulla del West*, but even though Caruso sang at its first performance it never attained the popularity of its predecessors, chiefly because it contains no show-stopping arias.

La Rondine didn't set the world alight, but the composer's ailing fortunes were restored by his penultimate work, *Il Trittico*, which comprised

LEBRECHT COLLECTION

Autographed photo of Puccini at home at Torre del Lago, 1909

three brief operas – a thriller, *Il Tabarro*, a sentimental religiose drama, *Suor Angelica*, and a comedy, *Gianni Schicchi*. Puccini's last opera, *Turandot*, remained incomplete at his death in 1924; however, Toscanini engaged Franco Alfano to complete the work and the opera received its first performance in front of an ecstatic Milanese audience on April 25, 1926.

Puccini was prone to glutinous sentimentality, and a sadistically misogynistic streak is evident in the casting of most of his heroines, who are generally helpless and weak creatures at the mercy of callous, domineering men. While he was unquestionably a verismo composer, his plots are often absurd or trivial, and many of his realistic details – such as the bells in *Tosca*, the Americanisms in *Fanciulla* – amount to little more than cheap motivic imitation. For most audiences, however, these objections ultimately don't matter. The important thing is that Puccini's twelve operas contain some of the most beautiful vocal music ever written, carrying into the twentieth century the bel canto tradition of Bellini, Donizetti and Verdi.

MANON LESCAUT

The plot of Puccini's *Manon* is more or less identical to that of Massenet's opera (see p.248), but Puccini's treatment of the story (based on a classic eighteenth-century novel by Prévost) is unremittingly intense. *Manon Lescaut* establishes Puccini's ultimate goal, which was the creation of a flexible, through-composed structure in which all the elements are subordinated to dramatic melody – where other verismo composers went for a continuous sequence of melodramatic shocks, Puccini tried writing an opera carried entirely by melodic high points. Rejecting Verdian structures of interspersed arias, recitatives and choruses, the gushing, momentous score of *Manon* takes a grand step towards Straussian opera. The problem with *Manon* is that Puccini keeps the tension consistently high, with no points at which the senses can recover before the next emotional crisis – the effect is rather like a banquet of desserts. To an extent all Puccini's music is prone to this weakness of excessive strength, but *Manon* is particularly concentrated. Nonetheless, it has a glut of good arias and the duets with Des Grieux and Manon are very effective.

◑ **Björling, Albanese, Merrill, Calabrese; Rome Opera Chorus and Orchestra; Perlea** (RCA GD 60573; 2 CDs).

This is about the greatest recording Licia Albanese ever made. Some find her technique mannered, but she is a remarkably intelligent singer and she reveals the different stages in Manon's decline with sometimes alarming naturalism. Jussi Björling is in splendid, velvety form, and – unusually – he conveys more than just the beauty of his voice, giving the character room to develop. Robert Merrill is a little blunt as Lescaut, but the voice is hard not to enjoy.

O Olivero, Domingo, Fioravanti, Mariotti; Verona Arena Chorus and Orchestra; Santi (Foyer 2-CF2033; 2 CDs).

This set was recorded live in Verona in 1970, when Placido Domingo was still barely known, and it captures him in fantastically exciting form – if you want proof that he's one of the century's greatest voices, just listen to this. He's placed alongside a fine soprano, Magda Olivero, and the sparks really fly. Nello Santi, never a first-rank conductor, was inspired by his singers on the night and this is an exhilarating show. Good sound, wild audience.

LA BOHÈME

La Bohème is the finest lyric opera ever written. Set in Paris around 1830, the drama unfolds amongst a group of impoverished students, one of whom – Rodolfo – is a struggling poet. He meets and falls in love with the seamstress, Mimi, but by the third act they have agreed to separate, largely because Rodolfo can't cope with the fact that Mimi is dying from consumption. At the opera's close, Mimi duly expires, leaving Rodolfo and his colleagues distraught, and not a dry eye in the house. Puccini's score is superbly constructed and littered with classic arias – including *Che gelida manina*, otherwise known as *Your tiny hand is frozen*. Lush orchestration and a cast of vividly defined sub-characters add to the pleasures of the ultimate operatic tear-jerker.

◑ **Tebaldi, Bergonzi, d'Angelo, Bastianini; Santa Cecilia Academy Chorus and Orchestra; Serafin** (Decca 421 049-2; 2 CDs).

The most famous *Bohème* is the Pavarotti and Freni account conducted by Karajan (on Decca), but the finest is sung by Bergonzi and Tebaldi, conducted in 1958 by Puccini's friend and Bergonzi's mentor, Tullio Serafin. The wondrous, meltingly lyrical voice of Bergonzi is perfectly suited to the part of Rodolfo. He may not have the ringing tone that Pavarotti boasted in 1976 but his sound is powerful and his characterization unmatched. He is ably matched by the equally fresh-sounding Renata Tebaldi, and they are well supported by Serafin's sense of pace and style.

O Te Kanawa, Leech, Titus; London Symphony Chorus and Orchestra; Nagano (Erato 0630-10699-2; 2 CDs).

The casting of Erato's 1995 recording seemed inauspicious (mature soprano, novice tenor and a conductor with no track record in this music), but it's the most successful *Bohème* for years. Richard Leech's Rodolfo has a powerful and honeyed Italianate style and injects just the right measure of emotion into his voice. Kiri Te Kanawa, sounding half her age, is a divine Mimi – kaleidoscopic in colour and

expressive in shape. Rounding off a fine achievement, Kent Nagano's conducting has a strong drive and yet is delicately phrased.

TOSCA

Based on a play that had been a great success for Sarah Bernhardt, *Tosca* was soon labelled "A shabby little shocker". It is indeed a heady mixture of sex and violence. The beautiful singer Tosca loves the painter Mario Cavaradossi, but she suspects him of having an affair with a local noblewoman. Meanwhile, Tosca is being lecherously pursued by the chief of police, Baron Scarpia (perhaps the most disgusting character in opera), who is consumed by hatred for the revolutionaries – one of whom, Angelotti, is being protected by Cavaradossi. For this Cavaradossi is arrested by Scarpia and horribly tortured (offstage). After murdering Scarpia with a table knife and seeing her lover executed by firing squad, Tosca hurls herself off the walls of Castel Sant'Angelo, one of Rome's most famous landmarks.

Puccini spent a long time working on *Tosca* and the effort paid off. The harmonies are even richer than *La Bohème*, and Puccini's leitmotifs – a feature of *Bohème* – are refined to the point that anyone can recognize, for example, the Baron's signature tune. The opera has a dozen classic moments, including the two arias for Cavaradossi, the Act One duet between him and Tosca, the Scarpia's *Credo*, the final duet *O dolci mani* – and, most famous of all, Tosca's Act Two aria *Visi d'arte*, in which she laments the misery of her fate. This "prolonged orgy of lust and crime", as it was called, is the perfect foil to the saccharine sadness of *La Bohème*.

O Callas, Gobbi, di Stefano; La Scala Chorus and Orchestra; de Sabata (EMI CDS 7 47175-8; 2 CDs).

Maria Callas recorded the work twice: once in the early 1950s, conducted by Victor de Sabata, and again in the early 1960s, conducted by Georges Prêtre. Do not confuse the two. De Sabata's Callas is at her thrilling, unselfconscious peak, Tito Gobbi's portrayal of the vile Scarpia is similarly convincing, and though di Stefano is miscast he manages a committed portrayal of Cavaradossi, relishing de Sabata's inspired conducting. Although the mono recording has its limitations, this blistering *Tosca* is a clear first choice.

◑ Nilsson, Corelli, Fischer-Dieskau, Maionica; Santa Cecilia Academy Chorus and Orchestra; Maazel (Decca 440 051-2; 2 CDs).

When, in 1966, Decca teamed two great operatic voices with a young, headstrong conductor the gamble paid off. This is the most impressively sung *Tosca* – if not the best characterized. Nilsson is clearly not Italian, but her power, range and colour are such that you overlook her lack of perception. Corelli's lyrical fluency and hammy masculinity make his Cavaradossi among the best. Supported by Maazel's urgent, temperamental conducting, the two stars set the performance alight. Fischer-Dieskau's Scarpia is the one limitation of an immensely entertaining account.

MADAMA BUTTERFLY

Butterfly is the archetypal Puccini woman, crushed by the selfishness and cruelty of a man. Based upon a David Belasco play which in turn was based on real events, *Madama Butterfly* is set in Nagasaki during the early part of the twentieth century. A geisha called Cio-Cio-San (Madama Butterfly) marries Pinkerton, an American naval officer, who duly deserts her shortly after the service. Butterfly, bearing their child, faithfully awaits his return. When Pinkerton does come back, it's in the company of Kate, his American wife; Butterfly kills herself with her father's ceremonial sword, leaving the child to the care of Pinkerton and Kate.

In one respect at least, *Madama Butterfly* is even more gruesome than *Tosca*, for the cruel drama is accompanied by some of the most seductive music Puccini ever composed – even when Pinkerton is finally revealed as a monster, the music is pleasingly light, reflecting nothing of his crimes. The growing sophistication of Puccini's technique is demonstrated by the first act's closing twenty-minute duet between Butterfly and Pinkerton, a gorgeous piece of writing in which the Japanese harmonic traits associated with Butterfly are blended with Pinkerton's more robust New World style. Although he dominates the opening act, Pinkerton hardly makes another appearance, leaving the opera almost entirely to Butterfly. When performed by a singing actress capable of impersonating the 15-year-old bride of Act One as well as the mature woman of Act Three, *Madama Butterfly* becomes one of Puccini's most moving operas.

◑ **Tebaldi, Bergonzi, Sordello, Cossotto; Santa Cecilia Academy Chorus and Orchestra; Serafin** (Decca 452 594-2; 2 CDs).

Both Tebaldi and Bergonzi recorded this opera twice but neither managed to recapture the glorious performances they produced in their first studio recording, in 1958. This is one of the great lyric partnerships of the postwar years, rising to rapturous heights of emotion – the duet is sung magnificently, even if Serafin's tempi do not quite generate a sense of sexual ecstasy. The Decca recording brings the orchestra too close, but otherwise this is an astonishing set.

◑ **Price, Tucker, Maero, Elias; RCA Italiana Opera Chorus and Orchestra; Leinsdorf** (RCA 74321 39497-2; 2 CDs).

This is the most energetically conducted *Butterfly*, with Leinsdorf concentrating less on line than on pulse, colour and gesture. Price, a vocally luscious Butterfly, revels in Leinsdorf's obsession for detail – the way she lightens then swells the tone during "Un bel dì" is amazing. Her Pinkerton, Richard Tucker, is a powerful, virile tenor – less seductive than Bergonzi but more exciting. The love duet – a feverish outburst of passion – trumps all others, not in elegance or sweetness, but in sheer theatricality.

TURANDOT

Pavarotti's rendition of *Nessun Dorma* was a great choice of signature tune for the 1990 World Cup, but it gave people the wrong idea about the opera from which it's taken. *Turandot* is a grand but profoundly unpleasant work, being the most disturbing example of Puccini's affection for violence against women. The action is set in Peking during "legendary" times. The evil Princess Turandot anounces that she will marry the first man to answer her three riddles – unsuccessful candidates will be decapitated. The deposed King of Tartary, Timur, recognizes his son, Calaf, in a crowd assembled to witness one of these executions. Timur is with the slave girl Liù, who loves Calaf. Calaf, however, loves Turandot and he resolves to solve her riddles. Turandot ridicules Calaf's quest for her hand, and is less than happy when he answers her questions correctly. In an uncommonly generous move Calaf tells Turandot that if she can guess his name before the following dawn, she may, after all, have him killed. Turandot promptly orders mass executions if his name is not brought to her, so the people turn against him. They capture Liù and Timur, and Liù kills herself rather than give up the name of the man she loves. Calaf then professes his love for Turandot and melts her icy heart.

The score shows Puccini's absorption of contemporary trends (Debussy and Schoenberg are recognizable in the orchestral textures), but *Turandot* is still essentially a work of committed romanticism. It contains some marvellous vocal writing apart from Calaf's *Nessun Dorma* – Calaf's *Non piangere, Liù* and *Principessa di morte*, for example, and Turandot's *In questa reggia*, one of the most powerful and chilling arias ever composed for a dramatic soprano. The use of exotic harmonies and melodies is more subtle here than in *Butterfly*, and the roster of leitmotifs is considerably larger. On the other hand, it lacks something with regard to dramatic cohesion, and the sadism of the opera might leave you with a bitter aftertaste.

○ **Nilsson, Corelli, Scotto, Mazzini, Ricciardi; Rome Opera Chorus and Orchestra; Molinari-Pradelli** (EMI CMS7 69327-2; 2 CDs).

This recording was made four years after Corelli and Nilsson headed the Met's first revival of *Turandot* for thirty years, and their performances were responsible for bringing the opera wider popularity in the US. Franco Corelli's stupendous, wildly emotional Calaf is the finest ever recorded, and the combination of him and the equally powerful Nilsson produces a performance that beggars description. Molinari-Pradelli might have kept a tighter grip on the reins, but he gets some lovely phrasing and colouring from the orchestra.

○ **Sutherland, Pavarotti, Caballé, Ghiaurov; John Alldis Choir; London Philharmonic Orchestra; Mehta** (Decca 414 274-2; 2 CDs).

This 1972 recording was one of Pavarotti's earliest ventures into the heavy repertoire and is among his most successful. His pure, easily produced voice lacks weight but he uses it with great musicianship. Sutherland never sang Turandot on stage and, like Pavarotti, her voice is best in lighter music, but she manages superbly, producing some meatily theatrical tone. Caballé's Liú suffers from some lazy pronunciation, but she gives a distinctive, potent reading. The supporting cast – including the aristocratic Sir Peter Pears as the Emperor Altoum – are all fine, and Zubin Mehta conducts with tremendous flair, encouraging some exquisite playing from the LPO.

HENRY PURCELL

(1659–1695)

Henry Purcell is the greatest composer England has ever produced, and his premature death, at the age of 36, was a terrible blow which curtailed the development of a specifically English musical identity until the emergence of Elgar (see p.136). In the intervening two hundred years, the high points of English musical life were achieved either by foreigners who lived here (like Handel) or by those who were merely passing through (Haydn and Mendelssohn). Not that Purcell was in any way an insular figure: though his youthful training was in the English choral tradition, he assimilated the latest trends of continental music that were so popular with the newly restored King Charles II. Purcell is therefore a pivotal figure, one through whom the art of the Renaissance polyphonists flows into the Baroque era of J.S. Bach, and his importance was fully recognized during his lifetime.

Like J.S. Bach (who was 10 years old when Purcell died) Purcell came from a family of professional musicians. His father, also named Henry, and his uncle Thomas were both musicians at the court of Charles II, and his brother Daniel was a composer and organist. Unsurprisingly the young Henry had very close connections with the leading English musicians of the day: first as one of the twelve Children of the Chapel Royal, and later as a student with Matthew Locke, whom he succeeded as court composer for the violins in 1677, and with John Blow, whom he succeeded as organist of Westminster Abbey in 1679. Purcell spent all of his life in the environs of Westminster, and his principal places of work – Whitehall Palace, the Chapel Royal at St James's, and Westminster Abbey – were all within walking distance of his home.

From 1680 he travelled further afield, supplementing his official income by writing music for the Dorset Garden Theatre in the City of London. From 1682 he was one of three organists at the Chapel Royal and in 1685 he produced his first major work – the anthem *My Heart is Inditing*, composed for the coronation of James II. Four years later, the Catholic James II was overthrown and Purcell had to provide music for the coronation of the new monarchs, James's daughter Mary and her husband William III – an occasion at which he fell out with the Dean and Chapter over his right to sell tickets to the organ loft. His theatrical activities intensified after the frugal William and Mary cut down on musical activities at court, and it was around this time that Purcell's opera, *Dido and Aeneas*, was staged at a girl's school in Chelsea run by the dancing master Josias Priest.

In 1690 both Purcell (and Priest) were engaged by Thomas Betterton, the leading actor-manager, to work on his adaptation of Fletcher and Massinger's play *The History of Dioclesian*. Though Purcell had written a substantial amount of incidental music for Betterton, this was his first semi-opera (a play with musical interludes). Staged at the Dorset Garden Theatre, it was an enormous success and led to three more: *King Arthur* in 1691, *The Fairy Queen* in 1692, and *The Indian Queen* in 1694–95, completed on Purcell's death by his brother Daniel. Of these three *The Fairy Queen* was the most ambitious, costing an extraordinary £3000, much of it presumably spent on the machinery needed to effect the spectacular transformation scenes that were required. Despite the fact that "the Court and the Town were wonderfully satisfied with it", the show lost money – the only semi-opera to do so.

Purcell's last years were extremely busy: as well as his work for the theatre, he produced a large amount of extraordinary church music, including the funeral music of Queen Mary – a work performed at his own Westminster Abbey funeral a few months later.

Like his French contemporary Charpentier (see p.103), part of Purcell's achievement was his success in synthesizing certain aspects of the French style – the two-part overture, rhythmically defined dances, and declamatory vocalizing – with the more lyrical and expressive style of the Italians. However, what makes his musical language unique is the way these elements are suffused by a sense of national identity, typified by heavy chromaticism, elaborate counterpoint, extended melody and, above all, an emotional immediacy.

THE OPERAS

In the history of opera, Henry Purcell is often presented as one of the great might-have-beens: though he was famed, in the words of a contemporary, for "having a peculiar Genius to express the Energy of English Words", his career coincided with a period in which opera repeatedly failed to establish itself in England despite the enthusiastic support of Charles II. Had he lived just fifteen years more, he would have experienced the London opera mania that was to bring the young Handel such extraordinary success. Instead Purcell wrote just one short operatic masterpiece, *Dido and Aeneas*, and four semi-operas which, though highly popular at the time, now tend to be treated as cumbersome, and largely unperformable, historical freaks. Fortunately, the tercentenary of his death brought a spate of recordings and performances that at last revealed the whole range of his genius, and brought some of his great theatre works from out of the shadow of *Dido and Aeneas*.

DIDO AND AENEAS

The first known performance of Purcell's *Dido and Aeneas* was at a Chelsea girls' school that had close connections to the court. The libretto, by Nahum Tate, was an adaptation of his own play *Brutus of Alba* and Book 6 of Virgil's *Aeneid*. Tate is regularly derided as a talentless hack but, in fact, he provides an admirably condensed version of the story (the opera lasts less than an hour), and observes Dryden's rules about texts for a musical setting: that verses should be short, with frequent stops, repeated lines, and not too many consonants.

Dido and Aeneas, perhaps more than any other of his works, displays Purcell's remarkable skill as a setter of words. This is particularly evident in his recitatives, in which emotional nuance is communicated by an arioso vocalizing of extraordinary subtlety. It can be heard in Dido's recitative "Thy hand, Belinda", which immediately precedes her famous lament, "When I am laid in earth". The recitative is highly chromatic – that is, it uses notes foreign to the key that it is in – with the voice moving in a series of small intervals on the syllable "dar" of the word "darkness". The effect is like someone feeling their way in the dark step by step, or, in Dido's case, coming to a true realization of the enormity of her imminent death. The opera is full of such telling details, with the lament having pride of place. This episode has almost talismanic status in English music, and its fame is justified: indeed the single-note repetition of the words "Remember me" must be one of the most agonized and vulnerable moments in the whole of opera.

◑ **Baker, Herincx, Clark, Sinclair; St Anthony Singers; English Chamber Orchestra; Lewis** (Decca 425 720-2).

Vocally, this remains the most gratifying recording of Purcell's opera. As epitomized by the closing lament, Janet

Baker's attention to the music's emotional substance has never been equalled: there is a nobility and a fragility about her interpretation that is extraordinarily affecting. Anthony Lewis's direction of the ECO is reliable and frequently lively, and Baker is ably supported by Raimond Herincx's baritone Aeneas and Patricia Clark's Belinda. Some will find the over-characterized Sorceress of Monica Sinclair irritating, although it is less peculiar than many.

○ **von Otter, Varcoe, Dawson, Rogers; English Concert Choir and Orchestra; Pinnock** (Archiv 427-624-2AH).

Trevor Pinnock's 1989 account is the best recent recording. Pinnock is especially good at registering the mood changes of the work, from public joy to private grief. Anne Sofie von Otter is a well-judged Dido – elegant and poised and possessing real gravitas. Her performance of the opening aria, with the cello continuo more forward than usual, is particularly affecting in its simple directness. She's well supported by Lynn Dawson's bright-toned Belinda, but Stephen Varcoe's Aeneas is solid rather than inspiring, and Nigel Rogers' doubling of the Sailor and the Sorceress is irritatingly arch. Where this performance loses out to the Lewis recording is in its failure to convey a real sense of theatrical excitement.

THE FAIRY QUEEN

Like the musical, the semi-opera was a populist extravaganza that mixed singing, dancing and speech with spectacular scenic effects. But it did not integrate its musical moments with its spoken ones, placing them, instead, at the end of each act in the form of a masque – a self-contained entertainment, with separate performers, that neither helped the narrative forward nor developed the characters. The problem for modern stagings (and recordings) is that if the play text is abandoned, you are left with five relatively incoherent scenes, each containing a wealth of beautiful music.

The quality of the music is especially high in *The Fairy Queen*, the spoken text of which is fairly closely based on Shakespeare's *A Midsummer's Night's Dream*. Without setting one word of Shakespeare, Purcell manages to convey the essential qualities of the play – its mystery, its anarchic humour, its sexiness. There is an astonishing variety of music, from the spine-tingling air "Hush no more", with its eloquent silences, to the knockabout comedy of the "Dialogue between Coridon and Mopsa" adapted in the 1693 revision of the work for a countertenor who specialized in comic drag roles. There is also a range of highly theatrical musical devices, such as the echo effect in "May the God of Wit Inspire", or the sopranino recorders imitating birdsong in the prelude to Act II. This last piece uses a ground bass, a form that occurs frequently in *The Fairy Queen*, most famously in Act V's "O let me weep", added in the 1693 revision to cover a scene change, and markedly similar to the lament in *Dido and Aeneas*.

⊙ Argenta, Dawson, Corréas, Deletré, Desrochers, Gens, Piau, Daniels, Randle; Les Arts Florissants; Christie (Harmonia Mundi HMC 1308.09; 2 CDs).

This is music-making of great vividness and immediacy, and it stands out from rival recordings precisely for that reason. Despite the lack of any real narrative in the masques, Christie never treats them as a mere collection of songs, but instead turns them into a real theatrical event. This is also true of the dance music, which always sounds spring-heeled and lively. The singers, mainly English and French, are fresh and committed.

SACRED MUSIC

As well as introducing continental practices into court music, Charles II was determined to liven up the music that he heard in the Chapel Royal. Not everyone approved. John Evelyn, on hearing a large body of violins playing "after the French phantastical light way", pronounced it to be music "better suited to a Tavern or Play-house than a church". Purcell had first-hand experience of the "new" music from an early age (he joined the Chapel Royal aged 8), so that when he came to write sacred music himself he had none of the dificulty of the older generation in embracing the new style. The result was the most opulent and expressive music ever written for the church in England, though in many ways it was untypical, since no other establishment could match the musical resources available at Westminster.

THE ANTHEMS

English church music in the seventeenth century made a distinction between the full-anthem, which was choral throughout, and the more dramatic verse-anthem, in which solo sections were contrasted with sections for chorus. Under the influence of French composers like Lully (see p.227) and Charpentier, the verse anthem became an ever more splendid display piece and included lavish orchestral preludes and ritornelli. These are sometimes known as festival anthems since they were usually produced for special occasions like a coronation. Purcell excelled in all three forms. One of the festival anthems, *My Heart is Inditing* (written for the coronation of James II), exemplifies the splendid heights to which the form could rise. It begins with a long instrumental introduction or "symphony" from which the tune of the verse emerges and which is repeated before the final chorus. In between – in the more delicate ensemble writing – Purcell shows that his brilliance as a word-setter was even in evidence for the most ceremonial of music.

⊙ Choral Works: Christ Church Cathedral Choir; English Concert; Preston (Archiv 447 150-2; 2 CDs).

Recorded in the early 1980s, these performances of a good cross-section of the major sacred choral works (including the *Te Deum* and *Jubilate*) still sound fresh and lively. If a two-CD set at full price seems an extravagant outlay, then bear in mind that the Argo disc reviewed on p.321 contains a selection of the anthems.

THE FUNERAL MUSIC FOR QUEEN MARY II

Queen Mary died of smallpox at the end of 1694 at the age of 32. Her funeral, held the following year, was one of the most lavish and grandiose ever accorded an English monarch and there was a great public outpouring of grief. As the Westminster Abbey organist, Purcell was responsible for the music and he responded magnificently, composing a special processional march and canzona – both for the recently introduced "flat" trumpets. This is music of amazing poignancy, profoundly melancholic but full of great dignity. It is followed by the choir singing a slow and reverential setting of *Thou Knowest Lord the Secrets of Our Hearts*, accompanied by the trumpets. The other Purcell music associated with the funeral – *Man That is Born of a Woman*, *In the Midst of Life*, and another setting of *Thou Knowest Lord* – may or may not have been sung at the royal funeral (scholars are currently at odds about this). All three of these funeral sentences are characterized by a stark simplicity and a chromatic foundation that is astonishingly advanced for its time. Additional musical obsequies included three elegies for the Queen – two by Purcell and one by John Blow. Of these, Purcell's duet for two altos *O dive custos Auriacae domus* is one of the most exquisitely beautiful works he ever wrote – highly Italianate in its interweaving florid lines and clashing dissonances.

⊙ Lott, Brett, Williams, Allen; Monteverdi Choir & Orchestra; Equale Brass; Gardiner (Erato 2292-45123-2; with *Come Ye Sons of Art*).

This is one of the finest of all John Eliot Gardiner's period performances. Absolute restraint and discipline are maintained throughout, accentuating the air of doom established by the opening march, and purging all sentimentality in the choral sections. The gravity and weight of this fine performance should leave you with a heavy heart.

⊙ Winchester Cathedral Choir; Baroque Brass of London; Brandenburg Consort; Hill (Argo 436 833-2; with a selection of anthems).

Winchester Cathedral Choir lack the finesse of the Monteverdi Choir but this is a performance of great feeling, with the resonant acoustic of the cathedral creating a suitably sepulchral atmosphere. The brass playing is beautifully poised and restrained.

⊙ Countertenor duets and solos by Purcell and Blow: Bowman; Chance; The King's Consort; King (Hyperion CDA 66253).

Purcell's two *Elegies for the Queen* are included on this marvellous disc, which brings together two of the finest English contertenors of recent years, James Bowman and Michael Chance. Their rendition of *O dive custos* is an utterly spine-chilling blending of voices which should help to make this great work better known. The disc also includes Blow's powerful *Ode on the Death of Mr Henry Purcell*.

THE ODES

The ceremonial splendour of the Stuart court led the poet and playwright Ben Jonson to revive the Pindaric ode – a celebratory lyric poem derived from the Greek examples of Pindar. Purcell's immediate forbears – Locke and Blow – both set odes to music, but it was Purcell who perfected the form, exploiting the expressive riches of the Baroque orchestra. He wrote them for a wide range of different occasions (including the *Yorkshire Ode* for an annual feast of Yorkshiremen in London), but the most important were written either for royal events or for the annual celebration of St Cecilia's Day (the patron saint of music) first organized by London musicians in 1683.

BIRTHDAY ODES FOR QUEEN MARY

For each of the six birthdays of Queen Mary's reign, Purcell composed a celebratory ode on a poem written especially for the occasion. All are contrasted in style, two of them are masterpieces. Sir Charles Sedley's rather stilted verses for *Love's goddess sure was blind* (1692) inspired an intimate, if rather mournful, setting from Purcell, dominated by the soloists. There's just one incongruous section when the soprano sings a solo verse over a bass line derived from a Scottish ballad (favoured by the queen), but the ode closes with a really magical moment – a quartet of soloists sing a lament, in canon, for Mary's inevitable death. *Come Ye Sons of Art* (1694) is a much grander and more festive affair with a large Baroque orchestra complete with trumpets and drums. The verses, possibly by Nahum Tate, are crude and unmetrical but, as is so often the case, the poorer the text, the more brilliant Purcell's response. There are no weak moments, just a wonderful series of contrasted solos and duets which include the sparkling "Sound the Trumpet" for two altos, an amazingly deft setting for bass and chorus of the clumsy fourth verse, and – best of all – a glorious melismatic soprano solo ("Bid the Virtues") with an ornate oboe obbligato.

⊙ Gooding, Bowman, Robson, Crook, Wilson-Johnson, George; Choir and Orchestra of the Age of Enlightenment; Leonhardt (Virgin VC7 59243 2).

Though more associated with German Baroque music, Leonhardt is a distinguished Purcellian who brings a new perspective to this music. In particular he emphasizes the ceremonial aspects with some slow tempi and some luxuriant orchestral playing.

ODE FOR ST CECILIA'S DAY – HAIL, BRIGHT CECILIA!

There was a certain competitive, as well as celebratory, aspect to the annual St Cecilia's Day festivities. Since Purcell's initial contribution of 1683 (*Welcome to All the Pleasures*), the music had become increasingly opulent, culminating in Draghi's grandiose setting of a new poem by Dryden in 1687 – which included trumpets in the orchestra. Purcell's 1692 ode *Hail, Bright Cecilia!* aimed to emulate this splendour. Once again, weak verses (by Nicholas Brady) elicit a highly imaginative response from Purcell. A long Italian sinfonia in eight parts functions as a kind of compendium of music's capabilities before a succession of solos, ensemble and choruses – extolling music's origins and its power – begins to unfold. The chorus plays a more forceful role than in the birthday odes: its first appearance is preceded by a dramatic and mysterious bass solo which leads into the first startlingly confident choral "Hail". Even more thrilling is the central chorus "Soul of the World", in which the divided choir overlap a broad, noble melody which then transforms into an animated fugue before the voices come together once more on the words "perfect harmony". A series of brilliantly drawn portraits of individual instruments follows before a final triumphant chorus closes this magnificent work. Such was the enthusiasm of the first audience that they demanded to hear the whole thing again – immediately.

Taverner Consort and Players; Parrott (Virgin VC5 45160 2).

There are several good recordings of this, the greatest of all Purcell's odes, but Andrew Parrott's is the most exciting overall. All his decisions – in terms of tempi and choice of soloists – seem to have been made to maximize the idea of the work as a homage to music's multifarious and seductive charms.

INSTRUMENTAL MUSIC

Purcell's instrumental music, mostly written in his early twenties, constitutes a minute fraction of his total output, but its quality is outstanding. As a pivotal figure, standing between two epochs, his instrumental music has proved difficult to classify and has, until recently, been unfairly neglected. His fifteen fantasias (or fancyes) for viol consort brought to an end a genre that had thrived in England since the middle of the sixteenth century, whereas his *Trio Sonatas* were the first attempt by a leading English composer in this "new-fangl'd" Italian form.

THE FANTASIAS AND SONATAS

Written for upper-class amateurs, the fantasia was essentially a free form in several movements performed by a consort of between three and seven players. It eschewed individual virtuosity in favour of a largely equal exchange of voices. Purcell's fantasias, composed at great speed during the summer of 1680, are an astonishing summation of the genre and possess a contrapuntal inventiveness that has been compared to Bach's *Art of Fugue*. They are shot through with a very Purcellian introspection yet at the same time have a restless energy and internal tension which often sounds extremely modern. In fact when Purcell wrote them, the fantasia was already regarded as old-fashioned, and had largely been replaced by the more formally tight trio sonata. Purcell wrote two sets of trio sonatas shortly after his fantasias. Scored for two violins, viola da gamba and keyboard, their textures are lighter, and the sound is much brighter due to the greater incisiveness of the violin. Even so there is still a melancholy quality to this music which one contemporary described as "very artificiall and good . . . " but "clog'd with somewhat of an English vein".

Complete Fantasias for Viols: Phantasm (Simax PSC 1124).

This recent recording is outstanding for the way the young performers create a perfect balance between the darkness of the music's clotted textures and its contrapuntal dynamism. It's a performance of such emotional power as to put in mind Beethoven's late quartets.

Sonatas Nos. 8–14: Purcell Quartet (Chandos CHAN 8663; with *Three Parts Upon a Ground*, *Chacony* and *Two Pavans*).

The excellent Purcell Quartet have spread the fourteen trio sonatas across three discs and augmented them with a selection of other chamber works. Volume 2, which contains the last seven, makes a good introductory disc. The sound is beautifully fresh and clear, a quality enhanced by the decision to employ a chamber organ for the continuo part.

SERGEY RACHMANINOV

(1873–1943)

Sergey Rachmaninov was a displaced person in more than one sense – a Russian who spent much of his life outside the mother country, and a Romantic who embodied a brooding stereotype that belonged to a previous era. A virtuoso of Liszt-like abilities, and a composer of music as expansive as any nineteenth-century symphony, he upheld the Romantic tradition – in particular the tradition of his idol, Tchaikovsky – with a granitic integrity, unmoved by the onslaughts of modernism or the disdain of pro-

LEBRECHT COLLECTION

Rachmaninov at the age of 24

gressive critics. Stravinsky summarized him thus: "Rachmaninov's immortalizing totality was his scowl. He was a six-and-a-half-foot-tall scowl . . . he was an awesome man."

Rachmaninov's doom-laden appearance and taciturn manner were acquired quite young: he was born into wealth but his father was profligate, so by the time Rachmaninov was 9 the family was left with nothing. In 1885 he moved to Moscow where he began piano lessons, which in turn led to his first attempts at composing. In 1891, after further studies with various teachers, he completed his *Piano Concerto No. 1*, following it a year later with his most celebrated work for solo piano, the *Prelude in C Sharp Minor.* His opera *Aleko* met with similar acclaim in 1893, but his first symphony was a complete disaster (see p.324). Rachmaninov's reputation as a pianist continued to blossom, yet from 1897 he put almost all his energies into his conducting position with the Moscow Private Russian Opera Company. It was in this capacity that he made his first professional trip abroad, when he journeyed to London in 1899.

Around this time Rachmaninov began to suffer bouts of self-doubt so severe that he lost all faith in his abilities as a composer. A doctor named Nikolai Dahl came to the rescue with a course of hypnosis, through which Rachmaninov overcame his insecurities and began work on his second piano concerto. The first performance in 1901 was an enormous success, and the work has remained his most popular. From then on, he composed fluently but for the next three years he was possessed by an enthusiasm for opera, an area of his output that's now all but forgotten. By 1906 he was becoming worried by Russia's social instability, and he spent extended periods of time outside the country – in 1909, for example, he toured all over America, playing nothing but his own music, including the recently completed *Piano Concerto No. 3.* Shortly after the 1917 Revolution, an invitation to conduct in Stockholm was the catalyst for the inevitable decision, and Rachmaninov and his family left Russia for the last time.

Shrewdly, if reluctantly, he recognized America as the answer to his financial worries and it was in New York that he finally settled in November 1918. His remaining years were dominated by performing engagements, with little time to spare for composing – apart from the fourth piano concerto, the *Paganini Rhapsody*, the third symphony and the *Symphonic Dances*, he produced little of note in the last third of his life. His last American home was a metaphor for his career and his music – it was a complete replica, down to the food and drink, of his home in Moscow.

◑ **The Complete Rachmaninov Recordings** (RCA 09026 61265-2; 10 CDs).

Rachmaninov had enormous hands (it's been suggested that he suffered from a rare bone disease), which enabled him play with ease what other pianists would find impossible. Thus much of his own music makes terrible demands upon the soloist, and very few recordings of Rachmaninov's works even begin to approach the composer's own. This dazzling set includes all four piano concertos, the *Paganini Rhapsody*, the third symphony (conducted by Rachmaninov) and a large selection of his solo piano music – but, sadly, there is no recording of the second sonata. In addition to Rachmaninov's incredible performances of his own music, this invaluable document also includes pieces by Beethoven, Grieg, Schumann, Mendelssohn, Schubert, Tchaikovsky, Scriabin, Liszt, Debussy and others.

SYMPHONY NO. 2

The premiere of Rachmaninov's first symphony was a spectacular failure, thanks to its conductor, Glazunov (see p.159), who arrived at the podium tanked up on vodka and turned the performance into a humiliation for the young composer. In the wake of this debâcle, Rachmaninov pronounced the symphony "weak, childish, strained and bombastic", withdrew it from public use, and never heard it again. The *Symphony No. 2*, however, is a work of immense power and maturity – coming, as it did, twelve years later. It may be over-long, but it's more disciplined than its predecessor, and the richness of its themes makes it the most absorbing of Rachmaninov's three symphonies. In particular, the Adagio is one of the greatest symphonic movements in all Russian music. A song for orchestra, the Adagio becomes perilously sentimental in places, but its lush harmony and exquisite orchestration are so genuinely felt that you'll forgive any excesses.

O St Petersburg Philharmonic Orchestra; Jansons (EMI CDC 555140-2; with *Vocalise and Scherzo*).

Perhaps the finest recording of recent years is Mariss Jansons' second account of the score, with the St Petersburg Philharmonic. It might be at times too slick and precise, but overall the passion of the interpretation is thrilling, and Jansons maintains a tight balance and responsive tempi throughout.

SYMPHONY NO. 3

The *Symphony No. 3* was composed in Switzerland between 1935 and 1936 – nearly thirty years after its predecessor. It's very nearly as powerful: a great blare of brass galvanizes the opening and finale alike, the singing interludes between the music's recurring motifs are of Rachmaninov's most alluringly heartfelt kind, and before the symphony's hovering ghosts are laid to rest a last fugato is wittily spun in which the composer's *idée fixe,* the Dies Irae, insinuates itself as a counterpoint. This is a work to stand by the best of Rachmaninov's Indian summer.

O St Petersburg Philharmonic Orchestra; Jansons (EMI CDC 54877-2; with *Symphonic Dances*).

Jansons repeats the success of the second symphony with a mesmerizing performance of the third, in which his close attention to detail does the work a lot of favours. It's coupled with a scintillating account of the *Symphonic Dances*, the last of Rachmaninov's orchestral works.

THE ISLE OF THE DEAD

The *Isle of the Dead* (1909), Rachmaninov's first orchestral masterpiece, owes its inspiration to Arnold Böcklin's famous painting of an upright shrouded figure being rowed by boat to a cypress-covered island. Through a steadily repeated rythmic motif, Rachmaninov brilliantly conveys the movement of oars across the water and the journey's inexorable progress. But this glowering early masterpiece also owes much to the Wagner of *Tristan* with its "immortal longings" for the oblivion and bliss of death (the Dies Irae makes another appearance). It's an amazingly powerful piece, whose simple repetitions and sepulchral air work their way insidiously into the memory.

O Concertgebouw Orchestra; Ashkenazy (Decca 430 733-2; with *Symphonic Dances*).

The sombre weight of Rachmaninov's tone poem is magisterially caught by Ashkenazy. The way in which he makes inflections surge and die, as if themselves caught on the waves, creates just the right atmosphere of brooding heaviness and tense expectation.

THE PIANO CONCERTOS

In view of Rachmaninov complete technical command of the piano, it's amazing that he should so rarely have succumbed to the temptation to write bravura music. His piano concertos are all very difficult to play, but, with the exception of the blatantly taxing third concerto, there are few moments where it sounds like it. Of the four, the *Piano Concerto No. 2* is understandably the most popular. Dedicated to Doctor Dahl, the hypnotherapist who restored Rachmaninov to composition, it is a wonderfully optimistic work, opening with a famous eight-chord progression and crammed with soaringly beautiful music. Remarkably, at no point in the first movement does the soloist take up the main opening theme, and there is a notable sense of self-denial throughout the solo part – which is not to say that the orchestral music doesn't have its moments of wallowing.

Rachmaninov's *Piano Concerto No. 3* is a production of the fruitful years following his aberrant "operatic" period. Commenced at the same time as the second symphony and completed in 1909, it is his grandest concerto, reflecting a confident mastery of melodic writing and the resources of the orchestra. Here he finally overcomes his habit of signposting the introduction of new material by bringing the music to a screeching halt, and his subtle metamorphosis of the first movement's thematic core into a leitmotif for the whole work gives the concerto a continuity unprecedented in Rachmaninov's work. However, the most important aspect of the *Piano Concerto No. 3* is its scale and violently Romantic vision: it was dedicated to the great Josef Hofmann (see p.105), and although Hofmann never played the piece it was clearly written with his thunderous abilities in mind.

◑ **Piano Concerto No. 2: Richter; Warsaw National Philharmonic Orchestra; Wislocki** (Deutsche Grammophon 447 420-2; with Tchaikovsky, *Piano Concerto No. 1*).

Sentimentality has no place here. Instead the powerful authority of Richter dominates the proceedings, above all in the sheer daring of an interpretation which hangs fire as if possessed of a deep despair and then explodes as if suddenly bursting into flame. Its coupled with a majestic performance of the Tchaikovsky piano concerto, and is also available un-remastered (and with a different coupling) at budget price.

◑ **Piano Concerto No. 3: Janis; Boston Symphony Orchestra; Munch** (RCA VD60540; with *Piano Concerto No. 2*).

This is absolutely stunning playing from Byron Janis, a pupil of Horowitz, that is matched in authority and grandeur only by his teacher and by the composer himself. Janis takes the first movement faster than most, but it pays off with an increased tension and sense of urgency that really gets under the skin. It's paired with a good performance of the second concerto by Alexander Brailowsky.

O Piano Concerto No. 3: Horowitz; New York Philharmonic Symphony Orchestra; Barbirolli (Appian APR 5519; with Tchaikovsky, *Piano Concerto*).

The third concerto was very much Horowitz's calling card and he made several recordings of it. Since the great 1951 RCA recording is not currently available, try this as nerve-tingling substitute. The sound is not good (it's from a 1941 radio broadcast) but what you get beneath the crackle is highly charged virtuosity at its most daring.

O Piano Concertos Nos. 2 & 3: Rachmaninov; Philadelphia Orchestra; Stokowski; Ormandy (RCA RD85997).

These exhilarating performances were made by the composer in 1939 and 1940. His fluidity and all-pervading magic, his refined understatement and even tempi, are revelatory correctives to the histrionics and ballooning phrases of many interpreters. Not only a unique historical document but musicianship of the highest order.

RHAPSODY ON A THEME OF PAGANINI

The last of Paganini's 24 *Caprices* (see p.295) has spawned more sets of variations than almost any other piece of music. Rachmaninov's response to it, the immensely popular *Rhapsody on a Theme of Paganini* (1934), is a set of variations for piano and orchestra, a sequence that's strictly constructed (the main theme is never far away) but has as strong a Romantic sweep as any of the symphonies or concertos – indeed, it's perhaps best described as a quasi-concerto. Particularly effective episodes are variation number seven, which invokes the Dies Irae chant so popular with Romantic composers (eg Berlioz), and the swoony variation eighteen, perhaps Rachmaninov's greatest hit. The last six variations form a highly charged coda, but the work ends with a barely audible flutter of notes that is almost as capricious as Paganini's original.

◑ **Ashkenazy; London Symphony Orchestra; Previn** (Decca 417 702-2; with *Piano Concerto No. 2*).

Ashkenazy is responsive to the music's exuberance as well as its nostalgia, and Previn's accompaniment is superbly attentive. The famous inversion of Paganini's theme, when it comes, is particularly simply done, and quietly moving in its intimacy.

O Pletnev; Philharmonia; Pesek (Virgin VC7 59506-2; with *Piano Concerto No. 1*).

Pletnev's performance is a thrilling and unsentimental reading. Tightly constructed and aggressive, it refuses all the music's invitations to self-indulgence.

PIANO SONATA NO. 2

Neither of Rachmaninov's piano sonatas has entered the standard repertoire, a neglect attributable to their extreme technical demands and to a *fin-de-siècle* opulence that many find offputting. In the case of the first sonata this is fair enough, but the *Sonata No. 2* is a different proposition. It was written between January and September 1913, and it soon became a mainstay of Rachmaninov's own concert programmes. In the 1930s, having doubts about the volume of "surplus material" in his early music, he cut the sonata down, but the revision did nothing to improve a work that succeeds by its very expansiveness. The opening is a declamatory and rugged movement that moves into a central Adagio in which the harmonies recall Scriabin. None of this prepares you for the breathtaking finale, a polyphonic Romantic drama of immense grandeur and virtuosity. The wild and jubilant final section is almost crazed with energy.

O Horowitz (Sony SK 53472; with a selection of the *Études tableaux* and *Preludes* and works by Scriabin and Medtner).

Vladimir Horowitz's playing of the sonata was monumental, as many recordings attest, and Rachmaninov certainly took the pianist's advice on how the score could be improved – he approved Horowitz's preparation of a version that restored most of the passages trimmed by the revision. This performance is not quite as daring as the now deleted RCA version, recorded live in 1980, but it is still tremendously exciting. Horowitz's rapport with the music is such that it frequently sounds like the most glorious of improvisations.

THE PRELUDES

Like Chopin's, Rachmaninov's *Preludes* comprise a sequence of miniatures in every major and minor key and, as with Chopin, the self-imposed constraints inspired some of the composer's most original ideas. Comprising the famous C sharp minor *Prelude* (Op. 3 No. 2) plus two later sets (Op. 23 and Op. 32), the *Preludes* are on the whole more economical than the ripe piano music of Rachmaninov's early career. Melody is a less dominant element than you might expect, for many of these pieces are built upon rhythmic patterns that lead towards the establishment of a melodic pattern that reflects the rhythmic pulse. This is not especially warm music – and you certainly shouldn't tackle the whole series in one sitting – but the *Preludes* are essential listening if you want to get a rounded picture of Rachmaninov.

O Weissenberg (RCA GD60568).

Alexis Weissenberg's punchy sound is well-suited to this frequently percussive music, and his searching approach highlights Rachmaninov's inner, contrapuntal voicing to great effect. This recording is presently without equal.

ÉTUDES TABLEAUX

Rachmaninov was as complex and contradictory a Romantic as Chopin had been. "My outlook is a product of my temperament, and so it is Russian music. I have never consciously attempted to write Russian music, or any other kind of music." He was equally reticent about illuminating the title of the *Études Tableaux,* which suggests pictures in sound, perhaps as Mussorgsky's *Pictures at an Exhibition* had. Pictures we know there were; but Rachmaninov commented, "I do not believe in the artist disclosing too much about his images. Let them paint for themselves what they most suggest." As with the Chopin of the *Ballades*, *Études*, and *Preludes*, the *Études Tableaux* take a motif or a technical challenge as their starting point, and weave poetically from that. Mordant, terse, visionary in their endless chromaticism, luminously simple or spectrally poignant, they are distinguished by a new brevity and a new, virtuosic level of pianism.

The first set was composed straight after the Opus 32 *Preludes*: chips from the creative block of the composer who had just written *The Second Symphony* and *The Isle of the Dead.* The Opus 39 collection was one of the last works Rachmaninov wrote in Russia, and one of his least Russian: his imagination was fast outstripping the straitjacket of any parochial idiom that others wanted to impose upon him.

O Shelley (Hyperion CDA 66091).

In the absence from the catalogue of Richter's classic account and Horowitz's 1960s recordings, Howard Shelley makes an excellent recommendation. This is a searching and distinguished account of these melancholy pieces.

THE CELLO SONATA

As with the majority of nineteenth-century Russian composers, Rachmaninov wrote a small amount of chamber music, and the only work in this field that shows him at his best is the *Cello Sonata* of 1901. It displays an exceptionally detailed knowledge of the expressive qualities of the instrument, a knowledge doubtless acquired with the help of his cellist friend Brandukov, to whom the work is dedicated and by whom it was first performed. After a brief introduction, the cello plays the opening movement's yearning first subject but the piano is given the responsibility of carrying the second. Thereafter, the piano is the dominant partner, and only in the elegiac Andante – one of Rachmaninov's greatest achievements – does the cello come back into its own.

O Starker; Neriki (RCA RD60598; with cello transcriptions of pieces by Brahms and Schumann).

Janos Starker is highly suited to music that thrives off the projection of a sweet tone. This is a surging, urgent vision of the score: the outer movements are dashed off with considerable passion, while the Andante's emotional assault course is traversed with great dignity, although Starker and Neriki sometimes indulge in a little too much structural flexibility.

THE VESPERS

Rachmaninov might have been ambivalent about the church, but he was far from irreligious; and taking his cue from Tchaikovsky he had already composed a succession of choral works when he began to write the *Vespers* during a concert tour in 1913. It is the culmination of a great tradition, outstripping all predecessors in terms of colour and choral virtuosity.

Rachmaninov clearly relished the sepulchral resonance of Slavic basses, the tolling of great bells, and traditional thematic material itself, which he quotes in both his *Symphony No. 1* and *Symphonic Dances*. By turns haunting, serene and magnificent, the *Vespers* proved an instant success, and were repeated four times in the 1915 concert season.

◑ **St Petersburg Cappella; Tchernouchenko** (Harmonia Mundi RUS 788050).

This is singing of extreme fervour, with an inner intensity which one seems to get only from Russian choirs. There is serene incandescence which lights up the longest passages, but also a polish and a quality of shading such as one does not always expect from a Russian source.

O Corydon Singers; Best (Hyperion CDA 66460).

This British alternative is completely different: lighter, sweeter and more elegant, yet at the same time sumptuous. A more than interesting complement to the St Petersburg Cappella's recording.

JEAN-PHILIPPE RAMEAU

(1683–1764)

Rameau achieved fame as a composer relatively late in his career. In 1733, when he was fifty years old, his first opera, *Hippolyte et Aricie*, created a storm of controversy because it dared to challenge the model for French opera established by Lully some fifty years earlier. In fact Rameau claimed to be a follower of Lully, but his music is much more dynamic and harmonically adventurous – qualities that his critics decried as being forced and unnatural. Success had been long in coming, partly because he had spent the first forty years of his life in provincial obscurity, and partly because what reputation he had made was as a music theorist, an occupation thought to be incompatible with the actual business of composing, though Rameau himself rated it more highly. Despite his academic background, his music does not sound especially intellectual – rather it has the charm and elegance of Couperin (see p.113), but with rather more bite and vigour.

Rameau was born in Dijon, the seventh of eleven children. His father – who taught him music – was the organist of the cathedral of Notre Dame in Dijon, a post to which Jean-Philippe succeeded in 1709. His early career was spent largely as an organist at a series of other French cathedrals, including Clermont-Ferrand, where in 1722 he published his *Traité de l'harmonie* (Treatise on Harmony), in which he examined the origins of harmony and the relationships of chords.

The following year he left for Paris but achieved only modest success writing light theatrical works and teaching the harpsichord, before being taken up by one of the city's greatest artistic patrons, the financier La Riche de la Pouplinière. One of the wealthiest men in France, La Pouplinière was prodigal in his expenditure on art. Among his several homes was a chateau at Passy near Paris, where he had a private chapel, kept an orchestra of fourteen players, and gave regular concerts and musical festivities. Rameau was his music director from 1731 to 1753, and it was La Pouplinière who provided the contacts and the money that launched his late-flourishing operatic career. Within just a couple of decades Rameau's status as a radical innovator had been reversed, and he was held up as exemplifying all that was best about the French operatic tradition in the quarrel that followed the performance of Pergolesi's *La Serva Padrona* in 1752 (see p.302).

CASTOR ET POLLUX

Rameau's operas conform to the general pattern of Lully's *tragédies lyriques*: they are in five acts, preceded by an overture and a didactic prologue, and in each act there is a lavish *divertissement* for dancing or spectacular scenic effects. The musical differences, however, are so great that audiences at the time were forced to take sides either as Lullistes or Rameauistes. For one thing, Rameau's orchestration is much more imaginative, using novel combinations of instruments to create specific descriptive effects (like the storm scene and its sunny aftermath in Act Five of *Castor et Pollux*) – indeed it was for this pictorial skill that he was most admired during his lifetime. As well as this, his harmonies were much richer and bolder than Lully's, and one moment in *Hippolyte et Aricie* was regarded as so bizarre and cacophonous that Rameau was forced to withdraw it after the first performance.

Castor et Pollux is Rameau's operatic masterpiece, but its initial reception in 1737 was unenthusiastic and Rameau made extensive revisions (mainly cuts) in 1754. The libretto is based on the classical tale of two half-brothers: one mortal, Castor (tenor), the other the son of Jupiter, Pollux (baritone). When Castor dies, Pollux intercedes with his father, who allows Castor to return to life only if Pollux takes his place in Hades. The story is a simple one of fraternal love and loyalty, made complicated by the fact that Pollux is in love with his brother's lover, Telaira, but not in love with the woman who loves him, Phoebe. Rameau clothes the story in extraordinarily rich and varied music, often juxtaposing profoundly contrasting moments, as when Telaira's meltingly tender lament for Castor's death in Act One (*Tristes apprêts, pâles flambeaux*) is immediately followed by the warlike music that heralds Pollux's arrival.

◑ **Jeffes, Huttenlocher, Smith, Buchan; English Bach Festival Chorus and Orchestra; Farncombe** (Erato 4509 95311-2; 3 CDs).

This 1982 recording of the revised version is beautifully sung, with Peter Jeffes' tenor and Philippe Huttenlocher's resourceful baritone bringing bewitching tones to their intelligent, emotive interpretations. The female cast are as impressive and, although the ECBO lacks the personality of Les Arts Florissants (see below), they play with real panache.

O Crook, Corréas, Mellon, Gens; Les Arts Florissants; Christie (Harmonia Mundi HMC 901435/37; 3 CDs).

The one dramatic failure of this opera (especially in the earlier version used here) is that the two brothers are just too good to be true, a drawback compounded on this recording by Howard Crook's rather watery Castor. This recording's strength are its women, with Agnes Mellon particularly convincing in the difficult role of Telaira, and there is some superbly atmospheric orchestral playing, particularly in the overture and in the Hades scenes of Act Three.

SUITES FROM LES INDES GALANTES

As well as writing opera, Rameau also wrote for that peculiarly French theatrical hybrid, the opera-ballet, in which each section has a separate plot and equal importance is given to both song and dance. Rameau's first venture into this genre was *Les Indes galantes* in 1735, a light-hearted work concerned with romance in exotic climes, and reflecting the vogue for the "noble savage" – a concept central to the philosophy of Rameau's fiercest critic, Jean-Jacques Rousseau. The work was so successful that Rameau arranged it for harpsichord and as four orchestral suites, in which form it has become one of his most popular works.

◑ **Suites from Les Indes galantes and Dardanus: Collegium Aureum** (Deutsche Harmonia Mundi 05472 77269 2).

Rameau's selection from *Les Indes galantes* begins with the opera-ballet's gloriously triumphant overture and ends, as the opera-ballet did, with a sombre chaconne. Though recorded in the mid-1960s the pioneering original-instrument group Collegium Aureum play with an energy and commitment that would put many more recent groups to shame.

SACRED MUSIC

Rameau is little known, even in France, as a composer of sacred music. But before achieving fame as a composer of operas, he wrote some outstanding *Grands Motets*, in the tradition of Lully and Charpentier, which seem to presage his achievements in the theatre. The French *Grand Motet*, with its mixture of solos, ensembles and instrumental writing, always has had a dramatic element, but in a work like *Deus noster refugium* (1715) there is a level of intensity and excitement (including a musical description of a storm) that is positively startling.

O Deus noster refugium; In convertendo; Quam dilecta: Daneman, Rime, Agnew, Rivenq, Cavallier; Les Arts Florissants; Christie (Erato HMC 4509-96967-2).

An outstanding release which displays all the characteristics which make Christie the doyen of conductors of French Baroque music. All of the more tender moments are exquisitely shaped, but what sticks in the memory is the richness of sound and the sheer excitement that is generated.

INSTRUMENTAL MUSIC

Rameau wrote four books of harpsichord pieces, amounting to 65 pieces, of which only books two and three – the best of them – were published during his lifetime. As with Couperin, many of these pieces are fancifully named miniatures, and they are among his most charming creations, less elusive and mysterious than Couperin's but no less beautiful. Among them is a late work, *La Dauphine*, which was extemporized for the wedding of the Dauphin to Maria-Josepha of Saxony, and is full of cascading runs and daring harmonies. Perhaps his finest achievement as a keyboard composer, though, is the glorious *Suite in A Major* from the third book – its powerful opening Allemande can stand comparison with the finest of Bach's Allemandes from the *English* and *French* suites.

◑ **Pièces de Clavecin: Christie** (Harmonia Mundi HMS92 6018).

William Christie is also a talented harpsichordist, and he has recorded all but the earliest Rameau keyboard works. This 22 minute selection from that set includes the whole of the *Pièces de Clavecin* in E minor published in 1724. It's a spirited performance on a firm-toned instrument that makes a good introduction to Rameau's brilliantly inventive keyboard writing.

O Pièces de Clavecin: Rousset (L'Oiseau-Lyre 425 886-2; 2 CDs).

If the above disc has whetted your appetite, then this set by the outstanding French player Christophe Rousset gives you almost all of Rameau's harpsichord works in sparklingly vivid performances. Just occasionally his speeds seem a little fraught, but mostly tone and style seem admirably judged. For added variety, he divides the music between two instruments.

EINOJUHANI RAUTAVAARA

(1928–)

Though the resurgence of religious spirituality in late twentieth-century music is usually attributed to the trinity of "holy minimalists" – Pärt, Górecki and Tavener – some of the most profoundly spiritual music of recent years has come from the elder statesman of Finnish contemporary music, Einojuhani Rautavaara. Unlike Pärt and the others, Rautavaara does not write "religious" works as such, yet his music is imbued with a powerful mystical quality that is largely inspired by the elemental qualities of his native landscape. Recently, Rautavaara has developed a near-obsession with the idea of the angel-as-archetype: "They repeat in my mind like a mantra that radiates musical energy." It's an idea that has inspired several works, including the serene and expansive *Symphony No. 7* (1994), subtitled by the composer "Angel of Light".

Rautavaara regards himself as a Romantic composer because of the stylistic freedom he insists upon: "A Romantic has no co-ordinates. In time he is in yesterday or tomorrow, but never in today." During his long career his music has, in fact, undergone several transformations. As a student of Aare Merikanto at the Sibelius Academy in Helsinki, his work conformed to the neo-classicism then prevalent in Finland. At the recommendation of the 90-year-old Sibelius, he was given a scholarship for further study in the US, where he enhanced his already considerable orchestral technique under Vincent Periscetti at the Juilliard School, and Roger Sessions and Aaron Copland at Tanglewood. Travel and yet more study in Europe in the late 1950s led him to embrace dodecaphony, but even in as serialist a work as the *String Quartet No. 2* (1958) there is an underlying emotionalism that shows a closer affinity to the Expressionism of Berg than the austerity of Webern. By the 1970s, however, Rautavaara had embraced an openly Romantic idiom exemplified by his best-known work, the extraordinary *Cantus Arcticus* (1972).

CANTUS ARCTICUS

Described by the composer as a concerto for birds and orchestra, it juxtaposes Rautavaara's own recordings of arctic birds with orchestral music of great subtlety and lyricism. The result is a mysterious and exotic sound-world, with the birds as soloists emerging and disappearing in the sombre half-light of Rautavaara's orchestral landscapes. This is music with a strong sense of place, which – while not being in any sense programmatic – conjures up vivid images of the great forests and lakes of arctic Finland.

O Leipzig Radio Symphony Orchestra; Pommer (Catalyst 09026 626712; with *String Quartet No. 4* & *Symphony No. 5*).

This CD makes the perfect introduction to Rautavaara's music: it contains the best of several recordings of *Cantus Arcticus* plus excellent performances of the *String Quartet No. 4* (its austerity in marked contrast to the sonorous textures of the *Cantus*) and the *Symphony No. 5*.

SYMPHONY NO. 5

Scored for a huge orchestra in one continuous movement, Rautavaara's monolithic *Symphony No.5* (1986) battles to reconcile the contradiction which lies at the heart of its opening statement – a major triad that slowly pulses and crescendos to fortissimo only to shatter into dissonance. This dramatic opening dissolves into a darkly chromatic theme for cellos and violas (reminiscent of the fugue in the first movement of Bartók's *Music for Strings, Percussion and Celeste*), which is gradually drowned out by a cacophony of babbling woodwind. Originally entitled "Monologue with Angels", this is a broodingly romantic work despite momentary outbursts of modernist angst. Its stark juxtaposition of conflicting elements encapsulates an important element of Rautavaara's style, one that he continues to explore in later works such as the *Symphony No. 7*.

⊙ Leipzig Radio Symphony Orchestra; Pommer (Catalyst 09026 626712; with *Cantus Arcticus* & *String Quartet No. 4*).

The meat of the disc is the *Symphony No. 5*, which under Pommer's sensitive direction has a Sibelian power and recalls Rautavaara's own definition of the symphony as "an epic flow of thinking".

SYMPHONY NO. 7 – "ANGEL OF LIGHT"

Rautavaara's angel fixation has nothing to do with the benign anthropomorphic figures of Christianity, but is more closely related to the stark and terrible presences of Rilke's *Duino Elegies*, or the visions of William Blake. It emerged after a visit to a former benefactor Olga Koussevitsky, who had suggested he write a double-bass concerto. On the flight home Rautavaara looked out of the plane window and saw a cloud formation shaped like an angel. Two works emerged: an overture *Angels and Visitations* (1978) and a double-bass concerto *Angel of Dusk* (1980). *Angel of Light* (1994) is the most incandescent and serene of all these "angelic" works. The opening music breathes in a slow pulse, like a huge astronomical clock with a gentle, undulating ostinato in the upper strings punctuated by icy vibraphone chords and granite-like pedal notes in the double basses. Equally impressive is the unfettered violence of the second movement, the fury of which stands in marked contrast to the luminous quality of the work as a whole.

⊙ Helsinki Philharmonic Orchestra; Segerstam (Ondine 896-2; with *Annunciations*).

Segerstam is a renowned interpreter of Romantic music – Sibelius and Mahler in particular – and he brings to Rautavaara's symphony a sense of vast empty spaces and controlled power. Any tendency to wallow in the sumptuous melodic writing is resisted and the result saves the work from displaying its transcendental aspirations too blatantly. The disc also contains an organ concerto, *Annunciations*, of a considerably more restless energy. It calls for playing of great virtuosity, which it here receives from Kari Jussila.

MAURICE RAVEL

(1875–1937)

Nineteenth-century France made a speciality of failing to recognize its home-grown talent (Berlioz being the most spectacular instance of neglected genius), thereby encouraging composers such as Gounod, Massenet and Saint-Saëns to look to Germany – and Wagner in particular – for inspiration. The inevitable consequence of this trend was a reaction against Wagnerism, a reaction which came to a head around the beginning of the twentieth century with the re-emergence of a completely French school of composition. At the head of this resurgence was Debussy; and the greatest of his lieutenants was Maurice Ravel.

Ravel's music might at times be redolent of Debussy's later work, but these two composers followed quite different paths. Whereas Debussy pushed his music into a world of extreme formal and tonal ambiguity, Ravel never renounced traditional tonality and form, and cultivated a style that combined the classical with the contemporary. He was fascinated by the grand pianistic tradition of Liszt (as shown by his *Gaspard de la Nuit*), and even more obviously drawn towards the purity of Rameau and the eighteenth century (as in *Pavane pour une infante défunte* and *Le Tombeau de Couperin*), an interesting enough hybrid without the addition of other enthusiasms, such as gypsy music, jazz, Spanish culture and the music of the Far East. This last major influence can be traced to Debussy's encounter with Javanese music in Paris in 1889, a seminal moment from which one can follow the thread of Orientalism through much of France's twentieth-century music, right down to Messiaen and, less obviously, Boulez.

Ravel bound all these strands together with brilliant wit and an unrivalled understanding of orchestration, though his mastery of instrumental colour has sometimes been used as a charge against him – Stravinsky, for example, suggested that something was missing in the substance of a work if the

LEBRECHT COLLECTION

Ravel (right) playing the piano score of Daphnis et Chloé with the great dancer Nijinsky

thing you noticed above all was the dazzle of its sound. This is to overlook Ravel's marvellous sense of melody and structure, but it's true that he often expended too much energy refining the surface of his compositions or orchestrating piano works that were already perfect in themselves. Ravel relied excessively on spontaneous inspiration, a precarious thing at the best of times, and perhaps made even more precarious by this perfectionism. As he himself admitted – "I can be occupied for several years without writing a single note . . . one must spend time in eliminating all that could be regarded as superfluous in order to realise as completely as possible the definitive clarity so much desired."

He spent his childhood in Paris, and enrolled at the Conservatoire in 1889. In the course of the next six years he studied with Fauré, among others, and developed a personal style that was characterized above all by unconventional harmonies. His progressiveness offended his conservative elders: in 1901, 1902 and 1903 he entered the Prix de Rome and was failed on each occasion, and his final attempt, in 1905, caused an outcry when Ravel was eliminated in the preliminaries. This setback did not inhibit Ravel's creativity and the next ten years saw the composition of his greatest works, including the *Rapsodie espagnole*, *Gaspard de la Nuit* and *Daphnis et Chloé*. With the outbreak of World War I he tried to enter the services, but neither the army nor the air force wanted him (he was two kilos underweight, and too short), so he became an ambulance driver. He wrote: "They tell me that Saint-Saëns announced that during the war he has composed theatre music, songs . . . If instead he had been servicing Howitzers, his music might have been the better for it."

Ravel, however, did not gain from his engagement in the war, even though his beautiful *Le Tombeau de Couperin* was written as a tribute to the dead. He was released from his duties in 1916 after suffering a complete physical collapse, and the death of his mother shortly afterwards seemed to push him into a slow but inexorable decline. From 1918, with the death of Debussy, Ravel was regarded as France's greatest composer, and was fêted all over Europe, but his creative powers were diminishing. The last two decades certainly produced some outstanding works – *L'Enfant et les sortilèges*, the *Piano Concerto*, *Tzigane*, the *Violin Sonata* and *Boléro* – but most of his time was spent tampering with earlier compositions. In the last year of his life he was struck by a virulently degenerative brain disease; eventually he could not even sign his name. In December he risked a brain operation, and never regained consciousness.

L'ENFANT ET LES SORTILÈGES

Ravel wrote two operas. The first was *L'heure espagnole* (The Spanish Hour), a one-act comedy which has wonderful rhythmic vitality and orchestral colour, but is ultimately too disorganized to work as a whole. His second venture, written in 1925 to a libretto by Colette, is an unqualified success, however. Described as a "lyrical fantasy", *L'enfant et les sortilèges* (The Child and the Spells) is one of the most entertaining operas written this century. The central character is a spoiled brat who gets his comeuppance when the household objects he has abused – the sofa, the armchair, the clock and others – come suddenly to life. The trees and animals in his garden are equally hostile, and only when the child attends to a wounded squirrel do they forgive him. He is then returned home and, by implication, restored to innocence. The pictorial clarity of the whole opera is astonishing but perhaps the most magical moments are the scenes in the garden in which, through highly original instrumental colour, Ravel creates an utterly convincing world that is both seductive and sinister.

O Ogéas, Collard, Berbie, Gilma, Herzog, Rehfuss, Maurane, Sénéchal; French Radio Chorus; French Radio National Orchestra; Maazel (Deutsche Grammophon 423 718-2GH).

Lorin Maazel is not renowned for his work in the opera house, but this is a fine performance of Ravel's shimmering score – come the reconciliation he is in his element, revelling in the opulent orchestral sonorities. The cast sings well, with the soprano Françoise Ogéas excelling as the child. You can also get this coupled with Maazel's excellent account of *L'heure espagnole* on a mid-price two-disc set from DG.

DAPHNIS ET CHLOÉ

Daphnis et Chloé, the finest of all French ballets, was commissioned by Serge Diaghilev for his Ballet Russe in 1909. Work on the score occupied the composer from then on until 1912, the same time that Stravinsky was working on another Diaghilev commission, *The Rite of Spring*. The two composers became friends at this point, and Stravinsky was later to recall that Ravel "was the only one to understand the *Rite*". Like Stravinsky's ballets, *Daphnis et Chloé* now survives not so much in the theatre as in the concert hall, through performances of the two orchestral suites into which Ravel split the ballet. However, the ballet really needs to be heard in its complete form, for *Daphnis et Chloé* is a tone poem in all but name, achieving, through adroit orchestration, vivid characterization of the two lovers, Daphnis's rival (the brutish Dorcon), and the gang of pirates who abduct Chloé (the story is taken from a third-century pastoral poem). In Ravel's words: "The work is constructed symphonically, according to a strict tonal plan by the method of a few motifs, the development of which achieves a symphonic homogeneity of style."

◑ London Symphony Orchestra; Chorus of the Royal Opera House, Covent Garden; Monteux (Decca 448 603-2; with *Rapsodie espagnole* and *Pavane pour une infante défunte*).

The fact that Pierre Monteux was the original conductor of *Daphnis et Chloé* is not the only reason for recommending this disc – he was also one of the greatest conductors of the century, a former string player who had a marvellous rapport with orchestras. In this 1959 recording, he creates a dazzlingly sensual array of sounds and really communicates the dramatic momentum of the narrative.

◑ Boston Symphony Orchestra; New England Conservatory Chorus and Alumni Chorus; Munch (RCA 09026 61846-2; with Roussel, *Bacchus et Ariane*).

Charles Munch was renowned as an inspired conductor of French music and his recording of *Daphnis* is a fine example of Euro-American collaboration. In 1955, the date of this performance, no French orchestra approached the standard of the Boston Symphony, yet no American conductor was the equal of Munch, who here achieves remarkable extremes of colour without affecting the intricate musical structure, and without recourse to sentimentality.

ORCHESTRAL MUSIC

Daphnis et Chloé might be Ravel's masterpiece, but he's better known for a number of smaller orchestral works, beginning with the *Rapsodie espagnole* of 1908. This four-movement evocation of Spain – all glittering colours and exotic atmosphere – manages to transcend a certain indebtedness to Rimsky-Korsakov and Chabrier, by way of its brilliantly dramatic orchestration – the first movement *Prelude à la nuit*, in particular, creates a wonderful air of mystery and expectation. It was followed a few years later by another ostensibly "Spanish" piece, the *Pavane pour une infante défunte*. Originally written as a piano piece, its distinctly eighteenth-century sound-world conjures up a kind of fairy-tale solemnity (an infanta is a Spanish princess). Popular from its first performance, it's an extremely tender piece, with an apparent simplicity that belies the demands it makes on the performers – especially the horn player.

It was largely thanks to Diaghilev's insistence that Ravel wrote the "choreographic poem" *La Valse*, a work he finally completed in 1920. This is a waltz of sorts, but it's waltz music scarred by the experiences of wartime, turning the dance form that had recently been the toast of decadent Vienna into a vehicle for biting satire. Diaghilev rejected it and in 1928 the dancer Ida Rubenstein (whose company first performed *La Valse*) asked Ravel to orchestrate some of Albéniz's piano music as a dance score. Instead he gave her *Boléro*, a piece that made his name internationally known. Commenting on its success, Ravel ruefully summarized the piece as "orchestration without music". It's built from an unwavering repeated phrase in C major, announced and maintained throughout by a snare drum, which the various orchestral instruments join at regular intervals until reaching the famous climax, a quarter of an hour later.

◑ **Rapsodie espagnole; La Valse; Boléro: Boston Symphony Orchestra; Munch** (RCA 09026 61956-2; with Debussy *Images*).

For *Boléro* and *La Valse* Munch is again a skilful advocate. *Boléro* is much more difficult to conduct than might be thought: the hardest task is for the snare-drummer to hold a steady tempo throughout. The drummer never loses concentration here, and Munch adopts a well-judged pulse, moulding a wonderfully rich orchestral texture. The performance of *La valse* is one of the very best available. The Monteux recording of *Daphnis* (reviewed on p.332) also contains beautifully poised accounts of the *Rapsodie* and the *Pavane*.

◑ **Rapsodie espagnole; La Valse; Pavane; Tombeau de Couperin; Alborado del gracioso: Detroit Symphony Orchestra; Paray** (Mercury 432 003-2MM; with Ibert *Escales*).

Like Munch and Monteux, Paul Paray was a great interpreter of French music, and his performances of Ravel for Mercury are no exception. As with Munch, the combination of French inspiration and American technique produces outstanding results – particularly in an intoxicating rendition of the *Rapsodie espagnole*.

SHÉHÉRAZADE

For French composers, Berlioz's *Nuits d'été* was the great example of how the orchestrating of songs could extend their emotional scope. Having several years earlier failed to complete an opera based on *The Arabian Nights* (he only managed the overture), Ravel turned in 1903 to the *Shéhérazade* poems of Tristan Klingsor, a young symbolist whose mildly perfumed verses conjured up a fantasy landscape of the exotic Orient. The first of the three poems Ravel set, *Asie* (Asia), is also the longest; its fluid vocal line is borne by an orchestral score that evokes a voyage of discovery, full of rich and colourful sights and sounds (a rocking boat, Chinese princesses, a fierce executioner). *La Flûte enchantée* is a simpler mood piece in which the sinewy arabesques of a flute remind Shéhérazade of her lover's kisses. The last song, *L'Indifférent*, is the most beautiful of all – its gentle languor feels close to the *Pavane pour une infante défunte*, as does its undertow of subdued melancholy.

○ **Hendricks; Orchestre de l'Opéra de Lyon; Gardiner** (EMI CDC7 49689-2; with *Deux mélodies hébraïques*, *Cinq mélodies populaires grecques* & Duparc's *Six mélodies avec orchestre*).

Ravel's *Shéhérazade* simultaneously contains both a languorous heaviness and a fresh innocence of vision. Both these qualities are beautifully and dramatically conveyed by Barbara Hendricks, whose slightly hard but focused tones are softened by some exquisite orchestral playing.

THE PIANO CONCERTOS

"The music of a concerto . . . should be light-hearted and brilliant, and not aim at profundity or at dramatic effects." Ravel's G major *Piano Concerto* certainly lives up to his dictum, and is one of his most lyrical and captivating scores. It was begun in 1929, when jazz was all the rage among the intelligentsia of Paris. The concerto is deeply infused with the idioms of jazz, but unlike Gershwin's *Rhapsody in Blue* (1924) this is a classically organized, three-movement structure, and it's this combination of opposites that gives the music such zest. It begins with a whip-crack, then hustles and gambols on towards the pivotal slow movement, whose opening unaccompanied tune suggests a Chopin nocturne in its purity and Rachmaninov in its breadth. A glittery yet brooding finale, less than half the length of its predecessor, is a perfect conclusion to this work of brilliant contrasts.

At the same time as he was working on the G major concerto, Ravel was writing a very different concerto for the pianist Paul Wittgenstein, brother of the philosopher. Wittgenstein had lost his right arm in World War I, and had begun to commission leading composers to write works for left hand alone. The astonishing achievement of Ravel's Piano concerto (for left hand) is that it is never apparent to the listener that just one hand is being used, such is the complete integrity of the solo part. If it doesn't quite contradict Ravel's concerto dictum, it is certainly one of the most serious of his works, permeated by a hard-driven energy and a sense of anxiety that borders on the tragic.

○ **Piano Concerto in G Major: Benedetti Michelangeli; Philharmonia; Gracis** (EMI CDC7 49326-2; with Rachmaninov, *Piano Concerto No. 4*).

This is one of the few records that do justice to the astonishing abilities of Arturo Benedetti Michelangeli. In the middle movement, he achieves a sonority and expressive range that is overwhelming, and throughout the punchily rhythmic outer movements you're borne along by his panache and unforced wit. He takes the finale at a fittingly brisk pace, but his technical mastery is so perfect that he almost whispers the piano part, barely touching the keys.

⦿ Piano Concertos: François; Paris Conservatoire Orchestra; Cluytens (EMI CDC5 56239-2; with *Gaspard de la Nuit*).

Samson François, one of the best French pianists of the century, is largely unknown outside of France. In this 1959 recording he performs both concertos in a manner very different from Benedetti Michelangeli: more rough-edged and improvisatory but with amazing energy and flair.

THE STRING QUARTET

Ravel was fast making a name for himself when he began composing the *String Quartet* in 1902, and it was this work – his first and most successful foray into chamber music – that established him as a mature composer when it was premiered two years later. In his autobiography he stated that the *String Quartet* "more than any of my earlier works, was in line with my ideas of musical structure". Indeed, though the enthusiasm of youth is still very much present, the formal poise of the writing is what strikes you above all. Legend has it that Debussy thought Ravel's quartet bore too close a resemblance to his own, and there are undeniable similarities – both open with a movement in sonata form, for example, and both use the opening theme as the basis for the material of the other movements. However, from the second movement onwards the Ravel quartet displays a rhapsodic, indulgent quality that's miles away from Debussy, and in fact the older composer was a great admirer of the piece; on hearing it for the first time, he wrote to Ravel, saying "in the name of God, you must not tamper with this string quartet".

◑ Quartetto Italiano (Philips 420 894-2; with Debussy, *Quartet*).

This is a classic recording, full of sinewy vigour and immense charm, recorded when the Quartetto Italiano were at their peak. There's a lot of spontaneity about their performance, which is particularly appropriate for Ravel's mercurial changes of mood and direction.

TZIGANE

Ravel always took a special interest in performers who embodied strong folk traditions, and one of these was the Hungarian violinist Jelly d'Aranyi, whom Ravel heard improvising gypsy music at the home of a friend in 1923, an event that proved to be the inspiration for *Tzigane*. Styled a "rhapsody for violin and piano", it was composed in the following year and dedicated to d'Aranyi, who gave the first performance. The violin part is vividly Hungarian in feeling but its virtuosity also makes a gesture in direction of Paganini – *Tzigane* begins

with a fearsome cadenza played solely on the G string, an improvisational-sounding passage that's reminiscent of Paganini's *Variations on a theme from Rossini's Moses*, which is written entirely for the G string. The cadenza culminates with the piano's first entry and the work's main theme (which was heard, in a distended form, in midst of the opening fireworks), setting up a white-hot exchange that continues right to the final bar.

⦿ Vengerov; Vinogradova (Biddulph LAW 001; with works by Schubert, Ernst, Ysaye, Waxman, Tchaikovsky and Debussy).

Maxim Vengerov was 15 years old when he recorded this album of violin showpieces, and his playing is some of the most remarkable ever captured on record. When you've got your breath back after his playing of *Tzigane*, listen to his performance of Ysaye's *Third Sonata* – it's the sort of playing that starts you thinking in terms of Faustian pacts.

PIANO MUSIC

The subtle colours and evanescent textures of Ravel's piano music is often compared to that of his older contemporary Debussy, but, in fact, Ravel got there first, defining a new distinctly French style of pianism with *Jeux d'eau* in 1902. The rippling arpeggiated figuration suggestive of water, which recurs throughout his piano works, is derived from Liszt, but Ravel imbues it with a new delicacy. In the six wistful pieces collectively called *Miroirs* (1905), the desire to convey an increasingly wide range of sensations, aural and visual, is even more refined and creates what are, in effect, miniature tone poems. An epic scale is realized in only one work, his piano masterpiece *Gaspard de la Nuit* (1908) – a set of three ferocious and morbid pieces derived from the macabre prose-ballads of Aloysius Bertrand. With its broad

washes of tonal colour and its gunfire-rapid repeated notes (a hallmark of Ravel's style), *Gaspard* is a barnstorming addition to the Lisztian repertoire, particularly remarkable for the way in which the overall texture is often made up of clearly delineated and individual strands of sound.

⊙ Gaspard de la Nuit: Pogorelich (Deutsche Grammophon 413 363-2: with Prokofiev, *Piano Sonata No. 6*).

In one of his very best recordings, Ivo Pogorelich brings all his idiosyncratic brilliance to bear on *Gaspard de la Nuit*. The variety of his touch and the extraordinary control of dynamics that he is capable of yields breathtaking results. The second movement *Le Gibet* (The Gibbet) can rarely have sounded spookier.

⊙ Gaspard de la Nuit; Miroirs; Jeux d'eau; Pavane pour une infante défunte: Perlemuter (Nimbus NIM5005).

Vlado Perlemuter worked closely with Ravel and developed a brilliant understanding of Ravelian nuance and textural layering so that, although these recordings were made when he was in his seventies, they have an extraordinary lightness and immediacy. Nimbus recorded all the solo piano music with him but this disc, volume one in the series, makes the best introduction both to the music and to a great pianist.

MAX REGER

(1873–1916)

Max Reger was the central figure of the "Back to Bach" movement, and devoted much of his life to the promotion and reinterpretation of Bach and his Baroque contemporaries. However, his neo-classicism was not simply a matter of the resurrection of the old ways of doing things, no more than the music of his Italian equivalent, Ferruccio Busoni (see p.94), was straightforwardly nostalgic. Reger may have come to dismiss Wagner as "perverted rubbish", but he grew up in his shadow and he remained essentially a Romantic, albeit a Romantic who drew his strength from the great tradition of Bach, Beethoven and Brahms.

Reger's devotion to heavy, Germanic polyphony led to his being labelled "the second Bach", a nickname that had some justice in the case of Reger's organ music, a field in which Bach's influence would have been almost unavoidable. Like Hindemith and Milhaud, Reger was far too prolific for his own good: he produced music with an amazing facility and it is sometimes hard to sort out the inspired from the merely proficient. There's also an element of truth to the stereotype of Reger as a rather joyless academic: much of his life was an uneventful succession of teaching posts at Wiesbaden, then Munich and finally Leipzig. This may sound a rather damning summary, but there is much more to Reger's music than an obsession with fugues and, in fact, he's a composer capable of assuming several different (often unexpected) guises. The late orchestral compositions in particular are worth a hearing for the way they clothe classical structures in lush, almost Wagnerian orchestration.

ORCHESTRAL MUSIC

Reger's finest music is to be found in the *Four Symphonic Poems after Arnold Böcklin* (1913), well-constructed pieces in which the composer goes some way to betraying his own principles. The influence of the decidedly unclassical Debussy is clear in the harmonies, and the style of Richard Strauss, another *bête noire*, can be heard in the melodies. Moreover, this is illustrative music, and Reger was forever proclaiming the supremacy of "absolute" music – that is, music that referred specifically to nothing outside itself. Their inspiration comes from paintings by the Swiss artist Arnold Böcklin, whose Symbolist paintings often depicted Romantic landscapes populated by mythical creatures. Reger's interpretation of these images is powerfully evocative: the opening picture of a hermit playing his violin is full of longing and sweet despair (with modal harmony that suggests Vaughan Williams's contemporary *Tallis Fantasia*), but best of all is Reger's haunting vision of the *Isle of the Dead* – a painting also admired and interpreted by Rachmaninov (see p.324). The weighted stillness of the scene brings an outpouring of rich, romantic sound, and the tranquillity of the closing music is some of the composer's finest. An uproarious bacchanal ends one of the composer's most engaging works.

Also enjoyable, in a less emotional way, are the sets of variations that Reger wrote on themes by Hiller, Beethoven and Mozart. The first movement of Mozart's A major piano sonata forms the basis to Reger's most popular and tuneful score, the *Variations and Fugue on a Theme of Mozart*, while the *Hiller Variations* (once advertised at the Proms as the *Hitler Variations*) are arguably his most impressive technical achievement – hugely inventive and abounding in rich (but never over-rich) orchestration. In all three sets there is a sense of Brahms's *Variations on a Theme by Haydn* having been refracted through a late Romantic sensibility. Only in the great fugal movements that close each one does a hint of academicism reveal itself.

⊙ Four Symphonic Poems after Arnold Böcklin; Hiller Variations: Concertbegouw; Järvi (Chandos CHAN 8794).

Järvi's account of the *Symphonic Poems after Arnold Böcklin* (part of a general survey of the composer's work on the Chandos label) is splendidly carried off, with the Concertgebouw in brilliant form. Clearly recorded, the performance comes coupled with an adventurous interpretation of the *Hiller Variations*, and makes the best introduction to Reger for anyone who doesn't want to swallow buckets of fugues.

⊙ Variations and Fugue on a Theme of Mozart: Bavarian Radio Symphony Orchestra; Davis (Philips 422 347-2; with Hindemith, *Symphonic Variations*).

When he conducted the BRSO, Colin Davis was something of a Reger advocate, and this sparkling account of the Mozart *Variations* is the most persuasive performance on disc. Davis clearly sees Reger as essentially a Romantic composer, and he brings out the radiance of Reger's orchestral colouring and pinpoints the more poetic details.

STEVE REICH

(1936–)

Though one of the most influential Minimalist composers, Steve Reich has not been his best publicist, acquiring a reputation for irascibility and moodiness. At one stage Reich was continually contradicting himself in interviews: one minute extolling Minimalism, the next decrying it; at times suggesting that microphones were the only acceptable electronic aids, while his home studio in Vermont was filled with the latest computers and sampling equipment. Yet, for all his "difficulty", Reich's uniquely detailed and ethnic-influenced music is some of the best of the late twentieth century.

Born in New York, Reich was reared on Schubert and Beethoven before encountering Stravinsky's *Rite of Spring* at the age of 14, an event that widened his horizons – soon he was delving into the sounds of African drumming, jazz, the Balinese gamelan and Hebrew chant. He has also acknowledged Bach as a crucial inspiration. After graduating in philosophy at Cornell University, he progressed to the Juilliard, where he met Philip Glass and Meredith Monk, then went on to study with both Berio and Milhaud.

In 1965, after a short spell in San Francisco, Reich moved back to New York, bought a batch of tape recorders and – while experimenting with identical tape loops of a street preacher – hit upon the technique of phase-shifting, in which the tapes move out of synch and then come back into unison. He produced *It's Gonna Rain* (1965) and *Come Out* (1966) for tape, then began to recreate the effect with instruments, starting with *Piano Phase* (1967).

Continuing to investigate tape-looping and phasing, Reich collaborated with Philip Glass until they fell out, then in 1970 he went to Ghana on a grant to study the music of the Ewe people. The subsequent *Drumming* (1971), written for bongos, marimbas, voices, glockenspiels, whistle and piccolo, marks the honing of Reich's technique – it's a bright and inventive piece with no melody or changes of rhythm or key, instead using slight changes in timing, pitch and timbre to maintain its momentum. Following on from that, the psychedelic *Music for Mallet Instruments, Voices and Organ* (1973) brought gushing reviews from American writers, while *Music for 18 Musicians* (1974–76) sold like rock music.

Yet Reich's approach had a greater intellectual seriousness than that of Philip Glass, the other high earner of American Minimalism. Restlessly refining his ideas, he followed the lead of Debussy in studying Indonesian music, and in 1979 went to Israel to study Hebrew chant. In 1983 he utilized the poetry of William Carlos Williams in the hugely symphonic *Desert Music*, then composed the interlocking orchestral piece *Four Sections* (1987) before switching direction again with the award-winning *Different Trains* (1988) for the Kronos Quartet, plus found sounds and voices. His most ambitious project to date is *The Cave* (1993), a four-year work in collaboration with his wife, video artist Beryl Korot, for which he was given a million-dollar grant. Recorded in Israel and America, it presents a series of talking heads whose views on Arab or Israeli history were projected onto five large screens, their speeches punctuated by melodies performed by strings, percussion and four singers. It's an enthralling multimedia experience and a new development in Minimalist music, and its success seemed to mellow Reich, who for once smiled in interviews.

EARLY WORKS

The astonishing early tape works, *My Name Is*, *Come Out* and *It's Gonna Rain*, prefigured *Different Trains*, *The Cave* and *City Life* and anticipated techniques now common in hip-hop and related styles, yet used them in ways those genres never caught on to. *Come Out* (1966) is a quintessential Reich work for a number of reasons: there is the repetition of a small "cell" of material; it is based on a fragment of recorded speech; its rhythms are derived from vernacular speech patterns; it develops by use of phase-shifting; and it has a polemical purpose. *Come Out* was produced for a benefit concert in support of six black youths who had been beaten while in police custody. One of them told how he squeezed his bruises "to let some of the bruise blood come out to show them" so that he could leave the cells and go to hospital. Reich focused on the five words "come out to show them" and subjected them to a simple phasing process. The result is a coruscating counterpoint of syllables and phonemes which gradually lose their meaning and develop into a dense, hypnotic, sibilant screen of abstract sound.

⊙ Come Out; Piano Phase; Clapping Music; It's Gonna Rain: Tilles, Niemann, Hertenberger; Reich (Nonesuch 7559 79169-2).

A crash course in early Reich, showing the discovery and development of the phase-shifting process, its application to live performers, and the beginnings of Reich's move away from simple phasing.

MUSIC FOR 18 MUSICIANS

Music for 18 Musicians is "classic" Reich, one of the works which moved the composer and American Minimalism into the mainstream. Composed between 1974 and 1976, it marked an expansion of Reich's vocabulary because of its more varied instrumentation (strings, woodwinds, voices, pianos, and wood and metal percussion), its structure, and its "harmonic speed" ("there's more harmonic movement on the first five minutes than in any other complete work of mine to date"). Previously, transitions in Reich's works had tended to be gradual but inexorable: pieces would conclude when the system on which they were based had worked itself through. But in *Music for 18 Musicians* Reich made "arbitrary" decisons about the shift from one section to the next, signalled by a phrase on the metallophone. The constant rhythms of piano and percussion are humanized by the voices and wind instruments, which sustain pulsing phrases for as long as their breath holds out. Based on a cycle of eleven chords, the piece is permeated by the spirit of the gamelan and of African pitched percussion, but Reich was also inspired by the music of the Notre Dame school (see p.303). Despite its insistent rhythm, *Music for 18 Musicians* is intricate and graceful, shimmering like sunlight on rippling water.

⊙ Reich (ECM New Series 821 417-2).

The predominantly bright textures and instrumental colours of this piece are well captured by ECM, though the CD has less "top" than the original LP issue. In compensation, the ebb and flow of the bass clarinets has a more elemental swell. While Reich's writing frequently has a hypnotic effect, it is not "trance" music and the details are important. As well as performing and directing, the composer had a hand in mixing this recording.

DIFFERENT TRAINS

During childhood, Reich shuttled from coast to coast, visiting his divorced parents. He later realized that, as a Jew, he would have ridden very different trains if he had lived in occupied

Europe. Responding to a commission from the Kronos Quartet, he took fragments from the taped reminiscences of his governess, a Pullman porter, and survivors of the Holocaust, and hand-notated the speech rhythms and pitches for the quartet to play. The Kronos made four recordings (in concert, the quartet plays alongside tapes of the other parts), which were combined with train sounds and the speech fragments, sometimes in unison, sometimes echoing and commenting on the memories in an evocative, multilayered antiphony. As in *Come Out*, Reich weaves magical art from grim real-life events, but the complexities of *Different Trains* mark the emergence of a new form of music, which was developed in subsequent works like *The Cave* (1993) and *City Life* (1995).

⊙ Different Trains; Electric Counterpoint: Kronos Quartet; Metheny (Nonesuch 7559 79176-2 **)**

Reich deservedly won a Grammy Award for this disc. The Kronos excel with their characteristic blending of technical precision and emotional commitment. It's coupled with *Electric Counterpoint* (1987), a work written for jazz guitarist Pat Metheny, which generates a complex, pulsing tapestry of sound from the interaction between the soloist and up to twelve taped parts.

OTTORINO RESPIGHI

(1879–1936)

Such was the success of Verdi and Puccini, and of lesser figures such as Leoncavallo and Mascagni, that by 1900 Italy had almost no composers of instrumental music. A career in music meant a career in opera. The burden of restoring the nation's instrumental tradition fell largely on two men – Ferruccio Busoni (see p.94) and Ottorino Respighi.

Respighi was born in Bologna, where he trained as a violinist. In 1891 he became a student of the composer Giuseppe Martucci (a favourite of Toscanini) then in 1899 left for St Petersburg, where he began composition lessons with Stravinsky's teacher Rimsky-Korsakov, who heavily influenced his approach towards orchestration. He came back to Italy in 1903 and embarked upon a fairly successful career as a solo violinist, but his rapidly developing interest in Baroque and Classical instrumental music eventually led him to concentrate on writing rather than performing music. In 1913, after a stimulating spell in Berlin, he returned to Rome where he was appointed professor at the conservatory of Santa Cecilia. Nine years later, he became the conservatory's director, but resigned within two years in order to devote all his time to composing.

The trouble with Respighi's music is that it wears its influences on its sleeve, and of these influences none is more pronounced than Richard Strauss. The habitual classification of Respighi as the "Italian Strauss" was dismissed by the composer's widow in her biography of her husband, where she stoutly defended his preference for classical structure. There are indeed many works by Respighi in which he upholds the values of his illustrious predecessors, re-creates the logical lines of the eighteenth century, but much of Respighi's neo-classicism amounts to little more than skilful pastiche. For the foreseeable future, the popularity of his overblown orchestral poems is likely to obscure Respighi's affection for formal clarity.

ORCHESTRAL MUSIC

Respighi's most famous compositions are his three technicolour portrayals of Italy's capital city: *Fountains of Rome* (1916), *Pines of Rome* (1924) and *Roman Festivals* (1929). The grandiose and tuneful first part of this "Roman Triptych" is the best, in the sense that it is the most idiosyncratic, even if it does reflect the styles of Debussy, Ravel and, inevitably, Richard Strauss. Melodically, the *Pines of Rome* is heavy-going, but the orchestration is viviacious enough to overcome the cumbrousness of the material. The gaudy *Roman Festivals* has been attacked for its fascistic undertones, and it doesn't stand up to comparison with Strauss's earlier treatment of a similar subject in *Aus Italien*.

Respighi had a genuine interest in earlier music, adopting a modal approach for some of his concertos and making a realization of Monteverdi's *Orfeo*. Several of his most popular orchestral works are transcriptions of Renaissance or Baroque pieces – albeit given an extremely lush and somewhat Pre-Raphaelite tint. *Gli Uccelli* (The Birds) takes five such pieces (two by Pasquini, one by de Gallot, one by Rameau, and one anonymous) and dresses them up in a manner that all but disguises their origins. In *Three Botticelli Pictures* he applies a spot of "archaic" colour to three works inspired by and named after paintings by Botticelli – *Spring*, *The Adoration of the Magi* and *The Birth of Venus*. The second is the most effective of the three, an evocative miniature tone poem through which Respighi skilfully weaves the Epiphany hymn "O Come, O Come Emmanuel".

⊙ Fountains of Rome; Pines of Rome; Roman Festivals: Montréal Symphony Orchestra; Dutoit (Decca 410 415-2DH).

A splendid recording that conjures every shade of the score: from the nightingale singing through the pines of the Janiculum, to the thunder of the Roman legions marching down the Appian Way. Dutoit's tempi are light enough for the thick orchestral treatment not to sound crass, and the Montréal orchestra plays with great passion.

⊙ Fountains of Rome; Pines of Rome; Roman Festivals: Royal Philharmonic Orchestra; Bátiz (Naxos 8.550539).

This budget recording is not very far behind its full-price rival in terms of quality. A top-class orchestra and conductor give inspired readings, spontaneous and full of character.

⊙ The Birds; Three Botticelli Pictures: Orpheus Chamber Orchestra (Deutsche Grammophon 437 533-2DH; with *Ancient Airs and Dances, Suites Nos. 1 & 3*).

The Orpheus Chamber Orchestra is a consummate group, with a miraculous sense of ensemble and a beautifully ripe tone. These splendid performances, refreshingly bright and energetic, are all the more remarkable for having been played without a conductor.

VIOLIN SONATA

Respighi's predilection for classical form is perhaps best realized in the *Violin Sonata* of 1916–17, a work championed by many soloists (including Jascha Heifetz), but still little known. Written on a grand scale and demanding a lot of both performers, it is characterized throughout by beautiful melodies, especially in the lyrical opening movement. The finale, a showcase for Respighi's technical dexterity, is a brilliantly written passacaglia, in which a set of twenty variations is built upon a ground first established in a ten-bar bass passage.

⊙ Chung; Zimerman (Deutsche Grammophon 427 617-2; with Strauss, *Violin Sonata*).

The CD from Kyung-Wa Chung and Kristian Zimerman does great service to a pair of unjustly ignored sonatas, giving a highly involved account of Respighi's *Violin Sonata* and a mighty performance of Strauss's opulent work.

NIKOLAI RIMSKY-KORSAKOV

(1844–1908)

Rimsky-Korsakov is honoured as an inspirational teacher and as a fine orchestrator of other composers' music, but of his own compendious output only one orchestral score – *Sheherazade* – has made a really lasting impact outside of his native Russia.

Born into the aristocracy, he received a standard musical education, but his primary ambition was to enter the navy, which he did in 1856, aged only 12. Based in St Petersburg, he was deeply affected by the nationalistic music of Glinka and was encouraged by Balakirev to begin a symphony despite his tenuous grasp of the basics of harmony and tonality. In 1865, after two and a half years at sea, he applied himself to the study of theory and resumed work on his symphony; four years later he completed Dargomyzhsky's opera *The Stone Guest* – the first of several such second-hand projects. In 1871, though still ignorant of the fine details of compositional technique, he was appointed a professor of composition and orchestration at the St Petersburg Conservatory, and worked in private to obtain a better knowledge of the subject he was teaching. It was not until 1876, when he began editing a collection of Russian folk songs, that he perfected his technique and developed a genuine musical identity of his own.

From 1882 he began revising Mussorgsky's music (see p.280) and after Borodin's death in 1887 he assisted Glazunov in the completion of *Prince Igor* (see p.68), a project that coincided with the composition of his own *Sheherazade*. After attending the first Russian performance of Wagner's *Ring* cycle, he devoted most of his remaining years to opera. These years were interrupted by illness, but in 1896 he managed to

LEBRECHT COLLECTION

The last photo of Rimsky-Korsakov (right), with Glazunov

produce an orchestration and revision of Mussorgsky's *Boris Godunov*.

In 1905 he ran head first into the authorities for openly supporting the revolutionaries, and the subsequent ban on his music spurred him to compose his last opera, *The Golden Cockerel*. Based upon Pushkin's satirical attack on autocracy, this too was banned and was not performed until the year after his death.

Rimsky-Korsakov's music is famous not so much for what it says but for the manner in which it says it. He was a brilliant orchestrator and contributed as much to the development of the craft within Russia as did Berlioz in France. Like Berlioz he was liberated by his lack of proficiency at the piano, and thought primarily in terms of orchestral textures, developing a style that made adventurous use of primary instrumental colours, progressive harmonies and innovative part-writing. *Sheherezade* is one of the greatest works of nineteenth-century Russia, but some have argued that Rimsky-Korsakov's influence is his most important legacy. Had it not been for him, the music of Mussorgsky may have remained unknown, and his efforts to promote Glinka's nationalist ideals proved extremely effective. Of those he taught, Glazunov, Prokofiev and Stravinsky were the most significant; the last of the three said of him, "he made me the most precious gift of his unforgettable lessons", and in *The Firebird* (see p.413) produced a powerful testimony to the depth of Rimsky-Korsakov's impact.

SADKO

Rimsky-Korsakov regarded opera as "essentially the most enchanting and intoxicating of lies", and most of his operas are an exotic blend of supernatural elements within a Russian folk setting. Few productions take place outside of Russia, even though they contain some of his most original and thrilling music. *Sadko* (1896), based on an episode in the eleventh-century epic the *Novgorod Cycle*, he regarded as his best work in the genre, but even here the emphasis is on spectacle rather than coherent narrative, and the work is more of a sprawling musical pageant than an opera. Made up of seven tableaux, it tells of the minstrel Sadko, whose adventures take him from Novgorod to the bottom of the ocean, where he almost marries the Sea Princess Volkhova. The interplay between fantasy and reality is handled with dazzling skill: chromaticism delineates the fantasy domain; diatonicism, the earthly world. Above all else, *Sadko* is a virtuoso display of picture-painting in music, with Rimsky-Korsakov equally adept at evoking the sombre beauty of Lake Ilmen (Tableau II) as he is at capturing an undersea party and a riot of storms and hurricanes (Tableau VI).

O Galusin, Tarassova, Alexashkin, Tsidipova: Kirov Chorus and Orchestra; Gergiev (Philips 442 138-2; 3 CDs).

This live performance is remarkable for its closely knit ensemble singing: even so, the muscular tenor of Vladimir Galusin as Sadko really stands out. Valentina Tsidipova's Princess and Sergei Alexashkin's Sea King play their supernatural roles with athletic flair, doing much to make Tableau VI seem like the best thing the composer ever wrote. Valery Gergiev gives a splendidly colourful reading of the score and the performance is captured with fresh and vibrant sound.

SCHEHERAZADE

Rimsky-Korsakov's decision to use *The Arabian Nights* as the basis for an orchestral work was symptomatic of the attraction that neighbouring Islamic cultures held for many Russian composers. Each of the "Mighty Handful" (Cui, Balakirev, Borodin, Mussorgsky and Rimsky-Korsakov) wrote Orientalist music, and Rimsky-Korsakov's output is particularly dominated by the trend.

Lasting some forty minutes, *Scheherazade* (1888) contains an abundance of beautiful melodies which are carried on a sensual wash of sound. Different moods and pictures are conjured by the music, but the composer denied that *Scheherazade* was a programmatic piece – it was, he insisted, merely a suite of fairy-tale images of the Orient, rather than a sequence of episodes relating to the stories told by the young Scheherazade to delay her execution. The beguiling, sinuous violin solo in the third of the four movements, *The Young Prince and the Young Princess*, is perhaps the most effortlessly beautiful moment in a work which in places sounds like an anticipation of Debussy's hedonistic sound-world.

O London Symphony Orchestra; Mackerras (Telarc 80208; with *Capriccio espagnol*).

A stunningly vivid and immediate performance directed by Charles Mackerras. All of the work's exoticism and drama are successfully communicated, and there is a luxuriant sensuousness to the playing which seems entirely appropriate. Rimsky-Korsakov's brilliant evocation of Spain, *Capriccio Espagnol*, gets an equally committed reading.

◑ Royal Philharmonic Orchestra; Beecham (EMI CDC7 47717-2; with Borodin, *Polovtsian Dances*).

This classic account from the late 1950s still holds up very well indeed, thanks to Beecham's remarkable sensitivity to the work's light and shade. In his hands it becomes a brilliant piece of theatre music (though Rimsky-Korsakov is known to have hated dancers interpreting his work).

ANTAR

Antar, another exotic fairy-tale with a Middle Eastern setting, was actually begun before *Scheherazade* in 1868, but Rimsky-Korsakov made several revisions to its transforming it from his second symphony into "a poem, suite, fairy tale, story, anything you like, but not a symphony". The first of its four movements tells how the warrior poet Antar saves a gazelle who has been attacked by a great bird. The gazelle turns out to be Gul Nazar, Queen of Palmyra, who promises him the three great joys of live – revenge, power and love – which are then depicted in the following three movements. The languid "big tune" that recurs in all three movements is employed somewhat in the manner of Tchaikovsky, though Rimsky-Korsakov lacked his colleague's febrile intensity and, if anything, rather underworks its potential. Nevertheless this is a beautiful piece, full of the subtle instrumental colouring that made Rimsky-Korsakov so revered as an orchestrator, even though it ultimately lacks the thrilling impact of *Scheherazade*.

O Philharmonia; Svetlanov (Hyperion CDA 66399; with *Russian Easter Festival Overture*).

Exquisite playing from the Philharmonia, enhanced by Hyperion's wonderfully natural sound. The veteran Russian conductor Yevgeny Svetlanov concentrates on colouristic detail and creating a genuinely fairy-tale atmosphere. It is coupled with a lively performance of the sparkling *Russian Easter Festival Overture*, a work meant to convey the joyous excitement and solemnity of the Easter morning service.

JOAQUÍN RODRIGO

(1902–)

Outside of his native Spain, Joaquín Rodrigo is one of twentieth-century music's one-hit wonders, although the beautiful *Concierto de Aranjuez* (1939) for guitar and orchestra is quite some hit. Inspired by the beautiful Rococo palace at Aranjuez in southern Spain, it succeeds in recreating something of the elegance and formality of Spain in the eighteenth century. Its slow movement, in particular, has assumed an almost talismanic popularity and has even inspired a brilliant jazz tribute by Gil Evans and Miles Davis,

Sketches of Spain, as well as a surprisingly effective version by the Grimethorpe Colliery Band.

Blind from the age of 3, Rodrigo revealed an innate talent for music in childhood and was sent to study composition with Francisco Antich in Valencia (1920–23). He later became a pupil of Dukas (see p.127) at the École Normale de Musique in Paris, where he met and received encouragement from his compatriot Manuel de Falla (see p.141). Following his marriage to the Turkish pianist Victoria Kamhi in 1933, he returned briefly to Spain but then, on receiving a grant, went back to Paris to study musicology. With the outbreak of the Spanish Civil War in 1936 he decided to stay in Paris, returning at the end of hostilities. Rodrigo's politics are something of a grey area. It has been argued by his friends that he was a canny individual who merely paid lip service to Franco's repressive regime; outward signs seem to indicate that his views were in accordance with those of Franco's government, and there is no doubt that he was the musician most favoured by the administration after the premiere of the *Concierto de Aranjuez* in 1940.

Thereafter he was firmly esconced as Spain's leading composer. In 1944 he was appointed music adviser to Spanish Radio, and two years later was appointed to the Manuel de Falla chair, which was created for him at the University of Madrid. Ever since he has led a full life as both an academic and a composer, though he has tended to repeat the musical formula of the *Concierto de Aranjuez* in his later concertos for piano, violin, cello and flute. But, conceding his conservatism in comparison with composers such as Falla, Rodrigo nonetheless did Spanish music an important service by helping to preserve the country's musical identity following the traumas of the Civil War.

THE GUITAR CONCERTOS

The guitar is the instrument that Rodrigo is most associated with and although he never learned to play it he had the advantage of close associations with guitarists of the calibre of Regino Sainz de la Maza and Segovia. His musical nationalism is in a different mould from that of Falla, Albéniz and Granados – the big three of modern Spanish music. Whereas they embarked on a deep exploration of the forms of Spanish popular and art music, and transmuted those forms into their compositions, Rodrigo's approach is more generalized, and he is generally content to create attractive melodies and rhythms that generally evoke Spain's sunny atmosphere and traditional culture without recourse to specific folk rhythms. The *Concierto de Aranjuez* is suffused with a Mediterranean spirit, and an underlying nostalgia for an older and more chivalrous Spain. This conservatism is even more marked in the beautifully poised *Fantasia para un gentilhombre* (1954), in which Rodrigo pays homage to the eighteenth century by transforming a selection of dances, collected by the Baroque guitarist Gaspar Sanz, into what is in effect a guitar concerto. The "gentilhombre" is the work's dedicatee, Segovia.

◑ **Concierto de Aranjuez; Concierto madrigal; Fantasia para un gentilhombre: Romero, Romero; Academy of St Martin-in-the-Fields; Marriner** (Philips 432 828-2).

The Spanish guitarists Pepe and Angel Romero deliver fine performances of three of Rodrigo's most celebrated works – the flamenco quality of Pepe Romero's playing could not be more perfect for the *Concierto de Aranjuez*. The balance between soloists and orchestra is highly satisfying, with every detail finely etched.

◑ **Concierto de Aranjuez; Fantasia para un gentilhombre: Bream; Chamber Orchestra of Europe; Gardiner; RCA Victor Chamber Orchestra; Brouwer** (RCA 09026 61611-2; with *Invocacion y danza* and *Tres Piezas españolas*).

Volume 28 in RCA's Julian Bream Edition, given over to works by Rodrigo, makes an excellent alternative to the above disc in what is an increasingly crowded field. Bream is not so hard-edged a player as Romero – his are dreamier, more romantic interpretations, with a distinctively ripe tone.

GIOACCHINO ROSSINI

(1792–1868)

Italian operatic life during the first half of the nineteenth century was dominated by one man – Gioacchino Rossini. Between *Demetrio e Polibio*, written before 1809, and *Guillaume Tell*, less than twenty years later, he completed nearly forty operas, taking the first decisive steps towards the establishment of Italian music drama. Donizetti and Bellini worked in his shadow, and it was only when Verdi reached maturity in the late 1850s that Rossini was replaced at the centre of Italian operatic life. His impact upon the development of opera was immense: he was, for example, the first to do away with unaccompanied recitative, thus making the opera a continuous musical fabric, and he was the first to write out all the embellishments for his singers, not leaving anything to chance. But the key to his success was the sheer tunefulness of his music, a quality which seemed to cause him no effort – "Give me a shopping list and I'll set it to music", he once said.

Praise for Rossini was not universal, however. Berlioz was speaking for many non-Italians when he raged against Rossini's conveyor-belt creations: "Rossini's melodic cynicism, his contempt for dramatic expression and good sense, his endless repetition of a single form of cadence, his eternal puerile crescendo and brutal bass drum, exasperated me to such a point that I was blind to the brilliant qualities of his genius, even in his masterpiece, the *Barber*, exquisitely scored though it is." Making an exception for the enduring popularity of the *Barber of Seville*, Berlioz's opinion has become increasingly common, for Rossini's operas do indeed seem simple after Wagner or Strauss. However, this simplicity is part of Rossini's strength. There is a directness and immediacy to his work that is missing from that of his Italian predecessors and contemporaries, whose plots seem ludicrously entangled alongside Rossini's, and whose characters appear bloodless in comparison.

Rossini was born the son of a trumpeter and a singer. Some time soon after his eighth birthday he composed his first opera and his first commission came before his eighteenth birthday. In 1812 he had a work performed at La Scala, Italy's most prestigious opera house, and in the following year *Tancredi* and *L'italiana in Algeri* established his name outside Italy. Before long he had been appointed music director of the opera houses of Naples and was producing an enormous amount of music for them, including *Otello* and *Il Barbiere*, *La Cenerentola*, *La gazza ladra* and *Mosè in Egitto*.

In 1822 he married, and soon after visited Vienna where, reputedly, he met Beethoven. Two years later, aged only 32, he moved to Paris, where he composed the epic *Guillaume Tell* (1829). Whether from doubts about his own powers or sheer exhaustion, he composed no more operas. He did write the extraordinary *Stabat Mater*, but for all its acclaim it did not inspire Rossini to return to full-time composition. Perhaps with the success of Verdi and the advances of Wagner, he thought himself incapable of producing any new opera worthy of his name and reputation.

○ Viva Rossini (Testament SBT 1008).

This album of classic Rossini recordings from between 1903 and 1940 features performances that put to shame nearly all modern singers, and makes a fine introduction to Rossini's operas. Tito Ruffo's grand and idiosyncratic singing of *Largo al factotum* ("Figaro là, Figaro qua" et cetera) beggars belief, but an even more astounding performance is Luisa Tetrazzini's agile singing of *Una voce poco fa* from the same opera. Also on this CD are Giovanni Martinelli and Giuseppe de Luca singing the thrilling Act Two duet from *Guillaume Tell*, plus Enrico Caruso and Francesco Tamagno, Verdi's first Otello.

◑ Fourteen Overtures: National Philharmonic Orchestra; Chailly (Decca 443 250-2; 2 CDs).

The overtures to Rossini's operas are among the most sparkling ever written and create a real frisson of excitement when heard before an opera. Unsurprisingly they are his most popular music and function perfectly satisfactorily out of a theatrical context. Chailly directs scintillating performances which include some obscurer ones as well as old favourites like *William Tell* and *The Barber of Seville*.

IL BARBIERE DI SIVIGLIA

Operatic folklore has it that *Il Barbiere di Siviglia*, Rossini's comic masterpiece, was composed in just a fortnight, a feat of which he was certainly capable, though the music is so original and the characterizations so rounded that the tale is unlikely. Nowadays it's one of the most popular Italian operas, but it wasn't an immediate hit – indeed the first performance, in Rome in February 1816, was one of operatic history's greatest disasters. Everything that could have gone wrong did go wrong, and by the second act the music was inaudible above the din of the audience. As the critic Castil-Blaze wrote afterwards, "All the whistlers of Italy seemed to have given themselves a rendezvous for this performance".

The source of the libretto is a play by Beaumarchais, covering events in the life of the libidinous Duke of Almaviva – the philandering aristocrat of the later Beaumarchais work that became the text for Mozart's *Le Nozze di Figaro* (see p.268). The world of *Il Barbiere* doesn't have the ambiguities and depths of *Le Nozze*, but as a straightforward, life-affirming comic opera it has no equal. Each of its arias is a highlight, and some of them are truly astonishing – Figaro's *Largo al factotum* is of course one of opera's great bravura set pieces, while Almaviva's *Ecco ridente* is one of the most beautiful things Rossini ever wrote. A characteristic device used to startling effect throughout the opera is the "Rossinian Crescendo", whereby the composer takes a theme and repeats it, each time at a higher pitch and with a larger orchestral accompaniment.

◑ **Gobbi, Callas, Alva, Ollendorff, Zaccaria, Carturan, Carlin; Philharmonia Chorus & Orchestra; Galliera** (EMI CDS7 47634-8; 2 CDs).

Perhaps the finest studio performance of *Il Barbiere* boasts the sublime partnership of Maria Callas and Tito Gobbi. The latter's Figaro is a deeply personal piece of vocal characterization with a waggish charm that all but overcomes the restrictions of the studio. Callas is only slightly less convincing (but then, so is the role of Rosina, the Count's love object), and Luigi Alva – a marvellous Rossini tenor – sings Count Almaviva with great elegance and charm, although at times he is rushed by the conductor. It may be old-fashioned in its romanticism, but this set has stood the test of time.

◑ **Berganza, Ausensi, Benelli, Corena, Ghiaurov; Naples Scarlatti Chorus and Orchestra; Varviso** (Decca 417 164-2DM2; 2 CDs).

Berganza's two readings of Rosina (1964, 1971) are generally thought of as the best-sung on record. This, the earlier version, is perhaps slightly the better: her warm and generous mezzo is ideal for the part and she tackles the coloratura with skill and finesse, dropping in a few high Cs for good measure. Her supporting cast is strong: Ugo Benelli gives a cultured portrayal of Almaviva, while Manuel Ausensi's wild Figaro introduces a devil-may-care frisson that's unrivalled even by Gobbi. Varviso's conducting is not the most exciting, but he has a fine ear for detail.

LA CENERENTOLA

Stendhal referred to Rossini's music as "seldom sublime, but never tiresome", a description that perfectly fits *La Cenerentola*, a semi-comic homily on the value of true love and the speciousness of rank, inspired by Charles Perrault's *Cinderella*. Perhaps the chief reason for its comparative lack of popularity is the florid writing for the title role, a part that demands the combination of a contralto's range with a coloratura's agility. Once in a while a suitable voice comes along – as has happened recently with the arrival of Cecilia Bartoli – and *La Cenerentola* sneaks back into the repertoire, but it's always going to be an opera to hear on disc rather than see onstage. In terms of the proportion of time allotted to them, ensembles predominate over arias in *La Cenerentola*, but, for all Rossini's concentration on multi-voice writing, the main attraction is the title role, one of the finest female roles in Italian opera.

○ **Bartoli, Matteuzi, Corbelli, Dara; Chorus & Orchestra of the Teatro Comunale di Bologna; Chailly** (Decca 436 902-2; 2 CDs).

Chailly is an inspired conductor of Rossini and in Cecilia Bartoli he has one of the great voices of recent years in a role that completely suits her light and flexible voice. Much more than her recording of *The Barber of Seville*, this is a performance that really works dramatically.

○ **Berganza, Alva, Capecchi, Montarsolo; Scottish Opera Chorus; London Symphony Orchestra; Abbado** (Deutsche Grammophon 423 861-2GH2; 2 CDs).

Abbado's recording for DG boasts the incandescent singing of Teresa Berganza, who transcends mere technical security to give her character life. Abbado and the LSO tend to smash their way through Rossini's score, but for Berganza's singing alone Abbado's recording is worth the money.

GUILLAUME TELL

Rossini's last and grandest opera, *Guillaume Tell*, like *Il Barbiere*, was not immediately popular, but unlike *Il Barbiere* it has never established a toehold on the opera-house circuit. The chief reason for this is that *Tell* is very uneven and far too long, as Rossini himself acknowledged: on being confonted by an enthusiast who had recently seen a performance of the second act, the composer replied, "What, the whole of it?" Performed in full it would last nearly five hours, and it still has lethargic patches in the extensively cut and revised version that's usually performed today. Nonetheless, this serious-minded celebration of Switzerland's great folk hero is worth the effort. Rossini knew well beforehand that it was to be his last opera, and he intended it to be his masterpiece – and in dramatic terms it is, for in its large-scale coherence it looks forward to the through-composed operas of Verdi.

The overture is especially powerful: the very start, scored for cello sextet, is one of Rossini's greatest inspirations but it is the trumpet theme, a third of the way through, that you'll recognize – it was the theme tune for both *The Lone Ranger* and for the *William Tell* TV series. Act One has an exciting finale but things get even better in the second act, which boasts a glorious aria for the female lead, *Ces jours, qu'ils ont osé proscrire*. Act Three is unbearably dull, but the final act, beautifully introduced by the magnificent tenor aria *Asile héréditaire*, is the opera's crowning glory, culminating in the Swiss nation's prayer of thanksgiving for the liberation of their land.

○ **Milnes, Freni, Pavarotti, Ghiaurov, Tomlinson, Jones, Connell; Ambrosian Opera Chorus; National Philharmonic Orchestra; Chailly** (Decca 417 154-2DH4; 4 CDs).

Rossini composed *Guillaume Tell* in France, in French for a French audience, and it should be performed in French if the opera is to receive a fair trial. Due to the absence of any great French singing talent, recent recordings have had to rely upon Italian artists and their dubious pronunciation, or – more usually – on a translation. This set, the finest of the latter category, is very good indeed, boasting an exceptional cast and highly tuned sound: Freni, Pavarotti and Tomlinson in particular are superb.

STABAT MATER

Just as Verdi's *Requiem* was his only major composition during a long period of inactivity, so Rossini's *Stabat Mater* was his first major composition for twelve years and the last he ever wrote. During a journey to Spain in 1831, Rossini was commissioned by Fernandez Varela to set the text of the Stabat Mater. He completed half the score before asking a friend to take over. This friend, Giovanni Tadolini, did as he was asked but ten years later, under pressure from his Parisian publisher, Rossini replaced Tadolini's work with his own. This revised draft was first performed in Paris on January 7, 1842, and was received with wild enthusiasm – an appropriate response to a composition that is not so much devotional music as lyric opera in liturgical attire. Leaving aside considerations of piety, the *Stabat Mater* is brilliantly written and contains some superb vocal music, notably the tenor's melodically sumptuous (but inappropriately jaunty) *Cujus Animam* and the unaccompanied quartet, *Quando corpus morietur*.

◑ **Lorengar, Minton, Pavarotti, Sotin; London Symphony Chorus & Orchestra; Kertesz** (Decca 417 766-2DM).

Decca assembled a fine cast for this recording: Pavarotti navigates the D flat at the end of *Cujus Animam* with great flair and is in magnificent form throughout, while Lorengar and Minton tone down their big voices to make light but heartfelt contributions to this remarkable piece of music. The overall performance is directed with equal measures of sobriety and ebullience by Kertesz, and Decca's engineers have produced an even and natural recorded sound.

POUL RUDERS

(1949–)

The music of Poul Ruders, Denmark's leading contemporary composer, has an elemental quality that is powerfully communicative. Largely self-taught, he uses the raw material of instrumental sound like building bricks, fashioning it – even in small-scale works – into strong bold statements in which structure is always clearly visible. Absence of complex thematic development can sometimes make his method seem reductive, but when it works – as it does most effectively in his 1989 *Symphony* – the result has the compelling eloquence and rugged primitivism of a prophetic utterance.

Born at Ringsted in central Zealand, Ruders' first sustained contact with music was as a chorister in the Copenhagen Boys Choir. He later trained as an organist and his first-hand familiarity with church music influenced his own writing, which often contains echoes of, or direct quotations from, liturgical music of the Renaissance and Baroque periods. Equally important was the impact on his musical imagination made by the composers of the Polish avant-garde in the 1960s and 1970s, especially Penderecki, whose *Threnody for the Victims of Hiroshima* (which Ruders heard when he was 17) uses large blocks of sound in a strikingly graphic fashion.

In the 1980s Ruders became a regular visitor to the US with a series of guest lectureships at various American universities. His first major work, *Manhattan Abstraction* (1982), dates from this period. Like much of his music, it has a strong visual dimension, being inspired by "the New York profile seen from Liberty Island, one icy cold January day". A definite sense of the city as both beautiful and repellent is expressed by way of starkly juxtaposed types of sound – harsh versus lyrical, heavy and block-like versus light and delicate, etc. It's a technique which can be heard in other orchestral works, such as the apocalyptic *Thus Saw St John* (1984), in which the fearsomely gyrating percussion of the opening moments suddenly subsides into an eerie stasis of extended chords.

SYMPHONY

A BBC Proms commission of 1989 resulted in one of Ruders' most striking and powerful statements. Subtitled with a quotation from Goethe's *Egmont*, "Himmelhoch jauchzend – zum Tode betrübt" ("To heaven rejoicing – cast down unto death"), it is an extreme work (it needs a large orchestra and extended percussion section) which is epic and indeed visionary in its aspirations. It demands a high level of virtuosity from the orchestral players, above all in its opening, where the incessant scurrying of every instrument conjures up a mood of anarchic, cosmic joy – a mood underlined by a quotation from the opening chorus of Bach's *Christmas Oratorio*. This gives way to a more contemplative section, evoking vast empty spaces, in which a sense of vulnerablity prevails despite an attempt to return to the movement's joyous opening. Tranquillity pervades the extraordinary second movement, which uses just two alternating chords (like slow regular breathing) to create a feel of time suspended, eventually interrupted by a high solo violin redolent of a frail human presence. A frenetic and short Scherzo moves straight into the last movement marked "Maschera funerale" (Funeral Masque), a nightmarish vision of long suspended chords and a steady inexorable pulse which gradually thins down into near-nothingness save for the final whisperings of a lone violin.

⊙ Symphony; Gong; Tundra; Thus Saw St John: Danish National Radio Symphony Orchestra; Segerstam (Chandos CHAN 9179).

This disc gives a pretty clear picture of Ruders' strengths and weaknesses as a composer. The sound quality is bright and natural and the performances are absolutely thrilling, but even an orchestra of this quality cannot make *Thus Saw St John* sound like anything other than a bombastic melodrama. *Gong* is a rather more effective piece, full of unexpectedly brilliant sounds, but it lacks the coherence of the *Symphony*, which under the vigorous direction of Segerstam has a coherence and a dynamic energy that is truly breathtaking.

CAMILLE SAINT-SAËNS

(1835–1921)

S

A lot of composers began as freakish children, but by any standards Saint-Saëns was an extreme case. As a two-year-old he could read and write, and was picking out melodies on the piano. Shortly after his third birthday he began composing, and by the age of 5 had given his first piano recital. At 7 he was reading Latin, studying botany and developing what was to become an eighty-year interest in lepidoptery. As an encore after his formal debut as a concert pianist, the 10-year-old Camille offered to play any of Beethoven's 32 sonatas from memory. In short, his childhood suggested Mozartian potential, and yet it was a potential that was never realized. Saint-Saëns once remarked that he lived "in music like a fish in water" and that composing was as natural as "an apple tree producing apples". And there lay the problem. As with Mendelssohn, the technique came so easily to him that it virtually extinguished the spark of originality.

That said, for many years he was considered by many to be France's greatest musical revolutionary, though his reputation grew more from his outspoken support of other composers' music – especially Wagner's – than from any work of his own. As well as promoting contemporary music, Saint-Saëns threw his energies into researching the work of his forerunners. Along with Mendelssohn, he was one of the first to re-establish the music of Bach (converting the sceptical Berlioz in the process) and he did much to restore Mozart to his rightful place, being the first to play a complete

GUS ONG

cycle of the piano concertos. Handel was another unfashionable composer to engage Saint-Saëns' attention, and (as with Berlioz) Gluck held a fascination that lasted most of his life.

By the time Saint-Saëns reached his mid-fifties, the past had won the upper hand over the present. Embittered, ill-tempered and restless, he became the arch-traditionalist, opposing the progressive music of Debussy and Ravel, bellowing outrage at the first performance of *The Rite of Spring*. And yet, for all his reactionary pomposity, he was one of the first neo-classicists, embodying many of the finest traditional qualities of French music – neatness, clarity, elegance and dignity. His best epitaph is the rueful one he wrote for himself – "I ran after the chimera of purity of style and perfection of form."

SAMSON ET DALILA

Of Saint-Saëns' thirteen operas, only *Samson et Dalila* has achieved any lasting popularity. Composed in the 1870s, this retelling of the biblical story was originally planned as an oratorio along the lines of Mendelssohn's *Elijah* (see p.253), which Saint-Saëns so admired, but it was cast as an opera on the advice of his librettist. The dramatization is not the most enthralling example of operatic stagecraft, but *Samson et Dalila* was a huge hit, holding its own for a long time against the tide of Wagnerism then rising in France. Its qualities are modest but genuine: the characters are tightly drawn, the orchestration has real finesse, and both leads are supplied with memorable, tuneful music – the last being the quality that attracted Liszt, who secured the work's first production in Weimar in 1877.

◑ **Vickers, Gorr, Blanc, Diakov: René Duclos Chorus; Paris Opéra Orchestra; Prêtre** (EMI CDS7 47895-2; 2 CDs).

A marvellous performance from the Canadian tenor Jon Vickers in a role for which he was famous. The power and commitment of his singing is staggering and he brings a genuinely tragic grandeur to his death scene. Rita Gorr as Dalila wisely chooses not to go over the top – it is her dignity as much as her sexuality that conquers the hero. Prêtre's reading is highly impassioned and there are few more epic performances of French opera on CD.

SYMPHONY NO. 3

Saint-Saëns' most popular orchestral work, the *Symphony No. 3*, was dedicated to the memory of Liszt and received its first performance in London in 1886. An upbeat, expressive work that revels in German bombast and French colour, it has stayed in the repertoire mainly on the strength of its last movement, with its resonant organ part – hence its subtitle, "The Organ Symphony". The preceding three movements are less expansive, but the symphony as a whole is still one of the most entertaining written by a French composer, and gives an accurate picture of Saint-Saëns' strengths.

O Preston; Berlin Philharmonic Orchestra; Levine (Deutsche Grammophon 419 617-2GH; with Dukas, *The Sorcerer's Apprentice*).

Levine's account, with Simon Preston, may be a little over-aggressive for some tastes but it is undoubtedly tremendously exciting. It is also very well engineered, with the last movement in particular a tribute to the wonders of digital recording.

◑ **Hurford; Montréal Symphony Orchestra; Dutoit** (Decca 430 720-2; with *Le Carnaval des animaux*).

A more subtle performance, and a cheaper one, comes from Dutoit and another English organist, Peter Hurford. Here the emphasis is less on sonic spectacle – though the last-movement organ entry still packs a real punch – than on clarity and momentum.

LE CARNAVAL DES ANIMAUX

It is a wonderful irony that Saint-Saëns, a man obsessed with his standing as a serious composer, should now be known chiefly for a piece that was dashed off as a joke. Written to entertain himself and his friends while on holiday in 1886, *Le Carnaval des animaux* – his "Grand Zoological Fantasy" – was never intended to be published, and Saint-Saëns forbade its performance during his lifetime. The carnival is in part a musical menagerie, caricaturing some thirteen types of "animal" (including *People with Long Ears* and *Pianists*), of which the thirteenth (*The Swan*), is the best known and most beautiful. It's also a barbed parody of the music of some of his contemporaries, including Offenbach, Mendelssohn, Berlioz, Rossini and, thankfully, himself.

◑ **Rogé, Ortiz; London Sinfonietta; Dutoit** (Decca 430 720-2DM; with *Symphony No. 3*).

There are over thirty recordings of *Le Carnaval des animaux*, most of them sounding very much like the others. Dutoit's performance has the merit of sharpening the satire, while pianists Rogé and Ortiz add to the flair. It's coupled with a muscular version of the third symphony (see above).

VIOLIN CONCERTO NO. 3

Composed in 1880 for the Spanish virtuoso Pablo de Sarasate, the *Violin Concerto No. 3* is a stunningly dramatic piece, which opens with one of Saint-Saëns' most striking melodies, a gypsy-like theme on the lowest of the instrument's strings. This hammer blow of an opening leads into a less characterful Adagio, but the finale is a stupendous creation that makes inordinate demands on the soloist.

O Wei; Philharmonia; Bakels (ASV CDDCA680; with Bruch, *Concerto No. 1*).

Xue-Wei's recording comes closest to fulfilling the music's dramatic potential. He uses gut strings, producing a fuller sound than that produced by the routine steel strings, and his playing is the most natural and instinctive performance currently available.

PIANO CONCERTOS NOS. 2 & 4

Saint-Saëns' *Piano Concerto No. 2* epitomizes much of the composer's output, being pleasant on the ear and murder on the fingers. It was also, typically, a quick job – commissioned in 1868 by the great Russian pianist Anton Rubinstein, it was finished in just seventeen days. Unusually for Saint-Saëns, it opens with an unorthodox gesture, a cadenza that runs into a particularly sumptuous first theme. Thereafter, things run pretty well to pattern: as with the third violin concerto, the central movement is the work's weak spot, but the Presto is a steamroller of a finale, demanding heroic virtuosity from the soloist.

⊙ **Biret; Philharmonia; Loughran** (Naxos 8550334; with *Concerto No. 4*).

Idel Biret's enthusiastic account displays great technical assurance and sense of forward momentum, with James Loughran giving more than adequate support. The delightful fourth concerto gets an equally spirited reading.

◑ **Rubinstein; Symphony of the Air; Wallenstein** (RCA 09026 61496-2; with Franck's *Symphonic Variations* & Liszt's *Piano Concerto No. 1*).

A legendary performance from Artur Rubinstein, a champion of this concerto, who recorded it several times. This is the best of them, and it still sounds fresh and alive some forty years on.

VIOLIN SONATA NO. 1

Most of Saint-Saëns's chamber music is doggedly formulaic, but the *Violin Sonata No. 1* (1885) shows him throwing off the shackles, especially in the last movement where for once he sets out to thrill. It's a brilliant if technically cruel moto-perpetuo, in which pianist and violinist really have to battle to stay together – an entertaining antidote to Saint-Saëns' habitual propriety.

O Wei; Lenehan (ASV CDDCA892; with *Violin Sonata No. 2, Berceuse* & *Introduction and Rondo Capriccioso*).

Xue-Wei proves himself as persuasive an advocate of the violin sonatas as of the *Violin Concerto No. 3* (see p.347). In partnership with pianist John Lenehan he finds just the right balance between the work's emotional overdrive and its technical virtuosity.

ERIK SATIE

(1866–1925)

Though dismissed in some quarters as a eccentric lightweight, Erik Satie was one of the most influential figures in twentieth-century music. Ravel never tired of paying tribute to a man he called simply "the precursor", and the young Debussy – for a time his closest friend – was encouraged by Satie to make the final break with Wagnerism and dispense with the heavy romantic "sauerkraut". Essentially a solitary figure, eking out a living as a pianist in the cafés of Montmartre (dressed always in a grey velvet suit and bowler hat), Satie became famed among the cognoscenti of Paris chiefly for his quirky piano pieces, with their mystifying titles and whimsical performance directions. Compositions such as *Pieces to Make You Run Away*, *True Flabby Preludes* and *Bureaucratic Sonata*, published with such unhelpful tips as "Wonder about Yourself" and "Be Clairvoyant", make Satie a forerunner of Dada and Surrealism, while their combination of wistfulness and satirical wit give them a unique – but distinctly French – flavour.

From the mid-1910s Satie was championed as the supreme anti-Romantic by that arch-trendsetter Jean Cocteau, with whom he collaborated on a ballet. *Parade* (1917) was the Russian Ballet's next big scandal after the furore caused by *The Rite of Spring* (1913). This time round, it was not so much Satie's music or Cocteau's scenario that people objected to so much as Picasso's three-dimensional Cubist costumes. The action took in front of a fairground booth and involves three showmen and their artists – a Chinese juggler, a pair of acrobats and a "Little American Girl". Satie presents them as a series of rather wittily impassive vignettes, "an everyday music" Cocteau claimed, which drew on popular music-hall style and found room for the sound of a typewriter, a revolver, sirens and a xylophone made up of bottles.

Satie himself was largely unstinting in his support of young musicians, most notably the group known as Les Six, two of whom – Poulenc and Milhaud – saw in his independence of traditional musical models a position to emulate. Satie collaborated with Cocteau (and Picasso) again on another entertainment, *Les Aventures de Mercure* in 1924, but then, for his final ballet *Relâche*, threw in his lot with the Surrealists. *Relâche* is the term used when a theatre is closed between performances, and when the audience turned up for the "first night" they found the theatre closed (the performance actually occurred three days later). The nonsensical scenario and designs (the set consisted of hundreds of suspended gramophone records) were by Francis Picabia, and a short film by René Clair (in which Satie appeared) was shown in the interval. As with *Parade*, the music is profoundly inoffensive and indeed somewhat innocuous.

Sadly, just as his star was really on the rise his health began to fail him, due in no small part to the strong drink he consumed in vast quantities over the years. He died of cirrhosis of the liver at the age of 59. Among the tributes heaped on him was this one from Darius Milhaud: "The purity of his art, his horror of all concessions, his contempt for money and his ruthless attitude toward the critics were a marvellous example for us all."

In fact Satie's legacy was more profound than Milhaud's words suggest. The timeless, directionless quality of his music was an important influence on John Cage (see p.97); his idea of *musique d'ameublement* (furniture music) anticipated Muzak by some fifty years; while the simplicity and repetition of much of his work (*Vexations* requests that the same chord be played 840 times without any variation) provided Minimalism with an inspiring historical precedent.

PIANO MUSIC

Satie's mysteriously poignant piano pieces, which make up about three-quarters of his output, are his most representative music. Their frequently absurd titles often have a parodic intention (sometimes poking gentle fun at some of the more absurdly poetic titles of Debussy's piano pieces). But despite their apparent frivolity these miniatures are often deeply lyrical, with a sound-world derived partly from the café-cabarets in which Satie played but also from his interest in the modal music of medieval Christianity. This emphasis on modal techniques and austere "white-key" harmonies is heard to particularly good effect in his two most famous sets of pieces, the languid *Trois Gymnopédies* (1888) and the haunting *Gnossiennes* (1890), which predate Debussy's exploration of such harmonic resources by some fifteen years. Debussy so much admired the *Gymnopédies* that he made orchestrations of two of them, emphasizing their dreamy quality but undermining their quirky incisiveness which is best rendered in their original piano form.

O Avant-dernières pensées and other pieces: Rogé (Decca 421 713-2).

O Gnossiennes, Gymnopédies and other pieces: Rogé (Decca 410220-2).

Pascal Rogé's two recordings of Satie's piano music perfectly capture the composer's mixture of knowingness and naïvety, drawing you into this unique sound-world in performances that are full of elegant poise. Rogé is just as successful at bringing out the underlying melancholy of a set like the six *Gnossiennes* as he is at catching the sharp wit of a collection like *Véritables préludes flasques*. If you want to pick just one CD as a sampler of Satie's music, go for the collection featuring the *Gnossiennes* and *Gymnopédies*.

ALESSANDRO SCARLATTI

(1660–1725)

Alessandro Scarlatti has become the obscure Scarlatti, but he was a figure of great historical importance. One of the major composers of opera before the generation of Handel and Gluck, he was immensely successful during his lifetime, when numerous editions of his works were published and his operas were frequently produced throughout Italy.

He began his musical studies in Rome with Carissimi (see p.99), under whose guidance he composed his first opera, *Gli equivoci nel sembiante*, in 1679. During the next 46 years he composed more than one hundred stage works (the precise number isn't known) and became a seminal figure in the world of opera seria – the principal operatic genre of the early eighteenth century. After working for the Queen of Sweden as *maestro di cappella*, he settled in Naples in 1684 where he was employed by the Spanish viceroy. He remained there until 1702 and for the remainder of his life floated in and out of various court appointments.

Scarlatti established Naples as the centre of Italian operatic life and made several technical advances to the genre, such as his development of the da capo aria, his skilful use of instrumental textures, and his adoption of subjects less high-flown than the mythological themes so loved by Monteverdi. Yet he was not a great innovator – rather, his work looks back to the declamatory Venetian tradition of Monteverdi rather then towards the dramatic school that followed. It was perhaps indicative of a recognition of his fundamentally conservative nature that Scarlatti composed fewer and fewer operas from the 1700s, and the overall pallidness of his style isn't likely to win many admirers nowadays. At the moment there is not a single complete Scarlatti opera in the catalogue.

But Scarlatti was also a major composer of other types of vocal music closely related to opera. He composed over six hundred cantatas - a genre which was to opera what the short story is to the novel. He also wrote about 34 oratorios, which were essentially sacred operas (though usually scored for fewer voices) – several of which were written during his time in Rome when the pope had placed a ban on the performance of opera.

THE MOTETS

Scarlatti's sacred works, which form a relatively small but important part of his output, were mostly composed during his time in Rome. As well as oratorios, he also composed a number of Masses and about one hundred motets. Of the latter, some are polyphonic and in a self-consciously archaic style while others (often for solo voice) employ the expressive range and variety that you find in the cantatas and operas, with the text divided into short musically contrasted sections. The *Salve Regina*, a hymn to the Virgin for two voices, falls into this category. Both the vocal and the instrumental writing is ornate and sometimes virtuosic and there's an effective but sparing use of dissonance. But above all it's the sense of a personally felt reaction to the words that makes such an impact – a musical emotionalism that was to be a major influence on Pergolesi's even more extreme *Stabat Mater* (see p.302).

⊙ **Lesne, Gens; Il Seminario Musicale** (Virgin Classics VC 5 45103 2).

This is the most wholly satisfying recording of Scarlatti's music to have appeared in recent years. Countertenor Gérard Lesne is something of a specialist in Italian Baroque vocal repertoire, and he emphasizes the music's warmth and sensuousness without overdoing it. He sings three solo motets and is joined by Véronique Gens for a moving account of the *Salve Regina*.

THE CANTATAS

In the seventeenth century the term "cantata" simply meant music that was sung as opposed to music that was played (sonata). During Scarlatti's lifetime the Italian cantata developed into a short dramatic scene, often for just one voice, that employed recitative, aria and arioso (a more lyrical recitative). Cantatas were privately performed by leading operatic stars before an aristocratic, and therefore classically educated, audience. Their brevity allowed for a concentration and emotional intensity for which Scarlatti became renowned, and which was heightened by expressive instrumental accompaniment (including an introductory sinfonia) close in feeling to the trio sonatas of Scarlatti's colleague Corelli (see p.111).

⊙ **Cantatas Vol. 1: Brandes; Arcadian Academy; McGegan** (Conifer Classics 75605 51293 2).

A number of recordings of Scarlatti's cantatas has appeared in recent years, and this is among the best. Four works are included, all on classical themes (apart from the first, *Già lusingato*, which is an allegory about James II's attempt to regain the English throne). Soprano Christine Brandes has a beautifully clear-toned voice and a range of vocal colour that allows her to communicate the often startling changes of mood that occur. Even so, it is probably not possible to listen to more than two of these cantatas in one go without a certain weariness setting in.

DOMENICO SCARLATTI

(1685–1757)

Although he composed in many genres, Domenico Scarlatti – son of Alessandro – is now known just for his keyboard sonatas. This is scarcely surprising, because between 1719 and his death Scarlatti wrote an incredible 555 of these single-movement works, in one of history's most remarkable musical marathons.

Born in Naples, he studied with his father before moving to Venice sometime in the late 1700s. While in Venice he met Handel, whose patron, Cardinal Ottoboni, arranged for a public harpsichord and organ contest between the two

GUUS ONG

composers. Handel was deemed the better organist, while Scarlatti was thought superior on the harpsichord. He moved to Rome in 1708, working as a church musician but also producing operas for the dowager Queen of Poland. In 1713 he was appointed Maestro of the Cappella Giulia at St Peter's in Rome, a position he maintained for four years until he moved to London to work as a harpsichordist in the Italian Theatre.

In 1721 he became court composer to King João V of Portugal, a position whose duties included teaching music to the king's daughter, the Infanta Maria Barbara with whom Scarlatti established a close relationship. When she became Queen of Spain in 1729, Scarlatti followed her to Madrid, where he remained in her service until three years before his death. In Madrid, Scarlatti was happy to be a backgound figure at court – apparently uninvolved in opera – and the majority of his massive keyboard output was composed solely for the private consumption of Maria Barbara.

THE KEYBOARD SONATAS

The keyboard of Scarlatti's day had a far smaller range than the modern piano, but within these confines he created music of extraordinary variety, ranging in character from helter-skelter urgency to the most delicate lyricism. Scarlatti may not possess the depths of his contemporary J.S. Bach, but he boasted a seemingly inexhaustible fertility, and was the first really to explore the limits of what ten fingers could achieve – his music is littered with jumps over two octaves, crossed-hand passages and rapid note repetitions. Indeed, like Beethoven, Scarlatti can be credited with the invention of a totally new keyboard technique.

Scarlatti's sonatas bear no resemblance to the multi-movement form mastered by Haydn, Mozart and Beethoven – to Scarlatti the term "sonata" signified nothing more precise than that a piece was purely instrumental. Scarlatti's one-movement compositions do not develop their material in the organic way that Classical sonatas mould their themes, but rather proceed by the interweaving and juxtaposition of motifs which reappear throughout the sonata. The charm of Scarlatti's melodies, the quick-wittedness with which he conducts his musical arguments, and the quasi-romantic expressive effects he achieves through sharply contrasted motifs, make these sonatas as absorbing as any instrumental music of the eighteenth century.

◑ **The Celebrated Scarlatti Recordings: Horowitz** (Sony SK53460).

Horowitz was one of the first pianists to regularly programme Scarlatti's sonatas, usually at the beginning of a recital. These performances, part of Sony's Horowitz Edition, highlight the quirkiness of the music and use the piano's full resources to produce textures beyond the scope of the harpsichord. The choice of sonatas is stimulating and the playing is enchanting – this is one of the mercurial pianist's greatest recordings.

○ **Seven Scarlatti Sonatas: Perahia** (Sony SK62785; with works by Handel).

This marvellous recording, made in 1996, fully deserves all the plaudits that have been showered upon it. Murray Perahia's playing is warmer and more fluid than Horowitz's, with a sinewy elegance which is completely captivating.

The Complete Masterworks Recordings · Volume II
HOROWITZ
THE CELEBRATED
SCARLATTI RECORDINGS
SBM

One of the highlights is the extraordinary *Sonata in B Minor* (K.27) with its mesmerizing repetitions of a single phrase, which Perahia handles with wonderful subtlety.

⊙ Twenty-Two Sonatas: Hantaï (Astrée Auvidis E 8502).

For those wanting to hear Scarlatti played on the harpsichord, this selection by Pierre Hantaï makes a good introduction (the Erato recording of all 555 sonatas by the harpsichordist Scott Ross is not currently available). Hantaï plays a big, bold-sounding instrument and, on the whole, has selected fast and virtuosic sonatas. His playing is suitably brilliant, but this disc should be dipped into – it can seem a little frenetic if taken in one sitting.

ALFRED SCHNITTKE

(1934–)

Alfred Schnittke, Russia's most celebrated contemporary composer, is widely seen as the successor to Shostakovich, but the generation gap makes them significantly different musicians. Whereas Shostakovich's music was forged in the heat of the early Revolutionary period and tempered in the ice of Stalinism, Schnittke was young during the Khrushchev thaw and matured under Brezhnev's stagnation. The other crucial factor in Schnittke's background is that his mother was German and his father German-Jewish – though born in the Volga Republic, he spoke German as his first language and always felt an alien in his native land. Thus it's scarcely surprising that, if there are any common elements running through his wide-ranging output, they are irony, parody, disguise and wild pastiche. His music can be uncomfortably dissonant and loud, and it does have a tendency to be ramblingly episodic, but Schnittke at his best is one of the wittiest musicians around, and his manifest sincerity has done a lot to secure him a wide following.

Schnittke began his musical studies in Vienna, where his father was posted as a journalist right after the war. The musical traditions of that city – both the classicism of Haydn, Mozart and Beethoven and the *fin-de-siècle* works of Mahler and Schoenberg – have had an enormous effect on him. In 1948 he settled in Moscow (where he was to stay until moving to Hamburg in 1990), and soon began writing music using serial techniques that were almost obligatory for composers in the West, but led to his marginalization by the Soviet establishment. Few official commissions came his way, and rare performances of Schnittke pieces were packed out, becoming more like sociopolitical events than concerts. Most of his income came from the cinema (he produced sixty film scores in just twenty years), and his work for directors such as Elem Klimov and Mikhail Romm, who were to become the leading lights when *perestroika* arrived, helped spread his reputation.

Schnittke was one of the first Russian composers to be influenced by post-Webern serialism in the 1960s. But his distinctive and postmodern "polystylism" or mixing of styles emerged in the 1970s, notably with the *Symphony No. 1* (1974). "The goal of my life", he wrote, "is to unify 'E' [*Ernste Musik*, serious music] and 'U' [*Unterhaltungsmusik*, light music], even if I break my neck in so doing!" A number of commissions from western Europe followed. These included the notorious opera *Life with an Idiot* (1992), a scathing "requiem for the Soviet Union" and one of the most provocative, idiosyncratic and lewd scores of the last years. Arguably, critical reaction in the West rather overhyped Schnittke's music as the Cold War came to an end. But this should not obscure the fact that, though uneven, his output includes some of the most incisive music of our time.

CHORAL MUSIC

Schnittke's 1983 choral masterpiece *Seid nüchtern and wachtet (Faust Cantata)* is Schnittke's adaptation of the concluding part of Goethe's *Faust* for soloists, choir and orchestra. Constituting the third act of his opera *Faust* (but written many years before the completion of that misbegotten project, and conceived as a freestanding work), this Gothic postmodernist fantasy opens with a liturgical combination of chorus and choir, but with a distant tango beat. The tango comes to the foreground in the climactic scene, where Mephisto describes Faust's blood-spattered room and corpse in a nightmarish monologue. Rather more approachable than this is the *Choir Concerto* (1985), a profoundly devotional score using settings of a tenth-century Armenian poet and owing much to the Orthodox choral tradition.

⊙ Faust Cantata: Malmö Symphony Choir and Orchestra; DePreist (BIS CD-437; with *(K)ein Sommernachtstraum, Ritual & Passacaglia*).

This vivid BIS recording of *Faust* powerfully communicates

the work's visceral energy and features an outstanding Mephisto from the countertenor Mikael Bellini. It comes coupled with some of Schnittke's best orchestral music.

O Choir Concerto: Dof-Fonskaya; Russian State Symphonic Capella; Polyansky (Chandos CHAN 9332).

Chandos have made two separate recordings of this work with different choirs. This is the better of the two, with the Russian State Symphonic Capella successfully communicating something of the authentic Orthodox atmosphere.

ORCHESTRAL MUSIC

Schnittke's landmark *Symphony No. 1* was premiered by Gennadi Rozhdestvensky in 1974 in Gorky, an emblematically out-of-the-way venue for this crazed mishmash of a work. "The First Symphony is the central work for me," says the composer, "because it contains everything that I have ever had or done in my life, even the bad and the kitschy as well as the most sincere . . . all of my later works are its continuations and are determined by it." Featuring theatrical entrances and exits for the orchestral players, free-jazz improvisation and undigested fragments from the classics, it's a raucously eclectic piece. By contrast, the consistently powerful *Symphony No. 2* – actually more a Mass than a symphony – was inspired by Austria and by Bruckner in particular; permeated by bell sounds and sonorous choral writing, it's a far more homogenous work than its predecessor. Schnittke's symphonic output now stands at eight, the later ones sparer and more chamber-like in texture.

The *Concerto Grosso No. 1* (1977) is quintessential Schnittke polystylism, with frenzied excerpts of Vivaldi, dissonant outbursts and a tango for harpsichord and violins; it has its moments, even if it doesn't quite add up. The *Viola Concerto*, by contrast, is romantic and expressionistic: its two, slow outer movements enclose a frenetic central section at the centre of which comes a moment of uneasy repose, with the viola playing a simple classical melody over a piano accompaniment. It's not easy listening, but in the right hands it's a mightily impressive piece.

O Symphony No. 1: Russian State Symphony Orchestra; Rozhdestvensky (Chandos CHAN 9417).

This is a live recording with a fairly noisy audience, clearly enthusiastic about the occasion. Rozhdestvensky (a consistent promoter of his music) does a brilliant job in giving a semblance of order to this unruly pageant of styles and genres. This may not be a great symphony, but as a musical spectacle it's compelling.

O Symphony No. 2: Mikaeli Chamber Choir; Stockholm Philharmonic Orchestra; Segerstram (BIS-CD 667).

The second symphony works far better on CD and has been given several recordings. This is the best of those currently available, with Segerstram completely in control of his forces, and managing to make Schnittke's rather heavy-handed symbolism sound less obvious than it actually is.

◑ Concerto Grosso No. 1: Kremer, Grindenko; Chamber Orchestra of Europe; Schiff (Deutsche Grammophon 445 520-2; with *Quasi una sonata & Moz-Art à la Haydn*).

If you prefer the eclectic Schnittke, the best basic introduction is the CD of the *Concerto Grosso No. 1*, which gets ideal performances from Gidon Kremer and Tatiana Grindenko; it's combined with *Quasì una sonata*, a strenuous rearrangement of his second violin sonata, and *Moz-Art à la Haydn*, a more playful reworking of Mozart.

O Viola Concerto: Bashmet; London Symphony Orchestra; Rostropovich (RCA RD60446; with *Trio Sonata*).

The *Viola Concerto*, one of Schnittke's most Mahlerian scores, is given a definitive performance by Yuri Bashmet, for whom it was written. It is coupled with Bashmet's orchestral arrangement of the *String Trio* (see p.354).

CHAMBER MUSIC

Although it shares the multi-stylistic character of his large-scale pieces, Schnittke's chamber music contains his purest and most intense expression. Out of his entire output, nothing makes such a powerful impact as the *Piano Quintet* (1976) and the *String Trio* (1985). Both works were written in memoriam. The *Piano Quintet* commemorates his mother and juxtaposes episodes of tortured longing with a bittersweet waltz, using conflicting elements to construct a statement that is imaginative and haunting. The *String Trio*, composed for Berg's centenary, contains a macabre and insinuating motif based on "Happy Birthday to You". It's a powerful, tortured work which seems simultaneously to acknowledge the past and point to a new way forward. The *String Quartet No. 3* is one of Schnittke's most performed works. Perhaps the use of quotation – from Lassus, Beethoven and Shostakovich – is more obviously stated than other polystylistic works, but this is immediately attractive and extremely powerful music.

O Piano Quintet; Piano Quartet; String Quartet No. 3: Borodin Quartet; Berlinsky (Virgin VC 7 91436-2).

This disc is highly recommended as a first step into Schnittke's music. The Borodin Quartet's close relationship with Schnittke really comes through on this disc, and with Ludmilla Berlinsky on piano they produce a towering performance of the *Piano Quintet*, one which grippingly captures the desolation of the work. The second movement, a haunting waltz, projects a deep foreboding from the very start.

⊙ String Trio; Concerto for Three; Minuet: Kremer, Bashmet, Rostropovich; Moscow Soloists (EMI CDC5 55627-2; with Berg/Schnittke, *Four-Part Canon*).

This stellar line-up offers a first recording of the *Concerto for Three* and a performance of the extraordinary *String Trio* that is at times of red-hot intensity. The passion and immediacy of the playing has an intensity that is almost claustrophobic.

ARNOLD SCHOENBERG

(1874–1951)

In 1909 Arnold Schoenberg wrote his *Three Pieces* for piano, Op. 11, the first wholly atonal piece of music and arguably the most significant composition of the twentieth century. In these three epigrammatic works, Schoenberg abandoned the time-honoured methods of musical expression – tonal centres, key signatures and the traditional application of harmony – in favour of one in which all the notes of the chromatic scale were assigned equal importance. As might be imagined, this brought the heavens down upon Schoenberg's head, and even today there are many people who find his subsequent work violent and incomprehensible.

Born in Vienna to Jewish parents, Schoenberg first learned the violin and cello, and taught himself theory until 1894, when Alexander Zemlinsky – whose sister he later married – began instructing him in counterpoint. By the time he was 25, Schoenberg had seen each of Wagner's major opera's more than twenty times, and although his earliest music reflects an admiration for Brahms's classical discipline, Wagner's influence soon became all-consuming, as was clear from the opulent string sextet *Verklärte Nacht* and the grandiose choral work *Gurrelieder*. With the latter project under his arm he applied for a teaching post in Berlin. On Richard Strauss's recommendation he was accepted at the Stern Conservatory, where he stayed for three years, a period during which he composed his Straussian tone poem *Pelléas und Mélisande*.

But, whereas Strauss and Pfitzner seemed content to live off the harmonic legacy of Wagner, to Schoenberg it seemed evident that Wagnerian chromaticism had exhausted the conventional vocabularies without offering any way forward. Schoenberg shared the preoccupation of many *fin-de-siècle* artists: how to find a way of expressing an inner vision – the subjective and the abstract. Between 1900 and 1910 Schoenberg set off in a new direction: developing a style from which he gradually moved away from the opulence of Symbolism towards the more economical and increasingly personal language of Expressionism. All his music of these years possesses a raw, passionate emotionalism that sometimes reflects his own troubled personal life and completely belies his later image as a dry intellectual. With the *String Quartet No. 2*, written in 1907, he came to the brink of composing music that was in no identifiable key, and with the *Three Pieces* of 1909 he finally made the complete break with tonality, following it up in the same year with the bleak atonal opera *Erwartung*.

By the following year, Schoenberg and Strauss (by now estranged) were the *enfants terribles* of European music, but whereas Strauss was hugely successful Schoenberg was the subject of venomous derision – though he had two devoted

LEBRECHT COLLECTION

Schoenberg's self-portrait, 1919

supporters in his pupils Anton Webern (see p.474) and Alban Berg (see p.49), the other key members of what became known as the Second Viennese School. The Viennese premiere of *Pierrot Lunaire* in 1912 produced outright hostility, in marked contrast to the premiere of the *Gurrelieder* early the following year, which was an unqualified success.

Schoenberg served in the ranks during World War I, and immediately after the war returned to Vienna, where, together with Berg and Webern, he organized and played in concerts of new music, events from which the critics of the Viennese press were barred. He composed little until 1924, when he announced his "re-emergence" with the creation of twelve-tone serialism, the method by which he brought order to the potential chaos of atonalism. Whereas pure atonalism gave the composer freedom to select notes at will from the entire chromatic scale, the twelve-tone technique arranged the twelve notes in a specific sequence (or tone-row) for each piece. The tone-row could be played note by note, simultaneously, even upside down, but no note could be repeated until the whole series could be played. By giving all twelve notes of the chromatic scale equal value, the conventional sense of movement to and from the tonic was eliminated, as it had been with atonalism, but this new method gave modern music a sense of focus that had been lacking in atonal works.

In 1925 Schoenberg moved back to Berlin, where he taught composition at the Academy of Arts, but with the advent of Nazism he was dismissed from his post. He left Germany in 1933 and eventually emigrated to the United States, where he settled in Los Angeles, and taught at the University of California. In the remaining years of his life he produced a large body of music in a range of styles. In 1944 he applied for a Guggenheim grant to enable him to complete his opera *Moses und Aron*, which he had begun in 1930; his application was refused, and he died leaving the third act incomplete.

Schoenberg is one of the most remarkable figures in the history of music, as inspirational in his dedication to his art as in his published work. Driven by an inner compulsion to create new foundations for Western music, he was spurred to ever greater determination by the hostility he encountered. In 1947 he accepted an award from the American Academy of Arts with the words, "That you should regard all I have tried to do in the last fifty years as an achievement strikes me as in some respects an overestimate. My own feeling was that I had fallen into an ocean of boiling water; and, as I couldn't swim and knew no other way out, I struggled with my arms and legs as best I could . . . The credit must go to my opponents. It was they who really helped me."

CHORAL, VOCAL AND STAGE WORKS

Of all Schoenberg's choral works, the most important is the mighty *Gurrelieder*, perhaps the greatest Austro-German choral composition of the twentieth century. After Mahler's *Symphony No. 8* it requires the largest forces of any concert work, and each of Schoenberg's subsequent stage works also demands a large-scale orchestra. However, these later pieces – *Erwartung*, *Die glückliche Hande*, *Von Heute auf Morgen* and *Moses und Aron* – are of completely different character from *Gurrelieder*, for they all come after his shift into atonality. Lyricism and melody are not wholly absent from the stage works (indeed, *Erwartung* is littered with moments of lush expressionism), but on the whole they are challengingly dissonant and extreme works. The orchestra is heavily subdivided, so that often only a few instruments are playing at any one time, while the vocal parts are typified by extreme leaps and the use of *Sprechgesang*, a style of declamation that is midway between speech and song, and is used to even more disconcerting effect in *Pierrot Lunaire*, a work described by Stravinsky as "the solar plexus" of twentieth-century music.

GURRELIEDER

Of all Schoenberg's scores, none has won such wide popularity as *Gurrelieder* (Songs of Gurre) – there is even a worldwide Gurrelieder Society. Its success has a lot to do with its scale, for *Gurrelieder* is a work that blasts you out of your seat. Deploying a veritable army of players, it calls for at least seventy strings, four choirs, five soloists, a narrator, eight flutes, ten horns, seven trumpets, seven trombones, five tubas, four harps, six percussionists and iron chains – and that isn't a full tally.

Schoenberg started it in 1900 but didn't complete the orchestration until 1911. Thus, when it was first performed in 1913, conducted by Franz Schreker (see p.360), audience and critics were astonished to hear such lush Expressionism from a composer who was by then immersed in work that denied everything that *Gurrelieder* stood for. Based upon a poem by the Danish romantic Jens Peter Jacobsen, the ninety-minute work dramatizes the love between King Waldemar and Tove, resident of Castle Gurre. Set in the fourteenth century, it's a tale that would have appealed to Wagner, and indeed the music of *Gurrelieder*, though in part a homage to Strauss, is especially indebted to Wagner, whose *Tristan and Isolde* is the prototype for the febrile emotionalism of Part One. This section is dominated by a long and luxuriant duet for Waldemar and Tove, which is interrupted after each verse by sumptuous orchestral commentaries, and is followed by the murder of Tove and a lament for her, sung by a wood dove. Part Two sees Waldemar cursing his fate (combative relationships with the deity were to recur in Schoenberg's work), but Part Three builds to a final, pantheistic chorus of outrageous, wondrous dimensions.

O Dunn, Fassbaender, Jerusalem, Becht, Haage, Hotter; Berlin St Hedwige's Cathedral Choir; Dusseldorf Musikverein; Berlin Radio Symphony Orchestra; Chailly (Decca 448 279-2; 2 CDs).

A superb achievement from both Chailly's combined forces and Decca's engineers. The sheer scale of this work makes it difficult to bring off: often something gets lost – either the vast epic sweep or Schoenberg's detailed scoring (clanking chains in the percussion section). In this superbly dramatic performance, everything is present and correct: the soloists are all excellent (Susan Dunn in particular) but it's the way Chailly creates such a thrilling sense of occasion that is ultimately so impressive.

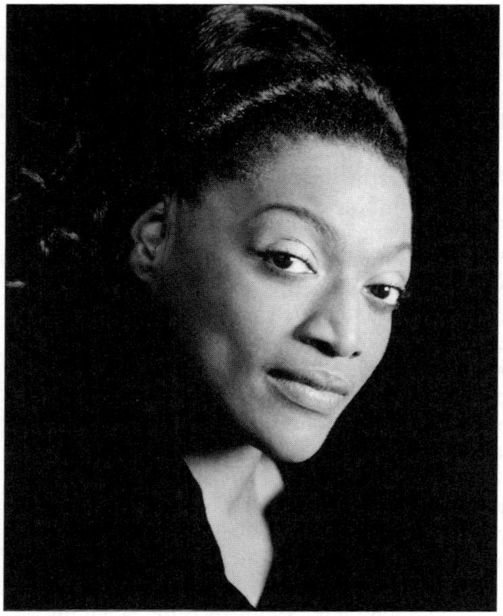

PHILIPS/DAVID SEIDNER

Jessye Norman

ERWARTUNG

Erwartung (Expectation), for soprano and large orchestra, is a thirty-minute monologue of gruelling concentration. Schoenberg wrote it in 1909, soon after the Op. 11 piano pieces, and *Erwartung* shows him applying the techniques he had developed in those atonal miniatures to a large, dramatic structure. Though moments of tonality and tantalizing classical motifs do punctuate the score, it's essentially a stream of dreamlike images and jagged musical gestures – one of the most extreme examples of musical Expressionism. It was written a year after the painter Richard Gerstl – who taught both Schoenberg and his wife Mathilde – committed suicide after Mathilde had ended their affair and returned to her husband.

The plot, if that is the right word, was created by Marie Pappenheim, a young doctor and poet, and is a typical product of Freud's Vienna. A lone, unnamed woman is seen wandering at night through a forest which may be real or may be the landscape of her subconscious. The woman is searching for her lover, whose corpse she stumbles across fairly early in the work; leaving unanswered the question of the motive and identity of the murderer, the rest of *Erwartung* is given over to the woman's disjointed, distracted recollections of their life together. The rapidity of the mood swings – moments of lucidity next to near-incoherence – are brilliantly communicated by the music's extraordinary rhythmic freedom, while the absence of a clear pulse, like the absence of tonality, contributes to a sensation of rootlessness and timelessness, as if the whole opera were taking place within the woman's head.

O Norman; Metropolitan Opera Orchestra; Levine (Philips 426 261-2; with cabaret songs).

Levine's performance of this dense score is a revelation, unleashing tremendous power at the climaxes as well as perfectly controlling the orchestra in the delicate, introspective passages. The disc is dominated, however, by a fearful performance from Jessye Norman – this is perhaps her greatest half-hour on record. The skittish, fragile cabaret songs are less suited to her massive voice, but she succeeds in bringing a smiling quality to the frequently witty texts. The recording is ideal.

PIERROT LUNAIRE

At the time of *Erwartung*, Schoenberg was almost equally active as a painter – indeed, he exhibited at the famous *Blaue Reiter* exhibition organized by Kandinsky in 1911. Many of his paintings from this period are preoccupied with nightmare images of staring mask-like faces, and he had little hesitation when the actress Albertine Zehme commissioned him to write her a vocal melodrama around the Pierrot poems of Albert Giraud. The result was *Pierrot Lunaire* (1912), another startling work of raw expressionism. Scored for a small ensemble (flute, clarinet, strings and piano) and a soprano employing *Sprechgesang*, *Pierrot Lunaire* focuses on a dislocated, splintered personality in the same way *Erwartung* did. This time, however, there's a strong element of grotesquerie – madness even – as Pierrot (traditionally a figure of pathos) rasps out his tortured and often violent fantasies. The lightness of the accompaniment (the instrumentalists were hidden at the original performance) means that it functions as a kind of ghostly commentary.

◑ **Manning; Nash Ensemble; Rattle** (Chandos CHAN 6534; with Webern, *Concerto*).

A tart, acerbic and uncompromising performance from Jane Manning, who growls and swoops her way through the increasingly disturbing verses. The Nash Ensemble, under Simon Rattle, provide virtuosic but discreet accompaniment.

MOSES UND ARON

An unresolved need for communication with God was central to Schoenberg's artistic personality, and for most of his life he was racked by the problems of self-knowledge and religious belief. His conversions to and desertions of Judaism were indicative of the anguish he suffered, and in his last opera, *Moses und Aron*, he wrestled with the issue of humanity's inability to deal with absolute truth, as given to Moses by God. The work was left incomplete at his death, not because of the shortage of time, but because Schoenberg found it impossible to find music for the final act, in which Moses berates Aaron for his devotion to the Image rather than to the Idea.

Moses und Aron is Schoenberg's largest staged work and the most complete dramatic expression of serialist techniques. The deeply philosophical libretto – written by the composer – is set to music of such complexity that Schoenberg doubted that a performance would be possible. The work is too hieratic to be completely successful on stage, but for all the difficulty of the music the emotional power of *Moses und Aron* is as direct as anything by any of Schoenberg's more traditional contemporaries. The baritone role of Moses is written in *Sprechgesang*, while Aron's part is fully scored for a very high tenor – as far from the style of Moses as could be imagined. An almost delirious intensity is generated by the resulting range of expression in their exchanges. The longest, most significant and most accessible scene comes in the second act, where Aaron leads the people to reject Moses (who is on the mountaintop communing with God) and descend into an orgy of debauchery, for which Schoenberg wrote music of sumptuous colour.

○ **Merritt, Pittman-Jennings; Netherlands Opera Chorus; Concertgebouw Orchestra; Boulez** (Deutsche Grammophon 449 1742; 2 CDs).

This is Pierre Boulez's second account of *Moses und Aron*; his 1974 set was very good, but this 1995 recording is really something special – especially for Chris Merritt's Aron, for it's rarely the case that the role is assigned to a tenor with the necessary range, which Merritt certainly has. As ever with Boulez, the orchestral textures and lines are fastidiously defined, but his conducting is never finicky.

ORCHESTRAL WORKS

It was his orchestral music that first earned Schoenberg his reputation as a dangerous radical. The premiere of the "tuneless" *Five Orchestral Pieces* caused an outrage at its first performance, as did the later *Variations for Orchestra*, an uncompromising example of fully developed serialism. To appreciate the origins of these works you should approach them via his early *Pelleas und Melisande*, which shows Schoenberg at his most romantic. These three works represent only a small selection of Schoenberg's orchestral output, but they will give you an excellent introduction to the composer's range.

PELLEAS UND MELISANDE

Debussy wrote his *Pelléas et Mélisande* in the mid-1890s; though unaware of Debussy's opera, Schoenberg also considered writing a stage work based on Maeterlinck's play at this time, but in 1902 he decided instead to turn the story into a symphonic poem. Whereas Debussy's opera is all about understatement and implication, Schoenberg's music is a tightly strung, blatantly hedonistic piece, explicitly portraying Melisande's illicit love for her brother-in-law – the love duet in particular is breathtakingly effective, containing some brilliantly dramatic counterpoint. In places *Pelleas und Melisande* does suggest that Schoenberg's grasp of the technicalities of orchestration was not yet complete, yet Schoenberg's only symphonic poem is obsessively involving, and contains some of the most erotic music ever written.

○ **Chicago Symphony Orchestra; Boulez** (Erato 2292 45827-2; with *Variations for Orchestra*).

Boulez's recordings of early Schoenberg do not stint on the unbridled Romanticism on display while underlining details that other conductors often miss. When that is coupled with magnificent orchestral playing in a clear and natural acoustic, the result – as here – is overwhelming.

CHAMBER SYMPHONY NO. 1

With the *Chamber Symphony No. 1* the grandiosity of *Pelleas und Melisande* has been condensed into a something much more spare and sinewy. This is a concentrated single-movement work for fifteen solo players: a semblance of classical four-movement structure still remains as does the passionately rapturous quality of the earlier orchestral works. Where the old fixities start to break down is in the way that melody is gradually undermined, rather than reinforced, by its underlying harmony. There is plenty of energetic momentum to this work (it's one of Schoenberg's most positive pieces), but it is sustained through lively contrapuntal writing against a background of unstable tonality which is both disconcerting and liberating.

Orpheus Chamber Orchestra (Deutsche Grammophon 429 233-2; with *Verklärte Nacht* & *Chamber Symphony No. 2*).

The conductorless Orpheus Chamber Orchestra is a phenomenally brilliant ensemble, who sometimes produce such a seamless, pristine sound that works can be rendered bland as a result. That is not the case here: the contrapuntal complexity of the *Chamber Symphony No. 1* is enhanced by this level of virtuosity and it is hard to imagine a better performance.

FIVE ORCHESTRAL PIECES

Composed in the *annus mirabilis* of 1909, the *Five Orchestral Pieces* shows Schoenberg moving further into the free-floating world of atonalism, yet this is not a schism so much as a transition. The rather unwieldy orchestrations betray an affinity with the *fin-de-siècle* aesthetic of *Pelleas*, as do some of the titles originally appended to each of the five pieces: *Premonitions*, *Yesteryears*, *Summer Morning by a Lake*, *Peripetia* and *The Obbligato Recitative*. The first and the last of the set are laden with the kind of angst associated with Expressionism, but the second piece is a restrained and essentially Romantic episode which in turn leads into the extraordinary *Summer Morning by a Lake*, the work's high point. Here Schoenberg explores the possibilities of what was termed *Klangfarbenmelodie* ("sound-colour melody"), in which a melodic effect is transformed simply by changing the timbre of a single note or a simple harmony. Just as colour can alter the eye's perception of an object's shape, so a chord or run of notes is here modified by playing with its tone-colour. The tranquillity of this third movement is extremely affecting, and its stylistic impact upon Webern and subsequent generations is incalculable.

London Symphony Orchestra; Dorati (Mercury 432 006-2; with orchestral works by Webern and Berg).

This is an amazing recording from one of the century's most perceptive conductors. Aware of every inflection of the music's colour and internal shape, Dorati makes the most of Schoenberg's orchestration; combined with other fine examples of the Second Viennese School, this brightly engineered recording serves as an excellent starting point for atonal orchestral music.

VARIATIONS FOR ORCHESTRA

The *Variations for Orchestra*, Schoenberg's most successful orchestral application of twelve-tone method, was premiered by Wilhelm Furtwängler on December 3, 1928, and prompted such tumultuous scenes that the concert came close to being abandoned. Nonetheless the critic Max Marschalk was moved to comment – "Schoenberg convinces us with the *Variations* that he has succeeded in discovering new vistas in music in which we can feel comfortably at home . . . The music he presents in the *Variations* is without precedent." This is not strictly true, for Schoenberg had created his own precedents, but this music certainly did mark a new direction in its rigorous formal cohesion. You cannot hear the variations taking place – Schoenberg himself said that this was impossible – but you can detect an underlying momentum generated by the music's complex rhythmic patterns, and the rich orchestral detail builds to a climax as fulfilling as that of any conventional variation sequence. The more often you listen to this piece, the more easily you'll be able to follow the many layers from which it is constructed and so appreciate its fundamentally classical architecture.

Berlin Philharmonic Orchestra; Karajan (Deutsche Grammophon 415 326-2GH; with *Verklärte Nacht*).

Karajan's finely crafted performance of this extraordinary unbroken 25 minute score is extremely persuasive. There is no question but that this is difficult stuff, yet Karajan's subtle and highly imaginative approach allows the music's lines to appear clearly, and the resonant recording brings out the richness of Schoenberg's textures.

CHAMBER AND PIANO MUSIC

Schoenberg's string quartets and his piano music comprise two categories of his output within which you can clearly trace the dominant pattern of his career, from chromatic Romanticism through atonality to serialism. Besides these works, one other piece is essential listening – the string sextet *Verklärte Nacht*, the composer's most seductive creation.

VERKLÄRTE NACHT

Verklärte Nacht (Transfigured Night) was one of Schoenberg's earliest pieces and it gave him his first taste of success when it was performed in 1903, four years after its composition. It was liked both by the public and by its creator, who produced orchestrated versions of it in 1917 and 1943, each of which proved as popular as the orginal sextet.

Verklärte Nacht was written shortly after Schoenberg's immersion in the Symbolist poetry of Richard Dehmel, whose words he used for a set of early songs. The Dehmel poem that specifically inspired the sextet concerned a woman racked by guilt and fear, like the figure portrayed in *Erwartung*. However, whereas *Erwartung* ends in unease, *Verklärte Nacht* ends with a resolution: she confesses to her lover that she is pregnant by another man; he replies that through their love the child will be born his, and thus the night is transfigured. However, no knowledge of this programme is really necessary to enjoy a piece of music that is one of the peaks of late Romanticism and which possesses a highly charged, near-neurotic expressiveness which is completely unique. In this work Schoenberg manages to achieve a sort of reconciliation between Brahms and Wagner: the lyricism, instrumentation and sheer tunefulness of *Verklärte Nacht* reflect the influence of the former, while its chromaticism and overall construction bear the marks of the latter.

⊙ Chamber version: Raphael Ensemble (Hyperion CDA66425; with Korngold, *Sextet*).

The Raphael Ensemble deliver a pulsating but sensitively drawn performance, in which the intricately balanced counterpoint is made to sigh with erotic yearning – in the final part, introduced by the second cellist's beautiful solo theme, the music seems about to burst its banks. Coupled with Korngold's equally sumptuous *Sextet*, this well-engineered and finely annotated set should be in any basic CD library.

⊙ Orchestral version: Orpheus Chamber Orchestra (Deutsche Grammophon 429 233-2; with *Chamber Symphonies Nos. 1 & 2*).

The Orpheus Chamber Orchestra produce beautifully lyrical playing of the 1943 version for string orchestra, bringing out all the work's textural delicacy and sensuality. There is also a shimmering opulence – like a Klimt painting translated into sound – that is utterly magical.

STRING QUARTETS

Schoenberg's *String Quartet No. 1* of 1905 is a Brahms-like piece, forward-looking in the sense that it is written as a single extended movement, but basically conservative in its language. In extreme contrast, the third and fourth quartets (1927 and 1936) are thorough-going serial works. Bereft of anything that could be termed conventional melody, they are immensely intellectual pieces that are best approached after you've become familiar with the earlier works. The *String Quartet No. 2* (1907) is the one most likely to excite you if you're coming fresh to Schoenberg. In the last two movements this amazing quartet steps over the line into the shifting, eerie soundscape of atonality, a move announced by a soprano soloist who sings Stefan George's prophetic words, "I breathe the air of other planets." More than any other of Schoenberg's works, the *String Quartet No. 2* dramatizes the transition from the old to the new.

⊙ Arditti Quartet; Upshaw (Auvidis Montaigne MO 782024; 2 CDs).

These are exceptionally fine readings of all the music for string quartet. The playing is rigorous and lucid without being merely efficient. Schoenberg's densely argued last two quartets have rarely sounded so impressive, and if the first two are given less Romantic accounts than usual they are still utterly compelling performances.

PIANO WORKS

Schoenberg was not a pianist and composed very little for the instrument – indeed he published only six works for solo piano. However, no part of his oeuvre provides so complete and so concise a survey of the composer's development.

The unpublished *Piano Pieces* of 1894 have a clumsy, embarrassed feel (as if Schoenberg were intimidated by his forebears) and he did not compose for piano again until 1909, when he produced the epoch-making atonal music of the *Three Piano Pieces* Op. 11. The first of this set is constructed as a set of variations, but in the absence of a home key it's impossible for the untrained ear to perceive the structure in the way it could perceive the musical argument of, say, Beethoven's *Diabelli Variations*. What the *Three Piano Pieces* is working towards is a sound-world that denies the sense of closure and hierarchy that the major and minor scales create, the sense that some episodes in a piece are more important than others. This movement towards an open-ended music in which every statement has equal space is furthered by the aphoristic *Six Little Piano Pieces* Op. 19 (1911), which rejects all motivic development in favour of a reliance upon tone colour and vertical relations between the notes, proceeding through clusters of tones that obey no other logic than Schoenberg's intuitive sense of what works. These pieces still attract dissent: some people find them insubstantial and uncomfortably dissonant; others regard them as masterpieces of expressive concision, in which everything happens in the present tense.

The next piano work, *Five Piano Pieces* Op. 23, concludes with a waltz (undanceable, needless to say) which was the first published example of rigorous serial music. The *Piano Suite* Op. 25, a distant relative of the keyboard suites of Bach, shows Schoenberg further refining the twelve-tone method, which he once declared – rashly, it turned out – would "assure German music of its pre-eminence for the next century". The two *Piano Pieces* of Op. 33, written while Schoenberg was at work on *Moses und Aron*, show the twelve-tone technique at its most polished. To really understand the formal intricacies of these works requires a fair amount of study. The non-specialist, however, simply needs concentration and open ears: the radical dynamic shifts, eventful rhythmic changes and startling juxtapositions of tones within these small-scale pieces make them as engrossing, if not as comforting, as any Chopin study or Schumann miniature.

◑ **Pollini** (Deutsche Grammophon 423 249-2GC).

Pollini's recording of the complete published piano music is a magnificent achievement. As ever, he is technically in a class of his own, and nobody has ever matched the intellectual and emotional cohesion he brings to this music. If anyone tells you that Schoenberg is all about composing by numbers or by random selection, just listen to this CD – Pollini reveals the passion behind the method.

FRANZ SCHREKER

(1878–1934)

In the 1910s Franz Schreker was regarded as the third member of German music's avant-garde triumvirate, alongside Richard Strauss and Arnold Schoenberg. Nowadays he is little more than a footnote to the history of modern music, even though his operas are among the most intriguing works of the early twentieth century. At times reminiscent of both Richard Strauss and Debussy, Schreker creates an impressionistic sound-world of ever-changing moods and colours, a style perfectly suited to the post-Freudian psychology of his subjects. But if his music deserves to regain its former reputation, his lurid and overwrought libretti – which he wrote himself – have always had their critics.

Born in Monaco to Austrian parents, Schreker lived most of his life in Vienna where, in 1892, he was enrolled at the conservatory. His first success as a composer came in 1908 with *Der Geburtstag der Infantin* (The Birthday of the Infanta), a ballet based on a story by Oscar Wilde. Four years later the premiere of the first of his major operas, *Der ferne Klang* (The Distant Sound) established him as a leading modernist with both Schoenberg and Berg expressed great admiration for the score. For a short time Schreker's influence on the development of new music was crucial. He conducted the premiere of Schoenberg's *Gurrelieder* in 1913, and in 1920 was appointed to the prestigious position of director of the Hochschule für Musik in Berlin, where he presided over an impressive teaching staff that included Hindemith.

Two more operas, both written during World War I, consolidated his reputation: *Die Gezeichneten* (The Stigmatized Ones) and *Der Schatzgräber* (The Treasure Seeker) were two of the most frequently performed operas of the immediate postwar period, but by the mid-1920s Schrecker's opulent style was rapidly going out of fashion as the more acerbic manner of composers like Weill and Hindemith began to find favour. He produced four more operas but his later works were not well received. The first performance of *Christophorus* in 1931 was cancelled as a result of Nazi pressure, but the premiere of *Der Schmied von Gent* (The Blacksmith of Ghent) the following year was allowed to continue – only to be shouted down by an anti-Semitic mob.

In 1932 the composer Max von Schillings became the new President of the Prussian Academy of Arts, accepting the task of purging the Academy of all "racially undesirable" members. Schreker was duly dismissed from his teaching post and he found himself at the mercy of some of modernism's most virulent opponents. Quite apart from any musical criticism, he was attacked for "sexual deviancy", with disastrous consequences. Condemned for his race, his homosexuality and his music, Schreker suffered a fatal heart attack, dying just two days short of his 56th birthday. Only in very recent years has there been any serious attempt to reassess his achievements as an opera composer.

DER FERNE KLANG

Der ferne Klang tells how Fritz, a young composer haunted by a magical sound, abandons his lover, Grete, to go in search of it. She falls into prostitution, but they are finally reunited as Fritz is dying – whereupon he realizes that the "distant sound"

– the natural world, the power of love, Grete – was within his grasp all the time. The opera's incredible success established Schreker as one of Germany's leading modern composers but for all the daring of its subject matter and Schreker's advanced harmonic language this is essentially a Romantic work, characterized by muscular instrumentation and extremely atmospheric sonorities that augment the moods and emotions of the protagonists. In terms of dissonance it is not as extreme as Strauss's *Elektra*, which was composed around the same time, and it was the opera's luxuriant and diaphanous textures that so appealed to contemporary audiences.

⊙ Schnaut, Moser, Nimsgern, Helm; Berlin Radio Chorus and Symphony Orchestra; Albrecht
(Capriccio 60 024-2; 2 CDs).

There are two recordings of *Der ferne Klang* but Gerd Albrecht's is preferable in most respects, with a rich, indulgent sound and a fine orchestra, to whom the music is clearly second nature. Gabriele Schnaut is a powerful, chesty mezzo and she copes well with Grete's difficult music. Thomas Moser is reliable in the baritone role of Fritz but no more, the remaining cast all give solid – if not top-flight – performances.

DIE GEZEICHNETEN

Die Gezeichneten (The Stigmatized Ones) is an even stronger brew. After the success of *Der Geburtstag der Infantin*, Alexander Zemlinsky asked Schreker to write him a libretto for an opera based on the same Oscar Wilde story. Zemlinsky did produce an opera of *Der Geburtstag* (see p.484), but he had to go elsewhere for his text, as Schreker became so fascinated by Wilde's theme that he composed his own exploration of it. Set in sixteenth-century Genoa, *Die Gezeichneten* is a tale of erotic obsession, physical deformity (the protagonist, Alviano, is a hunchbacked dwarf), self-sacrifice and madness, carried by some of Schreker's most lyrical and richly chromatic music. The extraordinary reaction to *Die Gezeichneten* suggests that its emotive depiction of moral stagnation through music of almost mystical euphoria struck a profound chord in war-ravaged Germany. One critic called it a "grand mental and moral house-cleaning in Germany".

The mood of *Die Gezeichneten* is immediately established by the opera's remarkable prelude, which alone deserves to guarantee its composer's reputation. It opens with a mysteriously shimmering chord before stating the main leitmotifs of the opera, motifs that evoke as much by dazzling orchestral colour as by melody. The orchestra remains the main musical protagonist, with the solo voices mostly adopting a free-flowing vocal style which is wrapped around by delicate and evocative instrumental detailing. As in *Der ferne Klang*, there is an implicit suggestion that art – and indeed the pursuit of pleasure – represents a flight from reality, and as such *Die Gezeichneten* makes an interesting parallel with the contemporary *Doktor Faust* of Busoni.

⊙ Kruse, Connell, Pederson, Muff; Berlin Radio Chorus; Berlin Symphony Orchestra; Zagrosek
(Decca 444 442-2; 2 CDs).

This is a magnificent recording, even if Zagrosek tends to wallow in instrumental texture to the detriment of the opera's shape – the prelude, for example, is never allowed to take off in the way it should. However, his ear for sonorities is acute, and he provides excellent support for his cast. Heinz Kruse is a Wagner tenor in the making and throws himself into the role of Alviano, tackling the high tessitura with ease and confidence. The highlight of the set, however, is Elizabeth Connell's glorious portrayal of the love interest Carlotta, and she captures the rise to (and fall from) emotional freedom with exquisitely controlled tenderness.

FRANZ SCHUBERT

(1797–1828)

The neglect that Schubert suffered for most of the nineteenth century now seems incredible. None of his symphonies was performed during his lifetime and not one was published until some fifty years after his death. In 1827 a music dictionary was published in which Schubert's name did not so much as feature once. A century later, another book attacked him as a "conventional music-machine, contentedly turning out work after work, day after day". A partial explanation for this situation is that – unlike Beethoven or Mozart – Schubert was not a virtuoso musician, and he found no other means of promoting himself. Ironically, however, his unfettered talent for melody and his attachment to classical forms also contributed significantly towards his neglect. In the high Romantic period, when

LEBRECHT COLLECTION

Franz Schubert

Holzer later wrote: "If I wished to instruct him in anything fresh, the boy already knew it. So I gave him no actual tuition but merely talked to him and watched him with silent astonishment." Every moment Schubert had to himself was spent composing, and in 1812 he was accepted as a student by Salieri, under whose guidance he composed his first symphony. Two years later, to Salieri's astonishment, the 17-year-old presented him with the 341 pages of his fully orchestrated first opera. (Despite repeated attempts, mastery of operatic form was always to elude him.) On October 19, 1814, Schubert wrote his setting of Goethe's poem *Gretchen am Spinnrade* (Gretchen at the Spinning Wheel) – his first real masterpiece. Unlike the young Beethoven, composing came completely naturally to Schubert. On the first anniversary of *Gretchen am Spinnrade* he composed no fewer than eight songs in one day, and in the course of 1815 he produced some 144 songs.

complexity and ambiguity were the order of the day, Schubert's lucid and tuneful music was often dismissed as the product of a naive mind. But even in the area of his output where melody predominated – his Lieder (songs) – there is so much more to his work than mere tunefulness. During a life of less than 32 years he composed over six hundred songs, and no other composer had ever displayed such an ability to match music to poetry so closely that the words seem to have been written expressly for this purpose. He remains the greatest of all songwriters, but that is not the limit of his achievement, for in his late chamber music, piano sonatas and symphonies Schubert created works that mark him down as the first great Romantic. The progressive element to this late music suggests that, had he lived longer, he would have gone on to produce music of daunting originality. The epitaph on his monument, written by his friend Grillparzer, says as much: "The art of music here entombed a rich possession, but even fairer hopes."

Schubert was born in Lichtenthal, a suburb of Vienna, and at the age of 9 or 10 was sent to study with the local church organist, Michael Holzer. As

From 1814 to 1817 Schubert worked in his father's school, spending all his spare time writing – students who interrupted him received short shrift. Towards the end of this period he began to gather around him a close and influential circle of friends (an essentially homosexual milieu it has been suggested) including the rich and rather disreputable Franz von Schober, the melancholy poet Johann Mayrhofer, and the operatic baritone Michael Vogl, for whom Schubert composed many of his greatest songs. Although his music was now sporadically performed in concert as well as at private gatherings called "Schubertiads", Schubert was regarded as an esoteric taste and he was in desperate need of money, a plight that was to dog him throughout his life.

In the summer of 1818 he moved to Zseliz in Hungary to take up the position of music tutor to the daughters of Count Johann Esterházy. Initially happy there (he particularly liked the girls) he soon started to miss Vienna and his friends. On his return the following year he took rooms with Mayrhofer and a new friend Josef Huttenbrenner, who devoted himself to the composer, collecting and cataloguing his music. This was an especially productive period, with two operas commissioned by the Court Theatre and an extended summer holiday with Vogl in the countryside at Steyr providing the inspiration for the *Trout Quintet*. In 1821 the song *Erlkönig* was published by Diabelli – his first published composition – and in the same year he sketched, but never orchestrated, a seventh symphony.

What seemed like the beginnings of a great career began to fall apart in 1822. The Court Theatre, which had continued to favour Schubert – despite his failure to produce a popular success – brought in new, Italian, management (Vienna had gone Rossini-mad) who cancelled two outstanding commissions. Worse was to follow: around this time Schubert contracted syphilis, then rife in Vienna, and in 1823 his health began to fail, resulting in his admission to the Vienna general hospital. Though the mental and physical shock was overwhelming, his illness and subsequent depression did nothing to inhibit his creativity and while in hospital he began work on his first song cycle, *Die schöne Müllerin*.

In 1825 he and Vogl spent five restorative months touring Austria, in the course of which Schubert is known to have sketched a symphony – possibly an early draft of *Symphony No. 9*. At some point during the next two years Schubert met Beethoven (by now totally deaf) and, although there are no details of any strong ties between the two men, Beethoven clearly recognized the younger man's talent and Schubert is known to have been one of the torchbearers at Beethoven's funeral in 1827. As with Beethoven, Schubert's last years saw him reaching a new level of achievement, as if the prospect of death had forced out of him the creation of his finest works. The *Quintet in C Major*, the *Winterreise* song cycle, the last three piano sonatas and his final symphony all plumb the most astonishing emotional depths. In March 1828 he gave a concert of his own music and, although the Viennese turned out in force, the concert's success was completely eclipsed by the Vienna debut of Paganini three days later. Eight months later Schubert was dead at the age of 31. His brother Ferdinand interpreted his dying words as a wish to be buried near Beethoven, and so he was; in 1888 both bodies were exhumed to be placed in the Zentralfriedhof in Vienna, where they now lie side by side.

THE SYMPHONIES

Schubert lived in Beethoven's shadow all his life and yet his symphonies owe less to Beethoven's style than you might expect. Devoid of the Promethean defiance so common to Beethoven's works, they generally have a lightness, openness and thematic profusion that owes more to Haydn and Mozart than to Beethoven. However, while it's true that Schubert's symphonies as a whole are not as individualistic as his smaller-scale works, the last two symphonies display an approach to orchestral colouring that looks forward to the expansive symphonies of the mid-nineteenth century – the opening of the *Unfinished Symphony*, for example, is more Romantic than Classical in feel. As with all his works, the symphonies are dominated by a succession of seraphic melodies, but unlike the highly melodic symphonies of Schumann and Mendelssohn, Schubert's are never facile, and their range of emotion, from capricious gaiety to deep melancholy, marks them out as one of the great cycles of the century.

The numbering of Schubert's symphonies can be confusing, as *Symphony No. 7* was never orchestrated by Schubert (though others had a go). Thus, although Schubert composed nine symphonies, only eight are played and some authorities label *Symphony No. 8* (the *Unfinished*) as *Symphony No. 7* and *Symphony No. 9* (the *Great*) as *Symphony No. 8*.

O Complete Symphonies: Concertgebouw; Harnoncourt (Teldec 4509-91184-2; 4 CDs).

Harnoncourt's Beethoven cycle reaped every award on offer, but his Schubert set is even better – refreshingly instinctive conducting that is at once lyrical and brisk. If you've heard more traditional recordings, the light-footed delicacy of the much-reduced Concertgebouw orchestra might surprise you, but nothing is done merely to surprise. These performances probably come as close as possible to how Schubert might have heard his symphonies. The only negative point is the pretentiousness of the sleevenotes.

SYMPHONY NO. 4 – THE TRAGIC

Composed at the age of 19, the *Symphony No. 4* shows that a dark strain was present in Schubert's music from the very beginning. Its epithet "tragic" was added by Schubert himself and it is indeed a sombre work, revealing more than any other the influence of Beethoven, not least in the choice of key – C minor. It opens with a slow introduction, which gives way to a development of great urgency and vigour that recalls the *Symphony No. 40* of Mozart. The subsequent broad-themed Andante is twice interrupted by agitated episodes, and this mood of restlessness is continued in the ensuing Minuet and Allegro.

O Chamber Orchestra of Europe; Abbado (Deutsche Grammophon 423 653-2 with *Symphony No. 3*).

Instead of overplaying the tragic element in this performance Abbado manages to generate an atmosphere of real tension and excitement from an orchestra who have, on previous occasions, sounded rather too suave.

SYMPHONY NO. 5

Begun a mere five months after *Symphony No. 4*, the *Symphony No. 5* is of an altogether sunnier disposition and has proved one of the most popular of all Schubert's orchestral works. It is certainly a work of far greater confidence than the previous four symphonies, with a Mozartian orchestral and architectural scale but a personality very much Schubert's own. The exquisite slow movement, characterized by poignant, uniquely Schubertian key modulations, features a magical duet between the strings and wind section near the end, while its coda is perhaps the most affecting conclusion in all his symphonic music. He was still only 19 when he completed this masterpiece, and its captivating finale embodies all the optimism and clear-sightedness of youth.

⊙ **San Francisco Symphony Orchestra; Blomstedt** (Decca 448 707-2DH; with *Symphony No. 8* and *Rosamunde Overture*).

Blomstedt's account is marked by finely judged balance and exquisite melodic colour, best shown in the slow movement, where a beguiling attention to detail creates a chamber-like intimacy. It's coupled with an excellent version of the eighth symphony (see below).

SYMPHONY NO. 6

Sometimes known as the "Little" C major symphony to distinguish it from *Symphony No. 9*, the *Symphony No. 6* is one of the least known of Schubert's major works. Its neglect probably stems from the fact that, though its orchestration is heavier than in earlier symphonies, it has a somewhat throwaway air despite several moments of grandiloquence. This insouciance can be traced to the influence of Rossini apparent throughout, but, in particular, in the opening introduction which recalls a Rossini opera overture and in the bustle of the dotted rhythms that dominate the last-movement Allegro.

◑ **Royal Philharmonic Orchestra; Beecham** (EMI CDM7 69750-2; with *Symphonies Nos. 3 & 5*).

Thomas Beecham's scintillating performance, made in 1955, should really have rescued this symphony from its unjustifiable neglect. It's poised, elegant and fleet-footed and comes with equally seductive performance of *Symhonies Nos. 3* and *5*. An irresistible bargain.

SYMPHONY NO. 8 – THE UNFINISHED

Schubert's *Symphony No. 8* was composed in 1822, and then abandoned for reasons about which one can only speculate. It may be that he was simply unable to find the inspiration to continue with the last two movements or, more likely, that he was repulsed by the symphony's association with the painful events that had accompanied its composition – arguments with Vogl, a regrettable publishing agreement, and the emergence of the symptoms of syphilis. Its truncated form has been no handicap to success, however, and this is now the best known of all Schubert's orchestral music.

The first movement is ushered in by the basses, playing a darkly hued theme of ominous power. This leads to a gentle rustle of strings over which an intensely yearning theme is played by oboe and clarinet in unison; then the movement's dominant idea is introduced, in the shape of a sweeping melody which, for extra weight, is given over to the cellos. It is one of the most profound openings in all symphonic music. The second movement is an open-air episode, in which the first movement's intimations of doom are transformed into radiant optimism. With this movement Schubert showed himself to be a master of orchestration as well as of symphonic form. From here on, no one could categorize him as a songwriter with unseemly aspirations.

◑ **Vienna Philharmonic Orchestra; Kleiber** (Deutsche Grammophon 449 745; with *Symphony No. 3*).

Carlos Kleiber's recordings are self-recommending: unwilling to tackle any piece of music without thoroughly thinking it through, he goes into the studio very rarely, and always obtains thrilling results. This account of the *Unfinished* is the most dramatic on record, highlighting the dynamic contrasts without impeding the flow. It's coupled with a quicksilver interpretation of the third symphony.

⊙ **San Francisco Symphony Orchestra; Blomstedt** (Decca 448 7072-2DH; with *Symphony No. 5* and *Rosamunde Overture*).

Blomstedt concentrates on the essentially lyrical nature of the *Unfinished* – nothing is forced and everything has its place. Something of the composer's contradictory psychology might be missed, but this is immensely accomplished playing, and it comes with the best available version of the fifth symphony.

SYMPHONY NO. 9 – THE GREAT

Schubert's orchestral masterpiece is the mighty *Symphony No. 9*, better known as the "Great". It was written in the year of his death for the Gesellschaft der Musikfreunde (Society of Friends of Music), who found the music too difficult for their tastes. The spurned manuscript went missing for a number of years until Schumann found it in 1838, whereupon he sent it to Mendelssohn, who gave the symphony its premiere in Leipzig on March 21, 1839.

Schubert's slow movements are frequently the high points, and the blissful, ardent slow movement of the *Great* is very special indeed. Schumann, for one, admired this movement immensely, extolling its "heavenly length". He was especially taken by the section leading towards the recapitulation of the main theme, when the horn plays a series of delicate repeated notes – the instrument, Schumann said, was "calling as though from . . . another sphere. Everything else is hushed, as though listening to some heavenly visitant hovering around the orchestra." The symphony as a whole is characterized by an exceptional rhythmic energy, while his radically advanced orchestration places much greater weight on the brass sections, anticipating the bias of much Romantic orchestral music. In brief the *Great* is Schubert's longest, most demanding and most eloquent symphony.

◑ **Berlin Philharmonic Orchestra; Furtwängler** (Deutsche Grammophon 447 439-2; with Haydn, *Symphony No. 88*).

This is not as exciting and emotionally charged as Furtwängler's live recording of 1942 (not currently available) but it still makes an incredible impact. Furtwängler's vision and discipline bring a dimension to this music that few other conductors have realized on disc.

O North German Radio Symphony Orchestra; Wand (RCA RD60978).

Gunther Wand's recording with the North German Orchestra is an extremely good modern version; his players might respond with less character and immediacy than do Furtwängler's, but the sound and balance are considerably better.

CHAMBER MUSIC

Schubert composed an astonishing amount of chamber music, much of it before the age of 20, but it's the work that he carried out in his last years which really justifies the use of superlatives. Overall his chamber music is marked by a vein of intensely lyrical melody to which, in the later works, is added a strengthening of resources on several fronts. Increasing chromatic boldness and a greater flexibility of form become notable, as do a scrupulous attention to the details of instrumentation, a more aggressive use of rhythm, and a sometimes overwhelming sense of urgency. Schubert's final chamber masterpieces – the last three string quartets, the piano trios and the *String Quintet* – were written about the same time that Beethoven was working on his final series of quartets. Both bodies of work are profoundly personal and, while Schubert's may not possess the same degree of discursiveness or complexity, not even Beethoven conveys the sheer implacable momentum that runs through these last works.

QUINTET FOR PIANO AND STRINGS – THE TROUT

In 1819, during a walking tour with Michael Vogl in Upper Austria, Schubert stayed in Vogl's home town of Steyr, a place he thought "inconceivably lovely". Here the two men met a wealthy patron of the arts named Sylvester Paumgartner, who asked Schubert to compose a work for one of his musical gatherings. Paumgartner made some stipulations: the piece should employ the same instrumentation as Hummel's *Quintet* (piano, violin, viola, cello, double bass) and at least one of the movements should be a theme and variations based upon Schubert's song *Die Forelle* (The Trout). The resulting *Trout Quintet*, completed the following year, is an irresistibly good-natured piece of music, and there is no better introduction to Schubert. The dramatic Allegro, soulful Andante, lively Scherzo, rippling variations and gypsyish finale all display a staggering wealth of invention and thematic contrast. The piano part is marvellously integrated with the textures of the strings, with a high, lightly written role that beautifully balances the weight of the double bass.

⊙ **Jandó, Tóth, Kodály Quartet** (Naxos 8550658; with *Adagio* and *Rondo concertante*).

The Kodály Quartet and Jenö Jandó have individually produced a succession of excellent recordings for Naxos. In 1992 they came together with István Tóth to make this warm and effulgent version of the *Trout*. Star-name recordings are often dominated by an overbearing pianist, but Jandó and the Kodály Quartet are brilliantly coordinated in their light-footed approach. A charming recording, and great value.

◑ **Curzon, Vienna Octet** (Decca 448 602-2; with Dvořák, *Piano Quintet*).

Recorded in 1957, this is an utterly winning account, full of wit and sparkle though the rather thin sound may deter some. Curzon was a natural Schubert performer and here his playing sounds particularly joyous and spontaneous – especially in the Variations. This is great chamber-music playing, with the players sounding in one mind but also clearly having a good time.

PIANO TRIOS NOS. 1 & 2

Schubert's two complete piano trios were probably composed in fairly quick succession in 1827. The first, in B flat, is one of his ripest creations: stuffed with long melodies of effortless lyricism, it is a perfectly balanced composition. Whereas Beethoven's trios give preference to the piano part, each of Schubert's three players is accorded an equal bite of the very sweet cherry. All four movements are immensely attractive but the second is its finest: a journey of musical discovery, it begins with one of the most marvellous of all his tunes, played first by the cello over rippling triplets and then by the violin. The *Trio No. 2 in E Flat* was performed at Schubert's public concert in March 1828. It opens with a similar flourish to the earlier work but, on the whole, it's a rather more delicate and sombre work full of passages of quiet yearning. This is especially true of the marvellous slow movement (used in the film *Barry Lyndon*) in which a plaintive song-like melody on the cello is heard against a repeated strumming accompaniment. The weakness of the work is its overlong last movement which, though full of glorious moments, seems to go around in circles.

◑ **Beaux Arts Trio** (Philips 438 700-2; 2 CDs; with *Notturno* and *String Trios*).

The Beaux Arts Trio may seem a predictable choice, but once again the amazing rapport between the players and their impeccable style yield winning results. The verve with which they attack the opening of *Piano Trio No. 1* justifies Schumann's comment that "A glance at Schubert's *Trio*. . . and all the world glows fresh and bright again." They even succeed in making you forget the prolixity of *No. 2*'s last movement. This two-disc set also includes fine performances by the Grumiaux Trio of the charming but slight *String Trios*.

ARPEGGIONE SONATA

This is the oddity in Schubert's chamber music. In 1824 the instrument maker J.G. Staufer of Vienna invented a new instrument, a kind of bowed guitar, which he called the arpeggione. The guitarist Vincenz Schuster seems to have been its only professional exponent, and in the same year he commissioned a work for it from Schubert. The result was a fine sonata, which is now performed mainly by cellists and occasionally by viola players. It remains an underrated work, although in the right hands it exudes enormous panache, beginning with an opening melody which seems to possess the seemingly contradictory qualities of swagger and melancholy. A beautiful Adagio – another quasi-song – leads into a thematically rich but slightly underdeveloped Allegretto.

◑ **Rostropovich; Britten** (Decca 417 833-2; with Debussy, *Cello Sonata*).

Stravinsky famously dismissed Benjamin Britten as "a talented accompanist", an enviable skill displayed at its best in the wonderful partnership he established with Rostropovich. There's a warmth and tangible sympathy on display here which brings out all the sonata's wit and sly charm. A classic recording.

OCTET IN F

Schubert's serenely confident *Octet* is doubly unique: it is is his only work for eight players, and no other major composer has written for the same combination – two violins, viola, cello, bass, clarinet, horn and bassoon. It was commissioned by a Viennese nobleman named Ferdinand Troyer, a fine clarinettist, who wanted a companion piece to Beethoven's *Septet*, a work of immense popularity at the time. Schubert completed his commission on March 1, 1824, but it was not performed until 1827 and did not appear in print until 26 years later.

The *Octet*'s six movements last over an hour, but the piece is so light-hearted that the time flies past. Similarities between Beethoven's and Schubert's works are few, and the only real acts of homage are Schubert's imitation of Beethoven's use of folk-based variation form for the fourth movement, and the use of a slow introduction to the finale – exactly eighteen bars in length, just like Beethoven's. Highly appealing is Schubert's delicate, unfussy counterpoint and, as ever, his concentration upon song-like melody, but the most remarkable feature of the *Octet* is his effortless unification of the potentially disparate instrumental colours, with the clarinet and violin taking the dominant roles.

◑ **Vienna Octet** (Decca 421 155-2DM; with Mozart, *Divertimento*).

There are a number of fine *Octet* recordings, but the Vienna Octet's performance is perhaps best suited to the music's optimistic nature, and their attention to ensemble playing produces an endearing through-flowing momentum. Excellently recorded and, at mid-price, good value.

STRING QUARTETS NOS. 13–15

In March 1824, despite describing himself as "the most unhappy and wretched creature in the world", Schubert completed the *String Quartets* in A minor and D minor – his first for over three years. He'd been inspired to write them through contact with the famous Quartet led by Ignaz Schuppaznigh who duly performed *No. 13* a few weeks later. It's the most intimate and highly concentrated of the quartets, with an opening theme of brooding sadness played by the first violin over a restless accompaniment. It's a work full of Schubertian ambivalence – sad songs interrupted by flurries of almost manic energy. This ambivalence is pushed to extremes in *Quartet No. 14*, which he wrote shortly after. This is arguably the greatest of the three late quartets, chiefly on account of its harrowing emotional honesty, which reaches an almost unendurable pitch in the second movement, a set of variations based upon Schubert's song *Der Tod und das Mädchen* (Death and the Maiden) – hence the quartet's customary title. The quartet is characterized by its unrelenting rhythmic force, which is introduced by the opening movement's furious principal theme, then carried by the desperate song of the variations, and in turn followed by a whirling Presto like a grim dance of death. Schubert's final quartet, in G major, is less driven than *No. 14* but it has a similar rawness with an unnerving tension set up between major and minor in its long first movement. An elegiac cello melody in the slow movement establishes a mood of calm, broken by angry interruptions, while another whirligig dance rounds the whole thing off – this one with a somewhat theatrical display of menace.

◑ **Lindsay Quartet** (ASV CD DCS 417; 4 CDs; with *Quartets Nos. 8 & 12* and the *String Quintet*).

The Lindsay Quartet are best known for their passionate performances of Beethoven, but if anything their Schubert recordings are even better, bringing out every gradation of light and shade with thrilling directness. There's an apparent spontaneity to their playing which, of course, comes from knowing the work so thoroughly that it sounds absolutely fresh and exciting.

◑ **Quartetto Italiano** (Philips 446 163; 2 CDs).

If it's just the late quartets you want, this is an excellent choice at mid-price. The Italian Quartet were always a tightly knit ensemble, and this set shows them at their best. As you'd expect from a mid-1960s set, the sound isn't quite as crisp as the ASV recordings, but it's more than acceptable.

THE STRING QUINTET

Schubert's *String Quintet in C Major*, his greatest chamber work, was also his last – on October 2, 1828, just seven weeks before his death, the composer wrote to a friend that he had "finally turned out" a quintet. Rather than compose for a string quartet plus extra viola, which is the conventional setup for a string quintet, Schubert scored his work for an extra cello, thus creating a darker, more sonorous tone for this tragically beautiful music. Every moment is magnificent – no other composer could surpass the lyricism of the cello duet in the opening movement, the simple grace of the third movement and the rhythmic bite of the finale. But the emotional centre of gravity is the Adagio, a desperately poignant, valedictory statement which seems to hover between two worlds.

O Lindsay Quartet, Cummings (ASV CDDCA537).

This wonderful performance is courageously restrained, with none of the self-indulgent emotionalism that mars many other recordings. Delicate yet full of intense contrasts, this intense but never overstated account does full justice to Schubert's masterpiece. The performance can also be obtained in the four-disc set discussed above.

◑ **Stern, Schneider, Katims, Casals, Tortelier** (Sony SMK 58992; with *Symphony No. 5*).

This 1952 performance is one of the most celebrated of all chamber music recordings. At the heart of it is the cello of Pablo Casals – a musician whose deep sensitivity and awareness of the music's emotional ebb and flow makes for an experience that is even more moving than usual.

LIEDER

Schubert's *Gretchen am Spinnrade*, written at the age of 17, announced the arrival of a songwriter of preternatural abilities. Nobody previously had brought such complexity and sophistication to this salon genre. In *Gretchen am Spinnrade* the piano is no mere accompaniment to the singer but a protagonist in its own right, playing its part in the creation of the emotional drama. Through the music you hear the motion of the spinning wheel and sense every fluctuation of Gretchen's ever-changing emotions, which build to a crisis at the extraordinary moment when the wheel stops, only to begin again as she recovers herself. Goethe, on whose poem the song is based, disapproved of the prominent piano part and found Schubert's harmonic style too bizarre; he returned the manuscript, unimpressed. However, the poet later had a change of heart regarding Schubert's songs. In 1830 he heard *Erlkönig* performed by Wilhelmine Schröder-Devrient (a favourite singer of Wagner), and was moved to remark – "I saw this composition once before, when it did not appeal to me at all; but sung in this way the whole shapes itself into a visible picture."

More than anything else by the composer, Schubert's songs live or die with the talents of their performers. Like the plays of Shakespeare (several of whose verses he set), the songs respond to a variety of interpretations while always needing a singer who can strike the right balance between characterization and vocal beauty, and a pianist who knows when to step into the limelight and when to withdraw. Broadly speaking, interpretative styles range between those who tend to let the music alone bring out the meaning and those who dramatize the songs – sometimes to an extreme extent. The brilliantly spooky *Erlkönig*, with its four different voices, makes a good yardstick for checking which approach you prefer. It's also typical in the way it combines memorable melodies with an acute sensitivity to the text's nuances of mood and feeling.

The habit of singing these songs in translation has, unfortunately, largely disappeared (the baritone Peter Dawson's 1936 performance of *Erlkönig* in English is one of the most exciting ever recorded). But do not be put off, as some are, if German is not a language you understand. Nearly all recordings provide translations, which are worth following until a song becomes familiar. This is not music to be rushed: its unique blend of directness and subtlety means that the songs' full range of pleasures is only revealed after many hearings.

There are many ways to enter the vast terrain of Schubert's song catalogue. Our selection below represents the tip of the iceberg. The two anthology discs by young singers make a good starting point (and there are equivalent individual recital discs by Dietrich Fischer-Dieskau). On the other hand, if you want to start at the top, then listen first to *Die schöne Müllerin* and *Winterreise*, where an unforgettable impact is created by the cumulative effect of one connected song after another.

O Favourite Schubert Songs: Terfel, Martineau (Deutsche Grammophon 445 294-2).

The Welsh baritone Bryn Terfel won the Lieder prize in the 1989 Cardiff Singer of the World Competition, since when he has pursued a glittering career as an opera singer. He still makes occasional forays into lieder singing and this disc of some of the most well-known Schubert songs would make a very good introduction for anyone new to this music. It's a big dramatic voice, some might think too big for song, but one with a wide range of colours which are employed with wonderful control – he's equally at home in the wild melodrama of *Erlkönig* as he is in the serene beauty of *Du bist die Ruh'*.

O Schubert Lieder: Bonney, Parsons (Teldec 4509 90873-2).

Schubert's lieder are not an exclusively male preserve – though it sometimes seems that way – and the American soprano Barbara Bonney makes an extremely persuasive case for them being performed by every type of singer. It's not just that she has a beautiful voice, but her interpretations communicate very strongly the meaning of the words. There is some overlap with the Terfel disc, but she includes a highly introspective account of *Gretchen am Spinnrade* as well as the famous *Shepherd on the Rock* with its clarinet obbligato.

⊙ Lieder: Fischer-Dieskau, Moore (Deutsche Grammophon 437 214-2GX21; 21 CDs).

Dietrich Fischer-Dieskau, the most popular of postwar lieder singers, has a declamatory and forceful style that is utterly unlike Souzay's. Nobody has lived with Schubert's songs for as long as Fischer-Dieskau, and he has produced scores of recordings of them, often returning to the same pieces several times, invariably bringing something new to them. Deutsche Grammophon's colossal budget-price boxed set, a splendid testament to a great artist, includes nearly all of Schubert's songs. The 21 CDs are also available in three mid-price volumes, covering the periods 1811–17 and 1817–28, with the three cycles comprising the three-disc third volume. Some of Fischer-Dieskau's finest single-CD recordings are recommended below.

O The Hyperion Schubert Edition: Graham Johnson (Hyperion; 36-CD series available individually).

Once you've got to know more than a handful of songs, it's worth investigating the wonderful Hyperion series. Under the guidance of pianist Graham Johnson – who provides highly perceptive annotations for each CD – Hyperion have set out to record all Schubert's songs. The novelty of this series is that the songs are grouped by theme, with singers selected for their suitability for each group of songs (not even Fischer-Dieskau is right for every song). Thus, to take two of the most outstanding contributions, Arleen Augér's recital concentrates on songs with a theatrical connection, while Brigitte Fassbaender has made a set of songs about death. Johnson has also enlisted the brightest of the new generation of lieder singers, in particular Ian Bostridge, Mathias Goerne and Christine Schäfer. Of course not every voice will necessarily appeal, so its worth taking advantage of the budget-price sampler by way of an introduction (CD HYP200).

DIE SCHÖNE MÜLLERIN

In 1823, during a time of great physical and mental distress, Schubert discovered a collection of verses – *Poems from the Posthumous Papers of a Travelling Hornplayer* – by a contemporary, Wilhelm Müller. The poems had a simple directness which clearly made a strong impact on him and he set twenty of them as a cycle entitled *Die schöne Müllerin* (The Fair Maid of the Mill). The verses outline a rather sketchy story about a young miller setting out on his travels. Constant throughout the cycle is the presence of the millstream, which Schubert evokes,

POLYGRAM

Brigitte Fassbaender

notably in the first six songs, through a torrent of rippling semi-quavers in the piano part. The cycle begins with an opening song, *Das Wandern*, of jaunty optimism, but gradually the general air of lightness begins to darken as it becomes clear that the young man's love for the miller's daughter is unrequited. Jealous anger is provoked by a rival, the hunter, and a new tinge of tragedy emerges with *Die Liebe Farbe* in which the miller meditates on the colour green – the favourite colour of his beloved. This, essentially conventional, tale of doomed innocence is transformed by Schubert into an acute study of the pain of disillusionment. Its unhappy denouement foreshadows the even darker world of *Winterreise*.

◑ **Fischer-Dieskau, Moore** (EMI CDC7 47173-2).

Fischer-Dieskau has recorded this cycle several times. Of his three versions with Gerald Moore, this 1961 account is the best as a first-time buy. His partnership with Moore produces some dramatically spontaneous singing and his wonderfully crafted voice comes into its own in the more sombre songs (he is slightly uncomfortable in the lighter, less furrowed works).

O Bostridge, Johnson (Hyperion CDJ 33025).

This is a high point of the Hyperion series and one of the most moving versions of the cycle. The choice of Ian Bostridge, a light-voiced English tenor, brings home how much *Die schöne Müllerin* is a young man's tragedy. Its a very detailed performance where every nuance and subtlety has been carefully pondered without a hint of contrivance or artfulness. All of the unset Müller poems are recited by Fischer-Dieskau, an interesting addition.

WINTERREISE

In *Winterreise* (Winter Journey), Schubert takes the despondency which closed *Die schöne Müllerin* and pushes it to extremes, creating a desolate landscape (both inner and outer) of unrelenting pessimism – indeed his friends, when they first heard the complete cycle in the autumn of 1827, were dismayed by its bleakness, while understanding the personal pain from which it was created. The 24 verses are again by Müller, but Schubert altered their order so that the occasional flashes of consolation offered by the poet in the original sequence are no longer visible. The protagonist, a rejected lover, seems on the verge of madness as we follow his lonely peregrinations through a snowbound landscape. Unlike the earlier cycle, nature is here represented as something cruel and unsympathetic to his fate. As his journey progresses, so his vision becomes all the more inward and the subjectivity of the songs all the more pronounced. The final song, *Der Leiermann*, is a masterstroke: the traveller meets a destitute hurdy-gurdy player, whose rustic music Schubert mimics with a drone and a quirky figure in the piano. The wanderer wonders whether he should go with him but his question is left hanging in the air and the song simply drifts away.

O Fischer-Dieskau, Brendel (Philips 411 463-2PH).

Fischer-Dieskau's dark intensity is best suited to these heavy-hearted songs, and he brings terrible poignancy to the plight of the friendless wanderer. This is perhaps the finest of all Fischer-Dieskau's Schubert recordings.

O Schreier, Richter (Philips 442 360-2).

Some people, however, find that a baritone voice rather overdoes the gloom of *Winterreise*, and that a tenor actually enhances the drama through the contrast between vocal tone and meaning. Peter Schreier's live recording, accompanied by the ever-thoughtful Sviastoslav Richter, is a most persuasive argument in favour of the tenor approach.

O Fassbaender, Reimann (EMI CDC7 498 46-2; with five other songs).

Brigitte Fassbaender's dark-hued mezzo is one of the most intense and affecting voices of modern times. Above all, she has the ability to wring every nuance out of a song's meaning and packs more incident into these microdramas than almost anyone else.

SCHWANENGESANG

The fourteen songs of the aptly named *Schwanengesang* (Swan-Song) were not conceived as a cycle by Schubert, but were cobbled together after his death by the publisher Haslinger, who had bought them from Schubert's brother. The songs set verses by three young poets – seven are by Rellstab, six by Heine and one by Seidl – and while there is no unifying narrative the selection and setting does creates a coherent psychological landscape. *Schwanengesang* isn't coloured by the unremitting grief of *Winterreise*, but the mood is fairly sombre. In particular the Heine settings have a pared-down style which is especially effective in the two vignettes of the uncanny – *Die Stadt* and *Der Doppelganger*. The one anomaly is the somewhat twee final song *Die Taubenpost*, in which the poet tells of his carrier pigeon – a rather cumbersome metaphor for constancy – but even here there's a suggestion in the music that the whole thing could just be wishful thinking.

O Terfel, Martineau (Sain SCDC 4035).

Bryn Terfel recorded *Schwanengesang* in 1991 for the Welsh company Sain. It's an outstanding performance and well worth tracking down. Sain favour a less forward sound than Terfel's Deutsche Grammophon disc, thus increasing the sense of tension and concentration – *Der Doppelganger* in particular gets a rapt and marvellously controlled reading.

◐ Holzmair, Cooper (Philips 442 460-2).

Sadly Philips have decided to delete Gerard Souzay's astonishing performance of *Schwanengesang* – one of the very best recorded – which until fairly recently was available in a four-disc box set. In the meantime they have issued this version by Wolgang Holzmair and Imogen Cooper which is extremely fine – more subdued than Terfel but no less convincing.

PIANO MUSIC

Almost alone among the great composers for the piano, Schubert was himself no virtuoso. This is reflected in the absence of bravura passages in his piano works which, with the exception of the *Wanderer Fantasy*, make no great technical demands on a performer. Instead Schubert translated his matchless lyric gift into practically everything he wrote for the piano – from the numerous light-hearted dance pieces to the profoundly personal late sonatas. It is with the sonatas that his reputation as a piano composer stands, even though they were completely neglected for a hundred years after his death until the pianists Anton Schnabel and Edward Erdmann rediscovered them. Schubert was the last great composer for whom the sonata was the primary genre of piano music. His loyalty to the form goes some way to explain his neglect in the era of Chopin, Liszt and Schumann, for whom the traditional imperatives of the sonata made it less attractive than the étude, prelude and other vehicles for spontaneous-sounding expression. However, Schubert's relationship to the sonata tradition was not one of straightforward allegiance. Most of his piano sonatas – especially the last three – display a flexibility of structure and an adventurous handling of harmony and tone that is the key to their profoundly dramatic character. Schubert the proto-Romantic is more clearly revealed in the *Wanderer Fantasy* and in his short lyric pieces, in which the minimum of formal constraints is placed on his melodic expansiveness.

◐ Complete Piano Sonatas: Schiff (Decca 448 390-2; 7 CDs).

Schiff is an outstanding Schubertian, particularly alive to the undercurrents of feeling that are a constant presence in the sonatas. He plays on a Bosendorfer piano precisely because its gentler, warmer tone and touch corresponds to his view of Schubert as, above all, a creator of multilayered and translucent texture.

◑ Complete Piano Sonatas: Kempff (Deutsche Grammophon 423 496-2; 7 CDs).

Not as sweet-toned nor as ingratiating as Schiff, nevertheless these are immensely assured performances – elegantly phrased and with a full, strong tone. Just occasionally, in the late sonatas especially, the internal drama seems underplayed but, with outstanding sound (from the late 1960s) and at mid-price, this set has no serious faults.

SONATA NO. 14

The *Piano Sonata No. 14* in A minor, written in 1823, a few months after the *Wanderer Fantasy*, signals a change of direction in Schubert's sonata writing. Though only in three movements, it possesses a breadth of feeling and a grandness of design which is positively symphonic in scope. The opening – a short phrase in stark octaves that manages to be both simultaneously expansive and reticent – sets the tone for a piece which abounds in startling contrasts. The most dramatic occur in the first movement, which travels from a mood of sombre yearning through agitated tremolandos into a rich melody shot through with resignation. It's an encapsulation of Schubert at his most quixotic.

◐ Cooper (Ottavo OTR C68608; with *Sonata No. 18* and *12 German Dances*).

Imogen Cooper, who has recorded all the major Schubert piano works for the Dutch company Ottavo, has emerged in recent years as one of the most dynamic and eloquent of Schubert interpreters. More than most she lets the music do the work for her, her acute musical intelligence bringing out the constant interplay of darkness and light through perfectly judged dynamics and deftly applied variations in colour.

SONATAS NOS. 17 & 18

In August 1825 Schubert was at the mountain spa of Gastein, halfway through his extended holiday with Vogl. This was one of the happiest times of his troubled life and it produced one of the most exuberant of all his piano sonatas, *No. 17* in D Major. The opening Allegro is especially energetic

with a bold fanfare-like figure followed by rapid triplets which scurry around for most of the movement. The subsequent three movements redress the balance by way of a series of sweet melodies that, at times, border on the simpering. *Sonata No. 18* in G Major, written a year later, is a work of more subtly shifting moods, quintessentially Schubertian in the way the lilting dreamlike opening is developed to incorporate angry outbursts and troubled asides without in any way upsetting the overall cohesion of the movement. This is piano music as discursive soliloquy – each idea clearly develops out of another – with an overriding sense of a rather fragile consciousness gradually revealing itself.

O Piano Sonata No. 17: Cooper (Ottavo OTR C128715; with *Moments Musicaux*).

Again what is impressive here is the variety of touch that Cooper brings to bear on this sonata, allowing her to be bold but unmelodramatic in the first movement, and delicate and playful in the other three.

O Piano Sonata No. 18: Cooper (Ottavo OTR C68608; with *Sonata No. 14* and *12 German Dances*).

The intimate, dreamy nature of *Sonata No. 18* is particularly difficult to bring off. Cooper judges the overall shape of the long first movement to perfection, controlling the sudden changes of musical and emotional direction with consummate ease.

THE LAST SONATAS

The last three sonatas – *No. 19* in C Minor, *No. 20* in A Major and *No. 21* in B flat Major – were all composed around the same time as the *String Quintet*, and Schubert died two months after finishing his work on the last of the group. Comparison with Beethoven's final sonatas are inevitable, and to an extent the comparison is just: like Beethoven's last five, these works are overcast by the imminence of death, and they represent the furthest extremity of the composer's keyboard music in more than a merely chronological sense.

But, whereas the late Beethoven sonatas are marked by a desperate need to communicate, to arrive at a means of conveying something that ultimately eludes expression, the Schubert sonatas look inward, constantly repeating and reformulating themes as if they were persistent memories. Deep pessimism pervades this music – the Andantino of *Sonata No. 20*, for example, is built on a melody that returns again and again to the same single note, as if to an unassuageable pain, and is then interrupted by a terrifying outburst of splintered motifs within which no melody can be found. The late sonatas are long musical soliloquies in which the forceful direction of Beethoven's music is replaced by structures that seem to circle round their subjects without ever coming to rest. This is not to say that these works are in any way self-indulgent or prolix. It is rather that the conventional perception of linear time is here suspended. The philosopher Theodor Adorno summarized what is astounding about these three sonatas when he talked about their "landscape-like quality"; they do indeed define an emotional terrain that is unique to Schubert.

O Late Piano Sonatas: Pollini (Deutsche Grammophon 419 229-2; 2 CDs; with *Drei Klavierstücke* & *C Minor Allegretto*).

This rapt, anguished and self-absorbed music requires not just sensitivity to each inflection but an analytical mind capable of bringing out the cogency of the longer spans. So perfectly judged are the tempi, tone and weight of Pollini's performances that there's always a point to each repetition; what can seem like meandering diversions in other hands here come across as essential qualifications and revisions. These superb accounts are coupled with four late Schubert miniatures, each as melancholy as the sonatas. Also available as two separate CDs.

O Piano Sonatas Nos. 20 & 21: Schnabel (EMI CHS7 64259-2; 2 CDs; with *Sonata No. 17*, *Moments Musicaux* and *March*).

These 1939 recordings, finely transferred, are by the man who, more than anyone else, revealed Schubert's piano music as essential repertoire material. Despite some odd tempi, these are still remarkable performances – convincing, above all, for their intellectual probity and resistance to any false sentimentality.

◑ Piano Sonata No. 20: Serkin (Sony SBK63042; with *Impromptus*).

In his prime Serkin was regarded as one of the great masters of the classical repertoire and this recording (from the mid-1960s) shows why. Concentration is so palpably intense, technique so much at the service of feeling that is hard, having heard it, to imagine this work played any other way.

◑ Sonata No. 21: Curzon (Decca 448 578-2; with Brahms, *Piano Sonata No.3*).

Curzon's recordings of Schubert are few and far between, which is a pity because, like Serkin, he had a real affinity with the composer. The approach is noble and expansive and reveals a singer-like sensitivity to Schubert's long arching phrases.

MOMENTS MUSICAUX

The concentrated poetic miniature for the piano was the mainstay of the Romantic piano repertoire. Schubert's major contribution to the genre consisted of six pieces published together, in 1828, under the title *Moments Musicaux*, and two sets of *Impromptus*. Most of the *Moments Musicaux* almost certainly date from Schubert's last years, though two of them were published separately at an earlier date: *No. 3* , with its jaunty rhythm, as *Air Russe*, and the melancholy *No. 6* as *Les Plaintes d'un troubadour.* All six pieces display Schubert's ability at distilling a feeling without recourse to the kind of virtuosity that you frequently find in the miniatures of Chopin and Liszt. And although their range is limited – the dominant mood is one of introspection – the emotional fine shading which the *Moments Musicaux* possess is unprecedented in its detail and intensity.

Cooper (Ottavo OTR C128715; with *Sonata No. 17*).

This is deeply sensitive and elegant playing which more than holds it own in comparison with those by better-known names. Every phrase is given just the right weight and emphasis to draw out its internal meaning. The elegiac *No. 3* gets an especially fine reading.

THE IMPROMPTUS

Schubert once wrote to his father, "people assured me that the keys became singing voices under my hands", and nowhere is the vocal nature of his piano writing more evident than in the two sets of four *Impromptus* he composed in the last year of his life. Perhaps best described as large-scale miniatures, these brief but expansive pieces have the appearance of spontaneous personal utterance, veering from one mood to another with all unpredictability that the title "Impromptu" suggests. The second set has sometimes been read as a loose-limbed sonata: it certainly is not one in any conventional sense, but certainly there's a sense of interconnection to the sequence, which culminates in a fierce, scherzo-like episode. In their roaming exploration of fleeting emotion and piano texture, the *Impromptus* are Schubert's most direct connection to the music of Chopin, Schumann and Liszt.

Perahia (Sony SK37291).

Perahia's recording of the *Impromptus* was deservedly hailed as a classic on the day of its issue, in the mid-1980s. Elegant and perfectly paced, Perahia's playing is so subtle and profound that you are left with something different after every hearing.

Brendel (Philips 422 237-2).

Brendel is another marvellous Schubert player, especially good in the smaller pieces, where his attention to detail and concentration create performances of poised perfection.

THE WANDERER FANTASY

Comprising four movements to be played without a break, the *Wanderer Fantasy* of 1822 is at once a homage to the classical sonata and a subversion of it. The overall shape resembles that of the great Beethoven sonatas, but it is used to contain quasi-improvisatory elements which, as it were, break down the ordained structure from inside. Thus the second movement is a set of variations that sounds more like a sequence of impressionistic mood pieces, while the finale opens as a fugue that evolves quickly into a blazing outbreak of unfettered passion. A degree of formal unity comes from the motif with which the fantasy opens, for it provides the basic material from which all the subsequent major themes are constructed. In the second movement this motif becomes recognizable as a theme from Schubert's song *Der Wanderer*, a link that introduces a Schumann-like element of autobiographical confession. The array of free-ranging ideas within a plan of overarching unity marks the *Wanderer Fantasy* as an ancestor of Liszt's B Minor sonata and, indeed, this is one of the few Schubert piano works about which the succeeding generation showed any interest.

Pollini (Deutsche Grammophon 419 672-2; with *Piano Sonata No. 16*).

Pollini's version of the *Wanderer* is an ideal performance: highly charged but not reckless, tautly structured but not inflexible. It's coupled with the virtuosic *Piano Sonata No. 16*, written three years after the *Fantasy*, which reveals a similarly ambivalent attitude towards sonata form. Pollini's *Wanderer* is also available at mid-price, coupled with a similarly great reading of the Schumann *Fantasie*.

Perahia (Sony MK4124; with Schumann's *Fantasie*).

Perahia makes an interesting contrast to Pollini: less aggressively tempestuous, he brings out the work's more poetic aspects without compromising its restless energy.

PIANO DUETS

That Schubert wrote so much music for piano duet is often taken as a measure of just how convivial a man he was. Much of it was written during his time teaching the Esterházy girls at Zseliz, and several pieces involve a fair amount of stretching over a partner's arms (implying, for some, a desire for intimacy irreconcilable with his alleged homosexuality). Of the half-dozen or so masterpieces that he wrote for piano duet, the outstanding work is the *Fantasie in F Minor*, written in the last year of his life and dedicated to his favourite Esterházy pupil, the Countess Caroline. Like so many of his piano pieces, it is technically unchallenging but demands an acute sensitivity from both players, particularly in the control of dynamics. The opening is one of the

most strikingly mysterious that he ever wrote, with a desparately yearning upper part set against a darkly murmuring passage below. Given the prevailing sadness, Schubert succeeds in communicating such a variety of feelings in its four continuous sections as to suggest a work of intensely personal significance.

MOZART SONATA FOR 2 PIANOS IN D MAJOR, K.448
SCHUBERT FANTASIA FOR PIANO, 4 HANDS IN F MINOR, D940
MURRAY PERAHIA
RADU LUPU

⊙ Fantasie in F Minor: Perahia, Lupu (Sony SK 39511; with Mozart, *Sonata in D for 2 Pianos*).

Only one other recording, by Ingrid Haebler and Ludwig Hoffmann, matches this for poetic insight and it has never been issued on CD. Both performances possess the essential prerequisite for the *Fantaise* – a real rapport between the players that allows for some immensely hushed and delicate playing from the very beginning. Perahia and Lupu invest the work with more tragedy than poignancy, but it's an utterly compelling and convincing account of one of Schubert's greatest works.

ROBERT SCHUMANN

(1810–1856)

Robert Schumann died a failure in his own eyes, yet he occupies a key position in the music of the nineteenth century. The first Romantic with a deep knowledge of literature and philosophy, Robert Schumann saw it as his mission to fuse all the arts in music that spoke profoundly of its creator. He once wrote: "I am affected by everything extraordinary that goes on in the world and think it over in my own way . . . then I long to express my feelings and find an outlet for them in my music: a poem, something infinitely more spiritual, the result of poetical consciousness." His music came to be the confessional for his inner life. Schumann composed four symphonies and some fine chamber music, but it is his transparently candid piano works that truly reveal this enigmatic, complex composer. Despite his respect for classical forms (he was in awe of Beethoven), Schumann was quick to break away from them, creating instead music which reads like the pages of a diary – fragmented, condensed and profuse in invention. Schumann's compositions have a uniquely changeable emotional climate, shifting from passion to nostalgia, or from pain to ingenuous optimism, in the passage of a moment.

He was a middle-class boy from the provinces, born in Zwickau, Saxony, in 1810. His father, a bookseller and novelist, died in 1826, whereupon Robert's sister committed suicide, an event from which he never recovered. He enrolled at Leipzig University to study law, enjoyed the good life and the customary Grand Tour of the continent, and was told by his professor that he had no talent whatsoever. Yet he continued with his musical studies under Friedrich Wieck, a notable teacher in whose house he took lodgings. There he met Wieck's daughter Clara, a 9-year-old who was already showing signs of extraordinary ability as a pianist. Robert's own hopes of becoming a virtuoso were soon wrecked by the crippling of his left hand – ostensibly the result of a machine designed to strengthen his fourth finger, but more likely due to poisoning by the mercury he took when he realized he had syphilis ("My whole house is like a chemist's shop," he told his mother). Fortunately he had already begun to show talent as a composer.

His Opus 1 *Variations* derived their central motif from the letters of the surname of Meta Abegg, an early love. Schumann would often use such codes to devise thematic fragments, which he then developed into musical dialogues between imagined characters who reflected the ambivalences of his nature. In Jean Paul's novel *Die Flegejahre* (Years of Indiscretion) he came across Walt and Vult, introvert and extrovert, from whom he derived his two creative demons, christened Florestan and Eusebius. The personae of Florestan and Eusebius recur in his work "in order to express contrasting

LEBRECHT COLLECTION

Robert and Clara Schumann, 1847

In that same year Schumann composed two great song cycles, *Dichterliebe* and *Frauenliebe und -leben*, both relating to his feelings for Clara. The following year his first symphony appeared, then in 1843 Mendelssohn offered him a piano professorship at the new Leipzig Conservatory. But Schumann's manic depression was now taking the form of increasing bleakness of vision and creative sterility, and led to serious breakdowns. He resigned and moved to Dresden, but Clara's triumphant concert tours, triumphs for herself as a concert artist, only emphasized how widespread indifference to her husband's music had become. He lacked the training to dash off musical money-spinners: operas, festival canatas, frothy salon-pieces. His spell as conductor in Leipzig, beginning 1850, ended in recriminations and disaster. In 1854 he attempted suicide by throwing himself in the Rhine and was committed to an asylum near Bonn. There he died in July 1856, in the final ravages of tertiary syphilis, having starved himself through depression.

points of view about art", as the composer explained, since he perceived music as having the cut and thrust of Hegelian dialectic. Then there was the Davidsbund (The Band of David), a fictitious band of musicians at war against the artistic philistines; their names swarm through his scores and their signatures peopled the pages of *Neue Zeitschrift für Musik*, an iconoclastic musical journal of which Schumann was editor.

The 1830s began with the "Abegg" variations and produced most of his finest music: *Papillons*, *Carnaval*, *Davidsbündlertänze*, *Fantasiestücke*, the piano sonatas, *Kinderszenen*, the *Fantasie in C Major*, the beginnings of the *Études Symphoniques*. Yet it was also a decade of despair, for his attempts to marry Clara were blocked by her father. There were good reasons for the obstructiveness: Clara's blossoming career (unquestionably sacrificed in later years by the demands of life with Schumann); and the frivolities of a young man who showed little sign of being able to establish a serious career. In 1840 Schumann won legal action to overturn Wieck's veto and the couple were married one day before Clara's 21st birthday.

Of all great composers, Schumann is perhaps the worst represented by the CD catalogue. There have been some wonderful recordings over the years – Artur Rubinstein's 1960s interpretations of *Carnaval* and the *Fantasiestücke*, for example, or Murray Perahia's brilliant debut recording of the *Davidsbündlertänze* and *Fantasiestücke*. None of them is available at the moment. You can get hold of Perahia's versions of *Papillons* and the *Études Symphoniques*, but only if you invest in an eleven-disc set of Perahia recitals. It's a similar situation with Horowitz's performances of Schumann, which are only available packaged with other music in volumes 1, 3, 4 and 7 of Sony's *Horowitz Complete Masterworks* set – a fascinating series, but someone coming new to Schumann might not want to buy two hours of additional music just to hear Horowitz play ten minutes of Schumann. Deutsche Grammophon have issued a mid-price four-disc survey of Schumann's piano music played by Wilhelm Kempff, a set that has many high points (eg a very fine *Carnaval* and a superb *Davidsbündlertänze*), but in places misses the evanescent quality of the music. If you want to familiarize yourself with the range of Schumann's output, buy the Kempff set. If you want the very best, however, keep an eye out for Perahia and Rubinstein reissues, and in the meantime take your pick of the CDs selected below.

THE SYMPHONIES

Schumann for years tinkered with sketches for a major orchestral work, but like Brahms he lacked the courage to pursue them further. His discovery of Schubert's ninth symphony gave him the encouragement to try again, and in January and February of 1841 he wrote his *Spring Symphony*. It's an exuberant work, as indicated by the titles Schumann originally gave to its four movements – *Spring's Awakening*, *Evening*, *Merry Playmates* and *Full Spring*. The second symphony, written in the wake of a nervous breakdown in 1845, is the darkest, most conventional and least popular of the cycle, but the third, the *Rhenish*, is his most joyous and spontaneous. Conceived as a celebration of the landscape, legends and history of the Rhineland, it progresses from a thrilling, syncopated opening to a stately polyphonic finale that was inspired by a Mass celebrated in Cologne Cathedral – he marked it to be played "In the manner of an accompaniment to a solemn ceremony". The *Symphony No. 4*, written in 1841 but massively revised in 1852, is an extremely intense work, and is of revolutionary originality, being through-composed as one seamless development – almost every significant theme is generated by the motifs that appear in the slow introduction to the opening movement.

It has to be admitted that Schumann's symphonies are not masterpieces of orchestration. Schumann's first thoughts came to him as piano music, and his efforts to reorchestrate them invariably make them more opaque. It may be that he was deliberately making the music easier for inept orchestras and conductors (Schumann had experience of both), but whatever the reason they sometimes sound clumsy. For all that, they are essential to a full understanding of the composer, and there's a great deal in the symphonies to dispel the myth that Schumann's final years were a period of unmitigated decline.

O Staatskapelle Dresden; Sawallisch (EMI CMS 7 64815 2; 2 CDs).

Of all the complete sets available, Sawallisch is the most consistent, with more control than most over Schumann's more slovenly moments (the *Symphony No. 2* really moves under his direction). But what really convinces is the sheer euphoric vitality of his readings, notably in the fourth, which travels along with all the inevitability of a wave.

◑ Berlin Philharmonic Orchestra; Kubelik (Deutsche Grammophon 437 395 2GX2; 2 CDs).

Rafael Kubelik offers stiff competition to Sawallisch, with playing of superlative resilience and poise which, on the whole, is better recorded. The full emotional compass of Schumann's cycle is realized with a radiant ease, almost as if it were magnified chamber music.

O The Hanover Band; Goodman (RCA 09026 61931-2; 2 CDs).

Roy Goodman has said that Sawallisch was the inspiration for his own recording on period instruments. Goodman may not quite match Sawallisch's incandescence, but, for all those who wants to discover what Schumann really meant to say, this set is a revelation.

THE PIANO CONCERTO

In 1841 Schumann composed a single-movement piece for piano and orchestra, "something between a symphony, a concerto and a large sonata". When it was turned down by the publishers, he decided to transform it into a full-length concerto, but it was not until 1845 that he completed its Intermezzo and finale, extracting the motifs for both added movements from the woodwinds' opening theme. Liszt called the end result "a concerto without piano" and, anticipating its rejection, Schumann had declared he was unable to write a display piece. It certainly is not a vehicle for hair-raising virtuosity, but the concerto is a supremely eloquent piece, placing its emphasis on intimate dialogue between the soloist and orchestra. Its most obvious antecedents are Beethoven's fourth concerto; its descendants are the concertos of Brahms and, especially, the concerto by Grieg.

◑ Kovacevich; BBC Symphony Orchestra; Davis (Philips 446 129-2; with Grieg, *Piano Concerto*).

This is a performance which stands out for its clarity of thinking, and gets right to the heart of the music. Kovacevich has a fine rapport with the orchestra, and between them they develop a sense of line that sounds as natural as breathing.

O Perahia; Symphonie-Orchester des Bayerischen Rundfunks; Davis (Sony SK44899; with Grieg, *Piano Concerto*).

Perahia brings a magical impulsiveness which, coupled with his bright tone, creates a sharp, crystalline surface. There's an effervescent spontaneity to this performance, but also a sense of constant qualification, of building effects and redefining them.

THE CELLO CONCERTO

In 1849 Schumann had been offered the directorship of the Dusseldorf Orchestra, but despite his new duties his composing continued unabated. The *Cello Concerto* was finished in two hurried weeks, "a concert piece for cello with orchestral accompaniment", the composer called it – revealing his affinity for the instrument to which he had turned since the crippling of one hand and an end to his hopes as a concert pianist. It is, indeed, a quietly revolutionary piece made up of three linked movements and an accompanied cadenza. Its most memorable virtue is a solo line embedded in the orchestral fabric as a leading voice amongst civilized equals; its highlights are the exquisitely poetic opening and the twilight song which makes up the slow movement. It's the only nineteenth-century cello concerto of substance until that of Saint Saëns's and yet it was not performed in public before 1860.

O Starker; Bamberg Symphony Orchestra; Russell Davies (RCA 09026 68027-2; with Hindemith's *Cello Concerto*).

Starker's subtle agitation and sophisticated phrasing draw real intensity from what can too easily seem Schumann's most sombre and four-square work.

PAPILLONS

Schumann once referred to himself as a chrysalis, and he spoke of his initial inspirations as butterflies – motifs which appeared and then as suddenly disappeared in a flitter of colour and uncertain shape. The image is perfectly suited to the Opus 2 *Papillons*, which were written as a suite of twelve waltzes inspired by *Die Flegejahre*. Beginning with a motif that fades past vanishing point at its end, *Papillons* contains the most capricious and diaphanous music Schumann wrote, a supreme instance of art concealing art: completed in 1831, they represent three years of intermittent but intense work, distilling countless sketches and rearrangements.

O Richter (EMI CDM7 64625-2; with *Fantasie* and *Faschingsschwank aus Wien*).

Richter's live 1963 performance is both majestic and mercurial. The prevailing spirit is one of mischievous reminiscence, in which grand rhetorical gestures can suddenly dissolve into an almost imperceptible whisper.

O Ashkenazy (Decca 414 474-2; with *Études Symphoniques* and *Arabeske*).

With Perahia's wonderful account not currently available, Ashkenazy's performance of *Papillons* is the obvious alternative to Richter. Ashkenazy finds the resilience of these pieces as well as their lightness, through playing in which subtlety and vigour are well matched. It's coupled with a good, meaty version of the *Études Symphoniques*.

THE PIANO SONATAS

Schumann's three sonatas were all started in the same year, 1833, but were completed at intervals over the next five years – the first in 1835, the second in in 1836, the third in 1838. Shortly after finishing the last one, Schumann thus expressed his thoughts on the sonata as a genre: "it seems that the form has outlived its life cycle. This is of course in the natural order of things: we ought not to repeat the same statements for centuries, but rather to think about the new as well. So let's write sonatas or fantasies" – adding the comment, "what's in a name?" In essence, Schumann's sonatas are fantasies braced by a desire to live up to the example of Beethoven's sonatas. They are not as episodic as his other major works for solo piano (there are, for example, numerous motivic links between the movements), but neither do they adhere to the principles enshrined in the great Germanic tradition – in the *Sonata No. 1*, for example, the four movements are so disparate that really there's no reason why the work couldn't just as easily have been six movements long, or three or five. With their sudden changes of key, dramatic thematic transformations, and juxtaposition of rapt self-absorption with outbreaks of expansive emotion, the sonatas are quintessential Romantic piano music. The first two are more rewarding than the third – a revision of an earlier work, it is far less frequently recorded.

O Sonata No. 1: Pollini (Deutsche Grammophon 423 134-2: with *Fantasie in C Major*).

Lesser players can make the first sonata sound like nothing more than a stream of fugitive ideas, but Pollini's precise articulation and his sense of overall form ensure that the music's impetuousness never degenerates into incoherence – every gesture has a context.

◑ Sonata No. 2: Argerich (Deutsche Grammophon 437 252-2; with Liszt's *Sonata in B Minor* and Brahms's *Rhapsodies*).

In the second sonata, Martha Argerich gives a performance of fearless virtuosity: whole passages of notes are at once perfectly transparent yet gorgeously coloured, and there's a sense of tightly disciplined improvisation about the entire piece.

CARNAVAL

Carnaval is the Schumann piece in which spontaneity, invention and superlative technique coexist most vividly. Written in September 1834,

Carnaval is a series of tableaux, a masked ball in which one character after another takes centre stage. It was described by the composer as "Little scenes on four notes", a reference to the exercise in creative cryptography by which Schumann proclaimed his love for Ernestine von Fricken through the music. The letters ASCH, which spell Ernestine's birthplace as well as a fragment of his own name, translate in German musical notation into the notes A, E flat, C and B. Permutations of these notes litter the entire score, generating the themes for the Carnival characters, some of them historical (Chopin and Paganini), others folkloric (Pierrot and Harlequin), and others incarnations of Schumann's various personae (Florestan and Eusebius). It concludes with a *March of the Davidsbündler*, in which the Philistines are put triumphantly to flight.

Benedetti Michelangeli (Testament SBT2088; 2 CDs; with *Faschingsschwank aus Wien* and pieces by Chopin, Debussy and Mompou).

This is a recording of a legendary Festival Hall recital given by Arturo Benedetti Michelangeli, and it captures the volatile perfectionist at the very peak of his form. Listen to this and you'll understand why the mere mention of his name makes some people go glassy-eyed with awe. And listen to the sound check that makes up part of the second CD and you'll understand why some people found him the most exasperating person on the planet. A fascinating, thrilling document.

Barenboim (Deutsche Grammophon 431 167-2; with *Kinderszenen* and *Faschingsschwank aus Wien*).

This disc is an excellent deal, with Daniel Barenboim playing not only *Carnaval* but also a sensitive *Kinderszenen* and the underrated *Faschingsschwank aus Wien*. It's not the subtlest presentation, nor the most charming, but there's a big personality at work here, and at modest price this CD makes a splendid introduction to Schumann.

DAVIDSBÜNDLERTÄNZE

Written three years after *Carnaval*, the *Davidsbündlertänze* (Dances of the Band of David) is an assembly of eighteen mood-pieces that epitomize the multifariousness of Schumann's art. The sequence begins with a musical motto composed by Clara, and most of the dances use this motto's interval of a falling second as their starting point. Schumann attached a traditional poem as the epigraph – "In all and every time, pleasure and pain are linked" – and each of the pieces bears a phrase sketching the atmosphere: "Rather cockeyed . . . wild and merry . . . as if from afar". If you don't find the *Davidsbündlertänze* irresistible, you're not going to get on with Schumann.

Ashkenazy (Decca 425 109-2DH; with *Fantasiestücke*).

Ashkenazy's performance is fervent and brightly characterized, even if it doesn't match the standards set by Perahia's sparkling performance on Sony which, unfortunately, is not currently available.

KREISLERIANA

"One hardly dare breathe whilst reading the works of E.T.A. Hoffmann", Schumann confided to his diary in 1831. The Kapellmeister Johannes Kreisler was Hoffmann's own fictional ego, and the "fragments" of Hoffmann's novel depict an ardent and overwhelmingly restless romantic personality, spun helplessly by secret visions and fancies as if "on through an eternally stormy sea . . . He seemed to seek in vain the haven that would finally give him the peace and tranquillity without which an artist can seek nothing". Such demons and glimpses of "heavenly luminescence" were also Schumann's creative byword, and nobody has given us a more compelling or rounded musical self-portrait than in these eight dazzling vignettes.

Horowitz (Sony S2K 53468; 2 CDs; with *Variations on a Theme by Clara Wieck* and works by Chopin).

Horowitz's vintage account from the early 1960s is a clear first choice, even though it's only available on this double-disc set. Never has *Kreisleriana* been played with greater imagination: its refinement and passionate enchantment make an overwhelming impression.

Argerich (Deutsche Grammophon 410 653-2; with *Kinderszenen*).

Though Radu Lupu has also made a fine record of the same repertoire as is featured here, Martha Argerich's version is perhaps the best single-disc account of *Kreisleriana*. There's a sense of brilliant fantasy in this high-voltage performance, tempered with intellectual rigour.

FANTASIESTÜCKE

The Opus 12 *Fantasiestücke* (there's another, less interesting *Fantasiestücke* set, Op. 111) was composed between May and July 1837, shortly after Clara had returned all Schumann's letters. The ever-volatile composer dedicated the work to a Scottish pianist by the name of Roberta Laidlow. The *Fantasiestücke* catches the fragility of inspiration, which Schumann felt sprang from hidden depths to vanish as consciousness was reached, and the titles of its chimerical scenes evoke the higher realities of Romanticism – the worlds of night, twilight and dreams. Some of Schumann's most touching and delicate writing is here: *Warum* (Why?), for example, in which the music is the subject of momentary dialogue rather than formal development, or *Des Abends* (Of the Evening), which moves into unexpected keys to create a sense of revelation within stasis.

⊙ Argerich (EMI CDM7 63576-2; with *Fantasie*).

In the absence of Murray Perahia's account, this is the version to go for. Argerich's quicksilver playing really penetrates to the soul of these pieces, capturing all of their elusive magic. At the moment it's only available as an EMI import, but it's worth the hassle of ordering it.

⊙ Rubinstein (RCA 09026 61160-2; with pieces by Beethoven, Chopin and Debussy).

Rubinstein's account is a live recording made towards the end of his life – his command of the ebb and flow of musical phrases is as alluring as ever it was. The occasional slip of finger is excusable, but the quality of the recording (lifted from a video soundtrack, complete with hiss and wow) is less so.

KINDERSZENEN

Written in February 1838, *Kinderszenen* (Scenes from Childhood) was suggested by Clara's comment that Schumann sometimes seemed to her like a child. These tiny, exquisite pieces are very much the recollection of an adult, yet one whose affinity with the innocence and vulnerability of childhood was painfully acute. *Kinderszenen* opens with *Of Strange Lands and People* (the storyteller's "once upon a time") and progresses through evocations of emotions in their purest state, until at last the adult steps forward in *The Poet Speaks* (the titles of the episodes suggested themselves after the music was written). Trance-like and apparently artless, *Kinderszenen* contains moments of disarming enchantment: the floating syncopations of *Almost Too Serious*, for instance, or the phrase with which *Entreating Child* opens and closes, so that the piece ends as it began, and hangs quizzically in space.

The Complete Masterworks Recordings · Volume I
HOROWITZ
THE STUDIO RECORDINGS 1962-1963
BEETHOVEN · CHOPIN · DEBUSSY
LISZT · RACHMANINOV · SCARLATTI
SCRIABIN · SCHUBERT · SCHUMANN
2 CDs
SBM

⊙ Horowitz (Sony S2K 53457; 2 CDs; with pieces by Chopin, Rachmaninov, Liszt, Beethoven, Schubert, Scarlatti, Debussy and Scriabin).

Kinderszenen is the perfect conjunction of naivety and experience, and to conjure it up you need to be a master of fleeting effects. Vladmimir Horowitz has this quality in abundance, but also brings a cohesive shape to the music.

⊙ Lupu (Decca 440 496-2; with *Kreisleriana* and *Humoreske*).

There's tender reticence and a spring-like freshness about Lupu's performance, which is illuminated by memorable asides. Not one of his gestures or insights is prosaic or superfluous.

FANTASIE IN C MAJOR

In 1838 Schumann wrote to Clara: "I have just finished a fantasy in three movements that I sketched in all but the detail in June 1836. The first movement is, I think, the most passionate thing I have ever composed – a deep lament for you." Possibly so, but the work's origins lie in an attempt to raise funds for a monument to Beethoven. Schumann thought he could contribute best with a commemorative sonata, and the original titles of its movements are suitably redolent of tribute: *Ruins*, *Triumphal Arch* and *Wreath of Stars*. The *Fantasie* has Beethoven-like drive and verve, and indeed draws part of its thematic material from a Beethoven song. But if its march – "it makes me hot and cold all over," Clara wrote – is worthy of Beethoven's *Hammerklavier* (see p.44), its ardent and tender finale reveals a different, more diffused world. In the words of the philosopher Theodor Adorno, it seems to "open upon an undefined vastness". Subtle chromaticism, cross-rhythms, syncopation, countermelodic chords and a host of other stylistic subtleties give substance to the Schiller quotation that Schumann appended to the score: "Through all sounds in the coloured earthly dream resounds a quiet sound drawn for him, who secretly listens."

Argerich (EMI CDM7 63576-2; with *Fantasiestücke*).

The perfect marriage of artist and repertoire: Martha Argerich was born to play this music, and she brings a spontaneous-sounding energy to what is Schumann's most driven and passionate work.

Richter (EMI CDM7 64625-2; with Schumann concert).

Superhuman playing, in which every phrase seems to have been rethought and made Richter's own. The song-like tenderness of this music has never been better brought out, and the finesse makes its great climaxes all the more telling.

Horowitz (Sony S3K 53461; 3 CDs; with pieces by Bach/Busoni, Scriabin, Chopin, Debussy and others).

Horowitz's recording is a document of one of the major concerts of the 1960s, his return to the platform after years of fearful introspection. The first movement is mercurial and dynamic, with the left hand providing surging motive force, while in the finale he creates a weightless shimmer of sound. Playing with the composure that almost flawless technical reserves make possible, this is Horowitz at his very best.

ÉTUDES SYMPHONIQUES

The *Études Symphoniques* began life in 1834 simply as variations on a theme written by Ernestine von Fricken's father. After years of dogged gestation, they emerged in 1852 as one of the cornerstones of Romantic piano literature, a dazzling exposition of the "symphonic" possibilities of the instrument for blending, contrasting and superimposing timbres. The variation technique still forms the structural armature of the *Études Symphoniques*, but at the heart of this work is the exhilaration of experiment – of clarifying dense planes of polyphony, presenting themes against a background of tonal reverberation (in a way that anticipates Debussy), exploring the borders of sound and silence.

Richter (Olympia OCD 339).

Richter thinks through the organic structure of this music in playing of extraordinary richness and power; there's an unflagging urgency to this account, yet Richter never loses the crucial sense of private meditation. This is a performance which thinks on the move.

Pollini (Deutsche Grammophon 445 522-2; with *Piano Concerto* and *Arabeske*).

Pollini's version doesn't project quite the same degree of personal commitment as Richter, but it has an even greater analytic rigour and range of tone. It's coupled with a fine version of the *Piano Concerto* and a touching account of *Arabeske*, a marvel of considered innocence.

Pogorelich (Deutsche Grammophon 410 520-2; with *Toccata* and Beethoven's *Sonata No. 32*).

This performance was largely slated when it appeared in 1983. Pogorelich was accused of self-indulgence and eccentricity, in particular for the slowness of the initial theme. But it remains a powerful and engaging performance, his wonderfully varied touch opening a Pandora's box of dazzling ideas.

PIANO QUINTET

Before Schumann, no composer of importance had attempted to combine piano and string quartet. But the piano was Schumann's instrument, and it gave him the foothold he needed to tackle and conquer the field of chamber music, which he had resolved to do after his 32nd birthday. The *Piano Quintet* was begun in September of 1842 and tried out privately less than a month later, with Mendelssohn as pianist stepping in for a heavily pregnant Clara.

That the sonata-form first movement surges with such high spirits is a tribute to Schumann's sheer bravura. Between this, and an ebullient Scherzo in which prodigies are accomplished through simple ascending and descending scales, lies a funereal sonata-rondo. The quintet concludes with an exhilarating finale, which reveals Schumann's increasing preoccupation with unity through thematic metamorphosis. A masterly piece of craftsmanship, yet also one of the boldest and most brilliant declarations of its composer's creative spirit – and by far the best of his chamber music.

Beaux Arts Trio, Bettelheim, Rhodes (Philips 420 791-2; with *Piano Quartet*).

This is vintage Beaux Arts: pianist Menahim Pressler is very much in the driving seat in a performance of probing dynamism in which the wide range of episodes is bound together as a kind of inexhaustible dialogue.

Argerich, Schwarzberg (EMI CDS5 55484-2; 2 CDs; with concert of Schumann's chamber music).

Martha Argerich's grand manner very much dominates this thrilling live version, which is distinguished by the superlative interplay between what is clearly a collection of soloists. Individual contributions are strikingly eloquent, and the slow movement is more tender than it is for the Beaux Arts, but contrasts are sometimes a little less persuasively shaded and held together.

DICHTERLIEBE

Dichterliebe takes its text from Heinrich Heine and introduces to German song a new mingling of sentiment and irony, much as Heine's poems had done for German verse – this is a world of disillusionment in which nature acts as an adjunct and reflection to a bittersweet love story. *Dichterliebe* takes the song to a higher level of evolution: the piano here becomes an equal partner with the singer, appearing sometimes as combatant, sometimes as commentator, and is given long solo preludes and postludes which add an extra dimension to the possibilities of the genre. In a sense *Dichterliebe* is a continuation of Schumann's character pieces for piano, adding a second layer of tone-colour, liberating the lyrical element and defining the emotional content more precisely. They offer, as the composer put it, "a deeper insight into my inner musical workings".

◑ **Wunderlich; Giesen** (Deutsche Grammophon 449 747-2; with Schubert and Beethoven songs).

Fritz Wunderlich, one of this century's finest tenors, made his recording in 1966, shortly before his premature death. His rich, honeyed tones bring out the sadness and tenderness of Schumann's settings to an almost painful extent.

○ Fischer-Dieskau; Brendel (Philips 416 352-2; with *Liederkreis*).

The baritone Dietrich Fischer-Dieskau has a profound perception of dramatic narrative, and in Alfred Brendel he has a creative partner rather than a mere accompanist. Where Wunderlich was all youth and freshness, Fischer-Dieskau impresses through valedictory power and anger.

FRAUENLIEBE UND -LEBEN

A Woman's Love and Life was written at a fraught time for Schumann: the courts had just given permission for him to marry Clara, but her father Wieck had ten days to appeal against the decision. Between July 11 and 12, 1840, in his anguish, Robert snatched a cycle of poems by Adelbert von Chamisso, depicting a woman who loves her husband and lives only for him. It is very much a nineteenth-century male's conception of womanhood: and Schumann edits the text so as to reinforce further the impression that the girl's happiness can exist only alongside that of her man. But, matters of self-abnegation aside, *Frauenliebe und-Leben* has maintained its key place in the repertoire as a supreme embodiment of *Innigkeit:* inwardness, intimacy and sincerity of feeling.

○ Otter, Forsberg (Deutsche Grammophon 445 881-2; with *Five Songs*, etc).

Supreme artistry from Anne Sophie von Otter, from the first tentative yearning through voluptuous delight to final disappointment. The emotion she can wring from a whisper is something to marvel at, and the living growth of each song is perfectly judged. The remainder of the recital, revealing the widest range of Schumann's writing and von Otter's sensibility, is magnificent.

HEINRICH SCHÜTZ

(1585–1672)

Heinrich Schütz was the greatest German composer before J.S. Bach, a status that has a lot to do with the four years he spent in Venice, assimilating the polychoral style of Giovanni Gabrieli (see p.149). Schütz took this declamatory and dramatic style back to Germany, where he applied it to the texts of the Lutheran Church to produce some of the most powerful and pious music of the seventeenth century.

Schütz was born in Kostritz in Saxony into a family of legal officials. He began studying law at Marburg University in 1608, but was encouraged to turn his attention to music by the Landgrave of Hesse, who sponsored his studies in Venice. Schütz returned in 1612 and was made organist at the Landgrave's chapel at Kassel before being poached by the more powerful, but less sympathetic, Elector of Saxony at Dresden. He was officially appointed the Elector's Kapellmeister in 1618, the same year that the Thirty Years' War broke out – a religious conflict that was to devastate northern Europe.

In 1628 Schütz returned to Venice to recruit new musicians for Dresden and to familiarize himself at first hand with the new style of Monteverdi. To escape further the ravages of the war, which had severely depleted the musical forces at Dresden, Schütz requested extended leave of absence, and between 1633 and 1635 he was at Copenhagen reorganizing the court chapel there. Back in Dresden his duties at the court became increasingly onerous, but the Elector was not prepared to pension him off, and much of Schütz's time was spent petitioning for funds to pay the few court musicians who remained. He finally retired when he was 72, to his sister's house at Weissenfels, where he spent the final years of his life occasionally composing but mostly studying and reading the Bible.

SACRED MUSIC

Schütz wrote several operas, including the first ever written in German (*Dafne*), but none has survived. Nowadays he is entirely known as a composer of a large body of magnificent sacred music. Though his 65 years as a composer were marked by some quite radical changes of style, notably the shift from the monumental choral works such the *Psalmen Davids* (1619) to the more intimate madrigalian style of the *Cantiones Sacrae* (1625), there is nonetheless a consistent tone of grave solemnity that runs through most of his sacred works, punctuated by many dramatic and highly expressive moments.

One of Schütz's greatest works is the *Musikalische Exequien* of 1636, a Lutheran Requiem composed for the funeral of one of Schütz's early benefactors, Prince Heinrich von Reuss. The prince had specified that certain texts should be inscribed on his coffin, and that these should be set to music for performance at his funeral. Schütz assigns these contemplative words to his soloists, and inserts them within a setting of the Kyrie, sung by a chorus. This is followed by a choral motet and culminates in an extraordinarily powerful setting of the Nunc Dimittis in which a spectral-sounding reduced choir periodically interrupts the main chorus with the words *Selig sind die Toten, die in dem Herren sterben* (Blessed are the dead who die in the Lord).

O Musikalische Exequien, Motetten und Konzerte: The Monteverdi Choir, English Baroque Soloists; His Majesties Sagbutts and Cornetts; Gardiner (Deutsche Grammophon Archiv 423 405-2).

This is a wonderful selection of some of Schütz's most startling and intense music, featuring the *Musikalische Exequien* and four short motets, which are remarkable for the richness of their sonority. One of them, *Auf dem Gebirge* (In the Mountains), has a spine-tinglingly mysterious opening in which the overlapping vocal lines of two countertenors seem to float across the dark, stolid tones of the sackbuts (early trombones). It is these subtleties of colouration that give so much of Schütz's music its power, and John Eliot Gardiner is brilliant at balancing and controlling his forces to bring out the finest gradations of light and shade. In the more complex *Musikalische Exequien*, the amazing variety of vocal and instrumental combinations is handled with a remarkable assurance.

ALEXANDER SCRIABIN
(1872–1915)

Alexander Scriabin was the embodiment of E.T.A. Hoffman's dictum: "Only in the truly Romantic does comedy mix so fittingly with tragedy that both are fused in a total effect". Scriabin's egomaniacal delusions – sustained by the attentions of countless adoring aunts, wives, lovers and nurses – grew to a grandiosity unrivalled even in the history of music. He came to believe that he was one with God and that he would ultimately be absorbed into the rhythm of the universe, becoming a revivifying deity who would one day unite the world. Grand ambitions for someone who died from a septic boil on his lip. However comical his writings and beliefs, there is no question about the merits of Scriabin's music. He lived out the transition from Romanticism to modernism, initiating a musical language that moved decisively towards a break with tonality. Only slightly less radical than Schoenberg or Debussy, he could have become one of the major figures of twentieth-century music had he not died so young.

He was Rachmaninov's immediate contemporary, attending the same class and graduating from the Moscow Conservatory in the same year. Like Rachmaninov he was a virtuoso pianist. But whereas Rachmaninov remained an ardent traditionalist, Scriabin quickly arrived at conclusions that placed him at the forefront of contemporary musical thought. His earliest piano music reflected his obsession with Chopin, although there are certain hints at what was to come. The *Sonata No. 1* bore reflections of Rachmaninov, Prokofiev and early Stravinsky, but by the *Sonata No. 3* his style was clearly shifting towards the shimmering exoticism with which he is now associated. The breakthrough came in 1907 with the completion of his *Sonata No. 5*, a single-movement work of extreme difficulty and tonal dissolution.

From then on, Scriabin's musical experimentation led him as far away from his peers as could be imagined, while his extreme hypochondria and his fascination with his own personality assumed Wagnerian dimensions. Influenced by the spiritual ideas of Theosophy, Scriabin was fascinated by synesthesia – the notion that all the senses stimulated each other – and the idea that musical keys corresponded to specific colours. In 1909, building on the success of his symphonic poem *Prometheus*, he unveiled a project more ambitious than anything Wagner ever dreamed up. The *Mysterium* was an extraordinary, cataclysmic idea, synthesizing all the arts and senses into a extravaganza involving a "colour organ", pianos, a huge orchestra, choirs, dancers, "visions" and clouds of perfume. His friend and publisher, the conductor Serge Koussevitsky, bought the rights. Scriabin designed a temple to be built in India expressly for the performance of the *Mysterium*, and in preparation for the great day bought himself a sunhat and a book on Sanskrit grammar. The project died with him.

THE SYMPHONIES AND SYMPHONIC POEMS

Completed in 1900, Scriabin's *Symphony No. 1* shows him thinking in typically immodest terms: lasting fifty minutes, it's in six movements, the last of which boasts a chorus and soloists singing "visionary" texts of his own writing. The circulation and repetition of thematic ideas is used to bind together the work's ambitious length, and Scriabin's extensive use of triple time (finally broken in the finale), progressive tonality and highly dramatic melody all contribute towards a sweeping fluency that makes this one of the most powerful of all Russian Romantic symphonies.

The *Symphony No. 2*, composed the following year, is the same length as the first and is similarly marked by religio-mystical inebriation, but it is neither as bombastic nor as engaging. It's chiefly of interest for its orchestration, for in its use of bold instrumental colour and its quotation of birdsong it looks towards the style of Messiaen, another composer for whom music was an aspect of the spiritual world. The extra-musical dimension of the *Symphony No. 3* or *Divine Poem* (1904) was helpfully summarized by its composer: "The *Divine Poem* represents the evolution of the human spirit which, freed from the legends and mysteries of the past that it has summoned and overthrown, passes through pantheism and achieves a joyful and exhilarating affirmation of its liberty and its unity with the universe." As you may imagine, this is his most opulent creation. There is a conservative, formal architecture beneath the gorgeous, kaleidoscopic

GUUS ONG

orchestral colour, but really it's best to treat the *Symphony No. 3* as an aural wallow.

Scriabin also wrote two single-movement symphonic poems, *The Poem of Ecstasy* (1908) and *Prometheus* (1910), which like his late piano music pushed tonality to its very limits. Melodies and conventional thematic material are conspicuously absent; instead harmonic progressions generate the material and Scriabin employs what he called a "mystic" chord of his own devising. *The Poem of Ecstasy* is a masterpiece of orchestration and harmonic modulation, with shifting sound colours that reflect the composer's intense interest in Debussy's music. *Prometheus* was the forerunner for the *Mysterium* and requires a "colour organ" to project coloured light, instead of sound, to correspond with certain chords.

⊙ Symphonies Nos. 1–3; Poem of Ecstasy; Prometheus: Myers, Toczyska; Philadelphia Orchestra; Westminster Chorus; Muti (EMI CDS7 54251-2; 3 CDs).

Muti's is the finest available set – he gives wonderful cogency to these massive works. The Philadelphia Orchestra plays with bright and responsive enthusiasm, while the solo soprano and tenor in the last movement of *Symphony No. 1* are suitably ecstatic.

THE PIANO CONCERTO

Scriabin's *Piano Concerto* is the most neglected of major Romantic concertos, which is not altogether surprising as it requires a very large and expensive orchestra and makes savage demands on the soloist. Completed in 1896 and scored in three lush movements, it's an extended piece of *fin-de-siècle* opulence, whose textures recall

Rachmaninov or, in the last movement, Tchaikovsky. Full of bewitching melody and counterpoint, this is Scriabin's most accessible work for orchestra.

◑ **Ashkenazy; London Philharmonic Orchestra; Maazel** (Decca 417 252-2; with *Prometheus* and *Poem of Ecstasy*).

Ashkenzay's mid-1970s recording with Lorin Maazel still makes the most convincing argument for this concerto. Ashkenazy moves unscathed through the work's technical minefields and, if Maazel's grip on the orchestra is not always as tight as it might be, he does produce some wonderfully luscious sonorities. This CD, including Maazel's equally grand readings of the *Poem of Ecstasy* and *Prometheus*, is the finest introduction to Scriabin.

THE PIANO SONATAS

Scriabin's extensive output for piano is dominated by his sonatas, which cover his entire creative life: he wrote his first (unnumbered) sonata in 1892, and his last in 1913. The first four of the ten numbered sonatas are for the most part routinely Romantic, relying heavily on the legacy of Chopin and featuring a lot of aimless, overripe material. As examples of turn-of-the-century expressionism they are fascinating, but the *Sonata No. 5* (1907) is extremely interesting in itself. A brooding creation, it poses severe musical challenges, not least the dissonant, violent introductory bars, in which the music rises from the growling bass to the uppermost reaches of the keyboard in a startling flash of inspiration. From this work onwards, the sonatas become increasingly fiendish in their technical difficulty, exploring every recess of piano sonority. Scriabin's extremely complicated chromaticism – effectively borderline atonalism – reaches its expressive extreme in the so-called *Black Mass Sonata* and in its successor, the tenth. Concentrating myriad themes into the span of a single, multilayered movement, these last two sonatas are as scintillating as the virtuosic piano works of Liszt.

◑ **Ashkenazy** (Decca 425 570-2DM2; 2 CDs).

Vladimir Ashkenazy's cycle of the ten sonatas, recorded in the 1970s, set the standards against which all other performances have been judged. His percussive, frequently belligerent tone is ideal for Scriabin's Mephistophelean music, and the recorded sound is excellent.

PRELUDES, OPUS 11

Scriabin write a total of ninety preludes, but the 24 selected for Opus 11 formed his first and most popular cycle. Sketched between 1888 and 1896, these pieces cover the years between his studies at the Moscow Conservatoire and his career as a travelling composer and virtuoso. Alternately daring and coy, but always with an awareness of the possibilities of the instrument, this is the work of a young man still finding his feet, and it would be another decade before his writing would take on its own peculiarly transcendental quality. But if the inspiration for the 24 *Preludes* is clearly Chopin's own *Préludes*, Op. 28, then it is given a Russian twist of mordant and far-sighted chromaticism. Already Scriabin's occasional moments of naivety are surmounted by a command of shifting harmonies and of complex, impassioned rhythmic pulses which seem, just as much as Liszt ever did, to shine a light into the future.

○ **Pizarro** (Collins 14962; with Shostakovich *Preludes Op. 34*).

Scriabin's sketches are fleeting, and the diaphanous quality of these supremely impressionistic pieces is captured by Artur Pizarro with an appropriate restraint and a sense of wonder.

THE ÉTUDES

With Chopin the étude ceased to be an exercise for the rehearsal room and became instead a celebration of what the the pianist-composer could achieve: an exploration and extension of language for the nineteenth century's greatest instrument. This is the agenda Scriabin inherited, an agenda given an added charge by the otherworldly brilliance of Liszt's *Transcendental Etudes*. Scriabin wrote études throughout his career and they lie at the heart of his imaginative world. Functioning as a means for experiment as well as for private pleasure, they evolve from an early happy innocence through to music which seems to exist only as some spectral coalescence of rhythm and timbre. Though his Opus 8 remains the set favoured most by virtuosos, the principal later collections, Opus 42 (1903) and Opus 65 (1912) are just as rewarding.

○ **Richter** (Melodiya 74321 29470-2; with *Piano Sonata No. 6*, Prokofiev's *Sonata No. 7*, Miaskovsky's *Sonata No. 3*).

In this superlative 1952 recital, Richter plays the whole of Op. 65 and substantial extracts from Opp. 8 and 42. Where other performers hammer the notes, Richter finds a dizzy and teeming world in which ideas float and dart like fish in an exotic lagoon.

VERS LA FLAMME

Lasting less than seven minutes, the strange piano essay of *Vers la Flamme* dates from 1914, when Scriabin was striving for a hedonistic fusion of the arts into a total sensory experience. This is powerful and progressive music, a breakthrough work inspired by theosophy and mysticism, in which Scriabin pushes tonality to its very limits and where deliberate harmonic irresolution opens up audacious and visionary possibilities. Throughout this late music there is an overwhelming sense of darkness made visible and of an attempt to suggest a dissolution of time itself.

⊙ Richter (Philips 438 627-2; 2 CDs; with *Poème Nocturne, Danses Op. 63, Fantasie Op. 28*, Prokofiev *Sonatas Nos. 4* and *6*, etc).

Scriabin's brooding mysticism has never been animated more brilliantly than it is here. The opening hesitancy of *Vers la Flamme* is handled through dissolving sonoroties which Richter makes to ebb and flow in an almost improvisatory manner. The inner lines and tensions are beautifully controlled, however, driving the music on to its ecstatic culmination.

DMITRI SHOSTAKOVICH

(1906–1975)

Dmitri Shostakovich died in 1975, four years after Stravinsky, and was the last composer whose qualities were acknowledged throughout the Western world, in both the modernist and the traditionalist camps. Within weeks of his death, memorial concerts were held throughout the world and he was being celebrated as the finest composer of the century. For many that claim still holds true, and even among those who rate him not quite so highly none would argue that he is one of modern music's most fascinating characters. Unlike Prokofiev, who grew up and was educated in Tsarist Russia, Shostakovich spent his entire life under the Soviet system, and he was the first successful composer to emerge because of and not despite the Communist regime.

Shostakovich was taught initially by his mother, but his first major musical influence came from Glazunov, who encouraged the boy when he entered Petrograd (St Petersburg) Conservatory in 1919. Four years later Shostakovich graduated from Glazunov's piano course and began giving concerts. In 1926, his diploma work – the *Symphony No. 1* – was performed in Moscow and Leningrad (the renamed Petrograd), earning the composer international fame before his 21st birthday. The idealistic Shostakovich believed that it was his responsibility to serve the state as an artist, and he settled down to composing "realist" music, albeit with a progressive edge. He was impressed by much of the music of the Second Viennese School, and by Berg's *Wozzeck* in particular, and developed an eclectic style that was rooted in tonality yet incorporated some more abrasively Germanic and avant-garde tendencies. His mission was to produce work that was accessible without being regressive, and it was to bring him into conflict with the musical arbiters within the government.

Two years after the successful 1934 premiere of his opera *Lady Macbeth of the Mtsensk District*, the work was savaged in *Pravda*, where an article titled "Chaos instead of Music" deplored *Lady Macbeth* for its "confused stream of sounds" and "petty bourgeois sensationalism". The state made it clear that "Soviet art can have no other aim than the interest of the people and the state" and, while Shostakovich sympathized in part with these vague dictates, he was appalled by the extremes to which the state was willing to go. When you have a country of over 180 million people, speaking 108 different languages, it is hard to find a common musical ground, but Shostakovich was relentlessly bullied for his deviations from the ill-defined path of Socialist Realism.

From 1938 until 1955 Shostakovich devoted himself chiefly to symphonic music, and also began his vast cycle of string quartets. Notably, he produced nothing for the stage. During the siege of Leningrad in 1941 he fought fires and helped the wounded, then in 1943 he settled in Moscow, where he was appointed a professor of composition at the Conservatory. Even though he toed the party line with humiliating obedience, Shostakovich still fell foul of the government in 1948, when he and many other prominent Russian composers were singled out and denounced for "formalism" and the creation of "anti-people art". He was dismissed from his teaching post, and subsequently composed almost nothing but film scores and patriotic music until after Stalin's death in 1953. The last twenty years of his life were much calmer: free from state intrusion, he produced some particularly fine music, and saw the first performance of several major pieces written during the Stalinist repression. One of his most consistent pleasures in later years was his friendship with Benjamin Britten and the group of Russian musicians for whom he composed, including Nikolayeva, Oistrakh and Rostropovich.

Shostakovich's style is heterogenous yet immediately recognizable, combining the three strands of "high-spirited humour, introspective meditation and declamatory grandeur", in the words of musicologist Boris Schwarz. As Schwarz goes on to say, in much of his music Shostakovich allows one of these elements to prevail, and the result can be monotonous and wearisome. But in his greatest works, notably the symphonies and string quartets, he encompasses exceptionally wide emotional extremes, juxtaposing tragic intensity and grotesque wit, sublimity and banality, folksy jauntiness and elemental darkness, in a manner that recalls Gustav Mahler, a composer he especially admired.

OPERA – LADY MACBETH

The greatest of Shostakovich's four full-length operas, *Lady Macbeth of the Mtsensk District* (usually abbreviated to plain *Lady Macbeth*) was heralded as a work of great power and originality after its premiere in Leningrad on January 22, 1934. Productions outside the Soviet Union soon followed, but in December 1935 Stalin himself went to see the show. The result was a *Pravda* editorial decrying this "fidgety, screaming, neurotic music" and deriding the composer for sympathizing with a thoroughly wicked heroine – a bored adulteress who murders her husband, is exiled to Siberia with her lover, and ends up committing suicide. The authorities entirely missed the opera's mordant social satire, and demanded a revision; Shostakovich duly toned down what he termed the "animal eroticism" of *Lady Macbeth*, and the work reemerged in 1956 under the new title *Katerina Izmaylova*.

The strength of *Lady Macbeth* is the orchestral score, a brilliantly garish creation of primary colours, cruelly driving rhythms and wild dissonances. It can be difficult listening even for modern audiences, but as a piece of sustained and intense dramatic writing *Lady Macbeth* warrants comparison with *Wozzeck*. Characterization and mood are created chiefly by the orchestra rather than by the vocal roles, for Shostakovich rarely wrote well for the voice. Perhaps that is one of the chief reasons why he never composed the rest of his planned tetralogy of operas about women, a cycle that was intended to end with a work concerning a hard-working employee of the Dnieper hydroelectric installation.

O Vishnevskaya, Gedda, Petkov, Krenn, Tear, Valjakka; Ambrosian Opera Choir; London Philharmonic Orchestra; Rostropovich (EMI CDS7 4995-2; 2 CDs).

Rostropovich might have a general tendency to be careless and lumbering, but here he gets it right, extracting vivid performances and generating a real erotic charge. The cast includes Rostropovich's wife, Galina Vishnevskaya, and the incomparable Nicolai Gedda.

THE SYMPHONIES

From the daring precosity of the *Symphony No. 1* (1923–24) to the anguished bitterness of the *Symphony No. 15* (1971), Shostakovich's symphonies display a range unequalled by any other modern cycle. His style, however, was largely consistent from the *Symphony No. 4* onwards: a harmonic language that borrowed a little from Prokofiev and a little from Russian folk song, a tendency (shared with Mahler) to juxtapose music that is startlingly different in mood and feeling, and a mordant sense of humour that often finds expression in the grotesque. Since the publication of the composer's supposedly dictated "memoirs" (*Testimony*) in 1979, and even more so since his death, critics have speculated at length about encoded messages in his symphonies which reveal his "true" feelings about the ideological and aesthetic constraints placed upon him. Such speculation is sometimes enlightening but more often tendentious: Shostakovich's work stands on purely musical grounds, irrespective of the always interesting circumstances in which it was written. There is currently no completely satisfactory cycle of the symphonies on CD, and they are best bought individually.

SYMPHONY NO. 1

Hackwork, and the onset of tuberculosis, frustrated Shostakovich's progress on the work planned for his graduation from the St Petersburg Conservatoire. His first symphony, the "symphony-grotesque", as he christened it, was begun early in 1923 and completed, after much hard grind, in June 1925. In Moscow, a crush of students, who came to blows in order to hear it, and its success was repeated in the West where it was conducted by Bruno Walter. It is indeed a tremendous debut: clean and deft, tightly integrated and structured with many of the resources that would serve Shostakovich well in later life, not least a natural symphonist's manipulation of interludes and anticlimax. It is the work of a composer turning his back on specifically Russian music to forge a new modern language (for new Revolutionary times) that was witty, ironic and bursting with energy.

⊙ **Philadelphia Orchestra; Ormandy** (Sony SBK 62 642; with the *Festive Overture* and selections from *The Gadfly*, *The Age of Gold*, *Moskow-Cheryomushki*, *Ballet Suites Nos. 1* & *2*).

This razor-sharp performance from Ormandy catches exactly the right element of burlesque and always allows the wit to shine through. There are hints at an undercurrent of sedition and a profound disquiet which runs through this work, and which unfolds in the later symphonies to give Shostakovich's cycle its unique contemporaneity. A well-played selection of Shostakovich's most flamboyant film and stage music completes an irresistible disc.

O Scottish National Orchestra; Järvi (Chandos CHAN 8411; with *Symphony No. 6*).

Järvi's is probably the best of the modern interpretations: it lacks the keenness and individuality of Ormandy but combines style and sensitivity in equal measure. It's coupled with a splendid performance of the underrated *Symphony No. 6* and the recording is excellent.

SYMPHONY NO. 5

Shostakovich began the *Symphony No. 5* a year after *Pravda* had attacked his *Lady Macbeth*, and the work was premiered on November 21, 1937. A journalist referred to it as "A Soviet Artist's Practical Creative Reply to Just Criticism" and Shostakovich let the description stand. It was a sensational success, for, in accordance with the Politburo's dictum that "all aspects of music should be subordinated to melody and such melody should be clear and singable", Shostakovich produced a work bursting with tunes. The treatment is less ambitious than in its immediate predecessor, but the symphony is still constructed along grand lines – though Shostakovich's confidants attest to the irony of its optimistic finale.

◑ **Leningrad Philharmonic Orchestra; Mravinsky** (Erato 2292-45752-2).

Mravinsky was for years Shostakovich's own favoured interpreter, and generally has no equal in his music. He conducts with incision and an utter lack of sentimentality or strain. Nobody else brings off the last movement as Mravinsky does.

O Scottish National Orchestra; Järvi (Chandos CHAN 8650; with selections from *The Bolt*).

Järvi's disc has more technical polish than Mravinsky's live recording, and there is no doubting the sincerity of this performance or the dignity with which its desolate vision is communicated. For those who might be concerned about Mravinsky's lack of gloss, Jarvi is ideal, though Mravinsky flows better – conspicuously so in the Scherzo.

SYMPHONY NO. 7 – THE LENINGRAD

The *Symphony No.* 7 was written during the siege of Leningrad when maybe as many as a million people died of cold and starvation. Shostakovich was evacuated near the beginning of the siege, by which time he had already written the symphony's first three movements. Once completed, it was performed (with the siege still going on) not just in Moscow and Leningrad but also in London and across America. It is therefore inextricably tied up with the war and comes with even more extra-musical baggage than usual (including a detailed programme by Shostakovich). To confuse matters the composer later declared: "I have nothing against calling the *Seventh* the *Leningrad* . . . but it's not about the Leningrad under siege, it's about the Leningrad that Stalin destroyed and Hitler finished off." Famously the long opening movement is dominated by a long, rather banal, march that builds ever more menacingly to a shuddering climax. This "War" or "Invasion" motif has divided critics, but the way the composer creates an atmosphere that is both cheap and exhilarating before having it subside into something spare and elegiac is highly effective. In the rest of the symphony there is an equally profound tension between bitterness and hope, not least in the beautifully judged slow movement, which resolutely refuses to succumb to sadness.

O Scottish National Orchestra; Järvi (Chandos CHAN 8623).

In Järvi's hands the *Seventh* becomes great music: this is a mesmerizing reading, in which the opening builds like a wave. Yet Järvi's crisp phrasing keeps the slower episodes nimble, allowing him to pull back the tempo without any sense of disruption. Rarely has the humanity of Shostakovich's desolate grotesquerie been more finely judged or so passionately communicated.

O Chicago Symphony Orchestra; Bernstein (Deutsche Grammophon 427 632-2; 2 CDs; with *Symphony No. 1*).

This live performance is a determined rethink, adding a level of gravitas beyond the usual rhetoric. Bernstein manages to create an extra breadth for Shostakovich's white-hot inspiration, even if more than once the work's overriding tension is somewhat reduced.

SYMPHONY NO. 8

Critics tend to consider the *Symphony No. 8* a more considered and effective reponse to the experience of war. It is certainly a work that exudes a profound feeling of tragedy, and when Shostakovich was criticised by Zhdanov in 1948 the *Eighth* was singled out for its "extreme subjectivism" and "unrelieved gloom". Its opening is immensely powerful: a long, inward-looking Adagio punctuated by a faster development that seems to mock the original material. There is little let up in this work but the third-movement Allegro is positively demented in its hard edge and its machine-like rhythms. It culminates in a fulsomely expansive passacaglia before leading straight into a final movement in C major, usually a key associated with joyous ceremonial, but here shot through with an unnerving ambiguity which suggests that hope is just too expensive a commodity to enjoy unreservedly.

O **Concertgebouw; Haitink** (Decca 425 071-2).

Haitink finds a highly satisfactory middle ground between the impassioned extremity of some Russian recordings and the sleek angst-free tones of many Western interpreters. This is one of the most successful of his complete cycle of Shostakovich symphonies – there's energy as well as pain in this hard-driven performance.

O **Leningrad Philharmonic Orchestra; Mravinsky** (Russian Disc RDCD 10917).

The sound is rather harsh and there are some irritatingly intrusive offstage noises in this live recording, but apart from that it's the most completely convincing account currently available – intense, anguished and powerfully dramatic.

SYMPHONY NO. 10

Shostakovich's *Symphony No. 10* is one of the least programmatic of his works but it was performed soon after the death of Stalin, and the bleak power of the first three movements could be taken as a commentary on the dark age that had just passed. Galina Vishnevskaya has called the *Tenth* "a composer's testament of misery, forever damning a tyrant". But what impresses most is the way in which this music commands and subverts symphonic decorum on purely abstract terms to produce a profound disquiet. It is a reinvention of the symphony at the hands of a master, whose thoughts here have undergone years of secretive gestation. There's an epic scope to it: indeed the first movement – an immense autumnal essay of gradually built momentum – could almost stand alone. As it is, its solemnity is shattered, in typical fashion, by a shrill and aggressive Scherzo. The finale is also built on a striking contrast, this time between the poignant Mahlerian Andante which begins it, and the frantic *danse macabre* which dominates the rest of the movement.

O **Berlin Philharmonic Orchestra; Karajan** (Deutsche Grammophon 439 036-2).

The second of Karajan's two recordings, with its marvellously rich sound, is the outstanding version of this symphony. He gives it a darkly lustrous and noble stature, spinning out the long lines, merging its interlocking structures in a sweeping but cohesive vision.

THE CONCERTOS

Compared with his fifteen symphonies and fifteen string quartets, Shostakovich's concerto output was relatively meagre. There are six in total (two each for piano, violin and cello) and all of them were written with a specific performer in mind – himself for the first piano concerto, his son Maxim for the second, David Oistrakh for the violin concertos, and Mstislav Rostropovich for the cello concertos. All have been recorded on several occasions, but only the two piano concertos and the first violin concerto have gained a permanent foothold in the concert hall.

THE PIANO CONCERTOS

Shostakovich's *Piano Concerto No. 1*, written in 1933, is scored for strings, piano and solo trumpet, a combination as unusual as the concerto's form, which consists of four through-flowing movements which sound like just one. Because of its wit, its clarity and its sharply etched contours it has been compared to the concertos of Poulenc (see p.305) but Shostakovich's humour is far more sardonic and barbed. It's always been a popular work, chiefly because of its plenitude of uplifting tunes, its frequent, provocative changes of mood and a wonderfully high-spirited last movement which is pure Keystone Kops. The second concerto, written for his son Maxim in 1957, is for the conventional combination of piano and orchestra, and is a lighter work than its predecessor. Like the *Violin Concerto No. 1*, it has a slow movement of exquisite pathos – its unabashed Romanticism would not be out of place in a concerto by Rachmaninov – while the last movement presents a corrective dose of Shostakovich's very own brand of flippancy.

◑ **Alexeev, Jones; English Chamber Orchestra; Maksymiuk** (Classics for Pleasure CFP4547; with *The Assault on Beautiful Gorky*).

This is the best modern coupling of both concertos, with Dmitri Alexeev a brilliant and assertive soloist. As a bonus there's a fine mini-concerto taken from one of the composer's many film scores.

O **Shostakovich; French National Radio Orchestra; Cluytens** (EMI CDC754606-2).

Quirky, frenetic playing from Shostakovich himself in 1958 – at times he makes the music rear up like a ferocious beast. A selection of the *Preludes and Fugues*, superbly laconic, completes a disc which is a delightful discovery and an indispensable historic document.

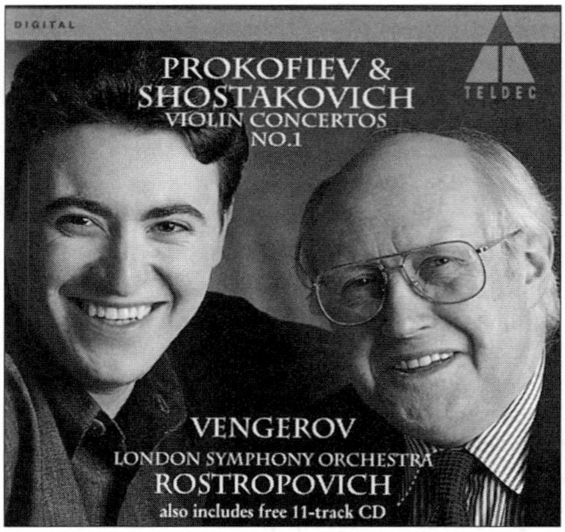

VIOLIN CONCERTO NO. 1

Shostakovich composed two violin concertos, both of them written for and first performed by David Oistrakh, one of the century's finest violinists. The first, the better of the two, was composed in 1947–48 but remained unperformed until 1955, and was perhaps altered during the intervening years. This concerto features some of the finest music ever written for the violin, and in its third movement Shostakovich created his most beautiful concerto episode – a deeply spiritual passacaglia, in which the timpani announce a regular rhythmic pattern against which the soloist plays a desperately mournful lament. The concerto as a whole is a multifaceted work of great difficulty for the soloist but of complete immediacy for the listener.

⊙ Vengerov; London Symphony Orchestra; Rostropovich (Teldec 4509 92256-2; with Prokofiev, *Violin Concerto No. 1*).

The spirit of Oistrakh seems to inform Vengerov's playing, which has a burnished intensity. The guidance of Rostropovich is also an influence that Vengerov has been happy to acknowledge. It shows in the breadth of his bowing and tone, which ranges from an anguished whisper to a raucous outcry – the finale has never been more brazenly demonic than it is here.

CHAMBER AND PIANO MUSIC

Many of Shostakovich's finest works were written for small instrumental ensembles that allowed for an intimacy and a directness of expression. The most celebrated of all his chamber music are the fifteen string quartets, which for several critics is the most significant twentieth-century quartet cycle after Bartók's. Shostakovich was a fine pianist – not as good as Rachmaninov or Prokofiev but good enough to enter the 1922 Chopin competition in Warsaw. His intensely idiomatic piano writing is very much concerned with classical forms, such as sonatas and preludes. Best of all are his *24 Preludes and Fugues*, which were inspired by hearing the pianist Tatiana Nikoleyeva play Bach preludes and fugues, and are worthy successors to them.

THE STRING QUARTETS

Shostakovich wrote fifteen symphonies and fifteen string quartets, but the numerical equality might be misleading – he didn't compose his first quartet until 1938, when he had already completed his fifth symphony, and waited another six years before embarking on the second. Each of the quartets displays an understanding of the interrelationship of string instruments that is as fine as that shown by Schubert or Beethoven, and as with the Beethoven quartets these pieces are a vehicle for the composer's most intimate utterances. In comparison with Bartók's quartets, the century's other great cycle (see p.21), Shostakovich's are extremely melodic and direct, sometimes to the point of obviousness, but his gift for the unexpected turn of phrase is evident in every one.

Two of the finest of this astonishingly sustained sequence are the first and the eighth quartets. The former contains some gorgeous melodic writing, particularly in the second movement, which possesses the sort of tune that sets you thinking of divine inspiration. The latter was written in 1960 but was inspired by the firebombing of Dresden, a disaster that was also a source for Strauss's *Metamorphosen*. Unlike *Metamorphosen*, however, this is a bleak creation that offers no sense of hope or reconciliation. Written "In Memory of the Victims of Fascism and War", it's also a coded autobiography, for the music quotes from Shostakovich's own *Piano Quintet* and from *Lady Macbeth*, while the dominating theme is his musical "signature" D-S-C-H (D-E flat-C-B), which he also used in the *Symphony No. 10* and in other places.

⊙ Complete String Quartets: Fitzwilliam String Quartet (Decca 43 078-2; 6 CDs).

The outstanding set of live recordings by the Borodin Quartet is not currently available. This, however, is an excellent alternative: the Fitzwilliams may lack that final, emotionally driven, edge that the Borodins have, but these are deeply felt and densely argued performances. More than the symphonies, this is a cycle worth exploring from beginning to end.

O Quartets Nos. 3, 7 & 8: Borodin String Quartet (Virgin VC 759041-2).

If you want to test the water, here is the Borodin Quartet in an electrifying account of *String Quartet No. 8*.

THE PIANO QUINTET

After the failure of his *Symphony No. 6*, Shostakovich's income was sustained by film commissions (for which he received the Order of the Red Banner of Labour). But in 1940 there was the chance to rekindle his fame with chamber music on a grand scale – the *Piano Quintet* in G minor. It's a work that is impressive, above all, for its propulsive force – the opening prelude is like Bach with a searing modernist edge. The second movement is music cut back to bare sinews, from which the piano is all but absent. The finale exploits the open diatonic intervals through which Mahler used to envelop music in buoyant euphoria, but for Shostakovich the emotions soon become more complex than that, as if optimistic resignation were the best one could hope for. When Shostakovich appeared in the Hall of the Conservatoire to give its first performance with the Beethoven Quartet, his audience rose and their final ovation had all the fervour of a political demonstration.

O Borodin Quartet; Leonskaya (Teldec 4509-98414-2; with *Piano Trio No. 2*).

Shostakovich was rarely more economical in his scores than he is here; and filled with such warmth as the Borodins give it, the sense of suffering is almost unbearable. It's a reading in whose machinery the heroic and the hopeless are equally realized, and it comes across with the biting intensity of an assault.

THE SONATA FOR VIOLIN AND PIANO

The *Sonata for Violin and Piano* was composed in 1968 to celebrate the sixtieth birthday of David Oistrakh. Abounding in private allusions and coded messages, this haunting sonata is written in Shostakovich's most sparse and desultory style. It's a work whose expressive compass ranges from a meditation on twelve-note chromaticism, through ironic vehemence, to a series of stratospheric variations, as noble as Bach – indeed, the finale repeats the passacaglia structure which had already been put to such powerful effect in Shostakovich's *Violin Concerto No. 1*.

O Mordkovitch; Benson (Chandos CHAN 8988; with pieces by Prokofiev and Schnittke).

Lydia Mordkovitch prevents this sardonic piece of writing from descending into crabbiness, deploying timbres that range from a crepuscular sotto voce to sinuous resilience. However much she holds in reserve, she keeps enough metrical buoyancy and power to drive on Shostakovich's bitter narrative.

PRELUDES AND FUGUES

Shostakovich's penchant for musical "signatures" derived from his study of the music of Bach, who wrote pieces in which the notes signified by the letters of his name were used as thematic material. A more interesting product of his immersion in Bach was the *24 Preludes and Fugues* Op. 87, which was written in 1950–51 for Tatiana Nikolayeva. Comprising a prelude and fugue in each key, this huge composition mirrors the structure of the *Well-Tempered Clavier*, but this music is a world away from the decorum of the Baroque era. These are intensely personal pieces, covering an emotional spectrum almost as wide as that of the quartets. From the simplicity of the first in C major to the quasi-symphonic grandeur of the last in D minor, the *Preludes and Fugues* bare the composer's soul with uncompromised honesty.

O Nikolayeva (Hyperion CDA66441/3; 3 CDs).

It was a Bach recital by Tatiana Nikolayeva that gave Shostakovich the idea of writing the *Preludes and Fugues*, and she advised him throughout its composition. Unrecognized outside Russia until only a few years before her death in 1993, Nikolayeva was a brilliant pianist who combined a sparkling unpredictability with a powerful technique. Powerhouse playing is required by these demanding scores and she plays them as if her life depended on it. A superb document and a lasting testament to a great musical personality.

JEAN SIBELIUS

(1865–1957)

Nineteenth-century Finland was a Grand Duchy of Tsarist Russia, ruled by the Swedish-speaking minority. It was one of Sibelius's greatest achievements to reassert Finnish culture as something distinct from that of both Russia and Scandinavia. Sibelius became the cultural figurehead of Finnish nationalism, a status he achieved largely through writing some of the greatest symphonic music of the nineteenth and twentieth centuries.

Johan (later Jean) Julius Christian Sibelius was born into a Swedish-speaking doctor's family in a small town in southern Finland, but spent much of his school life in a Finnish-speaking environment. He was composing by the age of 10 and at first saw his future as a violinist, though he entered Helsinki University to study law, before turning to music when he came under the influence of Ferruccio Busoni (see p.94), then on the university's staff. Sibelius continued his musical studies in Berlin and then in Vienna.

Returning to Finland in 1891, he completed his first major work, the choral symphony *Kullervo*, the first of many compositions based on the mythology of the Finnish national epic, the *Kalevala* – the closest Finnish equivalent to the Arthurian legends of Anglo-Celtic culture or the Nordic legends of Scandinavia. His *Symphony No. 1* (1899) consolidated a reputation in his home country, which had already honoured him with a small pension for life, partly as recompense for his not getting the post of Director of Music at Helsinki University. His fame now spread abroad and several ensuing works were first performed in Berlin, including the *Violin Concerto* (1903–05), which was given its premiere under Richard Strauss.

The first decade of the century also saw Sibelius develop a more personal style, away from the Tchaikovsky-inspired early symphonies towards something sparer, more refined and more organic in structure. When cancer of the throat was diagnosed in 1908, depriving him of his beloved tobacco and alcohol, he responded by darkening and paring down his style even further, a process

LEBRECHT COLLECTION

Jean Sibelius

clear in works such as the *Symphony No. 4* (1911). Further deprivation was to come: the outbreak of World War I obliterated his income from royalties, then an attempted Communist coup in Finland – which had achieved independence in the wake of the Russian Revolution – forced Sibelius to leave his home in the forests to the north of Helsinki.

After the war Sibelius composed the last two of his seven symphonies and the great tone poem *Tapiola* (1926). The following year, with restored royalties and his state pension giving him a secure future, he simply retired from composing and conducting, and for the next twenty years kept the musical world waiting for an eighth symphony that never materialized.

THE SYMPHONIES

Sibelius is the most original symphonist since Beethoven, in that he found unique solutions to the problems of symphonic form. The earliest work is a fairly traditional nineteenth-century Romantic symphony, but Sibelius soon went on to develop a highly complex structural approach, in which the music was conceived in terms of a great arch. As broad generalization, the mature symphonies of Sibelius progress from scattered and fragmentary ideas into fully formed themes and sections, as if the compositional process were happening in the presence of the audience. The high point of this process is the *Symphony No. 7*, where Sibelius manages to combine the usual four movements into a single continuity, in which it is impossible to tell where one section ends and another begins.

◑ **Complete Symphonies: Philharmonia Orchestra; Ashkenazy** (Decca 455 402-2 and 455 405-2; 4 CDs).

Complete sets of the symphonies have proliferated recently; each has its merits, but Vladimir Ashkenazy's mid-price cycle with the Philharmonia, recorded in the early 1980s, offers the most consistent rewards. Decca have recently repackaged the set as a pair of mid-price double albums.

SYMPHONY NO. 1

Sibelius was still under the influence of Tchaikovsky when he wrote his first symphony, but these Russian overtones coexist with assuredly individualistic orchestral textures and themes. At the very opening, for example, in a highly original stroke, a clarinet over a gentle timpani roll introduces the main theme, which achieves its apotheosis at the climax of the finale. An emphatically rhythmic Scherzo reveals the influence of Bruckner, a composer whose music he had first encountered in Vienna in 1890.

○ **Oslo Philharmonic Orchestra; Jansons** (EMI CDC7 54273-2; with *Karelia Suite* and *Finlandia*).

In the right hands, the first symphony can be an extremely exciting work. Mariss Jansons finds just the right level of energy as the symphony unfolds, and the Oslo Philharmonic respond with a brilliance that is never forced.

SYMPHONY NO. 2

The *Symphony No. 2* (1901), one of the most popular of the cycle, marks a transition between the youthful and the mature Sibelius. Much of it was composed in Italy, and the Russian influence has here been replaced by something more southern in feeling: textures are more open, the thematic writing more ingratiating and there is general atmosphere of warmth. That said, a darker element does emerge during the second movement, and a stirring "big tune" – that most Russian of concepts – appears at the crowning point of the finale.

○ **London Symphony Orchestra; Davis** (RCA 09026 68218-2; with *Symphony No. 6*).

Sir Colin Davis's second cycle of Sibelius symphonies is a thrilling achievement. What stands out second time around (especially in the second symphony) is the way he avoids any rhetorical flourishes and yet, by letting the music speak for itself, achieves the highest levels of expressive eloquence.

◑ **Philharmonia Orchestra; Ashkenazy** (Decca 430 737-2; with *Karelia Suite* & *Finlandia*).

This radiant performance is one of the best of Ashkenazy's Sibelius cycle. The Philharmonia is in rapturous form and really lets rip with the invigorating big tune of the finale.

SYMPHONY NO. 3

Perhaps because it lacks the broad sweep of the earlier symphonies, *Symphony No. 3* (1907) is one of Sibelius's least-known symphonies, which is a pity given its many attractions. It shows Sibelius moving in a new direction, with restraint, subtlety and clarity of texture the most obvious characteristics. The orchestra is now relatively small and the strings dominate the presentation of the main thematic material.

○ **London Symphony Orchestra; Davis** (RCA 09026 61963-2; with *Symphony No. 5*).

The third is one of the most difficult of all the symphonies to put across effectively. Colin Davis's reading is a triumph of concentration and control.

SYMPHONY NO. 4

The increasing austerity and reduction of scale is even more marked in the *Symphony No. 4*, a work that can be seen as Sibelius's riposte to the megalomaniac tendencies of Bruckner and Mahler. Sibelius's fear of death (more specifically, his fear of a recurrence of cancer) seems to be another strong factor in this symphony, which is characterized by a generally grey orchestral palette and an emphasis on themes and harmonic relationships based on the tritone, a musical interval traditionally called upon to represent the Devil or other sinister concepts – as in Liszt's *Mephisto* waltzes and Saint-Saëns' *Danse macabre*.

◑ **Berlin Philharmonic Orchestra; Karajan** (Deutsche Grammophon DG439 527-2; with *Symphony No. 7* & *Valse Triste*).

A classic performance from Karajan, who frequently performed the fourth and recorded the work three times. This one dates from 1966, and it has an intensity and prevailing feeling of welling despair that has rarely been equalled.

SYMPHONY NO. 5

The *Symphony No. 5* is one of Sibelius's most original reworkings of symphonic form and he had great difficulty in getting it completed to his satisfaction: he withdrew it after the premiere in 1915 (to celebrate his fiftieth birthday) and the final version didn't appear until 1919. Originally it was in four movements, but during the revision he merged the first and second into one, with a transition passage that miraculously glides from one into the other (given the right conductor). The formal concision of the fifth is astonishing – a horn call at the start of each movement defines a chord that then becomes the basis for that movement's material.

After the pessimism of *No. 4* this symphony is one of his most heroic and confident statements, with a triumphant finale whose main theme was memorably described by the writer Donald Tovey as "Thor swinging his hammer" – it culminates in a series of crashing chords that will have you on tenterhooks for the final cadence.

○ **London Symphony Orchestra; Davis** (RCA 09026 61963-2; with *Symphony No. 3*).

Again it's the restraint with which Davis handles this symphony that makes it so impressive. Too many conductors can overwork its compelling mixture of desolate elementalism and heroic grandeur. Davis always concentrates on the musical argument, leaving the listener to project any visual or poetic fancies onto its raw beauty.

◑ **City of Birmingham Symphony Orchestra; Rattle** (EMI 7 64112 2; with *Symphony No. 7*, *Nightride & Sunrise*, and *Scene with Cranes*).

Simon Rattle has recorded the work twice, once with the Philharmonia and later with the CBSO. Both versions display a refinement and structural integrity that is enormously impressive. The CBSO version comes coupled with an equally fine performance of *Symphony No. 7*.

◑ **Berlin Philharmonic Orchestra; Karajan** (Deutsche Grammophon 439 982-2; with *Symphony No. 6* & *The Swan of Tuonela*).

Another triumphant reading from Karajan and the Berlin Philharmonic recorded in the mid-1960s. There's a cumulative force to this performance, which makes the great brass climax a thoroughly overwhelming experience.

SYMPHONY NO. 6

The *Symphony No. 6* (1923) is another restrained work, more subtle and less physical than the others. It seems to combine the sound-worlds of the third and fourth symphonies, though it was actually conceived alongside the fifth – Sibelius even sketched passages for one that ended up in the other. The music is based on modal rather than traditional tonal harmonies and melodic lines, and the effect of this procedure on the work's mood is well summed up in Sibelius's suggested motto: "When shadows lengthen".

○ **London Symphony Orchestra; Davis** (RCA 09026 68218-2; with *Symphony No. 2*).

There's a directness and unfussiness to this performance which seems exactly on target. The strings of the LSO produce a vivid and resplendent sound and the slightly otherworldly quality of this work is beautifully communicated.

SYMPHONY NO. 7

After the formal experiments of *Symphony No. 5*, Sibelius finally went the whole hog and created a one-movement symphony that contains all the traditional four-movement symphony's characteristics of contrast and development. It's perhaps the greatest of all his works: extraordinarily fluid, expressive and even epic in character, and yet in its concision and brevity (it lasts twenty minutes) anticipates the structural rigour of Webern.

◑ **City of Birmingham Symphony Orchestra; Rattle** (EMI 7 64112 2; with *Symphony No. 5*, *Nightride & Sunrise*, and *Scene with Cranes*).

Simon Rattle again excels in this most complex of works, building it slowly but with an inexorable and steely logic. This is a performance of real integrity and the playing of the CBSO is absolutely first-rate.

◑ **Berlin Philharmonic Orchestra; Karajan** (Deutsche Grammophon 439 527-2; with *Symphony No. 4* and *Valse Triste*).

Karajan's seventh may not have the white-hot intensity of his recordings of the fourth and fifth, but it is still a highly impressive account, with a muscular energy and a probing intelligence that penetrates to the very heart of the work.

THE VIOLIN CONCERTO & ORCHESTRAL WORKS

Though Sibelius's music is dominated by his symphonies, these are by no means the sum of his orchestral output. In addition to his great *Violin Concerto*, he wrote a string of symphonic poems that are formally just as original as the best of the symphonies, and make especially vivid use of the orchestra to conjure up the atmosphere of the northern forests and Finland's mythical tales. There is also a wealth of music for the theatre, and orchestral pieces composed for specific occasions, of which the best known is *Finlandia*.

THE VIOLIN CONCERTO

Sibelius's *Violin Concerto* is now acknowledged as one of the top half-dozen concertos in the repertory, but its reputation was hard-won. By the time of its premiere in 1904 Sibelius already had two symphonies behind him, and he expected the concerto to be acclaimed. In the event, Karl Flodin, the country's most prominent music critic, pronounced it "a mistake", partly because the soloist made such a mess of the numerous tricky episodes in the work – in particular, the first movement has two full cadenzas. Sibelius seems to have taken Flodin's misgivings to heart, for in the following year he unveiled a smoother and trimmer version that was about five minutes shorter than the orginal. Boldly Romantic, with an intensely poignant opening movement which alternates a drawn-out and hauntingly Slavic melody with passages of rhapsodic yearning, the concerto progresses though a gently languorous Adagio and culminates in a lumbering finale which has been likened to polar bears dancing in the snow. This second draft is the version that is now almost invariably played.

○ Mullova; Boston Symphony Orchestra; Ozawa (Philips 416 821-2; with Tchaikovsky, *Violin Concerto*).

The brilliant Russian violinist Victoria Mullova has been criticized for insufficient emotion in her playing, but her performance of this concerto is thrilling in its depth and insight. The mysteriously, plaintive opening has a penetrating starkness which, far from minimizing its emotional impact, actually intensifies the poignancy.

○ Lin; Philharmonia; Salonen (Sony SK 44548; with Nielsen, *Violin Concerto*).

This is an immensely subtle reading from Cho-Liang Lin and the Philharmonia. If anything the sense of teamwork is more pronounced in this performance: there's an exemplary balance between soloist and orchestra – the first movement, in particular, conveys a powerful sense of the violin as an optimistic, but still troubled, voice emerging from the dark orchestral texture.

KULLERVO

Kullervo (1892) was classified by Sibelius as a choral symphony, but could be more accurately described as a symphonic poem, since its form is determined by a literary source – the five movements depict the exploits of the eponymous mythological hero of the *Kalevala*. Preceding his first "abstract" symphony by some eight years, it was *Kullervo* that first brought Sibelius to prominence in Finland. Sibelius himself withdrew it after the premiere, and it was not performed again until after his death, but it's well worth hearing – it could have been written by no one else, and its importance to his development is crucial.

○ Mattila, Hynninen; Gothenburg Symphony Orchestra; Järvi (BIS CD313).

Neeme Järvi's is the most successful of the handful of recordings in the catalogue: both the choral and solo singing have a dramatic urgency and the immediacy of the work is intensified by the spectacular recording.

KARELIA SUITE & FINLANDIA

Karelia, a region that spreads over eastern Finland and into neighbouring Russia, is the heartland of Finnish culture. In 1892 Sibelius wrote music to accompany a student production of scenes based upon its history, and the rousing three-movement *Karelia Suite* evolved from this music as a separate concert work. Sibelius's other well-known piece of nationalist banner-waving, *Finlandia*, evolved in a similar way. Originally written to accompany a series of tableaux staged in Helsinki in 1899, representing events in Finnish history, the show was put on in the guise of a charity event, but was designed to encourage anti-Russian sentiment. First known under the title *Finland Awakes*, it struck an immediate chord – so much so that the authorities banned people from whistling its melodies in the streets.

◑ Philharmonia Orchestra; Ashkenazy (Decca 430 737-2; with *Symphony No. 2*).

Ashkenazy is first choice in both these works: in *Karelia* the outer movements in particular have great sweep, while the performance of *Finlandia* is the most stirring available, with a ripe recording and a particularly pungent sound from the Philharmonia's tuba. It's coupled with good performances of *Tapiola* (see p.394) and *En Saga* (A Saga), a generalized

DECCA/VIVIANNE PURDOM

Vladimir Ashkenazy

evocation of the spirit of the Nordic sagas, written in 1893 and revised in 1901.

LEMMINKÄINEN SUITE

The *Lemminkäinen Suite* (1895), also known as *Four Legends*, is another early work based on the *Kalevala*. It's best known for its second movement, *The Swan of Tuonela*, in which a cor anglais, singing mournfully over sombre string and low wind harmonies, evokes the swan gliding on a dark river. The excerpt is heard far more often on its own than in its original context, but the other three movements are equally worth getting to know for Sibelius's distinctive way of creating drama and atmosphere.

⊙ Lemminkäinen Suite: Gothenburg Symphony Orchestra; Järvi (BIS CD294).

Neeme Järvi conducts a particularly satisfying performance of the whole suite, with the Gothenburg Symphony Orchestra, in a warm spacious acoustic.

⊙ The Swan of Tuonela: Berlin Philharmonic Orchestra; Karajan (Deutsche Grammophon 439 982-2; with *Symphonies Nos. 5 & 6*).

If you just want the highlight of the "Suite", *The Swan of Tuonela*, go for the Karajan version, which boasts the appropriately refulgent string tones of the Berlin Philharmonic.

THE TEMPEST & TAPIOLA

Sibelius composed a fair amount of music for theatrical productions (in those days many theatres had orchestras), and his finest piece of theatre music was his last, written for a production of Shakespeare's *Tempest* in Copenhagen in 1926. Beginning with a wonderful evocation of the storm, cleverly composed almost entirely of held chords and swishing cascades of chromatic scales, it consists of over thirty separate numbers, including character studies and settings of the play's songs. Written immediately after *The Tempest*, *Tapiola* was Sibelius's last work, and it's one of his greatest. Inspired by Tapio, the ancient Finnish god of the forest, this symphonic poem – like the early *En Saga* – is a broadly pictorial and atmospheric composition, rather than a musical depiction of a specific train of dramatic events. It's as tautly conceived as any of his symphonies and as evocative in its tone-painting as anything in his entire oeuvre.

⊙ The Tempest: Tiihonen, Paasikivi, Hirvonen, Kerola, Keinonen; Lahti Opera Chorus & Symphony Orchestra; Vänskä (BIS CD581).

There have been several recordings of the suites compiled from Sibelius's full score of *The Tempest*, but none matches the magnificence of this recording of the complete music. Vänskä has recently made a name for himself as an outstanding Sibelian and this performance is full of much exquisite detailing.

⊙ Tapiola: Gothenburg Symphony Orchestra; Järvi (BIS CD312; with *Pohjola's Daughter*, *Rakastava*, *Impromptu*).

The epic northern landscape is marvellously conjured up in Järvi's Gothenburg account of *Tapiola*, which is coupled with a luscious version of *Pohjola's Daughter* (1906), another Kalevala-inspired tone poem. Sibelius's command of the orchestra was never more clearly revealed than in this piece, and Järvi's stunning recording does full justice to its wide-ranging and sumptuous use of orchestral colour.

BEDŘICH SMETANA

(1824–1884)

Czech classical music did not spring into existence with the arrival of Bedřich Smetana – Prague, after all, was one of the great musical centres of the eighteenth century. However, Smetana almost single-handedly established Czech musical nationalism, being the first to integrate folk-based material into his compositions. His music may reflect a prominent Germanic influence – hardly surprising considering that he spent his formative years under Austrian rule – but his impact upon the more overtly nationalistic Dvořák, Janáček and Martinů is incalculable.

Born in Bohemia, the son of a brewer, Smetana showed incredible ability as a child: he was playing in a string quartet from the age of 5 and three years later produced his first symphony. He was educated at the Proksch Institute in Prague, where he wrote some Lisztian tone poems that received little recognition. Obliged to teach in order to make ends meet, he was almost penniless when Liszt prompted him to try his fortune in Sweden, away from the oppressive atmosphere of Austrian-ruled Prague. From 1856 to 1861 he lived in Gothenburg and it was there that he composed his first successful symphonic poem, *Richard III*; written as a tribute to Liszt, it was heavily Romantic and Germanic, giving no hint of a Czech national style.

In 1861, with the easing of the Austrian regime, Smetana returned home. His financial instability forced him to tour as a pianist for a while, but exciting possibilities appeared with the opening in 1862 of the Provisional Theatre, Prague's first theatre built exclusively for Czech use. Four years later Smetana's first opera, *The Brandenburgers in Bohemia*, was performed there, and its success led to Smetana's appointment as the theatre's chief conductor. Later the same year, a draft of Smetana's most remarkable opera, *The Bartered Bride*, received its premiere at the Provisional, but it was the performance of the definitive three-act version in 1870 that effectively created a Czech national opera.

It was to prove the apex of his public career. His subsequent operas were attacked for their Wagnerian tendencies, and Smetana's enemies plotted for his removal. In the event, he was forced to resign in 1874 when he went deaf as a result of syphilitic infection. He continued to compose (*Má*

GUS ONG

Vlast, his best-known work, comes from this period), and he became recognized as something of a national institution, but Smetana's life ended tragically. Suicidally depressed and ravaged by syphilis, he eventually went mad, and was committed to Prague's lunatic asylum early in 1884. He died in May, and was buried with full Czech honours.

THE BARTERED BRIDE

The Provisional Theatre was not the best-appointed opera house in Europe. Bewailing its meagre facilities, Smetana wrote: "How can we possibly play opera in a house as small as ours? In *Les Huguenots*, the armies barely number eight on each side . . . and thus provoke laughter. The singers are pressed so close together in the foreground that everyone must be careful not to hurt his neighbour when he turns." Yet it was in this theatre, in 1866, that *The Bartered Bride* heralded the birth of Czech opera.

Smetana later wrote that he had composed *The Bartered Bride* "out of spite, because I was accused after *The Brandenburgers* of being a Wagnerian who was incapable of writing anything in a lighter vein." Even though he was working on *The Bartered Bride* some time before *The Brandenburgers* was staged, there is something to Smetana's claim, for the style of this opera is indeed unlike the declamatory Wagnerian manner of *The Brandenburgers*. Set in a Bohemian village, *The Bartered Bride* is an engagingly direct love story in which boy gets girl after just the right amount of comic misunderstanding, and the music is full of broad strokes and bold contrasts, with plenty of Czech "numbers", such as drinking-choruses and polkas, to keep things moving. An equally important aspect of *The Bartered Bride* is Smetana's vivid characterization. Each of the leads is assigned clearly recognizable musical features that are maintained throughout the opera, and Smetana brilliantly uses key signatures to reflect their changing moods.

Beňačková, Dvorský, Kopp, Novák; Czech Philharmonic Orchestra & Chorus; Košler (Supraphon 103511-2; 3 CDs).

Many recordings of *The Bartered Bride* use a translated libretto, but Smetana's operas lose much of their musical style if not performed in Czech. The earthy qualities of the original are best heard in Supraphon's excellent recording under Košler with the the, fabulous Czech Philharmonic. Lyrical central performances from soprano Gabriela Beňačková and tenor Peter Dvorský, together with some exemplary chorus work, make this a highly entertaining production.

MÁ VLAST

The six symphonic poems of *Má Vlast* (My Homeland) were begun in 1872 and completed a full seven years later, but at the end of this process he had created his fullest expression of the Czech national spirit – although, ironically, the principal theme of *Vltava*, the second and most famous of the six, is a derivation of a Swedish (rather than a Czech) folk song. Characterized by expansive melodies and dramatic rhythms, *Má Vlast* presents a vision of Czech legend, history and landscape, packing an incredible array of battles, celebrations and other scenes into fifty minutes' music. Specifically, the first section is a graphic description of the river flowing through Prague; the second is a portrait of the Czech countryside; and the remaining four refer to episodes from Czech history, making repeated use of a nationalist hymn in the last two sections. It's heroic, astonishingly well-crafted music, meriting comparison with the orchestral poems of Liszt – Smetana's inspiration – and Richard Strauss.

Czech Philharmonic Orchestra; Kubelík (Supraphon 111208-2).

This recording was made on Rafael Kubelík's return to Prague in 1990 to conduct the Czech Phil after an absence of many years. The reunion inspired conductor and orchestra to put on a display of explosive emotional exuberance, captured on a recording of excellent quality. The playing is occasionally a little rough, but few CDs transmit such a sense of occasion.

Bavarian Radio Symphony Orchestra; Kubelík (Orfeo 115 841 A).

This 1984 recording is, arguably, a more musically satisfying, if less emotional account than the one discussed above. Both orchestra and conductor are so in control of the material that the smallest details are revealed in all their subtlety. A beautiful performance, and well recorded.

Boston Symphony Orchestra; Kubelík (Deutsche Grammophon 429 183-2).

Kubelík recorded Smetana's masterpiece on at least five occasions. This account, made in 1971, boasts the most luscious sonorities and strongest rhythmic bite, but the studio recording is slightly dry and overprecise.

THE STRING QUARTETS

The first of Smetana's two stupendous string quartets was composed in 1876, two years after he had gone deaf from the disease which eventually was to kill him. Subtitled "From My Life", the *String Quartet No. 1* is Smetana's autobiography in music; as he put it himself, the four movements comprise a "recollection of my life and the catastrophe of total deafness". The folk rhythms and rustic harmonies are allied to a heightened comprehension of the instruments' expressive potential, a development which, as with Beethoven, was surely connected with the composer's isolation. In a moment of desperate poignancy, the end of the jaunty last movement is interrupted by a shattering, dissonant high E on the first violin. This is the note which tormented the composer in his deafness; Smetana grimly referred to it as his "little joke".

The *Quartet No. 2* is not blatantly autobiographical, but the music does relate to the suffering of his later years, and its bittersweet themes can be deeply distressing. It was composed in 1882, when Smetana's mind was in such a state that he found concentration all but impossible, and he would frequently forget a theme within seconds of writing it down. The movements are therefore episodic and brief, but they constitute an amazingly advanced essay in the form. Schoenberg judged that in its treatment of rhythm, harmonic obscurity, melodic richness and tendency to terseness, Smetana's *Quartet No. 2* was decades ahead of its time.

○ Talich Quartet (Collins 13232; with Suk, *Meditation on an Old Czech Hymn*).

The Talich Quartet produce astonishingly imaginative performances that project all the composer's anxiety into a world of sumptuous colour. Perfectly recorded, and coupled with Suk's haunting *Meditation on an Old Czech Hymn*, this is one of the most rewarding CDs of Smetana's music.

ETHEL SMYTH

(1858–1944)

Ethel Smyth is finally beginning to achieve the attention she deserves, with much of her music now available on CD. The daughter of an army general, Smyth was a quite extraordinary woman, who was determined to study music at a time when professional careers for women were frowned on, fighting with a most unladylike tenacity for recognition as a composer and for performances of her powerfully vital music. After a fierce fight with her family, Smyth went to Leipzig to study composition. Her first works, chamber music and songs, were published and performed there, and show a decidedly Germanic flavour. On her return to England she had a few successful performances of various orchestral works and her compelling *Mass in D* (1891), but she found it difficult to interest most conductors and promoters in such large-scale music. Women were thought to be incapable of producing complex compositions, being expected to write nothing but pretty songs and delicate piano pieces. Undaunted, Smyth turned to opera, the most complex of all musical genres, even though at that time new operas had little chance of success in Britain, and her first three operas, *Fantasio* (1892–94), *Der Wald* (1899–1901) and *The Wreckers*, were first performed in Germany.

Smyth devoted two years to the militant suffragette campaign, spending a few weeks in Holloway prison for throwing a stone through the Colonial Secretary's window. It was Holloway where she wrote her best-known work, the rousing suffragette anthem *March of the Women*, which she used to conduct with a toothbrush from her cell window. After her release Smyth produced *The Boatswain's Mate* (1913–14), a comic opera with a decidedly feminist theme – Mrs Waters, the strong-willed heroine, constantly outwits a bumbling suitor who is determined to prove that she needs a man to protect her. Smyth also wrote two other operas, *Fête Galante* (1922), a neo-classic "dance-dream" set in the eighteenth century, and another comic opera *Entente Cordiale* (1925); works in other forms included the lively unaccompanied chorus *Hey Nonny No* (1911), the beautiful orchestral songs *Three Moods of the Sea* (1913), and *The Prison* (1930), an intense work for soloists, chorus and orchestra. Smyth had realized that she was beginning to lose her hearing during the 1910s and, although she continued to compose, in later life she concentrated more on her ten volumes of memoirs and essays, in which she expressed her views on subjects ranging from women's creativity to golf and sheepdogs.

THE WRECKERS

Smyth's greatest opera was first performed in Leipzig in 1906 and later received a production at Covent Garden, conducted by Bruno Walter. Set in a Cornish fishing village, where the inhabitants supplement their meagre livelihood by looting ships wrecked on the nearby coast, it tells the story of two lovers who, disgusted at the wrecking activities, light beacons to warn ships off the rocks. When discovered, they are forced into a cave where the rising tide drowns them. *The Wreckers* is a thrilling work: Wagnerian in its orchestration and use of leitmotifs, full of passionate vocal writing and powerful evocations of the raging sea and treacherous Cornish coast. In its depiction of an introverted coastal community, it anticipates *Peter Grimes* (see p.83) – in fact Britten studied the score before he embarked on his masterpiece.

○ Owens, Lavender; Huddersfield Choral Society; BBC Philharmonic Orchestra; de la Martinez (Conifer CDCF 250/1; 2 CDs).

This CD was recorded live at the Proms in 1994, when *The Wreckers* received its first professional performance in many years (although not a fully staged one). Odaline de la Martinez conducts with her usual vigour, while Anne-Marie Owens and Justin Lavender carry off the difficult second-act love duet with all the requisite intensity.

ORCHESTRAL WORKS

When Smyth's orchestral works, the *Serenade in D* and *Overture to Anthony and Cleopatra* (both written in 1889), were first performed in London, several critics expressed surprise that a woman had written such powerful and dramatic music. The *Serenade* is a large, four-movement work which is symphonic in scope and remarkably assured for a first orchestral work. Smyth did not write another purely orchestral work until the *Concerto for Violin, Horn and Orchestra* of 1927, although several interludes from her operas (such as *On the Cliffs of Cornwall* from *The Wreckers*) achieved widespread popularity in the concert hall. Skilfully orchestrated, the *Concerto* is a delightful work with another of Smyth's deeply felt slow movements but also a sense of fun as the unusual solo pairing of violin and horn weave with the orchestra an intricate and often joyful pattern of diverse themes.

⊙ Serenade in D; Concerto for Violin, Horn and Orchestra: Langdon, Watkins; BBC Philharmonic; de la Martinez (Chandos CHAN 9449).

A recording that provides two very different examples of Smyth's writing, separated this time by nearly forty years. Odaline de la Martinez has long been a champion of Smyth's music and brings energy and passion to these gripping performances, which clearly demonstrate Smyth's importance.

CHAMBER MUSIC

Most of Smyth's chamber music was written while she was at Leipzig in the 1880s, and the best of her work from this period is represented by the Brahmsian *String Quintet* (1883), an eloquent, large-scale composition with a beautifully poignant slow movement, and the impressive four-movement *Violin Sonata* (1887), which a contemporary reviewer found "deficient in the feminine charm that might have been expected of a woman composer". The dramatic and more strikingly individual *String Quartet* is one of her few post-Leipzig chamber works: the first two movements were written in 1902 but not performed until 1912, when they were heard at the first public concert of the Society of Women Musicians. On hearing them, Smyth decided to complete the work by adding two more movements, an expressive Andante and the exuberantly contrapuntal finale.

⊙ String Quartet; String Quintet: Mannheim String Quartet; Griesheimer (CPO 999352-2).

These two works are separated by nearly thirty years and putting them together on this CD clearly shows the development of Smyth's musical language. They are given thoughtful and fluent performances by the Mannheim Quartet, who are more convincing in the slower movements (especially the heartfelt Andante of the *Quartet*) than the faster ones, where they lack the sparkling vitality that is so much part of Smyth's music.

KARLHEINZ STOCKHAUSEN

(1928–)

In today's global village of information highways and cultural cross-pollination, no composer occupies so pivotal a place as Karlheinz Stockhausen, who way back in the 1960s was predicting "a music of the whole world". The iconic figure of postwar highbrow modernity, he has been admired by people right across the musical spectrum: Frank Zappa and a generation of German progressive rock musicians like Tangerine Dream looked up to him, as did John Lennon – the single *Strawberry Fields* as well as chunks of *Sergeant Pepper* were directly influenced by Stockhausen's electronic music of the 1950s. As the first electronic studio composer, he is revered by the newest generation of rock and pop producers, whose computer processes and sampling techniques owe much to Stockhausen's pioneering efforts.

Brought up in the environs of Cologne, Stockhausen spent his earliest years on the move, following the wanderings of his schoolteacher father, while absorbing music from his mother – who played piano and sang – and from the new media of radio and gramophone. The war shattered his childhood: his mother, who had been recuperating in a mental home, fell victim to the Nazi's inhuman euthanasia programme; his father was reported missing, and was never seen again. Conscripted as a stretcher-bearer, the orphaned Stockhausen witnessed the most brutal carnage, and many times came within an inch of losing his life. By the war's end he had become a devout Christian, and was playing jazz piano for American GIs to finance his courses at Cologne's music school and university, where he studied German literature, philosophy, piano and musicology.

HARALD FRONZECK FOTOGRAFIE

Stockhausen in his home studio

Under the influence of Schoenberg and the cell-like writing of Anton Webern (see p.474), Stockhausen composed some brilliant serial pieces, including *Choral* (1950), a haunting evocation of the bleak North Rhine landscape. By the following year he was attending new music courses in Darmstadt, where he was entranced by the work of Olivier Messiaen (see p.256), with whom he then studied in Paris – and by whom he was promptly proclaimed a genius. There he also met Pierre Boulez (see p.71) and Pierre Schaeffer, who were working on innovative forms of tape composition at the studio of ORTF radio.

Still fascinated by Messiaen and Webern, Stockhausen – like Boulez – went on to advocate a music of "total serialism", where every element would be determined by impersonal parameters. Performances of his work at Darmstadt were greeted with shock and dismay, as audiences struggled with music that just seemed to consist of an amorphous blob of notes, lacking any discernible melodic or rhythmic sense. In 1952–53 he spent three months in Paris splicing and processing two minutes and twenty seconds of taped "concrete" sounds (ie "real" sounds). On its presentation to Schaeffer, the resulting *Etude* was dismissed as sheer folly, but at the age of 24 Stockhausen was offered a job at the WDR radio station in Cologne to continue his search for a "pure electronic music". Later in 1953 he went on to create *Studie I*, the first piece of music constructed entirely of sine waves.

Stockhausen tirelessly experimented with white noise, feedback and chance operations, stimulated by his studies in phonetics and communications science at Bonn university. From this period came the mighty *Gruppen* for three orchestras, a piece that moved music through space as well as time, and the thirteen-minute *Gesang der Jünglinge* (Song of the Youths) for boy soprano and electronic sound, a *tour de force* which took more than a year to create in the primitive Cologne studio. The debut of *Gesang der Jünglinge* at WDR caused as much uproar as Stravinsky's *Rite* had done, for the audience were made to sit down and experience a performance of this "electronic space music" through loudspeakers alone. Fame quickly spread, as people such as Ligeti (see p.219) made pilgrimages to Cologne to see the inspirational German inventor.

Stockhausen's career now entered a stage of consolidations and expansions. *Kontakte* (1960) pushed the tape machine to its limits; *Momente* (1962) for choral groups and instrumentalists applied to acoustic instruments his electronic discoveries about the importance of such elements as sound-colour and silence-duration; in 1966, after a visit to Japan, he wrote *Telemusik*, a meta-collage of ethnic musics; after a visit to America in 1967 he completed the epic *Hymnen*, based on the world's national anthems; and his openness to world music was further explored in *Stimmung*, a vocal work inspired by Aztec and Maya mythology. In May 1968 the disintegration of his relationship with Mary Bauermeister precipitated a personal crisis from which Stockhausen extracted himself through the writing of *Aus den sieben Tagen* (Out of the Seven Days), a titanic sequence of fifteen works that he commenced during a seven-day fast. Termed "Intuitive Music" by the composer, *Aus den sieben Tagen* in its written form consisted of prose texts to be interpreted by its performers, who were required to bring the music into being through the filter of their own beliefs, moods and experiences. In its loosely structured procedures and its incorporation of raw material from its creator's life, this cathartic sequence foreshadowed much of Stockhausen's future work. Everything he saw, heard or in any way experienced – however trivial – was now assimilated into a continuous production system in which events were meticulously annotated, logged and transcribed into music. Stockhausen's presentation of a thousand hours of "musical space travel" at the Osaka Expo of 1970 was a typically audacious project.

The apotheosis of Stockhausen's inexhaustible ambition (or megalomania) came in 1977, when he announced the genesis of the twentieth century's closest equivalent to gigantic musical projects of Wagner. He had set himself the task of creating a *Gesamtkunstwerk* titled *Licht* (Light), a seven-part opera (one for each day of the week) for solo voices, solo instruments, solo dancers, choirs, orchestras, dancers, mimes and electronics. To date, six sections have been completed – *Donnerstag* (Thursday; 1978–80), *Samstag* (Saturday; 1981–83), *Montag* (Monday; 1984–88), *Dienstag* (Tuesday; 1977 & 1988–91), *Freitag* (Friday; 1994) and *Mittwoch* (Wednesday; 1998). Only *Sonntag* (Sunday) remains to be written, and the complete cycle is intended to be presented in its entirety at the dawn of the new millennium.

In 1991 Stockhausen returned to WDR to digitally remaster his entire 205-composition oeuvre on CD. The dazzlingly remastered works are now being issued by Stockhausen-Verlag, a company based at the composer's self-designed house in Kürten, and you can only get hold of them direct from there – the address for CDs, stock lists and other publications is Stockhausen-Verlag, Kettenberg 15, 51515 Kürten, Germany. Together with Stockhausen's own incisive insights into his music and life, detailed in his six-volume *Texte zur Musik* (excerpts translated as *Towards a Cosmic Music*, published by Element), the Stockhausen-Verlag series will amount to a definitive career statement. We've selected the three Stockhausen-Verlag releases that make the best introduction to Stockhausen's vast output, plus two of the few Stockhausen CDs from other companies.

ELECTRONIC MUSIC

Stockhausen is a crucial figure in the history of electronic music, and remains one of its most accomplished exponents. He first began his explorations in 1952 with *Etude,* a brief piece constructed by the complex splicing and overlapping of the sounds of piano strings struck with an iron beater. It caused a rift between him and Pierre Schaeffer, the father of *musique concrète*, who later commented: "All you heard was 'Schuuut'. He was terribly pleased with it; me, not at all." Consolidating his artistic independence from Schaeffer, Stockhausen produced two electronic studies (*Studie I*, 1953; *Studie II*, 1954) based on entirely synthesized material, which he used to experiment with the application of serial principles to timbre and frequency, elements which resist precise control in instrumental music.

Studie I, a piece constructed from the sine waves of a frequency generator, marked a major leap forward despite the limitations of the available technology, but the work that brought electronic music to maturity, and set the agenda for future developments, was *Gesang der Jünglinge* (1955–56).

Conceived as part of a projected but never completed Mass, *Gesang der Jünglinge* interweaves synthesized and natural elements – in this case, a boy's voice half-singing and half-reciting syllables and words from the third Book of Daniel (*preiset den Herrn* – "praise ye the Lord"). It was condemned as blasphemous when it was performed at Cologne Cathedral, but it is a devout, exultant and quite magical piece of music, with the voice sometimes emerging clearly from the mix of strange, unidentifiable sounds, then being submerged by electronic noises or altered in such a way that it seems alien itself.

Lasting some 35 minutes, *Kontakte* (1960) is by far the lengthiest of Stockhausen's seminal electronic pieces. Its fundamental concern is one that he explored in several works of this period: the way that frequencies are perceived differently – as pulsation, rhythm, focused note, etc – depending on their speed. Replete with previously unheard sonorities, *Kontakte* embodies the aesthetic of "Moment Form", in which each sound event is intended to be viable in itself, rather than deriving validity from its place in the overall process or structure.

O Elektronische Musik 1952–1960 – Etude; Studie I & II; Gesang der Jünglinge; Kontakte (Stockhausen-Verlag 3).

This CD collects Stockhausen's crucial contributions to the genre, and comes with exhaustive documentation by the composer. On record you get only an approximation of his intentions for *Gesang der Jünglinge*: he designed the piece for five channels, with the boy's voice assigned to its own overhead speaker, but had to reduce it to two channels for release on disc. Despite this limitation, it remains a breathtaking achievement. The version of *Kontakte* included here is purely electronic. Recordings of a version with piano and percussion soloists interacting with the tape are available on Stockhausen-Verlag 6 (paired with *Zyklus* and *Refrain*).

GRUPPEN

The gestation of *Gruppen* (Groups) began before the creation of *Gesang der Jünglinge*, and at the outset it was conceived as a work for tape and orchestra. Yet when Stockhausen recommenced work on *Gruppen* in 1957, it transmuted into a piece for three orchestras, each comprising six woodwind instruments, seven or eight brass, six percussion (including keyboards and electric guitar), and sixteen or eighteen strings. As with *Kontakte*, the music is underpinned by the perception of rhythm, tempo and pitch as aspects of the same phenomenon (slow any note far enough, for example, and you start to hear it as a beat). *Gruppen* is innovatory in the way it treats tempo to the sort of serial techniques that composers had been applying to tones since the breakthrough compositions of Schoenberg (ie subjecting tempo to systematic organization); but in performance, however, it's the spatial dimension of this piece that makes the immediate impact. Arrayed on three sides of the audience, and each with its own conductor (at the premiere the roles were taken by the formidable trio of Stockhausen, Boulez and Bruno Maderna), the three orchestras merge in accelerations and crescendos, then separate into a tripartite dialogue in which independent tempos are combined or fragments of sound fly between the groups – as in the work's climax, when a great brass chord swirls around the hall.

O Berlin Philharmonic Orchestra; Abbado (Deutsche Grammophon 447 761-2; with Kurtág's *Grabstein für Stephan* & *Stele*).

Claudio Abbado, one of the very few top-flight conductors to consistently champion the music of the postwar avant-garde, here gives a thrilling reading of *Gruppen*. No CD could adequately convey the experience of being hemmed in by Stockhausen's triple orchestras, but the DG engineers have achieved a superb illusion of space on this live recording. Equally exhilarating are the two coupled pieces by György Kurtág, who was one of several young composers in the audience for *Gruppen*'s first performance.

HYMNEN

Begun in 1965 and informed by trips to Japan and America, *Hymnen* is an ambitious two-hour work which some critics have called Stockhausen's *Sergeant Pepper* – and both works indeed appealed to many of the same people. Divided into four regions or movements, it juxtaposes forty songs and national anthems (shorn of their jingoistic baggage), mixing them with natural sounds, electronic interventions and the reactions of live performers. Listeners have to be content with meditating on the journey rather than fretting about the destination, as *Hymnen* unfolds slowly through the extended transformations (Stockhausen often puns with sound, as when crowd noises mutate into the calls of swamp-ducks) and passages of near-silence. Using short-wave radios he literally plucks sounds from the air, drawing on every culture to produce a genuine World music.

O Hymnen (Stockhausen-Verlag 10).

Like a number of Stockhausen's other works, including *Kontakte*, *Hymnen* exists in more than one version. It can be "performed" purely on tape, or with soloists who are encouraged to introduce improvisatory elements. Both versions are included here.

STIMMUNG

Written in Madison, Connecticut, during the early months of 1968, *Stimmung* (Tuning) is a hypnotically static work for six unaccompanied voices, in 51 brief sections. Using only a series of harmonics of a low B flat, the six singers recite and transform speech sounds based on various "magic names" (mostly gods and goddesses) and erotic texts written for Stockhausen's partner, Mary Bauermeister. The lyrics, when audible, are often pretty gauche, but the music is mesmerizing: beginning with overtone singing that produces sounds like a kind of softer, higher-pitched didgeridoo, it continues its bewitching journey with swirls of vowels, phonemes and chords, the luminous clouds of abstract syllables shot through with startling, clearly enunciated words.

O Singcircle; Rose (Hyperion CDA66115).

This brilliant performance was recorded in 1983, in consultation with the composer. Two different recordings are also available on Stockhausen-Verlag 12, both outstandingly sung by Collegium Vocale (who premiered the work), but non-aficionados are advised to go for the single-CD Hyperion account.

ALESSANDRO STRADELLA

(1644–1682)

Alessandro Stradella was a notorious womanizer whose sexual adventures led to his murder in Genoa at the age of 37. This has tended to obscure the fact that he was also a notable composer of opera and oratorios – one of the latter, *San Giovanni Battista*, being among the most dramatically compelling works of the seventeenth century. In both his oratorios and his purely instrumental works Stradella was one of the first composers to employ the concerto grosso form, in which the music was divided between the full ensemble and a smaller group within it, for the purpose of dramatic contrast.

Stradella was born in Rome into the minor nobility, a distinction that allowed him entry into exalted aristocratic circles. His patrons included the powerful Colonna and Pamphili families as well as Queen Christina of Sweden, who was living in Rome in voluntary exile and in whose household Stradella served from the age of 14. In 1669 the discovery of his involvement in a plot to embezzle money from the Church forced him, briefly, to leave the city, although he returned in time for the opening of a new theatre, the Teatro Tordinona, which was to perform several of his works.

In 1673 in Florence he attempted to abduct a young nun, Lisabetta Marmonari, who had been the object of his attentions for several years. Four years later in Venice, having been hired by Alvise Contarini to give music lessons to his young mistress, Stradella instead eloped with her to Turin. An incensed Contarini pursued the couple and eventually two of his hired thugs left Stradella seriously wounded after a murder attempt. He fled to Genoa early in 1678, but four years later yet another amorous involvement with a high-ranking lady led to his assassination at the hands of a hired killer in the city's main square.

SAN GIOVANNI BATTISTA

San Giovanni Battista was written for the Confraternity of Florentines in Rome, who in 1675 – declared a Holy Year by the Pope – commissioned fourteen oratorios on the subject of their patron saint, St John the Baptist. Stradella's is a masterpiece of dramatic sophistication, with fully rounded characters, a huge range of emotions and a remarkable immediacy that's increased by the fact that the text is in Italian rather than Latin. Though San Giovanni is the protagonist, it

is the corrupt and incestuous court of Erode (Herod) that generates the piece's psychological complexity. Stradella is helped by his librettist, who maintains the tension by dispensing with a narrator, but it is the music that builds up the atmosphere of degeneration and moral panic. In several arias Stradella seems to anticipate Handel's florid lines, but he doesn't have Handel's tendency to spin out the luxuriant moments at the expense of dramatic momentum – the mood often changes here within the space of a single aria. Thus when Erodiade (Salome) makes her request for the death of San Giovanni, she begins her exchanges with Erode nervously, becoming insinuating then petulant, and finally pleads with him in a beguilingly beautiful aria, *Queste lagrime*. Only Monteverdi's *L'Incoronazione di Poppea* (see p.264) creates such a splendid frisson from the apparent triumph of evil.

O Bott, Lesne, Huttenlocher, Batty, Edgar-Wilson; Les Musiciens du Louvre; Minkowski (Erato 2292 4573 92).

This performance is exceptionally well cast, with an emphasis on characterful rather than merely beautiful singing. Indeed the Erode of Phillippe Huttenlocher (bass) is a little woolly sounding, but he more than compensates by projecting the tyrant's mixture of bluster and fearfulness so convincingly. Gerard Lesne (countertenor) as San Giovanni is equally strong, with an incisiveness of tone that admirably conveys the incorruptible authority and dignity of the saint, while Catherine Bott's rendition of the demented aria *Su coronatemi* (Come now crown me) is one of the highlights of the disc.

THE STRAUSS FAMILY

When Johann Strauss died in 1849 at the age of 45, a Viennese obituarist suggested that the city should mourn not just because a great man had gone but because once again Vienna's resident genius had been struck down prematurely. Fifty years later the same writer made the same claim for Johann Strauss the Younger (1825–99), and again courted controversy by suggesting that waltz-manufacturers should command as much respect as Schubert, or indeed any composer of symphonies and sonatas. Admirers of the Strauss family still face an uphill struggle to convince people that their music is anything more than the froth of Viennese high society, but it's a mistake to patronize the talent required to write hundreds of memorable pieces within the extreme technical limitations of the waltz. Strauss senior's compositions may often have been convention-bound and short-winded, yet in his flamboyant *Radetzky March* he produced a work that became the very symbol of Habsburg military might, just as his son's *Blue Danube* was to epitomize the glittering hedonism of imperial Vienna.

GUUS ONG

In addition to the two Johanns there was also a Josef (1827–1920) – Johann the Younger's brother – who composed some 280 pieces, but couldn't match the fertility of his sibling, the so-called "Waltz King". Johann Strauss the Younger set the standards for every writer of "light" music in the next half-century, not just by enriching the Viennese waltz and other dance forms, but also through the creation of *Die Fledermaus* (The Bat), a magnificent operetta that has a claim to be his finest composition. Nobody would make out that there is any great depth here, but Johann the Younger has few rivals as uncomplicated melodist and orchestrator, and his music has retained the nostalgic attraction to which the obituary referred when it called him "the last symbol of cheerful, pleasant times".

DIE FLEDERMAUS

Premiered in 1874, *Die Fledermaus* is a brilliantly clever commentary on Viennese moral laxity, cloaked in sparklingly tuneful music that made it an instant hit – by the end of the decade, it was playing in some 170 theatres. On paper the plot is complicated to the point of unintelligibility, but on stage this tale of infidelity, mistaken identity and excessive champagne consumption works as well as any piece of music-theatre. Offenbach's witty, hedonistic operettas obviously influenced the musical style of *Die Fledermaus*, but Strauss's quintessentially Viennese decorum softens the edge of the satire. The most important stage work of its sort ever written, *Die Fledermaus* established a tradition that saw its apogee in the works of Lehár, and Richard Strauss paid homage to its waltz rhythms in *Der Rosenkavalier*.

◑ **Varady, Popp, Prey, Kollo, Weikl, Rebroff, Kusche, Gruber, List, Muxeneder; Bavarian State Opera Chorus & Orchestra; Kleiber** (Deutsche Grammophon 415 646-2GH2; 2 CDs).

For its flair and wit, Carlos Kleiber's superbly conducted performance of *Die Fledermaus* is the obvious choice. The reclusive, semi-retired Kleiber is the most remarkable Strauss conductor of the present generation, and there is no conductor alive today who's able to get such downright erotic sounds out of an orchestra. His cast isn't ideal, but Hermann Prey gives one of the best performances of his career, and Julia Varady and Lucia Popp are very, very good – their singing of Act One's *So muss allein ich bleiben* is completely wonderful.

THE DANCE MUSIC

Johann I's *Radetsky March* is played every year at the New Year's Day Concert at the Vienna Musikverein, an outbreak of white-tie jollity to celebrate the city's kings of dance music. Leaving aside the *Radetzky March*, however, it's Johann II's waltzes that dominate the dynasty's output, and pieces such as *Thunder and Lightning*, *Vienna Blood*, *Acceleration*, *Tales from the Vienna Woods* and *The Blue Danube* are among the best-known tunes of the nineteenth century. (*The Blue Danube* has now been recorded more than seventy times, putting it in the same league as many of Beethoven's symphonies.) Strauss once claimed that he merely took over the waltz form from his father, and indeed the structure of Johann II's waltzes is similar to the later works of his elders: slow introduction, five repetitions of the waltz and a quick coda. However, Johann II greatly increased the length of the central sections, introduced a greater sense of homogeneity to the whole piece, and enhanced the textural complexities, which makes his waltzes much more satisfying as concert music. But ultimately, of course, this is music to move to. If you don't have a ballroom at your disposal, sample the following CDs sparingly, because you can only listen to so many waltzes before going berserk. Taken in measured doses, however, they'll cheer you up in almost any circumstances. Schoenberg was so fond of them that he made transcriptions of two of them and set others as transcription exercises for his pupils Berg and Webern!

○ **New Year's Day Concert 1996: Vienna Philharmonic Orchestra; Maazel** (RCA 09026 68421-2).

It has long been a Viennese tradition to have a New Year's Day Concert in the Musikvereinsaal and many fine conductors have done the honours with the Vienna Phil over the years. Not surprisingly, for such spontaneous music, live recordings are preferable to studio efforts, and Lorin Maazel's 1996 concert proves one of the best of recent years. The selection mixes the popular (*Radetsky March*, *Emperor Waltz*, *The Blue Danube*) with some more unusual fare. The fresh and natural sound well captures the sense of occasion, and the versatile Maazel doesn't just conduct – he joins in with the occasional violin solo. There's an extra twenty minutes of encores thrown in on a separate disc, all for the price of one.

◑ **Favourite Waltzes: Vienna Philharmonic Orchestra; Boskovsky** (Decca 417 706-2).

This disc concentrates on the best-known waltzes of Johann Strauss II in performances with the VPO's concertmaster Wili Boskovsky. The sound is a little thin (it has been digitally remastered), but these are idiomatic and joyous renditions, with the orchestra at their most effervescent and uninhibited.

RICHARD STRAUSS

(1864–1949)

Richard Strauss was the last great German Romantic, but the trajectory of his career was more convoluted than such a definition suggests. Having burst onto the scene as the composer of feverishly ardent orchestral pieces, he went on to produce operas as progressive and discomforting as any of their time, before switching to decorous, slightly decadent and often ironic conservatism. However, through each phase of Strauss's long life – from the electrifying brilliance of *Don Juan* to the ersatz eighteenth-century charm of the late opera *Capriccio*, there runs a fundamentally consistent harmonic and melodic style, marked above all by a Mozartian tunefulness. Like Mozart, Strauss possessed an amazing technical facility, and if his abilities did sometimes lead to passages of superficial note-spinning, he was constitutionally incapable of writing anything slipshod. Often depicted as the traditionalist opponent of modernism, even the epitome of bourgeois complacency (few composers ever enjoyed Strauss's financial success), he has now come to seem like a prophet of the postmodern age, in which irony and pastiche are perceived as radical procedures. His work is dismissed as shallow kitsch in some quarters, but such critical disapproval has not affected his standing as one of the two most popular opera composers of the twentieth century (Puccini being the other).

Born in Munich, Strauss was the only son of Franz Strauss, the brilliant principal horn player in the Bavarian Court Opera, who instructed him in music's fundamentals. Strauss senior was an arch-conservative who hated Wagner and brought up his son with a profound reverence for Bach, Mozart and Beethoven. Strauss junior took piano lessons from the age of 4, began composing two years later and, requiring no formal musical tuition, received a traditional, rounded education. After the composition of his Brahmsian *Symphony No. 1* in 1880, he scored something of a success with his *Serenade* for wind instruments, which in turn induced the conductor Hans von Bülow to commission a suite from him in 1882. By 1885 he had succeeded von Bülow as principal conductor at Meiningen, a post he left the following year to journey to Italy, where he composed his first symphonic poem, *Aus Italien*. Upon his return, he was appointed conductor at the Munich Opera.

LEBRECHT COLLECTION

Strauss and a pair of admirers, Vienna, 1909

Having achieved provincial success as a conductor, Strauss struck international success as a composer in 1888 with *Don Juan*, a flamboyant tone poem that established him as the most exciting composer in Germany, a position secured by a string of virtuosic orchestral pieces written between 1895 and 1899. During the next six years he concentrated chiefly on conducting, though in 1901 he produced his first successful opera, *Feuersnot*. In 1905 he shocked audiences with his interpretation of Oscar Wilde's *Salome*, then four years later repeated the outrage with *Elektra*: both works were decried for their moral corruption, while the music was deemed dissonant and unintelligible. After *Elektra* it seemed inevitable that Strauss would cross over into outright atonality, but *Der Rosenkavalier*, composed only two years later, turned out to be a sumptuously tonal and charmingly elegant comedy. The volte-face caused much consternation, but *Der Rosenkavalier* established itself immediately as his operatic masterpiece, and its reputation has remained intact ever since.

In 1915 Strauss completed *Ein Alpensinfonie*, which, with the exception of *Metamorphosen* and the *Four Last Songs*, turned out to be his last large-scale non-operatic work. From then on, having completely mastered his craft, Strauss settled into the composition of opera, never looking back to the extremes of *Elektra*, and never tempted by the formal innovations of Schoenberg and the Second Viennese School. Living in a plush villa in Garmisch, not far from Munich, Strauss wrote prolifically and was amply rewarded for his work, but a problematic chapter in his life began in 1933, when the Nazis appointed him President of the Reichsmusikkammer, a job that effectively made him the national representative of German music. For two years he seems to have been content to fulfil the function required of him, disengenuously maintaining the belief that he could serve German music in the Reich without serving the Reich itself. However, two years later he had to choose between loyalty to the abstraction of German culture and loyalty to a Jewish individual, the writer Stefan Zweig, with whom he was working. He refused to condemn Zweig, was removed from his post, and from that point on was merely tolerated by the Nazis. He remained in Germany until the war's end, when he was investigated as a Nazi collaborator, and acquitted. In 1947 he took his first flight in an aeroplane to travel to London, where he was honoured as the greatest living German composer. Strauss died in his villa shortly after celebrating his 85th birthday.

THE OPERAS

The major part of Strauss's life was dedicated to opera, and of all twentieth-century operatic composers only Puccini could match his fluency. His first opera, *Guntram*, was a Wagnerian experiment, interesting solely for one glorious tune in the final act. Similarly, his Bavarian folk tale, *Feuersnot*, though showing Strauss's ever-increasing understanding of the orchestra and human voice, is little more than a Wagnerian homage. With *Salome* and *Elektra* he arrived at a unique expressionistic style, to which he returned – after the recidivistic *Der Rosenkavalier* and his delightful chamber opera *Ariadne auf Naxos* – in the extremely complicated and not altogether successful symbolist drama, *Die Frau ohne Schatten*, composed in 1919. After *Die Frau* Strauss produced nothing of comparable quality until 1933, when he wrote *Arabella*, a work along the same mock-classical lines as *Rosenkavalier*. Five years later came *Daphne*, followed in 1942 by his fifteenth and final work for the stage, *Capriccio*.

The vividness of characterization in Strauss's work is partly attributable to the quality of the writers with whom he collaborated. Of all these librettists the greatest was Hugo von Hofmannsthal, with whom Strauss established a relationship as productive as that of Mozart and da Ponte: four of the five operas they produced together – *Elektra*, *Der Rosenkavalier*, *Ariadne auf Naxos* and *Arabella* – represent the pinnacle of Strauss's operatic art. Precise delineation of character is only part of the appeal of Strauss's operas, however, for they provide some of the most hedonistic pleasures to be found in twentieth-century music. Above all, they are typified by lushly expressive harmony, elastic and extended melody, ingenious orchestrations and an unrivalled understanding of the female voice.

SALOME

It was the premiere of *Salome* on December 1905 that catapulted Strauss into superstardom. Oscar Wilde's drama, originally in French, translated into German by Hedwig Lachmann and cut into shape by Strauss himself, formed the basis for the shocking libretto. Herod arrests and jails John the Baptist (Jokanaan), who then rejects the advances of Salome, Herod's stepdaughter. Salome performs the "Dance of the Seven Veils" for Herod on condition that he give her anything she asks for. Herodias, her mother, tells her to ask for the head of Jokanaan. The severed head is brought out on a platter and in a final scene of immense length and power, she kisses its lips. In disgust, Herod has her crushed to death.

Salome is an intoxicating evocation of depravity and madness. The headily erotic decadence of the narrative is conveyed by music of unprecedented colour, and Strauss's portrayal of Herodias's necrophilic daughter is of awesome emotional strength. Strauss described the title part as a role "for a sixteen-year-old-girl with the voice of Isolde" and this is indeed one of the most demanding soprano roles, as Salome is rarely off stage during the continuous ninety minutes of the opera. Though *Salome* is not imitative of Wagner in the way Strauss's earliest efforts were, this through-composed opera still owes much to Wagner in its use of the orchestra (which is dominant throughout), in its system of leitmotifs and in its vocal writing, which alternates between declamation and sustained melodic lines of thrilling richness.

O Nilsson, Hoffman, Waechter, Stolze, Veasey; Vienna Philharmonic Orchestra; Solti (Decca 414414-2; 2 CDs).

Birgit Nilsson's Salome generates the sort of tension more commonly found in the theatre than on record, while Eberhard Waechter is a grand but lyrical Jokanaan and Gerhard Stolze is a revolting Herod. Solti's conducting is the best testimony to his gift for Strauss's music, and the Vienna Philharmonic make an indecently sumptuous sound, revelling in the sweatiness of Strauss's colossal score. A legendary performance, tightly recorded.

ELEKTRA

Elektra (1909) was the first Strauss opera with a text by Hofmannsthal, who here provided Strauss with a libretto (based on his own play) that remains one of the greatest of all operatic texts. The immediacy of Elektra's hatred for her mother Klytemnestra, her love for her brother Orestes and her disgust with her sister Chrysothemis inspired Strauss to heights even he could never equal. Elektra's savage desire for her mother's death (in revenge for Klytemnestra's killing of Agamemnon, Elektra's father) is realized in a characterization of chilling dramatic depth and, though all the characters are essentially grotesque, Klytemnestra, for whom Strauss composed his only atonal music, is the most disgusting creation in his entire output. Orestes is the opera's weakest portrayal but his contribution is of little relevance until the climax.

This astonishing one-act opera is sumptuously Romantic yet dissonant, so that its dozens of melodies are not immediately apparent, but rather blossom to surface as your ear becomes accustomed to the textures. The first audiences had problems with Strauss's complicated and heavy counterpoint, his virtuosic orchestrations and his insistent use of polytonality, but the superb vocal writing quickly made it a soprano's favourite. Especially memorable are Elektra's and Chrysothemis's monologues, the recognition scene between Elektra and Orestes, and the final duet for the two sisters, when Elektra performs a hysterical, fatal victory dance.

◑ Borkh, Madeira, Schech, Uhl, Fischer-Dieskau; Dresden Staatskapelle Chorus & Orchestra; Böhm (Deutsche Grammophon 431 737-2; 2 CDs).

Jean Madeira in suitably fragile as Chrysothemis and Fischer-Dieskau copes well with Orestes's extended range, but it is the instinctive partnership between Borkh and Böhm that marks this performance out as the finest on record. Inge Borkh is just about perfect in the title role, producing a fearsome mixture of hysteria, compassion, love and vehement determination. Böhm's tempi are very quick, creating a momentum that is only briefly stilled in the magical recognition scene, and yet this is a performance that makes much of the sweeping Romantic gestures. The Staatskapelle are in superb form and the recording is as realistic as can be imagined.

DER ROSENKAVALIER

After the excesses of the one-act shockers, Strauss and Hofmannstahl turned in 1911 to Mozartian comedy with *Der Rosenkavalier*, which has always been the most popular Strauss opera. Subtitled "A Comedy for Music", it is set in Vienna in the middle of the eighteenth century, and adopts a neoclassical framework for its bittersweet tale of romantic love, in which Baron Ochs (a "rural Don Giovanni", in Strauss's words) intends to marry the young Sophie, but is thwarted when she ends up falling for Octavian, the lover of the Marschallin and the "Rose Cavalier" of the title. In the end the young lovers are united, and the ageing Ochs and the Marschallin withdraw from the scene. Boasting a subtle and clever libretto, and Strauss's most delicate and seductively tuneful score, *Der Rosenkavalier* is a perfect combination of good humour, high farce, deep sentiment and pleasant sentimentality. The smoothness of the dramatic action, the fullness of characterization and the graceful profusion of melody make *Der Rosenkavalier* a worthy homage to the art of Mozart.

Central to *Der Rosenkavalier* are its waltzes, which are derived from the music of Schubert, Lanner and Johann Strauss the Younger, but are treated in so refined a way as to cheat the ear into believing they could have been a feature of eighteenth-century musical life. The enchanted atmosphere of these waltzes is sustained in moments of intense lyrical beauty: the tenor's "Italian" aria and final scene of Act One, the presentation of the rose in Act Two and the famous final soprano Trio of Act Three are among the most overwhelmingly beautiful music composed this century.

◑ **Ludwig, Troyanos, Mathis, Adam; Vienna Philharmonic Orchestra; Böhm** (Deutsche Grammophon 445 338-2; 3 CDs).

Karl Böhm recorded *Rosenkavalier* in the studio in 1958, but that set pales beside this 1969 live recording from the Vienna Staatsoper The beauty and warmth of Christa Ludwig's Marschallin, the urgency of Tatian Troyanos's Octavian and the fragile innocence of Edith Mathis's Sophie have never been bettered, while Böhm's feel for the opera's overall shape, orchestral texture and phrasing is unsurpassed. From start to finish this is the most consistently beautiful performance on record.

◑ **Schwarzkopf, Ludwig, Stich-Randall, Edelmann; Philharmonia Orchestra; Karajan** (EMI CDS7 49354; 3 CDs).

Schwarzkopf was famous in two of the principal female leads in *Rosenkavalier* but it was with the Marschallin that her name was most frequently associated. For Karajan's first account of the opera Schwarzkopf, Christa Ludwig (Octavian) and Theresa Stich-Randall (Sophie) produced an ensemble performance of deep humanity. Karajan presides over the glowing pit of sound with extreme sensitivity to the individual qualities of his singers' voices. Good sound for 1957.

ARIADNE AUF NAXOS

Ariadne auf Naxos (1916) is Strauss at his most economical, using a chamber-sized orchestra for large-scale effects. The opera began as an entertainment to follow a production of Molière's play *Le Bourgeois Gentilhomme*; Strauss then revised it, adding a prologue showing preparations for the performance of the opera in a Viennese nobleman's home. To save time before his big fireworks display, the patron insists that the opera be played simultaneously with a *commedia dell'arte* piece, and the ensuing mix-ups provide plenty of opportunities for musical pastiche and musings on the nature of operatic art. Containing lyrical outpourings for the soprano lead, interspersed with comic scenes and arias for the burlesque troupe, *Ariadne auf Naxos* is an entertainingly self-referential musical hybrid. As usual with Strauss, the most memorable parts are for women. Ariadne herself is an engaging portrait of Romantic excess, and her long, arching lines of song demand a voice of equal power and sensitivity, notably for one exquisite octave leap to a pianissimo top C.

◑ **Janowitz, King, Geszty, Zylis-Gara, Prey; Dresden State Opera; Kempe** (EMI CMS 7 64159-2; 2 CDs).

Kempe's performance is a joy from beginning to end. The orchestra is superb in this often subtle score, and Gundula Janowitz is a searing Ariadne, supported by a fine cast of Dresden regulars such as Peter Schreier and Hermann Prey.

ORCHESTRAL MUSIC

Strauss first achieved fame for his mastery of the orchestra, as demonstrated in the set of tone poems he produced in the last years of the nineteenth century: principally the sparkling miniatures *Don Juan* and *Till Eulenspiegel*, and the more epic *Tod und Verklärung*, *Also sprach Zarathustra*, *Don Quixote* and *Ein Heldenleben*. Notable for their flamboyant gestures, complicated counterpoint and remarkable melodies, these pieces are the lineal descendants of the tone poems of Berlioz and Liszt, but their musical stories are even more expansive and dramatic. The expressive, pictorial and narrative elements of these orchestral works paved the way for his operas, and once he had embarked on his operatic career Strauss rarely returned to purely instrumental composition. However, towards the end of his life he created possibly his finest orchestral work, *Metamorphosen*, then brought the full panoply of his orchestral skills to bear in his valedictory *Vier letzte Lieder* (Four Last Songs).

DON JUAN

Don Juan set the musical world on fire in 1888. In less than twenty minutes of music Strauss showed himself to be both a classical master of his craft and a radical innovator, for the demands upon the orchestra (especially the horns) were more strenuous than anything even in Berlioz, and the sheer scale and drama of the scoring was shocking. The piece recounts the loves and losses of the amorous Don Juan, who is characterized throughout the score by a horn call of Wagnerian intensity. Some gushingly exciting string writing leads to a love scene in which the oboe solo prefigures many of the sentimental tunes that were to come in Strauss's operas. The finale, leading the antihero's damnation, is a blazing crescendo that will knock your socks off.

○ **San Francisco Symphony Orchestra; Blomstedt** (Decca 421 815-2; with *Ein Alpensinfonie*).

Herbert Blomstedt's account of *Don Juan* for Decca is utterly exhilarating. It's coupled with an unbeatable performance of the *Alpine Symphony* which, while not the tautest of Strauss's orchestral works, has some glorious moments, including a lustrous depiction of the dawn.

ALSO SPRACH ZARATHUSTRA

Nietzsche's book *Also sprach Zarathustra* (Thus Spake Zarathustra) had only been published a few years when Strauss chose, in 1896, to write a tone poem inspired by it. Nietzsche's philosophy of the Superman and his celebration of human power and energy clearly appealed to Strauss's overwhelming self-belief and sense of destiny. His response was a work of enormous proportions, a free-flowing fantasia which, apart from its philosophical aspirations, creates some truly awe-inspiring orchestral sounds. Not least of these is the work's inspired "sunrise" opening used by Stanley Kubrick in his science fiction film *2001*. Nothing else quite lives up this and, taken as a whole, the work's eight episodes (each with a heading from Nietzsche) can seem a little meandering in all but the most brilliant performances. It's not without humour, however: Zarathustra's dance, towards the end of the work, is cast in the form of a Viennese waltz – albeit one with a decidedly rustic flavour.

◑ **Berlin Philharmonic Orchestra; Karajan** (Deutsche Grammophon 447 441-2; with *Don Juan* and *Till Eulenspiegel*).

This is a work well-suited to Karajan's flamboyant exhibitionism and the BPO's rich and refulgent tone, and in their 1973 recording both conductor and orchestra hit the mark in thrilling fashion.

◑ **Chicago Symphony Orchestra; Reiner** (RCA 09026 61494-2; with *Ein Heldenleben*).

A stupendous recording; the Chicago SO play with adventure and excitement under Fritz Reiner's dynamic leadership. Few other versions manage to give such a convincing sense of shape to this work. The early stereo sound of 1954 is amazingly good.

DON QUIXOTE

The following year Strauss turned to another literary character, Cervantes' *Don Quixote*, for inspiration. Subtitling his work "Fantastic Variations on a Theme of a Knightly Character", the unworldy Don Quixote is assigned to a solo cello, while his robust sidekick Sancho Panza is a viola. The work is thus a kind of concerto in variation form, each variation depicting an incident from the novel by developing new material out of the main themes. There's a chamber-music dimension to *Don Quixote*, which makes it the least draining of his long tone poems, but the orchestration is as brilliantly inventive as ever – the Don's battle with the sheep is full of disturbingly dissonant bleating – and Strauss's luxuriant side, most stirringly presented in Variation III, is never far away. A long and melancholy cello solo, representing the Don's death, brings this affectionate portrait to a close.

○ **Meneses, Christ; Berlin Philharmonic Orchestra; Karajan** (Deutsche Grammophon 439 027-2; with *Till Eulenspiegel*).

Don Quixote needs a cellist with a brilliant technique who can also characterize with wit and restraint. Paul Tortelier, who recorded the work at least four times, was such a one, but his best performances are only available in box sets. This recording makes a more than adequate alternative: Antonio Meneses has a beautiful tone, the death scene is touchingly conveyed, and Karajan and the BPO provide excellent support.

EIN HELDENLEBEN

When *Ein Heldenleben* was premiered in 1899 it caused a sensation, not because of its musical audacity but because of the arrogance of a composer who, at the age of 35, could present the world with an autobiographical piece titled "A Hero's Tale". There's no point trying to argue away Strauss's egotism – he did, after all, once remark that he found himself "every bit as interesting as Caesar or Napoleon". The music itself, however, is a vigorous affirmation of life, realized in orchestration of sensational colour and imagination. The hero battles against the critics, who are portrayed by a bleating and dissonant wind section, and is both soothed and frustrated by his wife, depicted by the lead violin. His victory is hailed in "The Hero's Works of Peace", an eight-minute section in which Strauss packs in some thirty excerpts from his own catalogue, including all his other tone poems. "The Hero's Retirement from the World" ends the work: its tender duet for horn (himself) and violin (his wife) is perhaps the most beautiful bit of music outside his operas.

◑ **Chicago Symphony Orchestra; Reiner** (RCA 09026 61494-2; with *Also sprach Zarathustra*).

Fritz Reiner, a friend and colleague of Strauss, gives a reading that is muscular and hard-driven (the battle scene is suitably cacophonous) without being brutal. He brings out the part-writing with exemplary lucidity, and in the final section he employs the sweetest of tones to create a great Romantic wash of sound.

METAMORPHOSEN

Strauss spent much of his life expressing the emotions of others; in *Metamorphosen* he expressed himself, pouring out his grief over the destruction of Dresden, Weimar and Munich in 1945. As he wrote shortly after: "history is almost entirely an unbroken chain of acts of stupidity and wickedness, every sort of baseness, greed, betrayal, murder and destruction. And how little those who are called upon to make history have learned from it." A single movement for 23 strings, *Metamorphosen* is based upon a motif taken from the funeral march of Beethoven's *Eroica*, and as the piece progresses its emotional state is transformed from grief-stricken sombreness to grudging reconciliation, via music of the most trenchant anger.

Berlin Philharmonic Orchestra; Karajan (Deutsche Grammophon 447 442-2; with *Tod und Verklarüng* and *Vier letzte Lieder*).

In the absence of Furtwängler's desperately moving live performance made shortly after the war, this is the version to go for. Karajan, who made the first recording of this work in 1947, controls and shapes the almost supernatural string sound of the BPO as if he were moulding it. The result is both mysterious and moving in its valedictory pathos.

FOUR LAST SONGS

Like Grieg, Strauss learned most about the quality and capacity of the female voice from his wife, for whom he wrote a great deal of music, including his finest group of chamber songs, the four Op. 27, which were composed as a wedding present for her. The great majority of his two hundred songs are for soprano, and Strauss ended his life as a composer with a grandiloquent piece for soprano and orchestra, the *Vier letzte Lieder* (*Four Last Songs*). They were not composed as a cycle – after Strauss's death, his publisher brought them together, gave them an opus number and saw to their first performance – but they indubitably work as one, for they share a mood of autumnal peace and absolute honesty in the face of death, and the music is of a consistent simplicity and clarity. After settings of three poems by Hermann Hesse, the *Four Last Songs* concludes with a text by Eichendorff, *Im Abendrot* (At Sunset), where Strauss alters the last line from "Is that perhaps Death?" to "Is this perhaps Death?" This final song portrays an ageing couple watching the setting sun: as they close their eyes, their lives end to the sound of trilling flutes, signifying skylarks and the liberation of their souls. Some might find it maudlin, but for many people it's an acutely moving conclusion to one of the most intriguing careers in the history of music.

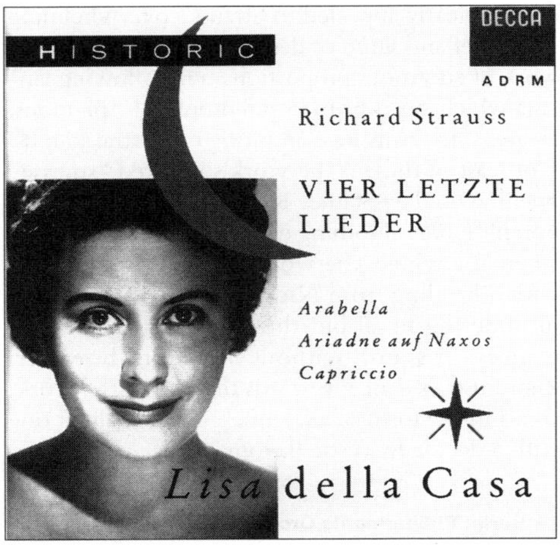

della Casa; Vienna Philharmonic Orchestra; Böhm (Decca 425 959-2; with excerpts from *Arabella*, *Ariadne auf Naxos & Capriccio*).

Della Casa's 1953 recording of the *Four Last Songs* is one of the finest ever made. Her limpid, tranquil tone is beautifully supported by Karl Böhm, who prevents the music from descending into sentimentality. A dry-eyed and dignified account, this recording is a wonderful testament to all those involved.

Janowitz; Berlin Philharmonic Orchestra; Karajan (Deutsche Grammophon 447 422-2; with *Metamorphosen & Tod und Verklärung*).

Gundula Janowitz is one of the most celebrated of postwar Straussian sopranos and this 1974 recording is justly famous. The rounded richness of her voice is never used in an indulgent fashion and her vocal strength allows the orchestra to play out. The one problem is that the CD transfer seems to have constricted the voice in the upper register.

IGOR STRAVINSKY

(1882–1971)

Like his friend Pablo Picasso, Igor Stravinsky became a modernist icon, an artist as well-known to the general public as he was to the cognoscenti. And, as with Picasso, people were never quite certain what Stravinsky was going to do next. He made his name with *The Firebird, Petrushka* and *The Rite of Spring*, Dionysian masterpieces that shocked and enthralled their first audiences. He then rejected the legacy of Romanticism and went into a neo-classical phase, an audacious change of direction, but not quite as extraordinary as the last volte-face of his career, when, in ripe old age, he threw in his hat with the serialist enemy. However, through all his metamorphoses Stravinsky remained a classicist at heart. Above all other things he loved precision, order and structure, and all his works have a consummate sense of poise. The Swiss writer C.F. Ramuz, who collaborated with Stravinsky on *L'Histoire du soldat*, once wrote: "His writing desk resembled a surgeon's instrument case. Bottles of different coloured inks in their ordered hierarchy each had a separate part to play in the ordering of his art . . . One was reminded of the definition of St Thomas: beauty is the splendour of order."

Stravinsky's early years gave little hint of the *enfant terrible* to come. Born near St Petersburg, he was a musical child and diligent student, but on the advice of his parents he studied law, thinking that profession a safer bet than a life devoted to music. In 1903 his encounter with the great pedagogue Rimsky-Korsakov (see p.339) changed the direction of his life. Rimsky took on Stravinsky as a private pupil, and Stravinsky soon resolved to try to make it as a composer, albeit against his teacher's advice.

By a stroke of good fortune Russia's leading impresario, Serge Diaghilev, happened to catch his first mature compositions – *Scherzo fantastique* and *Feu d'artifice* – at a St Petersburg concert in 1909, and promptly asked Stravinsky to write two numbers for a ballet he was producing. Stravinsky acquitted himself so well that Diaghilev commissioned from him a score for his new Paris-based dance troupe, the Ballet Russe – and, as Diaghilev had predicted, the *Firebird* made Stravinsky famous overnight. Knowing that he was onto a good thing, Diaghilev persuaded Stravinsky to write an even more exotic Russian-style ballet for the next season. The result was *Petrushka*, a work which caused a stir with its daring polytonality and tart rhythms. This was nothing compared to the impact of Stravinsky's next ballet, *The Rite of Spring*. A score of unprecedented rhythmic and harmonic ferocity, it caused a riot at its premiere on May 29, 1913, and established Stravinsky as the prince of the avant-garde.

LEBRECHT COLLECTION

Igor Stravinsky ponders his next move

During World War I Stravinsky and his family found refuge in Switzerland, where wartime deprivation obliged him to think in terms of writing for small ensembles. *Les Noces* (1914–17) and *L'Histoire du soldat* (1918) showed Stravinsky developing leaner textures, and he spoke of the latter as his "final break with the Russian orchestral school". With the coming of peace in 1918, Stravinsky and his family settled in Paris, where the composer took up French citizenship. (Their planned return to Russia became impossible after the Communists confiscated their property and blocked Stravinsky's royalties.) At the behest of Diaghilev, Stravinsky began fashioning music for a ballet called *Pulcinella* (1920) out of some pieces by the eighteenth-century composer Pergolesi, a commission that marked the beginning of his neo-classical phase. Whereas Schoenberg devised the twelve-tone method as a modernist discipline to supplant the prescriptions of the past, Stravinsky reinvented the past, using its conventions as vessels for modern ideas. His neo-classicism was immensely fluid, adapting Handel and Gluck for *Oedipus Rex* (1927), Mozart in *The Rake's Progress* (1951), but running through most of his work for the next thirty years was an emphasis on classical elegance and clarity.

By the end of the 1930s Stravinsky was tiring of Europe: his wife and one daughter had both died of tuberculosis, war was once again about to break out, and the French critics who had once vilified *The Rite* were now carping about his supposed sell-out to neo-classicism. The USA seemed the obvious place to go: he had wealthy admirers there, and the conductor Serge Koussevitsky was proving a hugely influential champion of his work, having already commissioned the *Symphony of Psalms* for the fiftieth anniversary of the Boston Symphony Orchestra. In 1939 he made the move, taking with him his mistress, the painter Vera de Bossett, whom he married the following year. In 1940 Stravinsky and his family settled in Hollywood, where the cell of exiled European artists included Arnold Schoenberg, whom Stravinsky seems to have avoided.

During the 1940s he composed some magnificent neo-classical works, including the *Symphony in C* and *The Rake's Progress*, but then came his dramatic conversion to the serialist cause. The young American conductor Robert Craft discreetly introduced him to various key serial works, and Stravinsky became particularly taken with the crystalline scores of Anton Webern, declaring that "the serial composers are the only ones with a discipline that I respect". He now turned to twelve-note techniques with characteristic inventiveness and a vigour that was typified by the creation of the astringent *Agon* (1957) at the age of 75. By now, such was Stravinsky's reputation that each new work was guaranteed several performances and a recording, however prickly its musical language. In his last decade he achieved a degree of celebrity unmatched by any composer since Mozart, being fêted by Pope John Paul XXIII, by the Kennedys and, in a triumphant visit to Russia in 1962, by Nikita Khrushchev. He died in New York on April 6, 1971, and was buried where he had asked to be – near to his old comrade Diaghilev, on Venice's cemetery island of San Michele.

◑ **The Igor Stravinsky Edition** (Sony SX22K 46 290; 22 CDs).

Towards the end of his life Stravinsky gave a lot of his time to conducting and supervising performances of his works. Sony have gathered all of Stravinsky's performances of his own music, supplemented by recordings of those pieces he didn't conduct himself, into this immense set, which is available as one box of 22 CDs, or as twelve separate volumes. It has to be said that Stravinsky was not an outstanding conductor, and there are better recordings of much of his music, but this is nonetheless a great historical document – and Stravinsky's output was so vast that in several instances the *Stravinsky Edition* offers the only opportunity of getting to know a piece on disc.

OEDIPUS REX

Based on Sophocles's most famous tragedy, Stravinsky's *Oedipus Rex* (1927) is a semi-abstract, ritualistic music drama that narrates its events in the simplest, starkest terms. The sense of Oedipus's story as the exemplar of inexorable fate is enhanced by the absolute detachment of the presentation, in which the arias and choruses are punctuated by short and simple texts delivered in French by a narrator who stands apart in modern clothes from the rest of the costumed cast, who are themselves not

empowered to act or express any individuality. For the text of the vocal parts, Stravinsky and his collaborator Jean Cocteau settled on Latin as "a medium not dead, but turned to stone, and so monumentalized as to have become immune from all risk of vulgarization". Narrative momentum and cohesion is created above all by the music: the drama of *Oedipus Rex* is static, but the score is awesomely powerful. This is also one of the most impressive displays of Stravinsky's allusive neo-classical technique, with its evocations of such composers as Monteverdi, Handel, Mussorgsky and Verdi.

O Cole, von Otter, Estes, Sotin, Gedda, Chereau; Eric Ericson Chamber Choir; Swedish Radio Symphony Orchestra & Chorus; Salonen (Sony SK48057).

The Finnish whizzkid Esa-Pekka Salonen conducts the finest account of Stravinsky's opera-oratorio yet committed to disc. It is gripping from the first bar to the last, with the chorus and top-class singers as incisive as the orchestra.

THE RAKE'S PROGRESS

Stravinsky's only full-length opera was inspired by Hogarth's *Rake's Progress*, and its libretto – by W.H. Auden and Chester Kallman – fleshes out the story told in Hogarth's series of eight paintings, charting Tom Rakewell's descent through dissipation into madness. Appropriately enough, the musical language of this eighteenth-century morality tale is heavily indebted to Mozart – *The Rake's Progress* is constructed from solo and ensemble numbers, which are accompanied by a small orchestra and strung together by recitatives accompanied by harpsichord. With its subtle anachronisms the music mirrors a world in which the natural order – epitomized by marriage – is subverted by Tom's feckless career, and in its extremely knowing (some might say cold-hearted) exploitation of opera's heritage, *The Rake's Progress* marks the culminating point of Stravinsky's neo-classical style. Almost everything in this opera appears in quotation marks, so to speak, and its libretto is perhaps the richest operatic text of this century. It demands a little effort but it does include some episodes of extraordinary directness: the final scene in Bedlam is saturated with desperate tragedy, and Anne Trulove's farewell to Tom is probably Stravinsky's most tender creation.

O Hadley, Upshaw, Ramey, Bumbry; Chorus and Orchestra of Lyon Opera; Nagano (Erato 0630-12715-2; 2 CDs).

Kent Nagano has made *The Rake's Progress* something of a speciality, and his studio recording pretty much redefines the standard, presenting an ideally cast and exactingly prepared performance that gets as close to the opera's mercurial character as anything yet recorded.

THE FIREBIRD

The Firebird (*L'Oiseau de feu*) is a straightforward fairy tale, in which the Firebird helps a young prince to rescue a beautiful princess from an evil ogre, and in the process win her heart. Aspects of its musical language would have been familiar to its first Parisian audience in 1910, for Stravinsky borrows much from his teacher Rimsky-Korsakov: for example, in his use of chromaticism for the ballet's magic creatures and of a modal-diatonic style for the mortals. Knowledgeable onlookers, however, realized that there was something much deeper here than another piece of Rimsky-style exoticism. Debussy for one was thrilled by its latent barbarism, and revelled in its "unusual combinations of rhythms".

O Chicago Symphony Orchestra; Boulez (Deutsche Grammophon 437 850-2; with *Four Études; Fireworks*).

Boulez's second recording of *The Firebird* is as colourful and vivid as his first, but even more tightly focused. The playing of the Chicago Symphony is characterized by great finesse and power.

PETRUSHKA

To quote Stravinsky, the central figure of *Petrushka* is "the immortal and unhappy hero of every fair in all countries"; more specifically, he's a "puppet, suddenly endowed with life, exasperating the patience of the orchestra". On June 13, 1911, the title role was danced by the legendary Nijinsky, ensuring that what was happening onstage was as remarkable as what was coming out of the orchestra pit. The ballet's burlesque and parodic elements are heightened by ever-shifting rhythms and a startling polytonal harmonic language – the juxtaposition of the two unrelated keys of C major and F sharp major in one section is typical of Stravinsky's brazen innovation. These advanced musical devices, which are primarily used for the appearances of Petrushka himself, are contrasted with the predominantly diatonic harmonies of the vivid crowd scenes.

◑ New York Philharmonic Orchestra; Boulez (Sony SMK 64109; with *The Rite of Spring*).

A brilliant, scintillating account from Boulez and the New York Phil which brings out the all the angularity and awkwardness in the score. Rarely has Petrushka's plight, and the sheer bustle of the fair, sounded so vital.

◑ Minnesota Symphony Orchestra; Dorati (Mercury 417 758-2DM; with *The Rite of Spring*).

As with his performance of *The Rite* (see below), Dorati gives a blazingly urgent reading of Stravinsky's second seminal ballet.

THE RITE OF SPRING

The idea for *The Rite of Spring* (*Le Sacre du printemps*) came to Stravinsky several years before he actually wrote it, as he was later to recount. "One day, when I was finishing the last pages of the *Firebird* in St Petersburg, I had a fleeting vision . . . I saw in my imagination a solemn pagan rite: sage elders, seated in a circle, watched a young girl dance herself to death. They were sacrificing her to propitiate the god of spring." In 1913 he unleashed the visceral music that this vision prompted, and the result was the most notorious premiere in the history of modern music. The catcalls started only seconds after the music, and soon Debussy was pleading vainly for people to calm down, while Ravel yelled "Genius, genius!" in the midst of fist-fights and screams of abuse so loud that the dancers were unable to hear the orchestra.

It is not difficult to understand why *The Rite of Spring* had such a profound effect. Written for a huge orchestra, it's unrelentingly barbaric in its dissonances and asymmetrical rhythms, jolting the listener into attention from first to last. *The Rite*'s defining quality is its thumping, irregular pulse, a rhythmic propulsion achieved through frequent changes in time signature – sometimes, as in the *Sacrificial Dance*, in every successive bar.

◑ **Minnesota Symphony Orchestra; Dorati** (Mercury 417 758-2DM; with *Petrushka*).

Dorati's fiery temperament made him an ideal interpreter of *The Rite* and his various studio recordings of the work have never been bettered. The finest of all is the recording he made for Mercury: fast, furious and dangerous, this account lets you hear what Stravinsky wanted you to hear – "the whole earth cracking". Including Dorati's fire-breathing *Petrushka*, this disc is extraordinarily good value.

◑ **New York Philharmonic Orchestra; Boulez** (Sony SMK 64109; with *Petrushka*).

Boulez's reading of *The Rite* brings out less of the work's primeval quality than Dorati. Instead we get a more analytical, though still exciting, account in which the radical, experimental nature of Stravinsky's score is made especially clear.

LES NOCES

Stravinsky had the idea for *Les Noces*, a dance cantata depicting a Russian peasant wedding, while working on *The Rite of Spring*. The text, arranged into four scenes, is derived from Russian folk poems and is meant to suggest "scraps of conversation without the connecting thread of discourse". It's one of the most Russian of his works, with a strong ritualistic element of repeated words and insistent rhythms, a quality reinforced in the first production of 1923 by Bronislava Nijinska's austere and abstract choreography. After much experiment, Stravinsky decided to accompany the predominant vocal part with a largely percussive accompaniment which included four pianos, xylophone, timpani and bells. It is this extraordinary instrumentation which gives *Les Noces* much of its unforgettably raw energy.

○ **Pokrovsky Ensemble; Pokrovsky** (Elektra Nonesuch 7559-79335-2; with *Traditional Russian Wedding Songs*).

There's no ideal version of this piece available, but Dimitri Pokrovsky and his ensemble get close with a hard-hitting account in which the authentic Russian vocal sound is an extra bonus. The odd, but effective, aspect of this disc is that the instrumental parts have been produced on a computer.

L'HISTOIRE DU SOLDAT

L'Histoire du soldat was devised by Stravinsky, in collaboration with the Swiss writer Ramuz, as a small-scale, low-budget theatre piece which could be toured around Switzerland on the back of a lorry. Although the story, a morality tale about a soldier who makes a pact with the Devil, is based on a Russian folk tale, the music turns its back on a distinctly Russian style in favour of a more contemporary and eclectic idiom – ragtime and tango both feature in typically acerbic guise. Because the soldier gives his violin to the Devil, the instrument leads the small ensemble of trumpet trombone, double-bass, clarinet, bassoon and percussion – an usual combination of instruments from which Stravinsky produces some wonderfully rich and acid timbres. Despite its vivid picture-book colours, *L'Histoire du soldat* is rarely staged partly because of its length but also because of its unusual mixture of music, spoken roles and dance.

○ **St Luke's Orchestra; Craft** (MusicMasters 67152-2; with various Stravinsky choral works).

Stravinsky arranged *L'Histoire du soldat* as a suite, which seems the best way to hear the music outside of the theatre. Robert Craft, for years the composer's right-hand man, directs a performance of great wit and verve.

PULCINELLA

The ballet *Pulcinella*, written in 1920 for Diaghilev and the choreographer Massine, inaugurated Stravinsky's neo-classical period. Stravinsky's source material was a melange of operas, cantatas, trio-sonatas and other pieces ascribed to Pergolesi (see p.302), which he turned into the music for a *commedia dell'arte* story. Although the orchestration of *Pulcinella* recalls a lean, eighteenth-century ensemble, Stravinsky gives the eighteenth-century melodies a modernist spin through a range of devices. The orchestration is wonderfully quirky (there's a rare double-bass solo in one movement); harmonies are decidedly non-authentic; its rhythmic accents shift about ceaselessly, while its melodies sometimes seem to start in midstream, or stop short of a satisfactory resolution. The whole effect of *Pulcinella* is of an oscillation between passages of giddy energy and elegant if tentative repose.

O Murray, Rolfe Johnson, Estes; Ensemble Intercontemporain, French National Orchestra; Boulez (Erato 2292-45382-2; with *Le Chant du rossignol*).

As a young man Pierre Boulez was fond of heckling at premieres of new works from Stravinsky, in his capacity as standard-bearer of the avant-garde. He went on to become one of the finest conductors of twentieth-century music, and this meticulously lucid and sprightly reading of *Pulcinella* is a marvellous example of Boulez's ability to think himself into an aesthetic that is miles away from his own.

APOLLON MUSAGÈTE

Apollon musagète (Apollo, Leader of the Muses), the most serene of all Stravinsky's ballets, was commissioned in 1927 for a festival of contemporary music at the Library of Congress in Washington DC. It's a paradoxical work in that, though Stravinsky conceived it as embodying a classical ideal, devoid of "many-coloured effects and of all superfluities", by restricting himself to an orchestra of strings alone he produced one of his warmest and most luscious-sounding works. Much of *Apollon musagète* really doesn't sound like Stravinsky at all, and it has none of the satirical edge of much of his other neo-classical works. Diaghilev thought it "extraordinarily calm, and with greater clarity than anything he has done so far . . . somehow music not of this world, but from somewhere above". It was the perfect vehicle for the clean, linear vision of choreographer Georges Balanchine, and the first of several marvellous collaborations between him and Stravinsky.

◑ Berlin Philharmonic Orchestra; Karajan (Deutsche Grammophon 415 979-2; with *The Rite of Spring*).

The svelte and refined string tone of the Berlin Philharmonic is well-suited to this ballet (here performed in the composer's 1947 revision), though it succeeds in making the work sound even less like Stravinsky. It's coupled with a sonically impressive version of *The Rite of Spring*.

AGON

Completed in 1957 for Georges Balanchine's New York City Ballet, *Agon* is as abstract a dance piece as it's possible to write. The title means "contest" in Greek, and the work is can be read as a kind of dialectic between tradition and modernity. Starting with neo-classical fanfares, it becomes increasingly chromatic until it reaches fully fledged serialism, then at its conclusion returns to the tonal fanfares. Along the way you'll hear some of the finest dance music written this century and, if any single piece is going to convince you that serialism does not have to be hard work, *Agon* is it.

◑ London Symphony Orchestra; Tilson Thomas (RCA 09026-68865-2; with *Circus Polka, Huxley Variations, Scènes de ballet,* etc).

Agon is strangely under-represented in the CD catalogue: Stravinsky gives an assured and atmospheric account in a Sony three-CD set of the later ballets, but this recent performance by the LSO has exceptional poise while maintaining a strong sense of theatre.

SYMPHONY OF PSALMS

The *Symphony of Psalms* (1930) is symphonic only in the loosest sense of the word, for in its treatment of chorus and orchestra it looks back to the choral works of the Baroque period rather than to archetypal classical models. Dedicated "to the glory of God", it was written not long after Stravinsky's conversion to Christianity and is imbued with the intensity of the first flood of faith. The Latin texts of the three movements are taken from the Psalms, which the composer saw as "poems of exultation, but also of anger and judgement", and he responded with music in which self-expression is expunged in favour of humble devotion. The sound-world of *Symphony of Psalms* is austere, due in large part to the absence of the "warm" sonorities of the violin, viola and clarinet.

O Suisse Romande Chamber Choir & Orchestra; Järvi (Chandos CHAN 9239; with *Concerto for Piano and Wind Instruments; Symphony in C*).

Järvi gives a performance of breathtaking beauty and power, inspiring his choral singers to pinpoint precision of ensemble. This is a strongly characterized reading, enhanced by first-rate recording quality.

SYMPHONY IN THREE MOVEMENTS

The *Symphony in Three Movements* (1943–45) was described by Stravinsky as his "War Symphony", and it is indeed one of the most significant compositions to come out of World War II – although, unlike the war music of Prokofiev,

Shostakovich and Richard Strauss, the *Symphony in Three Movements* reflects images seen on newsreels, rather than the direct experience of a country ravaged by armies. Stravinsky's hallmark techniques – prominence of wind instruments, rapid changes of time signature, astringent harmonies – are all employed to telling effect, and Stravinsky's loathing of fascism is nowhere better depicted than in the third movement, with its relentless march rhythms and sharp brass-band orchestration.

O London Symphony Orchestra; Tilson Thomas (Sony SK53275; with *Symphony of Psalms*).

Tilson Thomas conducts the *Symphony in Three Movements* with electrifying panache, and the LSO respond magnificently. The disc also contains a warm and heartfelt performance of the *Symphony of Psalms*.

THE VIOLIN CONCERTO

L'Histoire du soldat was the only work that Stravinsky had written with a substantial violin part when, in 1931, he was approached to write a concerto for the young virtuoso Samuel Dushkin. Stravinsky was reluctant to accept until he met Dushkin, who became an active collaborator in the technical detailing of the violin part. The composer studied other violin concertos, but the only apparent model seems to have been Bach. Stravinsky's concerto is in four movements with the pointedly Baroque titles of Toccata, Aria I, Aria II and Capriccio. Its parodic neo-Baroque characteristics include the bouncy motor rhythms of its opening movement, and the leaping violin line of the Capriccio. The second of the slow movements, an effusive Bach-inspired cantilena, belies many critics' insistence that this concerto is a purely abstract work with little emotional content.

O Mutter; Philharmonia; Sacher (Deutsche Grammophon 423 696-2; with Lutosławski, *Chain 2*).

Conductors frequently get the balance wrong between soloist and orchestra in this work, which is why it often fails in the concert hall. In Mutter's fresh and invigorating performance, the balance sounds just right (easier to achieve in the studio) and both soloist and orchestra exude enjoyment.

THE OCTET

With the *Octet* for wind instruments of 1922, Stravinsky completely embraced neo-classicism. Counterpoint and strong rhythmic propulsion are very much to the fore, though the inspiration seems more Bach than Mozart. Stravinsky claims the idea for the instrumentation came to him in a dream – whatever its origins, the combination of two trumpets, two trombones, two bassoons, a flute and a clarinet makes for a wonderfully transparent texture which, in Stravinsky's own words, "renders more evident the musical architecture". Objectivity was the point of the exercise and Stravinsky was adamant that the *Octet* was "not an 'emotive' work but a musical composition based on objective elements which are sufficient in themselves". All of which makes it sound dry, which it isn't. As in so many of his neo-classical works an element of witty subversion is constantly present – from the over-insistent bassoon ostinato that seems a foretaste of Minimalism to the syncopated coda in the finale with its heavy-footed but light-hearted rumba.

O London Sinfonietta; Salonen (Sony SK 45965; with *Pulcinella*, *Ragtime*, *Renard*).

Stravinsky thought that the issue of interpretation was irrelevant to this work (he conducted the premiere himself) because the almost mechanistic interaction of the voices didn't need to be emoted or nuanced in any way. That said, it certainly needs players of outstanding ability, and this performance by players of the London Sinfonietta is one of the most sparkling and vital on disc.

PIANO MUSIC

Stravinsky was a very accomplished pianist and composed a fair amount of music for the instrument, the best known being his stupendous arrangement of three movements from *Petrushka* for Artur Rubinstein. Of the other, woefully overlooked piano pieces, the best are the two piano sonatas, the *Four Études* and the offbeat *Circus Polka*.

The heavily Romantic early sonata was composed under Rimsky-Korsakov's guidance in 1903–04, and is extremely similar to the first sonatas of Rachmaninov, Prokofiev and Scriabin. The other sonata, written twenty years later, is also highly entertaining but in a rather more different manner – it's a fiendishly difficult piece, in places giving every finger its own clearly delineated role in the musical texture. The *Four Études* (1908) are just as difficult to play, with their complex rhythmic and polytonal experiments. They are by no means esoteric compositions, however. On the contrary, they are light, tuneful and immensely witty – the performer is the one who suffers, not the listener. Stravinsky at his wittiest appears in the *Circus Polka* of 1942, a piece commissioned by the Barnum and Bailey Circus, who wanted a work that could be danced by the troupe's elephants. Originally written for orchestra, it was later made into a wonderfully effective showpiece for piano.

◑ Three Movements from Petrushka: Pollini (Deutsche Grammophon 447 431; with music by Prokofiev, Boulez and Webern).

Maurizio Pollini's recording of the *Three Movements from Petrushka* is a bewilderingly brilliant performance, taking the music at a speed that defies belief. Coupled with equally stunning accounts of other key modernist piano works, this is a classic recording that nobody interested in twentieth-century music should be without.

O Sonatas; Four Études; Circus Polka; Serenade; Tango; Piano Rag Music; Scherzo: Sangiorgio (Collins 1374-2).

Victor Sangiorgio's recording of most of Stravinsky's piano compositions was one of the most entertaining piano CDs of the 1990s. His understanding of the composer's orchestral style of writing and his affinity with Stravinsky's humour are apparent in every item, and his technique allows him to navigate with ease this often horrendously difficult music.

JOSEF SUK

(1874–1935)

Before he had reached the age of 20, Josef Suk was being hailed as the musical heir of Antonin Dvořák, his father-in-law and teacher. He did indeed produce work that was remarkably similar to Dvořák's – the light-hearted and tuneful *Serenade for Strings* of 1892 shows a direct influence, for example. Yet the resemblances are less important than the differences between Dvořák and a composer he once accused of writing too much in the melancholic minor keys. Suk's music has amost nothing of the joyful pastoralism that's so common to Dvořák, and in his orchestral pieces – in particular *Asrael* – Suk's use of huge orchestral forces to create vast expressions of anguish suggest closer affinities with Mahler.

Suk received his first lessons from his father, a schoolmaster and choir director in Bohemia. In 1885 he entered the Prague Conservatory where, three years later, he began studying chamber music with the cellist Dennis Wihan – a friend of both Dvořák and Richard Strauss. After six years he graduated, but remained at the conservatory for a further year in order to pursue his lessons with Wihan and begin studies with Dvořák. It was at this time that Suk joined the Czech Quartet, an ensemble with whom he was to play some four thousand concerts until his retirement in 1933. In 1898, he married Dvořák's daughter Otilie, and was by then acknowledged as one of the most important Czech composers.

However, he never really established himself outside his native country and for the rest of his life he remained something of a peripheral figure, bathing in the light shed by his father-in-law more than in the glory of his own reputation. Nowadays, although sporadic attempts are made to bring his music to wider audiences, he is still widely known for just one work.

ASRAEL SYMPHONY

Suk was at his best working on a large scale, and his most popular work, the massive symphony of mourning called *Asrael*, is the finest example of his expressive, late Romantic style. Taking its title from the name of the Islamic angel of death, the symphony was written in response to the death of Dvořák in 1904 and the death of Suk's own wife a year later. The five-movement symphony, with its concentration of slow movements, is saturated with a sense of loss, conveyed in music of cathartic intensity – in the depths of his grief, Suk wrote that he was "saved by music". Though to an extent indebted to Mahler in its funereal idiom and to Strauss in its orchestration, *Asrael* is one of the finest orchestral works of its time.

O Royal Liverpool Philharmonic Orchestra; Pešek (Virgin VC7 59638-2).

The *Asrael* symphony has found considerable popularity in recent years and a number of recordings are now available. Libor Pešek's account with the RLPO makes a convincing case for this mighty work: his tempi brings heart-rending gravity to the symphony, and the work's plush sonorities are given fabulous colour and shape.

ARTHUR SULLIVAN

(1842–1900)

"They trained him to make Europe yawn", ran George Bernard Shaw's obituary of Arthur Sullivan, referring to the "serious" music – long since forgotten – which Sullivan had claimed that he always wished to devote more time to. But Arthur Sullivan hangs on as the composing half of Gilbert and Sullivan, creators of a uniquely English blend of social satire, burlesque and sophisticated musical parody.

He was born in Lambeth in 1842, and was accepted into the Royal Academy of Music in 1856. Studies at the Leipzig Conservatory between 1858 and 1861 culminated in a performance of his Mendelssohnian overture to *The Tempest*. He wrote a ballet and in 1867 visited Vienna, where he discovered a lost Schubert score, which did his credentials as a serious musician no harm at all. In the same year he met W.S. Gilbert.

The first fruit of their partnership, *Thespis*, closed to mixed reviews, and Sullivan returned to teaching and religious composition – including the hymn *Onward Christian Soldiers*. His permanent reunion with Gilbert was brought about by the impresario Richard d'Oyly Carte, who suggested the plot of what became *Trial by Jury* (1875), a work so successful that a string of collaborations followed, including *The Sorcerer* (1877), *HMS Pinafore* (1878), *The Pirates of Penzance* (1880), *Patience* (1881) and *Iolanthe* (1882).

In 1882 Sullivan was knighted. Honours notwithstanding, his frustration at his diet of musical frivolity came to a head with *Princess Ida* (1884), and off he stormed to tour Europe. Carte negotiated a truce between him and Gilbert, and after a lot more bickering *The Mikado* took shape. It was, in the view of Ethyl Smyth (see p.397), their masterpiece; within four years *The Gondoliers* and *The Yeomen of the Guard* were to follow.

A quarrel and lawsuit between Gilbert and Sullivan in 1890 was later patched up, but it ended their creative streak. Sullivan died ten years later, in his own estimation a shadow of what he should have been. A jaunty *Symphony in E* hints at what he might have achieved, had Gilbert never turned up. As it is, he's forever shackled to Gilbert, with whom he created a sequence of crisp, witty and untranslatable works of art. Sullivan represents the acceptable face of Little Englandism.

THE MIKADO

Librettist and composer were at their most epigrammatic and imaginative in *The Mikado*, which was their longest-running show. A hugely popular exhibition of Japanese products in Knightsbridge suggested the setting, but the work's orientalism is only skin-deep: the absurdly convoluted tale, tying together such characters as Ko-Ko the Lord High Executioner, Pooh-Bah "the Lord High Everything Else", the wandering minstrel Nanki-Poo and the lovely Pitti-Sing ("Pretty Thing" in baby talk), is a satire aimed at the absurdities of British society. The wit of Sullivan's music can be gauged by the fact that *The Mikado* manages to incorporate a genuine Japanese tune (used for the entrance of the Mikado himself), an English madrigal and a Bach fugue, while still sounding completely coherent. Victorian ballads are nicely set against the more acerbic pastiches, and the essential cruelty of much of Gilbert's text is perfectly balanced by the overall sunniness of Sullivan's sparkling music. Many of the work's best numbers have lodged in the English collective unconscious: Ko-Ko's "Tit-willow" refrain, for example, will be recognized by many who think they don't know any Gilbert and Sullivan.

O Adams, Rolfe Johnson, Suart, van Allen, McLaughlin; Welsh National Opera Orchestra and Chorus; Mackerras (Telarc CD80284).

This is the finest of Mackerras's G & S recording for Telarc, and is certainly the best-sung *Mikado* on disc, with a world-class operatic cast really letting their hair down. However, not only is the dialogue omitted, but the overture is cut as well and, though there's an economic benefit to editing the score to fit onto a single CD, you are left with a savagely trimmed object. That said, Mackerras is in sparkling form, the performances are all excellent, and no rival recording is complete anyway.

KAROL SZYMANOWSKI

(1882–1937)

Karol Szymanowski, the most prominent Polish composer of the twentieth century, is comparable to Bartók in the way he forged a distinctive style out of the folk music of his native land, but there's another important component to his achievement. Many of his visionary scores constitute a personal celebration of Dionysus and ecstatic love, exemplified by works such as the opera *King Roger, Symphony No. 3 – Song of the Night* and the two violin concertos, all of which create an opulent sound-world full of yearning melodies and filigree decoration. If any music could be said to be heavily perfumed, it's Szymanowski's.

Szymanowski was born in Tymoszówka in the Ukraine, to a musical family whose life seems to have been a continuous round of dances, plays and music. The poet Jarosław Iwaszkiewicz, with whom Szymanowski later worked on *King Roger* and the ballet *Harnasie*, left accounts of the elaborate fancy-dress balls for which Karol and his elder brother Felix composed the music. Of the five children in the family, three went on to become professional musicians – his sister Stasia became an opera singer and starred as Roxana in the first performance of *King Roger*.

Yet in his early years Szymanowski found little to inspire him in Poland, a country then partitioned between Germany, Russia and the Habsburg empire. His musical interests lay with foreign composers such as Richard Strauss, Debussy, Scriabin and Stravinsky, and he felt a deep affinity with Italy, Sicily and North Africa, regions he explored in 1911 and 1914 with Stefan Spiess, who was probably his lover. The cultures of ancient Greece, Norman Sicily and the Arab world had a huge and lasting impact on his music.

World War I and the Russian Revolution completely overturned Szymanowski's world – the house at Tymoszówka was destroyed by the Bolsheviks in 1917, and he was unable to compose amidst the upheaval. Instead he wrote a novel called *Efebos*, an exploration of homosexual love which was destroyed by fire in Warsaw in 1939.

An independent Poland emerged out of the chaos of World War I, and like many Polish intellectuals Szymanowski was determined to create a truly national art. In the exotic pieces for which he first gained international recognition – the *Symphony No. 3*, the *Violin Concerto No. 1* and *King Roger* – he resisted using folk material out of a fear of its limitations ("Poland's national music should not be the stiffened ghost of the polonaise or mazurka"). However, in the early 1920s a meeting with Stravinsky and the direct experience of *Le Sacre du Printemps* and *Les Noces* showed him a way to use folk elements in a completely unsentimental way.

During the 1920s he spent more and more time in Zakopane, at the heart of a distinctive folk culture of the Tatra mountains. A key member of a group who called themselves "the emergency ambulance service of Tatra culture", Szymanowski befriended the Obrochta family – one of the leading bands of village musicians – and began to notate the strange and idiosyncratic sounds of *gorale* (highland) music. The main work to come out of this research was the ballet *Harnasie* (1923–31), a tale of highland brigands culminating in a village wedding, a score which includes many genuine *gorale* dances. Alongside *Harnasie*, Szymanowski worked on his austerely beautiful *Stabat Mater* (1926), a piece that uses the ancient traditions of Polish church music, but in a much less self-conscious and bombastic way than *Harnasie* uses folk melodies.

During the last decade of his life Szymanowski took over the directorship of the Warsaw conservatory but suffered increasingly from health problems as the first signs of tuberculosis appeared. This was not a fruitful period as a composer, but he completed two major works, the *Symphonie Concertante* for piano and orchestra and the second violin concerto, both of which have characteristics of Polish folk music, combined with the lush exoticism of his earlier style. His last years were a sad story of failing health, financial hardship and neglect in Poland, but at least he had growing success abroad – *King Roger* was triumphantly received in Prague, and *Harnasie* likewise in Paris. Szymanowski died in a sanatorium in Lausanne and received a huge state funeral in Kraków, with the Obrochta family playing beside his tomb.

KING ROGER

The opening of *Król Roger* (1924) is one of the most extraordinary of any opera. The curtain rises on a service in the Palermo cathedral during the twelfth-century reign of King Roger, as choral music evokes clouds of incense and glistening mosaics. A mysterious shepherd arrives to preach a new faith of ecstasy and love ("My god is as young and beautiful as I am") – he is the embodiment of the union between Christ, Dionysus and Eros, a mystical idea sketched by Szymanowski in his novel *Efebos*. Roger's wife Roxana and many of his subjects find the shepherd's message intoxicating, and the opera culminates in a ritual in an ancient Greek theatre: the shepherd is transformed into Dionysus, while Roger – also transformed by the experience – salutes Apollo and the rising sun.

The opera is rarely performed, perhaps because it is essentially contemplative rather than dramatic. The music, though, has some breathtaking set pieces – the opening religious service, the arias of the shepherd and Roxana, a wild Dionysiac dance and the final hymn. Szymanowski was working on the score just after hearing Ravel's *Daphnis et Chloé* in America, and it shows the composer indulging in orientalist fantasy at its most full-blown.

⊙ Hiolski, Ochman, Zagórzanka, Grychnik; Katowice State Philharmonic Choir and Orchestra; Stryja (Marco Polo 8.223339-40; 2 CDs; with *Prince Potemkin*).

The newest *King Roger*, made in 1990 under Karol Stryja, is the finest: the score really benefits from a digital recording and the glittering sonorities come across well in a clear acoustic. The three principals are well characterized: Andrzej Hiolski's Roger has a suitably authoritative presence, Wislaw Ochman as the Shepherd is a good foil, and Barbara Zagórzanka just melts into her seductive aria. Unfortunately no libretto is supplied with the set, though there is a synopsis.

HARNASIE

Szymanowski is sometimes called the Polish Bartók, but he's far less rigorous and economical with his material, favouring a more rhapsodic and colourful approach. Typical of Szymanowski's style is *Harnasie*, his most ambitious attempt at reworking highland folk music in symphonic form. The music is scored for a massive orchestra plus tenor soloist and chorus, which often seems overblown for melodies and dances that belong to a small village ensemble, but there is no denying its vigour and local colour, with the orchestra recreating the typical melodies and harmonies of *gorale* music.

⊙ Choir and Orchestra of the Teatr Wielki, Warsaw; Satanowski (Koch Schwann 311 064; with *Mandragora*).

This is a wonderfully clear and vivid recording of Szymanowski's ballet, coupled with another interesting ballet score, *Mandragora*.

STABAT MATER

Szymanowski made a study of sixteenth-century Polish church music in preparation for writing the *Stabat Mater*, and the results are plain in the simplicity and purity of the piece, which makes an interesting counterweight to the lush scores of *King Roger* and *Symphony No. 3*. Gone is the over-chromatic harmony that dominates so much of his earlier work, replaced by simpler chords and finely placed tensions and dissonances. Szymanowski was not a religious man, and perhaps his indifference to the established church helped him to maintain the detachment that makes this his masterpiece. Szymanowski described the work as a peasant requiem (the text is in Polish, not Latin), and it has the same qualities of naive directness as the paintings that adorn some of the ancient wooden churches of southern Poland.

⊙ Szmytka, Garrison; City of Birmingham Symphony Orchestra; Rattle (EMI CDC5 55121-2; with *Symphony No. 3*).

The *Stabat Mater* contains some of Szymanowski's most beautiful music and this is the finest recording of it. The opening of the last movement, for instance, with the soprano solo rising from soft dissonances with the clarinets to a glowing major chord with the chorus, is a sublime moment. If this can't win new fans for Szymanowski, nothing can. Rattle controls the ebb and flow perfectly, moving from rapt intensity to outbursts of passion.

SYMPHONY NO. 3

Szymanowski's *Symphony No. 3*, subtitled "*Song of the Night*" (1916), is the most lavish of his large-scale compositions. Fascinated by Eastern mysticism, he turned for inspiration to the writings of the thirteenth-century Persian poet Jelal-ad-din Rumi, the founder of the Mevlevi (or whirling dervishes). Like other Sufi sects, the Mevlevi strove to attain an ecstatic relationship with God, and the poem from which *Symphony No. 3* is derived is typical of their art, celebrating the beauties and mysteries of an eastern night. Szymanowski was no Persian scholar, but his instinctive response to this text produced an opulent, intoxicating score full of langour and intense emotion.

⊙ City of Birmingham Symphony Orchestra; Rattle (EMI CDC5 55121-2; with *Stabat Mater*).

All Szymanowski's colouristic effects shine through on this wonderful recording, particularly the languorous melodies on the solo violin and the glittering flashes on piano, harp and percussion. After this performance you can understand Lutosławski's comment that listening to this music was like opening a gate onto a fantastic garden.

THE VIOLIN CONCERTOS

Along with the *Stabat Mater*, the violin concertos are probably the place for the Szymanowski novice to start. The first was written in 1916 and was inspired by a poem titled *May Night*, a fervent evocation of love amid the rich fecundity of nature. In this rhapsodic one-movement fantasy the solo violin part is characterized by filigree decoration or swooning melodies in a very high register, whereas in the second concerto (1933) – another one-movement piece – the solo writing is earthier and leaner, perhaps reflecting Szymanowski's immersion in Polish folk music. Both works show Szymanowski at his most sensuous and seductive.

⭘ **Zehetmair; City of Birmingham Symphony Orchestra; Rattle** (EMI CDC5 55607-2; with *Three Paganini Caprices, Romance*).

There are several very good versions of the violin concertos in the catalogue, but this one is in a league of its own. It sounds as though Zehetmair and Rattle have pondered long and hard over these superb works, to produce multidimensional readings which have an almost organic feel.

THE STRING QUARTETS

String quartets do not come much more febrile than Szymanowki's *Quartet No. 1* in C. Written in the autumn of 1917, it has the same rapturous quality as the slightly earlier *Violin Concerto No. 1* and *Symphony No. 3*, with the first violin seemingly possessed of a restless desire to pull itself away from its more earthbound colleagues. Sudden changes of mood abound, but the first two movements seem to occupy the same mental landscape as Schoenberg's *Verklärte Nacht* – the slow movement contains some of the most mysterious and exotic sounds you are likely to hear in a quartet. Ten years later Szymanowski entered his *String Quartet No. 2* for a competition in Philadelphia. The tone is fractionally bleaker and more astringent (the first movement alternates lushness with extreme spookiness) and may reflect both an awareness of the more aggressive quartet writing of Bartók (whose *Quartet No. 3* won the Philadelphia competition) and Szymanowski's study of Polish folk music.

⭘ **The Maggini Quartet** (ASV CD DCA 908; with Bacewicz, *String Quartet No. 4*).

Both quartets, with their kaleidoscopic changes of sonority and texture, are very difficult to play really well. The constant flow of ideas, and the different vocal groupings which seem to emerge from within the quartet, can tax the most experienced players. The Maggini Quartet capture all the shades of these colourful pieces with the greatest subtlety and an almost uncanny sense of ensemble.

TORU TAKEMITSU

(1930–1996)

Many of the poetic titles that Takemitsu gave to his pieces evoke the presence of water, and there is a recurring quality of purity and evanescence to much of his work. Largely self-taught, his wartime experiences initially led him to turn his back on Japanese music in favour of Western models. The textural delicacy of his work is clearly indebted to Debussy and Messiaen, and the eloquent silences recall Cage, yet his love of timbre for its own sake has always indicated the strength of his native musical heritage, which he eventually came to embrace openly. On occasions, his music can seem a rather glib fusion of East and West, but mostly it transcends such distinctions. At his best, Takemitsu is a refined sensualist whose shimmering soundscapes evoke a magical world that is both aurally precise and yet intensely dreamlike.

Western music was banned in Japan during the war and Takemitsu's first real contact with it came through the US Armed Forces Network which played both classical and popular music. Throughout his life he was to remain extremely receptive to a wide range of music (he even made arrangements of Beatles songs), but during the 1950s he was especially interested in the European avant-garde and set up an experimental workshop, Jikken Kobo, in 1951. Influenced by *musique concrète*, his electronic works included *Mizu no kyoku* (1960), a piece made exclusively from the recorded sounds of water. The first work to make a real impact in the West was the *Requiem for Strings* (1957), which was highly praised by Stravinsky, and in 1964 Takemitsu was invited to Hawaii to give a series of lectures with John Cage. The early 1960s was also the time when Takemitsu began a serious reassessment of traditional Japanese instruments, which he employed for the first time in the film score *Seppuku* (1962). The combination of the lute-like *biwa* and *shakuhachi* (bamboo flute) can be heard in his most famous orchestral score, *November Steps* (1967), and in *Ran* (1985) – one of the best of his 93 film scores.

ORCHESTRAL MUSIC

Takemitsu's work has often been criticized for a lack of structure and thematic development. But these are Western musical preoccupations and it is better, when listening to his work, to let the music unfold in its own unruffled way. The aesthetics of Japanese gardens (which Takemitsu loved) make a useful analogy when describing his music: there's a similar interplay between nature and artifice as well as a sense of an exquisite placing of aural elements to create a balanced and harmonious whole. In *November Steps* the two Japanese instruments are placed well in front of the orchestra, where their dialogue takes on an almost competitive edge. The orchestra, though large, has essentially a background role, ebbing and flowing in and out of the solos in the manner of multi-voiced and eloquent chorus. Their language is gestural and splintered (not unlike Boulez), greatly increasing the overall impression of highly coloured abstraction. Ten years later another large orchestral work proved a popular success. *A Flock Descends into the Pentagonal Garden*, inspired by a dream about Marcel Duchamp, is more cohesive in its orchestration, with an almost Mahlerian sumptuousness. Even richer than this is the *Viola Concerto* (1984). Subtitled "A String Around Autumn" because of the way the soloist functions as an observer in "an imaginary landscape", this is an appropriately warm-hued and mellow work which at times reaches a rhapsodic fervour reminiscent of Szymanowski.

O November Steps; Eclipse; Viola Concerto: Imai, Yokoyama, Tsuruta; Saito Kinen Orchestra; Ozawa (Philips 432 176-2).

Ozawa is a specialist in the more impassioned masters of early twentieth-century music, and when he approaches Takemitsu's work there is a similarly full-bloodied approach to his conducting. In *November Steps* he manages to make the often dense orchestral writing markedly clean and clear, while in the *Viola Concerto*, with its closer relationship between soloist and orchestra, he adopts a more relaxed approach, providing a vigorous counterpart to Nobuko Imai's splendidly ripe tone.

CHAMBER MUSIC

Arguably, the individuality of Takemitsu's voice can be heard best in his small-scale works, where his diaphanous textures and subtle colours make an intense and startling impact. Two of his most effective chamber works were written for Tashi, an ensemble comprising piano, violin, cello and clarinet. *Quatrain* was composed for them in 1975 following a performance the group gave of Messiaen's *Quartet for the End of Time* at which Takemitsu was present. In its quiet meditative stillness, it's very much a homage to Messiaen, with a range of understated but expressive gestures communicating a restrained anguish. Takemitsu originally wrote it for the group and a symphony orchestra, then in 1977 produced a version, *Quatrain II*, for quartet alone. In the same year he produced *Waves*, a much more dramatic work for the startling combination of clarinet, bass drum, French horn and trombones. This is a highly atmospheric piece, with the looming background presence of the drum – sometimes soft, sometimes loud – suggesting an impending but never realized violence. Throughout much of the piece the other instruments, the clarinet in particular, seem to simulate the breathy vitality of the *shakuhachi*. A more bluesy final section subsides into the ghostly sounds of the wind players breathing into their instruments. *Water-Ways* (1978) was written for Peter Serkin – Tashi's pianist. Inspired by watching the rich movement of a stream near his studio, Takemitsu overlays a Debussy-inspired piano part with delicate pulsating figures for the rest of the ensemble plus vibraphone and harp.

O Fantasmas/Cantos; Water-Ways; Waves; Quatrain II: Stoltzman, Tashi; BBC Welsh Symphony Orchestra; Otaka (RCA 09026 62537-2).

The disc is billed by RCA as a vehicle for Tashi's clarinettist Richard Stoltzman (who gives a rapturous performance of Takemitsu's clarinet concerto *Fantasmas/Cantos*), but in fact the musicianship of all the players is of the highest standard. Tashi brings to these works the rapt concentration and attention to detail which characterizes so much of the group's playing of contemporary music. It would be easy to overwhelm such delicate washes of sound if dynamic levels were not kept under careful control, and in this respect their judgement is that of performers both familiar and enamoured with the music.

THOMAS TALLIS

(1505–1585)

Tallis's powerful but ethereal sacred music was written during one of the most turbulent periods of English history. Each of the four Tudor monarchs whom he served possessed widely different attitudes to religious affairs. This not only meant that he was forced to write sometimes in Latin and sometimes in English, but also resulted in regular changes of musical style. His earliest music adopts a peculiarly English, florid style of polyphony, quite similar to Taverner (see p.425); then during the reforms of Edward VI he was obliged to write much more simple and direct music in line with the rationalization of the liturgy; finally in Elizabeth I's reign he developed a tighter and more lucid polyphonic manner, one which became increasingly sensitive to the meaning of the words being set.

Next to nothing is known of Tallis's early life, but in 1540 his livelihood was directly influenced by the volatile religious climate when he lost his job as organist at Waltham Abbey in Essex, following the dissolution. He received twenty shillings' payment and a further twenty shillings as compensation. After brief employment at Canterbury Cathedral, Tallis joined the royal household in 1543 as a Gentleman of the Chapel Royal, a position he maintained until his death. His duties as composer and organist earned him significant rewards from his royal patrons: in 1557 the Catholic Queen Mary granted him a 21-year lease on a lucrative property in Kent, and in 1575 the Protestant Queen Elizabeth gave him, and his younger colleague William Byrd (see p.95), the exclusive right to print and publish music. Their first publication, which came out in the same year, was the *Cantiones Sacrae*, a collection containing seventeen Latin motets by each composer. It was not a financial success, and the two men petitioned the queen as a result of which they were granted a joint lease on another property. Tallis died in 1585 and was buried in the church of St Alphege at Greenwich.

SACRED MUSIC

Among Tallis's most celebrated works are the two settings of the *Lamentations of Jeremiah*, sombre and heartfelt works that convincingly express the spirit of their melancholy words, and the extraordinary and unforgettable motet, *Spem in Alium*, for five eight-part choirs. Possibly written for the fortieth birthday of either Queen Mary or Queen Elizabeth (no one knows for sure), *Spem in Alium* uniquely combines complex and delicate polyphonic writing with clamorous tutti passages, and is one of the greatest achievements of all English music.

O Spem in Alium and other music: Winchester Cathedral Choir; Hill (Hyperion CDA 66400).

This recording, which contains both *Spem in Alium* and the *Lamentations of Jeremiah*, is remarkable both for the outstanding Winchester Cathedral choir and for the resonant acoustic of the vast cathedral, which adds an extremely dramatic quality to the sound. The opening of *Spem in Alium*, with its gradual accumulation of voices from just one voice is particularly thrilling. In the lighter-textured five-part motets, especially the austere first setting of *O Salutaris*, there is a quality of rapt concentration in the singing that perfectly matches the directness of the music.

JOHN TAVENER

(1944–)

If John Tavener seemed unexcited by the 1993 chart success of his sumptuous work for solo cello and strings, *The Protecting Veil*, it's hardly surprising – he has seen it all before, and it turned sour the first time round. Back in 1968 the critics pronounced Tavener the new composer to watch: the *Guardian* described the premiere of his *In Alium* as "nothing less than a musical love-in"; he found himself courted by the Beatles to record for their Apple label; London's Trinity College of Music invited him to join their staff as a professor of composition;

and, to cap it all, Covent Garden commissioned him to write a full-length opera, *Thérèse*, on the recommendation of Benjamin Britten. The pressure soon began to tell, and by the early 1970s Tavener was finding that it took a progressively longer time to compose each work, and there were worrying "dry" periods. He was in danger of burning out. Salvation came in the shape of the Russian Orthodox Church.

Ever since Tavener converted to the Orthodox faith in 1977, he has held the view that art is inseparable from religion – "Music is a form of prayer, a mystery." His fervent spirituality was not the result of some blinding revelation – on the contrary, he has been concerned with such things from the start. As a boy of 12 he was profoundly influenced by a broadcast of Stravinsky's *Canticum Sacrum*, a remarkable synthesis of ancient and modern, Eastern and Western, sacred and secular, with which he felt an instant affinity. His parents brought him up a Presbyterian and some of his earliest compositions were written for that church. Apart from the works produced in the late 1960s, when he became something of an apostle of flower power, Tavener has devoted himself to exploring the connection between art and the sacred.

Despite a conventional British musical training, Tavener is, by his own admission, "not very interested in Western art music", reserving special disdain for "angst-ridden serial music". Tavener instead looks for inspiration to Greek, Persian, Indian and Sufi music, exotic languages from which he has distilled a style that conveys spiritual depth through simple textures and forms. His music is non-developmental – "iconic" is his preferred term. For Tavener "the icon is the supreme example of Christian art", and the severe shapes and limited colours of a Byzantine icon are, in his view, analogous to the spartan means by which his music seeks to inspire a sense of spiritual wonder.

Tavener has his detractors, for whom his static simplicity is merely musical nostalgia of the most sentimental and retrogressive kind, but he's become one of the most frequently performed living composers, and recordings of his works sell in vast numbers. For the time being, at least, the unashamedly backward-looking music of Tavener, like the similarly devotional works of Górecki (see p.163) and Pärt (see p.298), seem to have struck a chord among people seeking refuge from the neuroses and struggles of postmodern times.

THE PROTECTING VEIL

Commissioned for a BBC Promenade Concert and written with the cellist Steven Isserlis in mind, *The Protecting Veil* (1987) for cello and orchestra takes its inspiration from the Orthodox feast of The Protecting Veil of the Mother of God, which commemorates the alleged appearance of the Virgin Mary in tenth-century Constantinople. The music is divided into eight sections, but there is little feeling of development in a Western sense; instead the intensely rhapsodic solo part rises, like a vocal lamentation, slowly but steadily against a subdued orchestral background. Tavener strives for an Eastern ideal of perfection in this music, a timeless spirituality untrammelled by the Western artist's struggle for individuality and self-advertisement. *The Protecting Veil* never grabs your attention (despite an insistent pealing figure in the high strings) but this is no mere background music: it demands an undivided attention, a willingness to surrended to its meditative atmosphere and devotional purpose.

O Isserlis; London Symphony Orchestra; Rozhdestvensky (Virgin VC7 59052-2; with *Thrinos*, and Britten, *Cello Suite No. 3*).

Over the last few years the creative partnership between Tavener and cellist Steven Isserlis has grown closer, but the impact of *The Protecting Veil* has not been surpassed by his subsequent works for cello. In this superbly produced disc, both soloist and orchestra manage to convey a rapt and inward-looking quality that many have found truly uplifting.

⊙ Wallfisch; Royal Philharmonic Orchestra; Brown (Tring International TRP 048).

The Protected Veil was almost as successful as Górecki's *Symphony No. 3*, and like that work there are now several recordings available. Raphael Wallfisch's performance is very different from that of Isserlis: less enraptured and contemplative, more upfront and forceful, the cello's voice struggles harder for the transcendent but gets there in the end.

CHORAL MUSIC

Even before his conversion to the Orthodox Church, Tavener's choral music (by far the most substantial part of his output) was striving for a more simple and direct form. The *Little Requiem for Father Malachy Lynch* (1972) makes a powerful impression through the way non-polyphonic choral singing (much of it in unison) is contrasted with the bright and animated sounds of a small orchestra of two flutes, trumpet, organ and strings. The *Akhmatova Requiem* (1980), a setting of Anna Akhmatova's poetic tribute to the victims of Stalinism, makes an even greater impact. Written for two soloists and an orchestra in which brass and percussion stand out, it's a stark mixture of the reassuringly simple and the harshly modern, at times reminiscent of Britten's *War Requiem*.

Much of Tavener's music has been prompted by the need to come to terms with death, and reflects the paradox, for Christians, of death being an experience of both loss and release. When his own mother died in 1985, Tavener was unable to write for several months but then responded with a number of deeply felt works which include the ritualistic *Eis Thanaton* and the *Two Hymns to the Mother of God*. This preoccupation with death continues with two very different works, both completed in 1995. *Syvati* (O Holy One) was shaped by the news of the death of a friend and includes some luminous writing for chamber choir as well as an important role for cello, an instrument which Tavener has come to regard as the perfect avatar for the spiritual essence of his music. *Innocence* spreads the net of his compassion further. A sombre eulogy to innocent victims of oppression throughout history, its startling theatricality is partly due to the way Tavener divides the vocal forces around the space it was written for – Westminster Abbey. Most famously the *Song for Athene* (1993) shows Tavener's ability to touch people by the most simple means. Written in memory of a young Greek actress, its slow processional quality and continuous underlying bass drone create a mood of both solemnity and serenity (and made it a fitting musical climax at the funeral of Diana, Princess of Wales).

O Innocence: Rozario; Westminster Abbey Choir; Neary (Sony SK 66613; with other Tavener choral works).

This recording presents a representative selection of Taverner's choral works in outstanding performances. The longest work is the title piece, the bleakness of which (Tavener instructs it should be performed in a "petrified manner") is moderated by Westminster Abbey's vast and resonant acoustic. The reverberant ambience works better in the larger works, as smaller pieces (like the exquisite *The Lamb*) tend to get slightly lost in the spaciousness. Nevertheless the disc makes a near-ideal place to start with this composer.

◑ Akhmatova Requiem: Bryn-Julson; Shirley-Qirk; BBC Symphony Orchestra; Rozhdestvensky (BBC Radio Classics 15656 91972; with *Six Russian Folksongs*).

A more abrasive – yet no less moving – side to Tavener is revealed by the *Akhmatova Requiem*, perhaps his finest work. It's a live recording from a 1981 Promenade Concert and, though the sound quality is not exactly perfect, Phyllis Bryn-Julson is in glorious voice and gets right to the heart of Akhmatova's searing verses.

JOHN TAVERNER

(c.1490–1545)

John Taverner was the outstanding talent of pre-Reformation English music and one of the greatest of all polyphonists. To a large extent his music was the culmination of an extremely rich English polyphonic tradition which employed highly florid vocal writing and a variety of contrasted voice combinations within the same piece. To this tradition Taverner added the continental device of imitation, whereby a phrase sung by one voice would be repeated by another, thus giving his works a greater sense of shape and direction than those of his English predecessors.

Taverner was probably born in Lincolnshire: the earliest record of his musical activities is in 1525 as a lay clerk at the collegiate choir of Tattershall, northwest of Boston. The following year, on the recommendation of the Bishop of Lincoln, he was appointed choirmaster to the newly founded Cardinal (later Christ Church) College, Oxford. This was a prestigious position but a short-lived one, due to the fall from power in 1529 of the college's founder, Cardinal Wolsey. The year before that, Taverner was briefly arrested for his involvement with a group sympathetic to Lutheranism, an incident treated with leniency at the time, but which gave rise to the legend that Taverner eschewed both Catholicism and music to dedicate his remaining years to the destruction of the monasteries. This is the subject of Peter Maxwell Davies's 1970 opera, *Taverner*, on the life of the composer, but the truth seems to be rather less dramatic. Taverner returned to Lincolnshire to become a lay clerk and possibly choirmaster at the church of St Botolph's at Boston. Once again it was not an appointment that he held for long – this time he left because of the collapse of the guild that paid his wages. From 1537 his musical activities seem to have ceased and the rest of his life was spent in the role of a well-to-do local dignitary, one well enough regarded to be honoured at his death with burial beneath the great tower of St Botolph's church.

SACRED MUSIC

Eight of Taverner's Masses have survived, of which the most beautiful is the early six-part *Missa Gloria Tibi Trinitas*. This employs a plainsong cantus firmus which is located in the alto part, thus making it more audible than usual since only the treble part is higher. The work is remarkable for its variety and for the liveliness of its counterpoint – there are several moments of richly florid writing, notably near the beginning of the Credo, when the treble line weaves ever more complex patterns above the bass part. Its most famous section, the *In Nomine* from the *Benedictus*, was used by subsequent English composers from Tallis to Purcell as the thematic material from which to write short pieces for viol consorts, which were duly known as "in nomines".

O Missa Gloria Tibi Trinitas; Leroy Kyrie; Dum Transisset Sabbatum; Western Wynde Mass: The Tallis Scholars; Phillips (Gimell 454 995-2).

The Tallis Scholars bring to the *Missa Gloria Tibi Trinitas* their customary precision and textural clarity, but with a greater degree of flexibility and warmth than is usual. The intimacy of the reduced voice passages is well contrasted with the radiant sound produced by the full choir. Occasionally the incisiveness of the female voices in the upper parts brings a slightly top-heavy quality to the sound, but this is a small distraction. The other works included on the disc are less animated, being made up of smoother, more drawn-out phrases which produce an altogether more solemn and serene impression.

PYOTR IL'YICH TCHAIKOVSKY

(1840–1893)

If any one composer can be said to encapsulate the essence of Russianness, it is Pyotr Il'yich Tchaikovsky, and yet he was the one major composer of nineteenth-century Russia who cannot be bracketed with the Russian nationalist school. Although he associated with prominent nationalist figures, particularly Balakirev, Tchaikovsky followed a fiercely independent path, and he paid heavily for his determination to be true to himself above all else – few major artists have ever suffered the sort of critical savaging that was meted out to Tchaikovsky. Nowadays it's difficult to understand why his music aroused such antipathy, for Tchaikovsky is the most powerful and direct of composers: characterized above all by its tunefulness and sweeping orchestral sound, Tchaikovsky's music appeals directly to the heart. Certainly he was prone to bombastic gestures and sentimentality, but these weaknesses are the obverse of his chief strength, which is his sincerity. The emotional fluctuations and contradictions of his work reflect the turbulence of an extraordinary life.

Tchaikovsky was born some nine hundred kilometres east of Moscow in the provincial town of Votkinsk, where his father was a mining engineer. His formal tuition began at home, where his parents played him pieces by Mozart and Rossini, and gave him lessons in piano and music theory. In 1848 the family moved to St Petersburg, and in 1850 he was sent to a boarding school in the city; nine years later, after intensive and extended law studies (and the death of his mother, a trauma that was to scar him for the rest of his life) he found employment at the Ministry of Justice. Aged 22 he left the ministry and entered the city music conservatory to study with Anton Rubinstein, a composer and stupendous pianist. In 1866 he went to Moscow, where Anton's brother Nikolai appointed Tchaikovsky professor of harmony at the conservatory.

In Moscow he came into contact with Rimsky-Korsakov and his cabal of young nationalists, and for a short while Tchaikovsky was swept up by their enthusiasm for Russia's folk heritage. He even composed a nationalist symphony – the *Symphony No. 2*, known as the *Little Russian* – but it was not long before his cosmopolitan instincts prevailed. By the time of the first performance of his *Piano Concerto No. 1* in 1875 he had created a style that was strongly individual while being equally accessible to any audience raised on the wider European tradition – indeed, the concerto at first found greater acclaim abroad than at home.

1877 was the most crucial year in Tchaikovsky's life, and the point from which his music radically expands its emotional depth and profundity. Bizarrely, this transformation was prompted by his contact with two women hitherto unknown to him. The first was Nadezhda von Meck, a wealthy widow who, impressed by some of his early music, now commissioned Tchaikovsky to produce some

LEBRECHT COLLECTION

Tchaikovsky (seated, centre) with members of the Kharkov Music Society, 1893

violin and piano arrangements of his more recent works. Thus began a relationship between the two that lasted fourteen years, during which time they never once met. Convinced of Tchaikovsky's genius, she supplied him with an annuity that would enable him to devote all his time to composition.

The second woman was Antonina Milyukova, who in May 1877 started sending Tchaikovsky infatuated love letters in which she threatened to take her life unless he responded. Initially cautious, Tchaikovsky seems suddenly to have seen in his unstable admirer a solution to the problem of his homosexuality (homosexual acts were punishable by death in Russia). Within seven weeks of meeting her, and unbeknown to most of his family, the two were married. Predictably it was an unmitigated disaster: Tchaikovsky immediately sank into an overwhelming depression and the couple separated after just a few weeks.

The love of his family and friends, in particular his increasingly intimate correspondence with Nadezhda von Meck, helped Tchikovsky over the breakdown caused by his marriage and, remarkably, this period corresponds with the composition of two of his greatest works, the *Symphony No. 4*, dedicated to "my best friend" (ie Nadezhda), and the finest of his nine operas *Eugene Onegin* which he completed in 1879.

By the 1880s his music was being played as far afield as the USA, and by 1885 he had made enough money to buy himself a country estate at Klin. He lived there in almost complete isolation until 1887, when he ventured back to Moscow to make his debut as a conductor. In this capacity he toured Europe in the following year, and then in 1889 he moved to Florence, where he composed the opera, *The Queen of Spades*. The work's triumph was marred by the collapse of his relationship with von Meck, but although he was deeply distressed by their falling out he made an incredibly successful visit to the USA in 1891, conducting at the opening night of what was to become Carnegie Hall. "I am a much more important person here than in Russia", he wrote, bewildered by his reception.

In 1893 his achievement was recognized in France, where he was elected a member of the Academie Française, and England, where Cambridge University awarded him an honorary doctorate. In August he completed his *Symphony No. 6*, the *Pathétique*, a creation that typifies the work of a composer who poured the whole of his life into his music. It was premiered in St Petersburg on October 28; nine days later he was dead.

The circumstances of Tchaikovsky's death remain controversial to this day. The official version was that he had died from cholera after drinking unboiled water. Many people surmised that Tchaikovsky had hoped this reckless act would bring about his death, but in the 1970s a Russian scholar produced a new account of Tchaikovsky's last days, a version which, it was claimed, established suicide as the incontrovertible cause of death. Shortly before his death, the story goes, Tchaikovsky had been caught in flagrante with a nephew of a high-ranking official. Tchaikovsky's law-school colleagues, determined to avert a scandal that would reflect badly on them, summoned Tchaikovsky before a "court of honour" on October 31 and ordered him to commit suicide. Two days later, he took arsenic.

THE OPERAS

Tchaikovsky's operas are the distillation of what he termed his "lyrical idea", the notion that everything can be characterized or made real through melody. His technique was always at the service of melody, and his music was first and foremost conceived for the voice – whether or not it was actually written for voice, all his music can be sung. Tchaikovsky was not, however, an effortless tune-writer in the manner of Mendelssohn or Strauss. He worked hard at honing his skills, making an intensive study of his European precursors, not just as a student in Russia, but also in later life as a touring celebrity. For his operatic music Tchaikovsky immersed himself in Italian bel canto as well as in the operas of Mozart, and the breadth of Tchaikovsky's schooling is a major distinction between him and his Russian contemporaries. He wrote no fewer than ten operas, though only two of them have found a regular place in the repertory – *Eugene Onegin* and *The Queen of Spades*.

EUGENE ONEGIN

Tchaikovsky was initially sceptical about a friend's casual suggestion to turn Pushkin's great verse-novel *Eugene Onegin* into an opera, but when he reread the passage where Tatyana, the heroine of the story, writes a declaration of love to Onegin, he was immediately struck by the similarity to his own situation and the letter he had received from Antonina Milyukova. His strong sense of identification with Tatyana prompted him to begin work on the "letter scene", which would become the emotional core of the opera. It also prompted his disastrously sympathetic response to Antonina, and by the time of their wedding he had already completed about two-thirds of the opera.

Despite the horrors of his brief marriage, *Eugene Onegin* contains some of the composer's most graceful, untroubled music. Where Pushkin's poem had explored at length the social and moral discrepancies between the world of Tatyana, the country girl, and that of the cynical aristocratic Onegin, Tchaikovsky keeps the spotlight on their aborted relationship. Onegin spurns Tatyana, then flirts with her sister at the party to celebrate the sister's engagement to Lensky. When Lensky protests, Onegin reluctantly fights a duel, in which Lensky is killed. Six years later Onegin returns from abroad to find Tatyana married. Realizing he loves her, he tempts her to leave with him, but eventually she rejects him.

Lensky is a particularly fine tenor role (his aria is one of the work's highlights) and Onegin is delineated with great subtlety, but it is the characterization of Tatyana that is the making of this opera. There are few more realistic or sympathetic heroines, and her "Letter Scene" is just about the most moving twenty minutes that Tchaikovsky ever devised.

O Allen, Freni, von Otter, Schicoff; Staatskapelle Dresden; Levine (Deutsche Grammophon 423 959-2; 2 CDs).

Levine's thrilling account for DG is the most impressive modern recording. Thomas Allen's Onegin is a perfectly shaped performance and the surprise casting of Mirella Freni works amazingly well – she is able to convey the requisite youthfulness for her first meeting with Onegin just as clearly as the maturity needed for their final confrontation, and her "Letter Scene" is particularly well drawn. The Dresden orchestra play with great fervour and the smaller roles are played with similarly convincing commitment.

THE QUEEN OF SPADES

The Queen of Spades (sometimes translated as *Pique-Dame*) is also based upon a story by Pushkin. Its protagonist is a young army officer named Hermann, who is trying to discover a secret to success in gambling, a secret known only to the Countess who is the grandmother of Lisa, the woman he loves. He breaks into the Countess's room at night in order to attain the secret of the "three cards", but so terrifies her that she dies of shock. The Countess returns as a ghost and tells Hermann the secret. He abandons Lisa (who drowns herself), and takes to the gambling rooms ready to make his fortune. However, the Countess reappears and, in revenge, drives Hermann into killing himself.

The opera was premiered in St Petersburg in 1890, over ten years after *Onegin*, by which time Tchaikovsky's technique had become far more sophisticated. In *The Queen of Spades* he combines nineteenth-century realism with the elegance of Mozart's world and the Rococo style of Catherine the Great's St Petersburg. Indeed, a generalized longing for the past permeates the score. The focus upon Fate – a recurrent idea in Tchaikovsky – is handled brilliantly, with the "three cards" motif strongly colouring the work's fabric. The roles of Hermann (a high, dramatic tenor) and the Countess (a dark and noble contralto) interact in some immensely impressive scenes – especially the blood-curdling episode where Hermann is confronted by the ghost of the Countess. But *The Queen of Spades* is littered with memorable moments; as he wrote to his brother (his co-librettist) – "Unless I'm terribly mistaken, the opera is a masterpiece."

○ Freni, Atlantov, Hvorostovsky, Forrester; Boston Symphony Orchestra; Ozawa (RCA 09026 60992-2; 3 CDs).

This is perhaps Ozawa's finest achievement on record. His direction is tight but flexible, the Boston Symphony makes a wonderful sound, and the cast is sensational. It's headed by the mighty Vladimir Atlantov as Hermann – frequently over the top but always powerful and committed. Freni was too old to be playing Lisa as Tchaikovsky intended her but she is still in glowing voice, while Margaret Forrester gives a fine portrayal of the Countess. Excellent recorded sound.

THE BALLETS

Russian ballet music before Tchaikovsky was vapid stuff, amounting to little more than background music for displays of the dancers' qualities. Tchaikovsky introduced a greater range of rhythms, an increased richness of melody and orchestration, and above all gave the ballet a sense of symphonic construction – in short, he gave respect to ballet music as an art form. Classical ballet owes more to Tchaikovsky than to any other composer, and if *Swan Lake*, *The Sleeping Beauty* and *The Nutcracker* met with little more than polite approval during Tchaikovsky's lifetime, they are now the world's most frequently performed dance scores.

◑ Ballet Suites: Berlin Philharmonic Orchestra; Rostropovich (Deutsche Grammophon 449 726-2).

This recording of the suites from *Swan Lake*, *The Sleeping Beauty* and *The Nutcracker* is a bargain at mid-price. Rostropovich is not the greatest conductor but his Tchaikovsky performances are always full-blooded and he is given ravishing support from the Berlin Philharmonic. Both he and the orchestra clearly enjoy every minute of the music.

SWAN LAKE

Tchaikovsky was commissioned to write *Swan Lake* at the end of May 1875 by the Imperial Theatre. He gladly accepted the work, partly because of his poor financial situation, and partly because, as he wrote to Rimsky-Korsakov, "I have long had the wish to try my hand at this kind of music." Tchaikovsky duly produced the first ballet that had overall musical coherence, for rather than being the customary series of dances strung together by the vaguest of plots *Swan Lake* is constructed of extended quasi-symphonic movements, unified by a system of themes and key structures. Tchaikovsky's brilliantly orchestrated musical narrative flows perfectly, and features more memorable tunes than any of the composer's other scores. The first production was nonetheless a resounding failure. Petipa, the pre-eminent choreographer of his day, and Drigo, a ballet composer of the old school, then set about revising the work, but it was still considered undanceable. Time has told a different story.

⊙ Philharmonia Orchestra; Lanchbery (Classics for Pleasure CD-CFPD4727; 2 CDs).

John Lanchbery, a ballet conductor who worked frequently with Fonteyn and Nureyev, made this budget-price recording in 1982, and it remains the best version on record. This is a delicate, flowing performance with fine orchestral playing and a spacious dynamic range that highlights even the subtlest of touches.

THE SLEEPING BEAUTY

Tchaikovsky's second ballet is a work of his maturity, coming between the fifth and sixth symphonies. It was premiered in 1890, with choreography by Petipa, and this time Tchaikovsky had learned his lesson – he allowed Petipa to guide him, section by section, through the ballet's composition. (On certain occasions Petipa would go so far as to specify the number of bars required.) Unlike its predecessor, *The Sleeping Beauty* is a happy-ending tale. But for all the sweetness of the story line, this is Tchaikovsky's finest ballet, for if *Swan Lake* marked the establishment of a symphonic style of ballet music, *Sleeping Beauty* went a stage further – it was even attacked at the time for being "too symphonic". Elaborately constructed, it contains movements within movements that are, effectively, miniature concertos for the orchestral section leaders.

◑ Concertgebouw; Dorati (Philips 446 166-2; 2 CDs).

Antal Dorati's recording of the complete *Sleeping Beauty* is magnificently coherent. Dorati's aggressive manner and almost impatient tempi, exemplified by his performances of music by Stravinsky, is a gift to music that can easily become sickly sweet.

THE NUTCRACKER

The Nutcracker, based on E.T.A. Hoffmann's story of a little girl and her Christmas presents, was written at the end of Tchaikovsky's life but it reflects nothing of his misery or self-hatred – rather it evokes a world of innocence where everything is as it should be. Again, Petipa worked closely with the composer on the production of a detailed scenario, and much of Hoffmann's ironic juxtaposition of reality and fantasy was lost in the process. Yet this is still an enchanting work, containing many of Tchaikovsky's best-loved tunes – notably the *Sugar-Plum Fairy*, which includes music for the celesta, a new instrument that Tchaikovsky was desperate to keep secret from his rivals, in particular Rimsky-Korsakov. The celesta's finest hour was to come courtesy of Bartók (see p.27).

◑ **London Symphony Orchestra; Dorati** (Mercury 432 750-2; 2 CDs; with *Serenade*).

The Nutcracker is shorter and considerably less ambitious than *Sleeping Beauty*, but it is in no way lacking in drama or colour. Dorati's calm direction is perfectly delicate but he produces a wash of sound such as few have achieved on record. A wonderful, superbly engineered recording.

SYMPHONIES AND ORCHESTRAL WORKS

Tchaikovsky viewed the symphony as the mould into which to pour his most profound thoughts and feelings, and his seven completed symphonies are the emotional graph of a lifetime, from the relative calm of the *Symphony No. 1* (*Winter Daydreams*) to the desolation of the *Symphony No. 6* (the *Pathétique*). They are uniformly revealing but not uniformly excellent. The first three have plenty of Tchaikovsky's outgoing melodies and thrilling rhythms, but they also have slack episodes that you won't find in the last three numbered symphonies. These represent the high-water mark of the Romantic symphony and are discussed below. The seventh, written between the fourth and the fifth, is known as the *Manfred Symphony* since it was inspired by Lord Byron's poem of the same name. It has some truly thrilling moments but is rather shapeless and tends to overwork its big tune.

When the level of Tchaikovsky's invention is below the standard of his finest works, his music can seem tremendously banal and short-winded. This perhaps explains why, out of the substantial body of other orchestral music that he wrote, only a handful of pieces have permanently entered the repertoire outside of Russia. Of the works that have, the *1812 Overture* is the best known, but *Romeo and Juliet* represents his highest achievement, both because it is rich melodically and because it succeeds in developing its thematic material in a dramatically convincing way.

◑ **Complete Symphonies: Oslo Philharmonic Orchestra; Jansons** (Chandos 8672-8; 7 CDs).

Mariss Jansons' survey of Tchaikovsky's symphonies is a remarkable achievement, bringing something fresh to each one. He and the Oslo players give a sense of conviction to the early symphonies that is lacking from the majority of alternative versions, and with the late masterpieces they are at least the equal of any rivals. These fine recordings are available on separate, full-price discs, or as a specially reduced set – in the latter format they represent a very good investment.

SYMPHONY NO. 4

The composition of the *Symphony No. 4* was interrupted by the breakdown of Tchaikovsky's marriage and by a consequent, pathetic attempt at suicide – he waded into a river, hoping to catch pneumonia. Yet when he completed the piece in December 1877, he was convinced that it was his greatest work: "in technique and form it represents a step forward in my development, which has been proceeding extremely slowly". The fourth symphony shows a greater control of the orchestral palette, and a stronger grasp of the means of integrating melodic material into an overall structure. The first movement is an expansive conception, dominated by a bleak "Fate" motif that colours the entire movement, while the second is a mournful song of poignant beauty. The third movement features some amazingly original scoring for plucked strings, but it is the charging, ebullient finale that justifies the use of superlatives – incorporating variations on a Russian folk song, this is the composer's most exciting symphonic invention, ending in a torrent of enthusiasm after the violent incursions of the "Fate" motif.

◑ **Leningrad Philharmonic Orchestra; Mravinsky** (Deutsche Grammophon 419 745-2; 2 CDs; with *Symphonies Nos. 5 & 6*).

Mravinsky was one of the finest of all Soviet conductors, whose Tchaikovsky performances were admired for their rigour and their athleticism. Under his baton, the Leningrad Phil became one of the world's great orchestras and this performance shows them at their very best. In this symphony the prevailing sense of tension created by finely shaded dynamics is breathtaking.

SYMPHONY NO. 5

Tchaikovsky wrote of the *Symphony No. 5* (1885): "I have become convinced that the symphony is unsuccessful. There is something repellent about it, a certain patchiness, insecurity and artifice . . . All this causes me a keen torment of discontent . . . it is all most distressing." This certainly is a distressing work, but chiefly because of its unguarded candour rather than because of any compositional failings. Fate is more cruel and implacable in this symphony than it was in its predecessor: it begins in despairing mood, and the frequent, massive emotional climaxes generate a sense of hysteria that rarely featured in the fourth. The symphony's "Fate" motif destroys even the song-like melody of the slow movement, and only at the close of the finale does the tragic atmosphere lift – even then, you feel it's a case of putting a brave face on things.

⭘ London Symphony Orchestra; Dorati (Mercury 434 305-2; with *Marche Slave* and excerpts from *Eugene Onegin*).

Dorati's discipline prevents the emotional climate of the symphony from becoming too oppressive, and the potentially cloying textures are balanced with precision and imagination. The first four movements are evenly paced, but the finale is driven with an insatiable energy that is well served by a clear and resonant recording.

◑ Leningrad Philharmonic Orchestra; Mravinsky (Deutsche Grammophon 419 745-2; 2 CDs; with *Symphonies Nos. 4 and 6*).

Mravinsky's fifth is as controlled as Dorati's, but he stresses the work's melancholy side more: the beginning of the slow movement is particularly poignant, with the dark brass sound – so characteristic of Russian orchestras – bringing a touching frailty to the first statement of the movement's big tune.

SYMPHONY NO. 6 – THE PATHÉTIQUE

"I give you my word of honour that never in my life have I been so contented, so proud, so happy in the knowledge that I have written a good piece." Within months of writing this to his publisher, Tchaikovsky was dead, possibly pushed towards suicide by the hostile reception accorded to his *Symphony No. 6*. The title *Pathétique* was added by the composer's brother, and is undeniably appropriate to a work which, despite a number of positive interludes and beautiful thematic writing, is overwhelmingly melancholic.

Although the opening movement contains one of Tchaikovsky's loveliest themes, a sense of intense internal struggle is conveyed by extremes of dynamics – no previous symphony had displayed such violent ranges between soft and loud. The second movement is a ghostly piece written in a rhythm that seems to be imitating a waltz but never quite becoming one. In the third movement a hectic march takes over, but any hints of momentary triumph are soon dispelled. Unusually the symphony ends with a slow movement, and it's the most anguished music Tchaikovsky ever composed – the emotional weight of this Adagio becomes ever more burdensome until, breaking down with grief, the music disappears into the darkness from which it emerged.

⭘ Russian National Orchestra; Pletnev (Virgin VC7 91487-2; with *Marche slave*).

The pianist Mikhael Pletnev's transition to conducting began with this staggering performance of the *Pathétique*, in which he achieves a perfect balance of strength and pathos. The orchestra's playing is breathtakingly urgent and the expressive range truly harrowing. It is disappointing to add that his subsequent Tchaikovsky symphony set for Deutsche Grammophon only hits such heights sporadically.

◑ Leningrad Philharmonic Orchestra; Mravinsky (Deutsche Grammophon 419 745-2; 2 CDs; with *Symphonies Nos. 4* & *5*).

Mravinsky recorded the *Pathétique* several times, and there is an authority to this performance which is awe-inspiring. The conductor's restraint pays great dividends: there is a convincing sense of emotional connection between the four movements which makes the final movement's despair all the more shattering.

ROMEO AND JULIET

The idea of a fantasy overture on Shakespeare's *Romeo and Juliet* was suggested to Tchaikovsky in 1869 by his friend and fellow composer Balakirev, who had no qualms about giving advice as to the exact form it should take. In fact Balakirev's suggestions were sound ones, and Tchaikovsky revised *Romeo and Juliet* twice, giving it its final form in 1880. It's rightly one of his most celebrated works, and possesses a vitality as well as a structural tightness that is very satisfying. Clearly its big love tune, with its rapturous swooping horn accompaniment, has become as big a cliché as the Mona Lisa. But it still retains its impact, largely because, before you get there, you travel through some startlingly vivid music in which tension and anticipation are brilliantly handled, first with the solemn, stately opening (a chorale represents Friar Lawrence) through more sunny expansive music into the feverish violence of the brawl scene. The work's relationship to the play is not a slavish one; nevertheless it's a highly sympathetic attempt to encapsulate in music the helter-skelter of emotions that Shakespeare drags us through and, on the whole, it's a highly successful one.

◑ London Symphony Orchestra; Dorati (Mercury 434 353-2; with *Symphony No. 6*).

Recorded in 1959, this fine performance still has enormous impact. Dorati's Tchaikovsky interpretations never push too hard on the throttle and this one is no exception. The pacing of the drama is always perfectly controlled and the final ringing chords bring to an end a perfectly integrated reading in which every element seems to grow out of another.

◑ Royal Liverpool Philharmonic Orchestra; Edwards (EMI CD-EMX 2152; with *Francesca da Rimini, 1812 Overture & Marche slave*).

Sian Edwards studied conducting with the great Russian conductor Evgeny Mravinsky, and her performances of the Russian repertoire have a genuinely idiomatic feel to them. This *Romeo and Juliet* has very strong contours and a firm sense of direction. It doesn't quite have the tautness of Dorati but it's still very impressive.

FRANCESCA DA RIMINI

It's hard not to see a special significance in Tchaikovsky's choice of Francesca da Rimini as the subject for his epic and sprawling tone poem of that name. In Dante's *Inferno* she and her lover Paolo are punished for their illicit passion by spinning for ever, locked in a permanent embrace. Written in 1876 at a time when Tchaikovsky was contemplating marriage as a means of providing a smokescreen for his homosexuality, it's an enormously passionate work which at times borders on the excessive. It begins with a kind of brooding horror which then rapidly builds to the brilliant depiction of the relentless whirlwind conveyed by a rich chromatic sweep of orchestral sound. Francesca's story appears as the still lyrical centre of the piece, a long cantabile melody (not dissimilar to Lensky's aria) which begins tentatively and goes through several guises before building to a richly passionate and intricately orchestrated climax. The storm music returns and culminates, with a terrible finality, in a coda of almost frantic desperation.

◑ New York Stadium Symphony Orchestra; Stokowski (Dell'Arte CDDA 9006; with *Hamlet*).

This work was a Leopold Stokowski speciality; one that matched his own oversized personality. He recorded it more than once, but this is the one to go for: a completely over-the-top performance, with some superbly deployed percussion, which vividly conjures up the Second Circle of Hell.

THE 1812 OVERTURE

The *1812 Overture* was composed by Tchaikovsky in 1881 with a great deal of reluctance. A state commission, the composer rattled it off in a week and was particularly scathing about it: "The overture will be very loud and noisy. . . but I wrote it with no warm feelings of love, and therefore there will probably be no artistic merits in it." Critics have tended to agree with him, but popular opinion deems it among his most thrilling works. Commemorating the Russian rout of Napoleon's forces, it weaves together a number of original and historically significant themes, including the *Marseillaise*, the Russian national anthem and an Orthodox hymn, into a veritable hodgepodge of breathless excitement culminating in the ringing of bells and the explosion of cannons. Bombastic vulgarity or history brought thrillingly to life? Who cares? In the right circumstances it's a supremely enjoyable and extravagant romp.

◑ Royal Liverpool Philharmonic Orchestra; Edwards (EMI CD-EMX 2152; with *Francesca da Rimini, Romeo and Juliet & Marche slave*).

Performances of the *1812 Overture* range from the sonically spectacular (Telarc warn that the cannon blasts may ruin your speakers) to the musically overserious. Edwards gets the balance right: in her performance the dances swing, the cavalry caper, and the cannons crash with the requisite degree of swagger and panache.

THE CONCERTOS

Tchaikovsky composed five concertos: three for piano, one for violin and the *Variations on a Rococo Theme*, which is for cello in all but name. The *Violin Concerto* and *Piano Concerto No. 1* are particularly grand conceptions, boasting an exceptional orchestral expertise in addition to the customary large-scale emotionalism. The second and third piano concertos, on the other hand, have never really entered the repertoire, but the *Rococo Variations*, Tchaikovsky's charming homage to the music of the eighteenth century, is something of a showcase for those cellists with the technique and style to play it.

PIANO CONCERTO NO. 1

Many of Tchaikovsky's best-known works received a rocky ride, but none came in for as much flak as the *Piano Concerto No. 1*, which Nikolai Rubinstein, the intended dedicatee, pronounced "worthless, unplayable and clumsy". He went on to declare the concerto so bad that it was not worth the effort of revision. Rubinstein later grandly agreed to play it on condition that Tchaikovsky changed the work to suit his requirements, but by this stage Tchaikovsky had rededicated the piece to his lifelong friend Sergei Taneyev. Tchaikovsky then changed his mind once more and replaced Taneyev's name with that of the German conductor Hans von Bülow, who cheerfully agreed to take on the responsibility for the premiere, which took place on October 13, 1875 in Boston. It went down a storm in the USA (though not at first in Russia), and in time even Rubinstein came to love it.

No one would argue that it's the most coherent of concertos – there's little discernible link between the opening movement and what follows, and the last movement is anticlimactic in all but the most sparkling performances. But Germanic rigour is not what Tchaikovsky is about, and the heroic bravado and typically Russian "big tunes" of the *Piano Concerto No. 1* have made it one of the most popular concertos. Incidentally, its most famous flourish, the grandiose piano chords which accompany the opening melody, was in large part the creation of Alexander Siloti (cousin and teacher of Rachmaninov), who helped arrange the score for its third edition. Siloti suggested that the repeated chords of Tchaikovsky's original be replaced by chords that covered the whole of the instrument's range; to his immense credit, Tchaikovsky agreed, thereby creating one of classical music's great attention-grabbing effects.

⊙ Argerich; Berlin Philharmonic Orchestra; Abbado (Deutsche Grammophon 449 816-2; with *The Nutcracker Suite* arranged for two pianos).

Perverse as it may sound, it is true to say that of the almost numberless recordings of this work that have been made, two artists dominate the field – Vladimir Horowitz and Martha Argerich. Both have recorded it several times and each performance has its own special insights. This recent live performance by Argerich is marked by a tumultuous drive – there's a feeling of the notes just tumbling out, but they're guided by a restless intelligence which, like that of Horowitz, is capable of making this music seem freshly written.

⊙ Horowitz; NBC Symphony Orchestra; Toscanini (RCA GD87992; with Beethoven, *Piano Concerto No. 5*).

In 1943 Vladimir Horowitz and his father-in-law Arturo Toscanini gave a performance of Tchaikovsky's *Piano Concerto No. 1* at the Carnegie Hall, to raise money for the war effort. Financially and artistically it was a stunning success. Ignore the constricted sound quality – this is the performance of a lifetime, bursting with energy and old-fashioned virtuosity, and there has never been a recording to compare with it.

THE VIOLIN CONCERTO

The history of Tchaikovsky's *Violin Concerto* is somewhat similar to that of the *Piano Concerto No. 1*. Written in just one month in 1877, it was intended for the violinist Leopold Auer (Heifetz's teacher), who promptly refused to perform it when he saw the difficulty of the solo part. Instead, it was Adolf Brodsky who gave the premiere in Vienna on December 4, 1881. Europe's pre-eminent music critic, Eduard Hanslick, was in the audience – "stinking music" was his verdict. The reaction was hardly unexpected, for the conservative Wagner-hating Hanslick was Brahms's biggest fan, whereas Tchaikovsky loathed everything that Brahms stood for – indeed, Tchaikovsky had been singularly unimpressed by the Brahms violin concerto, which had appeared in 1879. The two concertos are in the same key (the same key as Beethoven's masterpiece), but that's where the resemblance ends. Whereas tension and constraint are essential Brahms, Tchaikovsky creates a largely effortless, song-like part for the violin, while the orchestral score is packed with rumbustious energy and bold melodies. If the Brahms concerto is like a well-scripted dialogue, Tchaikovsky's is more like an uninhibited duet for soloist and orchestra.

⊙ Mullova; Boston Symphony Orchestra; Ozawa (Philips 416 821-2; with Sibelius, *Violin Concerto*).

Viktoria Mullova's thrilling interpretation is distinguished by ringing tone, impeccable technique and Russian flair; one of her first projects for Philips after winning the Tchaikovsky competition, it comes generously coupled with an equally fine account of Sibelius's concerto.

⊙ Perlman; Israel Philharmonic Orchestra; Mehta (EMI CDC7 54108-2; with a selection of solo pieces).

This live recording was made during Perlman's tour of Russia with the Israel Philharmonic. There's a palpable air of excitement and Perlman duly delivers with a thrillingly mercurial reading which ignites his audienc. The sound isn't brilliant, but this is music-making of the highest order.

⊙ Heifetz; London Philharmonic Orchestra; Barbirolli (Biddulph LAB026; with works by Wieniawski, Glazunov and Sarasate).

Heifetz recorded the work a number of times but the finest version is his first, made in 1937. With Barbirolli's sympathetic, flexible accompaniment, Heifetz hurls himself into the score, producing an extraordinarily exciting sound.

THE ROCOCO VARIATIONS

Tchaikovsky followed the unbridled passion and fury of *Francesca da Rimini* with the relatively cool and elegant *Rococo Variations*. As the title suggests, the inspiration is the eighteenth century, and the theme (Tchaikovsky's own) is a short and dainty dance tune similar to a gavotte. The seven variations which follow are refined and sophisticated, with only two of them – the one in C major and the one in D minor – really giving a glimpse of the composer's emotional side. Tchaikovsky originally wrote eight variations, but William Fitzenhagen, for whom they were written, discarded the last one and changed the order of the remaining seven – much to Tchaikovsky's annoyance. This is the most frequently performed version, although since its recent publication Tchaikovsky's original version is often preferred.

◑ **Rostropovich; Berlin Philharmonic Orchestra; Karajan** (Deutsche Grammophon 413 819-2; with Dvořák, *Cello Concerto*).

This is a wholeheartedly romantic account of Tchaikovsky's cello masterpiece, with Rostropovich wallowing in the slower variations while always keeping on the right side of mawkishness. His tone is warm but incisive and, if he doesn't quite make a convincing moment of the dreadfully difficult octave passage work in the coda (a Fitzenhagen addition), then few other cellists have managed it either. Karajan provides sympathetic support.

CHAMBER MUSIC

In the eyes of many of the Russian intelligentsia, chamber music was almost as trivial a genre as ballet, but Tchaikovsky created some fine work in this field, even without a strong indigenous tradition to support him. It's in his chamber music that Tchaikovsky's style is most clearly indebted to the great Germans, and to Brahms in particular but, as with everything he wrote, the overriding tone is quintessentially Russian. The three string quartets represent the best of his chamber music, and the sextet entitled *Souvenir de Florence* is also a splendid creation; his *Piano Trio* has quite a few admirers, but newcomers to Tchaikovsky are likely to find it a turgid exercise.

THE STRING QUARTETS

The *String Quartet No. 1* (1871) is Tchaikovsky's most attractive chamber work. The majority of the music is jauntily lyrical and folk-inspired, free of the melancholy and fatalism so common to Tchaikovsky. That said, its reputation rests on its incredibly mournful second movement, the Andante cantabile, which has become one of his most popular pieces – both in its original form and in orchestral transcription. The *Quartet No. 2*, written three years later, lacks the unity of the first and is notably less tuneful. The *Quartet No. 3* (1876), although well constructed, seems to strain for originality, and it is uncomfortably dominated by the first violin, no doubt in response to the death of the violinist Laub, the dedicatee of the quartet.

◑ **Borodin Quartet** (Melodiya 74321 18290-2; 2 CDs; with *Souvenir de Florence*).

The Borodin Quartet, widely acknowledged as one of the greatest chamber ensembles of the twentieth century, made these recordings between 1965 and 1980. The performances of the quartets approach perfection, especially the *Quartet No. 1*, and their account of the *Souvenir de Florence* sextet, with Rostropovich as the second cellist, is similarly superb, combining a supple instrumental balance and extraordinary fluidity of melodic line. Excellent sound quality and excellent value.

GEORG PHILIPP TELEMANN

(1681–1767)

Telemann was the greatest German composer of the first half of the eighteenth century – at least that's what they thought in Germany at the time. Nowadays his friend and colleague J.S. Bach (who became cantor at Leipzig only because Telemann turned it down) is regarded as infinitely superior, while Telemann is treated as an overproductive and superficial also-ran. He was certainly incredibly prolific, writing among other things about forty operas, forty-six Passions and five complete cycles of cantatas for the Lutheran liturgical year. And there's some justice to the charge of superficiality: able to write in pretty well any style that was demanded of him, he wrote no single work that stands out distinctly as his own. Yet, at its best, the music of Telemann has a bright melodiousness that looks forward to that of Haydn and Mozart.

Telemann was born at Magdeburg into an affluent middle-class background. Both his father and his brother, like several of their ancestors, were clergymen, and despite showing musical aptitude from an early age (he wrote his first opera aged 12),

Georg Philipp was intended for a similarly respectable career. In 1701 he went to the University of Leipzig to study law, but once his musical talents were discovered by others it was impossible for him to do anything else. He founded the Collegium Musicum (a society that gave public concerts and which Bach later directed), became organist of the Neue Kirche, then director of the Leipzig Opera, and so dominated the city's musical life that its ostensible music director, Johann Kuhnau, started to become extremely irritated. Telemann left Leipzig in 1705, and after positions at Sorau and Eisenach became music director of the city of Frankfurt, and Kapellmeister of the Barfusserkirche (church of the Barefoot Friars). He was there for nine years, from 1712 to 1721, before being invited by the city of Hamburg to be cantor of the Johanneum, the grammar school, and to be responsible for music at the city's five principal churches. A dispute with the civic authorities led to his applying for the Leipzig cantor's job in 1722, but things were patched up (his salary was increased) and he remained at Hamburg until his death, when he was succeeded in the post by his godson, C.P.E. Bach (see p.10).

CHORAL MUSIC

Telemann's prodigious output as a cantata composer is not quite so impressive once you realize that he was mostly writing solo cantatas, and not complex large-scale works like Bach's cantatas. Yet he did write plenty of big choral works, and among the most interesting of these is the oratorio, the *Hamburgische Kapitansmusik*, written to celebrate the centenary gala dinner of the Hamburg civic militia. The breezy and idiomatic text, which finally exhorts everybody to enjoy their food, is Telemann's own. Its recitatives, arias and chorales evoke an atmosphere that is sometimes solemn but more often festive, and at times sounds very close to Handel. There is also a distinctly Handelian feel to the delightful *Magnificat in C*, an early work probably written when Telemann was still a student in Leipzig.

⊙ Magnificat in C; Hamburgische Kapitansmusik 1730: van der Sluis, Pushee, Jochens, Langshaw, van der Kamp; Alsfelder Vokalensemble; Barockorchester Bremen; Helbich (CPO 999 109-2).

Both works get highly spirited and engaging performances on this CD, with outstanding contributions from the soloists. The *Magnificat* is more obviously appealing and contains some extremely beautiful arias, notably the alto's *Quia respexit* and the soprano's *Et misericordia*. The *Hamburgische Kapitansmusik* is very much more light-hearted, with several light and bouncy choruses, including a delightful "Chorus of the Joyful", which the Alsfelder Vokalensemble bring off with real aplomb.

ORCHESTRAL MUSIC

In Telemann's time the dominant orchestral forms were the concerto and the orchestral suite, which was made up of a French-style overture and a series of formalized dance movements. One of Telemann's employers, Count Erdmann II of Promnitz, distinctly favoured the French style of music and Telemann consequently composed several suites for him. It was while at the count's court at Sorau that he came into contact with the indigenous music of Upper Silesia, and folk elements – both rhythmic and instrumental – became a feature of his music throughout the rest of his career. In his concertos the influence is more Italian than French, with the model of Vivaldi particularly apparent in the way he frequently employs quite strange combinations of instruments as the solo group.

⊙ Concerto in D Major; La Bouffonne Suite; Grillen-Symphonie; Alster-Ouverture: Collegium Musicum 90; Standage (Chandos CHAN 0457).

This disc really shows off Telemann's versatility, from the rather formal and slightly bland elegance of the *Bouffonne Suite* to the inspired and bizarre scoring of the delightful *Grillen-Symphonie*, in which a double bass, a piccolo and a chalumeau (an early clarinet) combine with a string quartet to startling effect. Best and most striking of all is the *Alster-Ouverture*, a piece of light-hearted scene-painting with one movement of weird harmonies and unexpected key changes representing the music of the local peasantry, while another, full of spiky dissonances, conjures up the sounds of frogs and crows. Utterly compelling, and played with spirit and enthusiasm by Collegium Musicum 90.

CHAMBER MUSIC

Telemann published an enormous amount of chamber music for a wide range of musical combinations and in several different styles, including sonatas, quartets and Corellian trio sonatas. Much of it was aimed at amateur players and was not especially difficult. For this reason it was highly successful and his fame became so widespread that when his largest collection of chamber music, *Musique de table*, was published in 1733, 52 of the 206 subscriptions came from abroad. The predominant style is what the eighteenth-century dubbed "galant", meaning music in which simple melodies and clear textures convey a mood of easy-going elegance and charm.

⊙ Chamber Music: Ensemble Florilegium (Channel Classics CCS 5093).

The Ensemble Florilegium disc is a fine selection of consistently first-rate and beautiful music, even though much of it recalls other composers. Four of the five works use a recorder or flute to carry the melody, the exception being the *Sonata in F Major*, an uncannily accurate evocation of Corelli's chamber music. Other highlights are the stately elegance of the *Sixth Paris Quartet*, and the nervous intensity of the A minor concerto's opening movement – wonderfully atmospheric music, and this time sounding like nobody else.

SOLO INSTRUMENTAL MUSIC

Of the relatively small amount of solo instrumental music that Telemann wrote, the *Twelve Fantasies* for flute and the *Twelve Fantasies* for solo violin are outstanding. The latter pieces invite comparison with J.S. Bach's slightly earlier works for solo violin, but Telemann's approach is rather different. Though the first six fantasies have contrapuntal elements, including fugues, they don't have Bach's sense of organic development (the exception is the last one), placing more emphasis on contrast between the movements. Fantasies six to twelve are in more of a galant style, full of delightfully bright and sprightly melodies. They have neither the emotional range nor the musical complexity of Bach's solo violin pieces, but these fantasias are among Telemann's most personal and rewarding works.

Twelve Fantasies for Violin: Manze (Harmonia Mundi HMU 907137; with *Gulliver Suite*).

Andrew Manze's informative sleevenotes suggest that Baroque unaccompanied instrumental works derived from a lost tradition of extemporizing. His performance certainly possesses a refreshing air of spontaneity and élan, as well as a gracious wit and a seemingly effortless virtuosity. As a fill-up he performs, with Caroline Balding, a suite for two violins inspired by *Gulliver's Travels*.

MICHAEL TIPPETT

(1905–1998)

Michael Tippett was nearly 30 years old when Elgar died, yet he was more obviously a modern composer than his immediate contemporaries Walton and Britten. A late starter, he did not produce his first recognized score until he was 30, and attracted virtually no public attention until he was nearly 40. When he did, however, his neo-Romantic notions of self-expression attracted considerable, if far from universal, enthusiam. Tippett always remained a maverick belonging to no category except his own. On the one hand he had little sympathy with the ideas of modernity represented by serialism, but on the other he wrote music that is markedly more complex and demanding than that of a traditionalist like Malcolm Arnold (see p.8).

He did not begin to study music properly until he was 18 years old, but then applied himself vigorously to the mechanics and fundamentals of composition while at the Royal College of Music. In characteristic style he passed up the chance to study with Vaughan Williams, fearing to become a mere imitator of such a powerful figure. A spell as a schoolteacher and the first performances of his own works was followed by further study with R.O. Morris, a leading expert on counterpoint. It was only in the mid-1930s that his work began to develop a personality of its own, culminating in the remarkable *Concerto for Double String Orchestra* (1939).

Tippett was one of the most widely read and intellectually curious of modern composers, and his beliefs play a conspicuous part in much of his work. In coming to terms with his homosexuality he underwent Jungian analysis and this had the most profound and far-reaching effect on his music. Much of his work, beginning with the oratorio *A Child of Our Time* (1941), represents a quest for wholeness, a reconciliation of the dark and the light contained – he believed – within everyone. A committed pacifist, he had a spell in Wormwood Scrubs in World War II for refusing to carry out his non-combatant military duties.

Apart from composing, Tippett exerted a profound influence as a teacher, most notably in his eleven years as Director of Music at Morley College London. As great an encourager of amateurs as of professionals, he was a passionate if erratic conductor, with a special passion for the music of his great English forebear Henry Purcell.

In 1946, inspired by the success of his friend Benjamin Britten's *Peter Grimes*, Tippett began work on his first full-scale opera, *A Midsummer Marriage*. Though it contained some of the most refulgently lyrical music by an English composer, its libretto (which he wrote himself) was attacked by most critics for its alleged obscurity and pretentiousness – a criticism that was repeated for all his subsequent operas with the possible exception of *King Priam* (1961). Even so, by the 1960s he was at last beginning to be acknowledged as a major figure

SUZIE MAEDER/LEBRECHT COLLECTION

Michael Tippett conducting students at the Royal Academy of Music, 1985

in his native England and, following a trip to America in 1965, something of a cult figure in the US.

In the end it is the humanity that shines out of Tippett's complicated music, an essentially optimistic and affirmative vision that has attracted as many people as it has irritated: "I have to sing songs for those who can't sing for themselves. Those songs come from the torments and horrors that have happened. I can't lose faith in humanity."

THE MIDSUMMER MARRIAGE

The Midsummer Marriage is a quest opera inspired by two great fantasies: Mozart's *The Magic Flute*, in the way two sets of lovers undergo a trial before they can be united; and Shakespeare's *A Midsummer Night's Dream*, in the way that the lovers' world overlaps with a supernatural world which may be a dream. Tippett also pays tribute to T.S. Eliot by borrowing the Fisher King and the clairvoyant Sosostris from his poem *The Waste Land*. More important is the debt to Jung, whose concept of archetypes dominates the opera's supernatural landscape. In the opera the principal set of lovers, Jennifer and Mark, reach a spiritual maturity by recognizing those elements of each other that exist in themselves, and in this they are obliquely assisted by the He-Ancient and the She-Ancient – guardians of the temple in the woods – and opposed by Jenifer's father, the dark and materialistic King Fisher. Central to the work are the "Four Ritual Dances" that enact the constant seasonal cycle of death and rebirth.

Critics were initially baffled by all this symbolism, but what makes *The Midsummer Marriage* convincing is the sheer vigour and richness of the music, which conveys – more clearly than the words – a genuine sense of transcendence, and which reaches extraordinary heights of ecstatic lyricism. Tippett's score is determinedly tonal and lyrical, with its roots planted firmly in the English pastoral tradition – indeed the slow-moving peroration that Madame Sosostris sings in Act III sounds close to Elgar in the way its luscious harmonies maximize the spiritual intensity. It is true that Tippett sometimes adds more and more layers until the idea gets smothered, but ultimately this is one of the most joyous and affirmative of all post-war operas.

⊙ Carlyle, Harwood, Remedios, Burrows, Herincx; Royal Opera House Chorus and Orchestra; Davis
(Lyrita SRCD 2217; 2 CDs).

Recorded in 1971, this fine performance stands as one of Colin Davis's finest achievements. Resisting the temptation to wallow in the splendour of the writing, Davis's disciplined approach illuminates the often thickly Romantic orchestration. Alberto Remedios brings a true sense of impetuous vitality to Mark, and is nicely matched by the delicate beauty of Joan Carlyle's Jenifer.

⊙ Ritual Dances and Sosostris's Aria from the Midsummer Marriage: Hodgson; Chorus and Orchestra of Opera North; Tippett (Nimbus 5217; with *Praeludium for Brass, Bells and Percussion & Suite for the Birthday of Prince Charles*).

If you want a brief sample of the opera, then this disc is the place to start. The *Ritual Dances*, which are frequently performed as concert pieces, sound particularly mysterious and evocative under Tippett's direction, and Alfreda Hodgson gives a powerful account of Sosostris's aria (though unfortunately the sleevenotes do not include the words).

KING PRIAM

The initally negative reaction to his first opera failed to deter Tippett, but his second, *King Priam*, marked a quite radical shift from the lyrical and celebratory to the bitter and clamorous. The opera was first performed at the Coventry Festival of 1962, which celebrated the building of a new cathedral from the ashes of the old one destroyed in World War II. On the advice of theatre director Peter Brook, Tippett turned to an ancient legend, that of the fall of Troy after ten years of war. It is a story and a landscape filled with the suffering and pain of seemingly arbitrary and pointless killing, presented from the perspective of the losers and concentrating on the way individual choices have profound and far-reaching effects beyond those who made them.

The most obvious musical difference between *King Priam* and *The Midsummer Marriage* is the way the lush and largely contrapuntal orchestral writing of the earlier work has been replaced by something leaner and more focused. The raucous fanfare of brass with which the opera opens sets the dark background mood for the whole of the work, against which individual scenes are set in relief. In some instances Tippett allocates particular instrumental combinations for different characters, as in the sombre but sensual cello writing that he gives to Andromache. But for characters of greater complexity he employs a variety of musical signifiers. Achilles gets the most lyrical moment in the opera, the guitar-accompanied "O rich-soiled land", and also the most chilling, when – hearing of Patroclus's death – he puts on his armour and gives forth his terrible war cry.

⊙ Bailey, Harper, Allen, Palmer, Langridge, Minton, Tear, Roberts, Murray, Wilson-Johnson; London Sinfonietta Chorus; London Sinfonietta; Atherton (Chandos CHAN 9406/7; 2 CDs).

This outstanding recording was originally issued on Argo in 1981, and it's hard to imagine it being bettered. It boasts a cast that represents the cream of English singing talent, with Norman Bailey bringing both authority and vulnerability to Priam, and Robert Tear making a commanding Achilles. The extraordinary tension and violence of Tippett's score is brought out by conductor David Atherton with considerable energy and panache.

A CHILD OF OUR TIME

Tippett began his oratorio *A Child of Our Time* at the beginning of World War II but its first performance did not happen until 1944. During the Depression years Tippett had been profoundly affected by the social deprivation caused by unemployment, but it was the 1938 Nazi pogrom known as Kristallnacht that was the work's real catalyst. T.S. Eliot agreed to write the libretto but when he saw Tippett's scenario he felt that the composer's own text would be less distractingly poetic. Tippett modelled his composition on Handel's *Messiah* and the Bach *Passions*, employing recitatives, arias and dramatic choruses. In place of Bach's Lutheran chorales he had the inspired idea of punctuating the work with five negro spirituals, to which each episode returns. There's a wintery feel to the work and many of Tippett's operatic ideas are foreshadowed in the powerfully emotional and dramatic music. The most telling line – "I would know my shadow and my light, so shall I at last be whole" – stands as a kind of encapsulation of Tippett's beliefs.

⊙ Robinson, Walker, Garrison, Cheek; City of Birmingham Symphony Orchestra and Chorus; Tippett (Collins Classics 1339-2).

There are now six recordings of Tippett's choral masterpieces in the catalogue, all of which have good points. This one, conducted by the composer when he was 85, has the advantage of a straightforward directness and sincerity. It's a studio recording but the spacious sound creates the ambience of a live performance.

ORCHESTRAL WORKS

Beethoven was the young Tippett's musical idol and his first three symphonies (spread over nearly thirty years) are knotty contrapuntal reinterpretations of the classical, while the single-movement fourth (1977) is looser in form, closer to a symphonic poem. On the whole Tippett's smaller orchestral works have proved more popular, in particular the *Concerto for Double String Orchestra* (1939) and the *Fantasia Concertante on a Theme of Corelli* (1953). The former is Tippett's finest work from the 1930s, a rhythmically dynamic homage to the Baroque concerto grosso whose two outer movements have a gloriously spring-heeled linearity which frame the serenely melodious (and unmistakably English) Adagio cantabile.

Commissioned by the Edinburgh Festival in 1953 to celebrate the tercentenary of Corelli's birth the *Fantasia Concertante on a Theme of Corelli* is a densely elaborate set of variations for two violins and cello and double string orchestra on a theme from Corelli's *Concerto Grosso Op. 6 No. 2*. It's a less obviously neo-classical work than the *Concerto for Double String Orchestra*, having the same textural density of *The Midsummer Marriage* as well as a similar sense of symbolic transformation. The work progresses through five sections of increasingly fanciful flights of imagination, culminating in a Bach-quoting fugue that subsides into a radiant lyricism before returning to an almost exact replica of the initial variation.

Tippett's other major orchestral work from this period is the *Piano Concerto*. In the composer's own words, this piece "had its precise moment of conception years before, when I was listening to a rehearsal of Beethoven's *Fourth Piano Concerto* with Gieseking, who had just returned to England after the war. I felt moved to create a concerto in which once again the piano might sing." The first of the three movements (the longest at around fifteen minutes) sets smooth-flowing lines of melody against agitated orchestral effects, creating an engaging sense of momentum. Overall the concerto is a heavily contrapuntal composition, but in the slow movement it approaches a more rhapsodic sense of form; the last movement is basically an orchestral rondo, culminating in a marvellous duet for piano and celesta.

◑ **Concerto for Double String Orchestra; Fantasia Concertante on a Theme of Corelli; Piano Concerto: Moscow Chamber Orchestra; Barshai; Bath Festival Orchestra; Tippett; Philharmonia; Ogdon; Davis** (EMI CMS 7 63522-2; 2 CDs; with *Piano Sonatas Nos. 1 & 2, String Quartet No. 1*):

This double-CD set, from 1960s performances, is the best way to familiarize yourself with Tippett's range. There's a bright and exuberant account of the *Concerto for Double String Orchestra* form the Moscow Chamber Orchestra, while the composer's own recording of the *Fantasia Concertante* is easily the finest, with exemplary lightness and clarity. The two violinists, Yehudi Menuhin and Robert Masters, play with great refinement. John Ogdon's playing of the *Piano Concerto* is exceptional, and Colin Davis, a renowned interpreter of Tippett's music, conducts this piece with real energy – the sharply defined colours of the finale are especially marvellous.

STRING QUARTETS

Spanning his entire creative life, Tippett's five string quartets allow you to chart the evolution of his distinctive, essentially contrapuntal, style in which the example of Beethoven's chamber music is never too far away. The first three are the most appealing, especially the tuneful *Quartet No. 1* of 1935 (the first piece Tippett was prepared to acknowledge), which successfully reconciles the influences of Sibelius, Beethoven and English folk song. The second and third quartets, dating from 1942 and 1946, are grandly expressive creations, distinguished by close attention to the textures and intricacies of part-writing – three of the movements of *Quartet No. 3*, for example, are fugal in structure. The last two quartets are more difficult. The *Quartet No. 4* is an abrasive piece that illustrates a sometimes too obvious cradle-to-grave programme (also the theme of the *Symphony No. 4*), while *Quartet No. 5*, using material from the opera *New Year*, clearly aspires to a visionary radiance which is only fitfully achieved.

○ **Lindsay Quartet** (ASV CDDCS231; 2 CDs).

In general Tippett's energetic counterpoint is well-suited to the vigorous and exuberant style of playing of the Lindsay Quartet, for whom the fourth and fifth quartets were written specifically. Although other fine performances of the quartets exist on CD, these have an authority and a confidence that is extremely persuasive.

MICHAEL TORKE

(1961–)

Michael Torke, the brightest star to emerge on the American music scene in the past decade, has been described as both a post-minimalist and a post-modernist. The former label has been applied to him because his highly energetic music appears to have its roots in the tightly organized rhythmic systems of Glass and Reich, while the latter is due to his cool, polystylistic eclecticism. One of his first works to make a strong impact, *The Yellow Pages* (1986), typically combines a bass line taken from a Chaka Khan song with the bright, clean sonorities of Stravinsky's neo-classical phase carried along by a pulsating, toe-tapping beat. His music is an exhilarating mix that seems to work best in the textually uncluttered world of chamber music, although several of Torke's full orchestral scores have proved popular as ballet music – especially with the American choreographer Peter Martins.

Born and brought up in Milwaukee, Wisconsin, Torke was something of a prodigy, studying the piano and composing from the age of 5. As a teenager he won prizes for both piano and composition and began learning the bassoon. Surprisingly, considering his later development, popular music made very little impact on him at this time and it was only when attending the Eastman School of Music that he discovered jazz and rock and began attempting to instil some of their vitality and spontaneity into his own music. Further study took place at Yale University with Jacob Druckman and Martin Bresnick, and it was there that he wrote *The Yellow Pages* and his first "colour" work for orchestra, *Ecstatic Orange* (1985).

The many colour references in Torke's work reflect his interest in synesthesia – the ability to perceive one sensory stimulus in terms of another. Works like *Ecstatic Orange* and *Bright Blue Music* (1985) are his attempt to make a coherent aural equivalent of specific colour sensations. With their rich orchestration (the *New York Times* called him "the Ravel of his generation"), the "colour" pieces constitute Torke's most self-conscious mixing of disparate stylistic elements. In *Ash* (1989), for instance, it's as if the first movement of a rather nondescript nineteenth-century symphony has got permanently locked into its opening moments. This is postmodernism at its most pompous and banal, and fortunately an avenue of exploration that Torke seems to have abandoned. When his oddball stylistic matches and unpredictable rhythmic variations are applied with a lighter touch the results can be both thrilling and illuminating.

CHAMBER WORKS

In nearly all of Torke's music there's an implicit tension between a kind of free-form spontaneity and the tight structural control that he likes to impose on his material. An early work, the jazz-inspired *Vanada* (1984), bustles with a restless urban energy but, like fast-moving people in a modern city, each element knows precisely where it is

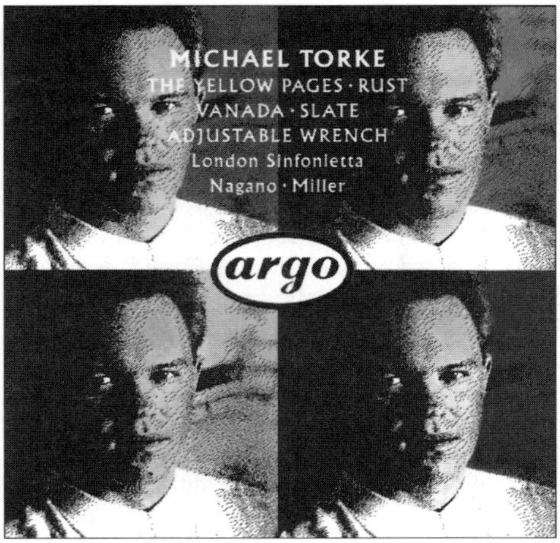

heading. It's one of Torke's harshest scores, close in spirit to the aggressive European minimalism of Louis Andriessen (see p.6). *The Yellow Pages* – all bright, breezy syncopation – is a more typical work, recalling Copland in its fresh-faced and unstoppable exuberance. An American tint can also be heard in *Adjustable Wrench* (1987), which introduces a new melodic element (it's easy to imagine a vocal line sung over the opening section), but also shows Torke the stylistic magpie, changing the mood by introducing the unexpected, such as a bass-guitar riff followed by sustained brass chords big-band-style. In *Rust* (1989) there's a return to the metallic sound-world of *Vanada*, but broken into by a section of surprising lyricism. Torke's great gift is that he can unify apparently contradictory material into coherent statements while maintaining the clarity and integrity of individual elements. Comparable to the collages of Robert Rauschenberg, it's a manner that in its unblinking confidence seems to encapsulate a very particular American optimism.

⊙ The Yellow Pages; Rust; Vanada; Slate: London Sinfonietta; Nagano; Miller (Argo 430 209-2).

Argo's beautifully balanced and crystalline sound is perfectly suited to Torke's high-energy music, permitting every strand of his often complex textures to emerge clean and true. The performances are hard to fault – the energy and chutzpah of the playing is completely winning, in *Adjustable Wrench* particularly.

MARK-ANTHONY TURNAGE

(1960–)

Mark-Anthony Turnage exploded into prominence in 1988 when his opera *Greek*, a brash and brutish vision of Thatcher's Britain, was premiered first in Munich and then in London. A retelling of the Oedipus myth set in the East End of London, *Greek* was attacked by some critics (including Steven Berkoff, on whose play it was based) for being crude, strident and simplistic. But even those who disliked it were impressed by the brilliance of the orchestral writing – music that pinpointed a mood or an emotion with more directness than the work's rather relentless vocal style. Since then, Turnage has expressed considerable ambivalence about opera as a genre, while steadily refining his orchestral writing into a powerful mix of smouldering colours and dark intensity.

Brought up in Grays, Essex (one of the gloomier London suburbs), Turnage began composition lessons with Oliver Knussen at the age of 15, later continuing his studies at the Royal College of Music, where Knussen taught. In 1983 a scholarship to Tanglewood led to further study with Gunther Schuller and Hans Werner Henze (see p.192), who commissioned *Greek* for the Munich Biennale. An even more profound influence on the evolution of Turnage's style was jazz. Increasingly, his orchestral scores seemed to occupy the same emotional terrain as the work of artists like Gil Evans and Miles Davis, and it is clear that Turnage regards the directness of expression and formal freedom of jazz as better able to communicate the anxieties and ambiguities of modern urban life than what he sees as the formulaic language of classic modernism.

Another catalyst in the development of Turnage's mature style was a four-year residency as Composer in Association with the City of Birmingham Symphony Orchestra. This afforded him the luxury of working out ideas in close collaboration with performers, and resulted in increasingly bold and complex orchestral textures. A similar arrangement with English National Opera has been rather more problematic. Despite the supportive environment of ENO's Contemporary Opera Studio, the first two works produced there were disappointing and Turnage's most effective recent score has been *Blood on the Floor* (1996), a powerful work for jazz soloists and orchestra. A full-length opera, an adaptation of Sean O'Casey's play *The Silver Tassie*, is scheduled for performance in 1998.

DECCA/DAVID SCHEINMANN

Mark-Anthony Turnage

ORCHESTRAL MUSIC

Night Dances (1981), the first orchestral piece to get Turnage noticed, already displays many typical stylistic touches. Written "to evoke feelings and emotions aroused by my first encounter with Black music", this is an overwhelmingly atmospheric work that employs a highly original mesh of instrumental voices – shimmering percussion, an amplified solo group and offstage string quintet – that manages to be both sensual and slightly unnerving. A more visceral side to the composer can be heard in *Three Screaming Popes* (1988), a reaction to the painter Francis Bacon's violent reworking of Velázquez. This is closer to the strident world of *Greek* – bold exuberant gestures are interspersed with moments of calm solemnity to generate a mounting mood of menace and foreboding, culminating in the raucous interruption of loud instrumental "screams".

Time and again, the raw and anguished eloquence of the saxophone – an instrument with which he strongly identifies – figures strongly in Turnage's work and in 1994 he wrote what is, in effect, a saxophone concerto, entitled *Your Rockaby*. Partly inspired by a Samuel Beckett monologue of the same name, *Your Rockaby* pitches the solitary voice of the saxophone against a kaleidoscopic orchestral backdrop which is part Ravel, part urban sleaze. This tendency to place the violent in close proximity to the tender can be heard at its most extreme in a recent, highly personal work. *Blood on the Floor* (1996) takes its title from another Bacon painting but much of it is a response by Turnage to his brother's death from a heroin overdose. Here the jazz element takes centre stage in the shape of three jazz soloists who interact, concertante style, with the bustling, abrasive sounds of the ensemble. It is Turnage's richest score to date, climaxing in the last of its seven movements, *Dispelling the Fears*, in a duet for two trumpets which gradually moves from harsh insistency to touching lyrical rapture.

O Your Rockaby; Night Dances; Dispelling the Fears: BBC Symphony Orchestra; London Sinfonietta; Philharmonia Orchestra; Davis, Knussen, Harding (Argo 452 598-2).

This is the first disc to be released by Argo following the company's exclusive contract with Turnage. It's not hard to see what he gets from the deal – the sound is stunning, combining amazing lucidity with warmth and naturalness despite being performed by different ensembles in different locations. The performances seem well and truly lived-in (contemporary works often suffer from under-rehearsal), in particular, the soloists – saxophonist Martin Robertson in *Your Rockaby* and trumpeters John Wallace and Håkan Hardenberger in *Dispelling the Fears* – bring a degree of finesse and nuance which raise both these works to a very high level of achievement.

VIKTOR ULLMANN

(1898–1944)

In 1938, mirroring the infamous *Entartete Kunst* (Degenerate Art) exhibition in Munich, the Nazis organized an exhibition of *Entartete Musik* in Düsseldorf, where the public was invited to sneer at recordings of the offending creations. "Degenerate" in this instance meant anything vaguely avant-garde, anything with jazz or black American associations, and absolutely anything written by a Jew. Blacklisted composers such as Korngold, Schoenberg, Weill, Zemlinsky and Hindemith soon emigrated; some of the lesser known were to endure marginalization and neglect, but at least they escaped with their lives. Others, such as Hans Krása, Erwin Schullhof and Viktor Ullmann, were not so lucky. A generation of composers was annihilated by the Nazis, and it's only in recent years that their music has been rediscovered, so that at last we can assess the true history of twentieth-century music in central Europe.

Ullmann was born into a German-speaking family in Teschen (now Těšín) on the Moravian–Polish border, but received his musical education in Vienna, where he joined Schoenberg's composition class in 1918. Schoenberg, Zemlinsky and Berg all became personal friends and strong influences, though Ullmann's highly chromatic music resisted the atonality of the Second Viennese School and always retained a strong tonal centre. In the 1920s he worked as assistant to Zemlinsky in Prague, then took up posts in Aussig and Zürich before giving up his musical career to run the Anthroposophic Society's bookshop in Stuttgart, devoting himself to the dissemination of Rudolf Steiner's philosophy of self-knowledge. Hitler's rise to power forced him back to Prague in 1933, but it was to prove a temporary haven.

After the Nazi occupation of Prague it is thought he tried, but failed, to emigrate. Soon after he was sent to the Jewish ghetto established by the Nazis in the town of Terezín, otherwise known as Theresienstadt. On his arrival in September 1942, Ullmann was excused the customary work assignment and asked to organize concerts and musical activities. He wrote reviews and set up a group to give performances of works by Terezín composers – Gideon Klein, Hans Krása, Pavel Haas and Ullmann himself – as well as by Mahler, Schoenberg and Zemlinsky. During his two years in Terezín, Ullmann was more prolific than at any other time in his life, writing three piano sonatas, the beautiful *String Quartet No. 3,* several songs and orchestral scores, and perhaps his most remarkable work, the satirical opera *Der Kaiser von Atlantis*. In October 1944, not long after the first performance of *Der Kaiser* had been banned by the SS, Ullmann and the majority of the composers and musicians in Terezín were transported to the gas chambers of Auschwitz.

DER KAISER VON ATLANTIS

Ullmann wrote two operas in Prague immediately before the war, *Der Sturz des Antichrist* (The Fall of the Antichrist) and *Der zerbrochene Krug* (The Broken Jug), but his most remarkable work, *Der Kaiser von Atlantis* (The Emperor of Atlantis) was written in the appalling conditions of the Terezín ghetto and designed for performance there.

The opera portrays a mad, paranoid Emperor, fighting wars on all fronts until Death, "an old-fashioned craftsman of dying", refuses to work any longer, in protest at the infernal mechanization of killing. With the sick and wounded now condemned to live on in agony, the Emperor pleads with Death to return to work, but he will do so only on one condition – that the Emperor agrees to be his first victim. The Emperor's demise in the final scene echoes the Nazi defeats on the eastern and western fronts.

Der Sturz des Antichrist had foundered because the antichrist could have been interpreted as a reference to Hitler, and *Der Kaiser* similarly fell foul of the authorities – the opera was rehearsed up to the dress rehearsal, but then banned after the slow-witted SS officers at last saw it as a satire of their leader. *Der Kaiser von Atlantis* finally got its first performance in 1975, proving to be a very powerful work on stage. Ullmann's score is an eclectic mixture of cabaret music, pastiche (there is a daring minor-key version of the German national anthem), operetta and lush Romanticism, for a band that includes saxophone, banjo and harmonium. Death is depicted in music of ecstatic beauty, dripping with sumptuous harmonies – not a fearsome character, but a reliable and faithful friend, merciful and welcoming. The ultimate message is one of hope mingled with resignation, as Death himself declares: "It's not the other side we need fear, but rather this world that is veiled in darkest shadow."

O Mazura, Kraus, Berry, Vermillion; Leipzig Gewandhaus Orchestra; Zagrosek (Decca 440 854-2; with *Hölderlin-Lieder*).

The premiere recording of *Der Kaiser* is extremely fine, though not ideal. The serious moments are very well done, but the lighter ones lack that final sense of dangerous fun that the score really needs. Walter Berry as Death is too old and crusty and doesn't bring over the lyrical seductiveness of his music. That said, the other voices are well-suited, and Michael Kraus is deeply powerful in the Emperor's farewell aria, which is very difficult to bring off (both versions are included). The closing chorale is unutterably moving. Included as a fill-up are Ullmann's three *Hölderlin-Lieder*, which are well performed by Iris Vermillion.

ORCHESTRAL WORKS

Ullmann wrote some impressive orchestral pieces before the war, including the uncompromising *Variations and Double Fugue on a Piano Piece of Schoenberg* (1934) and the powerfully lyrical *Piano Concerto* (1939). As with his operas, though, the extremity of Terezín produced his finest work.

The manuscript of Ullmann's *Piano Sonata No. 7*, which he completed only a few weeks before he was transported to Auschwitz, was covered with notes for its orchestration into a symphony. Now completed by the German composer Bernhard Wulff, this *Symphony in D* is a final summation of Ullmann's savagely curtailed career – including a quotation from *Der Sturz des Antichrist* and a waltz from Heuberger's operetta *Der Opernball*, which Ullmann worked on in Prague, it ends with an impressive *Variations and Fugue on a Hebrew Folksong*. The source tune for this resilient final movement, a Zionist song which would have been familiar to many inmates of Terezín, is transformed into a Czech Hussite hymn whose message of national liberation would also not have been lost on the symphony's intended audience.

O Symphony in D; Piano Concerto; Variations and Double Fugue on a Piano Piece of Schoenberg: Richter; Brno Philharmonic; Yinon (Bayer BR 100 228).

This premiere recording of the *Symphony in D* reveals it as a very fine work indeed. The conductor, Israel Yinon, keeps a grip on the symphony's very fluid scoring, in which melodic fragments dart from one instrument to another. This recording includes the *Variations and Double Fugue on a Piano Piece of Schoenberg* and the *Piano Concerto* – the latter given a fine performance by Konrad Richter, who finds just the right balance of power and gentle lyricism. This is the best all-round CD of Ullmann's works.

CHAMBER MUSIC

Ullmann's most accomplished piece in Terezín, and the one most likely to enter the standard concert repertoire, is the *String Quartet No. 3*, which was written in January 1943 although it isn't known whether it was ever performed in Terezín. It has a beautiful lyrical opening tinged with a melancholy typical of his Viennese background, while in the slow movement he ventures into the world of Schoenberg and Berg with a twelve-note motif, though he always retains an underlying sense of tonality. Ullmann's seven piano sonatas – three written in Terezín, four before his incarceration – are of more specialized interest, but they show him as a distinctive voice in the central European musical tradition. The writing can seem a little indigestible at first, but it mellows on further listening.

⊙ String Quartet No. 3; Piano Sonatas Nos. 5–7: Group for New Music; Kolben; Kraus (Koch International 3-7109-2).

The Koch CD – Volume 1 in the company's Terezín Music Anthology – presents Ullmann's chamber music from Terezín in very fine performances. In the luscious opening of the quartet the independent lines of the four instruments are beautifully blended, the melodic lines moving effortlessly from one player to another. Edith Kraus, who plays the sixth sonata, premiered this piece in the ghetto, and it's the most attractive of the three sonatas on this disc (the seventh sounds a bit awkward once you've heard its orchestrated version, the *Symphony in D*).

EDGARD VARÈSE

(1883–1965)

As early as 1917 Edgard Varèse spoke of instruments which could offer "a whole new world of unsuspecting sounds", foreshadowing the use of synthesizers and computers in contemporary music. He devoted his life to new ideas, new instruments and new music, and though his output is fairly meagre by comparison with many of this century's great innovators he was to be a prime influence on the postwar avant-garde, rejecting melody in favour of a rhythmically propelled aural abstraction. "I am not a musician," he once said. "I work with rhythms, frequencies and intensities. Tunes are the gossips in music."

Of Franco-Italian parentage (the pianist Alfred Cortot was a cousin), Varèse's serious musical studies began at the Schola Cantorum in Paris, where his independent spirit led to clashes with the director, Vincent d'Indy. By 1909 he was in Berlin, where he became friends with Busoni (see p.94) and was impressed by his ideas for "a new music". Varèse found employment there as a conductor but by 1913 he was back in Paris. He attended the riotous premiere of *The Rite of Spring*, a work with which he felt an immediate sympathy – the audience around him screamed abuse at the stage, but Varèse remarked: "The music seemed very natural to me."

Conscripted in 1914, he was discharged through illness and escaped to America the following year. Varèse's arrival in New York – where he was to spend the rest of his life – was the start of his career as an evangelist for new music. He organized an International Composers Guild for the presentation of works by Schoenberg, Stravinsky and Webern, and his first major composition, *Amériques* (1922), displayed his espousal of Stravinsky's anti-Romantic intensity, using plentiful brass and woodwind to invoke the pounding presence of the new world. "I refuse to limit myself to sounds that have already been heard," he declared. After labouring for years on *Arcana,* a huge work for 120 musicians but no string sections, his search for new sonorities led to *Ionisation* (1931), in which sirens, anvils, gourds and sleigh bells compete for attention.

In the 1930s and 1940s he explored the sonic potential of various electromechanical devices and new instruments such as the theremin and the ondes Martenot – the latter famously employed by Messiaen in a number of works (see p.256). In the 1950s Varèse went on to compose *Déserts* (1954), a pioneering work for magnetic tape and in 1958 the vast *Poème Électronique* for tape and 400 loudspeakers. This was co-created with Xenakis (see p.482) as the main feature of the Philips Pavilion at the Brussels World's Fair of that year. He died seven years later, hailed as a visionary by Stockhausen, the composer whose work did most to realize Varèse's vision of an electronic future.

AMÉRIQUES & IONISATION

Varèse's search for new sonic possibilities was influenced by Luigi Russolo, the Italian Futurist who created noise machines and whose manifesto *The Art of Noises* proposed a new world of organized sound which simulated the disparate soundscape of modern urban life. In *Amériques*, premiered by members of the Philadelphia Orchestra under Stokowski, Varèse calls for nine percussionists including two sets of timpani, a siren and the roar of a lion (later changed to ondes Martenot). It's a work of raw rhythmic energy, with the occasional moments of lyrical repose, which evokes the brash, angular and violent sounds of the city. Varèse described it as being about "new worlds on earth, in the sky or in the minds of men" and it marks the beginning of his fascination with the expressive possibilities of percussion.

In *Ionisation* (1931) Varèse dispenses with all conventional instruments in favour of percussion. The title rather unhelpfully comes from physics, and refers to the process by which an atom liberates an electron and assumes a positive electric charge. The 37 percussion instruments include bells, piano, glockenspiel, Chinese blocks, anvils, bongos, tam-tams, all manner of drums and two sirens. Its highly concentrated six minutes contrasts an astonishing range of sonorities with great virtuosity: a particular tension is set up between sounds that have a hard, abrasive quality and those of a more mellow and softer character. The result suggests an often terrifying dreamscape where images of primeval jungle, of modern urban bustle, and even of warfare, jostle for dominance in the listener's imagination. *Ionisation* was greeted with horror and alarm at its first performance at Carnegie Hall in 1933.

◑ **Amériques; Arcana; Density 21.5; Intégrales; Ionisation; Octandre; Offrandes: Beauregard; Yakar New York Philharmonic & Ensemble Intercontemporain; Boulez** (Sony SMK 45844).

Since Varèse's death, Pierre Boulez has been one of his greatest champions and he regularly programmed his music when conductor of the New York Philharmonic in the 1970s. This disc contains most of Varèse's major works in powerful and authoritative performances. It also contains some of the smaller, but no less challenging, chamber pieces like the meditative *Density 21.5* for solo flute and the haunting *Octandre* for wind instruments. High-definition remastering lends the music a deeper, more detailed sound than it had on vinyl. *Amériques* and *Ionisation* are also available on separate CDs in Erato's two-disc survey of Varèse's output (complete but for two minor pieces): the performances are fine, but the Boulez disc is preferable in its selection of pieces.

RALPH VAUGHAN WILLIAMS

(1872–1958)

With his friend and colleague Gustav Holst, Vaughan Williams spent many years researching and cataloguing English traditional songs that had never previously been written down, thereby spurring a resurgence in English music comparable to the similar folk-inspired movements within eastern and central Europe. He stands, alongside Elgar and Britten, as one of the most popular of twentieth-century English composers, thanks to music that is affirmatively humanistic and individual. Though an almost exact contemporary of Schoenberg, Vaughan Williams was never an experimental composer ("Why need music be original to be enjoyed?" he once asked). But it is wrong to categorize him – as do his detractors – as a nostalgic sentimentalist, forever evoking a fantasy idyll of a rural England that never was. His range is far wider than such a caricature, above all in his nine symphonies, the scope and invention of which can be compared to the seven symphonies of Sibelius – a composer he greatly admired.

As a composer Vaughan Williams showed an early talent but was something of a slow developer. Two bouts of study at the Royal College of Music (first with Parry, then with Stanford) were interrupted by a spell at Cambridge where he read history and obtained his Bachelor of Music degree. He then travelled to Germany for further study with Max Bruch, and as late as 1908 he was in France for lessons in orchestration from Ravel (three years his junior). Ravel, in particular, helped to make Vaughan Williams's sometimes cloggy textures much more transparent, and on his return to England he wrote one of his best-known and most beautiful works – the *Fantasia on a Theme by Thomas Tallis*. By 1914 he had produced a considerable body of music, including two symphonies, and was beginning to find an audience. After World War I – during which he served in the medical corps and the artillery – he threw himself into musical activity, not just composing but also conducting the Bach Choir and Handel Society, and teaching at the Royal College.

During the 1920s his music began to be heard overseas, with notable performances of his work being given in Salzburg, Venice, Prague, Geneva and the US. By the middle of the following decade he was established as the figurehead of English music, and was very much in demand as a conductor of his own work. His recordings – notably his 1937 version of the *Symphony No. 4* – testify to a greater talent than he would have admitted. He once began a concert saying, "You start and I'll follow", a self-deprecating joke typical of his modesty.

Success eluded him as an opera composer in spite of several attempts at the genre. Nevertheless much of his finest music can be found in his operas: in particular the short, bleak *Riders to the Sea* (1932) and the epic *The Pilgrim's Progress* (1951). The latter was based on John Bunyan's seventeenth-century religious "novel", a work Vaughan Williams was obsessed with for much of his life, and despite the fact that he referred to himself as an agnostic his several settings of Christian texts display a fervour and an intensity of feeling that seems almost mystical. Like his younger colleague Tippett (see p.436) – who he stood up for during World War II – he was a lifelong socialist and possessed an essentially optimistic and affirmative view of humanity. He once defined his role with the words, "the composer must not shut himself up and think of art; he must live with his fellows and make his art an expression of the whole life of the community."

THE SYMPHONIES AND ORCHESTRAL MUSIC

Without doubt Vaughan Williams's nine symphonies (which span a period of some fifty years) form the finest cycle ever produced in England. Ironically so because, as a young composer, he had no intention of writing any. All nine have a distinctive and individual voice, although the first two – the choral *Sea Symphony* and the exuberant *London Symphony* – reveal a small but discernible debt to Elgar. All are worth hearing, but two in particular – Nos. 3 and 5 – stand out as unquestioned masterpieces.

The reputation that Vaughan Williams gained for having a limited range exclusively based around folk-inspired modal melodies (what Elizabeth Lutyens called "cow-pat music") partly derives from the "rustic" opera *Hugh the Drover* (good tunes, patronizing libretto) as well as from a series of orchestral miniatures that do indeed conjure up an Edenic picture of England. Vaughan Williams certainly had a visionary (rather than a fantasy) picture of the countryside as a haven against the creeping industrialization that seemed to be destroying it. This vision is exemplified by the rhapsodic *The Lark Ascending*, and less poetically in the *Five Variants of "Dives and Lazarus"* based on a folk song that had greatly impressed him. His sense of a native tradition also surfaces in his interest in early English composers, finding expression in both his work on the English hymnal and in his much-loved orchestral masterpiece *Fantasia on a Theme by Thomas Tallis*.

O Complete Symphonies: Philharmonia Chorus & Orchestra; Slatkin (RCA 09026 61196-2; 6 CDs).

Vaughan Williams has been fortunate in interpreters of his symphonies. In his lifetime both Barbirolli and Boult were skilful advocates who consistently championed them. More recently both André Previn and Bernard Haitink have brought fresh insights to several of them, and there are currently no less than five complete cycles. Of these, the one conducted by Leonard Slatkin is the most consistently satisfying. Slatkin never flinches from the darker and more aggressive moments in these works – the fourth and sixth symphonies, in particular, have a violence that belies Vaughan Williams cosy pastoral image.

SYMPHONY NO. 3 – THE PASTORAL

Vaughan Williams's belief "that to attach meanings to music is a mistake" could well have been prompted by reactions to his *Symphony No. 3*. Completed in 1921, its four slow movements and modal melodies suggesting folk song (though none are present) were long taken to be a kind of homage to the English countryside. In fact the work was his highly personal and deeply felt response to the recent war: "a great deal of it incubated when I used to go up night after night with the ambulance waggon at Écoivres . . . and there was a wonderful Corot-like landscape in the sunset – it's not really lambkins frisking at all as most people take for granted." Neither is it the sound of guns and actual battle (though the second movement contains a distant bugle call), but rather an internal monologue encapsulating feelings of loneliness, pain and sorrow. But despite its slowness and introspection, its finale seems to offer an image of hope and reconciliation as a lone soprano intones a wordless text.

O Hohenfeld; Philharmonia; Slatkin (RCA 09026 61194-2; with *Symphony No. 4* and *Fantasia on "Greensleeves"*).

Under Slatkin the Philharmonia strings produce a marvellously rich and warm sound that seems to temper the elegiac mood of the work with an element of joyful rapture. This disc, one of the highlights of an outstanding cycle, also contains an uncompromisingly caustic account of *Symphony No. 4*.

◑ **Harper; London Symphony Orchestra; Previn** (RCA GD90503; with *Symphony No. 4*).

A wonderfully spirited, and yet controlled, performance from Previn and the LSO from the early 1970s. Textures are beautifully limpid and clear but there is also a greater sense of urgency and drama in this reading which is very revealing.

SYMPHONY NO. 5

The *Symphony No. 5* was commenced in 1938, while Vaughan Williams was at work on *The Pilgrim's Progress*. Beginning to doubt that he would ever complete his magnum opus, he used some of the opera's material for the symphony, which he completed in 1943 but then revised in 1951. The final version is perhaps the best of Vaughan Williams's nine symphonies. The first movement begins with a particularly haunting idea, stated softly by the horns, which is followed by ominously shifting music that foreshadows what's to come beyond the ghostly, muted Scherzo. Everything is leading towards the huge span of the wonderful slow movement, where Vaughan Williams introduces overwhelmingly emotive solos for oboe and violin. Its mood of reverence extends to the finale, a harmonic and rhythmic kaleidoscope that builds to an exalted climax before subsiding into a quietly contemplative state.

○ **Philharmonia; Slatkin** (RCA RD60556; with *Symphony No. 6*).

In Slatkin's performance of the *Symphony No. 5* the scale and sense of structure are brilliantly handled and the Philharmonia play with absolute conviction – there are few more moving accounts of the slow movement and the finale is realized with heartbreaking restraint. It's coupled with a similarly urgent and well-recorded account of the angry sixth symphony, a work that clearly bears the marks of the war years.

◑ **Royal Liverpool Philharmonic; Handley** (EMI CD-EMX 9512; with *Flos Campi*).

Handley's performance of *Symphony No.5* reveals a similar skill to Slatkin in the ability to present a broad view of the work's architecture and yet one with every important detail in place. It's part of a complete cycle which is outstanding value at mid-price.

FANTASIA ON A THEME BY THOMAS TALLIS

Termed a "Jacobean Fantasy" by the composer, the *Fantasia on a Theme by Thomas Tallis* (1910) is Vaughan Williams's homage to the music of Renaissance England. Specifically it grew out of his work editing the English Hymnal, in the process of which he came across a melody that Thomas Tallis had written as a psalm setting in 1567. Vaughan Williams took this basic theme and developed it into music that is both intensely devotional and sumptuously romantic. Commissioned for the Three Choirs Festival in Gloucester, the *Fantasia* is scored for two string orchestras, the smaller of which was arranged to produce an antiphonal effect, even in acoustics less resonant than the cathedral in which it received its first performance. The *Fantasia* also assigns separate parts to a string quartet, and the numerous independent voices confused many of those present at the premiere – one critic called it "a queer, mad work by an odd fellow from Chelsea". He was probably in the majority, but the work soon secured Vaughan Williams's place as the spiritual leader of English music, and nowadays it's by far the best known of all his works.

○ **New Queen's Hall Orchestra; Wordsworth** (Argo 440 116-2; with *The Lark Ascending, Five Variations on "Dives and Lazarus", Norfolk Rhapsody 1, In the Fen Country & Fantasia on "Greensleeves"*).

This account, played on period instruments and supposedly in period style, has a uniquely sweet sound, and conductor Barry Wordsworth encourages just about the right amount of gushing. Including performances of five other immensely engaging orchestral pieces (see below for *The Lark Ascending*), this well-engineered and generous CD makes a perfect introduction to Vaughan Williams.

THE LARK ASCENDING

Four years after the *Tallis Fantasia*, Vaughan Williams composed *The Lark Ascending* – one of his most simple and direct utterances but also one of the most effective. Described as a Romance for violin and small orchestra, the score was prefaced with some lines by George Meredith that conclude "Our valley is his golden cup/, And he the wine which overflows/To lift us with him when he goes./ Till lost on his aerial rings/In light, and then the fancy rings". A brilliant evocation of the song of the lark, the piece opens with a short orchestral introduction before holding a sustained chord over which the solo violin, tentatively at first, begins its short trilling birdsong phrases which gradually build into an upwardly climbing cadenza of great eloquence. The feel of a hot and hazy summer's day is created by the lilting phrase which marks the orchestra's return. The middle section culminates in a sturdy folk-like melody before the "lark-song" cadenza returns once more.

○ **New Queen's Hall Orchestra; Wordsworth** (Argo 440 116-2; with *Tallis Fantasia, Five Variations on "Dives and Lazarus", Norfolk Rhapsody 1, In the Fen Country & Fantasia on "Greensleeves"*).

Hagai Shaham is the beguiling soloist in an enraptured performance of *The Lark Ascending*. An extra summery glow seems to emanate from the orchestral sound, making a fitting backdrop for the violin's fluttering pyrotechnics.

VOCAL AND CHORAL MUSIC

Like Elgar and Parry, Vaughan Williams projected a rather hearty public persona that served to disguise an acute artistic sensitivity. He was a widely read man, and his choice of texts for musical setting reflect this. As an agnostic from a nonconformist background, he tended to favour writers with an intensely individual vision, most notably William Blake and John Bunyan. When a young man he was passionate about Walt Whitman (as was Delius) and used his verses on several occasions, notably for the choral *Sea Symphony*, the cantata *Dona Nobis Pacem* and *Toward the Unknown Region*. He also set – as did many of his contemporaries – several verses from A.E.Housman's *A Shropshire Lad*, but interestingly balanced the more morbid side of Housman's output with examples of his rarer rapturous moments.

SANCTA CIVITAS

Vaughan Williams wrote many choral works, but none have established the same kind of position in the repertoire as Elgar's *The Dream of Gerontius*, Walton's *Belshazzar's Feast* or Britten's *War Requiem*. His own favourite among his choral works, and the one that most exemplifies the emotional intensity of his beliefs is the oratorio *Sancta Civitas* (The Holy City, 1925). Unfortunately its shortness (it lasts about thirty minutes), its difficulty and the large forces required mean that performances are infrequent. Using words from the Book of Revelation and Walt Whitman, it presents an incredibly vivid vision of the afterlife which, though it begins and ends in a concentrated stillness, is far from the warm enveloping sound-world of *Gerontius*. *Sancta Civitas* contains some of Vaughan Williams's most startling and most sensuous music and its very concentration makes it an unforgettably powerful experience in performance.

○ Langridge, Terfel; St Paul's Cathedral Choir; London Symphony Chorus and Orchestra; Hickox (EMI CDC7 54788-2; with *Dona Nobis Pacem*).

This marvellous performance (one of only two in the catalogue) should do much to re-establish this work at the very centre of Vaughan Williams's achievements. Hickox marshals his forces brilliantly, keeping the textures ringingly clear, and it is hard to imagine two more incisive soloists than Philip Langridge and Bryn Terfel.

SONGS

Solo songs make up a substantial part of Vaughan Williams's output, of which the Housman settings *On Wenlock Edge* (1908) are the best known. Four years earlier he wrote another fine cycle, *Songs of Travel*, to words by R.L. Stevenson, which Vaughan Williams scholar Michael Kennedy has called "a kind of English *Winterreise*". They combine a typically Edwardian manly vigour with an element of melancholy. At their best (as in *The Vagabond* and *Bright is the Ring of Words*) they reveal an acute feeling for word-setting and a rare melodic gift.

On Wenlock Edge was written soon after returning from his studies with Ravel and it contains what Vaughan Williams referred to as "several atmospheric effects". These can be discerned in the scoring for piano quintet, and in certain delicate pictorial passages – the wind blowing in the title song, the chiming of bells in Bredon Hill. The latter is the longest and most telling song, in which the composer brilliantly captures the changes of mood from the joy of an English summer's day to the wintery presence of death, with the tolling of bells finally taking on a doom-laden oppressive quality.

○ Songs of Travel: Terfel, Martineau (Deutsche Grammophon 445 946-2; with songs by Butterworth, Ireland and Finzi).

There are several fine recordings of the *Songs of Travel*, but this performance by baritone Bryn Terfel has an extra dimension to it that makes the others seem pallid. He's almost unique among modern singers in making every word sound like a real expression of his thoughts and the result, here, is to make what is good (but not great) material sound absolutely first-rate.

◑ On Wenlock Edge: Partridge; Music Group of London (EMI CDM5 655589-2; with *Ten Blake Songs, Four Hymns* and *Merciless Beauty*).

The lyric tenor of Ian Partridge was at its prime in the early 1970s when this recording was made. It's a very English voice – not unlike Peter Pears – with a purity of tone and near-perfect control and understated fervour that is heard at its best in *Bredon Hill* and the short intensely beautiful *From Far, from eve, From Morning*. He is wonderfully supported by the Music Group of London.

GIUSEPPE VERDI

(1813–1901)

Verdi's operas are paragons of high Romanticism, with their lavish emotionalism, demanding vocal and instrumental writing, complex plots, high-voltage characterizations and so forth. Yet political engagement was not a notable feature of the lives of most Romantic composers, and Verdi was a supremely political artist. In the aftermath of the Napoleonic wars, Italy was divided into a mosaic of kingdoms and duchies, a situation that prevailed for most of the century, in the face of a burgeoning movement for national unifica-

LEBRECHT COLLECTION

Giuseppe Verdi

tion. Many of the plots of Verdi's earlier operas can be read as allegories related to the aspirations of the Italian people – the well-known *Chorus of the Hebrew Slaves* from *Nabucco* struck a particular chord in an audience living under the rule of countless princelings and foreign oppressors.

Censorship was a bugbear: although Verdi managed to smuggle a topical message into such works as *Nabucco* and *La Battaglia di Legnano*, where centuries of history provided a disguise of sorts, in other instances his plots had to be tampered with in order to ensure performance. Such interference achieved nothing, however. As the nationalist movement gathered force in the 1850s and 1860s, and Victor Emmanuel, liberal ruler of Piedmont, became the popular choice for king of united Italy, the chant "Viva Verdi!" was heard at performances of his work and on the streets – the composer's name being also an acronym for "Vittorio Emmanuele, re d'Italia" (Victor Emmanuel, King of Italy). Verdi himself came to be seen as a figurehead for the unification movement, and once the goal had been achieved he became an active politician, and was elected to the Italian senate in 1874.

There is little in Verdi's early upbringing that foreshadows the cosmopolitan operatic master. His parents ran a village inn in the northern plains of Parma, and everything about his education and early life suggests provincialism. After private studies in Milan (he failed to gain entrance to the city's conservatory) he returned to his home area as music director for the town of Busseto, where he yearned to get back to the Lombard capital. In the end he found it impossible to stifle his ambition to see an opera of his performed at La Scala: in 1839 he resigned his post in Busseto and headed with his family back to Milan. He was fortunate in that his first opera, *Oberto*, was almost immediately accepted for performance, even though his previous compositions of any consequence amounted to just a few academic exercises and liturgical works. *Oberto* was first heard in November of the same year, and it made the Milanese public sit up and take notice of the ambitious 26-year-old.

His second opera, *Il Giorno di Regno* (1840), was a flop, but two years later he produced *Nabucco*, which really saw his career take off. In the wake of its success came a steady stream of commissions from other Italian cities and from abroad, resulting in thirteen operas in just eight years: *I Lombardi alla prima crociata* (1843), *Ernani* (1844), *I due Foscari* (1844), *Giovanna d'Arco* (1845), *Alzira* (1845), *Attila* (1846), *Macbeth* (1847), *I Masnadieri* (1847), *Jérusalem* (1847), *Il Corsaro* (1848), *La Battaglia di Legnano* (1849), *Luisa Miller* (1849) and *Stiffelio* (1850). By the end of this sequence his mastery of the operatic stage was well established and he had earned so much money he could have retired had he wished. The pace of composition relaxed in the 1850s, but it was in this period that Verdi wrote his most popular operas, beginning with the trio of *Rigoletto* (1851), *Il Trovatore* (1853) and *La Traviata* (1853), followed by, among others *Simon Boccanegra* (1857), *Un Ballo in Maschera* (1859), *La Forza del Destino* (1862), *Don Carlos* (1867) and *Aida* (1871).

There then followed a gap of some fifteen years before the premiere of another Verdi opera, a phase during which he composed his only non-operatic work of any standing, the *Requiem* (1874), and otherwise concentrated on revising some of his earlier works, whenever new productions or new translations of the libretto brought an opportunity to tighten up structure or expand scenes. *Macbeth*, *La Forza del Destino*, *Simon Boccanegra* and *Don Carlos* were all overhauled at this time. The revised *Boccanegra* benefited from the involvement of the poet and composer Arrigo Boito, who provided the librettos for Verdi's last two operas, *Otello* (1886) and *Falstaff* (1893). His final years were spent on more religious music, the *Four Sacred Pieces*, and masterminding the foundation of the Casa di Riposa, a retirement home for musicians in Milan, funded by his royalties. He died of a stroke in January in 1901 and was buried in the grounds of the Casa di Riposa; a quarter of a million people attended his funeral cortège.

THE OPERAS

Verdi's fame rests as much on his stagecraft as on his music, for with Verdi, more than with any of his Italian predecessors, drama and music are fused into an indivisible entity. It's an indication of the speed of his advances that in his youth Rossini's operas were all the rage, with their concentration on vocal display and decoration at the expense of expressiveness. By the 1830s the trend had shifted, as more dramatic operas of Bellini (see p.45) and Donizetti (see p.123) swept Rossini's style aside, displacing light-hearted comedy with tragedies of star-crossed lovers and grandiose historical settings. During his time studying in Milan, Verdi had a subscription seat at La Scala and thus became thoroughly conversant with all the latest developments.

Accordingly, even his earliest operas revealed a mature knowledge of what was possible on stage. Admittedly, in his earlier work the style is not always up to the demands of the drama: *Macbeth*, for example, for all its wonderful tunes and its dramatic speed, often resorts to rum-tum-tum accompaniments that suggest comedy more than tragedy. It's a stylistic mannerism that even affects mature works such as *La Traviata* and *Rigoletto*, but the late works are masterpieces of consistency and continuity – by the time he came to write *Otello* and *Falstaff*, he could make each act a continuous flow from which it is virtually impossible to extract individual arias without destroying their meaning. By this stage, too, Verdi's music had gained a much broader harmonic vocabulary, with more subtlety and ease than the rather four-square harmonic language of the early works. And of course one skill he always displayed in profusion was his talent for melody, and it is the striking originality of Verdi's arias and choruses that have made him, with Puccini, the most popular operatic composer in history.

RIGOLETTO

Rigoletto was the work that revealed Verdi's operatic maturity, and it's always been one of his most popular. The tragic tale of the cursed hunchback jester Rigoletto, the heinous Duke of Mantua, and Rigoletto's daughter Gilda, was based on Victor Hugo's *Le Roi s'amuse*, but thanks to the Venetian censors the action had to be moved from the French royal court to the sixteenth-century ducal court of Mantua. This was admittedly closer to home for its audience, but at least the setting didn't depict a womanizing monarch – Venice was at that time ruled by the monarchist Austrians. *Rigoletto* is an immensely accessible opera, moving swiftly and coherently through a series of memorable arias, choruses and confrontations. Yet it's also a very dark work: Gilda sacrifices her life to the philandering duke, whose role is assigned to a tenor, normally the voice of the good guy. The villain gets the opera's best tune as well – La donna è mobile (Women are Fickle).

O Gobbi, Callas, di Stefano, Zaccaria; La Scala Chorus and Orchestra; Serafin (EMI CDS5 56327-2; 2 CDs).

Of the star Italian tenors of the 1950s who recorded the role of the Duke, only Giuseppe di Stefano achieved the right mix of licentiousness, cruelty and charm. The other lead roles on this recording are similarly superb: Callas is by far the most convincing Gilda on disc (the death scene is sickeningly real), and Gobbi is the most subtle Rigoletto – tormented and vengeful, but tender and loving. Serafin gives smooth and attentive support. The mono sound is perfectly acceptable.

◑ Milnes, Sutherland, Pavarotti, Talvela; Ambrosian Opera Chorus, London Symphony Orchestra; Bonynge (Decca 414 269-2; 2 CDs).

This 1971 recording was Pavarotti's first go at the Duke, and his firmness of tone, confident extension (listen to the unending high C in "La donna") and beautiful portamento make this Duke a dangerously beguiling villain. Sherrill Milnes is outstanding too – a wounded, roaring, spitting Rigoletto – and Sutherland produces some beautfiul sounds, even if her characterization of Gilda is rather thin.

IL TROVATORE

Best known for its supposedly incomprehensible plot, *Il Trovatore* (The Troubadour) is another fast-moving drama of revenge with a parent–child relationship at its centre, this time one of mother (Azucena) and supposed son (Manrico, the "troubadour" of the title). In some ways the opera backslides into pre-*Rigoletto* freestanding musical forms, in that the arias tend to hold up the action rather than move it on. Nonetheless the characterization is strong, and there is novelty in making a mezzo-soprano (Azucena) the centre of attention rather than a soprano, just as the baritone had usurped the lead role from the more glamorous tenors in *Rigoletto* and *Macbeth*. *Il Trovatore* too has one of Verdi's big tunes – this time the "Anvil Chorus".

◑ Bonisolli, Price, Cappuccilli, Obraztsova; Berlin Chorus; Berlin Philharmonic Orchestra; Karajan (EMI CMS7 69311-2; 2 CDs).

In Karajan's second version of *Il Trovatore*, recorded after a 1977 Salzburg production, passions are unrelievedly intense and the violence of the orchestral playing is electrifying. Such a background places enormous strain on the soloists, but Leontyne Price as Leonora is more than up to the challenge and gives a glowing performance, while Obraztsova is a forthright Azucena, rich in voice and vital in character. Bonisolli's tenor is too thick to give the music its natural ring, but he manages the notes and copes well with Karajan's intense direction.

O Corelli, Tucci, Merrill, Simionato; Rome Opera Chorus and Orchestra; Schippers (EMI CMS7 69311-2; 2 CDs).

Franco Corelli was the most famous Manrico of his day, and rightly so – the thrill of his voice is not easily forgotten and he makes a sultry, erotic and blisteringly powerful hero. Gabriella Tucci sings well but is too light for Leonora, and she's slightly lost next to Corelli; Simionato, a throaty Azucena, tries too hard; but Robert Merrill is grandly unpleasant as di Luna. There are some strange cuts, and the conducting is solid rather than inspired, but Corelli's performance would make up for greater weaknesses than these.

LA TRAVIATA

After a pair of operas with historic settings, Verdi wrote one placed in his own time. *La Traviata* (The Fallen Woman) is based on Alexandre Dumas the Younger's play *La Dame aux camélias*, about a consumptive "society hostess" (Violetta) whose love for upper-class Alfredo provokes the

disapproval of his class-conscious father, Germont. After the costume melodrama of *Rigoletto* and *Trovatore*, *Traviata* is a much more intimate piece, played out among the three principals against a high-society background. Nowadays this is perhaps Verdi's most popular opera, yet initially it was one of his few flops, though the reasons for its failure are to be found in the inadequacy of the original casting (including an implausibly unfrail Violetta) and in the fact that the director had for no obvious reason set it in the eighteenth rather than the nineteenth century. The role of Violetta is one of the most demanding in the repertoire, and there's scarcely a high-profile soprano who hasn't at some time in her career had a go at one of her poignant arias.

O Gheorghiu, Lopardo, Nucci; Covent Garden Chorus and Orchestra; Solti (Decca 448 119-2; 2 CDs).

Violetta was the role that established the international reputation of Angela Gheorghiu, and this 1992 recording shows what the fuss is all about – she has a gorgeous voice but, like Callas she does much more with that voice than merely convey the notes. She acts with every inflection. Her Alfredo is Frank Lopardo, whose youthful and warm voice mark him out as a potentially great tenor. Leo Nucci is a bland Germont, but Georg Solti gives a splendidly vital and well-paced account of the score.

O Callas, di Stefano, Bastianini; La Scala Chorus and Orchestra; Giulini (EMI CMS7 63628-2; 2 CDs).

Callas recorded the role of Violetta several times, but this live recording of the famous 1955 Visconti production stands out for its completeness and intimacy. At once naive and worldly, Callas creates an image as varied and contradictory as Verdi intended, and her voice contains a rainbow of tones, with none of the steel to which it was later prone. For all the forcing and curious diction, di Stefano is a worthy lover, and Bastianini's Germont is a powerful reading. Giulini shapes and phrases with intelligence, and the entire production hums with energy. The sound quality is as you'd expect, but really that isn't the main consideration.

SIMON BOCCANEGRA

Simon Boccanegra explores one of Verdi's favourite themes, the conflict between the private and public faces of rulers. Here the arena is fourteenth-century Genoa, where the action centres on the clash between its lowly born doge (Boccanegra) and the nobility (represented by Fiesco), with the complication that Boccanegra has fathered a daughter (Amelia) with Fiesco's daughter. The opera was not a great success when first staged, but was improved immeasurably in Verdi's 1881 revision and, although it is an opera perhaps more admired than loved, it comes close to the final Shakespearean operas in its scale and dramatic characterization – and it does have some of Verdi's most glorious duets.

O Cappuccilli, Freni, Carreras, Ghiaurov; La Scala Chorus & Orchestra; Abbado (Deutsche Grammophon 449 752-2; 2 CDs).

Made in 1977 and based around a La Scala production, this is a classic modern Verdi recording. The sound is warm, and it makes the most of the moments of high drama, with Piero Cappuccilli an intense, touching doge and Mirella Freni a fresh-sounding Amelia. Abbado's wonderfully fluent direction gives shape and life to this troublesome opera.

UN BALLO IN MASCHERA

Verdi had to change many things in his operas to suit the censors, and this happened most famously with *Un Ballo in Maschera* (A Masked Ball). It was originally based on a fictionalized account of the assassination of King Gustavus III of Sweden at a court ball in 1789, but the very idea of a king's murder being portrayed on stage was anathema to the Neapolitan censors. The action was duly transferred to Boston before the American War of Independence, with the king becoming Riccardo, the English governor. It is still performed in both versions – only the characters' names are different.

History records the incident as a motiveless killing by one of Gustavus's officers, but Verdi's opera suggests that Gustavus was killed in revenge for seducing the officer's wife (despite the historical evidence that his proclivities led elsewhere), and also throws in a few extra characters in the form of Oscar, the king's page, and the witch Ulrica, who foresees the murder. Much of the music emphasizes the dark inevitability of the king's fate, but the grimness is leavened by the mischievous character of Oscar (a soprano role), and by some wonderful ensembles and love duets.

◑ **Arroyo, Domingo, Cappuccilli, Grist; Royal Opera House Chorus; New Philharmonia; Muti** (EMI CMS5 66510-2; 2 CDs).

This mid-1970s recording benefits from determined, characterful direction, with Riccardo Muti generating animation through a close attention to detail and structure. Muti's cast is dominated by Domingo in a role that suited his youthful, technically secure voice, and the love duet is loaded with languorous eroticism. Arroyo is a fine Amelia, with an ideal balance of declamation and sweetness.

◑ **Price, Bergonzi, Merrill, Grist, Verrett; RCA Italiana Opera Orchestra and Chorus; Leinsdorf** (RCA GD86645; 2 CDs).

Apart from Carlo Bergonzi's gorgeous tenor voice, the charms of this set are Leontyne Price's husky Amelia, Robert Merrill's thrilling Renato and Shirley Verrett's overripe Ulrica. Some may balk at Leinsdorf's conducting, which seems in a perpetual state of nervous agitation, but it's an undeniably exciting ride, captured with bright if close sound.

LA FORZA DEL DESTINO

La Forza del Destino (The Force of Destiny) is another of Verdi's turbulent family dramas: the central character, Don Carlo, is tracking across country after country in pursuit of Don Alvaro, who has eloped with his sister, Leonora, and accidentally killed their father. He then unwittingly befriends the man he is seeking, ensuring calamity on all fronts. The opera was written to a commission from St Petersburg in 1862, but seven years later Verdi revised the ending and other passages for performances in Milan; it is this marginally less bleak version which is most often heard today. The time-spread of the action gives *La Forza del Destino* a rather disjointed narrative, and Verdi's use of recurring motifs (such as the fate themes in the well-known overture) doesn't create a cohesion comparable to that of Wagner's developmental leitmotifs, but it's an intriguing experiment in through-composed opera. It's not the place to start with Verdi, but you'll appreciate its boldness after you've heard his later work.

◑ **Price, Domingo, Milnes, Giaiotti; John Alldis Chorus; London Symphony Orchestra; Levine** (RCA 74321 39502-2; 3 CDs).

This 1976 production (of an uncut score) is among the most celebrated of all Verdi recordings. Levine shows a sure grasp of structure, giving the work's disparate elements a cumulative cohesion that no other conductor has managed. Domingo is the finest post-war Don Alvaro – his vocal weight and grand phrasing are nowhere better heard than in the big aria, which he pulls off with unflustered virtuosity. Leontyne Price sounds magnificent, singing Leonora with great intelligence and feeling, while Milnes gets the measure of Carlo's twisted, hateful personality.

○ **Callas, Tucker, Tagliabue, Rossi-Lemeni; La Scala Chorus and Orchestra; Serafin** (EMI CDS7 47581-8; 3 CDs).

Leonora is another of those roles that Callas was born to play: her kaleidoscopic range of inflection brings real tragedy to this portrayal, and her development of the character from lover to hermit is beyond comparison. Richard Tucker is by no means perfect as Alvaro but he is vigorous and smooth throughout. Serafin's direction is well balanced and quite energetic.

DON CARLOS

Verdi's next opera, a work on an even larger scale, was originally composed in French for Paris, but then was pruned drastically following its poor reception – hence the existence of two versions, the French-language *Don Carlos* and the four-act Italian-language *Don Carlo*. (To complicate things further, several recent productions and recordings have used an Italian translation of the Paris text.) Like *Un Ballo in Maschera*, its starting point is a fictional account of events in the lives of historical figures. Here Verdi adapts Schiller's play about the sixteenth-century Spanish king Philip II and his son Don Carlos, whose fateful love for his young stepmother, Elisabeth, leads to his downfall. The welter of political intrigue and emotional drama is most effective in the five-act version, from which Verdi later excised some scenes crucial to the dangerous relationship between Don Carlos and Elisabeth.

◑ **Carreras, Freni, Baltsa, Cappuccilli, Ghiaurov, Raimondi, van Dam, Gruberova; Berlin Opera Chorus; Berlin Philharmonic Orchestra; Karajan** (EMI CMS7 69304-2; 3 CDs).

Karajan's passion makes this 1978 recording of the four-act *Don Carlo* an unbelievably intense experience. The young Carreras is in magnificent voice, easily the most impressive Don Carlo on record, and the rest of the cast are almost as impressive, reaching almost hysterical levels of dramatic tension.

○ **Bergonzi, Tebaldi, Bumbry, Fischer-Dieskau, Ghiaurov, Talvela; Royal Opera House Chorus and Orchestra; Solti** (Decca 421 114-2: 3 CDs).

Despite the pushy direction of Georg Solti, this is the best of the various five-act versions – it's an Italian-language translation of the Paris score. Bergonzi is an excellent Carlo – powerful and authoritative, but sensitive enough to justify Elisabeth's love. Tebaldi and Bumbry generate a lot of excitement, though not as much as Freni and Baltsa, and the rest of the cast cannot match the Karajan team.

○ **Alagna, Mattila, Meier, van Dam, Hampson; Orchestre de Paris; Pappano** (EMI 5 56152 2; 3 CDs).

This recording of the French *Don Carlos*, following a production at the Chatelet, is superb. Roberto Alagna as Carlo and José van Dam as Philip are finely matched, but the outstanding performance is the gorgeous and very moving

Elisabeth of Karita Mattila. The orchestral sound isn't top-class, but that's the only problem with a interpretation that looks set to stand as the first-choice *Don Carlos* for many years.

AIDA

In November 1869 Khedive Ismail, the ruler of Egypt, announced plans to open a new opera house in Cairo as part of the celebrations surrounding the opening of the Suez Canal. He asked Verdi to compose a new work for its opening night, which was planned for November 1870; Verdi missed his deadline (the opera house opened instead with *Rigoletto*), but a year later, just weeks before the premiere in Egypt, he completed *Aida*, the spectacular successor to *Don Carlos*. Associated above all with its *Triumphal March*, it is regularly subjected to the most lavish treatment that stage technicians can muster – every year in Verona, for example, the Roman amphitheatre is turned into a replica of Pharaonic Egypt for a cast-of-thousands production of *Aida*. But, as with *Don Carlos*, the spectacle is essentially a backdrop to an intense emotional drama. In essence, *Aida* is another of Verdi's tragedies of divided loyalty, focusing on the Ethiopian slave girl Aida, daughter of the captured Ethiopian king, and her love for the Egyptian Captain of the Guard, Radames.

◑ **Tebaldi, Bergonzi, Simionato, MacNeil; Vienna Singverein; Vienna Philharmonic Orchestra; Karajan** (Decca 414 087-2; 3 CDs).

Karajan's first *Aida*, recorded in 1959, was also the first in stereo, and it has never been surpassed. Tempi are swift, but not unduly so, and Karajan elicits some gorgeous sounds from the VPO. Renata Tebaldi and Carlo Bergonzi, a well-matched pairing, produce consistently beautiful tone and both give unerringly stylish and intelligent readings.

◑ **Freni, Carreras, Baltsa; Vienna Philharmonic Orchestra; Karajan** (EMI CMS 7 69300 2; 3 CDs).

The second of Karajan's two recordings of *Aida* encompasses both the grandeur and excitement of the big public moments and the intimacy of the real drama beneath. His cast is equal to the conception, with José Carreras an ardently youthful Radames, Mirella Freni spinning out beautiful lines as Aida, and Agnes Baltsa sonorous as her rival in love, Amneris.

OTELLO

In 1879 Verdi began to sketch an opera based on Shakespeare's *Othello*, a project that was to take more of his time than any of his other works. *Otello* was completed in 1886, some sixteen years after *Aida*, and shows Verdi achieving an extraordinary level of dramatic sophistication. This opera marks the culmination of the evolutionary development

of the perfectly through-composed Italian opera (German opera already had Wagner), in which each act is a continual dramatic sweep within which the set pieces are intrinsic parts of the whole, intensifying the action rather than arresting it.

Some of this credit for *Otello*'s economy must go to Verdi's librettist Boito, who ditched the entire first act of Shakespeare's play to create a piece that focuses entirely on the characterization of the central trio, giving greater prominence to Iago than accorded by Shakespeare – indeed, for years Boito and Verdi used the working title *Jago*.

○ **Domingo, Studer, Leiferkus, Vargas; Paris Opéra-Bastille Chorus and Orchestra; Chung** (Deutsche Grammophon 439 805-2; 2 CDs).

This hard-driven and dramatic reading is the third time *Otello* has been recorded by Placido Domingo, who has effectively established a monopoly of the part since the 1970s. It's one of the greatest performances of his career, even if his vocal resources are not what they were. Studer makes a light, somewhat brittle Desdemona, but gives a touchingly vulnerable reading of the "Willow Song". The obviously Russian Leiferkus is a vulpine Iago, and easily the most interesting Iago to feature on a Domingo recording.

◑ **Vickers, Rysanek, Gobbi, Andreolli; Rome Opera Chorus & Orchestra; Serafin** (RCA GD 81969; 2 CDs).

This recording was made in 1960, before Jon Vickers performed the role onstage, but there is not even a hint of insecurity here. Although he possessed one of the most powerful tenor voices of his day, Vickers is is a vulnerable rather than a heroic Otello: the love duet is achingly moving, and his death scene has a haunting dignity. Leonie Rysanek is too grand for Desdemona, but Gobbi – using his open-throated voice to great effect – is a thrilling Iago, especially during his villainous "Credo".

FALSTAFF

Rossini once remarked that Verdi was "too melancholic and serious" to write a comedy. Verdi's riposte came right at the end of his life – premiered in 1893, the composer's eightieth year, *Falstaff* displays the wit and *joie de vivre* of a work created by a man half Verdi's age. He and Boito concentrate almost exclusively on the Falstaff of *The Merry Wives of Windsor*, and the fat knight's forlorn attempt to seduce Alice Ford and Meg Page simultaneously, with inevitable consequences. *Falstaff* has the formal perfection of *Otello*, yet was not immediately as successful – whereas the audience had packed the streets outside Verdi's hotel after the premiere of the latter, at the opening night of *Falstaff* the atmosphere was one of deep respect rather than spontaneous joy. It was mainly due to the efforts of Toscanini, who conducted the work in opera houses all over the world, that *Falstaff* achieved its due acclaim as one of Verdi's masterpieces.

⊙ Gobbi, Schwarzkopf; Philharmonia Chorus & Orchestra; Karajan (EMI CDS 7 49668; 2 CDs).

After the heaviness of *Aida* and the power of *Otello*, *Falstaff* requires an almost Haydn-like lightness of touch and this it receives in Karajan's classic first recording – one of the very first stereo recordings in the mid-1950s. Tito Gobbi was the greatest Falstaff of the age and he is joined by equally distinguished colleagues, including Elisabeth Schwarzkopf as Alice, Anna Moffo as Nannetta and Rolando Panerai as Ford. But the most impressive feature of this historic set is the superbly fleet-footed playing of the Philharmonia, dampened only by the lack of bloom in the recording.

THE REQUIEM

Apart from a string quartet, Verdi composed just one non-operatic work of consequence: his massive *Requiem*, written in 1873–74 in memory of the nationalist Italian writer Alessandro Manzoni. Verdi never had a particularly strong Christian faith, but intimations of mortality prompted a number of sacred works in his last years, notably the *Four Sacred Pieces*. However, none of these pieces stands up to comparison with the lavish *Requiem*, the most ambitious sacred work of the late nineteenth century. Hans von Bülow described it as Verdi's "latest opera, in church vestments" and, indeed, if you take Bach and Mozart as your standards, you'll find the Verdi *Requiem* more religiose than religious. Operatic gesture is never far from the surface and indeed irrupts into the foreground on more than one occasion, for example in the terrifying drama of the Dies Irae and in the aria-like lyricism of some of the solos.

⊙ Dunn, Curry, Hadley, Plishka; Atlanta Symphony Chorus & Orchestra; Shaw (Telarc CD80152; 2 CDs; with various opera choruses).

Robert Shaw was Toscanini's choral assistant and his account of the *Requiem* reveals his mastery in this territory, with superb choral singing, excellent young soloists who avoid the histrionics of some of their seniors, and alert orchestral playing. The overall sound quality is exceptional.

⊙ Orgonasova, von Otter, Canonici, Miles; Monteverdi Choir; Orchestre Révolutionnaire et Romantique; Gardiner (Philips 442 142-2; 2 CDs; with *Four Sacred Pieces*).

This performance also boasts a quartet of finely balanced soloists and some tremendous choral singing. Gardiner's speeds and dynamics are more dramatic than those of Shaw and there is a sense of the work having been rethought from scratch. The drawback (as with several Gardiner recordings) is that the dynamic levels will be irritatingly extreme for some tastes.

⊙ Filipova, Scalchi, Hernández, Colombara; Hungarian State Opera Chorus & Orchestra; Morandi (Naxos 8.550944/4; 2 CDs; with *Four Sacred Pieces*).

The best of the budget recordings (by a long way) and a fine performance by any standards. The chorus, though not as good as the other two recommendations, are spirited and sound genuinely involved. The soloists are even better (with the soprano Elena Filipova outstanding), while the conducting has both energy and warmth.

TOMÁS LUIS DE VICTORIA

(1548–1611)

Of all the great polyphonists of the sixteenth century, Victoria is the one whose music makes the most powerful impact. Whereas the music of his contemporary Palestrina (see p.295) creates a mood of serene repose and contemplation, Victoria transforms the polyphonic technique into a vehicle for more fervent and passionate feelings, ones that suggest a direct and personal relationship with God. It is a quality that has its roots in a particularly Spanish form of Catholicism, an intense piety that can be found in the writings of the mystic St Teresa of Ávila (whom Victoria probably knew), and in the visionary paintings of El Greco.

Victoria was born at Ávila, where he later served as a chorister at the cathedral and attended the Jesuit school of San Gil. Around 1565, with King Philip II as his benefactor, he was sent to Rome to complete his education at another Jesuit institution, the Collegium Germanicum. While there he would almost certainly have come into contact with Palestrina, who may even have given lessons to the younger man. Victoria held several important positions during his time in Rome, culminating in that of *maestro di cappella* at the Collegio Germanico (1573–78). Ordained a priest in 1575, he joined the community of Filippo Neri, the creator of the oratorio form (see p.99). The community was based at the church of San Giralmo della Carità and Victoria held a chaplaincy there between 1578 and 1585.

In the mid-1580s he expressed a wish to return to Spain and was made the personal chaplain to Philip II's sister, the Dowager Empress Maria, who was then living in retirement at the Convent of the Descalzas Reales in Madrid. He returned just once to Rome, between 1592 and 1594, to supervise the printing of his works and to attend the funeral of Palestrina; otherwise he remained in Madrid, serving the empress until her death in 1603, after which he continued at the convent until his own death eight years later.

SACRED MUSIC

Compared with Palestrina, Victoria's output is extremely small but it has a far wider emotional range, from the rapturous opening of the motet *O Quam Gloriosum* to the dark intensity of the *Tenebrae Responsories*. His greatest work is the *Requiem*, which he wrote for the Dowager Empress Maria in 1603, a piece which includes music for both the Mass of the Dead and the services that preceded it. Though at times solemn, there is nothing gloomy about this music. Its greatest moments – the swelling chords that open the Kyrie, the hushed intensity of the motet *Versa est in luctum* – rather give an impression of joyful acceptance and spiritual aspiration.

○ Requiem: Westminster Cathedral Choir; Hill (Hyperion CDA 66250).

The reputation of the Westminster Cathedral Choir received a major boost with their recordings of Victoria in the late 1980s. Intensely committed and sharply focused, these performances convey with complete conviction the spirituality of this music – a quality augmented by the cavernous acoustic. In the *Requiem*, to give some idea of the liturgical context, the recording has included some of the plainsong material that would have been sung with it.

○ Requiem: Gabrieli Consort; McCreesh (Archiv 447 095-2).

This is a very different performance from the one reviewed above but no less convincing. Paul McCreesh fleshes out the liturgical context – adding all the relevant chant material – and his choir is made up of just adult male voices (falsettists in the upper parts). The result, if anything, enhances the solemn, ceremonial nature of the music which seems to build in splendour as it progresses.

○ O Quam Gloriosum (mass & motet); Missa Ave Maris Stella: Westminster Cathedral Choir; Hill (Hyperion CDA 66114).

Surprisingly the *O Quam Gloriosum Mass* does not quote from the glorious opening phrase of the motet on which it is based (included on the disc), but it does have the same rapturous energy and variety – joyful in the Gloria, reverent in the Benedictus. The *Missa Ave Maris Stella* is more obviously soulful, and contains (at the close of the second *Agnus* setting) one of the most exquisitely beautiful moments in all Victoria's music.

HEITOR VILLA-LOBOS

(1887–1959)

Heitor Villa-Lobos was living proof that you do not need a conventional musical education to become a composer. He received most of his music lessons from his amateur cellist father, then taught himself to play many other instruments besides, including the guitar, on which he gained a remarkable facility. His close friend and compatriot, the conductor Burle Marx, once asked Villa-Lobos if there was anything he did not play. "Only the oboe," was the reply; but when the two men met again soon afterwards, Villa-Lobos was already well on the way to mastering the instrument. Villa-Lobos became Brazil's leading composer partly because his lack of academic training made him remarkably free-ranging in his approach to composition and in his selection of source material.

On his father's death, instead of pursuing the medical career his mother wished for, he preferred to spend his time playing guitar with the street bands of Rio, and for several years led a dissipated

Bohemian life. In his late teens and early twenties he undertook a long tour of Brazil to research its folk music. Villa-Lobos was fond of telling Rio's chattering classes that during his travels he had been captured by cannibals, who spared him only because of his musical capabilities; more plausibly, he claimed that the map of Brazil was his first harmony book. On returning to Rio he enrolled at the National Music Institute to further his technical studies, but soon found the atmosphere stifling, and decided to abandon his training in midstream. However, he gained the respect of the teaching staff, who continued to provide help, support and advice after he had left.

Although money was hard to come by, he spent the next few years building up a strong local reputation, and caused a sensation when his compositions were performed at a series of concerts in Rio in 1915. With scant concern for academic niceties, he had amalgamated a vast range of material into music that was eclectic and original. Indigenous Brazilian music went into the mix alongside Wagner, Puccini, Debussy, Milhaud, Stravinsky, Gregorian chant, Palestrina and Johann Sebastian Bach, the composer who meant most to him and who provided the inspiration for his most famous works, the *Bachianas Brasileiras* – a series of nine little suites that attempt to fuse the style of Bach with the idioms of Brazilian folk music. His fourteen *Chôros* were more populist but no less ground-breaking, representing, to quote the composer, "A new form of musical composition, synthesizing different types of Brazilian, Indian, and popular music".

The pianist Artur Rubinstein, on hearing some of the composer's work in Brazil in 1919, helped persuade wealthy patrons to sponsor Villa-Lobos's first journey to Paris in 1923. Parisian audiences immediately warmed to his music, and he was fêted by the press and artists of all descriptions, including people of widely different temperament from his own, such as Edgard Varèse (see p.444). On returning to Brazil he became a figurehead for young musicians. In 1930 he was appointed director of the National Music Academy and two years later he was given charge of the country's music education. In 1942 Villa-Lobos founded the Conservatorio National de Canto Orfeonico, with the aim of providing music teachers for Brazilian schools. Leaving aside the merits of his compositions, as a pedagogue and administrator, as well as folklorist and musicologist, Villa-Lobos made an incalculable contribution to Brazilian music.

BACHIANAS BRASILEIRAS

Villa-Lobos wrote music at all hours of the day and night, wherever he happened to be, jotting down ideas as they occurred to him, and rarely bothering to revise them. Thus his output is immense (around 1500 officially listed works) and highly uneven. At his best he achieved a romantic, strongly coloured amalgam of indigenous Brazilian music and the classical tradition of Western Europe, and nowhere is this better demonstrated than in his remarkable *Bachianas Brasileiras*. They're a fairly disparate collection of pieces, in which chugging Baroque motor rhythms will suddenly subside into lyrical effusion. *No. 1*, written for eight cellos, is a case in point; it's opening movement begins and ends with some hard-driven ostinati but also contains melodies of a more folksy complexion. *No. 2*, an arrangement of mostly cello pieces for a chamber orchestra, is much more overtly romantic music, being essentially a set of four exotic, and occasionally gushing, tone poems that attempt to evoke the colours and flavours of his native land – rather more Hollywood than Bach in evidence here – though its last movement, *The Little Train of the Caipira*, is justly famous as an exuberant picture of an energetic train journey across Brazil. Most celebrated of all, and Villa-Lobos's best-known work, is the *Bachianas Brasileiras No. 5* for soprano solo and eight cellos. It's in two movements: the first a rhapsodic and sensual night poem over pizzicato strings, the second an animated celebration of birdsong. It's a colourful and mysterious work, a showcase for a soprano able to communicate its uniquely rhapsodic fervour.

⊙ Bachianas Brasileiras Nos. 1 & 5: Gomez, Manning; Pleeth Cello Octet (Hyperion CDA 66257; with *Suite for Voice and Violin & arrangements of Bach preludes and fugues*).

This CD from Hyperion makes an excellent introduction to Villa-Lobos. Jill Gomez is in ravishing voice and the Pleeth Cello Octet provide a winning combination of expressive power and voluptuousness in the *Bachianas Brasileiras No. 5*, with Peter Manning giving warm and characterful support in the *Suite*. Completing a fascinating disc are Villa-Lobos' transcriptions of various Bach preludes and fugues.

⊙ Bachianas Brasileiras Nos. 2, 4 & 8: Cincinnati Symphony Orchestra; López-Cobos (Telarc CD-80393).

The Cincinnati Symphony Orchestra provide spirited accounts of three of the Bachianas Brasileiras – the luscious *No. 2* and two of the less well-known ones. They provide a warm and expansive sound which is at times a little too refined (the little train should surely clatter along in a rather more noisy fashion), but nonethleless these are very persuasive performances.

MUSIC FOR GUITAR

Villa-Lobos, himself a proficient guitarist from an early age, made the acquaintance of the great

Spanish guitarist Segovia during his stay in Paris in the 1920s. Segovia's brilliant technique had completely revolutionized guitar playing and the instrument was starting to be taken seriously by contemporary composers and in the concert hall. The *Twelve Etudes* (1929), the first result of this fruitful contact, function as a kind of compendium of what the instrument was capable of in the right hands: a range of techniques are explored – glissandi, arpeggiation, harmonics – but Villa-Lobos' idiosyncratic harmonies means that they rarely sound like mere exercises. The *Five Preludes*(1940) – less virtuosic and more emotional than the études – have proved his most popular guitar pieces. They are wonderfully fresh and imaginative poetic miniatures, whose prevailing melancholy is established at the very beginning with the yearning melody of *Prelude No. 1*. The guitar concerto (1951), commissioned by Segovia, is a rather more elusive work which rather suffers in comparison with the bright colours and seductive melodies of Rodrigo's concerto. There's a languid, almost throwaway quality to Villa-Lobos' work, which is permeated by an almost suffocating ennui that is only partly shaken off halfway through the final movement.

◑ **Guitar Concerto; Preludes; Etudes: Bream; London Symphony Orchestra; Previn** (RCA 09026 61604 2).

The warmth of Bream's playing and the variety of his tone and touch are well-suited to Villa-Lobos's guitar music which can be deadened by too technical an approach. These performances, which date from the 1970s, are justly celebrated. In particular the *Preludes* have a lyrical intensity which has rarely been matched. It is no surprise to learn that Villa-Lobos was himself an admirer of Bream's playing.

ANTONIO VIVALDI

(1678–1741)

"The same concerto four hundred times" is how Stravinsky dismissed him, but no reputation has mushroomed more in recent times than that of Antonio Vivaldi. Early this century he was an unknown name whose works were turned into salon pieces by the violinist Fritz Kreisler; now his *Four Seasons* are bought by people who have never listened to any other piece of classical music.

The life behind the music is elusive. His father was a musician at St Mark's in Venice, and Antonio – the youngest of six children – is said to have studied at the church under the *maestro di cappella*, Giovanni Legrenzi. Vivaldi was ordained as a priest of a minor order in 1703 (he was later known as the "Red Priest" on account of his hair colour) but he rarely celebrated Mass, due (so he claimed) to a debilitating illness which was probably asthma. In the same year he entered the service of the Conservatorio della Pietà, the most famous of four Venetian orphanages for foundling girls, all of which placed special emphasis on musical education. In addition to teaching the violin, Vivaldi composed music for the Pietà's outstanding choir and orchestra, and seems to have made himself well liked by the governors, who in 1713 granted him leave of absence to supervise the performance of the first of over 45 operas, *Ottone in Villa*, in Vicenza.

By now his fame was beginning to spread as a result of the publication of *L'estro armonico* in Amsterdam in 1711. These twelve concertos were greatly admired, especially in Germany, where Bach copied and arranged six of them. Much of Vivaldi's time was soon devoted to opera, both as composer and as manager of the Sant'Angelo and San Moisè theatres. Though he continued to work in Venice, from 1718 he was also in the service of Mantua and then spent several years travelling throughout Italy. The governors of the Pietà, trying to rein in their increasingly errant maestro, contracted him to provide two concertos per month, and for a while the scheme paid off. Shortly before Christmas 1725 he produced his last works for them – *Il cimento dell'armonica e dell'inventione* (Contest Between Harmony and Invention), another series of twelve concertos, of which the first four were *Le quattro stagioni* (*The Four Seasons*).

From this period stems his close association with a Anna Girò, a young soprano (and former Pietà protégée) who often took the principal roles in operas staged at the Sant'Angelo Theatre. Throughout the 1730s Vivaldi resumed his extensive travelling, accompanied by Anna and her sister Paolina, an arrangement that caused a fair amount of scandal and led to the Archbishop of Ferrara trying to ban him from that city.

He was invited to Amsterdam, where *Il cimento* had been published, and proved a major attraction there, but when he returned to Venice in 1739, to supervise a festival in honour of a visit from the son of the King of Poland, he found that his reputation – particularly as an opera composer – had considerably waned in his native city. The following year Vivaldi departed for Vienna in the hopes of gaining patronage from the emperor, but this plan came to nothing. At his death in 1741 he was almost a forgotten man, and he was buried a pauper outside the Vienna city walls. One of six choristers at his funeral was the young Joseph Haydn.

Characterized by dramatic contrasts of dynamics and harmony, Vivaldi's music was often criticized by his contemporaries as eccentric, and after his death it lay forgotten until the 1930s. Yet as a violin virtuoso he was fascinated by the range of possibilities in string sound, and he greatly extended the boundaries of instrumental technique: the slow movement of his B minor concerto for four violins, for example, is an exploration of different methods of spreading a chord and bowing it. Moreover, Vivaldi's contribution to the development of the solo concerto was immense, chiefly in that the structure of his concertos anticipated the three-movement plan of the classical concerto. His first movements are notable for their taut economy and the rhythmic drive of opening themes; his slow movements have the eloquence of operatic arias; and his finales anticipate those of the classical symphony in their buoyancy and pace.

L'ESTRO ARMONICO

Of one of Vivaldi's concerts a contemporary wrote, "At the end he improvised a fantasy which quite confounded me, for such playing has not been heard before and can never be equalled. He played with his fingers but a hair's breadth from the bridge, so that there was hardly room for the bow. He played thus on all four strings, and at unbelievable speed." The stupendous technique is confirmed by the concertos of *L'estro armonico*, yet there is much more than mere virtuosity to what has been called perhaps the most influential collection of instrumental music from the eighteenth century. The title is the key, for *l'estro* means "inspiration", and indeed the impersonal stateliness of Corelli's Opus 6, the precedent for these concertos, pales beside Vivaldi's music. The scholar H.C. Robbins Landon tallied the qualities of *L'estro armonico* when he wrote of the music's "freshness, the vigour, the variety and – in the slow movements – the mysterious tenderness". It was, he concluded, "unlike anything published before".

○ Standage; English Concert; Pinnock (Deutsche Grammophon Archiv 423 094-2; 2 CDs; with *La stravaganza*).

Where this account scores over its rivals is in its acknowledgement that a certain brusqueness is essential to Vivaldi's masterpiece. It was the metrical abruptness and crispness of *L'estro armonico* that lifted the composer above his predecessors, as Pinnock makes clear in this agile and exhilaratingly alert performance.

LA STRAVAGANZA

The *Capriccio stravagante* of Carlo Farina, published in 1626, was crammed with every trick of current violin technique. To the virtuosic Vivaldi the challenge must have been irresistible, and he rose to it in his Opus 4 set, *La stravaganza*, which he dedicated to Vettor Delfino, a former pupil and member of a celebrated Venetian noble family. "I cannot wish for a better protection of my feeble works", the composer wrote, "than that of Your Excellency." They have been neglected by comparison with *L'estro armonico*, but the concertos of *La stravaganza* are anything but "feeble". They display a winning flair throughout, with slow movements every bit as lyrical as their predecessors', and their astringent modulations, so bewildering to Vivaldi's contemporaries, make them vibrantly fresh for modern audiences.

○ Standage; English Concert; Pinnock (Deutsche Grammophon Archiv 423 094-2; 2 CDs; with *L'estro armonico*).

The same team as above tackle *La stravaganza* with the same level of flair and commitment. Once again there's an element of roughness to the playing, which contributes a certain raw immediacy.

◑ Kaine, Loveday; Academy of St Martin-in-the-Fields; Marriner (Decca 444 821-2; 2 CDs).

Marriner's vintage recording from the early 1970s still holds its own. The soaring contributions of his soloists and the verve of the Academy in its heyday create an account which is consistently thrilling.

LE QUATTRO STAGIONI (THE FOUR SEASONS)

Once a potent enough force to influence Haydn, *Le quattro stagioni* was not republished until 1950 but is now the most recorded piece of classical music, with over 150 versions issued to date. Each of the four concertos depicts a season, beginning with Spring, and takes its structure from four sonnets (possibly written by Vivaldi himself) – it is thus an early example of programme music. A bravura showpiece for its violin soloist, *Le quattro stagioni* is one of the most dazzling examples of musical scene-painting, evoking buzzing flies, drunkards and goatherds dozing in the sun, dripping rain and so on. The imagination with which Vivaldi manipulates rhythm and timbre to achieve each effect is crucial to its success, and the opening motif (a bouncy alternation of quavers and semiquavers) gives the work a sense of forward movement which is never lost.

O Drottningholm Baroque Ensemble; Sparf (BIS CD-275).

As an example of the "authentic" movement's capacity to strip away preconceptions, the brilliantly exuberant playing of the Drottningholm Baroque Ensemble is second to none. The sheer weight of ornamentation in "Spring" means that a little of the music's directness is lost and there should be a greater sense of fragility here, but overall this is bracing, challenging stuff. The lack of any coupling is the only serious drawback.

O Freiburg Baroque Orchestra; Goltz (Deutsche Harmonia Mundi 05472 77384-2; with *Violin Concertos Op. 8, Nos. 5 & 6*).

Not quite as hard-driven as the above recording but still pretty lively. This is a performance which really treats the work as programme music and the various representational "sounds" are effectively – but not unsubtly – indicated. The novelty of this version is the wide range of instruments employed in the continuo part and the inclusion of the four sonnets that originally inspired the work. A further bonus is the inclusion of the next two concertos from Opus 8.

◑ Huggett; Raglan Baroque Players; Kraemer (VER 5 61172-2; with *Violin Concertos Op. 8, Nos. 5, 6, 10 & 11*).

An absolute bargain at mid-price: not only do you get an exhilarating performance without excessive ornamentation and with Monica Huggett in sparkling form, but the generous length of the disc means that you also get another four violin concertos from Opus 8.

⊙ English Chamber Orchestra; Garcia (ASV CDQS 148; with other Vivaldi concertos).

Modern rather than original instruments on this budget release, but this is an exuberant account of great finesse and style, brilliantly led by José-Luis Garcia.

FLUTE CONCERTOS

In 1726 Venice played host to the virtuoso flautist Johann Joachim Quartz, and immediately afterwards the flute enjoyed an unprecedented vogue in the city. Vivaldi promptly wrote an ornate flute part into his opera *Orlando*, which was premiered in 1727, the year before an Amsterdam publisher commissioned the Opus 10 flute concertos from him. In a few cases Vivaldi was able to recycle music from existing movements, but the instrument also drew from him some of his freshest feats of imagination, and as a compedium of flute technique it had no rival at the time. The concertos' haunting evocations of night and birdsong compare with any of the onomatopoeic effects in *The Four Seasons*.

O Beznosiuk; English Concert; Pinnock (Deutsche Grammophon Archiv 423 702-2).

Liza Beznosiuk's fluidity of phrasing and articulation draws the best from this music, and minimizes any sense of routine in Vivaldi's less inspired patches. The English Concert provide fresh and vigorous support.

GLORIA IN D

It has taken a fair amount of time for Vivaldi's choral works to get the same amount of attention as his instrumental pieces. The exception to this rule is the *Gloria in D major*, catalogued as RV 589 (rather confusingly, he wrote another in the same key). This is the most popular of all Vivaldi's sacred music, and has been in the repertory since it was revived in 1939 by Alfredo Casella, a pupil of Fauré. Notable for its fusion of festive brilliance with moments of profound sadness, it was composed in Venice some time between 1713 and 1717 for two female soloists, choir and an orchestra that includes a prominent solo part. It's a highly theatrical work, full of unashamedly operatic excess, with the text divided between soloists and chorus into no less than twelve sections. The lack of male soloists confirms that it was almost certainly composed for the Pietà, but the *Gloria*'s bold contrasts and striking sonorities are also an acknowledgement of the Venetian polychoral tradition of Monteverdi and Gabrieli.

O York, Biccire, Mingardo; Akademia; Concerto Italiano; Alessandrini (Opus 111 OPS 30-195; with *Magnificat*).

This recording will irritate as many people as it thrills. Rinaldo Alessandrini, renowned for his Monteverdi recordings, attacks Vivaldi like a man possessed. The opening is taken faster than you would think possible, and with an incredible rasping attack from the strings. This is a highly theatrical performance in which startling contrasts abound, notably when a highly spirited Domine Fili (with the dotted rhythms pushed to extremes) is followed by a slow and sombre account of the Domine Deus in which the chorus respond to the soloist as if she were the protagonist of a classical tragedy.

◑ Nelson, Kirkby; Choir of Christ Church Oxford; Academy of Ancient Music; Preston (L'Oiseau-Lyre 443 178-2; with Handel *Utrecht Te Deum* and *Jubilate*).

This altogether safer and refreshingly joyful account of the *Gloria* comes from Simon Preston directing the Choir of

Christ Church, Oxford, in its heyday. There's a feeling of airy lightness to the performance which is enhanced by the light open tones of the two soloists.

STABAT MATER

Vivaldi also wrote a substantial amount of sacred music for solo voice, of which the most celebrated is the *Stabat Mater*, composed in 1712 for the church of the Oratorian Order in Brescia. The text, probably written by a Franciscan poet in the thirteenth century, is a meditation on the Virgin Mary's suffering as she stands at the foot of the cross. Vivaldi uses just over half of the text, but he pours into its setting some of his most intense and heartfelt music. It was written for a high male voice (either a falsettist or a castrato) and a string orchestra, and much of the pathos is derived from their exquisite interaction – in the penultimate stanza, for instance, where the harsh angularity of the dotted string introduction is followed by a legato phrase from the soloist, *Eia Mater* (O Mother), before the strings re-enter, nagging away underneath him. This is followed by a more ardent rocking arpeggiated figure in the strings, which is matched by the soloists' fulsome legato, which in turn leads into the relatively joyful (and fugal) Amen which closes the work.

ERIC LARAYADIEU

Andreas Scholl

⊙ Scholl; Ensemble 415; Banchini (Harmonia Mundi 901571; with other vocal and instrumental works by Vivaldi).

This is the disc which made the reputation of countertenor Andreas Scholl and it's not difficult to hear why. He has a beautifully clear and penetrating voice, with no hint of hoot, and he uses it intelligently, judging the many sequential runs that occur early in the work with an easy, natural grace. This is a well-projected and unsentimental account, and at times a bit more dynamic contrast from the string ensemble would have been welcome.

W

RICHARD WAGNER

(1813–1883)

No composer ever polarized opinion as violently as Richard Wagner. Nowadays, as in his lifetime, he attracts a cult following, and every year thousands of people make a pilgrimage to the small Bavarian town of Bayreuth, where in 1876 he inaugurated a festival entirely devoted to his own music. For many others, Bayreuth is the embodiment of the composer's megalomania, and the adoption of Wagner's music as a cultural and political icon by the Nazis is seen not as a propagandist perversion of his art but as the apotheosis of a man who prefigured the Teutonic, anti-Semitic triumphalism of the Third Reich. To his admirers, Wagner's vision of the *Gesamtkunstwerk*, the "total art work" in which music, poetry, drama and the visual arts were synthesized, is one of the mightiest achievements of European culture, on a par with the drama of ancient Greece. To the sceptics, the four-part *Ring des Nibelungen* is a boring tale of dwarfs and giants, while *Tristan und Isolde* is an impossibly long-winded love story with pseudo-medieval trappings. Yet none of Wagner's contemporaries was untouched by his music, even if they felt his influence to be malign, and to ignore his music is to turn away from a figure as seminal as Beethoven. You might never find Wagner appealing; it is equally likely that you'll hear the prelude to *Tristan* and be hooked for life.

Wagner was the archetypal Romantic artist, with a life story as fantastic as his plots. His true parentage has never been fully established: his father was either his mother's husband, Carl Friedrich Wagner, or her lover, the actor and painter Ludwig Geyer. (This uncertainty surely has some connection with the number of characters in his operas whose fathers were equally unknown to them – Siegmund, Siegfried, Parsifal.) Whatever the truth, Carl Friedrich died a year after Richard's birth, and his widow married Geyer. Wagner thus grew up in a theatrical milieu, and he was already writing plays in his early teens. His need for incidental music for these dramas sent him in search of composition teachers, and his first musical works (now lost) date from 1829, when he was 16. His first completed opera, *Die Feen*, dates from only four years later, a period when he was gaining his first experiences of working in the theatre as chorus-master.

LEBRECHT COLLECTION

Richard Wagner

By 1843 his reputation had been firmly established with the premieres of *Rienzi* and *Der fliegende Holländer* (The Flying Dutchman) in Dresden, where, as a result of these successes, he was appointed Kapellmeister to the Saxon court. There he worked on *Tannhäuser* and *Lohengrin*, and made preliminary drafts for *The Ring* and *Die Meistersinger*, at the same time becoming involved in the republican movement that swept across Europe in the late 1840s. In 1849 a warrant was issued for his arrest. With the help of Liszt, who was to be a devoted ally throughout his life, he fled to Zürich, where he wrote many of his most influential essays, among them *The Artwork of the Future* and *Opera and Drama*, in which he set out his theories of the *Gesamtkunstwerk*.

During this period of exile he finalized the libretto for the four dramas of *The Ring* and began composing their music, but he found himself distracted by his infatuation with Mathilde Wesendonck, the wife of one of his wealthy Swiss patrons. Showing his customary propensity for self-mythologizing, Wagner's thoughts now turned towards the Tristan legend, and soon he had interrupted work on his colossal operatic cycle to concentrate on *Tristan und Isolde*, a work he hoped would finance the building of the theatre he had realized would be necessary to stage *The Ring* as he had conceived it. The Wesendonck affair was the most damaging in a succession of infidelities that his wife, the actress Minna Planer, had been forced to endure since their marriage in 1836. Suffering from a heart condition, Minna spent much of her time in the 1850s either seeking cures or following Wagner around his various lodgings, with a dog and parrot in tow, trying to lure him back. But before long he was obsessed with yet another woman: Cosima von Bülow, Liszt's daughter and wife of the renowned conductor Hans von Bülow. Minna died in 1866, by which time Cosima and Wagner had been living together for a couple of years; in 1869 the Bülows' marriage was annulled, and the following year Cosima married Wagner, having already produced three children by him.

In the meantime, Wagner had found a new patron in King Ludwig II of Bavaria, the "mad King Ludwig", whose enthusiasm for Wagner's music was such that his fairy-tale castles in the Bavarian alps had interiors based on images from *Lohengrin*. It was through Ludwig's limitless largesse that Wagner could at last realize his planned theatre, though political intrigue made it impossible to build it in the first-choice location, Munich. In 1872 the foundation stone was laid in the backwater town of Bayreuth, and four years later the inaugural Bayreuth Festival opened with the first complete performances of *The Ring*. The ensuing financial loss, like most of Wagner's debts in his later years, were borne by Ludwig. The premiere of his last music-drama, *Parsifal*, took place at Bayreuth in 1882, a little over six months before Wagner died of a heart attack in Venice.

THE OPERAS

Wagner's reputation rests on the sequence of ten operas beginning with *Der fliegende Holländer*. These were preceded by a trio of works, each of which explored a different aspect of the operatic tradition as it stood in the 1830s. The first, *Die Feen* (The Fairies; 1833–44) is in the manner of the German Romantic operas of Weber; its successor, *Das Liebesverbot* (The Ban on Love; 1834–46) is a comic opera in the style of Bellini and his Italian contemporaries; and the third, *Rienzi* (1837–40), is an extravagant Meyerbeer-like historical tragedy. *Rienzi* occasionally receives a production, but none of these three apprentice works is anything like a match for what followed.

Der fliegende Holländer (The Flying Dutchman; 1840–44) is the work which marks the emergence of Wagner's distinctive stagecraft and musical style, a style that evolved through *Tannhäuser* (1843–45) and *Lohengrin* (1845–48) to achieve maturity in *Der Ring des Nibelungen* (text 1848–53, music 1853–74). Even though the same thematic material extends through the whole of this four-part epic, a growing sophistication of technique is manifest within the *Ring* cycle, as you'd expect of a work that was written over some twenty years. In the third episode, *Siegfried*, there is a stylistic shift between the second and third acts, for it was here that Wagner broke off composition of *The Ring* to compose *Tristan und Isolde* (1856–59) and *Die Meistersinger von Nürnberg* (1862–67), both of which are vast, single-evening works. His final drama, the "sacred stage festival play" *Parsifal*, occupied him from 1877 to 1882.

Superficially, the chief characteristic of Wagner's major operas is their length: ranging from three to five hours in duration, they require an unprecedented concentration on both music and text. However, Puccini's witticism that Wagner contains "wonderful moments but terrible quarters of an hour" is wide of the mark, for these massive creations are emphatically not composed as a succession of highlights padded out with narrative material. Containing very few arias, Wagner's works are not so much operas as vocal dramas structured symphonically. By the time he came to write *The Ring*, Wagner had mastered a means of weaving long spans of music into a continuous fabric, chiefly by the use of thematic leitmotifs ("leading motifs"), short phrases associated with either a character, an object or a dramatic idea. Debussy dismissed these leitmotifs as "musical calling cards", and at their most basic they are indeed little more than this – thus character X mentions character Y, and the leitmotif of character Y duly appears in the music. However, Wagner's technique became far more subtle than this. For example, in *The Ring*, the River Rhine has a swelling theme of arpeggios from which, ultimately, all the opera's other leitmotifs are derived – a horn call for Siegfried, a fanfare-like theme for his sword, an ominous motif for Alberich's curse of death on future holders of the ring, and so on. Furthermore, these leitmotifs are not static: each is modified by its contact with other motifs, thus mirroring and qualifying the action of the opera. The climactic destruction of Valhalla at the end of *Götterdämmerung* takes place against a sort of symphonic recapitulation into which some ninety leitmotifs are blended.

So you shouldn't be daunted by Wagner's epic scale. That said, it is perhaps better to start with his most concise mature work, *The Flying Dutchman*, before moving on to *The Ring* and the late works. *Tannhäuser* and *Lohengrin*, though once the most popular of his operas, are best appreciated once you have come to grips with Wagner at his best, as they do contain dull patches that may discourage further exploration.

◑ **Der fliegende Holländer; Tannhäuser; Lohengrin; Der Ring des Nibelungen; Tristan und Isolde; Die Meistersinger von Nürnberg; Parsifal: Bayreuth Festival** (Philips 434 420–2; 32 CDs).

Of all operas, Wagner's are best heard in live performances. Few conductors have managed to sustain the long spans of this music through the mosaic-like procedures of studio recording, and Wagner singers usually require the adrenaline of the stage to really get going. Hence a large proportion of our recommended recordings come from Bayreuth. Boasting the best Wagner orchestra in the world, as well as theatre acoustics specifically designed for this music, Bayreuth performances have for decades set the standards for others to follow.

The Bayreuth 32-CD bumper set features all ten mature operas in live Bayreuth performances of varying quality, ranging from an unsatisfactory *Ring* from Boulez (best experienced on video) to the best available *Holländer*, *Tristan* and *Parsifal*. This huge set offers a simple and relatively inexpensive way to get hold of Wagner's masterpieces, though for anyone new to Wagner his operas are probably best approached one at a time.

◑ **Preludes & other orchestral excerpts: New Philharmonia, London Philharmonic Orchestra, London Symphony Orchestra; Boult** (EMI CZS 7 62539 2; 2 CDs).

More than any other composer, Wagner is misrepresented by so-called "bleeding chunks" torn out of the operas, but you might nonetheless want to sample extracts before committing yourself. Adrian Boult's two-disc collection of the best-known preludes and orchestral passages contains performances of great drama and passion.

◑ **Siegfried Idyll & orchestral excerpts: Concertgebouw; Haitink** (Philips 420 886-2).

Bernard Haitink's strong single-disc selection features a warm account of the *Siegfried Idyll*, Wagner's lyrical reworking for chamber orchestra of themes from *Siegfried*. It was written as a birthday present for Cosima, and as a celebration of their belated marriage, while Wagner was completing the last act of the opera, and was first performed outside Cosima's bedroom window on Christmas Day 1870 by a gathering of their friends – including the conductor Hans Richter, who learned the trumpet specially for the occasion.

DER FLIEGENDE HOLLÄNDER

The idea of salvation through love is a common theme in Wagner's work, and it first emerges in *Der fliegende Holländer*, a work inspired by the legend of a Dutch sea captain whose blasphemy led to his being condemned to sail the seas for eternity, unless he could be redeemed by a faithful woman. The action begins in a Norwegian fjord, where a sailor named Daland is sheltering his vessel from a storm. A ghostly ship pulls in alongside and its captain, the Dutchman, offers Daland vast wealth in exchange for a single night's hospitality. Daland's daughter, Senta, is revealed to be obsessed by the tales she has heard of the Dutchman's fate and vows to be his salvation, forsaking her lover, Erik, in the process. When the Dutchman overhears Erik complain to Senta that she had once pledged to be true to him, the sailor believes he has lost her, but reasserting her fidelity she throws herself into the sea after him. In a climax that foreshadows the end of *Tristan*, the lovers are finally seen transfigured, rising above the waves.

Der fliegende Holländer is in three acts, but is often performed as a continuous two-and-a-half-hour whole. It is Wagner's most compact drama, though there is an imbalance between the rather leisurely first half and the swift pattern of events in the second. There is a certain imbalance too in the musical treatment, which ranges from strophic ballads and arias with definite Italianate overtones to more Germanically dramatic choruses and arias – something that was not helped by Wagner's piecemeal revisions in 1860, when parts of the opera were reworked in his more advanced *Tristan* style.

◑ **Estes, Balslev, Salminen, Schunk, Clark; Bayreuth Festival Chorus and Orchestra; Nelsson** (Philips 434 599-2PH2; 2 CDs).

This 1985 recording brilliantly captures the cohesion and fluency of *Der fliegende Holländer*. Made at the end of Harry Kupfer's long-running Bayreuth production, with Woldemar Nelsson conducting pretty much the same cast he had been directing since 1981, the performance has a conspicuous unity of vision. Simon Estes' full-voiced, bass-baritone Dutchman has an anguish and desperation rarely matched on record. Most of the remaining cast sing superbly, especially Matti Salminen's resonant Daland.

⊙ **Muff, Haubold, Knodt, Seiffert; Austrian Radio Symphony Orchestra and Chorus; Steinberg** (Naxos 8660025-6; 2 CDs).

This offering from Naxos is a powerful, beautifully recorded performance. Alfred Muff is a resonant, large-sounding Dutchman and the little-known Ingrid Haubold is more than a match for him. The big name here is Peter Seiffert, who sings Erik, a role that is usually given to too light a voice, but there are no real weaknesses in casting. At budget price, this is remarkably good value, even if it lacks the stature of the recording listed above.

TANNHÄUSER

At the heart of Wagner's next opera is another theme to which he was to return – the conflict between the sacred and profane, the spiritual and the sensual. Furthermore, its main protagonist, the minstrel-knight Tannhäuser, is saved by the love of a woman. He is condemned for having succumbed to the carnal temptations of Venus on the Venusberg, when supposedly in love with the pure Elisabeth, and is sent to Rome to seek the pope's forgiveness, which is refused. Meanwhile, Elisabeth has prayed for him and gone to heaven to intercede with God on his behalf, thus saving Tannhäuser's soul. It is not one of Wagner's most gripping plots, though it provides him with a number of marvellous musical opportunities, from the orgiastic opening scene through the drama of the central song contest (when Tannhäuser boasts of his experiences on the Venusberg) to the forward-looking narration of his experiences in Rome.

Tannhäuser exists in two versions. The so-called Dresden version is basically the form in which it received its premiere in that city in 1845, with a few later revisions, and is the one invariably performed at Bayreuth. When the opportunity for a production in Paris came up in 1861, Wagner expanded the opening bacchanal (pandering to the Parisian liking for operas full of ballets) and extensively revised other passages in the style of his recent *Tristan*, creating a work that's stylistically hybrid yet more potently brings out the conflict between the erotic and the spiritual.

◑ **Windgassen, Silja, Waechter, Bumbry, Greindl, Stolze; Bayreuth Festival Chorus and Orchestra; Sawallisch** (Philips 434 599-2PH2; 3 CDs).

Using a mixture of the Dresden and Paris editions, Sawallisch imposes secure direction and extracts some subtle singing from his patchy cast. Wolfgang Windgassen is a tired and emotional Tannhäuser, but Grace Bumbry is a compelling Venus and Eberhard Waechter as Wolfram is excellent. The star of the show, however, is Anja Silja's Elisabeth, a touching portrayal of innocence and conviction.

◑ **Kollo, Dernesch, Braun, Ludwig, Sotin; Vienna State Opera Chorus and Orchestra; Solti** (Decca 414 581-2DH3; 3 CDs).

This account of the Paris text is the best studio recording of *Tannhäuser*. In the title role, René Kollo gives the performance of his life, floating the languid line with ease and security, and portraying love, anger and despair with equal sensitivity. Helga Dernesch is too grand as Elisabeth, but Christa Ludwig is a glorious Venus, with all the mustard and none of the ham. Solti gives another one of those manic performances for which his work is generally celebrated, and often this is just what is required.

LOHENGRIN

Lohengrin, a tale of a Christian saviour overcoming the powers of darkness, has one of Wagner's more dubious plots. Lohengrin is Parsifal's son and a knight of the Grail, who arrives on a swan when called by Elsa of Brabant to defend her honour against Telramund, who has accused her of murdering her brother, Gottfried. Lohengrin promises to marry Elsa, on the condition that she never asks him his name or origin. Telramund's wife Ortrud fuels Elsa's curiosity and, after the wedding (featuring the famous "Bridal March"), the bride fatefully pops the forbidden question. Lohengrin has to fulfil his vow and leave forever, but not before miraculously restoring Gottfried to life, transforming him from the swan – a form to which the wicked Telramund and Ortrud had consigned him.

Whereas *Der fliegende Holländer* moves rather uneasily between the old-fashioned set-piece opera and through-composed drama, while *Tannhäuser* has protracted periods of inertia, *Lohengrin* marks a move on from both in the way each act is cast in a continual dramatic sweep. It's rather too one-paced, but it contains music of great range and lyricism, featuring some marvellously powerful choral work and expanses of orchestral splendour.

◑ **Thomas, Grümmer, Ludwig, Fischer-Dieskau; Vienna State Opera Chorus; Vienna Philharmonic Orchestra; Kempe** (EMI CDS 7 49017 8; 3 CDs).

This 1962 *Lohengrin* captures five of the finest Wagner singers at their peak. Jess Thomas is a formidably secure Lohengrin – powerful, confident and yet able to convey the human frailty and the inner quiet of the role. Elizabeth Grümmer was past her prime but she is a passionate force as Elsa, while Christa Ludwig is as vicious as Ortrud can get, and Fischer-Dieskau presents an almost charming face to the mad Telramund. The Viennese forces are as earthy as the characterizations, and they work superbly for the ever-inventive Kempe. There is one (traditional) cut, after Lohengrin's narration in Act II.

O Domingo, Norman, Randová, Nimsgern, Sotin; Vienna State Opera Chorus; Vienna Philharmonic Orchestra; Solti (Decca 421 053-2DH4; 4 CDs).

This studio production is a very sound performance – some even rate it as the best. Solti is comparatively restrained, directing a beautifully paced Act I Prelude, but he can't help himself during the third act, when the line is lost amid unwarranted surges and outbursts. Jessye Norman is too knowing, and her voice too luxurious, for Elsa, while Placido Domingo's warmth makes him too much the Latin lover, but the beautiful tone that flows out of this pairing is hard to resist.

DER RING DES NIBELUNGEN

Nothing in Wagner's output prefigures the sheer scale of *Der Ring des Nibelungen*, and indeed it was not initially envisaged on anything like the scale it ultimately attained. In 1848 Wagner began searching for a subject that could express the political fervour engendered by the Europe-wide uprisings of that year. He wanted a theme that would possess the power of ancient Greek theatre, with its emphasis on myth and communal experience, and he found it in the Norse-Germanic myth of the hero Siegfried, through whom an old, corrupt world was destroyed and replaced by one of hope.

Soon he had sketched the libretto for an opera called *Siegfrieds Tod* (Siegfried's Death), but then realized he needed to elaborate upon the events that led up to the hero's demise, and thus wrote a "prequel" called *Der junge Siegfried* (The Young Siegfried). Even that was not enough, so he drafted a scenario that added two more dramas, *Das Rheingold* (The Rhinegold) and *Die Walküre* (The Valkyries). Having written the libretti for the four dramas in reverse order he began composing the music in sequence, beginning with *Rheingold*, the shortest part of the cycle, described merely as a prelude to the main drama (though it's longer than many full-length operas). Having completed *Walküre* and much of *Siegfried* (formerly *Der junge Siegfried*), in 1857 he broke off composition of *The Ring* to write *Tristan* and *Die Meistersinger*. Resuming *Siegfried* in 1865, he then composed the gargantuan finale, *Götterdämmerung* (Twilight of the Gods), as *Siegfrieds Tod* had now become. From a single opera, his project had grown to a length of some fifteen hours, spread over four evenings.

Obviously enough, the plot is impossible to convey in a few sentences, though one wit summarized it as a moral tale about what happens when a god defaults on the repayments on his house. This might well sum up *Das Rheingold*, in which the ruler of the gods, Wotan, tricks a power-wielding ring from the Nibelung dwarf Alberich (who in turn has stolen gold from the Rhinemaidens), then is obliged to use it to pay the giants Fafner and Fasolt for building his fortress, Valhalla. In a nutshell, the rest of the cycle depicts the attempts of both Wotan and Alberich to retrieve the ring from Fafner (who guards it in the form of a dragon) by fathering offspring to do the deed for them. Wotan's grandson Siegfried kills the dragon and then, with Brünnhilde (his betrothed, and Wotan's daughter), foils Alberich's son Hagen's plan to gain the ring, which is returned to the Rhinemaidens as the old world is cleansed by fire and water.

In outline *The Ring* sounds a bit like a Dungeons and Dragons yarn, but it's in fact a drama so complex that it can bear – and has borne – scores of different interpretations. At Bayreuth, where they don't take kindly to frivolous cleverness, it has been presented both as a ritualistic exploration of such eternal verities as Love and Death, and as a quasi-Marxist study in power relations. The musical structure of *The Ring* is even more rich than its text, and includes some of the most powerful scenes in all opera: the very opening, for example, which conjures up the Rhine in a single, extended and elaborated chord; or the entry of the gods into Valhalla at the end of *Rheingold*; or the *Ride of the Valkyries* and *Magic Fire Music* in the third act of *Die Walküre*; or Siegfried's "Funeral March" from *Götterdämmerung*. But these are just moments of extreme intensity in an epic that is highly charged from start to finish. Take the plunge – this is one of the great musical journeys.

⊙ **Various artists; Bayreuth Festival Chorus and Orchestra; Böhm** (Philips 446 057-2PB14; 14 CDs).

Karl Böhm's *Ring*, recorded live at Bayreuth between 1966 and 1967, is the most viscerally exciting ever made. The casting is outstanding, the sound vital, and Böhm's identity stamped on every page. You might not like this identity – some find it too calculating – but few other performances

WARNER

Daniel Barenboim

carry such a weight of personality, and an overriding personality is essential to a convincing *Ring* cycle. Some of the casting overlaps with the Solti set below, but the live set captures these remarkable voices in richer, more theatrical form. The whole is considerably less beautiful than with Solti (the brass is too closely miked) but the feeling of narrative cohesion is unsurpassed.

◑ **Various artists; Vienna State Opera Chorus; Vienna Philharmonic Orchestra; Solti** (Decca 414 100-2DM15; 15 CDs).

The first studio *Ring* is for many the finest: the sumptuous orchestral presence, the superb singing, the sound quality and the special effects (eighteen real anvils for *Rheingold*) have never been bettered. As an overall conception it falls slightly short of the Böhm set, because incident rather than structure seems to have been the preoccupation of conductor and producer. But, with Wagner regulars Nilsson, King and Windgassen in outstanding form, there is no more impressive-sounding *Ring* on record.

O Various artists; Bayreuth Festival Chorus and Orchestra; Barenboim (Teldec 0630-10010-2; 14 CDs).

Recorded live in 1993 at Bayreuth, where Daniel Barenboim has been a regular since making his debut in 1982, this *Ring* is the most rewarding since Böhm's. The carefully prepared voices, sublime orchestral sonorities and clear, naturally balanced sound would satisfy the most pedantic score-follower, but the spirit of Wagner's Gothic imagination is also present throughout, thanks to some remarkably imaginative conducting. The jewel in the crown is the *Götterdämmerung* – perhaps the finest yet recorded.

◑ **Various artists; La Scala Chorus and Orchestra; Furtwängler** (Music and Arts CD914; 12 CDs).

Furtwängler's legendary La Scala performance (not to be confused with the Rome broadcast recordings released by EMI) is a grim and fatalistic vision of the *Ring*, saturated with a sense of tragic inevitability. Concentrating on the orchestra, Furtwängler allows his singers unusual freedom, an approach that leads to some inspired performances – not least from Kirsten Flagstad, whose exultantly regal Brünnhilde is the vocal highlight. Her colleagues rise to the challenge, flinging themselves with amazing energy into the music. There's a lot of ambiguous intonation and ragged ensemble work here, the mono sound is hazy and the Italian orchestra is woefully inferior to any Bayreuth band, but Furtwängler has everyone performing out of their skins in what remains a uniquely vital interpretation.

TRISTAN UND ISOLDE

Arthurian legend provided the raw material for Wagner's greatest opera, but his treatment of the story was inspired by the philosophy of Schopenhauer, specifically its contention that bliss can only be found through the negation of the will and of desire. Schopenhauer is certainly a presence in the completed opera, which ends in blissful annihilation, but desire is its governing force. *Tristan und Isolde* is in essence a five-hour love song.

The plot is refreshingly simple. Tristan has been sent to Ireland to bring back the Irish princess Isolde as bride for his uncle, King Mark of Cornwall. But Tristan has fallen passionately in love with Isolde himself and she reciprocates. They conclude that death is the only way out and on the voyage to Cornwall they take a potion they believe to be poison, but Isolde's maid Brangäne has substituted a love draught and their passion is only reconfirmed. They continue their affair until caught in the act, when Tristan is wounded by one of Mark's knights. He is taken back to his castle in Brittany, where he dies just as Isolde arrives. Mark forgives them for their love and Isolde sinks onto Tristan's body, united with him in death.

Right from the prelude, with its sinuous melodic lines and suspended harmonies, a sense of heady sensuality and physical longing saturates *Tristan und Isolde*. The long love duet of the second act is as explicitly sexual as any piece of music ever written, complete with a musical coitus interruptus when the two lovers are discovered. The ever-present unfulfilled yearning is only satisfied in the closing bars of the whole opera, as Isolde's famous *Liebestod* (Love-Death), in which she sings herself into ecstatic oblivion, finally achieves harmonic fulfilment. *Tristan* is revolutionary in its chromatic language, which stretches tonal harmony to its very limits, casting the listener adrift in a world that has no reliable markers. When you listen to the overture of a Mozart opera, its harmonic structure tells you how long the piece will last; with *Tristan* you don't have any idea which way the music is heading. The modernism of Schoenberg is just around the corner.

◑ **Windgassen, Nilsson, Ludwig, Talvela, Waechter; Bayreuth Festival Orchestra; Böhm** (Philips 434 425-2; 3 CDs).

Tristan's hothouse atmosphere is ideally caught in Böhm's live 1966 Bayreuth performance, featuring Wolfgang Windgassen and Birgit Nilsson at the height of their powers. Böhm directs the performance of his life: tempi are swift and the orchestra plays at white heat, never allowing the tension to flag. Not a recording for the faint-hearted.

O Flagstad, Suthaus, Thebom, Greindl, Fischer-Dieskau; Philharmonia; Furtwängler (EMI CDS 7 47322 8; 4 CDs).

For many people the greatest of all Wagner conductors was Wilhelm Furtwängler, and his 1952 account of *Tristan* has classic status. The sound quality doesn't match the Böhm set, the cast isn't ideal (even the legendary Kirsten Flagstad is past her best here), and the orchestra isn't in the same league as the Bayreuth players, but such is the cohesion and passion of this performance that these considerations really don't matter. You'll get to the end of this recording and be amazed at how quickly the time has passed.

DIE MEISTERSINGER VON NÜRNBERG

As if to cleanse his system of the excesses of *Tristan*, Wagner next turned to comedy and the purer world of C major. *Die Meistersinger von Nürnberg* is not, however, a simple comedy: it is a hymn to German art and a celebration of progressiveness in culture.

The setting is medieval Nuremberg and its society of trade guilds. The most revered of these is the guild of Mastersingers, one of whom, Pogner, has decided to offer his daughter Eva to the winner of the Midsummer Day song contest. Eva is already in love with an itinerant knight, Walther von Stolzing, who attempts to gain admittance into the guild. Only the cobbler-poet Hans Sachs, a widower who himself is not immune to Eva's charms, sees the potential in his modern style of song and promises to help him. Walther has a rival in the shape of the fussy, carping town clerk Beckmesser – a caricature of Wagner's arch-critic in Vienna, Eduard Hanslick. At the contest, Beckmesser is laughed off after his catastrophic performance of a song he believes to be by Sachs; but it is actually by Walther, who sings it properly and, of course, wins Eva's hand.

Although less musically extreme than *Tristan*, it is nonetheless a sublime work, particularly in its characterization – Sachs is Wagner's most sympathetic creation, and the pomposity of the Mastersingers is wonderfully delineated. There are several magnificent set pieces in this most social of Wagner's works: the nocturnal comedy of Act II, where Beckmesser tries to lure Eva with a serenade, is a bewitching piece of scene-setting; the first scene of Act III, in which Sachs relinquishes his claim on Eva, is an extremely moving episode; and the final song contest is genuinely funny.

◑ **Schöffler, Treptow, Gueden, Edelmann, Dönch, Dermota; Vienna State Opera Chorus; Vienna Philharmonic Orchestra; Knappertsbusch** (Decca 440 057-2DM04; 4 CDs).

This 1951 studio recording captured the uniquely creative but comparatively rare coupling of Hans Knappertsbusch and the Vienna Philharmonic Orchestra, and together they produce a light, swiftly moving platform for the cast. Paul Schöffler's Sachs is less beautiful than on his earlier recording of the role, but the intelligence and sensitivity are unmistakable. Hilde Gueden is a sweet, dramatically potent Eva and Anton Dermota makes a superb David, riding the high tessitura with ease and charm. Karl Dönch is a cartoon-character Beckmesser and Günther Treptow is a resonant Walther. The mono sound should not put you off, for this is a memorable version.

⊙ **Adam, Evans, Kollo, Donath, Hesse, Ridderbusch; Dresden State Opera Chorus and Orchestra; Karajan** (EMI CDS7 49683-2; 4 CDs).

Karajan's 1970 *Meistersinger* features a much less starry company than his 1951 version, but the atmosphere is noticeably more theatrical. Theo Adam (a celebrated Wotan) brings his usual weight and intensity to his performance as Sachs, while Karl Ridderbusch glows as Pogner, giving one of the performances of his life. Geraint Evans sings beautifully as Beckmesser, but doesn't give much to the characterization, while René Kollo sounds tinny as Walther. The women are uniformly superb, however, with Helen Donath swooningly lovely as Eva, and Ruth Hesse delightful as Magdalene. The stereo is excellent, the price appalling.

◑ **Frantz, Neidlinger, Grümmer, Höffgen, Schock; Chorus of the Berlin Municipal Opera and Deutsche Opera; Berlin Philharmonic Orchestra; Kempe** (EMI CMS7 64154-2; 4 CDs).

This 1956 mono recording is overall a superbly cast performance, from the principal roles right down to the minor part of the Nightwatchman, sung here with great beauty by a young Hermann Prey. Elizabeth Grümmer (Eva) and Marga Höffgen (Magdalene) are an exquisite, rich-sounding coupling, and Rudolph Schock is probably the finest studio Walther there has been. The only weakness – but a prominent one – is Ferdinand Frantz's Hans Sachs. The dignity and humanity are there, but the voice is not. Kempe draws some glorious tone from the Berlin Philharmonic.

PARSIFAL

Wagner's last opera has always divided even the composer's admirers. Some think *Parsifal* Wagner's masterpiece, others find it depraved in its celebration of ascetic virtue through music of sometimes overwhelming sensuality. The climactic scene of this Arthurian morality drama takes place on Good Friday, and the opera is replete with Christian imagery such as the Grail, baptism, Holy Communion and the Crucifixion. Into this scheme Wagner mixes Buddhist notions of self-denial and elements of Schopenhauer's grim philosophy, to produce a distinctively Wagnerian exploration of the theme of enlightenment through sacrifice.

As with Wagner's previous Arthurian opera, the action is more straightforward than the music. Amfortas, one of the senior knights guarding the Holy Grail, has succumbed to the temptation of lust and has thereby lost the sacred spear that pierced Christ's body on the cross. The spear has fallen into the possession of the magician Klingsor, who has inflicted on Amfortas a wound that can only be healed by a man "made wise through compassion". Parsifal at the start of the opera witnesses Amfortas's plight but doesn't understand it; eventually, having been similarly tempted by Kundry, he renounces sexuality in order to recover the spear and bring salvation to Amfortas and his knights.

Parsifal takes the harmonic experiments of *Tristan* one step further, dissipating the energies of tonal music to such an extent that the opera sometimes approaches the very verge of stasis. Though *Parsifal*'s slow-building crescendos and languid cadences express the seductiveness of spiritual goals and the duration of suffering, rather than the sexual ecstasy of *Tristan*, the overall dynamics of the two operas are very similar. In each opera a long prelude creates a state of suspension which lasts all the way through to the last moments – in the case of *Parsifal*, until the heavenward-reaching choral writing as the hero conducts Communion for the Knights of the Grail.

○ Thomas, London, Hotter, Dalis, Neidlinger, Talvela; Bayreuth Festival Chorus and Orchestra; Knappertsbusch (Philips 416 390-2PH4; 4 CDs).

This 1962 Bayreuth recording is a triumph of vision and execution. Not only are the performances faultless, but the early stereo is extraordinarily beautiful, capturing the Bayreuth sound to perfection. This is a more cultured and slightly lighter reading than Knappertsbusch's 1951 account (available on Teldec). It's also better sung, with a magnificent Parsifal from Jess Thomas and a remarkably moving Amfortas from George London. Hans Hotter's Klingsor and Martti Talvela's Gurnemanz are classic performances, while Irene Dalis's Kundry, hurling caution to the wind, is the most compellingly dislocated interpretation on disc.

◑ Goldberg, Lloyd, Schöne, Minton; Prague Philharmonic Chorus; Monte Carlo Philharmonic Orchestra; Jordan (Erato 2292-45662-2; 4 CDs).

This is the most convincing stereo recording of *Parsifal*. Jordan adopts quicker tempi than Knappertsbusch and voices the inner parts with great delicacy and detail – in short, where Knappertsbusch looks to the shadows, Jordan looks to the light. Yvonne Minton is breathtaking as Kundry, while Robert Lloyd comes across as the most commanding Gurnemanz since Hans Hotter. Reiner Goldberg is not really a Wagner tenor, but he tries hard and there are isolated episodes in which he manages both gravity and sweetness. The supporting cast (especially the Flower Maidens) are magnificent – as is the recorded sound.

WILLIAM WALTON

(1902–1983)

Although he dabbled briefly with atonality in his early *String Quartet*, William Walton was an unrepentant neo-Romantic for most of his life. By his late twenties he had settled on a style that reconciled the essentially lyrical Englishness of Elgar with the pungency of Prokofiev and Stravinsky, a style characterized by earthy rhythms, wide intervallic writing, colourful and unstable harmonies, and a predilection for melancholy. Walton may not be the most challenging of modern composers, but his music is always extremely well crafted and two of his works – *Belshazzar's Feast* and the *Symphony No. 1* – have proved to be among the most durable of the twentieth century.

Born in Oldham, Lancashire, the son of a choirmaster and singing teacher, Walton spent his formative years in Oxford, where he was a chorister at Christ Church Cathedral. It was there that he began to compose, and in 1918 he was taken up by the aristocratic and artistic Sitwell family who introduced him to the leading cultural figures of the day, including the composer Constant Lambert, who had a powerful influence on him. Four years later he he achieved notoriety with *Façade*, a self-consciously modernist "Entertainment" for six players and a speaker who recited poetry by Edith Sitwell through a megaphone. *Façade* gave Walton's name widespread currency, while his reputation was enhanced by his elegiac *Viola Concerto*, which Paul Hindemith (see p.195) premiered in 1929.

Walton's style reached maturity in 1931 with *Belshazzar's Feast*, a dramatic cantata which was acclaimed as the finest in English choral work since Elgar's *Dream of Gerontius*, while attracting accusations of modernistic and eclectic tendencies from some quarters. Less equivocal success was achieved with the *Symphony No. 1* (1935), and the *Violin Concerto* commissioned by Jascha Heifetz in 1939. During World War II Walton was encouraged to pursue his obvious gift for the dramatic, and he began an opera on the life of the composer Gesualdo, but the project foundered after a couple of years. A rather morer fruitful collaboration was with Laurence Olivier, for whom Walton wrote a number of brilliant film scores, beginning in 1944 with *Henry V*. Walton's music for Olivier reveals his acute sensitivity to narrative pace, as well as a sure touch in creating exactly the right mood for a particular scene.

His only full-length opera, *Troilus and Cressida*, was commissioned by the BBC in 1947. The troubled relationship between Walton and his librettist Christopher Hassall delayed work and it was not until 1954, after Walton had married and moved to the Italian island of Ischia, that the score was finally completed. *Troilus* was premiered at Covent Garden in the same year, but its dreadful reception proved a terrible disappointment. Walton spent the rest of his life in Italy, producing less and less music as his brand of Romantic traditionalism became ever more unfashionable.

BELSHAZZAR'S FEAST

Walton's reputation depends primarily upon *Belshazzar's Feast*, a fine piece of biblical Gothic, scored for baritone solo, full choir and large orchestra to a text selected by Osbert Sitwell. In his handling of these vast forces Walton displays remarkable abilities for orchestration and ensemble-writing, and his music is typified by ardent, sometimes violent, thematic material. There's an obvious nod to the English oratorio tradition, above all in the sheer scale of the piece, but there's a much more wild imagination at work here that produces an unbridled theatrical energy comparable to Orff's *Carmina Burana*. Indeed its pulsating quasi-paganism upset many of those present at the first performance in 1931, and the Three Choirs Festival wouldn't touch the piece until 1957.

O Terfel; Wayneflete Singers; Bournemouth Symphony Chorus & Orchestra; Litton (Decca 448 134-2; with *Henry V* & *Crown Imperial*).

There are several fine recordings of *Belshazzar's Feast* available, but the scales are tipped in this one's favour largely because of the powerful singing of Bryn Terfel as the narrator. It's a role absoultely suited to his direct and dramatic approach, and he's more than ably supported by Andrew Litton – one of the finest of recent Walton conductors. The sense of the sublime is enhanced by the resonant acoustic of Winchester Cathedral, brilliantly captured and controlled by Decca's engineers.

SYMPHONY NO. 1

Walton's next major score after *Belshazzar*, the *Symphony No. 1*, gave him such difficulties that it took three years to complete, and the work conveys a strong sense of personal victory and fulfilment. Opening with a gorgeous extended flute solo, the movement builds with an ever-mounting tension to a tumultuous climax. Ideas tend to be developed in a way similar to the symphonies of Sibelius: a sparky, colourful Scherzo (Walton marks it "con malizia") is followed by an Andante of an almost Elgarian melancholy. There is also a debt to Hindemith – in particular the fugal passage in the finale is almost a homage to Walton's German friend. With its broad emotional horizons, Walton's first symphony stands in the forefront of English symphonic achievement and stands comparison with Vaughan Williams' contemporaneous fourth symphony.

◑ London Symphony Orchestra; Previn (RCA GD 87830; with Vaughan Williams, *The Wasps*).

Previn has always been an inspired conductor of Walton and this is one of his finest achievements on disc. The air of tension is built with consummate skill but he also gives full rein to the symphony's more expansive moments.

⊙ English Northern Philharmonia; Daniel (Naxos 8.553180; with *Partita*).

Naxos's ongoing Walton series, with Paul Daniel and the English Northern Philharmonia, is one of the company's most successful projects, worth collecting in its entirety. This performance of the *Symphony No. 1* is extremely exciting. Like Previn, Daniel knows how to distil the drama of this symphony, although his approach is not quite so unrelenting. Only the slightly blurry sound mars this outstanding disc.

THE VIOLA AND VIOLIN CONCERTOS

It may not be a crowded field, but Walton's is the outstanding concerto for the viola, its introspective mood perfectly matching the mellow subdued tone of the instrument. It begins with a slow movement in which a long lilting melody for the soloist gradually takes on a rather edgy character before returning to its initial calmness. Another of Walton's spiky, mischievous Scherzos is followed by a broad Elgarian finale. The concerto was composed for the English viola player Lionel Tertis at the suggestion of Sir Thomas Beecham, but Tertis rejected it – which is why Paul Hindemith gave its first performance.

Arguably the most seductive of all Walton's music is the *Violin Concerto*, a work designed to display the virtuosity and beautiful tone of Jascha Heifetz. The soloist's opening theme, a lyrical idea which sets the emotional tone of the work, leads to a staccato section in which the violinist battles with the orchestra for dominance; having won, the violinist is rewarded with yet another captivating solo episode. This movement's sensuousness is carried through into the Scherzo, while the finale makes much of the composer's brilliant facility for orchestral writing.

⊙ Kennedy; Royal Philharmonic Orchestra; Previn (EMI CDC7 49628-2).

There are surprisingly few recordings that couple both these concertos, but even if there were it's difficult to imagine more sympathetic accounts than Nigel Kennedy's. He taps straight into the viola concerto's elegiac spirit and pulls out all the stops for the more extrovert and virtuosic violin concerto.

FAÇADE

First "staged" at the Aeolian Hall London in 1923, *Façade* was performed from behind a decorated curtain by six instrumentalists, plus Edith Sitwell reciting 21 of her verses. Her exotically surrealistic poetry now seems rather camply orchidaceous in a delightfully English way. Walton's music precisely matches its mood of quirky nostalgia, with a light parodistic mixture that includes suggestions of jazz, music hall and even folk music. There's an obvious formal debt to Schoenberg's *Pierrot Lunaire* (see p.356), especially in the way the reciter must follow precise rhythmic notation, but stylistically it is closer in feel to the similarly irreverent "Entertainments" organized by Jean Cocteau and his musical protégés, Les Six. Subsequent performances established the work's notoriety, assisted by Noel Coward's revue sketch "The Swiss Family Whittlebot", which parodied both it and the Sitwell siblings. A definitive version of the score was established in 1951 and a supplement of eight additional poems (*Façade 2*) premiered in 1979.

◑ Sitwell, Pears; English Opera Group Ensemble; Collins (London 425 661-2; with *Portsmouth Point*, *Scapino* & *Siesta*).

This mono recording from the early 1950s is still the one to have. Too many recent recordings have gone for celebrity reciters who tend to overact and can't quite manage the rhythms. There are no such problems here: Dame Edith has a finesse and an eccentric delicacy which sounds (as it should) completely appropriate, while Peter Pears brings a musician's precision to his rather more deadpan delivery.

CARL MARIA VON WEBER

(1786–1826)

If any single person can be credited with the creation of German Romantic opera, it is Carl Maria von Weber. His *Der Freischütz*, with its magical orchestral atmospherics and its use of Germanic folklore, established a lineage that would lead ultimately to Wagner. Weber was also in his time a highly regarded music critic, a pianist of international renown and one of the first to establish the importance of the role of the conductor.

He was born near Lübeck in northern Germany, into a musical and theatrical family (he was a cousin of Mozart's wife Constanze). He soon learned to play the piano and his subsequent training included a period with Joseph Haydn's brother Michael in Salzburg, where, aged 12, he wrote his first compositions. The following year he composed his first opera, the manuscript of which was destroyed by fire shortly after its completion. As a 17-year-old he secured the post of Kapellmeister at the theatre in Breslau, where he stayed for a couple of years until falling ill after accidentally swallowing some engraver's acid. His career as a travelling virtuoso pianist then took up most of his time until 1813, when he was put in charge of the Prague opera house. Here, resuming the efforts he had made at Breslau, he set about reforming the repertory, placing the emphasis on Mozart and contemporary French opera, in opposition to the prevalent taste for Italian opera.

This principle was taken further in his next major appointment, as Royal Saxon Kapellmeister

LEBRECHT COLLECTION

Carl Maria von Weber

DER FREISCHÜTZ

The structure of *Der Freischütz* (The Marksman), in which the musical numbers are linked by spoken dialogue, derives from the Germanic genre of music-theatre known as *Singspiel*, of which Mozart's *Magic Flute* is the best-known example. However, Weber's opera is an advance on its predecessors in its use of recurrent motifs to achieve musical continuity, notably in the use of horns to underline the huntsman theme. Furthermore, in its fusion of the supernatural, the folkloric and the rustic, *Der Freischütz* brought together some of the dominant strands of German Romanticism for the first time in the history of opera.

The hero of the piece is the huntsman Max, who makes a pact with the forces of darkness to gain some magic bullets that will allow him to win a shooting contest, and thus gain the hand of his sweetheart, Agathe. At the heart of the opera is the scene in which the magic bullets are forged in a gloomy, inhospitable mountain valley called the Wolf's Glen. This wonderful musical evocation of evil is Weber's most impressive creation, but his command of orchestral colouring is deft throughout the opera, especially in his use of folk-like melodies for his choruses.

in Dresden, a post he took up in 1817. Weber's endeavours to develop a German national opera company led to years of antagonism within the court, where the music of Rossini was greatly preferred. Until, that is, *Der Freischütz* was performed in Berlin in 1821. Its success was instant: it received dozens of productions throughout Germany within a year of its premiere, then was played throughout Europe. *Der Freischütz* was to remain the most popular German opera throughout the first half of the century.

Weber made two attempts to follow up his success with *Euryanthe* (1823) and *Oberon* (1826), but neither lived up to the promise of their predecessor, chiefly because of their terrible libretti. While in London to conduct the premiere of *Oberon*, his years of ill-health caught up with him and he died the day before he was due to return home to his family. He was buried in Moorfields Chapel, but in 1844, Richard Wagner (his successor in Dresden), arranged for his body to be returned to that city.

◑ **Grümmer, Schock, Otto, Kohn, Prey, Frick; Berlin Deutsche Opera Chorus; Berlin Philharmonic Orchestra; Keilberth** (EMI CMS7 69342-2; 2 CDs).

Joseph Keilberth was one of the finest opera conductors of his or any generation, but he made only a handful of recordings. Of these, this 1958 *Freischütz* is arguably the best. Elizabeth Grümmer's flowing soprano is applied to an urgent, sensitive characterization of Agathe, while Lisa Otto makes a delicious Ännchen and Rudolph Schock is a powerful, earnest Max. The young Hermann Prey and the old Gottlob Frick are matchless in the subsidiary roles of Ottokar and the Hermit. The dialogue is included and the sound is orchestrally thin but vocally sumptuous.

○ **Schreier, Janowitz, Weikl, Adam, Vogel, Mathis; Leipzig Radio Chorus; Dresden Staatskapelle; Kleiber** (Deutsche Grammophon 415 432-2; 2 CDs).

Carlos Kleiber adopts some extreme speeds in his recording of *Der Freischütz*, but he conveys the dramatic energy of the score like no other conductor. He gets sumptuous playing out of the Dresden Staatskapelle (from Weber's home territory), and his cast is generally good, though Peter Schreier's Max sounds a little strained at times, and Gundula Janowitz's Agathe, though exquisitely sung, might just as well be singing a shopping list. The theatricality of the spoken dialogue can take a bit of getting used to, but it is all done in the best possible taste.

◑ **Overture to Der Freischütz and other operas: Berlin Philharmonic Orchestra; Karajan;** (Deutsche Grammophon 419 070-2; with *Invitation to the Dance*).

If you want to sample Weber's operatic music first, get Karajan's CD of the overtures *Der Freischütz*, *Der Beherrecher der Geister*, *Euryanthe*, *Oberon* and *Peter Schmoll;* he distils the mood of each opera to perfection, and also includes Berlioz's exuberant orchestration of Weber's piano waltz, *Invitation to the Dance*.

CLARINET MUSIC

Next to his work in opera, Weber's principal claim to fame is as a composer of clarinet music. He wrote two concertos, a concertino, a set of variations (all 1811), a quintet (1814), and a showpiece for piano and clarinet called *Grand Duo Concertant* (1816), thereby extending the instrument's repertoire in a way comparable to the work of Mozart and Brahms. And, just as Mozart and Brahms were inspired by a particular musician – the former by Anton Stadler, the latter by Richard Mühlfeld – Weber's clarinet music was composed for his friend Heinrich Bärmann, the principal clarinet of the Munich court orchestra.

Weber's instrumental music is theatrically virtuosic on the whole, though the central movements of the concertos are beautiful slow episodes in which Weber highlights the vocal sonority of the clarinet's timbre. In the concerto finales, however, everything is subservient to display, while the *Grand Duo* – the most important work for solo clarinet and piano – is notable for its operatic brilliance and the extreme difficulty of the two evenly balanced roles. The finale is a sensational battle for supremacy.

○ Clarinet Concertos Nos. 1 & 2; Concertino Op. 26: Pay; Orchestra of the Age of Enlightenment (Virgin VC 7 59002-2).

Antony Pay plays a copy of an instrument of Weber's day and is accompanied by the period instruments of the Orchestra of the Age of Enlightenment. Weber's writing sounds even more fiendish than usual in this context, but everyone involved brings it off with great style and wit.

○ Clarinet Concertos Nos. 1 & 2; Concertino Op. 26; Grand Duo Concertant: Johnson, Back; English Chamber Orchestra; Tortelier/Schwarz (ASV DCA 747).

Emma Johnson's modern-instrument accounts of the same pieces are no less beguiling, and are combined with an outstanding rendition of the *Grand Duo Concertant* in which Gordon Back proves a stylish accompanist.

G. BRANDENSTEIN/DGG

Carlos Kleiber

ANTON WEBERN

(1883–1945)

Like Alban Berg (see p.49), Anton Webern began studying with Arnold Schoenberg (see p.354) in 1904, and soon realized that all his ideas about composition had to change. The path that Webern followed, however, took an entirely different direction from Berg's. Where the latter went on to write large-scale works in which the dictates of modernism were reconciled with the Romantic tradition of Wagner and Mahler, Webern worked relentlessly towards a state of absolute economy, compressing a vast range of emotions into a few wisps of music. He did, however, acknowledge links to Mahler, links which can be clearly heard in such works as *Six Orchestral Pieces* (1909), albeit worked out on a distinctly un-Mahlerian scale.

An assiduous, self-critical perfectionist, Webern assigned opus numbers to only 31 compositions, the vast majority of which last less than ten minutes, and some of which seem like mere splinters or tissues of sound. Yet these are among the most important works of the twentieth century. Webern once finished a lecture with the words "There is no other way", and in the aftermath of World War II the generation of Boulez and Stockhausen took this as truth in a quite fundamentalist way. It remains an open question whether Webern would have seen himself as their mentor.

Webern was born into prosperity in Vienna, and took his first piano lessons with his mother at the age of 5. He began composing at an early age, and from the age of 14 studied with Edwin Komauer in Klagenfurt, where the family had moved. In 1902 he entered the University of Vienna, where he quickly became dissatisfied with educational routine. He decided to take up studies with Hans Pfitzner (see p.304), but stormed out of his first meeting with Pfitzner when the older composer expressed a lack of enthusiasm for the music of Mahler. Instead he enrolled in Schoenberg's extracurricular classes in composition, and remained a Schoenberg student until 1908.

As with Schoenberg and Berg, Webern's early work revealed the influence of Brahms, Mahler and Strauss, but within weeks of joining Schoenberg's course he had begun to revise his ideas on tonality. The *String Quartet* of 1905 (one of the works to which Webern did not assign an opus number) already foreshadows his later style, and by the time he moved out from under Schoenberg's wing he was wholly committed to atonality (not a word either he or Schoenberg liked), as well as to a lifelong friendship with Berg. Webern's first major atonal work, the *Five Movements for String Quartet*, appeared in 1909 – the same year as Schoenberg's trailblazing *Three Piano Pieces*.

For the next nine years Webern devoted himself to composition and conducting. Much of the music he composed during this period was for voice, and all of it was of a revolutionary brevity: Schoenberg wrote that the *Six Bagatelles* for string quartet of 1913 (total duration less than four minutes) expressed "a novel in a single gesture, a joy in a breath". He served as a non-combatant during World War I before poor eyesight led to his being discharged. He renewed close contacts with Schoenberg, with whom he and Berg formed the "Society for Private Musical Performances" to promote new music (by no means exclusively their own). The Society's inauguration, in November 1918, followed closely after the end of the war.

When the Society ceased operating in 1922, Webern at last found himself in demand as a conductor. For twelve years he was the conductor of the Vienna Workers' Symphony Orchestra and Chorus, and he gave numerous concerts for the BBC between 1929 and 1936. Meanwhile he found time to produce an intermittent flow of predominantly vocal music, although when, following Schoenberg's lead, he adopted the serial method, he found himself able to return to writing for instruments alone, first with the *String Trio* (1927), then with the *Symphony* (1928). Always obsessed with structural precision (his works include the formal application of fugues, canons and passacaglias), Webern established a more complete form of serialism, applying rigorous principles not just to the intervals between the notes, but to aspects of timbre, rhythms and dynamics, thereby laying the foundations for the "total serialism" espoused by the modernist vanguard after World War II.

Although the Nazis banned his music as an example of "cultural Bolshevism", Webern had pronounced Nazi sympathies. He stayed in Austria throughout the war, earning his money by proofreading other composers' works, and completing three major works, *Cantatas Nos. 1 and 2* (1939 &

1943), and the *Variations for Orchestra* (1940). A terrible accident made him one of the war's last casualties, months after hostilities had ceased. On September 15, 1945, visiting his daughter, Webern stepped outside for a cigar and was shot by an American soldier in the mistaken belief that he was involved in the blackmarketeering activities of his son-in-law. He died before medical help arrived.

◑ **Complete Works: Harper, Rosen, Stern, Piatigorsky; Juilliard Quartet; London Symphony Orchestra; Boulez** (Sony SM3K 45845; 3 CDs).

In the 1960s and 1970s CBS (as they then were) recorded all Webern's orchestral works with opus numbers (Opp. 1–31), and these recordings provide a wonderfully concentrated overview of Webern's career at mid-price. Of the artists involved, Boulez has recently rerecorded several of the orchestral works in markedly more expansive interpretations.

PASSACAGLIA

The *Passacaglia* was the first work of which Webern felt sufficiently confident to assign it an opus number, and Opus 1 it remains, although earlier pieces are now part of the Webern canon (notably the "idyll for large orchestra" *Im Sommerwind*, written in 1904). The *Passacaglia* marked an enormous advance on the quasi-Romanticism of *Im Sommerwind*, being a highly individual interpretation of variation form. A theme of radical sparseness is stated in the strings, then followed by no fewer than 23 variations and a coda: all in the space of ten minutes. Already there is an impressive concentration on the quality of each note, and on the musical architecture. Webern later wrote to Berg that all his works from the *Passacaglia* on "relate to the death of my mother", and indeed there is a haunting and haunted sense of tragedy lurking just beneath its often suave surfaces.

O Berlin Philharmonic Orchestra; Boulez (Deutsche Grammophon 447 099-2; with *Five Movements*, *Six Pieces for Orchestra*, *Im Sommerwind* and arrangements of Bach and Schubert).

In the 1990s Boulez returned to Webern, and here presents more spacious and luxuriant performances than those he made with the LSO (see above). Webern's Bach and Schubert arrangements are fascinating tributes from one master to his forebears.

SYMPHONY

Webern adopted Schoenberg's twelve-tone method of composition in 1924 in *Three Traditional Rhymes*, but it was with the *Symphony*, written three years later, that the change truly registered. Here, in two compact movements, Webern returned for the first time in fifteen years to writing for orchestra, albeit one tailored to his own highly individual needs: strings (no double basses), a harp, pairs of clarinets and horns. There is a distilled clarity to Webern's scoring that was to sustain the rest of his career and, if it is built on a technical mastery that is dauntingly complex, the results are bracing, as if the ear is at last cleansed of the previous century's detritus.

O Oelze, Finley; Berlin Philharmonic; BBC Singers; Boulez (Deutsche Grammophon 447 765-2; with *Cantatas 1 and 2*, *Variations for Orchestra*, *Three Orchestral Songs*, *Das Augenlicht*).

Once again Boulez and the Berlin Philharmonic find a lustrousness in Webern that the earlier Boulez recordings sometimes missed. Strings and winds delicately caress the air as if reluctant to disturb the silence, yet there is no shortage of drama, and Boulez never allows the music to sag. Performances throughout are superb, not least from soprano Christiane Oelze. In the *Three Orchestral Songs* she finds beauty and tension where many others achieve only an antiseptic purity, and in the second cantata her feeling for the expressiveness of Webern's idiom is well matched by Gerald Finley.

VARIATIONS FOR ORCHESTRA

Webern heard very little of his music performed, and often overestimated how long it would last: the *Variations for Orchestra*, he calculated, would take "about twenty minutes". In the event, they last not much more than seven, but those seven minutes are packed with incident. Webern derives the whole piece from the briefest four-note phrase heard at the work's beginning. That fundamental material is then shaped and reshaped in six variations, as if one were to examine a tiny gem from every angle to see the light it cast. The composer described the work as an "overture", which suggests its dramatic potential, but for the composer it was all but a finale, and its 1943 premiere in Switzerland was the last time Webern heard his own work performed.

O Vienna Philharmonic; Abbado (Deutsche Grammophon 431 774-2; with *Passacaglia*, *Six Pieces for Orchestra*, *Five Pieces for Orchestra*, Bach arr. Webern, Schoenberg, *A Survivor from Warsaw*).

His reputation may be based on different repertoire, but Abbado excels in twentieth-century music. The same might be said of the Vienna Phil, which produces performances of airy transparency in music that can easily sound clogged. Abbado finds a restless tension in the score that makes Boulez's otherwise excellent version with the BPO (see above) seem almost demure.

STRING QUARTET OP. 28

Webern wrote comparatively often for the string quartet, although he only allowed four such works into his official oeuvre. None is more quintessentially Webern than the last, Op. 28, completed in 1938 to a commission from Elisabeth Sprague Coolidge. Its austerity is at first abrasive, yet the work grew from Webern's reflections on his daughter's pregnancy, and in the right hands there is warm eloquence as well as astringency in its three movements. As usual, the music grows from the smallest seeds (the metaphor appropriate here) as Webern manipulates rhythm, tempo and duration into mercurial patterns that shift even as we think we've managed to fix them in our mind.

Complete Trios and Quartets: Arditti Quartet (Auvidis Montaigne MO 789008).

The Ardittis, doughty champions of twentieth-century music, here present Webern's complete string trios and quartets (with and without opus numbers) in a typically authoritative survey. It's possible to imagine warmer performances, but the clarity of execution is exquisite. Yet again, and particularly in the Opus 28 quartet, Webern's musical miniatures prove to embrace a world of expression.

KURT WEILL

(1900–1950)

If Weill had lived and worked into a reasonable old age, the end of his career would have coincided with the beginning of Andrew Lloyd Webber's. What would Weill, whose work helped shape the modern musical, have made of what the form had become? A supremely practical composer, might he have adapted his style to suit the needs of the time? Perhaps we should be grateful that we shall never know. As it stands, Weill's oeuvre (and not only the stage works) remains one of the linchpins of twentieth-century repertoire, attracting audiences and interpreters far removed from the conventions of opera house and concert hall.

Weill was born in Dessau, where his father was cantor of the synagogue. His earliest musical studies were as a pianist. Later he studied composition with Humperdinck and Busoni. While still a teenager, he coached singers at the Dessau Opera, and in 1920 became Kapellmeister at the municipal theatre in Ludenscheid. His first compositions flirted with current styles, whether the neo-classicism of Hindemith or, as in the *Symphony No. 1* (1921), the atonality of Schoenberg. Nevertheless, something personal was already beginning to emerge.

In 1924 Weill met the actress Lotte Lenya and the two married in 1926. By the time Weill met Bertolt Brecht in 1927, he had already established himself as a successful theatre composer with acerbic pieces such as *Der Protagonist* (1926) and *Royal Palace* (1927). Now with Brecht, he embarked on one of the most significant collaborations in twentieth-century music. The first work they produced was *Mahagonny, A Songspiel* (1927), a setting for Lenya and five opera singers of pre-existing Brecht texts attacking American capitalism. This was the basis of the full-scale opera *Aufstieg und Fall der Stadt Mahagonny* (Rise and Fall of the City of Mahagonny; 1930), but before that Weill, Brecht and Brecht's largely unacknowledged collaborator Elisabeth Hauptmann wrote *Die Dreigroschenoper* (The Threepenny Opera; 1928), a "play with music" marvellously derived from John Gay's *The Beggar's Opera* (1728).

Acridly modern, bitingly satirical, it was a huge success. Within months of the Berlin premiere, European theatres were clamouring to stage the work: there were a reputed ten thousand performances by January 1933, and songs like "Mack the Knife" were international show stoppers. Brecht and Weill were now in demand, and another collaboration, *Happy End*, soon followed. The text for this "play with music" was again by Brecht and Hauptmann.

After *Mahagonny* came *Der Jasager* (1930), then *Der Burgschaft* (1932), for which Weill collaborated on the text with Caspar Neher. Shortly after the premiere he and Lenya broke up; and by now his relationship with Brecht had soured because, as Lenya later declared, Weill was not prepared "to set the Communist Manifesto to music"; but the darkest shadow of all was cast by the growing power of the Nazis. Hitler became Chancellor in 1933. Three weeks later, Weill's *Der Silbersee* (text and lyrics by Georg Kaiser) was premiered. Nazis demonstrated against the second performance, and hurled anti-Semitic abuse at Weill.

Weill knew what was coming, and fled to Paris. He never returned to his homeland. In Paris he wrote *Die sieben Todsünden* (The Seven Deadly Sins), his final and greatest collaboration with Brecht, and his *Symphony No. 2*. He and Lenya were reunited in London before sailing for New York, where the Manhattan Opera House was to premiere a version of the unperformed *Der Weg der Verheissung*, now called *The Eternal Road*.

Weill later confessed, "I never felt the oneness with my native country that I do with the United States; the moment I landed here I felt as though I'd come home." He thought America offered a way out of what he saw as the dead end of the European avant-garde. Here at last he could write music that would speak, not to the faceless masses of political philosophy, but to real audiences. He and Lenya remarried in 1937 shortly after the lavish premiere of *The Eternal Road*. New projects came thick and fast: besides the "musical play" *Johnny Johnson* (premiered in 1936) he wrote a score (not used) for the movie *Blockade*, as well as incidental music for several plays, a radio cantata and Broadway musicals like *Knickerbocker Holiday* (1938) and *Lady in the Dark* (1941).

Perhaps the greatest work of Weill's American period was *Street Scene* (1947), Weill's "Broadway opera": "75 years from now", he predicted, "*Street Scene* will be remembered as my major work." If it's customary to divide Weill's work into European and American periods, Weill himself saw no such discontinuity: his music was always a commentary on society in the most direct way possible. As he told an interviewer in 1940, "Schoenberg has said that he is writing for a time fifty years after his death . . . For myself, I write for today. I don't give a damn about writing for posterity."

THE THREEPENNY OPERA

The Beggar's Opera of 1728 was a scathing musical satire that played the realities of London's seedier side against the pompous conventions of opera seria. In the same way Brecht and Hauptmann's libretto for *The Threepenny Opera* set out to undermine the self-deluding niceties of Germany's bourgeoisie, while Weill's music aimed at "the complete destruction of the concept of music-drama", being cast in verse-song with pauses for spoken dialogue and any necessary action. The writers and first cast anticipated a flop, but in the event *The Threepenny Opera* proved to be Brecht and Weill's greatest success. It remains a savage work, too often betrayed by playing it purely as lowlife farce when its target is the bourgeoisie, every bit as roguish and thieving as the criminal underclass the piece ostensibly portrays. Brecht may have relocated the action to Soho, but Weimar Germany was clearly intended. Weill's insidious tunes were written for singers from cabaret, musical comedy and operetta, and in the right hands their suavity conceals their savage subversiveness: songs such as "Mack the Knife" and "The Song of Sexual Dependency" still pack a powerful punch.

○ Lenya, Neuss, Trenk-Trebitsch, Hesterburg; Chorus and Orchestra of Radio Free Berlin; Brückner-Rüggeberg (Sony MK 42637).

By the time Lenya took the role of Jenny in this 1958 recording, her voice was an octave lower than it had been in the 1930s. As a result, much of the music had to be transposed downwards. She also sang songs intended for other characters, somewhat mitigating their impact. If her contribution remains controversial, it's certainly characterful, and the rest of the cast responds well. Wilhelm Brückner-Rüggeberg directs a performance full of salty vigour.

BERLINER REQUIEM

Weill wrote his *Requiem* (for tenor, baritone, male chorus and wind orchestra) only weeks after the premiere of *The Threepenny Opera*, and it occupies the same musical world. Commissioned for radio, it takes its texts from poems by Brecht, but was never satisfactorily completed: the radio authorities refused to broadcast the section lamenting the murder of the revolutionary Rosa Luxemburg, and Weill himself added and subtracted sections, using the finale in *Mahagonny*. Nevertheless, in David Drew's performing version it's a powerful piece, as bitter in its wind harmonies as in its irony. The use of a very churchy organ only adds to the sarcasm.

○ Laiter, Kooy; La Chapelle Royale; Ensemble Musique Oblique; Herreweghe (Harmonia Mundi HM 901422; with *Vom Tod im Wald* & *Concerto for Violin and Wind Orchestra*).

Philippe Herreweghe is best known for his clean-cut period-instrument performances of Bach. Here he brings the same clarity of texture to Weill in a performance of ringing immediacy. He also includes the song "Vom Tod im Wald", which Lenya called "gruesome but powerful", and which was originally intended for the *Requiem*, and a spacious performance by Elisabeth Glab of the *Concerto* (see below).

CONCERTO FOR VIOLIN AND WIND ORCHESTRA

Weill wrote his *Concerto* in 1924 with a young man's open-minded approach to musical possibilities: the work partakes of the neo-classicism of Busoni and Hindemith, the atonality of Schoenberg, and the objective clarity of Stravinsky. Yet there are also foreshadowings of the mature Weill, not least in the decision to give the accompaniment to an ensemble of winds, brass, percussion and double bass. A youthful, but by no means immature, work.

O Glab; Ensemble Oblique; Herreweghe (Harmonia Mundi HM 901422; with *Berliner Requiem* & *Vom Tod im Wald*).

If Glab perhaps makes the *Concerto*'s solo part a touch more emotive than it needs to be, this is still a winning performance, full of grace and playful energy.

DIE SIEBEN TODSÜNDEN

Properly staged, *Rise and Fall of the City of Mahagonny*, with its slavetraders, its brothel and a climactic electric-chair execution, fully retains its power to shock. *Die Sieben Todsünden* is if anything even more powerful. Here Weill deploys his full armoury of spicy harmonic ambiguities, spiky instrumentation and witty dance rhythms, all in the service of a mordant attack on the hypocrisies of capitalist morality. There is arguably no more tragic figure in twentieth-century music than Anna, one woman split into two "sisters", a singer and a dancer, the former providing a commentary on the ruin of the latter while the family quartet (bass taking the role of the mother) look on, singing admonitory homilies. Although the piece works wonderfully well on record, it is a stage work, a *ballet chanté* (sung ballet) that reeks of the theatre.

O Fassbaender, Brandt, Sojer, Komatsu, Urbas; Radio-Philharmonie Hannover des NDR; Garben (Harmonia Mundi HMC90 1420; with songs).

Brigitte Fassbaender deploys all her considerable skill as a singer of both opera and lieder, but her performance lacks none of the theatrical intensity of the rasp-and-rant school of Weill intepretation. If her fellow interpreters are not quite so convincing, this remains the most searing of many distinguished recordings of the piece. Fassbaender also sings a selection of Weill songs, including the wonderfully slinky tango "Youkali", written in Paris in 1934 as part of the incidental music to *Marie Galante*, a play by Jacques Deval.

JUDITH WEIR

(1954–)

Judith Weir has the rare distinction of being as popular with audiences as with critics and she has produced vivid music for film, ballet and the theatre as well as numerous concert-hall works in a variety of genres. Her music, which uses modal or tonal techniques, is clear and direct yet always with hidden depths. She draws frequently on sounds and images from folk music, and like John Tavener (see p.423), with whom she trained, she also makes frequent gestures towards the music of the distant past. Her interest in medieval culture has led to two works based on the music of thirteenth-century composer Pérotin (see p.303): *Sederunt Principes* for chamber ensemble; and *Lovers, Learners and Libations – Scenes from Thirteenth-Century Parisian Life*, for singers and early-music consort. Homage of an even more direct kind is found in her reworkings of Mozart (*Scipio's Dream*, 1991) and Monteverdi (*Combattimento II*, 1992). But Weir's music is distinguished above all by her talent for lucid narrative structure, a talent most apparent in her operatic and music-theatre works.

Her first full-length adult opera, *A Night at the Chinese Opera*, was premiered in 1987 and was the first of her works to reach a wide audience. Weir wrote her own libretto from a thirteenth-century Chinese play about a collaborator with the Mongolian regime, and the music – which is mostly based around the fundamental intervals of the octave and the fifth – has a clear and open texture, showing Weir's abiding concern that her texts should be heard and understood. In 1990 came another opera, *The Vanishing Bridegroom*, retelling three traditional Scottish tales in which the supernatural obtrudes into everyday life. It's a work in which Weir's attachment to her Scottish heritage is especially noticeable, both in her use of Celtic folklore and literature, and in her quotations of fragments of Scottish music. Weir's third full-length adult opera, *Blonde Eckbert*, was first performed in April 1994; once again she wrote her own libretto, deriving it from an enigmatic German tale of incest, deception and betrayal.

In recent years Weir has turned increasingly to orchestral writing, with works such as her two pieces of 1995 for the City of Birmingham Symphony Orchestra (where she is composer in residence) – *Musicians Wrestle Everywhere* and *Forest*.

MUSIC DRAMAS

King Harald's Saga (1979), billed as a "Grand Opera in Three Acts" for solo soprano, compacts the story of King Harald's unsuccessful invasion of Britain in 1066 into less than ten minutes. The soprano sings eight clearly differentiated solo roles as well as that of Harald's entire Norwegian army, a technique which – combined with the matter-of-fact quality of Weir's text – emphasizes the absurdity of the violence depicted. The *Consolations of Scholarship* (1985) is a music drama for mezzo-soprano and nine instruments, and is based on the same source as *A Night at the Chinese Opera*. Like that later work, it carries much of the narrative through rhythmically notated speech, a style that recreates the transparent formality of classical Chinese theatre. In *Missa del Cid* (1988), a work for ten singers, Weir's text combines the medieval Spanish epic of El Cid with the liturgy of the Mass, each section being introduced by a speaker who tells the story of El Cid's bloodthirsty campaign against the Moors. Offsetting rich music for unaccompanied voices against the stark facts of slaughter, *Missa del Cid* shows Weir's predilection for simple, eloquent dramatic devices.

⭘ King Harald's Saga; The Consolations of Scholarship; Missa del Cid: Lontano; Combattimento; Manning, de la Martinez; Mason (CALA CACD 88040).

This CD provides the listener with a fascinating cross-section of Weir's earlier vocal dramatic music. The excellent performances are all given by the musicians for whom the works were originally written. Soprano Jane Manning is outstanding, presenting vivid portrayals of all the characters (including the entire Norwegian army) in *King Harald's Saga*.

BLOND ECKBERT

At one point in Act II, Eckbert sings of "The marvellous mingled with the commonplace", a precise description of Weir's imaginative world. She herself has called Ludwig Tieck's story "a psychological thriller", "a Gothic mystery" and "a crime novel", and there are elements of all three in her typically epigrammatic telling of the tale. At times, perhaps, her music (particularly the vocal lines) seems to be treading water so as to allow the story to catch up, but there are moments of striking colour: the Act II prelude can't be said to be illustrative in any conventional sense, but it paints a bewitching picture nevertheless; while the opera's last scene, plainly labelled "At the End", has an intensity that is chilling. There remains the suspicion that Weir's music can't quite take Tieck's story seriously, but there is no doubt that the opera is the work of a gifted musical storyteller.

⭘ Jones, Owens, Ventris, Folwell; English National Opera Chorus and Orchestra; Edwards (Collins Classics 1461-2).

This live recording does full justice to Weir's score. Sian Edwards, who conducted the premiere, gets the pacing and balance just right, and the cast's commitment is exemplary.

CHAMBER WORKS

Weir's chamber music, often written for musician friends, makes an excellent introduction to her absorbing and essentially melodic musical language, as well as demonstrating the range of her influences. Her piano pieces engagingly exploit the instrument's many different capabilities, with extremes of texture and attack in *The Art of Touching the Keyboard* (1983) – a title borrowed from Couperin – or vivid pictures of a remote Scottish landscape in *Ardnamurchan Point* for two pianos (1990). Echoes of traditional Scottish music can be clearly heard in works such as *The Bagpiper's String Trio* (1985) or *Distance and Enchantment* for piano quartet (1989). The folk music comes from further afield in *I Broke off a Golden Branch* (1991), a string quintet written for the same instrumentation as Schubert's *"Trout" Quintet*, which makes use of a haunting Croatian melody that gives its title to the work.

⭘ Distance and Enchantment; The Art of Touching the Keyboard; I Broke off a Golden Branch; Ardnamurchan Point; The King of France; The Bagpiper's String Trio: Tomes, Howard, Casén; Schubert Ensemble of London; Domus (Collins Classics 1453-2).

This disc presents a variety of Weir's chamber music performed by the musicians for whom the works were originally written. There is a palpable air of enjoyment about the playing, particularly in the delightful *I Broke off a Golden Branch*, the disc's highlight, which is given a convincingly spirited account by its dedicatees, the Schubert Ensemble of London.

HUGO WOLF

(1860–1903)

Hugo Wolf was the archetypal Romantic artist: manically driven, misunderstood, impoverished, mad and short-lived. He was also, after Schubert, the finest of all composers of German art songs. As a musician he was not in the same league as his great precursor, but where he arguably excelled him was in his sensitivity to words. Wolf conceived the music of his songs as exact translations of the poems that provided their texts: thus, unlike Schubert's songs, in which the music follows the mood of the text rather than the semantics, Wolf's make no sense without a complete grasp of what is being sung. He reconciled the dramatic and theatrical intensity of opera with the discipline of song, employing a Wagner-influenced style that took the form as far as tonality would allow. In short, Wolf's songs are highly wrought and complex creations, perhaps something of an acquired taste but deserving a far wider audience than they currently enjoy.

Born in Slovenia, Wolf was taught by his father until 1875, when he entered the Vienna Conservatory, where one of his contemporaries was Gustav Mahler. In December of the same year he met Richard Wagner, who encouraged him to concentrate on orchestral music, thereby condemning him to struggle at compositions for which his abilities did not equip him. He was a fractious student, and in 1877 – the year he contracted the syphilis that was to kill him – he was expelled from the conservatory, although Wolf maintained he had resigned over the college's inflexible conservatism. For the next decade he made his money chiefly from teaching, but in 1884 his songs aroused the interest of the greatly influential critic Eduard Hanslick, who recommended Wolf to two publishers, neither of whom was prepared to back the young composer. In emulation of Hanslick he began writing criticism, but in siding with the recently deceased Wagner against the very much alive Brahms he made many enemies in Vienna.

In 1888 he composed dozens of songs, including much of the *Spanisches Liederbuch* (Spanish Song Book), a work that established him in certain quarters as the finest songwriter of his time. By the mid-1890s a Hugo Wolf Society had been established in Berlin and even the Viennese were beginning to acknowledge his talent. In 1896 he completed his greatest body of songs, the *Italienisches Liederbuch* (Italian Song Book), but in the same year his mind began to collapse. The following year he fell into syphilitic dementia – he announced, for example, that he, and not Mahler, was director of the Vienna State Opera, and that the opera house would perform nothing but his music in future. He was committed to an asylum and remained incarcerated until his death, except for a brief period in 1898, when he was deemed to be cured, only to attempt suicide as soon as he was released. In belated recognition of his achievement, he was buried next to Schubert and Beethoven in the city's central cemetery.

LEBRECHT COLLECTION

Hugo Wolf

SONGS

Until the great explosion of songwriting that began at the age of 28, Wolf had composed extensively for chamber groups, solo piano and orchestra. Most of these pieces were left unfinished, and the few that Wolf did complete met with little or no success. He submitted his string quartet to the Rosé Quartet, who sent it back covered with derisory comments, and the Vienna Philharmonic were reduced to tears of laughter at the rehearsal for his tone poem *Penthiselea*. Wolf began to realize that, contrary to the advice given to him by Wagner, Brahms and Liszt, he was better suited to songs than to orchestral or instrumental music.

His most important work dates from the years between 1888 and 1898, and falls into several large groups. His preferred working method was to immerse himself in the works of a particular poet and produce nothing but settings of that writer's work until he had exhausted the material. Thus the clusters of Eichendorff, Mörike, Goethe, Michelangelo and Keller settings dominate his output, alongside two books of songs inspired by poetry from Spain (*Spanisches Liederbuch*) and from Italy (*Italienisches Liederbuch*). His settings cover an extraordinary range of moods and feelings, which he probes with the most acute psychological insight: the characters in his poems have a real living presence. For Wolf the words always come first, and his task as a composer was to clothe the words in music that most communicated their inner meaning, rather than simply letting the words inspire a generalized music interpretation of what they were about. In this he was closer to Schumann than to Schubert, and listeners with no German may find the songs initially rather dry. They are certainly worth persevering with, none more so than the songs of the *Italienisches Liederbuch*.

◑ **Selected Songs: Schwarzkopf; Moore** (EMI CDH 7 64905 2).

Elisabeth Schwarzkopf championed Wolf's music throughout her career, and her Salzburg recital from 1958 – when both she and her accompanist Gerald Moore were at the height of their powers – is a highly moving homage. Their selection consists mainly of Goethe and Mörike songs, plus some fine Keller pieces and excerpts from the Italian and Spanish books. Schwarzkopf's word characterization is as sensitive as any to be heard on disc, and she encompasses every gradation of tone between declamation and extreme tenderness without over-stressing. As an introduction to Wolf, there is nothing finer.

MÖRICKE LIEDER

Eduard Möricke was a Swabian pastor who wrote some of the finest German lyric poetry after Goethe. The tone of his poetry is ardent but never overstated, and he often dealt in the most fleeting of half-emotions inspired by the landscape or the coming of spring. Many of his verses touch on his own unhappy love life but he also wrote comic verses which appealed to Wolf as much as the lyric poems. Wolf's 52 settings did much to give Möricke an international profile as a poet and they are among his most inventive songs. They are not a cycle and vary considerably in mood from the solemn religiosity of *An die Geliebte* (To the Beloved), to the ridiculous comicality of *Storchenbotschaft* (Stork's Message), in which a stork's awkward gait is mimicked in a dissonant piano introduction. All the *Möricke Lieder* have a concentration that is highly communicative; there is nothing redundant in the music and very little repetition. Had Wolf written nothing else, he would still be regarded as one of the most gifted writers of German song.

○ 20 Möricke Lieder: Fischer-Dieskau; Moore (Orfeo C140401A).

Fischer-Dieskau has recorded these songs many times over, but this selection of twenty dates from the early 1960s, when his voice was still in fine shape and his interpretative skills had the effortless ease of a great actor.

ITALIENISCHES LIEDERBUCH

Of the 46 songs that make up the *Italienisches Liederbuch*, the first 22 were composed in 1890–91, while the remaining 24 were completed five years later. The texts were taken from a translation by Paul Heyse of anonymous Italian poems published in the year of Wolf's birth, and the obscurity of the verses evidently liberated him. Because these poems came with no burden of previous interpretation, Wolf was free to read himself into them and thereby produce his most profoundly personal music. The verses Wolf selected were mostly Tuscan love poems, which form a kind of narrative in which two lovers express devotion, quarrel, make up and generally carry on as lovers do. They are usually performed by a soprano and a baritone singing (mainly) alternative songs. Often very terse and to the point, these are not the most obviously engaging of songs, though the beauty of several is immediately apparent. Concentration brings great rewards, however, and their cumulative impact when performed by really good singers is overwhelmingly poignant.

○ Schwarzkopf, Fischer-Dieskau; Moore (EMI CDM7 63732-2).

Schwarzkopf, Fischer-Dieskau and Moore are again at their best on this milestone recording of the *Italienisches Liederbuch* from the mid-1960s. The delivery of both singers is incredibly subtle, and the nurturing of the often fractured melodic lines is unimaginably beautiful.

○ Bonney, Hagegård; Parsons (Teldec 9031 72301-2).

Of more recent interpretations of the cycle, none has displayed such a unanimity of mood and intention between the three interpreters as this 1992 recording by Barbara Bonney, Håkan Hagegård and Geoffrey Parsons. There's a real sense of the listener eavesdropping on intensely private and often painful moments.

IANNIS XENAKIS

(1922–)

Iannis Xenakis is known for three things: he's the only famous composer whose name begins with the letter X, he's the only Greek composer who's famous outside Greece and, most importantly, he's one of the crucial figures in the development of electronic music. Rejecting the straitjacket of serialism, Xenakis aimed to liberate sound from all a priori rules. His inspirations were the mythologies of Greek culture and natural phenomena such as the sounds of rain or the slow movement of shifting sand on a beach. His tools were chance operations, computer technologies and mathematical procedures, and at its best his music combines organic yet meticulously thought-out design with intense emotion.

Born into a wealthy Greek family in Romania, Xenakis went to school in Greece and then studied architecture and engineering in Athens. The next phase of his life reads like a parable of triumph over adversity. Deeply involved with the anti-Nazi resistance, he had half his face blown away in a street battle. After the war, his involvement in the Greek nationalist movement in British-occupied Athens led to a death sentence. In 1947 he escaped under a false passport to Paris, where he took a job with the architect Le Corbusier, for whom he worked for twelve years, most notably on the Monastery of Sainte-Marie de La Tourette. For the 1958 Brussels World's Fair Xenakis designed the futuristic Philips Pavilion, the venue for Varèse's groundbreaking *Poème Électronique* (see p.444), and for his own *Concret pH* for indeterminate mathematically generated sound. Le Corbusier's failure to acknowledge the extent of Xenakis's work on the Philips Pavilion led to the two men's estrangement.

BETTY FREEMAN/LEBRECHT COLLECTION

Iannis Xenakis

Varèse's radicalism was an important influence on Xenakis, and the younger composer's tribute to his colleague usefully encapsulates his own preoccupations: "Varèse worked on the very flesh of sound. He researched the architecture of sound itself . . . His music is colour and sonorous force. No more scales, no more themes, no more melodies, to the devil with music called 'musical', he delivers in the flesh that which is more generally called 'organized sound'."

After creating the orchestral sound-blast of *Metastaseis* in the mid-1950s, Xenakis took up composing full-time. Encouraged by Messaien to be true to his own vision, Xenakis set about applying probability theories and computer programmes to the processes of composition. He defined this method as "stochastic", meaning governed by the laws of probability. The pieces produced during the 1960s were often characterized by dense clusters and explosions of sound, and revealed a dazzling talent for stretching timbres to their limits. In 1966 he founded the Centre for Automatic and Mathematical Music in Paris and subsequently set up a similar unit at Indiana University, turning out work that impressed Pierre Boulez and led to his association with both IRCAM and the Ensemble Intercontemporain. Subsequent sound-and-light works such as *Hibiki-Hana-Ma* (1970), for twelve tapes and eight hundred speakers, displayed Xenakis's unparalleled technical virtuosity, but in later years the mythic and spiritual element of his music has come to the fore, expressing the composer's Christian faith and his profound feelings about his homeland, to which he returned after twenty years of exile.

CHORAL MUSIC

Xenakis's music is often linked with the harsh landscape of Greece and the bitter, fateful world of Greek tragedy. This aspect of his output is most directly expressed in his vocal and choral music which, like so much of his work, seems to aspire to the pure and the primitive. *Medea* (1967) is a setting of a classical text (albeit a Latin one) in which the ritualistic world of the original is conveyed by chanting male voices and struck stones, while various instruments – notably a cello, clarinet and rasping trombone – provide a kind of astringent commentary. In fact even in Xenakis's non-theatrical choral music, there is a highly dramatic quality. *Nuits*, written in response to the 1967 military coup in Greece, is a searingly intense work for twelve mixed unaccompanied voices, dedicated to the victims of the military junta. Adapted from Sumerian and ancient Persian, its synthesis of phonemes and syllables produces primitive sounds shorn of meaning and reference. Having experienced loss of freedom himself, Xenakis fully identified with the victims of oppression, and the result is a nine minute emotional cry for liberty – part lamentation, part political protest.

O Nuits; Medea; A Colone; Serment; Knephas: New London Choir; Critical Band; Wood (Hyperion CDA 66980).

This brave new recording of Xenakis's radical choral works is superbly animated and breathtakingly skilful. All of these works have an almost plastic quality, as if Xenakis were moulding shapes or creating blocks of sound from the dazzling range of vocal techniques on offer. These range from the declamatory to scarcely audible whisperings, and are carried off with incredible flair by the New London Choir.

CHAMBER MUSIC

Xenakis has pushed the range of music in all directions in more than a hundred compositions: multimedia, primitivism, spectacle, have all been absorbed into his sweeping vision. His larger-scale works are dense and exacting and demand a lot of work; perhaps the best place to start is with his smaller, but no less virtuosic, instrumental creations. *Nomos Alpha* (First Law), written in 1965 for Siegfried Palm, is a work for solo cello in which scales and traditional harmony are replaced by a sound continuum which places great demands on the player. It extends the dynamic range of the instrument by the use of simultaneous scales, rapid glissandi and the overlaying of low notes with high-pitched harmonics. The throbbing effect might sometimes recall the Bach suites for unaccompanied cello, yet the sound has an electrifying modern edge.

In his later chamber and instrumental – from the mid-1970s onwards – Xenakis abandoned the strict mathematical processes from which the formal outlines of his compositions were generated in favour of a more expressionistic, though still abstract, musical language. A work like *Ikhoor* (1978) for string trio is full of gratingly harsh sequences of sounds, and obsessively repeated rhythms whose raw but controlled energy recalls the pulsating dynamism and ethereal beauty of Bartók's late string quartets. *Evryali* (1973) for solo piano is more lyrical, despite its toccata-like propulsion. Here a restless, motorized energy forms a constant tension with ringing, and often delicate, sonorities. More recent works, like the 1990 string quartet *Tetora*, have an austerity and terseness of utterance which is occasionally tempered by fragments of melody.

O Chamber Music 1955–1990: Helffer; Arditti String Quartet (Auvidis Montaigne MO 782005; 2 CDs).

This recent set provides a revealing introductory compendium of Xenakis's work, including all the pieces discussed above. This is not easy music to come to grips with, but it has a rugged integrity and a focused intensity that is extremely impressive. The Arditti Quartet play to their customarily high standards and, in pianist Claude Helffer, Xenakis has an advocate with the technique and the insight to make his glittering piano works sparkle with an extra brilliance.

PLEIADES

Like Varèse, Xenakis is a composer particularly drawn to the sonic possibilities of percussion. Of several works for percussion ensemble, *Pleiades*, a strikingly beautiful quartet of pieces which evokes the richness of the Balinese gamelan, is the most exciting and aurally seductive. Written in 1978, it is divided into four sections, which group the percussion timbres by family – keyboards, metallophones, skins. The *Claviers* section is particularly rich, utilizing Indonesian scales and the bright timbres of vibraphone, xylophone and marimba to produce a fascinating ethno-Minimalist concoction.

◑ Dhalmann; Percussion Orchestra of Strasbourg (Harmonia Mundi HMC 905 185).

The Harmonia Mundi disc features the ensemble for which *Pleiades* was written and was recorded in the presence of the composer, who contributes a sleevenote analysis of the piece.

ALEXANDER ZEMLINSKY

(1871–1942)

Arnold Schoenberg once wrote: "I owe almost everything I know about composing and its problems to Alexander Zemlinsky . . . I always thought he was a great composer." Yet until the 1980s Zemlinsky was likely to feature in an A–Z of music only in order to justify its title, or in his secondary role as Schoenberg's mentor. Zemlinsky's essential problem was that he was too advanced for his conservative contemporaries, but not interesting enough for the radicals. To make matters worse, he was physically unprepossessing (Alma Mahler uncharitably described him as a "horrid little gnome – chinless, toothless and stinking of the coffee-houses"), and was uncomfortable pushing his own work. The result was relegation to the margins of history until the last decade, which has seen a reassessment of Zemlinsky's sumptuous *fin-de-siècle* Romanticism.

Zemlinsky was a typical example of Viennese multiculturalism. His father was Slovakian, his mother from a Bosnian Jewish family in Sarajevo, and Zemlinsky went on to become one of the cabal of Viennese musicians who formed around Gustav Mahler, the reforming force in the city's musical life. When Zemlinsky left the conservatoire in the 1890s, he became a member of the Wiener Tonkünsterverein (Viennese Society of Composers), whose honorary president, Johannes Brahms, encouraged the young composer.

Opera and song were to comprise the greater part of his output: *Sarema*, the first of his eight completed operas, was performed in Munich in 1897, and his second, *Es war einmal* (Once Upon a Time), was premiered by Mahler at the Court Opera in Vienna in 1900. His career as a conductor developed in parallel: from 1899 he was conductor at the Carltheater in Vienna, then he moved on to the Volksoper and was invited by Mahler to the Court Opera. He and Schoenberg founded a society to promote new music in Vienna, and his star seemed to be rising under the patronage of Mahler, who was going to present his next opera, *Der Traumgörge* (Görge the Dreamer). However, after numerous disagreements Mahler was forced out of the Court Opera in 1907, prompting Zemlinsky to walk out in protest. *Der Traumgörge* wasn't performed until 1980.

After another spell at the Volksoper, Zemlinsky went to work in the Deutsches Landestheater in Prague, where he was to remain for sixteen years. Under his direction it became one of the most important opera houses in Europe – Stravinsky, though usually begrudging in his praise, once described Zemlinsky conducting Mozart as one of the most satisfying experiences of his life. This was the most successful period of Zemlinsky's life as a composer too – it was in Prague that he wrote his best operas and the *Lyric Symphony*, his most famous work. In 1927 he went to work with Otto Klemperer at the Kroll Opera in Berlin, where his last completed opera, *Der Kreidekreis* (The Chalk Circle), was given a performance in 1934, before being suppressed by the Nazis. Zemlinsky fled first to Vienna and then, in 1938, to America, where he died a forgotten man.

DER GEBURTSTAG DER INFANTIN

The most remarkable of Zemlinsky's eight operas is the one-act *Der Zwerg* (The Dwarf), first given under Otto Klemperer in 1922 and the work most frequently performed in Zemlinsky's lifetime. Based on *The Birthday of the Infanta*, a short story by Oscar Wilde, it was revived in Hamburg in 1981 with a revised libretto that's closer to Wilde's original text – this version, renamed *Der Geburtstag der Infantin* (The Birthday of the Infanta), is the one you're most likely to see on stage. The opera tells of a dwarf given as a birthday present to a spoilt young girl. She adores him and he falls in love with her, but she eventually forsakes him, and he dies of a broken heart. *Der Geburtstag* brings out all Zemlinsky's strengths in orchestral colour, lyricism and highly charged emotion – the dwarf's achingly beautiful music no doubt gains some of its power from Zemlinsky's own feelings at his rejection by Alma Mahler.

○ Nielsen, Riegel; Radio-Symphonie-Orchester Berlin; Albrecht (Schwann 314013).

Sung by the cast of the Hamburg revival, this is the best introduction to Zemlinsky's operatic world. Kenneth Riegel has just the right qualities of innocence and vulnerability for the role of the Dwarf, while the contrast between his luscious music and that of the social whirl around him is finely drawn.

ORCHESTRAL MUSIC

Like Mahler's *Das Lied von der Erde*, Zemlinsky's remarkable *Lyrische Symphonie* (1923) is a cross between an orchestral song cycle and a symphony. A setting of seven love poems by the Bengali poet Rabindranath Tagore, it's typically Viennese in its fascination with yearning, parting and death, and clearly illustrates Zemlinsky's place between the classical Austro-German tradition and the innovative Second Viennese School. Alban Berg, one of the key figures of that school, underlined the work's importance by quoting it in his *Lyric Suite*, which he dedicated to Zemlinsky. Of Zemlinsky's other orchestral works, the best is the wonderful tone poem *Die Seejungfrau* (The Mermaid), which had the misfortune to be performed on the same programme as Schoenberg's *Pelléas and Mélisande* in 1905. Zemlinsky's piece was overshadowed and the composer lost interest in its future – it was not heard again until 1984. Also worth investigation are the masterly *Six Maeterlinck Songs* (1913), which display shimmering and unusual orchestrations and, once again, a strong preoccupation with death.

○ Lyric Symphony: Voigt, Terfel; Vienna Philharmonic Orchestra; Sinopoli (Deutsche Grammophon 449 179-2).

Of the seven recordings of the *Lyric Symphony* currently available, this one is the most satisfying, with the Vienna Phil at their most luxuriant. The songs form a dialogue between a heroic baritone and a dramatic soprano, and getting the right voices is absolutely imperative. Bryn Terfel finds just the right balance between the forceful and the sensitive, but Deborah Voigt, though in many ways superb, just lacks the equivalent range and sensitivity.

○ Die Seejungfrau: Berlin Radio Symphony Orchestra; Chailly (Decca 417 450-2).

In recent years Riccardo Chailly has become something of a Zemlinsky specialist, and his glorious recording of *Die Seejungfrau* was a major contribution to the current re-assessment of Zemlinsky. The shimmering woodwind and strings of this Mahlerian showpiece perfectly evoke the undersea world of its source – Hans Christian Andersen's *The Little Mermaid*.

GLOSSARY

Absolute music
Music that makes no references to events, paintings, literature and so forth; purely abstract music.

A cappella
Literally "in the church style". Unaccompanied choral singing.

Accelerando
Gradual increase in speed.

Accent
A stress on a particular note or beat, highlighting its place within a musical phrase.

Adagio
Slow and drawn-out tempo.

Alberti bass
In keyboard music, a running figure for the left hand that arpeggiates (see "Arpeggio") a simple series of chords, allowing the right hand to concentrate on melody. Highly popular in the eighteenth century.

Aleatory music
Derived from *alea*, the Latin word for "game of dice". Music composed by random procedures, often computerized. Very popular in the 1960s.

Allegro
Fast and lively tempo. The customary marking for the opening movement of a symphony.

Alto
1. The highest of the male voices.
2. The lowest of the female voices.
3. Prefix to an instrument that is lower in pitch and darker in tone than a treble instrument – eg alto saxophone, alto flute.

Andante
Moderate tempo. Slightly faster than Adagio – literally "walking pace".

Anthem
Brief, solemn composition for church choir; Protestant equivalent of the Latin Motet. Masters of the form include Purcell. Also used to define a patriotic vocal composition.

Antiphon
In the Catholic and Orthodox churches, a form of liturgical singing in which responses are exchanged between a solo voice and a choir, or between two separate choirs.

Aria
Term used since time of Alessandro Scarlatti to describe an independent solo vocal piece within an opera, frequently created to display the artist's vocal facility.

Arpeggio
Literally "like a harp". A chord in which the notes are spread, or played separately, either from top to bottom or vice versa.

Atonal
Music that is not in any key. With atonal music the traditional harmonic language no longer applies and the twelve notes of the octave function independently of any key centre. Atonality is associated above all with Schoenberg and his chief followers, Berg and Webern.

Authentic
Performance that attempts to reproduce, as accurately as possible, the way the music would have originally sounded. Many prefer the alternative terms of "period instrument" or "historically informed".

Ballade
Term used by Chopin to describe an extended single-movement piano piece in which narrative is suggested, without reference to any extramusical source. Later adopted by Grieg, Brahms, Liszt and Fauré.

Ballet
Dance form in which a story is told through the unification of music and dance. Originated in the French court of the sixteenth century. Used by Lully as an interlude in his operas, then evolved into hybrid opera-ballet. Later became an independent art form, dominated by the French until Tchaikovsky's emergence. Since the end of the nineteenth century many composers have written for the ballet, notably Prokofiev and Stravinsky.

Barcarolle
A composition (usually a song) that was originally associated with Venetian gondoliers' songs; usually has a gentle swaying motion, imitating the movement of the gondola.

Baritone
The male voice between tenor and bass.

Baroque
Music composed between 1600 and 1750, spanning the period from Monteverdi and Gabrieli to Bach and Handel. The period before Classical.

Bass
1. The lowest of the male voices.
2. The lowest part of a chord or piece of music.
3. The lowest of all instrument groups – eg double bass, bass clarinet, etc.

Bel canto
Literally "beautiful song". An eighteenth- and early nineteenth-century school of singing, characterized by a concentration on beauty of tone, virtuosic agility and breath control. Bellini, Rossini and Donizetti are the main bel canto composers.

Berceuse
A lullaby – the most famous instrumental example is by Chopin.

Binary form
A short work in two evenly balanced sections. Infrequently used since the death of Handel. Predated sonata form.

Bitonal
Music that uses two keys at the same time. It was a method favoured by Stravinsky.

Cabaletta
An heroic but brief aria (or end to an aria) built upon an unchanging rhythm. The most famous example is "Di quella pira" (for tenor) from Verdi's *Il Trovatore.*

Cadence
The closing sequence of a musical phrase or composition. The "perfect cadence" gives a sense of completion; the "imperfect cadence" leaves the music hanging in mid-air.

Cadenza
A solo passage designed to show off the soloist's abilities, occurring at the end of a concerto movement (generally the first), using material based upon the movement's main themes. Originally improvised, but composers began writing them out in the eighteenth century.

Canon
The strictest of contrapuntal forms. A work in which the same melody is played or sung by two or more voices, each beginning slightly after the preceding one. The most famous examples are "London's Burning" and "Frère Jacques".

Cantabile
A "singing" style. Generally applied to instrumental and orchestral music.

Cantata
Literally "sung piece". An extended vocal work with an instrumental accompaniment that tells a story through the use of arias, recitative and choruses. Distant relative of opera. First composed in the seventeenth century and mastered by Bach and Handel; Elgar, Bartók, Britten and Stravinsky – among others – created their own versions.

Cantilena
1. A melodic line which is smooth and lyrical.
2. In choral music, the vocal part that carries the main theme.
3. A vocal excercise which employs all the notes of the scale.

Cantus firmus
Literally "fixed song". A melody borrowed from a religious or secular source as the basis to a polyphonic composition in which other melodies are set in counterpoint against it. Popular between the fourteenth and seventeenth centuries.

Castrato
A male singer castrated as a child, developing a soprano or contralto voice. Very popular during the seventeenth and eighteenth centuries – the last castrato died in the twentieth century.

Cavatina
A lyrical operatic song or aria in one section, or an instrumental work in imitation of such a song – eg the fifth movement from Beethoven's *Quartet No. 13.*

Chaconne
A dance-piece in a slow three-beat time, consisting of variations upon a repeated theme in the bass part. Finest examples are the final movement of Bach's *Violin Partita No. 2* and Purcell's "When I am Laid in Earth", from *Dido and Aeneas.*

Chamber music
Instrumental music composed for a small number of players. Sometimes applied to solo instrumental pieces, but more commonly used for duos, trios, quartets, etc.

Chanson
French song form of the fourteenth to sixteenth centuries; generally polyphonic.

Chorale
Metrical hymn-tune, with its foundations in the Lutheran Church of sixteenth-century Germany. Originally sung in unison, but Bach extended the form into separate parts for soprano, alto, tenor and bass.

Chord
Any simultaneous combination of notes.

Chromaticism
Use of notes not belonging to the diatonic scale – ie using sharps, flats or naturals alien to the key. The chromatic scale comprises twelve ascending or descending semitones. Chromaticism is a strong element of Romantic music – Wagner's in particular.

Classical
1. The post-Baroque period, roughly between 1750 and 1830. Pre-eminent Classical composers were Haydn, Mozart and Beethoven, who refined the sonata, symphony and concerto forms.
2. General term used to distinguish Western music intended for a formal context, like a church or concert hall, from more informal, popular music (rock, folk, etc).

Coda
The closing section to a movement. Originally made a basic summary of what had gone before, but Mozart and Beethoven developed the coda into a substantial subsection, sometimes introducing new ideas.

Coloratura
Soprano voice capable of great agility and delicacy. Most famous coloratura role is the Queen of the Night in Mozart's *Magic Flute*.

Colour
Term used to describe the varieties and gradations of timbre that an instrumentalist or vocalist can produce.

Concertante
1. Like a concerto. A sinfonia concertante is a work for soloist(s) and orchestra which is closer in form to a symphony than a concerto.
2. Name for the group of soloists in a concerto grosso.

Concerto
Originally an orchestral work in several movements, with or without soloists, but in the eighteenth centuries it developed into a large-scale work in which a solo instrument is contrasted with an orchestral ensemble. The form was refined by Mozart, whose three-movement concertos became the model for the genre.

Concerto grosso
An orchestral work in which two bodies of instruments (one large and one small) play off against each other. Popular in the seventeenth and eighteenth centuries, and with twentieth-century neo-classicists.

Continuo
The same as figured bass (see p.489). Generally performed by a harpsichord, organ or any other chordal instrument.

Contralto
The lowest of the female voices – same as an alto, but alto is associated with sacred and choral music, whereas contralto is applied to opera singers.

Contrapuntal
Adjective derived from "counterpoint".

Counterpoint
The placing of two or more parts or voices against each other in such a way that they have both harmonic coherence and a degree of independence.

Countertenor
The highest male voice.

Crescendo
Gradual increase in loudness.

Cyclic form
The repetition or modification of a single theme in two or more of a work's movements. The most perfect use of cyclic form can be found in Franck's *D Minor Symphony*; Berlioz's *idée fixe* and Wagner's leitmotif are related concepts.

Da capo
Means "repeat from the beginning".

Diatonic
Music using the major and minor scales; music constructed exclusively from the notes defined by the key.

Diminuendo
Gradual decrease in loudness.

Dissonance (or discord)
A combination of notes that jars the ear, requiring swift resolution. Its opposite is consonance/concord.

Divertimento
A light and entertaining suite or movement. Mozart's are supreme examples; popular also with neo-classicists.

Dodecaphonic
See "Serialism".

Double-stopping
Simultaneous playing of two strings on a bowed instrument.

Dynamics
The qualities and degrees of softness and loudness.

Étude
A "study", or essay in technique. Paganini, Chopin, Liszt and Debussy – among others – developed the étude into an expressive form rather than a merely technical exercise.

Expressionism
As in the visual arts, a term used to describe works in which the artist's emotional or mental state is the primary subject. Applied to German music of the early twentieth century – above all to the pre-serialist works of Schoenberg and Berg.

Fantasia (or Fantasie or Fantaisie)
A loosely structured composition, allowing more freedom of expression than the classical forms. Mozart employed the term, but it is more closely associated with Schubert, Chopin and Schumann.

Figured bass
A bass part played on a keyboard or other chordal instrument, with detailed figures specifying the harmonies to be played above it. Extensively used during the Baroque period.

Fugue
A highly complicated contrapuntal form in which two or more voices are built around a single theme. Their entries are in direct imitation of the theme's opening, but each voice is developed independently so that ultimately the two or more voices are complete melodies in themselves. Bach was the greatest master of the form, which he characterized as resembling "people engaged in rational conversation".

Gavotte
An old French dance in 4/4 time, but beginning on the third beat of the bar. Popularized by Lully.

Gesamtkunstwerk
Literally "unified work of art". Wagner's term for his dramatic ideal in which music, drama and poetry would unite to create an unprecedented art form.

Gigue
A sprightly dance in binary form. Much used by Bach and other eighteenth-century composers as a finale to a dance suite.

Glissando
Principally applied to string instruments. The sliding of a finger over a number of consecutive notes, thus creating an extended slither of sound. Best used by Ravel and Strauss.

Gregorian chant
A type of solo and unison plainsong employed in the liturgy of the Roman Catholic Church. It was thought to have been codified during the papacy of St Gregory the Great (590–604), though his precise involvement is a matter of conjecture.

Ground bass
A brief, constantly repeated thematic bass pattern that serves as the foundation for the melody, counterpoint and harmony in the upper parts. The basis of passacaglias and chaconnes.

Harmony
The simultanous grouping of notes to form a musically significant whole; the basic unit of harmony is the chord. Harmony can colour any single melodic line in innumerable different ways and a composer's harmonic language is one of his or her most immediately identifiable characteristics.

Homophony
Music in which the parts move as one, in grouped chordal patterns, with no independent movement. The opposite of polyphony.

Hymn
A congregational work of praise in which the structure is invariably strophic and the words specially written.

Idée fixe
Berlioz's term for the motto theme that recurs throughout his *Symphonie Fantastique*. A forerunner of leitmotif.

Impressionism
Term taken from painting, to describe music in which suggestion and atmosphere were dominant considerations; typified by Debussy and his followers.

Impromptu
A short, improvisatory piece of song-like piano music – Schubert's are the best examples.

Instrumentation
The scoring of music for particular instruments – not the same as orchestration, which refers to a composer's skill in writing for groups of instruments. Thus Schubert's *Octet*, which shows a remarkable awareness of the qualities of each component, is a superb example of instrumentation.

Intermezzo
1. A brief instrumental or orchestral diversion performed during an opera's scene changes, to denote the passing of time. The Intermezzo in Mascagni's *Cavalleria rusticana* is perhaps the best known.
2. A single-movement concert piece, usually for piano. Brahms wrote many.

Interval
The distance between two notes. Intervals are expressed numerically – thirds, fourths, etc (though "octave" is used rather than "eighth"). Composers' preferred intervals are highly recognizable aspects of style – perhaps the most immediate are those of Puccini and Richard Strauss.

Inversion
The turning upside down of a chord or a melody. Employed in both traditional counterpoint and in the twelve-tone system.

IRCAM
Institut de Recherche et de Co-ordination Acoustique/Musique. Electronic studios attached to the Pompidou Centre in Paris, established in 1977 by Pierre Boulez as a research centre into new compositional techniques and methods.

Key
The basis of tonal music. The keynote is the foundation of the key, which classifies the notes lying at specified intervals from that keynote – thus the key of C major specifies the notes of the major scale, whereas C minor specifies the notes of the minor scale, which has different intervals from the major. As there are twelve notes in the chromatic scale, it follows that there are 24 keys. Each key has a certain number of flats and sharps, signified by the key signature. Notes other than those belonging to a work's key are referred to as "accidentals" – accidentals are the basis of chromaticism.

Klavier
German word for "keyboard" – can apply to harpsichord, piano or any domestic keyboard instrument.

Largo
Slow and broad tempo.

Legato
Instruction to play smoothly.

Leitmotif (or leitmotiv)
Literally "leading motif". First used with reference to Weber, to describe a short, constantly recurring musical phrase that relates to a character, emotion or object. Associated above all with Wagner, who turned the leitmotif into a means of blending numerous associations and making structural connections across vast spans of time.

Libretto
The text of an opera.

Lied
German word for "song", commonly applied to the songs of Schubert, Schumann, Brahms and Wolf.

Madrigal
A secular, polyphonic composition, frequently unaccompanied; at its height in sixteenth- and seventeenth-century Italy. Monteverdi and Gesualdo wrote outstanding examples.

Mass
The main service of the Roman Catholic Church. Most Mass settings use the so-called "Ordinary" of the Mass, the unchanging five-part core of Kyrie, Gloria, Credo, Sanctus and Agnus Dei. Settings of the "Proper" of the Mass have additional sections required by special circumstances – the best-known example being the Requiem.

Melisma
A group of several notes sung to the same syllable common in Gregorian chant.

Mezzo
The lowest of the soprano voices. One grade above contralto.

Minimalism
First used to describe a school of American music which rejected the complexities of nineteenth-century Romanticism and the twentieth-century avant-garde. Associated most famously with Steve Reich, Philip Glass and John Adams, the term usually denotes music which uses repeating cycles or additions of small phrases to achieve an hypnotic effect. It is now also applied to European composers such as Arvo Pärt, John Tavener and Henryk Górecki, whose music has affinities with the religious music of pre-Renaissance Europe.

Minuet
A brisk French dance in triple time, developed by Lully then highly popular during the eighteenth century. Became the standard third movement in classical sonata form, where it is coupled with a Trio. It later grew into the Scherzo, as mastered by Beethoven.

Modes
In essence, the scales used in European music prior to the seventeenth century, when they were reduced to the major and minor scales known today. Plainchant uses various modes as does much folk music.

Modulation
The movement from one key to another.

Monody
Term used to describe the style of writing in which a single line or melody is given a continuo accompaniment. Developed around 1600, in reaction to the complexities of polyphonic composition.

Motet
Sacred unaccompanied choral composition; the text is usually in Latin, but is never taken from the liturgy.

Motif (or Motiv or Motive)
A brief, recognizable musical idea, usually melodic but sometimes rhythmic.

Movement
A self-contained section of a larger work; so called because each section had a different, autonomous tempo indication.

Musique concrète
Music made from recorded sounds such as birdsong or traffic noises. Pioneered by the French sound technician Pierre Schaeffer (1910–96), it influenced electronic composers like Stockhausen.

Nationalism
The expression of distinctive national characteristics in music, usually through the adaptation of folk material. A prevalent tendency all over Europe in the latter half of the nineteenth century; associated with such diverse figures as Glinka, Liszt, Smetana, Dvořák, Bartók, Kodály, Grieg, Vaughan Williams, Janček and Sibelius.

Neo-classicism
A trend that became particularly strong during the 1920s, in reaction to the indulgences of late Romanticism. Typified by the adoption of Baroque and Classical forms, and the use of heavily contrapuntal writing. Much of Stravinsky's output can be classified as neo-classical.

Nocturne
1. In eighteenth-century music, a short serenade in several movements for a small group of instruments.
2. A brief, lyrical piano piece; associated especially with Chopin.

Note-row
The foundation of serialism; the order in which a composer chooses to arrange the composition's basic twelve notes, none of which can be repeated until the other eleven have been deployed (see "Serialism").

Octave
The interval that divides two notes of the same written pitch – eg C to C.

Opera buffa
A form of opera in which everyday characters are placed in comic situations. Mastered by Mozart in *Le Nozze di Figaro*, by Rossini in *Il Barbiere di Siviglia* and Donizetti in *Don Pasquale*.

Opera seria
The dominant operatic genre during the seventeenth and eighteenth centuries. Characterized by heroic or mythological scenarios, often with extensive florid writing for castrati. The last and

greatest example of the highly disciplined form was Mozart's *La Clemenza di Tito*.

Oratorio
A dramatic musical setting of a religious text, usually for solo voices, chorus and orchestra. Originated in Rome around 1600; later examples are Handel's *Messiah*, Mendelssohn's *Elija* and Elgar's *The Dream of Gerontius*.

Orchestra
The first regular orchestras appeared in the Baroque era, and consisted of strings, oboes and bassoons, plus a widely changing list of solo instruments. The layout became standardized during the Classical period, when Mozart and Haydn made specific demands regarding the number and quality of players for their symphonies. This Classical orchestra established the basic division of the players into four sections: strings; woodwind (flutes, oboes, bassoons and clarinets); brass (horns and trumpets); and percussion (kettledrums). Beethoven's symphonies demanded more (and better) players, and Berlioz, Wagner and Mahler required yet further expansions of the orchestra's resources. Though the instruments have changed over the years, the orchestra of today is not much different from the sort of array that sat before Mahler.

Orchestration
1. The art of writing for an orchestra, demanding an understanding of the qualities of each instrumental section, and an ability to manage and combine them.
2. The scoring of a work not originally intended for the orchestra – eg Mussorgsky's *Pictures from an Exhibition*, which was orchestrated by Ravel.

Ornaments (or Embellishments)
Notes added to the printed score in performance by a singer or instrumentalist. In the seventeenth and eighteenth centuries, composers generally indicated where such additions were required; by the start of the nineteenth century this improvisatory element had been virtually quashed.

Ostinato
A persistently repeated melodic or rhythmic figure (see "Ground bass").

Overture
1. An orchestral introduction to an opera, oratorio or play.
2. A single-movement orchestral piece composed for the concert hall, otherwise known as a "Concert Overture". Examples include Mendelssohn's *Hebrides Overture*, and Brahms' *Tragic* and *Academic Festival* overtures.

Parody
1. A work that ridicules the pretensions of another work by distorting its most characteristic features.
2. An already-existing piece of music which is used to set entirely different words.
3. A sixteenth- or seventeenth-century Mass in which the musical material has been derived from another source, like a motet or *chanson*.

Passacaglia
Instrumental work (originally a dance) with a continually repeated theme – not necessarily in the bass, and thus not the same as a chaconne.

Pedal point
A sustained bass note over which changing, and sometimes discordant, harmonies occur.

Pitch
The position of a sound in relation to the whole range of tonal sounds, depending on the frequency of sound waves per second (hertz). A high frequency is heard as a high pitch, a low frequency as a low pitch. In the US and the UK, pitches are named using the first seven letters of the alphabet.

Pizzicato
The plucking of bowed string instruments.

Plainchant (or Plainsong)
Medieval unaccompanied liturgical music in which a single vocal line (monophony) is notated in free rhythm, like speech. The principal form of plainsong in the West is Gregorian chant.

Pointillism
Term originally applied to the paintings of Seurat, in which colour is applied in small dots. Used by music critics to describe some serialist works in which the notes seem placed in isolation rather than in melodic phrases.

Polyphony
Music in which a group of voices are combined contrapuntally. The heyday of polyphonic music was from the thirteenth to the late sixteenth century – Palestrina, Lassus and Byrd are among the major polyphonists. However, Bach's music can also be described as polyphonic, even though it is governed by different harmonic principles from those of the Renaissance polyphonists.

Polystylism
Term applied to those contemporary composers (eg Alfred Schnittke) who employ a number of different styles within the same work.

Polytonality
The use of two or more keys at the same time. Stravinsky's music is full of examples.

Prelude
1. An introductory piece of music, eg one that precedes a fugue or an act of an opera.
2. A self-contained piano piece, as in the *Préludes* of Chopin.

Programme music
Music that relates to a specific story, painting, text, character or experience. Most often used in connection with "symphonic poems" or "tone poems" of Romantic composers such as Liszt, Berlioz, Tchaikovsky and Strauss.

Rallentando
Gradual decrease in speed.

Recitative
Semi-sung dialogue and narrative in opera and oratorio. In its rhythmic freedom it is closer to dramatic speech than to song.

Rhapsody
A Romantic term, applied to compositions suggestive of heroic endeavour or overwhelming emotion. Best-known examples are Brahms's *Alto Rhapsody*, Rachmaninov's *Rhapsody on a Theme of Paganini*, and Gershwin's *Rhapsody in Blue*.

Romanticism
The cultural epoch heralded in music by Beethoven and Schubert, and dominated by Chopin, Schumann, Liszt, Berlioz and Wagner. Characterized by the abandonment of traditional forms and structures, a predilection for extra-musical subjects, an increase in the scale of composition, and an affection for chromaticism.

Rondo
A structural form in which one section recurs at certain times throughout a work – thus (A) B (A) C (A) D (A).

Rubato
A subtle flexibility of pace that alters the shape of a phrase but does not affect its pulse, tempo or structure. A necessity in Chopin's music. Summarized by Liszt as being like the collective motion of the leaves of a tree.

Scherzo
Literally a "joke". Began as a lively movement derived from the Minuet, but developed into an autonomous genre in which the original humour is replaced by a free-ranging, rather tempestuous expressiveness – Chopin's piano *Scherzi* are the most famous examples.

Sequence
1. A type of hymn in the Catholic Mass which follows the Alleluia. The earliest, from the ninth or tenth centuries, were written in prose, later ones (eg the Dies Irae from the Mass of the Dead) were in rhymed verse.
2. The repetition of a phrase at a higher or lower pitch, much employed in Baroque music. In a "real sequence" the phrase is repeated exactly, whereas a "tonal sequence" is one in which the phrase is slightly altered to avoid a key change. In the chorus of the carol "Ding Dong Merrily on High" the word "Gloria" begins with a tonal sequence.

Serenade
1. A love song.
2. In the eighteenth century, an evening entertainment for orchestra – eg Mozart's *Eine kleine Nachtmusik*.

Serialism
Also known as twelve-tone or dodecaphonic music, serialism was developed by Schoenberg as a replacement for traditional harmonic and tonal languages. A serial composition is based on a twelve-note theme (the tone-row or note-row), which can then be used in different ways: forwards, backwards, upside down, upside down and backwards, or superimposed to create chords. Its most extreme form, in which predetermined rules govern every aspect of the piece, including volume and speed, is known as total serialism, and is associated primarily with the postwar work of Messiaen and Boulez.

Singspiel
Germanic genre – in essence comic opera with spoken dialogue instead of recitative. A good example is *The Magic Flute*.

Sonata
1. From around 1600 to the mid-eighteenth century, a solo instrumental composition not in any strict form – literally "sounded" rather than sung.
2. From the era of Haydn, an instrumental work in three or four movements for solo instrument and keyboard, or for solo keyboard. The form of the first movement became known as sonata form.

Sonata form
The crucial invention of the Classical era, sonata form was used in most instrumental and symphonic music until the Romantic era, and even then the likes of Brahms kept it alive, as did the great symphonists of the twentieth century. Sonata form is divided into the following three sections:
A. The exposition: here a first subject, the work's main theme, leads to a second subject in another key, in which fresh material is introduced.
B. The development: this consists of material already heard in the exposition, but develops it considerably.
C. The recapitulation: this presents a varied repetition of the material first heard in the exposition. Ends with a coda.

Sonority
A combination of different timbres which produce a specific sound quality.

Soprano
The highest female voice.

Spinto
Urgent, heroic Italian tenor voice.

Sprechgesang
Literally "speechsong", a singing style midway between song and speech. Invented by Schoenberg, the technique requires the singer to approximate the pitch of the note and deliver it with the right amount of colour. Used by Schoenberg in his *Pierrot Lunaire*, but the finest example is Berg's *Wozzeck*.

Staccato
The opposite of legato. A direction for a note to be played shorter than is marked, detaching it from the note that follows.

Stretto
1. In a fugue, the overlapping of the entries created by the subject starting up in one voice before the previous statement of it has finished.
2. Increase in tempo.

Strophic
Term used to describe a song which uses the same music for each new verse.

Study
See "Étude".

Suite
1. In the seventeenth and eighteenth centuries, a piece of instrumental music in several contrasting movements based on dance forms; in particular the Allemande, Courante, Sarabande and Gigue.
2. A set of movements assembled from a ballet or other stage composition.

Symphonic poem (or Tone poem)
Orchestral programme music, a genre devised by Liszt and perfected by Strauss.

Symphony
First used to designate an orchestral interlude or overture to a vocal work, but since the mid-eighteenth century the term has been used for a large-scale orchestral work, generally in four movements, sometimes in three or five. The Classical symphony was developed by Haydn, Mozart and Beethoven, and many of the greatest subsequent composers have added to the repertoire – Schubert, Brahms, Mahler, Bruckner, Sibelius, Nielsen and Shostakovich being notable masters of the form.

Syncopation
Accentuation of the offbeat (ie not the main beat). Characteristic of jazz, much used in jazz-influenced early twentieth-century music.

Tempo
The pace of a work.

Tenor
The second highest male voice.

Ternary form
An instrumental or orchestral composition in three sections, in which the first section is repeated – ie (A) B (A).

Tessitura
The natural range of a voice, or the range within which lie most of the notes of a role.

Texture
The quality of a composite musical sound or sequence of sounds as determined by the number of voices involved, and the timbre and spacing of those voices.

Timbre
The particular quality (literally "stamp"), or character, of a sound that enables a listener to distinguish one instrument (or voice) from another. Synonymous with tone colour.

Time signature
The numbers at the beginning of a composition, movement or section (or, indeed, midway through a phrase in some twentieth-century

scores) to indicate the number and kind of beats in a bar – 4/4, 3/4, 9/16, etc.

Tonality
Adherence to a single key.

Triad
A three-note chord consisting of a root note plus the intervals of a third and a fifth. The four types of triad are: major (eg C – E – G), minor (eg C – E flat – G), augmented (eg C – E – G sharp), and diminished (eg C – E flat – G flat).

Trio
1. Combination of three performers.
2. Work for such a combination.
3. Central section of a Minuet, so called because originally written in three-part harmony.

Triplets
A group of three notes of equal duration, played in the time of two.

Twelve-tone
See "Serialism".

Vibrato
Rapid but small vibration in pitch – most often used in reference to string players, singers and wind players.

Waltz
A dance in triple time. Especially popular throughout the nineteenth century in Austria, most famously through the music of the Strauss family.

INDEX OF COMPOSERS AND WORKS

Titles are listed in *italic*; composers are listed in **bold**, followed by the works discussed in the text, in the order in which they appear. Wherever a work is given a separate entry, the definite or indefinite article has been omitted from the title wherever it is the first word of the title – thus *La Traviata* is to be found under T for *Traviata*, *Der Freischütz* under F for *Freischütz*, and *A Midsummer Night's Dream* under M for *Midsummer*.

C

D

E

F

G

H

I

J

K

L

M

N

O

P

Q

R

S

T

U

V

W

X

Y

Z

WHEREVER YOU ARE . . .

ROUGH GUIDE TRAVEL:

Amsterdam
Andalucia
Antigua
Australia
Austria
Bali & Lombok
Bangkok
Barbados
Barcelona
Belgium & Luxembourg
Belize
Berlin
Big Island of Hawaii
Brazil
Britain
Brittany & Normandy
Bulgaria
Brussels
Budapest
California
Canada
Central America
Chile
China
Corfu & the Ionian Islands
Corsica
Costa Rica
Crete
Cyprus
Czech & Slovak Republics
Dominican Republic
Dublin
Egypt
England
Europe
Florida
France
Germany
Goa
Greece
Greek Islands
Guatemala
Hawaii
Holland
Hong Kong & Macau
Honolulu
Hungary
India
Ireland
Israel & the Palestinan Territories
Italy
Jamaica
Japan
Jordan
Kenya
Laos
Las Vegas
Lisbon
London
Los Angeles
Malaysia, Singapore & Brunei
Mallorca & Menorca
Maui
Mayan World
Melbourne
Mexico
Morocco
Moscow
Nepal
New England
New Orleans
New York
New Zealand
Norway
Pacific Northwest
Paris
Peru
Poland
Portugal
Prague
Provence & the Côte d'Azur
The Pyrenees
Rhodes & the Dodecanese
Romania
St Lucia
St Petersburg
San Francisco
Scandinavia
Scotland
Seattle
Sicily
Singapore
South Africa
South India
Southwest USA
Spain
Sweden
Sydney
Syria
Thailand
Tunisia
Turkey
Tuscany & Umbria
USA
Venice
Vienna

. . . ROUGH GUIDES READ BETTER

Vietnam
Wales
Washington DC
West Africa
Zimbabwe & Botswana

ROUGH GUIDE PHRASEBOOKS:
Czech
Egyptian Arabic
French
German
Greek
Hindi & Urdu
Hungarian
Indonesian
Italian
Japanese
Mandarin Chinese
Mexican Spanish
Polish
Portuguese
Russian
Swahili
Spanish
Thai
Turkish
Vietnamese

ROUGH GUIDE REFERENCE:
Classical Music
Country Music
English Football
European Football
Hôtels et Restos de France
The Internet & World Wide Web
Jazz
London Restaurants
Millennium
Music USA
Opera
Reggae
Rock
World Music

ROUGH GUIDE CDS:
Aboriginal Music
Brazilian Music
Cajun & Zydeco
Classical Jazz
Colombian Music
Cuban Music
English Roots Music
Flamenco Music
Irish Music
Music of the Andes
Music of Eastern Europe
Music of India & Pakistan
Music of Kenya & Tanzania
Music of Zimbabwe
Native American Music
North African Music
Portugese Fado
Reggae Music
Roots of Rock
Salsa Music
Scottish Music
South African Music
Tango
West African Music
World Music
World Music 2

ROUGH*NEWS* is Rough Guides' *free* newsletter giving you news, travel issues, music and website reviews and the latest dispatches from authors on the road. For a free subscription check out our website at www.roughguides.com or write to us at:

Rough Guides UK
62–70 Shorts Gardens,
London WC2H 9AB,
England
UK Orders: ☎ 0181-899 4036

Rough Guides US
375 Hudson St,
New York, NY 10014,
USA
US/International Orders: ☎ 1-800-253-6476

Trekking through **Costa Rica**?
Backpacking through **Europe**?
Cruising across the **USA**?
Clubbing in **London**?

Wherever you're headed, **Rough Guides** tell you what's happening – the history, the people, the politics, the best beaches, hotels, food, and nightlife on any budget

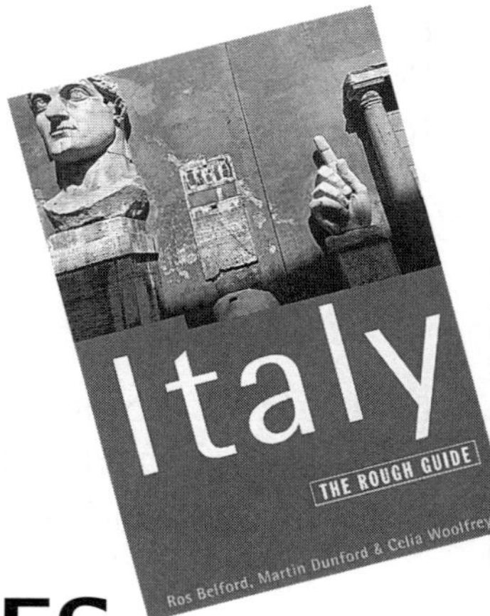

ROUGH GUIDES

Travel Guides to more than 80 destinations worldwide from **A**msterdam to **Z**imbabwe

AT ALL BOOKSTORES • DISTRIBUTED BY PENGUIN

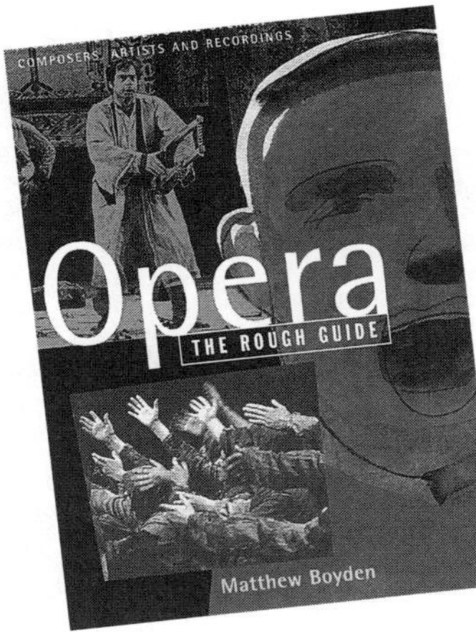

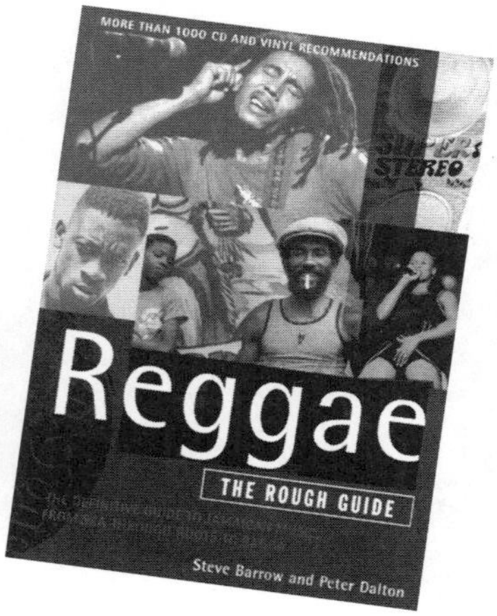

Good Vibrations!

ON PAPER AND ONLINE!

Visit Rough Guides' website www.roughguides.com for news about the latest books, online travel guides and updates, and the full text of our Rough Guide to Rock.

AT ALL BOOKSTORES • DISTRIBUTED BY PENGUIN